AF655386

2 EDITION

Sales and Distribution MANAGEMENT

Text and Cases with SAP Applications

An Indian Perspective

Taylor,
Terman,
Terrano

2nd EDITION

Sales and Distribution MANAGEMENT

TEXT AND CASES WITH SAP APPLICATIONS

AN INDIAN PERSPECTIVE

DR S L GUPTA

EXCEL BOOKS

Information contained in this work has been obtained by Excel Books from sources believed to be reliable. However, neither Excel Books nor its authors guarantee the accuracy of any information published herein and neither Excel Books, nor its authors shall be responsible for any errors, omissions, or damages arising out of use of this information. This work is published with the understanding that Excel Books and its authors are providing information but are not attempting to render engineering and professional services. If such services are required, then assistance of a qualified professional should be sought.

ISBN: 978-81-7446-870-3

First Edition: New Delhi, 2005
Reprint: 2006, 2007, 2008, 2009, 2010
Second Edition: New Delhi, 2010
Reprint: 2012, 2013, 2017, 2018

Copyright © 2010, Dr S L Gupta
All Rights Reserved

EXCEL BOOKS
Regd. Office: E-77, South Ext. Part-I, Delhi-110049
Corporate Office: B-25/5&6, Sector-59, Noida-201301
Sales Office: 81, Shyamlal Marg, Daryaganj, Delhi-110002
Bangalore Office: No.10, 1st Floor, Kalidasa Marg,
Gandhi Nagar, Bangalore-560009
+91-8130438484
info@excelbooks.com/projects@excelbooks.com
internationalalliance@excelbooks.com
www.excelbooks.com

Published by **Dr Rajan Chopra** for **EBPL**, B-25/5&6, Sector-59, Noida-201 301
and printed by Excel Printers, Delhi-110 002

BRIEF CONTENTS

Block V: Physical Distribution Management

Block VI: New Techniques of Managing Distribution

preface to the second edition

The second edition of this book, *Sales and Distribution Management*, is designed to serve the management students not only with updated text and cases but also with practical applications of SAP. The book will impart comprehensive knowledge to the marketing students and teachers of Indian Universities and Institutions.

Keeping in mind the changes in the field of sales management and distribution, this edition presents a thoroughly revised text in all the chapters.

Retailing, which is an important aspect in the distribution system, is growing at a fast pace in India. This edition includes many new aspects of sales and distribution concerned with organized retailing.

Further, this edition becomes updated with the addition of new exercises, activities and questions at the end of each chapter. Mandatory updations in chapters and additional information in the revised annexures make this book a complete resource book on Sales and Distribution Management. I welcome suggestions from all readers, teachers and students for improvement of the book.

S L GUPTA

preface to the first edition

Sales and Distribution is designed to serve as a textbook for Marketing students in Indian Universities and Management Institutes.

There are a number of books on Sales and Distribution, both Indian and foreign. Then why another book? A particular problem that Indian teachers and students are facing is that the existing books do not contain much about the Indian Market. This book is an attempt to fill in this gap. The book discusses the various Theories and Principles of sales and distribution in the context of Indian Products and Market, from a practical and result-oriented standpoint.

The importance of rural marketing in the Indian economy continues to grow day by day. With the rise in income of people in general, the overall demand for all types of goods has gone up. This has led to an increase in production of various types of consumer goods. The success or failure of a business now depends upon how effectively selling functions are performed. What is now needed is the intensive cultivation of sales to ensure proper utilisation of the productive capacities and to generate full employment.

Cultivation of sales needs accurate, factual information reasonably complete and timely, rather than hunches and guesswork, in making selling decisions. Hence, today sales and distribution has assumed an important place as an effective management tool for marketers.

Case methodology has now become a very popular technique for teaching the students how to handle business issues in various functional areas. For analysing various cases, one would require the help of concepts, precepts, tools and techniques. Broadly speaking, case studies involve both problem diagnosing and then taking a decision in the light of various facts of cases.

Case studies have been inserted in this book to give students an intimate insight into actual business situations. Although meant primarily for students, a study of the work will nonetheless enable even practising managers to systematize and improve their selling skills.

To sustain in the competitive world of today, one has to make systematic efforts to improve and upgrade his selling techniques. I shall be grateful if the readers send their comments and suggestions for enabling us to improve this book further.

S L GUPTA

about the author

Prof. (Dr) S L Gupta, MCom, MBA, PhD, PGRIM (IIM, Calcutta) is presently working as Professor and Coordinator – Academics and Doctoral Research at Birla Institute of Technology, Mesra, Ranchi, (Deemed University), Noida Campus. He has almost 20 years' experience in the field of teaching, training, consultancy and research. He has been teaching Marketing subjects (Marketing Management, Retail Management, Marketing Research, Sales and Distribution Management) to MBA, PGDBM, and MPhil students for last 20 years. Prof. Gupta has written 10 Books in different areas of Marketing Management. He has published more than 50 research papers and articles in the journals of repute. He is the Editorial board member of MAG *Scholars Journal* and Guest Editor of *International Journal of Retailing and Marketing.* He is an active member of the American Marketing Association (AMA), All India Management Association (AIMA) and AIMS International and ICMA. He is also an Accredited Management Teacher (AMT) by All India Management Association.

BLOCK I

Basics of Sales Management

Sales management is a challenging task. Management always holds sales managers responsible for obtaining sales volume, handling the selling operation so as to make contribution to profits and for ensuring that the business continues to grow. Sales managers have broad responsibilities. They recruit, select and motivate sales staff to optimum effort.

In spite of — or perhaps because of — severe pressure from political, legal, economic, social, technological and competitive forces on sales activities, there has been an exponential growth of sales departments at large.

This block focuses on the basics of sales management in the Indian perspective and in the Internet environment.

sales management strategy

learning objectives

On completion of this chapter, you should be able to:

- understand the role of sales management
- manage the sales force
- develop and formulate sales strategies
- define sales management in context to modern prospective
- analyse nature, scope and application of sales management
- explain selling process and sales force
- discuss the analysis of sales manager's duties and responsibilities in modern system
- understand the role of national sales manager

content outline

opening case

P&G's New Sales and Distribution System in India

It is a subject that is being discussed in hushed tones inside every fast moving consumer goods (FMCG) company today. Project Golden Eye – the code name for Procter & Gamble's (P&G) latest initiative in rationalising its sales and distribution system – isn't exactly an eyewash.

On the contrary, it raises some fundamental questions about channel design and network strategy – issues which are agitating the minds of a great many FMCG companies. For long, Hindustan Lever's famed distribution system was the only benchmark available. In other words, increased reach meant increased volumes. So the more the number of outlets you could bring under your distribution coverage, the better were your chances of hitting critical mass. So, almost every year, every FMCG company prided itself on setting ambitious targets to expand its distribution cover, appoint new distributors and plumb for volume growth. For almost a decade, P&G too strained every sinew to match the Lever juggernaut. It pushed for growth not just in urban markets but also tried very hard to establish direct coverage of rural markets. But in its quest for reach, P&G, like many other FMCG companies, overlooked one critical factor–the cost of extending distribution cover. After failing to aggressively challenge Lever in soaps and detergents, P&G has rewritten its focus areas: laundry (Ariel), sanitary napkin (Whisper) and Vicks. What's more, it has junked its original strategy of promoting top-end products. While the process of redrawing the organisational boundaries was on, two things became apparent. One, 85 per cent of its sales came from the top 30 towns. Two, its current volumes did not justify a large distributor network. Even in a market like Mumbai, there were close to six distributors. A large distributor network meant that no single distributor had large enough volumes to achieve an attractive return on investment. This resulted in each distributor trying to extend its reach to push up volumes. But with P&G's portfolio of high margin low volume products, merely extending reach only increased the cost of servicing, not the offtake per outlet. Today, P&G is busy slashing its number of distributors down to one-tenth of its size and reworking the margin structure. This has sparked off a debate among marketers whether it makes business sense.

In many ways, P&G's initiative raise two clear issues. One, is a large direct distribution cover necessarily a strength for every market? Can an alternate model emerge in India which results in large cost savings and, yet, is also effective in meeting marketing objectives?

More, not Less

At the heart of P&G's new system is the implicit assumption that lower reach does not lead to significantly lower offtake. 'My marketing objectives tell me that our brands are over-distributed', explains a P&G manager. If sales analysis shows that 95 per cent of Ariel or Whisper sales comes from 70 per cent of the outlets, then it counts for very little if distribution cover is actually reduced.

Given that the two prongs of FMCG distribution are cost and availability, P&G is likely to get a significant cost advantage, without losing out on availability, by cutting down on reach.

Apart from reducing costs by knocking down direct coverage, how does P&G hope to achieve significant cost saving in its supply chain? That's where P&G has started rationalising its distributors network. The intent–cut down the number of its distributors to about one-tenth of the current size. In Madhya Pradesh, for instance, P&G will now have just one distributor, who will operate like a superstockist. "So if 5 distributors were handling Rs 6 crore of business, now that entire business will be consolidated under one distributor," says a sales manager with Marico, who has been closely monitoring the new P&G system.

Earlier, since each distributor was working with small volumes, it wasn't economical for P&G to replenish them frequently. As a result, the average inventories lying with the distributor would be significantly high, forcing them to tread on the company's margins.

That is a dangerous loop for any distribution system; typically, channel design in any FMCG system is driven by distributor's economics. The key issue is: How effectively can you leverage your distribution? "For most companies, managing distributor inventory is not seen as critical to channel design. Primary sales is where companies hand off", explains a senior consultant. "So as long as the company has sold enough to the distributor, it is not interested", said he.

Now, a distributor evaluates a company on how it is faring largely on return of investment (ROI). Simply put, ROI, in a working capital intensive business, is the number of rotations (or the number of times that the distributor can turnover his investment in stocks) multiplied by the margin per rotation. The consequences of ignoring distributor ROI can be disastrous. Take the recent example of a leading FMCG company which attempted to benchmark its distributor economics with Hindustan Lever. The findings were startling. The distributor margin for the company was 6 per cent while it was 5 per cent for Levers.

Distributor stock levels for this company was an average of 4 weeks, while for Lever it is 2 weeks. Assuming that the distributors gave no credit to the market, the company's distributor ended up rotating his stock 13 times (52 weeks over 4 weeks) as against a Lever distributor who rotated his stock 26 times.

Now, given that the distributor aimed to hit a return of 30 per cent (the risk-free rate of return was 30 per cent if the distributor invested in the money market), the margin that had to be kept aside to achieve the above ROI was 2.5 per cent. The corresponding figure for a Lever distributor was 1.2 per cent. This effectively meant that the amount of money that the company distributor could spend on distribution (buying vans, investing in sales people, etc.) was 3.5 per cent, while for the Lever distributor it was 1.2 per cent. The writing on the wall was clear: despite its lower distributor margins, Lever was successful in getting higher distribution. So, even though the FMCG company in question spent Rs 14 crore more by way of higher margins, it ended up with poorer distribution. The reason: it fundamentally did not manage distributor ROI. The result can be disastrous. Even in healthy FMCG distribution systems, poor ROI usually results in distributor dropouts of around 10 per cent. The result? It leaves a vacuum in distribution, leading to obvious share losses.

Recently, a leading FMCG company in the household insecticides business could not find any distributors to service its key wholesale market in Begum Bazar for nearly three months, leading to a significant sharp drop. The company simply couldn't get any distributors to buy the economics of the business.

The other fall-out is that the distributor will stop extending credit in the market, resulting in retailers not picking up stocks. Gaps in distribution are then inevitable.

Competing on Size

Now, for P&G, by moving to a superstockist set-up, it could now replenish its distributors more frequently and hence reduce their average stock-level. Not only is its system complexity lower, it can also look at building stronger relationships with its superstockists. By ensuring a better return on investment, P&G will now be in a position to make the distributors invest more in their distribution infrastructure. Sources in P&G say that they will now be able to replenish stocks every three days.

Moreover, P&G hopes to make significant cost savings through the increased throughput available to be a superstockist. By offering him more volumes and reducing the distribution reach (hence his cost of operations), P&G is now trying to shave off distributor margins by a full 2 per cent. This shaving will then be channelled into building advertising. A larger advertising kitty will undoubtedly help it to fight competitors, particularly Levers, on mass media without being beaten on share of voice in media.

Additionally, with a limited number of distributors, P&G will also not need to invest in C&F agents. The superstockist will be expected to invest in storage and warehousing space, so that the stock transfer from the company can take place as soon as the stocks are shipped into the warehouse.

In the final scheme of things, P&G has another reason for reducing the distributor's margins. That's because of the peculiar distributor psychology at work. As in the earlier example, as soon as the company is able to reduce distributor stocks from 4 weeks to around 2 weeks, at 6 per cent margin, the distributor begins to earn almost 60 per cent of return. "That can be the starting point of trouble", says a senior manager.

The key is to keep the distributor's ROI in a band between 30 per cent to 40 per cent. The moment it falls below 30 per cent, the distributor is inclined to undercut in a bid to recover his money. On the other hand, if ROI is as high as 60 per cent, the distributor is tempted to aim for a higher turnover by undercutting the distributor in the next territory.

Of course, the only brand that will continue to need wide distribution cover is Vicks cough drops. The reason is simple. Vick's competitive set is impulse-driven confectionery. But for P&G to extend direct distribution cover for a single brand like Vicks is simply far too costly. So it has chosen to adopt wholesale distribution for the Vicks line. "If you don't have a portfolio to support a massive distribution thrust in the hinterland, there is very little point in aiming for direction distribution", avers a senior manager with an FMCG company.

However, for its future product launches, it is apparent that P&G has chosen to focus on key urban markets. "Reducing cover is in line with future plans" affirms a sales manager at P&G. The era of jostling with Lever across the length and breadth of the country is over. Focus is P&G's new name of the game.

***(Source: Business Standard,* Tuesday, 1st Dec. 1998)**

TRY YOURSELF

1. Analyse the sales and distribution system of P&G.
2. How does an FMCG's sales and distribution system differ from the industrial distribution system? Explain.

Introduction

Sales management is defined as "the planning, direction and control of personal selling, including recruiting, selecting, equipping, assigning, routing, supervising, paying and motivating as these tasks apply to the personal sales force".

The above definition of sales management has been given by the Definition Committee of the American Marketing Association. The main emphasis of this definition lies on management of sales force.

If we look back into the past, we find that business units used to be small in size, located near to the consumers, and shopkeepers were able to serve the consumers competently. But with the development of large business operations and an increase in the volumes of production, i.e. production on mass scale not only for local consumption but also to cater to the demand at national and global levels, the importance of sales management has increased considerably. Nowadays almost all business firms have an efficient sales department to look after the various aspects related to sales.

Sales force is responsible for the sale of products of a company and to add profit to the business operations and fulfil social obligations. Sales force should be hardworking, result oriented, well educated and competent to handle changing situations. Technical developments which are taking place at a rapid speed have made the task of sales force more challenging.

Nature and Importance of Sales Management

Selling concept is integrated with marketing management. Sales management helps to achieve the organizational objectives. The main objectives of sales management is that products should be sold at that price which realizes profits. Buyers and sellers both have same types of business relationships. This relationship is based on exchange of goods, services and money. Sales person develops a positive relationship with the customers. The role of sales team is interdependent and success of one team member depends on the other. The sales team continuously monitor the customer preference, competitors' situation, government policy and other regulatory bodies.

Relationship-based Selling

Relationship-based selling works because people would rather buy what they need to buy anyway from those they have come to relationship. Relationship-based selling means doing business in such a way that company is worthy of the customer's trust. Relationship selling is mainly personal not institutional, and buying is heavily personal as well. It is not selling centric. It's buyer-based. The objective of relationship selling is to help the buyer do the right thing for the buyer. Selling based on relationship goes beyond needs-based selling, constructive selling, or problem-solving selling. It is not about getting the transaction–it is about establishing relationship.

Managing the Sales Force

Many efforts are under way to make Indian companies more competitive. Typically, the focus is on internal processes and operational efficiency up to the factory gate, but no further. Unaddressed challenges lie in "factory forward" processes, often including competitive sales force management. For example, success in the intensively competitive consumer electronics industry today is decided at the dealer level, with each sales officer playing a crucial role in securing shelf space and dealer attention. Even in industrial goods, quality and low cost alone are not enough–an efficient and effective sales force approach focused on customer value is an effective competitive weapon. This acquires urgency because of the fact that new competitors typically poach the best members of the incumbents' sales forces at a time when the experience and dedication of star performers is most needed.

Consequently, for many Indian firms, a fresh approach to sales force management holds the key to translating efficiency gains in manufacturing to success in the market. Successful sales force management means:

- The right organisation and aggregation against product lines and geographies
- The right strength and qualification
- The right compensation and incentive system.

Organisation

The key to sales force organisation is the right level of aggregation against product lines and geographical coverage. The solution is not obvious. Even market leaders constantly experiment with different approaches. For example, at one time BPL sold its consumer electronics and refrigerator lines through the same sales force but has separated them recently. Philips, on the other hand, has traditionally had separate sales forces for its audio and colour television (CTV) businesses. The right organisation must triangulate between competitive levels of support for each product line (How much product know-how is required for selling a CTV versus a refrigerator?), exploitation of cross-selling opportunities (Do CTV dealers also sell audio?) as well as an efficient and economical coverage of the customers.

Strength and Qualification

Sales force strength and qualification significantly affect both the ability to provide competitive service levels and the economics of the sales force. A successful approach takes market requirements (service/qualification requirement by customer segment or channel), competitive benchmarks (organisation and strength of key competitor's sales forces) as well as target efficiency parameters (visits per day, face time with customer...) into account. The right starting points are benchmarks with leading competitors. However, in order to be helpful, these have to be analysed in considerable depth. For example, a major industrial company realised that its main competitor not only had 60% more salespeople on the ground but had also achieved a 25% higher turnover per salesperson. What seemed to be a contradiction at first was explained by an efficient back office organisation which gave each salesperson more time for intensive interaction with the customer and allowed for deeper service relationships.

Compensation and Incentive Systems

Compensation and incentives have a significant impact on the morale of the sales force and help in retaining successful salespeople. Incentives allow above-average compensation for the most successful salespeople while keeping overall compensation levels in check.

An effective incentive system sets aggressive but achievable targets, reflecting business priorities while being simple to administer and easy to understand. A major stumbling block for the implementation of incentive systems is often the quality of the forecasting system. The quality of the budget plans and the success of the incentive system are intricately linked, particularly in India's highly volatile markets, where, for example, demand for medium and heavy commercial vehicles grew by over 100% between 1993 and 1996 before plummeting back to the 1993 levels in 1998. Reliable forecasts, thus, are precious prerequisites for a successful incentive system.

In summary, sales force management holds the key for competitive success in India. The imperatives are:

- Tailor the approach to key segments. Start with differentiation for urban/rural markets, but go further and adjust for sophistication levels of customers/channels.
- Provide the right strength and qualification levels at your frontline interaction with the customer.
- Learn to meaningfully segment and forecast the market with limited data and adjust your incentives accordingly.

Many companies are currently taking the necessary steps towards successful sales force management and are achieving growth even in today's economic environment. Others have fallen further behind whether they will be able to participate in the next economic recovery is doubtful.

STEPS IN DESIGNING AND MANAGING A SALES FORCE

The main steps are as follows:

1. Objective Setting
2. Training for Sales Policies
3. Designing Sales Force: Structure and Size
4. Deciding Sales Force Compensation
5. Recruiting and Selecting Sales Force
6. Guiding and Motivating Sales Force
7. Performance Rating of Sales Force

Organising and Managing a Sales Force

Sales forces are regularly assigned particular sales territories. Various factors are taken into account when deciding the sales force for a particular territory. These include the physical size of the force for a particular territory, transportation links within a territory, purchasing power of consumers and their educational and living standards. Therefore, a sales force is deployed according to the geographical features of the territory and product or consumer requirements. A company should also devote considerable effort to the training and development of its sales force. There are two types of training which can be provided to sales force (a) In-house training, and (b) On-the-job training. It is also necessary for a company to arrange periodic meetings and discussions with its sales force. Finally, the performance of the sales force can be evaluated on the basis of targets and actuals.

SALES MANAGER'S DUTIES AND RESPONSIBILITIES

The sales manager is the most important person in a sales organisation. All activities are based on his functions and responsibilities. The following are some of the principal duties of a sales manager:

1. Organising sales research, product research, etc.
2. Getting the best output from the sales force under him.
3. Setting and controlling the targets, territories, sales experiences, distribution expenses, etc.
4. Advising the company on various media, sales promotion schemes, etc.
5. Monitoring the company's sales policies.

In the table that follows, Al Reid gives the steps necessary for getting success in-selling:

table 1.1 **Territory Sales Manager's Job Responsibilities**

To yourself	To your company	To your customers
Increase basic selling skills.	Be proud of your association with your company.	Work closely with decision-takers and influencers in each account.
Develop management abilities.	Maintain the company standing and standards with all customers.	Point out the advantages of an association with your company.
Keep pace with changes, trends and developments in your territory.	Inform the headquarters and your supervisors, through established channels, about changes and developments in your territory.	Keep accounts current and up-to-date on all company advertising and promotional activities.
Study the latest products, promotion policies and procedures.	Be prompt in handling records, reports, correspondence, etc.	Suggest ideas, methods, techniques and tips that can stimulate sales.
Be alert to new sales and merchandising ideas.	Cut selling costs by economical routing, good use of time, planning and greater awareness of opportunity.	Inform the customers about the trends in their areas.
Grow, so that you can assume greater responsibilities as opportunities permit.	Check demand and movement of products in the territory.	Handle complaints effectively and to the complete satisfaction of the complainants.
Maintain the appearance and goodwill expected of a territory sales manager.	Report activities of the competitors.	Suggest the best technique for selling your products to the customers.
Analyse your weak and strong points and then think about them.	Strive to reach the best goals.	Organise presentations to inform and save time.
	Ask for help, when you need it.	Make the customers aware of the changes in the company's policies or procedures.
	Cooperate with other departments of the company.	Stimulate and maintain enthusiasm for your products. Build and maintain goodwill.

Problems of Sales Management

1. ***Designing and Managing Sales Force***

The sales manager's control over the various activities of the sales force is a must. These activities may, sometimes, be beyond control, leading to intractable problems in a sales organisation. So the sales manager must maintain a vigilant check on the various activities of the sales force. Actual supervision of, and guidance to, individual salesmen is also a *sine qua non* of a sound sales manager.

2. ***Sales Force Authority***

If authority is not delegated to the sales force, they will not be able to deal with the customers who, in turn, do not like to deal with persons who have no authority. Therefore, the sales force requires delegation of authority with respect to the following:

- Changing or fixing prices
- Credit facilities to old and existing customers
- Assurance regarding quality and after-sale service
- Payment terms and settlement of claims.

In reality, powers in these areas are rarely delegated to salesmen.

3. ***Target-setting***

Target-setting is necessary for achieving organisational goals. Sales targets are fixed on the basis of past experience, time period and brand positioning in the market. In a competitive environment, targets can be based on the different aspects of sales strategies.

The targets should be fixed in such a manner that they are achievable and most of the sales force feels that if proper effort is put in by them, they can achieve the sales target. Where targets are fixed without taking into consideration past performance, present and the future business climate, then it invites frustration in the sales force and unhealthy comments. So the sales managers should be vigilant in fixing realistic targets and motivate the sales force to achieve those targets.

4. ***Sales Forecasting***

It is difficult to say how long consumers will continue to accept existing goods in a volatile environment which is changing fast with new competitors, new technologies, new fashion articles and new advertising strategies. Sales forecasts must change as conditions change. Accuracy depends on meticulous planning and dynamic strategies.

Sales Management — Formulation of Sales Strategy

The function of sales management includes the task of organising, planning and implementing the sales efforts so as to achieve corporate goals related to market shares, sales volume and return on investments. Tasks are performed by a sales manager both within the organisation and outside with other organisations. The following are key decision areas in sales management which are particularly relevant to strategy formulation:

- Determining the size of the sales force
- Decision regarding type and quality of sales force required

- Designing the sales organisation
- Territory designing
- Recruitment and training procedures
- Task allocation
- Compensation of sales force
- Performance appraisal and control system
- Feedback mechanism to be adopted
- Managing channel relationships
- Coordination with marketing departments.

DIFFERENT SALES STRATEGIES

Relationship Strategy

Establishing and maintaining a partnership-type relationship internally as well as with the customers is a vital aspect of selling. In this strategy, a major key to success in selling is the ability to establish working relationships with customers in which mutual support, trust and goals are nurtured over time. The sales force that builds effective relationships with the customer and provides valuable service are usually high-performers and top-achievers.

High-performance salespeople understand the importance of building relationships with customers as well as with others who interact with them. For example, the decision to buy a new computer may be made by a team of persons including the buyer and persons who will actually use the computer. Relationships with the support staff, product service, credit and training requirement, etc., are also important to understand. Most sales personnel will readily admit that their productivity depends on the contribution of these people.

A Selling Partner

P – Prepares strategically for a long-term, high-quality relationship that solves customer's problems.

A – Asks questions to get on the customer's agenda.

R – Restates customer needs with confirmation questions.

T – Teams with support people to provide the customer with solutions.

N – Negotiates double-win solutions with joint decision making.

E – Exceeds customer expectations whenever possible.

R – Re-examines the ongoing quality of the relationship frequently.

In this model, a customer is treated as a partner. Therefore, maintaining a good relationship with the customer is important.

The Double-Win Strategy

In this strategy, both the customer and the salesperson come out of the sale with a sense of satisfaction. The salesperson not only obtains the order but sets the stage for a long-term relationship, repeat business and future referrals.

They both come out of the sale feeling satisfied, knowing that neither has taken advantage of the other and that both have profited, personally and professionally, from the transaction. In the simplest terms, you know you have a win-win sales encounter when both the sales person and the buyer come out of it feeling positive.

The double-win strategy is based on such irrefutable logic that it is difficult to understand why any other approach would be used. However, some salespeople have still not accepted the merits of the win-win approach. They have adopted a win-lose approach which means that the salesperson wins at the buyer's expense. When a salesperson sells a product that is not the best solution to the buyer's problem, the win-lose strategy has been used.

We can adopt the win-win attitude which is one of the principles of partnering-style selling. The starting point to the development of a double-win philosophy is to compare the behaviour of persons who have adopted the win-lose approach with that of persons who have adopted the win-win approach (Figure 1.1).

figure 1.1
Double-Win Strategy

Win-Lose People	Win-Win People
See a problem	Help others solve their problem
Fix the blame	Fix what caused the problem
Let life happen to them	Make life a joyous happening for others and themselves
Live in the past	Learn from the past, live in the present and set goals for the future
Make promises they never keep	Make commitments to themselves and to others and keep both of them

There are a few companies in the developed world that have actually been able to establish lasting relationships of this kind, having survived and grown over a period of a century and half. In the 90's, however, with the impact of global competition on the corporate scene, a new dimension has been added to ensure satisfaction and happiness of the customer–time. It has been proved that those companies able to provide quality service/product at a competitive cost and most important of all, in the quickest possible time, are the ones that have grown by leaps and bounds.

Instant Service

It is in this context of providing almost "instant service" to the customer that the concept of "supply chain management" has caught the imagination of managements the world over. The philosophy behind this concept is simple. No matter how efficiently and effectively goods/services are produced, if they cannot be delivered to the customer in the quickest possible time, all efforts made earlier are in vain, particularly in the context of very short product life cycle, counted in months rather than years. Some of the IT products/services of recent times are reputed to have a life shorter than a case of fruits and vegetables and even fashionable clothes. As depicted in Figure 1.2, a combination of effective process plus supply chain management is what is required to cope with the challenges of the international marketplace. One cannot survive in a highly competitive market without conforming to the so called Q-C-D triangle – Highest Quality, Lowest Cost and Least Delivery times.

figure 1.2

Simplified Model for Ensuring Customer Delight

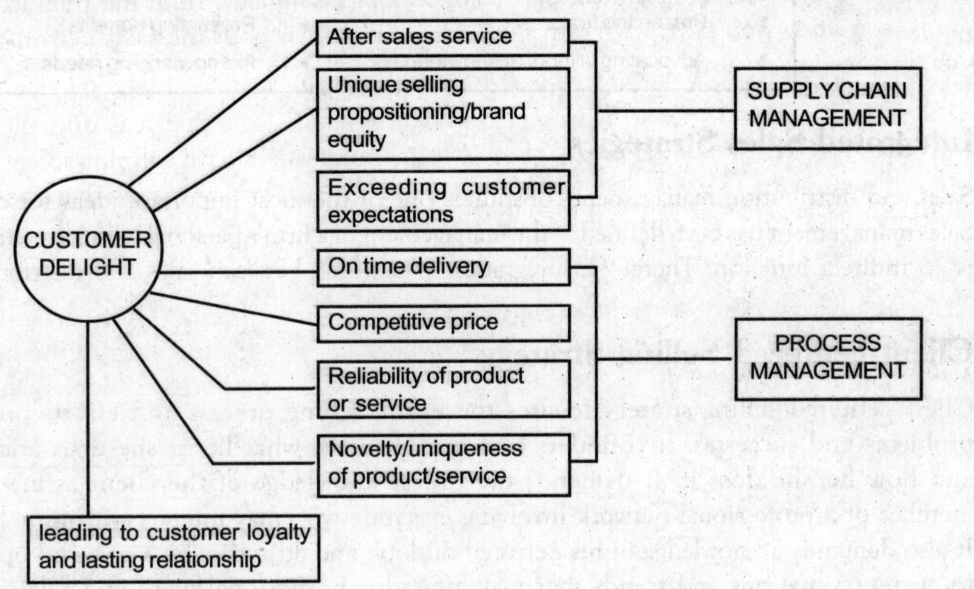

In their effort to "delight the customers", many of the companies in the developed world have adopted very creative, innovative ways of dealing with them. Not only that, they do not rest on their laurels but strive continuously to improve their service/product with a view to expanding not only their customer base but also to retain their loyalty.

Even as Indian industries prepare themselves to move into the "customer delight regime", there is a lot that they can learn from the experience of some of the most admired and efficient companies around the world. In fact, it would be worthwhile for Indian industries to benchmark their own activities with companies having similar business operations in the developed countries so that they can identify their own weak and vulnerable areas which need improvement.

Now that the permit-license *Raj* has virtually come to an end in our country and a new era is dawning upon Indian industries, the time has come to break away from the past and blaze a new trail of innovative, creative and, most importantly, ethical and transparent practices. These should be employed to achieve the goal of ensuring customer delight and for building a long-lasting customer relationship. Only then can Indian industries aspire to prosper in the next millennium.

Hard Sell Versus Soft Sell Strategy

The main purpose of a salesperson is not just to make sales but to create customers. Identifying potential customers is an important aspect of customer strategy. Every salesperson must cope with the inevitable loss of customers over a period of time, which can be attributed to a variety of causes. In identifying the customers, the salesperson can use two strategies which are explained in Figure 1.3.

figure 1.3

Strategies for Identifying Customers

Hard Sell	Soft Sell
▶ Concern for self	▶ Concern for customer
▶ Canned presentation	▶ Questions for discussion
▶ Talking	▶ Listening
▶ Pushing product	▶ Providing buying opportunities
▶ Presenting features	▶ Presenting benefits
▶ Advocating without acknowledging	▶ Acknowledging needs

Integrated Sales Strategies

Sales and distribution management constitutes one of the most important areas for customer satisfaction. Sales management has been defined as the management of a firm's personal selling function while distribution is an indirect function. Therefore, integration is required between sales and distribution functions.

Client-centered Selling Strategy

Client-centered selling strategy focuses the entire selling process and efforts on the client's needs, problems and successes. It considers who the client is, what he or she does and where, when, why and how he/she does it. It demands the fullest knowledge of the client as an individual and as a member of a professional network involving everyone who may interact with him/her in his/her work. It also demands a knowledge of his personal outlook and attitudes, his views and opinions, his reactions to current situations and trends that may affect his professional work and relationships.

Client-centered selling shifts the emphasis of the selling process away from the product and focuses, instead, on the client, whose wants and needs become the most important factor driving any selling process.

Client-centered selling is focused on the needs, interests, concerns and problems of the client rather than that of the company's or salespersons. Of course, the aim is to secure business for the products, ahead of the competitors, but this goal is achieved much more quickly and effectively by putting the client's needs first.

table 1.2 **Comparison Between Product-centered Selling and Client-centered Selling**

Product-centred Selling	Client-centred Selling
1. Seller puts in efforts for research and development of product.	1. Seller puts in efforts on research and development of relationship with clients.
2. Product centred selling emphasises knowledge of product.	2. Client centred selling emphasises knowledge of client.
3. Selling strategies and tactics tend to be most influenced by past performances of products and competition and present situations.	3. Strategies and tactics tend to be directed more to considerations of future growth and developments in the client's world.
4. Representative seeks to be accepted as a reliable, credible source of information and service.	4. Representative strives to raise client's expectations of personal excellence.

Source: *Premier Beyond 2000*, published by SB Academy.

Salespersons need to prove to clients that they are the people who can give them what they really need, whether it be information, support, service or product benefits to solve their problems. This ensures that clients are much more likely to turn to them for help in their decision making. In client-centered selling approach, the information you give, the product benefits you present or the service you are providing should be targeted and personalised to each individual client.

Example: The Aggressive Client

The first meeting with Buyer Y was scary. He was hostile and aggressive.

In this situation, the first and essential response should not be to react against the customer. This does not mean weakly submitting but keeping cool and trying to find out the reason behind the buyer's attitude. Tactful questioning and a relaxed and 'open' body posture should encourage the buyer to explain or justify his attitude. Remember that you are a professional too.

A rational and calm discussion of a complaint or objection is most effective when based on facts. Do not let your own attitude or opinions complicate the communication process.

If you can handle a hostile or aggressive customer skillfully, you will probably have converted him. His initial overreaction to you will swing in your favour in the long-term.

SELLING PROCESS

The selling process is defined as a process by which a salesperson identifies and locates the prospects, separates the prospects from the suspects approaches them and makes a sales presentation, handles their objections. He also follows up the existing customers to identify further sales leads and measures the success and customer satisfaction level of the current products and service offerings.

Selling concept refers to the exchange of goods or services for an amount of money or its equivalent in kind. Selling helps an organization achieve its organizational goals. Thus, managing sales in an organization is a critical activity. A sales manager needs to ensure that the salesman are motivated to give their best performance.

The sales team continuously look out the changes taking place in the external environment regarding competitors, customers, government policy and other regulatory agencies, advances in technology, and industry trends. This provides the sales personnel a vital information regarding trends in product sales, product development, and budgets.

By offering the management vital inputs pertaining to such information, the sales team helps the management to develop plans regarding sales, production, and design. Over the years, substantial changes have taken place in the selling environment, leading to changes in the sales function. The trends that have shaped the sales function include shorter product life cycles, longer and more complex sales cycles, reduced customer loyalty, intense competition among manufacturing firms, rising customer expectations, increasing buyer expertise, electronic revolution in communications, and the entry of woman into the sales force.

In addition to having a strong sales function, companies should also have efficient distribution channels to make the products available to the end consumer. Management of distribution channels involves efficient channel design, conflict management and implementation of sophisticated channel information systems which will enhance the process of making the products available to the end consumer in a timely manner.

Methods of Selling

Telemarketing: Selling Concepts on the Phone

What would you do to market your banking products, health, home shopping services or anything else you would like to sell? Easy. You advertise. Where? On television, radio, in the print media, hoardings and in exhibits. But how do you know if your advertisements are catching the attention of specific potential customers and not spilling over into unrelated areas? Moreover, how do you know that the customer will come back for a repeat purchase? The traditional way of benching and promoting products with a huge splash is still around. But now the economic slowdown is receding and budgets of companies are increasingly receptive to alternative direct marketing tools to sell their products. Tools are becoming more specific and comparably cheaper. Enter Telemarketing (TM), that is marketing products and services on the telephone, a direct marketing tool, which has touched a high in the last three years. The rising demand for telemarketing services has spun off a host of outfits like Direct Telephone Information Services Performance International (a joint venture by UK-based Teleperformance) and the IndusInd Media and Communications run Phone-In and several other TM companies. These companies count only multinational banks, finance companies, electronic and computer companies, also media and publishing houses, hotels for holiday resorts, airlines, telecom firms, relation firms and so on among their clients.

Apart from professional TM service outfits, many companies, including MNCs, have set up their in-house TM cells. Young energetic and self-driven people with excellent communication and persuasive skills are recruited and trained to hunt out prospective clients. Typically, a TM outfit works through a well networked team of trained telemarketers who make calls to potential clients and customers and establish direct contact with them. The key lies in convincing the customer about the value of the product or service and fixing up an appointment. The major challenge for the telemarketer is to talk to him on a one-to-one basis by telling him about the organisation, explaining the product so as to catch the interest of the customer and build a long lasting relationship for mutual profit. The back up team of field personnel then approaches the client and finalises the deal. Say, for instance, a team of telecallers of the in-house TM cell of a bank or its TM associate are put on the task of proofing banking products like car finance, hire and purchase schemes and so on. They are given a ready list of the company's client base, which comprises roughly 25 per cent of the target list. The remaining 75 per cent are cold calls in which potential customers are picked up at random from the telephone directory. Suppose the target customer is not available, then the telecaller has to interact equally effectively with the person who answers the phone so that the message is passed on to the actual person.

More than the salary, it is the added incentives that make the pay packets of telecallers lucrative. Salary usually hovers around Rs 2,500 and the added incentive of about 35 per cent for every clinched deal can net Rs 5,000 and above every month. In some cases, telemarketers are also allowed to go and meet the client personally and close the deal, which gets the executive a handsome incentive of around 65 per cent. As a field marketer, you can make an additional Rs 6,000 every month as incentives, which can take pay package to Rs 9,000. Some holiday resort chains even pay up to Rs 8,000 to Rs 12,000 a month, since the job involves a lot of concept selling and promoting timeshare holiday schemes in which telecallers have to almost educate the customer about a new idea and convince him to put in his money. Clearly, it is a profession where the go-getters walk away with the rewards. The marketing leads from the client base are equally distributed among the telecallers but it really depends upon how enterprising and motivated you are to seek out new buyers and expand the company's customer base. Telemarketing can prove to be a real test of patience and perseverance because customers can sometimes prove to be difficult, rude and argumentative. Telecallers must also process customer files and crosscheck their credentials. Computer knowledge is an added advantage. Educational qualification is a minimum 10+2 but more than that, it is fluency on the phone and selling abilities that count.

Concept selling through TM is also a favourite of the mushrooming holiday timeshare selling companies. Telecallers are also in demand for space selling, whether it is for newspapers and magazines or database information directories or any other publications. Some media houses and advertising agencies have their own space selling teams. Training for TM is usually provided on the job. The teams are handled by project managers who are responsible for setting up and managing a TM operation including manpower administration and training. TM also offers a wide entrepreneurial scope where you can set up your own outfit and provide service to the growing number of companies opting for the direct marketing route to sell their products and services.

Sales on the Internet

If your wife happens to be out of town and you do not have a clue about household management, Intercorp's new multidimensional distribution network could offer a solution.

An access to your wife's web page listing the previous month's purchases would supply all the information and an order placed through the Internet would instantly have the goods delivered at your doorstep.

After a market survey into the lifestyles of 250 people, Intercorp has identified a range of intermediate fast-moving consumer goods (FMCG's) which have been defined as products which a consumer would rather not dress up to buy. These include toothpastes, cosmetics, detergents and contraceptives. Convenience, price and assurance of quality are the prime considerations in buying these products.

"Our direct customer marketing system allows customers complete flexibility to purchase our products. Orders can be placed via the Internet, over the phone, by mail, through our catalogue or through the company personnel," says Anand Shrivastav, CEO of Intercorp.

Intercorp's marketing network seeks to eliminate the glitches that make existing distribution systems suspect.

"Network marketing is popular but we have observed that customers face problems as there is no guarantee that the salesperson is always going to be there".

"We are offering many avenues through which the customer can approach us by incorporating the latest that technology has to offer", says Anand.

"Teleshopping is limited to consumer durables, minimum purchase values are high, the telephone is the only means to place an order and the customer has to be watching TV."

However, Anand fears stiff competition from the unorganised sector.

"Home deliveries by retailers and grocers is popular among housewives. We will try to wean them away by offering an assurance of quality as well as corporate backing in case of any complaints", says Anand.

Intercorp has devised an uncomplicated system of hiring business directors.

Tenure based benefits would include home furnishing grants, child education scholarships, interest subsidy, life/medical contributions, superannuation contribution benefits, etc.

"We are going to tap housewives and single women initially on a part-time basis. The sales commission earnings are attractive and there is the added attraction of invitations to exclusive events and paid holidays, gifts and cash rewards," says Anand.

Currently there are 5,000 localities in Delhi where Intercorp business director's are operating. Their soft launch in May saw over 1,000 responses.

"Intercorp is going in for a full-scale launch from next month," says Anand. "Right now, only liquid cleaners, vegetable oils and mineral water are being offered. We are in the process of obtaining the franchise of leading multinationals, which will make a wide array of products available."

Mail Order Sales

Mail order houses are retail trading organisations engaged in the mail order business. This is also known as carrying on business through post or mail. In this method, customers do not visit the seller's business premises, nor do they make a personal examination of the goods before they are purchased. In this system, orders are received from customers by post and the goods are dispatched usually by VPP (Value Payable Parcel) or registered post.

In case of the mail order business, the selling function is performed without the intervention of the personal salesman. Therefore, it is obvious that not all types of goods are suitable for retail selling by mail.

- The goods should be known for their utility so that there is no need of convincing prospective buyers about their usefulness.
- They must fetch a sufficient price to have a wide profit margin.
- They must command wide demand.
- They must not be easily perishable.
- They should be available in large quantities throughout the year.

Goods of well-known brands are the most suitable articles for mail order business. Usually chemicals, patent medicines, footwear, jewellery, leather goods, watches, readymade clothes, fountain pens, toilet goods, books etc. are sold by mail order.

Sales through Large Scale Fixed Shop Retailers

Concentration of population in urban areas, increasing flow of manufactured goods and improved methods of organising business have led to the expansion of retail business. This expansion was effected in different ways, giving rise to different types of retail establishments, which operate on a large scale. More prominent among them are the following:

- Departmental stores
- Chain stores
- Mail order houses
- Hire purchase shops
- Super markets
- Fixed price shops
- Cooperative stores

Sales through Wholesalers and Retailers

Wholesalers perform a number of functions in the marketing of goods as listed below

- Assembling and buying
- Storing or warehousing
- Transporting
- Financing
- Risk-bearing
- Grading, packing and packaging
- Providing market information.

In the process of acting as a link between the wholesaler and the consumer, a retailer performs many functions. The more important of them are given below:

- Buying and assembling
- Warehousing or storing
- Selling
- Grading and packing
- Financing
- Supply of market information
- Advertising.

Direct Selling

Direct selling identifies the unfulfilled needs of ordinary customers. It is true that many companies believe that direct selling would work in this country. Amway, Avon, Modicare, Modi Telstra, Eureka Forbes, INDAL are a few examples of companies which are using direct selling and adding value for customer satisfaction. In this method, it only takes a minute to clinch a sale but choosing the right minute to contact the customer involves a day's work for a direct marketer. For example, 80 per cent of Eureka Forbes sales turnover came from the direct sales of vacuum cleaners, air purifiers and water purifiers. Direct marketing companies have an advantage over conventional marketers in that the relationship between the company and the customer starts building even before a sale is made. At Eureka Forbes too, the value addition continues at the follow-up stage. For example, Eureka Forbes does not make a sale beyond a radius of 60 kilometers from a service centre.

Figure 1.4 shows how to add value through direct selling. The following lessons are learned by direct marketers.

Lessons From Direct Selling

- THE STRATEGY: Eureka Forbes structures its demos according to the time at the customer's disposal.
- THE LESSON: Keep the process flexible enough to accommodate individual needs.

figure 1.4

How to Add Value Through Direct Selling

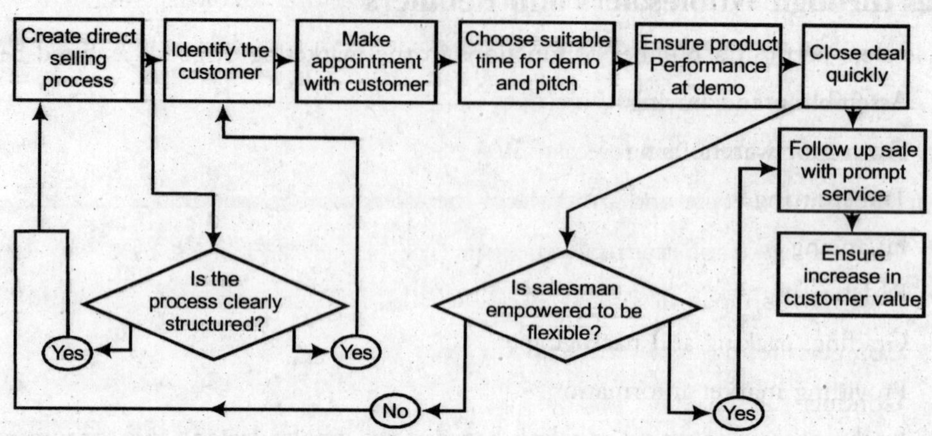

- THE STRATEGY: Modi Telstra uses a clearly structured sales call process to market its cellphone services.
- THE LESSON: Simplify the process of negotiation to save the customer's time.
- THE STRATEGY: Oriflame uses multilevel marketing to enlist direct sales agents from its customer base.
- THE LESSON: Use your customer to sell your product to other customers.
- THE STRATEGY: INDAL empowers its salesforce to take pricing decisions on the spot when closing sales.
- THE LESSON: Ensure that your direct seller can conclude a deal immediately.

Backdrop

Many producers do not sell their goods directly to consumers. They design a multi-channel system to reach final consumers. The design of marketing channel provides competitive advantage to the industry. Selection of marketing channel is the most critical ones facing by the marketing management. It is very complex by the fact that the channel system takes too much time to build. Generally Channel partners are not owned by the Industry. Sales management play a very important role in getting the best marketing channel. Integrated efforts of channel partners and sales efforts within the whole marketing effort becomes crucial in today's world.

NATIONAL SALES MANAGER

Many jobs in an organization are based on sales and the sales activity is the only activity that directly generate income, all other activities support this revenue-producing function.

Unless products and services can be profitably sold, the organization will not survive. Sales are one of the most exciting, financially rewarding and challenging of careers. It deals with human beings and their wants which are always changing. The perquisites offered for sales position are high earnings, frequent expenses-account benefits and tax write-offs for home office expenses. It is also a fastest way to reach the top of an organization. Sales managers are those persons who are paid to plan, lead and control the personal selling activities of an organization.

In carrying out these responsibilities, sales mangers do the following things:

1. Prepare sales plans and budgets
2. Set sales force goals and objectives
3. Estimate demand and forecast sales
4. Determine the size and structure of the sales force organization
5. Recruit, select and train sales people
6. Design sales territories, set sales quotas and define performance standards
7. Compensate, motivate and lead the sales force
8. Conduct sales volume, cost and profit analysis
9. Evaluate sales force performance
10. Monitor the ethical and social conduct of the sales force.

figure 1.5

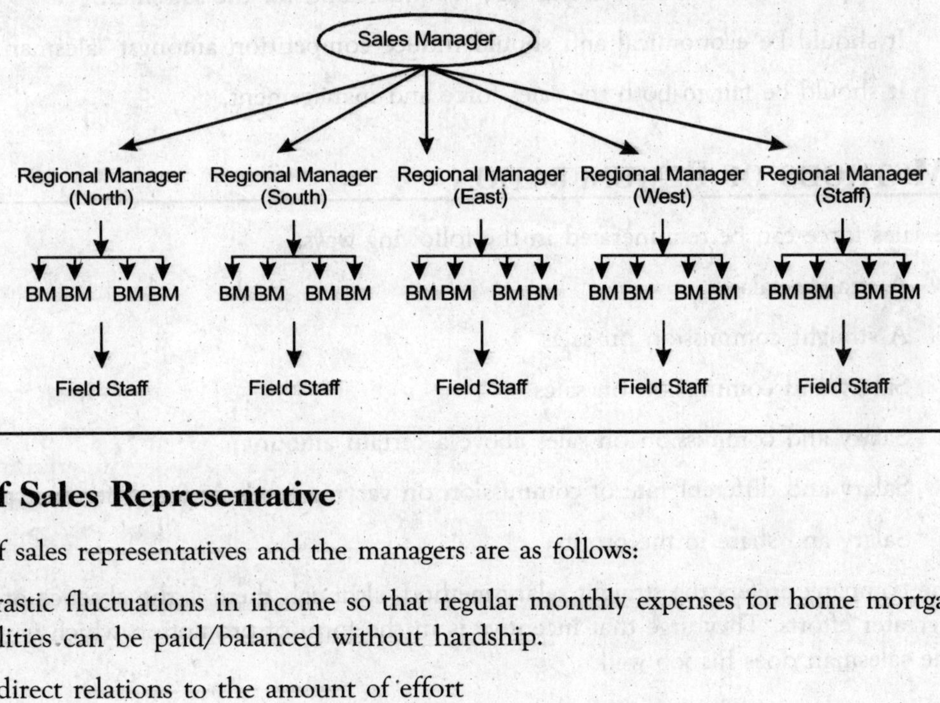

Stand Points of Sales Representative

The stand points of sales representatives and the managers are as follows:

1. To protect drastic fluctuations in income so that regular monthly expenses for home mortgage, food and utilities can be paid/balanced without hardship.
2. Expenses in direct relations to the amount of effort
3. Earnings to be equitable in terms of experience, ability, cost of living.

Sales representative should be able to calculate their own expected earnings over a given pay period to facilitate their personal financial planning.

EXPENSES ACCOUNTS AND FRINGE BENEFITS COMPENSATION

When we talk about compensation, we generally think in terms of money or financial incentives. But after reaching a certain level of income, it ceases to be an important motivator. Thus the question of psychic wages or non-financial incentives must also be considered in terms of motivating the sales force.

Organization uses two types of compensations:

1. Financial
2. Non-Financial

Financial includes compensation, salary, incentives and fringe benefits.

Non-financial includes motivation and its implications to sales management.

But monetary compensation is one of the most direct and least ambiguous ways of communicating to sales people about their performance.

REASONS FOR PROVIDING FINANCIAL COMPENSATION

The compensation plan is undoubtedly to reward the salesman for his performance. The plan includes.

1. The plan should provide a regular income at least at minimum level. In addition to this regular income, it should provide adequate incentive to induce minimum performance from the salesman.
2. The plan should be simple and easy to understand for the salesman.
3. It should be economical and should induce competition amongst salesman.
4. It should be fair to both the sales force and management.

METHODS OF REMUNERATION

The sales force can be remunerated in the following ways:

1. A straight salary
2. A straight commission on sales
3. Salary and commission on sales
4. Salary and commission on sales above a certain amount
5. Salary and different rate of commission on varying totals or for different types of goods
6. Salary and share in the profits

Some company prefers the straight salary method, although there is the absence of adequate incentive for greater efforts. They urge that incentive is in the form of promotion which would be forthcoming if the salesman does his job well.

The commission method provide incentives. However, a straight commission may not be fair to a salesman when sales decline.

Some organizations also realize that greater effort is required to keep selling more and more. Therefore they make the rates of commission vary upward according to the extra amounts sold. Sharing in the profits has so far not become popular as a method of remunerating salesman.

Compensation Plan

From the standpoint of sales representatives the compensation plan should offer:

- Income regularly

- Reward for superior performance
- Fairness

Expenses Accounts

The major sales expenses accounts are categorized as follows:

1. Salary accounts
2. Commission accounts
3. Bonuses
4. Meals and entertainment
5. Air travel
6. Automobiles rentals
7. Lodging
8. Travel accounts
9. Tour expenses accounts (Advance accounts)
10. Communication and services expenses accounts.

The expenses–accounts reimbursement policies must avoid legalistic language. Sales people should easily understand which expenses are reimbursable so that they have clear guidelines for making expenditures. These expenses accounts are generally In-house or external expenses.

1. ***Salary Expenses:*** Salaries should enable them to meet everyday living expenses which also encourages them to work more to perform tasks.

2. ***Commission and bonus expenses:*** These expenses are fixed and also easy to compute. The commission are paid only for measurable achievements for which a sales manager maintains an account. Sales person may receive commission on all orders written, accepted, shipped or paid for during a given period. It gets transferred to drawing accounts directly.

   Example: In Airlines industries, a sales manager maintains an account of how much tickets he has to sell in a day and how much commission he will get, like, if he sells 10 tickets, he will get 25% commission on that which goes to his commission. This commission can be any of nature like monetary (dollars, Rupee) or non-monetary as well.

3. ***Tours and Travel expenses account:*** This account includes the expenditures incurred due to tours and traveling:

   (a) **Lodging:** It includes the expenses done by the sales manager when he has to lodge himself in a hotel or rent a room outside the city, which is recorded in lodging expenses accounts.

   (b) **Automobile Rentals:** Car or light expenses or traveling; the separate account is maintained for the records.

   Example: (1) Taxi (2) Booking in any airlines.

   (c) **Entertainment:** This expenses account of a sales manager shows the expenses done during entraining the customer/parties.

4. ***Communication & Service Expenses accounts:*** These expenses accounts show the expenses incurred by a sales manager for the following items:

Communication: It includes:

(a) **Telephone/Telegraphic expenses account:** The expenses done for telephone calls or telegraphic messages which are sent to the concerned parties or to regular customers.

(b) **Telephone:** It can be subdivided into:

(i) Local (In-House)

(ii) STD

(iii) ISD (External)

(c) **Telegraphic:** It includes:

(i) Telegrams

(ii) Telex: It is also subdivided into Internal

- order forwarding
- order receipts

External with customer/buyer/party

(iii) Fax: Sending the message urgently to the concern parties.

- Drawing Accounts: The money paid against future commissions. It somewhat acts as a salary but is lower than a straight salary would be. It also gives a sales manager and his subordinates a fixed income.

Thus expenses accounts enables sales manager to carry out necessary selling activities. For this he has to have a well-designed expense plan having the factors such as flexibility, equitability, legitimacy, simplicity and affordability.

FRINGE BENEFITS

Types of fringe benefits are:

1. Company Car
2. Supplemental life insurance and medical insurance
3. Tax-return preparation
4. Personal tax and financial planning
5. Low or no interest loans
6. Deferred compensation
7. Supplemental retirement benefits
8. Air travel and First class A.C. for Train Travel
9. Relocation allowance
10. Stationary facilities

11. Laundry benefits, while on the tour
12. Special perquisites for outstanding performance by getting travel prizes recognition for outstanding performance
13. Medical expenses
14. Special business associations membership
15. Exclusive developmental programs by IIM, Ahmedabad, by Shiv Khera, etc.

SALES MANAGER AS COORDINATOR

The sales manager performs the function of a coordinator also. He ensures that the other departments in the company are well-informed of sales activities so that they can produce what is required, when it is required and whether the same can be produced with the existing facilities or it requires changes etc.

The sales manager also carries out coordinating work with the distribution network.

SALES MANAGEMENT AND CONTROL

Sales manager should act as per the objectives set by the organisation. He should analyse:

- present condition of the firm
- the plans for future
- ways to achieve those plans.

Sales manager's job is to exercise control over his staff so that on the one hand they may look for advice and on the other hand, they may give their best efforts and bring results.

GENERATING PROFITS

It is the responsibility of the sales department that the products of the company are sold at the best available prices in the given circumstances. While on the one hand the salesperson has to produce volume sales as per targets, on the other hand he has to sell the product at a price which may generate profit for the company. After all it is positive financial results that add position and power to the sales manager and bring credit to the sales department.

SUMMARY

In this chapter we discussed the nature, scope and importance of sales management. Sales department is vital for any organization because it converts the products into cash. The importance of marketing concept can be explained with the help of its integration with marketing concept. Organizing and managing a sales force is an essential part of any organization. Sales forces are continuously assigned to particular geographical area. The sales manager is vital for sales organization. The function of sales management includes the task of organizing, planning and implementing the sales efforts to achieve the organizational objectives.

The success of sales depends upon a good sales department headed by a competent, efficient and result oriented sales manager, who devotes his energies to fulfilling the targets with the help of other persons working in his department. It is a team work but the responsibility lies on the sales manager.

Sales Management is generally referred to as the backbone of marketing. It is overall management of selling activities and it refers to only as specialised application of the process of management as a whole. The ultimate objective of sales management is to influence the consumers of the target market to get sales orders. Sales force is regularly assigned particular territories. Various factors are taken into account in deciding on the physical links within territory, purchasing power of consumer and their educational and living standards.

The sales manager is the most important person in a sales organisation. All activities are based on his functions and responsibilities.

PROJECT WORK

1. Study the direct selling method used by M/s Eureka Forbes. What is the size of the sales force in this organisation? Discuss the strategy adopted by this organisation.
2. Study one concern from each of the following areas and their respective wholesalers and retailers. What are the strategies adopted by them?
   i. Book publishing
   ii. Car retail showroom
   iii. Food products
   iv. Furniture
3. You are the sales executive of Star TV and you sell TV connections which provide four channels for different programmes. You are required to answer the following questions:
   a. Who are your major competitors?
   b. What are your strengths and weaknesses?
   c. How do you contact the households?
   d What will be your sales strategy?

SHORT QUESTIONS

1. What do you mean by personal selling?
2. What is the importance of personal selling?
3. How is personal selling different from advertising?
4. What are the various techniques of motivating the sales force?
5. What are the basic principles of designing the training programme for sales force?
6. What do you mean by sales force?
7. Write different steps in designing and managing a sales force.
8. What is relationship strategy?
9. What is the role of national sales manager?

REVIEW QUESTIONS

1. What does the term 'relationship selling' imply and why has it become such an important concept?
2. What role does sales management play in the marketing function?

3. What is the difference between personal selling and sales management?
4. What is sales management? What are the various functions of sales management?
5. What are the various sales strategies and methods? Explain with suitable examples.
6. Explain sales manager's duties and responsibilities.
7. Explain different types of Relationship strategy.
8. Discuss different methods of selling.
9. Explain different methods of remuneration.

GO TO THE NET

- Using Internet search tools and other relevant resources, search information about the functions of sales manager, sales strategies and methods and prepare a brief report highlighting the above information.
- Using Internet search tools and other relevant resources, make a list of 20 companies involved in selling FMCG through the Internet. Bring out the strategies used by them.
- Using Internet search tools and other relevant resources, prepare a comparative analysis of the sales organization of top 5 automobile industries.

Caselet 1

Cool Heads

Cool Heads was established in 1985 to manufacture, distribute and market pharmaceutical soft drinks. It was purely an Indian company and had to face tough competition from multinational companies during the initial years. The company, in the last decade with the help of effective market strategies, has set up a place for itself, amongst the leading pharmaceutical companies in the country.

In 1995, the managing director of the company stressed the need for diversification and addition of new products to its existing product range. He floated the idea of manufacturing and marketing coffee with milk, coca and sugar. His advisers suggested that such products, enriched with cocoa, would be desirable and should be a big success, specially in view of its competitors brand. Marketing research department of the company also gave the green signal to the project after conducting a brief survey.

The company promoted its coffee with Choco-coffee brand name. It was supplied in a 400 gm. packet at the price of Rs 74. The product was heavily advertised in newspapers, health magazines, radio and television. The target audience was middle class who it was believed could afford 'Choco-coffee'. The ordinary coffee was available in the market at the rate of Rs 30 to Rs 40 per kg. The thrust of choco-coffee in the promotion campaign was that this coffee contains cocoa, milk and sugar.

The company has 50 stockists covering the entire country with a sales force of about 150 representatives, for promoting its products, through supermarkets and shops. The representatives of the company had a very good rapport with supermarkets and shops. To promote the coffee, its representatives gave discount coupons to the stockists for passing on to their customers for buying their coffee. The buyer was entitled to Rs 5/- discount per packet of 400 grams. The scheme continued for about six months.

Despite heavy advertisement and canvassing by its representatives, the product was unable to attract customers. It was observed that launching of this product did not affect the market position of other branded coffee at all which was being sold at Rs 90/- for a pack of 275 grams. Rather, it was observed that the sales of the other brands of coffee increased marginally consequent to the advertisement campaign by Cool Heads. The company could achieve only 25% of its sales target in the first year and it remained almost static for the next year.

Questions

1. What do you think are the reasons for the failure of the company to achieve its target?
2. Suggest a sales promotion plan for increasing the sales volume of the company.
3. Can a change in the distribution channel bring improvement in the sale of the product?

Caselet 2

NIRMA GETS LICENCE TO MAKE CAMAY SOAP

FMCG major Nirma is taking on arch-rival, HLL, in the premium soaps segment through an exclusive agreement to produce and market the Camay soap brand, which is owned by Procter & Gamble Home Products.

Nirma Consumer Care, a 100% subsidiary of Ahmedabad based Nirma, has secured a licence from P&G for using the Camay trademark for an undisclosed fee . The arrangement is valid for a rolling period of five years and covers toilet soaps.

Nirma will manufacture and market the brand and P&G will be paid a licence fee as per the agreement. Nirma, which is not present in the premium skin care soaps segment, will now have an international brand with a decent brand equity to take on Lever.

Camay is one of P&G's oldest brands and was launched in India nearly a decade ago. The brand was first promoted by Godrej Soaps (now called Godrej Consumer Care) which was P&G's first alliance partner in the country.

The Company later turned to haircare major, Marico Industries, for help when the Godrej alliance fell apart. But Marico, whose other main product was edible oil, merely marketed the brand even though it did not fit into the company's main scheme of things.

For P&G, its focus in India includes areas such as feminine care, health care, hair & fabric care in line with a global realignment, and away from soaps and beauty products.

Nirma, by contrast, is already a major player in the Rs 4,500 crore soaps market and has notched up a share of about 10% of the market share despite stiff competition from HLL.

Questions

1. What are the reasons for P&G to permit Nirma to produce and market Camay soap?
2. Who will benefit more from this agreement?

[illegible]

[illegible]

[illegible]

[illegible]

[illegible]

[illegible]

[illegible]

Questions

1. [illegible]

2. [illegible]

CHAPTER 2

personal selling

learning objectives

The objectives of this chapter are to:

- understand the changing face of personal selling
- understand the use of product price, promotion and distribution that the company uses to achieve its marketing objectives
- analyse the steps involved in personal selling
- role and responsibility of personal selling
- objectives, function and importance of personal selling
- analyse the process of personal selling
- understand the different theories of personal selling.

content outline

opening case

Suzuki may use Idle MUL Line for Scooters

Suzuki is considering using Maruti Udyog's Gurgaon facility for its proposed two-wheeler venture in India by converting one of the idle car lines into a two-wheeler line. MUL may then lease out the facility or sell it to Suzuki Motor. MUL has a total of three car manufacturing lines at its Gurgaon facility. However, a recent reorganisation resulted in one of the lines becoming idle. According to sources, Suzuki has already started the trial run for the production of scooters on this idle line.

However, when contacted, the Maruti spokesperson denied any such move by its Japanese parent, though he added, "there is now no difference between Suzuki and MUL as far as major strategic decisions are concerned." According to industry observers, though, Suzuki has the option to invest in a brand new facility to manufacture two-wheelers, it makes commercial sense for the Japanese major to leverage its majority holding in MUL.

"It would save Suzuki a lot of money and time if it piggybacks its two-wheelers venture on Maruti's extensive infrastructure," says a senior officer of a domestic two-wheeler company. The two-wheelers which are to be sold under Suzuki brand would be launched in the domestic market only after March 2004 as specified in its separation agreement with the TVS group. Suzuki has been permitted to re-enter the two-and three-wheeler market.

TRY YOURSELF

1. Do you think it will be possible to sell Suzuki two wheelers when there is stiff competition from other established brands?
2. Justify the action of the leading car unit to go for diversification.

INTRODUCTION

The importance of personal selling cannot be overemphasised. In pursuance of a prudent policy, an organisation can derive maximum benefit by giving personal selling the importance that it rightly deserves. It can help boost sales if wisely used and bring in a human touch when carrying out a transaction. Despite the beginning of e-commerce, personal selling is here to stay and continues to have a bright future. It is not just confined to promoting sales but also to personal service.

Some important aspects of personal selling are:

1. It enhances customer's confidence in the seller.
2. It promotes long-term business relations through personal intimacy.
3. It provides a human touch to business transactions.
4. It helps facilitate the seller to understand each customer's needs and preferences more clearly.
5. It helps satisfy a customer by modifying the product as per the customer's choice and preference.
6. Personal selling followed by personal service helps build long-term relations between the business and the customer.
7. It helps keep up with the competition in the market, based on product customisation as per customer's preferences.
8. It is a powerful and effective tool for convincing the customer about the product.
9. Through personal selling the time lag between introducing a product through the media and actually selling it is reduced.
10. It provides prospective customers with a better understanding of the product and an interactive opportunity to liaise with the sales personnel.

According to American Marketing Association, "Personal selling is oral presentation in a conversation with one or more prospective purchasers for the purpose of making sales".

OBJECTIVES OF PERSONAL SELLING

Personal selling objectives may be of short-term and long-term duration. Short-term personal selling objectives are more specific and of short-term duration. These objectives change very frequently as soon as there is change in production mix. Further, they are usually quantitative objectives. On the contrary, long-term personal selling objectives are broad and general. There is very little scope of change in long-term objectives. They are usually quantitative objectives.

FUNCTIONS OF PERSONAL SELLING

Personal selling is an oral presentation in face to face conversation with one or more prospective customers for the purpose of making sales. The main functions of personal selling are as follows:

1. ***Provide service to customers:*** The function of personal selling is to render services to customers, such as to introduce the product. Products explain the right use of the product by means of demonstration, convince the customers about the quality of the product, remove doubts of the customer etc.

2. ***To sell the product:*** The foremost function of personal selling is to make sales both to customers as well as consumers.
3. ***Maintain the sales record:*** Another function of personal selling is to maintain the record.
4. ***Executive Function:*** Personal selling also performs a number of executive functions, such as to provide training to salesman, to prepare short-term and long-term selling programs, to provide the information to the sales management about market trends etc.
5. ***Develop goodwill:*** Personal selling develop goodwill of the company in the competitive market.
6. ***Achieve sales target:*** Another function of personal selling is to achieve sales target by increasing profit through sales volume.

Personal selling followed by personal service helps to build long-term relations between the business and the customer. The salespeople, in personal selling, go far beyond realizing sales volume. Personal selling calls for an integrated approach devised from the experience of sales personnel. The salesman generally finds it very difficult to approach his prospect since the prospect are generally a busy lot. Sales people make special efforts to follow up with consumers to ensure that they are satisfied by or not.

CHANGING FACE OF PERSONAL SELLING

In today's competitive markets, a personal seller's role is not just confined to persuading prospective customers to buy products, it's scope has widened and corporations have begun to explore the efficacy of personal selling beyond the erstwhile sole objective of promoting sales. In view of the above, the modern sales approach is based on the following parameters

1. ***Value Sharing:*** The salespeople share the same values as their customers and perceive the customer's needs with the sole view to serve them better. This helps salespeople study the changing needs and preferences of their customers.
2. ***Relation Building:*** A value-based relationship helps the salespeople to constantly mobilise resources and modify the end product by catering to the specifics of the buyer. This culminates in building long-term relationships.
3. ***Role Playing:*** The salespeople, in personal selling, go far beyond realising sales volume. They act as consultants to their prospective customers constantly advising them of new products, their updates and impart knowledge to them with respect to product adaptation, training, installation, trouble shooting, etc.
4. ***Changing Approach:*** With a view to providing total customer satisfaction, a coordinated approach of salespeople with their colleagues, who are often the specialists in their own areas, is emphatically recognised. As a result, personal selling comes in a package containing the inputs of the experts from different areas such as maintenance, installation, trouble shooting, delivery staff, sales personnel, etc.

Benefits of Personal Selling

1. Availability of expertise
2. Early access to relevant market information

3. Availability to be flexible regarding processes, timing
4. Faster, shorter contracts
5. Economies of information sharing
6. Lower cost of selling
7. Knowledge of other uses or applications

EFFICACY OF PERSONAL SELLING

Product, price, promotion and distribution are the focal strategies that a company uses to achieve its marketing objectives. These factors are also known as the elements of marketing mix. In view of the fact that markets are growing increasingly competitive each passing day, experts are not only advocating a sensible mix of these factors but also propagating the efficacy of a personal touch to these factors. We will now elucidate the efficacy of personal selling in implementing selling strategies under different heads.

Personal Selling with Respect to Product Strategy

Since salespeople are in direct liaison with prospective customers, their input is valuable during product development. Their inputs help design the product based on customer preferences and needs. Products are changing very fast. Old products are being replaced. New products are tried. Some new products achieve acceptance from the customer, while some are forgotten and result in total loss to the manufacturer.

Personal Selling and Pricing Decisions

Sales personnel undergo requisite interaction with prospective customers to gauge their mood with respect to different price levels. Hence, their inputs are considered useful in formulating pricing strategies. The sales personnel are also well aware of the competitors' price and, based on the market reaction and customers' sentiments, they can advise a more prudent price policy to the management.

Personal Selling and Distribution

Whether the channel of distribution is direct or indirect, the sales force has a significant role to play. The end result of any distribution effort is the ready availability of the product to the customer, in the right quantity and at the right place. If the product is not available when it is actually required by the customer, then the whole business activity and all related efforts are rendered useless. In view of this, the sales force plays an important role in coordinating, liaisoning and advocating the product's utility to the end user.

Personal Selling and Product Promotion

The salesforce actually stimulates and generates enough interest in the customer and helps him make the final decision to buy the product. Sharing the same values that the customer does, a salesperson provides motivation and generates interest and confidence in the customer for the product. Without this effort the whole exercise of advertising and public relations would be futile. Advertising and public relations actually support the efforts of the sales force. And thus personal selling promotes a product.

Steps in Personal Selling

Successful personal selling calls for an integrated approach devised from the experience of the sales personnel. The approach comprises the steps as shown in the figure 2.1 here. Each of these steps are further described in brief.

figure 2.1
Steps in Personal Selling

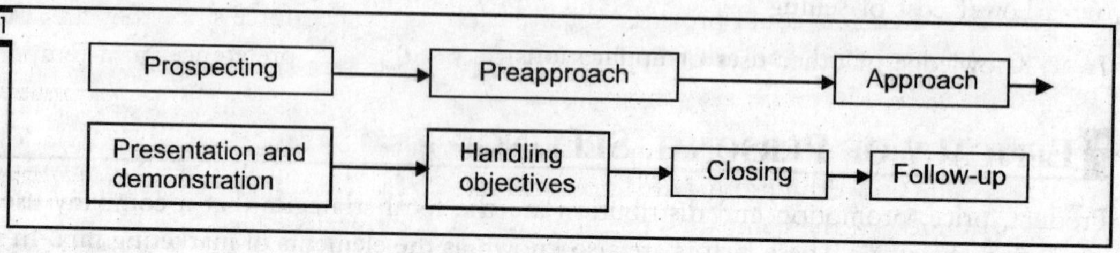

Prospecting

Prospecting is the process of identifying prospective buyers of the product. The prospects are those who have a need or will to buy and the power to pay. Prospects may be individuals or institutions. Hence, identifying the prospects and discovering newer customer needs and preferences is a part of prospecting. A prospect is qualified if he has the authority, need, ability and eligibility to buy.

There are different ways to identify prospects. Some of the most frequently used methods are described below:

- ***Acquaintance References:*** A satisfied customer can be a good source of information about the names, addresses and phone numbers of prospects who may be among his acquaintances, relatives or family members. In addition, the sales personnel can give the reference of a satisfied customer to motivate a prospect to buy, thus obtaining further references.
- ***Cold Calling:*** This method of prospecting identifies the customer segment to whom the sales personnel might call upon without any reference but with an anticipation of converting the call into a sale. This method is also called 'random prospecting'.
- ***Centre of Influence Method:*** Using this approach, the salesmen obtain the references for prospects from the eminent people of society. Using such references, the prospects are influenced to make a buying decision since the recommendations of eminent personalities such as politicians, actors, poets etc. are taken seriously.
- ***Personal Observation Method:*** A salesman has ample opportunity to identify prospects on several occasions such as interacting with friends and acquaintances, attending seminars, social gatherings, functions, travelling, etc. If the salesman is observant and vigilant, he can definitely find prospects and thus convert leads into sales.
- ***Direct Mail or Telephone Method:*** A salesman can contact prospective buyers on the telephone and inform them about the product range, plus the benefits and price of the products available. The salesman can also send mail/letters to old customers informing them about the modifications made in the existing range. For this method to be successful, the prospect must be educated in order to understand the contents of the letter. Secondly, the letter must contain a reply card to facilitate the prospects response or else the responses will be limited. Another source of identifying prospects is through the telephone directory and the prospective clients may then be contacted.

- ***Company's Records:*** The salesman can refer to the company's records and get in touch with several old and new contacts. Besides, there are chances of reviving many old lost contacts and thus sales may be promoted.
- ***Newspapers:*** There are several people who advertise their requirements through newspapers.
- ***Retailers:*** Retailers could provide valuable leads to the salesforce since they are in direct contact with the customers and are familiar with the taste, needs, preferences and temperament of the prospects.
- ***Other Methods:*** Among other methods could probably be leads given by the junior sales force. Trade fairs and exhibitions could be another source of finding prospects since the people who show interest in the company's products may be those leads which may be converted into sale at a later date.

Each of the methods described above has a different compatibility depending on the nature of the product and the kind of prospects who are likely to turn into customers.

Joe Girard, popular sales trainer, used the "Ferris Wheel" concept for prospecting. This is shown in Figure 2.1.

Pre-approach

Pre-approach is the second step in the selling process which emphasises that the salesman should know, after identifying the prospect in the prospecting stage, the prospect's likes and dislikes, his needs, preferences, habits, nature, behaviour, economic and social status etc. Based on all this information, the salesman has the necessary tools to plan his visit/interview with the prospect and can give an effective sales presentation. This kind of preparation to meet the prospect is called the pre-approach.

Significance of Pre-Approach

The following factors describe the importance of the pre-approach method:

1. It is a method by which a salesman concentrates only on the prospects and not the suspects, thus saving his time and energy.
2. It helps a salesman gain all the possible information about the prospect before approaching him. Hence any kind of loose talk or serious mistake can be avoided during the sales talk.
3. Because of the pre-approach method, the salesman gains ample knowledge about the prospect before approaching him. Hence, he is able to give a sales presentation more efficiently, effectively and with confidence.
4. It does not waste the prospect's time and energy since the salesman is already aware of the needs and preferences of the prospect. As a result the sales presentation is focussed around the needs of the prospect and is short, meaningful and to the point.

figure 2.2

The "Ferris Wheel" concept, which is aimed at supplying an ongoing list of prospects,

is part of world sales record holder Joe Girard's customer strategy

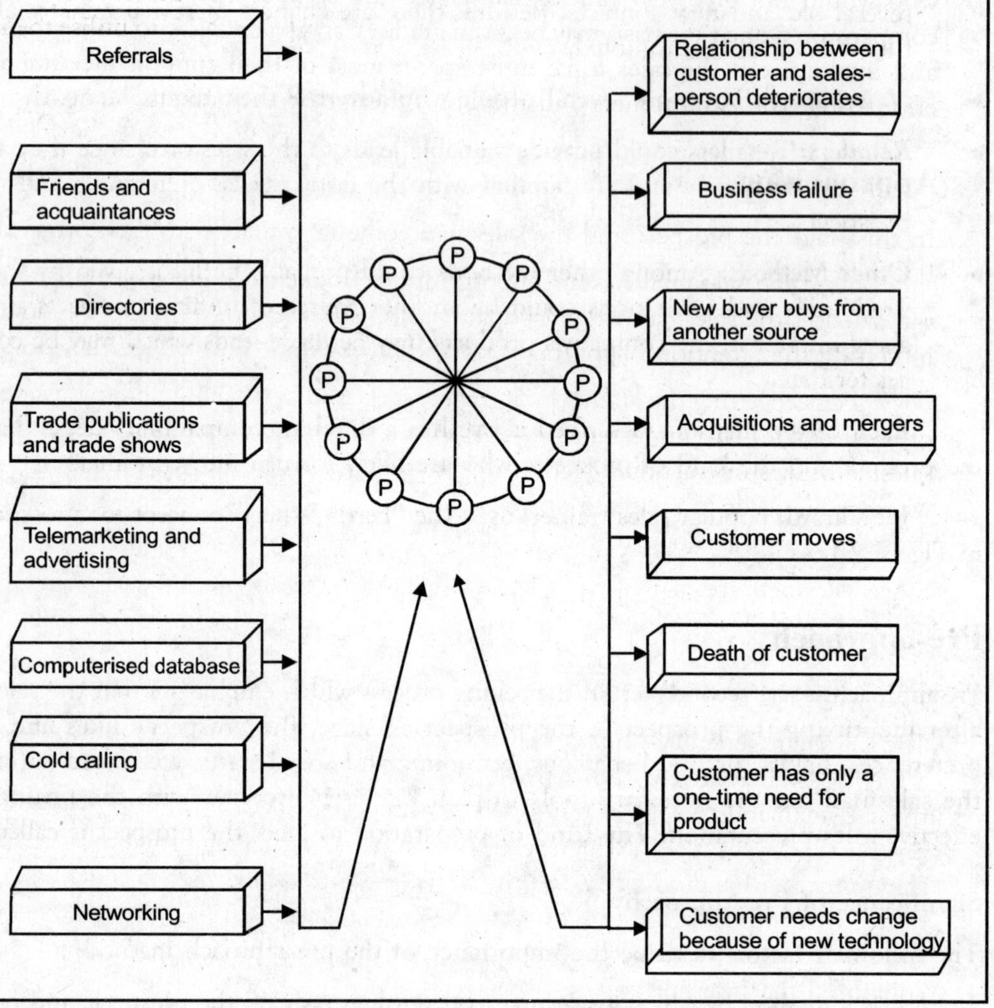

Usage of Prospecting Time

Quality usage of prospecting time means that the salesforce must plan its time in such a manner that maximum time is made available for those prospects who are likely to give a large volume of business to the company. It follows that the least time must be spent on activities that are required to support such objectives and devoting more time on significant prospects.

Experience says that more time than is desirable is spent by the salesforce in areas other than time spent with the most prospective clients. For instance, productive time which could otherwise be spent in meeting prospective clients is spent by the sales force in travelling, organising the documentation, completing paper work and attending meetings. With value time being spent in non-selling activities, the result is that, on an average, a salesman spends only $\frac{1}{3}^{rd}$ of his usage time in meeting prospects.

To avoid this wastage of time, the sales force has to be more organised. In this direction, what is known as the grading of the prospects will be an important step. Under such a system, each prospect may be allotted a specific grade based on the amount of business he is likely to give the company. For instance, the most important prospects are those who are likely to give a large volume of business to the company. Hence, such a segment should be categorised as grade A; on the same lines, those customers who would not give very much business to the company or those who are likely to deal with the company on a one time basis may be given grade B, and so on. Now to utilise their time more productively and qualitatively, the sales force must spend most of their time in meeting and concentrating their efforts on grade A customers and then on other graded customers.

Approaching

In this stage the prospect and the salesman come in contact with each other face to face.

Here the salesman has an opportunity to understand and interact with the prospect in a better way. Hence, the salesman should put forward his best efforts to make the best use of this opportunity in getting the attention of the prospect and to convince him to buy the product.

Hence, getting the attention of the prospect and persuading him to buy are the two main objectives of a salesman. The importance of the approach cannot be overemphasised since it is only after the salesman starts interacting directly with the prospect that the latter decides within the first few minutes whether he needs to purchase or not. Similarly, the salesman has the opportunity to judge whether the prospect is in the mood to buy or not.

Since salesmen are of two types, viz, the travelling salesmen and the counter salesmen, the approach adopted by each of these salesmen is obviously different.

1. Approach Adopted by Travelling Salesmen

The salesman generally finds it very difficult to approach his prospect since the prospects are generally a busy lot. Alternatively, they may not be interested in buying the product. Despite this major hurdle, the salesman must keep on trying to obtain an interview with the prospect. On gaining access to the prospect, however, the salesman must first impress and convince the prospect about the true value and the utility that his product offers. But if the prospect happens to be a high ranking executive or a senior officer then probably the task of the salesman becomes more difficult. He might first have to convince the subordinates of the prospect about the utility that his product offers. Once the subordinates are convinced that the salesperson is genuinely sincere, it is only then that the salesman can get access to the prospect. Hence, the salesman must be a little diplomatic and polite and convince the subordinates of his product.

There are different ways to gain access and thus interview the prospect:

- A salesman may directly approach the prospect without any introduction whatsoever and then conduct an interview. Suppose that even after introducing himself and making known the purpose of his visit, the company he represents and nature of it's business etc., the salesman is not able to arouse the prospect's interest. The salesman can then state the benefits his product has to offer which may awake interest of the prospect in the product.

- Another manner in which a salesman can seek an appointment with a prospect could be by sending an advance mailer explaining his product and its benefits vis-a-vis other products available in the market. Such mailers should be designed and written in a simple but attractive manner so as to arouse the interest of the prospect. In such instances, the salesman must be punctual or else he might lose the opportunity. This is especially true with busy executives who might not be interested in rescheduling the appointment, if the salesman does not reach in time.

- There is no better method of securing an appointment with a prospect than through a reference given by the friend, relative or business associate of the prospect. This not only facilitates an interview but also makes the task of selling the product to the prospect easier for the salesman. If the salesman already knows the prospect he may even write a letter requesting for an interview. Alternatively, if the prospect can spare some time, the salesman can even request for a tele interview.

- Another effective way of securing an appointment and interview with the prospect is for salesmen to give away gifts to the prospects before asking for an appointment. Such gifts may include diaries, calendars, pens, pen stands, key rings, etc. These gifts are also described as door openers since they open the doors of the prospect for the salesmen.
- Sale letters have proved to be another kind of door opener. Such letters provide ample detail about the product, benefits and schemes available with the product. These letters are different from letters of introduction since the latter describe the salesman who would be calling upon the prospect while a sale letter describes the product in general. When these sale letters are signed by senior executives and sent in advance, the salesmen find little or no resistance when they call upon the prospect.

2. **Successful Approach**

An approach can be described as successful only if it attains the twin objective of convincing the prospect about the product and a sale follows.

The following points specify the importance of a successful approach:

i. A successful approach enhances the sale and it is thus important for the running of a business.

ii. A failed approach will give an opportunity to the rival company. So a good approach will go a long way in building good relations with the prospect while a bad approach will not only result in losing business but will also make it easy for a competitor to tap new customers.

iii. The approach helps in enlightening the prospect by providing him ample information about the product, price, competitor's product, benefits etc. that he can derive from the product.

For an approach to be successful, given below are some key guidelines:

- ***Prior Appointment:*** It is best to meet the prospect with a prior appointment rather than paying him a surprise visit. No one likes to receive strangers. When an appointment is fixed, punctuality must be maintained. The salesman must never waste the prospect's time in giving unnecessary details but should straight away come to the point and keep the conversation brief and to the point.
- ***Timing:*** It is also vital to remember that the timing of an appointment is of great importance. An intelligent salesman tries to meet his prospect during slack hours rather than busy hours, or odd hours, such as late at night or too early in the morning. Similarly, when selling heaters, one must approach a prospect just when winter season has started rather than during summer, by the end of the month salaried individuals have generally exhausted their salaries, institutional or corporate prospects prefer not to make purchases during the close of the year since they are tight on funds and are generally busy closing the year, so that is not a good time to approach the prospects. The festival season is a good time to sell to individuals and to corporates. Hence, the timing of the appointment is of great significance.
- ***Command:*** Confidence, professionalism and complete command over the information about the product are some areas where the salesman can create an impression on the prospect. A formal business attire and a good dress sense certainly appeals to any person including the prospect.

It is, however, advisable that the salesman be cautious enough to keep the product in the forefront rather than his personality. Otherwise chances are that the prospect will remember the salesman more than his product. So a sensible balance has to be struck between the impact that he creates through his personality and the product that he is interested in selling to his prospect.

- ***Relaxed Atmosphere:*** It is very important for the salesman to make his prospect feel relaxed. The salesman should never give an impression that he desires to sell the product at that very moment or on the same day. Rather, he should convince the prospect that he would just give a sales presentation leaving the prospect with ample time to make his own decision about the purchase. The salesman should make him feel relaxed and not burdened. At the same time, the salesman should make the prospect feel important. After all it is the prospect who has to make a decision to buy.
- ***Open Mindedness:*** The salesman should respect the views of the prospect and should be open-minded to criticism of the product from the prospect. However, the salesman should not get dejected about the prospect's opinion of his product. Rather, he should accept the prospect's views and continue to stress and highlight the best points about his product. Such a positive attitude makes a sale possible, if not immediately, then in the future.

  So the salesman should not give in soon but be optimistic and keep on trying to influence the prospect to change his mind in the future.
- ***Courtesies:*** It is wrong on the part of some salesmen to apologise for taking up the time of the prospect. This makes the prospect subconsciously feel that his time is being wasted and the sales presentation is going to end in frustration for himself.

  As a result, the prospect becomes doubtful about the salesman and his attention is diverted to the idea of getting rid of the salesman as soon as possible. The salesman, therefore, must make the prospect believe that he has come to sell him a good product and he is not wasting his time.
- ***Effective Presentation:*** The salesman should give an effective presentation using sales figures, showing him videos or pictures of the product, giving a free sample of the product and a live demonstration of the product if possible, etc. to draw attention to the product or else the prospect shall busy himself in other jobs while listening to the salesman. Hence the salesman should draw the attention of his prospect so that he listens and not just hears the sales talk.
- ***Follow up:*** Despite a good sales presentation, the first meeting may not result in a sale for several reasons. Hence, an efficient follow-up will definitely lead to a positive response. The salesman must follow up and renew his prospect's interest in his product after a reasonable interval of time.

3. Methods of Approach

There are different methods of approaching a prospect and some of the most important ones are given below. No one method can be described as the best, since different methods are suitable for different prospects. It is, however, possible to start the approach with one method and end it with another.

- ***Cashing in on Brand Name or the Company's Reputation:*** This is the commonest of all the methods. The salesman here uses the influence of the brand name of his product or the reputation of his company to attract the attention of his prospect. In this method the prospect introduces himself as belonging to a reputed company and selling a reputed brand's product thus generating the prospect's curiosity. This method, however, is not suitable for lesser known firms or brands.

- ***Customer Benefit Approach:*** In this approach the salesman arouses his prospect's interest by making the prospect realise that buying the product will definitely benefit him. The salesman highlights those aspects about his product which would benefit the prospect. Statements such as "Would you like to cut down your telephone bills by 40%" or "Would you like to increase your productivity by 20%" or "Would you be interested in a free vacation every two years" etc. will definitely arouse the curiosity of the prospect and develop an interest in learning more about the product.
- ***Innovative Product Opens the Door to the Salesman:*** Under this approach the salesman hands over the product to the prospect so that the prospect satisfies himself by having a first hand knowledge and complete information about the product. Under this approach, the product examined must be new in the market, better designed, unique, attractive and appealing to the customer.
- ***The Premium Approach:*** Under this approach, salesmen generally give away small gifts or novelties to the prospect to draw attention to them and the product. This method is generally popular with housewives.
- ***The Shock Approach:*** Under this method, the salesman highlights rising crime rates, uncertainties, risks of old age etc. which forces the prospects into thinking about such factors. Generally, under shock and feeling insecure, they make a decision to buy. This method is useful for products such as life insurance, safety and security equipment and devices, health and fitness products, etc. This method is more popular for prospects in the middle or higher age groups.
- ***The Approach of 'Making the Prospect Feel Important':*** The salesman should always remember that it is the prospect who has to make the buying decision. Hence, he should make them feel important and pamper their egos.
- ***The Survey Approach:*** Before approaching a prospect, the salesman must survey the needs and preferences of the prospect so as to give an effective presentation. This will help the salesman focus on the exact needs of the prospect and ensure that the presentation is to the point and useful to the prospect.
- ***Interactive Approach:*** Under this approach, the salesman asks the prospect some questions and in this way interacts with him. The questions should be specific, appropriate and match the requirements of the prospect. This approach may also be combined with other approaches such as the Customer Benefit Approach and should arouse the prospect's curiosity.

The approach that a salesman resorts to will depend upon the product that he has to offer and the type of prospect. So, before the salesman thinks about the kind of approach to use, he must first be sure about the need of his prospect. He should also verify the desirability of the approach that he plans to use.

Presentation and Demonstration

A good presentation is as important as a good product. The significance of a good presentation of the product can be gauged from the fact that many a time an attractively packed presentation is sufficient to sell the product. A good presentation can be in the form of attractive packaging and display, conspicuous placement of the product in the display window, etc. A good presentation also includes the interior decoration of the shop and appearance of the article.

On several occasions a customer goes to a shop or a departmental store to buy a certain product but is attracted towards another product which is attractively displayed and packaged. This influences him to such an extent that he suddenly feels the need to buy that product and makes the purchase.

Essentially, a good presentation should fulfil the following requirements:

1. If the product is stored at a conspicuous location within the store or the shop, the salesman can promptly present it to the prospect. This quick presentation creates a good impression in the mind of the customer as he feels that he is being dealt with promptly and this satisfies his feeling of self-importance.

2. Attractively packaged, decorated and well-organised articles create a good impression in the mind of the prospect. Packaging sells more than the product. No doubt the product sells on its merits but the packaging plays a major role in enhancing the acceptability of the product.

3. The salesman should explain the product with its features and price advantage to the customer in simple and easy terms. The salesman must have a thorough knowledge about his product and also other competitive products available in the market. A well informed salesman would be able to satisfy all queries of the customer and answer them satisfactorily. The presentation can also be given through models, slides, pictures and videos if the product is voluminous. But, if possible, the customer should be given the opportunity to have a first hand feel of the product so that he can touch, handle, fondle, smell, taste and judge the product with his own perceptions and reach a conclusion. This will enhance the confidence of the customer in the product, facilitating his decision in making the purchase.

   An intelligent salesman should never compare his product with rival products. But if he is asked to talk about the competition, he should then highlight the best points of his product and emphasise the weak points of the rival. In no circumstances, however, should he criticise or condemn the rival products as this will leave a wrong impression in the mind of the customer.

4. It is very important that the customer be shown the kind of quality that he is looking for. Too many varieties will only confuse the customer, while too little does not help him make a choice. By showing the kind of quality demanded by the customer not only is time saved but also the customer tends to make a quick buying decision. When it is apparent that the customer has made up his mind on what he wants to buy, the salesman should remove the other product varieties from the customer's view. Also any further discussion on the product should be stopped. This may confuse the customer and the sale may not take place.

5. Demonstrating a product helps create a positive impression in the mind of the customer and increases his interest. This helps the salesman to prove the features of the product and emphasise its genuineness. Thus a demonstration of the product to the customer enhances his confidence in making a buying decision.

6. If the salesman is able to make the product appeal to the customer's senses then half the battle is won. When a product appeals to the senses of a prospect, he will make a subconscious decision to own that product; hence, the salesman's efforts should be to make it appeal to the prospect. Also, if the salesman is able to test the product successfully in front of the prospect then the buying decision is further reinforced in the customer's mind. During this exercise, the salesman can also make the customer handle the product, so that the prospect can have first hand information about how the product works, its characteristics and whether the product meets his expectations. This will further reinforce the prospect's desire to own the product.

Demonstration

Demonstration is an exercise to prove the characteristics of the product. It highlights various attributes of the product such as utility, performance, service and quality. During a sales presentation, the salesman describes the product to the prospect but it is only during the demonstration that the customer gets an opportunity to verify the facts about the product. Hence, demonstration is imperative and essential for a prospect to make a buying decision.

The salesman listens patiently to the points raised by the customer in purchasing the goods and then tries to reply with facts at his disposal. Avoid getting into arguments to supplement your point.

The Close

This is the last stage of any sales presentation. The whole exercise becomes useless if the sale does not take place. Therefore, it is the most crucial stage for a salesman. The main aim of the close is to convince the prospect to sign the order form or to place an order immediately rather than in the future.

The salesman should be alert and use his good judgement to spot an opportunity when he is in a position to close the sale. This requires judging the mood, attitude and perception of the prospect. Although this comes through experience and constant understanding of different types of prospects, the general rule remains that right from the start the salesman should be calm and should give due regard and importance to the views of the prospect. It is also important that through proper planning, prospecting, presentation and demonstration the salesman should try to capture the attention of the prospect and not let the prospect change his mind. This is possible only when the salesman is attentive and has an open mind, the ability to listen patiently to his prospect, facing every objection with a smile on his face and confidently answering any queries of the prospect.

RELATIONSHIP OF SALESMANSHIP WITH SALES MANAGEMENT AND PERSONAL SELLING

Selling is one of the most important marketing activities in most organizations. The scope for selling has increase substantially during the past few decades due to growth in the trade and industry. Persuasive selling skills are being used not only by organizations whose objectives is to earn profit but also by non-profit organizations. Because of this varied nature of the selling jobs professional selling has developed into a specialized area of management.

Salesmanship & Personal Selling

One of the most asked questions in the direct sales industry is: what makes a good salesman? It would seem to be an easy question to answer. Just go down to your local bookstore and you'll find stacks of books that claim to have all the answers. But in the real world of selling, what makes a good salesman is a little harder to answer.

The reason for this is that there seems to be as many different ways to be successful at sales as there are sale people. On the surface, they all seem to be completely different. But if you look a little closer, you will notice some similarities. The following are some of the traits that all good salespeople share:

1. The ability to quickly develop rapport with their prospective customers. Without rapport, your prospects won't trust you enough to feel comfortable doing business with you. What makes a good salesman is either an innate ability to bond with people, or more likely, working hard to study and acquire this ability.

2. A desire to truly help their customers. People can sense when the only thing you care about is your commission. What makes a good salesman is putting the customer's needs and desires first.

3. The habit of asking questions to gather information before making a pitch. The average salesman will just start right in with every reason they can think of why someone might want their product and hope that the customer will pick up on something and decide to buy. What makes a good salesman is their knack for finding out what is most important to each individual customer and showing them a product that gives them exactly what they said they wanted.

4. Sticking to a consistent, proven sales process. Good sales people don't just show up and "wing it". They know that even though they make some sales that way, in the long run their closing ratio is much higher when they follow a step-by-step process that consistently results in more sales. What makes a good salesman is his discipline in sticking to that process every time.

5. A never ending desire to learn more about how to sell more effectively. Most salespeople never take it upon themselves to further their own education in the profession of selling. What makes a good salesman is his drive to keep learning, keep improving even when he is already at the top of his game. Being successful at sales isn't really a big mystery. There are some basic fundamentals of interpersonal skills, selling techniques, attitudes and work habits that anyone can learn and apply. What makes a good salesman is simply learning and sticking to those basics.

Is salesmanship a Science or an Art?

What is Science?

Science means a body of laws or principles. It means characteristics of facts that can be analyzed systematically. Science is based on facts principles which can be universally accepted are called law of that science.

Salesmanship is also based on its own rule and principles which based on human psychology. A salesman has to study the psychology of the consumers. He should also have the knowledge of the product which he is going to sell. As a science salesmanship also follow some basic rules and principles which followed in a systematic way. Hence we can say that salesmanship is a science.

What is Art?

Art is practical science which is based on skills. If science is a knowledge then art is an action. Art is a skill which can be acquire by study, observation and experience. Art can be learned by the person who has some skill. Art makes the man exact. A salesman also possess some skill which can be acquired and developed. Every customer are different from another and salesman should have some skill to diagnose the customer expectation by using his skills. A salesman must have skill and knowledge to face the various types of customers. A salesmanship must have a knowledge of science and skill of art. Salesmanship is neither a science nor an art, but the combination of both. Therefore, salesmanship is based on art and science both.

Myths about Selling

Myths of selling: There are various myths about selling process which needs to be cleared for a sales person.

1. ***Buyers are liars:*** This is based on a assumption of sales people that customers mislead sales people. This usually happens when the sales person fails to earn the person's trust. To gain some one's trust it is very important to focus attention on their situation rather than trying to close the sale. Sales person should avoid not to push them into making a buying decision. Further more, to gain more trust, sales person should treat people with respect and dignity even if they are not prepared to make a buying decision at the time of sales presentation
2. ***Anyone can be persuaded to buy:*** In today's business world people have become more knowledgeable and aware than even before. The real key is to determine whether or not the person or company you are speaking to has a genuine need for your product or service. If they do not, then your best strategy is to move on to someone who does not AND want your particular solution. Even if a company could benefit from your product but they are reluctant to give you the opportunity to discuss, your time is better spent talking to other companies.
3. ***In buying decision, price is the primary reasons:*** Price is one of the factor in the buying processes, but not the primary reason. The whole process of selling can be failed unless the salesperson effectively carries the value of the products or services. Focus should always be to give solution to the customer's problem, in such situation price will not become roadblock in the buying process.
4. ***A technique that works well for one person will work for everyone:*** Selling techniques differ from person to person due to unique personality traits of people. A salesperson's natural style & approach should take care of this dimension while giving sales presentation.
5. ***Close the sales as soon as possible:*** As people move towards a buying decision, it is very important to gain commitments along the way. Salesperson should include a call to action in their proposals and conversations. At the same time salesperson should take care of the thing that not every sales decision will be made quickly. There can be various reasons for delayed decisions. Trying to push customers for sale can lead to non-closing of the deal.
6. ***The deal can be closed at any price:*** Too many salesperson feel they have to close every deal, even if it does not make good business sense to do so. Countless sales people will accept a deal that has virtually no margin just so.

BUYER-SELLER RELATIONSHIP

Conceptual Model of "sales-person-buyer" and their Dyadic Relationships

Salesperson plays the strategic role in buyer-seller relationships. Selling is often treated as order producing function. Ti measures sales function performance as sales volume, market share, or the attainment of a sales quota.

In established buyer-seller relationships, however, the buyer's demand is derived from customer demand, the ordering of product is governed by administrative routines, and the choices of supplier is often regulated by contractual arrangement. The outcomes used to evaluate sales function performance may therefore be primarily determined by factors not under the control of the salesperson, such as competitor actions, total market development, or the sales potential in a territory.

The salesperson does ply a strategic role, however, in achieving long-term sales from an established customer. By improving the buyer's motivation to continue the relationship, the salesperson can secure the continuity of the buyer-seller relationship.

Research on selling and sales force management has to large extent treated selling as an order-producing function and has measured sales function performance as sales volume, market share, or the attainment of a sales quota.

The salesperson has substantial influence on the buyer's motivation to continue the relationship, and thus on the long-term from these customers. In addition to the direct effect of perceived salesperson performance on buyer's motivation to continue the relationship, there is a strong indirect effect through the salesperson's influence on the perceived reliability of the supplier. The salesperson also affects the perceived value of supplier services, which differentiates that supplier from competing suppliers.

From the buyer's perspective, a high - performing salesperson in one who can foster an ongoing personal relationship with the buyer. A good personal relationship facilitates communication and mutual understanding. Skilled salespeople also manage conflict well and mediate planning information between the two organizations.

One of the strongest managerial implications of this study is that management should redefine the sale function as a long term marketing tool within established relationship. The salesperson's role is shifted from selling individual products to "selling" the relationship with the supplier. This implies, among other things, that the salesperson becomes responsible for coordinating internal functions and routines that will influence the reliability of the supplier and for orchestrating various value adding services.

Thus, within established buyer-seller relationships, the training and development of the sales force should emphasize relationship management in addition to sales techniques. These general marketing and organizational behavior skills include skills in negotiation and conflicts resolution, as well as thorough knowledge of both the customer's industry and the salesperson's own organization.

Within established relationship, the customer's environment, product and organization can be expected to change over time. In response, the seller's precuts and organization should adapt to maintain the relationship. Thus, the greatest challenge for sales management may be to develop a learning organization and to stimulate a learning orientation on the part of its salespeople.

Various Selling Theories

"SELL" Model

This is a simple model describing the various actions associated with the word itself, sales acronym for sales steps. Note, however, that there is another viewpoint which suggests that starting with features may turn the process less effective and generate more objections.

1. ***Show features:*** It is the very first stage; expected to show the features of the product, demonstrating how it works, and showing the results of using the product immediately.
2. ***Explain advantage:*** Immediately, after demonstrating the product, explain the advantage possibly related with the features, showing the advantages which ate derived from it.
3. ***Lead into benefits:*** Correlate the advantages with the benefits. This is simply highlighting the materialization of those benefits in conducting the set of activities due to having/using the product.

4. ***Let them talk:*** Then at the end, let them talk further about the product, its features and those future benefits. If the previous steps are done well, they will talk themselves for the sale.

"SLAID" Model

This is another simple model describing the various actions associated with the word itself, "Slaid" acronym for sales steps. Note, however, that there is another viewpoint which suggests that starting with demonstration may allow the selling to become more dramatic than rational one.

1. ***Show the product:*** Showing the product in full or showing specific function is also possible in the beginning, just to trigger the anxiety or curiosity in their mind. It is not a full product demonstration. Demonstration comes a bit latter state in this methods.
2. ***Listen:*** A partial demonstration flash triggers a lot of questions, or estimations or expectations, in case if the product is absolutely new concept. These are objections raised in challenge of the available framework in their mindset. Listen to them, show concern for those objections. In doing so, you may get a close view of their real needs and how important things and how important they are to them.
3. ***Acknowledge:*** Your hearing will endorse that you have understood and are ready to fulfill their needs. You may be given elaborative further deep information about their objection.
4. ***Identify:*** Identify the objections, and bring them on a squaring off situation with contents offered by your product. If possible, set up a concession clause, balancing the benefits of new product over the old objections, so that you can handle the objection and will get the sale.
5. ***Deliver:*** Ask the participants to repeat the demonstration to build the confidence about the product performance. Objections will be removed automatically. Show and endorse their problems and ask them to accept truth that those problems can be solved with your product. Deliver the same.

Theories of Selling

Stimulus Response Approach to Selling

This is the simplest approach to selling and is shown in Figure 2.3. It is up to the salesperson to provide stimuli, of any kind, initially. This is followed by an attempt to obtain a response from the prospective buyer a continued on until a decision is made.

figure 2.3

Stimulis response Approach to Selling

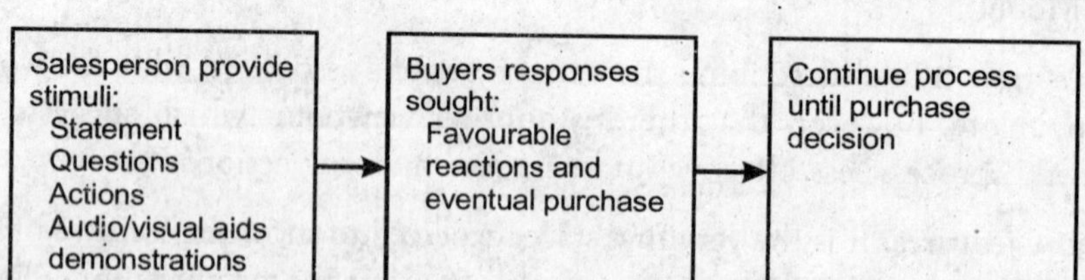

The early salesmen of the 1800's, the well-known traveling salesmen, and telemarketing salesmen normally use this approach. We all have heard of the various anecdotes of traveling salesmen asking to provide a demonstration. This is imperative in this approach as it provides stimuli, a point of discussion, and an entry point. Normally, it is essential as it is a part of the prepared script that the salesman will follow. If the salesman can show you how his vacuum machine works, or how well his soap cleans the cloth, or how thinly the slicer cuts the apple, it opens a situation where the prospective buyer has to say yes, continuously, to various statement of the product. If the buyer continuously says yes to all the stimuli, it is therefore anticipated that there will be an eventual purchase. In Malaysia, there are still many who employ this approach by carrying their goods, from honey, books, toys to various electrical goods, around with them to eating spots, trying to entice someone to look at the product and then to launch into script.

Mental State Selling

This approach utilizes the understanding of the AIDA (Attention, Interest, desire, Action) concept and its utilization in the selling process. It follows the same strategy of the Stimulus response Approach where a script is prepared and followed. What is different here is the timing. The timing refers to the mental state of the prospective buyer, whether at Attention, Interest, Desire, or Action. As such, the message changes according to the situation the prospective buyer is perceived to be in at the moment of the encounter. This means the salesman has to do some groundwork of the prospective buyer before the encounter, which is an improvement of the earlier approach. Nevertheless, reality indicates that while such scripts can be written, in many cases it is written for the seller and not the buyer.

Simplified tasks that the salesperson can do is as follows:

Mental State	Sales Task
Awareness	To get prospective buyers to be interested in the product
Interest	To get prospective buyers to want the product
Desire	To get prospective buyers to buy the product
Action	To close the sale

Need satisfaction selling

Salesman learnt very fast that customer didn't prefer the earlier two approaches. By the 1950s the essentials of marketing and management were being developed, to the point where recognition by salesman that men had their needs. Selling product that met those needs were easier than selling products that did not. Refer figure 2.4.

figure 2.4
Need satisfaction Approach to Selling

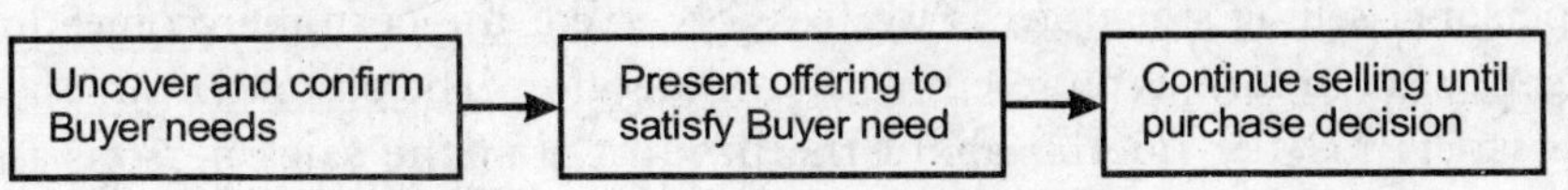

It was critical for salesmen to know what the needs of the customer were. This was done by various methods, including visit, studies of the customers, questioning and constantly probing. This will entails briefings by the customer of their needs, preliminary meeting they can get the sales. A store who quickly matched the prices of her competitor in order to prevent people from going to her competition. However, this seldom creates loyalty and only conditions that customer to continue asking for a better price. Decisions like this cost you or your company money. If you are not making your desired gross profit on a particular sale, then you need to consider whether it makes good business to accept it. Small business owners who will offer substantial discounts to a large company in the hopes of generating additional business from that client in the future. Unfortunately, they end up giving away their services and expertise because they don't get any more business from that company. They neglected to negotiated and upfront agreement.

7. ***Do whatever it takes to get the sale:*** Sales person should avoid certain behaviour traits like manipulation, high -pressure selling, aggression to close a sales deal. In this way they will not get loyal customers and clients. They may win the sales, but they can lose good customers. One time sales mentality should be avoided at all cost. Selling is an honorable career and sales professionals need to avoid falling prey to these myths. Focus on helping your customer make an educated buying decision. Concentrate on asking high - quality questions and positioning your solution appropriately and these myths will not affect you.

Characteristics of Sales Job

There are numerous models that describe the sales process. Nearly all have similarities. Yet over an over again, successful salesmen have shown similar behaviour and processes. These include preparation, approach customers by reference, customer-friendly language in their sales message, knowledgeable of the products, and ensuring post-purchase satisfaction of existing customers. The selling process discussed here includes finding prospects, opening the relationship, qualifying the prospect, presenting the sales message, closing the sale, and servicing the account. Refer figure 1. It must be understood that while the process here is detailed and presented in a linear fashion, it does not mean that this occurs in the real world. However, for the sake of brevity and conciseness, the process is presented as such.

Difference between Advertising and Personal Selling

Let us try to understand the difference between advertising and personal selling also, so as to clearly distinguish between these two important components of the marketing mix.

From a broad perspective, both–personal selling as well as advertising–are the means to communicate with the target customers for the product or service of an organisation. To be effective, i.e., to produce results, in terms of sales or orders, both should be understandable, interesting, believable and persuasive. We shall discuss the process of designing a personal selling effort involving all these four criteria of an effective communication.

However, there are some notable differences between these two means of communication. While the personal selling effort is a two-way communication process, advertising is a one way communication. In the personal selling situation, as we have observed, the customer comes in direct contact with the salesperson, who, in turn, is representing an organisation. The customer can ask any number of questions so as to satisfy his/her queries about the product that the sales persons is offering. It is the sales person's responsibility to satisfy his customer on the benefits of his product. If he does so, he gets the desired sales or an order. Thus, the result of the personal selling, whether positive in terms of an order or negative in terms of no order, is also quick and easily measurable.

In advertising, on the other hand, the customer does not come in direct contact with any representative of the organisation. Thus it is a one way communication. The reactions, attitudes or perceptions of the viewers cannot be immediately gauged in advertising.

Let us also understand a very interesting aspect of advertising and selling, about the relative importance of the two, during three different stages of a products/brand's market. The three phases can be pre-purchase phase, the purchase phase and the post-purchase phase. The pre-purchase phase is characterised by the phase where the organisation is trying to convince the targeted customers of the benefits of the product/brand. The purchase phase is the time/duration when the customer is making up his mind to actually buy the product. The post-purchase phase is one when the customer has bought the product and is evaluating the decision.

figure 2.5

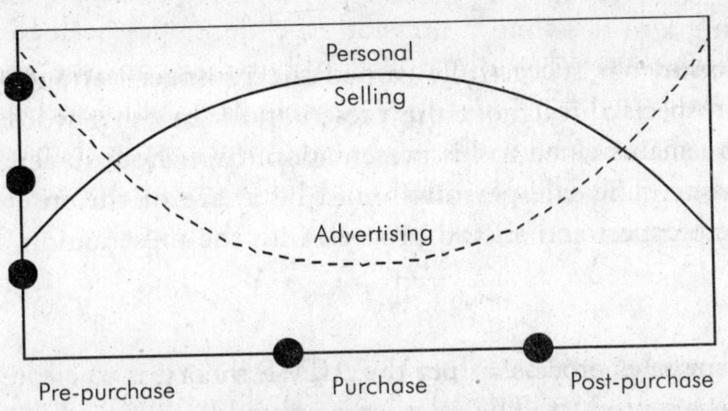

Advertising has a major role during the pre-purchase phase as the mass demand for the product has to be generated. Advertising also plays an important role in post-purchase phase as it gives sound reassurance to the purchaser that he has taken a sound decision in buying that product. Personal selling, on the other hand, has an important role to play in all the three phases. It plays a major role in the purchase phase.

THEORIES OF PERSONAL SELLING

There are three main theories of personal selling, which are as follows

- AIDAS Theory
- Right Set of Circumstances Theory
- Buying Formula Theory

AIDAS Theory

This theory is based on the premise that during a sales presentation, the prospect consciously goes through five different stages: Attention, Interest, Desire, Action and Satisfaction. In fact the name of this theory has been derived from the initial letters of these five words. The proponents of this theory believe that the salesperson should design his presentation in such a manner which takes care of all these stages of the process of selling. The details of five components of AIDAS theory are as follows.

Attention

The salesperson should attract the prospect to his presentation before he actually goes into the details of the same. This is to ensure that the prospect becomes receptive to the presentation.

Let us understand the need for securing attention. We would all appreciate the fact that usually the prospect may be busy in his routine jobs or his daily assignments. Thus, before meeting the salesperson, the prospect's mind may be engaged in something other than the concerned product, about which the salesperson in going to talk.

Unless the salesperson involves the prospect's mind in the presentation, his total effort may go unnoticed or unregistered. Drawing the prospect's attention, therefore, is tantamount to dissociating him from other assignments and involving him in the presentation, both physically and mentally, so as to gain maximum from the sales meeting.

Interest

Once the salesperson has successfully gained the prospect's attention, he/she should maintain the interest of the prospects throughout the presentation. In other words, the salesperson should ensure that the prospect remains glued to his presentation throughout its length and that he does not wander away from the same. The salesperson should be aware of the interest, likes, dislikes, attitude and motivation of the prospect and should proceed with the presentation, keeping in view all these factors.

Desire

The next step in the sales process, as per the AIDAS theory, is to create a strong desire in the prospect's mind to purchase his product. The salesperson should consciously try to bring the prospect into this stage of readiness to the point of buying his product. He should concentrate on projecting the benefits of his product to the prospect. He should go even to the extent of presenting benefits according to the motivation of the prospect.

The salesperson should also be prepared to anticipate the resistance to his sales presentation in terms of objections or questions from the prospect. Not only that, he should be prepared with several answers and explanations to the anticipated objections.

Action

Once the salesperson has been successful in taking his prospect through the three stages, as discussed above, he should induce the prospects into actually buying the product. It would be interesting for us to understand that even after going through the three stages of attention, interest and desire, the prospect may still have some doubt or some inertia which will stop him from taking the final decision of actually buying the product. Hence, it becomes an important task for the salesperson to help his prospect in taking the final decision.

At times, we ourselves have also experienced that inertia, as a prospect. We might have liked the vacuum cleaner of Eureka Forbes during its presentation at our home by the company's salesperson. He might have answered all of our objections quite satisfactorily. It is now up to us to take the final decision of placing an order to the Eureka Forbes' salesperson. But we keep on thinking whether to go for the same or not. Try to recollect what the salesperson told you at that time. He must have said, "Sir, should I send the machine tomorrow or today?" or "Sir, we also have an attractive finance option whereby you can pay in installments." or "Sir, only for you I can ask my sales manager for a 10% discount on the billing price."

As we have observed, the salesperson tries to push us into a situation to take a decision. And he has exercised the technique of closing very skilfully. This is what is expected of a salesperson in this stage.

Satisfaction

Once the prospect has placed an order, the salesperson ensures that the prospect carries the impression of having taken the right decision. He should always thank the prospect and even go to the extent of saying, "I appreciate your choice sir, you have taken an excellent decision".

The salesperson should also ensure that the delivery of the order takes place within the time frame and all other promises are kept, regarding installation, free servicing, etc. Moreover, the salesperson should try to keep in touch with his prospect and should keep enquiring about the efficient performance of his purchase.

Right Set of Circumstances Theory

The advocates of this theory opine that all the circumstances, which led to the sales, were appropriate or "right" for the sales to have taken place. In other words, if the salesperson is successful in securing the prospect's attention, maintaining his interest and inducing his desire to buy the product, sales will result. Moreover, if the salesperson is highly skilled, he will take control of the presentation, which would lead to sales.

Buying Formula Theory

In the earlier theories, emphasis was laid on the salesperson or the seller. In this theory the emphasis is on the buyer. This theory emphasises on the needs or problems of the buyer. The salesperson assists the buyer in finding an appropriate solution to the problem. This solution may be in terms of a product or service.

The buying formula theory is based on the analysis of the sequence of events that goes on in the buyer's mind during the sales presentation. Thus, the theory emphasises on the factors internal to the prospect and the factors which are external, i.e., influence of the salesperson on his prospect's decision to buy his product. The theory is based on the presumption that the salesperson will take care of the external factors.

The sequence of events in a prospect's mind can be represented as

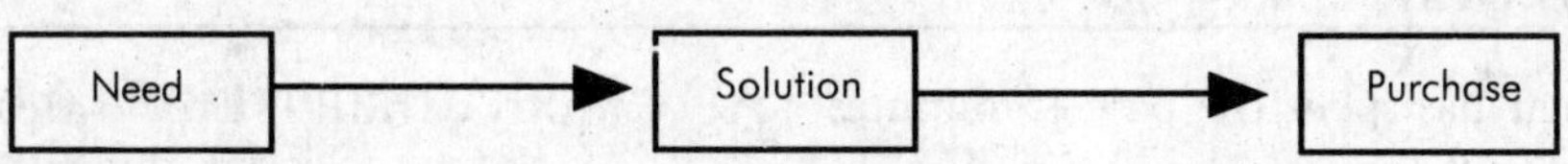

There are all the chances that a continuous relationship will develop between the prospect and the salesperson. As a result of sales, the satisfaction will also come in the sequence. This sequence can be presented as

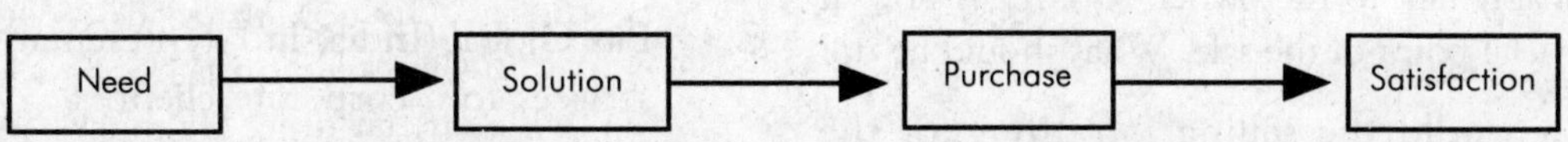

Furthermore, whenever a need is felt, the solution is available in the form of a product or service or both. A product or a service belongs to some manufacturer or a marketing agency. The product, service or manufacturing may also have a brand name.

For example, if someone is feeling hungry, he/she has a need. The solution lies in getting food. So the sequence of events in his/her mind will progress from need (hunger) to solution (food). The next step will be "What food,", whether it is Indian, Continental, or Chinese. This step will ensure the decision on the product (fast-food). Now the person will think about the brand in the fast-food category. It may be Nirula's, Wimpy's, Chotiwala's, Udipi's, etc. On taking this decision about the brand, the person will purchase the food. His satisfaction or dissatisfaction will depend on the delivery time, taste, quality, seating space, etc.

This sequence of events may thus be represented as

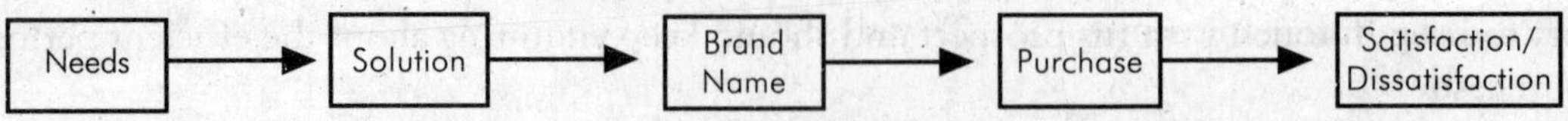

In practice, most of the sales presentations or the personal selling efforts are based on one or a combination of these theories.

SUMMARY

Personal selling is a two communication. Personal selling is flexible and extremely effective but costly form of sales promotion. It promotes long term business relations through personal intimacy. In today's competitive market's salesperson's role is not just to sell the product not know what modification consumer want in the product. In present globalized world products are changing very rapidly it depends on customer taste. So identify the customer tastes in typical job for sales department.

Today, personal selling has become a challenging and rewarding profession. In personal selling, a salesperson has to deal with an individual client, take account of the personal style and attitude of the client so as to make his approach and attitude acceptable to the client. If a salesperson is meeting clients in a group, then it is important to distinguish the different individuals who make up the group. In the interaction, the salesman should adapt his style and behave appropriately to the different group members who are present.

In order to be successful, a salesperson must possess a set of personal, product-related and functional qualities as a variety of analytical and administrative duties are important components of the job. Before approaching a prospect every salesperson is advised to do a bit of homework regarding the company's name, size, authority, concern and general requirements. The salesperson should introduce himself, his company, the product under promotion, product presentation and overcome any customer objections.

PROJECT WORK

1. Vasant Kumar has spent the past 45 minutes attempting to sell a new personal computer to an entrepreneur. The Purchase Manager tells Vasant Kumar, "I need to think about this, I am not ready to buy right now. I should probably talk to the owner". Vasant is now at a crucial point of the sale. What should he do?
2. How would the selling job differ for the following situations? What would be the most important activity for each job?

   A. Modi (India) Ltd. salesperson selling cameras to a photo studio?

   B. M/s New East Delhi Urban Society Ltd. representative selling services to government organisations?

   C. Bax Global (India) Ltd. representative selling services to a corporate client?

   D. Colgate (India) Ltd. salesperson selling soap and oil to a general merchant?

SHORT QUESTIONS

1. What is salesmanship?
2. What is the quality of good sales manager?
3. Define personal selling with the help of suitable example.
4. What is the scope of personal selling?

5. Write different steps of personal selling.
6. What are the different theories of personal selling?
7. What is the role of sales manager?
8. Write different methods of remuneration.
9. What is salesmanship?

REVIEW QUESTIONS

1. Explain AIDAS theory with the help of suitable example.
2. Explain different steps of personal selling.
3. Explain AIDAS theory of personal selling
4. Explain buying formula theory of personal selling.
5. Discuss the changing role of personal selling.
6. Personal selling is a two-way communication best suited to a company marketing consumer products with a poor brand loyalty. Discuss.
7. What is the difference between a suspect, a prospect and a qualified prospect?
8. How can a salesperson confront an objection in a sales presentation?
9. What are some sales closing techniques?
10. For selling FMCG in today's context, examine the role of personal selling as a tool of direct marketing.
11. What are the product and market situations conducive to the use of personal selling?
12. How would you handle these objections raised at the end of a sales presentation?
    a. The price is too high
    b. Your warranty period is too short
    c. I do not want to do business with your firm.
13. Differentiate between advertising and publicity. Highlight the role of public relations and personal selling in selling pharmaceuticals.
14. What is personal selling? Outline objectives and importance of each step in the selling process. Highlight the usefulness of personal selling in selling pharmaceuticals to doctors.
15. Briefly describe the personal selling process. How would the sales presentations differ in the following cases:
    a. Selling a life insurance policy
    b. Selling office computers
    c. Presenting a new drug to physicians.
16. Eureka Forbes uses personal selling as a major marketing communication tool than advertising or sales promotion for their vacuum cleaners and water purifiers. What is the relevance of such a strategy?

17. Explain salesmanship and personal selling with the help of suitable examples.
18. Discus different myths of selling.
19. Explain problem solving approach of selling.

GO TO THE NET

- Using Internet search tools or other relevant sources, search 10 companies using personal selling technique in India.
- Using Internet search tools or other relevant sources, search 5 companies using personal selling techniques for industrial products and make a report on selling strategies used by them.
- Using internet search tools prepare a comparative analysis of 6 insurance companies of India who are using personal selling strategy.
- Using internet search tools prepare a report of 5 Indian media industry report who are using personal selling concept.
- Using Internet search tools and other relevant resources, search information about functions of sales manager, their nature, scope and application.
- Using Internet search tools prepare a comparative analysis of 10 electronics goods company selling strategy.

Caselet 1

You are a sales executive working with M/s Rajeev Motors Ltd. Your showroom stocks various models of Matiz cars. You have been speaking to a prospect who is a senior executive in a reputed company. He has told you that one of the reasons why he looking for a small car is that he has not been claiming car allowance from his company.

He has a small family of five persons, which includes his wife, three small children—9, 7 and 5 years old—and of course, himself. He wants you to give him a stereo and other accessories free as these are being offered by another dealer. He is also very particular about after sales service.

Question:

1. What will you negotiate on?

Caselet 2

Would you like to tell me that why performance is lower than 25 percent in comparison to the last year. The General Manager of RT Steel Industry asked to his marketing manager. The marketing manager replied that it is due to recession in automobile industry. Can you analyse that which region is giving negative sale. Yes Sir, with the help of computerized data I would be able to give the accurate data that which region is giving negative sales.

Question:

1. If you are the General Manager, what course of action would be taken by you to increase the sales.

Caselet 3

You are a sales officer with DHL Ltd. The courier services offered by you are the cheapest in the market. You are going to meet a client who is representing a big business house. The client has mentioned that they need a courier who can adapt to the flexible requirements of the company—sometimes letters need to be sent early in the morning and sometimes late in the evening. He has also mentioned that your price is high.

Question:

1. What will you negotiate on? Please give reasons for your approach.

CHAPTER 3

sales organisation

learning objectives

The objectives of this chapter are to:

- understand and differentiate between the role of sales administration and sales organisation
- understand how to develop a sales organisation
- organise field sales.

content outline

- Opening Case
- Introduction
- Setting up a Sales Organization
- Factors Determining the Structure of Sales Organization
- Functions of Sales Organisation
- Role of Sales Administration
- Role of Sales Organisation
- Developing a Sales Organisation
- Field Sales Organisation
- Coordination
- Summary
- Project Work
- Short Answer Questions
- Review Questions
- Go to the Net
- Caselet

opening case

Sales Organisation in Thomas Cook (India) Limited Foreign Exchange Division

The Company in India

Thomas Cook first began operating in India in 1881 in Calcutta. Being a company which was incorporated abroad, it came within the ambit of Foreign Exchange Regulations Act, 1973, which imposed restrictions on the company's expansion.

The Thomas Cook Group thought that for the Indian operations to grow, it would first have to get out of the restraints imposed by FERA and become an "Indian" company. Thus, Thomas Cook (India) Limited was born and this company took the assets and liabilities of the branches of Thomas Cook Overseas in India w.e.f. 1st November, 1978.

For reasons beyond its control, the Indian company could make a public issue of shares only in February 1983.

The present pattern of equity holdings of the company is as follows

Thomas Cook Overseas Ltd.	-	40.0 %
State Bank of India	-	15.0 %
Public/Staff	-	45.0 %
		100 %

The company is managed by a board of directors with the chairman nominated by the Thomas Cook Group.

The company is involved in the following businesses

1. Travel
2. Retail foreign exchange
3. Wholesale foreign exchange
4. Tours—inbound and Indian horizon
5. Conferences
6. Leisure travel
7. Cargo.

Sales Organisation: [Foreign Exchange Division]

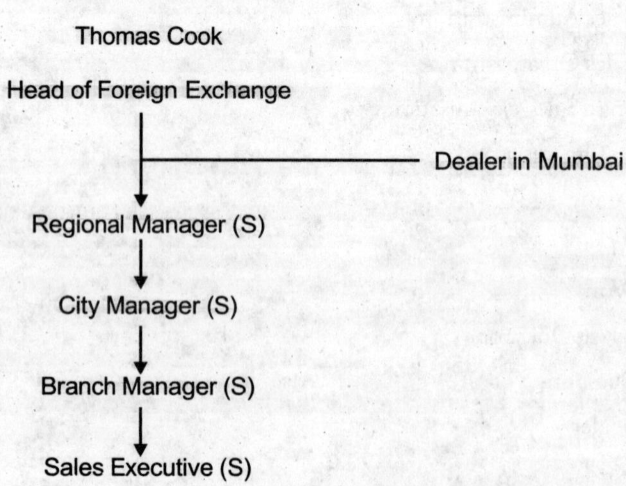

Staff Functions

1. Internal Audit
2. Finance and Accounts
3. Human Resources
4. Information Technology

The Thomas Cook foreign exchange division broadly operates under two major activities

1. Retail foreign exchange operation: includes walk-in-customers and corporate houses.
2. Wholesale foreign exchange operations: includes banks and stockists.

Under retail foreign exchange operations, the sales executive has to achieve his target by making clients from persons travelling abroad for business and/or personal purposes, that is under LERMS (Liberated Exchange Rate Management System) or BTQ (Basic Travel Quota).

The line manager often coordinates in close proximity with the sales executive for getting sales proposals from corporate houses by giving proposals.

The branch manager suggests the commission to be charged and incentives to be given to the corporate clients by the sales executive.

The city manager meets individual sales executives, on a monthly basis, of all the branches under him to review their performance.

The head of foreign exchange and regional manager communicates to the supervisors down the line through MIS. The MIS is prepared on a fortnightly and a monthly basis, which explains in detail all market-related activities, like total sales done by the branch, city or region, major clients made or lost and comparison of actual sales with the targets.

Under the wholesale foreign exchange operations, the wholesale executives have to make their sales strategy on a daily basis, according to the fluctuations in the foreign exchange market.

On receiving the rate list from the head office, the branch manager fixes the premium on the current rate, which is to be given to the banks for purchase of foreign currency.

The branch manager and city manager also decide upon the premium, if some bulk sale or bulk purchase of foreign currency is there.

In case the market is highly volatile or a large transaction is offered to the sales executives, they communicate directly or through the line manager with the dealer, who is operating from Mumbai, to decide on the premium to be offered.

The staff functions, though not directly involved in the operation, help in the smooth operations of the line function in sales organisation.

TRY YOURSELF

1. How has Thomas Cook (India) Ltd. improved its sales performance?
2. How do the staff functions help in the operations of the line functions in sales organisation?

INTRODUCTION

Organisation means the systematic coordination of the functions essential to achieving organisational objectives. The objective of a sales organisation, therefore, is the performance of various activities necessary to promote sales.

Sales Organization is a department of the organization which establish for the purpose of directing, coordinating and controlling the sales organization. It establishes coordination among various sales functions necessary for the achievement of sales and corporate goals. The organization structure of the sales organization depends on the objectives of the business enterprises. It is the most important department of the enterprises because the work of the enterprises is not complete until the product and services created are turned to the consumer.

A sales organization structure evolved in such a way that sales people and sales manager carry out their activity effectively and efficiently. It gives a blue print that "what activity is performed by which person". The basic concept include are following:

1. Centralisation
2. Specialization
3. Staff position
4. Marketing orientation
5. Co-ordination
6. Control

SETTING UP A SALES ORGANIZATION

There are five major steps in setting up a sales organization

1. Defining the objective
2. Delineating the necessary activities
3. Grouping activities into "jobs" or "positions"
4. Assigning personal to positions
5. Providing for coordination and control

1. ***Defining Objectives:*** The initial step is to define the sales department's objectives. Top management, of course, defines the long - run objectives for the company, and from these, the general, or long - run, objectives for the sales department are derived. Considered collectively, general objectives constitute top management's vision of the company at some future time. Top management, for instance, may want the firm not only to survive but to achieve industry leadership, develop a reputation for outstanding technical research, diversify its product lines, provide excellent service to customers, furnish investors with a generous return, establish an image of public responsibility for the sales department and articulates a set of qualitative personal selling objectives.

2. ***Delineating the necessary activities:*** Fundamental to sound organizational design is recognition that activities are being organized. Only after determining all necessary activities and estimating their volume of performance is it possible to answer such questions as; What executive positions

are required? What should be their relationship to other positions? What should be the duties and responsibilities of persons who fill these positions?

3. ***Grouping activities into positions:*** The activities identified as necessary are allocated to different positions. The planner must keep in mind that activities are aimed at achieving certain objectives- ultimately the composite provide the raw materials from which job descriptions are compiled.

4. ***Assignment of Personnel to Positions:*** The next step is to assign personnel to the positions. This brings up the question of whether to recruit special individuals to fill the positions or to modify the positions to fit the capabilities of available personnel. This is a question that has long been controversial. Compromises are frequent. On the one hand, some position requirements are sufficiently general that many individuals possess the necessary qualifications, or can acquire them through training. On the other hand, some individuals possess such unique talents and abilities that it is prudent and profitable to modify the job specifications to fit them. Nevertheless, planners prefer, whenever the situation permits, to have individuals grow into particular jobs rather than to have jobs grow up around individuals.

5. ***Provision for Coordination and Control:*** Sales executive who have others reporting to them require means to control their subordinates and to coordinate their efforts they should not be overburdened with detailed and undelegated responsibilities that they have insufficient time for coordination. Nor should they have too many subordinates reporting directly to them- this weakens the quality of control and prevents the discharge of other duties. Thus, in providing for coordination and control, consideration must be given the span of executive control.

Control and coordination is obtainable through both informal and formal means. Strong leaders control and coordinate the efforts of their subordinates largely on an informal basis. Through sheer force of personality coupled with unusual abilities to attract and hold the loyalty of followers, the strong leader tends to make minimal use of formal instruments of control and coordination. But all sales executives, whether strong leaders or not, can improve their effectiveness through formal instrument of control.

FACTORS DETERMINING THE STRUCTURE OF SALES ORGANIZATION

1. ***Price of Product:*** The price of the product also plays an important role in determining the structure of the sales organization. For instance, costly articles like motor cars, air conditioners, automatic machines etc. have a small sales organization. On the contrary, those products which are comparatively cheap but are of everyday use require comparatively large sales organization such as, vegetable ghee, blades, cloth, toothpaste, biscuits, cosmetics etc.

2. ***Nature of Product:*** The nature of the product occupies key position in determining the structure of the sales organization. For instance, consumer goods of everyday use like oil, ghee, cloth blade, soap, cosmetics that are bought repeatedly require comparatively more complex and a large sales organization. On the contrary, luxury articles like motor cars, color TV, air conditioners etc., the demand of which is hardly repeated, require a small sales organization. Further, if the products are of perishable nature such as fish, milk, vegetables, and milk products etc, in that case we will require a larger sales force along with close supervision.

3. ***Nature of Market:*** The nature of the market is also an important factor in determining the structure of the sales organization. If the product is such which is produced and consumed locally such as vegetables, the sales organization will be simple and a small one. On the contrary,

if the product is such which has international market like petrol, jute goods, cotton textiles etc. then it will have a complex and large market.

4. ***Size of the enterprise:*** The size of the enterprise also plays an important role in deciding the structure of the sales organization. For instance, the large enterprises like Tata Iron and Steel Company, Delhi Cloth Mills, Reliance Industries Limited will have a large and complex sales organization. On the contrary, the small enterprise with limited area of operation will have a simple and small sales organization.

5. ***Ability of the Executives:*** Ability of the executives would also determines the structure of sales organization. If an enterprise has a large number of able, honest and competent executives like Tata Group and Birla Group etc. then it will have a large and complex sales organization. On the contrary, if the executives of an enterprise are incomplete, dishonest and immoral, then it would have ultimately a small sales organization.

6. ***Sales Policies of the Enterprise:*** The sales policies of the enterprise also determine the structure of the sales organization. For instance, if an enterprise adopts aggressive sales policies then it should have a large, complex and extensive sales organization. On the contrary, if the enterprise adopts cold sales policies then it would have comparatively a small and simple sales organization.

7. ***Distribution System:*** The distribution system or method also determines the structure of the sales organization of enterprise. For instance, those enterprises which sell their products through multiple shops like Bata Shoe Company, Delhi Cloth Mills etc., require a large, complex and extensive sales organization. On the contrary, those enterprises which make purchases from manufacturers or wholesalers require comparatively a small sales organization.

8. ***Finance:*** Finance also plays an important role in deciding the structure of the sales organization. For instance, a manufacturer with a large capital affords to sell the goods to the retailers and also to the consumer directly. In such a case it would require a large and complex sales organization. On the contrary, a manufacturer with a comparatively small amount of capital would prefer to entrust the wholesale function to outside agents as he cannot afford to have such an expensive sales organization of his own.

9. ***Number of Products:*** Number of products or manufactured by an enterprise also play an important role in deciding the structure of the sales organization. For instance, if the enterprise is manufacturing a large number of products with different varieties such as Bata Shoe Company, Asian Paints Co., then it would require a large, complex and extensive sales organization. On the contrary, if the enterprise is manufacturing only one or two products then it would require comparatively a small and simple sales organization.

10. ***Miscellaneous:*** Besides above the following factors also determine the structure of the sales organization:
    1. Organization policy of the top management
    2. Customs and traditions
    3. Extent of Competition
    4. Types of Customers
    5. Volume of sales

FUNCTIONS OF SALES ORGANISATION

The functions of sales organisation can be classified as follows

1. Planning functions
   a. Sales forecasting
   b. Sales budgeting
   c. Selling policy
2. Administrative functions
   a. Selecting salesmen
   b. Training salesmen
   c. Control of salesmen
   d. Remuneration of salesmen
3. Executive functions
   a. Sales promotion
   b. Selling routine–execution of customers' orders.

Planning Functions

a. Sales Forecasting

Sales forecasting is the art that predicts the likelihood of economic activity on the basis of certain assumptions. The process of making certain estimates of future events is referred to as sales forecasting and the figure obtained from the process is known as a 'sales forecast'. Sales forecasting would be futile if the future were known. In order to determine the future course of events, aid is taken from an organised system of sales forecasting.

Different steps in sales forecasting are:

- Defining the objectives to be achieved
- Dividing the various groups into homogenous groups
- Analysing the importance of various factors to be studied for sales forecasting
- Selecting the method
- Collecting and analysing the related information
- Drawing conclusions from the analysis made
- Implementing the decision taken
- Reviewing and revising sales forecasting techniques from time to time.

b. Sales Budgeting

The sales budget is the final point of a sales organisation. All other budgets hinge on the basis of the sales budget. What then is a sales budget? It is a forecast of sales to be achieved in the stipulated period. The sales budget can be prepared on the basis of division, brand, products, dealers, territory and sales force.

The following factors need to be kept in mind when preparing a sales budget:

1. Past trends
2. Sales force estimates
3. Trade prospects
4. Present position
5. Potential consumers
6. Government policies
7. Changing business environment
8. Sales promotion strategies.

c. Selling Policy

The object of a selling policy is to place the right type of goods in the hands of consumers at the right time and at the right place. Further, it should aim at attracting customers and rendering them satisfactory services. A selling policy includes:

a. Method of distribution (sale)
b. Terms of sale
c. Guarantee and service

In case of products involving maintenance and repairs, the seller renders what is called after-sale-service. Technical representatives are sent to the user's place for repairing the machines/gadgets free of cost or at a nominal charge. Usually, free service is rendered during the "guarantee period". The after-sale-service policy is a strong selling point to push up the sales of industrial/durable goods. It enhances confidence in the buyers about the fitness of the product and impresses them with the seller's concern for the customer's convenience and satisfaction. It also helps in getting repeat sales orders.

Administrative Functions

a. Selection of Salesmen

Once an organisation has determined the number and kind of salesmen it requires, the next step is to get the right applicants, in sufficient number, for the positions. All the activities involved in securing applications for sales positions are referred to as recruitment. There are various sources of recruitment:

- Advertisements
- Employment agencies
- Educational institutions
- Salesmen of non-competing companies
- Internal transfers
- Recommendations of present salesmen.

The basic objective of the selection process is to gather information about the applicants for the sales job. This information is then used to predict their success/failure probabilities.

b. **Training of Salesmen**

The first step in designing a training programme is to assess the needs of the organisation. A need assessment begins with training requirements that focus on the organisation, the tasks and the personnel. Training methods can be very diverse and may include case studies, lectures, videos, behavioural simulations (role playing, computer simulations, interactive video, teletraining) and absorption training.

Basically, sales training is designed to change or reinforce behaviour that makes sales people achieve their sales goals more efficiently. Sales people are trained to perform activities they would not normally undertake. In addition, training is used to reinforce currently successful sales practices.

c. **Control of Salesmen**

Controlling the sales force is a critical part of the marketing/sales management process. Outstanding planning and implementation are important, but control is essential for a firm to achieve its sales objectives. Controlling extends to a firm's selling methods, distributors, customers and sales force.

An organisation must analyse its selling methods to determine whether they are using the most efficient means possible to reach their customers. Selling methods are analysed using marketing effort analysis as it allows a firm to directly calculate the comparative performance of alternative selling methods.

d. **Remuneration of Salesmen**

A majority of compensation plans for sales force combine two or more payment methods. The most widely used combinations are:

- Salary plus commission
- Salary plus bonus
- Salary plus commission plus bonus.

The purpose of a combination plan is to eliminate the weaknesses of individual components and, at the same time, retain their strengths. The salary element is usually most popular in reputed, more experienced companies that enjoy stable sales. These days, more emphasis is put on the commission component by companies that are concentrating on expanding their business. There has been a recent trend by companies to emphasise incentive over salary. The salary/commission combination is extremely popular, especially when earnings are divided equally between the two. The sales staff has the benefit of security and the company can offer strong incentives to the staff to excel. In addition, if salary is an important part of the compensation package, the company can exert considerable control over the salesperson.

Executive Functions

Sales Promotion

Simply put, sales promotion can be defined as "short-term incentives given to consumers to encourage their purchasing". The number of brands for almost all products is increasing, resulting in a highly competitive environment. This compels manufacturers to go in for sales promotion in either direct marketing or marketing of services. Sales promotion techniques in India are becoming quite common and effective. The following methods of sales promotion are generally used by marketers:

- Incentives
- Coupons
- Free samples
- Price-off
- Contests
- Refunds
- Point of purchase material (POP).

ROLE OF SALES ADMINISTRATION

- Total customer satisfaction by way of prompt and safe delivery.
- Proper maintenance of stock ensuring defect free delivery to customers.
- Effective coordination and communication between regional offices and dealers.

table 3.1

Work Purpose Chart

FIRST CLASSIFICATION	SECOND CLASSIFICATION	THIRD CLASSIFICATION
1. Order processing and vehicle dispatch	1.1. Domestic order processing and dispatch	1.1.1 Receipt and screening of orders
		1.1.2 Authentication from accounts for dispatch
		1.1.3 Processing of orders and communication for confirmation
		1.1.4 Allocation of vehicles
		1.1.5 Collection of toolkit/mats from store
		1.1.6 Arrangement of transit insurance
		1.1.7 Documentation for dispatch
		1.1.8 Excise challan
		1.1.9 Physical dispatch of vehicle
	1.2 Export order processing and vehicle dispatch	1.2.1 Receipt of export from export dept.
		1.2.2 Allocation and documentation for dispatch
		1.2.3 Coordination with excise for bond/AR4A
		1.2.4 Excise clearance and physical dispatch of vehicle
2. Production coordination	2.1 Spy/bus activities	2.1.1 Movement of chassis to body builders
		2.1.2 Movement of body built up vehicle from body builders to Surajpur and other destinations

Contd...

		2.2.1 Collection of production and data entry of production/ RGPIN
	2.2 Delivery of vehicle from plant/body builder to marketing	2.2.2 Inspection/checking of vehicle
		2.2.3 Parking in yard
		2.2.4 Communication to H.O. marketing/export
		2.2.5 Intimations of daily production details to excise
3. Logistics planning	3.1 Movement of vehicle	3.1.1 Coordination with transporters
		3.1.2 Ensuring safe and faster delivery
		3.1.3 Procuring of transport bills
4. Vehicle inventory control/maintenance to stocks	4.1 Inventory control	4.1.1 Proper control of inventory by preparing daily MIS
		4.1.2 Maintain manual FIFO system
	4.2 Maintenance of stocks	4.2.1 Visual inspection
		4.2.2 Periodic maintenance for tyre pressure, coolant, battery oils etc.
5. RTO coordination	5.1 Temporary registration trade certificate	5.1.1 Obtaining T/R No. and T.C.
		5.1.2 Remittance of monthly T/R and road tax payment to RTO
6. Office Administration	6.1 Maintenance of records	6.1.1 Preserving of old records of LCV
		6.1.2 Maintenance of general files, invoice, stationery and computer stationery
		6.2.1 Correspondence with dealers/R.O.
		6.2.2 Correspondence with sales dept.
		6.2.3 Correspondence with RTO etc.

ROLE OF SALES ORGANISATION

Once the sales plan has been formulated, the next logical step is to organise a sales force to achieve the organisational objectives. The qualified as sales objectives, which can be further divided, are shown in Figure 3.1.

Major Qualified Sales Objectives

figure 3.1

Overall Objectives	Break Up or Division
1. Total volume of products	1. Quarter, month and week
2. Total annual value of products	2. Product line and range
3. Total annual selling costs	3. Region and sales area
4. Total annual profit contribution	4. Type of customer

Sales organisation has the following basic purposes:

1. Define the line of authority
2. Ensure that all necessary activities are assigned and performed
3. Establish lines of communication
4. Provide for coordination and balance
5. Provide insights into avenues of advancement
6. Economics of executive time.

Sales organisation also depends on the type of sales force which is used, for example, field sales force, national account management, team selling, telemarketing, part-time sales forces, direct selling, etc.

DEVELOPING A SALES ORGANISATION

Sales organisation development refers to the formal, coordinating process of communication, authority and responsibility for sales groups and individuals. An effectively designed sales organisation has a framework that enables the organisation to serve its customers. Once the sales people know what their responsibilities are and who they report to, they can concentrate on doing their expected jobs to the best of their ability.

Thus, a sales manager must recognise and deal with some basic problems faced by organisations, when developing his own sales organisation. The five major issues are:

1. Formal and informal organisations
2. Horizontal and vertical organisations
3. Centralised and decentralised organisations
4. The line and staff components of organisations
5. The size of the company.

Formal and Informal Organisations

Every firm has a formal and an informal organisation. The formal organisation is that of the management whereas the informal organisation is often developed from the informal relationships existing within the organisation. Also called the grapevine, informal organisation is basically a communications pattern that emerges to facilitate the operation of its formal counterpart. Most formal organisations would be totally ineffective if it were not for a supportive informal organisation.

Figure 3.2 shows an informal communications pattern that might exist in a marketing organisation. Actual communications do not usually follow the formal organisational lines. This allows the formal structure to operate efficiently.

Consider the case of a field salesperson who is responsible for collecting certain competitive information such as prices and trade discounts. If this information were forwarded through the formal organisation (see figure 3.3) the data would be so backdated that it would be useless to the management. The informal communication system, however, allows the information to be transmitted directly to

figure 3.2

The Informal Communication System in a Marketing Organisation

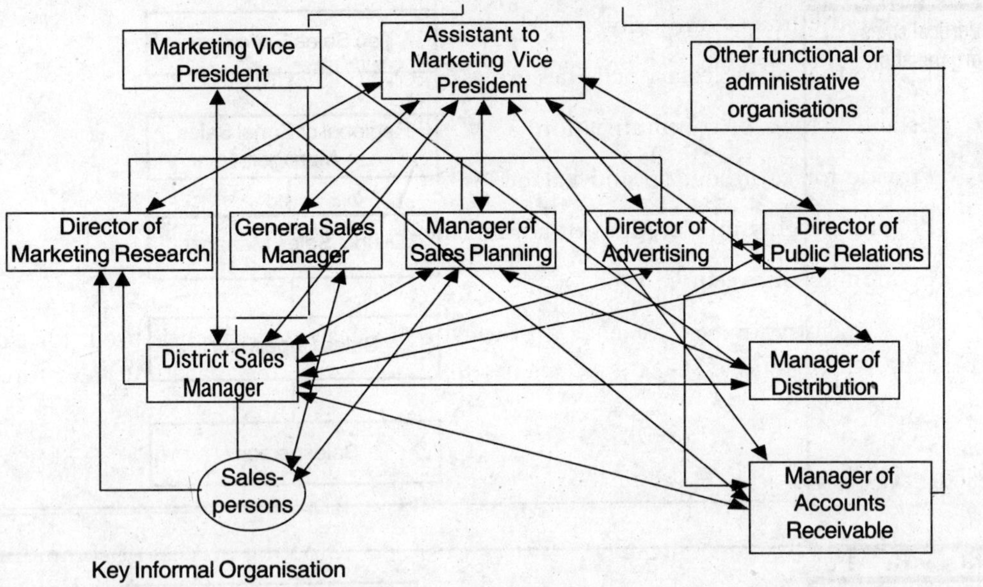

the director of marketing research. Similarly, consumer complaints over delays in correcting billing errors can be mitigated when the district sales manager directly contacts the head of accounts.

The development of an effective sales organisation requires that informal relationships and communication patterns be recognised as being equally useful in accomplishing sales objectives. They should be encouraged to the extent that they improve organisational efficiency.

figure 3.3

A Lengthy Formal Communications Channel

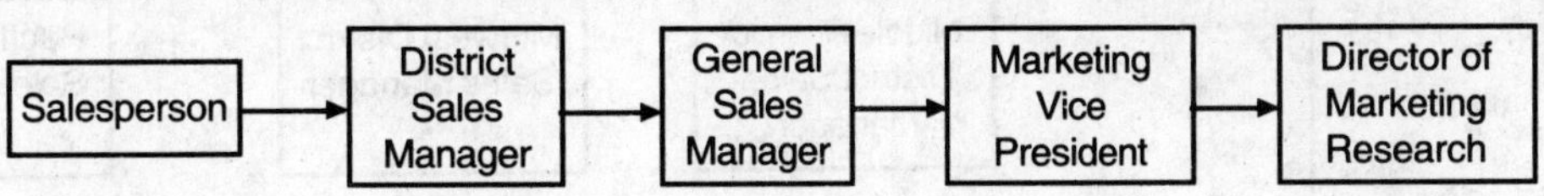

Horizontal and Vertical Organisations

A sales force can have either a horizontal or a vertical organisational format. This arrangement varies among companies even within the same industry.

A purely vertical sales organisation would be similar to the structure represented in Figure 3.4. In this structure, there are several layers of sales management – all of which report vertically.

The other extreme is a horizontal organisation, shown in Figure 3.5. Here the number of management levels is reduced appreciably, but the number of managers at any particular level is increased. Instead of two or three district sales managers, there may be seven or eight.

The factor that determines whether a vertical or horizontal organisational structure should be employed is the effective span of control. The span of control refers to the number of employees who report to the next higher level in the organisation. Horizontal structures tend to exist where larger spans of control are acceptable, while vertical organisations characterise cases in which closer managerial supervision is required.

figure 3.4
Vertical sales organisation

figure 3.5
Horizontal Sales Organisation

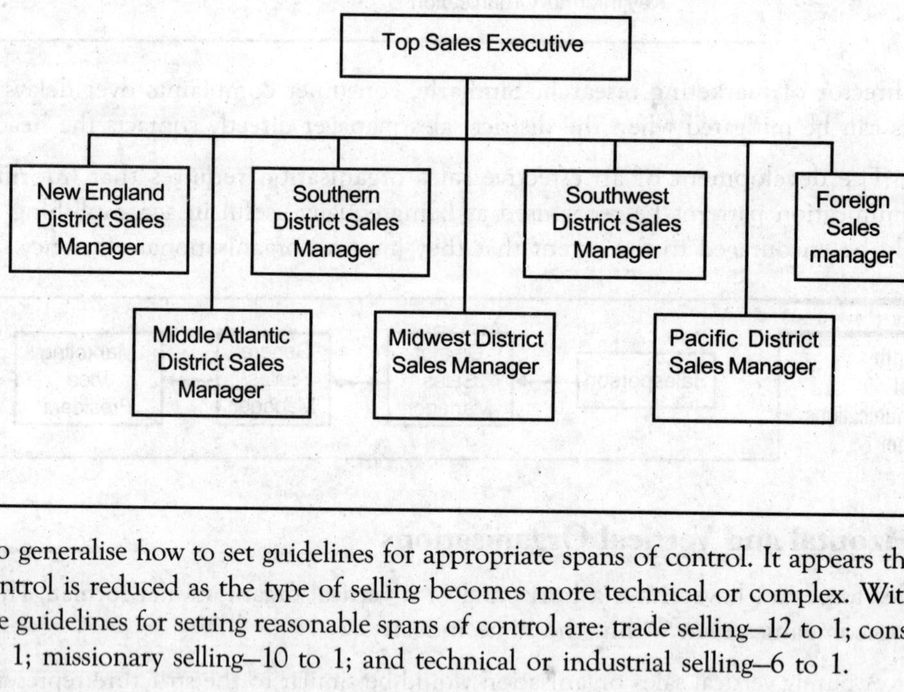

It is difficult to generalise how to set guidelines for appropriate spans of control. It appears that the optimum span of control is reduced as the type of selling becomes more technical or complex. With this in mind, approximate guidelines for setting reasonable spans of control are: trade selling–12 to 1; consumer service selling–10 to 1; missionary selling–10 to 1; and technical or industrial selling–6 to 1.

While these guidelines may seem appropriate, it must be remembered that they are only guidelines. Each company must determine the span of control that works best for its sales organisation. Once set, the span of control should be monitored periodically in order to assure maximum effectiveness.

Centralised and Decentralised Organisations

In a decentralised organisation, responsibility and authority are delegated to lower levels of sales management while in a centralised sales organisation, the responsibility and authority for decisions are concentrated at higher levels of management. A related concern is the degree of centralisation in a sales organisation. This issue has to do with the organisational location of the responsibility and authority for specific sales management tasks.

There is usually a higher degree of decentralisation as an organisation grows in size. Expansion results with top executives being less able to deal with the range of decisions that they handled when the organisation was small. By necessity, these decisions are then shifted downwards in the organisation.

A decentralised organisation structure is ineffective unless commensurate responsibility and authority accompany the assignment of decisions to a specific level of sales management. A classic mistake is for the top management to charge a field sales supervisor with the responsibility to perform a particular task, and then fail to grant the related authority to accomplish the same. This type of mistake should be avoided, since it results in poor morale as well as failure.

Line and Staff Components

Marketing organisations also feature line and staff components. A line function is a primary activity and a staff function is a supporting activity. In a marketing organisation, the selling function is the line component whereas advertising, marketing research, marketing planning, sales training and distributor relations are usually considered staff roles.

Although the use of the terms – line and staff – has been criticised in many quarters, the basic premise behind them remains applicable to marketing organisations. A modern sales force has to receive various types of support in order to accomplish its objectives. Advertising and sales promotional support is needed to precondition the prospect to accept the salesperson's presentation; marketing research and sales planning are required because they allow field representatives to concentrate their efforts on the largest potential markets; in-house sales correspondents relieve the field force of activities that would distract them from their basic efforts; and distribution, credit, and maintenance of personnel ensure that the customer is satisfied with the purchase.

figure 3.6

A Line Marketing Organisation

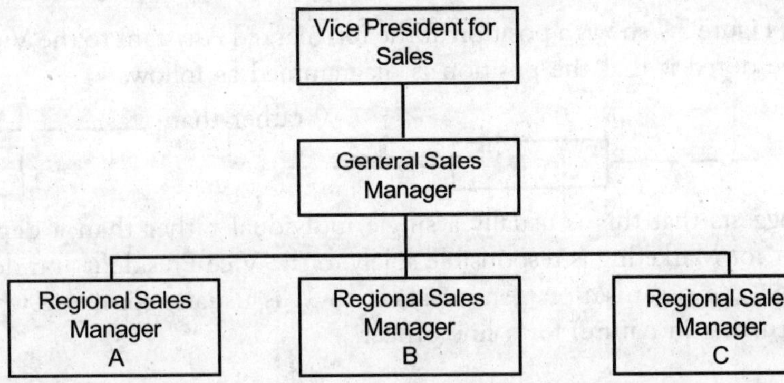

Some firms operate with a simple line marketing organisation such as the one shown in Figure 3.6. Here, a marketing organisation is simply the sales organisation. This type of arrangement may be satisfactory for small firms in basic industrial markets.

If the needs of the market place become more complex, or if the company expands, then there is usually a need to add specialists prepared to deal with these problems. Over time, these specialists become the staff departments found in most large organisations.

Figure 3.7 demonstrates several key aspects of a large-scale marketing organisation. First, the chief marketing officer is typically called the Vice President for Marketing or Director of Marketing, rather than Vice President of Sales. The title change is indicative of the person's added responsibilities under

figure 3.7
Line and Staff Marketing Organisation

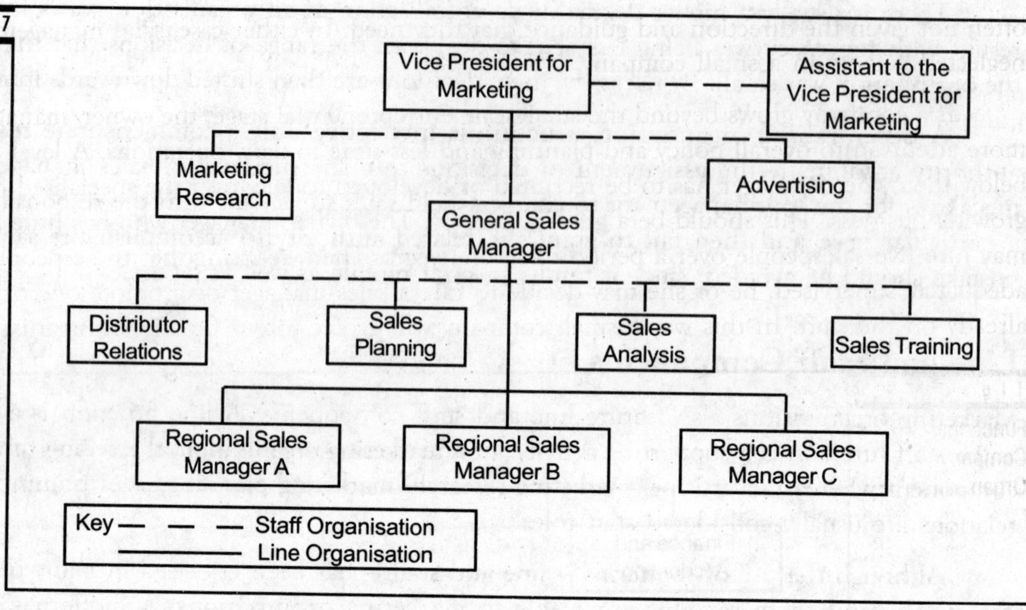

a line and staff structure. The Vice President for Marketing is in charge of more than just the field sales force. The line and staff organisation shown in Figure 3.7 indicates that all marketing activities have been grouped together, suggesting that the basic tenets of the marketing concept have been accepted.

Second, staff activities report to the line position that they support. Distributor relations, sales planning, sales analysis and sales training are considered to be directly supportive of the field sales effort so these departments report to the General Sales Manager. By contrast, marketing research and advertising are broader functions and they report to the Vice President for Marketing.

Finally, Figure 3.7 shows a position at the top marked Assistant to the Vice President for Marketing. The fact to be noted is that the position is diagrammed as follows

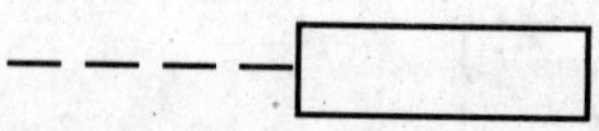

rather than:

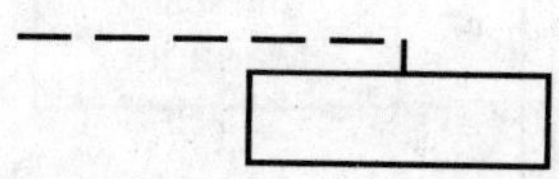

This suggests that this is usually a single individual rather than a department. The Assistant to Vice President for Marketing is responsible solely to the Vice President and does not have line authority over anyone in the organisation. An assistant to ... is usually someone who performs specific tasks (often non-recurring in nature) for a line officer.

Company Size and Organisation

The previous discussion suggests that the size of a company is a major factor influencing its organisational structure. For a small company there is likely to be no formal organisation structure. Rather, the owner/manager is involved in all aspects of the business–accounting, manufacturing, operations, personnel, sales and so forth.

The attention given to sales as a distinct function is primarily dependent upon the owner/manager's abilities and interests. In some cases, the owner/manager may have a strong sales background and, in fact, he or she may be the company's top (perhaps only) salesperson. In other cases, the owner/manager may not have a sales background and may hire one or more salespeople. These salespeople are often not given the direction and guidance that they need. In either case, sales management is usually a neglected activity in a small company.

If a company grows beyond the small-scale entrepreneurial stage, the owner/manager must devote more attention to overall policy and planning and less time to daily operations. A level of management below the owner/manager has to be recruited or developed to take over the specialised functions of the growing business. This should be a gradual process. The owner/manager who has little interest in sales may hire five salespeople over a period of several years. Then, realising that these people are not being adequately supervised, he or she may decide to hire a sales manager or promote one of the salespeople already on the staff. In this way a small company will evolve into a functional organisation.

figure 3.8
Functional Company Organisation

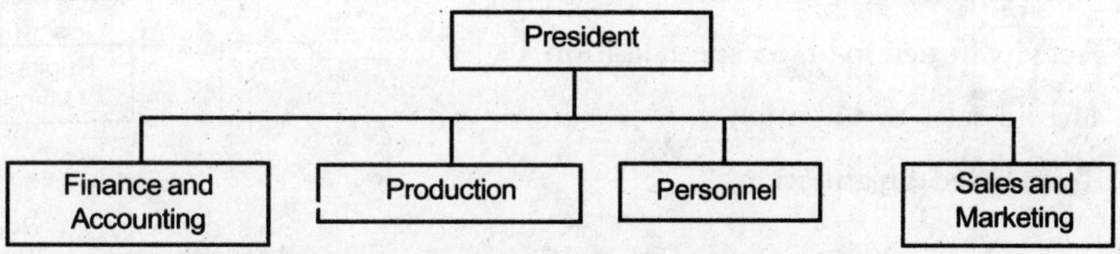

A simple functional company organisation is shown in Figure 3.8. This structure is appropriate for most small and medium sized companies. These companies have relatively few products or services and use a limited number of distribution channels. As each functional area grows larger, the functional organisation will be extended. A functional marketing organisation is shown in Figure 3.9.

figure 3.9
Functional Company Organisation

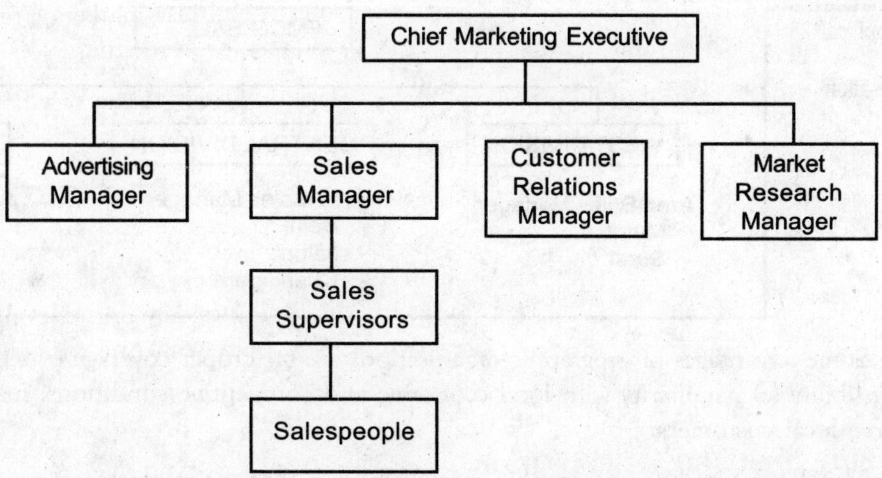

Coordination of a functional organisation becomes more difficult as a company grows. This is faulty because the manager of each functional speciality tends to think only of the function's own problems and needs. For example, the personnel department, in its desire for a uniform compensation plan for all employees, fails to recognise the need for a different compensation plan for salespeople. Another difficulty is that the company may be unresponsive to the changing needs of its customers because no one has overall responsibility for assessing the demand for each product. As a result of these and other difficulties, expanding businesses are likely to change to a more sophisticated form of sales organisation.

FIELD SALES ORGANISATION

Field sales force consists of salespersons who work primarily with customers in person, although they may also use the telephone or assistance from computer links to expedite orders and provide customer service. The structure of a field sales force is usually based on some means of specialisation, such as geography, market, product, or activity/function, or a hybrid of these types. The following are the important field sales:

1. Geographic sales specialisation organisation
2. Product-based sales specialisation organisation
3 Customer-based specialisation organisation
4. Activity/function-based specialisation
5. Hybrid sales organisation
6. Team-based organisation.

Geographic Sales Organisation

The most common means of specialisation of the sales force is by geographic region. In a geographically based sales force, a salesperson has to visit all current and potential customers in a given geographic territory. Figure 3.10 shows a geographic specialisation for the sales force of a large FMCG Company.

figure 3.10
Geographical Sales Organisation

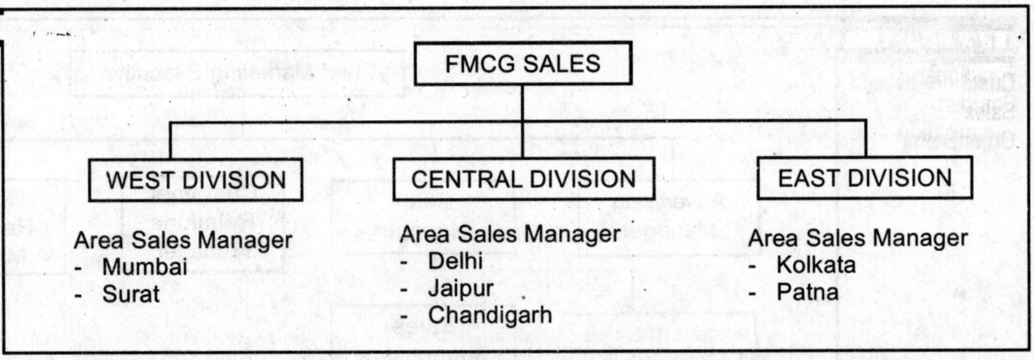

Some advantages of geographic organisations are (a) Proper coverage of territory (b) Defining the responsibility (c) Familiarity with local economic and competitive conditions, making them better able to serve local customers.

The disadvantages of geographic specialisation is that the salespersons need to be responsible for the entire product line in their territory even though they may not be having uniform knowledge about all products. Further, within their territory, they may choose to concentrate on products and customers that are easy prospects.

Product-based Sales Organisation

Organisations that specialise their sales forces according to the product line create a product-based sales force. Product-based organisations are useful for complex products because they require the sales force to concentrate on a limited product line. Product specialisation is generally combined with geographical specialisation at the higher levels, while at the level of field operators, different salesmen may be assigned to specific product lines. The disadvantages of product-based sales organisation include duplication of calls and buyer frustration. This duplication of coverage can lead to increased selling costs.

figure 3.11
Product-based Sales Organisation

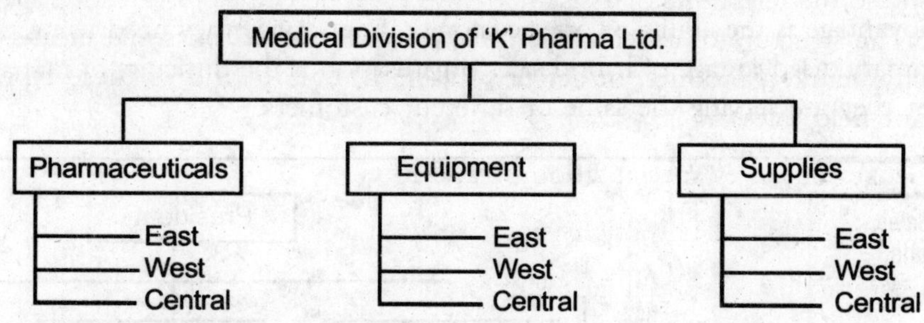

Customer-based Sales Organisation

Organisations with several separate and distinct markets, accounting for major portions of their sales, often organise their markets on the basis of customers. Organisations such as Hewlett-Packard, Xerox and IBM are customer-based organisations. Customer specialisation enables the salespersons to become more knowledgeable about the unique problems and needs of each group of customers. A customer-oriented sales force is consistent with the marketing concept with its increased emphasis on consumer satisfaction.

The main disadvantage of this form of specialisation is that geographical territories may typically overlap.

figure 3.12
Customer-based Sales Organisation

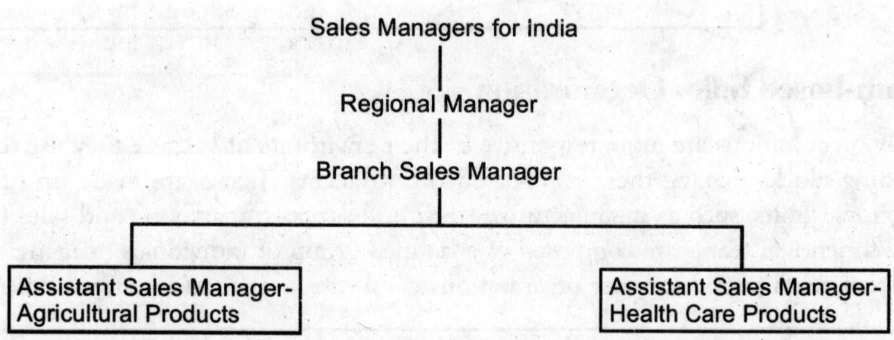

Activity/Function-based Organisation

An activity/function-based sales organisation is able to focus on the use of high-cost selling methods, such as face-to-face sales calls, during a selling process. An activity/function-based sales force can also be designed to meet the customer service issues that are most important at each stage of the selling process. A disadvantage of this type of organisation may be the overlapping of accounts by using different techniques.

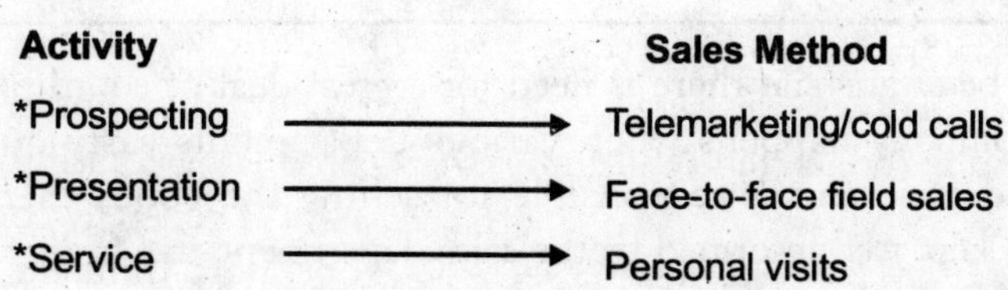

Hybrid Sales Organisation

A hybrid sales organisation is formed when two or more organisational types are combined. This type of organisation structure is designed to overcome the problems of individual sales organisations. Its main advantage is the ability to offer customers the service they need using the most efficient method. The primary disadvantage of hybrid sales organisation is the difficulty of managing multiple sales forces, whether they are serving the same or different customers.

figure 3.13
Hybrid Sales Organisation

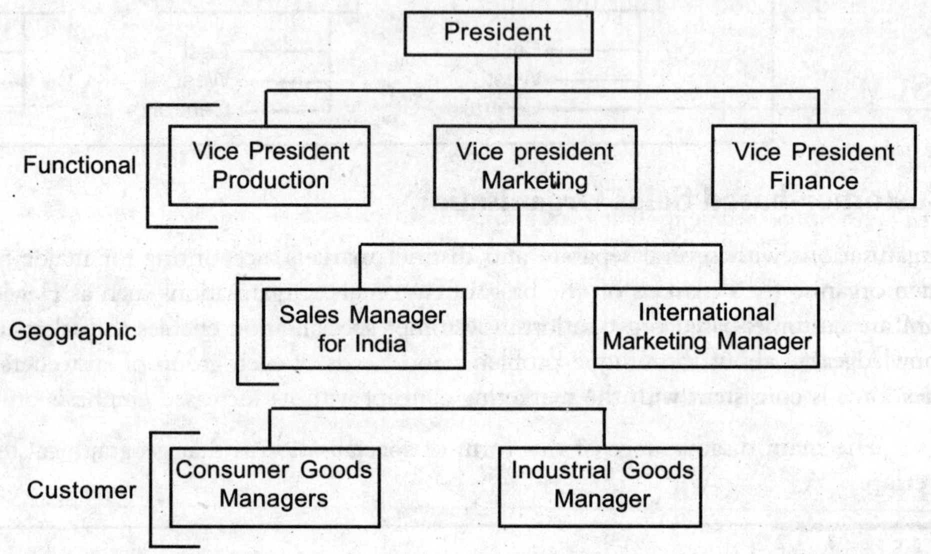

Team-based Sales Organisation

Many organisations are more responsive to their environment because they use team work as their basic building blocks making them team-based organisations. Teams are made up of people from different functional units, such as manufacturing, technical support, marketing and sales (see Figure 3.14). These cross-functional teams are composed of a defined group of individuals bringing together expertise from different parts of the supplier organisation to capture, retain and increase business with customers.

figure 3.14
Supplier Selling Team

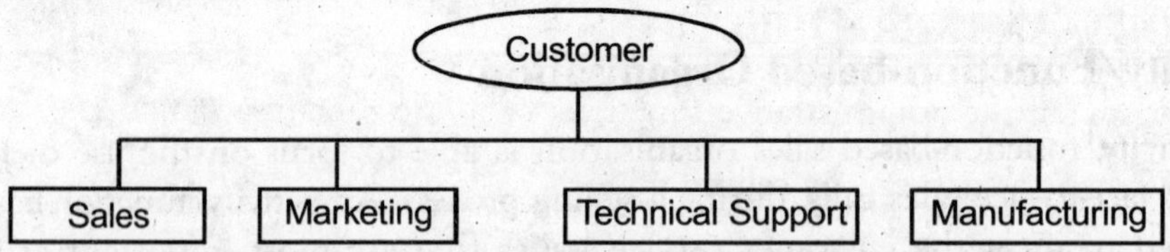

COORDINATION

Sales personnel should be aware that there is need for a great deal of coordination in the organization. The progress of the company happens when various departments carry out their jobs with proper coordination. If sales department is responsible for selling the goods then other departments like production, finance, are kept well informed by the sales department and from time to time meetings may be held to sort out any difficulty faced by them.

The coordination may be:

1. ***Formal:*** To group the allied activities.
2. ***General Administration:*** Where various officers discuss company related matters and find solutions.
3. ***Departmental:*** Where each department of the company attends the coordination committee meeting and a decision is taken in such meetings which is binding on all.
4. ***Informal Coordination:*** When an occasion or difficulty arises, the concerned personnel meet each other and sort out the matter.

SUMMARY

The performance of sales management depends on the effectiveness of the sales organisation. Sales managers are faced with some problems when designing a sales organisation. The decision depends on the type, structure and ownership of the sales force. Types of sales organisations include field sales organisation, team approach, telemarketing, part-time sales force and the Internet. Companies can structure their organisations in numerous ways. Most firms, however, use line organisation or a specialised design based on functions, geographic markets, products, customers, or a combination of these factors. Coordination plays an important role in a sales organisation because companies are not only dealing with domestic markets but are also competing in the international arena. Coordination is especially important for acquiring and retaining satisfied, long-term customers.

PROJECT WORK

1. Study two sales organisations each with product specialisation, geographic specialisation and customer specialisation. Then analyse and discuss the following
   a. Which factors resulted in the choice of this particular type of specialisation in each case?
   b. What are the specific benefits that the firms derive from their respective sales force organisation?
2. Obtain the sales organisation structure of any firm. Evaluate the design and structure of its sales force. Interview a sales manager of the company to determine how its markets and customers influence the design of its sales force.

SHORT ANSWER QUESTIONS

1. What are the administrative functions of a sales organisation?
2. What do you mean by selling policy?
3. What do you mean by sales forecasting?
4. What are the various sources of recruitment?

REVIEW QUESTIONS

1. Why is sales organisation important?
2. Give examples of line, coordinating, advisory and service responsibilities of a territory salesperson for refrigerators.

3. What are the various types of sales organisations?
4. How can a field sales organisation be organised? What are the advantages and disadvantages of each type?
5. What are the relative advantages of a line sales organisation and line and staff sales organisation?
6. Discuss the process of developing a sales organisation. Which factors affect the size of the sales organisation?
7. Discuss the factors favouring 'centralisation' of sales activities.
8. How do product complexity and special buying heads of the customers affect the design of the sales organisation?
9. What factors should be considered while designing the structures of the sales department in a large organisation selling financial services?
10. What are the major considerations that affect the choice of sales organisation structure?
11. What factors influence the choice of a sellers organisation?
12. What specific sales organisation structure would you recommend for the following? Give justifications for your recommendations.
    i. A publisher publishing specific trade magazines like A&M, Global etc.
    ii. A fast food outlet with home delivery as a major market.
13. Explain importance of sales organization with the help of suitable example.

GO TO THE NET

Using Internet search tools contact 50 customers of two sales organisations with different sales organisation and record how organisations provide different services to customers.

Using Internet search tools prepare a report of sales organization of Reliance Industries.

Caselet

ARTHUR ANDERSEN FINALLY DIES AT 89

After 89 years in business, Arthur Andersen LLP has ended its role as auditor of public companies.

The Chicago-based company was convicted in June of obstruction of justice for shredding and doctoring documents related to Enron audits. Afterward, Andersen told the Securities and Exchange Commission that it would cease auditing public companies. It already had given up its license to practice in several states.

"As of this day, Arthur Andersen LLP has voluntarily relinquished, or consented to revocation of its firm's permits in all states where it was licensed to practice public accountancy with state regulators," the company announced in a statement.

The company now has fewer than 3,000 of the roughly 28,000 employees it had before the Enron scandal. Of its more than 1,200 public-company audit clients, none will remain.

The firm's startling decline has come in less than nine months.

"It's like a family member who has terminal cancer," said Gary Brentlinger, human resources director for Andersen's offices in Houston, Austin, San Antonio and New Orleans. "We're watching the firm die."

As people have left and files have gone into storage, Brentlinger said Andersen staff members have removed papers from office in a downtown Houston skyscraper and turned off the lights, leaving only furniture and artwork.

Questions:

1. The most established and successful companies are prone to abrupt end — why?
2. Analyse how business stability can be achieved for longer periods.

CHAPTER

4

recruitment and selection

learning objectives

The objectives of this chapter are to:

- analyse and prepare the job description before recruiting the sales force
- understand the recruitment and selection procedures
- enforce sales force training
- understanding the role of performance appraisal.

content outline

- Opening Case
- Introduction
- Preparing the Job Description and Specification
- Recruitment Sources
- Selection Procedure
- Legally Workable Performance Appraisals
- Some Management Considerations
- Sales Force Training
- The Manager
- Summary
- Project Work
- Short Answer Questions
- Review Questions

opening case

Process of Recruitment and Selection in ABN AMRO BANK and AXIS BANK

Its carried in 9 steps:

1. ***Basic interview:*** Interviews are designed to probe into areas that cannot be addressed by the application form or tests. These areas usually consist of assessing candidates' motivation, ability to work under stress, interpersonal skills and ability to fit-in the organization.
2. ***Aptitude test:*** These tests measure whether an individual has the capacity of latent ability to learn a given job if given adequate training.
3. ***Typing test:*** It may or may not occur
4. ***Operation Round:*** It includes
   - Job Specifications
   - Person specifications
5. ***HR rounds:*** Assess the skills/competencies required in each area based on the various factors.
6. ***Selection:*** Once the recruiting effort has developed a pool of candidates, the next step in the HRM process is to determine who is best qualified for the job. This step is called the selection process. Selection involves mutual decision and prediction. The enterprise decides whether to make a job offer and how attractive the offer should be. The job candidate decides whether the enterprise and the job offer fit his or her needs and personal goals.

   The process also seeks to predict which applicants will be successful if hired. Success, in this case, means performing well on the criteria the enterprise uses to evaluate employees.
7. ***Reference:*** Information generated from the references can be vital in the candidate's evaluation process, should be carefully carried out. Some of the broad guidelines are;
   - At least two references should be taken from each candidate
   - The references should have known the candidate professionally and should not be blood relatives. Check on family background should also be made through such independent referees.
   - If the references given by the candidate do not provide enough/relevant information, the candidate should be contacted for additional references
   - There should be a standardized format for reference checks to help avoiding missing out on vital information.
   - Request comments from the references in writing. However, the same can be done telephonically also and documented.
   - In case the hiring is being done through Consultants/Search partners, the onus of conducting reference checks on the candidate lies with them which should at all points of time be taken in writing.
8. ***Medical checkup:*** All candidates who have been given firm job offers and who have accepted the same, will be required to undergo a comprehensive health check-up. Some of the guidelines to be followed are;
   - Unit HR should tie up with a reputed hospital/clinic for carrying out the health check-up for prospective employees.
   - Some of the suggested tests are;
     - Blood Tests
     - Complete Haemogram
     - Blood Sugar (Fasting & PP) cost towards the check-up will be borne by the Company
     - Only those persons who are certified as 'Medically Fit' by the Company certified doctor would be allowed to join.

9. ***Appointment letter:*** Finally deciding to hire a candidate, the final step in the process is to make a job offer. The following should be kept in mind while making an offer;

   - Job offers should be made face to face and not over the phone
   - Details of the candidates compensation and expectations should be taken well in advance to save time
   - Details of the offer should be kept ready before the candidate arrives (fitment in terms of salary to be in comparison with the salary band at that level)
   - The following documents/information should be provided to the prospective employee along with the job offer:
     - Company brochure
     - Latest Newsletter
     - Address of website
     - Details of joining formalities
     - Working hours, Dress code
   - The offer letter should be handed over to the prospective employee in an envelope. Close the offer in style.

AXIS BANK

Axis Bank was the first of the new private banks to have begun operations in 1994, after the Government of India allowed new private banks to be established. The Bank was promoted jointly by the Administrator of the specified undertaking of the Unit Trust of India (UTI - I), Life Insurance Corporation of India (LIC) and General Insurance Corporation of India (GIC) and other four PSU insurance companies, i.e. National Insurance Company Ltd., The New India Assurance Company Ltd., The Oriental Insurance Company Ltd. and United India Insurance Company Ltd.

The Bank today is capitalized to the extent of Rs. 358.97 crores with the public holding (other than promoters) at 57.59%. The Bank's Registered Office is at Ahmedabad and its Central Office is located at Mumbai. Presently, the Bank has a very wide network of more than 729 branch offices and Extension Counters. The Banks has a network of over 3171 ATMs providing 24 hrs a day banking convenience to its customers. This is one of the largest ATM networks in the country the Bank has strengths in both retail and corporate banking and is committed to adopting the best industry practices internationally in order to achieve excellence. Become a business consultant. This implies that he/she knows the business well enough to advise and utilize his/her own company resources as well as outside of his/her own company's resources. As the discussion implies, this is not a short-term fix, and a long-term is what a salesman should aim for if he/she uses this approach.

Adaptive Selling

The reality of selling indicates that most salesman do not just follow a single approach at all times. Even while using one specific approach, a salesman may integrate elements of other approaches and therefore adapt how they sell. This is done constantly. Adaptive selling refers to the degree that salesmen alter their sales presentation or approaches across and during interactions with customers. This is because salesmen are responding to what they perceive of the prospective buyers.

There are five facets of adaptive selling. They are:

1. Salesmen recognize that different sales approaches are required for different prospective buyers. No buyer is the same. A good salesman must be able to identify these differences, be it subtle or loud, and adapt accordingly.
2. Salesmen have the confidence in their ability to use a variety of approaches. If not, it will fail. This confidence must come from the salesman, perhaps through experience and backing from the company.
3. Salesman must have confidence in his/her own ability to alter approach during an interaction. This is the difficult part, where after speaking and utilizing a specific approach the salesman realizes that it is not working or the prospective buyer is not responding. The salesman must be able to react, and react fast. Here lies the issue of self-confidence.
4. Collection of information to facilitate the adaptation. Salesmen must be able to walk in a room, walk up to prospective buyer, and judge based on the surroundings and their prior knowledge of the buyer as to how to approach the buyer.
5. The actual use itself of the various different approaches.

Formulation of Personal Selling Strategies

Efficacy of Personal selling

Product, price, promotion and distributions are the focal strategies that a company uses to achieve its marketing objectives. These factors are also known as the elements of marketing mix. In view of the fact that markets are growing increasingly competitive each passing day, experts are not only advocating a sensible mix of these factors but also reports and resignation acceptance, if employed earlier (properly stamped by your previous employer, clearly Mentioning the designation and the contact no. of the officer accepting your resignation, last working day) Relieving letter if received, at the address as under.

TRY YOURSELF

1. Discuss the strengths and weaknesses of recruitment and selecting system of both companies.

INTRODUCTION

Recruitment is the process of locating and attracting job applicants. Recruiting and selecting a new sales force is an important aspect of the sales manager's job.

The basic objective of sales force planning is to balance supply and demand. This requires consideration of a wide range of variables, including (1) Market conditions such as increased competition in the form of new goods and services (2) Economic conditions, such as increased inflation or economic growth (3) Demographic conditions (4) Technological developments. One of the major considerations in this process is that of determining sources to tap in filling both new positions and those of individuals who are moving on to other jobs. Figure 4.1 shows variables which influence the forecasting of sales force requirements.

figure 4.1

Variables Which Influence the Forecasting of Sales Force Requirements

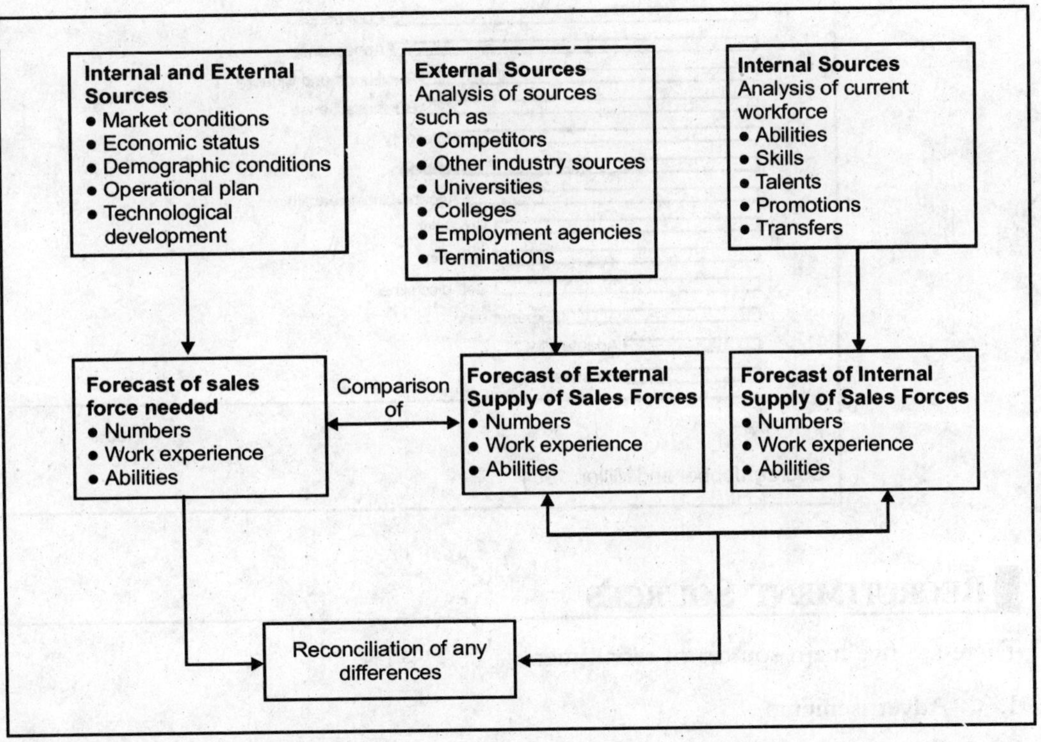

PREPARING THE JOB DESCRIPTION AND SPECIFICATION

The sales manager should prepare the job description before recruiting the sales force. The following factors should be included in any job description:

a. Title of the job

b. Duties and responsibilities

c. Reporting methods

d. Technical requirements

e. Territory to be covered

f. Degree of autonomy

Job description will act as the blue print for the personal specifications which describe the type of applicant the company is looking for.

Jobber and Miller have described certain important qualities of salespeople (see Percentage of respondents) as illustrated in Figure 4.2.

figure 4.2

Important Qualities of Salespeople

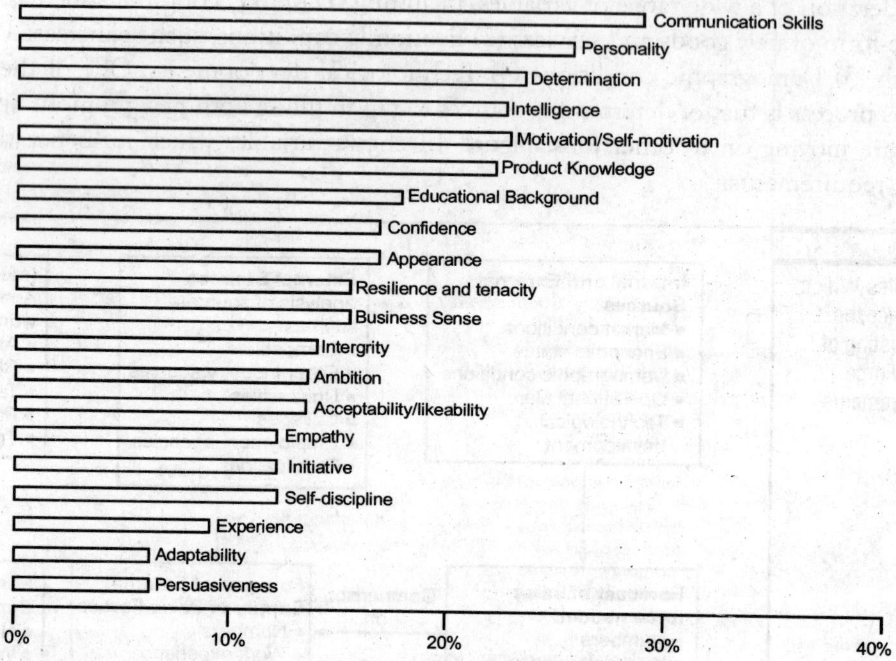

Source: Jobber and Miller, 1984

RECRUITMENT SOURCES

There are five main sources of recruitment:

1. Advertisements
2. From inside – the company's own staff
3. Recruitment agencies
4. Educational institutes
5. Competitors and other industries

Advertisements

Advertisements are both a source of recruits and a method of reaching them. Newspapers, magazines and trade journals are the most widely used media for advertisements which ordinarily produce large numbers of applicants in a very short time and at a low cost. However, this factor may be offset by the increased expense of carefully screening the large number of prospects. Also, the average number of applicants may be of questionable character.

The following are a few good advertisements for recruitment of sales force:

1. Manikchand Group recruitment for sales force
2. Times Multimedia recruitment for sales force.

figure 4.3

Manikchand

Offers rewarding careers for aggressive professionals in Sales

Traditionally a tobacco FMCG Company, the Manikchand Group with Rs.500 crores plus turnover and aiming at Rs.1000 crores in short span has successfully diversified into fields, such as Greeting Cards, Electrical Switches and Fast Moving Consumer Products like Mineral Water, Atta, Salt etc. To keep pace with the rapid expansion, we wish to recruit highly competent and experienced hardcore professionals who will provide the required impetus and at the same time assume key positions to lend vision and support which will effectively steer the company towards the demands of the next millennium. Each thrust area is considered as a separate profit centre, which will provide ample opportunities to the incumbents to scale new heights and reach the pinnacle of success. To take the quantum leap ahead, we wish to fill the following posts at our head office in PUNE.

ALL INDIA SALES MANAGER
(ELECTRICAL SWITCHES DIVISION)

To head the Sales and Marketing of our Electrical Switches division.

Job Profile: Will be responsible for all aspects of strategy planning and implementation of the wide range of products, right from the launching stage to locating established and new buyer markets. He will be responsible for all aspects of promotion and related day to day sales operations.

Requisites: An M.B.A. from a recognised institution with preferably a B.E. (Elec.). Excellent communication skills are necessary. Should have headed a similar profit centre for atleast 5-6 years. A proven track record in brand building is essential.

ALL INDIA SALES MANAGER
(GREETING CARDS DIVISION)

A savvy dynamic creative person with a flair for ideas, words and designs.

Job Profile: Must have thorough understanding of all intricacies of Greeting Cards market. The company aspires to become a market leader and only those who can meet the challenges to establish this division can fit the bill.

Requisites: A graduate with additional qualification of MBA is desirable. Around 5 years experience as a Visualiser in a similar capacity is an absolute must, as is a command over English.

ALL INDIA SALES MANAGER
(FMCG DIVISION)

A leader for our Fast Moving Consumer products including mineral water, atta and salt.

Job Profile: Candidate should have actually worked at consolidation of brands with vital inputs towards company's increased turnover. A sense of motivation is a must.

Requisites: An M.B.A. from a reputed institution with preferably a B.Sc. (Chem.). Experience of 6-7 years necessary.

The company is professionally managed and offers the right environment for realising potential and fulfilling growth.

Remuneration for all above posts would be at par with the best in the industry and not a constraint for the right candidate. Please mention present salary drawn and expectations. Selected candidates would have to make their own arrangement for accommodation.

All applications will be treated in strict confidence. Write with testimonials and C.V.s, superscribing the envelope with the post applied for, within 10 days to

The General Manager,
MANIKCHAND GROUP
Dealing Chambers, J.M. Road, Pune 411 004
Tel.: 321999, 322456, 322627, 323159 Fax : 322453

figure 4.4

TIMES MULTIMEDIA

The Times Group is a professionally managed diversified media conglomerate, which has grown more than 500 percent in the last ten years. The organisation culture promotes openness, innovation and excellence.

Times Multimedia, the latest in the new generation of Times Entertainment group, is poised to enter the market place with CDROMs, VCDs and DVDs. The division will be at the cutting edge of technology providing the market with Multimedia titles in the areas of entertainment, games, education and business,databases.

We invite people with Fire in their bellies to join this team who will make things happen :

Head - Sales & Marketing

This person will be in charge of Sales & Marketing. He/she will oversee the promotions, distribution and will be directly involved in strategic issues of the business. The person should be an MBA from a reputed institution and have experience in handling similar functions in Books/Toys/Music/other related industries.

He should preferably be under 35 years of age, with a good understanding of emerging technologies and should be a result oriented, self driven individual.

Product Managers

Candidates should be young MBAs from reputed institutes, tech friendly, creative individuals with business acumen. They should have an eye for identfying new opportunities in the market, scout for good business openings and have a good knowledge of consumer behaviour.

Manager - Promotions

He/she would be part of the Sales & Marketing team and would be responsible for branding, advertising, direct mail campaigns and all other promotion efforts. He/she should be a young creative person, an MBA from a reputed institution having 2-3 years relevant experience in coordinating with advertising agencies and running campaigns.

Sales Executives

He/she would be part of the Sales & Marketing team and be responsible for sales of the Multimedia products. Experience in handling channels like Music/Books/Toys/Computers will be useful. He/she will have to ensure that our products reach the shelves of all the targetted retailers across the country. Young, energetic, self driven individuals will find this assignment challenging and satisfying.

Accounts Manager

He/she will handle all Accounts and Finance related activities of the group. He/she should be conversant with Import procedures and be responsible for all commercial documentation and MIS of the group. He/she should be an ICWA/CA having atleast 2-3 years relevant experience and below 30 years of age.

Remuneration will be in line with the best in the industry. If you think your profile suits any of the above, please send your Bio-Data to :

Director - HR, Times of India House, Dr D N Road, Mumbai 400 fax your CV to 2652966. (Kindly superscribe the envelope with the position ap

THE TIMES GROUP

From Inside — The Organisation's Own Staff

The advantage of this source is that the candidate is familiar with the working of the company and its products. The company also knows the candidate much more intimately than any outsider or external candidate.

Recruitment Agencies

Recruitment agencies provide bio-datas of potential candidates for a fee. Normally, these agencies screen applicants for their suitability to various levels of sales positions. If the agency is selected carefully and good long-term relations are established with it, it pays in the long run.

Educational Institutions

This source includes management institutes, universities and technical institutes. This source is used for placement at the entry level. Recruits from educational institutions are more easily adaptable than their more experienced counterparts. The advantage of recruiting from institutes is that candidates are likely to be intelligent and possess the required technical qualifications.

Competitors and Other Industries

The advantage of this source is that the salesperson knows the market and its customers. Also the ability of the salesperson may be known to the recruiting company thus reducing the risk because the candidate is well acquainted with market trends and customers.

Friends and Relatives

Friends and Relatives can also be hired if they meet the necessary qualifications required for the job. It generates more confidence between employees when some known person is taken for the job. He can be relied upon.

Previous Staff

Many times previous staff which has served the organisation is willing to return. It may be either that he finds it more convenient to work with the old employer now or he is not adjusting with his present employer. Such cases may be considered carefully and if they meet the requirements then can also be considered for selection.

Selection of Key Executives from Outside

Nowadays organisations are trying to bring top executives from outside. The idea is to give a new look to the organisation and bring some famous name in the field. Such an approach is successful in same cases, while in many cases these selections are found unsuitable or good for a limited period only.

SELECTION PROCEDURE

Selection, as the name implies, involves picking and hiring a few people from the total number of candidates applying for the sales job. Selection is done by comparing the requirements of a job with the applicant's qualifications. The selection includes pertinent information on a recruit's mental abilities, physical characteristics, experience, personality and personal background. To collect that information, firms may incorporate the use of assessment centres and several selection tools including applications, resumes, interviews, testing, references and physical examination.

The following are some common steps in any selection process:

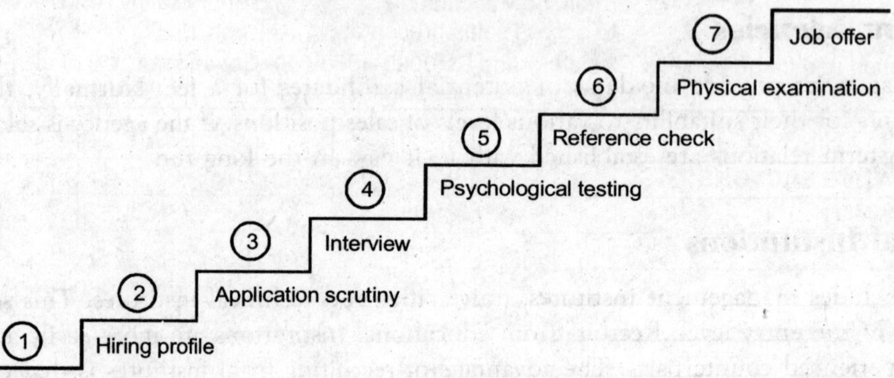

Hiring Profile

The aim of the recruitment process is to attract a number of qualified candidates. The sales manager must be careful here not to go to either extreme. The sales manager should develop a hiring profile system. Figure 4.5 shows the hiring profile form of a sales force.

figure 4.5
Hiring Profile Form of M/s VERO Cycles Ltd

JOB DESCRIPTION

1. Job title:
2. Basic job objectives:
3. Secondary objectives:
4. Responsible to:
5. Duties:
6. Performance evaluation:
7. Remuneration and fringe benefits
   (salary grade, commission system, bonus payments, car/fringe benefits)

JOB DESCRIPTION	
1. Job title	Territory sales representative
2. Basic job objectives	To achieve sales targets for all products each month.
3. Secondary objectives	To open at least six new accounts a month. To erect at least four displays a month.
4. Responsible to	Asst Sales Manager

Contd...

5. Duties	Operate the laid-down journey plan. Make at least eight effective calls a day. Always carry full range of product samples and literature. Report weekly on activities to Asstt Sales Manager. Report monthly on state of trade and competitive activity to Asstt Sales Manager. Collect overdue accounts as advised by credit department. Follow all laid-down administrative procedures on cars, expenses, etc.
6. Performance evaluation	Actual sales as targeted per product per month. Actual vs target call rates, new accounts display. Field appraisal by ASM, at least quarterly, to assess sales presentation.
7. Remuneration and fringe benefits	Salary grade Rs 3000-400-6000, Commission 4% of all revenue from territory. Average total expectations Rs 12,00,000 p.a.

1. QUANTITATIVE FACTORS	
a. Age	20-22 Years
b. Education	12th Standard
c. Experience	Cold canvassing, opening new accounts and field demo
d. Special qualifications	Must be scooter owner
e. Intelligence	No more than average (IQ around 100)
f. Availability	Immediate.
2. CHARACTER TRAITS	
a. Stability	Expect 2-3 years staff turnover, therefore fairly low
b. Industry	Must be willing to work very hard to build up territory
c. Perseverance	Must have high perseverance to continue opening new accounts
d. Ability to get along with others	Average ability required as low call frequencies and short calls
e. Loyalty	Average
f. Self-reliance	High degree required. Little field supervision. Must be self-starter
g. Leadership	No requirement.
3 JOB MOTIVATION	
a. Money	High — commission major factor
b. Security	Low — if territory sales not increased, must replace
c. Status	Low — junior member of a small company in non-prestigious trade
d. Power	Low — fixed price list, no decision making latitude
e. Perfection	Low — must sell and move on, product selling on price rather than high quality
f. Competitiveness	Low — will work and be paid as an individual
g. Service	Average — but must avoid doing retailer's job for him, e.g. delivery, shelf-filling.
4 DEGREE OF EMOTIONAL IMMATURITY	
a. Dependence	Low - must be on his own most of the time
b. Disregard of consequences	Average - not too relevant
c. Incapacity for self-discipline	Must be low — must be self-starter
d. Selfishness	Must be high to be motivated by individual achievement
e. Exhibitionism	Above average - must be capable of speaking in public at women's association, etc.
f. Pleasure-mindedness	Low - must wish to work hard and long
g. Unwillingness to accept responsibility	Average - little responsibility to accept.

Application Scrutiny

The sales manager can now review the completed forms he has received. The main purpose of scrutinising applications is to identify those candidates who fit the job specification and can be called later for an interview and testing sessions. The following format (see Figure 4.6) can be used to scrutinise application scrutiny for a sales job. The format has information such as applicant's sex, age, height and weight/ his educational qualifications, experience and his participation in extracurricular activities.

figure 4.6

Format for Application Scrutiny for a sales job

JOB APPLIED FOR

1. May I have your name? ____
2. Your address where you can be contacted ____
3. Telephone where you can be contacted
   Working hours ____
   Other times ____
4. What kind of a job are you looking for ____
   Must be sales
5. What do you expect to earn? ____
   Must be in line with what is being offered
6. What are you earning now? ____
   Compared with 5, is he being realistic?
7. What are you doing now?
   Whom for? ____
   How long for? ____
   Is it good experience for this job?
   Good company? Stable?
8. And before that? Whom for? How long for? ____
   Whom for ? ____
   How long for? ____
   Was it good experience? Had he shown progression?
   Good company? How long for?
9. How much time per month can you spend away from home? ____
   Is it sufficient?
10. Are you willing to move home? (at our expense) ____
    Flexible?
11. When can you be available? ____
    Is that soon enough?
12. Are you married? ____
    Children ? ____
    Stable?

Completed by ____

figure 4.7

Salesperson Profile Form of M/s VERO Cycles Ltd

1. Quantitative Factor

a. Age

b. Education (including professional qualifications)

c. Experience

d. Intelligence (as measured by test)

e. Availability

f. Health

2. Character traits

a. Stability - maintaining same jobs and interests

b. Industry - willingness to work

c. Perseverance - finishing what he starts

d. Ability to get along with others

e. Loyalty - to the employer

f. Self-reliance - self-starting, decisive

g. Leadership - ability to manage others

3. Job motivations (not already satisfied with the job)

a. Money

b. Security

c. Status

d. Power

e. Perfection

f. Competitiveness

g. Service

4. Degree of emotional immaturity

a. Dependence

b. Disregard of consequences

c. Incapacity for self-discipline

d. Selfishness

e. Exhibitionism

f. Pleasure-mindedness

g. Unwillingness to accept responsibility

Interview

The interview is the most used but least scientific of the various tools of selecting employees. A salesperson has to face three or four interviews before the final selection. The personal interview is used to help determine if a person is right for the job. It can bring out personal characteristics that no other selection tool is capable of revealing. In sales, different approaches are used in an attempt to elicit useful information. The approach used will depend on the sales manager's personality, training and work experience.

Types of Sales Interviews

Interviews differ, depending on the number of questions that are prepared in advance and the extent to which the interviewer guides the conversation. There are two types of interviews, (1) Structural interview or guided interview, and (2) Informal or unstructured interview.

Procedure of an Interview

The following steps are generally involved in an interview procedure:

a. Reviewing background information

b. Preparing a question plan

c. Conducting the interview

d. Concluding the interview.

The following format can be used for the purpose of rating:

figure 4.8

Format for Rating a Candidate

VERO CYCLES LTD

(Personnel Department)

(Confidential)

Interviewer's Rating Sheet

Name of Candidate ....

Position .... Deptt. ....

WRITTEN TEST

Give Ratings: A- Excellent, B-Good, C-Fair, D-Poor

Traits	Brief Notings	Rating
Background		
Conversational Ability		
Personality		
Qualifications		
Experience		
Overall Suitability		
Special Remarks		

Recommended for the Position: Yes/No

Signature of Interviewer

Date :

Rejected/Active Consideration/Selected

(Please return to Personnel Department after signing)

Psychological Testing

A psychological test is designed to measure such skills and abilities in a salesperson as are found to be essential for successful job performance.

Some important tests are: knowledge tests, ability tests, aptitude tests and simulation exercises.

a. ***Knowledge Tests:*** Tests measuring knowledge or information regarding sales job.

b. ***Ability Tests:*** Ability or proficiency tests are those which measure the skills and abilities already present in the candidate at the time of testing.

c. ***Aptitude Tests:*** These tests measure whether or not an individual has the capacity or latent ability to learn a given job quickly and efficiently.

d. ***Simulation Exercises:*** A simulation exercise is a test which duplicates many of the operations and problems confronting the sales job.

Reference Check

An organisation cannot be sure if it has all the information on an applicant until his/her references have been thoroughly checked. Reference checks allow an organisation to secure information not available from other sources. References are usually checked while the application form is being processed and before the final interview takes place. References from teachers and former employees are generally more helpful than other types of references.

figure 4.9

REFERENCE CHECK ON SALES APPLICANT____________________

Name of applicant

Person Contacted		Position
Company	Address	Telephone Number

1.	I wish to verify some of the information given to us by Mr........... who has applied for a position with our firm. Do you remember him? What were the dates of his employment with your company?	From______19_____To______19_______ Do dates agree?
2.	What was he doing when he started?	____________ Did he exaggerate?
	When did he leave?	____________ Did he progress?
3.	He says he was earning Rs ________ per ________ when he left. Is that right?	? Yes ? No Rs ________ Did he falsify?

Contd...

4.	How much of this was salary?	Rs ______
	How much commission?	Rs ______
5.	How was his attendance?	______ Conscientious? Health problems?
6.	How did his sales results compare with others?	______ To whom? How did get his contacts?
7.	How did his sales approach compare with others?	______ Industrious? Competitive?
8.	Did he supervise anyone else?	• NO • Yes How many? ______ Does this check?
	(If Yes) How well did he handle it?	______ Is he a leader or driver?
9.	How closely was he supervised?	______ Was he hard to manage?
10.	How hard did he work?	______ Is he habitually industrious?
11.	How well did he get along with other people?	______ Is he troublemaker?
12.	What arguments did he have with customers?	______ Does he like selling? Can he control his temper?
13.	What did you think of him ?	______ Did he get along with his superiors?
14.	Why did he leave?	______ Good reasons? Do they check?
15.	Would you re-employ him?	• Yes • No Why not? ______ Does this affect his suitability with us?
16.	Did he have any domestic or financial difficulties that interfered with work?	• NO • What? ______ Immaturity?
17.	How about drinking or gambling?	• NO • Yes What? ______ Immaturity?
18.	What are his outstanding strong points?	______
19.	What type of sales work do you feel he would do best?	______
20.	What are his weak points?	______

Checked by ______ Date ______

Physical Examination

Physical examination reveals whether or not a candidate possesses the required stamina, strength and tolerance needed under hard working conditions. The basic purpose of a physical examination is to place selected candidates on jobs which they can handle without any delay on health grounds.

Job Offer

When all other steps have been completed in the selection process, the company must decide whether or not to hire such an applicant. The applicant's goal and ambitions must be matched against present and future opportunities, challenges and other types of rewards that are offered by the job and company. A decision to hire is followed by a formal offer with no unspecified details or surprises; the terms should be in writing for the protection of both the recruit and the company. Some companies require that all new salespeople sign contracts containing all important job-related information.

LEGALLY WORKABLE PERFORMANCE APPRAISALS

A. A focus with respect to performance appraisal is the involvement of subjective judgments. In general, the courts have shown tolerance for subjectivity and performance appraisals, particularly when the positions involved are "upper level" jobs involving skills, attributes and abilities arguably not susceptible or at least less susceptible to objective measurement.

B. ***Elements of a Successful Performance Appraisal System:***

1. Clear instructions and training for performance raters.
2. Performance-rater familiarity with the nature and importance of job duties on which employee is being rated and with the employee's actual performance.
3. Use of an appraisal system that is as job-related and understandable as possible.
4. Precautions against improper bias by performance raters.
5. Some additional level of review and signature beyond the performance rater.
6. Some amount of monitoring to ensure uniform approach or application of the standards in the performance system.
7. Employee right to review and comment.
8. Employee signature to signify reading of review but not necessarily agreement with any rating.
9. Employee right of appeal if the system is oriented toward that.
10. Whether the system is numerical and traditional, or collaborative, some means to ensure specific and mutually agreed-upon goals.
11. Some statistical evaluation for adverse impact.

C. ***Practical considerations:***

1. Make sure the appraisals are actually done.
2. Try to ensure that the written text in the appraisal matches any numerical rating.
3. Use some form of review process to help ensure against arbitrary decisions.
4. Try as best as possible to ensure honest and candid appraisals so that, to the extent that the appraisal is set up to do this, it distinguishes between high and low performers.

D. Most truly effective performance appraisal systems are characterized by the fact that those administering the performance appraisals are well trained. Instead of offering simple instructions to performance raters, organizations that want the most from their appraisal process usually implement training programs to correct a rater's common mistakes. A list of common mistakes is as follows:

1. Halo effect – rating employees "excellent" in many categories when they excel only in one.
2. Leniency/stringency – very low or high ratings instead of finding any category in which the employee is average.
3. Contrast effect – evaluation an individual in relation to other employees' performance instead of on job requirements.
4. Similar-to-me effect – rating employees favorably because they mirror the rater's self-image.
5. Central tendency error – putting every employee's performance in the middle of the rating scale.
6. First impression – letting initial evaluations of employees overshadow actual performance during the rating period.

Some Management Considerations

A. As noted, a major issue with performance appraisal systems is defining the goals of the system and matching goals with the right tools and techniques.

   1. An emphasis on selection of employees for promotion or training and\or granting of compensation increases favors a traditional, quantitative appraisal with unilateral goal-setting by management.

      a. Managers may be more comfortable with numerical or scale rankings.

      b. Quantitative measures sometimes are easier to defend against legal challenges than qualitative appraisals.

B. If the emphasis is on communication, matching expectations between supervisor and subordinate, and mutual goal setting, then a collaborative approach aimed at helping employees develop and become more effective is preferable.

C. A system incorporating both traditional and collaborative approaches may be desirable, but such systems require sophistication and considerable attention to design. Employers should be wary, as noted, of imposing more goals on a performance appraisal system than it can be expected to accomplish.

D. Whatever system is used, a good measure of success is how those appraised and compensated perceive the accuracy and fairness of the program. A program that is seen as fair an personalized, regardless of sophistication, will likely be motivational. A good first step in deciding whether changes are needed in a performance appraisal system may be a survey of management and employee attitudes about appraisal practices and compensation.

Problems with Forced Ranking Approaches

1. With respect to discrimination issues, because forced raking presents the possibility that a satisfactorily-performing employee may nonetheless be ranked at the bottom and discharged as a result, the employer must be prepared to present a thorough explanation of the program, including its emphasis on comparative rather than actual job performance, in order to avoid findings of pretext and/or discriminatory intent.
2. To avoid disparate or adverse impact claims, the employer must ensure against disproportionate effect on employees in protected categories.

3. Such systems do not impose honesty in performance evaluations - more often they artificially deflate ratings. Because employee performance is rated in comparison with performance of other employees, it may have little to do with actual job performance.

4. Even if all employees are performing well, some will be ranked at the bottom, which may punish those organization that have recruited and trained well, but weeded out poor performers.

5. At the senior or executive-level, a company may not be accepting of the proposition that a certain proportion of employees are unworthy of retention.

6. If a forced ranking system is pushed too many levels down from senior and executive level positions, the tendency may be to impose the forced lower ranking on employees in positions which are less crucial, so that ranking becomes more dependent of job than quality of performance.

7. Forced ranking systems provide little allowance for market factors - some positions are difficult to fill because the labour market includes few persons with necessary skills. An employee in such a position may be marginal performer, but hard to replace, so that a discharge based on forced ranking be an unwanted result.

Sales and Cost of Sales Forecasting

Sales forecasting is basic to any business plan or budget and to some investment analysis. Essentially, you need to collect information for or make forecasts concerning as many as five related variables. For example, you typically need to collect the units and dollars of inventory that you already hold or that you estimate you will hold at the beginning of the sales forecast. In a manufacturing firm, these amounts are the sum of the work in process, or partially manufactured, inventory and the finished goods, or ready to sell, inventory. In a wholesaling or retailing firm, these amounts are the sum of those items purchased for resale. You need to collect both the units of inventory and the dollars of inventory. (In a service business, no inventory is manufactured or purchased, so these amounts are 0). Second, for each period in the forecasting horizon, you need to forecast the number of units produced if you're a manufacturer of the number of units purchased if you're a wholesaler or retailer. Typically, the amounts cannot be forecasted independent of sales, but sales isn't the only variable that affects production or purchases. Other important variables such as manufacturing capacities and availability of inventory items to purchases also impact planned production and purchases. Third, you need to forecast the costs of producing or purchasing the inventory for each period over the forecasting horizon. For a manufacturing firm, costs are often forecasted by classifications such as direct labour (the wages and employee benefits incurred in making the item), direct material (the raw materials and components that go into the finished product), and factory overhead (the miscellaneous and incidental costs associated with making the item, such as electricity to run the manufacturing equipment). For wholesalers and retailers, forecasted costs are the amounts paid to suppliers for those items purchased for resale. In a service business, no inventory is manufactured or purchased, so no production or purchase costs exist.

Fourth, you need to forecast the number of units sold and the price per unit sold for each period over the forecasting horizon. For manufactures, wholesalers, and retailers, the unit forecast simply is the number of cars, shirts, or basketballs sold; the unit price forecast is simply the price at which these items are sold to the customer. For service firms, the unit forecast simply is the number of times a service is provided or the hours of work performed; the unit price forecast is simply the price at which the service or work is billed to the customer. Fifth, you need to forecast any other variable costs associated with sales. For any type of business, these other costs might include sales commissions incurred as a result of the sale, taxes on the sale, and any other costs incurred and directly tied to the sale. With this information, you should be able to forecast total sales, cost of sales, and margins. Usually when you forecast sales and cost of sales, you use either the financial accounting or managerial accounting format. Using the financial accounting format, you calculate sales revenue, cost of goods sold, and gross sales margin. Using the financial accounting format, you calculate the marginal sales revenue, the variable costs, and the marginal contribution.

Given the complexity and size of today's organizations, sales forecasting is no longer an isolated exercise. Rather, it must be integrated into all facets of an organization to produce a business that urns more efficiently; thus saving money, increasing profitability and serving its customers better. Quality people, accurate data, current systems, relevant policies, and streamlined processes can support reliable sales forecasting, but it is a wasteful activity if it is not incorporated by management into the very core of decision making for all key business functions.

Financial Planning: Wall Street measures the success of a company by how well it meets its sales targets. Inaccuracies in the sales forecasts may lead to unfavorable earnings discrepancies, which result in a decline in share prices and puts the company's performance and management's ability under close scrutiny.

Sales Operations: Sales forecasts help enable an efficient and effective sales force through sales territory planning, refocusing limited sales resources on areas with maximum revenue potential, and fostering better sales collaboration. Manufacturing: Sales forecasts drive demand planning and inventory planning, aligning production capacity to avoid expensive and inflated inventories.

Human Resources: Sales forecasts also help in human resource planning by avoiding surprise layoffs or scrambling to find new hires needed to meet new business demands. An argument can be made that without incorporating accurate sales forecasts into decision making, companies are creating many of the serious problems that they will eventually struggle with in the near future. If accuracy is so important, then why is it that forecasts usually turn out to be wrong? The reasons behind the inaccuracies are best understood by examining the techniques employed in creating forecasts.

Judgment Based Forecasting: This involves a large degree of reliance on field sales personnel who are directly in touch with customers and understand changing buying behaviours and marketplace patterns. However, such forecasts are enriched by the application of gut feelings and wishful thinking using subjective, extrapolation and naive techniques. Without proper documentation of these judgments, large distortions in the forecast can occur when forecasts are passed up sales levels.

Statistical Forecasting: This involves relying on historical trends to predict short term and long term future performance. All statistical methods either even out the peaks and troughs in sales history to produce trend-based forecasts, or else they look for repeated patterns to create future forecasts. Mathematically, it is possible to forecast sales with some precision. Realistically, however, this precision can be dulled because of external market and economic factors that are beyond a business's control.

External Causal Factor-Based Forecasting: This involves relying on industry predictions for growth or shrinkage in market segments, economic predictions of consumer buying power, predictions of the effects of political change, and competitive intelligence regarding new product launches, new advertising campaigns and changes in pricing polices. None of the techniques mentioned above can provide a good forecast if used in isolation. The method most likely to succeed is forecasting from the 'bottom up', and reviewing forecasts from the 'top down'. This means building a robust forecasting platform that uses field knowledge of the business as the basis of the forecast and enriches it with informed management judgment that leverages statistical analysis of past sales performance, expected market conditions and external causal factors. But not all businesses are capable of adopting such a robust forecasting platform due to the time, effort and cost involved. The appropriate forecasting technique for a business or organization should be determined by its particular needs and must consider the following set of forecasting attributes.

Degree of accuracy required: If the decisions made on the basis of sales forecasts have a high risk attached to them, then the forecast should be prepared as accurately as possible. A combination of all three techniques may need to be used even though this involves more cost and effort. Management needs to think through what constitutes an acceptable tolerance of forecast error and what metrics/governance are in place to monitor accuracy. Forecast horizon - The time horizon that the sales forecast is intended to cover can affect the choice of forecasting technique. Is the company forecasting next week's sales, or forecasting what will happen to the overall size of the market in the sufficient for shorter time horizons.

Availability of historical data: Position in the product life cycle can affect the availability and hence the ability to use past sales data for statistical forecasting. For products at the "introductory" stage of the product life cycle, less sales data and information may be available than when products are at the "maturity" stage, when time series can be a useful forecasting method Access to competitive data - In some markets there is a wealth of available sales and competitor information, while in others it is hard to find reliable, up-to-date information, potentially limiting the ability to use external causal factor based forecasting. The relative importance of the different attributes listed above also varies given the nature of current economic conditions. In a recessionary economy where cost containment and resource optimization are a top priority, tolerance for sales forecast errors are lower. A high degree of forecast accuracy is required to ensure inventory control, optimize sales team allocation and plan channel flow. In such times, there is also a greater focus on longer forecast horizons that can guide long - term strategy and decision making, unlike in a growth economy where management is rarely worried about forecasting beyond the upcoming quarter. Forecasting in recessionary times also presents another problem; historical trends are not as relevant and may not be indicative of the numerous unknown variables sure to be present in times to come. To conclude, in current economic conditions, sales forecasting forces a business to look at the future objectively and can make the difference between just surviving and being a highly successful business. However, there is no denying that it is a tricky job because so many different factors can affect future sales.

SALES FORCE TRAINING

The purpose of sales training is to achieve improved job performance. In the absence of training, job performance improves with experience. Training substitutes for job experience so that trained sales personnel achieve high job performance levels faster.

The overall efficiency of a company's personal selling operation is influenced by the state of relations with customers and prospects. The sales force plays a crucial role in moulding and maintaining these relations. Contrasted with inexperienced sales personnel, experienced sales personnel maintain better continuing relations and make better impressions on prospects. Sales training contributes by accelerating the process of learning through experience.

Aim of Training

There may be a number of sales training programmes. It is desirable that before any training programme is imparted, its aim is clearly defined; whether the idea is to train the salesperson so that he may represent the company better in the market, or want higher turnover from him or to make him aware of new products that the organisation is going to launch. The defining of training aim will ease the planning of sales force training and bring better results. It will also help to evaluate the whole programme at a later date.

Building Sales Training Programmes

There are several types of sales training programmes. The most comprehensive and the longest is for newly recruited sales personnel. More intensive and shorter programmes on specialised topics, as well as periodic refresher courses, are presented for experienced sales personnel. Many companies provide sales training programmes for the sales personnel of their distributors and/or dealers.

Identifying Initial Training Needs

To determine the need for/and specific aims of an initial sales training programme, requires an analysis of three factors

- ***Job specifications:*** The qualifications needed to perform jobs are detailed in job specifications. The training has to be given according to job specifications.
- ***Trainee's background and experience:*** Each individual enters the initial sales training programme with a unique educational background and experience record. Training has to be given according to the sales personnel's background and experience.
- ***Sales-related marketing policies:*** To determine initial sales training needs, sales-related marketing policies must be analysed. Differences in products and markets mean differences in selling practices and policies which, in turn, means differences in training programmes.

Training on Market Place

Market place includes the wide client base upon which the selling process is focused. This is done in an environment which is subject to a range of influences and pressures which affect the final sales outcome. The market place is subject to constant change and these changes are opportunities to communicate to a varying and mobile audience.

During the training, sales staff should be informed about the location of the market where the company's products are already sold. It is desirable to inform the trainee about the important market places and areas in which the company wishes to put more efforts. (Figure 4.10)

figure 4.10

Training on Market Place

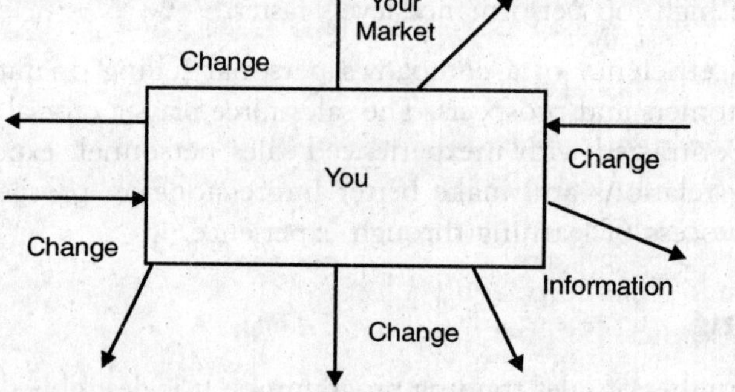

Training on Competitors

The sales force should have sufficient knowledge about the competition. By understanding the competition, you can ensure that you are fulfilling your customer's needs more closely than your competitors are doing.

How great is your awareness of competitors? The following checklist can help test your present knowledge of your competitors (Figure 4.11).

figure 4.11

Check List

A COMPETITOR CHECKLIST

1.	Competitor's Name	: ....
2.	Product Name	: ....
3.	What is the current percentage market share?	: ....
4.	What are the trends? Are percentage market shares and actual sales growing or declining?	: ....
5.	What added value, if any, does the competitor company add?	: ....
6.	Who is the competitor's representative in your territory?	: ....
7.	How are competitor's products promoted? Are you aware of their advertising, mailing service or educational or promotional items?	: ....
8.	What is the general image and prestige of the competitor?	: ....
9.	What could you learn from a competitor's representative?	: ....
10.	What are major markets of the competitor?	: ....

Training in Handling the Competition

The following four methods will help a salesperson to best handle the competition.

1. ***Create new needs:*** Through careful questioning techniques that the salesperson has developed using his previous selling skills training, he should try to uncover areas of need that the customer may not be aware of.
2. ***Present the product differently:*** A salesperson should present a company's products in different ways. His aim should be to bring about a change in the situation. His communication approach must also change.
3. ***Wait for the right opportunity:*** For example, the salesperson should invite the customer to a scientific or technical meeting where he/she may be influenced by peers or opinion leaders towards his product or offer.
4. ***Be prepared:*** The salesperson should use all information gathered previously to know his market and his customer. Be proactive!

Training on Communication

As we know, communication is a two-way process. It is an interaction between one or more persons. It is important to check that the message that the salesperson conveys is the same as the one his client receives.

There are different ways to communicate and the way chosen by the salesperson should match the message he is trying to convey. Communication may be by words, written or spoken, or by non-verbal means–by signs and symbols, by music or dancing, or by facial expressions, gestures or body movements.

The message may be an expression of an opinion or feelings, such as when a client expresses dissatisfaction with product performance or the level of service he has received from the company. There are some simple rules for communicating effectively. They include:

1. Decide the purpose and objectives of the communication before speaking.
2. Clarify your ideas and think about what you want to precisely convey.
3. Choose the words carefully.
4. Remember that your message will be affected by the receiver's attitude.
5. The only way to check whether your message is being received and understood correctly is to get feedback.
6. Be sensitive to feelings.

Training on Negotiating

Negotiating can be defined as the salesperson and his client, starting from opposing positions, settling for a satisfactory solution.

Remember these essential points in the process of negotiation

- To achieve the ultimate aim of both the salesperson and his customer of coming to a satisfactory solution, the negotiation process will almost certainly take some time. A satisfactory solution achieved is a single meeting which did not require negotiation.
- Effective negotiation takes place when it builds on good relationships founded on mutual respect.

Training Methods

- ***Lectures:*** The lectures feature passive rather than active trainee participation. Trainees mainly watch and listen. The main weakness of lectures is that teaching is emphasised more than learning.
- ***Personnel Conferences:*** In personnel conferences, trainer and trainee jointly analyse the problems such as effective use of selling time, route planning, call scheduling and handling unusual selling problems.
- ***Demonstrations:*** Demonstration is appropriate for conveying such topics as new products and selling techniques. Demonstrating how a new product works and its uses is much more effective then lecturing on the same product.
- ***Role Playing:*** This method involves trainees acting out parts in contrived problem solutions. The session begins with the trainer describing the situation and different personalities involved. Each trainee plays his or her assigned role and afterwards they, together with other group members and the trainers, apprise each player's effectiveness and suggest how the performance of each might be improved.
- ***Gaming:*** This method, also known as simulation, somewhat resembles role playing. It uses highly structured contrived situations, based on reality, in which players assume decision-making roles through successive rounds of play.

- ***On-the-Job-Training (Coach-and-pupil method):*** This method combines showing, telling, practising and evaluating. The coach begins by describing particular selling situations, explaining various techniques and approaches that might be used effectively. Next, accompanied by the pupil, the coach makes actual sales calls, discussing each with the trainee afterwards. Then, under the coach's supervision, the trainee makes sales-calls, each one followed by discussion and appraisal.

THE MANAGER

When a company selects a person for its requirements it should find out as much as possible about the person – his nature, good qualities and shortcomings. The information so gathered, should be checked and rechecked from more than one source. If a person is appointed and after some time it is found that he is not suitable for the role or his behavior is not liked by the salesmen members, it will create lots of problems for the organisation.

Managing is a difficult job and the managers should be right decision makers hence the importance of right staffing.

Self Improvement

Now we come to the most pivotal point of this sales training program. In order for a sales training program to be effective, it should increase sales profits. Out of all the strategies devised at anytime and is the only one guaranteed not to fail. This mysterious principle is the law of increasing return. Because of it simple nature, the principle is often overlooked by those who believe that achieving success is a complicated undertaking. It can easily be applied to increase income and enhance every other area of life.

A great deal of the screening process is done at a distance - through promotional materials available in print or on websites, through industry sources, through third party sources, and through initial rather scripted inquiry phone calls. The best screening materials consist of concise statements of focus and objective referent points of competence.

A common mistake made by salespeople is to continue behaving as if they are in the screening process when it comes time to work the selection process. They keep marketing the firm when they should be selling the salesperson.

Once you're in front of the client - in the selection process-it's time to stop reciting the company's experience and to begin applying it to the client's own issues. This is what selling by doing does. Don't talk about your capabilities and what you've done with other firms. Instead, talk about the client seated in front of you and about her specific issues. People are far more impressed with your capabilities if they can see them applied to their situation than if they can only hear about them secondhand from someone else's situation.

Selling by doing means giving samples-doing real client work, in real time. It makes all the abstract directly relevant. Selling by doing shows an other orientation, demonstration a willingness to take risk, and exemplifies collaboration, It adds value rather than talking about adding value. It shows a commitment to the client, feels genuine, is client focused and collaborative, and makes the abstract feel tangible.

SUMMARY

The selection of the right sales force is important for the long-term future of an organisation. It is a task which does not always receive the attention it deserves from sales managers. The goal of recruiting is to find and attract the best-qualified applicants. Recruiting begins with identifying the sources of candidates. Recruitment can be from within the organisation as well as from outside the organisation.

The selection process begins with the evaluation of recruited candidates which can include multiple interviews, tests, a day in the field and background investigation. The interviewing process attempts to find the right candidate for a challenging job. Psychological testing is used by many organisations as it determines intelligence, aptitude, personality, knowledge and interests. After the physical and all other screening tools have been implemented, the organisation selects the best candidate.

PROJECT WORK

1. Mrs K Lata is a recent PGDBM from All India Management Association. She has decided that she wants a sales job in the durable goods industry. She knows that there will be considerable competition from people with much better experience. She wonders how to approach the cover letter and resume to differentiate herself. What suggestions would you give her?

2. A General Manager (Sales) has been hiring 100 sales people a year for the past five years and has been keeping records of recruitment sources. A summary of this information is as follows

Recruitment Source	No. of Recruits obtained	No. of Recruits Hired	No. of Sales People after One Year
Employment Agency	80	24	16
Advertising	200	16	08
Competitors	120	60	15

Should the general manager concentrate on only one or two recruitment sources? If one, which one?

SHORT ANSWER QUESTIONS

1. What are main sources of recruitment?
2. Explain in brief seven steps in the selection process.
3. What are the four types of psychological testing?
4. What do you mean by training on negotiating?
5. What is self improvement?

REVIEW QUESTIONS

1. What information does a hiring organisation seek when evaluating recruited candidates?
2. What are the different forms of interviewing?
3. What is performance appraisals? Explain with the help of suitable example.

4. What are the primary sources of recruits?
5. Discuss the role of psychological testing in the selection process for sales people.
6. What tools does a hiring organisation have at its disposal when attempting to select a new salesperson?
7. Suggest criteria for selecting salesmen for the consumer products division of a company.
8. Design a sales training programme for two newly recruited salesmen of the consumer products division of a company.

GO TO THE NET

Using Internet search tools how will you recruit your salesforce for the following services

A - Education

B - Training

C - Consultancy

D - Airlines

E - Banking

F - Insurance

Caselet

On May 01, 2009, the McMillan Cast Company, applied for a 5,00,000 loan from the main office of the Bank of America. Jeorge the president of McMillan cast, applied loan in person. He told the loan officer that he had been in business since January 1975, and he had considerable prior experience in flooring and carpets since he had worked as an individual contractor for the past 20 years. Most of this time, he had worked in Frankfurt and Michigan. He finally decided to "work for himself" and he formed the company with the Dun and Bradstreet report obtained by the bank.

According to Jeorge, the purpose of the loan was to assist him in carrying his receivables until could be collected. He explained that the flooring business required him to expand considerable cash to purchase materials but his customers would not pay until the job was done. Since he was relatively new in business, he did not feel that he could compete if he had to require a sizeable deposit or payment in advance. Instead, he could quote for higher profits if he were willing to wait until completion of the job for payment. To show that his operation was sound, he included a list of customers and projects with his loan application. He also included a list of current receivables.

Jeorge told the loan officer that he had monitored his firm's financial status closely and that he had financial reports prepared every six months. He said that he would send a copy to the bank. In addition, he was willing to file a personal financial statement with the bank.

Question:

1. Prepare your recommendation on McMillan Cast Company.

CHAPTER 5

selection and training of representatives

learning objectives

The objectives of this chapter are to:

- understand, Selection of sales representatives.
- learn how to prepare of job description and personnel specification.
- understand training in personality development.

content outline

- Opening Case
- Introduction
- Selection of Sales Representatives
- Preparation of Job Description and Personnel Specification
- Short Listing and Interviews
- Consumer Sales
- Industrial Sale
- Training in Personality Development
- Conducting A Participatory Evaluation
- Sales Forecasting
- Summary
- Project Work
- Short Answer questions
- Review Questions
- Go to the Net

opening case

Sumit Products Ltd.

SUMIT Products Ltd. is a company that produces and markets steel cups, teaspoons, knives and forks for the catering industry. The company was established in 1958 in response to the changes that were taking place in the catering industry. The growth of the fast-food sector was seen as an opportunity to provide disposable eating utensils which would save on manpower and allow for speedy provision of utensils to cater to the fast customer flow. In addition, SUMIT Products has benefited from the growth in supermarkets and sells consumer packs' through four large supermarket groups.

The expansion of sales and outlets has led Rakesh Mohan, the sales manager, to recommend to S Kumar, the general manager, that the present sales force of two regional representatives be increased to eight.

Rakesh Mohan believes that the new recruits should be experienced in selling fast-moving consumer goods since essentially that is what his products are.

S Kumar believes that the new recruits should also be familiar with steel products since that is what they are selling. He favours recruiting from within the steel industry, since such people are familiar with the supply, production and properties of steel and are likely to talk the same language as other people working at the firm.

TRY YOURSELF

1. What general factors should be taken into account when recruiting salesmen?
2. Do you agree with Rakesh Kumar or S Kumar or neither?

INTRODUCTION

Selection and training of sales representatives is an on going procedure in all sales as organisations as sales managers cannot hold on to their staff forever and it is also not good to do so. Generally speaking, the sales representatives that stay on are not quality people. All the good people will either get promoted in the same company or move on to other companies for better prospects. So, it is not just the selection procedure but training which is imparted to the selected trainees that plays a very important role. We provide training to new people for doing the job and then keep them training than for doing the same job better and better. Let us now look at selection and training procedures in detail.

SELECTION OF SALES REPRESENTATIVES

Selection procedure starts from the search of the right candidate. The normal places to look for them are as follows:

i. ***Internal search:*** Look for the people inside your own organization who may be interested in joining the sales department. Many a times, some people join the service in any department only out of necessity when their inclination and aptitude is for something else. We may have such people in the ranks of other departments and can always get them shifted to sales.

ii. ***Competitor salesmen:*** We can always try to get salesmen from the team of competitors if we are convinced that they are eligible and willing.

iii. ***From the staff of your distributors:*** Sometimes it is found that the distributor staff is very promising. We may consider taking them into the service of the company. Remember, if we do not offer them job in our company someone else will do that and we will lose the opportunity.

iv. ***From the institutes:*** Educational institutes are a good source of getting good people.

v. ***From employment exchanges/agencies:*** We may contact the employment agencies when our requirement is for less number of people. The agencies take commission for every person employed.

vi. ***From the staff of other companies:*** We also observe different people working in the market. If we find someone good we can always offer them the job. Since he is already working, our training efforts too will be reduced.

vii. ***By advertising in newspapers:*** We can always go in for newspaper advertising where we get wider choice. Newspaper advertising is very successful if the reputation of your company is good.

Selection procedure involves two different activities (i) preparing job description and personnel specification (ii) short listing and interview. We will look at both in detail.

PREPARATION OF JOB DESCRIPTION AND PERSONNEL SPECIFICATION

Preparation of job description will involve the following activities:

a. Deciding the title of the job e.g., salesman, sales officer/ etc.

b. Deciding the duties and responsibilities.

c. To whom the person will report.

d. Technical requirements of the job e.g., travel for 20 days a month.

e. Location of the job i.e., place of work.

f. Degree of autonomy e.g., limits of authority.

Personnel specifications change from selector to selector. They can be:

a. Physical requirement e.g., strong physique to withstand travelling strain.

b. Attainments e.g. education experience.

c. Aptitudes and qualities e.g., communication skills, motivation levels.

d. Deposition e.g., maturity, sense of responsibility.

e. Interests e.g., hobbies etc.

f. Personal status e.g., married/unmarried.

SHORT LISTING AND INTERVIEWS

Short listing and interview become easy once you have a clear job description and personnel specification – all those who do not fit the description and specifications are not considered. These short listed candidates are then interviewed to find the best suitable candidates for your consideration and appointment.

The next step is training the selected candidate for job responsibilities. The training is again of two types (a) Induction training and (b) On job training. We will look into both aspects separately.

Induction Training

This type of training is given to a person who is joining the company from outside. It consists of:

a. Company profile

b. Position in hierarchy and job responsibilities

c. Introduction to the administrative staff and accounts staff

d. Reporting procedures and standards of reporting

e. Knowledge of products, their features and benefits

f. Knowledge of manufacturing units

g. Handing over stationery and kit etc.

The induction training is done at the sales office itself. Some companies arrange a visit to the manufacturing unit also to give assurance about the quality standards. In pharmaceutical companies, induction training is very important as all the companies have different formulations and detailing procedures.

On Job Training (Field Training)

On job training is a very important aspect of the sales managers job. This is an ongoing and continuous process for both the sales manager and his subordinates. It is directed towards improving job related skills and along with it the personality of the sales staff as these are the people who improve or spoil the image of the company by way of responsible or irresponsible behavior in the minds of the trade. The company image in the trade circle is very important in getting good channel members and their wholehearted support.

Training Skill Development

The skill development training, though similar in both industrial and consumer products, differs in emphasis on different aspects.

CONSUMER SALES

Consumer sales are generally divided into steps of a sales call. They are:

i. Planning and preparation
ii. Approach
iii. Stock check/need development
iv. Brand talk
v. Objection handing
vi. Close
vii. Detail work.

All the seven steps are very important for making a sales call productive. If the salesman is weak in any of the above aspects (steps), his performance will not be top class. Let us now look into the steps in detail.

Planning and Preparation

This is the most important aspect of salesmanship. In fact, planning and preparation is the most important aspect of everyone's life. This is the time when you decide your objective – where you want to go, how you want to go, what is the help you will need for achieving your objective, what are the difficulties you are likely to face, how you will overcome them, what are the contingency plans etc.

To take care of all the above aspects, a salesman is required to take the following checklist into consideration;

a. Prepare the day, target, in line with month's target.
b. Decide the route/market you want to cover as per your pre-journey planning.
c. Check the daily sales report for the previous visit which was executed, whether all the complaints and replacements were taken care of.
d. Check the available stock and the transit stock.
e. If you are operating ready delivery arrangements then check the condition of vehicle, the accompanying staff, the loading of proper stocks (to take care of targeted sales), POP materials, posters etc.
f. Check the manufacturing dates on stock and the MRP on it.
g. Check price list and carry the current and previous price lists.

h. Check the sales bag and kit.

i. Collect samples (important in case of new product launch).

j. Confirm that the route/market you are covering is open.

You are now ready for the visit to the market. The only aspect left is the contingency plan. For making contingency plan you need to be a very good planner or a regular planner. But do try to prepare the contingency plan.

Approach

Approach is a technique by which you attract the customer towards you and create a good impression of yourself. There are two aspects of approach:

1. Personality
2. Method

Personality is in the hands of the person himself. How he grooms himself, how he dresses, how he talks, how he presents himself etc. The other aspects of personality like communication skills etc. also play a very vital role so they become a separate aspect of on job training and not a part of selling skill training.

Method of approach keeps changing from area to area, but one thing is common–you should have a pleasant outlook and greet the person in such a way that he appreciates it. Following are the common techniques of greeting people that are accepted by all.

Common to all (present generation)	Hi, Hello, Good morning/evening
Sikhs	*Sat Sri Akal*
North	*Namaste/Jai Siyaram*
Muslim	*Salam*
Parsi	*Sahebji*
Bengal	*Nomaskar*
South	*Namaskara*
Marathi	*Ram Ram*
Gujarati	*Jai Sri Krishn Kem Choo*
Jains	*Jai Jeenendra*

When you get to know each other, you should start calling the customer by name only which brings you closer to the customer. Try to make him call you by your name so that he gets convinced of your close relation. This closeness gives you better access to the customer and hence better business.

Stock Checks and Need Development

Before the salesman starts his brand talk and demands an order, he must know what quantity the customer is in a position to buy, what is his need. It may so happen that you will undersell or try to oversell. If you undersell you are a loser, if you try to oversell you may not get the normal order in which case also you will be a loser. So you must avoid both the situations and check the stock before starting your brand talk.

Brand Talk

What is brand talk? Is it something to do with some good things about the product or is it something which will make the customer buy the product or is it something that is known as salesmanship and gives the profession a bad name i.e. talking anything to please the customer, even lies, and make the customer buy the product? Brand talk is definitely talking good about the product but the objective is not to fool the customer but to convince him of the goodness of the product and its superiority over competition. The salesman should never tell lies and false information. If you believe in sales and its continuity over a period of time and you do not plan to cheat people and then run away, you should speak the truth and only the truth about the product.

The modern day definition of sale under the AIDAS formula which this author likes to promote is as follows: sale is exchange of goods/services/or knowledge (consultancy) for money with long lasting satisfaction of both buyer and seller. AIDAS is short for Attention, Interest, Desire, Action (sale) and Satisfaction. With this definition, cheating is out of the question. If you are not going to cheat, you are not going to give false information. Then how do you sell? Yes, you can sell with proper brand talk.

To give proper brand talk one must know the brand (product) well. To know the product well you must know all its features and benefits. Now what are features and benefits? Whatever goes in the product to make it are features e.g. milk, malt, carbohydrates and minerals are the ingredients of Horlicks so these are features and whatever comes out of the product are the benefits i.e. the easy digestibility, the milk proteins etc. are the benefits that the consumer gets from Horlicks.

Whatever the product, it will have its own features and benefits and one must learn to highlight them in a proper way and convince the consumer with them. Sometimes the products, features and benefits are not very attractive. In such a case the salesman has to rely more on the service and the profitability they offer to the trade. Service and profitability are the features of the trader. If a salesman prepares himself properly with the features and benefit analysis there is little chance for him not to win.

Objection Handling

The salesman may do anything to convince the customer but still the customer will always have objections (queries) before he makes the buying decision. What should a salesman do? Should he ignore the objections? Should he avoid answering them? The answer is a big No. A salesman should never ignore or avoid the objections. The customer raises objections only when he wants to clarify his doubts (before making the purchase decision). So all the importance should be given to handling objections.

There are many different ways of handling objections. The important ones are as follows:

i. ***Listen and do not interrupt:*** While the customer is making a complaint, listen carefully to understand what he wants to say. The customer may get pleased to find someone listening to him. Answer only when the customer has finished talking.

ii. ***Agree and counter:*** Agree to what the customer wants to say and counter the argument to prove how it is wrong.

iii. ***Question the objection:*** Question the objection by saying "Do you mean to say that ———" and restate the objection in such a way that it is answered all by itself.

iv. ***Trial close:*** In this method the objection is turned into trial close like : "If I clarify the point will you buy——— This way if the objection is true the customer agrees to buy and if it is false he rejects. In case the objection is false you need not answer it.

v. ***Hidden objections:*** Sometimes the customer may not come out with the objections clearly, in such a case the salesman should probe and ask "Do you have any doubt about ——then be assured that it is not true" this clarifies any doubts in the minds of customer.

vi. ***Forestall the objection:*** If you feel that the customer may raise the objections for particular aspects of the product then clarify that point to avoid the objection.

vii. ***Straight denial:*** This is not an advisable method but sometimes you are required to deny the objection clearly.

Close

Close of call is securing the order and making the sale. A salesman should seek every opportunity to close the sale immediately after he has checked the stock to decide the need. Remember that the salesman is visiting the customer to get a sale and not to give him information about the product. Brand talk and objection handling are tools to get a sale. If one gets a sale without using the tools, nothing like it. Following methods are used to close the sale:

i. ***Ask for the order:*** You can explain the stock situation to the customer and tell him (if you are seasoned salesman) how much you are giving to him or ask him how much you should give him.

ii. ***Summarize and ask:*** Summarize the discussions you had with the customer and tell/ask him to order.

iii. ***The alternate close:*** In this, the salesman uses sentences like "Shall I send you ten units or five?" or "Shall I deliver stocks in the morning or in the evening?"

iv. ***Action agreement:*** In this the salesman agrees to something and says "I will do this and send you so much stocks".

v. ***The objection close:*** In this the salesman shows that he is not in agreement with what the customer is saying but accepts it to get the order.

vi. ***The concession close:*** In this the salesman offers extra concession to finalize the order.

Detail Work

This step is directed only towards the creation of good will, display and merchandising not to face unnecessary objections and problems. If a salesman follows these steps, he will always be successful.

INDUSTRIAL SALE

In an industrial sale, though the steps are the same, the emphasis shifts from brand talk to negotiating the terms of sale because in this case the buyer is the final user and he does not buy a brand but a need satisfier. If he is interested in satisfying his need, and saving costs in the process, and if your product is replacing an expensive product and satisfies the need effectively, you get the order. In industrial sales the formula SPANCO is in use. Its meaning is as follows

S = Survey of customers

P = Prospecting the customer

A = Approach the customer

N = Need development/negotiations

C = Close (order booking)

O = Order processing

We will look into the steps in detail.

Survey of Customers

In an industrial sale you are required to find out on your own who your customers are. So you are required to do a survey of the industries and find out your likely customers.

Prospecting the Customer

This is the most important aspect of industrial selling – to get an entry into an industry. You are required to find out how your product is going to be useful to the industry. Who is the person to decide on which product would be used? Who is the person to inspect the product utility and quality? What is the current product in use? What are the qualities of the product currently in use? How will you prove that your product is superior/cheaper than the current product in use? To find out answers to all these questions prospecting becomes very important.

Approach the Customer

This is the simplest aspect of industrial selling. The only precaution one has to take is to approach the right person and impress him sufficiently.

Need Development/Negotiations

This is the time when the salesman convinces the buyer how his product is most suitable for him and why he should start buying it. He may be required to give demonstrations of his product or he may be required to make modifications in the product to make it suitable for the customer. The process is long and needs patience. You may be required to face rejections several times but you should not lose heart and keep trying. After you develop the need for the product, negotiations are comparatively easier. The negotiations will cover the price, the payment terms and the delivery schedule.

Close

Close is the collection of purchase order. In industrial sale it is very important to collect the purchase order as it confirms all the terms and conditions accepted by the purchaser and there is no scope for dispute afterwards.

Order Processing

Since order processing in industrial sale is not done by the sales department, the dispatch department should be given proper instructions so that they do not create unnecessary problems for you.

TRAINING IN PERSONALITY DEVELOPMENT

In this part of training, the sales manager explains the following things:

i. Dress code
ii. Personal grooming
iii. Body language
iv. Communications skills (a) written (b) oral
v. Listening skills
vi. Manners and etiquette

A good understanding of each of the above will help one become a better salesman.

CONDUCTING A PARTICIPATORY EVALUATION

What is Participatory Evaluation?

Participatory evaluation provides for active involvement in the evaluation process of those with a stake in the program: providers, partners, customers (beneficiaries), and any other interested parties. Participation typically takes place throughout all phases of the evaluation: planning and design; gathering and analyzing the data; identifying the evaluation findings, conclusions, and recommendations; dissemination results; and preparing an action plan to improve program performance.

Characteristics of Participatory Evaluation

Participatory evaluation typically share several characteristics that set them apart from traditional evaluation approaches. These include:

Participant focus and ownership: Participatory evaluations are primarily oriented to the information needs of program stakeholders rather than of the donor agency. The donor agency simply helps the participants conduct their own evaluation, thus building their ownership and commitment to the results and facilitating their follow-up action.

Scope of participation: The range of participants included and the roles they play may vary. For example, some evaluations may target only program providers or beneficiaries, while others may include the full array of stakeholders.

Participant negotiations: Participating groups meet to communicate and negotiate to reach a consensus on evaluation findings, solve problems, and make plans to improve performance.

Diversity of views: Views of all participants are sought and recognized. More powerful stakeholders allow participation of the less powerful.

Learning process: The process is a learning experience for participants. Emphasis is on identifying lessons learned that will help participants improve program implementation, as well as on assessing whether targets were achieved.

Flexible design: While some preliminary planning for the evaluation may be necessary, design issues are decided (as much as possible) in the participatory process. Generally, evaluation questions and data collection and analysis methods are determined by the participants, not by outside evaluators.

Empirical orientation: Good participatory evaluations are based on empirical data. Typically, rapid appraisal techniques are used to determine what happened and why.

Use of facilitators: Participants actually conduct the evaluation, not outside evaluators as is traditional. However, one or more outside experts usually serve as facilitator-that is, provide supporting roles as mentor, trainer, group processor, negotiator, and/or methodologist.

Sales Forecasting

1. Forecasting methods: an overview
2. Direct extrapolation of sales
3. Causal approaches to sales forecasting
4. New product forecasting
5. Evaluating and selecting methods
6. Estimating prediction intervals
7. Implementation
8. Conclusions

Summary

Training of sales representatives is essential to make them skilled. Just as a gifted athlete needs coaching and practice to perform at his best, similarly a salesperson also requires proper training and development. After selection, sales representative should be given formal training which includes planned programmes complete with schedules, lesson plans, visual aids, other teaching devices and systematic reviews and evaluation.

Training varies with salesperson's career cycle, salespersons levels, learning abilities etc.

Project Work

Study the following organisations. Discuss and prepare the job description of sales representative required by them.

a. Apollo Tyres
b. Dabur India Ltd
c. Citibank

Short Answer Questions

1. Discuss in brief selection and training methods for sales representatives.
2. How do you prepare job description for sales representatives?
3. What are the various methods of personality development?

Review Questions

1. How do you prepare job description for sales representatives in an MNC?
2. How do you prepare job description for sales representatives in an industrial organisation?

3. How do you prepare job description for sales representative in an insurance company?
4. Explain participatory Evolutions and discuss its characteristics.

GO TO THE NET

You are the sales representative for a B2C e-business. Next week, you have to submit a report on the qualities of sales representative to your sales manager. Prepare the report.

CHAPTER 6

compensation and motivation of sales force

learning objectives

The objectives of this chapter are to:

- study the various compensation methods and modes of compensating the sales force
- understand the importance of motivation and its effect on the sales team
- analyses the different motivation theories and their application.

content outline

opening case

ABC Company

ABC Company was a producer of several kinds of industrial equipment listed in exhibit. It developed from the efforts, in the late 1940s, of a gifted engineer and inventor, Srirang Pandey, who patented several of his ideas for variations on standard products. He founded and was active in the firm for more than twenty-six years until his death.

Pandey had been very interested in the selling activity of his company and had a strong sense of professionalism that he used in personally selecting people for his sales force. He managed the sales force until it grew to a size of three men, at which time he secured the services of Hiren Shah as sales manager.

Before Shah's arrival, and for several years thereafter, Pandey told the salesmen expressly the names of firms he wanted them to call on. The founder was actually interested in the reputation of his young company. His concern for reputation included product characteristics as promised, delivery on time (critical to customers for these goods), and ethical, highly reserved business conduct by the salesmen. However, this concern for reputation was not restricted to these factors. Pandey also wanted to have, as his customers, those who employed the finest reputations. For example, he told his salesmen never to solicit the orders of a small firm then known by the name of Rohan and Lovely, for he considered the owners to be social climbers without proper backgrounds. In addition, he did not like an advertisement of theirs he once saw in a weekly business newspaper. He also instructed his salesmen not to call on Kapoor Glow Ltd because it had been turned down for a loan at the bank that Pandey used. This was despite the fact that Kapoor Glow Ltd found credit at another bank.

Not all the instructions were negative however. Pandey had the sales men, all of whom were engineers, visit Camden Mills, Stone & Kruger, and South Indian Metals time after time even though all three were committed to other sellers and other product designs. He wanted ABC Company to be a name that such firms knew and respected. He also cultivated several large national companies such as Combustion Engineering, Indian Machine and Foundry, Westinghouse and Melpar.

After Pandey's death, Shah continued these policies for the better part of a year. At that point Jevan Vats, the new president hired from outside, had a long talk with the sales manager and explained that he thought some changes were desirable. The firm should try to maximise sales and abandon all the "notions and pretentions', as he termed them. The salesmen should be put on a combination of salary plus commission. The two other executives in the company, the finance man and the production man, spoke up with a thorough endorsement of such changes. The existing policy was straight salary.

With some misgivings, Shah devised a new compensation structure for his four salesmen. Under this plan he estimated that a salesman would earn about 80 per cent of his compensation through salary and about 20 per cent through commission. The plan was announced on August 1 and the men were told it would go into effect in thirty days. Sales in August slumped about 17 per cent from the same month one year earlier and 14 per cent from the same month two years earlier.

After one month of use, the sales manager conducted a preliminary inquiry into the results of the new compensation policy. The results appeared to be that the easier to sell items in the product line were moving well, those of average difficulty to sell were moving adequately, and the one item that was rather difficult to sell (the dryer) was moving very poorly. The exhibit gives the comparison of September to the last month under the old policy (July) and to September one year before. Shah presented his analysis from these data. The sales manager said that he would repeat his comparison after another month. In the meanwhile, the president told the sales manager to urge the salesmen to solicit orders for dryers.

Exhibit 1

ABC Company Sales by Product, Selected Months

Product	September (Rs)	July (Rs.) last year	September (Rs) two years	September before (Rs)
Dryers	2,10,000	3,45,000	3,50,000	3,22,000
Sprayers	77,000	75,000	80,000	78,000
Planers	41,000	43,000	40,000	39,000
Power saws	32,000	30,000	30,000	31,000
Drills	42,000	41,000	40,000	39,000
Sanders	95,000	73,000	72,000	70,000
Metal buffers	75,000	49,000	50,000	48,000

TRY YOURSELF

1. **Do you think that as a promoter, Pandey was right in promoting the kind of sales policies he did ? Justify your comment?**
2. **Evaluate the compensation package in light of the facts given in the case. What are the suggestions that you would have for an ideal compensation plan in this case ? (IGNOU, June 1998)**

Introduction

Compensation plans for the sales force are designed to achieve several objectives. Some of these are: to assist the company in meeting its sales projections, to bring the earnings of the sales force to desired levels and to reward individual salespersons in direct proportion to their efforts and performance.

There are a number of ways in which sales force can be compensated. These range from salary to fringe benefits and perks. Each method can be employed to aid a company in achieving the desired results. Each method has strengths peculiar to it, but no single one is perfect. Unfavourable as well as favourable elements are implicit in each method of payment. In the following table, we will discuss and analyse attitudes toward a compensation plan.

Attitudes towards a Compensation Plan

Salespeople Look for	Company's Attitude
1. Adequate income for adequate performance.	1. No conflict, no argument on this point.
2. Superior income for superior performance.	2. None here either.
3. Incentives for special achievement.	3. All but a few reactionary companies agree.
4. A base of fixed-income for security purposes.	4. Many companies agree, but some cannot afford a fixed expense such as salary. In certain industries compensation ranges from 100 per cent salary to 100 per cent commission. Company attitude will depend on circumstances peculiar to it.
5. At least primary fringe benefits.	5. No argument here, but not all companies can afford full range.
6. Opportunity for advancement, promotion.	6. As much to the company's advantage as the salesperson's.
7. A yardstick to measure performance.	7. Equally important for the company to measure performance.
8. Equitable treatment to all sales people; pay based on performance — no free loaders, no favouritism or exploitation.	8. Equally important to the employer.
9. A sense of security because of the feeling that he is respected and regarded as a human being who is important to the company.	9. Just as important to the company which must rely on the morale of its sales force. The sense of security and well-being of sales force pay many bonuses to an employer.
10. Flexibility in a plan, sensitivity to changing conditions.	10. Equally important to a company.
11. Simplicity — easy to understand.	11. The company agrees — the simpler the plan, the easier and cheaper to administer it.

Determine Sales Force and Compensation Objectives

The sales manager must consider many factors when developing an effective reward system. Before embarking on a reward system it is important to establish the objectives. A compensation plan should have general and specific objectives for individual performers. The following diagram shows a formal compensation process in figure 6.1:

figure 6.1
Formal Compensation Process

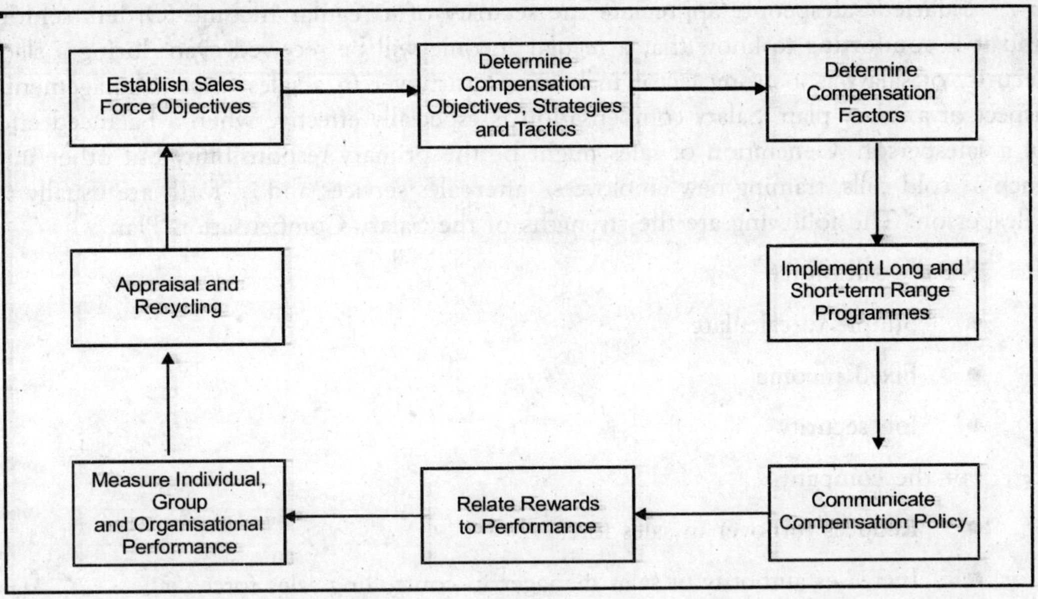

Once the compensation objectives are determined, the management should compare the compensation structure of the sales force with that of the industry and the sales organisation. After salaries are established, the procedures for administering compensation should be determined. Four basic compensation decisions affecting how compensation is structured for the sales force are made at the corporate level: salary level, salary structure, salesperson's individual salary, and administration procedures.

Various Modes of Compensating the Sales Force

Salary

A straight salary payroll is by far the easiest for employers to handle. Deductions for provident fund, income taxes and other fringe benefits are fixed and the work of accounting is reduced. In many industries, this method of compensation is generally used. There is always an overriding reason for choosing a salary plan. The following industries are using this method

- Highly seasonal industries
- High-tech industries
- Trade salespeople
- Route salespeople
- Missionary and educational salesmen
- Group selling

Salaried salespeople appreciate the security of a regular income. Orders seldom flow evenly and it is comforting to know that a regular income will be received even during a slack period. The security of salary is a strong factor in lowering turnover in a sales force. Management approves this aspect of a salary plan. Salary compensation is especially effective when a balanced effort is required of a salesperson. Generation of sales might be the primary responsibility but other important duties such as cold calls, training new employees/ after-sales services and so forth are usually required of the salesperson. The following are the strengths of the Salary Compensation Plan

1. For the sales force
   - Simple to calculate
   - Fixed income
   - Job security
2. For the company
   - Reduces turnover in sales force
   - Increases authority of sales manager in controlling sales force
   - An effective tool in case
     - ❖ Group efforts are required
     - ❖ Of business that is technical in nature
     - ❖ Hiring new staff
     - ❖ Of seasonal business

The following are the weaknesses of the Salary Compensation Plan

1. For the sales force
   - Lack of incentive to excel
   - Old sales force/under achievers tend to be overpaid
2. For the company
   - Fixed expenses, difficult to cut down expenses
   - Frequent adjustments in salary necessary, yet too many changes are as bad as too few
   - Requires excellent supervision which is not always available.

Straight Commission

Paying a commission is a variable expense rather than a fixed one. If sales are made, a commission is paid – no sales, no commission. This keeps sales expenses strictly in line. A straight commission pay plan has many advantages. It is desirable for a company suffering from a severe cash shortage since the commission need not be paid until proceeds are received from a sale. Flexible commission rates can be a strong incentive and many organisations are successful because the sales force enjoys a liberal commission schedule. Examples are real estate, automobiles, securities and insurance industries. Success of the Life Insurance Corporation is one example where commission is paid to agents on the basis of policies received. Sales force for a car dealership also works the same way; their job is to sell cars. Similarly, durable goods and services are sold on the same basis.

Salary levels are ,to a large extent, controlled by the overall performance of the company and the policies it operates under. A commissioned sales force, on the other hand, is the master of its own fate.

Target Commission

A straight commission is paid on sales volume. On a fixed commission base, a fixed percentage of sales volume is paid to the sales force. Other plans call for increase in rate as volume increases. A fixed rate commission is easy to figure and administer. If the rate is 2 per cent, it stays at that percentage whether the salesperson sells goods worth Rs 40,000 or Rs 4,00,000. A progressive commission rate accomplishes a major objective of most companies: it provides a constant incentive to the sales force to do better. The following example explains this:

	Sales (Rs)	**Commission Rate**
Up to	40,000	2%
From	40,000 to 1,00,000	3%
Above	1,00,000	4%

If a salesperson's quota is Rs 80,000, he would earn Rs 2,000 if he achieved that target exactly – a composite rate of 2.5 per cent. For example: Smith Kline Beecham is using this method in their worldwide selling.

Bonus, Profit Sharing, Fringe Benefits

Paying bonus is a method that a company adopts to reward special contribution and as an incentive to superior performance. Sales research has indicated that more than 50 per cent companies paying bonuses pay them annually, one-fourth pay quarterly and the balance pay half-yearly to earn bonuses, salespeople must work wholeheartedly for the entire year.

Profit Sharing

Many experts in the field of sales management disapprove extending profit sharing to salespeople. For once, companies agree with them. There may be an argument in favour of such a payment if no bonus plan is established for excellence in sales performance. The company can adopt a policy under which all managers – regional, divisional or branch – receive a fixed percentage of the profit made in their offices. They would be paid this irrespective of the condition of the company. Profit sharing, like bonuses, can be either discretionary or fixed.

Fringe Benefits

Fringe benefits have become a fascinating subject and an item of considerable expense to organisations. The costs of fringes can be as high as 30 per cent of direct compensation expense depending on what benefits are offered and whether a portion of the expense is shared with the employee. Many companies feel that the fringe benefits they provide must be in line with those offered by the competition. Fringe benefits are now a fact of life for all employers. These expenses are escalating and there appears to be little evidence that the future will see any reduction in either benefits or their cost.

Reimbursement of Expenses

Sales force expenses, as distinct from compensation, can range anywhere from zero to nearly 30 per cent of compensation costs. The "Zero" would of course relate to those companies that pay no expenses and the maximum probably would apply to employers of a small number of high-quality salespeople who travel the world to sell their products or services. The following are the major types of expenses normally incurred by salespeople:

- Travel – usually by car or scooter
- Meals
- Lodging
- Entertainment
- Miscellaneous

Companies may employ alternative expense allowances by which a salesperson would receive 3 or 4 per cent of his or her total sales amount to cover expenses.

Proper Sales Compensation Plan

Such a plan should:

- Provide a living wage
- Have performance Based pay levels
- Be adjustable to meet companys' goals and individual aspirations.

Such a plan not only helps in normal times but also takes care of special needs of a company.

Compensation plans are drawn after looking into the needs of the sales departments, its comparison or weightage as compared to other departments, availability of salespersons and nature of assignments – indoor/outdoors/outstations etc.

Change in Compensation Plan

Normally, compensation plans are not changed frequently; they are introduced in such a manner that there is minimum interference with established practices in the company.

But when there is low morale in the sales force, extra efforts are required regularly to meet the targets. So there is need to have a flexible compensation plan that can be suitably amended and adjustments made here and there to keep the sales force working with zeal and vigour.

Good Sales Compensation Plan

For preparing a good sales compensation plan, the following essential steps should be taken:

1. Define the sales job
2. Look to the company's payment scales to other staff.
3. Use grading or classification of jobs so that jobs may be compared.

4. Put in place a suitable job evaluation method to look into the relative importance of the job and decide the compensation.
5. Find out how much other companies are paying for similar jobs.
6. Give importance to local factors like place of work, distances etc.

Only after considering all the above factors, the company should prepare a compensation plan. This plan should encourage the sales force to bring results. Also there should be a system working simultaneously to punish those who fail to accomplish targets.

MOTIVATION TO THE SALES FORCE

Motivation is the force within us that directs our behaviour. Motivation is unique to every individual. A sales manager may adopt different methods to motivate his sales force. He should examine individual needs and use them as the basis for motivating his salespersons.

A sales manager can use the question guidelines suggested by Ginger Trumfio for motivating his salespersons (see Figure 6.2). In Figure 6.3, Sam Deep and Lyle Sussman suggest low-cost ways to motivate the sales force.

figure 6.2

Are you an Effective Motivator?

Keeping your sales force motivated is vital to execute ongoing sales. How effectively do you motivate your salespeople? Answer the following questions and you be the judge.

1. What are the three most effective techniques you use for motivating your entire sales force?
2. Do you know what motivates each person who reports to you?
3. Do you know what role compensation plays in the motivation of each salesperson?
4. Do you know what role recognition plays in the motivation of each salesperson?
5. Do you know what role "opportunity for growth" plays in the motivation of each salesperson?
6. Have you customised a motivational programme for each person who reports to you?
7. What have you done in the past week with the deliberate intention of motivating a salesperson?
8. Did you praise someone today?
9. Do you show your commitment to developing each salesperson by actively (at least once a month) coaching him on skills and techniques?
10. When a salesperson seems to be feeling stressed, do you ask questions and spend time listening to his concerns?
11. Do you ask your representatives, "What can I do personally to help your sales efforts?"
12. Do you review their monthly performance with them in a timely manner?
13. Have you done anything recently to "demotivate" your salespeople?

    For example: failed to give recognition; embraced a salesperson in front of peers or clients; taken over a sales call?
14. Do you treat your salespeople with respect?
15. Do you show your salespeople trust?

Source: Ginger Trumfio, "Are you an Effective Motivator?" *Sales and Marketing Management* (May 1994): 136.

figure 6.3

Low-Cost Ways to Motivate

- A pat on the back.
- A smile.
- A simple, sincere, thank you.
- A personal letter to the employee, with copies sent to your immediate supervisor and to the employee's supervisor.
- Public recognition in front of peers.
- Public recognition in front of one's boss.
- A letter of praise from a customer or vendor praising an employee, posted on the company's bulletin board.
- Listening to an employee who has an idea for improving efficiency and then acting affirmatively on that suggestion.
- Arranging employee discounts from your vendors or customers.
- Allowing the employee to work on an especially exciting project that he or she would not usually work on.
- Asking employees what non-monetary rewards they would like to have and, if possible, providing them.
- Issuing a "You Were Mentioned" certificate to employees whenever you hear something nice about them, whether from a customer, co-worker, or superior.
- Electing a high-achieving employee to a quality circle or to a company wide task force.
- Providing free lunch for employees caught in the act of victory by an appointed group of company wide "catchers"
- Rotating the "company flag" or other symbols of excellence from one deserving unit to another on a quarterly basis.

Source: Sam Deep, Lyle Sussman, *Smart Moves Reading*, Mass: Addison-Wesley, 1990

Sales Career Stages and Motivation

Are salespersons motivated by different rewards at different stages of their career? Do salespeople have different career and personal concerns based on career stages? The basic answer to both these questions is 'Yes'. A salesperson may be highly motivated throughout his or her career, but the desired rewards may be very different. Motivation based on career and personal concerns can differ. There are four career stages: exploration, establishment, maintenance and disengagement. Figure 6.4 summarises the characteristics of each stage.

figure 6.4

Characteristics of Different Stages in a Salesperson's Career

	Exploration	Establishment	Maintenance	Disengagement
Career Concern	Finding an appropriate occupational field.	Successfully establishing a career in a certain occupation.	Holding on to what has been achieved; reassessing career, with possible redirection.	Completing one's career.
Developmental Tasks	Learning the skills required to do the job well; becoming a contributing member of an organisation.	Using skills to produce results; adjusting to working with greater autonomy; developing creativity and innovativeness.	Developing broader view of work and the organisation; maintaining a high performance level.	Establishing a stronger self identity outside of work; maintaining an acceptable performance level.

Contd...

Personal Challenges	Establishing a good initial professional self-concept.	Producing superior result on the job in order to be promoted; balancing the conflicting demands of career and family.	Maintaining motivation though possible rewards have changed; facing concerns about ageing and disappointment over what one has accomplished; maintaining motivation and productivity.	Accepting carrer accomplishments; adjusting self image.
Psychological Needs	Support peer acceptance; challenging position.	Achievement esteem; autonomy; competition.	Reduced competitiveness; security; helping younger colleagues.	Detachment from organisation and organisational life.

Source: Adapted from William L Cron, "Industrial Salesperson Development: A Career Stages Perspective", Journal of Marketing (Fall 1984) 40; and William L Cron, Alan J Dubinsky, and Ronald E Michales, "The influence of Career Stages on Components of Salesperson Motivation", Journal of Marketing (January 1988); 79-92

IMPORTANCE OF MOTIVATION THEORIES FOR SALES FORCE

The sales executive's job is to make decisions and to see that others carry them out. The performance of sales executives, then, depends upon the composite performances of the individuals making up the sales force. Some sales representatives will put forth their best efforts without any special coaching from the management. To them, selling is the most fascinating job and they are ambitious self-starters, but the majority of sales representatives require encouragement and special incentives to perform at their best level. Thus factors influencing individual sales personnel to achieve given performance levels are:

i. ***Nature of Job:*** A sales representatives' job is usually tiring with irregular working hours. They do not often have the authority to do what is necessary to win an account and they sometimes lose large orders that they have worked hard to obtain.

ii. ***Human Nature:*** Most people operate below capacity in the absence of special incentives, such as financial gain or social recognition.

iii. ***Personal Problems:*** They are occasionally preoccupied with personal problems, such as sickness in the family, debt, etc.

High productivity in a sales force comes about neither naturally nor accidentally. It requires motivation.

The problem of motivating sales representatives has been studied by Churchill, Ford & Walker. They propose the following way (Figure 6.5):

figure 6.5

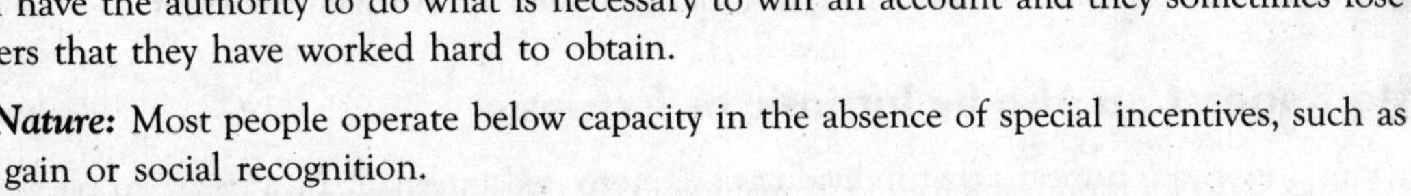

This model says that the higher the salesperson's motivation, the greater is his or her effort. Greater effort will lead to greater performance and greater performance will lead to greater rewards and this will lead to greater satisfaction which will reinforce motivation.

Specifically, for a sales force, motivation affects the amount of effort that the salesperson desires to expend on each of the activities, or tasks, associated with the sales job such as calling on potential new accounts, planning sales presentations and filling out reports.

A goods sales manager examines each individual's needs and uses those needs as the motivation for him.

DIMENSIONS OF MOTIVATION

Motivation has mainly three dimensions (Figure 6.6).

figure 6.6

XX XX

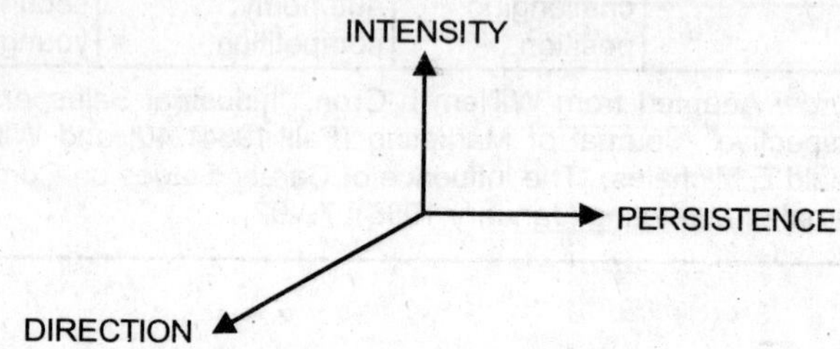

1. ***Intensity:*** It is the magnitude of mental and physical effort put in by a salesperson for his or her activity or goal. As this inner drive becomes more intense, more effort will be put in by him.
2. ***Persistence:*** It is the extension of effort over time. This works when first dimension 'intensity' is high and so the person has high persistence to expend the needed effort for the time period. In such a case, the person is said to be highly motivated.
3. ***Direction:*** It implies that the individual can choose how his or her efforts will be spent. Salespeople who are highly competitive and have high intensity and persistence will attempt to determine what activities are required to reach that goal and direct their behaviour.

Motivation Can Also be Intrinsic or Extrinsic

Intrinsic motivation means that individuals are motivated internally by a desire to please themselves or merely by the satisfaction of performing a job.

Extrinsic motivation means that someone else provides the motivation through methods such as pay, promotion or recognition.

A salesperson may be intrinsically or extrinsically motivated or motivated by both ways. The same intrinsically motivated salesperson may also be motivated extrinsically with the promise of more pay for an excellent performance.

MODEL OF THE MOTIVATION PROCESS

The motivation process consists of six steps (Figure 6.7):

1. Recognise need deficiency
2. Search for ways to satisfy needs

3. Establish goal-directed behaviour
4. Performance
5. Provide rewards or punishment
6. Process needs.

figure 6.7

The Six Step Motivation Process

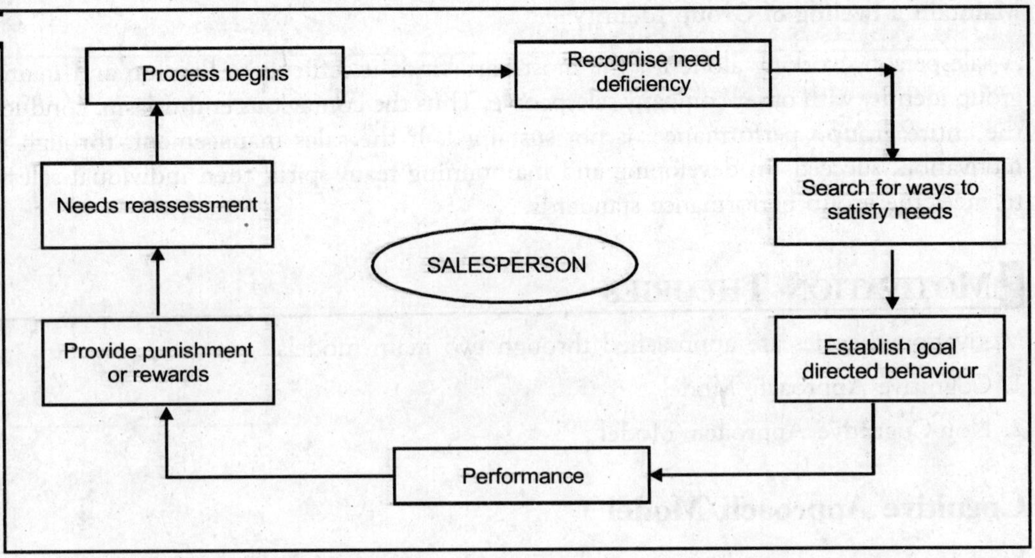

Reasons for Motivating Salespersons

As a member of a sales force, salespersons are targets for sales management efforts aimed at welding them into an effective selling team. Four aspects of the salesperson's job as discussed below affect the quality of his/her performance. Each aspect is an important reason why most sales personnel require additional motivation to perform their jobs satisfactorily.

Inherent Nature of Sales Job

To a greater or lesser extent, each sales job involves a succession of ups and downs, a series of experiences resulting in alternating feelings of exhilaration and depression. They usually meet unpleasant and rough persons in their daily job. Most of their time passes away from home due to which they miss out on family life. All these things combine to discourage and frustrate the salesperson which may affect his selling ability. Therefore there is a need to motivate salespersons.

Salesperson's Connective Role and Conflicts Due to this Job

A salesperson is an important member of the organisation's team. He has to satisfy customers as well as managers of the organisation. He has mainly four distinct groups with whom he must have cordial relations. These groups are (a) The sales management group (b) The balance of the company which is depending on him for orders (c) The customers and (d) Other company sales personnel. Sometimes the expectations of any one group may give rise to conflict. The conflicts that may occur in the firm may be due to conflict of identification or advocacy conflict. Thus, to remove divergent interests due to conflicts, additional motivation may be required to elicit acceptable job performance.

Tendency towards Apathy

Many sales personnel have a natural tendency to become apathetic as they have to cover the same territory and same customers continuously for a long time. So they tend to lose interest and enthusiasm. They feel that customers now know them so well that good salesmanship is no longer a necessity. Many salespeople require additional motivation to maintain a continuing enthusiasm for their work.

Maintain a Feeling of Group Identity

A salesperson, working alone for the most part, finds it difficult to develop and maintain a feeling of group identity with other company salespeople. Thus the contagious enthusiasm, conducive to improving the entire group's performance, is not sustained. If the sales management, through providing added motivation, succeeds in developing and maintaining team spirit, then individual salespersons try hard to meet the group performance standards.

MOTIVATION THEORIES

Motivation theories are approached through two main models

1. Cognitive Approach/Model
2. Non-Cognitive Approach/Model

Cognitive Approach/Model

Models of motivation which focus on internal states and mental processes are known as cognitive models (Figure 6.8).

figure 6.8

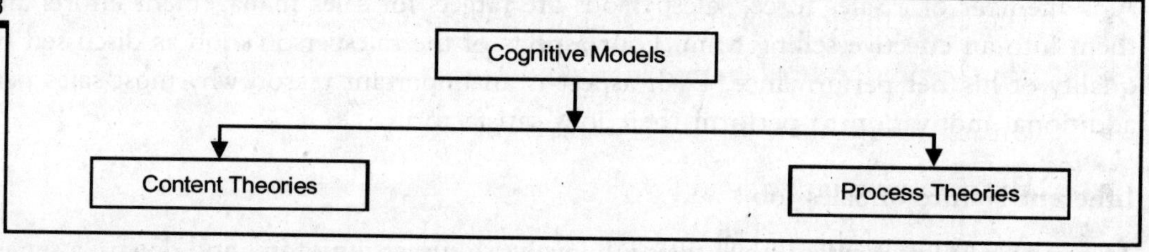

(A) Content Theories

These theories answer the question 'What motivates people?, To answer such a question most of the theories under this category focus on human needs and desires that are internalised and that give impetus to individual behaviour.

Some of the theories which are described further are:

i. March and Simon Model
ii. Maslow's Need Hierarchy Model
iii. Herzberg's Hygiene-Motivation Model
iv. Alderfer's ERG Model
v. McClelland Three Need Model
vi. McGregor's Participation Model

vii. Maturity and Immaturity Theory

viii. Theory Z: A Hybrid Model.

March and Simon Model

March and Simon defined motivation as a process or reaction which takes place in the memory of an individual. It is a combination of forces (motives maintaining human activity). They have established a positive correlation between productivity and motivation by means of the theoretical model shown here (Figure 6.9).

figure 6.9

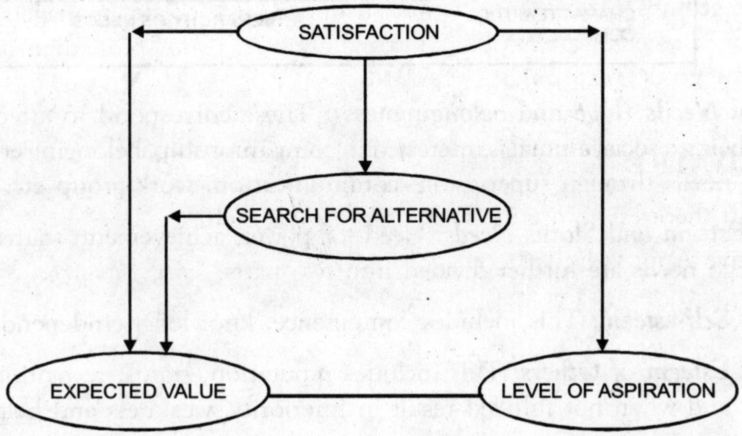

The main generalisations are

- The lower the individual satisfaction, the greater the search for better ways of doing the job.
- More search leads to greater expected rewards.
- Greater reward value gives a higher level of aspiration.
- Higher aspiration leads to lower satisfaction and thus continues the cycle.

According to this model, unsatisfied needs give birth to processes like motivation and if certain needs are fulfilled then it gives birth again to new needs, urges, desires, etc. This process never stops.

Maslow's Need Hierarchy Model

Abraham H Maslow developed a conceptual framework and defined a person's effectiveness as the function that matches man's opportunity with the appropriate position in the hierarchy of needs.

He assumed that the process of motivation is directed towards the achievement of the satisfaction of needs.

Maslow identified basic five level needs (Figure 6.10):

- ***Physiological Needs:*** Basic needs which relate to the maintenance of human life like shelter/ food, clothes, etc.
- ***Safety Needs:*** These include safety as well as security, i.e., the assurance of maintaining a given economic level through job security/provident fund/insurance/etc.

figure 6.10

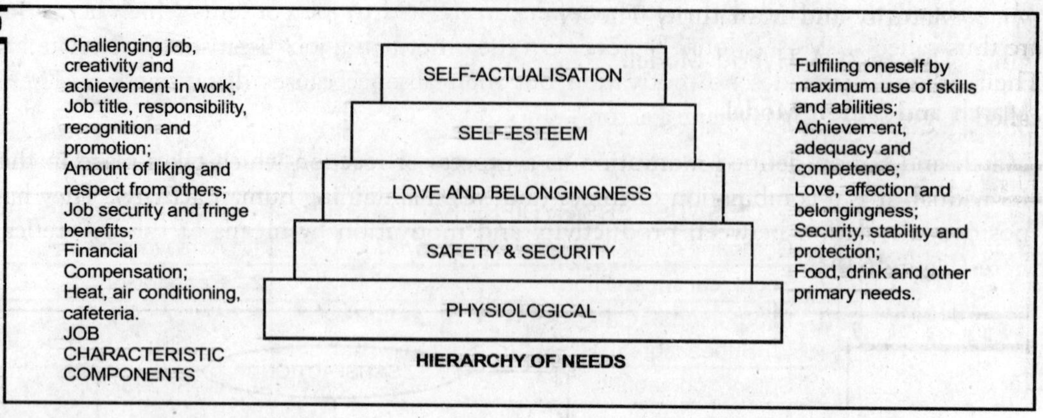

- ***Social Needs (love and belongingness):*** These correspond to affection and affiliation because man being a social animal is interested in companionship, belonging etc. Organisation can influence these needs through supervision, communication, work group etc.
- ***Ego/Esteem and Status Needs:*** Need for power, achievement, status, independence, competence etc. Ego needs are further divided into two parts:
  - ***Self-esteem:*** This includes competence, knowledge, independence, etc.
  - ***Esteem of Others:*** This includes reputation, status, recognition. These needs are infinite and when not fulfilled result in inferiority, weakness and helplessness.
- ***Self-actualisation:*** It involves realising one's potential for continued self-development and for being creative.

Salient features of this theory are:

- Urge to fulfil needs is a prime factor in motivation.
- Human needs are complex, multiple and interrelated.
- Human needs can be arranged in a hierarchy.
- Needs will be fulfilled in successive order from lower to higher, i.e., no higher need will act as an activator for motivation until the preceding lower need is fulfilled.
- As soon as one need is fulfilled, another need emerges.
- A satisfied need does not help in motivation. Rather, unsatisfied needs are motivational stimulators. Need hierarchy levels are interdependent and overlapping.

Herzberg's Motivation-hygiene Model (Two-Factor Theory)

Herzberg extended the work of Maslow to develop his theory. He conducted a widely reported motivational study on about 200 accountants and engineers employed in and around Pittsburgh, Pennsylvania.

The subjects in the study were given the following directions by an interviewer – "Think of a time when you feel exceptionally good or exceptionally bad about your present job or a previous one. Tell me what happened?" Responses obtained by this method were interesting and fairly consistent.

Reported good feelings were associated with job experiences and contents and reported bad feelings were associated with surroundings or job contexts.

Herzberg concluded that job satisfiers are related to job contents which act as 'motivators' and are thus called as 'Motivational Factors'. On the other hand, job dissatisfiers are related to job contexts. Their presence provides no motivation but their absence causes dissatisfaction. Therefore, they are called 'Dissatisfiers or Hygiene Factors'.

figure 6.11

DISSATISFIERS/HYGIENE FACTORS	MOTIVATIONAL FACTORS
1. Company policy and administration	1. Achievement
2. Technical supervision	2. Recognition
3. Interpersonal relation with (a) Supervisors (b) Peers (c) Subordinates	3. Advancement
4. Salary, job security	4. Work itself
5. Personal life, status	5. Possibility of growth
6. Working conditions	6. Responsibility

Salient features of this theory are

- Feelings of unhappiness or dissatisfaction were due to the environment or job context whereas feelings of happiness were due to job contents.
- It is necessary to maintain hygienic factors at a specific level because their absence leads to dissatisfaction.
- While the absence of motivational factors does not affect performance, their presence definitely leads to improvement in the performance.
- The above stated factors are unidimensional i.e. they flow only in one direction.
- The key to job satisfaction and high performance lies in job enrichment.
- Herzberg said that today's motivators are tomorrow's hygiene factors because they stop influencing the person's behaviour when they are obtained.

Alderfer's Existence-Relatedness-Growth Model (ERG Theory)

Clayton Alderfer formulated a need category model with three main core groups

1. ***Existence Need (E)***: Concerned with survival, i.e., physiological and biological needs, and safety needs, i.e., Maslow's first and second level needs.
2. ***Relatedness Need (R):*** Importance of interpersonal and social relationships, i.e., Maslow's third and fourth level needs.
3. ***Growth Need (G):*** These are concerned with the individual's intrinsic desire for personal development, i.e., Maslow's fifth and last level need.

Salient features of this theory are:

- It is an extended but brief model of Maslow's hierarchy.
- Consider the overlapping between various need levels, i.e., no need is separated by the other with clear demarcations.
- ERG needs do not have strict lines of demarcation.

- He distinguished between chronic needs which persist over a period of time and episode needs which are situational and can change.
- Along with satisfaction progression, we may experience frustration regression also, i.e., unable to satisfy one need, we may "drop back" and again focus on more concrete needs.

figure 6.12

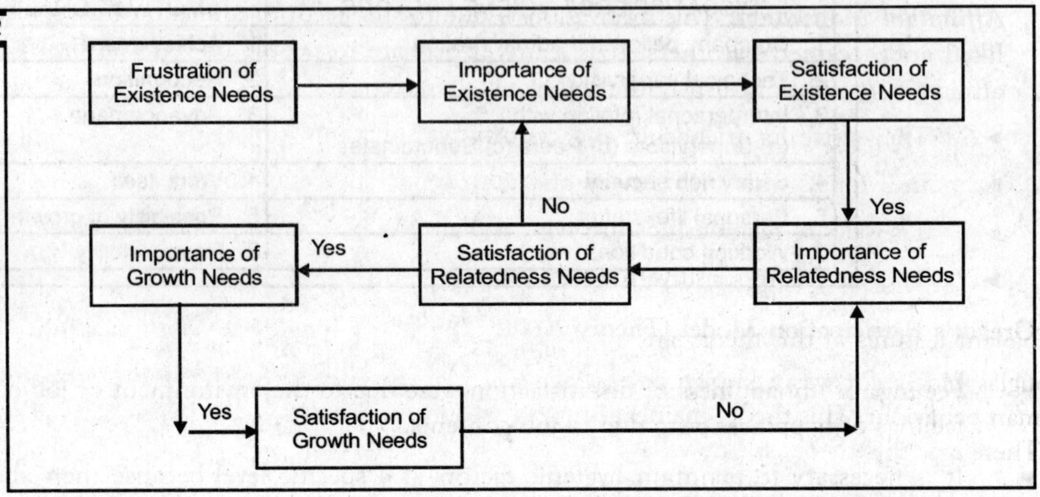

McClelland Three Need Model

David N McClelland, a Harvard psychologist (1961), used the Thematic Appreciation Test (TAT) to study various human needs. Through this test, he developed a model of motivation which is based on the three types of needs:

1. ***Need for Achievement (nAch):*** A drive to excel, advance and grow
2. ***Need for Power (nPow):*** A drive to influence others and situations
3. ***Need for Affiliation (nAff):*** A drive for friendly and close interrelationships.

On the basis of these needs he defined three types of motivation:

1. ***Achievement Motivation:*** Desire to do something better or more efficiently than it has been done before is the drive behind the achievement need (nAch). People with achievement motivation display the following characteristics:
   - They strive for personal achievement rather than the reward of success.
   - High achievers differentiate themselves from others by their desire to do something better.
   - High achievers are not gamblers. They dislike succeeding by chance. They accept challenging tasks in unknown areas.
   - They seek situations where they can attain personal responsibility for finding solutions.
   - They are goal-oriented people.
2. ***Power Motivation:*** This motivation supports the need for power which aims at making an impact, to be influenced and to control others. People with power motivation display the following characteristics:

- They want to influence others.
- They want to be in competitive and status-oriented situations.
- They are risk takers but only for the purpose of influencing or pressurising others.
- They are dominating people.

3. *Affiliation Motivation:* This motivation is due to the need for affiliation (nAff) which is being liked and accepted by others. It is a drive to relate to people on a social basis. People with affiliation motivation display the following characteristics:
   - They strive for friendship and cooperative situations.
   - Individuals with such a need are more cooperative than competitive.
   - They desire relationships involving a high degree of mutual understanding.
   - They are more sensitive towards people's feelings.

McGregor's Participation Model (Theory X and Theory Y)

Douglas McGregor was a known psychologist. He developed a theory of motivation on the basis of human behaviour. This theory mainly assumes that human behaviour is of two types– Type X and Type Y. Therefore, this theory is known as 'Theory X and Theory Y'.

In Theory X, he said that with respect to people management is a process of directing their efforts, motivating them, controlling their actions and modifying their behaviour to fit the needs of the organisation. Without the active intervention of the management, people would be passive, even more resistant to organisational goals. It shows a traditional approach to managerial motivation and control.

The assumptions considered are:

- The average human being is lazy and dislikes work.
- Lack of ambitions and lack of nAch.
- Little capacity for creativity to solve the organisation's problems.
- Their goals are mostly indifferent to organisational goals.
- Motivation occurs only due to physiological and safety needs.
- This theory utilises the carrot and stick approach to motivation.

The following propositions are put forward:

- The management is responsible for organising the elements of productive enterprise.
- Management directs, motivates and controls actions or behaviour to fulfil organisational needs.
- It suggests that the threat of punishment and strict control are the ways to manage people.
- It gives rise to an autocratic style of leadership.
- This theory suggests a high level of centralisation, close supervision and control of subordinates.
- Employees are treated merely as a commodity or passive production factors like machine, money, etc.

Since the above assumptions and proposition were challenged, McGregor developed another theory – Theory Y. This theory assumes that people are creative, not lazy and so it relates to self-fulfillment, ego satisfaction and satisfaction of the social needs of individual workers.

The assumptions considered are:

- The average human being does not inherently dislike work.
- The average man will exercise self-direction and self-control in the search of objectives to which he is committed.
- Commitment to the objectives is a function of reward with nAch.
- Average human beings learn, under proper conditions, not only to accept but also to seek responsibility.
- They have the capacity to exercise relatively high degrees of imagination, ingenuity and creativity in their solutions.

Theory Y is realistic and frequently used at different levels. This is why sometimes this theory is known as the Participative Theory of Motivation. The following propositions are made:

- The human being is effective, efficient and may even be creative.
- He can be motivated not only through physiological and safety needs but also by social, self-esteem and self-actualisation needs.
- There is decentralisation and delegation of authority.
- There is a scope of job enrichment because human beings are not a part of the passive production process.
- This theory allows for participation of management in the production process as well as cumulative management.

It can be safely concluded that theory X mainly pertains to unskilled and uneducated human workers whereas theory Y is for skilled and educated human workers.

Theory Z: A Hybrid Model

William Ouchi made a comparative study of the American and Japanese management practices and then suggested the adoption of theory Z which represents a hybrid model and is an integration of the American and Japanese management practices. Theory Z was adopted not only for analytical purposes but also for promotional purposes.

Japanese management is characterised by the following principles:

- Emphasis on the group rather than the individual.
- Emphasis on the human rather than functional relationships.
- A few of the top management people are generalists and facilitators rather than decision makers.

Theory Z represents the adoption of the Japanese management practices by American companies. The hybrid type of system incorporates the strengths of Japanese management (group decision making, social cohesion, job security, etc.) and American management (quick decision making, individual freedom, etc.).

Salient Features of theory Z are:

- ***Strong Bond between the Company and the Employees:*** Theory Z suggests life time employment in the company and that retrenchments, lay offs, etc. should be avoided. Financial as well as non-financial incentives should be used to motivate workers.
- ***Employees' Participation:*** In decision making, employees suggestions should be considered, which gives them due recognition.
- ***Mutual Trust:*** According to Ouchi, trust, integrity and openness are closely related. There should be trust between employees, supervisors, work groups, unions and management. To develop trust, there should be complete openness.
- ***Integrated Organisation:*** No formal structure is recommended by Theory Z, but organisation structure should be based on teamwork, without any chart etc. Employees develop a group spirit under such situations.
- ***Human Resources Development:*** The management must work to develop new skills which recognise the potential of human resource. The emphasis is on job enlargement, career planning, organisational socialisation, technical training and R&D.

Process Theories

These theories answer the question, "How are people motivated?" To answer this, most of the theories under this category focus on the dynamics of major variables that are interrelated in explaining the direction, degree and persistence of effort in human behaviour. Some of the theories which are described under this category are:

i. Vroom's Expectancy Model

ii. Porter and Lawler Expectancy Model

iii. Equity Theory

iv. Self-concept Theory

v. Vroom's Valence Expectancy Theory

Vroom's Expectancy Model

The first to formulate an expectancy theory directly aimed at work motivation was Victor Vroom in 1964. Vroom proposed his expectancy theory as an alternative to content models, which he felt were an inadequate explanation of work motivation.

According to him, a person's motivation towards an action, at any time, would be determined by the individual's perception that a certain type of action would lead to a specific outcome and his personal preference for this outcome. This can be taken as the assumption that "the choices made by a person among alternative courses of action are lawfully related to psychological events occurring contemporaneously with the behaviour".

The Theory states:

figure 6.13

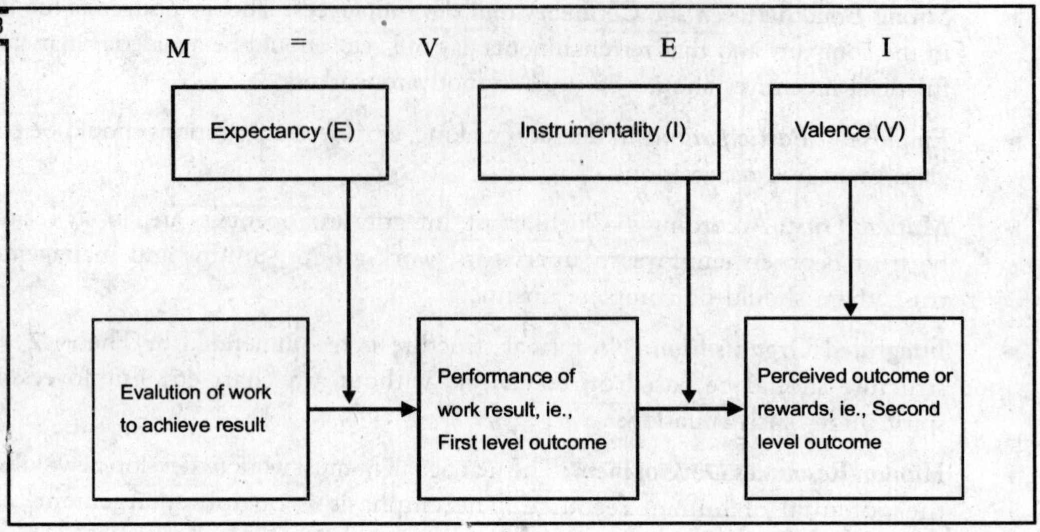

The importance of Vroom's Model is:

- It recognises the complexities of work motivation.
- It discusses how goals influence efforts.
- It finds out what is important to the perception and value that the individual places on certain goals.
- It emphasises the importance of individual perception and assessment of organisational behaviour.

Thus Vroom's model attempts to explain how an individual's goals influence his efforts and, like need-based models, reveals that individual behaviour is goal-oriented.

Porter and Lawler Expectancy Model

Layman Porter and Edward Lawler (1968) developed a version of Vroom's Model. They extended Vroom's model and discussed the relationship between satisfaction and performance.

The assumptions considered are:

- Behaviour is determined by a combination of factors from the individual and in the environment.
- Individuals makes conscious decisions about their behaviour in the organisation.
- Individuals have different needs, desires and goals.
- Individuals decide between alternative behaviours on the basis of their expectations that a given behaviour will lead to a desired outcome.

Various elements of this model are:

- ***Efforts:*** Refer to the energy exerted by a person on job.
- ***Valence/Value of Reward:*** Outcome of a particular behaviour has a specific valence for each individual.

figure 6.14

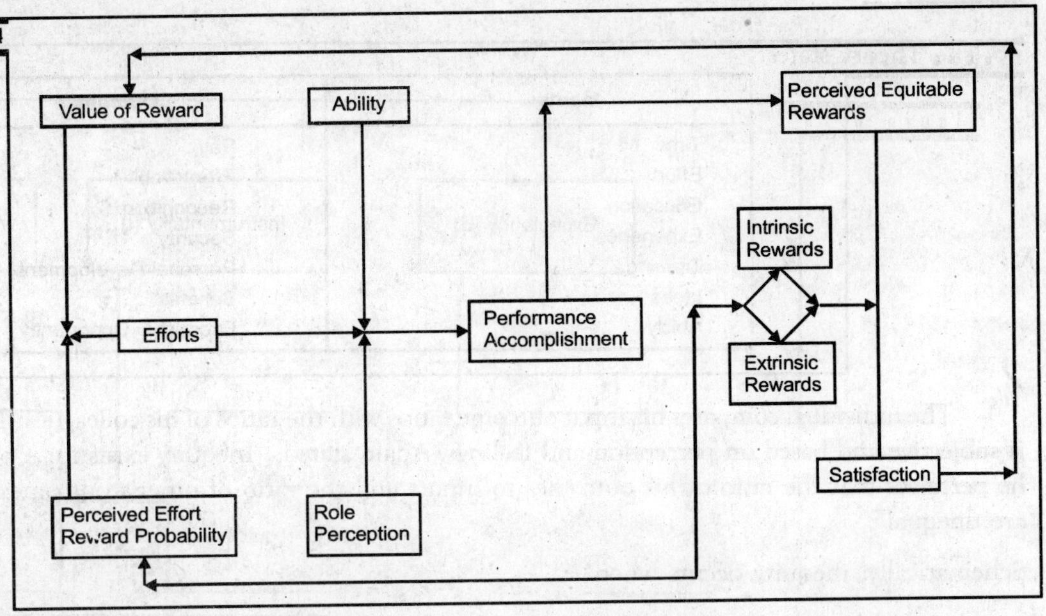

- ***Perceived Effort Reward Probability:*** Refers to the individuals perception of the probability that different rewards depend upon different degrees of efforts. Valence and this probability determine the amount of effort.
- ***Performance:*** Is determined by the amount of effort, ability and the role perception of the individual.
- ***Rewards:*** Performance may lead to two kinds of rewards, intrinsic and extrinsic.
    - *Intrinsic Rewards:* These are a sense of self-actualisation and much more likely to produce attitudes about satisfaction that are related to performance.
    - *Extrinsic Rewards:* These are related to working conditions and status.
- ***Satisfaction:*** The extent to which actual rewards fall short, meet or exceed the individual's perceived level of equitable rewards determines the degree of satisfaction.

The Porter and Lawler framework is, thus, a marked departure from the traditional analysis of satisfaction and performance relationships.

Equity Theory

Among the various theories of work motivation, credit goes to J Stacy Adams for his equity theory. The theory argues that a major input in job performance and satisfaction is the degree of equity (or inequity) that people perceive in their work situation. It is another cognitive based motivation theory in which Adams depicts a specific process of how this motivation occurs.

According to Adams, two variables are important, inputs and outcomes. Inputs are the effort skills which a member of an organisation perceives that he puts into his job. Outcomes are the rewards which a member receives from the organisation and his job.

figure 6.15

Inputs	Outcomes
Time	Pay
Effort	Promotion
Education	Recognition
Experience	Security
Training	Personal Development
Ideas	Benefits
Ability	Friendship Opportunity

The individual compares his input outcome ratios with the ratios of his colleagues. This comparison is subjective and based on perception and feelings. Adam stated, "Inequity exists for a person whenever he perceives that the ratio of his outcomes to inputs and the ratio of other's outcomes to their inputs are unequal".

Schematically, inequity occurs when

$$\frac{\text{Person's outcomes}}{\text{Person's input}} < \frac{\text{Other's outcomes}}{\text{Other's inputs}}$$

$$\frac{\text{Person's outcomes}}{\text{Person's input}} > \frac{\text{Other's outcomes}}{\text{Other's inputs}}$$

and equity occurs if the ratio is equal. The person strives to restore the ratio to equity and this striving is the basis of work motivation.

Equity perceptions are formed through four steps:

figure 6.16

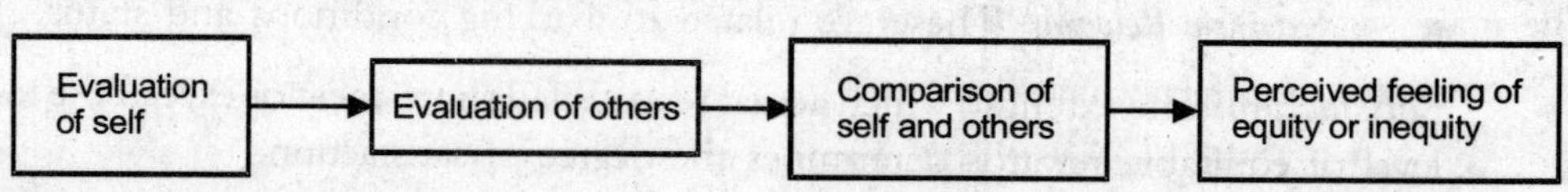

Self-concept Theory

This theory proposes that each of us, through our experiences, has developed ideas or concepts of who we are, what we can do and the type of person we are. These thoughts we hold and believe as true are called our 'real self-concept'.

We also develop our thoughts about who we would like to be, what we want to be able to do and the type of person we want to become. This is called our 'ideal self concept'.

These two self-concepts are internalised. On the other hand, there is an external behaviour which is called 'real other concept' and 'ideal other concept'.

There are mainly five principles, which explain the relations between various self-concepts and motivation. These principles are:

- A person will perform certain acts that he thinks will move his real self-concept closer to his ideal concepts.

- A person will reject all behaviour that he thinks will move his real concepts away from his ideal concepts.
- Many of a person's self concepts are in conflict with one another.
- People want to minimise the guilt involved in their behaviour.
- Success is achieving one's ideal concepts so that the real and ideal concepts become essentially the same.

Non-cognitive Approach

This approach concentrates on operating conditions, i.e., "Behaviour is a result of its consequences" and is explained through the Reinforcement Theory.

Reinforcement Theory

This theory is based on the operating conditions that behaviour is a result of its consequences. It has been developed by well-known psychologist, A F Skinner. According to him, individuals, having learnt from the past, develop patterns of behaviour to control future consequences.

figure 6.17

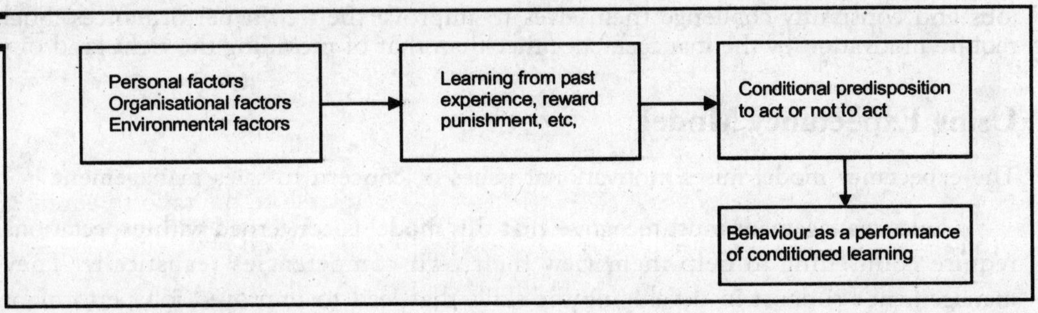

The main strategies of this theory are:

- ***Positive Reinforcement:*** Entails the use of rewards that stimulate repetitive behaviour.
- ***Negative Reinforcement:*** Also known as avoidance learning and implies the use of unpleasant consequences to condition individuals to avoid undesirable behaviour.
- ***Extinction:*** This is withdrawal of all forms of reinforcement to remove or extinguish undesirable behaviour.
- ***Punishment:*** This tool is used when an unpleasant behaviour needs to be reduced or eliminated.

APPLICATIONS OF VARIOUS THEORIES

Using Self-concept in Motivating Salespeople

In sales work, motivation begins with the selection process. The sales manager should not hire people for jobs in which they cannot achieve success. If a salesperson begins to think that he is not coming closer to his ideals by serving the company, his behaviour will digress from the management goals.

Throughout the selection process, the management must try to determine the individual's self-concepts. If a sales career is incompatible with the individual's self concepts, success is unlikely. Only people who can be motivated to produce on the job and who want what it can furnish, should be here.

Using Maslow's Theory

If the sales management is familiar with the unsatisfied portion of a salesperson's hierarchy of needs at a particular time, it could determine the best incentives to use in motivating his performance. Money rapidly loses its power as an incentive once an individual has gratified most of his physiological, safety and security needs. The promise of more money as an incentive becomes progressively weaker the further a particular individual's unfulfilled needs are pushed up in the hierarchy.

Using Herzberg's Two Factor Theory

The motivation hygiene theory has two important implications for sales management. First, the management must ensure that the job provides the conditions that prevent job dissatisfaction. This means that the management needs to provide an acceptable working environment, fair compensation, adequate fringe benefits and reasonable supervision. The second implication is that the management must provide opportunities for achievement, recognition, responsibility and advancement.

Using McClelland Theory

People with high need levels are self-starters. They require certain external incentives to succeed on their jobs and constantly challenge themselves to improve their own performances. Such people do not require motivation by the management other than that of providing the right kind of job environment.

Using Expectancy Model

The expectancy model raises motivational issues of concern to sales management.

Sales management must recognise that this model is concerned with expectations. Sales personnel require counselling to help them view their own competencies realistically. They also need sales management's support in developing the skills that lead to improved job performances.

There are two other types of factors that affect a salesperson's motivation:

Job Related Factors

- ***The Job Itself***
  - Skill variety
  - Task identity
  - Task significance
  - Job autonomy
  - Job feedback
- ***Leadership***
- ***Job Organisational and Involvement Commitment***
  - Job involvement
  - Organisational commitment
  - Institutional stars
  - Corporate citizens
  - Apathetics

Individual Related Factors

- ***Career Stages***
  - Exploration
  - Establishment
  - Maintenance
  - Disengagement
- ***Career Plateauing***
  - Performing deficiencies
  - Selection and training
  - Redesigning job to increase intrinsic motivation
  - Reducing stress and burnout
  - Increasing growth opportunities
  - Acceptance of growth opportunities

NON-FINANCIAL FACTORS AND THEIR IMPACT ON SALES FORCE MOTIVATION

Meetings between Manager and Sales Force

Meetings allow the sales manager to understand the personality, needs and problems of each salesperson. The sales manager can better understand the causes of demotivation/frustration in individual salespersons and respond in a manner which takes into account individual needs, problems and personality.

Clarity of Job

Job clarity and what is expected from the salesperson is a great motivation. The objectives, when duly quantified and well-defined, properly connected and linked with the reward and recognition, serve as a source of motivation to the salesperson.

Sales Contests

Competition by way of sales contests is also an important tool to motivate salespersons. Its purpose varies widely. It may encourage a higher level of sales, in general, to increase the sales of a slow-moving product or to reward the generation of new customers. It provides an incentive to show better performance and secure more satisfactory results.

Sales Conferences and Conventions

Sales conferences and conventions provide an opportunity to salespersons to participate, gain social satisfaction and express their views on matters directly affecting their work. They promote team work, dissolve social barriers, inspire and raise a salesperson's morale.

Positive Feedback

Responses in the form of praise, positive feedback and human warmth and understanding can impel others to perform to their full capabilities. This must be given genuinely and not be perceived as overtly self-serving.

Reward and Recognition

Although sales quotas, sales competition/contests, conventions and conferences have positive carryover effects, these are short-lived techniques to motivate salesmen. On the other hand, reward and recognition for a salesperson's accomplishments are more enduring and relatively economic methods of motivation.

Persuasion

One of the more common and recommended forms for inducing high levels of motivation is through persuasion. In this situation, managers use rational arguments to convince the salesperson that it is in their own best interests to act in a preferred way. Persuasion has the advantage of influencing people to conclude that their actions were performed out of their own free will.

Observations and Future Directions

Distribution channels have traditionally been monolithic; most firms in an industry used the same approach. In a stable situation, a strategy of following the others is simple to conceive and implement. However, few industries still have this simplicity. Both new entrants and existing firms are experimenting with new sales and distribution approaches in order to create competitive advantage. The framework of activities and their costs provides a strategic perspective on the sales and distribution process, helping manufactures understand and adapt to their changing environment. Innovations in sales and distribution have emerged from many directions. Improved logistics and delivery times by FedEx and UPS are reducing the requirements for local warehousing. Broader acceptance of electronic data interchange to monitor sales and inventory levels throughout the total channel is reducing inventories and speeding response to changing customer requirements. Low cost computer power moves product information, specifications and selection directly to the end customer. The Internet is emerging as a means to serve large numbers of customers at much lower costs. These new options create opportunities for manufacturers to restructure their sales and distribution approaches by performing activities in new ways which increase value to customers and reduce costs.

Manufacturers can gain competitive advantage by:

- Determining which activities are valued by the end customers
- Identifying new ways to perform high value sales and distribution activities so that they increase customer satisfaction
- Assessing alternative approaches to sales and distribution which lower costs and working capital investments throughout the total channel

SUMMARY

Reward system management involves the selection and utilisation of organisational objectives. Compensation is composed of financial and non-financial rewards. Financial rewards include current spendable income, deferred income, profit-sharing, retirement and various benefit packages. The popular and common forms of paying financial compensation are through straight salary, straight commission and bonus.

Motivation of sales force, which forms the other aspect of this unit, is among the most important responsibilities of a sales manager. Behavioural scientists have classified motivational needs. According to them each individual is a different entity and hence, to understand what would individually motivate the salesperson, the nature, character and needs of the individual have to be understood.

PROJECT WORK

1. Given below are certain types of selling jobs. Suggest a compensation plan which will be the most appropriate in each case.

	Job	Compensation Plan
a.	Salesperson employed with a bank and selling credit cards.	______________________
b.	Salesperson selling air conditioners to company dealers.	______________________
c.	Salesperson selling generators to industrial houses.	______________________
d.	Salesperson employed by a hotel, selling hotel services.	______________________

2. Critically evaluate the compensation scheme adopted by (a) M/s Shriram Honda Generators (b) BPL and (c) American Express Credit Cards.

SHORT ANSWER QUESTIONS

1. What are the various models of compensating the sales force?
2. What is profit-sharing?
3. What are the three dimensions of motivation?
4. Define Vroom's Valence Expectancy Theory.

REVIEW QUESTIONS

1. What are the basic components of a compensation package?
2. What are the various methods of non-financial compensation?
3. What are the advantages and disadvantages of a straight salary compensation plan?
4. What are the links among motivation, evaluation and compensation?
5. Which factors affect the motivational needs of salesmen?

6. Briefly discuss the alternative modes of sales force compensation.
7. On what basis are the sales force compensations decided?
8. What alternate sales force compensation schemes would you recommend for the salespersons of:
   i. A pharmaceutical company
   ii. Plastic gift items
   iii. Microwave ovens.
9. Suggest a compensation scheme for travelling sales persons for a marketer of soaps in the entire country.

GO TO THE NET

Using Internet search tools, study any five companies and the various compensation methods and models of compensating the sales force.

Caselet

This case tests the reader's skills in evaluation using marginal analysis. It exposes the reader to varying prices and costs and the results of these variations.

HARI lighting is an exclusive manufacturer of sensor executive desk lamps. The firm's manufacturing plant is centrally located in a large Midwestern state with access to a variety of transportation facilities, making product distribution less costly. The lamps, ranging from simple elegance to the most ornate, offer optional features such as a special sensor switch that allows them to move freely, yet be easily turned on or off. Lamps and lighting fixtures of Harper Lighting are available in a variety of sizes, styles, and colors to suit the discriminating executive who wants to add a touch of individually to an office.

HARI lighting's wide range of prices, reputation for quality, exclusive patented features, durability, ad superior craftsmanship have resulted in sustained success for the owners. In 1998, the firm sold 310,000 units of its basic sensor desk lamps at a market price of £ 40. For 1999, the firm anticipates a volume of sales of £ 330,000 units at the reduced price of £ 35. The increased demand for the sensor lamps will allow Harper to use its plant facility to capacity, thus reducing cost. This reduction in cost will allow Harper to pass the savings to customers in 1999 and still increase profits.

The firm's president, Mota, has made plans to continue the growth of the company by shipping the lamps to wholesalers in the eastern area. He arranged to meet with wholesalers form New York, Connecticut, and Pennsylvania on December 18, 1998 to discuss other measures to improve the level of sales and profits for Harper Lighting in 1999.

During the meeting in December, jhota, the vice-president of marketing, recommended lowering the prices of the basic of the basic model of sensor desk lamps further in the following year to increase the volume of sales. She had data showing that 290.000 units could probably be sold at £ 26 and 330,000 units could be sold at £ 24. It is expected that this action result in an increased share of the market for Harper.

Ron Carlse, vice-president of production, opposed jhota's price cutting suggestion and focused on an entirely different way to reduce expenses. Ron's plan was to offer an incentive bonus to distributors for the volume of sales. She had showing that 290,000 units could probably be sold at £ 26 and 330,000 units could be sold at £ 24. It is expected that this action result in an increase share of the market for Harper.

Ron Carlsen, vice-president of production, opposed jhota's price cutting suggestion and focused on an entirely different way to reduce expenses. Ron's plan was to offer an incentive bonus to distributors for the volume of sales reached. By automating several manufacturing processes, the result would be a reduction of the variable costs of the basic lamps from £ 22 of £ 18 per unit. Ron emphasized that his decrease in variable cost would be offset by a rise in fixed production and depreciation of £ 80,000 annually. The improvements would cost approximately £ 400,000 but would be worthwhile for numerous production and financial reasons, which Ron discussed thoroughly at the meeting.

Mota realized that Harper Lighting would have no difficulty in obtaining manufacturer's financing to cover the £ 400,000 capital improvement. The interest rate on the financing would be 11 percent. Harper has accounts payable of £ 42,000 other current liabilities of £ 79,000, and a long-term debt of £ 365,000, on which it plays 6 percent half yearly interest. Although the company does not have excessive debts outstanding, Mota feels that the recommendations from Jhota and Ron should be evaluated thoroughly in terms of the firm's reported profits since any drop in profits would be subjected to close skepticism by the major stockholders who control the board of directors who are overly conscious of the firm's reported earnings.

Question:

1. What price the firm should charge in order to earn highest net income after tax in 999 and which alternative is best under the present situation. Would there be any effect on firm's earning, if new machine is acquired.

[illegible]

[illegible] the reader's skill to evaluate using marginal analysis [illegible]

[illegible]

[illegible] the price of the lamps [illegible]

[illegible] on December 15, [illegible]

[illegible]

[illegible] that the [illegible] lamps from [illegible]

[illegible] per lamp [illegible]

[illegible]

[illegible] approximately [illegible]

[illegible] the [illegible] unit [illegible]

[illegible] 100,000 [illegible]

[illegible]

C H A P T E R

7

salesman's compensation and motivation

learning objectives

The objectives of this unit are to:

- understand compensation methods and modes of compensating the salesman
- understand sales contests
- analyse different sales contests

content outline

- Opening Case
- Introduction
- Motivation in Social Needs Level
- Motivation in Esteem Needs Level
- Cost and Value in Sales channels
- Summary
- Project Work
- Short Answer Questions
- Review Questions
- Go to the Net
- Caselet

opening case

Oriental Manufacturing Company is a public limited concern having its factory at Yaminanagar with its registered office in Delhi. It employs 1,200 workmen, who are organized into a union called the "Oriental Manufacturing Company Mazdoor Union". Ramjas, a fitter in the engineering department, is the president of the union, and he commands considerable respect among the workmen.

On 30 April 1983, about 20 employees of the company led by Ramjas met the works manager and asked him that may I be declared a holiday. The works manager expressed his inability to oblige the union. Then the situation took an ugly turn. There was exchange of hot words. Ramjas accused the works manager of being anti-working class and a callous despot.

The same evening, Ramjas addressed a gate meeting. He asked the workers to observe May Day in a fitting manner. A resolution condemning the attitude of the works manager was also adopted at the meeting.

At the start of the shift at 8.00 a.m. the next day i.e., may Day, Ramjas went to the factory, collected a number of workmen, including several office-bearers of the union, and went from department urging the workmen to stop work. Within a short time a large number of worker left their work place and streamed out. A flag hoisting ceremony was held outside the factory gate. Ramjas exhorted the workers to join the May Day rally later in the evening. The factory did not work for the rest of the day.

The management issued a charge sheet to Ramjas on 3 May 1983 giving details of the charges and stated that those acts amounted to gross misconduct.

You are herby required to submit your explanation to the above said acts of misconduct within 24 hours of the receipt hereof as to why you should not be dismissed from the service of the company.

It was stated in the charge sheet that Shri P.C. Gupta, the legal adviser of the company, would hold the enquiry on the charge-sheet at 11.00 a.m. on 10th May, 1983 in the Conference Room of the factory.

Ramjas refused to accept the charge sheet. Therefore, it sent to him by registered post on the same day and a copy thereof was displayed on the notice board of the company. The registered cover was received back with the remarks "refused to accept".

Ramjas, however appeared for the inquiry and asked in writing that he be permitted to be defended by a lawyer or alternatively by Pritam Singh, the General Secretary of the union, who was not an employee of the company. The request of Shri Ramjas was turned down by the enquiry officer. Ramjas walked out from the enquiry room stating that he could not expect justice from the legal adviser of the company who was biased in favour of the management and that he was not being proper opportunity to defend himself.

The enquiry officer recorded the statements of the management witnesses and concluded the enquiry proceedings. He found Ramjas guilty of all the charges leveled against him. He submitted his findings to the works manager. The works manager referred the same to the secretary of the company at the head office for advice. The secretary wrote back that Ramjas should be dismissed. Accordingly, the works manager issued a letter to Ramjas terminating his services with immediate effect stating that all the charges leveled against him were found proved and that he was guilty of misconduct for which dismissal was the proper punishment.

The punishment inflicted upon Ramjas was assailed by the union on the following grounds.

1. The charge of insubordination and subversive of discipline in passing resolution condemning the works manager was not a misconduct and, as such, no enquiry could be held against him.
2. The charge sheet was invalid inasmuch as the management being biased against him had already made up its mind to dismiss him and that holding of the enquiry was just a legal formality.
3. No opportunity was given to him to defend himself.
4. The proceedings of the enquiry recorded in his absence were not binding on him and no punishment could be awarded on the basis of the same.

5. The appointment of the legal adviser of the company as the enquiry officer was illegal and against the principles of natural justice.

6. The works manager, being himself involved in the incident, was interested in the outcome of the enquiry and could not act as the punishing authority.

7. The works manager in the circumstances could not and did not apply his mind independently in deciding the quantum of punishment.

8. He was victimized for his trade union activities and for being the president of the union.

INTRODUCTION

Salesman's job involves a lot of hard work; he has to face many disappointments and still continue to do his job. So salesmen need a lot of motivation to do their normal job also. Consider an example. A normal person working in an office will take holiday and stay home and nothing will happen. Everyone will understand and the officer loses only one casual leave and everything is normal. But, in the same situation, the salesman will not stay home. He will try to reach the place of work, and then he will report that the work was not possible due to heavy rains. He will not want to lose the day as casual leaves are very precious for him. He also does not want to lose that day's daily allowance which becomes payable only if he has worked or tried to work. The daily allowance acts as a motivator to the salesman. There are many such situations when the salesman is found to be working only to avoid losing a casual leave and the daily allowance. Let us now look into various ways that are used to keep the salesman motivated and his compensation is a part of it.

If we look into the psychology of the salesman, we find that people accept salesman's job for the following reasons:

- Liking for meeting new people all the time.
- Liking for travelling to different places.
- Liking for understanding different cultures.
- Eating exotic foods.
- Staying in good hotels at company cost.
- Earning good money.
- Getting freedom from constant bossing.
- Avoiding routine life (9 to 5 schedule).
- Wearing smart dress to work.
- Travelling first class.

The novelty of all these pleasures lasts for only a few days, and then the people continue working only for the sake of good money and freedom of time. So it is very important for companies to keep paying good money to its sales staff. The salesman's compensation package should be made up of two parts (1) His salary which should be higher than people who are in the same cadre like him but work in sheltered conditions and with much lower or no responsibility (2) His compensation towards his lost opportunities to be with his family in the moments of joy and sorrow and towards keeping him motivated to accept hardships that he is required to face constantly.

The salesman's compensation is given in the following ways:

- Salary only (plus travelling expense, allowances for food and lodging).
- Salary + commission (plus travelling expenses and allowances of food and lodging).
- Commission only (plus travelling expenses and allowance for food and lodge).
- Commission only.

In the Indian economy and culture where a young man is looking for a job and its inherent security, getting people to work only for commission is very difficult. Eureka Forbes continued to operate on the same terms for the last many years as strategy but, thereafter its sales staff as well as support staff is working on salary. So commission only method works well where it is used to employ people as part time workers e.g. insurance sector, textiles, etc. The other reason why it is difficult to get people to work for commission only is the attitude of the companies. There are many companies who appoint people on commission only basis, the person works very hard to establish the product and when he is about to earn high returns on sales because of contacts that he has developed, the company terminates his contract and appoints another salesman on low salary or asks the same salesman to accept revised terms. Because of this, the commission only method is used only to get commission agents and not salesmen for consumer goods companies.

The other methods – salary only and salary + commission–are very common and are acceptable to all. All the marketing oriented companies prefer salary only formula as they are assured of continued high volume sales generated by high volume advertisements and promotions. The responsibility of salesmen in such companies is not of selling but ensuring product availability at all possible outlets and creating and maintaining goodwill of the company in the minds of traders and consumers. The salary + commission formula is used by companies where efforts need to be made to make the trade accept the product and keep supporting it. The salary + commission formula is also popular in industrial and institutional sales areas.

It is important for any company to follow such a compensation formula which ensures that not only is the salesman compensated to his satisfaction but is also motivated if he is putting in reasonable efforts.

No company is happy with the work it gets out of its salesmen. No salesman works to his maximum capacity without additional motivation/rewards. In tropical countries like India even to get normal work done, one is required to use motivating efforts. Let us now look at the motivational methods used by different companies. A sales manager should use various methods to keep his sales team happy and motivated and understand them well to use them effectively. Normally salesmen are above the basic needs level in Maslow's hierarchy of needs and fall in the safety, security level or the social needs level or in esteem needs level depending upon the size of the company and the level of salary that they are being paid. Depending upon the level of the salesmen's needs, a sales manager will decide what type of motivational methods should be used.

Motivation in Social Needs Level

This is an easier level to handle. One has to be very cooperative and should mix with salesmen whenever possible and show solidarity with them. Be very strict about discipline and work standards but rest of the time be friendly and supportive. Keep giving tips for improvement in work standard and team building. Social functions and picnics are of help. If properly handled, you can have a highly motivated high standard winning team at hand.

Motivation in Esteem Needs Level

In this level, motivation comes from the urge to prove one's superiority amongst peers, so the motivation becomes easier. A sales manager should use peer rivalry to his benefit without actually disturbing the team spirit. Sales contests prove very useful for the same. The only precaution that should be taken is that nobody should get unfair advantage during the contest and everyone should have equal chance to win.

Sales Contests

One can devise different types of sales contests but their objective is always one and the same–achieve higher sales and motivate the salesmen. Achievement of higher sales has been particularly emphasized as that is more important to the company than motivation levels. Also, the expenditure on the contest is directly proportionate to the achievements. If you can generate high sales, then you can spend a higher amount of money. If you spend high amount of money you generate higher levels of motivation. Following types of sales contests are common:

- Daily productivity contests
- Monthly productivity contests
- Sales during a particular month contest
- Sales during promotional period contest
- Quarterly sales growth contest
- Half-yearly sales growth contest
- Annual sales target contest
- Growth in retail universe contest
- Level of distribution, width and depth contest
- Reduction in selling expenditure contest.

As said above, the contest should be fair to all participants and all the participants should have equal chance to win the contest.

Terms to Remember

Daily Allowance : Allowance paid to salesperson on days actually worked basis, to take care of his conveyance, tea/coffee, out of pocket expenses.

Ex. HQ Allowance : Allowance paid to the salesperson when he travels out of his HQ during the day but is back by evening.

Night Away Allowance : Allowance paid to salesperson when he travels out of his HQ and is required to stay away from HQ. This allowance takes care of salesperson's lodging, boarding and conveyance requirements.

Entertainment Allowance : Some salespersons are required to entertain their customers. Many companies pay entertainment allowance to take care of this need.

Example-1

PRODUCT XYZ LAUNCH CONTEST

Objective:

To achieve high degree of productive call average and high achievement of individual sales targets.

Places

Mumbai

Period

20th Jan. '99 to 20th Feb. '99

Number of Salesmen

Ten. All the salesmen in Mumbai team.

Eligibility

For winning consolation prize a salesman should achieve at least 60% productivity of targeted calls (not calls made) and achieve at least 80% of targeted sales.

Method

a. For every per cent of sales above 80%, salesman gets one point to his credit up to 100% achievement level. Afterwards he gets two points for every additional % e.g.

   For achievement of 90% he gets 10 points.

   For achievement of 95% he gets 15 points.

   For achievement of 100% he gets 20 points.

   For achievement of 105% he gets 20+10=30 points.

b. For every % productivity achieved above 60%, he gets half point till 100 % achievement, afterwards he gets one point for every additional % achieved (obviously new calls).

c. So a salesman with 70% productivity and 90% sales achievement has (10 × ½ = 5) + 20 × 1 = 20) = 25 points

Prizes

First Prize	:	One Philips audio recorder cum radio
Second Prize	:	Two Philips walkmans
Consolation Prize	:	All eligible salesmen will get Philips pocket radio.

Cost

Prizes: Rs 7000/-

Function: Rs 3000/-

Total: Rs 10,000/- (Rs Ten thousand only.)

Example-2

MUMBAI SALESMAN'S CONTEST

Objective

i. To achieve distribution objective of at least 80% outlets stocking product XYZ.

ii. To achieve sales objective of 25% sales growth over the current average during the contest period.

Scheme

During the contest period the product XYZ will be offered with a consumer offer of "Rs 2/- off" on each pack on sale.

Background

The product XYZ is unique and well supported by the company. But it is not achieving its sales objectives because of lesser support by the sales team. The sales team concentrates more on the company's major brand, which contributes to 85% of company sales and profits. The brand manager of product XYZ thinks that product XYZ has the potential to become a big brand given the right support which can be obtained once the product starts achieving reasonable level of sales. The sales are not coming, as the product is not widely distributed, not even in the company's normal outlets.

Working

i. Opening stocks at all the distribution points will be checked at the beginning of the scheme period.

ii. Entire opening stocks at the distributor points will be stickered with the promotional offer.

iii. Targets will be decided strictly on the basis of previous three months sales average.

iv. Sales achievement will be found from the actual closing stock verified at the end of the scheme period.

Eligibility

All those salesmen who achieve the minimum standard of 80% distribution and 25% growth are eligible for consolation prize. The first and second prizes would be decided on the basis of sales growth achieved (assuming that growth is not possible without distribution extension).

Prizes

First Prize: One Godrej 165 liter refrigerator.

Second Prize: Two Sumit mixer/blender.

Period

1st August to 31st October

Area	A	B	C	D	E	F	G	H	I	J	K	Total
Average	65	76	59	84	74	72	76	45	130	96	65	842
Target	81	95	74	105	93	90	65	56	163	120	81	1053

COST AND VALUE IN SALES CHANNELS

Situation

More and more companies are discovering that their accustomed approaches to selecting and managing sales and distribution channels no longer work. The channels cost too much and provide too little value. They meet neither the needs of the manufacturer nor the end customer. At the same time, competitors may be gaining position through innovative use of new channel options. Manufacturers need a new template to guide them to sales and distribution channel choices which better match channel costs with value and which offer the potential for competitive advantage. In most industries, sales and distribution channels have come as complete "packages"; manufacturers could choose among direct sales, manufacturers representatives, distributor, wholesalers, retailers, etc. Each package operates differently and a manufacturer has to select the one which seems most appropriate for its specific industry and situation. There has been little opportunity to disaggregate the sales and distribution process, so few manufacturers looked inside their chosen channel to understand the costs and value it brought. The clearest path for reaching such an understanding and for evaluating sales and distribution options emerges through analysis of the *activities* performed by the channel, assessing the costs of performing those activities, and matching the activities to customer needs and values. Based on an understanding of activities and their costs, manufacturers can evaluate whether the current channel is performing well and can assess whether new channel approaches are preferable.

Activities

One of the most useful insights to emerge from the quality and process improvement movements is a focus on *activities*. Prior to the identification of activities, managers often viewed their businesses as a set of concentrated on functions (marketing, sales, manufacturing, etc.) or organizational units. The reorientation to activities puts the emphasis on *what* actually gets done, and only then on *who* does the work. Functional approaches, on the other hand, tend to concentrate more on *who* is responsible. Both approaches are important, but for the purpose of understanding and building new sales and distribution channels, starting first with an understanding of the key activities, and then turning to who does them, provides the most fruitful path.

A company with direct sales to end customers, such as a machine tool or other durable equipment supplier, provides a simple example of a sales and distribution process because the manufacturer performs all of the roles itself rather than having a distributor or some other party involved. A common approach for a manufacturer using direct sales is a series of functional departments, each of which is partially responsible for the sales and distribution process. The sales group actually calls on customers, explains the benefits of the manufacturer's product and closes a sale. The sales force relies on leads and uses sales materials developed by the marketing department. Once a customer places an order, it is booked by the finance department and checked for credit limits. If the order is acceptable, it is then routed to manufacturing for production and shipment. If any follow-up is needed, the customer contacts customer service for help (Figure 7.1). All in all, at least five functional groups are involved in satisfying the customer and no single group has complete knowledge or control of the whole process.

figure 7.1

Typical Direct Sales Approach to Customers

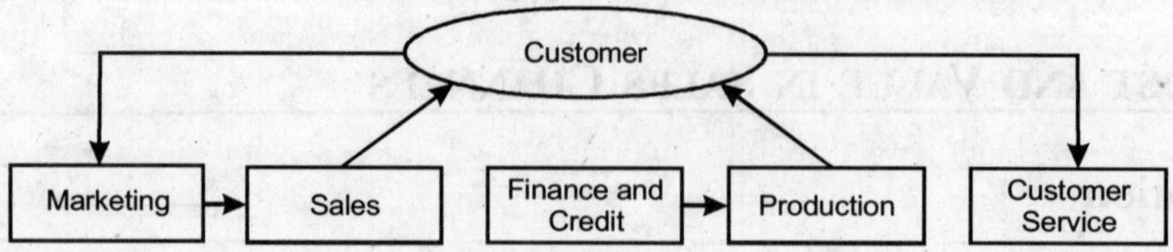

Channel Activities

Different sales and distribution channels exist because they allocate these seven basic activities in different ways between participants in the sales process. In other channel approaches, the distributor, wholesaler or retailer handles all customer-related activities. By selecting one of these channels, a manufacturer in essence "hires" a representative, a distributor, etc. to carry out some of the activities in selling and distributing products to end customers. Manufacturers "pay" the other channel participants by relinquishing some portion of the price paid by the end customer. Of course, in these more indirect channels, the manufacturer must still perform some of these activities itself in its dealings with its distributors, wholesalers or retailers (e.g. recruitment, credit decisions, logistics, etc.). The core question for a manufacturer is whether the channel partner provides sufficient value for the total price in terms of lost revenue from the customer and the cost to the manufacturer of the duplicated activities. The decision to cede activities (and margin) to distributors, wholesalers or retailers has been driven, in large measure, by the need to support increasing numbers of customers. Generally, a manufacturer selling directly to end users has several hundred customers. In industries where there are often ten of thousands of customers such as small contractors, distributors or wholesalers are a common approach to sales and distribution. When customers are in the millions, such as small businesses or consumers, retailers, direct mail or other mail or other forms of mass merchandising are the common sales channel Each channel organizes its activities to adapt to the number and geographic spread of the customer base.

Direct Sales

When a manufacturer chooses to use a direct sales channel, it intends to focus intense sales efforts on a relatively small customer base. The power of a direct sales channel is in the two activities of *Product/ Customer Matching* and *Closing*. A manufacturer with a direct sales organization is in a position to provide its sales force with the training, tools and motivation necessary to undertake complicated or long-cycle selling activities. Direct sales groups typically spend significant effort assisting customers with technical product selection, application engineering, demonstrations and other similar activities to assure the customer is selecting the most appropriate products. The sales organization may also write proposals, provide economic justifications and make multiple sales calls throughout the customer's organization in order to close the sale.

One challenge for companies using a direct sales approach is lead generation *(Customer Identification and Acquisition)*. The limited size of most direct sales forces and their focus on in-person dealings with customers make them costly and inefficient at identifying new potential customers. Direct sales forces work well with geographically limited customer territories, where leads come from either established customer bases or broad marketing approaches. In some industries, the overall sales and distribution process ends with product shipment and collection. For most manufacturers, though, post-sale activities (*Support*) are an increasingly important source of both customer loyalty and profit through sales of parts, service and follow-up for repeat purchases. In some instances, after-sales activities are the responsibility of the field sales organization. More and more, companies are raising the profile of the after-sales process and creating separate organizations of inside and outside groups to capture the full potential in this area.

Since the sales and distribution process cuts across several functional groups and budgets, companies rarely know its full cost. In a typical company, each functional group has its own separate budget built around head count and related expenses. From an expense control standpoint, budgets for functional groups are useful because managers who are close to the people doing the work can monitor and control costs. However, one certain consequence is that no one in the company has a clear understanding of how much it costs to sell and deliver products to a customer. Usually there is a well documented budget for the sales and marketing organizations, but the additional costs for the remaining activities are often buried in myriad other budgets.

Manufacturers often believe that a direct sales approach is expensive in both operating expenses and working capital. Actually, this channel approach has a relatively low total cost for the entire process because there are no additional costs, or investments, beyond the manufacturer's.

Independent Sales Representatives

From an activity and total cost standpoint, the distinction between direct sales and independent sales representatives (manufacturers representatives, etc.) represents only a minor variation. The activities of *Product/Customer Matching* and *Closing* and much of *Customer Identification and Acquisition* are transferred from the manufacturer to the independent representative. This produces only a minor change in total costs because the manufacturer sheds only the cost of the sales force and the commissions paid to independent representatives equals the cost of a direct sales force.

Independent representatives make sense in circumstances where a manufacturer cannot support a direct sales organization, or could not at the time the sales and distribution channel was created. Examples of common situations where independent representatives are useful include:

- Small companies or niche products which do not generate enough revenue to support a dedicated sales force.
- Accessory products which are easily sold in conjunction with a primary item and where secondary attention from the independent representative is not a significant issue.
- Entry into overseas markets where local knowledge and contacts are indispensable and where they are held by the independent representative, but not by the manufacturer.

Independent representatives serve principally to substitute variable costs for the fixed costs of the direct sales approach and to lower the minimum revenue level needed to support the sales and distribution channel. The fixed to variable cost trade-off is straightforward. Virtually all representatives are paid solely on commission so that approximately one-fourth the cost of sales and distribution channel management becomes variable. Scale effects occur because a manufacturer is only buying part of an independent representative's time and is, therefore, only paying part of the cost. At a given level of sales, a manufacturer can afford more "feet on the street" with independent representatives than with its own sales force. Unfortunately, the manufacturer only buys partial attention and support from those feet.

The distinctions between a direct sales organization and independent representatives yield little effect on the investment requirements for the sales and distribution channel. Since the manufacturer still holds all of the inventory and the receivables, it still has a working capital requirement similar to a direct sales approach.

Distributors and Wholesalers

The principle reasons for manufacturers to use distributors and wholesalers have been to shift the working capital responsibility from the manufacturer to a third party and to provide attention to many thousands of local customers. The primary emphasis in both the direct sales and the independent representative approaches is on the *Product- Customer Matching* and *Closing* activities. Distributors and wholesalers traditionally dedicate only a small portion of their efforts to these two activities; rather, they focus on the *Logistics* and *Finance* activities such as rapid delivery and credit decisions to small, local businesses. A distributor or wholesaler maintains a local stock of product and provides either a counter for customer pickup or frequent delivery services to its customers. While most distributors or wholesalers have a sales organization, it is usually dedicated to finding customers and to maintaining relationships *(Customer Identification and Acquisition)*. Some distributors have technically trained staff who can assist in *Product/Customer Matching*, but wholesalers rarely do. Wholesalers often have counter staff who can help the customer complete an order and who may answer some product related questions; few provide much real sales assistance. In addition, distributors and wholesalers will generally provide credit lines to their customers *(Finance)*. This is a critical element in the overall value provided by distributors and wholesalers because their customers are often small, undercapitalized firms who depend on free trade credit to finance their businesses. Deciding how much credit to provide and how long to ride with a troubled customer are functions where the local knowledge and business connections possessed by distributors and wholesalers create a strong basis for success. Many distributions and wholesalers create a strong basis for success. They have discovered that they are acting more like a bank than a sales or logistics organization.

Manufacturers must support their distributors or wholesalers in two major areas for the overall channel to operate effectively. First, manufacturers must supply selling tools and related training in order for the distributor, or more rarely the wholesaler, to perform the *Customer/Product Matching* activity. Few distributors or wholesalers have the technical knowledge to develop their own programs to explain adequately and help customers select products appropriately. Secondly, manufacturers still need to perform *Finance* and *Logistics* functions in order to serve the distributors or wholesalers. The manufacturer must process orders and ship to the distributors or wholesalers and must make credit decisions on whom to finance and to what degree. Post sales *(Support)* activities have emerged as a contentious issue in the relationship between manufacturers and the distributor or wholesaler channel. After-sale parts and service are often a key element in the lifecycle profitability of a product sale; distributors and wholesalers have traditionally controlled the aftermarket by virtue of their direct contact with the customer. As manufacturers have attempted to increase their own parts revenues and establish a service business, they have found themselves in conflict with their distributors or wholesalers, limiting the manufacturer's after-sale profit potential. The lost profit stream from after-sale parts and service raises the true cost of using distributors and wholesalers.

There is a fine line between wholesome self-appreciation, and self-centered egotistical conceit. Nothing will drive people away faster than a conceited person. And although someone with low self-esteem may not run others away, he or she would not draw people closer. Because sales is a people-oriented business, many salespeople neglect to cultivate a healthy self-love. While putting the customer first is noble, you don't have to leave yourself out of the picture altogether. You cannot have genuine love for others unless you first have some degree of love for yourself.

Taking proper care of yourself will help you better serve your customers. You are still the single most important sales tool that you will ever possess. Therefore, feed your body and mind a healthy diet of nutritional food and positive information. Maintain an optimistic attitude and a powerful spirit, and your self-love will inspire others to love you as well.

Sales Strategies

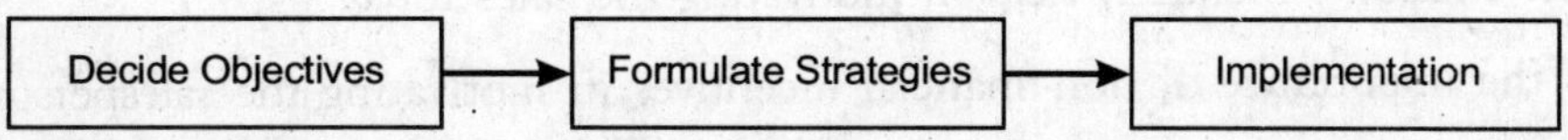

Strategies is the way to achieve the goal and implementation are the activities or course of action that should be carried out to achieve to implement the strategies.

Modern Approach in Sales Management

Global Perspective

Revolution in technology

Different sales force

Customer relationship management

Team selling approach

Managing multi-channels

Ethical and social issues

Sales professionalism

SUMMARY

Motivation of the salesman is important because he has a monotonous job to perform and he gets fed up very soon and wants a change. Through motivation, the salesman can be stimulated to action, so that he gets interested in the job and performs his duties to the best of his capability.

Salesman can be motivated through financial or non-financial incentives or both; while deciding the same, financial condition of the organisation has to be taken into consideration.

PROJECT WORK

Critically examine the compensation scheme adopted by (a) LIC of India (b) Citibank (c) Times of India Group (d) BPL.

Short Answer Questions

1. What do you mean by sales contest?
2. What do you mean by motivation at social needs level?

Review Questions

1. Why is motivation of sales force more important than for employees in any other sphere of activity?
2. How does Maslow's hierarchy help in motivating the sales force?
3. What is the importance of non-financial incentives in motivating the salesperson?

Go to the Net

Using Internet search tools, collect information for alternate salesman's compensation schemes for the salesperson of:

- A pharmaceutical company
- A plastic items company
- A microwave oven company.

Caselet

Premier Executive Packages

THERE is evil in genius — we commonly suppose. The star performer must, like the tempestuous footballer Roy Keane, have a character flaw that just comes with the territory. There is another way of viewing this, which is to say that it is nonsense. Nice people such as Gary Lineker can be just as successful. It is difficult to be a world beater if you are left to sit on the bench. The subject arises as an intriguing aspect of recent studies into how star business performers are rewarded. Those of an egalitarian disposition are uncomfortable with the fact that companies do better if they give higher rewards to their most talented people. But equality in some matters remains important.

A study by Hewitt Bacon & Woodrow, the human resources consultancy which looked at the development and rewards of business leaders, found a correlation between higher rewards for top performance and better business results. It is not a linear relationship, however: 40 per cent of the top performing companies paid high performers "significantly" more than average performers, but the majority of the best companies paid only moderately or slightly more.

The implication is that though the top people should be generously rewarded, the gap with the others should not be too great, and fairness remains important.

"There are some people who, by dint of their capability, are worth more to the organisation than others, and to pretend that these people do not exist is folly," says Neville Osrin, leadership specialist at Hewitt Bacon & Woodrow. But he adds: "The other aspect that is important is that because you see talented people make an extraordinary contribution to the business, sometimes their less desirable attributes are ignored. For example, they might be narcissistic or a bit of a bully. With people who are not seen as part of the star group that behaviour would not be ignored."

It serves no one any benefit if damaging behaviour goes unchallenged; and if there are double standards, the damage is multiplied. Indirectly, even a brilliant individual could be doing more harm than good if the influence of their character flaw is truly malign.

Managing high performers can be even more difficult than managing poor performers, because it is "less clear what needs to be done", says Mr. Osrin. Everyone is part of a team, in the wider scheme of things.

As Duncan Brown, a pay expert, reminds us in his book, *Reward Strategies*, the mistake is to pretend that pay is about formulae and systems. In reality it is about good and fair management.

Questions:

1. What do you think is the limit to which Indian companies can afford the compensating for top salespersons?
2. Should there be a parity between lowest paid and best paid staff? If not, how much difference is justified in compensation at the lowest level and highest level?

C H A P T E R

8

monitoring and performance appraisal

learning objectives

The objectives of this chapter are to:

- understand the essentials of sales force monitoring programme
- study the principles of evaluation and record performances
- understanding the role and Importance of sales performance.

content outline

- Opening Case
- Introduction
- Purpose of Performance Appraisal
- Essentials of Sales Force Monitoring Programme
- Principles of Sales Evaluation
- Evaluating Performance Standards
- Recording Performance
- Field Sales Reports
- Summary
- Project Work
- Short Answer Questions
- Review Questions
- Go to the Net
- Caselet
- Appendices

opening case

CEOs Under Fire

The five Pitfalls of CEO Succession

IT takes some effort to find CEOs who can make a difference. For a board of directors, no decision is more momentous. Yet many boards—perhaps even most—do a dismal job of succession planning. According to one survey, a stunning 45 per cent have no process for grooming potential CEOs. None! That sets them up for five big pitfalls.

1. Letting the CEO play kingmaker

Though many CEOs relish the process of cultivating a replacement, to others it's a threatening reminder of their own mortality or, worse, dispensability. Some develop a knack for driving off any promising heirs. Others back successors cast in the image of guess-who.

That's why boards shouldn't allow a 'choose your own successor 'approach'. Starting a minimum of six years in advance, they should demand a list of candidates plus regular briefings on how those candidates' skills are being tested. As the top contenders emerge, the outside directors have a duty to meet with them alone for open ended discussions. The larger goal is to create what former Fannie Mae CEO, James Johnson, has called a "succession culture." A periodic census of the leadership pools at all levels will help spot future stars earlier in their careers.

2. Using boiler plate criteria

When headhunters draw up their "specification sheet" describing the ideal candidate, the language tends to be hopelessly generic. Consider these passages from two actual spec sheets—one for a software firm, the other for a manufacturer—and try to guess which is which. One company seeks a "natural leader and mature communicator" with a "bias for action" and a "solid reputation for integrity, maturity, and energy." The other is looking for a "proven leader" who is "decisive, action-oriented, and personable, with the highest integrity and authenticity." Stumped? (The manufacturer is the first one, the software firm the second.)

Instead of wasting time with such boiler plate drivel, boards need to drill down to specifics. If the job opening is in the PC industry, the first question to a candidate ought to be—How are you going to cope with Michael Dell's attack on the business? If you can't cope with it, what's plan B? Remember a board's task is to find someone with the right skills for this job, not someone who meets central casting's idea of a "leader."

3. Letting headhunters run the show

Executive recruiters can play a valuable role in assembling a slate of candidates. But boards err by letting them rush the deal to a conclusion. At one major infrastructure company, the selection committee never even interviewed a second candidate—a blunder reflected in the company's subsequent sagging performance.

It's best for boards to set aside two days to meet with finalists. The directors may split into small groups, rotating candidates through at least three interviews. They shouldn't hesitate to grill them.

4. Succumbing to fads

Outsiders are in. Between the 1970s and the late 1990s, the proportion of externally recruited CEOs rose from 8 per cent to 19 per cent. (This despite studies showing that outsiders are more expensive than insiders— commanding roughly twice the starting compensation—and perform no better on an average.) Relying on external labour to fill the top slot should be seen for what it usually is: a second-best approach.

A fixation on outside saviors also undervalues in-house talent, often assumed to be bureaucratic, blinkered and beholden to the status quo. This view ignores the fact that some of the biggest corporate revolutionaries have been insiders. Jack Welch was already a 20-year company man when he put General Electric in the blender, while insiders also led dramatic transformations at Circuit City, Intel and Boeing.

Finally, outside hires are too often a symptom of the board's anxiety to please Wall Street and its bias for new blood. The day

AT&T signed Michael Armstrong as CEO, its market value surged $3.8 billion; the day Kodak signed former Motorola chief George Fischer, its value climbed $1.4 billion. Never mind that both appointments were the result of each company's failure to line up an internal successor (and that those one-day surges proved fleeting). The last people you want weighing in on the succession process are securities analysts.

5. Keeping Elvis in the building

So the board has picked a new CEO. Now make sure that the old one leaves the premises. Really, intentionally or not, ex-CEOs can end up undermining their successors when they linger around the building or the boardroom. That's why the safest policy is a clean break. It sounds harsh, but as the outgoing CEO surely knows, nothing succeeds like a smooth succession.

TRY YOURSELF

1. Analyse the reasons behind the poor performance of CEOs in India.
2. What are the ways and techniques used by MNCs for CEOs' performance rating?

INTRODUCTION

What essentially governs the evaluation of the performance of a sales force are the objectives of the company. Whether the objectives, with respect to the sales targets set by the management, have been achieved or not will determine the performance level of the sales force. It's a different matter, altogether, to achieve the desirable performance levels which fall under the purview of the sales force compensation policy of the company.

Whether a company will be able to achieve the overall organisational goals depends, to a large extent, on where the sales are heading. Whether the company will be able to compete in the market place and be able to sustain its market share and increase it substantially in the long run will also depend on the sales performance. Hence the role of the sales force cannot be over emphasised, making it imperative to constantly monitor the performance of the sales force.

In view of the above, a well designed, objective and pragmatic evaluation programme of the sales force and managing it effectively is equally significant.

According to Spriegal performance appraisal as the process of evaluating the employee's performance on the job in terms of requirements of the job. Performance appraisal is known by various names such as performance evaluation, progress rating, merit rating, merit evaluation etc. Performance appraisal is the systematic rating of an employee's according to their performance. Performance appraisal is process of evaluating the performance and qualification of the employee in terms of the requirements. Performance appraisal is a process of evaluating the performance and qualifications of the employee in terms of the requirements, promotion, providing rewards etc. It helps in identifying the difference among the employees in terms of their performance. Performance is used for taking personnel decisions such as promotion, demotion and transfer etc.

PURPOSE OF PERFORMANCE APPRAISAL

1. Identify the specific job criteria on the basis of performance.
2. Measurement of performance.
3. Rewarding the individual of their high performance.
4. Define the development experience the employee needs to both enhance performance in the current job and prepare for future responsibilities.

Importance of Performance Appraisal

In any organization performance appraisal is require to improve the personal qualities of every employee in the organization. Performance appraisal is the most important activity in many organization because it provides data of past, present and expected performance of the employee's.

The following benefits of performance appraisal justify the designing of an effective programme of performance appraisal

1. It gives us scientific base to with the help of which we can calculate the worth of an employees.
2. It helps us in finding out worthy and unworthy workers.

3. It helps the supervisors to evaluate the performance of the subordinates.
4. The record of performance appraisal are available help to protect the management against subsequent charges of discrimination.

Traditional Method of Performance Appraisal

Every organization whether it is big or small, have a performance appraisal system to do the rating of their employee's. The basic method of performance appraisal are discussed below:

1. ***Ranking Method:*** It is the simplest method of rating system. In this method we give the rank to every employee on the basis of their job performance. In this method all employees are judged on the factors and they are rated on the overall basis with reference to their job performance instead of individual assessment of traits. In this way the best is placed first rank and the poorest occupies last rank.
2. ***Graphic Rating Scale:*** In this method the management places a checkmark on a form next to the word or phase describing the degree of merit for each of several traits such as quality of work, quantity of work, dependability, attitude and so worth. A major drawback of Graphic rating is that the words like "excellent" and "poor" mean different things to different people.

Rating Sheet

Employee Name: Date;
Department: Job Title:
Instructions of Rate: 1
2
3

Performance Ratings

Performance Factors	Does not meets job requirements	Partially meets job requirements	Meets job requirements	Exceeds job requirements	Far exceeds job requirements
1. Quantity of work	Undue no. of errors	Occasional Errors	Normal Accuracy	Seldom inaccurate	Exceptionally Accurate
2. Quantity of work	Slow worker	Works in spurts	Consistent quantity	Above average quantity	Usually fast worker
3. Job knowledge	Needs to study job	More knowledge required	Possesses adequate knowledge	Good working knowledge	Exceptionally understanding of all phases of job
4. Dependability	Requires Constant supervision	Needs occasional supervision	Ordinarily can be depended upon	Needs very little supervision	Completely trustworthy
5. Attitude	Reluctant to cooperate	Occasionally uncooperative	Generally cooperative with others	A good team worker	Very cooperative inspires others to work

Forced distribution Method: In this method rated are distributed along the given scale and fixed percentages of employees are assigned to the best and worst ends of the scale and to the middle bracket. In this system a five point scale for job performance is used. One end scale represent the best job performance whereas the other end poorest job performance. The basic concept of this system is forced distribution that eliminates any room for subjective judgment on the part of supervisors.

Check List Method: In this method a list of statement is prepared which describe the performance of an employee. Each statement have a definite scale rate. The total of this statement gives the merit of an employee.

Checklist For Mechanics		
Characteristics	**True**	**False**
1. He is regular on the job.		
2. He has skills according to the job profile.		
3. He accomplish his assignment in the given time period.		
4. He is devoted to his job.		
5. He is efficient.		

In this method individual are rated on the basis of the weights. Statement should be prepare by the supervisor who have complete knowledge about the job.

Critical incident Method: In this method every supervisor prepare a record notebook in which all the successful and poor performance of an employee is mentioned. This record is maintained in a special designed notebook. The main problem with this method is that outstanding incident happens so infrequently that individual's appraisal may not vary markedly in any two time periods. In this type of system we generally find that employees neither come into positive category nor into negative category. The main drawback in this method is that if critical incident does not happen then it is difficult to rate an employee. The general procedure in this method is to construct the specimen checklist that collect behaviour incidents from a sample of experts in this area.

Field Review Method: In this method the supervisor are interviewed by an expert belonging to the personnel department. The expert questions to the supervisor to obtain information of each employee and takes a note in his notebook. There is no rating form in this method form. In this method the workers are mainly classified into three categories outstanding, satisfactory and unsatisfactory. The interviewer questions the supervisor about the requirements of each employee in his job. It also ensures a greater likelihood that the supervisors will give adequate attention to the appraisals because the personnel department largely controls the process.

ESSENTIALS OF SALES FORCE MONITORING PROGRAMME

A sales manager must design the complexity and sophistication of the sales programme based on the environment under which his company operates.

Sales force monitoring is a necessary procedure that is implemented by almost all companies, because it is the only tool with which salespeople are supervised. However, it's structure, design and scope may vary depending upon the size of the firm, whether the firm deals in goods or services and what is the nature of the business – whether the firm is dealing in consumer goods or industrial products, whether it's an exporting firm or selling to government agencies. It also depends upon the size of the sales force. Sales force monitoring may be informal as well as formal. It may also be simple or complex. The conclusions from a sales force monitoring programme, however, may be based on objective parameters or the discretion of the management. Whatever may be its structure, one must remember that a sales performance evaluation programme must be realistic in nature.

The inherent objective of a sales force motivation programme must be to improve sales. The scope of an evaluation programme is not just confined to ascertain as to who is not doing his job effectively but more positively and realistically to find why one is not able to perform at the desired level and then to find ways and means to devise and implement the corrective procedures to eliminate deficiencies. Hence, an evaluation programme must be positive in nature and not merely an exercise to find ways to criticise non-performers.

A sales evaluation and monitoring programme is only a means to an end and not an end in itself; it should be a realistic exercise aimed at attaining the broad organisational goals.

After a detailed study of the sales job is carried out and the job description of each salesperson is jotted down, the next step in devising a sales evaluation programme comprises of three stages, viz.,

- Establishing standards for performance appraisal.
- Identifying and evaluating reasons for performance under or above the laid down standards.
- To adopt measures to correct deficiencies leading to the lower performance and evaluate methods for further improvements.

PRINCIPLES OF SALES EVALUATION

Principles applicable to sales evaluation differ largely depending upon the factors governing a company at the micro level or an industry business environment at a macro level. It may be important for a soap manufacturing company to sell a certain number of soap cakes every week or every month but it may just suffice a car manufacturing company to call upon certain number of prospects and apprise them of their newer model and to book orders. Similarly, a good evaluation programme used in one type of industry or in one company may not be very good for yet another kind of company or industry. Further, whether the evaluation is to be done annually, biannually, quarterly or monthly is a matter of the factors governing at the micro and macro levels as well as the nature of the business and product that a company is dealing in. Whatever the evaluation programme may be it has certain underlying principles which make it more realistic and goal oriented. Some such principles are elucidated here.

1. ***Pragmatic:*** Evaluation should be on practically possible parameters rather than predecided goals. Sales force problems should be kept in mind while evaluating the performance.
2. ***Transparent:*** It should not be a classified document meant to judge a person's ability without his knowledge as to how and when he is being judged. Rather it should be a transparent affair in the knowledge of those being judged so that a participative spirit may be encouraged making this a better exercise.
3. ***Realistic:*** It should be based on actual facts and figures such as the competition in the market, sales potential, market segment, geographical boundaries, consumers' perception etc.
4. ***Positive in spirit:*** It must not be aimed at criticism but should aim at identifying the factors that lead to falling performance standards and ways and means to eliminate the same. In essence, it should be positive in spirit with the sole aim of achieving the sales targets.
5. ***Informative:*** It should be articulate and self-explanatory thus providing valuable inputs to make policies attain the sales objectives.
6. ***Participative:*** It should motivate the sales force to participate in and share their inputs in improving the methods and procedures of evaluation.
7. ***Objective:*** It should be based on benchmarks and standards and not on prejudices. Objectives should be measurable and realistic.

8. ***Flexible:*** It should have the necessary element of flexibility so that it can be moulded according to the changing market conditions.
9. ***Specific:*** It should not be vague but more focused and specific about the objectives to be achieved.
10. ***Cost Effective:*** It should be economical to devise and implement. It should also not be very time consuming.
11. ***It should be a means and not an end:*** A good sales evaluation is a means to an end and not an end in itself; hence, the sole objective is not to evaluate the sales performance but to find reasons why and where the sales force is lagging and the ways and means to overcome the same.

Evaluating Performance Standards

Quantitative Criterion

Performance evaluation may be quantitative as well as qualitative. Most organisations choose to have their standards set on quantitative measures. Any quantitative standard should be designed to compare the sales volume with the total sales volume potential. This objective, according to a sales manager's viewpoint, is even more important than the profit and growth of the organisation since higher sales volume automatically results in higher profit and growth rates.

The quantitative performance standards also help measure the profit objectives. Since the profit is the outcome of the interplay of many factors rather than just sales, it is imperative that the factors affecting profit must also be included under sales management control.

In view of the above, the selling expenses, the sales mixture, the call frequency rate, the cost per call, the size of the order, etc. must be given due weightage for assessing the true level of profits and the actual sales turnover.

More complex than gauging profit is the assessing of the growth objectives of an organisation using the quantitative performance standards. Although growth is directly related with the natural momentum that a company attains with maturity, the impact on growth of the performance of sales personnel cannot be underestimated.

In view of the fact that the impact of sales on growth and profit objectives is ever increasing, it is only logical and reasonable to expect growing sales every year. The attainment of this objective, however, depends largely on the cohesive policies of the sales and marketing management which should be supportive and not negative to each other. Against this backdrop, the marketing policies should be in line with changing market demand and continuously rising efficiency of the sales management.

Quantitative standards measure the nature and desirable levels of performance. They are used not only to stimulate good performance but also to measure it. Quantitative standards translate the management's expectations and aspirations in quantitative terms. Sales personnel with well-defined objectives make their activities more purposeful and they do not waste time, effort and energy in pursuing activities that do not help in attaining the objectives.

An individual's appraisal of his total performance cannot, and should not, be made merely on the attainment of sales volume. Unlike in the past when the attainment of sales volume was the sole factor used to appraise an individual's performance, sales managers today realise that it's no use making an unprofitable sale or current sale at the cost of future sales. At the same time there exist many uncontrollable factors over which the sales personnel have little or no control. These factors include competition, promotional support given to the sales personnel, the potential sales volume in a particular territory and the "windfall" business, cyclical tendencies of boom and recession. In light of these facts, merely attainment of sales volume cannot be a good judgement parameter in assessing the performance of the sales personnel.

In essence, therefore, each company sets and selects the quantitative performance standards that fit its given micro and macro level environment. An organisation may even customise those factors that suit the purpose of monitoring and evaluating its sales volumes. Some such standards or factors are briefly described as under. Figure 8.1 shows the format on quantitative performance standards.

- ***Quotas:*** This is a quantitative objective expressed in absolute terms assigned over a period of time to a marketing unit. It may be measured in monetary terms or units of products. Quotas are the popularly and widely used quantitative standards to measure sales volume, gross margin, net profit, expenses, performance of non-selling activities or a combination of these and similar items.

  Based on the general and specific objectives that are realistic and attainable, the management assigns a quota for a fixed period. Assigning quotas is based on several market conditions. For instance, the future market demand of a company's product in a particular territory will help determine the quota for that territory for a period of time.

- ***Selling Expense Ratio:*** The selling expenses vary depending upon the territory. Some of these expenses are controllable by sales personnel while some are not. Hence the selling expenses must be set individually for each sales personnel depending upon the territory of his operation and the sales potential of that territory. Using the selling expense ratio, a salesman can affect the profit by not only controlling the expenses but also making sales.

- ***Gross Margin Ratio:*** Assigning gross margin ratios as a quantitative measure has the objective of focusing attention on a particular sales territory and emphasising the need of selling a balanced line of products and for considering the relative profitability of a particular territory vis-a-vis other territories or for considering the profitability at one point with another time frame in the future. Using such a ratio as a quantitative measure, the management regards each territory as a separate organisational unit that should make a profit contribution. Hence the target here is to cut down on sales expenses and to achieve a certain given profit over a period of time.

- ***Territorial Market Share:*** Here the market share is the quantitative measure to monitor the performance of the sales force. A percentage of the target market is set to be achieved which becomes the standard to judge how the sales force is doing. At the end of the assigned period the industry sales are matched with the company sales in the particular territory based on which the efficacy of the sales force is judged.

- ***Sales Coverage Effectiveness Index:*** This measures the efforts of a salesperson to convert prospects into customers. In this method, the ratio of prospects to customers is set and the salesperson is apportioned a target among different categories of prospects for different range of products.

- ***Call-frequency Ratio:*** In this method the number of sales calls on a particular class of customers is divided by the number of customers in that class.

- ***Calls per Day:*** This is self-explanatory and is especially used in the consumer product field where sales personnel need to contact a large number of customers; it is therefore desirable to set a standard for the number of calls per day. The number of calls for each sales personnel will depend upon different territories, taking into account territorial differences as well as customer density, road and traffic conditions and competitor's practices.

- **Order Call Ratio:** This is measured by dividing the number of orders secured by the number of calls made.
- **Average Cost per Call:** This method is used to emphasize making profitable calls, hence a target for average cost per call is set. When the cost incurred on each call varies on different classes of accounts, standards are set for each category of account. To counter this problem, a target average cost per call standard is also used to keep checks on unwarranted costs per call.
- **Average Order Size:** This method is used to control the frequency of calls on different accounts. In this method different standards are used for different sizes and classes of prospects. This method, along with the average cost per call, is used to control the salesperson's efforts and energies among different accounts and the emphasis is also laid on increasing the average order size by applying a certain level of efforts, thus obtaining the maximum out of a given level of effort. This method emphasises more effort on those prospects where the possibility of large orders is greater than on those where such a possibility is less.
- **Non-selling Activities:** Appropriate standards are set whenever non-selling activities are likely to generate increased sales volumes such as meeting the customers of the distributor, dealer displays, training the distributor's personnel, etc.
- **Multiple Quantitative Performance Standards:** In this method different standards of monitoring and evaluating the effectiveness of the sales personnel are combined. This will depend upon the standards that the management considers important to understand the effectiveness in a multidimensional environment.

figure 8.1 Format on Quantitative Performance Standards of M/s Kapoor India Ltd

ASSIGNED STANDARDS OF PERFORMANCE

SALES PERSON:.. OPERATING PERIOD: ....

1. Sales during period:.................................(Target: Rs.............................)
   STANDARD: Meet or exceed target.
2. New customers obtained during period: ....
   STANDARD: 10 per period.
3. Sales to new customers during period: Rs. ....
   STANDARD: 20% of total sales.
4. Total calls during period:..............................Average calls per day: ....
   STANDARD: 10 calls per day.
5. Percentage of customers called on one or more times during period: .... %
   STANDARD: 90%
6. Total contacts during period:..............Average number of contacts per call ....
   STANDARD: 2 contacts per call.
7. Proportion of calls on retain ® accounts............%, wholesale (W) accounts .... %
   STANDARD: R 80%, W 20%
8. Total sales meetings held.........................Attended.......................
   STANDARD: Attend all,
9. Customers entertained during period:..........................Average per week: ....
   STANDARD: 2 or more per week.

Qualitative Standards

Such criteria are used to appraise those performance attributes that affect sales results. The attributes may affect the sales performance over a long run but they can only be evaluated subjectively and qualitatively and hence an exact definition of such attributes is not possible. Examples include customer relations. A detailed checklist of such factors is provided in the table marked 'Assessment on Qualitative Performance Standards' in figure 8.2. Since a quantitative measure cannot be applied to appraise such traits among sales personnel, generally an executive judgement plays a major role in such an appraisal system.

Hence written job descriptions are used to highlight such attributes that the sales personnel need to possess and to what extent, but the manner in which these criteria are applied depends upon the needs of the management.

RECORDING PERFORMANCE

The kind of information needed for evaluation purposes will depend upon the performance standards. The choice of performance standards is based not just on the desire to use certain standards but also on the information available.

figure 8.2

Quantitative Performance Standards

Sales force performance analysis

Name...date......................

		Problem	Fair	Average	Good	Superior
A.	Job factors					
1.	Product knowledge					
2.	Customer knowledge					
3.	Relationship with customers					
4.	Number of sales calls made					
5.	Quota performance					
6.	Service follow-up					
B.	Personal factors					
1.	Punctuality					
2.	General attitude					
3.	Dress and appearance					
4.	Diligence					
5.	Cooperation					
6.	Accuracy					
7.	Adaptability					
8.	Reliability					

Strengths: ______________________

Weakness: ______________________

Comments ______________________

Signature

The two basic sources of performance information are the sales and expense records and various kinds of reports. The in-house data available in a company's database can be used after reprocessing for sales control purposes. The reclassified sales and expense data is helpful in the measurement of actual performance.

The sales personnel and junior sales staff can make vital information available to the management. In addition, the sales forecasts contain information for setting standards such as sales volume quotas and target share-of-the-market percentage.

FIELD SALES REPORTS

The field sales reports are prepared for obtaining control information. A good field sales report depends upon the interaction between those preparing the report and those receiving it. Such reports provide a basis for discussion between the sales management and the sales personnel. They also serve as tools to supervise the sales personnel in matters such as: whether the salespeople are calling on and selling to the right people and whether they are making the proper number of calls. Such reports also help ascertain how to secure more and larger orders and provide the raw material to the management to make the long-term and short-term policies regarding the sales management.

A good field sales report helps the sales force in their self-evaluation and self-improvement. Self-evaluation always proves to be more valuable and effective than the evaluation done by others.

A field sales report contains the requisite information that serves the purpose for which it is made. Although the common purpose of all kinds of field sales reports is to gauge the performance of the sales force, yet it may be designed to include additional information so that it serves various purposes which are elaborated below.

- ***Sales Planning:*** A field sales report helps the sales personnel to plan their time and work with respect to the information requested in the report.
- ***Data for Evaluation:*** A field sales report provides valuable data for performance evaluation of the sales force such as number of calls made, number of orders signed, total days worked, total miles covered, total selling expenses, advertising arrangements made, training of distributors' personnel, details concerning accounts, prospects called upon, etc.
- ***Records:*** A field sales report is an excellent routine diary where suggestions, complaints and reactions of the customers with respect to newer products can be recorded. Similarly, the reaction of the customers with respect to the service policies, prices variations, etc. can also be recorded. All this information helps the management to frame the short and long-term policies in tune with the attainment of the overall objectives of the organisation.
- ***Market Information:*** A field sales report helps gather vital information about the competitors' moves in the market place. A report becomes an excellent record that provides vital information about competitors' activities such as launching new products, conducting market tests, promotional activities and introducing new pricing and credit policies.
- ***Barometer of Market/Economic Conditions:*** A field sales report provides information regarding essential parameters necessary to understand the pulse of the market place and the economy.

- ***Help Organise Logistics:*** These reports help in planning and stocking stores and making appropriate plans with regard to complete logistics solutions so as to perform with minimum possible working capital. Helps maintain the mailing list to apprise the customers of new products.

A field sales report can be devised to serve various purposes. Some typical examples are:

- ***Call Report or Progress Report:*** This report is prepared individually for each call or calls made during a week or a month. Such reports are used by the management to keep a watch on sales personnel's activities, give an idea of where the company stands in terms of each account being handled and company's relative position in each geographical territory. This report also helps to actively follow up on more serious prospects. It also helps judge the market sentiment and competitors' moves such as new product launching, promotional activities pursued by competitors, etc.

- ***Expense Report:*** An expense report has two purposes – one, for tax purposes and two, to keep a watch on the total expenses being incurred and their authenticity. It helps in monitoring and controlling the expenses of the sales personnel. Certain reports are linked with expense reports so as to find the trend between the sales and expenses. This helps the sales staff to keep a tab on the expense. By using such reports, the sales staff can establish a ratio of expense to sales which will keep the management happy.

- ***Sales Work Plan:*** This report helps the salesman to submit a work plan for a week or a month such as names and numbers of accounts and prospects to be contacted, the products to be introduced and discussed, areas to cover etc. This aims at planning a schedule within a given time frame and also gives the management an insight into what the sales personnel are doing and whether that needs any correction.

- ***New Business Report:*** This report highlights the prospects that have been converted into new accounts or the prospects who are likely to turn into new accounts and the effectiveness of the sales force in converting such prospects into accounts. It also highlights the reasons for the loss of such prospects such as the new policies ensued by competitors with regard to price, credit, discounts etc. considering which the management can consider changes in their own policies.

- ***Complaint Report:*** The purpose of such a report is to handle and analyse complaints arising from the performance of sales personnel, complaints from a customer etc. This helps the management to introduce desired improvements and devise training programmes for the sales force to meet such complaints.

The Top One

Nowadays performance appraisal has assumed importance because it is related to the performance of the CEO (Chief Executive officer).

Companies depend so much on the CEO's policy, personal liking, experimenting and undertaking unrelated risks that the real monitoring and performance appraisal becomes secondary with some organisations.

In order to cover such situations, the company should also be cautioned about various pitfalls which chief executive officers may face.

SUMMARY

The sales manager must understand and conduct a proper performance appraisal of his salespersons as it helps in motivation, cost reductions and reduces role ambiguity. The sales manager has two basic choices: outcomes or behaviours. Outcomes are specific, measurable results of selling efforts. Behaviour is a salesperson's activities that are related to accomplishing the firm's sales objectives. Behaviour includes product knowledge, presentation quality, closing ability, service performed, number of calls made, days worked and other activity measures. Behavioural activities are measured via scales, including traditional rating, forced-choice rating, call reports etc. Sales reports generated by the sales force give information on many decision making areas for the top management. Every company, in accordance with its requirements, sets standards of performance for specific criteria and develops a reporting system for comparing actual performance with the norms.

PROJECT WORK

1. Critically evaluate the monitoring and performance appraisal system followed by M/s CIPLA Ltd. State the criteria used for evaluation of the system.
2. Study five organisations which have field sales operations. Find out
   a. What are the criteria used to evaluate their sales performance?
   b. In case multiple criteria have been used together, how has the composite measure been derived ?

SHORT ANSWER QUESTIONS

1. What are the essentials of a sales force monitoring programme?
2. What are the principles of sales evaluation?
3. What are the purpose of performance appraisal?

REVIEW QUESTIONS

1. What are the different reports generated to monitor sales force ? How are they used?
2. Describe the importance of monitoring and performance appraisal of sales force.
3. What is the rationale for a salesperson's self-evaluation?
4. How can a sales manager determine whether a given level of a salesperson's performance is at, above, or below standard?
5. Explain different types of traditional method of performance appraisal.

GO TO THE NET

Using Internet search tools, study ten organisations which have field sales operations. Study the criteria used to evaluate their sales performance.

Using Internet search tools, prepare a report on performance appraisal process of 5 Indian companies.

Caselet

On the basis of the data given in the following two tables, make appropriate recommendations to management.

Table I Comparative Performance of Salesmen

Sales Area	Total Calls	Total Orders	Sales/Calls Ratio	Average Sales by Salesman	Average Salesman By Order	Total Customers
A	1,900	1,140	60.0%	4,56,000	400	195
B	1,500	1,000	66.7	3,60,000	360	160
C	1,400	700	50.0	2,80,000	400	140
D	1,030	279	27.1	66,000	239	60
E	820	165	20.1	31,000	187	50
TOTAL	6,650	3,284	49.4	1193,000	363	605

Table II: Comparative Cost of Salesmen

Sales Area	Annual Compensation	Expense Payments	Total Salesman Cost	Sales Produced	Cost/Sales Ratio
A	11,400	5,600	17,000	4,56,000	3.7%
B	10,800	7,200	18,000	3,60,000	5.0
C	10,200	5,800	16,000	2,80,000	5.7
D	9,600	12,400	22,000	66,000	33.3
E	10,000	16,000	26,000	31,000	83.8
TOTAL	52,000	47,000	99, 000	119,3000	8.3

appendix I

Customer Call Report of M/s Kapoor India Ltd

Date: ____________________

Customer: ____________________

Address: ____________________

Persons Contacted: ____________________

Type of Customer		Selling Steps Taken	
Doctor	____________	Catalogues	____________
Engineer	____________	Movie	____________
Software Professional	____________	Service	____________
Shopkeeper	____________	Demonstration	____________
Government Employee	____________	Entertained	____________
Housewife	____________	Product Information	____________
Other	____________	Other	____________

CUSTOMER INTERESTED IN

NEW ____________ USED ____________ RENTAL ____________

Follow-up Plan/Action ____________________

Date of next call ____________________

Remarks: ____________________

Name of the salesperson: ____________________

Signatures: ____________________

appendix II

Weekly Expense Report of M/s Kapoor India Ltd

Name________________ For the week __________

Date	From/To	Fooding	Lodging	Entertainment	Miscellaneous		Daily Totals
					Description	Amount	
Expense item totals for the week							
Amount to be reimbursed							

I hereby certify that the above expenses represent the amount spent legitimately for business related activities only.

Approved/Disapproved Signature: ____________

appendix III

Sales Work Plan of M/s Kapoor India Ltd

Days	Prospect	Location	Purpose of Contact
Monday			
Tuesday			
Wednesday			
Thursday			
Friday			
Saturday			

appendix IV

Weekly Activity Report of M/s Kapoor India Ltd

Salesperson ________________________ For the week ending ___________________

Branch ____________________________ PROSPECTS ________________________

Customer	New or Used	Make and Model	Engg.	Sale	Rental in months	Purpose	Status

CHAPTER 9

planning of promotions of sales force

learning objectives

The objectives of this chapter are to:

- know the mistakes made by appraisers
- understand how to set objectives in the beginning of the year
- know about planning of promotions
- know about setting up sales quotas.

content outline

- Opening Case
- Introduction
- Common Mistakes Made by Appraisers
- Appraisal Against Set Standards Decided at the Beginning of the Year
- Setting Sales Quotas
- Summary
- Project Work
- Short Answer Questions
- Review Questions
- Go to the Net

opening case

Cool-Heads was established in 1985 to manufactured, distribute and markets pharmaceutical soft drink. It was purely an Indian company and had to face tough competition from multinational companies during the initial years. The company in the last decade with the help of effective markets strategies, has set up a place for itself, amongst the leading pharmaceutical companies in the country.

In 1995, the Managing Director of the company stressed the need for diversification and addition of new products to its existing product range. He floated the idea of manufacturing and marketing coffee with milk, cocoa and sugar. His advisers suggested that such products enriched with cocoa, would be desirable, and should be a big success, specially in view of its competitors brand. The marketing research department of the company also gave the green signal to the project after conducting a brief survey.

The company promoted coffee with Choco-Coffee as the brand name. It was supplied in a 400 gm. packet Rs. 75. The product was heavily advertised in the newspapers, health magazines, radio and television. The target audience was middle class, who it was believed could afford Choco Coffee. Ordinary coffee was available in the market at the rate Rs. 30 to Rs. 40 per kg. The thrust and Choco Coffee in the promotion campaign was that this contained cocoa, milk and sugar.

The company has 50 stockiest covering all the country and has a sales force of about 150 representatives, for promoting its products, through supermarkets and shops. The representatives of the company has very good discount coupons to the stockiest for passing over to their customers to induce them to buy their coffee. The buyer was entitled over to their customers to induce them to buy their coffee. The buyer was entitled to Rs. 5 discount per packet of 400 gms. The scheme, continued for about 6 months.

Despite heavy advertisement and canvassing by its representatives, the product was unable to attract customers. It was observed that launching of this product has not affected the market position of other branded coffee at all which was being sold at Rs. 90 for a pack of 275 grams. Rather, it was observed that the sales of the other brands of coffee increased marginally, consequent to the advertisement campaign by the Cool Heads. The company could achieve only 25% of its target in the first year and it remained almost static for the next year.

1. What do you think the reasons for the failure of the company to achieve its target?
2. Suggest a sales promotion plan for increasing the sales volume of the company.
3. Can a change in the distribution channel bring improvements in the sale of the product?

INTRODUCTION

Most of the companies in both the Indian and MNC sector have started giving importance to performance appraisal. It is a key management tool for monitoring, controlling and improving the performances of subordinates. It also helps in preparing a second line of managers for future use.

Performance appraisal, if not done systematically, can lead to lot of frustrations, grumbling, reduction in performance levels and high turnover of manpower. What are the common mistakes made by the appraisers?

COMMON MISTAKES MADE BY APPRAISERS

▸ The appraisal is based on the performance 2–3 months preceding the appraisal

This is a common mistake found in all the companies. The appraiser makes his decision on the performance of previous 2-3 months only; the high performances during the first half or three-fourth of the year go unrewarded. So we see efficiency levels going up during the appraisal period in most of the companies. Subordinates suddenly become more obedient and subservient. They are ready to do anything and spend lot of extra hours without any compensation for it. But you cannot blame the people for this because the wrong method has been adopted by the manager in appraising them with a short memory period. They are at liberty to take full advantage of the situation; it is for the appraiser to correct his mistake.

▸ Appraisal based on personal bias

This is another common mistake. The appraiser prepares the appraisal based on his personal impressions about his subordinates and not on hard facts. Since he is not discussing the appraisals with the subordinates, they never come to know what is happening and why they are left out every time.

The appraiser often neglects the possibility that his impressions are based on his encounters with the subordinates on very few occasions and that too many a times not in actual work situation. Some instances have been known where a very good salesman lost his chance of getting higher increment because he did not wish the manager properly in the men's room during the appraisal period, and many such trivial reasons. The manager must give the subordinates a fair chance of proving themselves.

▸ Appraisal based on hearsay

Sometimes the appraisals are based on the opinions expressed by others about someone you are appraising. This is totally unfair. The people who are passing judgement may not be qualified to do so. It is also possible that they have their own grudges and scores to settle.

After looking into common mistakes, let us look into various methods followed for appraisals:

- Actual achievements vis-a-vis previous year
- Profits generated during the year by every subordinate in absolute terms
- Growth in percentage terms achieved by every subordinate
- Appraisal against set standards decided at the beginning of the year.

It has been found that the method based on standards set at the beginning of the year has no inherent flaws and gives equal opportunity to every individual. This method has the following steps.

Appraisal Against Set Standards Decided at the Beginning of the Year

Setting Objectives at the Beginning of the Year

At the beginning of the year you must choose 5-6 common parameters against which you wish to appraise the performance of your subordinates. The parameters can be any of the following:

- Achievement of set targets
- Adherence to budgeted expenditure
- Sending reports on time as decided
- Personal appearance and grooming
- Behaviour with colleagues
- Behaviour with distributors
- Behaviour with retailers
- Behaviour with distributor sales staff
- Punctuality in work
- Planning and preparation for the work
- Enthusiasm
- Merchandising and display standards
- Increase in retail universe
- Development of new markets etc.

Give weightages to each parameter and fix performance standards at say Poor, Fair, Good, Very Good, Excellent etc. levels. Discuss these parameters and performance levels and their respective weightage with your subordinates and take their acceptance to all the parameters.

Self Assessment by the Subordinate

At least a month before the appraisal interview, send blank formats of appraisal to all the subordinates for self-assessment. Inform the subordinates that the performance interview will be held on so and so date at so and so place at so and so time and the subordinate should come prepared with his self assessment and supporting documents/facts to prove his point of view. This gives them time for preparation so that the discussions at the time of performance interview become meaningful.

Fixing Appraisal Interview

It is very important that appraisal interview is fixed well in advance. If possible, it should be fixed in some neutral area with absolutely no tension of workload. The atmosphere should be free and relaxed

– possibly a secluded restaurant where you can have lunch/breakfast without much disturbance and talk with each other without interruptions.

Advise the subordinate to talk freely as this is a very important opportunity for him which is available once in a year and he should not waste it. Also advise him that in case he cannot prove his point, your opinion will prevail. There should not be any heated discussions and losing temper will go against the subordinate. With this background start showing him your views and ask him to prove his point if he does not agree to your viewpoint and not vice versa. You can, on your own, give him the facts on the basis of which you have made your views and opinion. To help you do that keeping a diary of events both good as well as bad for each member of your team throughout the year proves very useful.

After the interview is over it is advisable to take the subordinate's signature on the points as accepted.

Discussion on Appraisal with Your Superior

It is very important to have discussions with your superior on the appraisals you have made. Your report, along with the appraisal forms, may not be accepted by your superior, so it is better to have personal discussions on this important issue. It is advisable that you show the appraisals to your superior before holding appraisal interview so that you can take your superiors' approval before you commit yourself in front of your subordinate. You can also get his views about your subordinates, which will be helpful for future planning.

If the appraisals are carried out in this manner there is very little room for disagreements and ill-feelings. The shortcomings pointed out about the subordinate can very well be termed as training needs and a plan can be made to act upon the same.

Example

Form of Performance Appraisal (Specimen)

(To be submitted in duplicate at the time of appraisal interview)

Objectives:

(To be decided and agreed upon at start of appraisal period)

STANDARD OBJECTIVES	YOUR RATING FOR SELF	AGREED RATING
▶ To achieve agreed sales targets		
▶ To achieve agreed reporting standards		
▶ To achieve agreed retailing standards		
▶ To achieve agreed merchandising standards		
▶ To achieve agreed budget adherence levels		

Special Individual Objectives:

- ▶ To improve distribution in Pune
- ▶ To appoint distributors in all district/taluka place
- ▶ To increase retail universe by 20%

RATING CAN BE IN PERCENTAGE OF SET STANDARD OR ON FIVE POINT RATING SCALE

AGREED ACTION POINTS:

S. NO.	ACTION POINT	BY WHOM	BY DATE

NAME OF APPRAISEE: SIGNATURE:

DESIGNATION:

Q.:

DATE OF INTERVIEW:

CONDUCTED BY: SIGNATURE:

DESIGNATION:

SETTING SALES QUOTAS

Their process of setting sales quota includes the following:

- ***Establish parameters for setting quotas:*** The start of the quota - setting process is to look at history to determine what sales success your team has had in the past or what sales success your team is likely to have in the future. Common parameters that can be used to define quota include:
  - *Historical trends*: How much of which product lines have been sold in your various sales territories over time?
  - *Last year's revenue:* What was the total revenue from all products and sales territories?
  - *National standards*: How much did all vendors (selling the same types of products) sell?
  - *Territory analysis*: How much does each salesperson think can be sold in his or her territory based on the existing pipeline and recent successes?

  The best quota-setting practices include looking at several of these parameters. For example, you might look at historical trends while your staff members go through their own records for a detailed territory analysis.

- ***Add a Growth Expectation:*** Step one helped you understand history. Now you have to take the next step to predict revenues for the next year (and then convert that revenue into quotas for your sales team). HUL has its own method for determining how much growth in revenue should be achieved. That expectation should be:
  - *Realistic*: What is doable for your products in the current state of your market? Some industries can realistically expect sales growth of 5% while others may see 100%.
  - *Challenging*: The goals you set should require each member of your team to work hard to meet the assigned goals.

- ***Adapt the Quota to Each Sales Representative:*** Adding the figures from steps one and two, you have the total revenue expected from your sales force. You could now be tempted to divide this total revenue by the number of salespeople to define the quota for each person. But in fact, not all salespeople are created equal. And not all sales territories are created equal.

Instead, look at each salesperson individually before determining the appropriate quota to assign. Some factors you need to consider are:

- *Tenure:* Sales representatives who have been with your company for several years have well-developed pipelines and contacts within their territories. They are more likely to sell more than those who have just joined your sales team.
- *Assigned job:* If you have different types of salespeople within your team, you may need to adjust quotas based on the type of job. The potential for sales of telemarketing people may be different from that of outside salespeople.
- *Sales skills:* Face it - some members of your team just have better sales skills than others. Having better sales skills is more likely to result in higher sales results.
- *Market potential:* Each territory may be different in its needs and appetite for acquiring each of your products.
- *Competition:* In some territories, the competition may be strong and thereby reduce the potential for sales. In other territories, competition may be weak or non-existent.

Using these factors (and others that might be unique to your company), assess your expectations for each of your sales representatives. Then use those expectations to determine the right quota for each person.

► ***Get buy-in from your sales team:*** If quotas are imposed on your salespeople without an explanation of how they were defined, the result could be resistance. It's important to have your staff buy in to your process for setting quotas, believe that these goals are achievable and work toward meeting or exceeding their assigned quotas.

To increase the buy-in of your sales staff to your quota-setting process:

- *Start with a planning meeting:* In one of your sales meetings, outline the process you'll be using to set quotas. Describe each of the steps you will be taking and the likely completion date. Most importantly, explain how team will be involved in this process.
- Have your representatives help gather information for the quota-setting process. Let your salespeople gather the information about their individual territories that you will use as one of the parameters for setting your quotas.
- Meet with each person to determine an individual quota. In the meeting, discuss any factors that might influence setting of that person's quota. Make it a joint decision, if possible, to assign a specific quota.

► ***Adapt Quotas to market realities:*** No matter how careful we are in our plans to set revenue targets or break these targets into quotas, we cannot predict what will happen in the economy. Changes in market conditions are inevitable. That means that quotas may have to be changed accordingly.

SUMMARY

Performance appraisal, if not done systematically, can lead to a lot of frustrations, grumbling reduction in performance levels and high turnover of manpower. Sometimes appraisals are based on opinions expressed by others about someone you are appraising, this is totally unfair. Sales quotas have been setup to increase the sales performance. The people who are passing the judgement may not be qualified to do so. It is also possible that they have their own grudges and scores to settle. It is very important that appraisal interview is fixed well in advance. If possible it should be fixed in some central area with absolutely no tension of work load.

PROJECT WORK

1. Critically evaluate the promotion policy of the following organisations:
   - AIR-INDIA
   - HDFC Bank
   - Maruti Udyog Ltd.
   - CIPLA Ltd.

SHORT ANSWER QUESTIONS

1. What do you mean by self assessment by the subordinate?
2. What are the parameters used for the beginning of promotion policy.

REVIEW QUESTIONS

1. What are the common mistakes made by appraisers?
2. Design a form of performance appraisal for your sales force.
3. What are the steps involved in planning of promotions?
4. Discus the parameters of setting sales quotas?

GO TO THE NET

- Using Internet search tools, study five organisations on their promotion policy for sales force.
- Using Internet search tools, design a new form of performance appraisal for sales force as per the Indian environment.
- Using Internet search tools, prepare a report of setting a sales quotas of 5 pharmaceutical companies.

CHAPTER

10

sales forecasting, quotas and territory management

learning objectives

The objectives of this chapter are to:

- understand the steps involved in sales forecasting
- difference between long run and short run forecasting.
- analyse the different methods used in sales forecasting
- appreciate the importance of sales quota and territory management.

content outline

- Opening Case
- Introduction
- Sales Forecasting
- Methods of Sales Forecasting
- Sales Quotas
- Territory Management
- Sales Forecasting and Global Factors
- Summary
- Project Work
- Short Answer Questions
- Review Questions
- Go to the Net
- Caselets

opening case

Raj Tyres is a company involved in the import and marketing of car tyres manufactured in the Far East. Raj Tyres established the business in 1990 when a friend living in Singapore told of the supply of tyres from that area which substantially undercut European prices. Although tyres from the Far East were not as long lasting as European (average 20,000 miles compared with 30,000), they were produced in accordance with high standards which meant that problems like weak spots, cracks and leaks were less serious than with European tyres.

Raj Tyres believed that a viable target market existed for the sale of these tyres in India. He was of the opinion that a substantial number of people were primarily interested in the purchase price of tyres. This price-sensitive target market could roughly be described as the mid-lower income, working-class family man who owned a secondhand car which was over three years old.

He decided to buy a consignment of tyres and visited tyre centres to sell them. Initially, business was slow but, gradually, as distributors began to believe in the quality of the tyres, sales picked up.

By 1999, MacLaren had taken on the role of general manager and had recruited five salespeople to handle the sales function. A brief personal profile produced by MacLaren of each of his salespeople is given below.

Profile of Raj Tyres Salesmen

Raj Mani

Joined the company in 1995. Has an MBA (Marketing) and has previously worked as an insurance salesman for three years. Aged 27. Handles the South area. Gregarious and extrovert.

Raj Lata

Joined the company in 1996. No formal qualifications but sound track record as a car salesman and, later, as a toy salesman. Aged 35. Handles the North area. Appears to be hard-working but lacks initiative.

Raj Laxmi

Joined the company in 1996. Has an MBA (Marketing). Was a technical representative for an engineering firm. Aged 28. Handles the East area. Appears to enjoy his work but lacks the necessary 'push' to be really successful in selling.

Rajan

Joined the company in 1997. Has a degree in Industrial Management. Previous experience includes selling bathroom suites and textile fabrics. Aged 29. Covers the Western area. Appears to lack enthusiasm but sales record is about average.

Raj Kumar

Joined the company in 1997. Has a degree in Business Studies. Only previous experience is as a marketing assistant during the industrial training period of his degree. Aged 25. Handles the Central area. Keen but still very raw.

Sales Force Data

Raj Tyres decided that the time had come to look in detail at the sales records of his men. The plan was to complete a series of statistics which would be useful in evaluating their performance. Basic data for the year 1997-98, relevant to each man, is contained in the following table

	Sales (Rs 000's)	*Gross Profits (Rs 000's)*	*Live accounts (1997.98)*	*Calls made*	*Number of different customers called upon*
Raj Mani	298	101	222	1,472	441
Raj Lata	589	191	333	1,463	432
Raj Laxmi	391	121	235	1,321	402
Rajan	440	132	181	1,152	211
Raj Kumar	240	65	296	1,396	421

Market Data

From trade sources and from a knowledge of the working boundaries each man operated in, MacLaren was able to produce estimates of the number of potential accounts and territory potential for each area.

	No. of potential accounts	*Territory potential (Rs 000's)*
Raj Mani	503	34,620
Raj Lata	524	36,360
Raj Laxmi	711	62,100
Rajan	483	43,800
Raj Kumar	646	38,620

TRY YOURSELF

1. Evaluate the performance of each of Raj Tyres salesperson.
2. What further information is needed to produce a more complete appraisal?

INTRODUCTION

Demand forecasting is a useful tool for planning. It helps estimate and forecast the market share of a firm. Most firms are very often confronted with the task of projecting future sales of their product. Identifying future sales problems is no easy task for companies, small or big. In some cases, it is very difficult to get any information about future market sales. Sales forecasting is not just an estimation of sales; it is also matching sales opportunities – actual and potential–with sales planning and procedures.

SALES FORECASTING

Sales forecasting, according to Cundiff and Still, is "an estimate of sales during a specified future period which is tied to a proposed marketing plan and which assumes a particular set of uncontrollable and competitive forces."

Purpose of Sales Forecasting

Steps in Sales Forecasting

1. Defining the objectives to be achieved.
2. Dividing various products into homogeneous groups.
3. Analysing the importance of various factors to be studied for sales forecasting.
4. Selecting the method.
5. Collecting and analysing the related information.
6. Drawing conclusions from the analysis made.
7. Implementing the decisions taken.
8. Reviewing and revising the sales forecasting from time to time.

Meaning and Types of Forecast

The term forecast is ordinarily used to refer to a prediction for a future period. Although this usage is technically correct, it is too general for managerial value.

	Best Possible Results	Expected Results for given strategy
Industry Level	Market Potential	Market Potential
Firm Level	Sales Potential	Sales Potential

A useful way for viewing what is being forecast is presented in figure above. This figure suggests that it is important to differentiate between industry and firm levels and to determine whether the prediction is for the best possible results or for the expected results given a specific strategy. Four different types of forecasts emerge from this classification scheme:

1. ***Market Potential:*** The best possible level of industry sales in a given geographic area for a specific period.

2. ***Market Forecast:*** The expected level of industry sales given a specific industry strategy in a given geographic area for a specific period.
3. ***Sales Potential:*** The best possible level of firm sales in a given geographic area for a specific period.
4. ***Sales Forecast:*** The expected level of firm sales given a specific strategy in a given geographic area for a specific period.

Meaning of Sales Forecast: The sales forecast is a prediction of expected sales for a specified period. It is an estimate for sales in rupee or units for a specified future period. In other words, it is basic tool for anticipating the nature of future sales or sales prediction.

According to Cundiff and Still, is "an estimate of sales during a specified future period which period is tied to a proposed marketing plan and which assumes a particular set of uncontrollable and competitive forces".

According to Stuits, "A sales forecast is an estimate of the amount or unit for a specified future period under marketing plan or programme".

According to American marketing Association "forecasting is an estimate of sales in dollars or physical units for a specified future period under a proposed marketing plan or program and under an assumed set of economic and other forces outside the unit for which the forecast is made. The forecast may be for a specified item of merchandise or for an entire line."

Objectives of Sales Forecasting

The objectives of sales forecasting may be studied under the following two major heads

1. Short - run (range) objectives.
2. Long - run (range) objectives.

1. ***Short - Run objectives:*** Short - run sales forecast short period, ranging from three months to twelve months it has generally been accepted that forecast for a short period is more accurate than for long period. Short run sales forecasting is undertaken for day to day operations. The short run objectives of sales forecast may be summarized as under:
    1. Formulation of suitable production policy so as to meet the demand as per the sales forecast.
    2. To make provision for the regular supply of raw material etc. for the production on the basis of sales forecast.
    3. To make the best utilization of machines on the basis of sales forecast.
    4. To make the regular supply of labour force as per the sales forecast.
    5. To determine an appropriate price policy for a given period.
    6. To estimate and provide the requisite working capital on the basis of sales forecast.
    7. To establish sales quotes targets for different market segments.
    8. To estimate stock requirements for unfinished semi-unfinished and finished products for a specified period of time.

2. ***Long Run objectives:*** Long run sales forecasting is mainly concerned with planning and policy decisions bearing on production and distribution. Under this type of forecasting the growth of the business enterprise attains its highest point of importance. The long run objectives of sales forecasting may be summarized as under:

   1. Estimating cash inflows from sales.
   2. Provision for capital expenditure.
   3. Planning of plant capacity so as to meet the future demand.
   4. Manpower planning so that production and distribution may not suffer in the long run.
   5. Planning for acquisition of raw materials so as to meet the future demand.
   6. Determining the dividend policy.
   7. Establishing coordination between various functions of on organization.
   8. Reducing selling costs and thereby reduces the final cost of the product.
   9. To estimate future profits of the business enterprise.

Factors Affecting or Influencing Sales Forecasting

There are a number of factors affecting or influencing sales forecast.

The main factors affecting or influencing sales forecast.

1. ***Business Environment:*** The term business environment refers to the general business conditions prevailing in the country under which the business enterprise has to affect the sales. He can do so when he is fully aware of economic, political and business trends. An adequate knowledge of general conditions which are likely to affect the sales, such as population growth and its density, level of national income and per capita income, government policies affecting trade and industry, general customs and traditions of the society, distribution of income and wealth in the society, fashion and styles, seasonal fluctuations etc., will enable him to predict sales forecast with accuracy and precision. These factors decide the general aggregated demand also.

2. ***Conditions within the industry:*** The conditions prevailing in the industry affect the sales forecast to a great extent. For instance; industrial unrest, rigid government rules and regulations, shortage of raw materials, shortage of finance, outdated machinery etc., disturb industrial activity and generate uncertainties regarding profits, sales and production. Such unstable conditions in the industry as a whole forecast may get out of gear.

3. ***Internal Conditions of the business Enterprise:*** Internal conditions of the business enterprise also affect the sales forecast. These may include price policy, promotion policy, publicity campaign, sales promotion, selection of distribution channel etc. These factors are within the control of the business enterprise. Hence, the sales manager should analyze these factors while preparing the sales forecast. Any change in organizational structure will directly affect the sales forecast.

4. ***Socio Economic Conditions:*** Socio economic conditions of the country also affect the sales forecasting. They may include total national income, per capita income, standard of living of the masses, education, inflation, deflation etc. For instance, if the prices are rising sharply and the production is not increasing to cope with the demand and thereby the sales forecast will be

affected. On the contrary, if there is a rapid increase in the per capita income along with increase in production, the demand will increase and thereby the sales forecast will be affected.

5. ***Factors Affecting Export Trade:*** If the business enterprise is engaged in the export "trade", the sales manager should take into account the factors which the export trade uses in making forecast of export sales, such as import and export policy of the government, export finance, export agreements of the country with foreign countries, market condition of the importing countries etc.

Steps in sales Forecasting: Sales forecasting procedures involves three sequential steps, which can be undertaken by the sales management team.

1. ***Forecasting of General Economic Conditions:*** General economic conditions within the boundaries of the nation, do effect the purchasing power of the individual customer. The standard yardstick for assessing general economic conditions will be: gross national product, per capita income, personal income, personal consumption expenditure, level of employment and the consumer price index.

   The general economic conditions the world over too need to be considered, as many a times the imports substitution and the export boom or recession could have a direct impact on the home industry.

   Such forecast could be available through the secondary data published by various private foundations, government agencies, universities export associations, trade associations and chambers of commerce. The budgets presented by the state governments also reflect on the general economic conditions as the backdrop while preparing the industry and product estimates.

2. ***Forecast of Industry Sales:*** Though the industry forecast are available from the trade associations and chambers of commerce, a SWOT analysis of the competition prevailing could throw much light on the competition within the industry.

   The sales manager can seek the help and counseling of professional forecasters in predicting more accurate sales of the industry who will base their projectionist on more sophisticated techniques.

   The indicators used for predicting general economic conditions, become helpful in estimating industry productions and sales to a large extent.

3. ***Preparing Forecast of Company Sales:*** The sales manager, while preparing the sales budgets of the company has to forecast the company and product sales for the coming year. The entire planning of the organization for production, manpower, financial arrangements, and revenue calculations will depend upon the accuracy of the sales manager's forecast.

   The sales manager will be seeding the help of the other experts and the salesmen, field sales executives involved in the activity of sales. A combination of many such opinions and methods will be used by him to forecast as precise and accurate as possible.

Some entrepreneur really understand what drives their markets, their industries, or their images. Without understanding this, it is not possible to predict the future, explain the past, or develop the plan for the future. Typically, Decision Analyst approaches demand forecasting at the industry level first and recommends including as much historical data as possible. What are the different components for the growth of an industry? Forecasting is based on marketing research and analytical consulting firm, has the experience and expertise to conduct sophisticated demand forecasting analyses for businesses, governments, universities, and nonprofit organizations. Sales forecasting can be focused on an industry, an industry, an individual company, or specific brands. Typically, these forecasts are updated monthly or quarterly and provide national as well as regional projections. These short-range and long-range analyses and forecasts can help companies understand the fundamental forces that drive their sales-nationally and regionally.

Choice Modeling

Discrete choice, volumetric choice, and conjoint models are analytical methods used to understand the behaviour of consumer purchasing behaviour. Our Advanced Analytics Consultants set up carefully controlled experiments in which consumers are simply asked to choose how many of each product to buy, given predetermined sets of realistic conditions.

Discrete Modeling

Discrete choice modeling is ideal for each product categories where only one purchase is made over a longer period of time. In these carefully controlled experiments, current and potential customers are asked which one product they would buy, given a realistic scenario including all of the products of services that compete with one another in the marketplace. In each scenario, the respondent is presented with a different set of marketing stimuli and asked which brand or product would be purchased. The type of decision that the respondents make in each scenario is designed to mimic the real market, and again each variables' importance is being determined implicitly.

The terms Management Science refers to scientific methods applied to the solution of complex business problems. The main objective of Management Science is to create a mathematical model that simulates, real-world processes and systems so that optimal solution can be achieved.

Marketing Mix Modeling

In recent times, we have seen the proliferation of new media (Internet, viral marketing, event marketing, sports marketing, product placement, cell phones, etc.), decreased television and similar technology where viewers can skip through commercials, and increased cost-cutting pressures. All of this has combined to increase demands for Marketing Departments to maximize the return on their marketing investment: that is, to optimize the combination of marketing and advertising investments in order to generate the greatest sales growth and/or maximize profits. Marketing mix modeling measures the potential value of all marketing inputs and identifies marketing investments that are most likely to produce long-term revenue growth.

Typically, Marketing Mix Modeling involves the use of multiple regression techniques to help predict the optimal mix of marketing variables. Regression is based on a number of inputs and how these relate to an outcome such as sales or profits. Once the model is built and validated, the input variables can be manipulated to determine the net effect on a company's sales or profits.

The data that go into creating a Marketing Mix Model include:

- ▶ Economic data
- ▶ Industry data
- ▶ Category data
- ▶ Advertising data
    - Promotional data

- Competitive data
- Service data

▶ Product Data

- Pricing Data
- Features & Performance

▶ Market Outcome Data

- Sales
- Revenues
- Profits

METHODS OF SALES FORECASTING

Survey Method

The survey method is based on the opinion of buyers and consumers. It is useful with respect to industrial products but not as far as consumer goods are concerned. According to this method, a company first of all selects potential buyers/consumers. It then collects their opinions for forecasting.

Expert Opinion

According to this method, a company invites the opinions of executives and consultants who are acknowledged experts in studying sales trends. On the basis of their opinions, it forecasts future sales. This estimate is also made on the basis of past performance. However, the method suffers from the drawback of not taking into consideration changes in the future business environment.

Market Studies Method

This method is commonly used by marketers for consumer goods. It is also known as the Market Test Method. A market test provides data about consumers and the marketing mix. Some people use this method as a market experiment method. According to this method, market experiments are conducted on changing consumer behaviour, prices, advertising expenditure, etc. This method lets the management know how people might actually buy the product in question.

Sales Force Opinion Method

This method estimates the buyers intentions from experienced personnel in the sales force. They can easily forecast for their respective territories. Territory-wise forecasts are consolidated at the branch level and the branch level forecasts are consolidated at the corporate level. This method can be used only when the firm has competent high-calibre sales personnel.

Statistical Methods

Statistical methods are considered to be superior techniques of sales forecasting because their reliability is higher than that of other techniques. Some commonly used statistical methods are given below:

a. *Trend Method*

This method provides a rough trend of the forecast on the basis of past experience. It does not, however, take into account the changing environment. It is a simple method for business forecasting on the basis of past performance.

b. *Graphical Method*

According to this method, sales data are plotted on graph paper and a graph is drawn for a number of years. This is a simple and inexpensive method.

c. *Time Series Method*

This method is used for long periods duly taking into account cyclical changes, seasonal variations and irregular fluctuations.

figure 10.1

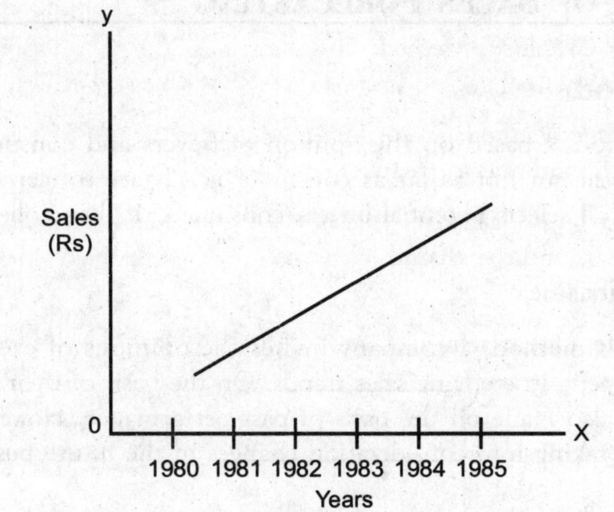

"A time series may be defined as a collection of magnitudes belonging to different time periods, of some variable or composite variables, such as production of steel, per capita income, gross national product, price of tobacco, or index of industrial production."

Ya-uin-chou

The Time Series Method shows the future trends of sales. The various techniques that can be used for determining these trends are:

- Freehold or Graphical Method
- Semi-average Method
- Moving Average Method
- Method of Least Squares.

figure 10.2

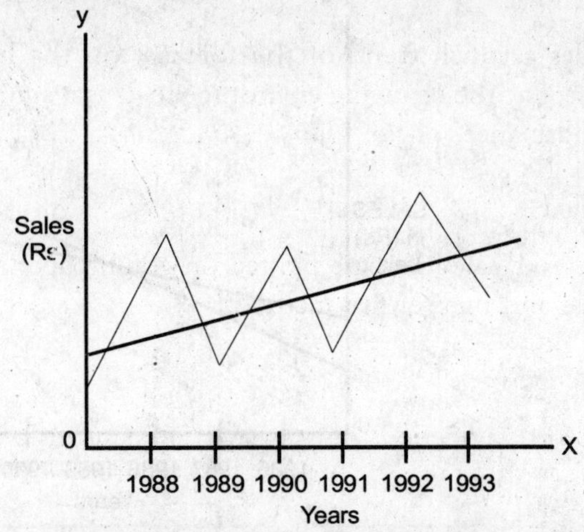

i. ***Freehold or Graphical Method:*** This is the simplest method for obtaining a straight line. A trend line is fitted by freehand to know future sales.

ii. ***Semi Average Method:*** According to this method, data are divided into two parts, preferably with the same number of years.

Example: If we are given data from 1983 to 1992, i.e., over a period of 10 years, the two equal parts will be the first five years and the second five years. This means that two semi-averages will be calculated and joined by a straight line.

For example, (3-year semi-averages)

Year	Sale (Rs. Lakhs)
1986	12
1987	13
1988	12
1989	14
1990	13
1991	16

Solution

First semi-average $= \frac{12+13+12}{3} = \frac{37}{3} = 12.33$

Second semi-average $= \frac{14+13+16}{3} = \frac{43}{3} = 14.33$

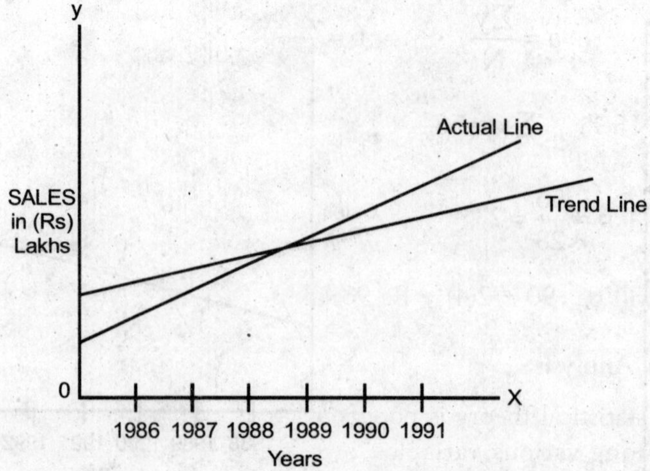

iii. ***Moving Averages Method:*** According to this method, a trend is determined by moving averages. Therefore, out of the averages such as 3-yearly moving, 5-yearly moving and 7-yearly moving average, the five-yearly moving average will be computed as follows:

$$\frac{A+B+C+D+E}{5} \qquad \frac{B+C+D+E+F}{5} \qquad \frac{C+D+E+F+G}{5}$$

iv. ***Least Squares Method:*** This method is most commonly used in practice. The straight line is represented by the equation:

yc = a + bx

For example: Fit a straight line trend for the following series. Estimate the value for 1994.

Year:	1987	1988	1989	1990	1991	1992	1993
Sales:	80	90	92	83	94	99	92

Solution

Year	Sales (Rs) Lakh	X	XY	X^2	Trend Value YC
1987	80	-3	-240	9	84
1988	90	-2	-180	4	86
1989	92	-1	-92	1	88
1990	83	0	0	0	90
1991	94	+1	94	1	92
1992	99	+2	198	4	94
1993	92	+3	276	9	96
N=7	$\Sigma y=630$	$\Sigma x=0$	$\Sigma xy=56$	$\Sigma x^2=28$	$\Sigma yc=630$

The equation of the straight line trend is

yc = a + bx

Since $\Sigma x = 0$, $a = \dfrac{\Sigma y}{N}$, $b = \dfrac{\Sigma xy}{\Sigma x^2}$

$\Sigma y = 630$, $N = 7$, $\Sigma xy = 56$, $\Sigma x^2 = 28$

$a = \dfrac{630}{7} = 90$ and $b = \dfrac{56}{28} = 2$

Sales for 1994 will be 90 + 2(4) = Rs 98 lakhs

d. ***Regression Analysis:***

This branch of statistical theory is popularly used on the principles of sciences. It helps determine the relationship among various variables. According to Ya-uin-chou, "Regression analysis attempts at establishing the 'nature of the relationship' between variables, that is, to study the functional relationship between the variables and thereby provide a mechanism for prediction, or forecasting."

SALES QUOTAS

A sales quota refers to an expected routine assignment to sales units, such as territory, districts and branches, etc. Sales quotas are also assigned to individual salespeople over a particular time period and are used to plan, control and evaluate the selling activities of a company. Sales control is facilitated by setting quotas to use in appraising the performances of sales force. Sales control is tightened by setting quotas on expenses and profitability of sales volume. They are tactical in nature and are thus derived from the sales force strategic objectives. Strategies stem from marketing and sales plans, sales forecasts and budgets. Thus, quotas are guides for what needs to be done and a means of evaluating how well they have been done.

Importance of Sales Quotas

Sales quotas serve several purposes. The important objectives are shown in the diagram below:

figure 10.3

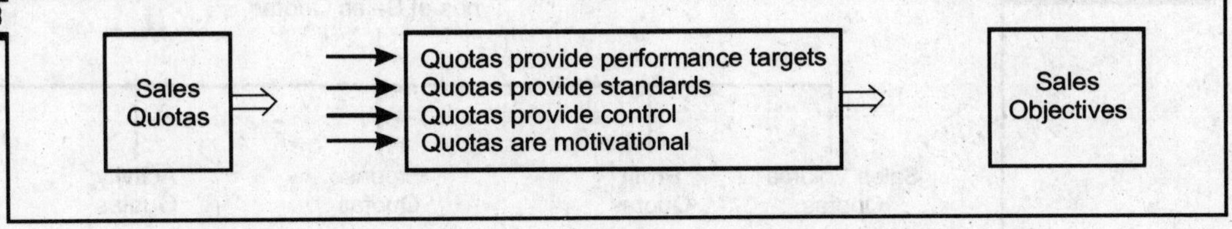

Purpose of Setting Sales Quotas

- Provides Goals and Incentives.
- Evaluating performance.
- Controlling the sales person activities.

- Uncovering strengths and weaknesses in the selling structure.
- Improving the compensation Plan's effectiveness.
- Controlling the Selling Expenses.
- Enhancing sales Contests,

1. ***Provides Goals and Incentives:*** A Quota provides salespeople with a standardized measure of their sales ability. In many companies who surpass the quota receive increased competition through commissions or bonuses and are recognized for superior performance.
2. ***Evaluating performance:*** It provides management with a tool to use in measuring the salesperson's performance.
3. ***Controlling the sales person activities:*** Quotas enable management to direct and control the activities of the sales force. Salesperson are responsible for certain activities like calling on a minimum number of accounts per day, calling on new account.
4. ***Uncovering strengths and weaknesses in the selling structure:*** If sales fall significantly short of the quota in a particular territory, the cause must be determined. It may be that a typical environment or market conditions exist only in that territory.
5. ***Improving the compensation Plan's effectiveness:*** Quotas can play an important role in the company's sales compensation plan. In some companies, salesperson must exceed the quota before they start to receive any commission.
6. ***Controlling the Selling Expenses:*** Quotas are also designed to keep selling costs at minimum. By restricting the amount of money that may be spent on meals, lodging, and entertainment, management can control the cost of selling.

Types of Sales Quotas

A sales organisation can set many types of quotas. The most common quotas are shown in the following diagram:

figure 10.4

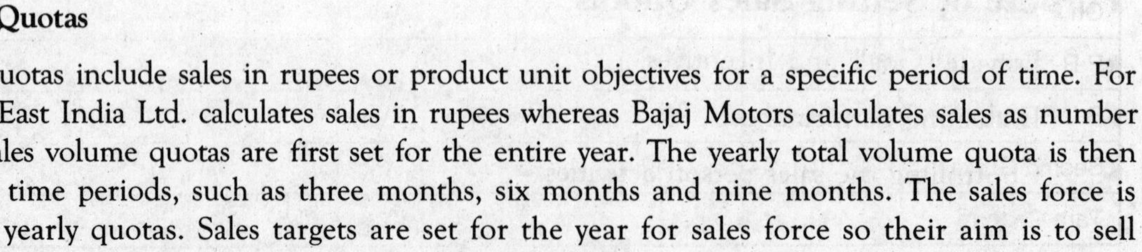

Sales Volume Quotas

Sales volume quotas include sales in rupees or product unit objectives for a specific period of time. For example, New East India Ltd. calculates sales in rupees whereas Bajaj Motors calculates sales as number of cars sold. Sales volume quotas are first set for the entire year. The yearly total volume quota is then set for shorter time periods, such as three months, six months and nine months. The sales force is assigned their yearly quotas. Sales targets are set for the year for sales force so their aim is to sell throughout the year to achieve the total sales objective. The sales volume quotas can be set in the following areas:

figure 10.5

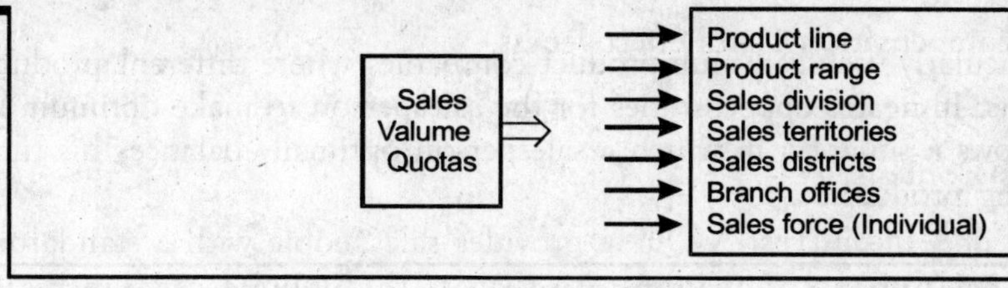

Example

The following example of M/s South India Ltd. shows sales volume quotas for Bangalore territory.

Sales Volume Quota of M/s South India Ltd. for Bangalore

Sales force	*Sales Quota (in Rs)*	*Actual Sales (in Rs)*	*Difference*	*Performance Index*
P Kumar	43,10,000	43,34,000	24000	100.6%
	2,16,02,000	2,10,14,000	-58800	

Sales Quota and Actual Performance for Month, Year: Another Example of Sales Volume Quota.

Salesperson	Current Month				Year to Date			
	Quota	Sales	Per cent	Rank	Quota	Sales	Per cent	Rank
Ajit Kumar								
Basant Kumar								
Chetan Kumar								
Utkarsh								
F Singh								
G P Singh								
H R Sharma								
I L Gupta								
J K Jain								
K L Gupta								
L L Singh								
Mona Sharma								
N L Verma								
Oh P Aggarwal								
P R Singh								
R L Gupta								
Seema Gupta								
Tara Chand								

Profit Quotas

Profit quotas are particularly useful in multiproduct companies where different products contribute to varying levels of profits. It creates opportunities for the salesperson to make optimum use of time. The following example shows a situation in which a salesperson optimally balances his time between high and low profit yielding products.

Product	Sales price per unit	Profit margin per unit (%)	Volume per month (Mr. Raj Kumar)	Net profit per month (Mr. Raj Kumar)
Product A	Rs 400	Rs 280 (70%)	60,000	168,00,000
Product B	Rs 200	Rs 80 (40%)	25,000	2,00,000
Product C	Rs 100	Rs 20 (20%)	10,000	2,00,000

Expense Quotas

Expense quotas are related to selling costs within reasonable limits. Some companies set quotas for expenses linked to different levels of sales attained by their sales force. Salespeople may receive an expense budget that is a percentage of the territory's sales volume. The salesperson must spend only this amount as expenditure.

Activity Quotas

These quotas set objectives for job-related duties useful for attaining salespeople's performance targets. Activity quotas are required to make the sales force perform other activities which have long-term implications on the goodwill of the firm. A sales organisation must set a target level of performance for salespersons. Some common types of activity quotas prevalent in Indian companies are as follows

figure 10.6

Common Types of Activity Quotas

- → Number of sales presentations made
- → Number of service calls made
- → Number of dealers visited
- → Number of calls made for recovery
- → Number of new accounts opened

Activity quotas typically should not be a basis for rewards. Rather, their attachment helps the manager better understand why salespeople do or do not meet their sales volume quota.

Quota Combinations

Many companies use a combination of these quotas. The two most commonly combined are sales volume and activity quotas. These quotas influence selling and non-selling activities.

It is also important not to have too many quotas; otherwise, the salespeople may become confused as to what is expected of them. Several quotas can be used but they should be on the most important activities – total sales volume and the products – that result in the most sales.

TERRITORY MANAGEMENT

A sales territory comprises of a group of customers or a geographical area assigned to a sales unit. The territory may or may not have geographic boundaries. A sales territory represents a group of customer accounts, an industry, a market or a specific geographical area. Territory management includes the market potential, number of customer accounts, the firms experience and market share in the territory, the capability of the salesperson assigned and the frequency of sales calls made.

The following diagram outlines the activities of territory management

figure 10.7

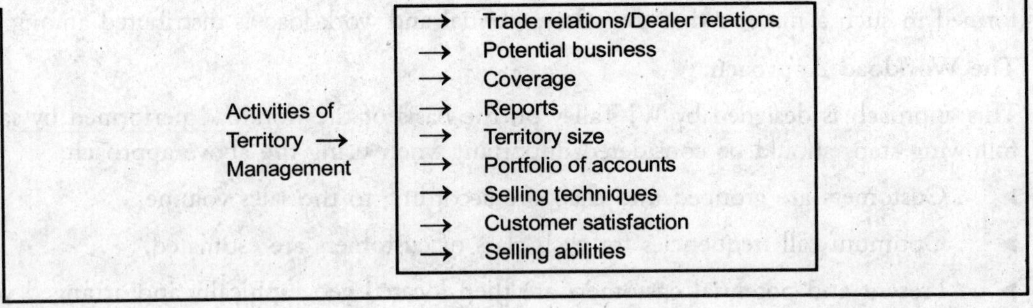

Why Establish Sales Territories?

A company can develop and use sales territories for various reasons. Some of the reasons are as follows:

- To obtain entire coverage of the market
- To establish a salesperson's responsibility
- To evaluate performance
- To improve customer relations
- To reduce sales expenses
- To allow better matching of salesperson to customer
- To benefit salespeople and the company.

Factors to be Considered when Designing Territories

In setting up or designing sales territories, these four steps must be followed:

1. Selecting a basic geographical control unit
2. Determining sales potentials in control unit
3. Combining control units into tentative territories
4. Adjusting for coverage difficulty and reallocating tentative territories.

The two basic approaches commonly used for designing sales territories are discussed below.

Market Build-up Approach

In this approach, an estimation of the present and potential products/services demand is made by looking at how the market is built up, who are its present/potential users, how much do they consume and at what frequency.

In this approach, information from trade directories, state publications, etc. is consolidated and then aggregated to understand an all India market potential for the product. For example, if the market potential for a new deluxe car in Maharashtra is 1,00,000, Gujarat is 60,000 and Rajasthan is 50,000, it shows that the total market potential is of 2,10,000 cars in the country. This leads to an estimation of total sales calls required per area and number of salespersons required. Sales territories are then formed in such a manner that the sales potential and work load is distributed among areas.

The Workload Approach

This approach is designed by WJ Talley on the basis of the workload performed by salespersons. The following steps should be considered important when using the above approach:

- Customers are grouped into class size according to the sales volume.
- Optimum call frequencies for each class of customers are estimated.
- Present and potential customers are then located geographically and arranged volume-wise and value-wise.
- The number of present and potential customers in each volume/value group is then multiplied by the desired call frequency to get the total number of planned calls required for each geographical control unit.

Assigning to Territories

Some salespeople can handle large territories and the travel associated with them, some territories require experienced salespeople, and some are best suited to new people. There are a few factors a manager needs to consider when assigning both new and experienced people to territories.

In today's complex selling situation, the presence of a well-thought-out daily and weekly route plan is required for effective management. The following may be considered basic route patterns of a territory.

Straight Line Pattern

figure 10.8

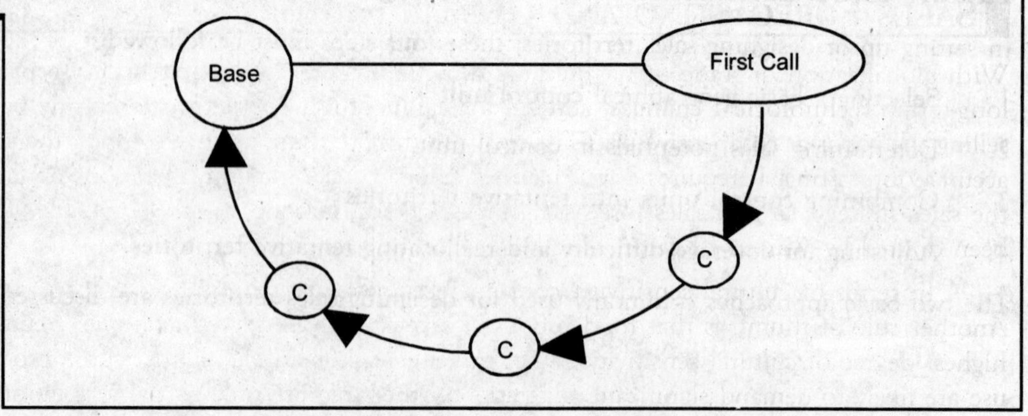

Clover Leaf Pattern

figure 10.9

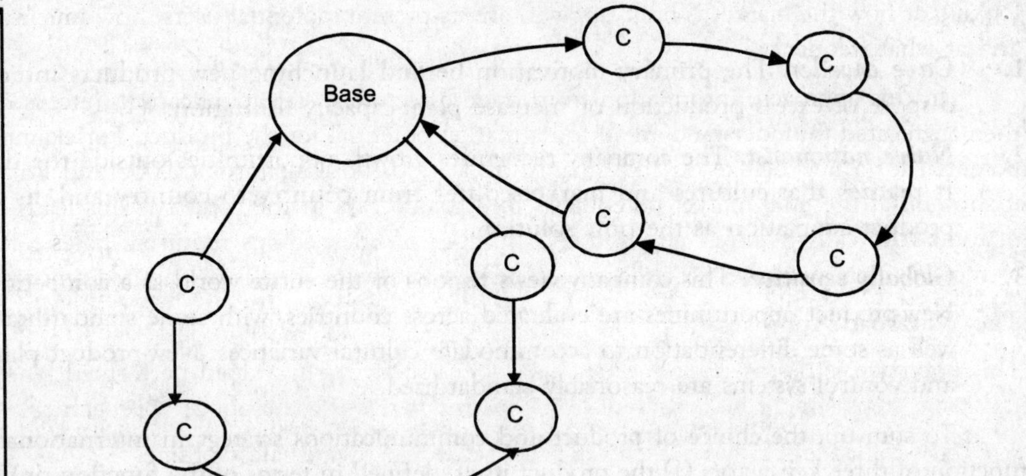

Major City Pattern

figure 10.10

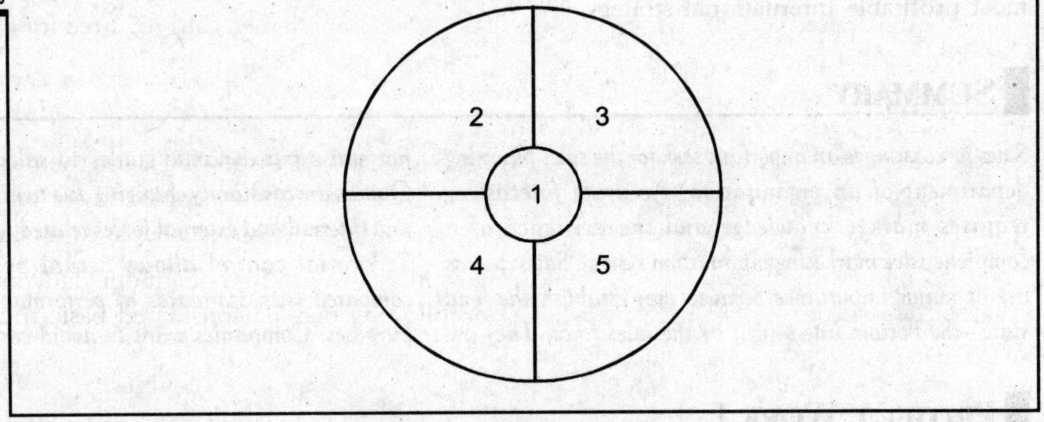

Sales Forecasting and Global Factors

With globalization of trade, it has became difficult to forecast accurately, more particularly for the long-term. Technological changes, sudden appearance of a competitor from any part of the world, selling the goods at competitive prices or even resorting to dumping, are some of the problems faced in accurate forecasting. It requires a well planned effort to take into consideration the factors influencing the sales strategy, so that sales forecasting may be a realistic one, as far as possible. This situation has been drafted by Warren J Keegan as follows:

In terms of cultural sensitivity, consumer products are more sensitive than industrial products. Another rule of thumb is that food products, especially those served at home, frequently exhibit the highest degree of cultural sensitivity. What this means to managers is that some products of daily life use are likely to demand significant adaptation. Others require only partial adaptation and still others are best left unchanged.

Companies differ in both their willingness and capability to identify and produce profitable product adaptations. Unfortunately, too many stage one and stage two companies are oblivious to the foregoing issues. One new-product expert has described three stages that a company must go through as follows

1. ***Cave dweller.*** The primary motivation behind launching new products internationally is to dispose of excess production or increase plant-capacity utilization.
2. ***Naive nationalist.*** The company recognizes growth opportunities outside the domestic market. It realizes that cultures and markets differ from country to country and, as a result, it sees product adaptation as the only solution.
3. ***Globally sensitive.*** This company views regions or the entire world as a competitive marketplace. New-product opportunities are evaluated across countries, with some standardization planned as well as some differentiation to accommodate cultural variances. New-product planning processes and control systems are reasonably standardized.

To sum up, the choice of product and communications strategy in international marketing is a function of three key factors (1) the product itself, defined in terms of the function or need it serves (2) the market, defined in terms of the conditions under which the product is used, the preferences of potential customers, and the ability to buy the products in question and (3) the costs of adaptation and manufacture to the company considering these product/communications approaches. Only after analysis of the product/market fit and of company capabilities and costs can executives choose the most profitable international strategy.

SUMMARY

Sales forecasting is an important task for the sales planning department of an organisation. Accurate forecasting requires market knowledge and the existence of a comprehensive marketing information system. Sales quotas are of major importance because they establish the 'end state'–the bottom line sought by the sales force. They are not static but dynamic guides to sales force behaviour. Quotas are constantly changing due to experience, feedback and internal and external forces related to the organisation. Territorial control allows actual performance to be compared with standards of performance for evaluation purposes. Companies want to avoid costly sales leakages.

PROJECT WORK I

K Lata is a salesperson of M/s New Delhi Ltd. Her manager suggested that she should keep a time log of her activities. Her last Saturday's time log is as follows:

1. Reached the distributor's office — 9.30 am
2. Had tea at distributor's office and general discussions — 9.30-10.45 am
3. Asked distributor to make unit ready — 10.45 am
4. Unit ready to move to the market — 11.00 am
5. First call made in the market — 11.20 am
6. 12 shops covered — 11.20 – 1.30 pm
7. Lunch break, market partially closed — 1.30 – 2.30 pm
8. 16 shops covered — 2.30 – 5.30 pm
9. Shopkeepers having busy time after 5.30 pm
10. Tea break — 5.30 - 6.15 pm
11. Returned to distributor godown — 6.45 pm

Evaluate utilisation of time by K Lata.

PROJECT WORK II

Sunil Mahajan is a salesperson of M/s MBA Ltd.

He covers the market for a distributor named Pooja Trading Co. Sunil Mahajan has made a one day time-log which is as follows

1. Reached the distributor's office 9.00 am
2. Unit ready the previous evening as per prior advice of Vivek Rai 9.00 am
3. Unit moves to the market 9.45 am
4. First call made in the market 10.05 am
5. 20 shops covered for selling 1.30 pm
6. Lunch break, reviewed the sales, balance stock and the distributor canvassers' evaluation of functioning 1.30 – 2.15 pm
7. Restarting shop coverage, covered 16 shops 2.15 – 5.30 pm
8. Shopkeepers busy with customers. However, quick visit to balance 4 big shops 5.50 pm
9. Returned to distributor godown and office 6.30 pm
10. Had tea at distributor's office. Reviewed past week performance. Booked orders, passed instructions for the next day coverage and unit loading 6.30 – 6.45 pm
11. Left distributor's office
    Study the time logs maintained by both K Lata and Sunil Mahajan and identify time wasting/time saving areas. Also, analyse which of the two salespersons were more productive and why? 6.45 pm

PROJECT WORK III

Can you join these nine dots with four straight lines without lifting your pen?

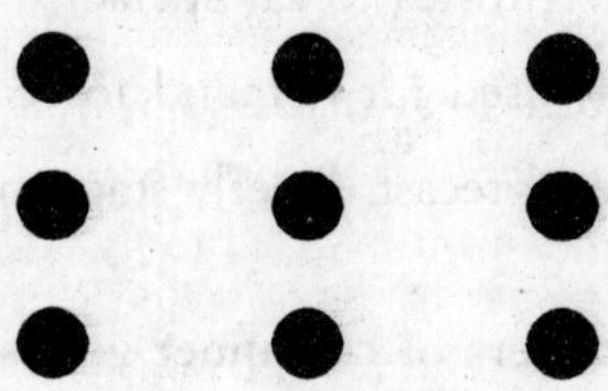

SHORT ANSWER QUESTIONS

1. What is sales forecasting?
2. What do you mean by expert opinion method?
3. What do you mean by sales quotas?
4. What are the different stages of sales forecasting.
5. What is the purpose of setting sales quotas?

Review Questions

1. What functions do quotas perform and why are they so important to a firm?
2. On the basis of the table given below compute the three salesperson's orders to sales call ratios and average size of order for the year. Why might the three salesperson's performance differ?

Name of territory	Name of Salesperson	Number of calls	Number of orders	Actual sales (Rs)
A	Raja Singh	1400	350	6,00,000
B	A K Singh	1600	800	7,00,000
C	S P Singh	1800	700	12,00,000

3. What is a sales territory? Why do firms establish sales territories? Can you think of a reason why a firm might not want to have sales territories?
4. What major factors do organisations consider while designing sales territories?
5. Briefly explain the various techniques of sales forecasting.
6. Discuss the workload approach for designing sales territories.
7. 'Quotas' can act as a 'motivator' as well as demotivator. Comment.
8. Identify the factors you would keep in mind for deciding the sales territories of an industrial product company like Crompton Greaves.
9. Critically analyse the various methods of sales forecasting used for industrial as well as consumer products.
10. Which method would be suitable to forecast the sale of a new brand of tetra pack fruit juice for the Indian market? (You can make your assumptions but state them clearly).
11. Which points are essential for finalising the allotment of territories to salespersons?
12. Define demand forecasting and discuss the various methods used for demand forecasting.
13. Explain the terms: market potential, sales potential and sales forecast. Briefly state the subjective and objective methods of sales forecasting.
14. What are the sales forecasting techniques used by manufacturers of consumer goods?
15. What are the forecasting methods that you would suggest for:

    i a kitchen appliance to be newly introduced in Indian market?

    ii. a fitness machine targeted at the urban middle class?
16. What is the difference between long-run and short-run forecasting?

Go to the Net

Using Internet search tools, study the forecasting methods used by various companies in introducing a new product.

Using Internet search tools' prepare a report on comparative analysis of 5 Automobile Industries.

Caselet 1

SWATANTRA COMPANY

Swatantra Company was established in 1940 to market office equipment in the entire country. They carried the entire product line manufactured by its parent company in UK. After the partition of the country, the company's activities were confined to India. In keeping with the government's policy, the company started manufacturing some of the products in the country. However, it continued to market the products under the brand name of the company. The company had a sales force of more than 100 sales representatives who were responsible for promoting the sales in their respective territories.

With a view to keeping the sales force sufficiently motivated, the company compensated the salesmen on the basis of salary-cum-commission. The salaries varied according to the length of service, experience and performance of non-selling functions. The commission, on the other hand, was calculated on the basis of the percentage of the quota achieved. Thus, if a person achieved 130 per cent of the quota fixed, his commissions worked out to 30 per cent of his salaries for the year. But in case a person failed to accomplish his target, he was not entitled to any commission.

The quota in case of a new territory was fixed at Rs 10,00,000 per annum and in subsequent years it was raised by 10 per cent of the quota achieved.

Mr. Kapur had joined the company in 1970 immediately after his graduation. After an initial training period of three months, he was allotted the newly created territory of South Delhi. During the period 1970-80, Kapur was consistently successful in achieving the sales quota fixed for the year. In 1980, Mr. Arora, a young man of 21, joined the company and after 3 months of training in Faridabad, was given the new territory of Faridabad. During the year 1981, Mr. Arora, who was employed on an initial salary of Rs 500/- per month, received a pay packet of Rs 1,000/- which consisted of his salary (Rs 500/-) and a commission of Rs 500/- (since he achieved a sales target of 200 per cent). Mr. Kapur's emoluments for the same year, however, worked out to Rs 950/- only, since he was just able to achieve the target fixed for the year.

Mr. Kapur (on entering *the room):* Sir, I am sorry to say that it is no longer possible for me to continue with this company any further where ....

Branch Manager: *(interrupting him)* Hold on, Kapur, calm down. Have a seat.

Mr. Kapur: (sitting on the chair) Sir, how can you expect me to keep calm, if I find that after 10 years of my service in this company I am no better than a youngster, who has joined only a year ago?

Branch Manager: Oh, you are referring to Mr. Arora's performance this year.

Mr. Kapur: Sir, don't tell me that his performance was better than mine. Anyway, I don't care since I have decided to quit the company. I am sure if you were in my position you would not have accepted a pay packet of Rs 950 — against Arora's pay packet of Rs 1,000/-.

Branch Manager: I fully appreciate your viewpoint but I am helpless. You know the fixation of quotas is done at the head office and I have no say whatsoever.

Mr. Kapur: Sir, I am sure you will agree that the present system of quotas fixation is absurd. Just look at me. When I joined the company I was given a target of Rs 10,00,000 but today I am supposed to achieve a target of 60,00,0000 from the same territory despite the growing competition in the industry.

Branch Manager: You are right, but .....

Mr. Kapur: (interrupting him) Sir, let's cut it short. All I wanted to say was that it would no longer be possible for me to continue in this company: In fact I have already got two offers (taking out some papers from his pocket).

Branch Manager: Hang on. How about seeing the Zonal Manager, who is coming to Delhi tomorrow? I shall definitely put a word for you.

Mr. *Kapur:* I won't mind, but I must repeat that I am determined to quit unless I get more than Arora and I am assured that the system of quota fixation would be changed to avoid such situations in the future.

Questions:

1. Critically evaluate the present system of quota fixation. Suggest a suitable method.
2. As the Zonal Manager, how would you handle the situation?

Caselet 2

An international company sells a large number of products, which are accessories for a certain class of machine. In India, it has nine salesmen, each of whom is responsible for sales in a separate territory.

Estimates of total market potential are Rs 12 crore and Rs 14.2 crore for the years ended 31st March 1997 and 1998, respectively. Data for two individual salesmen and "for the company as a whole are:

	Territory 1	Territory 2	Total India (including territories 1 and 2)
Territory area ('00 sq.km.)	10.4	21.9	328.8
No. of machines (lakhs)	16.5	8.3	128.0
Potential number of accounts	699	423	5965
Year ended 31.3.1997	Amal	Bimal	
Sales (Rs '000s)	1940	2020	24220
Customers (Number of accounts)	412	323	3318
Gross Margin (Rs '000s)	680	780	8520
Calls Made	1410	1163	10901
Year ended 31.3.1998			
Sales (Rs'000s)	2240	2460	29200
Customers (Number of accounts)	398	364	3271
Gross Margin (Rs '000s)	780	940	9960
Calls Made	1450	1220	11030
Salary (Rs '000s)	142	120	1216
Commission (Rs '000s)	34	37	432
Total Remuneration (Rs'000s)	176	157	1648
Expenses (Rs'000s)	39	64	561

You are required to do the following:

- For the average of all the nine salesmen and for any one salesman between Amal and Bimal, for the year ended 31st March 1998, calculate
  - Sales potential
  - Sales penetration percentage
  - Sales potential per account
- Any seven relevant indices that would help to assess the performance of salesmen under the following headings
  - customers
  - gross margin
  - calls made
  - remuneration
  - expenses

  At least one index should be calculated for each heading.
- Assess the performance of Bimal for the year ended 31st March 1998, based on a combination of the data in (a) above plus any other data that you may consider relevant.

CHAPTER 11

sales budgeting and control

learning objectives

The objectives of this chapter are to:

- prepare a sales budget and understand its significance
- appreciate the techniques of sales control
- understand the importance of sales auditing.

content outline

- Opening Case
- Introduction
- Sales Budget
- Significance of a Sales Budget
- Factors Affecting Sales Budget
- Sales Control
- Sales Audit
- Credit Control
- Budget Purposes
- Budgetary Control
- Market Share Analysis
- Summary
- Role Plays
- Short Answer Questions
- Review Questions
- Go to the Net
- Caselet

opening case

Komal Food Products Company Limited

Komal Food Products Company Limited, which was founded in 1965 to manufacture grocery and other food products, had, in the course of years, grown into a vast enterprise having offices and branches in almost all the important cities of India. Annual sales amounted to between Rs 50 and 60 lakhs a year.

The company's head office and factory were situated in Calcutta. Its products were distributed through five zonal sales offices which directed 25 district sales offices. The administrative responsibility of each zonal office was borne by a manager whose duty was to promote sales in his zone. He was advised and instructed by the head office from time to time.

Under the control of each zonal manager there were four functional heads, viz., personnel manager, accounts manager, sales manager and office manager. These executives advised and assisted the zonal manager on various functions relating to the zonal administration. Each functional head enjoyed considerable freedom and independence with respect to his work.

On matters relating to sales, the zonal manager received advice from the sales manager. The latter formulated policies; planned schedules for sales operations; suggested improvements in district sales administration; and submitted his views on all matters concerning sales to the zonal manager. At times he issued orders and instructions to the district sales manager but these were typically routed through the zonal Manager. Ordinarily, his views and advice were accepted and approved by the zonal manager.

The sales manager was assisted in his work by three product managers who were considered to be experts in their respective fields. Their duty was to travel with the sales supervisors of the various districts and study the market for the company's products, survey the competitive position of the company's products, study dealer and consumer reactions, sales trends and advise the district sales manager and sales supervisors regarding the steps to be taken for promoting sales in the districts. Every month each submitted a report on the sales activities of the company to the sales manager. The relationship between the product manager and the sales manager is the same as that between the zonal manager and sales manager.

Also directly responsible to the zonal manager were five district sales managers each of whom was responsible for sales in his territory. Each district manager was, in turn, assisted by five sales supervisors besides several salesmen. The duties and functions of district sales manager were to:

i. Select, train and supervise his sales supervisor and salesmen following the policies and procedures laid down by the zonal manager

ii. Make a study of the nature of consumer demand, changing market conditions, existing stock and to formulate sales campaigns, promotional methods

iii. Fix the sales targets to be attained in his territory from time to time

iv. Formulate the credit policies to be followed after consultation with the zonal manager

v. Develop better teamwork among the sales supervisors and salesmen

vi. See that the customers were satisfied with the company's service

vii. Undertake such other functions and duties as might be assigned to him from time to time by the zonal manager.

Every month, each district sales manager submitted a detailed report on the sales activities of the company in his district to the zonal manager. Ordinarily, these reports were passed on to the sales manager for necessary action to be taken with respect to each district.

On the morning of June 1991, the following conversation took place over phone between Mr. Rajan, the sales manager at the South Zonal Office and Mr. Shankar, one of the district managers in the Zone.

Shankar: I wish to bring to your notice an important matter that needs your urgent consideration.... The product mangers are interfering too much with the sales activities of my district. I receive frequent complaints from my supervisors that they are not able to carry out my instructions due to unnecessary interference from these people. If this state of affairs continues it will be very difficult to maintain our sales. The morale of the supervisors will be seriously affected. I will not be responsible if sales drop this time in our area on this account. You must take some steps to see that the relationship between the line and staff is maintained on good terms.

Rajan: Mr. Shankar, you need not worry. I shall call the product managers and see that they maintain the proper relationship with you...

Next day Mr. Rajan called all the product managers and after discussing routine matters he said, "... I was told by Mr. Shankar that his sales supervisors are complaining that you are interfering with their activities... Definitely you are expected to advise them on the steps to be taken for increasing sales. But at the same time please remember that you have to play only an advisory role. While advising these people you must also see that the line authority is respected...."

The product manager did not say anything.

In the subsequent months Mr. Rajan did not ask him why there was so much decline in sales in his territory while all the other districts showed very good progress.

Shankar replied: "..... During the past three months the product managers have not advised our men properly. In fact they did not advise the supervisors of the recent changes and trends in the market. They seem to be unwilling to cooperate with our sales force. What can I do ? Even then, we have done our best to maintain sales..."

When asked about this by the zonal manager, one of the product managers said,"... We used to give advice to this district office also as we usually do with other district offices. On a complaint, it seems from Mr. Shankar, we had been told by Mr. Rajan that we were exceeding our authority and unnecessarily interfering with the activities of this district. We had been asked to restrain ourselves... The district manager takes advice directly from the zonal manager. We have got nothing to do in this matter...."

TRY YOURSELF

1. Evaluate the organisation structure of the company and comment whether any changes in the reporting relationships should be made to affect better cooperation between line and staff.
2. Identify the reasons for conflict between product managers and field sales staff at Komal Food Products Limited. Suggest possible ways of resolving or minimising the conflict.

INTRODUCTION

A sales budget is a programme designed for a stipulated time frame that highlights the selling expenses and anticipated sales, quantitatively and in value terms. This helps in making an objective estimate of net profit on the selling operations. In a real sense, it is a statement aimed at comparing the revenue, net profits, sales volume and the selling expenses relating to a particular product or the entire business.

Since the volume of sales and selling expenses have their bearing on personal selling strategy, it is important to consider the following key issues:

a. The quality of sales force, and

b. The size of the sales force.

The sales volume for the period in question is estimated by the sales forecast. The sales volume derived at through sales forecast is classified to highlight the quantities of products that are to be sold, sales personnel who would handle their sales and the respective sales districts, the prospective buyers, and the quantities to be sold at different time periods during the stipulated period.

After arriving at this broad-based classification, the likely selling expenses that would be incurred in the implementation of the year round sales programme are then estimated.

The first point in designing a sales budget is the anticipated sales volume. The top sales executives would be involved in this to the extent of their participation in the sales forecast.

There are three types of sales expenses:

- ***Fixed Expenses***: These expenses pertain to the compensation of salespersons, office rent, insurance and interest on fixed assets like vehicles, office space, office equipment, etc.
- ***Performance-related Expenses***: These include commissions, incentives, bonus and awards, etc.
- ***Activity-related Expenses***: These include travel and communication expenses, etc.

SALES BUDGET

The sales budget is the amount of money available or assigned for a definite period. Usually one year. It is based on estimates of expenditures during that period and on proposals for financing the budget. Thus, the budget depends on the sales forecast and the amount of revenue expected to be generated for the organization during that period. The budget for the sales force is a valuable resource that the sales manager redistributes among lower level managers. Budget funds must be appropriate wisely in order to properly support selling activities that allow sales personal and the total marketing group to reach their performance goals.

Significance of a Sales Budget

The importance of a sales budget cannot be overemphasised. Its significance can be gauged from the factors given below:

- It serves as a scale, or a yardstick, to measure the performance/progress of the company in terms of the performance of the sales personnel, regions, products, marketing channels and customers.
- It helps identify the areas in which the company needs to strengthen or improve its performance.

- It serves as an indicator to control the expenses associated with the sales activity and to keep a constant watch on the net profits of the company.
- It helps in comparing the actual performance with the budgeted performance and takes corrective measures if drawbacks appear or to follow the strategy if the performance is good.
- It helps the planners to frame policies for actual market situations and provides the platform to establish ways and means to get the business where they want it to be.
- It provides vital statistics to relate and dedicate the resources in an effective manner so as to realise the forecasted sales and convert these figures into reality.
- It helps keep expenses under control so that by using scarce resources, the objective of net profits may be achieved.

FACTORS AFFECTING SALES BUDGET

The sales manager should take into consideration the following factors while preparing the sales budget:

- Past sales figures and trend
- Salesmen's estimates
- Plant capacity
- General trade prospects
- Orders on hand
- Proposed expansion or discontinuance of products
- Seasonal fluctuations
- Potential market
- Availability of material and supply
- Financial aspect
- Other factors
    - The nature and degree of competition within the industry
    - Cost of distributing goods
    - Government controls, rules and regulations related to the industry and
    - Political situation – national and international – as it may have an influence upon the market.

The sales manager, after taking into consideration all these factors, will prepare the sales budget in terms of quantity and money, distinguishing between products, periods and areas of sales.

Example

Sales Corporation Ltd. has three sales divisions at Delhi, Jaipur and Lucknow. The company sells two products – Product A and Product B. The budgeted sales of the year ending 31st December 1998 at each place are given below

Delhi : Product A 2,00,000 units @ Rs 16 each

Product B 1,40,000 units @ Rs 10 each

Jaipur : Product B 2,20,000 units @ Rs 10 each

Lucknow : Product A 3,00,000 units @ Rs 16 each

The actual sales during the same period were as follows:

Delhi : Product A 2,50,000 units @ Rs 16 each

Product B 1,50,000 units @ Rs 10 each

Jaipur : Product B 2,50,000 units @ Rs 10 each

Lucknow : Product A 3,10,000 units @ Rs 16 each

From the reports of the sales personnel, it was considered that the sales budget for the year ending 31st December 1999 would be higher than the 1998 budget in the following aspects

Delhi : Product A 16,000 units

Product B 10,000 units

Jaipur : Product B 26,000 units

Lucknow : Product A 20,000 units

Intensive sales campaigns in Jaipur and Lucknow are expected to result in additional sales of 50,000 units of Product A in Jaipur and 36,000 units of Product B in Lucknow. You are requested to prepare a sales budget for the period ending 31st December 1999.

Solution

table 11.1 **SALES BUDGET**

Division	Product	Budget for 1999			Budget for 1998			Actual for 1998		
		Qty	Price Rs	Value Rs	Qty	Price Rs	Value Rs	Qty	Price Rs	Value Rs
Delhi	A	2,16,000	16	34,56,000	2,00,000	16	32,00,000	2,50,000	16	40,00,000
	B	1,50,000	10	15,00,000	14,0,000	10	14,00,000	1,50,000	10	15,00,000
		3,66,000		49,56,000	3,40,000		46,00,000	4.00.000		55,00,000
Jaipur	A	50,000	16	8,00,000	—	—	—	—	—	—
	B	2,46,000	10	24,60,000	2,20,000	10	22,00,000	2,50,000	10	25,00,000
		2,96,000		32,60,000	2,20,000		22,00,000	2,50,000		25,00,000
Lucknow	A	3,20,000	16	57,20,000	3,00,000	16	48,00,000	3,10,000	16	49,60,000
	B	36,000	10	3,60,000	—	—	—	—	—	—
		3,56,000		54,80,000	3,30,000		48,00,000	3,10,000		49,60,000
Total	A	5,86,000	16	93,76,000	5,00,000	—	80,00,000	5,60,000	—	89,60,000
	B	4,32,000	10	43,20,000	3,60,000		36,00,000	4,00,000		40,00,000
		10,18,000		136,96,000	8,60,000		116,00,000	9,60,000		129,60,000

SALES CONTROL

Control is a function of every management to ensure that operations are being carried out as per the plan to achieve the objectives. Sales control ensures the achievement of personal selling objectives. Sales coordination is very essential to ensure proper conduct of sales operations by different functionaries in the field.

The sales manager's position in the company can be compared to the commander of an army unit on the war front; his success or failure will decide the fate of the war. The sales manager has to produce tangible results and for this to happen he has to have a clear view of his job responsibility. His position is unique in the sense that he represents the company in the market which treats him as the company. Sales control is the most important task for the sales department of a company. It is the control tool for ensuring that the marketing activities of a company are directed towards the marketing objectives.

Types of Sales Control

	Type of Control	Prime Responsibility	Purpose of Control	Approaches
1	Annual plan control	Top level managers	To examine whether the planned results are being achieved	- Sales analysis - Market shares analysis - Marketing expenses to sales ratio
2	Profitability control	Sales controller	To examine where the company is making or losing money	Customer attitude Tracking profitability by - Product territory - Market share - Trade channel - Order size - Sales audit

Steps in Designing a Sales Control System

- Objective setting
- Designing different control levels
- Designing a reporting system and a feedback system
- Deciding tools and techniques of control
- Variance analysis and reasons thereof

SALES AUDIT

Sales audit is a comprehensive, systematic, independent and periodic examination of a company's environment, objectives, strategies and activities to determine problem areas and opportunities and recommend a plan of action to improve the company's sales performance. The job of sales audit is performed by a sales auditor.

The Aim of the Audit

The Aim of the sales audit in any sales organization is to :

i. Find out the true and accurate position of sales.

ii. To exercise control over future planning and over the results of the company.

iii. To analyse the past performance and learn from mistakes made in the past or shortcomings in any operation of the sales department.

iv. To bring alertness to the organization. The staff should know that their functions are under the watchful eyes of the management and they cannot take liberty with their working or responsibilities.

v. To award increments, promotions, giving extra rewards in case of exceptional performances and to punish those whose actions have resulted in loss to the company.

Therefore, auditing is called an instrument of further controls.

Koontz and O' Donnell have said that controlling implies "the measurement and correction of the performance of subordinates in order to make sure that enterprise objectives and the plans devised to attain them are being accomplished".

And the real aim of sales audit is to scrutinize and improve performance of the sales department.

Sales audit can be conducted in two ways:

- By internal staff of the company.
- By outside auditors like chartered accountants or consultants – experts in particular type of business activities.

Timely sales audit at a regular interval and follow up of the recommendations as given by the auditors can result in excellent results for future and help in devising timely safeguards.

Auditor's Plans

An auditor can ask a number of questions.

After getting responses to his questions, he can put forward his suggestions to the management to implement new strategies or plans.

The following questions can be considered by a marketing auditor:

- What are the strengths, weaknesses, opportunities or threats to the company (known as SWOT analysis)?
- What are the changes in consumer behaviour?
- What are the major changes in market segmentation?
- What are the changes in the major competitors' strategies?
- What are the changes in the competitive environment?
- What are the pricing strategies of the competitors?
- What are the main channels of distribution?
- Have the marketing objectives been achieved or not?
- What major advertising media are being used by the competitors?

Format of Customer Satisfaction Audit, which is part of Sales Audit, is shown below:

	MARKETING SERVICE (Weightage = 1.25)	*CODE*	*SCORE*
01	How is the response to enquiries?		
	Response to enquiries after reminders	0	
	Prompt response to enquiries	1	
	Effective pre-tendering followed by prompt response to enquiries	2	
02	How is the quality of offer?		
	Incomplete and lacking detail	0	
	Matter of fact - complete to the extent required	1	
	Highly informative and complete in all respects	2	
03	Is the company technically and commercially competent?		
	No	0	
	Somewhat	1	
	Yes	2	
04	Does the company have good engineering capability?		
	No	0	
	Somewhat	1	
	Yes	2	
	TOTAL	T1	
	ORDER HANDLING (Weightage = 1.0)		
05	How is the quality of documentation?		
	Poor	0	
	Average	1	
	Good	2	
06	Are the orders executed on time?		
	Never	0	
	Sometimes	1	
	Always	2	
07	How is the quality of packing?		
	Poor	0	
	Average	1	
	Good	2	

08	How is the project and site management?	
	Poor	0
	Average	1
	Good	2
	TOTAL	T2
AFTER-SALE SERVICE (Weightage = 1.75)		
09	Is there a prompt response to complaints/commissioning calls?	
	Never	0
	Sometimes	1
	Always	2
10	Is there a timely supply of spares?	
	Never	0
	Sometimes	1
	Always	2
11	Are the complaints resolved to the customer's satisfaction?	
	Never	0
	Sometimes	1
	Always	2
12	How is the product training and briefing on new developments?	
	Poor	0
	Average	1
	Good	2
	TOTAL	T3
	PRODUCT (Weightage = 2.0)	
13	How is the quality of the product?	
	Poor	0
	Average	1
	Good	2
14	Is the product easy to install and maintain?	
	No	0
	Somewhat	1
	Yes	2

15	Is the price competitive?	
	No	0
	Somewhat	1
	Yes	2
16	Is the product appealing?	
	No	0
	Somewhat	1
	Yes	2
	TOTAL	T4

TOTAL CUSTOMER SATISFACTION SCORE = T = (1.25 × T1) + (1.0 × T2) + (1.75 × T3) + (2.0 × T4)

T (MAX) = 48

T(MIN) = 0

table 11.2 **RATING**

0-24 (upto 50%)	24-31 (50% - 65%)	31-38 (65%-80%)	38-48 (80% -100%)
Below Average	Average	Good	Superior

CREDIT CONTROL

Credit rating of distributors, wholesalers, dealers and customers is necessary for sales control. It enables a company to determine what credit facilities it can allow to these groups.

Steps in Designing a Credit Control System

1. Identifying credit distributors and wholesalers or consumers on the basis of past experience.
2. Processing the credit sanction.
3. Circulating and implementing the credit sanction.
4. Aging analysis (see the format given below).
5. Reviewing credit sanctions from time to time.

table 11.3 **Aging analysis statement of M/s ....**

Customer Code	Customer's Name	Credit Amount (Rs)	Sanctioned Days	Total Outstanding (Rs)	Below 60 days (Rs)	60-120 days (Rs)	Above 120 days (Rs)
0005	M/s A.S Ltd	10,000	60	50,000	30,000	5,000	15,000
0008	M/s Tara Ltd	5,000	30	40,000	30,000	—	10,000
0014	M/s Gulati Bros	10,000	60	12,000	4,000	6,000	2,000

The following factors should be taken into consideration in the credit rating of dealers/distributors:

- Organisational set-up of the firm
- Market reputation
- Trade line of dealers/distributors
- Financial position of dealers/distributors
- Analysis of financial statement
- History of payments.

BUDGET PURPOSES

The budget is an extremely important factor in the successful operation of the sales force. Top sales managers spend a great deal of time attempting to convince corporate management to increase the size of their budgets. Budgets are formulated for many reasons, including the major ones of planning, coordination, and control.

1. ***Planning:*** Corporations and their functional units develop objectives for future periods, and budgets determine how these objectives will be met. For example alternative marketing plans, the probable profit from each plan, and the individual budget for each will be considered before management is able to decide on future marketing programs.
2. ***Coordination:*** The budget is a major management tool for coordinating the activities of all functional areas and subgroup within the entire organization. For example, sales must be coordinated with production to ensure that enough products are available to meet demand. The production manager can use sales forecasts and the sales department's marketing plans to determine die necessary production level. Budgeting allows the financial executive to determine the firm's revenues and expenses and have enough capital to finance all business operations.
3. ***Control:*** Allocation of budgeted funds gives management control over their use. Sales managers estimate their budget needs, are given funds to operate their units, and then are held responsible for reaching their stated goats by using their budgets effectively. As the sales program is implemented and income and expenses are actually generated, managers assess results against the amount budgeted and determine whether they are meeting objectives.

Factors to be Considered while Preparing Sales Budget

The sales manager should take into consideration the following factors while preparing the sales budget.

1. Past sales figures and trend
2. Salesmen's estimates
3. Plant capacity
4. General trade prospects
5. Orders on hand

6. Proposed expansion or discontinuance of products
7. Seasonal fluctuations
8. Potential market
9. Availability of material and supply
10. Financial aspect

Budget Analysis (Reporting)

Budgeting Analysis cover the following application areas:

- Sales Analysis
- Sales Orders
- Finance – Accounts Receivable
- Finance – Accounts Payable
- Finance – General Ledger
- Inventory
- Purchasing
- Manufacturing

BUDGETARY CONTROL

The Institute of Cost and Management Accountants of the UK has defined Budgetary Control as "the establishment of budgets relating to the responsibilities of executives to the requirements of a policy and the continuous comparison of actual results with budgeted results, either to secure by individual action the objective of that policy or to provide a basis for its revision."

Budgetary control has become an essential tool of management for controlling costs and maximising profits. The technique of budgetary control is, in fact, a must for every business enterprise. To exert control over the budgets, every organisation has to set up an effective budgetary control system. The following factors should be examined at the time of budgetary control reporting:

- What changes are most likely in the business environment?
- What are the major objectives to be achieved?

MARKET SHARE ANALYSIS

This is another sales control tool that is undeniably very useful. It helps in marketing planning and achieving marketing targets. Market performance can also be evaluated on the basis of the market share analysis. If the market share of a company is increasing, it is a sign of progress; if it is decreasing, the company must take the necessary measures to arrest, and possibly push back, this trend.

Ratio Analysis

Ratio analysis is a powerful tool of marketing control. It helps in correctly identifying the financial strengths and weaknesses of a company. Different ratios can be calculated for different purposes. For example, profitability ratios help determine the profitability of a company. Several ratios can be calculated from the accounting data contained in financial statements. The following ratios are useful for management control:

i. Current ratio
ii. Liquidity ratio
iii. Proprietary ratio
iv. GP ratio
v. NP ratio
vi. Operating profit ratio
vii. Earnings per share
viii. Dividend payout ratio
ix. Dividend per share
x. Debtors turnover ratio
xi. Average collection period
xii. Working capital turnover ratio

The following are some of the advantages of ratio analysis:

- Ratio analysis helps in planning and forecasting.
- It helps in intra-firm comparison.
- It simplifies financial statements.
- It helps in coordination, control and communication.

Variance Analysis

Comparison of standards with actual performance is required to understand the performance of sales. The difference of the actual from the standard is known as variance. The variance may be favourable or adverse according to circumstances. Sales variance is used in marketing control. It has many types.

figure 11.1

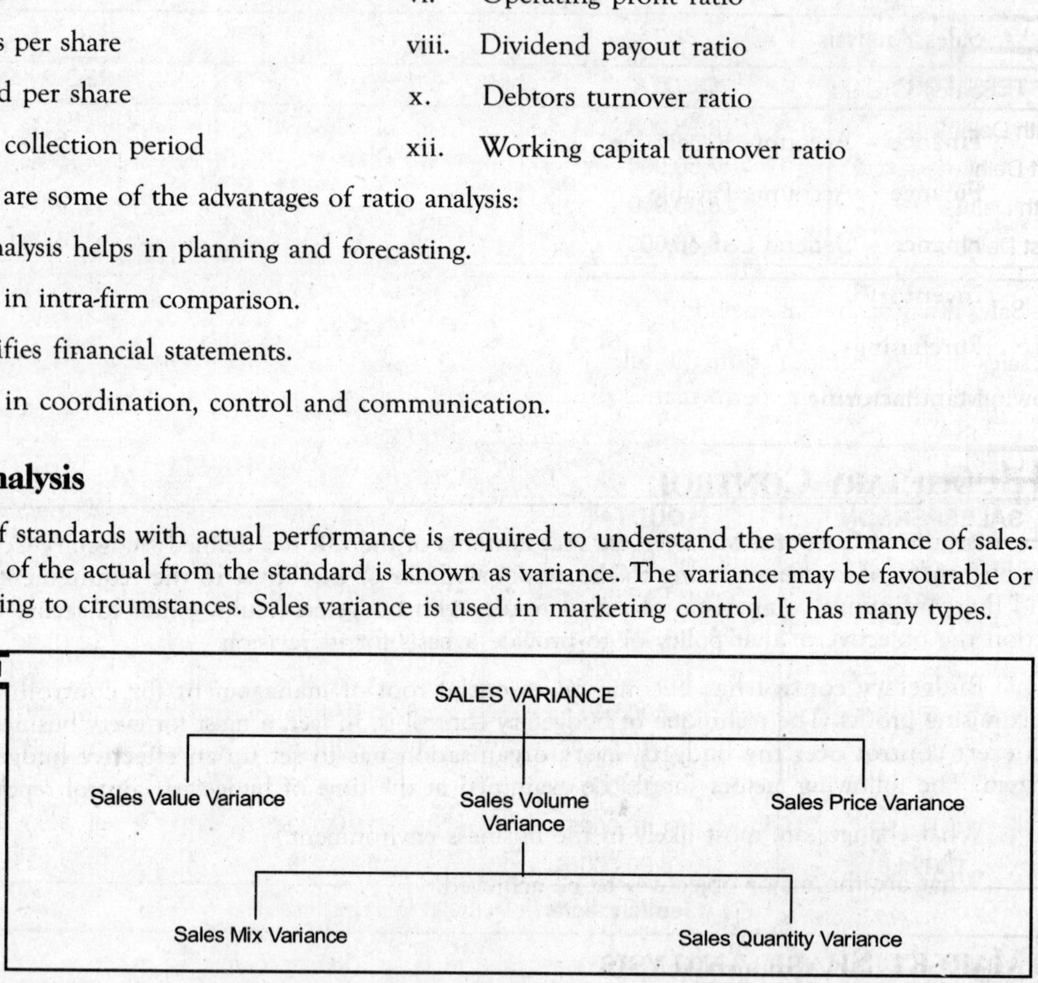

Sales Price Variance	:	Standard Sales - Actual Sales
Sales Volume Variance	:	Budgeted Sales - Standard Sales
Sales Value Variance	:	Budgeted Sales - Actual Sales
Sales Mix Variance	:	Standard Price × (Revised Standard Quantity - Actual Quantity)

Sales Analysis

Sales analysis is the detailed examination of sales volume by territory, salesperson, customer, product line, etc. It works on the basic principle that the trends of the total sales volume conceal rather than reveal the market reality. The following methods are used for sales analysis.

a. Sales Analysis by Territory

In this method, the sales force is controlled on the basis of territory. It assumes that each quota assigned to each salesperson is based on fair and sound measurement i.e., potential. The following example will explain sales analysis based on territory.

table 11.4

TERRITORY	QUOTA	ACTUAL	PERFORMANCE
South Delhi	8,25,000	8,50,000	103%
East Delhi	7,50,000	7,50,000	100%
North Delhi	8,90,000	8,70,000	98%
West Delhi	8,50,000	9,20,000	108%

b. Sales Analysis by Salesperson

The sales manager should study the sales performance of all salespersons working in the territory. The following table shows the performance of salespersons

table 11.5

SALESPERSON	QUOTAS	ACTUAL	PERFORMANCE
A	95,000	93,000	98%
B	1,15,000	1,17,000	102%
C	1,10,000	1,09,000	99%
D	1,06,000	1,10,000	104%
E	1,08,000	1,07,000	99%
F	1,10,000	1,12,000	102%
G	1,30,000	1,06,000	82%
H	1,16,000	1,16,000	100%
TOTAL	8,90,000	8,70,000	98%

Territory: North Delhi (Sales by Salesperson)

c. Sales Analysis by Product Line

The sales manager should also see the performance on the basis of product line where the performance is poor. The following example explains performance on the basis of product line

table 11.6

PRODUCT	QUOTA	ACTUAL	PERFORMANCE
Scooters	2,20,000	23,00,000	104%
Motorbikes	2,80,000	28,00,000	100%

d. **Sales Analysis by Customer**

Customer-wise break up of sales helps to understand the target market and where the sales manager has to put more emphasis.

Sales Cost Analysis

Sales cost analysis is a detailed examination of the costs incurred in the organisation and administration of the sales and marketing functions and its' impact on sales volume. The following are the important sales costs which should be kept in mind by a sales manager:

- Cost of goods per rupee of sales
- Profit per rupee of sales
- Cost per segment
- Cost per territory
- Cost per salesperson
- Cost per channel member
- Average cost per order.

Sales cost analysis is an important tool for controlling the various sales costs. It also helps in profitability analysis.

SUMMARY

Sales budget is the statement of revenues and costs that are expected for a given time period and are among the most important control devices available to sales managers. The process of developing a sales budget involves identifying ways of optimal resource allocation to various selling activities. A sales budget aids in sales planning and acts as both a standard of performance and a tool of control. Control is a function of every management to ensure that operations are being carried out as per plan to achieve the objective. Sales control ensures the achievement of personal selling objectives.

ROLE PLAYS

Role Play (1)

Assume that you are a territory sales manager. What characteristics would you look for or what criteria would you use for promoting a sales person to the position of district sales manager?

Role Play (2)

Assume that it is year 2001 and you are a senior level sales manager. Tell us something about your job profile.

Role Play (3)

As a sales manager, you are required to prepare an annual operating plan. What would you include in the plan?

Role Play (4)

"Salespersons are born, not made". Do you agree? If so, why does a firm need a training programme for sales supervisors? If you do not agree, why is so much importance given to good selection? Perhaps a firm should spend far less time and money on selection and instead place the effort on the training programme.

Role Play (5)

If a person wants to be a top-notch professional career sales representative interested in being a manager, is a college education necessary? Discuss. If your answer is no, why do so many firms recruit salespeople from colleges and why is a college education so often listed as a qualification for a sales job?

Role Play (6)

Assume that a company wants to hire a sales engineer, that is, fill a position where the major emphasis is on technical product knowledge. Should this firm recruit engineers and train them to sell, or recruit sales representatives and teach them the necessary technical information and abilities?

SHORT ANSWER QUESTIONS

1. What do you mean by sales budget?
2. What are the various types of sales expenses?
3. What are the steps in designing a sales control system?
4. What is sales audit?
5. What is sales budget?
6. What are different factors to be considered while preparing sales budget?

REVIEW QUESTIONS

1. Topaz manufactures two products A and B and sells them through two divisions, North and South. For the purpose of submission of sales budgets to the Budget Committee, the following information has been made available.

   Budgeted sales for the current year were

Product	North	South
A	200 at Rs 4.50	300 at Rs 4.50
B	150 at Rs 10.50	250 at Rs 10.50

   Actual sales for the current year were

Product	North	South
A	250 at Rs 4.50	100 at Rs 10.50
B	350 at Rs 4.50	200 at Rs 10.50

   Adequate market studies reveal that product A is popular but underpriced. If the price of A is, therefore, increased by Rs 1, it will find a ready market. On the other hand, B is overpriced and the market could absorb more, if the sales price of B is reduced by Rs l. The management agrees to give effect to the above price changes.

From the information based on these prime changes and reports received from salesmen, the following estimates have been prepared by the divisional managers. The percentage increase in sales over the current budget is

Product	North	South
A	+10%	+5%
B	+20%	+10%

With the help of an intensive advertisement campaign, the following additional sales over and above the estimated sales of divisional managers are possible:

Product	North	South
A	60	70
B	40	50

You are required to prepare the sales budget.

2. What do you understand by a sales budget? Explain the various steps in preparing a sales budget.
3. What is a sales budget? Discuss the principal factors that must be taken into account while preparing a sales budget.
4. Explain the budget process with the help of suitable example.

GO TO THE NET

1. Using Internet search tools, study the balance sheet of six organisation's and find out sales cost analyses on the following basis:
   a. Cost per segment
   b. Cost per territory
   c. Cost per person
   d. Cost per channel member.
2. Using Internet search tool prepare a data of 10 companies to analyses their sales budget.
3. Using Internet search tool prepare a report on the objectives of preparing budget process.

Caselet

Sales manager use diverse system to motivate their team. It is the responsibility of the sales manager that their team should achieve the target at the given interval of time. So sales manager inspire and motivate their team to achieve the target. A good sales manager appreciate their team by providing them financial incentives for their performance.

Carpet products Limited manufactures a special variety of industrial carpet which are used by other manufacturing units to produce shoes and chappals. The market for the company's product comprises a few large public limited companies and a number of small units run as proprietary or partnership concerns. The sales had in the past proved to be seasonal, with peak sales being recorded in the period January to July.

One year back the company had expanded its production capacity from 3,000 to 8,000 MT per annum. However, the actual production in the financial year just ended was restricted to 5,000 MT, mainly on account of lock of orders. The Cost Statement for the year indicated the following:

	Rs/MT
Raw Materials	1,500
Direct Labour and Supervision	700
Indirect Materials, Fuel, etc.	400
Depreciation, Insurance, etc.	1,700
Factory Cost of Production	5,500
Administrative, Selling and Interest Charges	400
Selling Price per MT	6,000
(exclusive of all discounts, allowance for Freight, etc.)	

The Managing Director was not satisfied by the under utilization of installed capacity and its effect on the profitability of the company. He called his senior managers to discuss the situation and means of improving the profitability of the concern. The Sales Manager, on whom the pressure was really on, tried to attribute the limitation of sales to norms for grant of credit followed by the company. He argued that under the strict norms for grant of credit followed by the company, only the larger public limited companies among the customers were put on the cash and carry list. This he maintained, led to an overdependence on the larger customers and an almost complete neglect of a section by offering them consisting of the small manufacturers came to this company only if the market was starved of the product. The Sales Manager pleaded for a more liberal credit policy which would also help increase the sales volume. He ruled out the possibility of procuring additional volume of business from the big customers who had already evolved a scheme sharing out their business among the different suppliers. Any attempt to obtain more business by offering discount to the bigger firms, the Sales Manager argued, will only lead to a retaliatory action by competitors and ultimately escalate into a price war which will only prove disastrous for the company. On the other hand, granting credit to the smaller customers will bring the company's policy in the line with competitors and will actually stimulate growth in the consuming industry with beneficial effects to the company.

The Managing Director, obviously undecided about the wisdom of extending credit to the smaller customers to boost sales volume, called for a detailed note from both the Sales Manager and the Credit Manager. He, however, pointed out that any such change of credit policy, even to boost sales. The Sales Manager, at this point, conveyed to the Managing Director, an offer he had just received from the Shoe Plast Limited, one of the receivables that this transaction would entail and reckoning interest at 18 percent per transaction would involve an interest burden of Rs. 1,54,150 whereas the profits from Shoe Plast Limited would pay for these additional supplies to be effected in the next three months, in the seventh month from date. It was, however, unwilling to pay any Limited ranked high in the ratings by the Credit Department and therefore, there should be no hesitation in accepting this offer for additional business.

The customer company was carrying out an expansion scheme at that time using partly its current resources to finance the same and was, therefore, finding itself in a difficult liquid situation. It however, expected this to be only temporary and anticipated that the position would improve considerably after six months. Shoe Plast Limited had and above the regular off-take if Plastic Products Limited agreed to give special credit among the smaller firms. He read out a long list of the smaller

Contd...

firms in the industry which include excellent record of the company in the matter of credit management and to the fact over as credit manager. Extending sales to the smaller manufacturers, he argued, was fraught with grave risks and the company, if it close to adopt such a policy, should be reconciled to an incidence of bad debts of about 6 percent each year, which he was quick to point margin the company appears to have its products.

Questions:

1. What consideration he should take into account, while revising the credit policy of a company?
2. Advice the Managing Director how he should take the circumstances.

BLOCK II

New Techniques of Sales Management

Direct Marketing is demassified marketing. It deals with customers on a one-to-one basis. In conventional marketing, the marketer sells to a multitude of customers treating them as a mass. He uses mass production, mass communication and mass distribution devices. While mass marketing targets the average customers of the chosen segment and develops its offer for the average customer, new techniques target the individual customer and develop its offer for them.

The block focuses on various new techniques of sales management through 5 chapters.

Chapter-12	Sales Management Information System and Sales Training
Chapter-13	Relationship Marketing
Chapter-14	Internet as an Emerging Selling Technique
Chapter-15	Direct Marketing
Chapter-16	International Sales Management

CHAPTER 12

sales management information system and sales training

learning objectives

The objectives of this chapter are to:

- understand the sales information system
- describe various reports
- discuss sales training and presentation techniques
- understand role and importance of sales Promotion.

content outline

- Opening Case
- Introduction
- What is Sales Management Information System?
- Planning and Control
- Reports
- Monthly Performance Review
- Sales Training
- Presentational Techniques
- Ensuring that Learning Takes Place
- Summary
- Short Answer Questions
- Review Questions
- Go to the Net
- Caselet

opening case

Disposable Crockery — A New Concept

Concept — Product Research

Packaging (I) Pvt. Ltd. was in the business of manufacturing packaging materials made of biodegradable thermocol for the last six years. In the year 1994, it was thinking of diversifying into a technology-related product.

Product Concept

With nuclear families increasing in numbers, consisting of more number of working women, coupled with the difficulty of finding domestic help, entertaining at home has become a bane for every housewife. Food can be ordered from outside but cleaning up after the party is not easy. The available crockery range can extend from expensive Chinaware to inexpensive disposable paper crockery. However, most housewives are reluctant to use their Chinaware for large gatherings in view of breakages and other problems like washing up.

That leaves them with the option of disposable crockery/cutlery especially for large parties, children's parties, etc. The quality of disposable plates/glasses, etc. available in the market is not very good and, therefore, unsuitable for buffet meals, or are esthetically unappealing. This leaves the average middle class housewife in a dilemma.

In this context, the product concept that Packaging (I) Pvt. Ltd. brought out was of disposable designer crockery made of thermocol. A pack size of 12 would include 12 dinner plates, 12 quarter plates, 12 bowls, 12 glasses, 3 serving bowls, 1 rice plate, 4 serving spoons and 12 spoons. The crockery would be made up of microwave-safe thermocol. Spoons would be made of plastic. Three pack sizes, viz., 12 plates, 20 plates and 25 plates were envisaged.

Also, the company was wondering whether the pack should include designer disposable, matching, high quality paper napkins, a matching table cloth (disposable) along with the napkins or simply the crockery. A preliminary exploratory survey had indicated that the consumer is willing to spend Rs 125-250 for the purpose of party crockery which is disposable. Three price intentions—Rs 125, Rs 200 and Rs 250 – were to be considered.

Try Yourself

1. Which technique of product research would you use to recommend for the pack combinations that the company must introduce?

INTRODUCTION

Tactical information systems are designed to support recurrent decision making situations– this means that the information requirements can be determined ahead of time. This allows for reports to be produced regularly and in predetermined format(s).

Generally aimed at operating and control levels of the organization, this precludes that they are being prepared by top level management.

Example of the type of recurrent decisions supported by these reports include: daily call report, expense statement etc. Online retrieval is achieved through invoking programmes which incorporate the routines necessary to retrieve the data and the predetermined formats for presenting it.

Situations that cannot be anticipated or call for information that is not anticipated require the production of unscheduled reports – sometimes referred to as ad hoc reports.

These reports may be needed to provide information for situations that have not been foreseen or to accommodate changes in information requirements or differences in decision making styles between managers.

WHAT IS SALES MANAGEMENT INFORMATION SYSTEM?

To achieve the sales goals set by senior management, the sales manager must make tactical decisions about

- shape of sales territories
- allocation of sales staff to territories
- what product to push
- which customers to contact
- incentive schemes
- which market segments to emphasise and with what products.

In addition, they must also monitor the sales effort and make changes to the tactics in response to changes in the market.

Much information about past sales is required for analysis – from the sales management information system. Data provided can be analysed in a variety of ways to assist in tactical decision making.

Such a tactical information system would provide the sales manager with a variety of statistical analysis tools that could be used to look for trends by segment product, salesperson, geographical region, customer etc.

In addition to these requirements, the sales manager needs information to control current activities. We will be examining some of the reports in this chapter on Sales Management Information System.

Sales Promotion

Sales Promotion refers to motivate customers to purchase more, manufacturer to produce more and seller to sell more. The sales promotion manager use different tools and techniques to increase their sales volume. The sales promotion manager trained his people how to handle different types of sales promotion activities. The sales promotion use incentives as a tool to motivate their team.

Sales Management

A motivated sales team always achieve profitable goal for their organization. In today's globalized world the success of an organization depends on the success of its employees. Selling concept refers the profit through sales volume but it also ensure that customers should satisfied by the product. According to American Marketing Association "Sales Management defines as the planning, directing and controlling of personal selling including recruiting, selecting, equipping, assigning, routing, supervising paying and motivating as these tasks apply only to the sales force".

PLANNING AND CONTROL

Planning

Planning is looking ahead on the basis of the present and the immediate past. The plan of action is the result envisaged, the line of action to be pursued, the stages to be gone through and the methods to be employed. Planning includes the objectives and scope of the business.

In large businesses, we usually have an annual plan. In conformity with this annual plan, monthly, weekly, daily plans also simultaneously operate. These forecasts all merge into a single plan operating as a guide for the whole concern. The plan should be one and continuous and flexible and as exact as possible.

The plan given beforehand makes the manager responsible for its execution and forces a comparison between anticipated progress and actual achievements and also searches for means of proper implementation.

"It Reduces Hesitancy and False Steps" - Henry Fayol

Control

The next important task of the manager is control. Control ensures that the programme and standards laid down are adhered to by planning. It operates on all fields of management including sales. Control operates on everything – things, people, actions.

For control to be effective, it must be done within a reasonable time and must be followed by rewards and/or punishment.

Importance of Data

To be useful, the various information systems must be integrated—the factor that best relates the various systems is data.

A tactical information system is constructed around a common core of data collected because of its potential use to the area that collects it and also because this data is a resource for the entire organization.

Data is often organized in a database; since the database receives inquiries from all over the organization, it acts as a centre for the network of information flows. Not all data is maintained in a database – some information is needed only within the department that collects it. Therefore they may keep it separately within their own files. If the data is required by other sections within the organization then it is wise to incorporate it into the corporate database(s). We will now study some important aspects of sales management information system.

REPORTS

Daily Report

This is a very vital tool for any organization. As the salespeople are mostly in the market, it is very difficult to actually see them working. Thus daily report helps in informing the company about the customers met by each rep on that particular day and the business transacted.

The daily report helps in assessing the number of customers met by the salesperson on a particular day. Normally each organization has a list of pre-identified customers for a particular territory, be it a multinational company, or a small company; FMCG or a Pharmaceutical company; consumer durables company or a particular territory based on the past information or the past sales. But this list is constantly updated from time to time depending on the feedback by the salesperson working in that territory.

The daily reports can be of different types for different companies depending on the products. But the basic information of a daily report remains similar. A daily report always contains the name of the sales rep or the employee code number, the date, the market worked during the day, names of customers met or the code numbers of the customers, the products for which the rep met the customers or the codes of the products and the orders taken during the day. In addition to these basic things, some companies have a special column for competitor activities seen during the day (for e.g., pharmaceuticals, soft drinks, industrial products, etc.) where there might be an urgent need for the company to alter its marketing strategy for that particular territory as the profit margins are low and loss of even a single customer might be difficult to bear. As the salesperson is away from the company office, this report acts as a communication link between the salesperson, customers and the market in general with the company.

Unlike in an office atmosphere where a person can punch his card or sign the muster, and his supervisor can observe him from 9.00 a.m. to 5.00 p.m., sales personnel's activities need to be monitored continuously and the Daily Report is a tool which can be used for continuous monitoring.

Daily Report: A Sample

1. Name of sales rep
2. Employee code number
3. Date
4. Market worked during the day
5. Names of customers met
6. Products for which met
7. Orders taken during the day
8. Special column for competitors' activity during the day.

General format of Daily Report:

Name of the Rep. : Sr. No:

Market covered: Date:

Rep. Code: ASM Code:

Name of the Distributor/Dealer Place Activity Output/Result

Work Started at: am/pm

Signature

Weekly Report:

Rep. Code: ASM Code

Dates From: To:

Name: H.Q: Date:

THE WEEK-IN-A-NUTSHELL

Date	Time From	Time to	Places Visited	Night halt Place	Distributors	Dealers	Others	Volume (MT/LTS)	Value (Rx.)	Signature

* Others include C&F agent/unit/branch/H.O. govt. officials/univ. etc. Please mention.

* Product wise, packwise details:

In short the week was:

Competitors' activities (enclosed schemes, prices, products etc.)

Signature

Tour Programme

This report informs the company about the customers and towns to be covered during the given campaign. This report is sent to the immediate boss by every sales rep in advance or prepared together with the boss. It informs the sales manager about the day-to-day working and the division of target for that period.

The tour plan also indicates the various expenses that are likely to be incurred by the sales rep and the various programmes that might be conducted for the promotion of the product in a particular market. On conformation from the sales manger, the sales rep goes ahead with the work. Thus the travel expense statement depends upon the tour plan submitted.

Normally an area of conflict occurs between the sales rep and front line manager on the mode of travel. It should be resolved at the beginning of the year itself so that it need not recur during campaign meeting.

Tour Programme: Two Months or a Full Campaign

Date	Place visited	Daily Allowance	Other Allowance	Postage & Telegram	Sundries	Total
1						
2						
3						
4						
5						
6						
7						
8						
9						
10						
11						
12						
13						
14						
15						
16						
17						
18						
19						
20						
21						
22						
23						
24						
25						
26						
27						
28						
29						
30						
31						

Signature

table 12.1 Monthly Sales Performance Value (in Rs) and Product wise

	JAN	FEB	MAR	APR	MAY	JUN	JUL	AUG	SEP	OCT	NOV	DEC
MONTHLY												
CUMULATIVE												
PRODUCT A												
MONTHLY												
CUMULATIVE												

Thus, at a glance, it is possible to find out what's happening in a given rep's area for rupee value sale and productwise sales. Similar format can be developed for a variety of products, in a multi product company.

table 12.2 Sales Performance Value (In Rs) and Quarter wise

	1st Quarter			2nd Quarter			3rd Quarter			4th Quarter		
	JAN	FEB	MAR	APR	MAY	JUN	JUL	AUG	SEP	OCT	NOV	DEC
Monthly Budget												
Monthly Sales												
Performance												
Growth												
Cum. Sales												
Cum. Performance												
Cum. Growth												
Call Target												
Call Performance												
O/s. Value												
O/s. Days												

Thus, at a glance, one would know how a sales rep is performing on the sales front as well as on the collection front.

MONTHLY PERFORMANCE REVIEW

Frequency : Monthly/Quarterly/Annual performance at office by Sales Rep.

Guidelines

Each sales rep to report personally to the branch office once in a month to review the following:

- Previous tour cycle date wise
- Plan for next tour cycle to be sent one week before reporting
- Managers to ensure complete availability for each sales rep.

SALES TRAINING

Any training is dependent for its success on a number of factors. These include how well it relates to identified needs, how relevant it is to the real day-to-day job of participants, how participative it is, and more.

- Presentational techniques
- Techniques to prompt and handle participation
- The methodology of role-playing, which as has been said in the previous section can be of valuable assistance in developing sales skills
- The use of training films.

PRESENTATIONAL TECHNIQUES

Whoever is putting across the training workshop, how it is received will be dependent, in part, on the way it is presented. So presentation is important. But there is more to it than simply putting on a performance that is stimulating and sends people away with a warm glow as it were; you are seeking to ensure that learning takes place and which when put into practice results in change. So the details of how things are done is also important.

This section is designed to highlight key factors which can be used to make your presentation more effective. If you look at what you are doing as helping people to learn, which in any case is an excellent definition of training, then it makes sense to keep the group in mind and consider what helps people to team.

ENSURING THAT LEARNING TAKES PLACE

There are several classic ways of positively assisting this process:

- ***Making the message relevant***: You need to keep the nature of the group in mind throughout, to make sure that what is said is in their language, rotates around the real job that they have to do and fits into their frame of reference. If the group sees the training message as tailored to them, representing their situation and if, above all, they think it will help them do the job better or more easily–or both–then they will take an interest and learn. Having clear, stated objectives for the session and seeking participants' agreement to them is also important.
- ***Use a logical order***: Any message is going to be easier to take on board if it is not a struggle to work out, so creating a good, clear and logical path through the content is important. The material provided should have a clear structure and the working method should be logical.
- ***Use appropriate emphasis***: The training message must prompt a concentration on it. This is helped by a number of things, such as varying the pace and also by repetition. Never be afraid to repeat, albeit in a different way, the key elements of the content. It is the combination of methods–lecture, discussion, an exercise etc.–which can do this and really enhance the likelihood of participants retaining the essentials of the message.

Do Not Assume it is Easy

Any kind of communication can be perhaps surprisingly, difficult. The difficulties stem from various factors, which, taking a positive view, means that you must:

- Vary the pace and keep up the interest as the natural tendency of people is to let their minds wander rather than concentrate continuously.
- Work at achieving an understanding by avoiding too much unfamiliar jargon, using visual aids to reinforce points, choosing your words carefully and fighting peoples' instinct to make judgments too soon by anticipating–often inaccurately–the totality of the message before it is even complete.
- Accept that change is always seen as threatening until its usefulness is clear; if you advocate change, make sure that you explain both how it can be achieved and what good results will flow for the members of the group.
- Accept also that there will be plenty of preconceived views and existing memories that act as filters to what you are saying; these may have to be aired and disposed of along the way if a new way is to replace them.

All these points speak of care being necessary and also flexibility.

Preparation

The difficulties mentioned above dictate the three key rules for a successful presentation: prepare, and prepare. It is that important. There is no substitute for being truly familiar with the material in front of you. It will not only facilitate progress through the material but make you more confident and thus more able to fine-tune, respond to questions and digress where appropriate and useful. A key part of preparation is creating guidelines that you can keep in front of you and which act as an effective prompt and make it easy to work through the content.

The Group

It may seem obvious but the session is not yours, it is the group's and all the focus of its preparation and delivery must reflect that. Ask yourself how it will be seen, does it reflect their needs, can it be used in their jobs – any question that will enhance this focus. The presenter who prepares only to make it easier for themselves is not so likely to create a session that will work well for others.

A second important point here is how the group will see you. Any lesson is more likely to be taken on board coming from someone the group respects rather than from someone perceived as 'trying to teach their grandmother to boil eggs'. A well-prepared presentation, even a well-turned out presenter, makes a difference. Your knowledge and your professionalism can enhance learning. On the one hand, you need to be perceived as the 'expert', at least to some degree; on the other hand' you should talk about the 'opportunities we have to improve sales performance', rather than saying something that comes across as 'you people must get your act together'. As was stated earlier, training is helping people to learn.

The third point is to bear in mind that training is often perceived as a cure for weak performance. In order to create an atmosphere where training is welcomed by the group, it is vital to ensure that the event is seen as other than being criticism. Stating that you intend to build on strengths, listing successes, talking about even better results, all help this process. The need for sales training is often linked to external change. This may range from increased competition to new customer expectations. Whatever the situation, even if there are some weaknesses of performance, you must start the exercise in a way that will make it more likely that people will listen and participate with an open mind.

Structure

The oldest maxim about communication is also one that offers good advice here: Tell'em, tell'em and tell'em. This means that you should tell people what you are going to tell them (introduction), tell them (the main content), and then tell them what you have told them (summary). Whatever else you aim to do, this one thought will help to keep you on track. However, it is not sufficient to have a structure, you must make sure that it is visible and develop it as you go along, a process sometimes referred to as 'sign-posting. Frankly it is hardly possible to indulge in too much sign-posting as a session proceeds; it is a technique which allows the group to keep everything you say in context. They know the objectives, they know the structure and where you are in the sequence, how it fits in with what has been covered to date and what will come later, and can follow the thread that much more easily than with less information of this sort. So, the overall structure is classic: a beginning, a middle and an end. Consider the three in turn.

The Beginning

It is a common cliche that you only get one chance to make a good first impression; but it is true. It is always right to get off to a good start. People make rapid judgments at the start of the session ('Am I going to like this? Will it be useful?'); a good start gets them in the right frame of mind and is also good for the presenter's confidence.

At the beginning of the whole session all, the preliminaries need to be dealt with – the welcome, the administration and so on – and, at the same time, you must:

- Gain the group's attention
- Create (or begin to do so) the necessary rapport. The first can be helped by a striking start
- Ask a question (even a rhetorical one)
- Use a quotation (to make a point in a memorable manner)
- Tell a story, an anecdote, or a true, recent or memorable occurrence
- State a striking fact, say a statistic
- Use something visual, a slide, a gesture to create impact or something just downright intriguing to give the necessary impact.

The second is helped by an immediate display of empathy, a focus on the group and how they see things and sheer enthusiasm – always potentially infectious – for the event and the topic.

Using an OHP

Some care should be taken in using overhead projectors to begin with; they appear deceptively simple, but present inherent hazards to the unwary. The following hints may be useful

- Make sure that the electric flex is out of the way (or taped to the floor); tripping over it will improve neither training nor dignity.
- Make sure that you have a spare bulb (and you know how to change it) – though many machines contain a spare you can switch over to automatically test both.

- Make sure that it is positioned as you want; for example, on a stand or a table on which there is room for notes, etc. Left-handed people will want it placed differently from right-handed people.
- Stand back and to the side of it; it is easy to obscure the view or the screen.
- Having made sure that the picture is in focus, look primarily at the machine and not at the screen; the machine's prime advantage is to keep you facing the front.
- Only use slides that have big enough typefaces or images and, if you plan to write on acetate, check that the size of your handwriting is appropriate.
- Switch off while changing slides, otherwise the group will see a jumbled image as one is removed and replaced by another.
- If you want to project the image on a slide progressively, you can cover the bottom part of the image with a sheet of paper (use paper that is not too thick and you will be able to see the image through it, although the covered portion will not project).
- For handwritten use, an acetate roll, rather than sheets, fitted running from the back of the machine to the front will minimise the amount of acetate used (it is expensive).
- Remember that when something new is shown, all attention shifts, at least momentarily, to the slide: as concentration on what you are saying will be less, stop talking until this moment has passed.
- It may be useful to add emphasis by highlighting certain things on slides as you go through them; if you slip the slide under a sheet or roll of acetate you can do so without marking the slide.
- Similarly, two slides shown together can add information (this may be done with overlays attached to the slide and folded across); alternatively, the second slide may have minimal information on it, with such things as a course title, session heading or company logo remaining in view through the whole, or part of the session.

If you want to point something out, this is most easily done by laying a small pointer (or pencil) on the projector. Extending pointers are (in my view) almost impossible to use without looking pretentious, and they risk you having to look over your shoulder.

The middle

This is the core of the session, and must:

- Review the content in detail
- Ensure acceptance of the message
- Maintain the attention of the group.

This structure and 'sign-posting' referred to above will keep the content unfolding logically and smoothly. Sufficient examples and anecdotes will exemplify what is said, add credibility and make it live; they will also help maintain interest especially if the session is kept reasonably participative with questions and discussion acting as raisins in the bread. Make sure that the words you use are sufficiently descriptive, for example you cannot say: "This is like ...." too often. As the details of the core content come through here, the visual aids used will help maintain concentration and memory (and have an additional advantage as an extra aid to the presenter's memory).

In research carried out on behalf of Kodak, it appears that people take in information in a way that is made up of:

- Visual–55 per cent
- Tone of voice–37 per cent
- Words–8 per cent.

Assuming that this is correct, it is vital to create visual inputs for as much of the message as possible to increase the chances of more being taken in and remembered. It is because of this that this workshop suggests that so much be put up on the flip chart, which is the easiest form of visual aid likely to be available. Other methods make visuals – rather than words – easier to handle and the overhead projector (OHP) is the next most readily available device with this characteristic. So it is perhaps worth a short digression – checklist style – to set out some of the principles of using the ubiquitous but initially somewhat awkward piece of equipment.

The End

Whether of the whole session or just of a segment of it, the final stage is an important one. There is a need to summarise and a need to end on a high note. The end is a pulling together; there should be no loose ends or unanswered questions, and, particularly, participants should leave confident that they have found something useful and, moreover, are well placed to implement what they have reviewed. The very end may consist of some sort of flourish. A quote, a punchy remark, an injunction to act, a little humour perhaps may all be appropriate on occasions. And the final word will often be a 'thank you'. If the group have worked hard, paid attention and you feel action will follow then this is not all your doing, it is theirs too, so thanks are certainly in order.

Key Principles of Presentation

Overall have

- Clear objectives
- A sound, and stated, structure
- A focus on the audience's point of view
- The right tone of voice and plan to earn a hearing not expect one.

The Beginning

This must respect the audience and make it clear that you will be accurately directing your message at them and their needs. Here you must:

- Get off to a good start
- Gain attention
- Begin to build rapport
- Make the group want to listen by starting to satisfy expectations, yet ensure that they keep an open mind for what is to come

- Position the speaker appropriately (e.g., as confident, expert, credible)
- State your theme, outline how you will go through it (structure) and make it clear that this will suit the group (you may also feel it appropriate to say how long you will take – If the timetable does not – and then stick to that time).

The Middle

This is the longest section; it must:

- Maintain and develop interest
- Develop the case through a logical sequence of sub-themes and points
- Illustrates, as necessary, with descriptive language and visual aids
- Overcome doubts and scepticisms, anticipate specific objections and deal with them and ensure that the building message is seen as of value to those listening.

The End

There is a need to finish on a high note, maybe with a flourish. The concluding part of the presentation must:

- Summarise and pull together the arguments
- Stress benefits to the group
- Make clear what action is now appropriate (and often actually ask for a commitment)
- Finish on a memorable note.

Throughout the presentation, the language and gestures (how you appear and the animation with which you go about the task is just as important as how you sound) used must be:

- Clear
- Natural
- Positive
- Courteous.

Remember to put emphasis on key points so that the overall impression is of out-and-out professionalism--your goal is to get your professional approach prompting people to think: 'This is the sort of person I could do business with' (or learn from).

Participative Techniques

Presentation must be blended with participation to make any training session truly successful. Quite simply, involvement makes it more likely that learning will take place and that practice will change as a result; long ago also when Aristotle said–What we have to learn to do, we learn by doing'–this principle was understood.

This principle is now backed up by research and this shows clearly that learning is more likely if participation is involved, and that retention of what is put over is much more likely. Because of this the more you can create involvement in the session–especially if this takes the form of actually practicing new techniques–the more likely it is that learning will be carried over and change real work practices for the better.

Prompting involvement can utilise a number of techniques, some as simple as asking a question, others more complex to set up, such as role-playing which is very much part of the proceedings.

Role playing is not always well conducted. It is important to address any concerns the group may have about it, perhaps based on prior, and poor, experience. Stressing the positive benefits, making it clear that they will be well briefed and that it is an opportunity will help get over any misapprehensions. The key benefits should be seen as useful.

A number of factors within the overall introductions and initial formalities can be used to break the ice and begin to get people involved. It is often important for people to realise early on that they will not be able to simply sit and listen; they will be expected to contribute. Such initial initiatives include:

- Issuing a simple instruction: 'May I ask you just to fill in the name card in front of you before we continue.'
- Asking for individuals to speak, perhaps to each other (where they do not all know each other): Introduce yourself to your immediate neighbour', for example, or: 'Ask the person next to you what they think is the most important objective today.'
- Using discussion of the brief for the course to get people talking: 'Now that I have run through the objectives, can you think of anything else.'
- The use of a formal 'icebreaker' exercise (as set out at the beginning of the workshop material).

During the review, the following needs to be discussed thoroughly:

- Area wise/district wise/taluka wise budget vs. actual sales with respect to potential
- Distributor wise sales
- Outstanding along with collection plan
- Sales rep performance review
- Expenses on travel/vehicle/telephone etc.
- Vehicle (2 wheeler/4 wheeler) utilization/log book/fuel efficiency
- Market development activities/plan.

At the end, action plan in writing with time frame which is to be reviewed during an implementable next cycle is prepared. Copy of action plan should be sent to regional sales manager.

SUMMARY

Sales reports are used to monitor sales performance. A weekly report or daily report is submitted depending on the products and its movement. It assists in product planning, cost planning and portfolio planning. A summary of daily/weekly report for all branches is made on a monthly basis and its variance for estimated sales is studied and accordingly budget is prepared.

SHORT ANSWER QUESTIONS

1. What are the basic contents of a sales report?
2. How does monitoring help in performance evaluation of sales force ?
3. What are the needs of monitoring and what are the parameters used in monitoring the sales force?
4. What is sales promotion?
5. What is sales management?

REVIEW QUESTIONS

1. Describe sales information system as a communication process. Illustrate with examples.
2. Discuss information needs for the sales management process.
3. Classify information needs of sales information system design.
4. What are the components of sales information system? Discuss with an example.
5. What are the objectives of a sales information system?
6. Discuss the role and importance of a sales information system.
7. What are the characteristics of a good sales information system?
8. Distinguish between data and information.

GO TO THE NET

Using the Internet, locate three website of major corporations. Which companies did you choose? How effective were the websites as a form of sales information applications.

Using the Internet prepare a report on nature, scope and importance of sales promotion with the help of suitable example.

Caselet

The rubber industry in India has both been dominated by branded as well as unbranded rubber (generally more dominant in the unbranded category). Consumption of rubber has been in the form of solid rubber as well as in the form of rubber profiles made up of solid, sponge and flocked rubber. Generally, the rubber sold in the Indian market in the form of natural rubber has been in price range Rs. 13 to Rs. 22 per kg. These qualities are sold from Delhi to other parts of the country with sales amounting from hundreds of kgs to a few hundred tons per month. In contrast, rubber profiles are also sold lengthwise i.e., in rupees per meter. Such rubber are being used in metal frames, windows etc. and also along with fabricated parts sent from Delhi to U.P., Punjab, Vijayawada, Rajasthan etc. The other application of such rubber and rubber profiles include shipping containers, building profiles, bus/truck body buildings, solar panel equipments, control panels, air conditioning units, helmets etc. There have been numerous players in the market with major unbranded players thriving in this highly price sensitive market.

Anand Nishikawa Co. Ltd. was started by Iqbal Singh Anand with very limited capital resource. Its plant was set up in Rudrapur near Nainital district in Uttarakhand. The company was pioneer in introducing synthetic EPDM rubber (Ethylene Propylene Diene Monomer, as it is chemically known) with manufacturing capability brought from Lescuyer, France in an effort to convert customers from natural rubber products to synthetic rubber (EPDM) products users. The company also collaborated with Nishikawa Rubber Co. and Sumitono Corporation of Japan for upgrading technology and extending its product range.

The advantages of synthetic rubber profiles is numerous. Some important one's are:

The life of EPDM rubber is much more than that of natural rubber.

The finish of EPDM rubber is much better than natural rubber.

Most important, the length of profile per kg for the same profile is approximately 45 percent longer in EPDM than natural rubber. This reduces cost/meter for EPDM substantially (for varieties sold in meters than in kgs).

In addition to the above, the EPDM rubber is weather resistant, ozone resistant, heat resistant, acid and alkali resistant, has colour stability and does not crack as we see in natural rubber contains more clay content.

Anand Nishikawa Company would like to conduct a marketing research study to evaluate the synthetic rubber product opportunities that the rubber markets would offer. The present market offers a potential of Rs. 1300 million in the organized sector with an annual market industry growth of 15 percent. However, the potential threat to the company is offered by unbranded players in the delivery schedules. The branded category also witness key players such as ASP, NER, Gold Seal, WADCO and others (including local players) having significant market share of 17, 11, 12, 12, and 40 percent respectively.

Questions:

1. What are the issues discussed in the case.
2. What marketing information could help ANCO decide whether the consumer would be ready to use the new product?
3. Should only a few case be studied or a large sample be surveyed?
4. What action plan could ANCO adopt after the result of the research? Give alternate action plans.

C H A P T E R

13

relationship marketing

learning objectives

The objectives of this chapter are to:

- understand the meaning of relationship marketing
- identify applications of relationship marketing
- describe transaction marketing
- understand nature, scope and importance of customer relationship management.

content outline

opening case

Never Again

Manmohan was a Professor of Science and his son Adhish was a student of the eighth standard. Manmohan and Adhish had never travelled by air and were accustomed to local train and bus journeys. Only once had they experienced a long train journey between Delhi and Calcutta when they had the opportunity to visit one of their relatives.

For the past three years, Adhish's mother, Mrs Tirath, was doing her doctorate in philosophy in South India and she was being conferred this honour on December 20, 1998. On December 18, Mrs Tirath talked to her husband and expressed her desire that both he and Adhish should be present on this occasion. To make it, Manmohan and Adhish had no alternative but to travel by air. They had never travelled by air before. Both were enthusiastic as they had heard the wonderful experiences of friends and were anxious to feel the experience themselves.

They contacted Western Express, an air ticketing agency, to book two tickets for them for the destination airport and through a direct flight as they were new to flying and did not want to face any hassles enroute. The Western Express promised to deliver the tickets at their house four hours before the scheduled departure time and took all the fare money in advance. Both father and son were delighted. The flight was scheduled to depart for destination airport at 2 pm on December 18, 1998.

At 10 am the doorbell rang and Manmohan looked at his watch and was all praise for Western Express and asked Adhish to open the door for the boy and collect the tickets. To the great surprise of both of them a it was Courier boy carrying some books ordered by Mrs Tirath. Till 12 noon there was no positive response from Western Express and at about 1.15 pm it was informed that no confirmed tickets were available for December 18, and they had been booked for the 19th instead for a flight leaving at 12 noon. They were also asked to collect the tickets from the office as no delivery boy was available to deliver the tickets.

The office of Western Express is not enroute to the airport but in the opposite direction. So both Manmohan and Adhish had to travel to Western Express office located 15 km in the opposite direction and then another 20 km to the airport. In order to reach one hour before the departure time, both of them had to leave home at 8.30 a.m. to catch a flight at 12 noon to avoid traffic congestion.

They arrived at the 'originating airport' at 11 am, one hour before the scheduled departure. They tried to contact the reception counter to find out the details of the flight, check in window number but preferred to stay away as there was a heavy rush. There were no queues, windows were crowded, and people were shouting to gain the attention of the enquiry attendant who was smoking and talking in an unbusiness like fashion to some acquaintance for a longtime on the telephone. They moved to the passenger information board on which the flight number, time of departure and window number for check in was clearly displayed. For 'Destination Airport' passengers, it was clearly stated to check in at window no. 19.

They started looking for window number 19. They went from window to window and could not locate window 19 and there were no directions or guide maps available near the passenger information board giving the location of check-in counters. They approached a uniformed employee working at window number 6 and enquired about window 21. He asked them to contact the assistance counter for this. When they were moving towards the assistance counter they chanced upon a security officer who was not an airline employee but a private security services employee. This agency provided security personnel in the departure lounge. He was very polite and personally escorted them to window 19 and also asked them if he could provide any more assistance to them.

To reach window 19 they had to make their way through many trolleys of luggage haphazardly parked and luggage unsystematically piled up. They could see long queues of passengers on each check-in window. As they reached window 19, they felt the first relief. There were hardly four passengers at this counter. This relief was short-lived as the counter boy informed them to move to window 20. The window 19 was meant for first class passengers only. They had to shift to window 20 and they had to join a queue where already more than 50 passengers were ahead of them.

Both Manmohan and Adhish were non-smokers. After great persuasion they managed two seats in the non-smoking area. This was very crucial for Manmohan because he was a non-smoker and also allergic to cigarette smoke. Despite all these hassles both of them were still pleased to travel by air which symbolised exotic travel but Adhish was quite upset at the treatment for the price of the travel.

Half an hour before the scheduled departure, the security check was announced and passengers were asked to move to the security check area. The voice of the announcer was inaudible as if she was speaking with food in her mouth.

Interestingly the police officers on duty were discussing the passengers in their respective rows and the area looked quite ruly. As soon as they reached the security area they were asked several embarrassing questions. Anyway they were only doing their job. After security check they proceeded towards the western lounge and anxiously awaited the announcement of the flight for departure. It was still half an hour for the flight to take off and they preferred to seat themselves at a position where they could see the TV screen on which flight information is displayed. The seating plan of this lounge was such that only twenty to twenty five per cent passengers could have a look at the single TV screen provided in the lounge. Passengers were frequently craning their necks to look at the TV screen and no announcements were made along with the information on the TV screen. The information on screen was displayed only in English". The system of displaying information made the area quite congested as passengers seated in front of the screen often raised their head obstructing the visibility of people seated in back-rows. As announcements were made along with information displayed on TV, some passengers left their seats to see the information on the monitor. Some of the passengers were quite uncomfortable as the moni**tor** displayed information in English only. Manmohan was quite perturbed over all this **but** Adhish looked unconcerned as he glued himself to his walkman listening to Hindi songs.

At 12.15 hours there was an announcement that their plane had developed some technical snag and the new flight departure schedule would be intimated shortly. There was no news about the rescheduling of this aircraft for about one hour and passengers started getting impatient. It was already lunch time and no one was there to look after the passengers.

At 14.15 hours the announcement for the flight departure was announced and all passengers bound for "destination airport" stood up to form a queue for the bus to take them to the aircraft. After about five minutes wait the passengers were told to walk up to the aircraft which was about 400 meters away from the main building. The plane could be seen from a distance. As soon as they entered the plane, they started looking for their seats. No assistance came from the cabin crew and this created considerable confusion and crowd in the corridors. Adhish soon occupied his seat and started looking around at the fellow passengers who were a mix of young boys and girls, old people, businessmen and some film stars.

Adhish settled himself in the flight by putting on the headphones and running through the music provided on the plane. He never bothered to go through the demonstration emergency procedures. Refreshments were served on board.

At 16.00 hours came an announcement to tighten the seatbelts as the plane had started descending for the "airport enroute." It came as a shock for both of them as they had instructed the travel agent to book them on a direct flight. On seeing the airticket, they realised that Western Express had booked them on a flight with a stopover. They had also asked Mrs Tirath to receive them at 'destination airport' as they were coming by a direct flight. She had rescheduled all her engagements for the day to receive them. She was quite tense for all the confusion going on.

At 16.30 hours the flight took off for 'destination airport' with a new crew and landed at destination at 15.15 hours. The landing was very smooth. The cabin crew lined up at the gates to give parting smiles. They were all elegantly dressed, polite and helpful. They even helped an old couple in disembarking the plane. The bus was parked just near the plane. The passengers were directed by a smart, uniformed young man to the bus and driver of the bus helped the people in getting seated. The driver drove the bus smoothly and stopped it in front of the gate. The passengers were greeted by the airport staff and guided towards the luggage area. The airport was well lit. The passenger information provided on the screen was accompanied by related announcements in a pleasing voice. Important information regarding flight schedules, instructions for proceeding to various gates, check in counter details were being flashed through electronic display media. Pleasing Indian music was being played. All important locations had TV monitors displaying the current information, changes if any and distances and taxi fares to different places from the airport.

Manmohan and Adhish finally made it to the destination to be with Mrs Tirath and share in her ceremony. All of them preferred to return home by train.

Try Yourself

1. What is the service which a customer pays for?
2. When does a service start and when does it finish?
3. How do Manmohan and family contribute to the service experience?
4. Are the provisions of service different for Manmohan and Adhish?
5. How do employees affect the service experience?
6. How does physical evidence affect the service experience?
7. How do other customers affect the service experience?

INTRODUCTION

The term relationship marketing was first coined in America in the early 1980s. Although it has no single, agreed meaning, most definitions have common factors defined in the dictionary of marketing terms of American Marketing Association (1995), "Relationship.Marketing is marketing with the conscious aim to develop and manage a long-term and/or trusting relationship with customers, distributors, suppliers, or other parties in the marketing environment".

The building and management of relationship with customers has always been a key approach to marketing practices and some companies habitually market on a relationship basis without consciously calling it that. However, use of the term relationship marketing suggests that deliberate efforts are being made to retain customers, provide effective communication with them and use different approaches to marketing that are:

- based on development of two way communication between suppliers and customers
- affordable by technology
- usually guided by highly technical analysis of customer purchasing and profitability.

The building of a good personal relationship with the customer is usually integral to small business management and the example of the owner of a small corner shop is often used to illustrate the essence of relationship marketing. The small shopkeeper has direct knowledge of all regular customers and becomes familiar with their needs and their likes and dislikes. This enables the shopkeeper to provide services tailored to individual needs, planned on the basis of known customer requirements. Over time, a bond of loyalty is likely to develop between shopkeeper and regular customer.

Why Relationship Marketing?

Because of the deregulation policies of the government and competition because of internationalization, many industries have faced far reaching effects on the competitive environment like:

- The ability to replicate physical products at lower and lower costs has facilitated price undercutting by domestic and international competitors. This encouraged many manufacturers to augment their physical products with services in order to compete and even to survive. Many large firms have been transformed from predominantly manufacturing organizations into predominantly service organizations by bundling services with products.
- The need to keep existing customers became a priority in the face of intense competition and the higher comparative marketing costs of acquiring new customers.
- Increased competition and deregulation in many service-dominated industries has resulted in emphasis on service quality as a means of achieving a competitive advantage.

Definition

Pathmarajah (1993) has defined relationship marketing as "the process whereby the seller and the buyer join in a strong personal, professional and mutually profitable relationship over time".

5 Es OF RELATIONSHIP MARKETING

Relationship marketing is characterized as having the following properties:

- Effective
- Efficient
- Enjoyable
- Enthusiastic
- Ethical.

Companies which are genuinely committed to the 5 Es are far less common than one may expect, but those who are aim to

- Offer the most value, personally and professionally
- Become a unique source in helping the buyer build something better, e.g. better peace of mind
- Become a partner with the buyer in his or her objective and establish a long-term trusting relationship with the buyer.

Levitt has opined that sale transaction should be regarded as a start rather than an end of relationship. As shown in the table below, even now, many firms' reaction to a sale is the exact opposite of the customer.

table 13.1

Seller	Buyer
• Objective achieved	• Judgement postponed; applies test of time
• Selling stops	• Shopping continues
• Focus goes elsewhere	• Focus on purchase; wants affirmation that expectations have been met
• Tension released	• Tension increased
• Relationship reduced or ended	• Commitment made; relationship intensified.

In fact, even today, many firms still practice transactional marketing rather than relationship marketing. Pathmarajah has provided a summary of the key differences in two approaches

table 13.2

Transactional Marketing	Relationship Marketing
• Do the deal and disappear	• Negotiate a win-win sale situation and stay around, being a resource for better result
• Push price	• Promote value
• Short-term thinking and acting	• Long-term thinking and acting
• Building the business on deals	• Building the business on relationships
• Getting new customers	• Keeping all customers and clients
• No structure for on-going business	• Structure created to support business relationship; special club and memberships for frequent users/buyers
• Selling focused	• Relationship focused for results

Contd...

• Short-term empathy	• Long-term empathy and rapport
• Incentive for doing the deal	• Incentive for long-term relationships and revenue
• Foundation of sale telling and selling	• Foundation for revenue trust selling
• Race for a sale result	• Swift, strong, safe and enduring in results through relationship building
• After-sales support and service poor — seen as cost	• After-sale support and service' seen as an investment in the relationship
• Product-service focused	• People expectations and perception focused
• Rewards-incentive for' doing deals'	• Rewards incentives for maintaining and growing relationship and revenue
• The deal is the end. Pursuit of deals.	• The sale just the beginning. Pursuit of long-term relationship and result.

Companies with transactional marketing approach constantly search for new customers because they fail to satisfy existing customers rather than retaining the existing customer base by demonstrating an unequivocal commitment to total quality customer care. Transactional marketing leads quickly to corporate decline. Your most expensive customer is the new customer because you have probably had to advertise to get him or her. You have no relationship with each other as yet. Getting an order from the new customer can be five to six times more costly than getting one from the previous one.

The latter contributes to enduring corporate prosperity. Why are your most profitable customers – your old customers – consistent repeat purchasers? Answer – because their value sharply rises with each subsequent order. Not only do their subsequent orders defray your front end advertising costs but, also, the more they buy from you, the more they trust you. And more likely they are to buy again and again.

According to Groonroos, marketing aims to establish, maintain and enhance [usually but not necessarily always long-term] relationships with customers and other partners, at a profit, so that the objectives of the parties involved are met. This is achieved by a mutual exchange and fulfillment of promises.

He suggests that relationship and transaction marketing are opposed on a marketing strategy continuum and equated with the marketing of services and consumer packed goods respectively. In other words, transaction marketing is common in the consumer packaged goods sector and service marketing performance is purely the type of relationship with the consumer.

APPLICATION OF RELATIONSHIP MARKETING

Table 13.2 highlights the contrast between transactional and relationship marketing. When faced with such contrasting outcomes, it becomes imperative for marketers to practice relationship marketing.

The relationship marketing concept varies with the customer, as some are more disposed towards it than others. Jackson's identification of three type of customers was based on 'the time horizon within which a customer makes a commitment to a vendor and also the actual pattern that the relationship follows over time'. The three types of customers identified are:

- The lost-for-good customers
- The always-a-share customer
- The intermediate type.

The Lost-for-Good Customers

The lost-for-good customer makes a series of purchases over time, faces high costs in switching to a new supplier, and views the commitment to a particular supplier as relatively permanent. The buyer adopts this position because switching costs are high. For example, airlines are unlikely to change lightly the type of aircraft which they purchase. Even at a more mundane level, an organization will have some reluctance in changing its office automation systems because of the costs and disruption that ensues.

It is argued that since the buyer faces high switching costs, it is looking to form a long-term relationship with the seller. Hence, the seller needs to adopt a similar approach, and be prepared to make a substantial up-front investment to win new or greater commitments from such customers. It suggests that relationship marketing is apt for the buyer who might be lost for good. In short, the big plus of this type of account is that once won, customer loyalty can be expected. The down side is that if lost, it is unlikely ever to be regained.

The Always-a-Share Customer

At the other end of the customer behaviour spectrum, lies the always-a-share customer who purchases regularly, has little loyalty to a particular supplier, and can switch easily from one vendor to another. Both parties recognize such relationships as short-term. For example, if an Indian firm wishes to send a package by courier to England, it is unlikely to attach any special importance as to which courier operator it last used, but instead obtain quotations from a number of equally acceptable operators. Any operator who can offer an attractive package immediately (i.e., a combination of the marketing mix) has a chance of winning business from always-a-share customers. Thus, Jackson suggests that transaction marketing– marketing that emphasizes the individual transaction – is most appropriate for the always-a-share buyer. Table 13.3 summarises the typical characteristics of customers at the end point of the account behaviour spectrum: lost-for-good and always-a-share customers.

table 13.3

Time Account Behaviour and Marketing Approach

Long time Horizon	Short Time Horizon
• Typified by lost- for-good customers	• Typified by always-a-share customers
• High switching costs	• Low switching costs
• Substantial investment actions, especially in procedure and lasting assets	• Smaller investment action
• High perceived exposure	• Lower perceived exposure
• Focus on a technology or a vendor	• Focus on a producer or a person
• High importance: strategic, operational and personal	• Lower importance

The Intermediate Type

Most of the customers belong to this category. Wide range of factors–like the characteristics of the product, category, the customer's pattern of product usage and the actions of the customer and the supplier – affect the relationships. Such relationships are more applicable for organizational buyers than consumer products, where regular buying is a norm.

MARKETING STRATEGY CONTINUUM

Transaction marketing is common to the consumer packaged goods sector but as a company is forced to become more service oriented in approach, relationship marketing increasingly displaces transactions based marketing. The driving force behind this displacement are

- Better or more diverse technologies
- Growing consumer satisfaction
- Customers' access to more options
- Competition.

It is observed that all firms are on a continuum with transaction and relationship marketing representing the two extremes and the need for relationship marketing being dependent upon the line of business e.g. transaction marketing is best suited to commodities, and relationship marketing to services. While a series of factors may influence the status of a particular product and customer behaviour, it is surely essential to select a proper blend of type of marketing for consumer durable and industrial goods.

table 13.4 **Marketing Strategy Continuum**

Marketing strategy continuum	Transaction Marketing			Relationship Marketing
Dominating marketing function	Traditional marketing mix dominated			Interactive marketing dominated
Quality dimension most important for competitive advantage	Outcome-related technical quality dominating			Process-related functional quality dominating
Price sensitivity	Customers very price sensitive			Customers less price sensitive
Interface between marketing and other functions e.g. operations and personnel	Limited or nonexistent; interface of no significant strategic importance			Substantial interface of strategic importance
Typical marketing situations continuum	Consumer packaged marketing	Consumer durables marketing	Industrial goods marketing	Services marketing

CUSTOMER RELATIONSHIP MANAGEMENT

Customer Relationship Management is mainly oriented towards customer loyalty. CRM helps customers to get information at any time from any source. Implementation of CRM helps in getting feedback from customer whether it is positive or negative. Providing all the information to the customers is a complicated process but essential part of CRM.

Customer Services Capabilities

- ***Call Center Management:***
  - Provide automated, end-to-end call routing and tracking

- Capture customer feedback information for performance
- Measurement, quality control, and product development

▶ ***Field Service Management:***

- Allocate, schedule, and dispatch the right people, with the right parts, at the right time
- Log materials, expenses, and time associated with service
- Orders
- View customer history
- Search for proven solutions

▶ ***Help Desk Management:***

- Solve the problem by searching the existing knowledge base
- Initiate, modify, and track problem reports
- Provide updates, patches, and new versions

Definitions of CRM

Traditional marketing strategies focused on the four Ps (price, product, promotion, and place) to increase market share. The main objectives to increase the volume of business between seller and buyer for the performance of marketing strategies and tactics. CRM is a business strategy that goes beyond increasing sales volume. Its objectives are to ease profitability, sales volume, and customer loyalty. CRM is a business process strategy which is use to achieve the greater customers satisfaction and loyalty.

CRM consists of three components:

▶ customer,

▶ relationship, and

▶ management

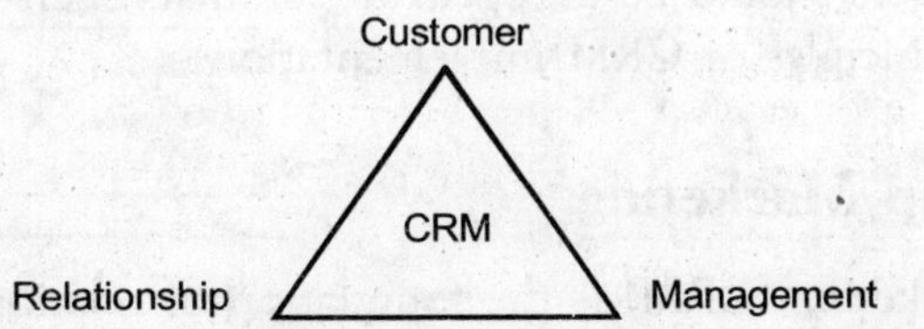

Information Technologies and CRM

CRM differs from the previous method of database marketing in that the database marketing technique tried to sell more products to the customer for less cost. The database marketing approach is highly company centric. However, customers were not kept loyal by the discount programs and the one-time promotions that were used in the database-marketing programs. Customer loyalty is, indeed, very difficult to obtain or buy. The CRM approach is customer-centric. This approach focuses on the long-term relationship with the customers by providing the customer benefits and values from the customer's point of view rather than based on what the company wants to sell.

The basic questions that CRM tries to answer are:

1. What is the benefit of the customer?
2. How can we add the customer's value?

1. ***Customer Identification:*** To serve or provide value to the customer, the company must know or identify the customer through marketing channels, transactions, and interactions over time.
2. ***Customer Differentiation:*** Each customer has their own lifetime value from the company's point of view and each customer imposes unique demands and requirements for the company.
3. ***Customer interaction:*** Customers demands changes over time. From a CRM perspective, the customer's long-term profitability and relationship to the company is important. Therefore, the company needs to learn about the customer continually. Keeping track of customer behaviour and needs is an important task of a CRM program.
4. ***Customization/Personalization:*** "Treat each customer uniquely" is the motto of the entire CRM process. Through the personalization process, the company can increase customer loyalty. The automation of personalization is being made feasible by information technologies.

Principles of CRM

The Applications of CRM are based on the following basic principles.

- ***Treat Customer Individually:*** Remember customers and treat them individually. CRM is based on philosophy of personalization. Personalization means the 'content and services to customer should be designed based on customer preferences and behaviour.
- ***Acquire and Retain Customer Loyalty through Personal Relationship:*** Once personalization takes place, a company needs to sustain relationships with the customer. Continuous contacts with the customer especially when designed to meet customer preferences - can create customer loyalty.
- ***Select "Good" Customer instead of "Bad" Customer based on Lifetime Value:*** Find and keep the right customers who generate the most profits. Through differentiation, a company can allocate its limited resources to obtain better returns. The best customers deserve the most customer care; the worst customers should be dropped. In summary, personalization, loyalty, and lifetime value are the main principles of CRM implementation.

Customer Relationship Marketing

Customer Relationship Marketing (CRM) is the foundation of relationship marketing. In Extension, the goal of CRM is to convert the target audience into loyalists and loyalists into enthusiasts, advocates, and donors. Here is a useful strategy:

Step 1

You will first need to identify the diverse customers to whom you would like to establish a relationship.

Step 2

Find out the customers who are favourable towards your organization then you will have to keep maintaining a good relationship with that customers by keeping in touch with them through impersonal marketing techniques like mailings, etc.

Step 3

Actively solicit the increased participation and involvement of community members, which will foster greater loyalty to the program.

Step 4

Encourage greater support from community members. Loyal individuals are more likely to advocate for the program and/or donate resources to the program. Each of these steps takes time and attention, Relationship marketing must be nurtured.

Conclusion

Relationship marketing is one of the most time-consuming, but most effective strategies for marketing Extension programs. Relationship marketing is a process, not a one-time event; clientele must understand that you are committed long-term and that they can depend on you to provide education.

CUSTOMER RELATIONSHIP

It is important to keep and improve relationships with customers for the following reasons:

1. There are higher marketing costs associated with generating interest in new customers. The costs involved in creating an informed new customer far outweigh those involved in making the relationship necessary to continue exchanges between buyer and seller (Barnes and Glynn,1992).

   It has been estimated that the cost of attracting new customers can be as high as six times that of retaining existing customers (Desatnick, 1987; Sellers, 1989; Congram, 1991).

2. Close and long-term relationships with customers imply continuing exchange opportunities with existing customers at a lower marketing cost per customer (Gronroos, 1990b). Reichheld and Sassier observe:

   'Across a wide range of business, the pattern is the same: the longer a company keeps a customer, the more money it tends to make (Reichheld and Sasser 1990)'.

3. Viewing customer exchanges as a revenue stream, as opposed to a compendium of isolated transactions, enables cross-selling of related services over time and premium pricing for the customer's confidence in the business (Reichheld and Sasser, 1990; Congram 1991).
4. Strong customer relationships with a high degree of familiarity and communications on both sides can generate more practical new product ideas from customers and contact personnel (Kiess-Moser and Barnes, 1992).
5. Good relationships with customers can result in a good word-of-mouth from successful exchanges and minimal bad word-of-mouth in the event of unsuccessful exchanges. Service quality cracks can often be papered over where good relationships have existed previously.

SUMMARY

The marketer must determine what customers want and then give it to them. This can be done in several ways. One is by getting feedback regarding buyer preferences and then using the information to customize the services.

Customers make sales, and sales make profits and cash flow, therefore, customers are the most essential component of the business. Can you afford to annoy them?

PROJECT WORK

1. Make groups of three students. Select a service industry you are familiar with and conduct the customer satisfaction survey. Submit your findings and make a presentation.
2. Conduct Survey through focus interviews and collection of secondary data etc. and draw the complaint handling model for the following services:

   a. Airlines industry
   b. Fast food restaurants
   c. Railways
   d. Management school
   e. Courier industry

SHORT ANSWER QUESTIONS

1. What are the 5 Es of relationship marketing?
2. What is CRM?
3. What is transactional marketing?
4. What do you mean by "lost for good customer"?
5. What are different components of CRM?

REVIEW QUESTIONS

1. Why is it necessary to identify the customer and understand him?
2. The most effective way to meet quality challenges is to determine what customers want and then give it to them. Comment.
3. Explain the term "customer relationship". What are the techniques of customer relationship?
4. How information technology helps in influencing the efficiency of CRM?

GO TO THE NET

Using Internet search tools or other relevant sources, identify several e-businesses in different markets that use Internet technology to maximize their customer relationships. Then select one of the e-businesses and write a one-page paper describing the e-business and the way it maximizes its customer relationships.

Caselet

This case has been drafted to test the reader's ability to make planning decisions in terms of maximizing profits. The reader must also develop a proforma income statement.

The Harold Manufacturing Company is a small, family owned manufacturer of household ornaments and novelty items. It was founded in British Columbia in 1942 by James Marris an immigrant from Rotterdam. The present facility employs 12 people in a small plant 32 miles north of Vancouver. Shone Morris the grandson to the founder, is the principal owner of the business and conducts the day to day operations. Most of the planning and profit decisions are shared with his sister Levis who spends 6 days a week at the plant.

In recent years, the Morris have severely reduced the variety of products available from their firm. In an effort to achieve volume, they have concentrated on the craze for antique style ornaments that has been weeping Canada and the United State. The firm's product's are ordered from catalogue found in a variety of stores and specialty shops in western Canada and some parts of the western and southern United States.

Two years ago, the Morris decided to concentrate on producing two fairly popular item:

1. "Rustic" candlesticks - a matched pair of frontier style bronze candlesticks.
2. "Pioneer" door knockers - a bronze, western style door knocker.

Since specialization in these two items, the firm has dropped the many custom items previously produced. This has not hurt business, as the two items are selling well. Levis has projected sales for each item on a unit basis for the next fiscal year. The firm should be able to sell 6000 pairs of candlesticks, and 5,900 door knockers. These figures represent the maximum demand for each item at Levis planned selling prices, and the firm should be close to these figures.

In order to achieve the projected sales figures, the firm must operate at 57 percent capacity. The candlesticks and door knockers will require 32 percent and 25 percent of firm's capacity respectively.

Levis has projected next year's income statement, which includes a break down by products area, as shown in the projected income statement. To achieve her statement, Levis applied basic cost accounting techniques. The manufacturing costs would include depreciation on the firm's machinery, repairs and maintenance, insurance, taxes and the production foreman's salary and benefits. Sales costs are basically the salary and expanses of an office clerk who deals with retail customers and distributes by mail or phone. Advertising and promotion are included at a £ 5,000 figure. The administrative fixed costs cover items needed to run the company with a major item being the costs involved with providing information and materials in support of catalogue operations. These fixed costs were allocated to the products on the basis of a ratio of fixed costs to total sales. For example, Levis noted that fireplace kits will make up 62 percent of the total sales. Thus she allocated 62 percent of the fixed costs to fireplace kits.

In an effort to use 100 percent of capacity Levis has considered lowering the price of both the products. At a £ 51 selling price, 8,200 Rustic candlesticks could probably be sold. At £ 11,7000 door knockers could be sold.

Another alternative to use the excess capacity would be to produce a third product. The firm once sold" "Ye Old Lantern" kits did fairly well this item. The firm could probably sell 3,100 lanterns at a £ 26 selling price. The raw materials would cost about £ 9 and the labour £ 5 per lantern kit. Levis has estimated that producing 210 of the lantern would use 2 percent of the firm's productive capacity. Drucker has often remarked during planning sessions, "In these uncertain times, we must produce for profit if we are to survive".

Assignment

In order to maximize the profit what is price of a product should be charged by the firm. Which product will give the maximum profit.

Contd...

Harold Manufacturing Company Ltd.
Pro Forma Income Statement

		Fireplace	
	Totals	Kits	Candlesticks
Doorknockers			
Sales 70,000	510,000	280,000	60,000
Variable cost			
Raw materials 30,000	150,000	50,000	70,000
Labour 10,000	60,000	90,000	15,000
Marginal contribution 5,000	100,000	30,000	40,000
Fixed cost			
Manufacturing 5,000	62,000	30,000	7,000
Sales 8,000	18,000	10,000	9,000
Administrative 4,000	30,000	14,000	7,000
EBIT and EBT 5,000	50,000	36,000	10,000

CHAPTER 14

internet as an emerging selling technique

learning objectives

The objectives of this chapter are to:

- understand the role of Internet in selling
- describe Internet advertising as a selling technique
- discuss methods of maintaining online public relations
- understanding the role and importance of E-commerce.

content outline

- Opening Case
- Introduction
- Internet Marketing
- Mammoth Size of the Internet
- Internet Advertising Methods of Selling
- Evolution of Banners
- Sponsorship
- Methods of Online Public Relations for Selling
- Summary
- Project Work
- Short Answer Questions
- Review Questions
- Go to the Net
- Caselet

opening case

Rethinking the Sales System

At the beginning of 1999, Eckhard Pfeiffer, CEO, Compaq Corp, declared that the company's objective for the year was to become the 'Internet leader' in the infotech industry.

Clearly, the future was going to be networked rather than desktopped. Once again, marketers had to prepare for non-linear growth on the base of shifting tectonic plates, the kind of thing that management guru Ron Schultz has been talking about.

Since then, Pfeiffer — who took the company to No 1 in the PC market in 1995 through commodity-price aggression — has been ousted as CEO. And Compaq Worldwide's Internet plan, which was taking too long in the making, now seems in even greater disarray.

Take PC sales over the Internet. Dell, say market watchers, is way ahead. The rival takes just over three days to deliver a built-to-specs machine ordered via the Net in the US.

Compaq, meanwhile, has behaved all muddled up about it. The company made a tentative start, but recently announced that it has stopped selling its computers to Internet-only retailers worldwide, a move that has had a drastic effect on major players such as Cyberian Outpost and Shopping.com, which derive much of their revenue from the sale of Compaq PCs through their websites.

On the other hand, Compaq plans to purchase Shopping.com and merge it with the Alta Vista search engine on the Internet. The move to stop Internet retailing may not be permanent, as Compaq is sort of testing the waters and will re-examine this policy after three months.

So what exactly prompted Compaq to move away from what is apparently the direction in which all others are headed?

Apparently, Compaq's regular stores were being hurt through onlines sales. Many online retailers sell items at just above procurement cost, since they maintain low inventories and have hardly any overheads to take care of. This was turning out to be competition to Compaq's brick-and-mortar retailers, which simply couldn't match those prices because of the slow operations and high overheads. So Compaq's move was partially a concession to these stores. In any case, Dell is the brand that online buyers tend to prefer, since it has the slickest Internet sales system up and running, not to mention its online customer service, which is also rated highly and is reputed to be based on sound marketing insights and principles (for details, see '*The Delight Doctrine*', A&M, September 15, 1994).

For months now, Compaq has been debating whether it can match Dell's prowess in direct Internet sales, from its own website.

The logic is flawless. With the Internet becoming a selling medium for PCs, it's best to do the retailing oneself, most of all because of the instantaneous collection of data on real time trends and preferences. The website, then, behaves as the eyes and ears of the company's digital nervous system. This speeds up response and keeps the company well in touch with its market.

In the future, when technology permits, such a website could even create a digital character (as in advertising) to play online salesman, hand-holder, PC guide and troubleshooter.

The friendlier, the better. After all, the advantage of dealing with huge numbers is that it's easy to track consumer behaviour accurately. A website designer can use statistics to pre-guess (on the basis of a representative sample) and then classify the most common kinds of queries and problems. This can be used to create a series of canned responses kept in memory. In fact, corporate annual reports (online versions) might soon be designed similarly, with interactive zones that contain capsuled responses from top executives to common questions from the media.

What that means is that sooner or later, real world PC sellers might start developing real world cobwebs.

The Internet, simply, is far more efficient as a sales medium. It transfers information instantaneously. And PCs, as Compaq had successfully gambled in the early 1990s, are fast turning into commodities, with product differentiation having collapsed (barring the odd Apple iMac). When this happens, pure bargaining takes over. So low-cost manufacturing and low-cost trading skills have to be combined. And it is price and speed of delivery that matter most. Other than that, customer service is what gives marketers the edge over rivals.

Unless, of course, the buyer needs to go through the touch-and-feel process, which is why analysts feel that Net selling of PCs can't really succeed in a country such as India.

TRY YOURSELF

1. Keeping the Indian consumer psyche in mind, do you feel that Net selling will succeed in India? Why or why not?

Introduction

By and large, Internet has emerged as the most powerful communication medium so far known to human kind. The explosive growth of the Internet advertising industry is very reminiscent of the early days of television advertising. A report from the Internet Advertising Bureau of UK, on statistics for the fourth quarter of 1999, indicates a revenues surge of 161 per cent in spending on Internet advertising.

It is estimated that in United States alone, by 2004, citizens will spend $16 billion a year on health care over the Internet. In 1999, $450 million was spent on purchasing prescription drugs online alone. More than 32 million adults a year currently go online for game related content. Advertising expenditure on the Internet in 1999 was £4·7 billion in United States alone and is expected to rise to £ 5·4 billion by the year 2002.

Internet Marketing

People use the Internet for nearly everything, including buying and selling. The Internet has the advantages of worldwide distribution, potential for excellent colour and graphics, capacity for large amounts of information in a single ad (Website) and relatively low cost. It also has the potential of direct purchases through the Website itself. The main downside of posting a Website is that there are many millions of them already posted, and it is a challenge to position yours in a way that it can be found by the people who are looking for your product. There are numerous tricks for making your site attractive to the search engines that potential customers use and, generally, it's best to hire a pro to optimize your site. Also, many of the businesses that use the Web have found that Internet into their overall ad campaign and use print or broadcast advertising to drive customers to their Websites.

E-Commerce

The Internet has revolutionized small-business marketing and leveled the playing field for small businesses by lowering promotional costs while concurrently expanding the businesses' reach. Few companies can ignore the Internet as a marketing tool and not suffer consequences. One of the biggest impacts the Internet has had is something called "disintermediation," which describes the reduction in the cost of direct communications between producers and consumers. This has allowed the bypassing of middlemen and expensive distribution networks. E-commerce is the use of computers to support business activities, particularly marketing and promotion. Increasingly, e-commerce encompasses a variety of business functions, including "back office" tasks such as order-processing and fulfillment, inventory management and accounting tasks. E-marketing describes using the internet and related technologies that assist with marketing. This includes promotion, research, advertising and a host of other activities. The most ubiquitous e-marketing application is the business website. Web sites are beacons announcing a business' presence. Website features can range from a simple electronic brochure to a fully interactive site that dynamically adapts itself to the needs and preferences of individual customers. Setting up a company website can be more challenging than a traditional brick and mortar shop. Another e-marketing technique is e-mail promotion - e-mail directed at a specific target market. Thousands of listservs link to Internet communities with some shared interest or cause.

Since listserv membership is voluntary, members receive e-mail and can view postings and announcements by other members or outsiders.

MAMMOTH SIZE OF THE INTERNET

It is impossible to measure cyber space accurately and many experts disagree on which metrics should be used for sizing the web, but everyone agrees that Internet growth is a phenomenon. Websites appear faster and faster everyday. Currently, the rate of growth of commercial Internet websites is estimated to be more than 4400 sites per day. The number of web pages, which is may be the best way of sizing the Internet, has skyrocketed in the past. A research study by NEC research estimates that there are over 1.5 billion web pages at the current time. Roughly 2 million web pages are created everyday. It is estimated that by the year 2002, the number of web pages will be more than 8 billion, a number that will exceed the world's population.

Cyberspace is a very big place and there is almost unlimited amount of competition looking for customers.

The mixed usage of the Internet, with commercial sites, pages to deliver information and research and personal pages designed to communicate with others, add complexity for the potential advertiser. The Internet grew from purely academic origins, it is still a mixture of things, and even though it is today predominantly commercial, it is not exclusively a commercial environment.

The paradigm shift in Internet usage from an academic to a commercial environment is taking place, however, and the advertising world now has a new medium to make use of.

Marketing communication consists of both planned and unplanned messages between firms and customers, as well as those from customer to customer. Planned messages originate from a firm that is attempting to inform or persuade its target stakeholders. Unplanned messages include things such as word of mouth among consumers and publicity in media.

Firms try to manage messages but, as consumers gain more control, it becomes impossible. Thus firms are well advised to spend their efforts on creating positive customer product experience so that unplanned messages will be positive.

The following is a brief review of the definitions for key promotion mix elements along with Internet examples:

- ***Advertising*** is non-personal communication of information, usually paid for and usually persuasive in nature about products or ideas by an identified sponsor through various media. Banner ads and buttons are currently the predominant forms of online advertising. Sponsorships and other forms are also important.
- ***Sales Promotion*** are short-term incentives of gifts or money that facilitate the movement of products from producer to end user. Some firms e-mail coupons, sweepstakes information and other sales promotions to customers and potential customers. Promotions may also appear in banner ads or on a site's web page itself.
- ***Public relations*** consists of activities that influence public opinion and create goodwill for the organization. Many websites are designed to serve as public relations vehicles. The Cricinto site is a great example of public relations (www.cricinto.com) where comprehensive information is offered about all facets of the sports of cricket.
- ***Personal selling*** is a direct face-to-face presentation to potential buyers. By definition, personal selling is not possible on the Internet, though the Internet can be used to generate sales leads.

- *Direct marketing* is direct communication through non-personal media with carefully targeted individuals to obtain an immediate response. It includes such techniques as telemarketing, outgoing e-mail and postal mail–of which catalog marketing is a big part. In some ways, targeted banner ads and other forms of advertising and sales promotions could be considered as direct marketing.

INTERNET ADVERTISING METHODS OF SELLING

Two methods of Internet advertising are: through e-mail and on websites. Both have useful applications. E-mail advertising is most often text based, tagging along on a consumer's incoming messages. Conversely, web advertising usually includes multimedia content, utilizing banners, buttons, interstitials and sponsorships on websites. Neither e-mail nor websites are limited, however, website advertising can be as small as a line of text with an embedded hyperlink to the advertiser's site and e-mail advertising can include graphics.

E-mail Advertising

By far the least expensive type of online advertising, e-mail advertising is generally just a few sentences of text embedded in another firm's content. Advertisers purchase space in the e-mail sponsored by others (e.g., Hotmail).

Website Advertising

Anything goes with web advertising: text which can be from a sentence to pages of story, graphics, sound, animation, and hyperlinks. A website consists of special files with text, video, graphics and sound. Browser programmes like Navigator and Explorer take the user to a new site. A website can be established for a few thousand rupees. The message can be served to a large body of net surfers. Websites are of three types–information and product driven, recognition and association websites for promotion with slogans and tag lines and experimental websites which involve a viewer through sensory experience and aesthetics.

Banners and Buttons

Banners and buttons occupy designated space for rent on web pages. This is similar to the print advertising model used by magazines and newspapers, except on the Net there are video and audio capabilities in that few square inches of space. Buttons are square or round and banners are rectangular. The Internet Advertising Bureau (IAB) and the Coalition for Advertising Supported Information and Entertainment (CASIE) have proposed standard dimensions for buttons and banners. Eventually the industry will standardize on a couple of ad sizes, as did traditional media, because it is easier for websites selling space and the agencies designing ads.

Electronic commerce, in short e-commerce, consists of the buying and selling of products or services over electronic systems such as the Internet and other computer networks. The basic requirements to sell over the Internet are principally the same as in an off-line business, Registration. Your business needs to have a name, a seat (real address) and must be registered (according to national rules, depending where the seat is). Upon registration, you receive a VAT number, your unique business identity. Observation of common business rules: Law on unfair commercial practices, know-how and trade secrets, accounting etc. Requirements specific to e-Commerce: A difference is made between B2B = business to business, or business among "equals", as apposed to B2C = business to consumer, where the consumer is considered the weaker part and, therefore, enjoys special protection.

B2C Consumer Protection Rules

Online commerce applies the rules for distance selling (like buying from a catalogue; without the presence of the seller and buyer at the same time). These rules can mean considerable hardships to small and micro enterprises (e.g. not knowing when a contract is final!). Thus, a quick look to these rules can save long troubles!

B2C Requirements

Need to provide full information on the website. If this is not observed, the consumer has a longer period to cancel the contract (3 month instead of the ones laid down in the cooling off periods. For details, see consumer protection. Cooling-off periods: periods during which the consumer can cancel the contract without giving any reason Applicable jurisdiction is that of the consumer (where the consumer lives) and not the seat of the commerce (as in B2B if not otherwise negotiated)

How is your Online Contract made?

It is essential that you explain how the contract with your online customer will be made. This is achieved by Internet legal Terms & Conditions. They will cover a number of issues including details of the precise point the contract is accepted by you. For example, under the E-Commerce Regulations you must acknowledge online orders by electronic means almost immediately. Be careful. It is important that you do not formally accept an offer until you know you can fulfil the order. There may also be other reasons why you should not accept until you are satisfied it is safe to do so. Unless you explain fully in your Terms when Acceptance occurs you might be in breach of contract with your online customer. Other things your Internet legal Terms and Conditions will cover include, which country's law applies to your online sale? There are laws which give online consumers the right to sue in the country of delivery of the goods or services if they live in the EU. There are certain things you might wish to exclude as legal liability. For example, you will not want to be liable for computer viruses which your online user alleges they contracted by visiting your website.

EVOLUTION OF BANNERS

Banner advertising has evolved substantially since the first banner ad on *Hot Wired* in 1994. The first stage featured banners that called out "click here", "free", and "download" in bright colours. This was to train users that banners were indeed interactive and that by clicking on them the user would be transported to another website. Most banners are hyperlinked to the advertiser's site. Users have since become savvy to the notion that banners have click-through capability, though some marketers still feel that the "click here" message is effective. Like everything else on the web, when the novelty wears off, content is what captures the user's attention. The same is true for banners. To distract users from the site itself, the message in the banner must appeal to their needs.

The second stage of banner advertising featured banners with animation. Movement captures attention on an otherwise static page. Many banner ads today feature animation. A file called an animated GIF (Graphic Interchange Format) usually provides the animation. Animated GIF files consist of a series of frames each containing a separate picture. The animation results from rotating the frames with very short time delays between each one. The animation can be either continuous (which is somewhat annoying) or can loop through a fixed number of times, stopping on the final frame. Some animation is used to stimulate movement while other animation is designed simply to expose the user to a sequence of messages.

The third stage of banner advertising features the interactive banner. There are many varieties of interaction. Some banners sense the position of the mouse on the web page and begin to animate faster as the user approachés. Other banners have built-in games Still other banners have drop-down menus, check boxes and search boxes to engage and empower the user.

All of the ads examined up to now have functioned via click-through. By clicking on the ad, the user is transported to the merchant's website, where the transaction or other objective is actually achieved. This means that the user must leave the site that he is browsing.

SPONSORSHIP

The banner emerged as a simple mechanism for explicitly transporting a web user from a sponsored page to those pages belonging to the sponsor themselves : an obvious doorway linking the two sites, and one that was knowingly used by the web browser. However, as reluctance to use those links has gradually increased – even if the links themselves have been granted a degree of legitimacy of presence – and even as the banner technology itself has progressed, advertisers have began to question the fundamental assumptions inherent within the very banner advertising model itself.

Sponsorships integrate editorial content and advertising. Most traditional media clearly separate content from advertising. Food advertisers sponsor many other stakeholder groups. It is important to remember that many different stakeholders will view an organization's website : for example, prospective employees will check out a firm by viewing and even submitting electronic resumes at the site, and community members who may be displeased with local pollution caused by a firm may look for evidence at the website. Exhibit below displays six important stakeholders along with the type of public relations content that is well suited for the web.

Stakeholder	*Online Content*	*Stakeholder*	*Online content*
Shareholders	Financial reports Management changes Company activities	Consumers and business buyers	Online events Brochureware Product information Store locators Testimonials Customer service activities
Employees	Employee accomplishments Employee benefits Employee directory Company information Training materials	Suppliers	New-product information Company news
Media	Press releases/news Media kit material Contact information	Community	Social programmes Local news relating to firm Employment opportunities

Exhibit: online Public Relations contest for Selected Stakeholders
Source: E-Marketing by Straum & Frost

METHODS OF ONLINE PUBLIC RELATIONS FOR SELLING

Content Sponsorship

Web content that is not advertising, sales promotion, or transactional is public relations: that is, most web content. Most free online content published by corporations that is meant to inform, persuade, or entertain is public relations (PR). By public relations we mean content that attempts to create a positive feeling about the company or its brands among various publics.

Brochureware is used to describe sites that inform customers about products or services without providing interactive features. They are the equivalent of a PR product brochure placed online. Many of the early corporate sites featured brochureware. The greatest advantage of brochureware is that it is a low-budget method to establish a web presence and, thus, serves as a public relations vehicle. In addition to product information targeted to consumers, brochureware sites can meet the needs of other stakeholders. Press releases can be provided for the news media and corporate reports can be provided for investors. Employment information can be showcased for potential employees and employee benefit information can be served out to current employees. Brochureware sites need routine maintenance in order to make sure that the information does not grow stale. Old information, like yesterday's news, has little value in the eyes of the public and may actually create an overall negative impression of the corporation.

Community Building

Many websites build community through online chat rooms, discussion groups and online events. Discussion groups allow users to feel a part of the site by posting their own information and responding to other users. Amazon.com (one of the largest website on books) allows users to write their own book reviews and read reviews of others.

Online Events

These serve to generate user interest and draw them to a site. Perhaps the most memorable commercial online event occurred in 1999 when Victoria's, Secret held an online fashion show. The firm announced it in a television ad and the 1.5 million user response was so great that its servers could not handle it. Companies and organizations hold seminars, workshops, and discussions online.

SUMMARY

Growth in online trading and popularity of e-commerce has opened up a new vista for commercial activities. With universal accessibility and ever increasing penetration of the PC, networking transactions over the Net are increasing at an exponential rate. Advertising on the web has quite clearly become a major part of our modern commercial environment and as we move towards new and more advanced interactive media, such as on demand digital television, it will become even more important. Two most widely used communications tools for Internet marketing are advertising and public relations. E-mail, website, banners and buttons are some of the forms of online advertising. In addition to dot-com companies, old economy companies have also moved to online advertising to augment their total communication effort. Content sponsorships, community building, brochureware etc. are commonly used public relations methods for e-marketing.

Project Work

You are planning your start-up B2C e-business and are evaluating various traditional and electronic payment methods. Using Internet search tools or other relevant sources, research security or potential fraud issues with traditional paper checks, credit, debit, or charge cards and various forms of electronic cash. Then write a one to two page paper ranking each method, from most secure to least secure, and give your reasons for the ranking.

Short Answer Questions

1. What is Internet advertising?
2. What is e-mail advertising?
3. What do you mean by sponsorship?
4. What is E-Commerce?
5. What is Internet research?

Review Questions

1. What are the major problems of Internet advertising in India?
2. What are the main concepts of e-mail advertising?

Go to the Net

Using Internet search tools or other relevant sources research current B2B payment methods. Write a one-page paper giving examples.

Using Internet search tools Propose a defect on online selling strategy of Amazon.com.

Caselet

INTRODUCTION

The Internet is an increasingly expanding medium of interaction that has virtually eliminated geographical boundaries and overcome previously existing obstacles of global business. It can be considered to be an accidental mega-market born out of technology and that of economic needs. The Internet, the single most sophisticated on line service, is relatively simple and immediate to use; however, these attributes may not enjoy a perceived status of usability for those new to and somewhat hesitant of advances in computer technology. The Internet today offers India the best opportunity to expand its market on an even larger global scale. This network of computers represents a perpetually open market without geographical barriers to prevent any business from reaching customers all over the world via a virtual market where trade, transactions, cash and commodities flow in the form of electronic consumption.

The boom in computer, telephone and television technologies has had a major impact on the way businesses produce and market their products. As technology has delivered new and better foods, clothes, housing, vehicles and entertainment possibilities, our lives have changed dramatically. Telecommunications is the driving force that is simultaneously creating the huge global economy and making its parts smaller and more powerful. At the heart of this phenomenon is the Information superhighway and its backbone, the Internet. Philip Kotler, one of the most prominent figures of marketing, warns that even though alert marketers see this technology as producing an endless stream of opportunities, taking advantage of it entails walking a thin line (i.e., companies must avoid jumping in too soon — before the market is ready — or too late — after the market has been conquered [Kotler 1997].

The Internet is an inter-networked system of computers linked by telephones that allow free flow of information from one part of the network to any other, provided the information is packaged according to certain conventions. It was born out of a vision of universal connectivity and global community. Created as a data link among a sprinkling of academic communities, the Internet has last been embraced by business. Companies are using it to link employees in remote areas, stay in touch with customers and suppliers, distribute sales information more quickly, as well to sell and distribute goods and services.

The Internet began to grow dramatically in 1994 with the advent of a new, more user friendly application — the world wide web — which provides companies access to millions of new customers at a fraction of the cost of print or television advertising, and in many cases, distribution. The web uses a technology called hypertext which allows users to leap from one computer data base to another by simply clicking on highlighted images or text. It employs easy-to-use browsers to capture the public's imagination with the promise of a navigable world of a seemingly infinite amount of information. The world wide web's popularity, in turn, has caused the entertainment media and the communication industries to reevaluate their business models. The use of the Internet to carry real time data, such as voice and video, in addition to traditional forms of data, which lent themselves more readily to packet switching technology, is on the horizon (Lewis and Lewis 1996).

The number of computers in the world grew from less than half a million two decades ago to 200 million in 1996. The number of websites are doubling every 53 days and the number of non-US users is projected to grow from an estimated 40 million in 1997 to 500 million in the year 2000. In India, the Internet subscribers in August 1995 were only 703, but by June 1998 the number had grown to 1,20,000 (*Outlook* 1998). However, Jay Forrester, the inventor of random access memory, expects that for at least three four generations, people will use computers for what they've always done, only faster (*Advertising and Marketing,* 1997).

A profession, no less than a craft, is shaped by its tools. The profession of marketing, its theories practices, and even the basic sciences that it draws upon, are determined by the tools at its disposal at any moment. When the tools change, the discipline adjusts, sometimes quite profoundly and usually quite belatedly.

Impact of Internet on Marketing

Clearly, marketing's tool kit is experiencing an unsettling amount of change. The boom in direct and database marketing, the dawning of electronic commerce, new ways to automate sales force management and the sudden blossoming of the world wide web all suggest that the discipline is under pressure to redefine itself. The stock market is well aware that something important is developing; venture capitalists and technology companies are making large bets; and students at business schools, alert to any hint that their investment in the development of personal skills might have to pay off in a changed environment, show particular interest in new methods of market making. Mass marketing concepts and practices are taking advantage of new ways to become more customized, more responsive to the individual.

Contd...

The challenge facing the companies today is how to take strategic advantage of these opportunities to build more desirable products and services, build brand equity and increase revenues and profits (Tarafdar 1998). The Internet represents new opportunities for the marketers and sales people because it provides a wide reach for all marketing efforts conducted on it. International markets can be opened up at low costs. Advertising and promotion costs in other countries can be significantly reduced, if not eliminated.

With the use of the Internet there can be continuous customer support. Services can be made available through interactive e-mail systems on the net. This saves time and money. In addition, feedback (i.e., research data) from the marketplace can be likewise collected on an ongoing basis and, in may cases, in the form of "real-time" data. New products and services can be tested through interactive questionnaires on the Internet. This feedback forms the basis of market identification and segmentation that enables marketers to better position their products.

Increased Interactivity

The term interactive, as we interpret it, points to two features of communication (1) the ability to communicate to an individual/ business or an entire marketplace, and (2) the ability to gather and remember the response of that individual in a way that takes into account the context of his or her unique response. Thus, we see interactivity as a tool that allows good marketing to become good conversation.

Interactivity has already made major inroads into marketing budgets in the past decade in the form of direct mail, catalog retailing, telemarketing and the incorporation of response devices into broadcast advertising. Developments in data storage and transmission, however, hold out the promise of new and better interactive tools to manage relations with customers to link the networked corporation to its channels and its collaborators. For example, when a broadcast advertisement elicits a response such as a toll-free call, which is then stored in a computer database and which triggers a personalized direct mailing, it represents a form of low-tech interactivity. A sales representative calling on customers is also engaging in low-tech interactivity.

The web, however, promises high-tech interactivity. When a consumer visits a website, many cycles of messages can be exchanged in a short time. Then, when the consumer visits sometime later, the dialogue can resume where it left off. The web medium is as subtle, flexible, pertinent and persuasive as one-to-one dialogue. It boasts a better memory than the most diligent salesperson and has none of the salesperson's distaste for repetitive tasks. Direct marketing and distribution channels, aided by electronic commerce, can be used to substantially augment sales through conventional retail and distribution systems.

Interactivity is a powerful hook, which enables the customer not just to passively view the pages, but also to answer questions, play games and involve him/herself with the website. Interactivity can be leveraged by ensuring that the website is designed to accept feedback, usually in the form of electronic questionnaires which visitors can fill in on screen, so that companies can tailor their content according to their customer's needs.

The Market-space and Cyber Consumers

The mega-network is now a mega market. The frontiers of the Net are dotted by shopping windows wherever in the world there is a computer, a modem and a telephone line. Cyber space is fused with markets and the result is — the market space. This market space is truly global with its main commodity — data — not restrained by international borders, no custom duties, no import barriers. While the old Net viewed surfers as mere cyber-pros, business is looking at them as customers who can visit this market space simply by switching on their computers and using their modems to connect to the Net. The customers come and go in this cybermart at the click of a mouse. Seated at their computer terminals all over the globe, ordinary people — who use soap, drive cars, and eat breakfast in everyday life — are being converted into cyber- consumers as soon as they enter the market-space.

CHAPTER

15

direct marketing

learning objectives

The objectives of this chapter are to:

- understand the meaning of direct marketing
- describe the direct mail techniques
- discuss trends in telemarketing.

content outline

opening case

Not Delivered as Promised: Don't Pay for It

Sunny and his wife Rekha both had degrees in Hotel Management with specialisation in catering and hospitality respectively. Both were working at Host, a restaurant located in the midst of a busy business locality. Just hundred meters away was the stock-exchange where hundreds of people gathered every day to exchange business transactions. The one kilometer market had offices of many prestigious companies of India, reputed business houses, consultants, multinational companies and industrial houses. The area was known as the financial district of the city.

Because of the educational and work experience, Sunny worked in the restaurant kitchen and Rekha supervised the dining area and handled the billing and cash register. The restaurant, having space limitations, had no scope of expanding its operations. So, for the past ten years they were doing the same routine work.

Sunny and Rekha were keen on starting an enterprise of their own and were looking for the right type of business opportunity. Rekha, being in the dining area, was always observing the guests coming to the Host. She observed that most of the guests coming for lunch were people belonging to the financial trade like investors, stock brokers, bankers and their business operations were concentrated at the stock exchange. Since the lunch break was only for half an hour, they could not afford to be out of their business premises for more than half an hour. Since half of the break time was wasted in the to and fro movement to the eating place, they were always found to be intent on finishing their lunch rather than enjoying it. Many of the guests were seen talking on their cellular phones even while eating.

Sunny and Rekha once visited the stock exchange to know the work place of their guests and realised how hard pressed for time they were. They were convinced that if they could offer these customers an appealing lunch at their workplace, they could certainly develop a clientele. Moreover, the customers will be able to relish their lunch as they will be able to better utilise the to and fro movement time to the restaurant.

They started talking to a select list of potential customers about the service they wanted to introduce. They found that their concept was acceptable to most of them. A demand for onsite food service was established. Sunny and Rekha worked on the economies of this service and established that they could build a very profitable business.

They decided to quit their jobs and open a small kitchen at their home exclusively to cater to customers requiring onsite food delivered as per their requirements. The focus of the service was 'quality food delivered on time'.

The operational strategy was very simple. They had met the potential clients and asked them to give their requirements by 10 am and also the time at which they would like the food to be delivered in their office. Normally 1.00 to 1.30 p.m. being lunch time gave them enough time to prepare food and deliver the packets.

The procedure followed by Sunny and Rekha was this.

a. The service delivery start time fixed at 11 am. So all food must be filled, packed labelled and sorted by this time.

b. The delivery boys must report at 11 am to pick up their packs. The delivery boys were selected on the basis of their location in the customer area, their knowledge about topography and distribution skills.

c. The client base of 70 people, located at seven different places, was served by seven delivery boys each handling 10 customers whose offices were located either in the same building or in the immediate vicinity. The distribution strategy and mode was designed on the basis of client dispersion in the segment. On an average, one delivery boy was supposed to handle 8 to 10 clients.

d. The work study had indicated that each delivery boy can deliver the food and drop back the empty cases within one and half hour from the start of service. The kitchen was located five kilometers from the business offices.

In the same area there are four more organisations providing similar food delivery service and Sunny and Rekha had to compete with them in the same area. To have a proactive approach, they started providing a service guarantee stating "Not delivered as promised — don't pay for it." Their main focus was speed of service (SOS).

As a consequence of this service guarantee, their service started getting recognition and gained the reputation of reliability, accessibility and responsiveness. More and more customers were willing to enroll themselves as regular members for this service. The other suppliers in the same area were not willing to match the service and guarantee offers of Sunny and Rekha. Their customers started defecting thereby causing economic strain on their business. "How long can they offer this guarantee," commented one supplier as he felt it would be very difficult to continue this. In fact, this was also the concern of Rekha as she was incharge of customer management and Sunny was looking after the kitchen management.

The increased flow of customers was alluring them to expand the business but the type of guarantee was forcing them not to expand. But the experience of both convinced them to go ahead for expansion and cater to the segments they had identified and they were sure of winning without problems.

TRY YOURSELF

1. How could Sunny and Rekha create a market niche for their service offerings? What are the characteristics of the niche? What is the customer base?
2. What value-added services did they start offering their clients? Explain at least three of them.
3. What distribution strategies were adopted by them to deliver the food within the promised schedule? Did this build up customer satisfaction? Explain how customers and service providers benefited?

INTRODUCTION

Peter F Drucker has rightly observed that there is only one valid definition of business purpose–to create and keep a customer. "Companies are not into business to make things", he said, "but to make customers". The essence of keeping a customer is to stay in touch. This is also fundamental to direct marketing.

WHAT IS DIRECT MARKETING?

On a simplistic note, we can say that direct marketing is nothing but getting the message through, directly. However the Direct Marketing Association (USA) defined it as "an interactive system of marketing which uses one or more advertising media to effect a measurable response and/or transaction at any location."

In the above definition, we identify some key words, which differentiate Direct Marketing (DM) from other marketing communications disciplines. These key words are:

- ***Interactive:*** One-to-one communication or interaction between the marketer and the prospect/ customer.
- ***One or more advertising media:*** A combination of media used to synergize. Often more effective than any single medium.
- ***Measurable response:*** Possible to measure response quite accurately.
- ***Transaction at any location:*** May take place by phone, at a kiosk, by mail or by personal visit.
- ***Direct Marketing, Direct Mail, Mail Order, Direct Response Advertising:*** Many relate Direct Marketing to a medium (Direct Mail) or a technique (Direct Response Advertising) or a channel of distribution (Mail Order). In fact DM is all the three, and much more.

Direct Response Advertising in any medium, including mail, is that which offers a measurable response and/or transaction at any location. It is any advertising used to sell directly to customers: be it an advertisement with a coupon in a newspaper or magazine or even a telephone solicitation.

Direct Mail is a medium through which a predefined and predetermined number of selected consumers are addressed through mail. Using computers, letters are easily personalised to make the maximum impact on the person receiving it. This medium becomes very effective in respect of selectivity of consumers, timings and the ability of the customer to respond using coupons or prepaid reply envelopes.

Direct mail is only one of the media, the others being newspapers, magazines, television, radio, telephone and such others used for Direct Marketing.

Mail Order is a method of selling that relies on Direct Response Advertising to effect a measurable response and/or transaction by mail, telephone or other interactive media. Mail Order usually means the sale of products or services to a customer or to industrial users by means of catalog or Direct Response Advertising. In many cases, the medium used is Direct Mail and the fulfillment is also by mail.

The buyer personally visits the sellers' location to effect a transaction. The seller calls at the buyer's location in person or by telephone to effect a transaction.

The ups and downs in business frustrate producers who are in favour of maintaining good relationship with customers. This lesson taught the producers to take control of the price received through the direct marketing of their products. The person selling goods in Direct marketing act as a "middle man" and producers sell directly to customers.

What Kind of Direct Marketing is best for any organization?

The main concept of direct marketing is to sell the product directly to the final customer? If so, you become a retailer and you may spend a lot of your time sitting in a shop, on your boat in harbor or at a roadside stand, with a scale and a cash box, meeting your customers face-to-face. Even if you ship or deliver your fish to your buyers, you will have to be a salesman, talking up the quality of your product, answering lots of questions, making lots of calls. Don't have time for that? Maybe you want to wholesale your product, delivering to individual restaurants or fish markets. If so, you won't have to sit in your pickup by the side of the road, day after day, but you probably will have to meet a delivery schedule of one or several days a week. And you'll have to produce the size, quality, species and form of product your buyer demand. Maybe you would rather sell to a wholesaler and let that person worry about making the sales, delivering the product and collecting payment. Of course, the amount you get for your fish will be lower, but your time commitment will be less. The further up the distribution chain you choose to sell, the greater portion of the total retail value of the product you get to keep for yourself, but the more time, complexity and risk is involved. The only way to completely avoid some level of additional complexity is to sell ex-vessel to your processor and avoid direct marketing altogether.

Which Link in the Chain?

In the distribution chain, to which link do you want to select? If you have large number of product, it may be best just to engage a broker or to sell to a distributor. If you have small amounts of product, you may want to sell to individual restaurants or small retailers. Some people get the greatest satisfaction by selling directly to consumers. Keep in mind these general principles:

- The farther along the chain you go, the greater your potential return per unit of product, but the greater the risk you assume.
- Consumers have the most precise needs in terms of volume, quality, grade, etc. Generally, they buy to provide a meal for a person, a couple or a family and may want a particular item, such as a steak or filet.
- Retailers and foodservice are also pretty choosy, but they use more per day or week, and they may be able to firm imperfections, to cut h&g fish into steaks or fillets and to hold excess product for a few days.
- Distributors and traders will buy larger quantities and may be able to use different species and grades.
- Brokers work for pennies per pound, so it's not worth their time to deal with small quantities, However, they might be able to sell a large load, possibly by parceling it out to several other middlemen.
- The farther along the chain you go (with the exception of selling off the boat or out of your pickup), the more service you'll have to provide in terms of sorting and grading, packaging, transportation, delivery and maintaining communication with your buyer. If you let a broker handle the deal, or if you sell to a trader, either person will arrange some of those services.

DIRECT MAIL

Even though direct mail is only one of a number of direct response techniques, yet it is the category most associated with direct response advertising in terms of both format and execution. It is rare that major advertising campaigns do not at least consider direct mail as a media vehicle.

According to the American Association of Advertising Agencies, direct mail offers five primary advantages. They are

1. ***Selectivity:*** The market that the marketer wants to tap can be identified and covered in the way he wants it to be. Elimination by region, by state, by market, and by individuals is possible. The medium offers the benefit of minimum waste and maximum efficiency. The entire market can be hit with a single mailing or the market can be segmented and some prospects can be mailed six times as often as the others. Through a continuous process of selecting mailing lists, testing them and segmenting them, targeting can be made more effective.
2. ***Ideal for Response:*** A ready to use, pre-addressed, postage paid reply card or envelope can be included to promote maximum response. Hence, it is an action-oriented medium.
3. ***Personal Impact:*** The personal "one-at-a-time" quality of direct marketing implies that the prospect reads the communication without competing intervening messages.

   When mailing is done by name, copy and offers can also be adjusted to fit things known about the recipient. The computer letter has made a number of creative possibilities available to copywriters who want to individualise the letters they write. Addressing the person by name instead of addressing him as "Dear friend" can make a significant difference in bridging the gap between the sender and the receiver of the message, leaving an enormous impact.
4. ***Flexibility of Format and Timing:*** Minimum standardisation of format is required and each direct mail package can be made interesting through the use of various devices.
5. ***Measurability:*** Direct mail lends itself to precise calibration of results. In a lead getting effort, the number of prospects converted into sales can be found out.

The four primary objectives of an effective direct mail campaign are.

i. ***Building Sales:*** It can be used to introduce sales people, promote other forms of advertising or announce a product introduction. It can also be used to make a sale.

ii. ***Cultivating Customers:*** It should be effectively used to build customer relationships in the long run.

iii. ***Supporting Dealers:*** Direct mail can alert dealers to future customer promotions, educate them on service problems and survey them concerning their needs.

iv. ***Providing International Benefits :*** It can also be used to build company morale. Internal newsletters and other employee communications are often used to personalise large corporations.

To depict two direct mail packages, we would like to take examples of the *Reader's Digest* and of Marico Industries (for Sweekar Refined Sunflower Oil).

The key to successful direct mail is reaching the right person; the best product, the most creative message and even the lowest price are all wasted on a non-prospect.

Information about who the prospective buyers are, what they buy, how often they buy, whether they buy by phone or by mail, how much they spend and by what methods they pay becomes crucial to any direct marketer. These databases are the secret weapons of most of them.

In the '90s, the key word in direct marketing was 'database marketing'. The process is one of feedback between the sellers and their customers to more precisely define the latter's interest and purchase intentions and its constant updation. In its simplest form, database marketing is a method of identifying the best prospect for a product from a larger pool of prospects. Outfits like *Reader's Digest* and Bull Worker have built up exhaustive databases which are very closely guarded. The Kamat's Club has built its database by asking the consumers to staple their business cards to the coupon response advertisements which are to be mailed back. This technique has also been applied by the Travel Corporation of India.

The major sources of input for databases are the mailing lists. They are simply a way to organise otherwise random material into market segments.

There are basically four types of lists:

1. ***Compiled Lists:*** This is a list of names, addresses and information about prospects–combined usually by some common interests. Examples of such lists include telephone directory listings, the newly born records and public records such as voters' lists. There are other extensive compilations in the business, professional, educational, technical and agricultural markets. These lists are generally less valuable and less expensive than response lists as they do not offer a previous record of direct response purchase. Many see them as a supplement to response lists. They represent a source of external data.

2. ***Response Lists:*** Mailing list houses may rent lists of people who have ordered something by direct mail or who have responded to an advertisement for further information. The people on response lists are those who are prone to order by mail and therefore these lists are more productive than compiled lists. A mail-derived list can either be a house list (internal data) or a list of customers/inquiry rented from other companies.

3. ***House Lists:*** These are the finest asset of any direct marketer. The customers on these lists are those who may have bought by mail, have dealings with the company, have confidence in its integrity and merchandise. Such house lists' which list active customers, inactive customers, inquiries and referrals represent additional value at no extra cost. House lists can be made more productive if these are looked at as specific segments in terms of geographic, demographic and psychographic segmentation.

4. ***Rental Lists:*** In effect, these are house lists of other business houses. Magazine publishers like the *Reader's Digest* can be a valuable source of information for such lists since they tend to reach certain demographic groups.

Within the response lists, there are certain factors which determine the likelihood of getting a response. Catalog giants, Sears and Wards, have suggested the RFM – Recency, Frequency, Monetary – formula as a criterion to effectively and cost efficiently promote such an effort. It is based on the premise that recent responders are better prospects than prospects from long ago. Again, frequent responders are better than less frequent responders and last, but not the least, high volume purchasers are better than low volume purchasers.

The RFM formula forms a basis for manipulating the databases to extract the more profitable segments.

Another important factor affecting responses is seasonality for most products. The same direct mail package sent to the same list may have widely varying responses depending upon the time of the year it is mailed.

Reader's Digest are pioneers in running direct mail campaigns during Diwali and New Year seasons.

Regardless of the nature of the lists, they should be clean and up-to-date. The contents of the list must be 'as described' or wasted mailing will occur. Names and addresses that are undeliverable clearly result in wasted expenditure.

Such a file maintenance procedure will involve continuous updation with regard to addition of names, change of addresses, recording new orders and requests etc.

A serious problem faced by direct marketers in compiling and maintaining lists is the potential for duplicating the same individual or organisation not only within the house list but also between the response lists and even between the house lists and response lists.

Such a problem is removed by the data-processing operation of "Merge-Purge" wherein the computerised lists are merged together and duplicate names are purged so that what is obtained finally is only a list of net names and addresses along with a unique source key that will enable responses from each list to be tracked. This also avoids damage to the goodwill of the public.

Other Direct Mail Techniques

1. ***Package Inserts:*** These are used to promote additional purchases of products sent to customers or to promote other items in their product line. They do not involve additional postage costs and are directed at proven customers who have just made a direct mail purchase since they are sent along with the packages of the recently ordered goods.

   'Ride alongs' are inserts which are sent along with packages of other companies after careful negotiations with them, at a fraction of the original costs.

2. ***Cooperative Mail Advertising:*** This may be pursued in an attempt to share expenses keeping in view the high cost of mailing. However, such a mailing may be highly impersonal since each advertiser's message will have to be very short. Secondly, it is difficult to reach specific customers through joint mailing and hence this also decreases the value of mailing.

3. ***Syndicated Mailing:*** Here the marketer may prepare the piece himself but may make financial arrangements with other mail order companies to mail the offer under their letterhead.

Direct mail can be used appropriately under any of the following circumstances:

- When sampling would be both practical and desirable.
- When the advertising message is too complicated or too detailed to be conveyed efficiently in other media.
- When a specific, selected market is desired and other media can provide it only at the cost of waste circulation.
- When personal, personalized, or confidential communication is desired.
- When the format or colour that an advertiser's marketing strategy requires can't be carried in other media.
- When a specific market area needs to be covered with a minimum of slop-over into adjacent areas.
- When specific timing or frequency of contact is desired.
- When couponing is desirable.

- When controlled research is called for (for example, measuring of effectiveness within certain markets; ascertaining prospect profiles; or testing price, packaging or logical users for new products).
- When controlled mailing is desirable (mailings will go only to certain income groups, owners of certain makes of cars, boat owners, etc.).
- When mail order (sale of the product directly to the prospect, without retailers, dealers or other media in between) is desirable.

As suggested above, the variety of forms or devices that can be mailed is limited only by one's imagination. Among the more popular forms are the following:

Letters	Programs
Folders	Sales, research and informative bulletins
Broadsides	
Booklets	Charts
Brochures	Posters
Self-mailers	Blow-ups
Postal cards	Coupons
Mailing cards	Calendars
Catalogues	Reprints
House magazines	Memorandums
Blotters	Printed novelties
Price lists	Business cards
Sale and informative manuals	Order forms
Invitations	Reply cards and envelopes

TELEMARKETING

Effective communication is vital for corporate survival and success and the telephone is becoming the most important part of the communications strategy. In many areas, it is replacing post and personal contact as the most efficient way to send, receive and process information. The combination of database information and effective telemarketing techniques can help in developing a powerful competitive edge. Many companies now recognize that telemarketing can help them make the most effective use of the telephone –increasing revenue, reducing costs and improving customer service.

Although telephone technology is advancing rapidly and sophisticated telemarketing systems are available for small, medium and large businesses, companies are still reluctant to take advantage of the marketing opportunities.

Trends in Telemarketing

- 34% of marketers have a dedicated inbound telemarketing team, compared with 45% in sales and customer service.
- 29% of marketers have dedicated outbound telemarketing teams, compared with 35% in sales and customer service.

- By the year 2005, inbound calls are likely to exceed 800 million per annum–a fivefold increase in current levels.
- 12% of packaged goods companies in the UK now offer their customers a helpline service compared with 43 % in the US.

BT's Business News quotes research that shows that people are increasingly keen on buying by phone. 67%-80% of those interviewed claimed that they found telephone ordering easy and convenient. Telephone ordering is used successfully in a wide variety of industries, including computer hardware and software, car insurance, office stationery components and catalogue-based products.

The telephone is probably the most important interface between your organization and your customers. It is vital for increasing sales, taking orders, handling enquiries, delivering customer service or collecting payments.

The Importance of the Telemarketing Database

Telemarketing offers considerable business benefits but the database is crucial to success. It has three main roles:

1. To provide customer information to operators so that they can improve customer handling.
2. To provide a basis for proactive selling to the customer.
3. To help gather and use additional customer information via the telephone.

At a minimum, any telemarketing database should contain the following information

- Name
- Address
- Account number
- Purchase history
- Preferences/special requirements
- Products and services bought
- Frequency of purchase
- Contact history.

The tele operator has all the key information at hand whether it is an outbound sales call or an inbound call handling orders or enquiries. By linking telephones and computers, for example, staff can handle calls quickly and efficiently and provide a highly personalized service. With Computer Technology Integration (CTI), calls can be coordinated with computer-based business application. Information screens can be transferred simultaneously. This improves both productivity and customer service.

CTI can also be used to generate outgoing calls automatically and intelligently, again with screen information. This can increase the productivity and efficiency of telemarketing staff, particularly in intensive outbound applications.

THREE BASIC PROPERTIES OF DIRECT MARKETING

i. A definite offer to the consumer

ii. All the necessary information provided to make a decision and

iii. A mechanism to respond to the offer. Within this framework fall all direct marketing options—sales letters, catalogues, telemarketing, direct response TV advertisements, and the Internet.

Direct marketing is an effective tool for both consumer and business-to-business marketing. Businesses that rely heavily on direct marketing include magazine and newsletter publishers, mail-order merchandisers, fund raisers and book clubs. Marketers often find that employing a combination of various direct marketing options in a given campaign works best.

Customers are getting used to the concept of personalised delivery. Direct marketers customise their products and services to satisfy their clients. With the increase in travel time and pollution, more and more customers are being attracted to the facility of direct marketing.

Entrepreneurs and businessmen also find direct marketing attractive for several reasons

- Investment required is low
- It does not require any specialised skills either
- All that is required is a database with consumer profiles
- Returns are quick and its effectiveness can be measured to the last rupee and
- Customer reaction can be known immediately.

If one is a little more enterprising, he could start something on his own with just a telephone.

An interesting example of direct marketing is the case of a person who started his business in a locality of Delhi with 1,500 apartments. He got leaflets printed announcing free home delivery of any product required with his residential address and phone number. That cost him Rs 2,000. He also paid Rs 150 each to the newspaper vendors for inserting this leaflet in every newspaper they delivered. Once a week, he went to Sadar Bazar to stock goods at home. He not only earned enough money to quit his job but also substantial goodwill in the locality.

Of course, everything depends upon trust. If one misuses the trust bestowed and overprices his product he will soon find his business collapsing.

Also, the Internet has made direct marketing more exciting. Some of the world's biggest retail shops are offering millions of products on the Internet.

Customers can browse through the product list and order from the comfort of their homes. Businessmen can also build their business on the Net.

According to the Direct Marketing Association (DMA), "Direct marketing is an interactive marketing system that uses one or more advertising media to effect a measurable response and/or transaction at any location."

table 15.1 Mass Marketing versus Direct Marketing (One-to-One Marketing)

MASS MARKETING	DIRECT MARKETING (one-to-one marketing)
Average customer	Individual customer
Customer anonymity	Customer profile
Standard product	Customised market offering
Mass production	Customised production
Mass distribution	Individualised distribution
Mass promotion	Individualised messages
Share of market	Share of customer
All customers	Profitable customers
Customer attraction	Customer retention

Source: Adapted from Don Peppers and Martha Rogers, *The One-to-One Future* (New York: Doubleday/currency, 1993).

Don Peppers and Martha Rogers have listed the main differences between mass marketing and direct marketing (One-to-one Marketing Techniques – table 15.1). Organisations that know their individual customers, can customise their product offer, message, shipment and payment methods to maximise customer appeal. Today's companies are building customer databases. These database help in maintaining and using other databases and information (products, suppliers, resellers) for the purpose of contacting and transacting. Database marketing is exhaustively used by business marketers and service retailers (hotels, banks and airlines). A well-developed customer database is a proprietary asset that can give the company a competitive edge.

ADVANTAGES AND DISADVANTAGES OF DIRECT MARKETING

Advantages

- ***Focused approach.*** It is possible to identify a very specific target market using direct marketing techniques. This makes it a very useful promotional tool for niche products because it is possible to target only those who are likely to respond to the promotion – there is less wastage.
- **Cost *effective.*** Although cost per thousand people reached may be high as compared to other mass marketing promotional techniques, direct marketing can be very cost effective for niche products.
- ***Measurable and attributable*.** It is possible to link a particular sale as being a response to a particular direct marketing activity. This is very useful information since, over a period of time, it is possible for an organisation to build up a picture of the kind of marketing messages to which a particular group of customers is more likely to respond.
- ***Immediate and flexible.*** Some promotional activities can take a great deal of time to develop from first idea to final execution – TV ads for example. Direct marketing is flexible and there are short lead times associated with its use because of which it often has an immediate impact on customer responses.
- ***Ability to test, re-test and measure the impact of single variables.*** Its flexibility also means that a number of pilot versions of a direct marketing campaign can be run before the final version is rolled out on a large scale.
- ***Easy international reach.*** It is relatively easy to adapt a direct marketing campaign to an international target market.

- ***Tailored messages.*** Direct marketing also offers greater opportunities for developing tailor-made messages for particular groups of consumers.
- ***Alternative distribution channel.*** Many organisations are realising that direct marketing not only offers the opportunity to communicate with customers but it is also a means of getting their products to the customer as well. In other words, it is a mechanism for distribution as well as promotion. For example, shoe retailers such as the Bata Group see direct marketing as a way of making their merchandise available to customers who, for some reason, are unable to get to its retail outlets.
- ***Opportunity to build a database.*** Over time, the details on customers– what they bought, when and so on – can be used to build up a detailed picture of purchasing patterns.

Disadvantages

Despite all these advantages there are a number of problems associated with direct marketing. They are:

- ***May be seen as competing with existing intermediaries.*** May upset marketing intermediaries as sales through direct marketing may be taking sales away from them. In effect, you may end up competing with your own customers, that is, the intermediaries.
- ***May be seen as intrusive by consumers.*** Especially a problem for door-to-door and telemarketing.
- **Costs.** Initial customer acquisition costs are high – high cost per thousand reached; and database development can be expensive.

SUMMARY

Direct marketing is a move away from mass marketing, which starts with a product and finds customers to buy it, towards an information led, one to one marketing, which may ultimately sell each individual a customised product.

The catalyst for this is computer technology. Its falling costs and increasing power are allowing "mass-customised" manufacturing, the gathering and manipulation of vast amounts of personal data and, for the first time, a ready way for customers to tell producers directly what they think. The consequences are huge. With near perfect information, direct marketing has the potential to deliver near perfect customer service.

The transformation of direct marketing from its origins into advertising's downmarket cousin dates from the birth of mass production, which enabled manufactures to produce goods in large quantities for sale by chain stores to unseen buyers. The first mass produced shoes in America were called 'Straights'.

As advertising costs have risen and the media have fragmented, mass marketing has become harder and more costly. That, plus new computer technology, has pushed direct marketing into the limelight. Its full potential is only just being grasped. By manipulating information, including data over the Internet, direct marketing can be targeted and personalised. It can even be intelligent learning – what customers like from what they buy and where they browse, as well as soliciting feedback via the telephone and e-mail. The result can be more effective than mass advertising.

1. *Direct mail can be used for direct-response advertising, but all direct-response advertising do not use direct-mail. Explain.*
2. *Direct response advertising is an effective device for a two-step marketing strategy. Explain.*
3. *The keystone in the arch of direct mail advertising is the mailing list. Explain.*
4. *Interactive systems of direct marketing are the wave of the future. Do you agree or disagree ? Explain.*
5. *Enumerate in brief the various forms of direct marketing.*
6. *What do you understand by database management ?*

PROJECT WORK

Interview sales managers of three industrial organisations selling same industrial services and bring out a brief report highlighting the marketing strategies used by them.

SHORT ANSWER QUESTIONS

1. What is direct marketing?
2. What is telemarketing?
3. What are the three basic properties of direct marketing?
4. Write a note on direct selling.

REVIEW QUESTIONS

1. What are the differences between direct marketing and direct selling?
2. What are the methods of direct selling?
3. What are the advantages and disadvantages of direct marketing?
4. What kind of marketing is best for any organization?

GO TO THE NET

Using Internet search tools or other relevant sources, research famous network and website hacking events over the past three years. Then create a timeline of these events, including a description of each event.

Caselet

HMT made a humble entry in the wrist watch segment about four decades ago. At that time the competition was from local/small manufacturers and some foreign/smuggled watches. HMT was virtually in monopoly and customers were to wait for their preferred models. The intensity of distribution was limited as there was tremendous 'pull' the product enjoyed. Since it was a public company, HMT started distributing watches through cooperative stores and Canteen Store Department (CSDs). Soon the company opened its own showrooms in metros and large cities.

As the market grew, the company started building up its dealer network and appointed about 300 authorized sales service agents (ASS) who primarily acts as wholesalers but also sold watches in retail.

These authorized sales and servicing agents service about 5000 retailers in every nook and corner of the country. The compensation to these intermediaries is linked to different levels of achievement. As of now, HMT deals directly with the authorized sales and servicing agents. In addition to wholesale of watches, these authorized sales and servicing agents provide after sales service facilities both during and after guarantee period.

Since they developed a multichannel distribution system, the company developed. Over three decades into a distribution situation where watches are sold directly by the headquarters to bulk institutional buyers, 30 showrooms of the company in retail and institutional segments, CSD, cooperative stores, ASS and dealers.

Question:

1. Evaluate the multinational distribution system of HMT. Identify the likely areas of conflict and make recommendations to gain channel cooperation.

CHAPTER 16

international sales management

learning objectives

The objectives of this chapter are to:

- know the challenges faced by international sales managers
- understand international sales strategies
- understand role of sales management.
- understand role of ERP in sales management.

content outline

- Opening Case
- Introduction
- Sales Management Objectives
- Challenges Faced by International Sales Managers
- Formulating Sales Strategies at the National Level
- Summary
- Project Work
- Short Answer Questions
- Review Questions
- Go to the Net
- Caselet

opening case

Marketing Across Boundaries

F Rozen, President of the Best Frozen Foods Company, was reviewing the latest sales figure for his company. He noticed that the greatest profit margins came from sales in the military commissary system in Europe. The commissaries are essentially no frill American type supermarkets that sell grocery products that Americans want and need. The commissary system encompasses food stores run by the American Army to serve military soldiers assigned to Europe. Most of the commissaries and the personnel are located in Germany. Only military and American civilians connected with the US government, and their dependents, can shop at these stores.

F Rozen called his vice-president, NEW Market, into his office and said, "Our frozen foods are making profits in the German commissaries, especially without giant-size meals. As in America, our frozen corn is the best seller. Family meals with corn as a vegetable are outselling meals that have vegetables other than corn. Sales of frozen corn have exceeded our highest expectations. I remember that when I was with the American Army in Germany, you could not get frozen food. This will make a great market for us to expand our frozen food line. Since then our warehouse and transportation network have been established and the additional distribution costs are negligible."

"Whenever expanding our market area, we have used a massive television campaign, going with a successful theme "Better than Fresh". Since the German population drinks a lot of beer, let us use local actors drinking a cold beer while eating a meal. I want you to go to Germany, get the shelf space, arrange the television advertising, promotion and everything else involved an introducing the frozen food line in Germany. The food will be shipped next week and will be available for shipment to the stores in three months."

"In the US, refrigerators are large and have very large freezing compartments. Many Americans even own separate freezers. The typical German refrigerator is smaller and there is little room for frozen food; Germans are not used to frozen foods and even drink their beer warm. You have to request for ice in the restaurant. There are many food stands in front of grocery stores that sell sausages and french fries. Grocery stores sell plenty of fresh meat, fish, cheese, etc. There is plenty of help in the shops who give out samples and conduct demonstrations. But there is little refrigerator or freezer space."

"I showed the package to potential customers. We had forgotten to print instructions in German. Most packaging is printed in four or five languages, including German, English, French and Spanish. People said they could not follow the English instruction on our package. They were also not sure how large a pound or ounce was."

"The product also met with some advertising problems. A major problem exists with television advertising. The only advertising occurs between 6.30 and 7.00 pm. There is an all advertising show that is one of the most popular shows; but to get space you have to bid for it at least 18 months in advance. There is no guarantee when the commercial will be shown. Comparative advertising is banned. The food industry will not let us use the theme 'better than fresh'. This is considered derogatory to the fresh food industry."

"I cannot find shelf space for our product. Stores do not have freezer space, nor do they want an untried product. Please advise what action should I take. What should I do with the product which is arriving?"

TRY YOURSELF

1. Summarise the problem involved in marketing frozen foods in Germany.
2. What should F Rozen advise NEW Market to do?
3. Should the product be introduced? What suggestions would you make if the product is introduced?

INTRODUCTION

Sales management has increasingly taken on international dimensions. The multinationals and other companies with foreign production and marketing operations look to sales management to implement sales related marketing policies in each national market. In companies with sophisticated exporting operations, sales management obtains international distributors and dealers, maintains relationships with their distributors and dealers, maintains relationships with their distributive networks and monitors continuing changes in marketing conditions and needs in national markets.

International sales managers have to guide and coordinate the efforts of the sales organisation in countries where the company does business. Personal selling plays an important part in international markets. Promotion mix, distribution strategy, etc., are governed by rules and regulations of the foreign country. Environmental challenges in the international market have to be identified and tackled by the sales managers.

When the global business is firmly developed, international markets have to adopt information and marketing strategies, employ the latest information and communication technologies. The sales managers must understand the environmental changes, risks difficulties and obstacles which they do not have to encounter in their own country markets.

SALES MANAGEMENT OBJECTIVES

- Understand the marketing concept and be able to explain the salesforce manager's contribution to a marketing orientation.
- Have an overall model for sales activity management and tools to gather, analyse and use activity data.
- Know the major options for salesforce organization and be able to create a suitable structure for their market.
- Understand and use the principles of Behaviour Analysis to make their management interactions more effective.
- Be able to create effective motivation plans and policies for individual salespeople and the team as a whole.
- Have understood the difference between leadership and management and considered the leadership functions of a salesforce manager.
- Be able to explain the function of appraisal in the performance management cycle and have practiced using appraisal as a management tool.

Different types of Sales Orders

- Cancelled sales order by customer
- Last sales orders by customer
- Late sales order shipments by customer
- Open sales orders by customer
- Overdue sales orders by customer

- Sales order returns by customer
- Sales orders shipped not invoiced by customer
- Last sales orders by product
- Late sales order shipments by product
- Open sales orders by product
- Overdue sales orders by product
- Sales order returns by product
- Sales orders shipped not invoiced by product

ERP in Sales Management

Distribution: ERP is used for fast moving environments and totally integrated to reduce costs and build customer loyalty.

E-Business: A comprehensive integrated ERP solution integrate customers, vendors and employees.

Manufacturing: Address functions across the entire enterprise and supply chain, increase your ability to compete successfully. Contact Centre - Instant access to information on contacts, providing a consistent view of the customer/vendor across the business.

Maintenance: All aspects of company maintenance often overlooked by other ERP systems, improve productivity and increase profit.

Warehouse: Based on the concept of Random Storage, this is a fully integrated ERP solution made as flexible as possible to manage all situations.

Financials: Comprehensive accounting functions, from simple to highly complex for you to take control with a minimum of effort.

Rental & Hire: Automate all hire activities, from initial customer enquiry to final invoice, equipment purchase planning to servicing.

Challenges Faced by International Sales Managers

- **Economic Factors**

A country's economic sources includes sources of domestic livelihood and the allocation of resources. Because not all of the world's economies operate at the same level of efficiency, it is necessary to form a clear idea of the economic situation of a particular host country in order to develop an appropriate marketing strategy.

The economic system of a country is another important economic factor that marketers must understand. Traditionally, there are two types of economic systems: capitalist systems and state-owned systems.

- **Cultural Factors**

The cultural traits of a country have a profound effect on people's lifestyle and behaviour patterns, and the same are reflected in the market place. Culture is a complex term, and its precise definition is difficult. Cultural differences have an impact on marketing decisions affecting product price, distribution and promotion.

► **Political Factors**

An international marketer needs to examine carefully the political environment of a country before making major commitments in that country. The political situation of a country may or may not be conducive to profitable business there.

Political problems related to foreign business occur mainly because of political sovereignty, a country's desire to assert its authority and political conflict – either internal ones such as civil war or external troubles with another country. Such troubles may lead a country to intervene in the affairs of private business, particularly those of foreign firms. Intervention may range from takeover or expropriation which is official seizure. Other forms of intervention include exchange rate control. Political intervention, mainly encountered, in developing countries. Now even industrially developed countries seek to control foreign enterprises in various ways.

► **Legal Factors**

International marketers must be aware of treaties and international conventions. By and large, the relevant laws of the host country would be those concerning tariffs, dumping, export/import licencing, foreign investment incentives (provided by the government to attract foreign business) and restrictions on trading activities.

Some international treaties and conventions are concerned with property such as patents, trademark models and the like, in foreign countries. Some international laws have provisions for the encouragement of both worldwide economic cooperation and prosperity and the realization of international products and processes standardization.

► **Qualities of the International Sales Force**

The managing of the sales force is a difficult task for the sales manager. An expert salesman possesses many qualities which are essential for his success.

► **Cultural Adaptability**

In the host country, a salesman has to work without supervision. He must be able to discharge his duties and show a great amount of responsibility. He should also have credibility.

► **Physical Fitness**

A salesman should be physically fit because he has to travel across the country. He should take a balanced diet at all times as he has a lot of strain on him.

► **Knowledge**

The salesman should have proper knowledge of the area that he has to visit. Search and research is a part of his task.

► **Decision Making Ability**

The salesman should be able to take decisions as per the requirement of the customer. He should also possess adequate selling techniques as risks are much greater in international selling if proper decisions cannot be taken at the right time.

► **Language**

The salesman should be able to follow the language that is spoken in that country so that he can clarify the queries of the customers.

FORMULATING SALES STRATEGIES AT THE NATIONAL LEVEL

▸ **Sales Job Description**

Different types of job descriptions should be developed for different countries.

Duties and responsibilities are different for different countries. In some countries job description does exist, e.g., in Japan it is considered that job description can come by learning therefore it is suggested that sales managers job should be properly described for the international market.

▸ **Recruitment and Selection**

Selection of proper salesperson is very important to avoid disappointment for both the employer and the employee. A company should use a multi-step selection system for different international markets. The purpose of selection of salespersons differs from company to company and country to country and depending upon the requirement, it is important for the company to find the suitable candidate and ensure that he is an asset to the company for making proper international brand image.

▸ **Sales Training**

Training of the salesperson can never become absolute. As long as technology changes, new people enter the work force, businesses strive to improve, organizations will need training. The term "training" may change but the concept remains the same; people continually need help in mastering new skills, applying new knowledge and/or adjusting their attitudes.

What many people fail to realise is that training is itself a skill that needs to be learned. Expert trainers are aware of the hours involved in learning how to train. Novice trainers also realise that training is not an easy endeavour and non-trainers often do not know where to begin.

Sales reports are the basic tools used for monitoring of salespersons. They help sales managers to know that the salesperson is calling on the right people, making the desired number of visits and ensuring customer satisfaction.

SUMMARY

International sales management is not simply domestic sales management transplanted overseas. Long-standing cultural forces dictate that the management of overseas sales operations be locally directed in large part.

All countries and all individuals have to sell something to survive.

Selling activities are carried on all over the world and the emergence of global markets has opened new vistas for resourceful growth of international selling jobs.

PROJECT WORK

You and five classmates are working on the international marketing plan portion of an e-business. Working together, create a name and description of the e-business, then create an outline for a sales plan including advertising strategies.

SHORT ANSWER QUESTIONS

1. Discuss in brief the various tasks of an international seller.
2. Discuss why products should be adapted to the needs of foreign markets?
3. Discuss the role of trade fairs in export promotion.
4. What are the points of difference in domestic and international selling?

REVIEW QUESTIONS

1. What models can be used in the overseas market for international selling?
2. What qualities must be possessed be salesman engaged in international sales?
3. What factors must be considered while preparing for international trade?
4. Discuss the objectives of sales management with the help of suitable example.
5. Explain the role of ERP in sales management.

GO TO THE NET

Using Internet search tools or other relevant sources, locate three e-business related international groups and their selling strategies.

Using Internet search tools prepare a report of 10 industries of international level using ERP.

Caselet

Mahakushal Engineering works, a heavy Engineering unit was established in 1992. To haul the steel and other materials from the finished products to the nearby railway station, and for the transportation of materials from one department to another within the works, the company had eight locomotives. These stream locomotives posed many repair and maintenance problems.

The company decided to have phased programme of replacing them by six diesel locomotives. These had several advantages over stream locomotives. Diesel locomotives could be easily switched on and off and were economical to operate. Besides providing cleaner working conditions for that loco crew, by this replacement the company would be relieved from providing stream coal and treated at different points in the works.

When the first diesel locomotives was received in the company premises, the management initiated a programme for training diesel drivers. First preference was given to the drivers of stream locomotives. Arrangements were to relieve them from duty for training for period of two months Log sheets were translated into Marathi who did not know English.

Each steam locomotives had been manned by a driver and a fireman. As there was a greater degree of automation in diesel locomotives and there was no need to maintain the fire and clean ash pans, these were not provided with fireman. What was more, in some of the smaller diesel locomotives to relieve each regular driver for the additional responsibility as for the charge in the job content, they were placed in a higher pay scale. Management also agreed to absorb the surplus fireman in other vacancies without any loss in their earnings.

The recognized trade union was kept informed of all changes and had raised no objection at the time. However when the new diesel locomotives were commissioned with one driver each to man them, the secretary of the Union wrote to argued that this change had effected the promotions of fireman, their group relationships and concern for safety. Management was aware that loco crew could, if they wanted, bring all operations in the works to a stand still. They therefore agreed to discuss this issue with the union.

Questions:

1. As a Manager how will you justify the Management's view point.
2. As a union, how will you justify union's stand.
3. As Personnel Manager, prepare a plan of Action to bring amicable settlement between management and union.

B L O C K

III

Sales Promotion Management

Sales promotion serves three essential roles – it informs, precedes and reminds prospective customers about a company and its products. The most useful product or brand will be a failure if no one knows that it is available. Therefore, a producer has to inform channel members as well as ultimate consumers about the attributes and availability of products. The cutthroat competition among different products puts tremendous pressure on their manufacturers and they are compelled to undertake sales promotion activities.

The block focuses on sales promotion activities which highlight product availability and its potential to satisfy customer needs through four chapters.

CHAPTER 17

sales display and sales promotion

learning objectives

The objectives of this chapter are to:

- analyse the objectives and types of sales displays
- understand the process of sales display management
- appreciate the role of retailers in sales displays and the tools of sales promotion
- study the factors influencing sales promotion.

content outline

opening case

Indra Pharmaceuticals

Indra Pharmaceuticals was established in 1985 to manufacture, distribute and market pharmaceutical drugs. It was purely an Indian company and had to face tough competition from multinational companies during the initial years. The company mainly survived on institutional buying i.e. buying from various government and charitable hospitals and in the last decade, with the help of effective market strategies, has set up a place for itself, amongst the leading pharmaceutical companies in the country.

In 1995, the managing director of the company stressed the need for diversification and addition of new products to its existing product range. Looking at the success of 'Threptin' brand of high protein biscuits, he floated the idea of manufacturing and marketing the biscuits rich in protein, minerals and vitamins. His advisers suggested that since most of the people in the country were suffering from protein deficiency, such a product enriched with protein, would be desirable, and should be a big success, specially in view of its competitors brand. Marketing research department of the company also gave the green signal to the project after conducting a brief survey.

The company promoted its biscuits with 'triple plus protein' brand name. It was supplied in a 400 gm. packet consisting of 60 biscuits at the price of Rs 75/-. The product was heavily advertised in newspapers, health magazines, radio and television. The target audience was middle class, who it was believed suffered most from protein deficiency and could afford triple plus protein biscuits. Ordinary biscuits were available in the market at the rate of Rs 30/- to Rs 40/- per kg. The thrust of triple plus biscuits in the promotion campaigns was that these biscuits contained 3 times more protein and have additional mineral and vitamin value.

The company has 50 stockists covering the entire country and has a sales force of about 150 medical representatives, for promoting its products, through doctors and registered medical practitioners. The medical representatives of the company had a very good rapport with government and charitable hospitals. To promote the triple plus brand of biscuits, its medical representatives gave discount coupons to the doctors for passing over to their patients for buying their biscuits. The buyer was entitled for Rs 5/- discount per packet of 400 gms. The scheme continued for about 6 months.

Despite heavy advertisement and canvassing by its medical representatives, the product was unable to attract customers. It was observed that launching of this product had not affected the market position of Threptin biscuits at all which was being sold at Rs 90/- for a pack of 275 gms. Rather, it was observed that the sale of the biscuits had increased marginally consequent to the advertisement campaign by Indra Pharmaceuticals. The company could achieve only 25% of its sales target in the first year and it remained almost static for the next year.

TRY YOURSELF

1. How do you account for the failure of the company to achieve the sales target ?
2. Critically evaluate the advertising and sales promotion strategy.
3. Suggest a suitable promotion plan which can increase the sales of the company.
4. Do you think that change in the channels of distribution can improve the sales of this product ? If yes, please elaborate.

INTRODUCTION

Sales display is the act of putting things for view or on view. In sales management, sales display means "arranging systematically saleable goods so as to attract the attention of the customer". Advertising helps in awareness, reminding and informing customers about products and services. The actual product is not displayed in advertising. Sales displays fulfil that need by appealing to the eye of the prospects. Through a sales display, the manufacturer shows the goods or services to the customer. In the past, sales display was the only media for exhibiting products and inducing prospects to buy the same. Sales display is actually advertising at the point of purchase.

SALES PROMOTION OBJECTIVES

The objective of the sales promotion activities is to promote the brand image of product. The first thing which you should consider is from where those sales comes. In what kind of sales you are interested? More new customers trying to purchase the product? Present customers buying and using more? Getting store owners to stack it in the aisle, so that you get more impulse purchases? Experiment of your new or modified product?

Sales Promotion Tactics

Sales promotion tactics are, essentially, all the different kinds of incentives that you can think of. If it adds value and has the potential to increase sales, it is a way for a sales promotion tactic.

OBJECTIVES OF SALES DISPLAY

The following are the major objectives of any sales display

- It shows the products or services to the potential customer.
- It gives an idea about every detail of the product such as variety, quality, size, colour, etc.
- It helps the customer to see and examine the goods before they actually buy them.
- Sales display appeals visually to the prospects and induces them to purchase.
- Sales display reminds the customers about their need and subsequently they are attracted to buy.
- Wholesalers and retailers are satisfied by display tactics undertaken by manufacturers and they buy the goods.

TYPES OF SALES DISPLAYS

There are three forms of display:

i. **Interior Display** includes displays on the floor, walls, in show cases and show boxes. Goods should be neatly arranged and displayed inside the retail outlet. In this type of display, proper lighting and colour matching should also be ensured so that the overall effect of interior display becomes pleasing and attractive.

ii. **Exterior Display** is the display of products in the show window of the retail outlet. It creates that long lasting first impression. It also attracts the attention of passers-by as well as prospects and invites them to enter the establishment. Window dressing is one example of exterior display.

iii. **Other Displays** like showrooms, show cases, glass boxes, cupboards, etc. form part of display. They are used not only for sales display but also as a publicity device for enhancing sales. The success of showrooms and show cases depends, to a great extent, on the location, decoration, lighting and such other devices.

There are various classes of sales display of which the following are important:

1. ***Product Unit Display:*** Such unit displays use merchandise that is identical in size, colour, shape, use, etc. This type of display is used for bags, readymade garments, shirts, etc. Efficient merchandising is of interest to both the dealer and the manufacturer. The following would probably matter to the dealer

    - Creation of a stocking point for his establishment based on an intelligent assessment of turnover and profitability.
    - Careful planning of shop floor layout–placing of shelves, display cabinets, etc.– and ensuring maximum speed of customer traffic during peak period, thus avoiding overcrowding and bottlenecks.

2. ***Life-style Displays:*** Using the market segmentation approach, life-style displays are used by retail stores which focus on life-styles of customers. The purpose is to make the retail store appear homely for the target customer and give him the feeling that he has come to the right place to shop. Example - Retail stores of Bajaj Scooters and Motorbikes.

3. ***Assortment Display:*** In this type of display, the retailer puts a large range of products for display. Assortment displays can be classified into two categories

figure 17.1

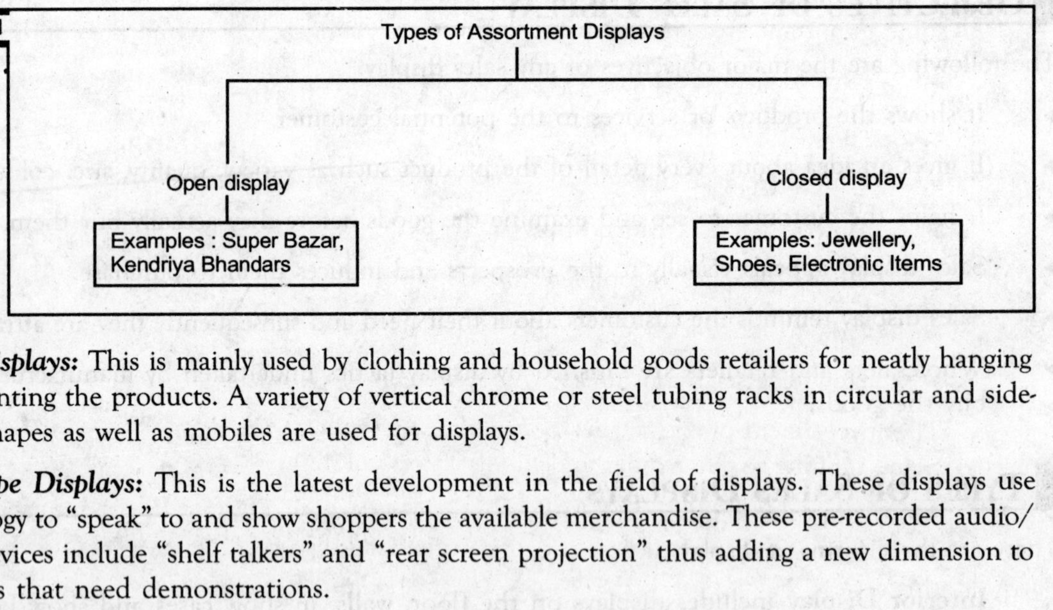

4. ***Rack Displays:*** This is mainly used by clothing and household goods retailers for neatly hanging or presenting the products. A variety of vertical chrome or steel tubing racks in circular and side-wards shapes as well as mobiles are used for displays.

5. ***Videotape Displays:*** This is the latest development in the field of displays. These displays use technology to "speak" to and show shoppers the available merchandise. These pre-recorded audio/video devices include "shelf talkers" and "rear screen projection" thus adding a new dimension to products that need demonstrations.

PROCESS OF SALES DISPLAY MANAGEMENT

In order to get the maximum advantage from sales displays, it is necessary that they are organised and managed effectively. The process of sales display can be divided into two parts:

figure 17.2

PART-I

Planning of sales displays

- Proper use of display space
- Use of cost-effective fixtures for display
- Layout of display
- Cost and frequency of display

PART-II

Planning of sales displays

- Managing adequate inventory for displays
- Earmarking specific space for different displays and fixtures
- Organising resources for the display including selection of outside experts
- Instructing store staff on handling of displays and merchandise
- Arranging for timely advertising and publicity of store.

It, therefore, requires the use of outside experts as well as search]for newer materials to achieve a distinctive edge in product display. MNCs are known to change their displays quite frequently and, for this purpose, even employ interior decorators and designers. Some even have an in-house merchandising and display department.

ROLE OF RETAILERS IN SALES DISPLAYS

Retailers act as a link between the wholesaler and the customer. Sales displays are handled by retailers. Thus, retailers have to manage the sales display task. For this, a retailer requires space in his outlet. Effective management of sales displays has two major aspects as discussed below:

1. ***Training to Retailers:*** A retailer can make the sales display a success or a failure. Therefore, if a company wants to make it successful, it has to impart training to retailers. The following are some important areas in which retailers can be provided training for sales displays:
   - How to match the display space available at the store and display requirements?
   - How to put up complicated display fixtures and material?
   - How to replace old and monotonous displays?
   - How to set up creative displays?
   - How to manage incomplete display kits?
   - How to make a good position for sales displays?
   - How to attract consumers by sales displays?

   The involvement of the retailer becomes necessary in the organisation to conduct sales displays. Some training to the retailer and his staff, for making the display a success, is always required.

2. ***Motivating the Retailer***: Retailers need to be properly motivated by the sponsoring organisation so that they can put their best efforts into the sales displays. The following are a few directions in this area:
   - Organising of display contests among retailers.
   - Publicity through newsletters mentioning retailer's name.
   - Provision of display goods and fixtures at special subsidised prices.
   - Photo-flashing of retailer's displays to other retailers.

- Cooperative advertising and sales promotion, i.e., promoting the retail store as well as the manufacturer's product on cost-sharing basis.

For example, Bata India Ltd. in India attaches considerable importance to the retail trade. The company spends nearly 25-50 per cent more money on shelf space than almost any other company.

SALES PROMOTION

Sales promotion serves three essential roles: it informs, persuades and reminds prospective customers about a company and its products. Even the most useful product or brand will be a failure if no one knows that it is available. As we know, channels of distribution take more time in creating awareness because a product has to pass through many hands between a producer and consumers. Therefore, a producer has to inform channel members as well as ultimate consumers about the attributes and availability of his products. The second purpose of promotion is persuasion. The cutthroat competition among different products puts tremendous pressure on their manufacturers and they are compelled to undertake sales promotion activities. The third purpose of promotion is reminding consumers about a product's availability and its potential to satisfy their needs. Some promotions are given below:

Definitions of Sales

- "Sales promotion consists of a diverse collection of incentive tools, mostly short-term, designed to stimulate quicker and/or greater purchase of a particular product by consumers and traders"

  Kotler

- "Sales promotion represents those marketing efforts that are supplementary in nature, which are conducted for a limited period of time and seek to induce buying".

  Davis

In simple words, sales promotion can be defined as "short-term incentives given to consumers to encourage their purchasing".

Choosing a Push or a Pull Strategy of Sales Promotion

- ***Push Strategy:*** A sales promotion programme, aimed primarily at channels of distribution, is called a push strategy. The marketer will promote his products heavily among distributors, wholesalers and retailers. At the last stage, the retailer promotes them among consumers. A push strategy usually involves a lot of personal selling and sales promotion including contests for salespeople and display at trade shows.

  Producer → Distributor → Wholesaler → Retailer → Consumer

- ***Pull Strategy:*** With a pull strategy, promotion is directed at the ultimate consumers. The objective is to motivate them to ask retailers for the product. This strategy relies heavily on advertising and various forms of sales promotion such as samples, free gifts etc.

figure 17.3

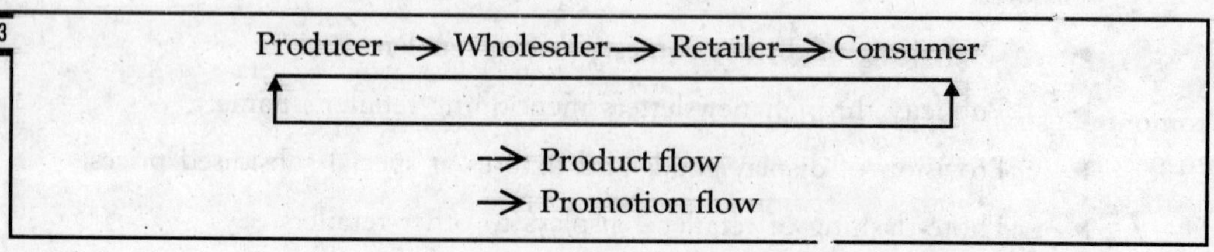

FACTORS INFLUENCING SALES PROMOTION

Four factors should be taken into account when determining the promotional programme:

- Target market
- Nature of product and services
- Stage of the product life cycle
- Budget available for promotion.

1. Target Market

A target market can be in any of the six stages of buying readiness. These stages–awareness, knowledge, liking, preferences, conviction and purchase – are called the hierarchy of effects because they represent the stages a buyer goes through in moving towards a purchase and each defines a possible goal of promotion.

- *Awareness:* The seller's task is to let buyers know that the product or brand exists.
- *Knowledge:* An attempt is made to let the potential buyer learn about a product's features.
- *Liking:* It refers to how the market feels about the product or brand.
- *Creating Preference:* It involves distinguishing among the various brands that are available in the market. It is not uncommon for the customer to like several brands of the same product but he cannot purchase a product until one brand is preferred by him over other alternatives.
- *Conviction:* It entails the actual decision or commitment to purchase.
- *Purchase:* It can be delayed by the customer due to non-availability of money. But through promotion or by incentives, the customer can be motivated to purchase immediately.

2. Nature of the Product and Services

There are various product attributes which influence promotional strategy. The most important of them are

- *Nature of Pre-sale and Post-sale Services:* When the products are demonstrated, the customers also ask the marketers regarding services offered by them e.g. personal computers, washing machines, etc.
- *Unit price:* When the unit price is low, the manufacturer as well as the customer has low risk but he can get the benefit of mass marketing. Therefore, mass marketing requires mass sales promotion schemes.
- *Degree of customisation:* If a product is marketed on the basis of individual customer's needs, no sales promotion is necessary.

3. Stage of Product Life Cycle

Promotional strategies are influenced by the life cycle of a product. When a new product is introduced, prospective buyers must be informed of its existence and benefits and middlemen must be convinced to stock it. Thus, both advertising and personal selling are critical in a product's introductory stage.

Later, if a product becomes successful, competition intensifies and more emphasis is placed on sales promotion to increase its sales.

4. Budget Available for Promotion

The funds available for promotion are the ultimate determinant of the promotional programme. A business with ample funds can make more effective use of sales promotion programmes than a firm with limited financial resources. The budget for sales promotion can be prepared by the following methods :

a. Percentage of sales
b. Fixed funds available for sales promotion
c. Following the competition, and
d. Budgeting by objectives.

TOOLS OF SALES PROMOTION

The following tools are used for sales promotion in India:

1. ***Prize Schemes:*** Prize schemes are an important method of sales promotion. A prize scheme is designed for both the public and the dealers. To make the scheme effective, it should be advertised through packages or retailers. The latest method of advertising is through the press, posters, etc. For dealers, sales competitions are arranged, prizes are announced or special offers are made if they show a substantial progress in sales.

2. ***Trade Fairs and Exhibitions:*** Trade fairs or melas are very common in India. They play a substantial role in selling goods of different varieties to different people in places where such fairs or melas take place. District exhibitions have been arranged on an annual basis since the early 1930s to promote sales of Indian products. These exhibitions attract a lot of people specially from rural areas who find them to be convenient places to make purchases of goods in general and durable consumer goods in particular. Many state governments announce relief or concessions in sales tax in such fairs; for example, a passenger car can be purchased in the Gwalior Mela without payment of any sales tax.

   The main objectives of trade fairs and exhibitions are:

   ▶ Meeting potential customers
   ▶ Making direct sales
   ▶ Discovering new applications for existing products
   ▶ Introducing new products.

3. ***Free Samples***: These are used for the sales promotion of consumer goods and the sale of many types of fast-moving consumer goods. Free samples are generally used to introduce a new product and as a sales tool to attract the attention of prospects. They are also shown to prospective buyers when sales contacts are established with them. Under this arrangement, not only is time saved, but it also eliminates the need for inspection or testing of goods by the buyer.

As a promotional device, it has been criticised on the following grounds

- It is costly.
- When buyers receive samples, they generally pay no attention to them.
- Generally, persons who are not genuine prospects collect free samples.

4. ***Correspondence:*** This could be an effective device for sales promotion. A specialised correspondence section will be more advantageous as it can communicate very effectively with prospects as well as potential customers and established for it is better equipped to write letters.

5. ***Catalogues:*** These play a dominant role, both in advertising and sales promotion campaigns. They are largely used when a firm manufactures different types of products, distinguishable by size, shape and other features. It is from the catalogue files that one can get information required about different products of a particular manufacturer. The following purposes can be served by catalogues

   - To get orders
   - To make the customers aware about the specifications
   - To provide detailed information
   - To solicit product sales.

6. ***Advertising Novelties:*** Small, interesting, or personally useful items, etc. can be used for sales promotion. To be effective, an advertising novelty should meet the following requirements

   - It should not be a high cost item
   - The item should be eye-catching
   - It should be useful.

7. ***Entertainment of Customers:*** Entertainment is essential when a standardised product is sold in bulk lots. In such a case, entertainment of customers acts as a primary promotional device. But when the product is sold on a routine basis, customer entertainment is neither necessary nor justified.

8. ***Sales Contests:*** The main aim of sales contests is to motivate the sales personnel, increase sales and bring more profit to the company. Under this scheme special incentives in the form of prizes or awards are offered. The following are different kinds of contest prizes

   - Cash awards
   - Merchandise prizes, and
   - Special honour, e.g. winners could be requested to appear in a TV show.

9. ***Price-off:*** This is simply a reduction in the price of the product to increase sales and is very often used when introducing a new product. A reduction in price always increases sales but the use of this technique should be carefully considered in the current market situation.

   According to various researches on sales promotion, price-offs should generally be considered

   - For introducing new brands or giving existing brands new uses.
   - For products/brands which are already doing better than the competing brands.
   - In conjunction with sales activities aimed at increasing retail distribution.

In 1997, price cuts of as much as Rs 4,000 to Rs 5,000 on almost all product lines, led to a whopping growth of 25 per cent in television and refrigerator sales. Again, in 1998, Videocon announced a reduction in colour TV and refrigerator prices. This happened even when other manufacturers as varied as Maharaja, Allwyn, Sony and LG were thinking of announcing a price increase induced by a 4 per cent import levy and the weakening rupee. BPL decided not to change its prices.

Coupons can also be used to provide 'price-offs' to consumers, specially at the product launch stage. Henkel, the German toiletries major, gave Rs 10 off on a Rs 40 pack when it introduced *Pril* scouring concentrate. Both, Colgate Palmolive and Hindustan Lever, offered coupons for a free tube of toothpaste.

10. ***Refunds:*** A refund may consist of straight cash, coupon values or a product offered to the consumer in return for a proof of purchase of a specified product or service. Refund is also an effective tool of sales promotion. It is an offer made by a manufacturer to give back a certain amount of money to a consumer.

11. ***Point-of-sales Materials:*** Point-of-sales (POS) materials are elements of sales promotion displayed at the point of sales. The POS display persuades, reminds and gives details to the consumers about a specific brand. Companies using this method are Procter & Gamble, Nestle and Parle.

12. ***Boosters for Dealers:*** In a bid to reduce its mounting inventories and boost the sagging morale of its dealers, Telco offered a 2 per cent discount to dealers on purchase of a truck if payment was made up front. Also, concessional interest rates were offered to expedite payments. These incentives were drawn up after getting a feedback from Telco dealers.

SUMMARY

Sales displays are very important in modern retailing. These help in enhancing the retail store image as well as attracting customers to the stores. Effective sales displays increase sales and profitability. Proper management of sales displays requires an eye for detail on the part of sponsors as well as retailers. Dealers and retailers play a critical role in the success of sales displays and hence require careful handling and proper motivation.

PROJECT WORK

Bounce Sales Bulletin

To All the Field Force

Sub: Display Scheme to Operate in Wholesale and Retail for the period 1/12/98 to 15/1/99

The Management has taken a decision to operate a Display Scheme for Nataraj Colour Pencils in the wholesale and retail markets for the period 1st December 1998 to 5th January 1999, the details of which are as follows

For the wholesale

On purchase of 50 Boxes of Colour Pencils– 5 Boxes of Colour Pencils FREE

Slabs will operate in multiples of the above. This scheme will be in addition to the existing trade scheme of One Set Free on purchase of 10 sets of colour pencils.

For the Retail

On purchase of 5 boxes of colour pencils–5 sets of colour pencils FREE

On purchase of 10 boxes of colour pencils– 1 box of colour pencils FREE

Slabs will operate in multiples of the above. This scheme will be in addition to the existing trade scheme of one set free on purchase of 10 sets of colour pencils.

Other Details

1. The purchase by each wholesaler/retailer to participate in the scheme should be on or before 31st December 1998.
2. Each participant must display Nataraj Colour Pencils along with the POP material for a period of 45 days from the date of purchase of the goods.
3. Acknowledgement of participation from the retailers along with the purchase quantity, signed and stamped by the participants and confirmed by the sales supervisors, must reach the respective depots by 25th December 1998 in the attached format (Format No.1).
4. On receipt of all acknowledgements of participation from the dealers, the RDS will send, in the attached Format No. 2, the details of primary purchase of Nataraj Colour Pencils as well as the total secondary sales made for colour pencils in the scheme in Format No. 3 to the respective depot by the 31st December 1998.
5. On completion of the display period, each RDS should give the free item to the participants in the required quantities and the confirmation of receipt of gift items from the participants to reach the depots by 25th January 1998.
6. The depots will despatch 80% of the stocks of colour pencils to be given as gifts to each RDS *by* 31st December 1998 on the basis of the estimated sale given by the SS/ASM for each RDS.
7. Each display must be supported by a photograph to qualify for reimbursement of free gift. We hope that you will strive to ensure the success of this scheme.

Good Luck.
With regards,
Sd/-
(Kirtibhai Sanghvi)

Q. Study the above communication which is directed by the sales manager to all the field force regarding display scheme and answer the following questions

a. What is the nature of display?

b. What is the major principle of display used in the above sales bulletin?

c. What is the reason of display?

SHORT ANSWER QUESTIONS

1. Explain the various methods of sales promotion.
2. What are the limitations of sales promotion in a sellers market?
3. What are the objections to sales promotion?
4. What is promotional mix?
5. What is sales promotion?

REVIEW QUESTIONS

1. Discuss the various objectives of sales display.
2. What types of display would you suggest for a toy store specialising in electronic toys?
3. What are the basic concepts of sales promotion? List the types of promotion directed at

   a. Middlemen

   b. Consumers.

4. Explain the role of public relations in sales promotion.
5. Draft a public relations strategy for a company marketing agro-based products for sales promotion.
6. What are the different types of sales presentations ? Discuss them giving suitable examples.
7. What approach would you follow in developing a sales presentation for a computer software package on financial management? Give justifications for your answer.
8. What is the percentage of a sales budgeting approach for advertising and sales promotion? Why is it so widely used? In what circumstances may it be considered inappropriate? Why ?
9. What are the various elements of a promotion mix? Is promotion different from marketing communication? Give reasons.
10. Suggest a promotional strategy for any two of the following:
    - i. Dish Washers
    - ii. Colour Television
    - iii. Detergent Powder
    - iv. Electronic Toy.
11. What are the different objectives of sales promotion?

GO TO THE NET

Using Internet search tools, or other relevant sources, locate several lists of best and effective websites which are used for sales promotion.

Using Internet search tools, or other relevant sources, make the report on the sales promotion activities of any 5 FMCG companies.

Caselet

Sales Promotion : Godrej-GE Appliances

Company Profile

- Godrej is one of the leading white goods producing company.
- Every year the company announces various promotional schemes to increase its products, frequency of purchase.
- Such schemes are more active during the festive season.

Scheme

- Keeping the festive season in mind, Godrej has announced "No. 1 Super Hit Dhamaka."
- This scheme includes various offers for customers such as free gifts, monetary discounts, etc.
- Duration — 20th-31st Sept. 1998

Strategy of Promotion

- High value promotion strategy
- Competitive promotion strategy
- Consumer promotion strategy

Advantages of the Scheme

- Induce trial
- Increase in frequency of purchase
- Utilisation of existing resources
- Optimum use of Festive season.

Competitors Analysis

- **Whirlpool:** (Offer for the season)
  1. Sony Cordless worth Rs 3445/-
  2. Philips Iron worth Rs 745/-
  3. Titan Watch worth Rs 445/-
- **Kelvinator:** (Offer (off season)
  1. Rs 125 off on a purchase of fridge.
  2. Free gift such as Prestige 31 Pressure Cooker. Valid till stocks last.

Questions:

1. Critically analyse the sales promotion scheme of Godrej-Ge Appliances.
2. Compare the scheme with competitor's scheme.
3. Would you like to give any suggestions for the improvement of the scheme?

CHAPTER 18

sales promotions strategies

learning objectives

The objectives of this chapter are to:

- understand sales promotions objectives
- describe sales promotion and consumer behaviour

content outline

- Opening Case
- Introduction to Sales Promotion Objectives
- Launch New Product and Increase Trial
- Encourage Repeat Purchase
- Sales Promotion and Consumer Behaviour
- Consumers' Price Perceptions
- Perceived Risk and Attitudes
- Consumer Decision Making
- Profiles of High and Low Involvement Consumers
- Rate of Discount, Terms and Conditions
- Protection from Competition
- Summary
- Project Work
- Short Answer Questions
- Review Questions
- Go to the Net
- Caselet

opening case

Godrej vs. Samsung Sales Promotion Scheme

Godrej:

Godrej is one of the oldest companies in India. It is a multinational company. Godrej is approximately 50 years old. Godrej is having a wide range of products. Some of its products are refrigerator, steel furniture, washing machines, office related items (typewriters, etc.), soaps, etc.

Samsung:

Samsung is also a multinational company. It is one of the world leaders in electronic goods. It has entered Indian market just about a year back and is trying to set its feet here. Some of its products are television, stereos, washing machines, etc.

Type of Scheme

Godrej:

1. **Customer Promotion Scheme:** Customer promotion scheme means that the customer is benefited.

   We can say that Godrej is following this scheme because it is giving rebate in the original price of the product (on its fully automatic washing machine worth Rs 14,999 which is now costing Rs 13,000) and is also giving a free gift (a VIP suitcase). It is also giving special loans to its customers. It is giving 0% interest loans for its products to the customers. All these state that customers are at benefit. By providing these benefits to the customers the company is actually increasing its sales.

2. **Trade Promotion Scheme:** Trade promotion scheme means that the middleman (retailer) is benefited.

   Godrej is giving 10-15% of the profits to the retailers, if they are able to meet a definite set target. Thus, in this way retailers are also benefited.

   Godrej started this scheme in the first week of October.

Samsung:

1. **Customer Promotion Scheme:** Samsung is following this scheme because it is giving rebate in the original price of the product (on its fully automatic washing machines worth Rs 21,000, which is now costing Rs 18,000) and is also giving a free gift (a camera). All these state that customers are at benefit. By providing these benefits to the customers the company is actually increasing its sales.

   Samsung started this scheme on 9th October and would last till Diwali (19th October).

Comparisons

	Godrej	Samsung
Loans	0% interest loans for its products (started in NA mid-August)	NA
Free Gift utility	VIP suitcase (has more utility, is necessity, is required by all class of people)	A camera (doesn't have much utility as a luxury item; is required only by specific classes)
Service	More service points and better service (since the company is old and is fully established)	Limited service points (since the company is new and people have less confidence in it)
Price	Less	High
Product Range	Large (semi-automatic washing machine, fully automatic washing machine, soaps, steel furniture, etc.)	Limited (fully automatic washing machine, televisions, stereos, etc.)

Result of Scheme: The sales of Godrej went up by 70%. The sales of Samsung went up by 30%.

Strategies Followed

Godrej – WIN-WIN Strategy

We can say that Godrej is following this strategy because it is giving rebate in the original price of the product and is also giving a free gift (a VIP suitcase). It is also giving special loans to its customers. It is giving 0% interest loans for its products to the customers. All these state that customers are at benefit. By providing these benefits the company is actually increasing its sales. Thus, the seller is also at benefit. They were the initiators.

Samsung—Defensive Strategy

We can say that Samsung is following this strategy because it is giving rebate in the original price of the product and is also giving a free gift (a camera). By providing these benefits to the customers the company is actually increasing its sales. They are defensive because they launched their scheme after Godrej to protect their market.

TRY YOURSELF

1. Make a comparative analysis of sales promotion strategies adopted by the Godrej vs. Samsung.
2. What are the factors which influence the formulation of sales promotion strategy?

INTRODUCTION TO SALES PROMOTION OBJECTIVES

Sales promotions are increasingly being used to accomplish an ever-expanding list of marketing objectives. The company's marketing objectives and strategies influence the development of sales promotion objectives and strategies. There can be a number of sales promotion objectives, depending upon the firm's policies, marketing objectives, nature of the product and its stage in product life cycle, level of existing and anticipated competitive activity, consumer response pattern, economic conditions and the target group (consumers, traders, or sales force), etc.

Sales promotion objectives could be either proactive or reactive. The most common objectives under proactive category are

- To gain additional market share or additional revenue.
- To expand the target market.
- To develop favourable consumer experience with the product.
- To add extra value to the product and develop brand franchise.

Reactive sales promotion objectives are developed in response to some unfavourable market situation, or where the objectives are essentially short-term, such as the following

- In response to competitive moves.
- When excessive inventory piles up.
- To generate short-term cash.
- When the decision is to discontinue a product, or close down the business.

In a dynamic and rapidly changing marketing environment, unfavourable conditions may appear with little or no warning. It is difficult for the management to anticipate and plan for such exigencies; however, hasty decisions regarding sales promotion objectives may sometimes produce adverse effects for the firm in the long-run.

An important area that concerns sales promotion objectives is directly related to the specific promotional techniques to be used. The techniques could be those where the measurement of results is straightforward, or difficult to measure. For example, it is easy to measure the impact of discount offer on sales, but it is very difficult to measure the impact of premium on the perceived value of the promoted brand.

The company can use sales promotion to achieve many objectives; however, every offer must start by being specific as to what objectives are intended to be achieved. According to Schultz and Robinson *in Sales Promotion Management* (Chicago: Crain Books, p. 149 1982.), the objectives should be:

1. Specific
2. Measurable
3. Clear and concise
4. Practical and realistic
5. Affordable, and
6. Attainable.

Perhaps, the most difficult part in managing sales promotion is to decide which particular sales promotion tools should be used for achieving the specific objectives, which of these tools can be and should be combined to produce a synergistic effect, and how can these be delivered to the target audiences, that is, consumers, resellers, or the sales force.

table 18.1 Examples of Three Options of Marketing and Promotion Objectives and Strategies

	Option 1	Option 2	Option 3
Marketing objective	Increase market share from 4% to 6% by the end of the current year	Increase sales by 15% in the current year	Increase profit by 10% over last year's
Marketing strategy	Promotion will use "pull-push" combination, while only "pull" advertising will be used	Increase purchase rate of product by trade and consumer	Decrease marketing cost while holding sales as high as possible
Promotion objectives	Increase purchase rates by consumer and gain 85% distribution for the brand	Decrease inter-purchase duration from 8 weeks to 6 weeks	Maintain distribution at 85%
Sales promotion strategy	Use trade and consumer deals, specially in low consumption and distribution markets	Use "pull-push" sales promotions to encourage faster usage rate, and frequent price-cuts	Stop consumer promotions which are unprofitable. Trade promotions only if necessary to maintain distribution.

(Adapted, with changes, from Blattberg and Neslin, 1990 pp. 384)

When objectives are expressed in numerical terms, these are called goals; strategies are broad action plans to achieve the stated goals. Marketing objectives and strategies are related to the marketing-mix of a company while the promotion objectives and strategies are related to the promotion-mix only. What would be the role of promotion-mix depends directly on the marketing strategy, and on the marketing objectives. All the three different options presented in the example in Table 18.1, show different marketing objectives in case of each option, and in each case a number of different promotion objectives and strategies can be developed. For instance, take option 1, given above. Once the marketing strategy assigns promotion-mix the role of using "pull-push" in case of sales promotion and only "pull" in case of advertising, the promotion objectives have consumer as well as trade orientation and the sales promotion strategies focus on different consumer promotions and trade deals.

Some of the important sales promotion objectives are mentioned below, and the more important ones have been discussed briefly.

- Increase sales volume
- Speed up the sales of slow moving products
- To check the fluctuations in sales
- Attract new customers
- Launch new product and increase trial
- Encourage repeat purchase
- Clearance of excessive inventories
- Motivate dealers
- Encourage dealers to participate in display and sales contests

- To gain advantageous shelf-space and increase store traffic
- Improve relationship with dealers
- To block competitors' moves
- Motivate sales force
- To supplement advertising and personal selling efforts and deflect customers' attention from price.

Increase in Sales Volume

The sales volume of any product depends on many basic factors of marketing, such as product quality, its price, distribution, effectiveness of marketing communications, and macro-environmental factors (demographic, economic, technological, political/legal, competitive, etc.).

Definitely, sales promotion cannot be a substitute for weaknesses in marketing strategy. There could be a number of reasons for companies to go for short-term increase in sales volume:

- To reduce inventories before financial year-closing
- To increase the stockholding of retailers, or even consumers, before the introduction of a competing brand, or
- To push stocks of the old brand before the introduction of new model.

Generally, the brand switchers or marginal buyers, who buy when a product is on promotional deal, contribute more towards increasing sales volume. One possibility, though, cannot be ignored that these brand switchers sometimes get exposed to better products and some of them may become repeat purchasers. Almost every sales promotion that offers immediate value at the time of purchase may contribute to increasing sales volume. These immediate value promotions can be directed toward those who like trying new products, and those who are regular users of the product. Such promotions can be particularly useful in new markets, and can also be used to introduce a sense of urgency in the consumer or the trader to buy the product now.

Launch New Product and Increase Trial

Small budget companies that cannot afford sustained advertising expenditures to introduce new products, or match the competitive advertising blitz, find sales promotion to be more cost-effective and helpful in generating sales volume. Companies, that have a small market share, cannot match the substantial advertising budgets of market leaders in the same industry. It is also difficult for smaller companies to obtain shelf-space in retail shops without offering incentives to re-sellers, or encourage trial by consumers without offering some immediate or extra benefit. A free sample, along with a coupon of some value, may prove to be more effective in inducing trial of a new product by consumer, and may also lead to purchase of the regular pack from the market. A free sample is generally welcome to almost all consumers and increases the probability of trial and, in some cases, purchase as well. A number of personal care products, such as shampoos, cosmetics, toilets soaps, or laundry products, such as detergent powders, cakes, etc., have been introduced successfully in the last few years.

Colgate Palmolive launched 'Palmolive' toilet soap in 1989. Its sales in Chennai, which is one of the largest markets for toilets soaps, were below all India levels. Market research studies revealed that the cause of below-level acceptance was inherent conservatism of the consumers in this market. They do not change brands easily, and consumer awareness and trial was low, despite heavy advertising. The trial-retention-ratio suggested that once consumers tried 'Palmolive' soap, they liked the quality and stayed with the brand. During a four-month period (February-May 1990), promoters called on about half a million households in this city. To encourage consumers to buy from the promoters, a stainless steel teaspoon was given with only one cake of 'Palmolive' soap and subsequent cakes were sold on a marginal discount. The focus was on an incentive, which would ensure trial of even one cake. For this period dealers were hired to place attractive displays to make 'Palmolive' soap a highly visible brand in the windows of retail stores. Sales increased substantially in March, and informed people say, it almost doubled by the end of April 1990. Product adoption increased just by stimulating trial rate by consumers, leading to growth in sales which was maintained subsequently.

Samples distributed free, with or without a coupon, are often used to introduce a new product or induce trial of even an existing product by consumers. Small budget firms have to exercise extreme caution and use such a promotion judiciously, because it may prove to be quite an expensive proposition. For them, it would be appropriate to choose selected markets with high potential.

ENCOURAGE REPEAT PURCHASE

Repeat purchase by customers leads to increased sales volume. Such sales promotions are undertaken to encourage existing consumers to forward-buy, for example, promotions, such as "get one free on purchase of four". Frequent-flier offer by some airlines is one such scheme, where the customer is allotted certain number of points, and on collecting specified points, gets a free offer of value. Some promotions offer free merchandise or cash refund offer by collecting tokens on purchases of a specified value.

In the month of January 1983, 'Nescafe' announced a consumer contest. Contestants were required to suggest one word as a prefix or suffix to describe 'Nescafe'. There was no limit on the number of entries one could send. The only condition was that with each entry the contestant must enclose an empty pouch of 50 gm 'Nescafe' as proof of purchase. There were 1565 prizes to be won.

An independent panel of judges was to select the most appropriate entries for different categories of awards. The first prize was Rs 200,000. Regular users of coffee, or even occasional users, responded with enthusiasm, because not only was the contest exciting, the prize money too, was quite substantial.

To Block Competitors' Moves

In business warfare, it is not uncommon that sometimes challengers resort to offering discounts. New product launches by competing companies are backed up by aggressive advertising and sales promotion campaigns. A firm that feels threatened would like to protect its loyal customers from switching to the new competing brand. Such a threatened firm would plan to load consumers so that they are in no need to go shopping for that product category. The firm may also announce some attractive trade-deals so that shelf space in retail shops is blocked. To accomplish the objective, normally a combination of "push-pull" strategy is used. To pre-empt competition, presence of certain favourable conditions is necessary. The inter-purchase interval, that is, the interval between two successive purchases should be long for the consumers. The product should be such that it can be stocked without occupying much space. There should be reliable information about competitor moves, and the inventory holding costs should not be high. Detergent powders and cakes, toilet-soaps, shampoos, oral care products, and other non-durable products, which are consumed everyday, may respond well to such promotions. This objective may also be accomplished for certain consumer durable goods in case of the trade segment.

Encourage Dealers to Participate in Display and Sales Contests

An important objective of sales promotion is to encourage re-seller participation in displays and contests. Display is a powerful tool to enhance sales. Displays attract consumers who are passers-by, or window-shoppers, by serving them as reminders. They encourage unplanned purchases and increase store traffic. Since the space available for displays in retail stores is limited, in an average store there may not be more than ten or fifteen items that get major display space at any given time. Generally these displayed items generate a higher sales volume.

Contests are used to motivate dealers. A certain sales quota is fixed for dealers and those who exceed the quota by a specified margin, or by the largest margin, are awarded cash or merchandise, and often a certificate too. Everything about a contest, whether display or sales, should convey the idea that it is something special. Such contests should be held infrequently and not become a routine feature, which would reduce their importance and lead to decline in interest. Contests can help in attaining short-term objectives and improve the company-reseller relationship.

Deflect Customers Attention from Price

Price increase can often have a negative effect on sales. Marketers can develop an appropriate sales promotion to accomplish the objective of reducing the negative impact of increased price on sales. If the price of the product was Rs 50 before the price rise, and the new price is Rs 60, then a coupon with a face value of Rs 5 is provided that places the product's price between Rs 50 and Rs 60, making the effective price only Rs 55. When the coupon is made available, the new price does not appear to be as high relative to the new price of the product. Consumers develop a new reference price for the product and the increase does not appear to be as high as it was perceived earlier. Of course the coupon should be of immediate value, instantly redeemable "on-package", or the discount should be given at the time of purchase.

To Supplement Advertising and Personal Selling Efforts

A company's objective can be to enhance the attention getting power of advertising and put power in personal selling efforts of the sales force. A coupon or a premium offer in a print advertisement increases the attention getting ability of the ad. When consumers see in bold print "FREE", their attention is focused on the advertisement. They may read not only the headline but also the copy, and may get exposed to the advantages and benefits associated with the brand. Bowman (1980) cited the evidence indicating that print advertisements containing coupons are more likely to be noticed and recalled than are the same advertisements not containing coupons.

SALES PROMOTION AND CONSUMER BEHAVIOUR

It is interesting to study and understand why consumers respond to sales promotions in certain ways. The implications for practitioners are clear.

Those who better understand as to how and why consumers respond to different sales promotion in certain ways, are likely to have an edge and would be able to meticulously design more appropriate and effective promotions. There are quite a few behavioural theories and concepts that help in explaining the responses of consumers towards promotions. Some of these theories focus only on the consumer's environment and behaviour and do not consider the internal mental processing, which may often be the case in some situations. Some other theories are concerned with cognitive aspects, such as perceived risk, attribution, and price perception, etc.

Classical Conditioning

This is a very well-known theory, described by Pavlov, a Russian psychologist, who conducted experiments with dogs. He demonstrated that hungry dogs would always salivate in the presence of food, when a bell was sounded almost immediately following the food, after sufficient number of times, the sound of the bell alone caused the dogs to salivate. Dogs had "learned" that the sound of bell was an indicator of food. The dogs associated the sound of bell (conditioned stimulus) with food (unconditioned stimulus) and made the same response (salivation) to the bell alone. A strongly conditioned stimulus can become unconditioned stimulus and can be used to 'condition' another stimulus.

Unconditioned stimulus – Food

Conditioned stimulus – Sound of bell

Response – Salivation

Many sales promotion techniques make use of this classical conditioning in practice. For customers, a brand frequently associated with premiums and contests may serve as the unconditioned stimulus and the resulting response could be excitement and the development of favourable brand attitudes among customers and, hopefully, purchase behaviour. Displays also explain as to why they lead to increase in sales even when there is no price or any other kind of incentive. Over a period of time, customers learn that displays are often associated with price discounts and hence become conditioned stimulus. 'A display becomes the ringing bell in Pavlov's experiment and the customers respond as per the conditioning'. Price cuts, coupons, premiums, etc., can serve as the unconditioned stimuli for consumers.

For the incentive associated with sales promotions, customers get conditioned by performing a certain type of behaviour repeatedly in ways which lead to reward. This reward becomes the unconditioned stimulus. Customers have learned to be smart shoppers because of this conditioning.

table 18.2 **Examples of Classical Conditioning**

	Unconditioned	Conditioned	Response
Classical conditioning	Food	Bell	Salivation
Sales Promotion	Premium, prize, price discount	Product display, contest	Excitement, purchase

Instrumental Conditioning

Such conditioning is also called "operant conditioning". The name most closely associated with instrumental conditioning is that of B.F. Skinner. The basic principle involved in this theory is best explained in one sentence.– "Behaviour is a function of its consequences". If a behaviour is reinforced, it is more likely to occur. In consumer behaviour terms, purchase behaviours that result in more favourable outcomes are likely to persist. Favourable experience as the outcome becomes instrumental in encouraging the consumers to repeat the behaviour in future.

In a "Skinner Box", there is a small lever which can be pressed easily by a small animal, such as a rat or pigeon. If the experimental animal does press the lever, food is delivered as a reward to reinforce the behaviour, which in this case is pressing the lever. When this response-reinforcement is repeated several times, there is more likelihood of the animal pressing the lever in a reasonable period of time when it feels the need for food. Once the reward to reinforce the behaviour is withdrawn, the chances of pressing the lever decrease, that is, when a learned response is not reinforced for some time, it diminishes to the point of extinction. In terms of consumers' purchase behaviour, the marketers wish to teach consumers to purchase a particular brand, and a premium, coupon, or prize becomes the reinforcement tool. The purpose is to use sales promotions to encourage purchase frequency, but in a manner that would considerably reduce the probability of extinction effect.

A coupon inside the product pack serves as a good example of operant or instrumental conditioning. The coupon is the reward that the consumer receives. In this case the response of the consumer is the purchase of the product, which occurs first and then is reinforced by the coupon, which is reward. Purchase behaviour of the consumer is reinforced and is likely to be repeated. In case of classical conditioning, if a premium is given first it becomes the stimulus and leads to response, which is excitement and purchase of the product. In this example of classical conditioning, the premium or the discount serves as the unconditioned stimulus that comes before the purchase response or excitement.

The difference between classical conditioning and operant conditioning approaches is that classical conditioning is based on stimulus-response theory. The stimulus occurs first, and a response is elicited. The operant conditioning is based on response-reinforcement theory. In this case the response is first emitted and then reinforced.

Through sales promotions, perhaps marketers are trying conditioning of consumers, but the important question is 'whether they are reinforcing the deal proneness in consumers (through price-cut or added value) or the brand usage'. Michael L Rothschilds (1987) is of the opinion that deal usage behaviour gets reinforced, not the brand usage. Consumers learn that by buying on deal they save money and that products bought on deal are not necessarily of lower quality, such as many consumer durable brands of well-known multinationals. Deal proneness appears to be shaped behaviour and the resulting behaviour of consumers is to seek and buy on deals.

Attribution and Dissonance Theories

Attribution theory is a group of interrelated psychological principles. The theory attempts to describe various approaches that consumers adopt to explain their own and others' behaviour. These explanations are called "attributions". Attributions have direct affects on attitudes, but have no direct effect on behaviour. Attitudes may affect behaviour significantly and hence the theory has considerable relevance to sales promotions. Mizerski, Golden, and Kernan, (1979) have distinguished three types of attribution theories: self-perception, object perception, and person-perception. Attributions regarding ones own motives are considered under self-perception, direct attributions, toward product relate to object perceptions, and attributions made about the other person relate to third theory.

1. Self-Perception

According to this theory (Bern, 1972), attitudes of individuals are formed by observing their own past behaviour and are consistent with those past actions. The key question that consumers ask is whether the action that they take is due to external causes (sales promotion), or internal causes (favourable brand attitude). For example, a lady who regularly purchases the *Femina* magazine is likely to conclude from her behaviour that the she likes *Femina* because the magazine is very good in its class. The same lady, in case of *Reader's Digest,* may conclude that she subscribes annually because she gets substantial discount on annual subscription. In case of *Femina,* it is her favourable brand attitude while in the case of *Reader's Digest* it is sales promotion, which is the external cause.

In case of defensive attribution, consumers are more likely to take total credit for any success (internal attribution), and consider others or outside factors responsible for failure (external attribution).

When significantly strong external causes are present, such as attractive promotional incentives, the consumer invokes the "discounting principle" and internal causes, such as favourable attitude, are disregarded.

Self-perception theory is certainly applicable to repeat purchase situation after a sales promotion. According to the theory, if the deal incentive is sufficiently strong, the consumer will attribute the purchase to an external cause. Internal causes, such as favourable brand attitude, will be discounted and the probabilities for repeat purchase would remain the same or may even diminish. Another application of this theory is to induce the customer to use a sample (an intermediate behaviour). If satisfied, then the customer is more likely to involve in a more complex behaviour, such as purchase of the brand on full price. The consumer is more likely to rely on internal cause for this action by convincing herself/himself that she/he conceded to a small request of trying the sample to have firsthand experience and satisfy curiosity.

2. Object Perception

This theory (Kelly, 1967) considers the distinctiveness, consistency, and observations of others about the event that involve the object in making attribution. For example, customers may judge the quality of a brand on promotion by considering the event. If this brand alone is on promotion, the event is significant. If this promotion is frequent enough over time, it is consistent. The consumers may draw an attribution about the brand that this brand must be low quality relative to the price. If a friend or acquaintance, or a neighbour also forms a similar opinion after the event, the attribution becomes strong. The implication for low-involvement consumer goods, which are frequently promoted, is that the customer does not form a negative image about the brand because most such brands are promoted quite often and any single sales promotion is hardly a distinct event for the consumer. Sales promotion of a consumer durable from high-involvement category does have the risk of degrading the brand image, if the promotion in that category is the first announced by a manufacturer.

3. Other-person Perception

In all those situations where a person asks "why' about an action or statement of another person, attribution theory is relevant. For instance, a customer is contemplating the purchase of a stereo system and visits a store. The sales person recommends brand 'A' while brand 'B' was advertised as available on discount. The customer considers, why did the salesperson recommend brand 'A', and not the brand 'B'? Perhaps, brand 'B' is of low quality and they cannot sell it on regular price, or by selling brand 'A', the salesperson will get more commission.

Dissonance Theory

According to this cognitive dissonance theory (Festinger, 1957), dissonance or discomfort is felt by consumers when they are exposed to information that conflicts with their original belief or attitude. This is particularly true in almost all cases of expensive high-involvement product purchases. Generally, after a high-involvement purchase, the customer recalls that some other brands with unique features were not selected. This often leads the customer to suspect that perhaps the choice made is not the wisest one. Post-purchase dissonance is quite normal and creates in the customer a feeling of uneasiness about prior beliefs or actions. However, the consumer needs to resolve this uneasiness or dissonance. One way the consumer can resolve dissonance is to change the original belief which is the source of discomfort. For example, if the brand bought on promotion is not satisfactory, the consumer may attribute the purchase decision to sales promotion. Here, according to self-perception theory, an external cause is available that explains the contradiction. The consumer may also feel dissonance when, according to her/his belief, a high quality brand offers a promotion. If other brands in the same product category do not offer promotion, then the consumer may change the belief that the product is of low quality and resolve dissonance.

table 18.3 **Sales Promotion Concepts Theories**

Concepts/theories	Type of sales promotion	Type of effect on sales
Classical conditioning	Premiums, displays, contests	Brand switching, repeat purchase, unplanned purchase
Instrumental conditioning (Operant conditioning)	Rebates, coupons, discounts, sweepstakes	Repeat purchase, multiple purchase, purchase timing accelerated
Self-perception	Price-cuts, premiums, rebates, coupons, trying a sample	Repeat purchases, multiple purchases
Object-perception	Discounts, rebates, premiums, end-of-season sale	Brand switching
Consumer decision making process	All types of sales promotion	Brand switching, repeat purchasing, purchase acceleration

CONSUMERS' PRICE PERCEPTIONS

There are many sales promotions that involve price concessions. For this reason, the process by which consumers' perceive prices becomes quite important to determine the appropriate size of price reduction, as this would have a significant influence on many types of sales promotions.

Considering Weber's Law, the amount of difference between the list price and the promoted price should be sufficient enough to be noticeable. For example, if the regular price of the product is Rs 3000, then what would be the amount of price reduction that would be noticeable to the customer to make the offer attractive. The minimal difference (in this case of price-cut) that can be detected between two stimuli (between the list price and the promoted price), is called "just noticeable difference or j.n.d.". To state differently, the law states that the stronger the initial stimulus (higher the list price) the greater the intensity needed (larger the size of the price-cut) for the second stimulus to be perceived as different. If the size of the price cut is too small to be noticeable, for example, only Rs 50 in this case, then probably this will not be noticeable enough to attract the customers. This means that price-cuts within a given small range may not be effective at all.

According to Hariy Helson (1964), perceptions of new stimuli are formed relative to a standard of "adaptation level". Factors that affect the level of adaptation include the past and present stimuli and, for this reason, this adaptation level changes according to the new inputs of stimuli to which people are exposed. The adaptation level for judging the price of a particular product is called the "reference price". Consumers develop a reference price for different products based on their earlier purchases of the same or similar products, prices of other available comparable products during recent shopping trips, or some subjective judgement about the worth of the product. The important implication is that consumers judge the prices of different products relative to their formed reference prices. Some researchers consider the reference price as the "expected price", "fair price", or the "target price".

The ideal situation for marketers, producers as well as re-sellers, would be that consumers' reference price should be high, so that any price-cut appears attractive to them. If consumers do make use of reference prices, then how are promotions likely to affect the reference prices ? If promotions decrease the reference price of products then it is a matter of concern for marketers, because they would like to sustain the high reference prices.

In case of sales promotions, probably a small price-cut is unlikely to change the consumers' reference price. But this small price incentive is also unlikely to motivate consumers to buy the product on promotion. A moderate price-cut may serve as an attractive incentive but is also likely to decrease the consumers' reference price. A large price-cut is unlikely to be beneficial for the marketer because the lost revenues will be too much.

To protect this shift in consumers' perceived reference price, marketers often provide a reference price in their communications of sales promotion. Retailers generally use the words "sale" or "special discount" to denote that this price reduction is temporary and that consumers should not infer that the list price has decreased. If the suggested price of the product is kept moderately higher than consumers' perceived reference price, then even a moderate price-cut would appear large and is likely to mean much to consumers. In some sales promotions a regular price is printed and is then crossed. Beneath this cancelled price is mentioned the promotion price. For example, in a recent promotion of Timex watches, the regular prices of the promoted models were printed and crossed and the reduced prices, applicable during the promotion period were printed underneath the crossed prices. This is an attempt to protect the consumers' reference price from decreasing.

PERCEIVED RISK AND ATTITUDES

Whenever consumers purchase any new brand, there is an element of risk in most such purchases. Perceived risk is defined as, "the uncertainty that consumers face when they cannot foresee the consequences to their purchase decisions" (Schiffman and Kanuk, *Consumer Behaviour* Prentice-Hall India, 4th Ed. 1991). According to this definition, there are two important dimensions associated with the purchase of a new brand–uncertainty and consequences. Only the risk, which is perceived by the customers, will affect the purchase decision; risks, no matter of what type or seriousness, will not affect the purchase behaviour of the consumer, if not perceived. The purchase decision of risk is not directly related with the amount of money involved. The selection of right ink-jet printer or a lipstick may present equal risk for a consumer. The reasons for risk perception can be many, such as the consumer has no previous experience with product category or it is an entirely new product launched in the market, or the consumer has limited knowledge and perceives risk in making a decision. Another possibility is that the consumer may lack the confidence in her/his own ability to make the "correct" decision.

Major risks faced by consumers fall under the following categories:

- ***Financial risk*** is perceived when it is suspected that the product is not worth the money {will this diploma really help me in getting a good job?)
- ***Functional risk*** may relate with the doubt that the purchased product will really perform as expected (will this ink-jet printer really print 10 pages in a minute?)
- ***Physical risk*** may be for self and others who would use the product (does the computer monitor screen emit harmful radiation?)
- ***Social risk*** may be felt with poor choice of the product resulting in social embarrassment (will that new toothpaste really check bad breath?)
- ***Psychological risk*** relates to wrong or bad product choice hurting the consumer's ego (would this purchase really mean that I am intelligent?)

An individual consumer's risk perception may vary with product categories and shopping situation. There are consumers who are high-risk perceivers and would limit their product choices to just a few alternatives that are perceived as safe to them. There are also low-risk perceivers who do not mind making choices from a wider range of product alternatives.

There are two ways that consumers use to reduce risk – either by reducing uncertainty or reducing the consequences of a wrong choice. Free samples are considered as an effective tool in reducing the perceived risk, more so in case of new products with which consumers may be unfamiliar. Free samples may reduce the risk of embarrassment and financial loss. High-risk perceivers also reduce the risk by purchasing only well-known brands of non-durable or durable products, or buying the same brand that proves satisfying. To reduce the risk, consumers also make purchases of smaller quantities, or smaller pack sizes.

Attitudes

Different models of attitudes developed by researchers show that the consumers' decision to behave in a certain way is a culmination of subjective beliefs, attitudes and intentions concerning that specific behaviour. The most recent attitude model is referred to as the "theory of reasoned action". According to this theory, it is not only the beliefs and attitudes of the concerned consumer but also the beliefs and attitudes of others that concern the specific behaviour. Social pressures and consequences of buying on promotional deal may have an important influence on the consumers' decision to buy on promotion. For example, if the relatives or friends, whose opinion is important to the consumer, have negative beliefs and attitudes towards buying on deal, this will affect the consumer's decision to buy on deal.

A price deal on a brand which consumers view as being expensive, may be looked at favourably and the brand may be purchased. Here, the price perception of the consumer is altered favourably. A low price because of sales promotion may also compensate for the low perceived quality of a product, more so if the quality is not as important as the price.

Deal Proneness

Are there a type of consumers who can be considered as deal-prone? The knowledge and understanding of this issue can be very helpful to managers in targeting the promotions to particularly attract this group, if there is deal proneness.

Definition

According to Blattberg and Nesline, "Deal proneness is the degree to which the consumer is influenced by sales promotion, in terms of behaviours such as purchase timing, brand choice, purchase quantity, category consumption, store choice, or search behaviour".

It is clear from the definition itself that sales promotions can produce some varying degree of "influence" on consumers' behaviour. Sales promotions may affect brand switching in some, while in some others it could be the timing of purchase, trying new products, or the quantity of the product purchased. For example, if there is an attractive discount (same for less), on a brand of toothpaste, the consumer may buy this brand instead of the regular one that he intentioned of buying. Another consumer, who was planning to purchase a refrigerator during the summer months, notices a promotional offer and buys this product during winter. When a certain promotion says, "buy three shirts and take one free", the customer might buy six shirts and gets two shirts free. A free sample of a new detergent may encourage the consumer to try the product. All these behaviours might pertain to the same consumer, or this consumer may not mind switching the brand, but may not change the purchase timing. The point emphasised here is that different consumers will be influenced in many different ways in response to the same sales promotions.

There are no definite answers as to who are those who may be characterised as deal prone or not deal prone. Researchers, in this area of consumer behaviour, have tried to study demographic, psychographic and behavioural variables of consumers to study the deal proneness to find any correlation. Consumers, who are brand loyal, generally may not qualify as deal prone. However, if the deal happens to be on some preferred brand (low-involvement product category), they may avail this opportunity and buy more than their immediate requirement. In fact, many producers, in an attempt to reward the brand loyalty of the consumer, announce promotions on such brands. An important question arises – is it the trait of deal proneness of consumers that leads to brand switching, or is it the sales promotion that makes consumers deal prone? It seems that price-sensitivity of consumers has a strong relationship with deal proneness. Other factors that perhaps may influence consumers in becoming deal prone are education and the level of income. Research conducted so far has provided strong support to the view that characteristic of deal proneness does exist in consumers for many product categories. However, the findings so far do not reveal who are those consumers that possess the trait of being deal prone.

Observations, in general, point to a few things. There are brand loyal consumers for certain products but these very consumers, at times, may behave as deal prone. There are others a who are brand loyal to products in high-involvement category but are brand switchers in other low-involvement category products and hence, deal prone.

Sales promotions affect by encouraging consumers to try new products, brand switching, repeat purchasing, and purchase acceleration, etc.

A consumer who tries a sample and, if satisfied, might become a regular user of the brand, for example, a new shampoo or many other non-durable products, which are consumed on a regular basis. Promotion offers encourage the consumers to switch brands, particularly in case of low-involvement product category. The probability of purchasing the same brand by the consumer increases after the use of the promoted brand. Promotion also affects the quantity of product purchased, for example, frequent use of noodles bought on promotion or other similar products.

CONSUMER DECISION MAKING

In the field of consumer behaviour, researchers have developed some fairly elaborate models of consumer decision process. Some well-known models are Nicosia Model, Howard-Sheth, and Engel-Kollat-Blackwell (EKB) model. No single model, from among the above mentioned, is accepted unanimously by people in academic circles. One important feature of EKB model is that it considers the concept of high and low-involvement of consumers in a purchase situation.

The consumer decision process starts with the recognition of need, that is, the consumer must recognise the need to purchase a product, only then does he go through the process of choosing the product. A display or any other promotion may remind the consumer that she/he needs the product, or may awaken the latent demand for the brand or product category. Because of the sales promotional communications, need or problem recognition may get triggered in both high-involvement as well as low-involvement products. It may be triggered by an attractive exchange offer, or interest-free installments for consumer durable products, such as refrigerator, oven, washing machine, and colour television set, etc.; however, it is more likely to result in extensive problem solving effort rather than immediate purchase. The sales effect in case of a low-involvement situation is likely to be immediate because of impulse or unplanned purchase, or because of familiarity or top-of-mind recall of the brand. The consumer may think that it is not worth devoting time and effort to the purchase situation in question. The low-involvement consumer may have visited the retail store with the intention of purchasing a certain product, but an in-store display attracted her/his attention and led to brand switching, or impulse buying. According to some researchers (Deshpande et al., 1982), this type of behaviour is an attempt towards reducing the amount of mental exercise by using simple decision rule in making a purchase decision. Some experts believe that price-cut and in-store displays are more effective for low-involvement than high-involvement consumers.

In a severely competitive market, where brands are considered as having no real differences, consumers learn that any of the many brands will meet the requirements, the purchase behaviour is likely to become one of low-involvement and the brand on promotion has more chance of being purchased.

One can distinguish between four different types of behaviours depending on the degree of perceived differences among brands and the level of consumer's involvement in a purchase situation.

1. ***Complex Buying Behaviour*** is shown by consumers when they perceive significant brand differences and they are highly involved in the purchase situation. Such a situation may be the result because the product is expensive, ego intensive, risky in some way, or infrequently purchased the consumer may not possess any meaningful information about the product and is in need of much information, to make a well-considered purchase.
2. ***Dissonance Reducing Buying Behaviour*** results when the consumer's involvement in the purchase situation is high because the product is expensive, risky, self-expressive, or infrequently purchased or the differences among brands are perceived as not significant. After the purchase, the consumer experiences dissonance. As all the brands would not have all the features, the consumer suspects the correctness of her/his decision. This causes uneasiness and the consumer looks for reassuring information and avoids disconcerting information.
3. ***Habitual Buying Behaviour*** occurs when the consumer's involvement is low and there are no significant differences among brands. This is generally the case with most low-priced and frequently purchased products. In this category, sales promotions can lead to considerable brand switching. Consumers buy these products as routine purchases and do not consider them to be important. They reach for certain brands because of familiarity and not because of any brand loyalty.
4. ***Variety-seeking Buying Behaviour*** results in product categories where there are significant differences among brands but the consumer has low involvement in these products. There is much brand switching due to variety seeking, or boredom. Sales promotions can encourage increased brand switching because of premium offer or due to some contest.

When the information requirements are high and there is an absence of any established criteria for evaluating the product category or specific brands in the category, the decision making would be one of extensive problem solving (EPS). Typically the purchase situation would be one of high-involvement.

If the consumers have already established some criteria to evaluate the product category or the brand, they are likely to engage in limited problem solving (LPS) and would collect some additional information to reach a decision. They may not have any preference for a particular brand and hence would like to know a little more about the differences among brands. This would be more like "fine tuning" their decision.

When consumers have some experience with the product category and have established criteria to evaluate different brands, they may buy the product as a matter of routine. This is routinised response behaviour (RRB). In some cases the consumers may search for a small amount of additional information but, in general, they only review what they already know. Sales promotions can lead to significant increases in the sales figures of the products if the consumers'[1] buying behaviour is routine type (habitual buying behaviour).

PROFILES OF HIGH AND LOW INVOLVEMENT CONSUMERS

The concept of consumers' involvement in a purchase situation is important. However, it is also important to realise that involvement is a matter of degree, and identifying or measuring low involvement against high involvement is a difficult task. Even then one can make certain distinctions between high and low involvement decision making. Consumers who are highly involved in a purchase situation actively seek and process information about the product or service. Consumers with low involvement rarely seek information and if the information is provided the processing is passive. To maximise the satisfaction from their purchases is the purpose of highly involved consumers. Consumers with low involvement seek only an acceptable level of satisfaction after the use of the product. In most cases, consumers with low involvement purchase products may or may not give any thought to product evaluation after use. At most this evaluation may be just cursory.

figure 18.1

A Model of Consumer Decision Making Related to Sales Promotion

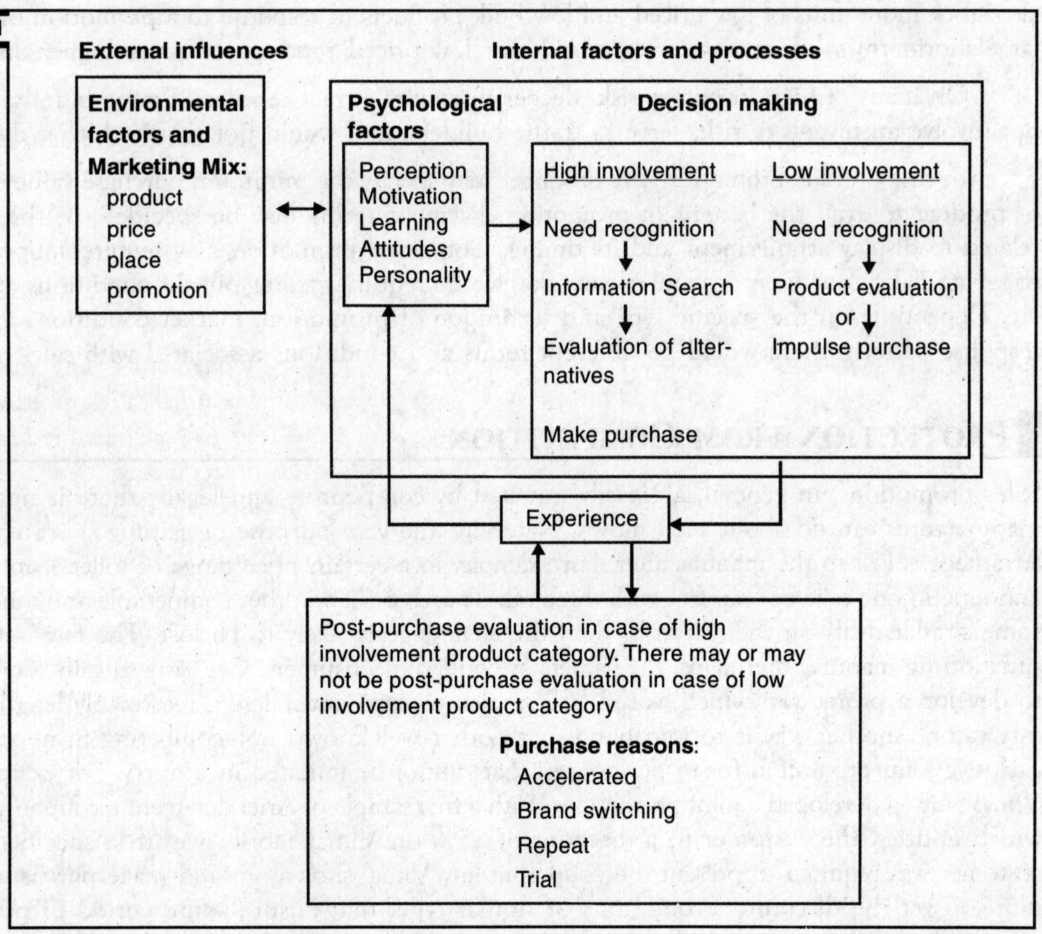

RATE OF DISCOUNT, TERMS AND CONDITIONS

Except for interest promotions, such as contests and sweepstakes, or free samples, where no purchase is involved, marketers offer either a straight price-cut or extra value ("same for less" or "more for the same"). What should be the minimum level of benefit in terms of price-cut or value addition that would attract the attention of the target customers (consumers and re-sellers) 'to induce the desired change in purchase behaviour? Planners have to ascertain the j.n.d. (Weber's Law) and answer this question.

If the proportion of goods which is sold through trade at the list price is low, then the resellers would want a deeper discount to "push" the product. Another aspect to be considered relates to the norms established by other brands in the same product category within a certain price range. If the benefit is far too low compared to what has been the practice, then the desired response is unlikely to be induced.

Except in the event of a clearance sale, the rate of discount on expensive, high-involvement products generally should not be as high as on low-involvement products. A smaller discount figure on high priced products would translate to a high monetary figure and would appear significant enough to attract customer attention and is likely to influence purchase behaviour. In case of low priced products, a higher percentage figure can be associated with the purchase of multiple units of the product (for example, detergent, bras and ready to wear garments), which looks attractive but in real monetary terms would be low. Generally price elasticity of low priced products is high because consumers do not perceive much difference between brands, and do not mind switching to another band. Customers can also stock more units of low priced and low bulk products in response to a promotion offer. To achieve large short-term sales, managers responsible for low priced products consider higher discounts.

On items of high inventory risk, deeper discounts attract re-sellers. Strong brands, in general, do not involve an inventory risk, serve as traffic builders, and would not require higher discounts.

In case of trade promotion, the producer may specify the minimum purchase value or the quantity of product to avail the benefit of promotion. Payment terms may be specified, or the terms may be related to display arrangement and its timing. Consumer promotion may require coupon expiry date, or rebate claim date. Contests and sweepstakes would require spelling out the conditions of participation, etc. Depending on the specific type and technique of promotion, market conditions and consumers response pattern, there would be different terms and conditions associated with sales promotion.

PROTECTION FROM COMPETITION

Sales promotions, in general, are easily imitated by competitors and legally there is nothing that any manufacturer can do about such moves. Naturally, the very purpose of gaining short-term competitive advantage is lost to the manufacturer. For example, in a certain price range of toilet soaps, if a marketer announces "one cake of soap free with three cakes purchase" and other competitors announce the same or some similar deals on their brands, then the advantage is likely to be lost. The fact is that in such a situation no manufacturer gains; the gainers are only the consumers. One way to gain some protection is to develop a promotion which would be complex to copy and allow a reasonably lengthy start to the innovator. Another way is to join hands with other well-known non-competing firms and develop an exclusive joint promotion (tie-in promotion) that cannot be imitated in a hurry. For example, Ariel and Vimal Suiting developed a joint promotion. With a free sample of Ariel detergent a coupon was distributed which entitled the customer to a discount of 15% on Vimal fabrics within a specified period. The customer was required to present the coupon at any Vimal showroom and make purchase of Rs 200 or more to get the discount. Promotions of similar type, that ensure some period of protection from competition, are announced by manufacturers of consumer durable as well as non-durable products. A&M magazine announced an offer on its subscription, those customers who would subscribe for one, two or three years would be entitled for a gift and also would participate in a draw. The participants had a chance of winning a Honda City car, 450 litre refrigerators, air-conditioners, and washing machines from Videocon; LML Vespa Scooter; colour television; holiday package from Club Mahindra, etc. These two examples show that joining with two or more non-competing companies cannot be copied in a hurry.

SUMMARY

Sales promotion aims directly at inducing purchasers to buy a product. It involves demonstrations, contests, prices-off, coupons, free samples, special packaging and money refund offers. Sales promotion activities are designed to encourage resellers and sales people to sell the product. It is different from personal selling and advertising in the sense that is non-recurrent in nature and is for a short period. Sales promotion objectives are consistent with marketing objectives. However, they may vary with the type of target market and points of channels. The objectives for retailers may be to carry new items, encourage off-season buying, offset competitive promotions, build brand loyalty, and so on. Sales promotion alters the market share permanently. It persuades buyers of competitors' product to shift to the product of the company.

PROJECT WORK

1. Collect five advertisements of the industry you are familiar with and analyse the context of its promotional themes.
2. Explain whether personal selling is likely to be the main element with promotional mix for each of the following services?
   a. Kitty parties
   b. Event management

SHORT ANSWER QUESTIONS

1. What are sales promotion objectives?
2. Explain the Dissonance theory.
3. What do you mean by consumer price perceptions?
4. What is the difference between high and low consumer involvement decision?

REVIEW QUESTIONS

1. What is Sales promotion? How is it different from other elements of the promotion mix?
2. What are the objectives of sales promotion?
3. How are conditioning theories useful in defining consumer behaviour towards sales promotion?
4. With contemporary examples, explain how sales promotion can be a source of short-term to medium-term competitive advantage?

GO TO THE NET

Using Internet tools, make a sales promotion programme for a tourist resort. Briefly describe the role you would assign to advertising personal selling, sales promotion and publicity in your campaign.

Caselet

The Indian government has implemented the scheme of Public Distribution System (PDS) for foodgrains and other essential consumer items. The main objectives of this scheme had been to ensure the supplied of the essential consumer items to the 'vulnerable' sections of society. However, it has been found that the scheme has not been very efficient and many of the 'vulnerable' society members could not avail of the services of this distribution system.

The government is now proposing to launch a new Targeted Public Distribution Scheme (TPDS). This scheme shall be particularly targeted at the lowest income consumers. This scheme shall segment the lower and higher segment consumers through separate ration cards and prices for the items sold.

Questions:

1. Suggest the possible marketing reasons for the inefficiencies of the PDS.
2. What marketing actions should be undertaken to ensure the success of TPDS?

CHAPTER

19

sales promotion budget and evaluation

learning objectives

The objectives of this chapter are to:

- understand sales promotion design issues
- describe sales promotion budget
- discuss sales promotion evaluation.

content outline

- Opening Case
- How are Sales Affected by Sales Promotions?
- Sales Promotion Design Issues
- Testing the Sales Promotion
- Types of Promotion
- Guidelines to Planning Sales Promotion
- Development of Promotion Budget
- Summary
- Project Work
- Short Answer Questions
- Review Questions
- Go to the Net
- Caselet

opening case

Sales Incentives

Lucknow Electronics manufactured power generating equipment and were in business for only about five years. They sold directly to consumers as well as through a distribution network. They expanded their sales force to cover a greater part of the market and to expand their activities in the entire country. The objectives were to increase sales revenue by 30% over the previous year.

The marketing manager felt that to achieve these objectives, the salesmen have to be motivated and there is an urgent need of introducing an incentive programme. For this he suggested that the goals be set in consultation with the sales managers. The principle of MBO (Management by Objectives) was suggested. The power generating business was highly competitive and although the company had a fixed price list, the sales managers would tend to ask for reduction in price on the approved list. In deciding whether or not the concessions should be given, a lot of valuable time of the marketing managers was being wasted and he wanted to stop this practice. The only way he could discourage salesmen from asking for concessions was to give them price flexibility (a range of price over which they could quote their clients a price that would win business). There was a danger that the sales people would arbitrarily drop prices to generate more revenue at lower prices and obtain greater incentives as bonus.

The marketing manager, after discussing with sales managers, devised an incentive programme as under:

a. Incentives bonus would only start after the salespersons had achieved 80% of their targets.

b. Although flexible pricing was allowed, but it was to be exercised by the discretion of the salesperson himself in genuine cases.

c. If the goods were sold at the minimum price, the incentive would also be minimised. It would increase in proportion to sales at higher prices.

The marketing manager presented this incentive programme to the sales force expecting enthusiastic support. However, there was no positive response from the sales force.

Try Yourself

1. Do you feel that this incentive programme will achieve the results expected by the marketing manager?
2. Can you suggest an alternative incentive programme to motivate the sales force?
3. Why was there no positive reaction from the sales personnel on the incentive programme?

HOW ARE SALES AFFECTED BY SALES PROMOTIONS?

It is Interesting to explore how sales promotions affect sales. Mostly, it is thought that there are four basic mechanisms involved

1. ***Brand switching:*** The objective of some sales promotions is to induce brand switching, which is encouraging consumers to purchase the promoted brand instead of the regular brand that would have been purchased had there been no sales promotion.
2. ***Repeat buying:*** Sales promotions influence the consumers in a manner that increases the chances of purchasing the same brand again in future.
3. ***Purchasing more, or accelerating timings:*** Consumers purchase more quantity than their immediate requirements, or the purchase timings are changed.
4. ***Increasing category expansion and consumption:*** Consumption of total product category is increased by the consumers as a result of sales promotion.

Brand Switching

Some promotions encourage consumers to buy a different brand than the one that they bought on an earlier purchase occasion, or had the intention of buying now. This type of brand switching is often termed as "aggressive switching". The second type of promotion effect on brand switching considered as "defensive switching". In this case the objective is to retain the customer by encouraging her/him to buy the same brand as was bought on earlier occasion instead of switching to a different brand on this purchase occasion.

The manufacturer's concern is to compete with other similar brands, while the concern of re-seller is to encourage customers to buy from her/his store (not especially the manufacturer's brand). When a retailer promotes, consumers respond by switching stores, that is, they purchase from the store that is promoting instead of the regular store. This store switching would not have happened had the retailer not offered a promotion. It is clear that from the retailer's point of view store switching is more important than brand switching.

Promotions, offering price deals, influence the attitudes of consumers towards buying the brand. Much would depend on the size of the discount and the consumers' sensitivity towards price and how much importance consumers place on price than quality. If the attitude towards the brand has been quite low as compared to some other brands, then a price promotion is likely to encourage a switch to the promoted brand.

Such price promotions may also encourage consumers to buy an otherwise expensive brand, which they could not afford on the normal list price.

Displays at the point-of-purchase may induce brand switching because they serve as conditioned stimuli associated with price promotions (classical conditioning theory). Over a period of time consumers get trained to associate displays with price reductions and respond even when the price reduction is not there.

Both high and low-involvement decision situations provide some explanation. A display shows a low priced, low-involvement product and the consumer buys it because it is convenient. In high-involvement situations, the consumers' search activity may lead to some other brand, which was displayed, and led to purchase. An example would illustrate the point. A customer goes to the market with the intention of buying a Philips colour television. In the dealer's showroom, Thompson brand is displayed prominently and the customer ask the dealer to switch the set on. What the customer sees impresses her/him and the customer buys it.

Consumer's price perception may also have significant effect on brand switching. Say the consumer has a coupon of some value for a certain brand but on reaching the store he sees the 'on sale' sign for another brand. For this brand on sale, the consumer has only slight preference. The extent of price reduction on this brand with slight preference would be influenced by the customer's perceived reference price of that brand. If the disparity is high then the consumer is likely to buy the brand for which she/he has the coupon. Consumers do not completely accept the suggested reference prices and at times they are suspicious of "sale" signs.

If the amount of price reduction is equal, then consumers prefer to use the coupon in switching the brand compared to in-store price reduction, that is, coupons are more effective in inducing brand switching. There is another aspect to coupons. Consumers having a coupon find themselves in a controlling position, with a sense of pride in using the coupon.

If most of the consumers are inclined towards low prices because of economic conditions, the majority of them are assumed to be buying low priced brands. However, if the price on an expensive item is reduced because of promotion, then some consumers from low quality category will switch to the promoted brand. But when the low quality product is promoted, there is no switching because the consumers have been buying the brand without promotion. The consumers from high-income group are unlikely to switch to low priced brand because of promotion and the sales gains would not be there.

Repeat Buying

When a consumer buys a product on promotion, this may lead to developing the habit of purchasing that brand and some evaluation about the performance of the brand. It may also happen that since the brand is purchased on promotion the consumer's attitude toward the brand weakens and the probability of purchase in future declines. Repeat purchase may result because of habit formation that may develop because the brand is bought more than once due to sales promotion. Much depends on the satisfaction of the consumer with the brand purchased on promotion. For example, if a customer purchased Godrej refrigerator on promotion and was satisfied, it is very likely that next time when the need arises, the customer would purchase the same brand again on promotion, or other products of the same manufacturer when available on promotion. Instrumental conditioning (operant conditioning) views sales promotion as rewards and the consumer learns to continue buying the product. However, the nature of reward may have a significant effect on behaviour reinforcement. The reward should be strong enough to encourage and reinforce the purchase behaviour to sustain it.

Repeat purchasing is often the result of habit formation and learning. Sales promotions stimulate the consumers to buy a product and this becomes the first step towards establishing a habit. Another route is not to allow the brand user to shift to some other brand by rewarding and reinforcing the already established behaviour.

In case of low-involvement products, habit plays an important role. Since the consumer does not want to devote much time to thinking and pre-purchase evaluation in making a purchase decision, habit helps the customer avoid any cognitive effort and helps as a simple and convenient way to decide which brand to purchase.

In case of high-involvement products, it is assumed that learning takes place when the consumer experiences the actual performance of the product and makes an evaluation. A favourable evaluation is likely to help sustain the habit. In some cases, even consumers with low-involvement often make evaluations that may have repercussions with regard to developing the habit.

Purchasing More, or Accelerating Timing

Purchasing more and accelerating timing refers to those situations when consumers buy more than their immediate requirement or change their purchase timing as a result of promotions. When resellers buy more than their normal requirement, it is called "forward buying". Building excessive inventories in this manner often leads to stock diversion in non-deal areas. Another important repercussion of this purchase bahaviour is that it merely shifts the purchases, which would have occurred anyway. For example, if a consumer buys more than the immediate requirements, than in the next purchase period he will buy less or abstain from buying. For example if the consumer buys the refrigerator now, though the intention was to buy after two months, this is purchase acceleration. Another effect of promotion can be that consumers who have bought in excess of their requirements should be out of the market. Similar would be the case when the retailers' shelves are full. This can help in preventing brand switching and, in some cases, increase consumption of the product (such as Maggi noodles or similar products).

The reverse may also be true in certain situations, that is, negative acceleration when the consumers buy less or decide to purchase later rather than now. This may happen when the sales promotion stimulates brand switching. The consumer wants to try the product and buys a smaller quantity to reduce the risk associated with using something new. The consumer may also postpone the purchase of a product because she/he learns from some source about the forthcoming sales promotion, or anticipates it.

Increasing Category Expansion and Consumption

Sales promotions are likely to stimulate demand by creating new occasions for purchase, or by increasing the consumption rate of consumers. In certain situations, the purchase of a product category gets accelerated.

Sales promotion, such as displays, can create new purchase occasions by reminding the customer that the displayed product is good for growing children (protein biscuits). Other products, for example noodles or potato chips, purchased on promotion in multiple units, can increase the consumption rate, which is often the objective of many promotions. One example can be of condensed milk, 'Milkmaid'. An attractive display of this brand is arranged and a free recipe book is given on purchase of two packs. This is quite likely to increase the rate of consumption of this product, as consumers will be tempted to try different recipes.

In cases of many high-involvement products, promotions can help consumers to realise that a certain product would serve as a good gift item (a silk sari, camera, Rayban sunglasses, etc.). In some cases, there is a certain price limit beyond which the customer would not buy a product, however, since a price promotion offer lowers the price of the product below the customer's price limit, a purchase occasion is created. Many customers buy autos when available on promotion, such as interest free installments, which otherwise they are not in a position to buy on down payment. Of late, this is happening in case of almost all known brands of computers.

Observations made in the market place point to the likelihood that brand switching, repeat purchasing, purchase acceleration and consumption, all occur simultaneously. The net result, however, is that sales promotions work.

SALES PROMOTION DESIGN ISSUES

There are a number of internal and external factors that influence sales promotions design. These factors include (1) place of sales promotion in marketing strategy (2) allocation of budget (3) present and expected competitive moves and (4) significant external macro environmental factors. The starting point in developing the promotional design is to specify the sales promotion objectives. The range of sales promotion objective is fairly large because the target groups involved can be consumers, trade and sales force. In general, managers do not face any difficulty in deciding the appropriate sales promotion objective, however, the confusion often may arise in determining what type of promotion will best produce the desired result, and this is a key decision area concerning the promotion design that must be taken up one after the other, in a sequential manner.

1. Promotion Choice

There are different types of promotions that can be used, singly, or in combination :

a. Consumer promotion

b. Trade promotion, and

c. Sales force promotion.

There are two major approaches for consumer and trade promotions:

1. Same for less, and
2. More for the same

The type of promotions for consumers and the trade can be usefully put under two headings– immediate value offer vs delayed value offer, and price-cut vs extra value offer.

Immediate Value Offer vs Delayed Value Offer

In case of sales promotions that offer immediate value to consumers or re-sellers, incentive is offered right at the time of purchase, include discount, extra goods, or a premium. In contrast, delayed value offers, such as a rebates, contests and sweepstakes, frequent flier offer, after making multiple purchases, and at the year end on target completion. Promotions that reward the buyer at the time of purchase produce a stronger impact and stimulate customers for unplanned purchases and encourage brand switching at the point-of-purchase. In case of low priced products, or brands having no significant feature or quality differences, or products purchased frequently and consumed on regular basis, such promotions can lead to significant brand switching. For example, there is significant brand switching in toiletries, laundry products, soft drinks, and cooking oils, etc.

Delayed value offers produce a weaker response, compared to immediate value offers, because the reward is not at the time of purchase. However, the effect of delayed value offers is longer lasting. When a customer is required to collect proof of multiple purchases, the product sold to a single customer is more in quantity or number. Every time the customer makes a purchase, there is a reminder of the product, and the customer is also exposed to longer duration of product usage. These promotions are often used to reinforce and reward the loyalty of regular users of the product.

Price Cut vs Extra Value Offer

One important feature of sales promotion is that there is an incentive associated with purchase of the product or service. In some cases of sales promotion, even purchase of anything may not be required, such as some type of contest or sweepstakes. However, the participants in these contests sweepstakes have a chance of winning some prizes. So, every sales promotion always may not involve a purchase, but an incentive may still be there. The manufacturer or retailer may offer "same for less" in the form of a price discount on the promoted product. On the other hand, there could be an offer of extra value, which would be "more for the same". For example, a special bonus-pack that contains more quantity of the same product without any increase in price, or a premium offered free with the purchased product. This extra value offered is independent of the promoted product and has more value to the customer than the cost to the marketer. For instance, there are many such offers these days on the purchase of almost all branded computers available in the market. Some are offering a printer, while others are offering valuable software, all free of cost. Such premiums can be quite helpful in building the long-term brand strength of certain brands. Consumer promotions, which frequently offer price cut, or extra quantity of the same product, generally degrade the perceived value of the brand and may weaken its brand strength. For brands having smaller market share, large price-cuts are required to make the offer appear attractive to customers.

Manufacturers of high-involvement products prefer not to offer straight price discounts because this approach may disrupt the price-quality perception of customers who may develop some negative evaluation of the product. Straight price reductions may be used only if this type of promotion is common to the category. For instance, this practice is fairly common in India among marketers in the electronic entertainment industry. In the international market, manufacturers of mass-market cameras that require particular type of film are using this type of promotion. In general, these price-cuts are limited to low-end products in a product-line and prove to be more effective. A variety of "more for the same" or extra-value promotions can be used for expensive high-involvement products. For example, some computer manufacturers are adding accessories in their offer, such as printer, modem, useful software, etc. Camera manufacturers can offer added value by offering consumables, such as films, or accessories, such as flash, lens, or extended warranty. Bundling of accessories along with the core product in consumer promotion encourages them to buy more than the core product at the time of purchase, increasing the total value of sales on items for which the consumers infrequently visit the market. Bundling accessories with the core product also helps consumers in decision making.

In case of low-involvement products, major portion of sales promotion budget is allocated to rewarding the consumers at the time of purchase by cutting the price or offering extra quantity of the product (immediate value offer). This is especially true if the product category is susceptible to unplanned or impulse buying and variety seeking; offers that encourage consumers to buy multiple units continue promotions, such as in-pack or on-pack coupons; and interest promotions that excite consumers, such contests and sweepstakes.

Sales promotions of strong brands are generally of the type, "more for the same price". Promotion offers of added value to consumers, such as bonus-packs, encourage increased usage by consumers. The same would not be the case if the offer is "same for less" (price reduction) because this is likely to focus the attention of consumers on price of the product. Weak brands have to emphasize trade promotions to gain "push" and maintain distribution.

2. Product Choice

This step focuses on choosing the products for sales promotion, their pack sizes, or models, and different variations of the product, etc. For example Hindustan Lever Limited markets many brands of toilet soaps and detergents. VIP bags are available in different sizes, quality and price range.

Sales promotion planners have to decide whether to run promotions on the entire product-line, or only selected items in the line? Should the promotions be run on higher priced or lower-priced products, the products that contribute more to the sales or those that contribute less? In case of consumer non-durable products, would it be advantageous to come out with special promotion packs, or the promotion should be run on regular packs ? Answers to these questions are likely to be significantly influenced by taking into account consumer and trade behaviour, competitive situation and coordination with advertising and personal selling.

Re-sellers' are concerned about the inventory risk associated with stocking or not stocking the product on promotion. If they are out-of-stocks, then there is an opportunity cost, and if residual stocks are left, they cannot be sold on list price to consumers, then the traders are concerned with lost margins. Inventory risk is higher for many reasons, such as, when the consumer demand for the product is unpredictable, when the inventory holding costs are high, when the product is seasonal, when the product is likely to go out of fashion quickly, and when the producer does not agree to accept unsold stocks. Manufacturers of high inventory risk items generally promote the more popular items during the peak period of consumer demand.

Inventory risk is less severe or milder if the manufacturer has more control on distribution channel, as in the case of exclusive distribution, or when the delivery is direct to the store.

This gives the marketer access to more control and the inventory can be managed more accurately to minimize risks with over or under stocks.

Some brands enjoy high awareness and loyalty. These brands may have a dominant share in the product category and their sales may be growing. These factors are important to the trade because they contribute to high sales turnover, profits and the image of the store, more so if the intensity of competition is low. Traders view such brands as good traffic builders and they do not hesitate in allocating advantageous shelf placing to such brands. In promoting such strong brands, it is preferable to offer price discount to traders, as they are more likely to pass through part of the benefit to the consumers. If price cuts are offered in the form of coupons to consumers, it is advantageous to mail coupons to non-users rather than existing users.

Brands, which are weak, do not have many options. Promotions requiring trade "push" are generally not available for such brands. A higher percentage of promotion budgets goes to price-deals for consumers to reward them immediately at the time of purchase to create any impact. It is a good idea to go for tie-in promotion with a strong brand that can attract greater consumer and trade attention. Sales force is also unlikely to pay much attention to weak brands unless they are offered some incentive (sales force promotion).

3. Choice of Market Areas

Promotion planners have the option to select national or regional markets. When promotion programmes are developed for regional markets, they provide some degree of protection from competitive moves. However, developing different regional promotional deals can complicate sales forecasting, production scheduling and physical distribution; this may also lead to cost escalation.

As already mentioned, strong brand are good traffic builders, however, they are promoted generally infrequently. When such brands are inexpensive and low bulk to transport and store, such as a popular toothpaste, toilet soap, or detergent, etc., there is considerable forward buying and diversion in non-deal areas by the trade. In such situations, it is advisable to avoid differences in timing of the promotions in different regions or states. Sales promotions of similar value should be announced at the same time everywhere.

In case of strong high-involvement category brands, such as computers or entertainment electronics, etc., promotion managers should observe caution about deal variations in different regions on nationally distributed brands (if these brands are sold through national chain stores, or the dealers are having their branches in different cities or states). In case of expensive products, such as cars, the customers may do their own diverting by reaching those places or outlets where they can buy at the lowest possible prices. Some years ago there was a car mela (fair) in the city of Gwalior every year and the reduction in car prices used to be in excess of Rs 5000 compared to the regular prices. Large number of customers visited the mela and purchased cars by paying less than what the prices were in places where they came from. In case of low-involvement products, diverting to non-deal markets is the domain of traders.

Higher inventory risk would require that promotions be developed for separate markets. Excess product stocks from one market can be shifted to another market where the sales potential is more.

4. Promotion Timing, Duration and Frequency

When the product or brand inventories are less than normal in trade channels, the objective of the promotion would be to build inventories, but when the inventories with the traders are high then the objective would be to clear the inventories. It is inadvisable for the producer to announce a promotion when the retailer shelves are full with the competitive brand because the promotion is quite likely to prove unprofitable. If the product use is linked to weather conditions (such as creams and lotions used during winters to protect skin from dryness or woolens etc.), then it would affect the consumer demand and hence the timing of promotion.

Ideally, some manufacturers plan their promotions when annual marketing plans are developed. However, sometimes marketers face compulsions like unexpected moves by competitors (for example, when there is reliable information that a competitor is ready to introduce a new competing product), or when excessive inventories pile up due to unexpected slow sales. As promotions grow in complexity and creativity, and producers desire more support from trade, trade cooperation in planning becomes more important.

How long should a particular sales promotion last ? There are no precise answers to this question. The duration of consumer promotion should be such that a larger percentage of customers get exposed to the promotion offer. In case of some product categories, interval between two successive purchases may give an idea about the duration. Low-involvement products are usually purchased more frequently and hence the duration of the deal for this category can be shorter.

In case of high-involvement category products, to induce a sense of urgency, the duration of the offer can be short. To attract the second wave of customers, it may prove to be advantageous to announce an extension of the deal period (sales promotion by A&M magazine was extended more than once in the recent past). If the brand is weak, then the deal period usually is longer.

Frequency of promotion depends on competitive situation, deal sensitivity of customers, the interest of the trade, and the complexity of the promotion offer. Very frequent promotions of high-involvement category product may create negative impressions about the quality and price relationship of the product. However, if the high-involvement purchases relate to "think" category, such as real estate, then promotions are unlikely to have any impact on price quality relationship.

For low-value, low-involvement products, deals are quite common in different product categories and are frequently used by some marketers. Trade deals often become necessary to motivate dealers to arrange displays and participate in contests.

figure 19.1 Promotion Planning Process

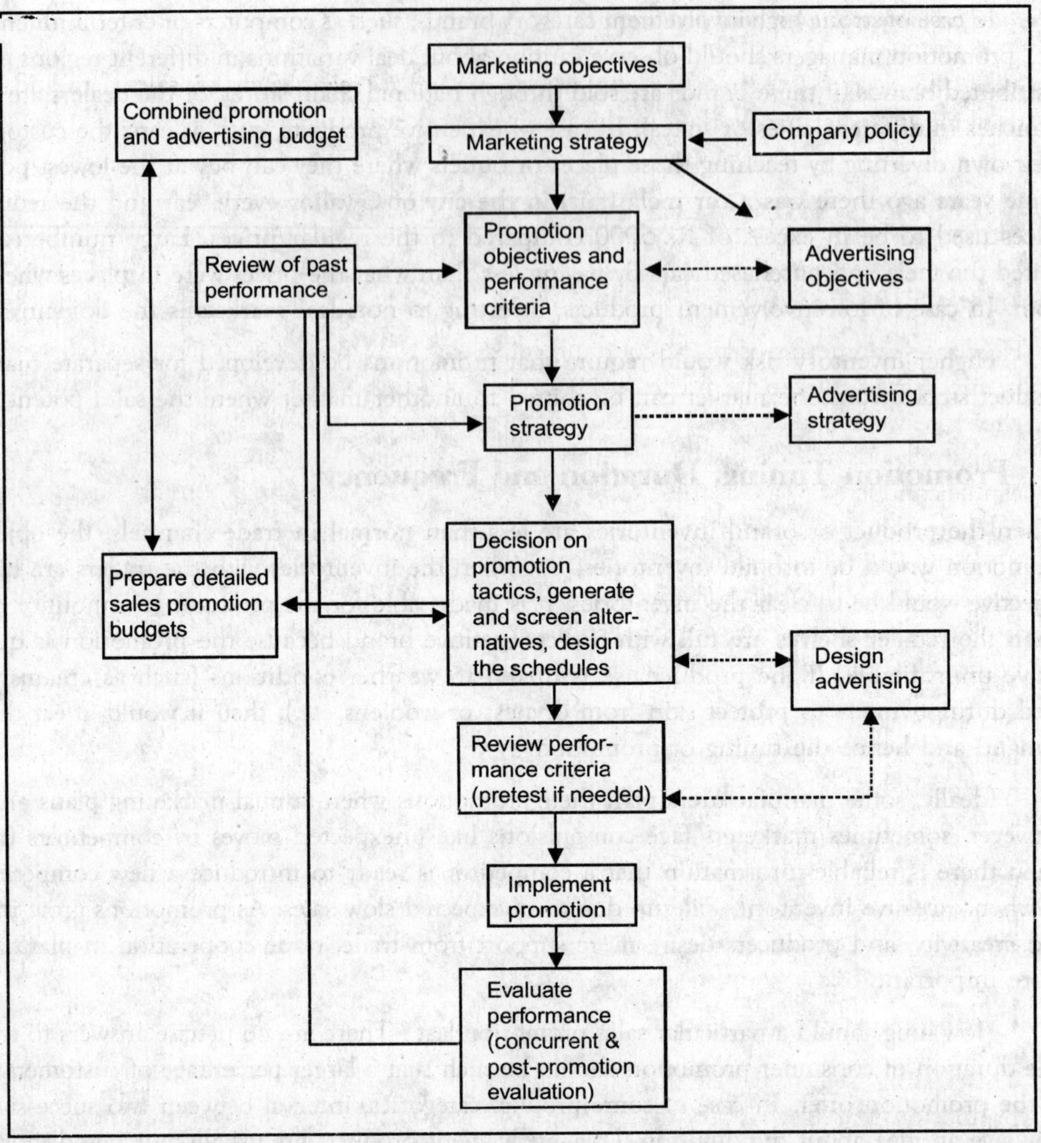

Measurement of results in any area of business activity is related to the objectives that are set. To accomplish this, a set of evaluation criteria is laid down before the implementation of a sales promotion programme. Measuring the success, or otherwise, of sales promotion can pose some difficulties because the nature and variety of objectives. In the topic "Sales Promotion Objectives" (Chapter 18), it has been pointed out that sales promotion objectives can be either proactive or reactive. A number of these objective are directly related to sales. In all cases, the measurement does not pose any complexity and the sales based techniques can be used with relative ease. For instance, it is quite easy to measure the sales effect before, during and after the sales promotion. In case of objective not related to sales, such as trial purchase, or change in consumer awareness and attitude as a result of increase in perceived value of the product, measurement is more difficult. In certain types of promotion, the re-seller support is important and can have significant effect on marketer's promotion performance.

In general, marketers can use sales data, experiments and consumer surveys to evaluate promotion progress and results. Promotion managers are generally reluctant to use experiments because in many cases of promotions there is only a short lead-time. Experiments also involve the risk that competitors would be alerted. For these reasons, managers tend to rely heavily on sales data and experience. The thinking is, "what has worked in the past will work again".

TESTING THE SALES PROMOTION

Pre-testing

How sales promotion is to be communicated and what would be communicated to the target groups is important and can be pre-tested. For example, the pre-test may find out what is likely to be the perceived value and the risk. A customer considers whether it would be wise to buy an unknown brand of sports goods at 45% discount. Is this offer worth the risk of buying an unfamiliar brand? The pre-test can be conducted to assess these factors by using 'focus groups and consumer panels'. Another approach, ballot method, consists of mailing a ballot paper to a list of consumers. They are requested to evaluate different illustrated promotions and vote for the most likely and return the ballot to the firm. A relatively expensive but more accurate method is portfolio test in which a portfolio of sales promotion is prepared and shown to consumers in person and their responses are noted. Other methods that can be used are jury method and mall intercept.

To test consumers behavioural response, such as trial purchase, or repeat purchase, etc., pre-testing consists of experimenting in certain markets or individual stores in a market. All other factors remain the same, only the sales promotion device being tested in the variable is manipulated.

It is often quite helpful to evaluate the response of re-sellers before implementing the promotions programme. The simplest way is to visit several important retailers and wholesalers and discuss the programme and seek their opinion and suggestions. This may prove to be quite favourable in case the support of re-sellers is considered to be of paramount importance for promotion results.

Concurrent Testing

This testing is done when the sales promotion is in progress. Concurrent testing may permit the promotion manager to modify the sales promotion, if needed. This type of testing is conducted in terms of sales data, which can be obtained on a weekly or monthly basis. If the promotion is a consumer contest and the consumer is not required to purchase anything, the response to the promotion can be adjudged by the number of entries received at some interval, and if need be the contest period can be extended. In case of coupon distribution programme, similar approach can be adopted by keeping a track of coupons redeemed.

Post-testing

Post-testing is done after the promotion period is over. To assess the change in consumer awareness and attitude, telephone calls, questionnaires mailed to consumers and personal interviews can be used. In these methods, the most expensive is the personal interview method and least expensive is the mail. The information sought pertains to the promotion event. In case of samples or premiums distributed through retail stores, intercept interviews at the point-of sale can reveal more reliable information.

To measure the sales effect, sales figures before the promotion period can be compared with figures at the end of the promotion, and one month after the promotion ends. If the promotion objective was to increase sales by 30% in a certain period and the pre-promotion sales for a similar period were worth five million rupees and the sales jumped to in excess of 5.6 million in the promotion period, this would show that the objective was achieved. It is very likely that in the ensuing month after the promotion, the sales will come down to, say 3.5 million rupees. If the sales return to five million rupees in the long run, then perhaps the sales jump was because of brand switchers and deal prone consumers. However, if the regular sales settle at 5.5 million rupees in the long run, then definitely the promotion proved successful in increasing the long run sales by attracting new customers, and may have also attracted customers away from other competing brands.

figure 19.2

Post-Testing Sales Effect

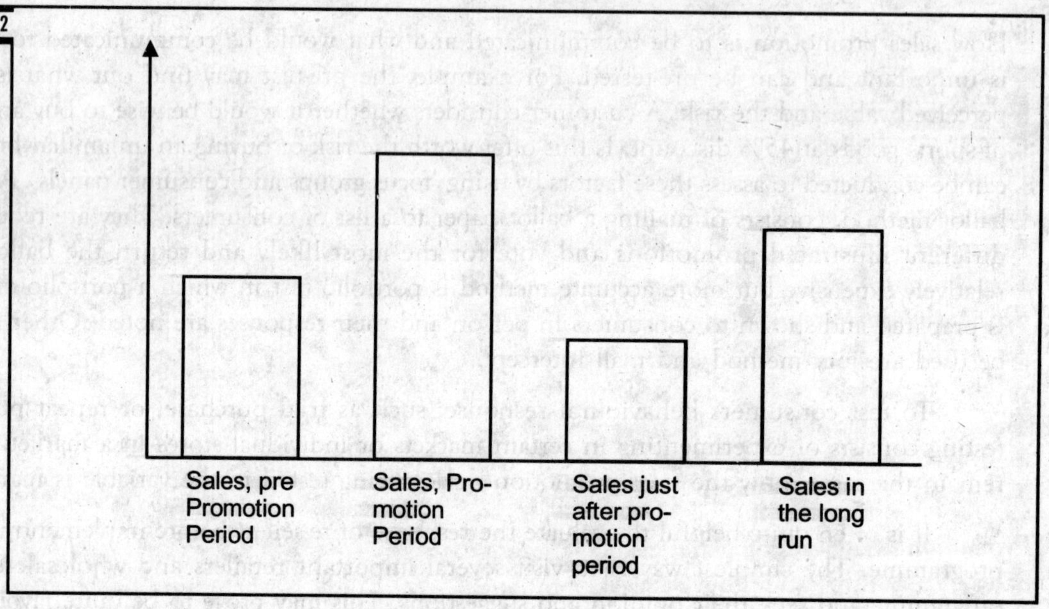

Example

In case of consumer durable goods promotion, the following evaluation method can be used before implementing the promotion :

M = amount of money spent on advertising

N = average number of units sold without sales promotion

P = number of product units expected to be sold if promotion is implemented

S = gross margin per unit in Rs

D = size of discount per unit in Rs

Profit without promotion will – NS

profit, with promotion will be – P (S – D) – M

In order to break-even or do better with promotion, we set and solve for P/N, yielding –P (S – D) – M ≥ NS

$$P/N \geq \left(1+\frac{M}{NS}\right)\left(\frac{S}{S\text{-}D}\right)$$

For example presume that normal sales were 4000 units, and margin of each unit is Rs 200. The Marketer offered Rs 50 per unit discount to dealers and decided to spend Rs 800,000 in advertising then

$$\frac{P}{N} = \frac{P}{4000}\left(1+\frac{800.000}{(48000000)}\right)\left(\frac{200}{200-50}\right)=1.50$$

For the sales promotion to be profitable, the marketer would have to sell 6000 units, instead of 4000 units, which are the normal sales without promotion. This amounts to an increase of 50% in sales. For some reason if this is not feasible, the marketers can reduce the advertising expenditure, or the discount rate, or both. (Adapted, with changes from John A. Quelch, *Sales Promotion Management*, Prentice-Hall. 1989).

TYPES OF PROMOTION

Promotion stands for personal selling, advertising, promotion mix., and customers relations. Personal Selling involves direct selling. In it there is face-to-face contact between firm and their respective customers. Advertising is form of "bulk selling" or communication to large numbers of customers instantaneously. Sales Promotion have some to specific activities (such as point-of-purchase displays, brochures, coupons) which can generate particular buying behaviour. Customer Relations is any free form of "bulk selling." All of these methods try to inform, persuade and remind the target large no. of audience about your product or service. They are complementary to each other and should be integrated with your profit. There are some other different forms of these types of promotion such as broadcasting, printing, direct mail and electronic devices advertising that offer many advantages, disadvantages, costs and paybacks. The similar message may be evaluated based on the source of the message in terms of reliability.

Promotion Mix Decision: There is no any unique promotion mix (between Personal Selling, Advertising, Sales Promotion, and Public Relations) for all situations. The promotion mix for your company should be designed to fulfil your overall objectives. The specific mix depends on a number of factors, including (1) the budget of the promotion mix., (2) Different stages of a particular product of its life cycle, (3) nature of the complicated situation, (4) the customers, and (5) the characteristics of the product.

Push, Pull or Push-Pull Strategy? There are three basic promotional strategies or philosophies push, pull or push-pull. A company that follows a push strategy is specifically sales-oriented, trying to push the product through the allotment of different channels. A pull strategy is generally a very marketing-oriented company that would spend all their marketing funds on advertising to pull the product through the distribution channel. A push-pull strategy is that where the company may spend upto 50% on trade promotion and 50% on end-user advertising Promotion is a critical factor in any marketing mix. To be successful you must offer a good product or service at a adequate price, and you must tell customer about the features of the product. Deciding the right promotional mix is obviously difficult task decision making process. It requires proper judgment and experience in the respective types of organization. You must consider the industry, the customer and your competition.

GUIDELINES TO PLANNING SALES PROMOTION

Planning process starts with situation analysis. To start with, the promotion planners must first consider the corporate policy with regard to sales promotion. The policy may exist in written form or may be part of the top management's attitude towards sales promotions as followed over the years. Joseph S Mair has recorded one such policy statement in *Handbook of Sales Promotion*, ed. Stanley M. Ulanoff, p.43. The policy was

1. "Sales promotion is an integral part of the marketing mix".
2. "Sales promotion should be used as an offensive weapon in the brand's marketing arsenal. Promotion should be used as a defensive reaction when a problem arises".
3. "Sales promotion should extend and reinforce the brand's advertising and positioning, whenever possible".
4. "Sales promotion should be developed as campaigns, not as single, unrelated events".
5. "Good sales promotions are built upon sound strategic planning".

These five policy statement concerning sales promotion do not appear to be harmful in any way; however, not many business houses share these views. Some companies believe that sales promotion is an unavoidable and costly evil to business. If possible, it should be avoided, or used as a defensive technique to attract particularly those who are brand switchers. In most organisations, advertising is thought as having better status than sales promotion because it builds the brand company image. (Recall the statement made by David Ogilvy in Chapter 1). Possibly the most widely accepted view about sales promotion is that it cannot build long-term brand following. In spite of these diverse views, company philosophy towards sales promotion affects the objective setting and the criteria for evaluation. For instance, it is only in the last few years that an increasing number of sales promotions are being observed in consumer durable and service industries. And since the company philosophies are formed gradually, based on experience or belief, it is quite in the nature of things that perhaps, there is no accepted philosophy on sales promotions in these companies.

In post-independence India, pharmaceutical industry has been using sales promotion as a regular feature and many companies, in their annual marketing plans, include sales promotion as an integral part.

Economies which are developing and where competition of some intensity has started in consumer goods and service industries, the companies may not have any definite policy towards sales promotion. Sales promotions may be purely in response to immediate business situations.

The first step in promotion planning is situation analysis. This would include product or brand performance analysis, competitive situation including the promotion activities of major competitors, distribution situation and consumer behaviour with respect to sales promotions. Political/legal aspects concerning sales promotion are also considered. The analysis would reveal possible opportunities and problems that the firm would like to address to. Based on marketing objectives and strategies, the promotion objectives would be developed and should be put into writing, along with the evaluation criteria. It is critically important to set unambiguous and measurable objectives, such as by stating the desired sales volume, market share, profitability, product trial among non-users, or inventory clearance, etc. In view of integrated marketing communication philosophy, sales promotion should not be developed in isolation from advertising or other promotion mix elements. The next step would be the allocation of budget to sales promotion, out of the combined total budget for advertising and sales promotion. In a multi-product company, individual product or brand managers may have to negotiate among themselves and reach a compromise about the budget and promotion slots. Promotion plans by most companies are generally prepared covering a period of two or three years. Managers often face difficulty in deciding about the type of sales promotion most suitable in a certain situation, or what combination of promotion techniques they should use to accomplish the desired objectives. Considering the objectives and the budget allocation, each promotion event must be carefully created. There is vast choice of promotion tools, and the combinations of these tools seem to be endless. Each sales promotion tool has its own advantages and disadvantages, and these may change when different tools are combined. A clear understanding of various tools and techniques is essential for the planners to make the winning choice from among alternatives.

The subsequent steps relate to sales promotion design issues (for a detailed analysis, the reader should refer to the second topic in this chapter). As already pointed out, there are six steps that focus only on the design issues of sales promotion. The managers should address each step one at a time and in a sequence. Answers to the following questions, duly considered, would be of immense help in creating a powerful promotion

A. Promotion Choice

- What promotion to use ? There are three types to choose from – trade promotion, consumer promotion, and sales force promotion. Each has a different potential and can be used to accomplish different objectives, alone or in combination of "pull-push".
- Should the promotion be "same for less", or "more for the same", an "immediate value" or "delayed value?" Should a combination of these be developed to accomplish the desired objectives ?

B. Product Choice

- Which product candidates, and what pack sizes, or models should be chosen to promote? Should we choose a high or low-priced brand ? What would be the effect on brand and company image ?

C. Choice of Market Areas

- Should the promotion be for regional markets ? Or the total national market?

D. Promotion timing, duration and frequency

- What should be the timing of promotion (when the trade inventories are low or, when the inventories are high)? How long should the promotion last? How often to promote?

E. Rate of discount, terms and conditions

- What should be the rate of discount ? What would the terms and conditions for participation, prizes, or premiums, etc.

F. Protection from Competition

- Is competition proofing required ? What strategies will be used ?

Answers to these questions would lead to the final shape of the promotion design. In many cases of contests sweepstakes, lotteries and premiums, permission from the sanctioning authority is needed. In India, before a consumer contest can be offered, permission from the Licensing Authority of the state is required. With the amendment of MRTP Act, and incorporation of Unfair Trade Practices therein, the sponsor must ensure that their sales promotions do not violate the provisions of the Act.

table 19.1 **Some Important Objectives and Suitable Promotional Types**

Objectives	Types of Promotion
Increase market share among brand switchers, or increase sales	Coupons in print media, coupons to other brand users, retail promotions, discounts, sweepstakes and contest premiums
Increase repeat-purchase	Continuity promotions, in-pack coupons
Increase trial among non-users	Free samples, trial packs, cross-couponing
Increase category consumption	Multiple-pack promotion coupons
Liquidate excessive inventories	Various trade deals.

DEVELOPMENT OF PROMOTION BUDGET

Marketing is often listed as a unique item on a business expenses. This may define that expenses for marketing process are easily categorize. To the contrary, marketing is one of the most important and complicated tool for planning and running a business. Marketing is often referred to as a "necessary evil" for a business. Without it, sales will likely struggle and with it can come significant costs. Sometimes marketing expenditures are needed just to insure product awareness and to stay even with the competition rather than greatly expanding sales. Marketing experts often prefer to consider expenses for marketing as investments rather than expenses because successful marketing efforts will increase sales. Marketing may be defined as the process of selling, purchasing or sending goods into a market. Marketing is often thought of as any or all of the functions involved in transferring title and moving goods from producer to consumer including buying selling, storing, transporting, standardizing, financing, risk bearing and supplying marketing information. The American Marketing Association's official definition of marketing provides a good working definition of the term. "Marketing is the process of planning and executing the conception, pricing, promotion and distribution of ideas, goods, and services to create exchanges that satisfy individual organizational objectives." Simplistically, marketing can be thought of planning and executing a set of objectives related to bringing buyers and sellers together so that a sale can take place. Marketing a product takes planning to be successful. The marketing plan is a process that identifies the steps necessary to implement a successful marketing strategy. Promotion, on the other hand, may be considered activities that are specifically aimed at advancing, increasing and boosting awareness, interest or sales. Because marketing can be such a complex issue in the management of a business, it should not be dealt with lightly. In fact, a thorough understanding of marketing and promotion options should be one of the first steps in the evaluation of a new business or enterprise. Once this understanding is gained, promotion options should be narrowed to those best suited for a particular project. Then, a promotional campaign should be planned. While a marketing budget is a listing of all the expenses planned for marketing a promotional budget is the part of the overall marketing efforts devoted specifically to promotion. Because marketing is more than advertising, a marketing budget should include expenses for marketing personnel, marketing training, marketing consultants, market research, market development and promotion. A promotion budget should include expenses for marketing personnel, marketing training, marketing consultation promotion. A promotional budget should include those expenses for promotional activities such as advertisements, brochures, direct mailings, samples, trades shows, displays and sponsorships. A promotional budget can be prepared by allocating a certain amount of expected sales to promotion activities or by planning certain promotion activities and allocating expenses for them. A promotion budget should be developed at the beginning of the year. For the existing business, a good place to start is using the past year's expenses. Additional promotional costs can then be included based on any new promotional strategies that are to be implemented in the upcoming year.

Promotion can be defined as any method that communicates to the target market about the right product to be sold in the right place at the right price. What the marketing manager communicates is basically determined when the target customers' needs and preferences are known. How the information is communicated in order to obtain action - a purchase - depends on a number of factors.

SUMMARY

Some promotions encourage consumers to buy a different brand than the one they bought on earlier purchase occasion, or had the intention of buying now. Promotions that offer price deals influence the attitudes of consumers toward buying the brand. Sales promotions are likely to stimulate demand by creating new occasions for purchase, or by increasing the consumption rate by consumers. In certain situations, the purchase of a product category gets accelerated. Measurement of results in any area of business activity is related to the objectives that are set. To accomplish this, a set of evaluation criteria is laid down before the implementation of a sales promotion programme.

PROJECT WORK

Collect literature on sales promotion methods used by various service providers and make a comparative assessment.

SHORT ANSWER QUESTIONS

1. How are sales affected by sales promotion?
2. What is sales promotion budget?
3. What are sales promotion design issues?
4. What do you mean by promotion choice?
5. What are the different types of promotion?

REVIEW QUESTIONS

1. What are the different types of sales promotion ? Illustrate with examples.
2. "Regional promotions often create problems for markets." Comment and substantiate with examples.
3. How does the marketer determine upon issues of timing, frequency and duration of promotion?
4. What are the methods of measuring the effectiveness of sales promotion?
5. Suggest suitable sales promotion strategies for different stages of the PLC to a marketer offering:
    i. Herbal shampoo
    ii. Photocopier
    iii. Computer software for accounting purpose
    iv. Holidays in a village resort.
6. Explain push pull strategy with the help of suitable corporate example.

GO TO THE NET

Using Internet resources study the following organisations about sales promotion techniques

a. CRY

b. Help Age India

c. World Vision

Using Internet search tools prepare a report on different types of promotion mix with the help of any 10 companies.

Caselet

A small scale manufacturer of consumer durables who has spent years with a reputed overseas manufacturer of similar products and who is a technocrat, wishes to introduce a complete range of kitchen appliances in the domestic market. The company does not have its own sales offices and as such depends on Distribution/Dealers for its entire marketing effort. The first product he has identified is a Microwave Oven for which he has obtained ISI certification and is the only brand to get that. The product is reasonably priced but the brand has little or no market awareness. His friend who is assisting him with the marketing effort feels the trade holds the key to their being able to establish their brand in the market. They turn to you for help-what advice you give him? Substantiate your recommendations.

C H A P T E R 20

types and techniques of sales promotion

learning objectives

The objectives of this chapter are to:

- understand various sales promotion schemes
- describe advantages and disadvantages of various schemes
- discuss examples of sales promotion.

content outline

- Opening Case
- Types of Sales Promotions
- Sales Promotions – Tools and Techniques
- Performance Criteria
- Price Deals
- Consumer Sales Promotion
- Refunds and Rebates
- Coupons
- Contests and Sweepstakes
- Premiums
- In-pack, On-pack and Container Premiums
- Free-in-Mail Premiums
- Summary
- Project Work
- Short Answer Questions
- Review Questions
- Go to the Net
- Caselet

opening case

Sales Promotion Scheme

(Advertised in the Times of India, *A&M* Special Subscription Offer dated 7th October, 1998)

Introduction

A&M, one of the leading Indian magazines in the field of marketing and advertising, has recently launched a sales promotion scheme to give the much required boost to sales. The sales promotion scheme is advertised in the print media i.e. newspaper (TOI).

About the Scheme

The scheme is an attractive subscription offer launched for the purpose of increasing the readership of *A&M*. The scheme offers heavy discount on the subscription rates of the magazine for the periods of 1, 3 and 5 years. Not only this, the scheme also offers free gifts with subscription of 3 and 5 years duration. The free gifts include a Videocon Digital Organiser with a 5-year subscription and a Braun Pocket Shaver with a 3-year subscription. The details are as follows

Subscription Term	No. of Issues	Newsstand Price @ Rs 50	You Pay Rs	Effective Saving	Plus Free Gift
5 years	120	6000	1995	66%	Videocon Digital Diary
3 years	72	3500	1395	61%	Braun Pocket Shaver
1 year	24	1200	695	42%	–

Highlights of the scheme are

- 25 early bird prizes of Videocon KT 3113 walkies.
- Fabulous prizes to be won by a lucky draw of all the new subscribers. The prizes include a Honda City car, Holiday packages to Goa and Mussoorie, Videocon refrigerators, washing machine, air conditioner, Toshiba colour TV, LML scooters and Kenwood car music systems.
- The scheme also offers flexibility in the mode of payment for the subscription. The payment is accepted either in the form of cheques, demand drafts or credit cards. The delivery of the first issue is on receiving the subscription form.

Why to Launch Scheme?

The main reasons behind launching of the scheme is to boost the sales of the magazines and to increase its readership. The magazine's owners, Spectrum (India) Limited, thought of introducing a special subscription offer for *A&M*. They realize that the customers would prefer to subscribe to an expensive magazine if an attractive offer is placed in front of them.

Secondly, its nearest rivals — *Business Today*, *Business India* and *Business World* — have also recently launched their respective subscription offers: so to counteract this action, it became necessary for *A&M* to come out with its own subscription offer, much more attractive than other magazines.

Thirdly, *A&M* realizes that it is the only magazine which specializes in advertising and marketing and there in no close competitor for the same, so it could easily snatch away normal reach (e.g., Students of marketing and advertising etc.).

Scheme Duration

The scheme was launched on the 6th of October, 98, and will last till 15th of November, 98. The duration is of sufficient length — neither too short, nor too long. This duration is proper because it gives the readers sufficient time to think about whether to avail the offer or not. The scheme has been launched keeping in mind the festive season of Diwali when the consumers are keen to buy new things or enter into new ventures.

Advantages of the Scheme

The scheme might prove to be very advantageous to *A&M.* It might increase the readership of the magazine to a great extent because of its attractive nature. Also, since the scheme is launched in the festive season, it might prove more fruitful. By offering free gifts and a huge lucky draw, A&M has attempted to hit the consumer sentiments, thereby trying to convince the consumer to take a positive step.

TRY YOURSELF

1. Critically analyse the sales promotion scheme adopted by M/s *A&M.* What objectives are achieved by using the above scheme? Discuss.

Types of Sales Promotions

One approach to categorise sales promotion is to look at the sources that are offering the promotion and the fundamental appeals. Generally, there are two major groups that offer sales promotion (our concern focuses on business activities) – manufacturers and retailers. When promotional deals are announced directly by manufacturers, these are termed as 'manufacturer promotions' and may be directed toward the consumers or the trade, or both these groups. Promotions offered by retailers to increase store traffic or sales, etc., are called 'retailer promotions' (also called as store promotions), and are offered only to customers or end-users. For example, when Akai announces sales promotion on its brand of entertainment electronics for consumers, this would be manufacturer promotion. On the other hand when one or more dealers carrying Akai products offer a promotional scheme, this would be termed as retailer promotion. Promotion offer by retailers may or may not be the outcome of promotion offered to trade by the manufacturer.

This types of appeal focuses either on price or interest. Price-cuts, coupons, rebates, bonus packs, exchange offers, financing programmes, etc. are examples of price appeals. The appeals of interest category include premiums, contests and sweepstakes, and free samples, etc. Besides manufacturer promotion and retail promotion, another approach to distinguish the type of promotion is to call them consumer promotion, trade promotion, and sales force promotion (sales force promotions are directed at the sales force). Sales promotions directed at the trade and sales force date back earlier than consumer promotions. Promotions are powerful competitive tools for getting new products in re-seller stores, inducing consumer trial, gaining shelf space and motivating salespersons and re-sellers.

Sales Promotions — Tools and Techniques

All techniques and tools of sales promotion are fairly simple and can be reduced to twelve in number. Almost all promotions make use of one or more of these tools, alone or in some carefully developed combination.

- Price deals (price-off, price-cut, cents-off, denote the same thing)
- Bonus-packs (price-pack)
- Refunds and rebates (both terms are used interchangeably)
- Coupons
- Contests and sweepstakes
- Premiums
    - In-packs, on-packs, near packs and container premiums
    - Free-in-mail premiums
    - Self-liquidating premiums
- Sampling
- Continuity plans
- Trade coupons
- Trade allowances and deals

- Exchange offers
- Displays, trade fairs, exhibitions and event sponsorship.

The list apparently appears to be short, however; considering the possible combinations, the figure reaches to about eight million different approaches. In most cases a combination of two or more techniques will combine the strengths of one and compensate for the weaknesses of the other and will produce better results as compared to either technique used alone.

As mentioned earlier, promotions directed at the ultimate consumers are called consumer promotions. These promotions can be developed for durable as well as non-durable goods. Most of these products are typically used by individuals or households and are generally sold by retail stores. The same techniques which are used for consumer promotions are also used to promote products to business users, such as stationery, computer systems and consumables, machinery, automobiles and many other products. Most of these techniques can be used both for consumer as well as trade promotions.

There is plenty of variety, flexibility and motivation to action. A judicious combination of techniques can be used to achieve almost any promotion objective. The flexibility of sales promotion has the potential of being used by small and large companies selling goods or services, and by profit and non profit organisations. Customers are motivated, stimulated and influenced to respond in a predictable manner to sales promotions.

PERFORMANCE CRITERIA

1. Process of measuring effectiveness of sales promotion programmes are identified in accordance with organizational procedures. Range may included but is not limited to - observation; research; monitoring of sales; analysis of results; self-evaluation; feedback from customers, manufactures, suppliers, staff.
2. Effectiveness of sales promotions is evaluated in accordance with agreed procedures. Range may include but is not limited to - targets, products, promotional strategies, marketing, focus, resources, incentives, value to customers, response to promotional tools, programme length, distribution method, achievement of objectives, profitability, implications for future sales promotions.
3. Procedures for improving effectiveness of sales promotions are implemented in accordance with organisational procedures. Range may include but is not limited to - setting development objectives; upskilling; training; coaching; motivating; encouraging; providing resources; changing strategies; adjusting procedures; providing incentives; seeking feed assistance.

PRICE DEALS

Price deals are probably the most commonly used promotional techniques. A price deal for customers means a reduction in the price of the promoted product which means that the customer saves money on purchase. Such a deal is designed to stimulate customers to try a new product, to encourage new users to try an existing product, or to encourage customers to continue product patronage, increase purchase quantity, purchase multiple units, and accelerate usage rate, etc. Such deals are suitable when brand loyalty is low, product category is considered a commodity and price is the primary consideration of the customers.

Price Discounts

A price discount can be used as a defensive as well as an offensive tool. More often, discounts are offered to match or beat the competitor's prices. When used as an offensive weapon, the objective is to generate additional sales and increase market share and long run profits.

Price discounts (also called cents-off deals) are communicated to the consumers through advertising, at the point-of-purchase, by listing the reduced price on the package or signs near the product or window display, or by the sales people. Such discounts may appear in newspapers, magazines and television advertisements. Similar discounts are often advertised by retailers in the local media (called feature advertising) and by manufacturers in national print and audio-visual media.

Manufacturers often offer extra incentives to retailers to gain their cooperation. Retailers may announce price discounts for a variety of reasons. By announcing a price discount on some popular consumer item, the retailer's intention is to increase store-traffic. Whenever the store-traffic increases, customers visiting the store not only buy the promoted product, but some of them buy other products as well. It is also possible that the retailer bought excessive stocks when the manufacturer offered the trade deal and to clear this excess inventory, the retailer offers a price discount to consumers. Yet another reason can be that when the retailer feels threatened, then the only way to respond to the competitive situation is to offer a price discount to consumers to move the product off the shelves.

Determining the quantum of discount depends on the consumers' price perceptions and may be difficult to decide. There is no precise answer; however, experts generally agree that the discount should be at least 5% to 20% of the normal price. Of course, the discounts may differ across product categories. Price discounts generally do not stimulate consumers to buy a product in large quantities if the unit value is low, product is not bully, and the holding cost is not high. If advertising support has been effective, or prior to offering price discount there has been a sample drop of the product, then even first time buyers may purchase the product.

Such promotions work very well in gaining the attention of consumers, particularly at the point-of-purchase (POP) among similar brands and may also encourage unplanned or impulse buying. If there are three different models of a product and because of the discount offer the price of the higher end model appears not too high to the consumer, compared to the lesser priced model, then the consumer may buy the higher end model. For example, if the price of a more expensive wristwatch is Rs 3000 and the next model is priced at Rs 2400 and the discount offer on higher model is 12% then the effective price of the higher end model would be Rs 2640, and the customer may buy the higher end model.

Advantages

The basic advantages that price discounts offer include the flexibility and convenience of implementation. They can be used to retain present customers as well. Such discounts offer immediate value and hence produce stronger consumer response. These discounts can lead to accelerated purchases (buying more than the immediate requirement) because they are for a limited period and keep the consumer out of the market for a longer period, thereby discouraging competitors.

Price discount offers are announced for the consumers (pull strategy) and hence pass through of savings to consumers is assured at the time of purchase. Such consumer discounts, when combined with similar type of incentive (push strategy) for the re-sellers, produce remarkable results. Often, competitive products are displayed next to or near each other. A properly displayed price can set the promoted brand quite apart from the competition. This combination is quite strong for the retailers, more so if the promoted brand happens to be a popular product.

Price offers are extremely flexible in the sense that the producer has total control on the number of units being promoted and the market area in which the offer will be given. If different packs of the same brand are available, the marketer can choose the one size that is not selling well. A price discount can be helpful in blocking the competitor's move to introduce a similar new product by loading the trade and consumers. A discount, coupled with display, arouses attention and the effect on consumer decision making can be significant. Experts estimate that something like 30% to 60% purchase decisions are unplanned in certain product categories, leading to impulse purchase.

Disadvantages

A discount offer may rapidly lose its advantage if competitors announce a similar offer. In fact, competitors are very likely to retaliate, leading to the danger of triggering a promotion war, in which no one benefits except the consumer (Prisoner's Dilemma). Such discounts are short-term and are unlikely to produce any long-term gains because the incentive is to purchase now by creating a sense of urgency. When the discount is withdrawn, the sales may fall bellow the level of pre-promotion period. The consumers are encouraged to switch brands, and this poses problems in sales forecasting. Many consumers have strong perceptions regarding price-quality relationship. A price discount can make them suspicious about the quality of the item and they may reject the product (Don E Schultz, Marketing News, August 1990). As mentioned earlier, many experts are of the opinion that price discounting is the primary cause of decrease in brand loyalty. Once there is doubt in the consumers' mind about the price-quality relationship of some brand, the trust in that brand takes a nosedive.

Price-pack Deals

Price-packs are also called value-packs. These may take any of the two forms, bonus pack and banded pack. In case of bonus pack offer, an additional quantity of the same product is offered free when the standard pack size of the product is purchased at the regular price. This type of deal is often seen in case of laundry products, food products and personal care products, etc. This is a way to reward the present consumers and may not have any impact on the users of competitive brands. A variation of this offer, more commonly observed, is when the marketer develops special packs of the product containing more quantity, but the price is proportionately low. For example, the regular price of a standard pack of a product is Rs 50 and the quantity contained in the pack is 100 gms. For the purpose of sales promotion the company offers a special pack containing 150 gams, and the price is Rs 62 only. This is a method to "load" the consumer up with the product. This technique is often used to introduce a new large size back of the product, or to encourage continued usage, and also to increase consumption. Many offers of this type are seen in consumer non-durable products consumed on a daily basis.

Banded pack offer, when two or more units of a product are sold at a reduced price compared to the regular price (couple of months ago, Lux International offered a similar deal. The pack contained four cakes of soap at the price of three). The products are generally banded together physically, or put together in a blister pack, such as razor-and-blade, toothpaste and toothbrush, or a smaller size of the same product may be attached to the regular size.

Another variation of this technique is "buy-one-take-one-free", or some similar offer (it could be "same for less" or "more for the same"). This is a fairly popular technique in cases of footwear, shirts, jeans, towels and many other varieties of products. Akai offered a 14" colour television on purchase of 21" colour television.

Bonus packs are generally limited to low bulk, low-price products. However, of late, exceptions such as the Akai offer have been observed. Additional quantity of the same product or additional unit of the product is appreciated as a reward by the consumer. This also offers the consumer the satisfaction of being a "smart shopper".

Advantages

Such offers are generally effective in converting product triers into users. The extra quantity may encourage increased usage and help sustain the habit. Among other similar brands, a bonus pack stands out at the point-of-sale. Extra quantity is an incentive and a reward. In consumer durable products, as in the example of Akai colour television, an additional 14" television is a big incentive to the buyer and as the deal is for a short period it may induce a sense of urgency. Consumers, who buy bonus packs of consumables, stay out of the market and are not exposed to competitors' offers.

Disadvantages

The cost of the additional product may be small to the manufacturer but the cost of the larger new pack may make the offer expensive. When bonus packs are branded together, in certain instances, retailers break the banding and sell the bonus product at regular price if the product happens to enjoy brand strength. In such a situation, the purpose of promotion is defeated, as the offer does not reach the consumer. In case of consumer durables, such a deal is quite likely to hurt the brand image and disrupt price-quality perceptions of customers.

CONSUMER SALES PROMOTION

The specific consumer oriented sales promotion are following:

- ***Consumer contests:*** Some pitches are to be made to promote the brand of the product. For example Britannia use a pitch line tin-tin- tin-tin.
- ***Consumer Premium:*** The extra offers deals with the shake of the organization, discount on the product, offering extra benefits along with the product, future purchase behaviour.
- ***Trading stumps:*** It is deal with the future offering of the product. What extra advantages given to the particular product in compare to other competitor.
- ***Subsidised sampling offers:*** Final product reach into the hand of consumer with the help of retailer, mall, store home delivery or through mail.
- ***Price of offers:*** The consumer deals with different offers time-to-time which influence the consumer to purchase the product. It deals with the concept of larger and bigger quantity.

REFUNDS AND REBATES

The terms 'refund' and 'rebate' are used as meaning the same thing. Long ago, the term rebate was made popular by the automobile industry in developed countries. There is a subtle difference between these two terms. *The Random House Dictionary* defines a refund as repayment of money, and a rebate as a return of part of the original payment for some service or merchandise. This means that a refund is repayment of total money paid for purchase, while the rebate represents repayment of only part of the money paid for purchase. However, both these terms are used interchangeably in the real world of marketing.

A promotion offering refund or rebate by a marketer is a promise to give back a certain amount of money after the purchase. The offer may be for a product purchase alone or in combination with other products. Depending on the objectives, refund offers are used to encourage trial of a new product, purchase of increased quantity, or increasing the frequency of purchase, or to encourage the customers to purchase those products whose purchases can be postponed, such as refrigerators, microwave ovens, air-conditioners, and other consumer durable products. Refund offers seem to work very well in guaranteeing the trial of a product or service, since there is no risk involved for the customer because of the promise of total refund of the purchase amount.

Evidence suggests that customers look at refunds as rewards for purchase. This appears to build brand loyalty rather than diminish it (Louis J Haugh, *Advertising Age*, May 1980). For example, Maruti announced a gift cheque of Rs 1,30,000 as a loyalty reward on purchase of a Maruti Esteem car, if the family already owned any other Maruti car. The offer was valid for a month only.

Gillette announced a refund offer. A customer was required to buy a pack of 7 O'clock P II for Rs 55.50. On returning the empty pack, the customer gets Rs 55.50 off on Gillette Sensor excel.

A computer magazine, *Chip*, offered a refund of Rs 350 on sending a one-year subscription, which the customer could use to purchase special issues of the magazine.

When consumers increase purchase quantity, they carry more stocks of the product and stay out of markets. This dampens the competition for a while.

In diverse product categories, such as exercise equipment, mixers and juicers, hair dryers, ceiling fans, inkjet printers and magazines, etc., refund offers are fairly common. Some of these promotions appear in audio-visual or print media. *'Readers Digest'* regularly makes this offer. Some of them offer a free trial period, and in case the customer is not satisfied, there would be total refund or money and no questions asked. The customer has to send back the product within a specified period of time. In these situations, the refund offer is used to encourage trial at no risk to the customer. This is a powerful method to ensure trial.

Refunds are quite effective in competitive situations where consumers, perceive little or no differentiation among brands. The refund offer may sway the decision in favour of the promoted product. When the product is good but the brand share is low, a refund seems to work very well. There are occasions when the company decides to move into new geographic markets. Such refund promotion may prove to be quite effective in motivating high-risk perceivers to decide in favour of the promoted product as the perceived risk is likely to appear manageable.

In local-convenience stores, shopkeepers recommend certain products of commodity type, such as rice flour, or cooking oil to consumers. The assurance given to customers is that if the product is not liked after usage for any reason, total money will be refunded or the customer will have the option to buy any other product of choice. This type of refund policy builds store loyalty among consumers who continue their a patronage.

Refund offer is limited only by the imagination of the promotion planner and the budget allocation. Such offers can be used to achieve a variety of promotion objectives, such as to guarantee trial, to reward loyal consumers, to load consumers, to increase purchase frequency, to introduce new products, to enter new markets, to encourage the purchase of related products, etc.

Advantages

Refund offers can induce excitement in consumers at relatively low cost. A higher percentage of customers forget to claim the refund, unless the amount is very significant. This phenomenon of forgetting is called "slippage", and hence an attractive offer can be made but the cost will still be low. Slippage is an interesting aspect associated with refund offers. Some refund offers are associated with only one purchase, while others may require multiple purchases. In both types of cases, proof-of-purchase is required to claim the refund. This ensures that the marketer pays only when the product is purchased. Besides the value of refund, slippage varies depending on the number of purchase proofs required and the procedure of claiming the refund. The reasons that consumers cite for failing to claim the refund are that they forgot, they lost the claim form, and the procedure for claiming the refund seemed to be cumbersome. Consumers generally perceive refund offers as rewards increasing brand loyalty. Requirement of multiple purchase helps load the customer at a relatively low cost. Refund offers, when combined with some trade incentive, can help gain in-store displays.

Disadvantages

If the refund offer is not large enough to increase sales significantly, profitability may be hurt badly. Refund offers are used often by consumers who would have not otherwise purchased the product. For immediate sales response, refunds are not very helpful. The difficulty in collecting the proof of multiple purchases often discourages participation.

COUPONS

Coupons can be considered as certificates offered by retailers or manufacturers that entitle the owner to some stated savings or claim the specified thing. Coupons bear a date of expiry and cannot be redeemed after the cut off date. Offer of a coupon is a very versatile technique and can be used to achieve many different sales promotion objectives. When coupons are offered by the manufacturer, all the costs associated with advertising and distributing the coupons, redeeming their face values and paying retailers a fee for handling, are borne by the manufacturer. When retailers offer coupons of their own, they have to bear all the above mentioned costs themselves. Coupons originating from the manufacturers are redeemable at any retail shop that carries the promoted product. The retailers serve as agents of the manufacturer in accepting and redeeming the coupons and send the collected coupons to the concerned manufacturer along with their claims of reimbursement. Retailer-originated coupons are redeemable only at a particular store or a group of stores (for example, a chain store having many outlets). The retailer-originated coupons generally have one objective – to encourage the consumers to shop at a particular store. Their interest is not tied up with any brand or manufacturer, unless there has been an agreement with the marketer of some cooperative venture. In such a case, the objective would be to encourage shopping at a particular store and buy a certain manufacturer's brand. Coupons are particularly attractive to consumers who are price sensitive. Research has shown that the tendency to use coupons rises under certain conditions

- When consumers perceive that there is need to control the budget
- Consumers are inclined to experiment with new products or services
- Consumers use coupons for products which are consumed regularly, such as tea, coffee, laundry products, etc.

Consumers who are strongly loyal to brands, or those who consider that collecting coupons is not worth the effort, are least likely to use coupons. Coupons generally attract older, better educated, urban, middle-income families. Comparatively, coupons seem not to be so popular with young, less educated, unmarried individuals. In case the coupons happen to be related to some current fashion or fad, then younger, middle-income individuals are likely to be attracted.

Manufacturers distribute their coupons by using print media, direct mail, product packages, or through retailers. Some manufacturers and service providers also distribute coupons during trade fairs (some on Internet access time). Media distributed coupons are common as part of an advertiser's print ads, or a more effective vehicle, "free-standing insert" (FSI) is sometimes used. A 'free-standing insert' is a leaflet inserted in a newspaper. When the reader opens the pages, the FSI falls out.

Distribution of Coupons

Direct to Consumer

Coupons can be delivered direct to consumers by hiring a team of promoters. They can also be distributed to consumers at a point where the product demonstration has been arranged, at retail stores, check out counters, passengers in an airline flight, in a club, in schools, exhibition or trade fair, and by direct mail, etc.

Marketers have the flexibility to be very selective with the target market on the basis of some selected criteria. Direct distribution is quite effective to ensure rate of coupon redemption. By using direct mail, a large population can be reached in India in urban and small towns. In some western countries, 90% of the population can be reached by using direct mail. However coupon distribution by using direct mail or door-to-door distribution is quite expensive.

Media Distributed

Coupons are included in ads appearing in newspapers, magazines, FSI, etc. Coupons that are distributed by a single advertiser are called "solo", and where two or more non-competing manufacturers join hands for several brands, they are called "co-op-coupons". Newspaper distributed coupons cost much less to the marketer. Based on the choice of newspaper, some selectivity can be exercised. For example, in India and other countries some newspapers are national, or regional in character. Some other newspapers cater to the needs of those who prefer a particular language (for example, in India, besides national newspapers, there are regional and local ones in Hindi, Urdu, Sindhi, Bengali, Tamil, Telugu, Malayalam, Kannada, etc.). Newspaper coupons offer flexibility in terms of size, shape, location, and timing of distribution, and all this can be done with limited lead-time. This is an effective method to mass distribute the coupons, however, the redemption rates are generally low and there can be much wasted circulation.

In case of magazines, coupons appear along with the advertisement on a page, or in case the coupon relates to subscription of the same magazine, the size may be smaller than the page. For example. *Reader's Digest, India Today. Business India, Femina, Chip, PC Quest, and Computer @ Home,* and many others, distribute coupons to encourage subscription.

Magazines offer certain advantages through regional or special editions, such as higher reproduction quality, audience selectivity, pass-along readership, long exposure and reasonable area selectivity, etc.

However most magazines have long lead times and cannot be used in a hurry to distribute coupons. This requires that promotion be planned much in advance. Also it is not possible to reach as large an audience as with newspapers.

Product-Distributed

Product-distributed coupons are delivered with the product. They can be "in-pack", or "on-pack". In-pack coupons are inserted within the product package. There may be an attention-getting message on the package informing consumers about the coupon.

On-pack coupons are attached to the outside of the product pack in some way. The coupon may be printed as part of the carton or wrapper. A type of coupon, called "cross-ruff, is also sometimes used. This coupon can be for a related or totally unrelated product. For instance, inside the pack of a shaving cream there could be a coupon for razor blades, a perfume, or a totally new product to encourage trial.

One major advantage of in-pack coupon is that it involves no extra distribution costs– the product bought by the consumer becomes the vehicle. Another advantage is that such coupons get distributed only to those who purchase the product. These coupons can be used to reward the consumers and encourage repeat purchase and trial of a related or new product. When such coupons are combined with a likely draw or sweepstakes, they can create much excitement and enhance repeat purchase of the vehicle product. It is also possible to control the areas of distribution and reach the desired customer segment in a geographic area through in pack coupons.

However, coupons that encourage brand users to buy the same brand on the next purchase occasion produce slower sales response because the coupon may get redeemed only after the usual inter-purchase interval. Also in-pack or on-pack coupons generally do not attract substantial number of new triers.

Each type of coupon irrespective of its face value or distribution method, can offer some specific advantages. In India, the use of coupons, as a tool of sales promotion, is growing at a rapid pace. Coupons can be used to achieve diverse consumer and trade sales promotion objectives. Some important promotion objectives that can be achieved by using coupons are discussed in brief.

Coupons can be used to Serve many Objectives

1. To Encourage Product or Service Trial

A consumer who has not tried an existing product or service, or one who tries a new product or service can be considered as a trier. A coupon can enhance the chances that such a consumer will make an initial purchase of the product, more so if such an offer is combined with a lucky draw.

Effective advertising, through a variety of emotional and rational appeals, tries to motivate consumers to purchase the product. Despite this, consumers face uncertainty and hesitate to purchase an untried brand. They may be uncertain as to how the brand will perform and the related consequences if the brand performs badly. A coupon can compensate the consumer in reducing the risk to some extent. If the consumer makes use of the coupon, it meets the objectives of inducing trial and also helps in communicating the reference price to the consumer. A free sample, in contrast, fails to develop reference price in the consumer's mind. Research shows that coupons help in inducing trial, particularly direct mail coupons. Heavy users of coupons are more likely to try new and different products.

2. To Encourage Brand Switching

Coupons are a direct economic incentive to encourage brand switching; the consumer feels exclusive and important, a smart shopper, and these are important economic and psychological reasons to encourage a switch. A coupon is a more tangible, believable proof of price cut than just a "heavy discount on list prices" as this does not communicate anything tangible.

3. To Encourage Repeat Purchase

Coupons can serve to achieve a long-term promotion objective by increasing repeat purchase of the brand by regular consumers, new triers, or infrequent users. It is believed that if the product category happens to be low-involvement, a coupon would encourage repeat purchase. For many consumers, coupons serve as a reward to keep on using the brand and as per the "instrumental conditioning" theory of learning, a rewarded behaviour gets reinforced and is likely to be sustained in the long-term.

Defending market share when the product category is fairly crowded with many brands is not easy; every brand is vulnerable to competitive moves. Most marketers are generally concerned with at least maintaining their market share of the brand. Coupons are a sure way to reward and retain the loyal consumers. Coupons also serve as a preemptive promotional move to make it tough to snatch away the loyal users of the brand. Consumers who are brand switchers or heavy coupon users are particularly attracted. A firm's objective to defend the market share can be seen in the light of "prisoner's dilemma". Market share of a company's brand can be affected when a coupon promotion is offered by competitors. The realization makes them to act in anticipation of competitor's move, or in response to competitor's move. However, the result is that competing firms succeed only in protecting their market share, but sacrifice part of their profits.

4. To Supplement Print Media Advertising

Unless the ad is noticed and read, it does not serve the purpose. A coupon included in a print advertisement increases the attention getting power of the advertisement. Research indicates that advertisements appearing in print, which include a coupon, are more likely to be noticed and recalled by consumers than the same ads without a coupon. Consumers are also more likely to read the headline and copy as a result of their attention and interest is increasing, provided the programme is implemented intelligently. The new price may be much higher than the present reference price that the consumers have, and hence the product may be perceived as unjustifiably expensive. To avoid the rejection of the product by the consumers, the marketer may issue a coupon of the value that would reduce the price to a level that is between the consumers current reference price and the new price. The consumers get adapted to the new price and when the coupon is withdrawn, the new price does not appear to be high relative to the new reference price of the consumers. The timing of coupon distribution should be such that the loyal consumers do not get enough time to switch to a different brand because of the price increase. The coupon should be of immediate value, preferably on the-package, so that the consumers get an immediate reduction on the price.

5. To Use Price Discrimination

Price discrimination produces a positive effect on total sales. The strategy is to charge different prices for the same product. Consumers who happen to be more price-sensitive are motivated to use coupons and pay less. Another group of consumers who do not make the efforts to redeem the coupon, pay a higher price for the same product. In another situation, where the coupons have been distributed selectively, only coupon owners have the advantage of buying the product at less than the list price, and all others buy the product at the normal list price. Coupons can be used as a highly effective tool to use price discrimination.

Advantages

Coupons are considered as a very versatile promotion tool as they can help in inducing trial of an existing or new product. A marketer can use coupons to encourage those who have tried a brand to become regular users. It is fairly convenient to reach a large number of prospects with coupons in a short time. Coupons can help to load-up the consumers and this may help in blocking the moves of competitors when there is reliable information. Line-extension products can be introduced easily by enclosing or banding the coupon with the vehicle product.

Disadvantages

One major disadvantage of coupons is wrong redemption. This happens when the retailer, by mistake or with intent, pays the consumer the face value of the coupon even though the product for which the coupon is meant is not purchased (the consumer, in connivance with the retailer buys some other product of the coupon's value). This type of redemption leads to wasted costs and adversely affects the achievement of objectives. Response to coupon promotion may be unpredictable because of factors such as media, timing, value, brand share, competitive moves, etc. In-pack or on-pack coupons generally do not attract new tries. Coupons for products, whose value is unknown, generally are not quite as effective as for known and established brands.

Louis J Hague, *Advertising Age*, 1979, has developed some suggestions

- Treat coupons as money.
- Discourage bulk redemptions through design, distribution, and handling.
- Don't use excessive values in coupons. Keep them within reason.
- The coupon value should not exceed the cost of the media in which it is distributed or the value of the product if it is a solo coupon.
- Keep the offer clear and uncomplicated. Cute and clever approaches make it more difficult for the retailer to understand the offer.
- Have no less than 50% product distribution in the area in which the coupon will be distributed.
- Make it easy to for the retailer to handle the coupon and to be repaid.
- Set a policy and stick to it. Don't hesitate to refuse payment for redemptions that are clearly fraudulent.
- Test your programmes and methods to educate the consumer. Don't go national or even regional without some sort of test to make sure that the coupon works.

One more suggestion, seemingly important but not mentioned in the list, is

- Due care should be taken to make the coupon difficult to counterfeit.

CONTESTS AND SWEEPSTAKES

These are part of interest promotions because such sales promotions create not only interest but also produce excitement and enthusiasm in consumers. There seems to be quite a bit of confusion in understanding these terms. A contest requires the participants to perform some task. For example, the participants may be required to write a slogan, choose a name, or create a design, etc. To decide which entries are first, second, or third, etc., an expert or a panel of experts examines the entries and judges the winning ones. The prizes, depending on the announced number of prizes, are declared. A contest is based on testing skill or ability and may not involve proof-of-purchase (this is called a "consideration") to enter the contests.

A sweepstake is a random drawing and is sometimes called a chance contest. This too may or may not involve the purchase of any product or service.

A lottery prize is decided on the basis of chance and requires a "consideration" for entry that may be proof-of-purchase of ticket or a product.

According to the American Association of Advertising Agencies, "A contest is an event that invites the customer to apply skill to solve or complete a special problem". The same agency says, "A sweepstake does not call for the application of skill on the part of the consumer. Winners are determined by a drawing from all entry forms. In other words, prizes are awarded on the basis of chance".

Often, a combination of contest and sweepstakes is employed in some promotions. The winners are decided in two stages. The first part involves a contest in terms of skill, or knowledge. If more correct entries are received, the second stage then involves a draw of chance to decide the winners. A well-known television programme in India, "*Surabhi*, is an example of this type of promotion. In the programme, anyone could send answers to questions that were asked on a postcard. Generally correct entries, running in thousands, were received. Out of these correct entries, depending on the number of prizes to be given, some were picked up on a random basis to declare the winners. In India, contests and sweepstakes are very popular promotional techniques and are frequently used in diverse product categories and services. The range covers low as well as high-involvement products starting from such low-priced product as "Pan Masala" or expensive products such as cars, and to almost everything in between. Even sporting events use contests and sweepstakes.

Among all the sales promotional devices, probably the most exciting and highly rewarding are the contests and sweepstakes. Every imaginable prize or reward is used to excite and attract customers to participate. The prizes may be gold or silver jewellery, hefty sums of money, cars, two-wheeler autos, colour televisions, computers, music systems, free air tickets, stay in five star hotels, holidays in health resorts, and anything else depending on the imagination of the marketer.

To add an element of extreme urgency and to speed up the response, early bird prizes are announced for the first 25 to 50 or 100 entries. In certain cases, all those who furnish the proof-of-purchase are given some specified premium.

Experience shows that everyone concerned – consumers, trades people and sales force – get a share of excitement when the contest or sweepstakes is well planned and executed. The prizes seem to be much larger to contestants than the money spent by the sponsor. For instance, in case the manufacturer plans to distribute free samples of a product, it can cost far more than the total money spent by the manufacturer for the prizes. Contests and sweepstakes generate considerable interest and awareness and can be used to gain large sales increases.

The success, or otherwise, of a contest or sweepstakes depends largely on the selection of prizes and prize structure. In most cases, the structure represents a typical pyramid, that is there is a bumper prize of very high value at the top, for instance, a car worth Rs 3,00,000 or more, or jewellery of the same value, followed by a number of prizes in the immediate value range, a large number of prizes of small value, and a larger number of consolation prizes. To make the contest or sweepstakes more tempting, there may be more than one winner of first prize (such as 10 first prizes for ten lucky winners). Different combinations of prizes are evolving. The duration of contests and sweepstakes varies considerably, depending on the objectives set for the sales promotion.

A producer of branded wheat flour, *Shakti Bhog Atta*, announced an interesting promotion. Grocery stores owners informed the consumers regarding the possibility of prizes that consumers can win with continued use of the brand. There were no first of second prizes, the top prize was a Santro car, besides many other prizes. Each pack of flour contained a coupon with certain half-word or one-third word printed on it. For example, to win a Santro car, the consumer was required to collect three coupons that would complete the name of the prize, that is, Santro. On one coupon would be 'SA', the other two coupons should have 'NT and 'RO', thereby completing the word Santro and entitling the consumer to win a Santro car by submitting the three coupons. No final date of promotion closing was announced. Consumers kept on buying the same brand and collected many coupons, most not winning anything because in most cases the coupons had the same or different letters, not fit to complete the desired word. Letters on some coupons were part of either a brand of washing machine, television, or wristwatch, etc. Because of the nature of the product, consumers did not mind continued purchase of the brand and kept on collecting the coupons. This is an example of a very clever sales promotion of a product which is considered a commodity. However, the technique proved to be extremely effective in retaining the customers and motivating them to continue using the same brand for an extended period of time.

In case of consumer durable products, Bajaj Auto announced a promotion to encourage the purchase of any Bajaj scooter. The promotion named *Crorepati Hungama* lasted one month (1st December to 31st December 1999). The promotion said, "buy any scooter, scratch a card and win a sure prize". The prizes were around 8000, the top prize being rupees ten million followed by hundred prizes of Rs 1,00,000 each, seven hundred prizes of Sansui music systems, seven thousand prizes of Kodak cameras and many Timex watches. A very tempting promotion, and simple too. Just buy a scooter, scratch a card and win a sure prize. The factor of chance limited only to what one gets, no losers, all winners.

These two examples present the use of the same method of sales promotion. The first example presents the use of 'chance' in case of a consumer non-durable good, which is a low-involvement category product and there is hardly anything like brand loyalty. In fact, in most Indian households the flour comes from flourmills where people take their wheat to be converted into wheat flour. Such service providing flourmills are located in almost all localities. The same element of chance has been used in case of a consumer durable product of high-involvement category. The promotion planning shows how effective the sweepstakes can be in increasing sales, and block competition.

Advantages

Contests and sweepstakes can create a high level of awareness and build or reinforce the image of the product or service. Consumers may associate the impressive prizes with the product or service. The promotions are more successful in getting the print advertisement read, or the audio-visual ad seen. This is becoming an increasingly difficult task because of audience boredom, apathy, disinterest, or even irritation towards advertising in general. Contests and sweepstakes can help gain store displays, generate store traffic and encourage the trial of a product if the prizes are sufficiently attractive.

Disadvantages

Contests and sweepstakes generally are not effective in generating trial of a new product. Heavy media expenditure is often required to make these events successful. It is generally not possible to pre-test a contest or sweepstakes programme and could prove to be quite risky. The promoter has to check thoroughly the rules and regulations that may vary from state to state. Designing a contest or sweepstakes requires lengthy lead-time. This may entail the risk that competitors may come to know about the event sufficiently in advance and may take steps to sabotage the efforts.

PREMIUMS

A premium (gift) is a reward given to the consumer for performing a particular act, generally purchasing a product or service. The premium may be free or available to the consumer by paying a price well below the regular market price. Getting a printer free with the purchase of a computer, or getting a bar of detergent free with the purchase of four cakes of toilet soap, or getting a Swiss knife well below the market price when the consumer purchases a microwave oven, are typical examples of premiums. Marketers choose premiums that have much appeal to the consumers, or products that are related in some way to the products of the marketer. For example, Kellogg's Chocos packs contained small plastic toys like different types of dinosaur replicas or sometimes, a plastic lunch box. As the product is primarily targeted at kids, these premiums had great appeal to them. Computer magazines often include a compact disc with each issue.

There are many varieties of premiums which are sometimes referred to as direct premiums and mail premiums. Direct premiums are used to reward the customers immediately at the time of purchase, and mail premiums require the customers to take some action, such as mailing the proof of multiple purchases to the marketer. After the receipt of the proof, the marketer sends the premium to the consumer.

IN-PACK, ON-PACK AND CONTAINER PREMIUMS

These various terms for premiums are primarily used to distinguish between methods of rewarding the consumers. Such premiums are attached either to the product, enclosed with the product, or otherwise available with the product when the consumer buys the product. The premiums can be used to solve a competitive price advantage or to counter the competitor's coupon promotion. Depending on the consumers' value perception of the premium, the consumers may even be agreeable to purchase the product at a slightly high total price for the combination of the product and the premium. When all similar products in a certain price range are perceived as basically alike, a premium offer, with the purchase of the product, is quite an effective method to gain shelf space or even display. Premium offers provide a point of difference, more so when the product category is fairly crowded. These are all different approaches to offer immediate reward to the consumer at the time of purchase. The premium is likely to offer a reason and an incentive to buy the product.

- ***In-pack premium:*** The premium is enclosed inside the product pack. Such premiums are generally small and low priced, such as a toy, steel bowl, face towel and many other items. These in-pack premiums are often used by manufacturers of ready-to-eat cereals, health and beauty aid products, or incense packs, etc.
- ***On-pack premium:*** As the name suggests, on-pack premium is attached to the outside of the product package or to the product itself if no outer package is used. The premium might be banded with a cello-tape, rubber band or it could be blister pack. It is also sometimes referred to as banded premium. At times these are related to the product, such as toothbrush with toothpaste, blades with razor, compact disk with computer magazine, etc.
- ***Near-pack premium:*** Sometimes the premium is bulky in size and hence cannot be enclosed inside the pack or put on the pack it is kept near the promoted product and the consumer takes one with the purchased product. For example, with the purchase of 4kg pack of Surf, a fourteen-litre plastic bucket was given as premium. In case of certain products, though, the premium is not bulky compared to the product on promotion, yet the premium is kept near the pack. For example, near the five-litre pack of a certain brand of sunflower cooking-oil was kept a pack of mosquito repellent product containing the electrical plug-in gadget and refill tablets.
- ***Container-premium:*** In this type of premium the product itself is packed inside the premium, which is a container, and this container can be used for some other purpose after the product has been consumed. For example, in a promotion, Bournvita was offered in an attractive glass mug,

Nescafe was available in good looking crystal jars, similarly tea and many other consumable items are offered in Pet jars. A brand of tea was offered in decanters. After the product is consumed, the container is used as water jug, and Pet jars are used to store other consumable items, such as pulses, or sugar, etc. These reusable containers are put to other uses at no extra cost to consumers and serve to keep reminding them about the product long after it has been consumed.

Advantages

Premiums are widely used to reward consumers. They serve as a powerful means of differentiating the offer at the point of purchase where all the products are similar and the competition is at parity. Depending on the preferences, premiums can be selected to appeal to the target groups in a market. For example, container premiums are quite popular among house ladies in middle class homes. If the target group is children, certain type of premium such as toy or chocolate is likely to be more useful. Likewise, if the target group is women, then a totally different type of premium would be more attractive. This kind of matching is possible with careful selection.

If the promotion objective is to increase usage, some product related premium would be more useful. For instance, to increase the usage of condensed milk in families, a recipe book to prepare different types of desserts can be attached. With packs of coffee or tea a mug can be given as a premium, which perhaps may increase consumption. If the premium is chosen with care, its appeal is generally greater than a discount. In consumers' assessment the value of the premium is more because of its market price, though the cost of the premium item is less for the marketer.

Near-pack premiums are a strong motivation for retailers to display the product with premium at a prominent place in the store. There is considerable flexibility; larger and more impressive items can be chosen as premium. In case, of container premium, if it is attractive and valuable from the consumers' point of view, the price of the offer can be increased thereby reducing the cost of the premium for the marketer. For example, a good quality container can be used to pack tea and the price of this container premium can be increased to offset part of the premium cost.

Disadvantages

If the premium selection is poor, it may hurt product sales. The appeal to the consumer is an important factor and this aspect must be pre-tested in some way. This would, of course, add to the cost of the promotion. Even regular consumers may shy away from the product if the premium does not measure up to their likes. This fact should not be overlooked that the consumer might have had a bad experience with this type of premium. Too frequent use of premium with any product is likely to lessen the importance of the product in the eyes of the consumer.

- ▶ Premium selection should be based on pre-testing in some way.
- ▶ The premium appeal strength is important to encourage consumers to make unplanned purchases.
- ▶ The premium preferably should be a known brand name.
- ▶ Premium should communicate its good quality and value.
- ▶ If possible, the premium should be related to the promoted product or the promotion theme.
- ▶ Premium should be as distinctive as possible, otherwise in the present day clutter of advertising and promotion, consumers are unlikely to take any notice.

Free-in-Mail Premiums

Free-in-mail premiums are unique because the promotion objectives may be quite different. In-mail premiums do not provide an immediate reward at the time of purchase, as do the premiums already discussed. Consumers have to take some action to claim the premium, such as sending the proof of a single or multiple purchases and wait for some period of time for the delivery of the premium through mail or courier.

When consumers do not perceive any meaningful persuasive differentiation between brands and the market is competitive, such promotions work very well. The motivation to purchase and continue purchasing the product gets shifted to the incentive of premium as the purchase situation is one of total low-involvement as far as the product category is concerned. Considerable brand switching is possible if only one proof-of-purchase is to be sent to the marketer. Another factor that may contribute to brand switching is the attractiveness and value of the premium as perceived by the consumers. Where multiple purchases are involved as proof of purchase, generally the usual inter-purchase interval is more, and consumers are more likely to stay with the brand.

If the premium is particularly attractive, there would be a number of consumers who would want the premium in a hurry and make the required number of purchases. This would help to load-up the consumer. Or, there may be some flexibility in conditions, such as the consumers may have the option to send one, two, or more proofs of purchase along with a specified sum of money to obtain the premium quickly. Much depends on the ingenuity of the promotion planner.

Advantages

Free-in-mail premiums reward present consumers and encourage them to stay brand loyal and may also increase usage. Consumers will be less tempted to switch brands as they would be collecting the required number of purchase proofs to get the premium. If the objective is to encourage multiple purchases, free-in-mail premiums could prove to be quite effective because the consumers will have to build up stocks in collecting multiple proofs-of-purchase to get the premium quickly. Rate of redemption is generally low in this type of promotion and hence more expensive premium can be offered. Low redemption occurs because of "slippage" effect.

Free-in-mail premiums also increase the attention getting capability of the advertisements. Attractiveness to the premium may motivate consumers to read the advertisement with more attention.

A premium that serves as "dealer-loader" is a premium that is kept as display in the store and after the promotion is over, this "dealer-loader" is given to the store manager/owner free. The purpose is to reward the dealer for stocking the promoted product. To set up and manage such promotions is relatively easy. As soon as the required proof-of-purchase is received, the premium is mailed to the consumer. Often the arrangement is made with the distributors or dealers (if the premium is bulky) in cities and towns to hand over the premium to consumers whose names are sent by the company and the concerned consumers are informed and requested to collect the premium.

Disadvantages

It is not possible to measure the sales increase which can be directly attributed to such a sales promotion because the redemption rates are usually low. In some cases the company may be left with more residual stocks of the premium. There is need to make some agreement with the premium supplier to accept surplus stocks otherwise the cost of promotion would be unnecessarily high. There is also the possibility that the premium stocks may fall short of the demand, and unless some arrangement has been made with the supplier for such an emergency, there would be problems.

Multiple proofs-of-purchase do not encourage new consumers, only existing consumers are attracted. To pre-test such a premium promotion is extremely difficult because no one can tell accurately in advance as to how they will react to multiple proof-of-purchase to get the premium.

An example. Way back in the late Sixties, Swastik Oil Mills had a very low share of detergent market. The brand of detergent marketed by Swastik Oil Mills was Sway. The dominant detergent brand was Surf, with a very high market share. Sway's objective was to capture, say, 15% market share. A promotion was planned that required multiple purchases of the product to get the premium. Sway's packet tops were printed with serial numbers and the promotion period was three months in 1969. The deal for the consumers was to collect six printed tops from Sway packets as proof of multiple purchases. Arrangements were made with retailers to handle the distribution of premium, which was a plastic bucket of fourteen litres, to consumers who made a claim to the premium with proof of six purchases. Print ads communicated the offer to consumers. The estimate of informed sources was that nearly 200,000 buckets were given to consumers against the expected 100,000 (the difference between planned figure and the result is too wide).

In this case the premium selection was very appropriate. Plastic bucket was a newly introduced item in those days and was very attractive to most housewives in middle-income households. The consumers' perceived value of the premium was high (plastic buckets in retail market were more expensive that the usual galvanised buckets), a bucket is the kind of product which can also be used for other purposes besides washing clothes or storing water. The promotion period of three months was considered to be right enough to develop regular usage of the product and collecting six packet tops was adequate.

SUMMARY

One approach to categorise sales promotion is to look at the sources offering promotion and the fundamental appeals. The types of appeals focus either on price or interest. Price-cuts, coupons, rebates, bonus packs, exchange offers, financing programmes, etc., are examples of price appeals. The promotions are powerful competitive tools for getting new products in re-seller stores, inducing consumer trial, gaining shelf space and motivating salespersons and resellers. A promotion of offering refund or rebate by a marketer is a promise to give back a certain amount of money after the purchase. Refund offers can induce excitement in consumers at relatively low cost. Coupons can be considered as certificates offered by retailers or manufacturers that entitle the owner to some stated savings or claim the specified thing.

PROJECT WORK

Study the following services. Collect relevant data and bring out the details of strategies used for sales promotion.

a. McDonald's fast food services
b. Postal Services
c. Insurance Services

SHORT ANSWER QUESTIONS

1. What do you mean by price deals?
2. What are the various types of coupons?
3. What do you mean by trade allowances and deals?
4. What is consumer premium?
5. What are trading stumps?

REVIEW QUESTIONS

1. Explain the various methods of sales promotion. What are the limitations of sales promotion in a sellers' market?
2. "Promotion has been the target of considerable criticism." Discuss.
3. Suggest various sales promotion measures for consumer goods to be introduced at
   a. The consumers' level, and
   b. The dealers' level.
4. What is promotional mix ? Explain the different sales promotion tools and compare them with one another.
5. Analyse the distinctive features of the various elements of promotion mix. Illustrate with suitable examples.
6. Explain consumer sales promotion with the help of suitable example.

GO TO THE NET

Using Internet tools, collect six advertisements of FMCG industry and analyse their sales promotion schemes.

Using Internet search tools, prepare a sales promotion activity of 10 companies.

Caselet

A small scale manufacturer of consumer durables who has spent many with a reputed overseas manufacturer of similar products and who is a technocrat, wishes to introduce a complete range of kitchen appliances in the domestic market. The company does not have its own sales offices and as such depends on Distribution/Dealers for its entire marketing efforts. The first product he has identified is a Microwave Oven for which he has obtained ISI certification and is the only brand to get that. The product is reasonably priced but the brand has little or no market awareness. His friend who is assisting him with the marketing effort feels the trade the key to their being able to establish their in the market. They turn to you for help - what advice would you give him/ Substantiate your recommendations.

Flash: Airport to Airport

Flash Airport to Airport offers delivery deadliness to customers, faster transport and transit handling using bar code technology, comprehensive insurance be in it.

Flash airport to airport is the core of Lufthansa cargo activities of ensure delivery of goods to reach the right person at the right place - be it hitech, equipments or sensitive pharmaceuticals.

Flash: Airport to Door

Flash airport to door service plays a critical role in reaching the customer on time. There supplement the worldwide network of on line destinations with range of reliable partners. These services are offered also on non working days. It also provides services of customs clearance, domestic transport this relieving the customers from the burden off handling these complex formalities.

Flash is having a transparent pricing one country one price a charge collect option and the tremendous support of Lufthansa's worldwide cargo.

On Board Courier

On board courier branch mainly concentrates on the sensitive document transportation. Accompanied by escorts, the shipment is checked is as baggage at origin and delivered on the belts at the destination. This mode of operation ensures speedy delivery and paperless transactions.

Question:

1. How Lufthansa cargo with its branded service. Flash is meeting the delivery requirements of the global customers. Discuss logistics and strategies?

B L O C K

Basics of the Distribution System IV

The availability of the product in the market depends on the efficacy of the distribution channel, therefore the distribution channel plays a significant role in the marketing activities. In fact the success of a company's marketing effort depends on its command over the distribution network.

The arena for competition in a free market system is the marketing channel. It is the marketing channel which determines the success or failure of an enterprise or of individual initiatives.

This block focuses on the distribution channel structure in which the producer, wholesalers and retailers act as a unified system through 8 chapters.

CHAPTER 21

distribution system

learning objectives

The objectives of this chapter are to:

- understand the basic concepts of the distribution system
- know the different modes of transport in India
- describe the distribution channel scenario in India.
- understand the role and responsibilities of Logistics.

content outline

- Opening Case
- Introduction: Basic Concepts of the Distribution System
- Setting Distribution Objectives
- Developing Channel Design
- Logistic Needs
- Definitions of Physical Distribution
- Summary
- Project Work
- Short Answer Questions
- Review Questions
- Go to the Net

opening case

New Paradigm of Distribution for FMCG Companies

Money talks. Or it must, if it hasn't been doing so. Today, it talks in bottom lines and profits. Among FMCG companies, this is precisely what's driving a serious soul search on the right marketing and distribution strategies, questioning established beliefs in target consumers and figuring out afresh what the Indian market means for their brands and products.

You can call it the search for a paradigm, specific to each company. Clearly, a move away from the traditional marketing and distribution paradigm, which FMCG companies in India earlier believed was the mantra for success— the Hindustan Lever model. With about a million retail points, 7,500 distributors and a basket of products focused on every possible price point, HLL straddles virtually every income and geographical segment in the country.

The challenge for the others was to replicate the HLL juggernaut in as short a time as possible. But mimicking HLL is no easy task. The basic problem which confronts every marketer trying to get on the HLL curve is the heterogeneity of the Indian market, in terms of geographical diversity and the spread of incomes.

Given this heterogeneity, HLL's task of building mass markets comes with associated costs. Setting up rural and small town marketing distribution networks or establishing new product at different price points takes both time and money. This, in turn, means that at the initial stage of establishing a product or a distribution network, companies have to take a hit on their bottomlines.

Analysts point out that the main reason for multinationals, other than HLL, going in for a revamp of their strategies, is a renewed emphasis by their parents on shoring up bottomlines rather than concentrating on topline growth. "The model of the parent's deep pockets supporting sales growth at the cost of low margins is becoming passe. For Indian companies, too, profits are becoming paramount, forcing them to take a second look at their existing models," says one.

So Procter & Gamble, in a marked shift from its earlier obsession with chasing sales targets by aggressively expanding the distribution cover, is streamlining its distribution network, in an exercise code named Operation Golden Eye.

Says Ashok Chhabra, public affairs director at P&G, "The traditional distribution systems in India operate on the lines of a command economy. Companies decide on a supply target and then somehow push this to the consumers. This leads to a tremendous waste of resources, which ultimately hurts the consumer. We are moving to a demand based model, which enables us to reduce the quantum of waste."

While company officials are unwilling to comment on the specifics of the revamp, industry insiders point to the fact that P&G is cutting the size of its distribution cover to roughly one-tenth and is getting out of rural markets. "The company is focusing on class A and B towns and getting out of smaller population clusters," says a competitor. Only for a limited set of products, like Vicks Action 500 and some detergent sachets, P&G will not have much of a distribution presence in rural areas, he points out. "The company is reducing the number of price points at which it offers its products. For example, it has reduced the number of pack sizes in which it markets its detergent, Ariel."

Then there's Nestle. An analyst, who tracks FMCG companies for a foreign brokerage, points out that between 1993 and 1996, Nestle added on roughly 3,50,000 retail points to its network," the bulk of them in smaller towns and rural areas. It also added a slew of new products and variants to its portfolio — 31 in 1997 as compared to just three in 1993. Operating margins dipped sharply in 1992, when they were at around 13.5 per cent. By 1996 they had dropped to 11.6 per cent.

Nestle is now reworking its product and marketing strategies. The emphasis is on products in which it was traditionally strong — milk products and beverages. This would be accompanied by a strategy of weeding out low profitability products from the portfolio. The soya based health drink, Bonus, was discontinued from 1998; the axe is likely to fall on other products too.

Instead of trying to reach its product to as many consumers in as many markets as possible, a la Lever, Nestle has identified a sharply defined target segment that it would focus its marketing and distribution efforts on. According to company sources, Nestle has identified about 1,443 million households as its target group, or roughly 55 per cent of the urban population. These would, in turn, be split into two groups: 63 million individuals in the primary target group comprising 11.5 million households; and 81 million individuals in the secondary target group comprising about 15 million households. These target groups currently have a per capita annual consumption of Nestle's products of a value of Rs 77 (the urban average consumption is Rs 42).

If HLL and P&G are at two ends of the spectrum, Dabur is thinking of a strategy which falls in between. It plans to follow the basic HLL track "Because we have entry level FMCG products, we are trying to catch the consumer at the point where he is transiting from unbranded to branded products," says Sunil Duggal, Vice President (health care business). Yet, Dabur has taken a leaf out of P&G's book by reducing the number of distributors. For towns with population of less than 20,000, the company has cut down on the number of distributors because it was uneconomical. Instead, it has appointed what Duggal terms "super stockist." A super stockist differs from a distributor in that he services 10 to 15 sub stockists, who, in turn, supply the retailers. If there is a central theme in the way companies are reworking their distribution and marketing strategies, it is a focus on the products that they are trying to market. Each product has an associated customer profile which, in turn, determines its demand, "instead of expanding distribution to increased demand for a product, demand should drive distribution", points out chairman of Quadra Advisory, Shunu Sen.

Hasit Joshipura, General Manager (Sales) at HLL elaborates, "HLL has been a pioneer in creating and evolving a market of products like soaps and detergents. Our product portfolio has been geared towards the mass market. It is not necessary for a company with a different kind of product portfolio to follow our marketing and distribution model."

And where does it leave HLL? With less competition in the non-urban markets? Is its first mover advantage so strong that it can sit back and rake in the money without much effort? Joshipura is emphatic, "No competitive advantage is permanent. We have to constantly change and innovate to stay afloat."

The Alternatives

If the Hindustan Levers' marketing and distribution model is not everybody's cup of tea, however tasty it may be, what are the alternative models that companies could look at? One option is clearly to stop looking beyond the city lights as P&G seems to have done for most of its products and keep the product space confined to the higher ends of the urban income spectrum. The other option is to concentrate on specific demographic segments and focus marketing and distribution efforts on them, as is the Nestle model. A third option lies in the choice of a distribution channel. "Companies which don't want to build large distribution and retail networks beyond the urban areas can fall back on wholesale distribution," suggests Hasit Joshipura, General Manager (Sales), HLL.

In a wholesale distribution system, companies off-load their products on a large wholesaler, usually at a larger discount than they would offer their regular distributors. Smaller retailers buy the product directly from the wholesaler. This obviates the need for a distributor with a large sales force, ultimately resulting in lower cost for the manufacturing company. Shunu Sen, CEO Quadra Advisory, gives the example of Nirma soap which is distributed largely through the wholesale segment, and contrasts it with price peer, Lifebuoy, which goes into the same markets but through a large distributor and retail network.

While each of these options have their inherent advantages, there are disadvantages too. Industry insiders point out that while wholesale distribution does lead to a reduction in costs, brand building and customer recognition suffer in the long-term.

The experiences of consumer companies in developed markets have thrown up models which provide for streamlining distribution and sales networks in tune with consumer needs. Proctor & Gamble executives tout the Efficient Consumer Response (ECR) model, which they claim forms the basis for P&G India's strategic revamp.

P&G India CEO, Helmut Meixner, described the ECR model in a recent speech thus: "The ultimate objective of ECR is to maximise consumer satisfaction by optimising the entire supply chain, rather than potentially sub optimising the total by focusing on one element at a time." May sound a tad jargony, this, but the model does throw up some specific recommendations like reducing the number of product variants.

Ultimately, it's all got to do with the product and the consumer it can successfully proposition. Surely, more models will emerge or evolve out of existing ones.

Source: Brand Equity, *The Economic Times*, 7-13 April, 1999

Try Yourself

1. What are the strengths and weaknesses of HLL's distribution model?
2. Compare HLL's distribution model with that of other FMCG companies.

Introduction: Basic Concepts of the Distribution System

Distribution of goods and services plays an important role in the sales system. Distribution system varies from company to company and region to region. The distribution system gives strength to the company by helping to increase the reach of the product to various parts of the region, country or even in foreign markets. An effective distribution system helps in making available goods in the right quantity at the right time when they are required and giving a reasonable earning to those who are associated with the distribution system like wholesalers, retailers, departmental stores, etc.

We present a robust approach for reviewing distribution strategies across industries. This approach, summarised in the Andersen Consulting Distribution Strategy Pyramid, focuses on answering the following strategic questions

- Given the value proposition, who are the end customers and, therefore, what are the distribution objectives?
- What channel structure will achieve these distribution objectives at the lowest cost to serve?
- How do we manage our physical network to achieve objectives at lowest costs?
- What processes and organisation structure will help sustain the distribution network's performance?

This approach aims to

- Ensure that a company's distribution strategy is based on zero-based distribution objectives derived from end customer needs.
- Ensures complete integration across channel structure and supporting processes with the zero based distribution objectives and
- Results in the lowest cost to serve across product markets.

Setting Distribution Objectives

What are distribution objectives? For a product market, they are defined in terms of availability of the product (for example, percentage of total outlets reached). Most companies do not explicitly set distribution objectives. Of those that do, distribution objectives often have no linkage to end customer requirements. Often companies fail to ask questions like, "How many and what kind of outlets do I need, to be available to a given target audience and their buyer behaviour?"

There are also regional differences in category development to be taken into account. For instance, will extending distribution in a region with a low level of category development help me boost sales? Finally, the objectives should take note of the marketing initiatives planned for the year.

The Andersen Consulting Distribution Strategy Pyramid recommends explicit setting of distribution objectives based on end customer needs.

In most FMCG (fast moving consumer goods) categories, distribution objectives are heavily focused on retail availability – how many outlets and what kind of outlets. In prescription drugs, the objectives would include, apart from outlet availability, coverage for doctors. Agro chemicals, on the other hand, may require objectives in terms of share of tonnage by leading wholesalers.

What is the basis for this difference? The difference lies in the definition of the end customer, which may be different from the end consumer. The end customer is the last entity in the supply chain who makes the brand decision. For FMCG industries, where the end customer is the consumer, retail availability becomes the distribution objective. In prescription drugs, however, the end customer is the prescribing doctor. Thus, the objectives need to ensure appropriate coverage of doctors, without which no amount of wholesale push will drive volumes.

In agro chemicals, distribution objectives depend largely on the land holding pattern in the market. Markets with large land holdings and geographic concentration require focus on a smaller number of large wholesalers whereas those with small land holdings and geographical fragmentation require availability to a large number of small traders.

Distribution extension decisions depend upon relative category development by the market . In a highly penetrated market, it is not possible to drive offtake merely by increasing availability beyond a point. Similarly, in a low penetration market, merely increasing availability without addressing the fundamental drivers of low penetration may not lead to volume growth.

figure 21.1

The Andersen Consulting Distribution Strategy Pyramid

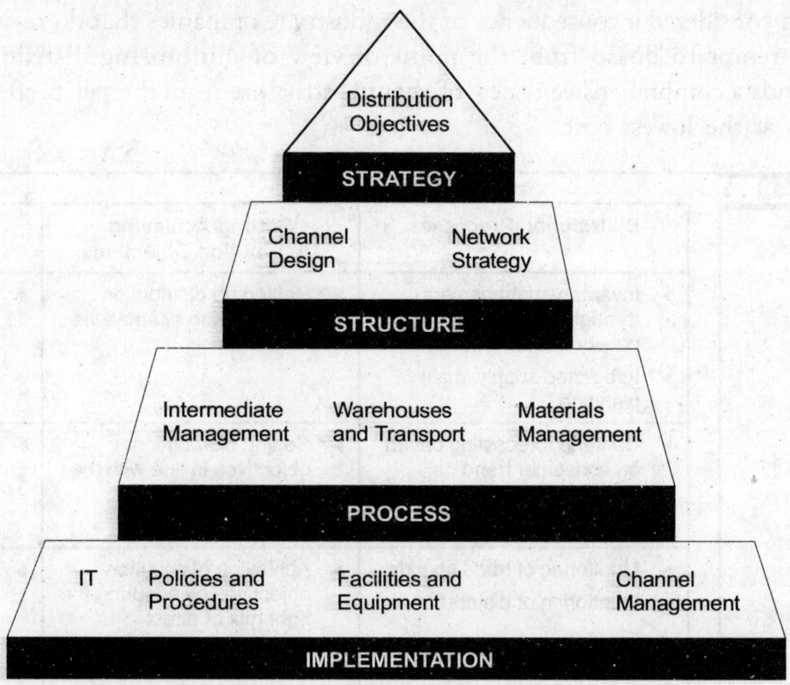

The Distribution Development Index (DDI) is defined as the availability of a brand/category in the market relative to that of a benchmark brand/category. The Category Development Index (CDI) is defined as the per capita consumption of the category in that market relative to the national per capita consumption of the category. The relative level of DDI and CDI will determine the extent of the opportunity to actually extend distribution (Figure 21.2).

figure 21.2

Distribution Development		Low (Category Development)	High (Category Development)
	High	Concentrate on demand generation activities	Concentrate on quality of distribution, service level, frequency etc.
	Low	Develop integrated sales and marketing package	Extend distribution immediately

Category Development

DEVELOPING CHANNEL DESIGN

A number of companies do not develop a channel structure; they inherit it. Channel structures are thus often considered a consequence of the industry. Companies that do review their channel structures do not attempt to do so from the point of view of minimising distribution costs. The Pyramid recommends a comprehensive review of channel structure from the perspective of achieving distribution objectives at the lowest cost.

figure 21.2

Distribution Processes	Setting/Achieving Distribution Objectives	Controlling Distribution TDC
▶ Inventory management through a periodic review of network ▶ Integrated supply chain planning	▶ Setting up distribution strategy with alternatives	▶ Consistently lower inventory levels in changing demand
▶ Demand forecasting based on consumer trend secondary	▶ Setting distribution objectives in line with the demand potential	▶ Lower inventories ▶ Lower trade spends (no attempts to boost sales where demand)
▶ Monitoring of trade spends ▶ Monitoring of distributor	▶ Achieving distribution objectives by ensuring the right mix of direct coverage and reach.	▶ Controlling trade spends ▶ Controlling distributor expenses and service evils to prevent distributors from making sales.

An optimal channel design requires the organisation to understand the following:

- ▶ What activities and functions need to be performed (redistribution, stocking, collections and disbursements to company)?
- ▶ Which channel intermediaries can perform these functions (C and F agents, distributors, wholesalers)?
- ▶ What are the service level requirements that channel intermediaries require from an organisation (credit, inventory levels, infrastructure, lead times from order placement to receipt of goods)?

- What are the service levels that an organisation would require from our channel intermediaries (number of outlets covered, frequency of coverage, etc.)?

Given service level requirements of the company and the intermediary, what minimum returns should intermediaries be making for them to deliver sustainable distribution objectives at the least cost? With C and F agents, it will be per cent commission/flat fees, with distributors/wholesalers, it will be gross margins, return on investment.

Optimal channel designs are heavily dependent on distribution objectives and the functions that need to be performed to achieve these. For typical FMCG categories, availability in over 5 lakh outlets requires services of credit, readily available stock and redistribution. This would typically require 1,500-2,000 distributors who, in turn, would need to be serviced by depots/CFAs for inventory freight economies.

Multinational FMCG players have thus established that the lowest cost distribution channel is the factory CFA distributor (wholesale) retailer route. For high value medical diagnostics products, where the customer base is a few hundred hospitals and diagnostics labs, the key service requirements are high credit, low supply lead times/inventories (since most products have a limited shelf life) and cold chain transportation and stocking.

Developing Physical Network Strategy

Most companies take the location and capacities of their depots and manufacturing units as given. The Pyramid recommends a comprehensive optimisation exercise for the TDC of distribution. This requires the optimal channel design to be populated with a plan for the flow of goods and information in terms of the following

- How many facilities (manufacturing units/depots/CFAs) are needed and where?
- Which customers/regions and which product lines should be served from each facility?
- How much inventory should be maintained in each facility?

  The populated network needs to be optimised with respect to the total delivered cost of distribution. Using linear optimisation, several companies have managed to cut distribution costs by as much as 10-15%.

Reviewing Distribution Processes

Most companies do not monitor the ability of the distribution network to achieve distribution objectives, or the cost of distribution.

The Pyramid recommends continuous monitoring of the ability of the distribution network to achieve objectives at the lowest cost through robust action oriented monitoring processes. A two step approach is required to formalise these principles.

It is a one time exercise to bring the distribution system (strategy, structure, processes) in line with distribution objectives. Subsequently, annual reviews of the distribution system, as a part of the annual strategic planning process, should be undertaken.

LOGISTIC NEEDS

All the activities related to distribution of goods may be said to be logistic needs or logistic management. Logistic means art of moving. The modern industrial organizations have need of

1. Land – Sufficient land so that industrial or business operations may be conducted smoothly.
2. Water – distribution
3. Energy – Sufficient electric power or alternative resources of power so that operations may go unhindered.
4. Storage for equipments, construction goods.
5. Machinery and spares.
6. Warehousing space for movement of goods/temporary storing till the goods reach final destination.
7. Transport equipments, trucks, trolleys, etc.
8. Telephones, telefax and other communication equipments.
9. Adequate supply of manpower
   a. Staff supervisory, managerial
   b. Workers – skilled and unskilled
   c. Specialised nature of persons to provide their services to the company.
10. Many other requirements like pollution control, energy saving measures etc.

All these requirements take us to a stage where a company has to devote time and energy to bring up a good logistic system.

Logistic Management

Logistic management is a field of management which primarily deals with the co-ordination of resources in an organization.

The term logistic is used in the army for supplying/meeting the requirements of the troops. It means 'art of moving'.

In the present times the term is applied to the movement of store activities, important not only to the military, but also to every business activity in the economy.

The term is common in the field agriculture, industry, trading

Logistics make the work effectively. This is required by the customers and industry also. For effective management of logistics, there are five important issues:

- ***Movement of product:*** This is the way that logistics is viewed in many companies. Rush ship on order. Expedite in a component. Products movements is according to the corporate strategy. In it we focus on cost reduction, lower inventories, customer service or whatever, then products must move in such a way that is consistent with the emphasis. Product must also flow, not just move, from, to, between and among vendors, manufacturing sites, warehouses and customers. If it does not flow, then there is not an adequate supply of products instead of there are imbalances in inventories with components and finished goods not being where they should be.

  The movement may be broad in geographical scope. Raw materials and finished goods can move among all parts of the world. While other departments in the company may focus on select geographical regions for sourcing, manufacturing or sales, logistics should deal with all of these.

  The movement plan must be flexible. Forecasting should be based on corporate planning and execution. So the movement must deal with the flow in business cycle. This require a multi-planning program to keep the global supply chain moving smoothly.

- ***Movement of information:*** It is not enough to move product and materials. You must know where they are. You must know what inventories are where and if critical action is required. You must know what orders are coming in and when they must be delivered. Information-timely and accurate-is vital for sound decision-making.

  The information must flow between the company and its suppliers continuously. It must also move internally among purchasing, customer service, logistics, manufacturing, sales, marketing and accounting. And doing this goes beyond Email, faxes and phone calls. Investment in information technology is not an alternative source; it is a requirement for logistics and corporate effectiveness.

  Systems should exist at the macro or corporate level and view. Since logistics is a process which interacts with many other groups in the company, it is fundamental that a corporate system be in place. It has to be dynamic for handling customer orders, production planning, material requirements planning, distribution requirements planning, finance and sales forecasting. There must also be systems at the micro, or logistics level and view. Programs are needed for warehouse management, cross-docking, shipment tracking for example. Each in turn takes technology, with bar-coding and scanning. These satisfy the operations and the planning needs.

- ***Time/service:*** The ability to give response to the dynamic of the global marketplace-changing forecasts, customer requirements, new product introductions, and how to manage all these changes-must be done quickly and fastly. Raw materials and components must be ordered and arrive completely, accurately and quickly. Orders must be filled completely, accurately and quickly. It is no longer months or weeks for lead times. It may not even be days. Hours may decided customer service, competitiveness and value-added. If your company cannot properly response to the customer, your customers will look for the other alternative.

  The concept of service is more than having to expedite a shipment. Time/service is a factor of competition, customer requirements, your company's reputation in the industry, your corporate culture, how well everyone in the global supply chain works together, and how well everyone works together in your company. Logistics is the interlink among all this. And the more diverse the geographical scope of vendors, manufacturing, warehouses and customers, the more critical is time. Distance means time. Yet time delays are not acceptable. Smoothly flow of good and information is essential for logistics.

- ***Cost:*** Cost is the key factor which measure the effectiveness of logistics. The high price of a product do not ensure the quality of the product. The highest price does not mean the best service, and it may not be the service you need. Nor does the lowest price necessarily meet your needs.

  There is no double that how important costs are. But the company must be careful about keeping the low cost of the various logistics elements, such as freight and warehousing. The effectiveness of the logistics group and of the company in satisfying its customers.

  Cost has a relation to service. They go hand-in-hand. As you define your service against your costs or costs against service, the give take develops into your operating costs and budgets. Then you have to make sure that the cost can be managed. Otherwise costs can go out of control, or seem to.

  However, there is no ready mechanism which really makes proper recognition in costs for time/service or for adjustments in any part of the company plan. There is no item in the P&L or balance sheet for Time/Service, which is the driver of a company's logistics efforts. Logistics cost measurement is a tool of measuring the shortcoming in the present accounting systems.

In addition there may be other issues such as conversion of currency and fluctuations. Air freight is quoted in the currency of the origin country. Ocean terminal and other accessorial origin charges are also in origin country currency. Warehouses in other countries will invoice in origin currencies. Currency conversion is a dynamics process which can create unfavourable or favourable cost variances which have nothing to do with logistics performance.

- ***Integration–within your company:*** Between you and your customers and between you and your vendors, integration–brings all of them together. Logistics is a process. Effectiveness requires that each relevant element is a part of its organization. However there is a problem with doing so. The traditional organization with its boxes and defined responsibilities is a collection of functional silos. Each silo segments and collects different parts of the vendor purchase/manufacturing/sales activity and stores it. Hence there is no process. There is a compartmentalization or a fragmenting in the process. This creates an anti-process effect.

  In addition to internal integration, you must bring together and work with the external players. Your vendors, including your carriers and warehouses, must understand what you are doing and why. You must share your logistics vision and plan with them. This sharing and understanding will better enable them to cooperate with and assist you. They may be able to offer ideas and gain sharing to further improve the logistics effectiveness and the key issues with it.

  Integration with customers is vital for any organization. You and everyone in your company must be working and satisfy your customers. You should review written customer requirements with everyone in the logistics department and with everyone in the company. It is not enough to a company to tear apart the written requirements and hand them to various departments. That is not integration. That is functional silos.

  Meeting with customers is very good for the growth of any organization. A face-to-face discussion with him about his requirements and how you will meet them is important. This shows how much you value him and want to work with him or not. What does he need? How does he need it? Why does he need it? When does he need it? The more you know about your customer and his needs, the more valued of a supplier you are to him. This is a competitive advantage. Partnerships and alliances can be developed or enhanced.

DEFINITIONS OF PHYSICAL DISTRIBUTION

There are various ways in which Physical distribution is defined. Some of the definitions are given below

1. "The term 'Physical Distribution Management', is employed in manufacturing and commerce to describe the broad range of activities concerned with the efficient movement of finished products from the end of production line to the consumer and, in some cases, includes the movement of raw materials from the sources of supply to the beginning of the production line".

   These activities are

   - Freight
   - Warehousing
   - Material handling

- Protective packing
- Inventory control
- Selection of site for various activities
- Marketing
- Forecasting.

2. "Physical Distribution is the art and science of determining requirements, acquiring them, distributing them and, finally, maintaining them in an operationally ready condition for their entire life".

3. "Physical Distribution Management is specifically concerned with the flow of goods through the economic system. In the business firm, the logistician is concerned with the inbound movement of goods to supply the production process of the firm. In this setting, the firm is the customer and anticipates a certain level of distribution services from the suppliers. The firm is also a supplier of finished or semi-finished goods and the logistician must provide a level of distribution service to the firms customers. The customer may be another firm or a final customer."

Functions of Physical Distribution

In main, physical distribution functions may be listed as follows:

1. Locational analysis
2. Transportation
3. Material handling
4. Warehousing
5. Packing
6. Order processing
7. Packaging
8. Inventory control
9. Customer sales service.

An organisation can achieve its objectives of sales by creating an efficient, looking forward system of physical distribution. In the coming chapters, we shall discuss the importance of these functions in detail.

SUMMARY

The task of distribution is concerned with the exchange process and gears itself to matching the demand and supply within a given periphery.

It is important to assess how the distribution task is being performed in India. This task can be undertaken by measuring the number of functionaries in each class, their organisational structure and their capital structure. The profit margin charged by them would be a function of the quantum of goods moved. The population served by them and services rendered by them would also assist in the task of measuring their performance.

Project Work

1. Recommend distribution channels for:
   - A new brand of cosmetics
   - PVC irrigation pipes
   - Branded packaged pasteurised milk
   - Computer Hardware
   - Photocopying machines.
2. What types of distribution channels are utilised for the following products? Give justification for your answers.

Short Answer Questions

1. What do you mean by channel design?
2. What do you mean by physical network strategy?
3. What do you mean by selective distribution?
4. What is channel strategy?
5. What is logistics?
6. What is the concept of Integration in supply chain management?

Review Questions

1. Mention the main control issue in the management of distribution channels.
2. What performance considerations would you use in the selection of channel structure for a newly introduced brand of frozen vegetables?
3. "Demographics decide the Indian distribution pattern." Discuss.
4. How does a marketing manager select a distribution channel? What are the various choices available to him?
5. Discuss the importance of "Marketing Channels".
6. Design marketing channels for cellular phones showing channel levels.
7. An efficient dealer network plays a crucial role in marketing consumer durables. Discuss.
8. Explain the terms extensive, selective and exclusive distribution. What considerations would you keep in mind in deciding whether to have extensive or selective distribution?
9. Suggest the distribution system for a manufacturer of library furniture. Justify your answer.
10. Examine the different channels of distribution presently operative in India, explaining their merits and demerits.
11. Design a distribution system for a new brand of computer hardware to be marketed globally.
12. Identify and discuss the factors affecting the selection of a distribution channel.
13. How logistics made the work more efficient? Explain it with the help of suitable example.

Go to the Net

Using Intenet resources, collect data about the following services and draw their distribution system:

1. Indian Airlines
2. ITDC Hotels
3. DHL.
4. Using Internet search tools, prepare a report on the role and importance of 10 Indian Logistic Companies.

C H A P T E R

22

distribution costs, control and customer service

learning objectives

The objectives of this chapter are to:

- understand the need for proper analysis of distribution costs
- analyse the elements of total cost in physical distribution system
- appreciate the control systems for efficiency.

content outline

opening case

Flash

The globalisation phenomenon of bringing the world together necessitated the need for reliable and experienced associates to provide express services to meet customer's requirements. Accuracy, responsiveness and reliability were the key requirements. Many cargo firms started offering tailor-made services in this field: Lufthansa Cargo, a premier cargo firm, offers several types of tailor-made services in this field.

The Lufthansa Cargo express concept focuses mainly on speed of service which fits into a definite time frame in the global environment. Lufthansa Cargo introduced services brand named FLASH which are available in 70 countries covering more than 200 destinations.

These services are broadly as under

Flash: Airport to Airport

Flash: Airport to Airport offers flexible delivery deadlines to customers, faster transport and transit handling bar-code technology, and comprehensive insurance.

Flash: Airport to Airport is the core of Lufthansa Cargo activities. It ensures delivery of goods to the right person at the right place, be it hi-tech equipments or sensitive pharmaceuticals.

Flash: Airport to Door

Flash: Airport to Door service plays a critical role in reaching the customer on time. These supplement the worldwide network of on line destinations with a range of reliable partners. These services are also offered on non-working days. It also provides services of customs clearance and domestic transport, thus relieving the customer from the burden of handling these complex formalities.

Flash has a transparent pricing system.

On Board Courier

The on Board Courier branch mainly concentrates on sensitive document transportation. Accompanied by escorts, the shipment is checked in as baggage at origin and delivered on the baggage belts at the destination. This mode of operation ensures specific delivery and paperless transactions.

TRY YOURSELF

1. How is Lufthansa Cargo with its branded service FLASH meeting the delivery requirements of global customers? Discuss logistics and strategies.

INTRODUCTION

Selling and distribution costs, no doubt, broadly represent marketing cost. Selling costs seek to create and stimulate demand, secure orders and retain customers. Distribution costs cover the sequence of operations from where the packed product is made available for dispatch ending with marketing the reconditioned returned empty package available for reuse. Distribution costs are those costs which are incurred in getting finished products from factory to customer – those involved with filling orders. The order-filling costs arise from answering that proper goods are in the proper place. These could be subdivided into the following:

1. Transportation such as freight and insurance, operating expenses, depreciation of delivery vehicles, etc.
2. Warehousing and storage rent, insurance and depreciation of warehouses, loss in warehouse, stock record - keeping costs, etc.
3. Administrative costs such as cost of carrying and buying of supplies, administration overheads apportioned to distribution costs.

NEED FOR A PROPER ANALYSIS OF DISTRIBUTION COSTS

The necessity for a proper classification and analysis of distribution costs arises due to the following reasons

- To determine cost of sales of different jobs and products, and the extent of profitability of each of them.
- To help in fixation of optimum sales level.
- To control costs of efforts in different areas of distribution activities, to determine the profitability of various sales outlets under different conditions in different markets and by different methods.
- To help in guiding marketing policy both in the short and in the long-term.

ALLOCATION OF DISTRIBUTION COSTS

Distribution costs are usually common to several functions and there is no easily measurable and assignable output. Also, standards of performance are much difficult to set and, therefore, distribution overheads are similar to manufacturing costs which could be identified with the product, division, unit, etc.

Some important bases of allocation of selling and distribution costs to products and customers are given in Table 22.1.

table 22.1 **Allocation of Selling and Distribution Costs to Products**

Functional Cost Group	Bases of Allocation
1. Inventory investment charge such as insurance and taxes	Average inventory value
2. Storage of finished goods handling	Floor space occupied
3. Inventory record-keeping	Number of invoices made/requisitions/orders handled

Contd...

4. Finished goods handling	Number of standard units handled
5. Packing and shipping	Number of standard shipping units, time studies
6. Transportation	Weight, number of standard shipping units
7. Sales promotion programmes	Direct where possible, analysis of promotion
8. Sales solicitation	Time studies; analysis of sales efforts
9. Order entry – processing of orders and preparing invoices	Numbers of invoices; number of orders
10. Billing – time spent in processing orders and preparing orders	Number of invoices; number of orders
11. Credit extension – costs related to numbers of handled customers, orders processed, posting, invoices	Not allocated to products
12. Accounts receivable record-keeping.	Not allocated to products.

table 22.2 **Allocation of Selling and Distribution Costs to Customers**

Functional Cost Group	Bases of Allocation
1. Inventory investment charges	Generally not allocated to customers
2. Storage of finished goods	Generally not allocated to customers
3. Inventory record-keeping	Generally not allocated to customers
4. Finished goods handling	Number of invoices; number of orders; standard units handled
5. Packing and shipping	Number of standard shipping units
6. Transportation	Preferably direct; weight handled
7. Sales promotion	Analysis of promotion programmes
8. Sales solicitation	Time studies; number of sales calls; analysis of sales efforts
9. Order entry	Number of invoices; number of orders
10. Billing	Number of invoices; number of orders
11. Credit extension	Average amount outstanding; number of orders
12. Accounts receivable record-keeping.	Number of posting; number of invoice.

Source: Crowningshied Gerald R and Gorman, Kenneth A. Cost Accounting: Principles and Managerial Applications (Boston: Houghton Mifflin Company, 1974), R 486.

Analysis of Distribution Costs

Selling and distribution costs can be analysed in a variety of ways, depending upon the needs and desires of management. If profit is to be maximised, sales efforts should be directed towards the most profitable of products and customers through the most economic channels of distribution. The analysis of distribution costs can be discussed on the following lines:

- Product or products lines
- Individual customers or groups of customers
- Channels of distribution
- Salesmen
- Geographical area or territories

- Terms of sales
- Order sizes.

ELEMENTS OF TOTAL COST IN PHYSICAL DISTRIBUTION SYSTEM

Transportation costs

Railway Cost

Railway costs can be classified into fixed cost and operating cost. Fixed costs are large, sunk, irreversible, risky, technology dependent, scale influencing, environment influencing and so on. Operating costs include maintenance of track, upkeep of rolling stock, repairs of buildings, renovation of facilities, fuel and lubricant cost, salary and wages, administrative cost, etc. Fixed costs remain constant upto a certain range of activity. Initially, marginal cost might decline resulting in the average cost per unit service declining. Costing in railways needs to be computed with respect to passenger kilometer, tonne kilometer run and wagon load kilometer. For better control, route-wise and round-trip wise costing would do well.

Freight Rate Structure in Road Transport

Freight rate refers to charges levied on the user for carrying and handling his cargo by the carrier. Freight rate in road transport is generally fixed on the basis of cost of service rules. Freight rate should be based on the cost of service. There are two types of transport costs (i) Standing Cost (ii) Operating Cost.

- Standing Costs includes the following costs:
    - Cost of vehicles
    - Capital cost for premises and buildings needed for garage, office, repair shops, etc.
    - Expenditure on miscellaneous.
- Operating Costs includes the following costs:
    - Repairs and maintenance cost
    - Depreciation and renewal expenses
    - Taxes
    - Insurance
    - Licence fee, administrative expenses.

The cost of service, the value of service and the paying capacity of the customer influence freight rate. Besides these, the nature of commodity to be transported, the demand and supply conditions in the transport industry, the competitive conditions in the transport industry, state regulations, etc., also influence the freight rate. The 'cost plus' method is adopted by private operators.

Cost of Airways

Cost of airways includes capital cost and operating cost. Capital cost includes huge cost which is involved in airport construction with all modern radar equipments, meteorological devices cost, the runway cost, cost of air traffic control tower, etc.

Operating cost includes ground expenses and flying expenses. Ground expenses include interest on investment in ground facilities, rent for office space, depreciation and maintenance of buildings, wages of ground personnel, traffic and advertising expenses, insurance tax, etc.

Costing of Seaways

Fixed cost and operating costs are two major cost components in seaways costs. Operating cost includes motive power, salary and wages, office costs, advertising and promotion costs, repairs and maintenance costs, electricity, etc. Fixed cost includes vessels and port buildings, loading and unloading equipments, lighthouses, cost of port land, etc.

Inventory Costs

There are three types of inventory costs:

1. ***Ordering Cost:*** It includes cost of stationery, postage, telegram, etc., in placing an order.
2. ***Cost of Materials:*** It is the purchase price plus transport and insurance during transit and taxes if any.
3. ***Carrying Cost:*** It includes space cost, storage cost, insurance, taxes, theft and pilferage, wastage and loss, etc.

Inventory control aims at reducing both the ordering cost and carrying cost. As these move in opposite directions, minimising the total of both these costs is the crux of the inventory management exercise. Economic order quantity technique of inventory management is based on this minimisation effect.

Warehouse Costs

The costs of maintaining a warehouse building are largely fixed and independent of the amount of stock it holds or the amount of handling required. These fixed costs include land, building cost, administrative cost, material handling, insurance and taxes. There are very few variable costs at warehouses.

Material Costs

The cost of material handling includes the cost of protective packaging, the costs of material handling equipment and of goods damaged in handling. The most important cost is that of labour associated with packing, loading and unloading the inventory.

Packaging Costs

Packaging cost is influenced by mode of transport and material handling equipments. On the other hand, the selection of a particular mode of transport determines the characteristics of packaging.

Customer Service Costs

A producer or a supplier cannot always ensure the availability of goods whenever they are demanded by the customer. It may increase the inventory carrying costs; in some cases, this cost may even be prohibitive.

The producer or the marketer has to set certain limits upto which he will satisfy customer demand and trade off the cost of lost sales against the inventory carrying costs.

CONTROL SYSTEM FOR EFFICIENCY

Logistics system should function efficiently. Efficiency is the ratio of output to input. A logistics system requires the following efficiencies:

- Operating efficiency
- Financial efficiency
- Service level efficiency
- Marketing efficiency
- Personnel efficiency
- Organisational efficiency.

For example, operating efficiency can be measured in terms of fuel consumption rate per tonne kilometer, maintenance cost per tonne kilometer, etc. Financial efficiency is known through operating profit to gross earnings, operating profit to capital employed etc. Service level efficiency is measured through number of door-to-door services rendered to total number of services made, number of on-time services to total number of services, etc. Marketing efficiency depends on market share, rate of growth in gross earnings, etc. Organisational efficiency is seen in the adherence to schedule, wider community coverage, flexibility, etc.

Logistics system should have a strategic orientation, i.e., linkages with inner and outer environments. A strategic logistics system must first of all be planned, organised, executed and controlled. The managerial functions need to be conducted with regard to raw materials, work in-process inventory as well as final goods. For all this, we require, human resources committed to the system.

table 22.3 **Output of Logistic System**

Inputs	*Process*	*Outputs*
Physical Resources — Land, Facilities, etc.	Management Actions	Consumer
Human Resources	Planning, Execution; Control	Time Utility
Financial Resources	Vendors	Place Utility
Information Resources	Raw materials, In Process: Final Goods	Efficient Movement
	Logistics Activities	Competitive Edge
	Inventory, Order processing, Warehousing, Transporting, Packaging, Communication Returns; Tracking	Consumer Satisfaction

Productivity Aspects and Logistics Management

The following ratios are suggested by the Asian Productivity Organisation (APO) for physical and financial productivity measures

1. Right Delivery Ratio = $\frac{\text{No. of deliveries on time/year}}{\text{Total no. of deliveries/year}}$

2. Route Potential Ratio = $\frac{\text{Tonne kilometre run/route}}{\text{Tonne kilometre capacity/route}}$

3. Accidents Ratio = $\frac{\text{No. of accidents/year}}{\text{No. of trips operated/year}}$

4. Service Ratio = $\frac{\text{No. of consignments booked/year}}{\text{No. of consignments planned/year}}$

5. Vehicle Utilisation Ratio = $\frac{\text{Vehicle kilometre actually run/day}}{\text{Vehicle kilometre planned/day}}$

6. Breakages Ratio = $\frac{\text{No. of consignments damaged in transit}}{\text{Total no. of consignments}}$

7. Business Efficiency Ratio = $\frac{\text{Tonne kilometre achieved/year}}{\text{Tonne kilometre planned/day}}$

8. Operating Express Ratio = $\frac{\text{Total operating expenses}}{\text{Total earnings}}$

9. Net Profit Ratio = $\frac{\text{Net profit}}{\text{Total earnings}}$

10. Promptness Ratio = $\frac{\text{No. of prompt deliveries/year}}{\text{Total no. of deliveries/year}}$

Distribution and Customer Satisfaction

Excellent quality of service will lead to customer satisfaction, which creates customer loyalty. Satisfied customers help in retaining market share. The marketer needs to understand what the customer needs from a service. Whether the buyer is satisfied after purchase depends on the offer's performance in relation to the buyer's expectation. In general, satisfaction is a function of perceived performance and expectations. Nowadays companies are aiming for high satisfaction because customers who are just satisfied still find it easy to switch when a better offer comes along.

In customer services, there are three elements, which are important for the marketer, in decision making.

table 22.4 **Elements of Customer Service**

PRE-TRANSACTIONAL ELEMENTS	TRANSACTIONAL ELEMENTS	POST-TRANSACTIONAL ELEMENTS
– Statement of policy Organisation	– Working Relations – Staff Training in handling customers	Installation, warranty Repairs,
– System Development		Spare parts, customer claims and complaints
– Technical services		

One important dimension of customer service is service after sales. It is an obligation on the part of a manufacturer to render service assistance to his customers by attending to breakdowns or failures in the case of consumer durable items, or replacing the items free of charges during the warranty period, and repairs on charge once the product is out of warranty. Hopkins and Bailey have very precisely described the functions involved in service after sales. These functions are:

- Information service to customer
- Warranty administration
- Maintenance repair
- Preventive inspection
- In-warranty repair
- Out-of-warranty repair
- Repair service centres
- Maintenance contract
- Parts standardisation
- Stocking of obsolete replacement parts.

SUMMARY

The distribution costs have been described and analysed in respect of each area of distribution, viz., transportation, warehousing, inventory material handling and information technology. One of the most important influences on customer service is the company's distribution policy, which has been viewed by many as a source of cost–admittedly a necessary cost – but a cost nevertheless.

A prerequisite for customer service oriented distribution management is an appropriate organisational structure. Customer service failings are often due to organisation problems. Effective customer service management requires that all those activities, involved from the time the order is placed until the goods are delivered, are managed in an integrated way.

PROJECT WORK

How do you control costs in the following services:

1. Courier Services
2. Fashion Designing
3. Home Delivery Services

SHORT ANSWER QUESTIONS

1. How do you allocate distribution cost?
2. What are the elements of total cost in a physical distribution system?
3. What are the various types of inventory costs?
4. What is customer satisfaction?

REVIEW QUESTIONS

1. Discuss the various costs associated with the physical distribution of a consumer durable product.
2. What kind of cost elements would be most critical in the following cases:
   a. Distribution of milk products
   b. Distribution of heavy duty capital equipment
   c. Distribution of textbooks for schools.
3. Discuss an integrated distribution effort to show how it has a major effect upon marketing performance and cost of company operations.
4. How does a marketing manager select a distribution channel? What are the various choices available to him?
5. How do you control channel members? Discuss the tools for the same.
6. What are the elements of total cost in the physical distribution system?
7. How can physical distribution be used to gain critical customer service advantage? Use examples from the Indian market to illustrate your answer.
8. Explain the terms – distribution channels, physical distribution and customer service and identify how they together relate to distribution strategy.
9. How should a company making electric home appliances determine the customer service components and their level?
10. Is it possible to measure channel performance realistically? If yes, how?
11. Suggest an approach to measure the channel performance of the following:
    a. A wholesaler in electrical fittings (switches, sockets, cutouts, MCBs, etc.) covering an entire state.
    b. An authorised sales and servicing (ASS) agent for a wrist watch manufacturer.
12. Explain productivity aspects and Logistic management with the help of suitable corporate example.

GO TO THE NET

Using Internet search tools and other relevant sources, suggest the cost control system for the following products and services:

1. Industrial products
2. FMCG products
3. Consumer durables.
4. Using Internet, search tools, prepare a report on the management of inventory control with the help of 10 Indian MNC.

CHAPTER 23

selection of channels

learning objectives

The objectives of this chapter are to:

- understand channel management and channel strategy
- discuss key issues in determining channel requirement
- understand role, responsibilities and need for distribution channel.

content outline

- Opening Case
- Channel Management and Channel Strategy
- The Need for Distribution Channels
- Types of Channels
- Types of Distribution within Channels
- Channel Strategy Decisions
- Key Issues in Determining Channel Requirement
- Manufacturing Strategies
- Wholesaler
- Retailing
- Summary
- Project Work
- Short Answer Questions
- Review Questions
- Go to the Net

opening case

Channel Management At Maxwell

The President of Maxwell Corporation is considering whether the company should set up its own distribution system or whether it should outsource the entire distribution and logistics function to a third party service provider. The company has set up a manufacturing plant at Vizag where wide range of orthopaedic equipments, *viz.,* crutches, wheel chairs, walkers, back braces, heating pads, elastic bandages, canes, knee braces, shoulder braces and so forth are manufactured. Presently, the finished goods warehouse is located at Vizag itself and the products are sent to all major towns in India as a point-to-point dispatch. The company is supplying these equipments directly to retail stores at all these locations. Marketing activity is headed by a general manager-marketing based at Vishakapatnam who is supported by a sales team comprising of sales officers. The company is not resorting to advertisements and publicity though the products of the company are fairly well known. But, it is felt that all the customers want quick response to their orders as the products are catered to emergency patients. However these retail outlets carry only very limited inventories. This is due to the fact that most of the products come in a variety of styles, shapes and sizes and the requirement is more customer driven and keeping even a moderate inventory of all types is economically not viable and leads to development of dead stocks in the long run. The company is looking at various options which include.

1. Setting up of a hub and spoke type of a distribution network wherein it proposes to set up a stock point or mother warehouse in each zone, —East. West, North and South — and respective retail outlets which are to be fed from the mother warehouse located in that zone.
2. Setting up of a central warehouse anywhere in central India and feeding retail outlets from this location.
3. Changing the distribution channel from the present numerous retail outlet system to a more efficient system.
4. Outsourcing the entire distribution and logistics to a third party wherein the entire activity of transportation and distribution till the ultimate retail outlet will be taken care of by this service provider so that the company can focus more on activities related to marketing and sales.

Try Yourself

1. Out of the given options, which should Maxwell Corporation follow for maximum benefit and why?
2. What should be the distribution channel for Maxwell and what advantages would having such a type of a set-up have?
3. What type of a marketing and sales set-up would you recommend for Maxwell Corporation?

   For successful sales of products and services it is desirable to be associated with a good distribution channel.

   The company should first study the methods of selling prevalent in the market and then select a channel.

Channel Management and Channel Strategy

Channels of distribution are of vital importance to all types of firms – producers, wholesalers and retailers. Each member of a channel is a link in a distribution network of organisations that extends from the producer to the end users of products or services. Although some firms perform all channel functions, typically, several organisations are linked together in a distribution channel to carry out the various activities of storage, transportation, warehousing, material handling service. Sorting and re-packing organisations that perform these marketing functions between producers and end users are called middlemen, intermediaries or resellers.

Marketing Intermediaries

The people and organisations that assist in the flow of goods and services from producer to customer are known as marketing intermediaries. The following are the common types of intermediaries

- ***Middlemen:*** Middlemen refers to just about anybody acting as an intermediary between the producer and the customer.
- ***Agent or Broker:*** Intermediaries with legal authority to market goods and services and to perform other functions on behalf of the producer are called agents or brokers. Agents generally work for producers continuously, whereas brokers may be employed for a particular deal. In some cases, agents sell to another intermediary such as an industrial distributor. In addition, an agent or broker can work for the buyer rather than the seller. This situation is becoming more common in real estate business.
- ***Wholesaler:*** Wholesalers are organisations that buy from producers and sell to retailers and organisational customers. They primarily deal in bulk and will ordinarily sell to the retailer or other intermediaries.
- ***Retailer:*** As the last link in many marketing channels, retailers sell directly to final customers. They purchase goods from wholesalers or, in some cases, directly from the producer.
- ***Distributor:*** Distributor is a general term applied to a variety of intermediaries. These individuals and firms perform several functions, including inventory management, personal sale and financing. The basic difference between an agent and distributor is that while agents work on a commission basis, distributors deal on their own account. Distributors are more common in organisational markets, although wholesalers also occasionally act as distributors.
- ***Dealer:*** Another general term that can apply to just about any intermediary is dealer. Basically, the same type of intermediary acts as a distributor, although some people distinguish dealers as those intermediaries that sell only to final customers and not to other intermediaries.
- ***Value-added resellers (VARs):*** They are intermediaries that buy the basic product from producers and add value to it or, depending on the nature of the product, modify it and then resell it to final customers.
- ***Merchants:*** They are intermediaries that assume ownership of the goods that they sell to customers or other intermediaries. Merchants usually take physical possession of the goods that they sell.
- ***Facilitating (C&F Agents) Agents:*** They are people and organisations that assist the flow of products and information to marketing channels and include banking and insurance functions. The following are the services where assistance is required:

- Transportation and Storage (C&F Agent)
- Covering the risk (Insurance)
- Financial services.

THE NEED FOR DISTRIBUTION CHANNELS

Why are all these layers needed in distribution? Why can't a producer simply sell to a retailer, who sells to a consumer? It's a fair question, and in some cases, that is exactly how it happens. But the fact is that many producers are either too small or too large to handle all the necessary functions themselves to get their products to market. Consider the small, specialty manufacturer who is terrific at making fine leather handbags but may not have the expertise to market its products as well as it makes them, or they may not have the money to hire a team of full-time salespeople to court the customers and secure the orders. An intermediary who works for several small, non-competing firms can easily handle those functions cost-effectively. An intermediary who specializes in importing and exporting can handle the intricacies of customs paperwork, overseas shipping, and foreign markets, too. Conversely, large companies need intermediaries because they are also in the business of manufacturing, not marketing. Turning out tens of thousands of cases of soft drinks, for instance, do you think Pepsi has take and fill individual orders from households? Channel members like wholesalers and retailers are useful because they are best at specific aspects of sales in their markets, leaving the manufacturers to do what they do best-which is turn out the best possible product. Having a distribution channel breaks the whole buying and selling process and all its related negotiations into manageable tasks, each performed by companies that specialize in certain skills.

Direct channel: This is when the same company that manufactures a product sells it directly to the consumer or end user.

Retailer channel: This is when the producer sells to the retailer, and the retailer sells to the consumer.

Wholesaler channel: Intermediaries play a role here, as the manufacturer sells to a wholesaler.

Agent or broker channel: The most complex arrangement involves several transactions, often because the merchandise is being imported.

Dual channel or multiple channel: This term refers to the use of two or more channels to sell products to different types of customers. A lawnmower manufacturer, for example, might sell some product lines at retail and others to commercial lawn care companies, each requiring different intermediary services.

How Channels are chosen although retailers drive distribution channels, it is not usually the retailer who makes the decision to utilize one channel over the others. Another advantage of the distribution channel is its ability to even out the natural ebbs and flows of a supply chain. This comes from the ability of some channel members to store excess goods until they are needed, and to stockpile goods in anticipation of seasonal sales peaks. Depending on how close their relationships, channel members may also work together to purchase goods or services in greater quantity at discounts, passing the savings on to customers. Even for consumers, the distribution chain is handy–beyond handy, in fact! It has become a necessity in our society. What if there were no supermarkets, for instance? Can you imagine how much more time and money you would spend having to buy every item at its source? How practical would it be to run out to the nearest farm to pick up a quart of milk and some salad ingredients on your way home from work?

TYPES OF CHANNELS

Because of the wide variety of channel arrangements that exist, it is difficult to generalise the structure of channels across all industries. However, distribution channels are usually of two types

- Direct Marketing Channel (or Zero Level)
- Indirect Marketing Channel.

Direct Marketing Channel (or Zero Level)

This type of channel has no intermediaries. In this distribution system, the goods go from the producer directly to the consumer, e.g., Eureka Forbes.

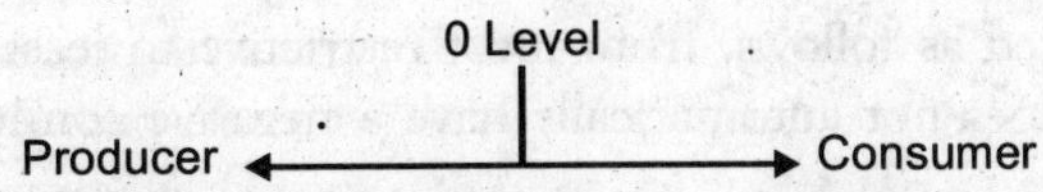

Indirect Marketing Channel

This may further be classified into the following categories

1. ***One-level Channel:*** In this type of channel there is only one intermediary between producer and consumer. This intermediary may be a retailer or a distributor.

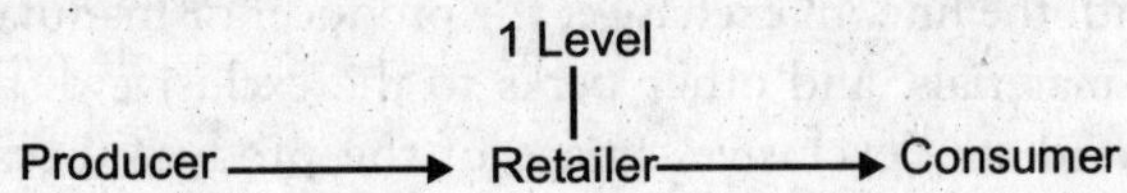

If the intermediary is a distributor, this type of channel is used for speciality products like washing machines, refrigerators or industrial products.

2. ***Two-level Channel:*** This type of channel has two intermediaries, namely, wholesaler/distributor and retailer.

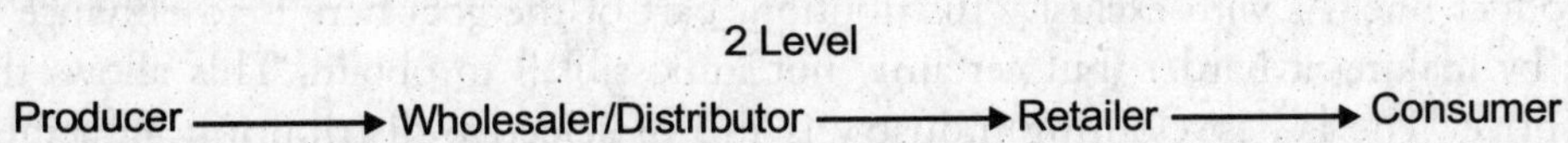

3. ***Three-level Channel:*** This type of channel has three intermediaries, namely, distributor, wholesaler and retailer. This pattern is also used for convenience products.

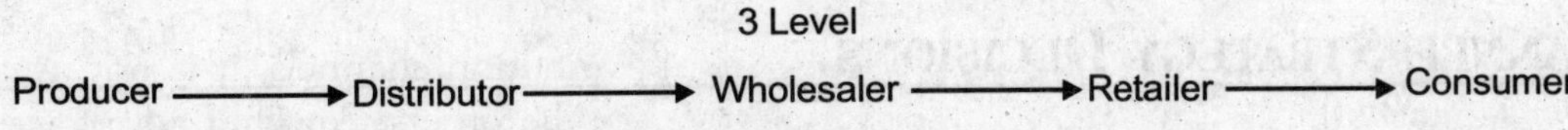

4. ***Four-level Channel:*** This type of channel has four intermediaries, namely, agent, distributor, wholesaler and retailer. This channel is similar to the previous two. This type of channel is used for consumer durable products also.

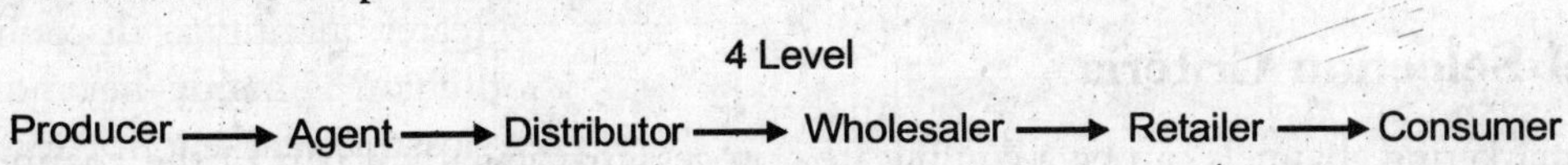

In addition to the above mentioned channels, some different types of channels are also possible. There is no watertight classification of channels. The use or selection of a channel also depends upon the product under consideration. Basically there are three or four types of products, viz. (i) Consumer non-durables (ii) Consumer durables (iii) Industrial products and (iv) Agricultural products.

Distribution channels of different types also depend on the nature of product and services. Therefore, we can say that for different products, there are different types of channels.

TYPES OF DISTRIBUTION WITHIN CHANNELS

The channel members may handle different portions of the transaction, but they must all agree on the end result-that the product(s) will be placed in the market in the manner desired by the producer or manufacturer, and that placement of the product(s) meets the contractual agreements of producer, retailer, and everyone in-between. Once a channel is selected, the distribution strategy can take three different forms. They are listed as follows, from most restrictive to least restrictive-and remember, in retail, the term "restrictive" does not automatically have a negative connotation.

Exclusive distribution is thought of most frequently for high-dollar products such as luxury cars or Rolex watches, but the fact is that even small-ticket items like toys are considered exclusive when they are in high demand. In an exclusive distribution agreement, one retail store or chain of stores has the legal right to market and sell the product line in a geographic area. Exclusive distribution is sometimes requested by the retailer, not the producer, to ensure that the retailer has something unique, that customers can't get anywhere else. This may also mean the retailer commits to not selling any products that are going to compete with the line. In exchange, the producer or manufacturer offers sales assistance, training, point-of purchase materials, and other perks to the exclusive distributor. Such a distribution arrangement can work toward the "exclusive" image of the product (because it's harder to get), the retailer (for having "the only ones" available), and the manufacturer (by implying that the company is interested in marketing "quality, not quantity.")

In B2B commerce, exclusive distribution works well for extremely specialized product lines, such as heavy equipment or high-tech products, ordered to the customer's specifications and budgeted for in advance of the purchase.

Selective distribution means the retailers are carefully screened, and only a few are permitted to carry the product line. As with exclusive distribution, part of the goal here is to enhance the image of the product by making it harder (but certainly not impossible!) to obtain. This allows the retailer to charge full price. The ladies' clothing industry is full of selective distribution agreements between designer labels and so-merchandise lines to sell to discounters; but these are generally sold under separate, secondary brand names.)

CHANNEL STRATEGY DECISIONS

Marketing managers face two sets of decisions when considering marketing channels. The first set leads to a selection of one or more channels. The second set deals with the selection criteria and examines the three levels of distribution. The final step is plan finalisation.

Channel Selection Criteria

Selecting marketing channels can be a complicated process, particularly if part of the channel is outside the producer's direct control. In addition, there is no endless supply of available intermediaries sitting around waiting for producers to give them a call. The elements that managers examine as they define channel strategies can be grouped into market factors, product factors and producer factors.

Market Factors

Analysing and understanding the target market is the first step in selecting marketing channels. There are several factors that an analysis of the market should explore, ranging from customers to the types of competitors:

- ***Customer preference:*** The channel which is most preferred by customers.
- ***Organisational customers:*** Organisational customers frequently have buying habits that are different from those of other consumers.
- ***Geography:*** Customer location is another important factor determining the type of channel to be used.

Competitors

Often a good channel choice is one that has been overlooked or avoided by competitors. In some cases, the marketer may try to duplicate his competitors' channel in order to have his products replace that of a competitors'.

Nature and Availability of Intermediaries

A question that arises very often in the channel decision is "Are there enough of the right kinds of intermediaries to build the desired channel?" We need to find intermediaries that can handle the products capably and provide adequate service to final customers. For new entrants, it is better to find the best available intermediaries in the market.

Product Factors

Even products that end up at the same retail location may need different intermediaries earlier in the channel.

- ***Life Cycle:*** A product category's stage in the life cycle can be an important factor in selecting a channel and channels may have to be adjusted over time. Customers require less support once the product has established itself.
- ***Complexity:*** Some products are so complicated and require so much support that producers need to stay closely involved. This indicates either a direct sales force or a limited number of highly qualified intermediaries. Scientific equipments, jet aircrafts, nuclear reactors, pharmaceuticals and computers are products whose complexity affects the way in which they are marketed.
- ***Value:*** The value of the product also affects its distribution channel choices. Items with low cost and high volume are usually distributed through large, well-established distribution networks such as grocery wholesalers.
- ***Size and Weight:*** A product with significant size and weight can face restricted distribution channel options, particularly if it is also of low value.
- ***Consumer Perceptions:*** The perceptions customers have of products and producers also play a role in channel decision making.
- ***Other Product Factors:*** Depending on the product in question, other factors may enter into the decision as well. Some of these include whether a product is fragile or perishable and whether or not it requires significant customer satisfaction.

Key Issues in Determining Channel Requirement

While a manufacturer faces an agenda of issues related to finance, marketing and industrial relations, attention is focused on selected topics that directly impact marketing channel arrangements. The key issues related to this are:

- Product proliferation and dynamics; and
- Total-quality initiatives.

These two issues are significant drives for a typical firm in determining how channel requirements will be delineated.

Product Proliferation and Dynamics

A major concern throughout industry is the rapid expansion that firms are experiencing in the number of stock keeping units that they maintain in their product list. Fully understanding basic customer needs through marketing research is viewed as a key to a successful new product launch. In practice, few firms have a highly successful new product track record. A large number of new products fail resulting in conflict within the distribution process and the need to remove obsolete inventory. The product life cycle is useful for planning a marketing and distribution strategy.

Numerous examples are available from the food industry to illustrate the product proliferation dilemma. The industry is characterised by a constant effort on the part of manufacturers to introduce new products for distribution. Retailers and wholesalers want to enter into an agreement with manufacturers in which they agree to buy all unsold inventory back at the retail price if a product fails. Independent of the fairness of such agreements, the fact is that the inventory mistakes must be cleared from the channel.

Total Quality Initiatives:

Total quality initiatives represent the primary focus of the revitalisation drive. The concept of total quality is "do it right the first time". The general concept of total quality is to focus managerial attention on the three key concepts of manufacturing: People, Process and Design.

Manufacturing Strategies

There are two popular manufacturing strategies (1) Flexible and (2) Focused.

The goal of flexible manufacturing is to increase responsiveness of production to consumer demands. Having the capability to manufacture what is needed reduces the amount of inventory. For this strategy to succeed, a manufacturer must have an efficient marketing channel so that the demand of the product can be fulfilled effectively in time.

The goal of focused manufacturing is the lowest possible per unit cost and fail-safe quality. The basic idea is to adopt leading edge manufacturing technology and utilise it to the maximum capacity. Focused manufacturing requires building of significant inventories in anticipation of future sale. The trick is to plan manufacturing schedules to keep anticipatory inventories balanced to market demand.

Each of these strategies requires a different type of channel management support. The modern concept of manufacturing seeks to involve employees at all levels of the organisation to effect process improvement and to take initiatives related to customer service. Manufacturers, because of the nature of their brand products, are typically held responsible for the performance of the entire marketing channel. Both consumers and channel trading partners expect manufacturers to maintain a high quality product. It is clear that with emerging manufacturing strategies a premium is placed on gaining and maintaining customer's satisfaction through speed and quality. Quality is dependent on manufacturers but the speed depends wholly upon the channels.

WHOLESALER

Wholesale trade is defined as "all establishments or places of business primarily engaged in selling merchandise to retailers; to industrial, commercial, institutional or professional users or to other wholesalers; or acting as agent in buying merchandise for or selling merchandise to such persons or companies".

Wholesaling is concerned with the activities of those persons or establishments which sell to retailers and other merchants, and or to industrial, institutional and commercial users, but who do not sell insignificant amounts to ultimate consumers.

It is important to understand that there are many different kinds of wholesalers, all of which differ in product categories handled as well as in specific marketing functions performed. There are three basic types of wholesale institutions:

- Merchant wholesalers
- Agent wholesalers
- Manufacturers' sales branches and offices.

Merchant Wholesalers

Merchant wholesalers take ownership of goods in which they deal; they are independently owned, separate from suppliers on the one hand and from the retailers on the other hand. The distinguishing feature of merchant wholesalers is that they take ownership and associated risks related to the goods in which they trade. Merchant wholesalers are of two general classes: full function or service wholesalers and limited function wholesalers.

- ***Full Function or Service Wholesalers:*** This type of wholesaler is also referred to as a distributor or a jobber. Merchant wholesalers perform all or most of the marketing functions normally associated with wholesaling. They may carry a broad variety of goods. Generally, service wholesalers specialise in a narrow range of goods. The extent of product line specialisation depends upon the particular needs and wants of the wholesalers' target markets by taking ownership of the product possession flow. Service wholesalers maintain inventories of their product line. From these stocks, customer orders are filled in and delivered. Personal selling, advertising and sales promotion are functions in the marketing channel. Negotiation with buyers and determining terms of sale along with extending credit to buyers, are other tasks undertaken by full function wholesalers. Of course, these customers pass along market information to their suppliers and accept payment for their customers' purchases. Generally, service or full function wholesalers participate in most aspects of the marketing channel flow.
- ***Limited Function Wholesalers:*** These merchant wholesalers perform only some of the functions typically associated with wholesaling. Among the more common limited function wholesalers are cash and carry wholesalers, drop shippers, truck wholesalers, mail order wholesalers, products, retail cooperatives and rack jobbers.

- *Cash and Carry Wholesalers:* Such wholesalers do not offer small business customers credit or delivery. Nor do they provide their customers much in the way of managerial assistance. They emphasise on the small business market.
- *Drop Shippers:* These wholesalers do not take possession of the goods they handle; therefore, they do not store inventory nor do they provide delivery facilities to their customers. Commodities like grains and natural resources like coal are typically marketed through drop shippers.
- *Truck Wholesalers or Wagon Jobbers:* Such wholesalers perform limited functions because their inventories are carried on their trucks. They provide their customers with a high degree of locational convenience.
- *Mail Order Wholesalers:* This type of wholesalers operate in a similar manner as mail order retailers. The wholesalers serve the business, governmental and institutional markets.
- *Products and Retail Cooperatives and Rack Jobbers:* Independent farm producers often band together to market their output jointly and to buy farm implements and supplies at quantity discounts. Associations of independent retailers are sometimes formed to gain the advantages of quantity buying and joint advertising. These associations are called producer cooperatives and retail cooperatives respectively.

Agent Wholesalers

Unlike merchant wholesalers, agent wholesalers do not take ownership and rarely take possession of the products that they market. They are primarily involved in the buying and selling of goods and services. They typically negotiate sales as representatives of other firms and do not take title to merchandise. They also participate in the collection of market information, promotion and ordering. Agents receive a commission for performing these functions. Among different types of agents are manufacturers agents, brokers, commission merchants, selling agents and auction companies. On the one hand, these agent wholesalers are largely involved in domestic trade and on the other hand, agent wholesalers also play an integral role in international trade.

- ***Manufacturers' Agents***: These are independent firms which typically handle non-competing lines of a variety of manufacturers and are often used in place of a manufacturer's own sales force. New companies use manufacturers' agents when they have neither the expertise nor the resources to develop their own sales force. Established firms rely upon manufacturers' agents when they wish to concentrate upon manufacturing and prefer to subcontract their distribution activities or when they wish to enter new markets. Manufacturers' agents are generally more familiar with the market and can provide more immediate representation than the producer could by developing his own sales force.
- ***Brokers:*** Brokers are commonly used in the real estate industry where they negotiate the buying and selling of property as well as negotiate its rental and leasing. They are the middlemen whose primary activity is to establish contact between the buyer and the seller. They negotiate and facilitate sales and are compensated by a fee or commission. They do not take title of merchandise. Brokers play a key role in the distribution of food products as well. Many small food producers and small food wholesalers rely heavily upon food brokers to provide them with outlets for their products and sources of supply respectively.
- ***Commission Merchants:*** Sometimes called "factors", commission merchants receive products on a consignment basis and then sell them on a commission basis. They typically operate on an

autonomous basis. They often participate in the physical possession, promotion, negotiation, financing, risk-taking, or ordering, payment and market information flow. They are most often used in distribution channels for farm produce, lumber products, etc., where the manufacturers' identity is relatively unimportant to the buyer.

- ***Selling Agents:*** Selling agents differ from manufactures' agents and brokers in that they normally carry a suppliers' entire product line. Unlike manufacturers' agents and brokers, they usually set prices and terms of sale, and also undertake promotional activities. Thus selling agents, in effect, act as the manufacturers' sales force. Note that, as with other agent wholesalers, selling agents do not take title possession of the goods that they handle.
- ***Commercial Auction Companies:*** Unlike other agent wholesalers, auction companies invite buyers and sellers to a single physical location, either at the seller's location or at the auction company's site. In addition to bringing buyers and sellers together, auction firms promote the goods that they handle and actively negotiate the sale of those goods. These wholesalers participate to a lesser degree in the other marketing flows, except for ownership. Their participation in a channel is typically limited to facilitating a transfer of ownership. They are often used in marketing channels for such products as real estate, household goods, used automobiles and equipment and machineries of all kinds. These firms also play a role in the marketing of some commodities such as tobacco.

Manufacturer's Sales Branches and Sales Offices

These are wholesaling operations owned and operated by a manufacturer and maintained separately from the producing plant to sell and market its products. The sales branches include a warehouse with inventory, whereas sales offices do not have any inventory. Manufacturers' branch stores selling to consumers and individual users are classified within retail trade. These are also, sometimes, called, captive distributors.

Manufacturers use sales branches and offices for a variety of reasons, particularly when (1) Independent wholesalers are unable to provide the technical support to the customer (2) These intermediaries cannot handle the quantities involved (3) The manufacturer wishes to achieve more control over the promotion and physical possession activities of marketing and (4) The wholesaling operations provide the manufacturer with additional profit opportunities.

Selecting Wholesalers

A wholesaler is generally selected on the basis of his performance evaluation. Before selecting wholesalers, manufacturers' analyse a wholesaler on the basis of the following questions:

- How can a wholesaler serve a supplier?
- How can a wholesaler serve a retailer?
- How can a wholesaler serve business users?

Issues in Using Wholesalers

A manufacturer cannot ignore wholesalers if he wants to make his distribution channel effective. A manufacturer can neither give up responsibility for effective marketing nor can he expect the wholesaler to respond to all of his suggestions when he turns to a wholesaler for assistance in making his products available for sale and for stimulating demand among industrial, institutional, or commercial end-users or among retailers. A manufacturer must assume the responsibility of making the wholesaler more effective through programmes of product development, careful pricing, promotional support, technical assistance, order servicing and training for wholesalers' salesmen and management. In the long run, the manufacturers have to deal with a larger and stronger wholesaling organisation. The development of mutual dependency will produce a more adhesive channel system.

Strategic Management of Wholesalers

The success of a wholesaler firm depends upon the following major factors:

1. ***Effectiveness***: Effectiveness of a wholesaler depends upon: (i) identifying target market needs, (ii) developing a product and service mix to satisfy those needs and (iii) adjusting the product and service mix to meet changes in the target market needs. Understanding target market needs is the main criterion for the success of any marketing institution. Without a clear understanding of the product requirements of the target market, wholesalers would have no idea how best to approach their customers or how to maintain long-term supplier-customer relationships with them.
2. ***Profitability***: Profitability of a wholesaler is mainly based on two factors
   - Managing net profit margins, and
   - Achieving high rates of assets turnover.

   The margins of wholesalers are highly dependent upon the prices they negotiate with suppliers, the prices they charge their customers, the mix of products they carry, the target market and their growth rates. Net profit margin is a function of gross margin. A small change in gross margin will carry directly through to net profit, producing a disproportionately large change in wholesaling. Due to this fact, gross margin is widely used as a critical decision variable at the wholesale level of distribution. Generally, gross profit margin varies from 10 to 25 per cent.

   Wholesalers generally invest their capital in accounts receivable and inventory. They exercise control on short-term credit and inventory to achieve desirable asset turnover levels. Ninety per cent of wholesalers' sales are made on credit basis for the maximum asset turnover. Fast asset turnover creates maximum profit in wholesaling.
3. ***Niche Marketing***: Several wholesalers owe their success to niche market strategy that specialises in limited or unique product categories.
4. ***Proprietary Brands***: Generally, successful wholesalers have developed strong proprietary brand products for gaining and maintaining a sustained competitive advantage.
5. ***New Technology***: Mechanisation and automation of warehouses strengthens relations with both customers and suppliers. Computer linkage among distribution channels is becoming a prerequisite for success in wholesale trade. Therefore, new technology adoption has deep significance in the wholesaling business.

RETAILING

Retailing is the final connection in the marketing channel that brings goods from manufacturers to consumers. In other words, retailing is the combination of activities involved in selling or renting consumer goods and services directly to ultimate consumers for their personal or household use. In addition to selling, retailing includes different diverse activities like buying, advertising, data processing and maintaining inventory.

Some retailers primarily carry the products of a particular manufacturer only. For example, a Ford dealer may carry a variety of cars but the majority of them are made by Ford. Most of the time, however, merchants are not compelled by manufacturers to create the product mix they believe will fill the needs of their customers.

Importance/Role of Retailing in Marketing Channels

In organisational marketing, producers often sell directly to their final buyers and so are linked to them in marketing channels. Such direct channels are much less common in consumer product marketing. Ultimate consumers make most of their purchases in retail stores that are independent of the producer. Retailing, therefore, is the final stage in marketing channels for consumer products. Retailers provide the important link between the producer and the ultimate consumer.

Retailing is a lot more than simply buying and selling. It is important to consumers because it creates economic utility. It is important to manufacturers because it is the major connection in the marketing channel between manufacturers and end-users. And it is important because of its contribution to the economy.

Retailing and Economic Utility

Retailers go beyond merely selling products off the shelf. They add value to the goods and services that they sell by creating time, place, possession and form utilities. Retailers' create place utility by opening stores in convenient locations. News-stand operators locate near train and bus stations because these are convenient places for their customers to purchase magazines and newspapers. Retailers also create possession utility when they put products in the consumers' hands. Retailers add value to their offerings by developing product and form utility or changing the form involved and these products and form utilities constitute the basis of the service that customers are paying for.

Retailing Functions in Distribution

In general, retailers perform four distinct functions. They participate in the sorting process by collecting an assortment of goods and services from a wide variety of suppliers and offering them for sale. They provide information to consumers through advertising displays and signs and sales personnel. They provide marketing research support to other channel members. They store merchandise, mark prices on it, place items on the selling floor and otherwise handle products. Generally, they pay suppliers for items before selling them to final consumers. They complete transactions by using appropriate store locations and hours, credit policies and other services.

figure 23.1

Functions of Retailing

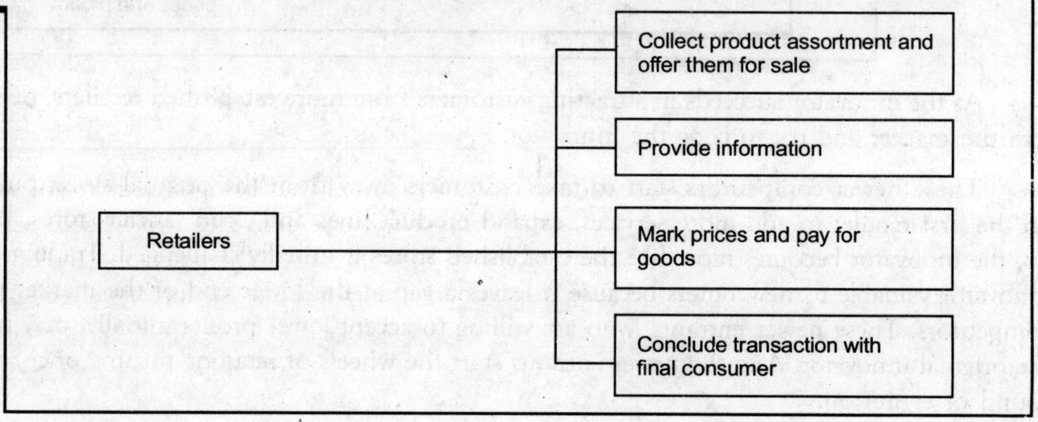

The Relationship Between Retailers and Suppliers

Retailers deal with two broad categories of suppliers (1) Those who are selling goods or services for use by the retailers and (2) Those selling goods or services that have to be resold by the retailers.

Store fixtures, data-processing equipment, management consulting and insurance are examples of goods or services used by the retailer. Suppliers must have knowledge of their retailer's goods, strategies and methods of business operation in order to sell and service accounts effectively.

Evolution of Retailing

The history of retailing is very old. Small stores play a key role in the nation's economy. Generally, most of the retailers are small one-man or proprietary stores. Retailing is a dynamic form of marketing. In some developed countries one-man or small stores are disappearing and have been replaced by departmental stores. Discount stores are few and are found in abundance in urban markets. But, in India, such stores are fewer and are found in urban areas only. In rural areas, only general stores exist in India. Most of the retailers in Indian suburban and rural markets are of the form of general stores. To explain the continuous evolution in retailing, several theories have been proposed including the wheel of retailing, the dialectic process and the retail life cycle.

The Wheel of Retailing

Harvard Professor, Malcolm P Mcnair, developed a theory in 1958 to explain the continuous evolution of retailing. His theory is known as the "wheel of retailing". This theory divides the cyclical patterns of retail evolution, trading up and vulnerability. According to this theory, a new retailer enters the market place with low prices, low margins and limited product line.

figure 23.2

The Wheel of Retailing

INNOVATION
New retailer enters the market with low prices, low profit margins and limited product lines.

VULNERABILITY
In trading up, innovator leaves gap at lower end of market place for new low price entrants.

TRADING UP
Responding to competitive pressure, innovator opens fancier stores, expands product lines and raises both prices and profits.

As the innovator succeeds in attracting customers from more established retailers, new competitors join the market and try to copy the innovator.

These newer competitors start to take customers away from the original store, putting pressure on the first retailer to add more services, expand product lines and open fancier stores. But in trading up, the innovator becomes more like the established stores it initially challenged. Trading up makes the innovator valuable to newcomers because it leaves a gap at the lower end of the market place for new competitors. These newer entrants, who are willing to accept lower profits initially, may now challenge the original innovator. And the newer entrants start the wheels of retailing turning once again in a new round of evolution.

The Dialectic Process

The dialectic process is the second theory which has been proposed to explain the changes that occur in retailing. According to this theory, when a new competitor uses an innovation that gives it an advantage over an established retailer, the established retailer will adopt a strategy that brings it closer to that innovation. By making the innovation its own, the established retailer negates some of the innovator's appeal. The newcomer, in turn, changes its strategies in a fresh attempt to gain competitive superiority, generally by upgrading, adding product lines or otherwise modifying the original retail concept. These changes result in a new type of retailing that blends the best of the established retailers and the newcomers.

In the dialectic process, the established retailer is the thesis, the newcomer is the antithesis and the newly revised format is the synthesis. The thesis retailers have full product line and full price, and the antithesis retailers have limited product line, self-service and discount price in the dialectic process. Soon a synthesis retailer emerges, blending the full product line approach of department stores with the self-service and discount prices of the discount store.

The Retail Life Cycle

The third theory of the evolution in retailing is the retail life cycle. According to this theory, retailers undergo a life cycle divided into four distinct stages: introduction, growth, maturity and decline. When a retailer first opens his store, it is in the introduction phase, during which it challenges established retailers through new competitive advantages such as price, product-line or service. During its introduction stage, it opens as a discount store loaded with low-priced appliances and other brand-name merchandise. In the growth stage, the retailer avails itself of its competitive advantage and adds new product-lines. Maturity comes when growth slows and sales reach a plateau. In this stage, retailers fight for market share and may cut prices, resulting in lower profits. Both sales and profits are low in the decline stage of the retail life cycle. Retailers are in this stage suffering from a lack of competitive advantage.

Some of the retailing gurus believe that the retail life cycle is accelerating, leading to shorter periods of time between each stage. Recent retailers move quickly from the introductory stage to maturity stage. This acceleration indicates that intensely competitive pressures in retailing, coupled with changes in the marketing environment, have resulted in retail formats that must adapt rapidly to service.

Retail Marketing Strategy

Retailers start their business and want to be successful. So they develop a marketing strategy to address two critical issues: identifying the target market and positioning themselves to reach that market and to be perceived as being different from competitors. Retailers must be responsive to survive, so a retail marketing strategy cannot be a one-shot affair. Good retailers continually examine their strategies adjusting their marketing mix and repositioning to keep customers happy and to stay ahead of the competition.

Target Market

Retailers start the marketing process by identifying specific customers of the stores. They generally consider demographic factors such as age, sex, residence, income and family situations as they focus on one or more narrowly defined customer groups that will become their target market.

SUMMARY

In this unit, we have explained the procedure for developing the sales and distribution strategy and the major determinants of each. As these two functions have a high degree of mutual dependence, the qualitative and quantitative objectives can be achieved by joint efforts. The following objectives have been discussed in the unit

- *To provide a high level of customer care*
- *To present an image of professionalism*
- *To gain prime position in stores*
- *To establish and maintain point of sales displays*
- *To provide continuous market/competitor reporting.*

Distribution channels must be responsive to the changing needs and wants of customers and to the development of new channel systems by competitors. Moreover, marketing management must monitor channel effectiveness and improve distribution networks to match changing conditions and potential market opportunities.

PROJECT WORK

1. Study the direct selling method used by M/s Eureka Forbes. What is the size of the sales force in this organisation? Discuss the strategy adopted by this organisation.
2. Study one manufacturer each of
   i. Text books
   ii. Cars
   iii. Food products
   iv. Furniture

   and their respective wholesalers and retailers. What are the strategies adopted by them?
3. You are the sales executive of Star TV and you sell TV connections, which provide four channels for different programmes. You are required to answer the following questions
   a. Who are your major competitors?
   b. What are your strengths and weaknesses?
   c. How do you contact the households?
   d. What will be your sales strategy?

SHORT ANSWER QUESTIONS

1. What do you mean by telemarketing?
2. What do you mean by direct selling?
3. What are the different types of channels?
4. What is retailing?
5. What is distribution channel?

REVIEW QUESTIONS

1. What does the term 'relationship selling' imply and why has it become such an important concept?
2. What role does sales management play in the marketing function?
3. What is the difference between personal selling and sales management?
4. What is sales management? What are the various functions of sales management?

5. What are the various sales strategies and methods? Explain with suitable examples.
6. What is meant by 'marketing channel'? What are the objectives of channel or distribution management?
7. What are the various types of channels? Elaborate?
8. How do sales objectives affect the designing of a sales strategy? Explain the above by taking an example of a five star hotel located at a hill station.
9. As a distribution manager of a new entrant for industrial/hand tools, you are given the task to study and recommend appropriate channels of distribution for the Indian market. What factors would you consider before designing the channel strategy? Explain clearly giving your argument in support of the viewpoint.
10. Discuss the major factors affecting channel strategy. What factors would you keep in mind for developing channel strategy for a company that wants to sell premium quartz watches in the market?
11. In what ways do the 'sales' and 'distribution' functions complement each other?
12. It is said that the objective of negotiations is to create a win-win situation. Discuss what specific preparations you would make before calling on a "customer' who is complaining about the poor after-sales service, whereas you have been servicing his purchase as per the company's laid down standards.
13. What are the factors which determine the allocation of specific sales and distribution tasks between the company's sales organisation and channels of distribution? Taking the example of a shampoo, which is set for a national launch by an established market leader, illustrate your answer.
14. Explain role and responsibilities of the need of distribution channel in any organization.

GO TO THE NET

Using Internet tools, select 25 retail products and their distribution channels.

Using Internet search tools prepare a report on the need of distribution channel of any 5 FMCG companies.

CHAPTER

24

selecting a suitable channel partner

learning objectives

The objectives of this chapter are to:

- understand the trends in wholesaling
- discuss factors for selecting the most appropriate channels
- describe analysis of cost structure.

content outline

opening case

An MNC's Merchandising Problem

Merchandising is an important part of the selling process. Yet there were problems: tardiness, wastage and mounting costs. What was going wrong, the GM (sales) wondered?

In the summer of 1998, Dinesh Mehta, 38, general manager (sales) of a large, diversified FMCG MNC in India, sat at his table looking at the reports before him. The reports were strictly speaking not sales reports. They were in fact concerning data relating to the various merchandising processes in the company. The reports had been delivered to him at his behest and they bewildered him no end. It was apparent to him that the merchandising system was plainly failing to serve its purpose. He wondered that if stocks could reach each part of the country on time without fail and with minimum wastage and that too on higher volumes, what could be wrong with the merchandising system? As he was waiting to convene the meeting of brand managers and sales managers, to be based on the reports, he tried to put his thoughts in place.

Company Background

Dinesh is with a company that has some of the best brands in the country. The company is reputed to have among the best distribution networks in the country, which is adequately leveraged by the sales force to make the company a shareholder's delight. Dinesh heads the sales of the personal products division. This division has been recording the highest rates of growth and is the star in the company's portfolio.

Theoretical Background

Any value addition that is done to the product at the point of purchase (POP), is known as merchandising. This is done to enhance its sales through higher visibility achieving top of the mind at the time of purchase. Visibility need not only be that of the product itself. Any advertisement of the product in the form of posters, dispensers, danglers and visuals are known as elements of merchandising. This is to gain prominence in the extremely cluttered marketplace and in the minds of the customers.

Merchandising can be used effectively in the following cases

- **New brand launches.** Visibility is of utmost importance when a new brand is being launched. The customer must be able to relate the advertisement seen on TV to the posters, etc., which are displayed in retail outlets.
- **Brand relaunch.** Often a brand is relaunched to boost sagging sales. The same theory, as stated above holds good in such cases too.
- **Brand activity.** There are periods when the focus is on a particular brand so as to increase its sales. This is done on a periodic basis and merchandising is also a key tool for the success of this exercise.

Historical Perspective

Indian consumers never had as much choice as they have today, especially after the post 1992 economic liberalisation. The use of international brands such as Pantene or Organics (shampoos) are no more esoteric. Competition has become fierce for companies both, in the air as characterised by aggressive advertising, and in the market place. The battle in the market place for the mind is through visibility and all marketers agree that there is tremendous clutter. Today, merchandising is a key component in the successful sale of any product. Consumer goods in India are looking at a quantum leap in the quality of their merchandising. To achieve the same, a system needs to be set up which takes care of the merchandising requirements from A-class outlets down to the pop strata.

The Merchandising System

The existing merchandising chain in the company started with the brand manager who gave a creative brief to the agency to develop a 'look' for the merchandise. More often than not, this was kept consistent with what was advertised through other media. The agency also selected the material for the various merchandising elements. The selection of the material and the design of the merchandising elements was a function of the image of the brand, the look that was to be conveyed, the durability of the material chosen vis-a-vis the length of the campaign and the ease of transport and storage. Once the merchandising elements had been finalised in both conception and form, it was sent to the printer/manufacturer. Typically, in a campaign, a number of merchandising elements were used.

For example, one campaign may involve posters, danglers, dispensers, etc. The numbers to be manufactured were decided by the brand manager depending on the coverage desired. Coverage was decided by the brand itself because each brand was sold through a different mix of outlet type. This estimation of the numbers was very crucial as merchandise was expensive and shortages/excesses were potentially harmful.

Once the merchandise were produced in the desired numbers, they are sent to the Quality Control (QC) department for approval. The QC department compared the material with the specifications given by the brand manager. They were then sent to a centralised godown for sorting. This sorting was in the nature of distinguishing the merchandise on the basis of destination, language and contents. As the merchandise travelled towards its destination (the retail outlet), the smaller godowns had to differentiate on the basis of type of merchandise (contents), as all merchandise was not displayed in all the shops. They were put up selectively depending on the sales and the customer profile of the shop. The details were often maintained and should have been maintained in the corresponding godowns, so that distribution was efficient. To see this process to an efficient conclusion, the field sales force had to be alert to the need of the merchandise and ensure that the right merchandise was being put up at the right shop.

Realisation Dawns

Dinesh could not say that he had not seen it coming. When Dinesh had gone to Hyderabad a month ago, he had seen that posters printed in Kannada, instead of Telugu, had been put up. He had reprimanded his sales force but they had given him the impression that this was an exception rather than the rule. Similarly, his wife had often complained that she never knew when a new brand arrived in the market place because the products were not prominently displayed, neither were posters or other display material to be seen. The product had to be asked for. He had not paid much attention to it. He himself was witness to it in Mumbai and it was true that the stocks were not arranged prominently on the shelves and the POP material that had been a part of the launch strategy was also missing. He had been briefed by his sales officer that the material had not arrived. Also when he had visited a distributor in Delhi, he had seen piles of merchandising material lying around. These materials mainly concerned brand activities that had happened sometime in the past but what baffled him was the issue of wastage. If the brand manager, in his calculations, had accounted for them, then where was the problem? Also, there was the common refrain from the brand managers that the merchandise was not being put up by the field force as per instructions. Often, there was a mix-up of merchandising elements between shops.

The Picture

Dinesh went over the select tables that he had shortlisted for the presentation from the huge volumes that lay before him. Time taken at the various stages are summarised in the following table

Stage	*Present Scenario*
Printer/manufacturer	11 days
Delivery to central godown	1 day
Printer to central godown	**12 days**
Quality control report	14 days
Delay due to non-availability of trucks	5 days
Reach regional depots (if sent by lorry)	5 days
Regional depot to local depot	8 days
Central godown to local depot	**32 days**
Local depot to distributor	4 days
Total	**48 Days**

Is my merchandise serving its purpose?

Brand activity	*Date of launch/relaunch/brand material at distributor*	*Date of receipt of POP*
1	25.03.97	07.04.98
2	25.03.98	04.04.98
3	15.03.98	23.04.98

Are the figures, on which the brand manager allocates, realistic? The following are the figures collected for Nagpur for four brands during different times of the year in the last sales period.

Particulars posters at Nagpur depot	*Actual requirement of depot*	*Poster received at Nagpur*
Brand A	16	150
Brand B	16	45
Brand C	16	32
Brand D	16	30

The Future

For the first time, Dinesh was trying to set right a system that he had thought was infallible. Merchandising is a key issue and, moreover, the other business divisions of the company are looking at personal products to show the way as far as merchandising is concerned. He felt a greater responsibility; as he puzzled over a series of questions:

- Why wasn't the merchandise reaching the shop on time? Where along the whole chain could he possibly cut lead times?
- Could any of the activities be done differently? If he remembered right, at the time of setting up, they had taken into consideration such lead times at various phases. Had the times changed making those benchmarks obsolete?
- Merchandising was becoming an increasingly costly affair. The hiring of shelves and displays in metro cities was especially costly. The cost of the merchandise itself was also high. Yet he had been witness to wastage. Was the field force not aware of the implications of merchandising as a marketing tool? In that case did they need training?
- To the best of his knowledge, performance, as far as merchandising was concerned, was part of the appraisal of the field force. Was it not being followed or was something more relevant required to motivate the field force?
- Merchandise was reaching the wrong destinations, a wasteful proposition. Why such carelessness? Are the communication lines properly drawn?

TRY YOURSELF

1. Critically examine the role and issues involved in merchandising.

BASIC CONCEPT OF RETAILING

The concept of retailing includes all transactions directed towards selling goods or services to the customer. It does not include purchases for resale activities or for business, industrial or any other kind of institutional use. The ultimate consumer is the buyer who makes the purchase for his own or family consumption.

Although small retailers still make up a major part of the retailing scene, the future could be different – it appears uncertain, with slow growth and low investment returns. The percentage growth has been fairly low for many years. The sector is oversupplied with retailers compared to the existing demand. This state of things is likely to continue until a major re-organisation takes place. Some specialised types in retailing may continue to enjoy growth, particularly mail order ventures and direct mail companies.

Despite this forecast, some retailers, who cater meticulously to consumer demand and provide good service with reasonable price, will continue to prosper. The losers will be those who continue in the conventional paths. The costs associated with property/sites will be a major issue in the face of high interest rates and inflation.

The retail revolution has been mainly concerned with changing the pattern of services available to the consumers. This is because retailing is one of the most labour-intensive industries. By finding out what level of service the customers can be happy with, the retail operation can he designed around that level. The growth of the suburbs and the number of cars has made it possible to site large stores in comparatively cheap localities with free car-parking facilities. In turn, this has slowed the growth of city centre shopping precincts. The shortage of time available for shopping and cooking, etc., has caused the development of mail order and similar shopping facilities as well as that of convenience foods. Demographic trends also play a part in retailing. An ageing population requires different varieties of retail goods than a young population: a wealthier society needs more luxury goods: and so on. There is also more competition between different types of retail establishments than before. For example, some drug stores are now selling foodstuffs.

The retailer's strategy mix is made up of product mix, location, service level, shelf stock/inventory and margins. Facilities are poor in most of the country where retailing is still mainly done through small businesses.

Distribution of products constitutes an important element of marketing mix of a firm. After development of the product, the entrepreneur has to decide channels of routes through which the product will flow from the factory to the potential customers. He has a number of alternatives available to him. The entrepreneur may choose to distribute the product directly to customers without using any intermediaries. Alternatively, he may use one or more middlemen including wholesalers, selling agents, and retailers. Big firms have their zonal or regional authorized agents or dealers spread over the entire country. The dealers, in turn, work with distributors and retailers. On the other hand, small firms cannot afford to have zonal offices, but are devising their own ways of doing business. They also receive regular orders for goods. Entry may be difficult for the small firms. It has been observed that many authorized dealers of known brands also stock other unknown or new brands of goods. They also insist on the customer buying the lesser known brand because of higher margin of profit. The small entrepreneur, with fewer overheads and low labour costs along with better planning and management may be able to earn good profits.

Meaning of Channels of Distribution

A channel of distribution or trade channel is the path or route along which goods move from producers to ultimate consumers. It is a distribution network through which a producer puts his products in the hands of actual users. A trade or marketing channel consists of the producer, consumers or users and the various middlemen who intervene between the two. The channel serves as a connecting link between the producer and consumers. By bridging the gap between the point of production and the point of consumption, a channel creates time, place and possession utilities. A channel of distribution represents three types of flows:

a. Goods flow from producer to consumers;

b. Cash flow from consumers to producer as payment for goods; and

c. Marketing information flows in both directions, from producers to consumers in the form of information on new products, new uses of existing products, etc. The flow of information from consumers to producers is the feedback of the wants, suggestions, complaints, etc.

Kinds of Distribution Channels

Channels of Distribution

A brief explanation of different channels of distribution is given below:

1. ***Manufacturer Customer:*** This is also known as direct selling because no middlemen are involved. A producer may sell directly through his own retail stores, for example, Bata. This is the simplest and shortest channel. It is fast and economical. Small producers and producers of perishable commodities also sell directly to the local consumers. Big firms adopt direct selling in order to cut distribution cost and because they have sufficient facilities to sell directly to the consumers. The producer or the entrepreneur himself performs all the marketing activities.

2. ***Manufacturer Retailer Customer:*** This is one stage distribution channel having one middleman, i.e., retailer. In this channel, the producer sells to big retailers like departmental stores and chain stores who in turn sell to customer. This channel is very popular in the distribution of consumer durables such as refrigerators, TV sets, washing machines, typewriters, etc. This channel of distribution is very popular these days because of emergence of departmental stores, super markets and other big retail stores. The retailers purchase in large quantities from the producer and perform certain marketing activities in order to sell the product to the ultimate consumers.

3. ***Manufacturer – Wholesaler – Retailer – Customer:*** This is the traditional channel of distribution. There are two middlemen in this channel of distribution, namely, wholesaler and retailer. This channel is most suitable for the products with widely scattered market. It is used in the distribution of consumer products like groceries, drugs, cosmetics, etc. It is quite suitable for small scale producers whose product line is narrow and who require the expert services and promotional support of wholesalers.

Choice Channel of Distribution

While selecting a distribution channel, the entrepreneur should compare the costs, sales volume and profits expected from alternative channels of distribution. In order to select the right channel for distributing his product, a small-scale manufactures should keep in mind the following considerations:

1. **Market Considerations:** The nature of the market is a key factor influencing the choice of channels of distribution. The following features of the market should be considered to determine the channels:

    a. *Consumer or industrial market:* If the product is meant for industrial users, the channel of distribution will be a short one. This is because industrial users buy in a large quantity and the producer can easily establish a direct contact with them. But in case for goods meant for consumers, retailers may have to be included in the channels of distribution.

    b. *Number and location of buyers:* When the number of potential customers is small or the market is geographically located in a limited area, direct selling is easy and economical. In case of large number of customers, use of wholesalers and retailers becomes necessary.

    c. *Size of order:* Direct selling is convenient and economical where customers place order in big lots as in case of industrial goods. But where the product is sold in small quantities, middlemen are used to distribute such products. A manufacturer may use different channels for different types of buyers. He may sell directly to big retail stores and may use wholesalers to sell to small retailers.

    d. *Customers buying habits:* The customer buying habits like the time he is willing to spend, the desire for credit, the preference of personal attention and one stop shopping significantly affect the choice of distribution channels.

2. **Product Considerations:** The type and nature of the product influence the number and type of middlemen to be chosen for distributing the product. The important factors with respect to the product are as follows:

    a. *Unit value:* Products of low unit value and common use are generally sold through middlemen, as they cannot bear the cost of direct selling. On the other hand, expensive consumer goods and industrial products are sold directly by the producers.

    b. *Perishability:* Perishable products like vegetables, fruits and bakery items have relatively short channels, as they cannot withstand repeated handling. Goods which are subject to frequent changes in fashion and style, are generally distributed through short channels, as the producer has to maintain close and continuous touch with the market.

    c. *Bulk and weight:* Heavy and bulky products are distributed directly to minimize handling costs. Coal, bricks, stones, etc., are some examples.

    d. *Standardisation:* Custom-made and non-standardised products usually pass through short channels due to the need for direct contact between the producer and the consumers. Standardized and mass-made goods can be distributed through middlemen.

    e. *Technical nature:* Industrial products requiring demonstration, installation and aftersale service are often sold directly. The consumer products of technical nature are generally sold through retailers.

    f. *Product line:* An entrepreneur producing a wide range of products may find it economical to set up its own retail outlets. On the other hand, firms with one or two products find it profitable to distribute through wholesalers and retailers.

    g. *Age of the product:* A new product needs grater promotional effort and few middlemen may like to handle it. As the product gain's acceptance in the market, more middlemen may be employed for its distribution.

3. **Middlemen Considerations:** The cost and efficiency of distribution depend largely upon the nature and type of middlemen as given in the following factors:

   a. *Availability:* When middlemen as desired are not available, an entrepreneur may have to establish his own distribution network. Non-availability of middlemen may arise when they are handling competitive products, as they do not like to handle more brands.

   b. *Attitudes:* Middlemen who do not like a firm's marketing policies may refuse to handle its products. For instance, some wholesalers and retailers demand sole selling rights or a guarantee against fall in prices.

   c. *Services:* Use of those middlemen is profitable who provide financing, storage, promotion and aftersale services.

   d. *Sale Potential:* An entrepreneur generally prefers a dealer who offers the greatest potential volume of sales.

   e. *Costs:* Choice of a channel should be made after comparing the costs of distribution through alternative channels. After deciding the number of middlemen, an entrepreneur has to select the particular dealers through whom he will distribute his products. While selecting a particular wholesaler or retailer, the following factors should be taken into consideration:

      a. Location of dealer's business premises;

      b. Financial position and credit standing of the dealer;

      c. Knowledge and experience of the dealer;

      d. Storage and showroom facilities of the dealer;

      e. Ability of the dealer to secure adequate business and to cover the market;

      f. Capacity of the dealer to provide aftersale service;

      g. General reputation of the dealer and his sales force;

      h. Willingness of the dealer to handle the entrepreneur's products;

      i. Degree of co-operation and promotion service he is willing to provide;

      j. Nature of other products, if any handled by the dealer.

TRENDS IN WHOLESALING

The main function of a wholesaler in distribution is to obtain supplies from a variety of sources and distribute the wide variety of goods to different buyers according to their needs. The more efficiently this function is performed, the more success is achieved. For the manufacturer, selling to a wholesaler removes the difficulties and costs of selling in small quantities and to varying locations and holding inventory for that purpose. The wholesaler deals in a wide variety of goods and can spread costs over goods from many sources. Wholesalers can also maintain better contacts with their retail customers. They are naturally more concerned with their customers than their suppliers and often offer them assistance, such as credit extension.

The average size of wholesaling distribution companies is expected to rise significantly, aided by acquisitions and mergers. New technology will help these businesses to reach new market areas at reasonable costs. The areas covered by wholesale organizations are expected to increase considerably.

The role as well as the size of the sales force in wholesale distribution companies is expected to change; there will be a much bigger emphasis on marketing, promotion, merchandising and space management. The use of computer technology will mean significant changes in marketing and sales strategies, with the use of online order entry systems and other systems for analyses of marketing and sales.

The proportion of goods carried by outside carriers is expected to rise significantly, while that carried by internal delivery vehicles is expected to drop. The proportion of businesses using online information systems for inventory and purchase is expected to rise dramatically. On the whole, the future of wholesaling is bright for those willing to change and to make full use of the new technology which is available. It may be possible to remove a wholesaling firm from a channel of distribution, but only if some other member of the channel is willing to perform the same functions.

For consumer goods, retailers are the end of the chain, which can be quite lengthy in some cases. Between them, the various channel members perform the services of transporting and storing the goods, transferring the title to the goods, supplying the necessary information regarding the goods, standardizing, grading and processing them, avoiding stockouts, running the risks associated with volatile demand and fulfilling the financial requirements for credit, etc.

Distribution has become more complex in the consumer goods area. The number of ways of marketing a product as well as the number of potential customers is increasing all the time. While the goal must be to satisfy consumer demand, discovering the size of the consumer demand is extremely difficult. There may be one to three links in the distribution chain reaching from the manufacturer to the consumer. It is not feasible for a manufacturer of consumer goods to sell through their own outlets because of high costs and limited distribution. The retailer chooses which products to sell and manufacturers can only try to persuade the retailer to stock their products.

The packaging, advertising and promotion, and brand name may be more important to a sale than the product itself. It is necessary to give some thought to the effects of a manufacturer's actions on each of these links. The following factors are important in motivating consumers to buy and motivating retail personnel to sell:

- Informative packaging
- Good quality manuals, catalogues and literature
- Displays
- Training
- Audio-visual materials
- Incentives in various forms.

The manufacturers of consumer goods are generally concerned that the image they are trying to project should tally with the image of the outlets which sell their goods. This matters more if the distribution is limited or selective. The pricing of the goods, their shelf location, displays and availability also influence the image of the goods in the minds of consumers. It has to be remembered that the relationship between the retailer and the manufacturer is forced upon them because of their interest in selling to the end-user. Otherwise their interests diverge considerably. The manufacturers are interested in distributing their products widely, displaying and selling their own products, maximising their own profits, low retail margins and consumer loyalty to their brands. The retailers are interested in being exclusive distributors, selling from their shops, retail profits and high margins, display of the most profitable items and consumer loyalty to their shops.

The Special Characteristics of High Technology Marketing Channels

In this context, a high technology marketing channel means a sales and service organization concerned with

1. Identifying prospective markets/customers in a territory in need of the benefits of the applications of a high technology product.
2. Promotion by a variety of means which include at least one channel concerned with direct face-to-face communication with the customer presenting the latter with arguments and reasons to show how they will benefit and persuading them to buy the product.
3. Offering satisfactory after-sale technical service.

The channel members need to be fully conversant with the changing technology and its applications and also technically competent to make what, in effect, is a technical sale. The products themselves may not be different in appearance or performance from what is generally available in the market – in such situations, the sale of the product is effected through competence, confidence, comprehension of customer needs, relationship, communication and professional application, counselling and consultancy.

The background, training, experience, know-how and technical skills of the staff members engaged by the channel often make the important difference between a good high technology channel and a bad one. The technical competence resident in the channel is one of the most critical factors to the success of high technology marketing.

MARKETING AND CHANNEL FLOWS

The above analysis of a company's SWOTs must be augmented by similar analyses of the other channel members. The number of members in a particular channel can vary according to the length and width of the channel strategy that a company adopts.

A CHECKLIST FOR SELECTING THE MOST APPROPRIATE CHANNELS

Product Factors

Four product variables must be weighed in channel selection:

1. ***Physical nature:*** the variations that influence the decision are
   - perishability of the product, whether physical or due to fashion
   - seasonal variation, causing inventory problems
   - unit value of the product
   - inventory investment required and
   - customer service requirements.
2. ***Technical nature:*** whether
   - a simple or complex product

- advice is needed on product use
- installation is needed or
- special training is needed.

3. ***Length of product line:*** This consists of a group of products related either from a production or a marketing standpoint. Intermediaries are preferable to own sales force when the line is short. Decisions must be made whether to use a single channel for the entire line or split the line and use multiple channels.
4. ***Market position:*** An established product made and promoted by a reputable manufacturer may have a high degree of market acceptance and can be readily sold through more channels than a lesser known product.

figure 24.1

Competitive advantage: SWOTs

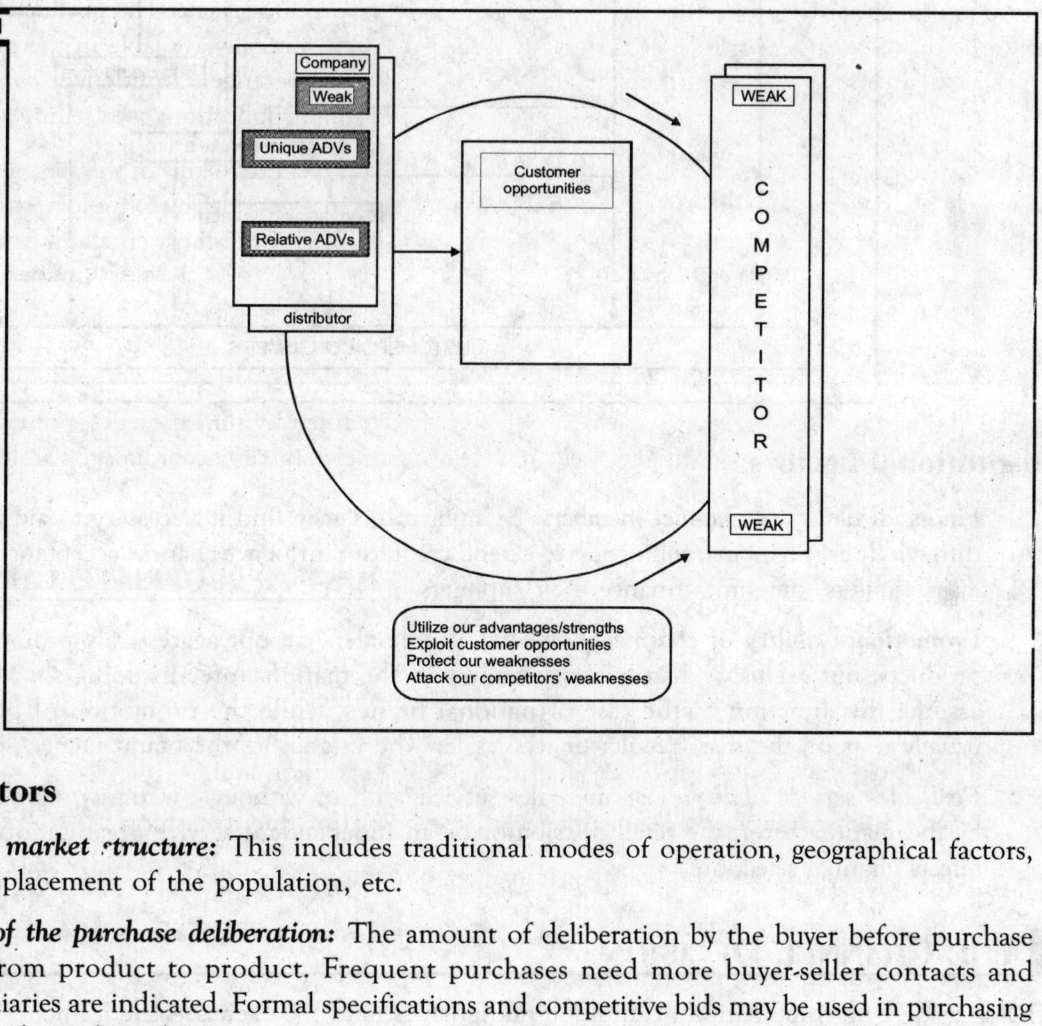

Market Factors

1. ***Existing market structure:*** This includes traditional modes of operation, geographical factors, size and placement of the population, etc.
2. ***Nature of the purchase deliberation:*** The amount of deliberation by the buyer before purchase differs from product to product. Frequent purchases need more buyer-seller contacts and intermediaries are indicated. Formal specifications and competitive bids may be used in purchasing certain industrial products.
3. ***Availability of the channel:*** Existing channels may not be interested in new products. The promoter can either persuade them or use aggressive promotion to stimulate consumer demand on the theory that this will force the intermediaries to carry the product in order to satisfy the customers.

figure 24.2
Marketing Factors Affecting Channels

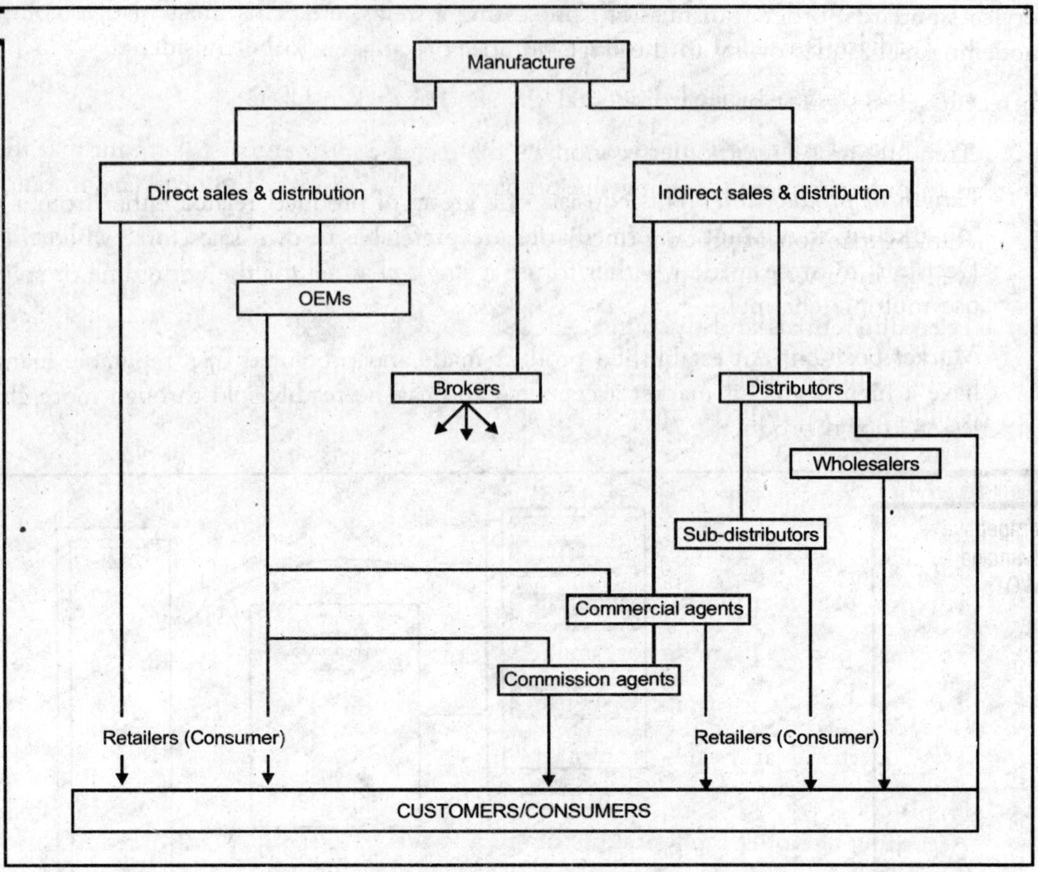

Institutional Factors

1. ***Financial ability of channel members:*** Manufacturers may find it necessary to aid their retailers through direct financing; willingness to extend credit can influence channel acceptance. Conversely, mass retailers sometimes finance their suppliers.
2. ***Promotional ability of channel members:*** Wholesalers cannot aggressively promote particular products, but exclusive distributors usually join the manufacturer in doing so. Manufacturers assume this function in the case of national brands, while the promotion of private brands usually rests on the mass retailer or wholesaler who establishes the brand name.
3. ***Post-sales service ability:*** The after-sales service, with or without a warranty, may be performed by the manufacturer, the retail distributor or an independent service organization. This ability affects channel selection.

THE CHANNEL DECISION

This is made by a combination of intuition and analysis, and the exercise of judgement. The decision is complicated by the interdependencies existing between relevant factors. While it is difficult to quantify the many trade-offs associated with channel decisions, certain tools can be applied to them. Cost analysis techniques will give reasonable estimates of each channel cost. System analysis involves trade-offs in time, service and costs in order to maximize profits in the long run. Quantitative comparisons are made between alternative production runs, inventory holding levels, transport modes, customer service standards, order transmission, processing systems, etc. This must involve computer oriented modelling techniques owing to the large number of variables to be considered.

In recent years, significant environmental changes have taken place:

1. Trend towards a short-order economy – the increase in inventory has meant that the best decision is to order frequently, forcing the primary supplier to carry the necessary inventory.
2. Rapid expansion of product lines – this generates obsolescence and stock availability problems as well as inventory imbalance.
3. Price differentials and discounts – legally speaking, these have to be cost-justified.
4. Competitive strategies – at one time they centered on product features and price; now the emphasis is on indirect competition such as outperforming competitors on logistic planning and customer service.

The members of a marketing channel are interconnected by several different factors:

1. The product line from manufacturer to end-user
2. The flow of ownership from member to member
3. The cash flow as payments are made by one member to another
4. The exchange of information between channel members
5. The advertising and sales promotion directed by channel members towards other members or end-users.

According to Kotler a physical distribution system can be said to be efficient if no re-organisation of logistical inputs could reduce the costs while maintaining the present service level'.

The distribution manager must consider the interrelated functions and their costs as a total entity when costs are being cut. Otherwise, cost-cutting by one function can end up with higher total costs. For example, capital costs of investing in new transport may be reduced by keeping the old trucks in use but their repair costs and lost orders due to delays in deliveries may end up by costing the company far more in the end. The number of possible distribution strategies increases as the complexity of the manufacturing company increases, from the simple options available to the single plant supplying a single market to the large number of possible choices faced by the company with many factories and a large number of markets.

Inventory decisions form an important part of the strategy because of the costs involved and the effect they have on many functions, especially the marketing function. The inventory decisions consist of deciding when to order and the amount to be ordered. The inventory maintenance costs can be as high as 30 per cent of the actual value of the inventory. It is possible to determine the optimal order quantity by using mathematical methods.

The location of warehouses and retail outlets is also an important part of physical distribution strategy in which the marketing function has a keen interest. They affect the speed and cost of delivery to customers and the number of potential customers:

The channel decisions depend upon the characteristics of

- customers
- products

- company
- intermediaries
- competitors
- industrial/legal environment

The alternatives available differ according to

- the types of channel members involved in the industry.
- the number of channel members to be used at each stage of distribution.
- the functions performed by these channel members.
- the mutually agreed terms and conditions and responsibilities of the company and its channel members.

The following criteria should be considered in the selection of the best possible channel:

1. Economically, the channel chosen should yield the most profit
2. The role of marketing is important in a channel, the relevant skills and enthusiasm for the role must be present in the channel
3. If there exist significant marketing objectives for the company, then the channel members' goals must be compatible with those objectives
4. In respect of the control exercised over the channel and the vertical and horizontal interaction, possible conflict between different channels and legal difficulties should be considered
5. There must exist the requisite management capability to make the business and trading relationship work for the success of both parties
6. With regard to the future relationship, the adaptability of the system is also important.

PROFITABILITY OF A DISTRIBUTOR

The profitability of a distributor has to be measured in terms of:

- The return on sales as a percentage
- The return on capital employed as a percentage per annum.

If one takes the first ratio, the return or profit is the result of the distributor's sales in a period less all the costs of operation, namely

- the cost of goods sold (this is the landed cost of the goods purchased from the manufacturer) plus any costs incurred in the process of value-addition
- advertising and promotion costs
- sales costs including any commissions paid to the sales staff and commission agents
- storage, transportation and handling charges
- training and administration costs and
- costs of capital employed (warehouse, transports, office, working capital, etc.).

The second ratio is the real return on investment and this is often expressed as:

a. Return on sales % multiplied by

b. Turnover of assets.

The first part has been described earlier; the second part reflects the efficiency with which the inventory and other assets are turned over. The first part indicates the margin on sales achieved, and the second part indicates the administrative and managerial aspects of the distributor's business management skills.

OTHER FINANCIAL CONSIDERATIONS

Level of Investment

The level of investment needed in the marketing channel depends very much on the type of channel and the goals set for it. A channel which merely acts as the sales agent may only need investment in the form of skilled sales resources, sales material, sales training and perhaps demonstration equipment. On the other hand, an independent channel, which acts as an importer/distributor covering a large territory, may need to invest in inventory, warehousing, transportation, outbound logistics, and marketing sales and supporting resources. What level of resources is needed and whether some of these call for capital investment on a longer term basis, depend on the nature of the product, the agreed goals and the task in hand.

In general, fixed capital investment and working capital requirements are treated differently. Financial soundness of the channel is important for the manufacturer as well as the channel. A good financial strategy is a must. A professional financial approach to evaluating investment requirements and their sourcing is very important in setting up any channel operation.

Inventory Management

The level of inventory appropriate for the type of product can be established by examining the industry statistics. In the case of a new innovative product, an initial estimate has to be based on the experience of a 'close-benefit' product and a view of the market characteristics, the launch programme and the product availability to meet customer demand. However, high inventory carrying costs must be avoided. A reasonably high inventory turnover rate is a prerequisite to getting a good rate of return on investment. As a high turnover rate has the effect of decreasing the operating costs (e.g. carrying costs, cost of capital, insurance, warehouse space, property costs, etc.) and reducing the need for a large amount of invested capital, it also leads to improved profitability and a better ROI. Yet inventory control and financial management have proved to be a problem for many channels. These are areas to which high technology channel management needs to pay particular attention.

The cost of obsolescence can be very high if unsold items continue to remain in inventory. High inventory may lead to two side effects. If a product remains for a long time in inventory, it may be ageing and, therefore, some provision may need to be made to cater for obsolescence, to the detriment of profits. If the product remains in inventory because it is unsalable, then a write-off provision may be required – this may be due to a competitor launching a new product which gives more advantages and better benefits to the customer. Channel management must include monitoring and controlling inventory and maintaining it at the appropriate level. In addition, high inventory in an obsolete product ties up capital and therefore prevents a channel from investing in the currently demanded product.

Debtor Management

The level of debtors outstanding at any given point indicates the degree to which customers are being financed by the channel. It is important to note whether the customers are being given credit in excess of the industry average, or if the customers are not being chased for payment, or if the problem is one of competing with others by giving extended credit. The more the number of days the debtors (receivables) are outstanding, the more is it likely that the channel is running out of cash. In any case, the terms of payment must include a clear assessment of the number of days of credit being given.

The age profile of the debtors, therefore, is an important factor to monitor. If customers are paying promptly, it is a good thing as it could mean that the customers are efficient and profitable, or it could point to inefficient financial management on their part. If the latter, problems may be accumulating only to surface later on. It is vital to recognize what is happening before it is too late. There is a danger that the long overdue debtor can become a bad debt. The nature of this adversity could also mean that the channel member is unable to make payments to the manufacturer.

ANALYSIS OF COST STRUCTURE — THE VALUE CHAIN

An important concept that highlights competition is the 'value chain'. This divides a company's activities into the technologically and economically distinct activities, 'value activities', which it performs to do business. The value a company creates is measured by the amount the buyers are willing to pay for its product or service. A business is profitable if the value it creates is greater than the cost of performing the value activities. To gain competitive advantage over its competitors, a company must either perform these activities more cheaply or in a way that leads to differentiation and earns the ability to change a premium price (i.e. the company's products or services command more value).

A company's value chain is a system of interdependent activities. Linkages exist between these activities when the manner of performing one activity affects the cost/effectiveness of others and creates trade-offs that should be used for optimization. For example, more costly product design and/or raw materials may reduce after-sales service costs. Careful management of trade-offs can be a powerful source of competitive advantage as it is difficult for competitors to copy.

The 'value system' of a company includes the value chains of suppliers and of distributor channels. The product passes through the latter on its way to the ultimate buyer and itself becomes a purchased input to the value chains of its buyers, who use it to perform one or more buyer activities. Linkages occur between the value chains of such a system and can be used to create competitive advantage and savings which can benefit all value chains in the system.

Competitive scope is a powerful tool for creating competitive advantage. It can be broad based with a coordinated national or international strategy or narrow-based to serve particular or unusual needs.

Every value activity has both a physical and an information processing component, which can be either simple or complex, a different mix being required for each activity. Metal stamping uses mostly physical processing whereas dealing with insurance claims needs just the opposite. Information technology is progressing faster than technologies for physical processing, so that the opportunities widen faster than management can explore them. The number of variables a company can analyze or control has grown dramatically. Information technology is creating new linkages between activities and enhancing a company's ability to exploit such linkages; e.g., by coordinating activities more closely with suppliers and buyers or in far-flung locations. The problem of dealing with too much information also means information technology is needed to store and analyse this information for the management. Most products have always had both a physical and an information component.

There is an unmistakable trend towards expanding the information content in products as well as processes. Together with the changes in companies' value chains, this emphasises the strategic role of information technology; the role and intensity of information will continue to differ in different industries.

The structure of an industry is embodied in competitive forces that collectively determine its profitability.

- The power of buyers/intermediaries
- The power of suppliers/feeders
- The threat of new entrants
- The threat of substitute products
- The rivalry among existing competitors
- The pressure from the investors
- Governmental/external influences.

Information technology can alter each of these seven components and affect industry attractiveness. It has had an especially strong impact upon the first two. The cost of tailoring products to market segments is falling, affecting the pattern of industry rivalry. Reduction of the personal element has made many service industries less attractive. Management must look carefully at the implications of new technology to realize its advantages and be prepared for its consequences.

In any company, information technology has a powerful effect on competitive advantage in either cost or differentiation. It affects value activities or allows companies to gain competitive advantage by exploiting changes in competitive scope through:

- lower cost
- enhanced differentiation
- change in competitive scope
- spawning new industries.

The information revolution is creating interrelationships between industries that were previously separate. The merging of computer and telecommunications technologies is an important example. This convergence is having a profound effect on the structure of both industries. AT&T used its position in telecommunications as a staging point for entry into the computer industry. IBM, having acquired Rolm, the telecommunications equipment manufacturer, joined the competition from the other direction. Broadline companies are increasingly able to segment their offerings in ways which were not feasible for them before. Telecommunications can profoundly affect each one of the value activities of a company, sometimes simply by improving effectiveness and sometimes by fundamentally changing the activity. In this process, the value chains of key customers and of competitors may change as well. In this context, the distributor's contribution to the process of value-addition must also be explored.

A Checklist on Commercial Risk

When a decision is being taken on selecting a trading partner and getting involved in commercial risk together, it is important to undertake appropriate research into commercial risks and to assess them before the relationship is finalised. Constant monitoring is equally important when the partnership is in existence. The following checklist is taken from a seminar conducted in 1991 by Phillip Day, director of finance, Booth & Co and a Director of EMSA.

Research implies making full use of all available sources (including a vital personal visit to discuss business with the prospective distributor), such as:

- Credit reference agencies
- Statutory returns
- Trade missions
- Commercial attachés
- Trade associations and Chambers of Commerce
- Other suppliers
- Insurance brokers/associations
- Police
- Customer references.

Commercial risk assessment is best done by:

- comparison with others in the same industry.
- comparison with others among your distributors.
- identifying any differences.
- explaining the differences.
- discussions with the distributor, if appropriate.
- discussions with your credit manager.
- assessment in relation to the business being contemplated.

It should be recognised that the financial strengths and weaknesses of a distributor will be different from those of a manufacturer.

A decision on taking commercial risks in a specific situation can be 'yes' or 'no' or 'perhaps'.

1. If the decision is 'yes', agree with the distributor on
   a. frequency of delivery
   b. credit terms–currency value
   c. insurance
   d. forfeiting.
2. If the decision is 'no', tell the distributor to explore cash alternatives.
3. If the decision is 'perhaps', discuss the matter further with the distributor.
4. Regarding monitoring, agree on the following with interested parties:
   a. The criteria for monitoring
   b. Frequency of monitoring
   c. The internal systems requirements
   d. Responsibility for monitoring
   e. Escalation procedures when things go wrong
   f. Diary of visits and review dates.

5. In avoiding exchange risk.
   a. Determine what risk you are prepared to take?
   b. Define when you are on'risk'/
   c. Quantify the risk elements.
   d. Take action to:
      - sell local currency forward
      - 'hedge' receivables in your own country
      - forfeit (sell receivables).

A CHECKLIST TO GUARD AGAINST OVERTRADING

Overtrading occurs when a business expands quicker than it can make money. An increase in sales and profits may have happened, but there may also be a disproportionate rise in inventory, receivables and capital expenses, all of which contribute to a drain on the cash resources. The overtrading so caused is also referred to by some bank managers as the dark shadow of the expanding business. In the short-term, the working capital cycle may not have been properly managed by the company management. The danger of overtrading in times of high inflation must be guarded against.

Do:

- Set conservative credit limits
- Monitor the settlement profiles
- Guard against sudden order increases
- Talk to the distributor
- Talk to the credit controller
- Recognise the problems that you can cause.

Don't:

- Fool yourself – it can happen to you!
- Accept orders without thinking
- Sell without caring if the distributor can pay
- Accept silence as a sign that all is fine
- Ignore the problem after you have recognised it.

SELECTION CRITERIA CHECKLIST

- Local presence
- Financial soundness
- Knowledge of the marketplace
- Contacts with target customers
- Appropriate reputation in the market

- Shared values and aspirations
- Sales area coverage
- Competitive service skills
- Complementary lines
- Required skills and competence
- Appropriate facilities for inventory, warehousing and transportation
- Motivation to succeed
- Capable of marketing support to the manufacturer
- Capable of discharging the responsibilities
- Appropriate ethical practice
- Necessary leadership qualities.

SUMMARY

Distribution is the process that brings a product from production location to the consumer or the end user. The distribution process should follow all the rules of good marketing. As part of the marketing process, it has to satisfy customers needs. It must also help establish a stable and predictable market for the product and provide those participating in the distribution process an optimum design. The distribution process includes the major function of selling and coordination of all the functions involved in moving the product from the factory to the end user. To establish a product satisfactorily in the market, many factors such as the quality of the product, the reputation of the manufacturer, the brand image, the quality of the packing and presentation, play an important part and not the least important is an effective channel of distribution. Many a product, which was intrinsically good, has died in infancy because it literally never found the right road to the market. Now one may well ask as to what is the right road to the market. This is a rather difficult question, because the right channel will depend upon the nature of the product to be soled.

While for one type of product a particular channel of distribution would be the ideal channel, for another type, an alternative channel may be more suitable. It is therefore obvious that much of the success of a product depends on the selection of a distribution channel, a selection done with a measure of scientific determination and logic strongly seasoned with judgment that comes from experience.

PROJECT WORK

What type of distribution will be applicable in the following services:

1. Home delivery Services
2. Courier Services
3. Electric appliances repair service.

SHORT ANSWER QUESTIONS

1. What do you mean by debtor management?
2. How do you calculate profitability of a distributor?
3. What do you mean by channel of distribution?

REVIEW QUESTIONS

1. What are the basic concepts of a channel member?
2. Discuss the trends in wholesaling and the special characteristics of high technology marketing channels.
3. Write short notes on:
    a. Profitability of a distributor
    b. Checklist of debt management
    c. Industrial goods.
4. Explain different kinds of distribution channel with the help of suitable example.

GO TO THE NET

Using Internet search tools or other relevant sources, locate information on selecting a suitable channel partner.

Using Internet, search tools or other relevant sources prepare a report on the process of channel distribution of 5 Indian companies.

CHAPTER 25

role and function of channels of distribution

learning objectives

The objectives of this chapter are to:

- understand the objectives of channels of distribution
- describe flows in channels of distribution
- discuss patterns of distribution.

content outline

- Opening Case
- Introduction
- Objectives of Channels of Distribution
- Flows in Channels of Distribution
- Patterns of Distribution
- Distribution of Mutual Funds
- Capital Structure
- Participants in the Channel System
- Summary
- Project Work
- Short Answer Questions
- Review Questions
- Go to the Net
- Caselet
- Appendices

opening case

Raymond's Retail Shops

RAYMOND — a success story that began six decades ago. In 1944, Raymond changed hands to become a member of the JK Organisation. Traditional product lines were dropped and high quality became the watchword, also the diversification programme got a head start. Backed by sound R&D, newer non-traditional blends of natural and man-made fibres were introduced. The result: greater consumer satisfaction, both at home and abroad. 1964 marked the beginning of vertical integration at Raymond. In 1968, a readymade garment plant was set up. Within 18 months, Raymond had become India's only exporter of sophisticated trousers and suits to the most sophisticated markets of the world. In 1979, Raymond established a new unit at Jalgaon with REPCO spinning machines with the latest in worsted spinning technology. In the early '50s, a completely new field – Engineer Files. Today it is the second largest file making company in the world and about 50% of its production is exported to almost all the countries of the world. JK (Mumbai) Ltd., another Raymond establishment was established in 1948. The company enjoys leadership in the domestic market for its line of manufacture, namely men's readymade garments. Currently its products are marketed throughout India under the brand name "Park Avenue".

In 1966, Raymond joined hands with Helene Curtis (International) to manufacture high quality cosmetics and toiletries and the Park Avenue range of exclusive men's toiletries was started.

In 1979, Raymond commenced work on a cement project. Today, it has a capacity of 12 lakh tonnes per year. This plant is the most efficient in the country, both in terms of overall productivity and energy consumption.

Overseas, Raymond's multinational line includes a composite textile mill and a readymade garment plant in Kenya, and a steel file plant in Indonesia.

Raymond today is one of the leaders in exporting Indian wool-worsted and blended textiles. From a small order in 1956, Raymond is, today, a major player in the global market. It has carved a niche for itself in the fiercely competitive market.

Today Raymond is a symbol of excellence and quality throughout the country and stands as India's premier textile manufacturer. It has a turnover of Rs 6 billion, a family of more than 6000 employees, high-tech manufacturing units and an annual output exceeding 15 million metres of pure wool, wool blended and polyester-viscose fabrics, and 0.5 million pieces of blankets and shawls. It's got an extensive distribution network, including 150 Raymond retail shops, India's finest men's shops in over 70 cities.

TRY YOURSELF

1. What are the channels of distribution available for M/s Raymonds?
2. Critically analyse the Raymond's Retail shops' success story.
3. Make a comparative analysis of Raymond's retail shops in India vs global market.

INTRODUCTION

A major focus of channels of distribution is delivery. It is only through distribution that public and private goods and services can be made available for use or consumption. Producers of such goods and services are individually capable of generating only the form or structural utility for their products and services. They can organise their production capabilities in such a way that the products they have developed can, in fact, be seen, analysed and sold in the market. The emergence and arrangement of a wide variety of distribution oriented institutions and agencies, typically called intermediaries because they stand between production on the one hand and consumption on the other, can be explained in the following terms

- Intermediaries can improve the efficiency of the process.
- They help in the proper arrangement of routes of transactions.
- They help in the searching process.
- They help in the sorting process.

Definitions

1. "Channel of distribution is a path traced in the direct or indirect transfer of the title to a product as it moves from a producer to ultimate consumers or industrial users".

   – EW Cundiff and RS Still

2. "The course taken in the transfer of the title to a commodity constitutes its channel of distribution. It is the route taken by the title to a product in its passage from its first owner, an agricultural producer, or a manufacturer, as the case may be, to the last owner, the ultimate consumer or the business user."

   – Beckman and Others

3. "A channel of distribution or marketing channel is a structure of intracompany organisation, units and intracompany agents and dealers, wholesalers and retailers through which a commodity product or service is marketed".

   – American Marketing Association

OBJECTIVES OF CHANNELS OF DISTRIBUTION

- To ensure availability of products at the point of sale
- To build channel members' loyalty
- To stimulate channel members to put greater selling efforts
- To develop managerial efficiency in channel organisation
- To identify your organisation at the buyer level
- To have an efficient and effective distribution system, to make your products and services available
- Readily
- Regularly

- Equitably, and
- In a fresh form.

FLOWS IN CHANNELS OF DISTRIBUTION

A flow is a set of functions performed in sequence by channel members. In the flow process, producers, wholesalers, retailers and consumers are linked. The functions that need to be necessarily performed in a channel system include transfer of ownership through transportation, order processing, inventory carrying, storage, sorting negotiations and promotions. The same function in a given channel system, may be performed at more than one level and, in such a case, the workload for the function would need to be shared between channel members.

A channel symbolises the path for the movement of title, possession and payment for goods and services. Figure 25.1 below gives a representation of these marketing flows:

figure 25.1
Marketing Flows in a Channel System

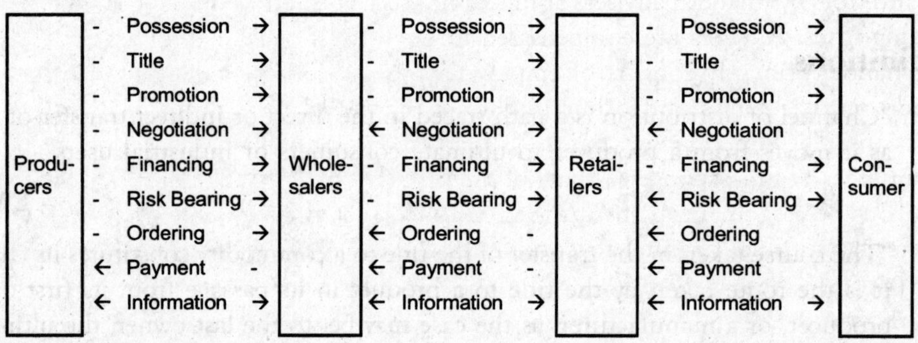

Source: Adapted from RS Valie, TS Grether and R Cox, "*Marketing in the American Economy*" (NY-The Ronald Press)

PATTERNS OF DISTRIBUTION

After a producer has selected the type of channel that makes the most sense for his products, the next step is to determine the level of distribution intensity, which specifies the number of marketing intermediaries that will carry the products.

Depending on a firm's product, objectives and customers, the levels of intensity may differ from case to case. Also, distribution intensity is frequently modified as a product progresses through its life cycle. Marketers have three basic levels of intensity to choose from: Intensive, Selective and Exclusive.

- ***Intensive Distribution***: A channel strategy that seeks to make products available in as many appropriate places as possible.
- ***Selective Distribution:*** A channel strategy that limits availability of products to a few carefully selected outlets in a given market area.
- ***Exclusive Distribution***: An extreme case of selective distribution in which only one outlet in a market territory is allowed to carry a product or a product line.

DISTRIBUTION OF MUTUAL FUNDS

Mutual funds are sold with the help of five principle distribution channels:

1. The direct channel,
2. The advice channel,
3. The retirement plan channel,
4. The supermarket channel, and
5. The institutional channel.

The first four channels primarily serve individual investors. In the direct channel, investors carry out transactions directly with mutual funds. In the advice, retirement plan, and supermarket channels, individual investors use third parties or intermediaries that conduct transactions with mutual funds on their behalf. Third parties also provide services to fund investors on behalf of mutual funds. The most important feature of the advice channel is the provision of investment advice and ongoing assistance to fund investors by financial advisers at full-service securities firms, banks, insurance agencies, and financial planning firms. Advisers are compensated through sales loads or from asset-based fees. The retirement plan channel primarily consists of employer-sponsored defined contribution plans in which employers provide mutual funds and other investments for purchase by plan participants through payroll deductions. The supermarket channel is made up of discount brokers that offer mutual funds from a large number of fund sponsors. Many of the fund offerings are subject to no transaction charges or sales loads. Businesses, financial institutions, endowments, foundations, and other institutional investors use the institutional channel to conduct transactions either directly with mutual funds or through third parties.

CAPITAL STRUCTURE

The capital structure of mutual funds has changed over the past two decades from solely single-class funds to a mixture of single- and multi-class funds. The majority of funds are now multi-class. The change in capital structure partly reflects the broadening of the distribution system. In particular, the multi-class structure enables funds to offer different distribution and service arrangements to investors with differing needs. As a consequence, investors benefit by obtaining preferred distribution arrangements typically at a lower cost. Because each share class is part of the some portfolio, investors benefit from the economies associated with the management of a single portfolio. Each share class is charged the same base fee for the fund. Differences in fees, expenses, and sales charges reflect differences in the distribution and service arrangements available to investors in a particular share class. The vast majority of funds sold through full-service brokers in the advice channel have multi-class structures. The most common use involves a group of three classes – A, B, and C shares – that are sold to individuals through stock brokerages. Each share class offers a different method for compensating brokers for advice and assistance other important share classes include an institutional share class for defined contribution plans and institutional investors, and an adviser share class that is sold through financial advisers who charge their clients directly for advice and services. Fund companies that sell funds directly to shareholders typically offer a distinct to retail clients might also offer separate share classes to institutional clients and financial advisers.

PARTICIPANTS IN THE CHANNEL SYSTEM

The next important stage is channel strategic decision. Plan finalisation includes the development of a framework to help, analyse and select the most desirable channel structure arrangement. The planning and analysis framework introduces a range of tools available to assist managers in the finalisation of a channel plan.

Primary Participants

Primary channel participants are defined as "participants that acknowledge their dependence upon one another in a channel arrangement and assume the risk during the value addition distribution process". The primary participants are manufacturers wholesalers and retailers.

SUMMARY

Channels of distribution are mainly concerned with the physical distribution of goods and services they also help enhance promotion and selling and import marketing control. It is the set of marketing institutions or intermediaries who participate in distribution of goods and services from the point of production to the point of consumption.

A channel symbolises the path for movement of title possession and payment, for goods and services. Depending on a firm's product objectives and customers, the levels of intensity may differ from case to case.

PROJECT WORK

You have decided that you are an entrepreneur and that you want to create a new e-business. Considering the current trends in e-business, the current status of the economy, recent changes in technology and other forces, create of list of five new e-business ideas you might like to pursue.

SHORT ANSWER QUESTIONS

1. What are the objectives of channels of distribution?
2. What are the patterns of distribution?
3. Who are the participants in the distribution system?

REVIEW QUESTIONS

1. What are the basic functions being performed by channel members at various levels?
2. Do you think that the channel participants also have "power"? If yes, then how does the retailer's power differ from that of the wholesaler?
3. What are the implications of retailer-power for channel management in case of the following products
   i. A locally made detergent powder?
   ii. Unbranded electrical appliances?
4. Explain distribution of mutual funds with the help of example.

GO TO THE NET

Using Internet resource tools, design the distribution channel for and give reasons thereof?

a. Image Consultancy

b. Management Consultancy

c. Insurance Services.

Using Internet, search tools, prepare a report on the application of 10 distribution channels of 10 Indian companies.

Caselet

ROLE OF CHANNELS OF DISTRIBUTION [A CASE OF BAJAJ AUTO LTD.]

Bajaj dealers handle a wide range of products. Each of these products cater to different segments of customers and require different selling techniques. Running a Bajaj dealership, in this sense, is equivalent to running dealerships of four independent manufacturers under one roof, i.e., of a scooter, motorcycle, scooterette and a three wheeler manufacturer. Added to this complexity, is the necessity of having an efficient spare parts and after-sales operations catering to each of these product groups and their model variations.

The only way a Bajaj dealer can do full justice to each of these product groups is by focusing on each of these groups separately, and treating them as independent centres. Since all these products are sold under one roof, the only way to focus on each product separately is by assigning exclusive manpower to each of these products with complete accountability for sales of that product. There should be an exclusive set of people (teams) handling scooter sales, motorcycle sales, scooterette sales and M-80 sales.

The above will take care of show room sales. However, apart from showroom sales, there are various other channels of sales which also need to be looked at exclusively for maximising their potential, e.g., command area sales, retail finance sales, institutional sales and sales through direct marketing activities. Therefore, as with showroom sales, there should be separate teams to handle command area sales, institutional sales and sales through direct marketing activities. For ease of monitoring and reporting, one person from each of the specified sales team should be designated as a group leader, who should be accountable for his team's performance.

Once the showroom as well as the field teams are in place, there should be a marketing manager to coordinate the activities of these various teams and be responsible for strategy formulation, target setting, monitoring and evaluation of the performance of each team, in line with the overall objectives of the dealership.

A dealership, where the sales functions are organised in the above manner, will have a reasonably better chance to function more effectively and increase sales across each product category.

Sales Planning

Sales planning involves the following component:

A. *Target Setting:* Targets for the month for all product categories need to be defined and communicated to each and every member of the sales team. This will give each member of the sales team a goal to strive for and help in quantifying his performance. In the absence of any clear targets, the sales team will have a tendency to wait for sales to happen instead of striving to make sales happen.

B. *Enquiry Targets:* For achieving the desired sales volume, it is important that adequate number of enquiries are generated. Depending upon the Enquiry to Conversion (sales) ratio, the target for the number of enquiries for the month should be defined. For example, if the Enquiries to Conversion ratio is 5:1, i.e., for every five enquiries 1 no. sales is to be generated, and the monthly sales target is 100 nos. then to achieve targeted sales, at least 500 enquiries need to be generated. This is the 'Enquiry Target'. Enquiry generation will, of course, depend upon the publicity level (press, hoardings, wall painting, promotional schemes, direct marketing efforts, etc.). Therefore, a well planned target setting and monitoring system for enquiries will make the task of achieving sales targets much easier.

Mid Course Corrections

Monitoring achievements against targets at regular intervals is of immense importance. It allows you to take stock of the situation every ten days and helps in initiating corrective actions well before the month end.

Contd...

Dealership Sales Organisation			
DEALERSHIP:............................			MONTH: ....
City			
Team	*Area*	*Req.*	*Name*
Counter			
T1	SCOOTERETTE		
T2	SCOOTER		
T3	MOPED		
T4	MOTORCYCLE		
T5	FINANCE		
COMMAND AREA			
T6	SCOOTERETTE/ SCOOTER		
T7	MOPED/ MOTORCYCLE		
INSTITUTION			
T8	ALL 2-WHEELERS		
DIRECT MKTG			
T9	SCOOTERETTE		
	SCOOTER		
	MOPED		
	MOTORCYCLE		
T10	MIS		
GL	SCOOTERETTE		
GL	MOPED		
GL	MOTORCYCLE.		
MARKETING MANAGER			
REQ. = REQUIRED NOS. AS PER SSIP-II-NORMS			

Monitoring Contribution of Channels of Sales

What are 'Channels of Sales'? Normally vehicle sales take place through one of the following methods

Contd...

Showroom Sales

- Cash or finance
- Sales through 'Direct marketing' activities
- Exchange.

Outside Showroom Sales

- Sales through Sales Service Outlets (SSOs) and other channel members, i.e. Command Area Sales.
- Institutional Sales (including DGS&D, CSD and bulk sales).

The above mentioned avenues are termed as 'Channels of Sales'. To increase the total sales, contribution of each of these channels should be maximised. This, however, is possible only if we have the required system to monitor each of these channels separately.

MONTHLY SALES PLAN VS ACHIEVEMENT
(SCOOTERS)

DEALERSHIP: MONTH:
CITY:

				SHOWROOM	COMMAND AREA		INSTITUTION		DIRECT
			ENQUIRIES	SALES	SSO SALE	SP/LMP/ SD SALE	DGS& D/CSD	PVT. SECTOR	SALE
SUPER	SALES	1-10 1-20 1-END							
	VARIANCE VS TARGET								
CHETAK	TARGET								
	SALES	1-10 1-20 1-END							
	VARIANCE VS TARGET								
CLAS-SIC	TARGET								
	SALES	1-10 1-20 1-END							
	VARIANCE VS TARGET								
TOT. SCTRS	TARGET								
	SALES	1-10 1-20 1-END							
	VARIANCE VS TARGET								

Contd...

For a Baiaj dealer, it is essential to work out in advance each month's publicity plan for the following reasons

1. Multiplicity of Products

A Bajaj dealer handles a wide range of products and each product needs to be marketed well. Lack of proper publicity planning may lead to over exposure, or under exposure of a particular product leading to unfruitful expenditure or opportunity lost. Apart from this, each product not only needs a different means of communication, but is also targeted at different segments. For example, if the dealership's command area is mainly rural then wall paintings may be a better means of advertising the product rather than through press. Or, if, M-80 needs to be advertised, it may be better to have wall paintings. Similarly advertising of Sunny needs to be addressed to a very different segment than that of KB 125.

2. Targeted Enquiry Generation

As mentioned earlier, for achieving sales targets, generation of targeted number of enquiries is of vital importance. This enquiry generation will not be possible until and unless a detailed product-wise publicity plan is worked out for each month.

DEALER MONTHLY PUBLICITY PLAN - PRESS PUBLICITY

DEALERSHIP : MONTH :

CITY :

PLANNING AREAS RESULT AREAS

PRODUCT	CAMPAIGN	NEWS PAPER	SIZE	PLANNED DATES	ACTUAL DATES	CAMPAIGN ASSESSMENT

ENCLOSURES = Copies of Campaign Ads.

Bulk series or institution sales is another channel of sale, which, if properly tapped, can boost sales very quickly.

The key to success in the institutional sales business is meticulous planning, patience and consistent follow-up. A dedicated team for procuring institutional sales can do wonders and very quickly pay back their cost. A haphazard approach to institutional sales will only result in set-backs. For effectively implementing institutional sales activities, a thorough assessment of the existing potential must be done, i.e., a comprehensive list of all the prospective institutions within the command area should be drawn up along with an estimate of the potential. Within this list, the institutions should be clearly segregated into

a. Institutions which source their requirements through their own funding, e.g., government departments.

b. Private industrial/commercial organisations purchasing for self use.

c. Institutions which provide loans to their employees for purchasing two-wheelers either directly or through societies.

Contd...

d. Institutions with large prospective customer base, where group finance schemes will be required to generate customer interest and enquiries.

From this list, a monthly schedule of tapping these institutions should be drawn up and implemented in a systematic manner with close monitoring of the progress made in each case.

MASTER LIST OF INSTITUTIONS

DEALERSHIP:

CITY:

S. No.	Institution	Address	Contact Person	Employee Strength	Exp. Potential (p.a.)	Previous Business Done (Nos.)

Need For Direct Marketing

Direct market as an enquiry/sales generation activity (in 2-wheeler business) is gaining increased importance as the market has shifted from being a seller's market to that of a buyer's market. The increasing competition has made it mandatory for dealers to seek out prospective customers rather than wait for customers to walk into the showrooms. Thus the direct marketing activities are aimed at seeking out and converting the passive customer segment.

Direct Marketing in the Context of Two-wheeler Business

In two-wheeler marketing, the term direct marketing encompasses the following sales/enquiry generation activities:

i. ***Direct Mailers:*** This activity is aimed at eliciting response from specific organisations and their employees (schools, colleges, companies, government departments, old customers, etc.). The methodology adopted is sending mailers giving special schemes, special finance packages, new product introductions, etc., to generate interest among the target audience. For example, old customers can be sent mailers relating to new product introduction, exchange offers, etc., or employees of an organisation can be sent special group finance schemes. Direct mailers can also be sent to cold call enquiries in an effort to sustain their interest level.

ii. ***Leaflets/Posters***: This exercise is aimed at increasing product knowledge and generating interest about the products in the target audience. This can be clubbed with mailers or can be physically carried out by distributing the literature at commercial complexes, educational institutions, factory gates at shift changes, etc.

Contd...

iii. ***Tagging:*** This exercise involves development of tags with specific messages and dealer's address/telephone number, which are then affixed to targeted 2-wheelers at selected sites. The messages carried by these tags may be varied. For example, if the dealer is conducting an exchange mela, then tags highlighting this may be prepared and attached to all old Bajaj vehicles or vehicles of competing brands within the same product category parked in the parking lot of a railway station, cinema house, college, etc. The same procedure can be followed in the case of new product launches, attractive finance schemes, etc.

iv. ***Door Tap Operations:*** This activity involves selection of a residential or commercial complex which houses prospects of the desired socio-economic profile and then approaching them directly with product literature, special schemes, free gifts for test rides, etc. with the aim of generating enquiries. Housewives of a particular residential colony may be targeted for creating awareness about Sunny by distributing product literature and by offering free test rides.

v. ***Product Demonstrations/Displays:*** This direct marketing activity aims at generating interest and, subsequently, enquiries for a particular product by exposing the target audience directly to the product through product demonstrations and displays. For this activity, a suitable spot with high visibility is selected and vehicles are displayed there. Such a display is generally accompanied by distribution of product literature or offers of free test rides.

DIRECT MARKETING PLAN

DEALERSHIP: MONTH:

CITY:

A. DIRECT MAILERS

Product	Message	Target Audience	Plan Qty.	Tgt. Date	Completion Date	Effectiveness

B. LEAFLETS/POSTERS

Product	Message	Target Audience Distributed at	Plan Qty.	Target Date	Completion Date	Actual Qty	Effectiveness

appendix I

COMPARISON OF THE SELLING DISTRIBUTOR'S AND COMPANY'S DISTRIBUTION SYSTEM

DISTRIBUTION THROUGH SELLING DISTRIBUTORS	DIRECT DISTRIBUTION
SD'S WS.	Company's WS
SD appoint wholesellers	Company appoints wholesalers
Good WS doesn't want to work with SD. (SD always sees his interest while passing commissions, incentives schemes, etc. Sometime appoints his relative for his sake.)	WS is always interested in working with direct Co
SD always appoints his regular/traditional WS.	Co appoints proper and right WS as per the product category
Sales force appointed by SD	Sales force appointed by Co
SM quality is not up to the mark (Good SM does not want to work with SD banner/low remuneration)	SM quality is always better and can be improved by proper training and guidance from time to time
SM reports to SD (information to Co. comes after filtration and fabrication)	SM reports to Co. (accurate and proper information)
SD does not provide SM, in proper quantity and quality	Co. appoints SM in terms of quality and quantity
SD is responsible for sales and collection from WS	Co is responsible for sales and collection from WS
SD does not take proper interest in all Co's promotional activities	Co does this through its SM directly
MIS is improper and time consuming	MIS is proper and very fast
SD reports to Co maximum on weekly basis (in a nut-shell)	Reporting from SM is on day-to-day basis (informative)
Loyalty of SM is always with SD	Loyalty of SM is always with Co .
Co controls only a single person to SD	Co controls a no. of SM and WS
SD works on a fixed percentage on sales value	Initially cost high to CO until the volumes are there
Co reaches upto SD level	Co reaches upto ground level (retailer) directly
Co Cannot command the trade very smoothly.	Co can command the trade in its own way directly.

appendix II

RETAILING TRENDS

It will be a big plan if shoppers find it cheaper to go to big shops. This can happen if large-scale retailing progresses beyond the cosmetic phase, perhaps when computer networking shakes up the cost structure. The success of US-style retailing (Wal-Mart being the best example) lies in price competitiveness. This is achieved through central purchasing (and warehousing), efficient logistics and computerised stock management.

Information on bar-coded products, for instance, can be read within seconds off a pack into computer memory. At a warehouse, the manager gets quick information on what's what and headed where, what's about to perish when, and so on. At checkout counters, shoppers do not have to wait for their bills.

But the real benefit of online operations is the information on what product is being sold and the speed at which this information can be transmitted across a network to all other links in the supply chain. So, if demand for mosquito mats spurts, manufacturers and stockists can respond immediately. This weeds dead stock out of the system and cuts down inventory costs and working capital needs. Says Bikosh Kumar, consultant, Retail Marketing Consulting, Bangalore, (RMC): "A foreign store like 7-Eleven replenish stock six times in a day, holding inventories of just half a day".

The data also allows the retailer to change things around to maximise turnover per sq.ft. In supermarkets, just rearranging the display pattern on shelves alters the rate of pick-up.

Unfortunately, bar-coding and networks are taking too long to settle in, largely because consolidated large-scale operations haven't begun and the assorted parties are too poor to cough up the money needed for such systems. However, isolated computerisation has already helped efficiency levels. At Crossword, the bookshop at Ebony, a plush departmental store in Delhi, there is a data-bank of all books, indexed by author, title and so on, and books move quite quickly.

Of course, price competitiveness is not all. Well-designed shops do add value to the products they sell. There is plenty, apart from air-conditioning, that the shopper will pay for. As mentioned earlier, stores selling lifestyle products to the rich, or which offer good service, get higher margins. Take specialist stores. Just as antique stores can command a premium by virtue of all that history narration by their glib attendants, so can others. Predicts Tony Smith, Vice-President, KSA, "Specialists will emerge in product categories like fashion-related products, lingerie, footwear and so on". Already in operation: Tangerine, which retails home computers and Underlines, which intends to make lingerie selling a fine art. Spencer & Co., in a technical tie-up with Hong Kong-based Dairy Farm International, has started Health & Glow, its chain of cosmetics and pharma products, in Chennai.

Most players are bullish on a gradual metamorphosis of the retail environment. Says Dev Desai, General Manager, Banaras House (Hyderabad), 'This is the right time for entry. We are at the beginning of a retail boom.' By 1997-98, Banaras House plans to have 15 more outlets in Andhra Pradesh and two in Bangalore. Rapid expansion, all agree, is necessary. Raghunandan estimates that a chain should have at least 40 stores to be viable.

What about mail order and teleshopping? Companies such as Otto Burlington, though claim to be doing well, have not significantly altered the way people like to shop. TSN and other teleshops have the advantage of wide reach (satellite TV viewers) and ability to demonstrate. Teleshopping seems to be picking up with offbeat products, but still is not a 'phenomenon'. Attribute some of the strengths of good old retailing to the consumer's desire to go out and do the look-touch-feel routine before putting down money.

In the US, Wal-Mart and others are now pondering the question of whether they are under threat from Internet shops, which allow people to pay by card and pick stuff to be delivered straight to their doorsteps. Amazon.com, an online bookshop which provides candid book reviews (from customers), is already being hailed as an outstanding success. By year 2000, about 46 million consumers are expected to be shopping online, with an average annual spend of about $350 (Rs 12,250) per head! Impressive!

But nothing for retailers here to worry about. In India, retailing will continue to thrive. The fact is that small corner shops are still popping up like nobody's business in small-town India, where proximity is everything.

Contd...

Footpath selling and iron-trunk shops are multiplying too. Like with so many other things in this land of multifarious co-existences, everything will evolve together.

In developed countries, innovation comes in small ways. Often, these look like tiny improvements to those on the spot, but combine to make a massive difference. Take an example from cold chain management: instead of having different trucks with different temperatures, someone figured it would be better to have assorted temperature zones in each truck. A minor capital expense, but since trucks were always running full now and items in each cool zone could be delivered more frequently, the cost and freshness benefits were enormous. Almost everyone in the US has replicated the idea.

Take another from a supermarket chain. While it had '10 items or less' express checkout counters (a standard), the staff observed that it was not quite enough. People dropping in for immediate need items (cigarettes, milk, eggs, et al. tend to park rashly and be fidgety and impatient at checkout counters. So, for such products, it stole McDonald's idea of a drive-through window service.

How does Indian retailing compare?

Innovation is seen chiefly in the form of promotions run either by the shop or in association with a manufacturer. Shoppers' Stop, for instance, has a loyalty club called First Citizen Club which offers rewards and other discounts to its customers. Nanz has a discount card for people whose monthly bills go over a certain limit. Crossword regularly invites authors and music idols to make speeches and sign autographs at its outlets. It is a start.

Others have been pushed by marketers to create space for special counters and demo tables. This activity has risen dramatically in recent years. Silk Epil and Satinelle have been at it in big departmental stores since they were launched. Sony Music launched its first music album in India at Delhi's Ebony. Says Anil Kumar, Manager (Operations), "We experimented in retailing computers for the first time in a departmental store with HCL Beanstalk. It was a success".

CHAPTER 26

selection and motivation of distribution channels

learning objectives

The objectives of this chapter are to:

- analyse the factors influencing the selection of distribution channels
- understand the various channel decisions through the use of examples of marketing channels
- study the points which motivate the intermediaries.

content outline

opening case

'In 1998, Classic refrigerator had a great year in northern India. It swept the whole market winning every single one of the first ten places except ninth. The fact is that the company had a moderate product. The Chief Executive Officer of Classic decided to go directly to the customer. The idea—instead of concentrating company efforts and resources on improving the relations with the dealers—was to focus on enhancing relations, with the final consumer. With this strategy, the plan was to eliminate the dealer completely and replace him or her with agents.

To say that the plan did not work well is an understatement. 'Northend Co.' distributors, who had represented Classic in north India, initiated legal action against Classic in four districts. All 120 Classic dealers felt betrayed by the elimination of their franchise. In spite of the fact that they were offered the opportunity to become agents, they were so opposed that they sued Classic and sought damages exceeding Rs 10 crores. Classic's top management decided that perhaps their original distribution system was not so bad after all.

TRY YOURSELF

1. What channel alternatives were available to Classic?
2. Did Classic fail to properly evaluate the existing distributors? Comment with reasons.
3. What do you know about channel selection and management that the Chief Executive Officer did not give full consideration to in the above case?

INTRODUCTION

Marketing channel decisions are among the most crucial decisions that a company has to take. But a large number of companies in India do not have sufficient information regarding types, locations and number of channel members. The company's chosen channels intimately affect various marketing decisions. There are a few specific reasons which show the need for channel members.

- When a new product is launched.
- When an existing product is aimed to enter the new market.
- Where there is change in marketing environment.

CHANNEL DECISIONS

Channel decisions refer to various decisions related to the selection of right channel member for distribution of goods as well as services from the manufacturer to the ultimate consumer. The following decisions are considered important while making policy:

- Marketing mix variables
- Long-term commitments
- Degree of channel control
- Level of customer services
- Price of the product/services.

PARTICIPANTS IN THE DISTRIBUTION CHANNEL

There are several types of participants that make up a distribution channel.

Retailers

The retailer is a part of distribution channel who sells the product to the final consumers. After a retailer the product finally comes into the hand of final consumers. As you know if in anytime, anywhere, you shop for some products from the retailer you find out that they are different according to their location and geographical area. Retailers may be grouped according to any of the following four categories:

Ownership: The retailers can be classified on the bases of number of ways as such as, national chain store; a smaller, regional chain store; an independent retailer; or a franchisee.

Pricing philosophy: Stores are generally based on discounters or full-price retailers. Within the "discounter" category, there are several subcategories such as factory outlets, consignment stores, dollar stores, special discount stores, membership clubs, and so on.

Product assortment: Assortment of products is very vital important for any retail industry, merchandise management is responsible for assortment of products. The breadth and depth of product lines carried by the store depends a lot on its ownership. An Ann Taylor store, for example, sells Ann Taylor branded clothing-not much breadth of product line there, but extensive depth in that line. A Kmart, on the other hand, carries thousands of brands, but perhaps does not have much depth (not many brands) in any given category of product.

Service levels: The more exclusive or specialized the store, the more types of services it will generally offer-from a name-branded credit card, to on-site alterations, to liberal return policies for its loyal customers. With the "big box" discounters, on the other hand, customers pay for convenience and bypass traditional service, by bagging their own groceries and the like. These distinctions between various types of stores will be important as we discuss their participation in certain distribution channels.

Wholesalers

Wholesalers act as a middlemen between the manufacturer and the final consumer products from manufacturers and resell them to the retailers. They take the same types of financial risks as retailers, since they purchase the products (thereby taking legal responsibility for them), keep them in inventory until they are resold to retailers, and may arrange for shipment to those retailers. Wholesalers can gather product from around a country or region, or can buy foreign product lines by becoming importers.

The term "wholesale" is often used to describe the discounting principle of retailers (as in "wholesale clubs"), but discounters are retailers, not technically wholesalers. And in B2B channels, wholesalers may be called distributors.

Agents and Brokers

Agents (sometimes called brokers) are also act as an intermediaries between suppliers and retailers (or in B2B channels), but their agreements are different, in that they do not take ownership of the products selling. They are independent on the sales executives who typically work on commission based Participants in the Distribution Channel on sales volume, and they can sell the product to wholesalers as well as retailers. In business to business arrangements, this means they sell to distributors and end users. Resident sales agents are good examples in retail. They reside in the country to which they sell products, but the products come from a variety of foreign manufactures. The resident sales agent represents those manufacturers, who pay the agent on commission. A resident sales agent does not always have merchandise warehoused and ready to sell, but he or she does have product samples for which orders can be placed and is responsible for bringing the items through the importation process. Retailers that don't have the money, time, or manpower to send someone overseas for manufactures' site visits to check out the new product lines can depend on a resident sales agent to do the job. Buying offices can also be considered a type of agent or broker, since they earn their money pairing up retailers with product lines from various manufacturers.

Factors in the Selection of Distribution Channels

Selection of appropriate distribution channel is very important because several elements of the marketing mix, like price and promotion, are closely interrelated with and interdependent on the distribution channels. Each channel member involves some cost which enters into the price of the product that the ultimate consumer has to bear.

The choice of the appropriate channels of distribution is not a simple task. Douglas M Lambert has suggested some criteria for selecting intermediaries as given in Table 39.1.

table 26.1 **Criteria for Selecting Intermediaries**

1. Size of prospective channel member	Sales, financial strength
2. Sales strength	Number of salesmen, sales and technical competence
3. Product lines	Competitive products Compatible products Complementary products Quality of lines carried
4. Reputation Leadership well-established	Leadership
5. Market coverage	Geographic coverage – Outlets per market area Industrial coverage Call frequency or intensity of coverage
6. Sales performance	Performance with related lines General sales performance Growth prospects
7. Management	
8. Advertising and sales promotion	
9. Sales compensation	
10. Acceptance of training assistance	
11. Transportation savings	
12. Inventory	Kind and size Safety stocks Reduction in manufacture's inventories
13. Warehousing	Supplied in files Ability to handle shipments efficiently
14. Lot quantity costs	

Source: Dougles M Lambert, '*The Distribution Channels Decision*' National Association of Accounts, New York, 1976, Page 37.

Prof William J Stanton has suggested a large number of factors in the choice of distribution channel

Market Consideration:

- Consumer or industrial market
- Number of potential customers
- Size of order
- Buying habits of customers
- Geographical concentration of market.

Product Considerations:

- Unit value
- Product line
- Standardised product
- Technical nature

- Bulk and weight
- Perishability.

Company Considerations:

- Volume of production
- Financial resources
- Experienced and competent management
- Services provided by the channels
- Desire for control of channels.

Middlemen Considerations:

- Availability of desired middlemen
- Financial ability
- Attitude of middlemen
- Sales potential
- Cost
- Competition and legal constraints.

SELECTION OF CHANNEL

The channel representation allows the construction of soft histograms, where peaks can be detected with a much higher accuracy than in regular hard-binned histograms. This is critical in e.g. reducing the number of bins of generalized Hough transform methods. When applying the maximum entropy method to the channel representation, a minimum-information reconstruction of the underlying continuous probability distribution is obtained. The maximum entropy reconstruction is compared to simpler linear methods in some simulated situations. Experimental results show that mode estimation of the maximum entropy reconstruction outperforms the linear methods in terms of quantization error and discrimination threshold. Finding the maximum entropy reconstruction is however computationally more expensive.

CUSTOMER SERVICE

The key mechanism in which Wholesale Distributors employ to differentiate themselves is customer service. Often competing wholesales carry identical items and the means to build customer loyalty is through exceptional service. Without a sound strategy for providing differentiated services upon which to compete, shortsighted wholesalers will find themselves forced to compete on price alone. Competing on price alone is clearly a path to extinction, as the most desperate distributor will always set the lowest price. Thus the tactic of chasing the lowest price will drive the price down to loss making levels for those wholesalers that cannot compete with service and are forced to follow the terminal strategy of price competition alone. Exceptional service includes having the items in stock as requested, at a competitive price and delivering when promised. Additionally, wholesalers are asked to perform value added services, such as kitting and labelling. Finally, another means by which wholesalers are differentiating themselves is to increase their product offering, creating a one-stop shop for retailers. Although this strategy has its drawbacks as wholesalers see their inventory costs rise with each additional SKU. For this reason it is of paramount importance to have systems in place that provide exceptional control over inventory levels.

Examples of Marketing Channels

1. ***Vertical Marketing System (VMS);*** It is the result of failure of marketing channels where each – manufacturer, wholesaler, retailer – is one independent separate identity seeking to achieve its own objectives.

   Examples are BPL, ONIDA, Philips, BATA, DCM, etc.

2. ***Horizontal Marketing System:*** Here two or more businesses, which are otherwise unrelated, put together their efforts to exploit an emerging marketing opportunity. Examples are Maruti Udyog, HDFC Bank, GE Capital, Auto Finance Ltd., Kotak Mahindra Finance Ltd.

3. ***Third Party "Delivery":*** In which specialised agency is providing logistics and distribution services. Examples are ACE which is providing door-to-door service for Godrej and McDonald's.

4. ***Multi-Channel Marketing System:*** In which distribution is performed by company's showrooms as well as channel members.

   Examples are BATA, Philips, Raymonds.

Criteria for Selection of a Distributor by M/s "RICOLA"

- Experience in FMCG (as per product clientele)
- Good financial status
- Adequate/proper storage
- Retail network in the area
- Good market reputation
- Administration arrangements
- Proper delivery arrangements.

Functions of a Distributor of M/s "RICOLA"

- He should place orders with the company 15 days in advance
- He should extend credit facility to retailers
- He should assist the company in market support activities
- He should maintain proper sales records
- He should assist the company in extending retailer network in his area.

Proposed/Potential Retail Outlets for "RICOLA"

▶ Departmental Store	A Class
▶ General Store	A Class
▶ Confectionery Shop	A Class
▶ Soft Drink/Paan/Cigarette shop	(Selected top of the mind)
▶ (Inside/Outside Restaurants/ Hotels/Cinema Halls)	
▶ Chemist	A Class

Minimum Infrastructure Requirements for a Dealer of M/s Bajaj Auto Ltd.

- *Front Window Display System:*
  - ***Glass Front:*** All showrooms to have a glass frontage.
  - ***Show Window for Product Display:*** For an active product display, show windows are to be provided.
  - ***Glass Entrance.***
- ***Netted Shutters for the frontage:*** For continued product display even after closing hours, netted shutters are to be provided.
- ***Lighting Arrangement:*** Adequate lighting to be provided inside the showroom, on display clusters and show windows for product visibility.
- ***Display Stands for Products:*** At least 1 no. display stand to be installed. Orders for the same to be placed with the approved vendor (address given below) through Mr GN Hemrajani at Bajaj Auto Ltd, Pune.

  Mr Sudhir Sharma/Mr Ashish DeshpandePh.: 0212-364781 /364431

  C/o M/s Elephant Design Pvt. Ltd Fax: 0212-365564 324,

  Pragati Complex,

  17/1B, Kothrud,

  Pune (MAH.) - 411 029.
- ***Colour Scheme:*** The showroom interior and exterior to be painted in the prescribed colours.

Minimum Manpower Requirement (Two-Wheelers)

Manpower, as specified, to be provided and organised as per the dealer sales organisation.

Sales Systems

- ***Command Area Activity Planning:*** This will involve formulation of plan of activities to be carried out in the command area on a monthly basis, their implementation and monitoring vis-a-vis plan vs achievement. This will also involve detailing of the route plan of the command area team.

- ***Publicity Planning:*** The publicity plans for each product (press as well as outdoor) need to be clearly spelt out on a monthly basis to ensure adequate coverage for each product in the Bajaj range and to maximise returns from each rupee spent on advertising.

Test Ride Vehicles

One test ride vehicle, clearly marked so (one of each product category), is to be kept ready for providing hands on riding experience to prospective customers. Special care is to be taken, that the vehicle earmarked for test rides is in perfect working condition.

MOTIVATION OF INTERMEDIARIES

After selecting the channel members for company's services, the company must keep motivating them to realise their potential. A company should make use of the following strategies.

Relationship Marketing

Relationship marketing starts on the premise that in a variety of products, mass marketing has run its course and that conventional methods of advertising are not delivering the kind of results they are supposed to. Companies like Tupperware, AVON, Amway, Modi Care do not distribute their products through the traditional distribution system. Relationship marketing puts stress on the company's relations with the distributors. A good relationship with the distributor will create long-term relations and improve sales.

Benefits and Costs Offered to Intermediaries

The company should offer various benefits to a distributor. These, as well as reimbursement of expenses, will create a positive impact on the distributor.

The company can offer the following benefits to a distributor:

- Reduction in the amount of capital employed by the distributor
- Lower operating costs
- Availability of specialists' services
- Reduction of overall risk
- Customer finance schemes
- Increased sales promotion.

Cooperative Programmes

Cooperative approach is a traditional method of motivating to intermediaries. It includes advertising allowances, training salespeople, payment for displays, free goods, commission on extra sales, etc. These programmes will help in the increase of sales of intermediaries.

Distributor Advisory Councils (DAC)

In this method, a council of distributors is formed, which gives the opinion of distributors, to the company. Normally, in these councils, top management discusses the company's problems with channel members. DAC results in an overall improvement of channel communication which, in turn, helps the manufacturer learn more about the needs and problems of his channel members.

Distribution Channel Control

The concept of power in channel relationships has been defined as 'the ability of a channel member to control the decision variables in the marketing strategy of any member in a given channel at a different level of distribution'. In most channels, one member will emerge as the leader. Traditionally, it was assumed that the manufacturer, as the most powerful member, was always the channel leader. Currently, however, this assumption appears less valid. The power wielded by retailers in the food and grocery industry is a classic example. As more and more merchandise is distributed through fewer and fewer outlets, the balance of power has shifted from the manufacturer to the distributor. Many manufacturers now have little choice but to accede to the demands of the major retail chains. This trend alone, which has continued worldwide for the last decade, dictates the need for cooperation and an end to the 'independent organisation' model. Figure 26.1 depicts the differing objectives that might apply to a typical manufacturer-distributor channel relationship.

Distribution Channel Conflict

The following are the areas where normally conflicts start between the company and its channel members:

- Product range mixes
- Ordering procedures
- Delivery schedules
- Enhanced communications (EDI)
- Trading terms and credit arrangements
- Packing and handling
- Special packs and pack sizes
- Selling aids and point-of-sale material
- Just-in-time logistics
- Credits, returns, breakages and empties
- Joint product development
- Joint promotion
- Trade-off opportunities.

Partners have common objectives and strategies for achieving them. They also have a common defence against any intrusion into the partnership. They are allies and advertisers. This is the way forward for progressive organisations in the 2001 as they seek platforms for long-term prosperity rather than short-term gain which is quickly dissipated.

Examples: Motivation to Retailers

In India, the consumer is very value conscious. Brown believes that better supply chain management will cut down costs as it will make for higher-efficiency and cutting down of unnecessary layers of middlemen. "The consumer wins if the supply chain is good". So the retailers win. In retail activity, the Tatas, RPG group and Piramal's are doing very well.

Manufacturer – Marketing strategy

Distributor – Marketing strategy

Product positioning – Price, quality, variety, convenience

Identify issues – Product ranges, pricing, promotions, distribution

Corporate positioning – Assortment trading style target segments, customer profiles

Objectives – volume, distribution, profit, brand loyalty

Joint Planning Activities

Objectives – Customer sales, size, frequency, volume, profit, store loyalty

Mutual profitability

Customer satisfaction

Source: *Handbook of Logistics and Distribution*, Page 96-98.

figure 26.1
The Distribution Channel

MANUFACTURER/SUPPLIER CHANNEL OBJECTIVES

- Market share by segment
- Profit/Contribution Goal
- ROI
- Distributor loyalty
- Market development

Consumer Satisfaction

CONSUMER OBJECTIVES

- Choice
- Availability
- Value
- Convenience

Manufacturer/Distributor Cooperation/Conflict

DISTRIBUTOR'S OBJECTIVES

- Turnover
- Gross Margin
- ROI
- Promotional assistance
- Technical Support
- Exclusivity
- Market development

SUMMARY

A smart company has to create a relationship with its intermediaries and strive towards creating a memorable and enjoyable experience for every single intermediary. A good company should keep distribution "lifelong" and should, therefore, look upon customers as "lifelong customers". A reputed company should try to delight its distributors by empowering them and creating a proprietary feeling among them.

Project Work

Select five distributors of your area and study their motivation level. If not motivated find out the reasons.

Short Answer Questions

1. Why do you believe that product considerations are important for selection of distribution channels
2. What are the benefits and costs offered to intermediaries?
3. What do you mean by distributor advisory channels?
4. What are distributors' objectives?
5. What is selection of channel?

Review Questions

1. Why should companies care for motivating channel members and what problems do they face in this exercise?
2. Can "power" always motivate channel members? Discuss, taking the example of a company which has a high market share as compared to competitors.
3. What are the major criteria used to select channel members?
4. A company selling high fashion garments is adding to its product line 'designer watches'. Would it be possible for it to continue with the same channels as being used for its earlier product line? Explain with reasons.
5. What are the criteria that can be used for the evaluation of channel members? Illustrate your answer with appropriate examples.
6. Explain the types of participants in the distribution channel.

Go to the Net

Using Internet sources, locate 20 websites of various distributors and study their material level.

Using Internet search tools prepare a report on the process of selection of channel of 5 Automobile companies.

CHAPTER

motivational tools of distribution channels

27

learning objectives

The objectives of this chapter are to:

- identify various motivational tools and control areas
- describe factors affecting the majoring of a manufactured product
- discuss remuneration of salespersons.

content outline

- Opening Case
- Introduction
- Types of Channels
- Motivational Tools and Control Areas
- Motivation of the Distributor and Motivational Tools for Distributor's Sales Force
- Remuneration of the Salesperson
- Risk Management
- Summary
- Project Work
- Short Answer Questions
- Review Questions
- Go to the Net

opening case

Motivation of Dealers

Study the following motivation schemes and answer the questions that follow:

1. **Product Training:** WIPRO provides training to dealers about the functioning of the product so that they are able to use and explain to the customers about its functions and its special features by working on it. WIPRO also provides training to its dealers about the different parts of the product and their uses are also told to them so that they can answer customers' query. It gives a feeling of security to the dealer.
2. **Demo Setup:** Demo setups are also a motivating factor for a dealer because under this WIPRO provides a system to the dealer at very low price so that he can demonstrate the function of the system. Otherwise it is very difficult for the dealer to unpack the system again and again for demonstration. Under such a setup WIPRO provides a computer of Rs 40,000 at Rs 15,000 – a discounted value. The dealer feels very enthusiastic under this procedure.
3. **Target Incentives:** These are additional incentives given to the dealer if he fulfils the target, e.g., if a dealer fulfils the monthly target of Rs 15 lakhs, then he will get 2.5% or 3% of it. These are mainly on monthly basis. It is one of the highly motivating factors for the dealer.
4. **30 Day Money back Offer:** Under such type of schemes, the company puts up a condition like, if a dealer is able to sell 15 computers or 40 printers in a quarter, then he will be entitled to a gift. The gift may be fridge, TV, microwave oven, washing machine, etc. A dealer showing top performance among all of them will again be getting some gift, e.g., foreign travel, etc.
5. **Financial Assistance:** It is one of the major motivating factors for any dealer. Under this scheme, financial assistance is provided by the sister concern of WIPRO, i.e., WIPRO Financial Ltd. in case of government or corporate orders of higher value.

Try Yourself

1. Examine the impact of various promotional schemes aimed at improving the dealers' performance.

INTRODUCTION

Channel objectives determine channel strategy. Making a major change in an established channel structure is difficult and often risky. Therefore, it is desirable to set up the objectives properly in the first place. They should be dictated by the service level output, which is desired by the ultimate consumer, and the global vision and mission of the company in terms of long-term return on investment, market share, absolute level of profits to be achieved and sales growth.

The specific objectives of any channel, apart from the global aspirations of the company, should be firmly based on the service outputs demanded by its customers. Different levels of these outputs may be required in different segments of the market and these need to be determined. The use of multiple channels, catering to different segments of the market, is common in marketing today.

Once the service levels are decided upon, then the market coverage needed has to be determined. This, in turn, determines the support, which can be expected from the channel in the event of different coverage strategies. Here the company should also decide whether it needs to own the entire channel or parts of it and what the costs of full and part ownership are going to be in terms of possible consequences.

Three choices are possible: intensive, selective or exclusive distribution. It is worth mentioning in this context that they are all possible in case of vertical or non-vertical integration although the costs may be prohibitive in case of full ownership of a channel specialising in intensive distribution.

Intensive distribution is generally used for products which are frequently bought and which need to be easily available, like newspapers and sweets. Selective distribution is usual for products which buyers like to choose with some effort, e.g., clothing. This type of distribution can range from expensive items which are almost exclusive, to items like cosmetics, which are almost intensively distributed. Exclusive distribution implies a mutually dependent relationship between seller and re-seller and is used for large or expensive items such as farm machinery or very expensive clothes or jewellery.

It is appropriate to check and verify that the strategy adopted is in line with current circumstances when considering how to motivate a channel member. The channel structure and the type of distribution are also interdependent to some degree. A 'long' channel structure, which possesses many intermediate wholesalers, allows for greater spread and therefore more intensive distribution. Conversely, a 'short" structure has more direct channels and tends towards exclusive distribution.

It is obvious that the more intensive the distribution, the greater the sales in the short-term. However, over a long-term, adverse effects such as lower margins appear, followed by unwillingness on the part of the distributors to sell the product, consequent necessity of an increase in promotional efforts by the manufacturer and deterioration of service levels. As a business executive once remarked, 'you can take fifty years to build a brand and you can ruin it in three years through careless distribution'.

However, intensive distribution is successfully followed in the case of innumerable products, through a well-formulated marketing programme, which fulfils the requirements of distributors and consumers alike. The various factors should be carefully considered before deciding on a distribution strategy, in particular, the relation between the products marketed and the last selling point for them.

TYPES OF CHANNELS

We'll set aside business-to-business channels for now and look at the four simple types of retail distribution channels for consumer products:

Direct channel: This is observed when the same company that manufactures a product sells it directly to the consumer or end user, a direct channel marketer. Mail-order catalog sales companies, like Lands' End, are also direct channel sellers.

Retailer channel: This is observed when the producer sells to the retailer, and the retailer sells to the consumer.

Wholesaler channel: Intermediaries play a role here, as the manufacturer sells to a wholesaler who sells to a retailer who sells to the consumer.

Dual channel or multiple channel: This term refers to the use of two or more channels to sell products to different types of customers. A lawnmower manufacturer, for example, might sell some product lines at retail and others to commercial lawn care companies, each requiring different intermediary services.

How Channels are Chosen?

Although retailers drive distribution channels, it is not usually the retailer who makes the decision to utilize one channel over the others. The producer of the product makes this decision. There are several characteristics of product lines that make them more or less appropriate for a particular type of channel.

Briefly, these characteristics can be summarized as follows:

The products themselves: If a product is perishable, like many grocery items, it requires the shortest, most direct distribution channel-which means the fewest possible intermediaries along the way. If a product is customized, like an expensive assembled-to-order computer system, it also benefits from a short distribution channel. There is no need for intermediaries when a customer orders a custom product directly from the company that makes it. Long distribution channels correspond to small purchases, either because the retailer doesn't carry much inventory or the consumer buys the item in small quantities.

The type of customer: Who are the customers, what do they need and expect from their shopping experience, and where are they willing to go to buy this type of product? How much quantity do they buy at a time? A channel may be chosen because it best reflects the end users' buying habits. Business-to-business customers have completely different needs and buying habits than individual consumers.

Market size: This factor encompasses two things: the population of an area and whether it is urban or rural. It is easier to sell direct to customers in a large city with lots of potential outlets for a product line. The more widely dispersed the stores. The more logical the dependence on agents and wholesalers—or on multiple retailers in different cities-to keep product sales strong and steady.

The producer's level of control: Most top-dollar clothing designers and fragrance manufacturers do not want their products showing up anywhere and everywhere. They've worked hard to build an exclusive reputation, and they expect their distribution channel to work just as hard to protect and enhance their upscale image. These producers will choose a distribution channel that ensures no discount merchants have access to their lines, and they will count on the members of their channel to honor their wishes and not make bargain "deals."

The size of the producing company: A producer is likely to sell direct when the company is large enough to handle the additional responsibilities that intermediaries would otherwise provide-credit to customers, warehouses for their own goods, the ability to hire and train their own sales representatives. Smaller producers require a larger distribution chain in order to fill these roles.

The size of the retailers: A segment of the industry that is fragmented, with most of the stores operating as single units, requires the distribution channel to be longer.

MOTIVATIONAL TOOLS AND CONTROL AREAS

The following means of persuasion are available to channel members to influence the decision making or behaviour of others.

1. ***Reward:*** If A possesses some resource which B wishes to obtain and B believes this can be obtained through conforming to A's wishes, this amounts to reward power. Specific rewards to channel members could include wider margins, granting of exclusive territories and various promotional allowances.
2. ***Coercion:*** This exists if B believes that A will punish anyone who does not conform to A's wishes. Coercion amounts to negative sanctions or punishment including reductions in margins, withdrawal of rewards granted earlier and slowing down of shipments. This brings less results over the long-term than other tools and should therefore be considered as a last resort.
3. ***Expertise:*** This occurs when B perceives A to possess some special knowledge, which would help B. Small retailers often rely heavily on their wholesalers for expert advice. However, once transferred, expertise is considerably reduced in power. If a business wishes to retain expertise over a long-term, the following options are open to it:
    a. It can ration its advice to small portions and keep back sufficient vital knowledge so that the others remain dependent upon it. This could be detrimental to efficient working of the channel, as every member should work to its capacity for the channel to function successfully. A member starved of vital information cannot contribute effectively.
    b. A better, though somewhat expensive, option is to collect accurate information regarding market trends, threats and opportunities, and other ongoing matters which individual channel members would find difficult to obtain themselves. The benefits of this option can be high in terms of channel goal achievements.
    c. Another way is for channel members to invest in specialized transaction expertise, which is difficult to transfer to other products or services and so hinders the members from leaving the channel.
    d. The ability of a channel member to acquire information, which is necessary for another channel member to function efficiently, confers power on the acquirer. For example, retailers hold a privileged position with respect to manufacturers because of their close customer contacts.
4. ***Identification:*** This occurs when B identifies with A or desires to do so. For example, given equal returns from two different dealerships, one may well choose that which one would like to identify with, perhaps the more prestigious one. Here the company reputation or image confers an advantage on the business.
5. ***Legitimacy:*** It results from B feeling that A has the right to exercise power over them. This would be the case between workers and their supervisor, for example. In a channel relationship, such a power may be assigned to the largest firm. Or the retailers and industrial suppliers may believe that they have the power since they are in contact with the end-users and the others are not. However, the amount of power thus exerted is usually small.

In real life situations, all these powers are used simultaneously in most situations. Sometimes, the use of one power may enhance another power base; or the opposite may happen. Environmental conditions and the effect of such a use of power on them must also be considered in this situation. The norms of the channel systems also prohibit the use of some of these powers.

The degree of success that a channel member will have in influencing the behaviour of other channel members will depend on its leadership behaviour. When the channel members have common goals, the use of information exchange and/or recommendations will probably produce positive results. In other situations, promises, threats, legalistic strategies and requests are used with varying success.

An international business manufacturing paints, which is based in Italy, has the policy of treating its agents like its own employees. They are required to submit progress reports every month just like the company sales force. All these reports are fed into a computer and analysed. The company management keeps an eye on the stocks bought by key customers and the price they paid. Any falling off in an agent's performance results in rapid identification of the problem and support provided by a senior staff member on the spot.

Focusing Channels onto Specific Products and Target Markets leads to Motivation of Channel Principals and Sales Force

Ensure that the traditional distributor attitude and priorities are recognised by you and dealt with. Distributors:

- always feel that a high price is charged by the manufacturer
- think that manufacturer's mark-up is high
- think that the manufacturer does not invest in the market

Avoid the traditional manufacturer attitude – the manufacturer:

- is interested in volume sales
- is interested in profits
- wants distributors to make stock investment.

How to Ensure that a Manufacturer's Product is majored

For mutual benefit the relationship should produce:

- Acceptable profit margins to the distributor
- Acceptable volume and rate of growth to the manufacturer, at optimum profit margins

table 27.1 **Factors Affecting the Majoring of a Manufacturer's Product**

Distributor principal has:	Distributor sales executive has:
1. Quality product	1. Quality product
2. Reliable delivery dates	2. Reliable delivery dates
3. Fair profit margins	3. Technical information as and when required
4. Good communications, physical and written	4. Ad hoc bonuses, e.g., money, travel, trip to manufacturer's head office, etc.
5. Reasonable advertising and sales promotion support	5. Good communications with manufacturer's 'field'
6. Willingness of manufacturer to assist with distributor's general problems.	6. Fair evaluation of performance.

The manufacturer's 'link person' must try and assist the distributor in upgrading their entire operation; allow the distributors to consult the company's financial director; let individual, interested distributors have the use of the director's time for a day or two; run seminars on relevant subject, e.g., 'modern warehousing'. A distributor should be able to call on the manufacturer's experience when trying to solve any problem related to their business.

Control Systems

First and foremost, a system to establish an annual campaign plan must be introduced. This campaign plan should cover, at a minimum.

- The common goals to be achieved in the first year at least
- What this would mean realistically in terms of the quarterly volumes of sales to the channel's customers and shipments from the manufacturer
- The recommended price at which the product would be marketed
- The price/discounts/terms of trading at which the manufacturer will supply the product
- What this would mean in terms of market share
- Levels of sales and supporting staff resources to be deployed
- A schedule of training to be provided by the manufacturer
- Promotional materials, campaigns, etc., to be undertaken by the manufacturer and the channel
- Specific actions to be taken concerning inventory/logistics, etc.
- Key event action review calendar
- Secondly, regular monitoring and review sessions must be held to ensure that the performance is on course and that, if needed, corrective actions are taken on time.

Motivation of the Distributor and Motivational Tools for Distributor's Sales Force

The link person to the manager can do the following to motivate a distributor

1. Attempt to categorise and understand all the distributors
2. Discover their wants as well as their needs: this will help in your dealings with them.
3. Remember that monetary rewards serve many needs and are, therefore, the best rewards.
4. Bear in mind, however, that recognition, praise, promotion and successful achievement of a task can also be effective motivations and are sometimes more needed than money.
5. If people know that good work will earn a reward, this makes the reward more effective. The expectation should be clearly set out on a payment-by-results basis, with an appropriate bonus or commission scheme. Achievable targets and standards should be set. Praise should be bestowed when deserved, at not too frequent intervals. The rewards and efforts required should be clarified. The penalties also should be stated, if targets are underachieved or if substandard results are recorded.

figure 27.1

The Link Person Likened to a Master of Ceremonies

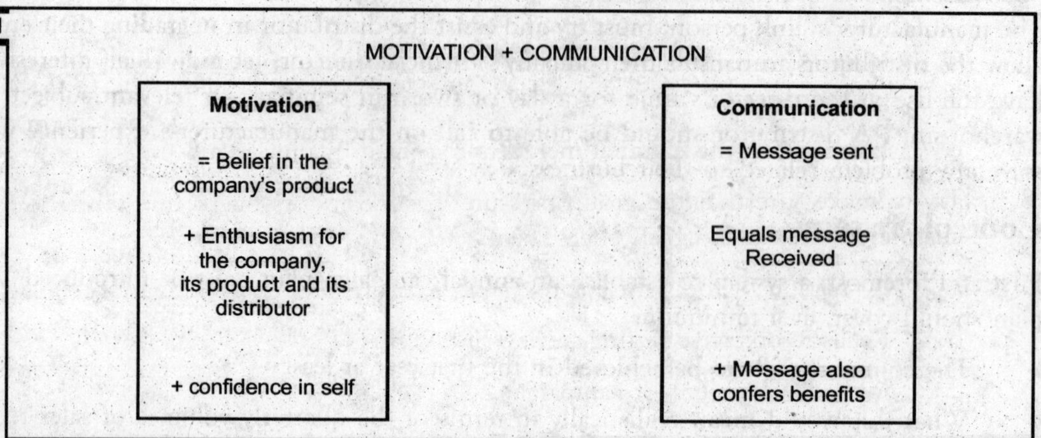

figure 27.2

This process calls for an understanding of the relationship, mutual SWOTs, mutuality of benefits and a commitment to working together for common goals

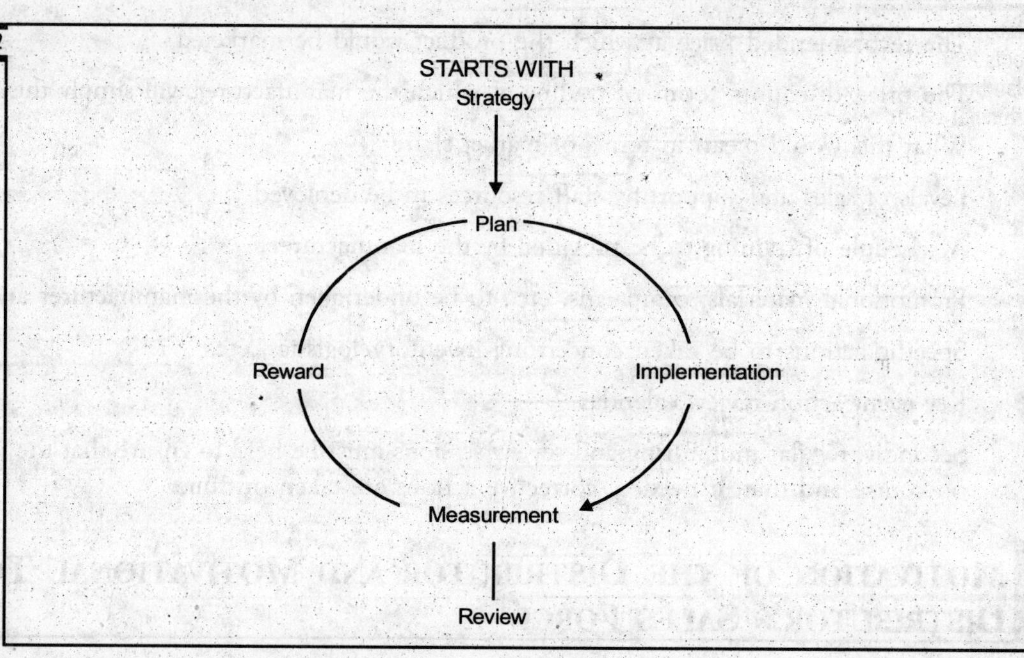

6. Paraphrasing what Douglas McGregor said in another context, conditions should be such that the members of the channel system should be able to achieve their own expectations by working for the success of the channel system as a whole. It is necessary to identify the needs of the members so that appropriate rewards can be devised and to set targets and standards with all the members.

7. People can be motivated by the work itself if their needs for achievement and responsibility are thereby satisfied. This can result from:

   a. Giving people more responsibility where called for and more scope for variations in methods and speed of work

   b. Giving groups a unit of work to perform, thus reducing specialization and increasing the sense of achievement and responsibility and the expertise

   c. Relaxing overhead controls while setting targets and/or standards to make members accountable

d. Making available all the necessary information so that members can monitor their own performance

e. Encouraging the channel members to join in planning and innovation.

8. Try to make sure that the group pressure is working for you by involving the members of the channel in decisions, which affect them.

a. A creation of the right environment - nature, scope and style of operation

b. Realistic objective setting, review and control

c. Joint development of campaigns.

figure 27.3

Motivational Tools for a Distributor Principal

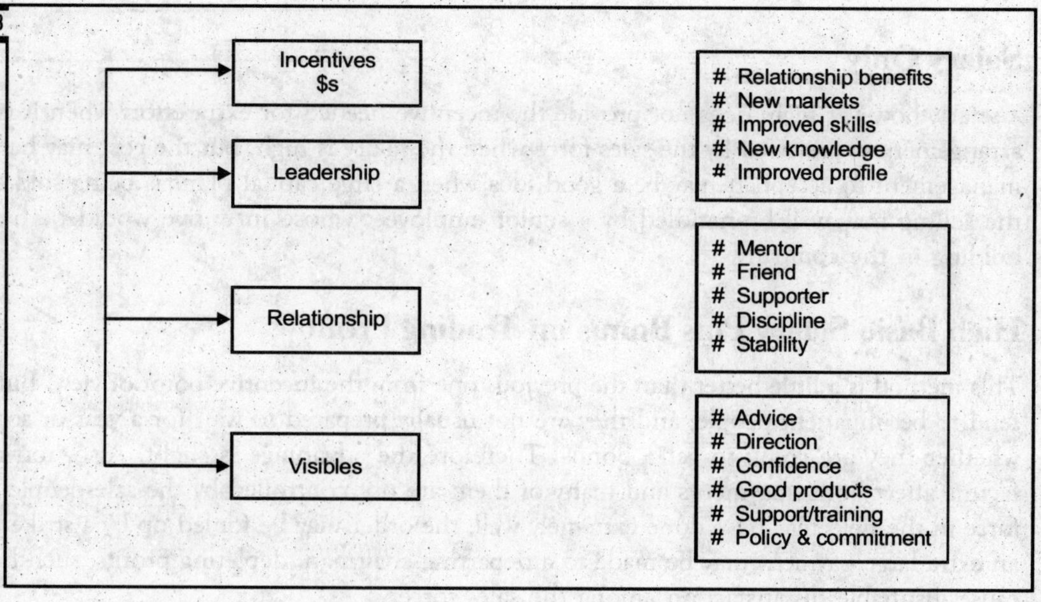

figure 27.4

Motivational Tools for a Distributor Sales Force

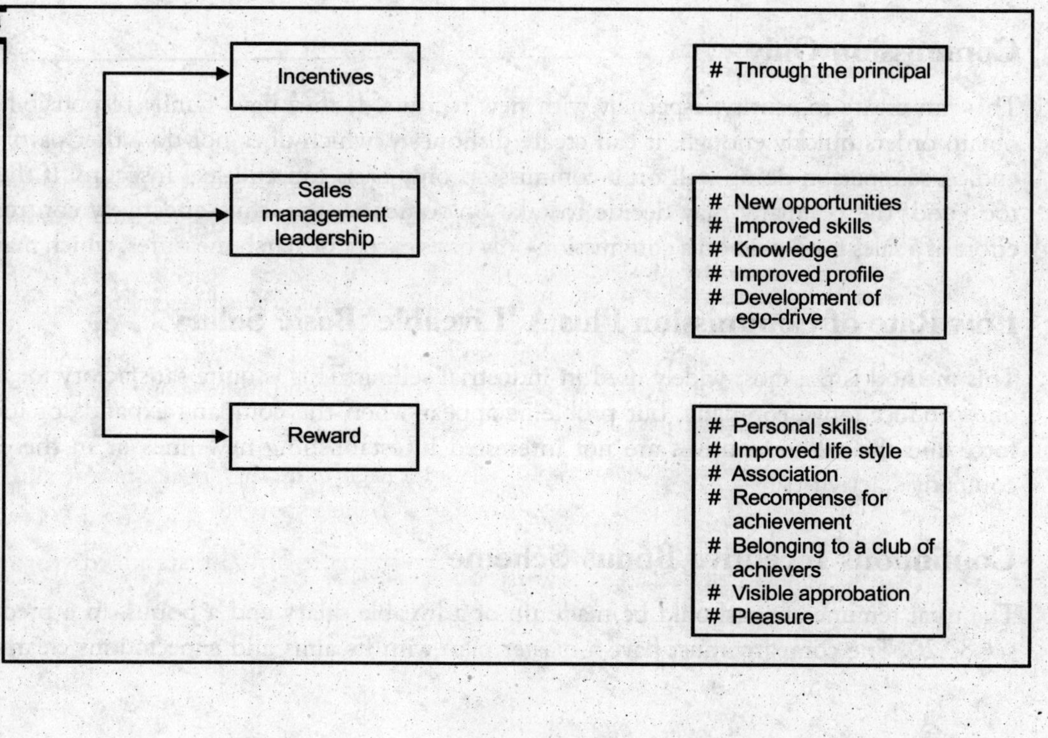

REMUNERATION OF THE SALESPERSON

Remuneration of sales executives always provokes a great deal of lively discussion whenever the topic is raised. So it should – it is an important motivational factor as far as the sales force are concerned. Companies use various methods to calculate the amounts paid to their sales force, depending on their number or the product they sell or other factors. However, any method of remuneration must be of mutual benefit to both the sales executives and the company employing them; if either party feels that it is not getting a fair deal, then the association will eventually, if not immediately, break down. A sales executive, who is dissatisfied with the remuneration, will leave the company, while a company that is unhappy with the salesperson's performance, in view of their total costs, may discharge him. We will briefly examine the methods of remuneration in current use.

Salary Only

A salary, however high, does not provide the incentive needed for extra effort when it is necessary. This arrangement is preferred by the sales force when the salary is high, but the cost may be too high for the management to accept. It may be a good idea when a large capital plant is being sold, but in that case the selling may well be handled by a senior employee, whose incentive would perhaps be an equity holding in the company.

High Basic Salary Plus Bonus on Trading Profit

This method is a little better than the previous one from the incentive point of view. But sales executives tend to be impatient people, and they are not usually prepared to wait for a year or so before knowing whether they are going to get a bonus. Therefore the advantage is slight. Also, too many intangible factors affect bonus payments and many of them are not controlled by the salespeople. While the sales force in the field may have done extremely well, the order may be fouled up by a strike in the factory or an extra large payment may be made to a departing chairman, depleting profits; such happenings could cause justifiable dissatisfaction among the sales force.

Commission Only

This can create insecurity, especially with new recruits. If they have family responsibilities, and cannot obtain orders quickly enough, it can create dishonesty, which does not do either party any good in the end. A salesperson doing well on a commission only basis can still feel insecure. If the performance is too good, the company may decide to take on someone else, thus effectively control and direct the effort of a sales force paid on a commission only basis except by harsh measures, which may be undesirable.

Low Rate of Commission Plus A 'Liveable' Basic Salary

This method is the most widely used in industrial selling. This is quite satisfactory for a one product or one product range company, but problems appear when the company expands or increases the sales force and the sales executives are not interested in establishing new lines or in the expansion of the company's activities.

Continuous Incentive Bonus Scheme

The total remuneration should be made up of a liveable salary and a bonus, in a predetermined ratio, say 80:20. The company must have a master plan with its aims and expectations clearly defined. At the beginning of every financial year, the company should set out, in the form of an overall company sales target

- The total sales target for the next twelve months
- The target for each salesperson in the achievement
- The share of the total sales target to be borne by each product range, particularly if a multiplicity of products are to be sold.

It is one of the functions of senior management to determine the target proportions carried by each product range and it is one of the sales executive's major functions to attain those objectives. It is vital that the sales force sell the product range that makes the highest gross contribution to the company profit. Others may be easier to sell, so incentives should be tied to selling those lines which enhance the bottom line of the business and maximize the return on capital employed, which is the true measure of the efficiency and helps in achieving objectives. This ensures that the goods are sold according to the overall company targets and in the right product range proportions. Every sales executive is given a mutually agreed sales target overall and by product range, and points are allocated to the targets set. For example, over a year, a typical profile may be similar to that given in Table 27.2.

table 27.2 **Setting Sales Targets by Product Range**

Product range	$	Points
A	40,000	20
B	30,000	15
C	20,000	13
D	20,000	13
E	10,000	10
F	10,000	10
G	10,000	10
General work		9
Total	140,000	100

In this example, nine points are allocated to general work. This covers punctuality, grooming, accuracy of records, etc. The percentage of target achieved, up to a maximum of 100 per cent, but not beyond, will qualify for that percentage of points allocated to the product group target; i.e., 75 per cent of twenty points, equal to fifteen points. In the case of general work, points received will be based on the recommendation of senior management.

At the end of the period, the points achieved per product range are added up and a total arrived at. A bonus is then paid according to a previous scale laid down, e.g., (for twelve months) it may be as given in Table 27.3.

table 27.3 **A Bonus Scale Based on Target Achievement**

	$
95 points and above earns	1500
95-94 points earns	750
75-84 points earns	375
74 and below earns	nil

It should not be necessary to point out that a sales executive does not qualify for a bonus unless all the product ranges are sold, not just a few. The executive should be kept informed of progress by the regular issue of progress information. This scheme combines flexibility with a fixed basic method and level of bonus payment. It can cope with changes in territory or in targets. Product range F may be more important than product range B, even though the target is lower; the profitability may be higher or it may be a new product. Therefore, the former may carry more points than the latter.

Note that:

1. Sales should be equal to invoice sales less credits.
2. All sales targets must be achievable, for the system to work, so management must plan ahead with due care.
3. The scheme can be operated by the company over any time period, viz., twelve, six, three or even one month.
4. The scheme is not difficult to operate and makes use of paperwork, such as invoices, which should already be produced by the company.
5. Sales costs could be significant (total costs against net sales turnover). The cost depends on marketing objectives and other factors, which should be considered before costing.

Finally, while remuneration is the most important motivational factor for sales executives, job satisfaction, security, etc., also count. Remember your salesperson's role: to maintain personal contact with customers and buyers for the purpose of obtaining sales.

RISK MANAGEMENT

Good management is all about anticipating events and planning for action before the event happens. This is where understanding the sorts of risks which are likely to arise is very important. The risks may be of one or more of the following types

1. The usual product risks, political risks, economic risks, etc., that exist in any international marketing operation – these are not being explored here.
2. A chosen channel member may turn out to be a misfit. This is where careful planning and selection of the right partners is vital. A good channel member of yesterday may not be a good channel member tomorrow. A mutual understanding of the roles of the channel members and their responsibilities to each other is a must.
3. At least one channel member is not pulling their weight. The performance expectation must be made clear right from the start. Mutual monitoring of performance is vital to the continuing success of the 'venture'. Mutual reliance must be recognized. All campaign planning must be undertaken jointly so that no motivation is lost due to inadequate planning.
4. Breakdown of 'relationship'. Where independent members form a significant part of the channel, the relationships are based on individuals, their interpersonal behaviour, trust, mutual understanding of a set of common objectives and other objectives based on the needs of the parties concerned. 'Mutuality' of interest must be maintained to avoid the risk of damaging the position of the two parties.

In all these cases, rapid contingency planning is crucial to safeguard the company's position.

SUMMARY

Channel objectives determine channel structure. The specific objectives of any channel, apart from the global aspirations of the company, should be firmly based on the service outputs demanded by its customers. Intensive distribution is generally used for products which need to be easily available. Selective distribution is usual for products which buyers like to choose with some effects. The desired success that a channel member will have in influencing the behaviour of other channel members will depend on its leadership behaviour. A manufacturer's support person must try and assist the distributors in upgrading their entire operations.

PROJECT WORK

Make a group of five students and study the various motivational tools which are useful for following:

a. FMCG Distributors
b. Industrial Goods Distributors
c. Services Distributors.

SHORT ANSWER QUESTIONS

1. What are the motivational tools for the distributors, sales force?
2. What do you mean by industrial selling?
3. What are the comfort systems for distributors?
4. What do you mean by continuous incentive bonus scheme?
5. Define remuneration of the sales person.

REVIEW QUESTIONS

1. "Channel objectives determine channel strategy". Explain the statement with examples.
2. What are motivational tools and control areas for a distributor?
3. How can a line manager motivate the distributor?
4. Explain different types of channels with the help of suitable examples.
5. Discuss how the process of selection should be taken.

GO TO THE NET

Using Internet sources, search information for the following motivation schemes:

1. DEMO setup
2. Target incentives
3. Money back offer.

Using Internet search tool prepare a report on the process of selection of 10 Indian companies.

CHAPTER 28

distribution analysis, control and management

learning objectives

The objectives of this chapter are to:

- analyse the scope of control
- understand the systems concept, management and the standards of performance
- differentiate between controlling the distributor and the retailer
- analyse the different tools and kinds of control devices.

content outline

- Opening Case
- Introduction
- Scope of Control
- Standards of Performance
- Systems Concept and Management
- Controlling the Distributor
- Controlling the Retailer
- Tools for Control
- Kinds of Control Devices
- Distribution Cost Control
- Summary
- Project Work
- Short Answer Questions
- Review Questions
- Go to the Net

opening case

Success Story of Two Intermediaries

This case study depicts how adapting (or not adapting) to the changing economic and business scenario can lead to the rise or fall of even giant business corporations. In view of the fact that appropriate strategic management, with respect to the volatile business environment, can go a long way in sustaining and substantiating the growth of business, it is imperative that in pursuance of a prudent policy one must make all provisions against any possible contingency.

In light of the above, the case study presents the rise and fall of two giant wholesale corporations which were doing very well during the mid 70s. The Classic Watches and Business Machines (or CWBM) was a wholesaler of wrist watches and calculators. In 1975 the company was only twelve years old and its sales were already touching Rs 1.3 crore per annum. The company was mainly catering to South India with its distribution facilities located at Chennai and Hyderabad.

During the same year, another company called Malhotra Home Appliances (or MHA), which had completed 20 years in business, was doing exceedingly well in the business of wholesaling home appliances. In 1975, it posted its sales at a whopping Rs 3.2 crore per annum. Malhotra Home Appliances was mainly catering to the North Indian markets with a single distribution facility and a very large warehouse cum distribution centre located in the suburbs of Chandigarh.

Both these companies were doing fine until such time as the market conditions and wholesalers started to change and this called for an urgent policy review and strategic introspection with respect to the changing scenario to be able to maintain the past growth rate.

The next 20 years saw both the companies on two different platforms. The following indicators highlight the standing of the two companies in the mid 90s

- By the end of 1995, the CWBM posted a sales figure of Rs 260 crore which was a two hundred times increase as compared to its 1975 sales, whereas MHA's sales were posted at Rs 35 crore, approximately ten times its sales back in 1975.
- By this time the CWBM had developed and expanded its infrastructure and facilities at the national level and was actively considering exporting by tapping the South Asian markets, while MHA still remained a regional wholesaler, undergoing a tough time to cope with rising pressures from its competitors.
- Despite the three-fold increase in its sales, the MHA's profits were not growing at an increasing rate but rather they were decreasing, while CWBM not only grew in sales and assets but its profits also increased rapidly.
- The CWBM had a good credibility in the market and it enjoyed good liquidity with diverse and substantial business interests, while MHA remained in the same business of home appliances with tight liquidity, considering to sell-off its assets and converting its distribution facilities into retail outlets.

The two companies, despite having promising futures back in 1975, were now (at the end of 1995) in two different situations which were not only very extreme in themselves but also very opposite to each other. The reasons attributed to their situations could be many such as:

1. The flexibility in approach
2. Adaptability to changing business climate
3. Diversification to spread risk
4. Modernisation
5. Expansion to reap economies of scale
6. Modern management practices.

In the case of the two companies, the management of CWBM looked at the changing business scenario with an open mind and changed its approach to business thus giving due consideration to the aforesaid factors, while the management of MHA remained traditional in its approach and did not show any inclination to change in time with the changing business climate, still using its age old strategies to do business. By the time MHA geared up to respond to the situation, it was already too late and the damage had already been done. A bird's eye view of how the management of the two companies perceived and acted in changing business conditions is highlighted here.

The CWBM Success Story

In 1976, the concept of merchandising was gradually picking up. Merchandisers were big players with substantial capital backup and with sound business acumen. Their strategy was to buy in bulk directly from manufacturers as middlemen. Merchandisers thus posed a threat to the existence of wholesalers especially in the consumer goods industry, which had its impact on all the wholesalers including those of the CWBM and MHA.

The CWBM management immediately prepared a contingency plan to gear itself up to meet the ensuing situation. The strategy adopted by CWBM included:

- Growth in the existing lines
- Diversification into unrelated lines
- Takeover, mergers
- Growth in areas where the company's core strength could be utilised.

Growth in Existing Business

The suboptions were:

- Globalisation
- Changing product mix
- Adding new facilities to cater efficiently to all the regions
- Setting up an assembling facility abroad to export computers to other countries.

In the backdrop of volatile conditions in the Indian market and CWBM's plans to maintain its growth rate, it was felt by the management that the company must venture into global markets. The company had immense scope of increasing its exports to European countries. The CMD strongly felt that the realisation of their growth rate with a target of doubling their sales every two years was impossible to achieve without significant global presence.

From wristwatches and calculators, the company decided to venture into assembling computers, telephone instruments and other telecom products such as walkie-talkies and selling computer hardware peripherals. There was an estimated demand of Rs 30 crore p.a. On the export front, there was a demand for computer peripherals, wrist watches and pocket calculators.

Not only this, some managers were of the view that setting up new distribution centres in West, North and East India and making franchises all over the country could give a boost to their sales. In view of this, the company acquired several distribution facilities and gave away franchises to all those interested in the company's products.

Some managers were of the view that the larger global demand could be satisfied by establishing distribution centres abroad, especially in the Gulf, to service the Middle East.

Another option was to get into a joint venture with a Saudi Arabian company, which had sent a preliminary inquiry in view of the rapid industrial growth in the region. An advantage in collaborating with this company was that their government was encouraging local entrepreneurs; thus, importing the latest technology and sophisticated computer hardware with cheap Indian labour would make production very cheap and ready for export in Europe and USA.

Thus the Gulf was a unanimous choice as it was closer to home which made controlling operations easier. This move was also accepted because it would give the company MNC status. Earning foreign exchange through this plant would also benefit the country.

In view of the above, the company set up an Import House in partnership with a Saudi based import house. The idea was to import peripherals from the overseas markets and use cheap Indian labour to assemble the computers and export them to the lucrative European and American markets.

Diversification into Unrelated Areas

This was especially in the growing computer and peripheral market abroad. This helped spread risk on account of business fluctuations and take advantage of the growth in the industry in which CWBM dealt.

Takeovers/Mergers

The company pursued an ambitious plan of takeover and merger by taking over certain sick or potentially sick units, turning them around and merging them with good performers. This increased and expanded the sales of the company with bare minimum investment.

Growth in Areas of Core Strength

The company could use the existing and expanding distribution network established to market wrist watches, pocket and desk calculators etc. to sell its telecom computer related products in the future. Further, importing peripherals from abroad and assembling in India to export abroad increased the business of the company manifold.

Beside the above, CWBM drastically cut down its stocks and kept the bare minimum, thus releasing precious money which was used as working capital. This made the company enjoy liquidity status and meet up all its recurring expenses.

All the above measures helped the company cope with and compete successfully with giant merchandisers or discounters. By the end of 1995, the company was an entity to reckon with in the wrist watch, calculators, telecom and computer products segment.

The MHA Failure Story

MHA did not bother much with entry of big merchandisers. The management of MHA did not perceive any threat from merchandisers even when profits were falling, anticipating the trend to reverse. The management was very upbeat about the reputation they enjoyed in the North Indian market and hoped to maintain their growth rate without even considering the changes that were marking the business environment.

The emphasis of the MHA was on procuring more and more appliances in different varieties and increasing quantities. This added up the cost of maintaining such huge inventory and overheads. Besides, the MHA management did not pursue any major overhaul to cut down on rising costs, but rather recruited a giant sales force of one hundred people to take care of selling the rising inventory levels. The conservative management retained old employees who had even crossed the retirement age and their sons and daughters were given employment in the company.

Throughout the 80s, the management continued with its traditional management and service policies. While most household appliance companies had begun to examine their merchandise assortment to help in controlling inventory, MHA continued to offer some 75 different appliances to its retailers – double that of its competitors.

By the end of the 80s, its retailers had already joined the mass merchandisers and some had defected to the new cooperative groups. As a result, its market share declined, operating costs increased and profit was squeezed. At this time, Mr Ravi Malhotra, the Chairman cum Managing Director who was already 79 years old, expired leaving the management with no choice but to appoint a new CMD. The management appointed an outsider, Mr Krishnamurthy, as the new CMD of the company. The new CMD had new ideas to cope with the situation. These were not welcomed by the employees and the management since they were used to the traditional and old practices of the company.

This resulted in the company becoming a likely takeover candidate; it was eventually taken over by the Manchanda Group who tried to restructure the company. The new management cut down on inventory from 75 to 26 and reduced stocks. This meant closing down two out of three distribution facilities. This eroded customer confidence in the company. In addition to this, suppliers to the company started to ask for advance payment to supply goods to MHA.

In a bid to cut down costs, the company retrenched some 125 employees and converted its distribution facilities into retail outlets. By this time, the merchandisers had already overtaken the market, so the company had no choice but to lose its giant status that it enjoyed back in the mid 70s.

By the early 90s, there were five big players in the market including CWBM while MHA was nowhere even in the first twenty.

Try Yourself

1. Critically analyse the distribution pattern of these two wholesalers.
2. What are the reasons of the success or failure of these two wholesalers?

INTRODUCTION

Planning sets forth the objectives that a manager intends to pursue. Organisation helps in providing the structure, people and responsibility to attain those objectives. Control is the measurement of progress towards objectives in accordance with the established plan. Controlling is seeing that actual performance is guided towards expected performance. Control is also a comparison and verification process and with the help of this process, a balance in the organisation activities directed towards predetermined goals can be achieved and maintained.

According to George R Terry "Controlling is determining what is, being accomplished, that is evaluating the performance and, if necessary, applying corrective measures so that the performance takes place according to plans".

SCOPE OF CONTROL

The scope of control is very wide. It covers all the areas of business, namely production, finance, inventory, marketing, etc. Control may be (i) physical or (ii) financial. Physical control may be either quantitative or qualitative. Control is influenced by personal supervision and checking.

STANDARDS OF PERFORMANCE

A standard is a criterion against which performance results of the individual are measured or judged. It should possess the following characteristics:

- Standards should be capable of achievement with reasonable amount of effort and time
- Standards should concentrate on results and not procedures
- Standards should be flexible
- Standards should be as per the objectives of the organisation
- Standards should be expressed in physical terms or monetary terms.

SYSTEMS CONCEPT AND MANAGEMENT

Managers are needed to convert the disorganised resources of men, machines and money into a useful and effective enterprise. Essentially, management is the process whereby these unrelated resources are integrated into a total system for objective accomplishment.

A system is composed of three basic elements: input, component or sub-system and output. A system is stimulated into action by impact. A system may be classified as structured system or a semi-structured system. Only semi-structured system in physical distribution is used in our country.

System Mission

A mission is usually market oriented and product oriented. In order to define the mission, the firm needs to define the desired system output and the costs associated with achieving the output. A mission would, therefore, look something like this example below.

Example

Product "ALPHA", to serve all India market with a 98% delivery within five days at the lowest possible cost.

Having defined the channel mission, we will discuss the control techniques with examples for distributors and retailers.

EXAMPLES OF DISTRIBUTION SYSTEMS OF BAJAJ AUTO LTD
(Communication to Dealer by the Company)

Markets are becoming extremely competitive with the introduction of new models by existing manufacturers as well as their entry into new segments of the two-wheeler business. The manufacturing capacity in the industry is also rapidly increasing and the customer will have a wider choice of two-wheelers to meet his specific requirements.

In view of the above, the success of the manufacturer and dealer network will depend entirely upon their marketing ability. This includes good models, quality, price, product positioning and communication, geographical spread of the network including SSOs and the ability of dealers to work on all segments and achieve success in their respective command areas.

Bajaj Auto is playing its role as a manufacturer by introducing a large number of new models which were on display at 'Auto Expo'98. Substantial steps have been taken successfully on the quality front. The pricing is always competitive for all Bajaj products and the distribution system and logistics are also being improved considerably. With CLASSIC SL, they have started aggressive launches of new products. They have also started aggressive sales promotion, direct marketing efforts, etc., in key states. In short, the company is doing its bit on several fronts.

As a dealer, you have to play your role properly by providing an appropriate infrastructure, competent manpower, adequate working capital, installing good sales systems and developing command areas by supporting and motivating SSOs.

Sales systems form one of the important aspects of day-to-day operations. It is only with the backing of a good sales system that a company is in a position to succeed in a competitive market. Though Bajaj network is considered to be the strongest in the two-wheeler industry in the country, they are very weak in their systems. Their dealers are unable to appreciate the importance of the systems and their implementation is very weak. Observations reveal that good systems were installed in a number of places, but within few months the systems became inoperative. This is primarily due to the managerial weakness in their dealerships.

CONTROLLING THE DISTRIBUTOR

A distributor is a firm or organisation which acts as the company's sole selling agent in a particular area which is known as his territory. He maintains stocks of the company's products, redistributes them in his area, collects payments and remits money to the company in a stipulated time. And he is given a certain fixed percentage of total amount of goods received by him towards his commission for his services.

The big question is how to identify a suitable distributor in a new town? Here is a general guide.

Contact five shops in the main market and ask them about suitable parties for distributorships, keeping in view your products range and your options and preferences, whether you would like to have a well established party, medium sized party, or a newcomer. Then find out the common names in all the lists from the shopkeepers and identify your most suitable parties and contact them to finally short list your distributors.

Ask questions based on the following:

- Product range
- Coverage
- Rapport with retailers
- Visits of S/M – regular or irregular
- Reputation in market – good or so-so
- Financial background
- Location of office/godown
- No. of salesmen and delivery vehicles.

Now, after shortlisting distributors, meet the party; ask questions on the above lines and brief him about:

- The company
- Present product range
- Price structure – MRP and margin of retailer
- Margin for distributor
- Conditions for distributions
- Your working days
- Advertisement support by the company
- New products in the pipeline.

Simultaneously take information on the following aspects:

His coverage, total number of retailers, blacklisted retailers and reasons for doing so, expected sales turnover keeping in view your target for that market.

Finally collect one blank, fully signed and stamped cheque from him, of a nationalised bank only, along with security DD. Ask him to sign and stamp a copy of distribution appointment letter towards his acceptance.

Salesperson's job at the distributor's place is made up of the following:

1. Ensure that the distributor opens his shop/office at the proper time, to avoid loss of your market work hours.
2. Ensure that the distributor maintains 45 days' stock of your products.
3. Ensure that the distributor maintains stocks by rotation enabling stock movement by freshness and batch-wise.
4. Ensure that the distributor maintains a separate stock register for your range of products and all the entries are updated. Physical check of stocks must be done on a monthly basis and the register must then be signed by you. It should also carry the date.

5. Ensure that the distributor redistributes the goods within 24 hours in the same town and within 48 hours in suburbs. The time frame refers to the time since the orders were booked by you and orders received directly by him.
6. Ensure that any scheme for retailers always reaches them with 100% interest and the distributor does not withhold a part of it.
7. Be on guard always. Never take any money from the distributor or accept any favour which will have to be repaid at the company's interest.
8. Always maintain friendly relations with the distributor and his men and listen to their suggestions carefully for it may help increase sales of products.
9. Always keep your paper work updated and send in reports, expense statements on time.
10. Always be fair in all dealings and stand by commitments.
11. Check stock level of POP material with the distributor.

Distributor's Objections

1. Product sales are very slow
2. Ratio of damaged stocks is high
3. Repeat orders are few and far between
4. Advertisement budget is negligible
5. Less working days
6. Food products, oil leakage, damages other products as well
7. Replacement slow by company
8. Claims not settled in time
9. Goods are not dispatched in time
10. Profit margin is less.

DAILY REPORTING FORMAT

(Used by M/s Godrej-GE India Ltd)

DATE-> Day	MON	TUE	WED	THU	FRI	SAT	SUN	TOTAL
WASHING MACHINES								
GODREJ-GE								
VIDEOCON								
WHIRLPOOL								
BPL								
VOLTAS								
ONIDA								
IFB								
OTHERS								

Contd...

REFRIGERATORS								
GODREJ-GE								
WHIRLPOOL								
BPL								
VOLTAS								
VIDEOCON								
ALLWYN								
SAMSUNG								
KELVINATOR								
OTHERS								
COOKING RANGES								
GODREJ-GE								
INALSA								
SUNFLAME								
SUPERFLAME								
HOMEAID								
FINANCIAL CASES								
ATTENDANCE								

DISPLAY: ____________________

LEAFLETS. ____________________

AVAILABILITY: ____________________

DISPLAY: ____________________

LEAFLETS AVAILABILITY: ____________________

P.O.P. MATERIAL: ____________________

ANY OTHER POINT: ____________________

CONTROLLING THE RETAILER

Retailing is the most important factor in the entire selling process because actual sale of products takes place at retail shops. A retail shop is a place where products are sold to actual users, known as consumers, in units.

So, to win the trust and confidence of a retailer, it is most important to make products available at retail shops and initiate their sale.

Retailers always select products for their shelves on the following grounds:

- Products awareness
- Product reputation among consumers
- Product quality
- Product's shelf-life

- Product's packing
- Retailer's margin
- Regular availability.

So if retailers are convinced on most or all the above points, products will always be there on retail outlets ensuring good sale.

Jobs to be Done at Retail Shop

1. The moment the salesman enters a retail shop, he should wish the retailer, even if he is busy, making him acknowledge the salespersons presence.
2. If the retailer is busy (on the phone) with customers, utilise the precious time in the shop. Observe the following:
    - Stock pressure of competitors' products in the shop.
    - Total stock pressure of all products in the shop to assess potential of the shop.
    - Location of stocks of salesman's interest; ideal location of product stocks in a shop will be from where they are easily located by customers.
    - Check POP material of competitors and your organisation as well and note down new POP introduced, new products launched. Also note pricing, packs, stock pressure and customers' response.
    - On a regular visit, salesperson should note the products, stock pressure, and find out reasons for good/poor sale; it will help to mentally outline the order to be placed by the shopkeeper.
3. Now, when the shopkeeper is free to interact, the salesman should introduce himself properly by giving his surname, name of the company and purpose of visit. Then display one product at a time, allow the shopkeeper to take the product in his hand to judge it while the salesman explains different packaging quality, selling points (USPs), margins/profits, benefits, etc. Ask retailers to cooperate, otherwise goods will not be sold.
4. After booking orders, the salesman should wish the retailer again and leave the shop.

Don't's For a Salesman

1. Don't show all the products to the retailer at the same times because he will lose interest and an order will be lost.
2. Don't show him the order book at any cost.
3. Don't make false commitments just to book an order. Not only will the salesman lose him next time, but also his image in the market will be that of an unreliable person.

Retailer's Objections

1. Packaging of products is not good
2. Quality complaints
3. MRP is high compared to local brands

4. Profit margin is less
5. Schemes are not there
6. Advertisement in TV/magazines is absent
7. Delivery is late
8. Customer does not ask for it
9. Distributor's credit is squeezed up
10. Dealer boards/shop painting is not done
11. Brand is local, he deals in reputed brands
12. Damage is high during transit
13. Range is not complete
14. Replacement is not done instantly.

TOOLS FOR CONTROL

There are three conventional methods for the purpose of controlling channel members. These are contract, power and structure.

1. ***Contract:*** Contract is considered one of the oldest and the most commonly used tool for control in the Indian context. It can be defined as 'an agreement enforceable by law'. It may be in writing or oral or even exemplified. In relatively long-term relationships, like channel contracts, the agreement is generally put in writing so as to impart clarity and avoid ambiguity.

   This tool of control is most commonly used for controlling channel systems. A contract as a tool for control must be very carefully drawn up. Some of the major elements of contracts can be enumerated as under:

   - Product handled
   - Classes and types of customers
   - Territory to be covered
   - Inventory
   - Installation and repairs/replacement
   - Prices and margins
   - Advertising and sales promotion obligations
   - Term
   - Payments.

2. ***Power:*** This is another tool available for controlling the channels of distribution. Power arises out of the dependency of one member upon another such that either one of them or both are capable of affecting the achievement of objectives of the other.

3. ***Structure:*** Structure of an organisation is important for distribution.

KINDS OF CONTROL DEVICES

There are three kinds of control devices, which are used by the marketing department, viz., Reports and Budgets, Dealer Relations Index and Distribution Audit.

1. ***Reports and Budgets:*** These are perhaps the most obvious and frequently used control devices. An established reporting system brings information on a daily, weekly or monthly basis. Such reports share experiences with other dealers. The daily visit report format of M/s Godrej-GE India Ltd is given in Figure 28.1 as an example.

2. ***Dealer Relations Index:*** This is a quantitative technique of measuring the overall effectiveness of the entire distribution programme. In this technique a composite index is prepared taking into account a number of strategic items, such as sales quotas, after sale-services, sales displays, etc.

3. ***Distribution Audit:*** Distribution audit is a systematic and comprehensive analysis of all activities and results of a distribution programme. It assumes that appropriate policies and programmes can produce positive results which can be identified and evaluated and are achieved by the distributor.

figure 28.1 **DEALER VISIT REPORT OF M/S GODREJ-GE INDIA LTD**

Current O/S	Cheque bounce details	Last month B.S	Current month D.S	Current B.

	100 L	165 L		Ultra					Frost Free			
		165 L Cold Gold	165 L Dl. Dlx.	165 L	200 L		230 L	300 L	185 LFF	250 LFF		400 L FF
Display												
Sale												
Order												
SCPR												
Stock												
Stock/Def												

GE Refrigerators

	320 L	357L	386 L	410 L	558L		568 L	754 L
Display								
Sale								
Order								
SCPR								
Stock								
Stock/Def								

Contd...

Competitors/Activity

	Whirlpool Conv/FF	BPL Conv/FF	Videocon Conv/FF	Voltas Conv/FF	Allwyn Conv/FF	Kelvinator	Samsung Conv/FF	Daewoo Conv/FF	LG Conv/FF
Display									
Sale									
Order									
SCPR									
Stock									
Stock/Def									

Sales Issues

Service Issues

POP/Catalogue Requirements	General Market Information

Observation on Display of Product/POP

DISTRIBUTION COST CONTROL

Distribution is one of the basic functions of marketing. The marketing job remains incomplete until the product reaches the consumer's door for ultimate use or consumption. This process of distribution involving different kinds of products and services is achieved at some cost. The nature and dimensions of these costs may vary with the product, manufacturer, channel and area. Concomitantly, these costs are reflected in the price for the customers and the profit for the manufacturer.

A significant and increasing part of many companies' expenditure is that which is incurred in keeping their products on the move through the channels of distribution to the final consumer. Physical distribution covers a broad range of activities concerned with this phase of corporate operations, such as transportation, warehousing, material handling, packaging, inventory control and administration.

It is at those points in the distribution flow where the products stop moving that they accumulate costs. But it is also found that physical production developments have not kept pace with developments in physical distribution management. Physical distribution is an important aid to marketing and must, therefore, be oriented towards meeting customers' requirements and securing the attainment of profit/ market share objectives. This link adds great emphasis to the need for effective planning and control of distribution activities. However, distribution costs should be kept at a level that ensures an efficient system of operations. This follows from the inability of any distribution system to simultaneously maximise customer service and minimise distribution costs.

Analysis and Control of Distribution Costs

In essence, a manufacturer must be concerned with ensuring that his products are where the customer expects to buy them and when he wants them, at the lowest cost. The provision of a high level customer service (for example, availability in a high proportion of possible sales outlets, or speedy delivery to the customer involving perhaps greater stocks and more vehicles) may increase sales. However, the cost involved in dispatching small quantities of the products to retailers, who are widely dispersed geographically, together with costs of ensuring quick delivery from the manufacturer's plant or distribution depots, may exceed any marginal benefit involved. The manufacturer has to balance the marginal costs of increasing service against the marginal gains he obtains.

Method of Fixing a Budget for Distribution Expenses

The manager in charge of the distribution function must be provided with the cost data for a given level of distribution volume with respect to the past period. The cost data should clearly be classified into its basic characteristic as to whether the costs are fixed or variable. The actual cost incurred should be given before the distribution function starts its plan for the planning period in question. A presentation of the actual cost incurred is given in Figure 28.2.

figure 28.2

Actual cost incurred in past 12 months related to level of activity

Item of Expenditure	Total
Dispatch warehouse	
Fixed costs	
▶ Salaries	
▶ Premises	
▶ Plant and equipment	
▶ Depreciation	
Variable costs	
▶ Wages	

Contd...

- Plant and equipment
- Running cost/freight

Motor lorries and vans

Fixed costs

- Drivers' wages
- Manager's salary
- Vehicle depreciation
- Insurance
- Licence fees, etc.

Variables

- Fuel
- Oil
- Repairs

Total

The level of performance for each month is to be expressed in some convenient units of measurement.

Based on these past data, the distribution manager would be in a position to calculate his budget of expenses giving due allowance for variable factors depending on the level of performance expected in the planning period. This budget, when approved by the marketing manager and the board, would form the criteria for judging the actual distribution cost incurred in two ways: first, to control the actual distribution cost in relation to the budget; second, to evaluate the cost incurred in relation to the physical performance of the distribution function. Any variation in the actual from the budget has to be further analysed to find answers to "What", "Why" and "Who" has been responsible for the variations and in terms of controllability aspects. The comparison of actual costs in relation to the budget should be prepared on a monthly basis and communicated to the distribution manager to enable him to control the distribution cost. The presentation could be as given in Figure 28.3.

figure 28.3
Suggested format for control of Distribution Costs

Month...........2004

Budget Rs

Actual Rs

A. **Fixed costs:**

Salaries

Premises (Rent)

Depreciation (P&E)

B. **Variables Costs:**

Wages

Contd...

Running cost (P&E)
Motor lorries and vans
Fixed costs:
Drivers' wages
Mgmt Salary
Depreciation
Insurance,
licence fees, etc.
Variables:
Fuel, oil
Repairs, etc.
Total Costs:

Source: Management *Control Systems*, P Saravanavel, pp. 472-475

This type of feedback information, when presented on a monthly basis with the least time lag, enables the functional managers to control costs in relation to the budget. The other advantage of such a periodical review is that it enables the management to evaluate functions and achieve the goals of the organisation.

Optimum customer service demands the existence of such facilities as high inventories, a large number of warehouses and means of transportation. The level of service is usually defined in terms of either the number of days it takes to deliver an order, or the percentage of orders that can be filled from stock at any point in time. The desired level of service is one which is at least equivalent to that of the firm's competitors, but it is extremely difficult to measure the value that consumers actually place on the level of service in selecting a supplier.

SUMMARY

The success of a firm using independent channel members to serve its target markets is dependent upon the effective and efficient performance of its intermediaries. Thus, analysis and control of channel member performance is of critical importance in channel management. There are various control techniques–reporting, budgets, performance index and distribution audit. To control the marketing efforts of channel members, a variety of strategic approaches like franchising, control of sales prices, handling competitive products, sales territories and reseller promotional efforts is looked at in competitive performance.

PROJECT WORK

Study any one distributor of the following companies and make your presentation on the controlling of distributor:

1. SAMSUNG
2. Ranbaxy
3. Maruti Udyog Ltd.
4. HMT

SHORT ANSWER QUESTIONS

1. What do you mean by standards of performance?
2. How do you control the retailer?
3. What are the retailer's possible objections?
4. What do you mean by distribution cost control?
5. What are the objectives of the distributor?

REVIEW QUESTIONS

1. Explain the dynamics of the channel system, its inputs and outputs.
2. Discuss the control issues in a channel system.
3. What are the criteria that can be used to evaluate channel members?
4. What are the strategic and functional implications of control of channels?
5. How can channel profitability analysis aid in the management of distribution channels?
6. Explain different kinds of control devices.
7. Explain the method of cost control of distribution with the help of suitable example.

GO TO THE NET

Using Internet websites, study any one distributor of the following companies and make your report on the controlling of distributor:

1. CIPLA Ltd
2. ITC Ltd
3. Bajaj Auto Ltd.

Using Internet search tools prepare a report on the controlling methodology of 5 giant Indian companies.

BLOCK V

Physical Distribution Management

Distribution interacts with product design in three areas: physical products attributes, packaging and competitive differentiation. The physical distribution concept is based on a total system view of the material and goods flow activity from the source of supply through to the final point of consumption.

The physical distribution task is concerned with the integration and coordination of marketing activities so that the markets are served in the most effective way.

Block 5 deals with in depth study of the physical distribution management.

CHAPTER 29

logistics for customer satisfaction

learning objectives

The objectives of this chapter are to:

- understand the functional areas of logistics
- study the physical distribution of petroleum products.

content outline

- Opening Case
- Introduction
- Functional Areas of Logistics
- Description of the Whole Chain
- Warehousing and Distribution Solution
- Logistical Integration
- Marketing and Physical Distribution of Petroleum Products
- Summary
- Project Work
- Short Answer Questions
- Review Questions
- Go to the Net
- Caselet

opening case

Dairy Development Corporation

Introduction to the Country

1. Nepal is a small landlocked kingdom situated between two big countries — India in the south and Republic of China in the north. It has a total land area of 1,47,181 sq. kilometres (56,000 sq. miles) and it is 700 miles away from the nearest seaport of Calcutta, India.

2. Geographically, Nepal is divided in 3 regions, i.e., Himalayan region in the north, hill region in the middle and plain land of Terai belt in the south. Similarly, the country is also divided into 5 development regions, 14 zones and 75 districts for administrative purposes. The total population of the country, as estimated in 1991 census, was 18.49 million, with the annual growth rate of 2.1%. The distribution ratio of population is 7.8% in Himalayan region, 45.5% in mid-hills and 46.7% in *Terai* region. The total land area covered by Himalayan and mid-hill regions is 83% and only 17% of land lies in *Terai* region. Hence Nepal Is basically a mountainous Himalayan country with the world's highest mountain peak, Mt. Everest.

3. Economically, Nepal falls under the list of least developed countries on the basis of low per capita income of about US $ 180. Agriculture has still remained the mainstay of the Nepalese economy with 80% of the people being dependent on it. The growth of Nepalese economy can be boosted with the optimum utilisation of production potentialities in agriculture and agro-based industries. It is necessary to deliver adequate agricultural inputs to rural areas like fertilizers and improved seeds, cattle feeds, etc. and provide marketing facilities to their products like foodgrains, fruits, vegetables, milk and milk products as well as other cash crops plus raw materials for agro-industries.

Status of Physical Distribution in Nepal

1. To facilitate physical distribution, every country should have the basic infrastructural development of air, road and sea-way transport as well as adequate storage facilities. For a land locked nation, with a predominantly difficult mountainous topography, the development and extension of transport infrastructure in Nepal has become difficult and high cost-oriented. The total length of road network in Nepal is 11,109 km, out of which only 3,432 km are blacktopped pitch, 2,439 km are gravelled and 4,238 km. are transportable only in fair weather. In total, 15,776 trucks/tankers and 12,505 tractors/trailers are registered for transportation of goods.

   The physical distribution of commodities is mainly dependent on porters or on mule back where motorable roads are not developed. This is very time-consuming and costly.

2. Air transport is available to 44 districts and 6 other domestic airports are under construction. To facilitate air transport, the government has recently encouraged private sector airlines to start operating. As a result, a number of private airlines, freight forwarders and transport agencies have come forward in the private sector which has facilitated the distribution of goods to some extent. Besides the road and air transport, one ropeway line of 42 km from Hetauda to Kathmandu and one railway of 52 km length in *Terai* region have been operating to carry goods.

3. Inadequate storage facilities, difficult transportation all over the country, lack of knowledge of modern cost-effective marketing management systems and lack of mechanised loading and unloading provisions have been the cause for high cost in physical distribution. The government, through its liberal and market-oriented economic policy, has encouraged the private sector to build-up cold storages, refrigeration plants and to develop the modern system of packaging. As a result, attractive packing materials are coming up in the market and a few storages have been constructed.

4. Nevertheless, private enterprises are unwilling to market the basic need consumer goods to rural, remote areas due to high cost involved in physical distribution. The public enterprises in the government sector are supporting the distribution of basic need goods such as fertilizers, foodgrains, salt, sugar, fuel, medicines, etc., to such remote mountainous rural places bearing high distribution cost on subsidy. The cost of distribution of such products comes up to 25 to 50 per cent depending upon the area and the nature of products. In consideration of this, the government has announced a policy to emphasise development of transport system and construction of roads and storage with allocation of budget at top priority. It is hoped that this will have a positive effect on the distribution system.

Physical Distribution System at Corporate Level

1. In Nepal, milk production is an integrated part of traditional production system of small non-commercial holdings. People in the rural area keep cattle at their households for consumption of milk of their family and use the manure as fertilizer as well as a source of energy for cooking the meals. In the past, most of these small farmers have been selling their milk to urban areas directly, by themselves, carrying it on bicycles or on their shoulders which is very time-consuming, costly and sometimes causes spoilage of milk during transit.

2. The dairy development activities in Nepal, at an organised level, started in 1952 when the government established a small milk processing plant at Banepa near Kathmandu valley under the department of agriculture. Later, it was converted into Dairy Development Corporation (DDC) in 1969 under the Corporation Act as a public enterprise. At present, this Corporation handles about 80 per cent of the urban market share of milk. The main objectives of the Corporation are to:
   - Provide a guaranteed market for rural milk producers with a fair price at their doorstep.
   - Supply pasteurized milk and milk products to urban consumers.
   - Develop an organised milk collection system, i.e., bring the rural milk to urban areas.
   - Develop an organised marketing and distribution system for pasteurized milk and milk products in urban areas.

3. To boost the level of milk production at the rural farm level, commensurate with growing milk demand in urban areas, the government implemented the ten-year dairy development plan in 1991. It assessed the present situation of milk production, marketing systems, the structural development of dairy industries and outlined the appropriate policy and strategies. National Dairy Development Board has also been constituted to streamline the dairy development activities in Nepal.

4. Distribution system of milk and milk products can be classified into two parts:
   - Collection of raw milk, i.e., acquisition of raw milk from the rural milk producers and
   - Marketing or distribution of pasteurized milk and milk products to ultimate consumers mainly in urban areas.

Milk Collection Network and Processing

1. The raw milk produced by rural farmers is carried in small containers and delivered to the nearest Milk Producers Association (MPA). The MPA/MPCS carries the milk in milk cans through porters, tractors or mini-trucks and through rope way at some hilly places and delivers the milk to the nearest chilling centre established by DDC. The milk so collected from MPA/MPCS is stored and chilled in the chilling centres to preserve the quality of milk. The chilled milk is again transported to processing plants situated at urban areas through insulated milk tankers. The collection net work at present is as follows:

MPA/MPCS	Chilling Centres	Collected milk quantity
772	42	44.1 million litres

2. The collected milk is pasteurized, standardised and processed for different products. At present, 4 milk processing plants in different parts of Nepal and one milk products production and supply scheme are operating to produce and market the pasteurized milk and milk products under DDC.

Distribution of Milk and Milk Products

1. Pasteurized milk is distributed daily to ultimate consumers directly by the above-mentioned four milk supply schemes (processing plants) through their 761 milk selling booths. No other middleman is involved. Distribution vehicles are annually contracted on hire to transport the milk.

2. Milk products such as butter, ghee, yoghurt, cheese and ice creams are marketed through dealers, retailers and DDC's own sales centres. Cheese is produced in 11 cheese factories situated in Himalayan areas mainly from yak and cow milk. Most of the cheese plants have no road accessibility. The porters carry the cheese to the nearest motorable roads and transport it to Kathmandu by trucks or bus for storage and marketing. The pasteurized milk and major milk products marketed by DDC for the last 3 years have been reflected below:

Products	Units	1993	1994	1995
Milk	Million Ltr.	52	57	62
Cheese	Tonnes	185	168	134
Butter	Tonnes	956	1,068	1,041
Ghee	Tonnes	360	591	797

Since last year, DDC has also produced Skimmed Milk Powder (SMP) from a plant established at Biratnagar in eastern Nepal. At present, SMP is not sold in the market but only used for reconstitution to meet the demand for liquid milk during the lean season particularly in Kathmandu valley.

Packaging, Loading and Unloading

Till a few years back, the pasteurized milk was packed in milk bottles. But with a change in consumer choice and in consideration of the high cost for loading, unloading and transportation, as well as difficulty in cleaning the bottles, DDC replaced the packing of milk in bottles with polythelyne pouches, filled and packed by automatic filling machines. The pouch packets of milk are distributed to milk selling booths and are kept in plastic sachet crates. Packaging of other products is almost completely manual. Ghee is packed in plastic as well as in tin containers. Butter is primarily packed in parchment vegetable butter paper. Ghee and butter have secondary packing in cardboard boxes for easy storage and distribution. The storage and loading of the milk in plants is facilitated through conveyor chain systems. However, loading in distribution vehicles and unloading at the market is handled manually.

Problems and Constraints

Nepal dairy industry has a peculiar problem. Dairy farmers are not able to market all their milk during peak period of production whereas sizeable quantity of milk powder and dairy products is imported in the country every year. This situation is mainly caused by:

- Lack of required milk chilling and cold storage facilities
- Clustering of small private dairies around Kathmandu valley
- Inadequate processing and powder milk making plants in potential areas
- Lack of knowledge about appropriate marketing management techniques
- High cost incurred in marketing rural milk in comparison to imported products
- Lack of finance to promote and develop the infrastructural facilities needed for physical distribution

These problems are prominent and common, applicable to other product industries too.

TRY YOURSELF

1. What alternative methods of distribution should DDC consider for mine and milk products?
2. What are the alternative solutions of problems which are faced by the dairy industry in Nepal?

INTRODUCTION

"Logistics is the process of planning, implementing and controlling the efficient, effective flow and storage of goods, services and related information from the point of origin to the point of consumption for the purpose of conforming to consumer requirements".

Logistics is not a new area of marketing management. It has been around since the beginning of civilisation. It describes the entire process of materials and products moving into, through and out of the company. The actual work of logistics is supportive in nature. It involves the integration of transportation, inventory, warehousing, materials handling, packaging and information technology.

Logistics helps the inflow of materials into the manufacturing process. It also helps in the distribution of products to consumers through various marketing channels. Hence, logistical support is a must for marketing and manufacturing operations, and materials handling cannot be avoided in the performance of logistics.

Logistical management includes the design and administration of systems to control the flow of material, work-in-process and finished inventory to support business unit strategy.

FUNCTIONAL AREAS OF LOGISTICS

There are seven important functional areas of logistics (Figure 29.1).

figure 29.1
Functional Areas of Logistics

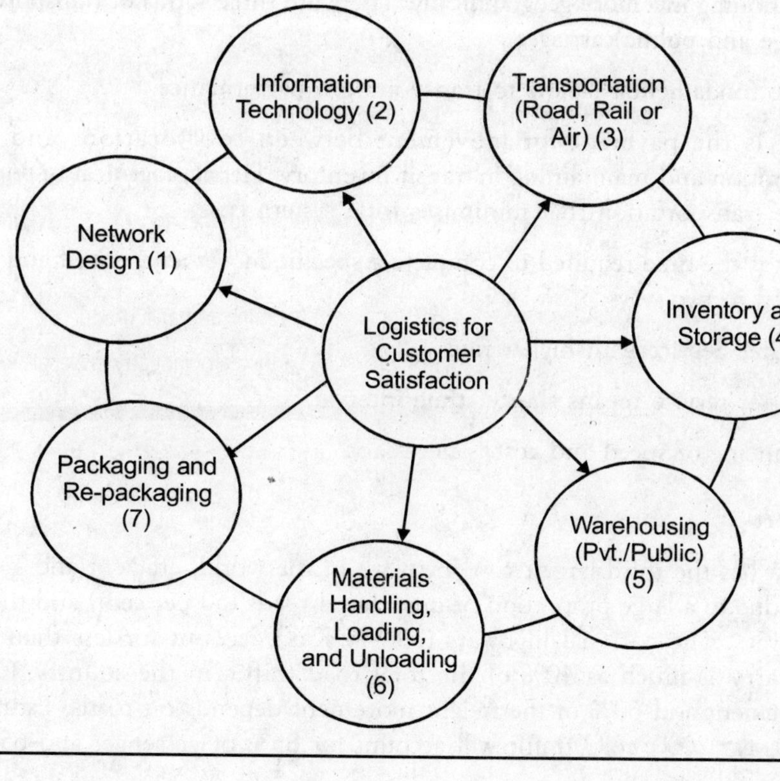

Network Design

Manufacturing plants, warehouses, material handling, distribution and after-sale services are typical logistics facilities. Network design is one of the prime responsibility of logistical management. It is required to determine the number and location of all types of facilities required to perform the logistics task. The selection of a superior locational network can be the first step towards competitive advantage. Logistical efficiency directly depends on the proper design of network and infrastructure.

Information Technology

Two major areas that depend on information are:

- ***Sales Forecasting:*** It is done to estimate the future requirements of logistics. It helps inventory management to satisfy anticipated customer requirements.
- ***Order Management***: Customer's order is very important in logistics. Logistics services are required for external and internal customers. External customers are those that consume the products or services and any trading partners that purchase products or services for resale. Internal customers are organisational units within a company.

The more efficient the design of a company's logistical system, the more sensitive it is to information accuracy. Incorrect information and delays in order processing can cripple logistics performance.

Transportation

It helps in positioning inventory geographically. There are three forms of transport, i.e., private carriage, contract carriage and public carriage.

There are three fundamental factors to transportation performance

- ***Cost:*** It is the payment for movement between two locations and expenses related to administration and maintaining in-transit inventory. Hence, logistical systems should be designed to utilise transportation that minimises total system cost.
- ***Speed:*** It is the time required to complete a specific movement. Speed and cost of transportation are related in two ways
  - Faster Service with higher rates.
  - Faster service means shorter time interval.

Therefore, balancing of speed and cost is necessary.

Road Transport

Although India has the third largest road network in the world, efficient and speedy transportation is not facilitated due to a large proportion of unsurfaced roads (50 per cent) and the over dependence on national highways. The national highways (38,445 Km.) account for less than 2% of the total road network but carry as much as 40% of the total road traffic in the country. Currently, 80% of the passenger movement and 60% of the freight movement depends on roads. Estimates indicate that, by the end of the year 2000, road traffic will account for 85% of passenger and 65% of goods traffic.

table 29.1

	1950-51	1994-95
1. Length of Roads (Thousand Km.)		
Total	400.0	2884.0
Surfaced	157.0	About 50%
2. Length of National Highways (Thousand Km.)		
Total	22.0	38.45
Surfaced	22.0	38.45
3. No. of Regd Vehicles (Thousand)		
All Vehicles	306.0	30287.0
Goods Vehicles	82.0	1796.0
Buses	34.0	425.0
4. Revenue from Road Transport (Rs Crore)		
Central	35.0	6918.2
State	13.0	4424.7

The Plan of Super National Highways

After the national highways, there is a plan under the consideration of the Central Road Transport Ministry to create Super National Highways. Through these super national highways of about 14,000 km. length, there is a plan to link big sea ports of the country with important cities. In the building of these highways, the role of the private sector will be important. This will be done on the basis of BOT (Build-Operate-Transfer) by the private sector. The Government of India has received 22 feasibility reports for the building of Super National Highways estimated to cost about Rs 1,50,000 crore. Out of these, 10 proposals have come from multinational companies.

After the amendment in Clause 9 of National Highway Ordinance 1956, the Rajya Sabha passed the National Highway (Amendment) Act 1997 on March 11,1997 through voice vote. This has given the central government the right of enacting laws regarding land acquisition for the development of national highways. By this, the process of land acquisition has been simplified.

Water Transport

Under water transport, coastal transport and overseas transport have their own importance. In the coastal areas, navigation by sea is comparatively cheaper. On the 5,560 km long sea coast of India, there are 11 big and 139 small and medium sized seaports. The development and management of big or major ports is the responsibility of the central government, whereas other ports are in the concurrent list. Among the big ports, Kandla, Mumbai, Majhgaon, New Mangalore, Cochin and JNPT (Jawahar Lal Nehru Port, Mumbai) are situated on the western coast and Tuticorin, Chennai, Visakhapatanam, Paradeep, Calcutta and Haldia ports are situated on the eastern coast. Jawahar Lal Nehru port is the latest big port equipped with most modern facilities. The ports of Mumbai and Cochin are natural seaports whereas the Kandla Seaport is used in tides. Visakhapatanam is the deepest port of India. Chennai is the oldest seaport. Calcutta port is situated on the river bank.

India has 11 major ports which handle around 90% of the sea borne trade. These ports are managed by Port Trusts under the central government. In addition, there are 139 minor working ports which are under the state governments. During 1996-97, the total cargo handled at major ports was 227.3 million tonnes, registering a growth of 5.6% over 1995-96. About 85% of the total volume of port traffic handled was in the form of dry and liquid bulk, while the remaining 15% consisted of general cargo, including containers. During 1997-98 (April-February), 228.1 million tonnes of cargo was handled by major ports, registering a growth of 11.6%. Maximum growth was recorded for fertilizer and raw material (28.4%), iron ore (18.6%) and others (22.7%).

The country has the largest merchant shipping fleet among developing countries and ranks 17th in the world in shipping tonnage. As on December 31, 1996, the net operative tonnage consisted of 484 ships totalling to 70,51,546 GRT.

Shipping Companies

There were 84 shipping companies in the country in operation as on 31st March, 1997, including the Shipping Corporation of India, a public sector undertaking. Of these, 48 are engaged exclusively in coastal trade, 21 in overseas trade and the remaining 15 in both coastal and overseas trade. The Shipping Corporation of India, which is the biggest shipping line of the country, had a merchant fleet of 179 vessels of 30-39 lakh GRT as on 31st march, 1997 and operated on almost all maritime routes. Its tonnage accounts for about 44% of total Indian tonnage.

Gopalpur Seaport Project

Orissa government had signed an agreement on 15 February, 1996 with MMTC (Mineral and Metal Trade Corporation) for the development of Gopalpur small seaport into an international seaport but, later on, the MMTC went back on its assurance in view of its financial difficulties. Now the state government has invited tenders from internal and foreign companies to complete the Project on BOT (Build-Operate-Transfer) basis. It is worth mentioning that, at present, coal and fertilizer are being exported and imported from this seaport.

At present, there are 12 major private sector shipping companies which own one lakh or more GRT. Great Eastern Shipping Company Limited is the biggest private company having the capacity of 8.73 lakh GRT, followed by Essar Shipping Limited (4:54 lakh GRT).

In the budget of 1997-98, an amount of Rs 1,354.22 crore was approved for the development of seaports.

National Waterways

The Inland Waterways Authority of India was set up on October 27,1986. This statutory body is entrusted with the responsibility of development, maintenance and regulation of national waterways.

The government has identified 10 important waterways for consideration to declare them as National Waterways. The following have so far been declared as national waterways and the same are being developed for navigation by Inland Waterways Authority of India – The Ganga between Allahabad and Haldia (1620 km.) on October 27, 1986, the Sadia-Dhubri stretch of river Brahmaputra (891 km.) on Oct. 26, 1988 and the Kollam-Kottapuram stretch of west coast canal (168 km.) along with Champakare canal (14 km.) and Udyogmandal canal (22 km.) in Kerala with effect from February 1, 1993. It is also proposed to consider the declaration of some more waterways like the river Godavari, Sunderbans and waterways in Goa as national waterways.

Air Transport

For civil aviation, Air India, Indian Airlines, Vayudoot, Pawan Hans and private air services are available. Air India and Indian Airlines were established under the Air Corporation Act, 1953. Air India was established with the purpose of international air flights and Indian Airlines for flights within the country. Air India has extended its air services to five continents. After showing a loss for two consecutive years in 1995-96 and 1996-97, Air India was hopeful of earning a net profit of Rs 91.26 crore and total profit of Rs 145.35 crore in 1997-98. Its main office is situated in Mumbai. For international flights, the aerodromes of Delhi, Mumbai, Calcutta, Chennai and Thiruvananthapuram have been declared as international aerodromes. The responsibility for the management and development of these aerodromes was entrusted to International Airports Authority of India. With effect from April 1, 1995, the responsibility of maintenance of international aerodromes along with internal aerodromes has been entrusted to International Airways Authority of India.

The head office of Indian Airlines is situated in Delhi. Basically, it is responsible for domestic flights but at present it also provides flights for 14 countries – Nepal, Pakistan, Sri Lanka, Singapore, Bangladesh, Afghanistan, Thailand, UAE, Qatar, Oman, Myanmar, Kuwait and Malaysia. In 1995-96, Indian Airlines had a fleet of 59 aeroplanes but showed a loss of Rs 110 crore.

Vayudoot was established on January 20, 1981 as a Corporation. Basically, it was established to fulfil the requirement of air services in the north-eastern area, but, by and by it has extended its services to other areas also where the services of Indian Airlines are not available. Vayudoot had 16 aeroplanes in 1992-93. It too showed a net loss in 1991-92 and 1992-93 amounting to Rs 30.6 crore and Rs 24.2 crore, respectively. Since 1992-93, Vayudoot has merged with Indian Airlines.

The Recommendations of the Rakesh Mohan Committee on Infrastructure

In Oct., 1994, under the Chairmanship of Shri **Rakesh Mohan,** Director General of NCAER (National Council of Applied Economic Research), a 17-member committee was constituted by the government. The committee handed over its report to the Finance Minister on June 22, 1996 which was released on Jan. 8, 1997. The committee, in its Report, has said that it is possible to increase the investment in basic infrastructure area from the present level, 5.5% of GDP, to 7% by 2000-06. This will increase to $ 30 billion by 2000-01 and further TO $50 billion by 2000-01 and 8% by 2005-06 in place of present annual investment of $ 17 billion. The committee has recommended wide concessions in taxes to promote private investment in basic infrastructure areas.

In order to fulfil the financial needs of basic areas, the committee has recommended the use of funds available with Insurance Companies, Assets Management Companies, Employees' Provident Fund. The committee has said that it is better to create small insurance companies and divide GIC and its four allied companies. The other recommendations of the committee are as under

Telecommunication

- To open the long distance inter-circle services to private sector by 2001.
- To create a company named 'India Telecom' for the Telecommunication departments.
- To consider the increased privatisation of MTNL (Mahanagar Telephone Nigam Ltd).
- To deposit all the license fees connected with telecommunication into one basic fund so that loans and equities may be provided to projects concerned with basic infrastructure.

Contd...

Electricity

- The formula of fixation of electricity charge should be based on investment and there must be a possibility of the increase in levy, on an average per year, in addition to adjustment for inflation.
- In order to promote entry of private sector, a minimum charge of electricity should be fixed.
- The state electricity boards should be reconstituted at an early date.
- The Central Electricity Tribunal should be decentralised.

Roads

- To establish a 'Highway Development Fund' by levy of surcharge of 50 p. per litre on diesel and Re 1 per litre on petrol.
- To construct Super National Highways, bypasses, etc., on an extensive scale in collaboration with private sector.
- To begin 'Highway Infrastructural Savings Scheme' on the lines of National Savings Schemes.
- To create a Road Board for the development of integrated main routes.
- To have 'Four Lanes' for some present national highways.

Seaports

- At least 2 'Mega ports' should be developed in the country. There should be at least one on both the coasts
- To exempt the private collaboration for seaports from corporation taxes.
- The financial arrangements for seaports should be done through primary market or financial institutions.

Pawan Hans was established on Oct. 15, 1985 as a Corporation. Its original name was Helicopter Corporation of India which was later renamed as Pawan Hans. Basically, it was established to provide helicopter services to ONGC (Oil and Natural Gas Commission) in the exploration of oil. Apart from this, it also provided services to certain state governments and public sector undertakings. The company achieved total flying task of 22,047 hours during 1996-97 as compared to 19,250 hours in the previous year.

In recent years, the permission to operate private air taxis in the field of air transport has been given by the government as a result of which the sole right of public sector in air transport has come to an end. Air taxi services can be operated as non-scheduled flights both on 'chartered' and 'non-chartered' basis to all airports in the country open to civil operations. The air taxi operators are free to charge any fare on their own commercial discretion.

Merger of NAA and IAAI

The two Airport Authorities — National Airports Authority ('NAA) and International Airports Authority of India (IAAI) —have been merged on April 1, 1995 as a new organisation named as Airports Authority of India (AAI). This newly created AAI is presently controlling both domestic and international airports of the country. Prior to it, NAA was controlling domestic airports, while IAAI was managing international airports of the country.

Just-in-Time (JIT) Transport Management

Just-in-Time transport management is an increasingly popular method used to manage inventory levels. Manufacturers, in a number of industries, employ it to help them reduce the amount of production supplies that they keep on hand. Discussed below are the benefits for implementing JIT concept in transport and inventory management.

A multitude of JIT benefits have been identified in the early JIT literature. However, some of them seem inappropriate in practical life. Some are elements which have been advocated as components of the implementation process itself (i.e., some authors say that a variable is a component of the implementation process itself, while some say that it is a result of JIT implementation; e.g., transport improvement or inventory reduction are prerequisites to JIT implementation or results of implementation?). To describe a variable as a component of JIT implementation and then designate it as a benefit utilised in measuring the level of success of JIT implementation is circular logic. Specifically, if reductions in lead time, set-up time and lot sizes are seen as a part of the implementation process itself, can these reductions be seen as success factors? Apparently, a more "cause-and effect-type" relationship is desirable for measuring successful implementation.

Seven results were selected for this study as benefits of JIT implementation:

1. Downtime reduction
2. Inventory reduction
3. Workspace reduction
4. Increased quality
5. Increased manpower utilisation
6. Increased equipment utilisation
7. Increased inventory turnover

Each of these is discussed below.

Downtime Reduction

In order to make the lot size cuts proposed by JIT advocates, equipment must be readily available for use. The demise of buffer stock means that product machinery must be capable of running what is needed, when it is needed, if current demand is to be met. If there is no "just-in-case" inventory, unexpected downtime can lead to the inability to respond to demand. In addition, the increased use of preventive maintenance in a JIT environment can also result in decreased downtime.

Inventory Reduction

In a JIT environment, total inventory levels fall. Raw material is reduced by smaller purchased lot sizes and more frequent deliveries. Work-in-process is reduced by the shift to smaller lot sizes, which are, in turn, made possible by shorter set-up times. When the firm produces at a rate demanded in the market, finished goods are shipped as they are finished. Nothing need accumulate in the finished goods warehouse. Even very early JIT literature contains numerous examples which support the contention that inventory reduction is an indicator of JIT implementation success. Inventory reduction benefits, can be as high as 97 per cent.

Workspace Reduction

Less workspace is needed in a JIT environment owing to smaller lot sizes and reduced inventory levels. This reduction is mostly due to the absence of stored inventory, both between and within work centres. This absence of inventory, in addition to the use of group technology techniques, has allowed some firms to move work centres closer together, freeing space and reducing material handling distances. This results in a neater, more organised facility, which provides for speed, identification of bottlenecks and fewer lost parts. Japanese plants are typically one-third the size of US plants providing a comparable output. An average company adopting JIT should be able to reduce workspace by 25 to 50 per cent.

Increased Quality

Reduction of "in-house" sizes of lots promotes rapid feedback from downstream work centres, when there is a quality problem. This feedback results in a reduction of scrap, rework and ultimately, a higher overall level of quality. Further, the cross-training of workers as an element of JIT implementation provides workers who are able to assist one another when a quality problem arises. For purposes of this study, increased quality is measured as a decrease in scrap and rework.

Increased Manpower Utilisation

Cross-training of employees allows less worker idle time when a machine is not needed for production. Having workers with the ability to move from one work centre to another results in increased manpower utilisation. The number of workers needed can then be reduced with no consequential drop in output.

Increased Equipment Utilisation

The introduction of total preventive maintenance, the cross-training of workers, smaller and more flexible machinery and the use of group technology techniques–all combine to increase equipment utilisation.

Increased Inventory Turnover

Reduction in inventory and lot sizes results in increased inventory turnover. Inventory turnovers at Haworth doubled in one year after implementing JIT, while other examples include threefold, fourfold and even sixfold increase.

Inventory Management

The interest of management in better inventory management is much more than it was a few years back. Management knows the need, importance and practicability of scientific inventory management.

table 29.2

S. No.	Title	Basis	Main Uses
1.	ABC (Always Better Control)	Value of Consumption	To control raw material components and work-in-progress inventories in the normal course of business.
2.	HML (High, Medium, Low)	Unit price of material	Mainly to control purchases.
3.	XYZ	Value of items in storage	To review the inventories and their uses at scheduled intervals.
4.	VED (Vital Essential Desirable)	Criticality of component	To determine the stocking levels of spare parts.
5.	FNSD (Fast, Nominal, Slow, Dead, etc.)	Consumption pattern of the component	To control obsolescence.
6.	SDE (Scarce, Difficult, Easy to obtain)	Problems faced in procurement	Lead-time analysis and purchasing strategies.
7.	GOLE (Government, Ordinary, Local, Foreign sources)	Source of the material	Procurement strategies.
8.	SOS (Seasonal, Off-season)	Nature of supplies	Procurement/Holding strategies for seasonal items like agricultural products.

The conflicting objectives of inventory control are reflected in the seemingly conflicting demands which are made on an inventory manager from time to time. For example, stocks are to be kept at a low level but not too low; turnover is to be increased but only at a satisfactory profit rate; bulk purchases are to be attempted to obtain better prices but over buying is to be controlled; special attention is to be paid to the disposal of obsolete or near obsolete items but not before the point of obsolescence is identified; and so on.

Economic Order Quantity (EOQ)

Economic order quantity is the quantity for which orders are placed when stock reaches the re-order level. In other words, EOQ is the quantity which is most economic to order, or, EOQ is that size of the order which gives maximum economy in purchasing material and ultimately contributes towards maintaining the material at the optimum level and at minimum cost.

With EOQ, two types of costs should be taken into account

1. ***Ordering Cost:*** This is the cost of placing an order with the supplier. Because of so many factors involved, it is quite difficult to quantify this cost.
2. ***Inventory Carrying Cost:*** It includes the following:
   - Cost of operating the stores
   - The incidence of insurance costs
   - Interest on capital locked up in store
   - Deterioration and wastage of materials

figure 29.2

Analytical marketing research system

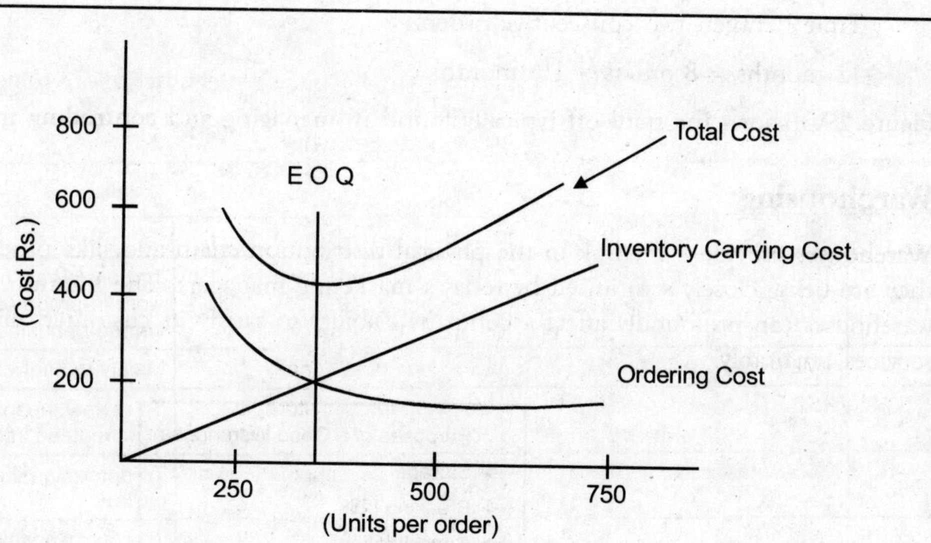

Mathematical Formulae

EOQ can also be calculated with the help of a formula as given below

$$EOQ = \sqrt{\frac{2.A.B}{C.S}}$$

Where E O Q = Economic Order Quantity

A	=	Annual Consumption in units
B	=	Cost per unit
C.S	=	Storage or carrying cost as a percentage of average inventory.

Example

The annual demand for a product is 64,000 units. The unit cost is Rs 6 and inventory carrying cost is 25% per annum. If the cost of one procurement is Rs 75, determine:

a. EOQ

b. No. of orders per year

c. Time between two consecutive orders.

Solution

a. $$\text{EOQ} = \sqrt{\frac{2.A.B}{C.S.}}$$

$$\sqrt{\frac{2\times 64000\times 75}{6\times 25\%}} = 8000 \text{ units}$$

b. No. of orders per year = 64000 ÷ 8000 = 8 orders in a year

c. Time between two consecutive orders

12 months ÷ 8 orders = 1½ months

Figure 29.3 shows the trade-off typically found in managing and controlling inventory levels.

Warehousing

Warehouses provide a key link in the physical distribution chain and, like other stages of distribution, they are being closely scrutinised by today's marketing managers. The location, size and capabilities of warehouses can profoundly affect a company's ability to satisfy its customers and deliver products and services profitably.

Purposes of a Good Warehouse

→ Storage
→ Breaking bulk
→ Consolidation
→ Unitisation

Types of Warehouses

The basic purpose of warehousing in distribution logistics is to arrange placement of products and supply storage facility to store them, consolidate them with other and similar products and divide them into smaller quantities on the basis of ownership. There are two types of warehouses (i) private warehouses (ii) public warehouses. The following decision variables can be considered.

figure 29.3

Trade-off typically found in managing and controlling inventory levels.

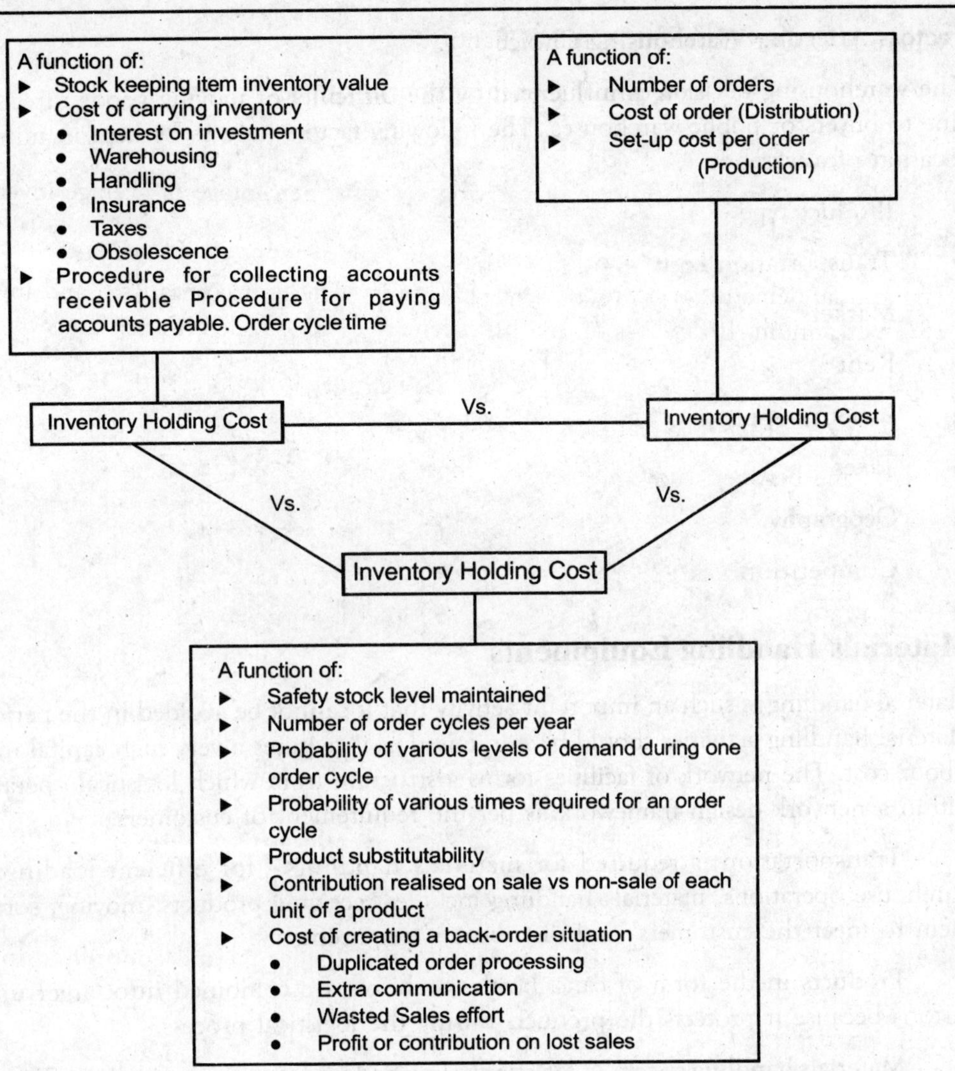

figure 29.4

Decision Variables in Choosing Among Types of Warehousing

	Types of Warehousing Arrangements		
	Private		
Decision Variables	Owned	Leased	Public
1. Fixed investment	Very high	Moderate, depends on the lease's terms	No fixed investment is involved
2. Unit cost	High	High, if volume is low	Low, since facilities are on "for hire *as* needed" and fixed costs are widely distributed among users
3. Control	High	High	Low managerial control
4. Adequate product line	Highly adequate	Moderately adequate	May not be convenient
5. Flexibility	Low	Low	High; termination of usage can be easily arranged.

Factors Affecting Warehousing Choice

The warehousing decision is influenced by the difficulty of moving goods directly from the assembly line to buyers or public warehouses. The following factors have to be kept in mind when deciding the location of a warehouse:

- Product type
- Transportation cost
- Markets
- Rent
- Labour supply
- Taxes
- Geography
- Competition.

Materials Handling Equipments

Material handling is such an important activity that it cannot be avoided in the performance of logistics. Material handling activities should be minimised as it requires a very high capital investment and direct labour cost. The network of facilities forms a structure from which logistical operations are performed within a network design framework as per the requirement of customers.

Transportation is required for materials handling – for efficient loading and unloading. In warehouse operations, materials handling includes receiving products, moving, sorting and assembling them to meet the customers' and distributors' requirements.

Products in the form of cans, bottles or boxes are combined into larger units to make master cartons because it protects the products during the logistical process.

Materials handling system in logistics is designed under certain guidelines. These are very important to assist management. These are:

- Equipment for materials handling and storage should be standardised
- The system should be designed to provide maximum continuous product flow as per the requirements of the company
- Handling equipment should be properly utilised.

Classification of Materials Handling Systems

Materials handling systems in logistics are mainly divided into 5 categories.

1. ***Mechanised Systems:*** These systems utilise a combination of labour and handling equipment to facilitate receiving, processing, and/or shipping. Mainly labour constitutes a high percentage of overall cost in mechanised handling. Even then, mechanised handling systems are very common. They employ a wide range of handling equipments. These are:
   - Forklift trucks
   - Walkie-Rider pallet trucks

- Townlines
- Tow tractors with trailers
- Electric hoists or cranes
- Conveyors

2. ***Semi-automated System:*** When selected handling functions are performed using automated equipment and the remainder of the handling is completed on a mechanised basis then the system is said to be semi-automated. It can be called as a mixture of automated and mechanised handling.

   The main equipments used in semi-automated system are:

   - Automated Guided Vehicle System (AGVS)
   - Sortations
   - Robotics.

3. ***Automated System:*** Automated System attempts to minimise labour as much as practically possible by substituting capital investment by equipment.

Packaging

Packaging includes handling and storage of finished goods. It also emphasises on protection from loss and damage.

Hence, we can say that logistics management is the framework of 7 'R's–Right quantity of the Right product or service to the Right place in the Right conditions at the Right cost and the Right time with Right impression.

Excellence in each aspect of functional work is relevant and must be viewed in terms of improving the overall efficiency and effectiveness of integrated logistics.

DESCRIPTION OF THE WHOLE CHAIN

The purpose of the chain model is to describe all the agents that perform functions in the chain distribution, from suppliers to final consumers. If a company is operating in the poultry business, red meat business, sugar business, milk, or beer, for example, just one system will be described. But for companies operating in more businesses, all the systems (chains) should be described, inserting the agents that perform negotiation functions (suppliers, farms, industry, wholesalers, retailers and others) at the product flow. With the recent trends of traceability, it is even more important to have this complete picture of the chain.

Distribution Managements delivers broad and deep functionality:

- Requirements Planning
- Enterprise Facility Planning
- Advanced Forecasting
- Quality Management
- Advanced Stock Valuation

- Inventory Management
- Bulk Stock Management
- Sales Order Management
- Procurement
- Advanced Pricing
- Warehouse Management
- Project Costing
- Agreement Management
- Customer Self Service
- Supplier Self Service

Warehousing and Distribution Solution

Experts can develop the so many concept of warehouses from planning stages to implementation process. Using proven warehousing and distribution solutions. The approach to implementing solutions ensures project success. Implementation support is provided in the following areas:

- ***Warehouse Strategic Planning:*** Selecting the efficient storage designs, material handling systems and warehouse management systems to ensure high operations performance.
- ***Distribution Center Design and Implementation:*** Creating, maintaining and administering budgets and schedules; assisting with obtaining proper permits; overseeing installation; developing product slotting configurations for maximum material handling and storage efficiency; conducting equipment acceptance testing and providing start-up support when operations go live.

  Distribution Network Configuration: Determining the number and location of distribution centers and manufacturing plants.

  Location Selection: Evaluation existing structures and Greenfield sites, utilities, fix-up costs, support services, community desirability and incentive packages.
- ***Construction Services:*** Providing total project management for facility construction and renovation, including site selection, employee selection and on-site project management.
- ***Systems Integration:*** Integrating computerized and manual warehousing systems through system configuration and set up, acceptance testing start-up and implementation.
- ***Inventory Management:*** Analyzing inventory levels throughout the supply chain.
- ***Transportation System Planning:*** Selecting the best transportation configuration and suppliers to minimize costs.
- ***Maintenance:*** Changing the maintenance operation into a profit oriented center by improving the quality of product, utilization of equipment resources, overall equipment performance, throughput capacity and equipment life.

LOGISTICAL INTEGRATION

The logistical integration process is composed of two interrelated efforts, i.e., goods flow and information flow. Information from and about customers flows through the enterprise in the form of sales activity, forecasts and orders. This information is refined into manufacturing and procurement plans. A value-added inventory flow results in transfer of finished products to customers.

The following are the major components of logistical operations:

a. ***Physical Distribution:*** It refers to those activities which are related to providing customer service. It requires performing order receipt and processing, deploying inventories, storage and handling and outbound transportation within a channel of distribution. It coordinates with market planning such as pricing, promotional support, customer service levels, delivery standards, handling returns and life-cycle support. Its main objective is to assist in revenue generation by providing desired customer service levels at the lowest total cost.

b. ***Manufacturing Support:*** These activities are related to planning, scheduling and supporting manufacturing operations. It requires master schedule planning and performing work-in-progress storage, handling, transportation and time phasing of components. It is responsible for storage of inventory at manufacturing sites and maximum coordination between manufacturing and physical distribution activities.

c. ***Procurement:*** It is related to obtaining products and materials from outside suppliers. It performs resource planning, supply sourcing, negotiation, order placement, inbound transportation, receiving and inspection, storage and handling and quality assurance. It is responsible for coordination with suppliers for better scheduling, supply continuity, hedging and speculation, as well as research leading to new sources or programmes. Its main objective is to support manufacturing or resale organisations by providing timely purchase at the lowest total cost.

d. ***Inventory Flow:*** It is concerned with the movement and storage of materials and finished products. It starts with the shipment of materials or component parts from a supplier and ends when a manufactured or processed product is delivered to a customer.

   The logistical process adds value by moving inventory when and where needed. Work-in-process inventory must be moved to support final assembly, thereby it gains value at each step of its transformation into finished inventory.

e. ***Information Flow:*** Information integrates operating components. These components contain the actual logistics work and information facilities, coordination of planning and control of day-to-day operations.

MARKETING AND PHYSICAL DISTRIBUTION OF PETROLEUM PRODUCTS

Marketing and physical distribution of petroleum products in India is quite developed and most of it is under public sector organisations. Recently, the government gave permission for the import and distribution of cooking gas and kerosene oil to the private sector. This permission opens the field foı import of these petroleum products from foreign countries and to sell it in the open domestic market. This type of open sale is still excluded from government price control.

Associated Units

1. ***Indian Oil Corporation Ltd (IOCL):*** This corporation was set up in September 1964 by amalgamating Indian Refineries Limited (established in 1958) and Indian Oil Company Ltd (established in 1959). This corporation has three divisions: Marketing Division (Headquarter Mumbai), Refining and Pipeline Division (Headquarter Delhi) and Assam Oil Division (Headquarter Digboi).
2. ***Bharat Petroleum Corporation Ltd (BPCL):*** Following the government's acquisition of two Burmah-Shell companies in January 1976, the name of Burmah-Shell Refineries Limited was changed to Bharat Refineries Limited on February 12,1976. Being an integrated refining and marketing company, the name of the company was changed to Bharat Petroleum Corporation Ltd (BPCL) from August 1, 1977. The company is engaged in processing of crude oil in its refinery at Mumbai and storage, distribution and marketing of petroleum products in the country.
3. ***Hindustan Petroleum Corporation Ltd (HPCL):*** HPCL was established in July 15, 1974 by acquiring the assets of US company, ESSO Eastern. On December 31, 1976, the government acquired Caltex Oil Refining Ltd and merged it with HPCL.
4. ***Gas Authority of India Ltd (GAIL):*** GAIL was established in August 1984, for handling post exploration activities relating to natural gas, viz., transportation, processing, distribution and marketing. The company was assigned the priority task of setting up the cross-country HVJ (Hazira, Vijaipur and Jagadishpur) pipeline. This project has been completed by GAIL. Presently, GAIL is the largest company in India for marketing of natural gas.

SUMMARY

The design of a logistics system depends on management information system. It has to serve two conflicting requirements. An effective logistic system requires a total cost approach instead of a fragmented cost approach. For the total cost approach, the logistics require enough data pertaining to the various key elements of the total cost and also such other information as would help to design and execute alternative physical distribution systems.

An effective physical distribution system ensures an efficient administration of the total system for controlling the flow of raw materials and finished goods.

PROJECT WORK

Make a group of 3 students and study the functional areas of logistics for the following goods and services:

a. Washing Machines
b. Banking Services
c. Electrical Fans
d. Mobile Phones.

SHORT ANSWER QUESTIONS

1. Name any five functional areas of logistics.
2. What do you mean by logistical integration?
3. What do you mean by physical distribution?
4. What do you mean by inventory carrying cost and ordering cost?
5. What is distribution solution?

REVIEW QUESTIONS

1. What is the role of inventory management in the overall distribution task?
2. What are the relative advantages and disadvantages of various transportation modes?
3. What do you understand by logistics management? Define its scope and objectives and discuss the key decision areas.
4. What are the factors to be considered for deciding the location of the manufacturing plant? Discuss the importance of materials management during this period.
5. 'Physical distribution is the better half of marketing'. Discuss and show the major elements of physical distribution.
6. Discuss the importance of warehousing in physical distribution. What are the important decisions that managers must make when establishing warehouses?
7. Suggest alternatives for the physical distribution of washing machines.
8. Describe the factors that determine the decisions about the locations of warehouses for a consumer durable product.
9. How would you decide on levels of inventory for electric motors primarily used in agriculture?
10. What modes of transportation would you use for a company manufacturing personal computers? Also give justifications for your recommendation.
11. Differentiate between 'Channel Management' and 'Physical Distribution Management'.
12. What are the advantages and disadvantages of the different transportation options for a company?
13. Discuss the description of the whole chain with the help of example.

GO TO THE NET

Using Internet resources, study the logistics system of five reputed companies.

Using Internet search tools prepare a report on the distribution management of 3 small car manufacturing companies.

Caselet

Mission

LG intends to achieve on-time delivery and realise customer satisfaction by implementing a swift and flexible Global Logistics System and utilising it as a strategic tool.

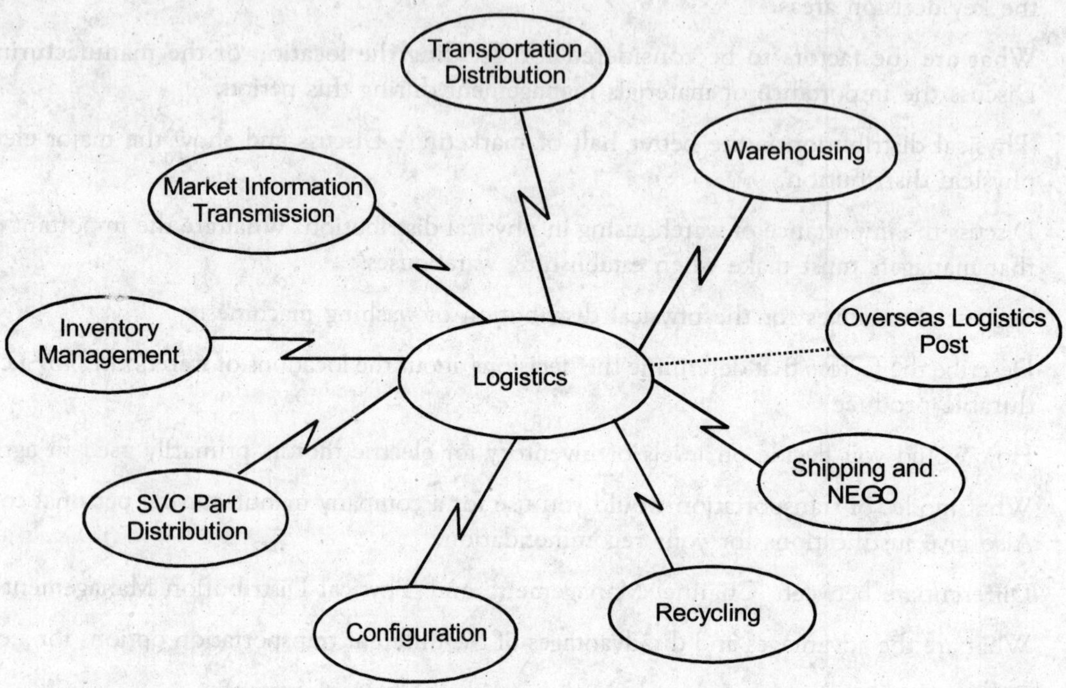

Vision and Slogan

LG considers hospitality one of its main values and aims to be the world's top logistics company that can satisfy varied customer needs by creating a new culture based on promise-keeping and autonomy.

Vision

Slogan

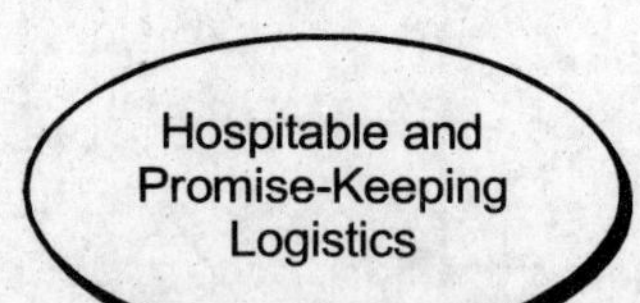

Organisation's History

LG's logistics function had been dispersed in the production and sales department and had performed such simple functions as storing, transporting and distributing manufactured/sold products until 1991 when it began to make considerable progress by starting logistics innovation activities of its own.

Contd...

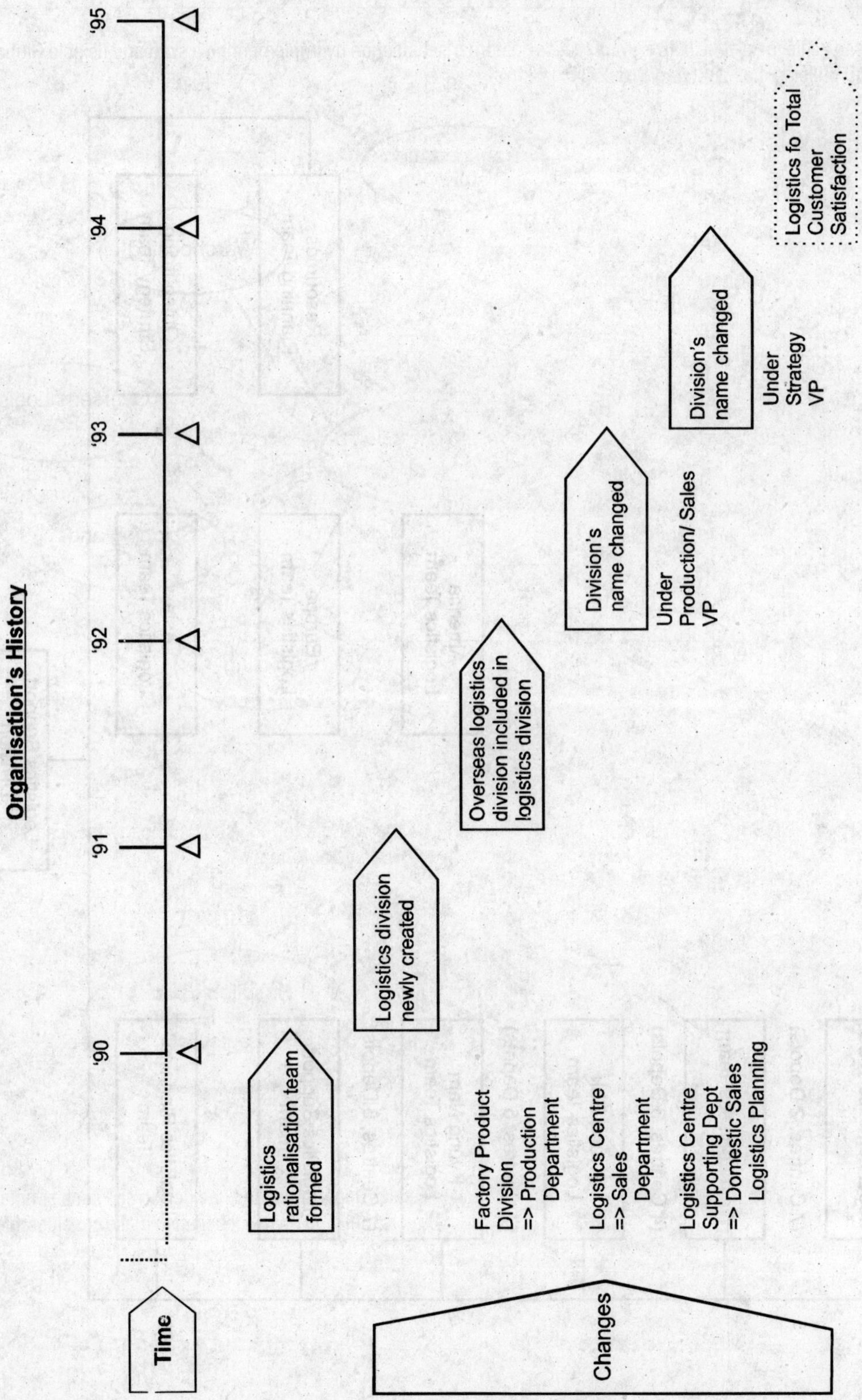
Organisation's History
Time
'90
'91
'92
'93
'94
'95
Changes
Logistics rationalisation team formed
Factory Product Division => Production Department
Logistics Centre => Sales Department
Logistics Centre Supporting Dept => Domestic Sales Logistics Planning
Logistics division newly created
Overseas logistics division included in logistics division
Division's name changed
Under Production/ Sales VP
Division's name changed
Under Strategy VP
Logistics fo Total Customer Satisfaction

Contd...

Organisation

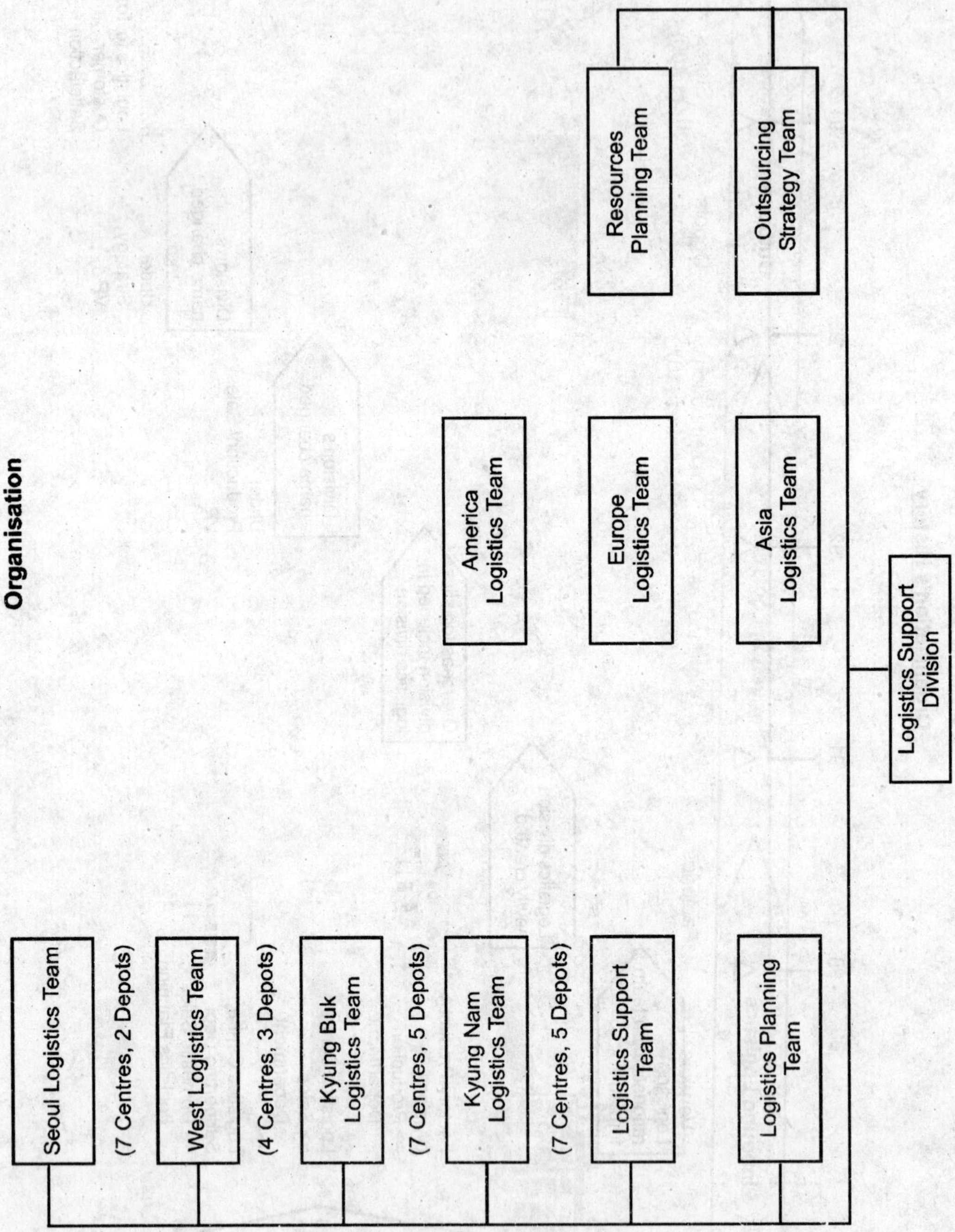

Contd...

Logistics Hubs

LG has vendors, factories, warehouses, logistics centres, depots, and stores as its logistics hubs.

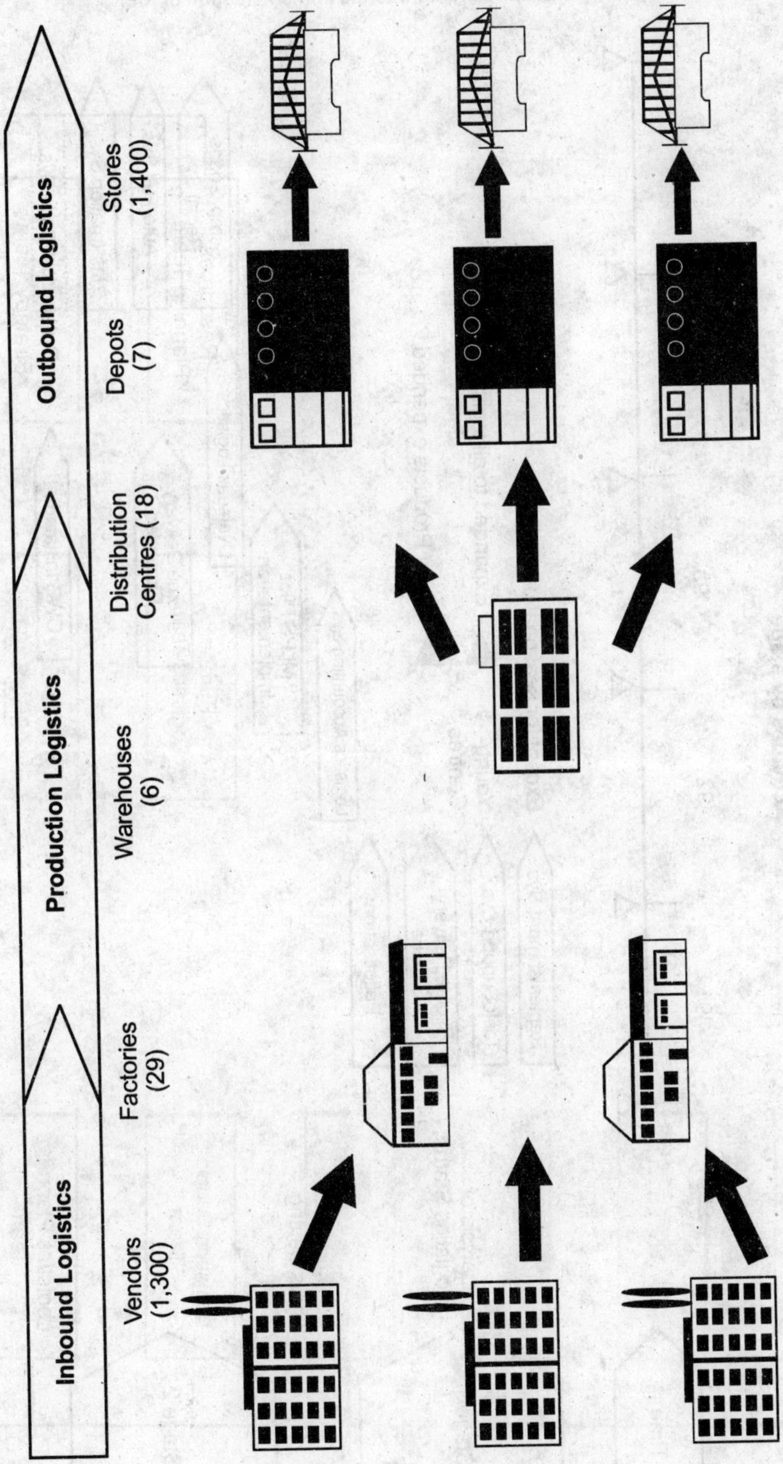

Contd...

Performance of Logistics Innovation

LG set the SVC level that customers require and performed a series of logistics innovation activities ranging from the analysis of logistics status and consolidation of logistics infrastructure to the implementation of MLPS.

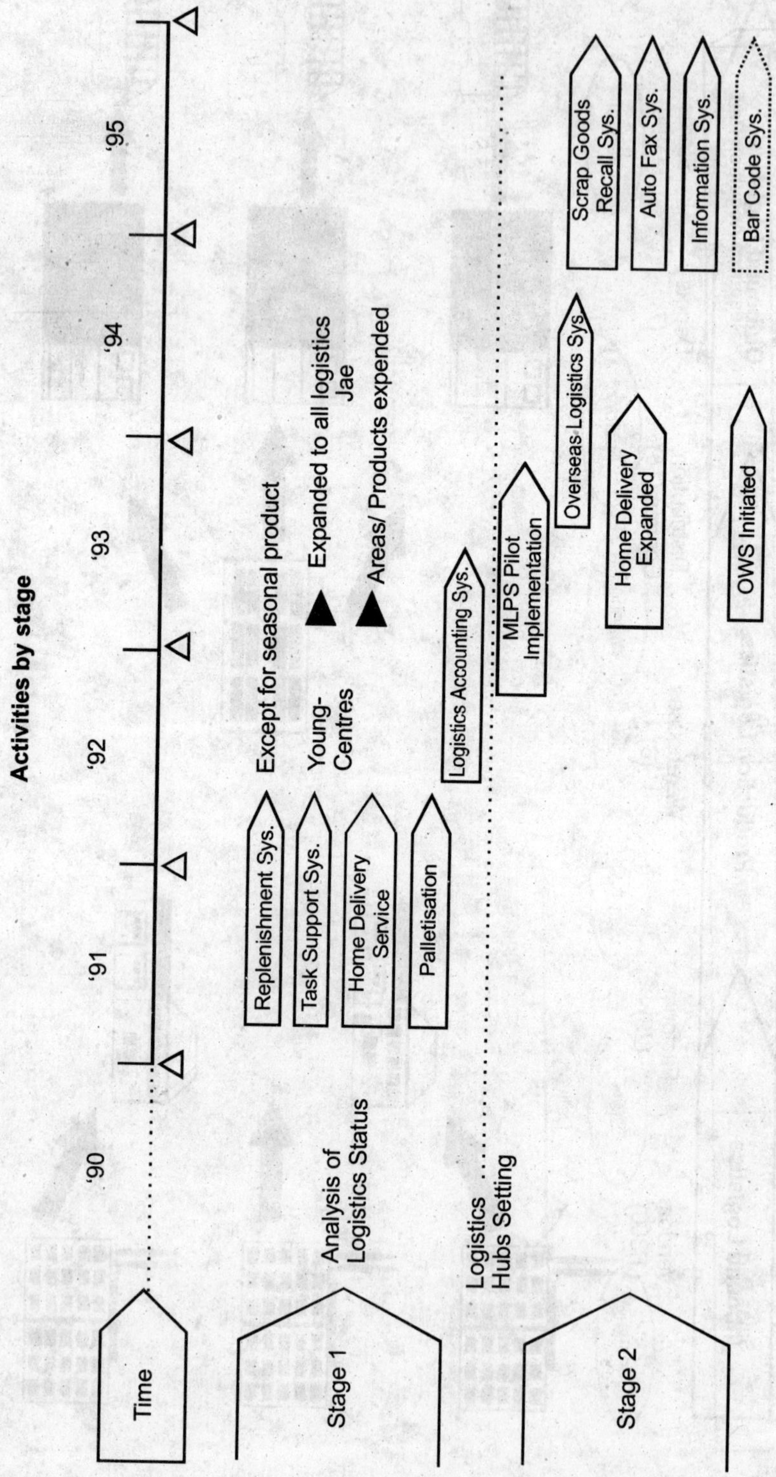

Contd...

Logistics Information System

LG has implemented a logistics system that can deliver required goods at the right time by combining the whole process from the resource acquisition of vendors to product sale and managing the entire information in an integrated way.

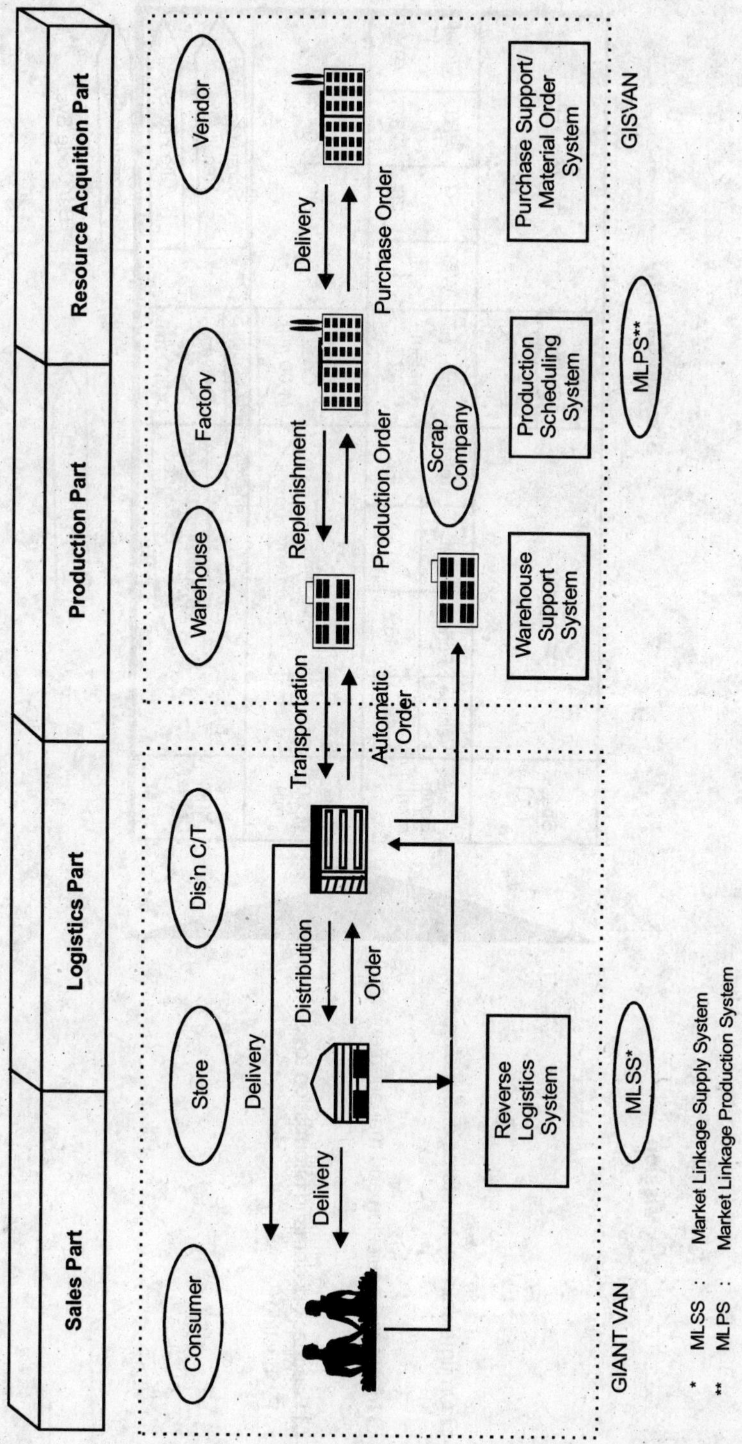

Contd...

Mission and Capacity of Yangjee Distribution Centre

Yangjee Distribution Centre, the largest distribution centre in Korea, aims at enhancing the SVC level for customers by realising feedback of demand information, efficient inventory management and on time delivery for stores and customers.

Mission

- ❑ On-time delivery for stores and customer
- ❑ Inventory acquisition and management
- ❑ Feedback of demand information to Production

Size and Capacity

Space (m^2)	3,830				Daily Transport Capacity (2.5 ton)	130			
Equip-ment	Vehicle	Forklift	Host	Total	Info. System	W/S	CRT	PRT	Total
	49	16	1	66		1	25	23	49
Sales (1,000 mil)	5,068				Transport Cost (1,00 mil)	15.6			
Home Delivery	25,900				Home Delivery Sales (1,000 mil)	142			

Contd...

Job Process and Information System (1)

The whole process from receiving an order to its delivery is connected in the information system so that the sales and production part may be linked efficiently.

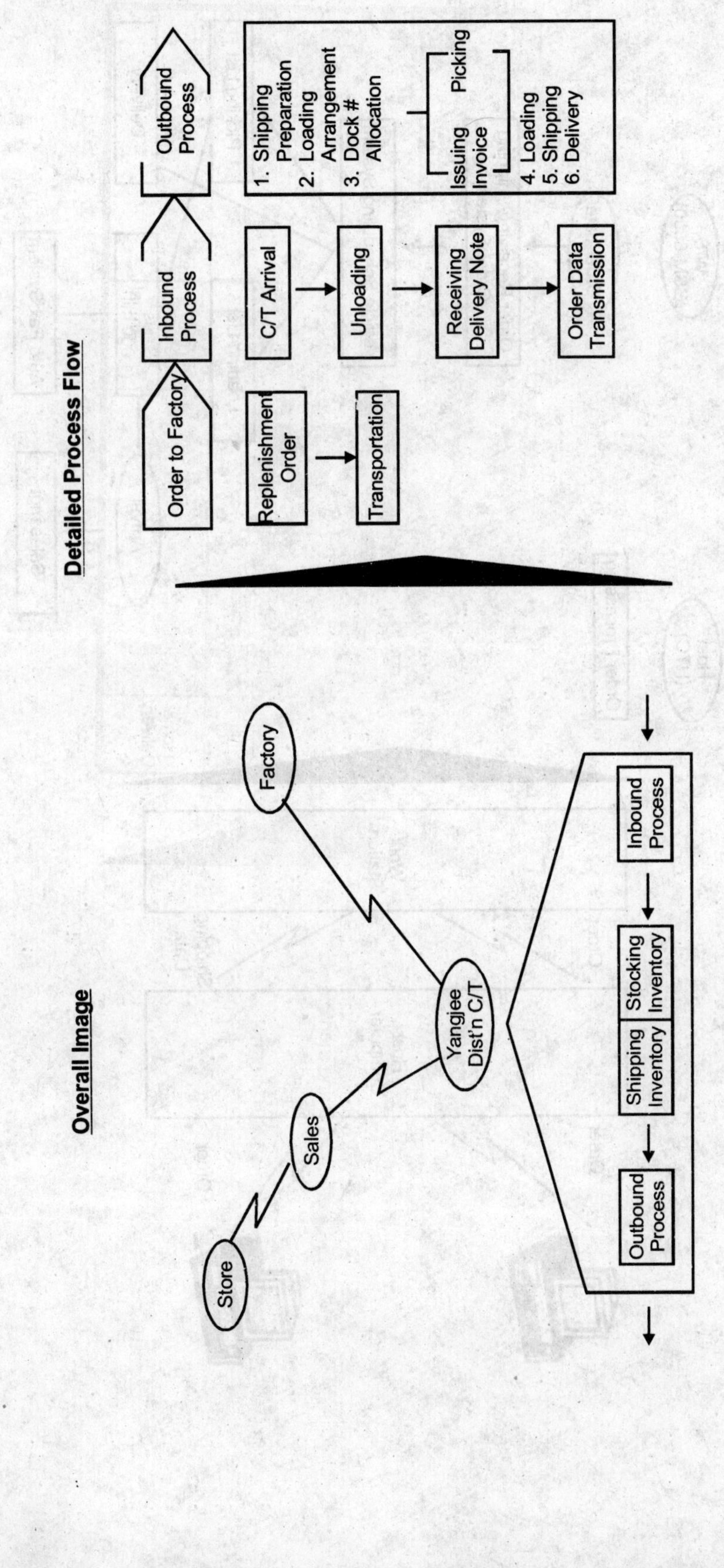

Contd...

Job Process and Information System (2)

LG has implemented and utilised an information system which reflects the current market status and customer needs and properly meets them.

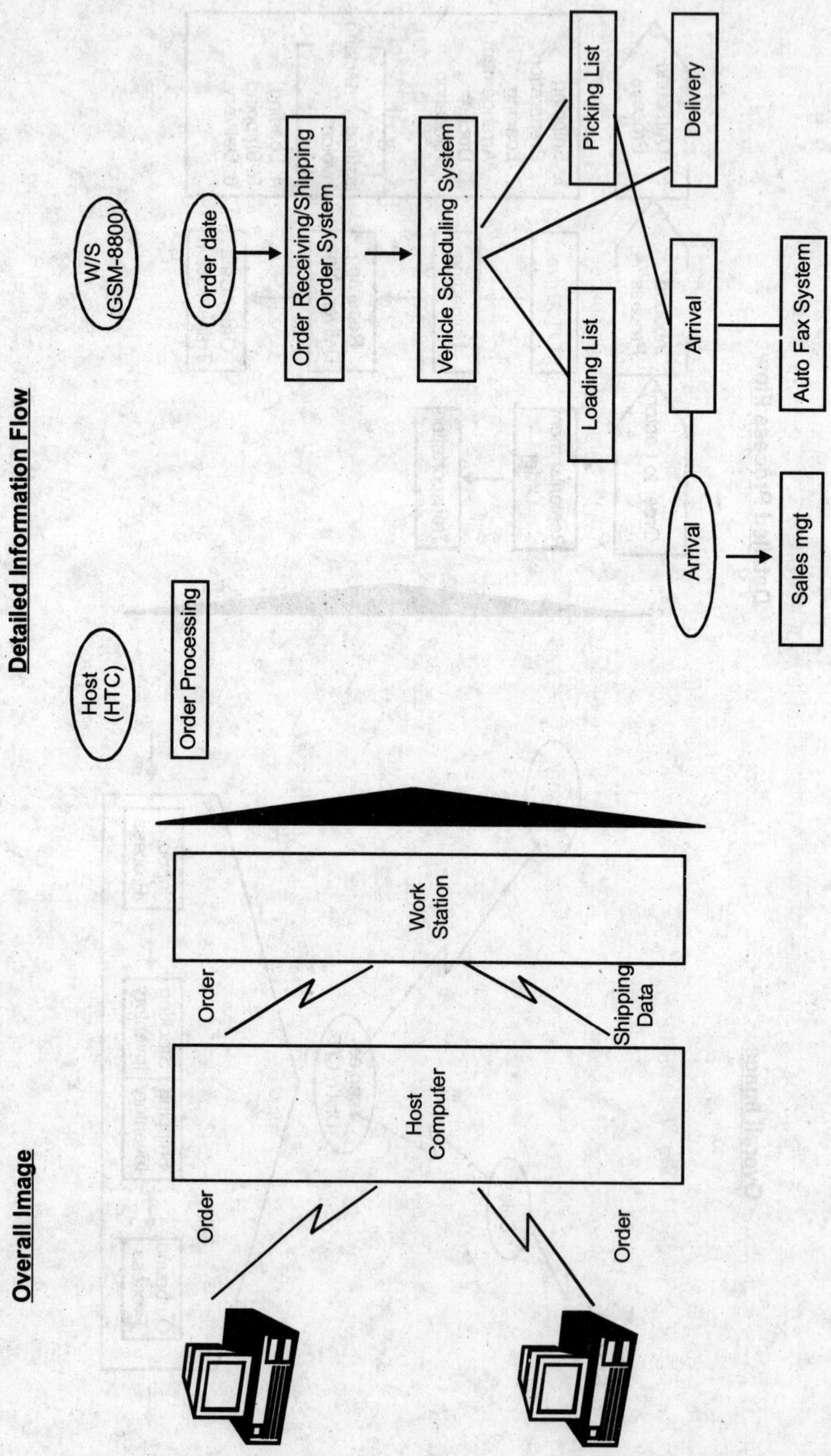

Contd...

Innovation Cases

LG has performed various innovative activities to properly cope with the changes in market environment and customer needs. As a result, the SVC level for the customer has been heightened and the competitiveness in the logistics division has been strengthened.

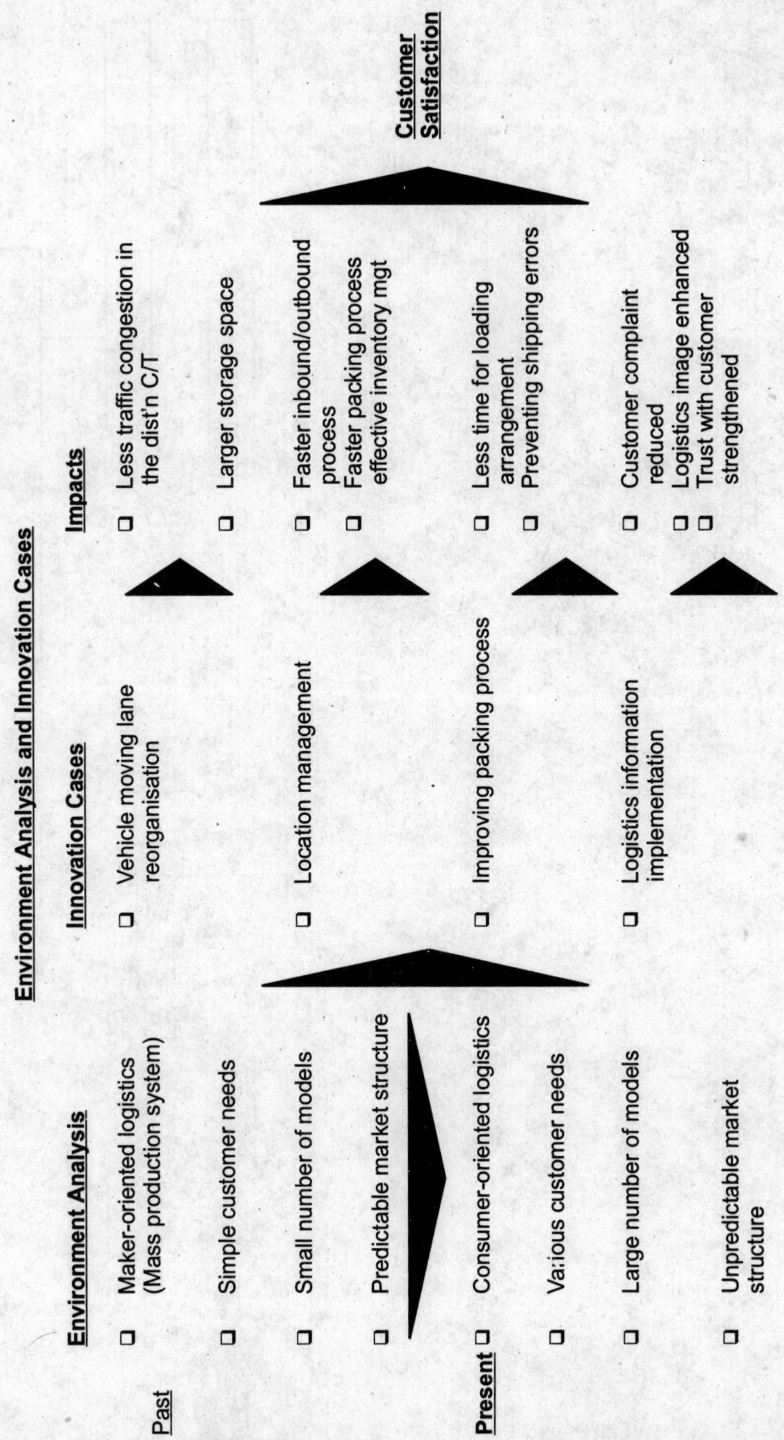

CHAPTER

30

physical distribution management – transportation and warehousing

learning objectives

The objectives of this chapter are to:

- understand activities of physical distribution
- describe transport infrastructure
- discuss distribution agreement specimen.

content outline

- Introduction
- Transportation
- Modes of Transportation
- Distribution Agreement Specimen
- Warehouses
- Summary
- Project Work
- Short Answer Questions
- Review Questions
- Go to the Net

INTRODUCTION

Sales service requires that a company should have a good infrastructure to make its goods' services available at the required time at the desired place.

For this purpose an infrastructure has to be created with the following objectives in mind:

1. To use the existing set up in any company towards the distribution of goods.
2. To minimise the cost of such a set up so that distribution costs are in no way higher that the competition's.
3. To have a maximum reach, so that goods are available far and wide and customers are able to buy them as and when they require.
4. To minimise time in distribution of goods from company's premises to the distributor or the consumer.
5. To take care of the future requirements of the distribution system, using modern handling devices and reducing cost in delivery times.

Hence, the physical distribution should fill all the logistic requirements needed for any product, that is why it is called logistic management.

Definition

Physical distribution management refers to:

"The management of all activities which facilitate movement and coordination of supply and demand in the creation of time and place utility in goods."

A more comprehensive definition of the physical distribution management may be:

"The term physical distribution management employed in manufacturing and commerce is used to describe the broad range of activities with the efficient movement of finished products from the end of production line to the consumer and, in some cases, includes the movement of raw materials from the source of supply to the beginning of the production line."

The above activities can be summarised as:

1. Transportation
2. Warehousing
3. Packing and packaging
4. Handling of materials
5. Maintenance of stocks, inventory controls
6. Orders, processing, dispatch
7. Customer services, complaints, redressals
8. Maintenance of records related to these activities.

These activities have been illustrated in Figure 30.1 below.

figure 30.1

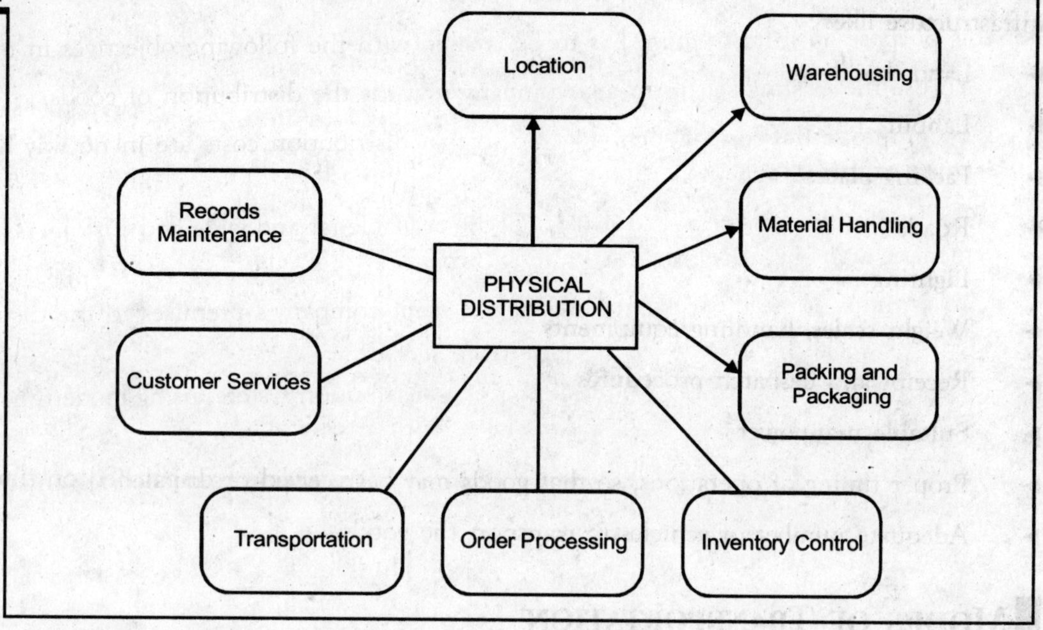

Therefore, in order to be a successful company in physical distribution, it is essential that efforts should be coordinated in such a manner that maximum utilisation of resources/activities takes place with minimum costs.

TRANSPORTATION

Transportation is an essential feature for any business activity. Goods need to be transported from one place to another. They are manufactured in the factory and afterwards they are sent to various destinations and then to the actual user or consumer.

Transportation system in an organisation should be:

- Efficient
- Economic
- Reliable
- Meeting customer needs in a timely manner
- Experienced
- Capable of meeting emergencies, special needs.

The job of transportation is usually handled by the marketing manager, who gives direct responsibility to the godown incharge/warehouse superintendent or an officer entrusted with such work solely. In big organisations, where movement of goods is very quick and volume is high, this activity is carried out by a separate department, the transportation department.

Transport Infrastructure

In order to be successful in managing a good transportation system, a company has to plan for a proper infrastructure like:

- Land, building
- Labour
- Packing places
- Roads
- Lighting
- Weight scales, handling equipments
- Receipt and despatch procedures
- Suitable manpower
- Proper timing of operations, so that goods may be received or dispatched on time.
- Adequate number of vehicles to transport the goods.

MODES OF TRANSPORTATION

The following modes of transportation are used keeping in mind the goods and places where they are to be sent and the volume of goods:

1. Railways
2. Road Transportation
3. Air Transportation
4. Sea Transportation (Marine)
5. Inland Waterways
6. Ropeways
7. Postal
8. Courier
9. Hand carts, Thelas, Rehres, Cycle Rickshaws,
10. Bullock carts, etc.

Railways

Railways are most established and spread throughout the country. They have a wide network. Good transportation is one of the important activities of Indian Railways.

Thousands of railway stations, located in various parts of the country, accept goods which are taken to the desired destination and special loads, or special cargo are handled by them efficiently. There is a continuous stream of goods trains, covering thousands of kilometres, every day.

Bulk cargo like coal, cement, wheat, agricultural produce, export cargo, import cargo are specialities of railways.

The major benefits of railway transportation are:

- Fast in service, specially when it is full load or export cargo
- Freight rates are lower
- Goods are kept in sealed wagons/boxes, so chances of breakage are less
- Small consignments can also be booked through railways
- Railway receipts are authentic documents and are acceptable for negotiation purpose by banks
- Minimum barriers/check posts and so much time is not lost in hold ups.

Road Transportation

Road transportation is very well developed in India. There are thousand of kilometres of roads. There are state and national highways on which trucks are plying uninterrupted from east to west and north to south and in all directions.

Main vehicles used in road transportation are:

- Trucks (HMV- Heavy Motor Vehicles)
- Tempos (Medium vehicles)
- Tractors
- Containers.

The main advantage of transporting goods through motor vehicles (road) may be summarised as follows:

- Speedy
- Warehouse to warehouse delivery possible
- Competitive freight rates from many commodities
- No need of transhipment/loading or unloading
- Minimum breakages, damages to goods
- Easy to settle claims with transport companies, as they care for clients.

Airways

Transporting the goods through air is also very common, when the goods are required urgently or where other modes of transportation either do not exist or they are equally costly.

Airline companies carry the goods in their usual flights, depending upon the load factor. They also run cargo flights on national and international routes.

Air cargo is very suitable when the goods are of high value, perishable or small in volume.

The most important thing to remember about air services is that they are quite costly, particularly when the goods are heavy.

Marine Transportation (Sea Routes)

Sending goods through sea routes has been going on for centuries. Most of the international trade is carried by sea vessels, who pick the cargo from one destination and deliver them to the other.

Sea transportation is economically suitable for bulk consignments and heavy goods. The major problem arises when the goods are needed urgently. In such a situation the sea route may not be convenient because it takes too long.

Inland waterways:

Where rivers are navigable, this mode of transportation is quite popular. In our country, inland waterways are existing in eastern India, particularly Bengal and Bihar. Small vessels carry goods as well as passengers. Since India is rich in water resources and there are number of rivers which are navigable, there is great scope for this mode of transportation which can prove to be quite economical.

Ropeways

Transportation of goods through ropeways is common in hilly areas where other modes of transportation may not exist.

Postal Authorities

Postal authorities have created their network throughout the country where they accept goods which are sent to destinations in India and all over the world.

Postal transportation uses various modes like aircrafts, trucks, vans, tempos, railways to carry their goods. Postal authorities have certain restrictions on the volume of one consignment or its measurements which can be found out from the department concerned.

Courier Services

Private courier services have developed a speedy and efficient network to transport the goods from one destination to another. They also use the various available modes of transport including manpower to cater to the needs of their clients and their urgency.

Hand Carts, Bullock Carts, etc.

These are various other means by which goods are transported from one destination to another. These may include

- Hand carts
- Bullock carts
- Tongas
- Rehras
- Cycle rickshaws
- Camel, etc.

Much depends upon the needs of the goods and distances involved. For small distances, and small loads these are the most appropriate means of transportation.

Selection of any mode of transportation, therefore, will depend upon the nature of the goods, distances involved, time at the disposal and security and safety of the goods. A good system should possess all these qualities.

Therefore, in order to be a successful company in physical distribution, it is essential that efforts should be coordinated in such a manner that maximum utilization of resources/activities takes place with minimum cost.

DISTRIBUTION AGREEMENT SPECIMEN

(Between a fast moving consumer goods company and its distributor)

From:

M/s ABC+ Co
New Delhi

To

M/s XYZ + Co
Ghaziabad (UP)

Dear Sirs,

We have pleasure in appointing you as one of our Confectionery Division Distributors at Ghaziabad w.e.f. 21.05.98 on the following terms and conditions:

1. The goods will be supplied to you in bulk treating the same as outright purchase by you prior to their distribution and you shall pay for the same by means of a banker's draft in advance (bank commission to your account) at New Delhi payable within two days of invoicing.

2. Price: The confectionery products of the company will be sold to you at the company list price applicable from time to time. This will, however, be subject to the following deductions:

   a. For products sold with a 'tax inclusive price', a deduction representing the element of taxes applicable to the product in your state/town, which, for the purpose of identification, has been designated by the company as Price Equalisation Discount.

   b. For all products, where applicable, a deduction on account of other trade discounts in accordance with the schemes which may be in operation from time to time.

   The discounts available under (a) and (b) above will be intimated to you in advance by our Field Staff.

3. Discounts: You will be entitled to a general trade discount of 6% on all products which will be calculated on the net price consideration after deducting the other trade discounts if and where applicable, as mentioned under price above.

4. Payment Terms: As per the general policy of the company, the payment is required to be made by a demand draft to be deposited in advance of supplies. However, the company, has, in your case, extended special facility as mentioned in clause (l) above. It is, however, clearly understood

that such special facility will continue to remain in force only so long as the company, at its discretion may vary or withdraw the same totally without assigning any reason.

5. The appointment does not give you any territorial right and we reserve the right to increase the number of distributors in your own town.

6. You shall, at all times, endeavour your best efforts to promote the business interest of the company and shall fully cooperate with the company in all its sales promotion schemes.

7. The basic prices chargeable by you to the trade can be less but in no circumstances more than the company's list price plus local taxes if and as applicable to the goods. The condition should be read as part of every price list that may be issued by the company from time to time.

8. You shall fully comply with the operating instructions of the company relating to proper storage, transport, distribution, payment, etc., of the company's goods supplied to you (Detailed instructions overleaf).

9. It is clearly understood that either of us will be free to terminate this agreement at will, simply by one party giving to the other, one calendar month's notice in writing and any such termination will not entitle either party to any indemnity, damage or compensation whatsoever.

   Provided the company shall be entitled to terminate the agreement with you if:

   a. You are found to be indulging in any undesirable trade practices which are contrary to the interest of the parties to this agreement such as overcharging, etc.

   b. Any legal dispute arising out of this agreement on any matter incidental or ancillary thereof shall be subject to the jurisdiction of the Courts situated at Delhi.

Please signify your consent to the above terms and conditions by signing and returning to us the duplicate copy of this agreement.

Thanking You,

Yours very truly,

Accepted

For XYZ +Co.	For ABC + Co.
sd/-	sd/-
Partner	Zonal Manager

Operating Instructions

Terms of Payment

As you are aware, the company supplies its goods to you on the basis of your ex-godown or shop. For your better understanding of the terms, we would like to give clarifications as under:

a. **Cost/Charges to Be Borne by the Company**

   1. Expense, if any, incurred by you in clearing and transporting the consignments from railhead/ transporter's godown to your godown.

2. Freight, non-refundable or non-revertible octroi or such expenses which are not in the nature of expenses at (b) below in respect of outstation despatches.

   The above expenses will be reimbursed to you through a credit note and you will be entitled to adjust the same against remittances that you will be making for the supply of goods.

b. Cost/Expenses to your Account

- Expenses by you in loading, unloading, cartage of your outstation despatches upto the railhead/transporter's godown.
- Expenses by you in loading, unloading and delivering the consignments in your town.

c. Interest on Delayed Payments

If you fail to make payments as per the terms stipulated, you will be liable to pay interest in the form of penalty at the rate of 0.1 % per day of default subject to a minimum penalty of 1 %.

d. Payment for Short/ Damaged Delivery

In the event the consignments are received by you in damaged condition or if you notice any shortages at the time of delivery, it will be absolutely necessary for you to make the relevant remarks on the accompanying documents, which should be countersigned by the person delivering the goods. This will enable you to recover the amount from the transporter. If you fail to follow this procedure and if the company is not able to recover the amount from the transporter, the company will not be liable to make good such shortages or damages.

Proper Storing of Goods

As you are aware, the company's goods supplied to you for resale are governed by the Food Legislations and other standards relating to proper storage, hygiene, date of expiry, etc. To enable you to ensure proper compliance with all these requirements, you are requested to strictly adhere to the following guidelines

1. Stocks should be sold strictly on the principle of, 'First In First Out' so as to avoid older stocks remaining unsold.
2. The goods should be properly stacked on wooden pallets and the stacking should be slightly away from the walls so as to protect them against damage by heat, leakage of monsoon water, fungal growths, pests or odorous material, etc.
3. You must also undertake regular pest control measures where company's products are stored on the basis of the guidelines issued.
4. A signboard reading 'The stocks of products stored in this godown are for distribution subject to the terms and conditions of the agreement subsisting between us and the company have no lien on these stocks" should be prominently displayed where goods bought from us are stored.
5. The stocks which are badly dented or damaged or where the date of expiry is over or which are returned as bad or complained goods should be stored in a separate room with a signboard reading "Not For Sale". This is absolutely essential with a view to avoid the sampling of such bad goods by the food inspector. Please note that if you fail to comply with this condition, you will

not be protected by the company's warranty regarding the quality of goods in respect of such dented/damaged goods, etc.

6. Wherever the date of expiry or shelf life in number of months and year of manufacture is printed on the container, it shall be your responsibility to dispose of the goods before such expiry date and the company will not be liable for any action that may be taken against you by the concerned authorities for the storage or selling of such expired goods.

The company will be at liberty to depute representatives to visit your premises where the goods supplied by the company are stored by you so as to ensure proper compliance with the above guidelines and the instructions issued in this regard by such representatives shall be carried out by you immediately.

WAREHOUSES

A warehouse plays an important role in the physical distribution system; it is used to make the best possible arrangement for keeping the goods for some time till they are sent to the final destination.

"A warehouse is a location with proper facilities where shipments are received from a factory or production centre, broken down, reassembled, and shipped to the customers as per their orders ," It is also defined as:
"a building in which goods are stored, bonded or displayed for sale."

Advantages

The warehouse provides the following main advantages

1. Reduces distribution costs.
2. Is easily accessible to the customers or is located near the market, resulting in better and finer distribution.

Cost of Warehouse

A warehouse costs money. It should be located near to the market, where good roads exist and there are minimum traffic movement restrictions. Some other factors affecting costs of warehouses are

1. Availability of cheap land
2. Easy accessibility
3. Low construction costs
4. Availability of power
5. Availability of water
6. Convenient connection
7. Safety/security of goods
8. No danger of floods/(higher plinths)
9. No water/dampness.

Types of Warehouses

The warehouses can be classified into two categories

1. ***Public warehouse:*** These are those which can be used by the public at large. They are constructed by government agencies and corporate houses to meet the needs of a particular type of goods. Businessmen can rent out the space which they need from the warehouse owners, who keep the goods stocked properly at the required temperature and deliver back the goods when they are demanded by the owner of the goods.
2. ***Private warehouse:*** These facilities are created by individuals or companies to meet their requirements. If they have extra space available, they let it out to others also. Many private warehouses are quite modern, systematic, strategically located in areas where goods are safe from the safety point of view.

Strong

Goods are stored in a warehouse at the demarcated place. There are different compartments for storing different types of goods. It is desirable that there be clear pathways to ensure checking of goods from time to time so that they do not lose their commercial value. Maintaining of proper temperatures, lighting, protection from rains, heat, cold and moisture are the other arrangements which the cold storage/warehouse owners are supposed to make.

Facilities Offered by a Warehouse:

Warehouse is supposed to provide the following service to its customers/users:

a. Temporary storage facilities

b. Proper stacking of goods

c. Ease of accepting/handling the goods at the warehouse premises.

d. Easy to deliver goods after the storing period

e. Informing the customer about any deterioration in the condition of the goods and taking remedial measures

f. To install proper safety measures including fire fighting equipment and to see that they are in working order

g. Safety from insects and rodents

h. To provide sales promotional services

i. To charge reasonable fees/charges for the services rendered.

Classification of Warehouse

Warehouses can be classified into the following categories

1. General warehouse
2. Bonded warehouse
3. Cold storages

4. Warehouses meant for agricultural goods
5. Buffer storage warehouses
6. Import-export warehouses.

Warehouse Capacity

Warehouse capacities are decided after keeping various factors in mind such as :

1. Type of material handled
2. Period for which it is handled (storage period)
3. Existence of similar warehouse
4. Scope for future expansion
5. Handling system used
6. Requirement of office and other space requirements
7. Parking space for vehicles.

Retail management is aware of the selling strategy. To establish the good team, managers search for the good professional, and pay them good salary and trained them. Them people who want to make their career in retail industry should start their career with sales. Apart good capability of selling, most retail sales people would like to move towards areas of the industry as soon as possible for them. In a retail store, the professional which hired mostly belong to the sales background.

Sales Process

Analysis of Retail Marketing and Sales Gap

Since last centuries, city are functioned as the commercial hub, government, and social hubs of the places where people came together to conduct their business, administrator government, share their experience, and celebrate their festival. But western communities have found new series of transformations over the past several decades that have changed the economies of the nation's downtowns. Many of these transformations are due to the expanding highway system, which enhance suburban development and made it possible for person to move farther away form town centers. As people have moved outward, the retail industry - always a market follower, rather than a market leader - has moved outward, also. With the adverse regional shopping malls and discount superstores, retailing store - the bedrock of a traditional main street district's economic foundation has slowly eroded. This market erosion is largely the result of retail overbuilding over the past five decades, as retail space has expanded at a rate far beyond the ability of most communities to absorb it. In addition to the change in the practical approach of retail space over the past five decades, retail has also become more systematic and strategic.

Generally Retail are classified into three categories.

Destination: Retail goods and services for which shoppers will travel significantly distances. These might include special types of business, large clusters of related businesses, or businesses that offer exceptional service and that have developed a very loyal clientele.

Convenience: Retail goods and services for which shoppers tend to patronize the closest business, like gas stations, dry cleaners, and grocery stores. "Impulse" retail - like card shops, florists, and gourmet cookies - also fall into this category.

Comparison: Retail goods and services for which shoppers like to do compare in styles, brands and prices before making a purchase, like apparel, shoes and furniture. For this reason, comparison retail businesses tend to cluster together, and a comparison business is likely to be more successful if located in a cluster than if it is freestanding, without related businesses nearby.

Sales gap analysis is initially a measurement of the extent to which a community's own residents are making retail purchases locally, the basic tools and techniques involved in sales gap analysis can also be used for finding out potential retail sales to people who live outside the community and for establishing sales goals and benchmarks over a period of time. While online shopping expanding exponentially every year, the marketplace for many downtown businesses is shifting from local to global, making it possible for businesses that would have been dependent almost exclusively on purchases by community residents and visitors a decade or two ago to reach customers almost anywhere worldwide. This means - among other things - that, with a good marketing plan and a solid understanding of e-commerce, highly specialized retail businesses can locate in historic downtown districts without necessarily needing to rely primarily on locally-generated sales.

Sales gap analysis provides the detail information about commercial district realization programs, offering insight both into the current condition of the district and also into areas for possible development and economic expansion. But, just as it answers many questions about how to economically restructure the district, it also opens up many more questions that can be answered only with further research (by conducting consumer surveys, for example). Even so, a sales gap analysis provides a solid starting point for defining the market-based strategies the district's revitalization initiative will pursue in the coming years.

Distribution of the products and services depends on supply chain management. Distribution channel builds many advantages, since marketing channels are of long-range planning an implementation, and to build them needs a consistent structure and due also to the fact that they are focused on people and relationships.

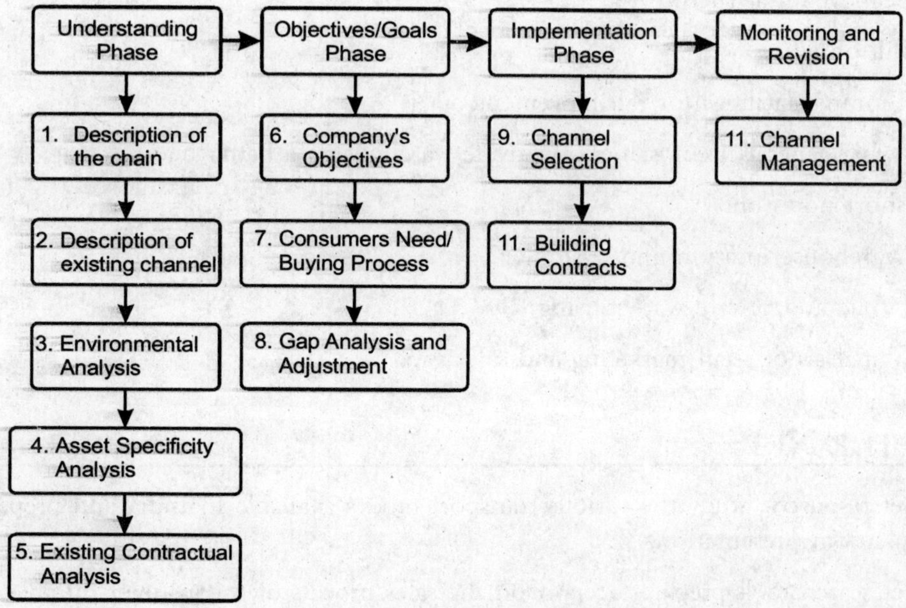

SUMMARY

The important role that transport plays in national economy has generally not been appreciated by national planners and managers in developing countries.

Transport of the finished product is often left to marketing managers. However, a marketing manager is oriented more towards marketing of the product and development of market than towards optimisation of cost, time or effort.

The concept of a distribution warehouse or a distribution centre is vastly different from the earlier concept of a godown for storage. The godown is usually a dumping place. In India, the subject of physical distribution management has been neglected by the industry, business as well as the government because there is no adequate infrastructure.

PROJECT WORK

Study the five types of warehouses and make a report on their facilities.

SHORT ANSWER QUESTIONS

1. What are the modes of transportation?
2. What are the types of warehouses?
3. What is the difference between logistics and physical distribution?
4. What is sales process?

REVIEW QUESTIONS

1. Write short notes on:
   a. Goods movement on Indian Railways
   b. Seaport infrastructure
   c. Bill of lading
   d. Terminal facilities for rail movement.
2. Under what general circumstances is private warehousing a better choice?
3. Write short notes on:
   a. Warehouse location and customer
   b. Public and private warehousing
4. Explain analysis of retail marketing and sales gap.

GO TO THE NET

Using Internet resources, study the various transport modes available in India and prepare a detailed report for classroom presentation.

Using Internet search tools prepare a report on the sales process of 5 consumer durable goods.

BLOCK

New Techniques of Managing Distribution

VI

In organisational marketing, producers often sell directly to their final buyers and so are linked to their final buyer in marketing channels. Such direct channels are much less common in consumer product marketing. Ultimate consumers make most of their purchases in retail stores that are independent of the producer. Retailing, therefore, is the final stage in marketing channels for consumer products. Retailers provide the important link between the producer and the ultimate consumer.

Retailing is a lot more than simply buying and selling. It is important to consumers because it creates economic utility. It is important to manufacturers because it is the major connection in the marketing channel between manufacturers and end-users. And it is important because of its contribution to the economy.

The block covers two chapters which highlight the importance of new techniques of managing distribution.

CHAPTER

retail management

31

learning objectives

The objectives of this chapter are to:

- understand role and importance of Retail Management
- discuss different types of Merchandise
- describe function and importance of Retail Market Strategy.

content outline

- Opening Case
- Introduction
- Retail Industry
- Characteristics of Retailer
- Types of Merchandise
- Food Retailers
- Non-stores Retail Formats
- Types of Ownership
- Retail Market Strategy
- Growth Strategies
- The Strategic Retail Planning
- Summary
- Project Report
- Short Questions
- Review Questions
- Go to the Net
- Caselet

opening case

Just when most of the new multinational cosmetic players are taking a hard look at their Indian business, the £ 12 billion French company, L'Oreal, is slowly and steadily making a splash. If there is any serious competitor to the established Lakme-Lever it is L'Oreal, industry watchers say.

Already, while most of the players have been reworking their India strategy, L'Oreal with an estimated turnover of Rs. 12 crore has been working to script. A script which has seen it gradually unfurl a portfolio in the various categories of the Rs. 1,300 crore Indian cosmetics market. From shampoos to skin care to hair colour, it has taken competition head on with the Maybeline range of coloured cosmetics.

L'Oreal's Indian strategy is simple; identify the gaps and plug them. Instead of launching a clutch of products at the same time, it has gone in for a slow and steady, well-paced portfolio expansion. After establishing an equity with premium products, it is now attacking the mass markets. Says Geoof Skiingsley, Managing Director Indelor, the fully owned subsidiary of the L'Oreal group. "Our strategy is largely product features driven. We are trying to introduce new products and categories that are already existing in other markets.

In a way, L'Oreal used niche products to test the market before plunging headlong with mass based brands. Like after the high priced skincare and haircare brand, the newly launched maybeline colour cosmetics is clearly competitively pitched. And this has got competition worried. "After Hindustan Lever, L'Oreal has the largest portfolio of brands which is making us very alert to market demands," says a Lakme manager.

Worldwide, the L'Oreal group has over 900 brands in cosmetics alone. In fact, last year cosmetics with brands in hair care, skin care, make up, sun care, toiletries and perfumes accounted for 81.3 percent of the total turnover. This was followed by producers in pharma 17 percent, dermatology 1.1 percent and others (0.6 percent).

In India, too, cosmetics and toiletries has been their mainstay. This when competitors are reshuffling portfolios and abandoning the market. A few months ago, the £ 4.5 billion Benckiser pulled out of India after slogging it out for four years. Recently, Modi Revlon deserted the skincare segment and is reworking its marketing strategy to focus on colour cosmetics. It is also developing the beauty parlour channel. Delhi based Oriflame and Avon's direct marketing strategy has not made much of a dent with the consumer. Most of these players have realized the need for differentiated products at different price points to survive in the extremely fragmented Indian market.

And L'Oreal hasn't been in a great hurry. It has entered Indian with two of its mainline umbrella brands- Laboratories Garnier and L'Oreal Paris. Lancome, another umbrella brand is being imported and retails at some of the upmarkets stores in Mumbai and Delhi. But the launch pad was Garnier's Ultra Doux shampoo in 1991.

Today, the brand has only a one percent share in the Rs. 550 crore shampoo category. This was followed by the Garnier's Synergie skin care range and the Excellent.

Syas Binita Kripalani, marketing director, Indelor, "We decided to get into skin care first because hair colour is very difficult of manufacture and we would have had to import the product which was not allowed. "The foray into skin care helped build the distribution channels and establish the L'Oreal name. Apart from one or two basic moisturizers and a facewash, the Synergie range consisted of differentiated products like anti-wrinkle cream, day cream and night wear cream.

By staying clear of the extremely competitive basic category, L'Oreal evolved products focus helped it gain a toehold in the Rs. 750 crore skin care segment. It did so by launching only non-basic, special benefit offerings. It concentrated on building entirely new categories according to the needs that were tapped by continuous research. Says Skingsley, "The degree of persuasiveness required to build new categories based on entirely new products is immense.

Although Synergie has been able to garner only three percent of the Rs. 850 crore skin care market, certain product in the line like the wrinkle free formulation is used by around one third of the two million targeted users. Says Skingsley," According to the needs tapped we have launched a select portfolio of products and our effort is to create product features led categories.

There was a distinct need for an age controlling product among the 40 plus consumers in the 13-19 million urban educated women segment. In this Rs. 250 crore niche segment, lakme is the market leader with a 34 percent share. It is followed by Synergie at 27 percent and Pond's at 23 percent.

Last year L'Oreal made a foray into the Rs. 48 crore hair colour category. Internationally, hair care accounts for 45 percent of the entire L'Oreal portfolio. The Indian hair dye market was largely dominated by Godrej which had 78 percent market share and JK Helene Curti's Trutone, besides a range of herbal dye from the unorganized sector. Hair dye was perceived as an undesirable but necessary product with no aspiration or pleasurable associations.

The L'Oreal strategy for hair colour was similar. Says Kriplani, "Our objectives was to change the existing perceptions about hair colour and to expand the segment in India. Earlier hair colour addressed only those who were greying but we wanted to expand the user base to those who used colour for style. "Which meant appealing to entirely new users".

To make this happen, booklets and leaflets were given to retailers and around 50 sales persons spent time educating the retailers about the products and destroying existing myths about hair colour. Excellence Cream and Castings is now available in around 3,000 retail outlets. Currently the hair colour products have achieved around 12 percent penetration in the category, even as Godrej dominates the market with a share of 78 percent.

Realising the optimism over such product and the lack of awareness and research on the category, L'Oreal decided to tap the influencers. Last year, it set up the salon division and launched L'Oreal Professional. World over, the Professional Division was introduced to rope in the beauty parlours and hairdressers. This was not in keeping with their international trend of taking the professional route before the consumer. Says are more in touch with our target customer and to provide exclusively of product portfolio. We decided to launch separate brands under the professional division. There products Majirel, Diacolour and Osmose came under the hair colour, hair care, perm and cutting categories."

Research conducted by the company revealed that there was serious need for technical training. So, L'Oreal decided to cultivate this very important channel through which they could tap the beauty needs of their target segment. So far, L'Oreal has around 2,500 hair dressers which stock its product – Majirel, Diacolour (non – ammonia which it launched recently), Perm and hair care and Osmose conditioner, Osmose was launched when customers using L'Oreal products expressed the need for a hair care shampoo or conditioner.

Having established a presence, L'Oreal has how positioned Maybelline as a technologically, superior product in the Rs. 500 crore cosmetics market. Says Kingsley, "Quality aspirations of Indian consumers are the same. The three sub areas of differentiating are price value perceptions, choice and the retail experience," Adds Sunita Bagard, product manager for Maybelline, "The price premium is very reasonable given the value provided by each of the products in the basket." In fact, it is the cheapest of all the new foreign brands and is today, in the Rs. 500 crore colour cosmetics market, Lakme, along with its sub-brands Elle 19 and Orchids has a 54 percent share. It is followed by Tips and Toes at seven percent and Revlon at three percent. In the next three years, L'Oreal wants to be the number one or two player in each of its product categories. And it knows that talking of Lakme Lever is not going to be carewalk.

TRY YOURSELF

1. What research design has been for this study?
2. Prepare a sample questionnaire which might be used to collect data for this study.

INTRODUCTION

Retailing is the final step in the distribution of merchandise – the last link in the Supply Chain – connecting the bulk producers of commodities to the final consumers. Retailing covers diverse products such as fruits and vegetables, food and grocery, apparels, jewellery, utensils, books, stationery, consumer goods, financial services, hotel and tourism and leisure.

A retailer, typically, is someone who breaks the bulk, makes products or services available to the consumer whenever required and thus offers a value proposition to a consumer by creating easy availabilities of the desired product in the desired sizes at the desired times.

The retail industry has developed into a full-fledged industry in America and Europe where more than three-fourths of the total retail trade is done by the organized retailers. The Table 31.1 below gives a list of world's top ten retailers.

table 31.1 **Top 10 Retailers**

Ranking by annualized USS retail sales	2005	2006
Wal-Mart Stores Inc.	1	1
Carrefour SA	2	2
Tesco Plc	3	3
Seven & I Holdings Co. Ltd.	5	4
Kroger Corp.	4	5
Target Corp.	6	6
The Home Depot Inc.	7	7
Walgreen Co.	12	8
Aldi Group	10	9
Royal Ahold NV	8	10

RETAIL INDUSTRY

The retail industry is changing rapidly. Some of the most important changes discussed in this section involve (1) the greater diversity of retailers, (2) increasing industry concentration, (3) globalization, and (4) the use of multiple channels to interact with customers. The first three trends are discussed below. The development of multichannel retailing-retailing through stores, catalogs, and the internet-to better serve their customers and compete in today's complex retail environment.

About half of the consumers in a recent survey made at least one catalog purchase in a year. Over half of the women surveyed made surveyed made at least one catalog purchase, compared to 36 percent of the men. The average household receives 1.9 catalogs and a similar number of direct mail solicitations per week. However, households that patronize catalog retailers receives three times as many catalogs as the average household.

Types of catalog and Direct mail retailers' two types of firms selling product through the mail are (1) general merchandise and specialty catalog retailers and (2) direct mail retailers. General merchandise catalog retailers offer a broad variety of merchandise in catalog that are periodically mailed to their customers. Direct mail retailers typically mail brochures and pamphlets to sell a specific product or service to customer at one point in time. In addition to the focus on a specific product or service, most direct-mail retailers are primarily interested in making a single sale form a specific mailing, whereas catalog retailers typically maintain relationship with customers over time.

Issues in Catalog retailing: Catalog retailing can be an attractive business opportunity because the start-up costs are relatively low. On the other hand, catalog retailing can be very challenging. First, it is difficult for smaller catalog and direct-mail retailers to compete with large, well-established firms that have embraced a multichannel strategy. The internet has become a natural extension to most catalogers selling strategy. Ninety five percent of catalogers describe themselves as multichannel retailers, with 53 percent defining their companies as catalog/Internet/retailer and 42 percent as catalog/Internet. Second, the mailing and printing costs are high and increasing. Third, it is difficult to get consumers attention as they are mailed so many catalogs and direct mail promotions. Finally, the length of time required to design, develop, and distribute catalogs makes it difficult for catalog and direct-mail retailers to respond quickly to new trends and fashions. Most analyses believe that the future will bring a seamless multichannel offering that integrates catalogs, the Internet, and often bricks-and-mortar stores.

Direct Selling

Direct selling is a retail format in which salesperson, frequently an independent businessperson, contact a customer directly in a convenient location, either at the customer's home or at work, and demonstrates merchandise benefits, takes an order, and delivers the merchandise to the customer. Direct selling is a highly interactive form of retailing in which considerable information is conveyed to customers through face-to-face discussion with a salesperson. However, providing this high level of information, including extensive demonstrations, is costly.

Almost all of the 11 million salespeople who work in direct sales are independent agents. They aren't employed by the direct sales firm but act as independent distributor, buying merchandise form the firms and then reselling it to consumers. Eighty three percent of the salespeople work part-time (less than 30 hours per week). In most cases, direct salespeople may sell their merchandise to anyone.

Retailing is a labor-intensive business. Employees play a major role in providing services for customers and building customer loyalty. Knowledgeable and skilled employees committed to the retailer's objectives are critical assets that support the success of companies. Recruiting and retaining great employees does not come easy. Retailers gain a sustainable competitive advantage by developing programs to motivate and coordinate employee efforts, by providing appropriate incentives, by fostering a strong and positive organizational culture and environment, and by managing diversity.

Distribution and Information System

All retailers strive for efficient operations. They want to get their customers the merchandise they want, when they want it, in the quantities that are required, at a lower delivered cost than their competitors. By so doing, they will satisfy their customer's needs and, at the same time, either provide them with lower-priced merchandise than their competition or decide to use the additional margin to attract customers from competitors by offering even better service, merchandise assortments, and visual presentations.

Retailers can achieve these efficiencies by developing sophisticated distribution and information systems.

Unique Merchandise

It is difficult for retailers to develop a competitive advantage through merchandise because competitor can purchase and sell the same popular national brands. But many retailers realize a sustainable competitive advantage by developing private-label brand (also called store brands), which are product developed and marketed by a retailer and available only from that retailer.

Vendor Relations

By developing strong relations with vendors, retailers may gain exclusive rights (1) to sell merchandise in a region, (2) to obtain special terms of purchase that are not available to competitor who lack such relations, or (3) to receive popular merchandise in short supply. Relationships with vendors, like relationships with customers, are developed over a long time and may not be easily offset by a competitor.

Customer Service

Retailers also build a sustainable competitive advantage by offering excellent customer services. But offering good services consistently is difficult. Customer service is provided by retail employees – and they are less consistent than machines. Retailer that offer good customer service instill its importance in their employees over a long period of time. It becomes part of the retailer's organizational culture.

Definition of Retail Formats

A retail format represents a specific configuration of the retail marketing mix (store size, typical location, merchandise, price and services offered) and it often forms the core of the retail strategy.

A retail format is the overall appearance and feel that it represents to the customers, primarily its look and layout, the sort of product range and the approach adopted for pricing.

It is basically the arrangement of overall retailing adopted by the retailer.

Retailers have various ways of meeting customer needs through organizing and designing their retail outlets.

From a managerial point of view, it is very important to understand the different types of retail institutions because they have a competitive impact on the retail business. There are several types of retail formats. Each format represents a specific retailing strategy.

Growing Diversity of Retail Formats

Over the past 20 years, many new retail formats have been developed. Consumer now can purchase the same merchandise from a wider variety of retailers. The initial category specializes in toys, consumer electronics, and home improvement supplies have been joined by a host of new specialists. The Internet has spawned a new set of retailers offering consumers the opportunity to buy merchandise and services at fixed prices, participate in auctions or submit "take-it-or-leave-it" bids.

Each type of retailer offers a different set of benefits, thus consumers patronize different retailers for different purchase occasions. For example, a consumer might purchase a pair of cargo pants from a catalog as a gift for a friend in another city and then visit a local store to try on and buy the same pants for himself. The greater diversity of retail formats increase competition in the industry and also enable consumers to buy merchandise and services from a retailer that better satisfies their needs for specific purchase occasions.

Increasing Industry Concentration

While the number of different retail formats has grown, the number of competitors within each format is decreasing. A few national retailers dominate most formats.

Globalization

Historically, retailing has been a local business. Stores were owned and operated by people living in the community and patronize by local residents. Today, however, some retailing concepts that are successful in their country of origin have successfully developed a global presence. The reason why some retail concepts work globally, and why some do not, are usually dependent on what provides their sustainable competitive advantage in their home country. McDonald's and KFC appeal to hungry people everywhere. For every successful global retailer, there is another that has failed.

Some factors stimulating retail globalization are the maturation of domestic markets, the development of skills and systems to effectively manage global operations, and the removal of trade barriers.

Maturation of Domestic Markets: Most large retailers have saturated their domestic markets. Growth oriented retailers often see greater opportunities in other countries.

Skills and Systems: Today's retailers are better prepared to effectively manage stores in non-domestic markets. Their expertise in managing information and distribution systems is easily transferable to market. Many have learned that global merchandise sourcing can provide their customers with a better selection and value. Global sourcing and sophisticated information and distribution system make global expansion easier to do.

Trade Barriers: Finally the relaxation of trade barriers makes global expansion easier. While there are millions of retailers across the globe, there are limited numbers of retail institutions.

CHARACTERISTICS OF RETAILER

Each retailer survives and prospers by satisfying a group of consumers' needs more effectively than its competitors. Over time, different types of retailers have emerged and prosper by satisfying a group of consumer's needs more effectively than its competitors. Over time, different types of retailers have emerged and prospered because they have attracted and maintained a significant customer base.

The most basic characteristic of a retailer is its retail mix- the elements used by a retailer to satisfy its customers' needs. Four elements of the retail mix are particularly useful for classifying retailers: the type of merchandise sold the variety and assortment of merchandise sold the level of customer service, and the price of the merchandise. Retailers often shop at their competitors' stores to compare their retail offering with the competition.

Price Cost Trade off

As you read about the different types of retailers, notice how patterns among retail mix element arise. For example, department stores appeal to consumers looking for fashionable apparel and home furnishings. Typically, department stores have higher price because they have higher costs due to stocking a lot of fashionable merchandise, discounting merchandise when errors are made in forecasting consumer taste, providing some personal sale service, and having convenient but expensive mall locations. On the other hand, discount stores appeal to customers who are looking for lower prices and are less interested in services and a wide range of merchandise sizes and colours.

This difference between the retail mix of department and discount stores illustrate the trade-off retailers make between the price and assortment of merchandise they sell and the service they offer to their customers. Offering more sizes, colours, and brands; making the store atmosphere more attractive and entertaining; and increasing the staff of knowledgeable sales associates raises the retailer's costs. To make a profit and provide these additional benefits to their customers, department stores have to increase the price of their merchandise to cover the additional costs.

TYPES OF MERCHANDISE

The classification scheme for food retailers: The first two digits 44 and 45 denote the retail sector. (Restaurants have been moved to sector 72 accommodation and food services). The third digit denotes the sub-sector. The fourth digit represents the industry group. Thus, under sub-sector 448, clothing and clothing accessory stores, we have 4481 (clothing stores) and 4482 (shoe stores). The fifth digit provides a further breakdown-44811 is men's clothing stores, whereas 44812 is women's clothing stores. The last digit, and not always used, may differ between the three countries. The annual sales of the larger categories as reported by the retail trade.

While retailer's principal competitors may be other retailers with the same, there are many exceptions. For example, clothing's primary designation is sub-sector 448. But clothing can be purchased in sporting goods stores (45111), department stores (4521), warehouse clubs and superstore (45291), and sports clothing, they satisfy different consumer needs and thus appeal to different market segments. Sporting goods stores have a large variety of sports clothing at relatively high prices and knowledgeable sales assistance. Department stores are equally expensive and service-oriented, but they don't offer the same broad assortment of sporting goods. Warehouse clubs may have a narrow assortment of relatively inexpensive sports clothing. Finally, a wide variety of sports clothing is available at an Internet shop.

The degree to which retailers compete against each other isn't simply based on the similarity of their merchandise. The variety and assortment of the merchandise they offer and the services they provide must also be considered.

Variety Assortment

Variety is the number of merchandise categories a retailer offers. Assortment is the number of different items in a merchandise category. Each different item of merchandise is called a SKU (stock keeping unit).

Warehouse club stores, discount stores, and toy stores all sell toys. However, warehouse clubs and discount stores sell many other categories of merchandise in addition to toy. (They have greater variety). Stores specializing in toys stock more types of toys (more SKUs). For each types of toy, such as dolls, the specialty toy retailers' offers more assortments (more models, size and brands, and deeper assortment) than general merchants such as warehouse clubs or discounts stores.

Variety is often referred to as the breadth of merchandise carried by a retailer; assortment is referred to as the depth of merchandise.

Customer Services

Retailers also differ in the service they offer customers. For example, the bicycle shop offers assistance in selecting the appropriate bicycle, adjusting bicycles to fit the individual, and repairing bicycles. Customers expect retailers to provide some services: accepting personal checks, providing parking, and being open long and convenient hours. Some retailers charge customers for other services, such as home delivery and gift wrapping. Retailers that cater to service-oriented consumers offer customers most of these services at no charge.

Cost of offering Breadth and Depth of Merchandise Services

When a retailer offers customers many SKUs, inventory investment increase because the retailer must have backup stock for each SKU.

Similarly, services attract customers to the retailer, but they're also costly. More salespeople are needed to provide information and assist customers, to alter merchandise to meet customers;' needs, and to demonstrate merchandise. Child care facilities, rest rooms, dressing rooms, and check rooms take up valuable store space that could be used to stock and display merchandise. Offering delayed billing, credit, and installment payments requires a financial investment that could be used to buy more merchandise.

A critical retail decision involves the trade-off between costs and benefits of maintaining additional inventory or providing additional services.

FOOD RETAILERS

What companies are food retailers? Ten year ago this would have been a silly question. People purchase food primarily at conventional supermarkets. Today, however, discount stores and warehouse clubs are significantly changing consumers' food purchasing patterns because they too sell food.

Surprisingly, the world's largest food retailer is Wal-Mart, with supermarket type sales of $77 billion in 2000.

Types of Retailers

There are different types of retail formats that exist today. Studying these types shows the relative sizes and diversity of different kinds of retailing and indicates how various retailers are affected by their respective environments.

Retail formats can be classified on the basis of:

Conventional Super Markets

A conventional supermarket is a self service food store offering groceries, meat and produce with limited sales of nonfood items, such as health and beauty aids and general merchandise. Superstores are larger conventional supermarkets (20,000 to 50,000 square feet) with expanded service deli, bakery, seafood and nonfood section.

Big Box Food Retailers

Supermarkets have increased in size and have begun to sell a broader variety of merchandise. Big box food retailing formats: supercenters, hypermarkets, and warehouse clubs.

Supercenters: By offering broad assortments of grocery and general merchandise under one roof, supercenters provide a one-stop shopping experience. Customer will typically drive farther to shop at these stores than to visit conventional supermarkets (which offer a smaller selection). General merchandise items (nonfood items) are often purchased on impulse when customers' primary reason for coming to the store is to buy groceries. The general merchandise has higher margins, enabling the supercenters to price food item more aggressively. However, since supercenters are very large some customers find them inconvenient because it can take a long time to find the items they want.

Hypermarkets: are also large (100,000 to 300,000 square feet) combination food (60-70 percent) and general merchandise (30-40 percent) retailers. Hypermarket typically stock less than supercenters, between 40,000 and 60,000 items ranging from groceries, hardware, and sports equipment, to furniture and appliance to, computers and electronics.

Hypermarkets were created in France after World War. II. By building large stores on the outskirts of metropolitan areas, French retailers could attract customers and not violate strict land-use laws.

Supercenters versus Hypermarkets: Both hypermarkets and supercenters are large, carry grocery and general merchandise categories, are self-service, and are located in warehouse-type structures with large parking facilities.

Hypermarkets are often larger, but they carry fewer items. The merchandise mix is different as well. Hypermarkets carry a larger proportion of food items than supercenters. Further, fresh food-product, meat, fish, and so forth– is their specialty, provides a profit center, and if the primary reason why many people shop there. Supercenters, on the other hand, have a larger percentage of nonfood items. Further, on the food side, their specialty is dry grocery, such as breakfast cereal and canned goods, instead of fresh items.

Warehouse club: A warehouse club is a retailer that offers a limited assortment of food and general merchandised with little service at low prices to ultimate consumers and small businesses. Stores are large (at least 100,000 square feet with some over 150,000) and located in low rent district. They have simple interior and concrete floors. Customers pick merchandise off shipping pallets, take it to checkout lines in the front of the store, and pay with cash.

Merchandise in warehouse clubs is about half food and half general merchandise. Specific brands and items may differ from time-to-time because the stores buy merchandise available on special promotions from manufacturers. Warehouses club reduce price by using low-cost locations and stores designs. More warehouse clubs have two types of members: Wholesale members who own small businesses and individual member who purchase for their own use.

Convenience Stores

Convenience stores provides a limited variety and assortment of merchandise at a convenient location in a 2,000 to 3,000 square foot store with speedy checkout. They are the modern version of the neighborhood general store.

Convenience store enables consumers to make purchase quickly, without having to search through a large store and wait in a long checkout line. Over half the items bought are consumed within 30 minutes of purchase. Due to their small size and high sales, convenience stores typically receive deliveries every day.

Convenience stores only offer a limited assortment and variety, and they charge higher prices than supermarkets. Milk, eggs, and bread once represented the majority of their sales.

Issues in Food Retailing

The primary issue facing food retailers in general, and supermarket and convenience store retailers in particular is the increasing level of competition from other types of retailers. Fast food restaurant like subway sandwich shops have positioned themselves as a healthy food alternative. Convenience stores are also developing new concepts emphasizing prepared meals.

Traditional grocery chains are fighting back by making significant investment in providing meal solutions, either hot food or partially cooked entrees. The market for prepared foods can be quite profitable. Profit margins on prepared foods are higher than most other grocery categories. Also, although shoppers rarely visit a supermarket in search of prepared food alone, those who do spend almost 40 percent more than those who seldom or never purchase prepared foods?

General Merchandise Retailers

The major types of general merchandise retailers are discount stores, specialty stores, category specialists, department stores, home improvement centers, off-price retailers, and value retainers. Many of these general merchandise retailers sell through multichannel, such as the Internet and catalogs.

Discount Stores

A discount store is a retailer that offers a broad variety of merchandise, limited service, and low prices. Discount stores offer both private labels and national brands, but these brand are typically less fashion oriented than brands in department stores.

Discount stores face intense competition form specialty stores that focus on a single category of merchandise. To respond to this competitive environment, discount store shave created more attractive shopping environments, placed more emphasis on apparel, and developed strong private-label merchandise programs.

Specialty Stores

A specialty store concentrates on a limited number of complementary merchandise categories and provides a high level of service in an area typically under 8,000 square feet.

Issue in specialty store retailing: In recent years, a specialty apparel store has been one of the weakest, slowest growing areas in retailing. One reason is the aging population: older people typically don't spend as much money on clothing as teenagers. A soft economy and a shift to more casual apparel in the workplace have further dampened apparel sales.

Category Specialist

A category specialist is a discount store that offers a narrow variety but deep assortment of merchandise. These retailers are basically discount specialty stores. Most category specialist uses a self-service approach, but some specialists in consumer durables offer assistance to customers.

By offering a complete assortment in a category at low prices, category specialist can "kill" a category of merchandise for other retailers and thus are frequently called category killers. Because category specialists dominate a category of merchandise, they can use their buying power to negotiate low prices and are assured of supply when items are scarce. Department stores and full-line discount stores located near category specialists often have to reduce their offerings in the category because consumers are drawn to the deep assortment and low price at the category killer.

Issues for Category Specialist

Most category specialist chains started in one region of the country and saturated that region before expanding to other regions.

Now competition between specialists in each category is very intense as the firms expand into the regions originally dominated by another firm. In many merchandise categories, the major firms are now in direct competition across the nation. This direct competition focuses on price, resulting in reduced profit because the competitors have difficulty differentiating themselves on other element of the retail mix. All the competitors in a category provide similar assortment since they have similar access to national brands. They all provide the same level of service.

Department Stores

Department stores are retailers that carry a broad variety and deep assortment, offer some customer services, and are organized into separate departments for displaying merchandise. These are those that carry relatively inexpensive products and compete closely with discount stores.

Each department within the store has a specific selling space allocated to it, a POS terminal to transact and record sales, and salespeople to assist customers. The department store often resembles a collection of specialty shops. The major departments are women's, men's, and children's clothing and accessories, home furnishings and furniture, and kitchenware and small appliances.

In some situations, departments in a department store or discount store are leased and operated by an independent company. A leased department is an area in a retail store that is leased or rented to an independent firm. The lease holder is typically responsible for all retail mix decisions involve in operating the department and pays the store a percentage of its sales as rent. Retailers lease departments when they feel they lack expertise to efficiently operate the department.

Department stores are unique in terms of the shopping experience they offer– the service they provide and the atmosphere of the store. They offer a full range of services from altering clothing to home delivery. To create excitement, apparel is displayed on mannequins; attention is drawn to displays with theatrical lighting; and sales associates are frequently stationed throughout the store demonstrating products. Department stores also emphasize special promotions such as elaborate displays during the Christmas seasons.

Issues in Department Store Retailing

Department stores overall sale have stagnated and market share has fallen in recent years due to increased competition from discount stores and specialty stores and a decline in perceived value for merchandise and services. Department stores which started in the nineteenth century, attracted consumers by offering them ambience, attentive service and a wide variety of merchandise under one roof. Department stores also offer designer brands that are not available at other retailers.

Unfortunately, many consumers believe that department stores are no longer convenient. Many believe that they are difficult to get to because they are located in large malls, that it is difficult to find specific merchandise because the same category is often located in several designer departments, and that it is difficult to get professional sales assistance because of labour cutbacks. At the same time, they typically charge higher prices than there discount and specialty store competitors.

Drugstores

Drugstores are specialty stores that concentrate on health and personal grooming merchandise. Pharmaceuticals often represent over 50 percent of drugstore sales and an even greater percentage of their profits.

Issues in Drugstore Retailing Drugstores, particularly the national chains, are experiencing sustained sales growth because the aging population requires more prescript drugs. Although the profit margins for prescription/pharmaceuticals are higher than for other drugstore merchandise, these margins are shrinking due to government health care policies. The non-prescription side of drugstores is also being squeezed by considerably competition from pharmacies in discounts stores and supermarkets, as well as from prescriptions mail order retailers.

In response, the major drugstore chains are building larger stand-alone stores offering a wider assortment of merchandise, more frequently purchased food items, and drive-through windows for picking up prescriptions. To build customer loyalty, the chains are also changing the role of their pharmacists from dispensing pills (referred to as count, pour, lick and stick) to providing health care assistance such a explaining how use a nebulizer.

Drugstore retailers are using system to allow pharmacists time to provide personalized services.

Off Price Retailers

Off-price retailers offer an inconsistent assortment of brand-name, fashion oriented soft goods at low prices. Off-prices retailers can sell brand-name and even designer-label merchandise at low prices due to their unique buying and merchandising practices. Most merchandise is bought opportunistically from manufacturers or other retailers with excess inventory at the end of the season. This merchandise might be in odd size or unpopular colours and styles, or it may be irregulars (having minor mistakes in construction). Typically, merchandise is purchased at one-fifth to one fourth of the original wholesale price. Off price retailers can buy at low prices because they don't ask suppliers for advertising allowances, return privileges, markdown adjustments, or delayed payments.

Due to this pattern of opportunistic buying, customers can't be confident that the same type of merchandise will be in stock each time they visit the store. Different bargains will be available on each visit. To improve their offerings' consistency, some off price retailers complement opportunistically bough merchandise with merchandise purchased at regular wholesale prices. Two special types of off-price retailers are closeout and outlet stores.

Closeout Retailers: closeout retailers are off-price retailers that sell a broad but inconsistent assortment of general merchandise as well as apparel and soft home goods.

Outlet stores: Outlet stores are off-price retailer owned by manufacturers or by department or specialty store chains. Outlet stores owned by manufactures are frequently referred to as factory outlets.

Manufactures view outlet stores as an opportunity to improve their revenues from irregulars, production overruns, and merchandise returned by retailers. Outlet stores also allow manufacturers some control over where their branded merchandise is sold at discount prices.

Value Retailers

Value retailers are general merchandise discount stores that are found in either lower-income urban or rural area and much smaller than traditional stores (less than 9,000 square feet). Many value retailers target low income consumers, whose shopping behavior differs from typical discount stores or warehouse club customers. For instance, although these consumers demand well-known national brands, they often can't afford to buy large-size packages. Since this segment of the retail industry is growing rapidly, and known to pay its bill on time, vendors are creating special smaller packages for them. Value retailers follow a variety of business models. Although most cater to low-income groups.

NON-STORES RETAIL FORMATS

In the proceeding sections, we have examined retailers whose primary modes of operation are bricks-and-mortar stores. In this section we will discuss types of retailer that operate primarily in non-store environments. The major types of non-store retailers are electronic retailers, catalog and direct-mail retailers, direct selling, television home shopping, and vending machines.

Electronic Retailing

Electronic retailing (also called e-tailing and Internet retailing) is a retail format in which the retailers communicate with consumers and offer products and service for sale over the Internet. The rapid diffusion of Internet access and usage and the perceived low cost of entry stimulated the creation of over 10,000 entrepreneurial electronic retailing ventures during the last five years of the twentieth century.

Electronic retailing entrepreneurs develop innovative retail business models. These electronic retailing entrepreneurs were able to raise significant venture capital to support their concepts.

The growth and profitability expectation for electronic retail entrepreneurs diminished in 2000. When the Internet bubble burst, electronic retailers could no longer raise funds to support their unprofitable businesses were forced to declare bankruptcy. Although electronic retail entrepreneurs – retailers that only offer an electronic channel for purchasing merchandise and services- have faced difficulties, consumer interest in electronic retailing continues to increase.

In 2001, billion of merchandise and services were purchased electronically. Electronic retail sales were 16 percent greater than in the previous year, while the growth rate for retail sales in stores was less than 3 percent. Books, CDs, DVD, videos, apparel, computer software, and toys are the bestselling merchandise online.

The continued consumer interest in buying electronically is the result of traditional store-based and catalog retailers beginning to offer merchandise through an electronic channel. While the electronic retail innovators had superior skills in using the new technology, they lacked retailing expertise and a deep understanding of customer needs. Traditional retailers have incorporated an Internet channel into a multichannel offering that provides more value to customers. The success of multichannel retailing is reflected in the rating of retail websites. Each year, Internet Retailers the best Internet sites. In 2002, only 4 of the top 25 websites were pure electronic retailers, whereas in 2001, 14 were pure electronic retailers.

Catalog and Direct-Mail Retailing

Catalog retailing is a non-store retail format in which the retail offering is communicated to a customer through a catalog, whereas direct mail retailers communicate with their customers using letters and brochures. Historically, catalog and direct mail retailing were most successful with rural consumers who lacked ready access to retail stores. Today's customers enjoy the convenience of shopping by catalog. The major catalog retailers have embraced a multichannel strategy by integrating the Internet into their catalog operations. Customers often get a catalog in the mail, look it over, and go to the Internet for more information and to place an order.

Two special of direct selling are party plan and multilevel selling. About 28 percent of all direct sales are made using a party plan system. In a party system, salespeople encourage customers to act as hosts and invite friends or coworkers to act as hosts and invite friends or coworkers to a "party" at which the merchandise is demonstrated in a party like atmosphere. Sales made at the party are influenced by the social relationship of the people attending with the host or hostess, who receives a gift or commission for arranging the meeting.

Almost three quarter of all direct sales are made through multilevel sales network. In a multilevel network, people serve as master distributors, recruiting other people to become distributors in their network. The distributors either buy merchandise from the firm and resell it to their distributor or receive a commission on all merchandise purchased by the distributors in their distributor or receive a commission on all merchandise purchased by the distributors in their network. In addition to selling merchandise themselves, the master distributors are involved in recruiting and training other distributors.

Some multilevel direct-selling firms are illegal pyramid schemes. A pyramid scheme develops when the firm and its program are designed to sell merchandise and services to other distributors rather than to end users. The founders and initial distributors in pyramid schemes profit from the inventory bought by later participants, but little merchandise is sold to consumer who use it.

Television Home Shopping

Television home shopping is a retail format in which customers watch a TV program demonstrating merchandise and then place orders for the merchandise by telephone. The three form of electronic home shopping retailing are (1) cable channels dedicated to television shopping (2) infomercials, and (3) direct response advertising. Infomercials are TV programs, typically 30 minutes long that mix entertainment with product demonstrations and then solicit orders placed by telephone. Direct-response advertising includes advertisement on TV and radio that describes products and provide an opportunity for consumers to order them.

The major advantage of TV home shopping compared to catalog retailing is that customers can see the merchandise demonstrated on the TV screen. However, customers can't examine a particular type of merchandise or a specific item when they want to, as they can with catalogs. They have to wait for the time when the merchandise shows up on the screen. To address this limitation, home shopping network schedule categories of merchandise for specific times so customers looking for specific merchandise can plan their viewing time.

TV home shopping retailers appeal primarily to lower-income consumers. Forty percent of TV home shopping sales are inexpensive jewelry. Other major categories are apparel, cosmetics, and exercise equipment.

Vending Machine Retailing

Vending machine retailing is a non-store format in which merchandise or services are stored in a machine and dispensed to customers when they deposit cash or use a credit card. Vending machines are placed at convenient, high-traffic locations such as in the workplace or on university campuses and primarily contain snack or drinks.

Technological developments in vending machine design may result in long-term sales growth. New video kiosk vending machines enable consumer to see the merchandise in use, get information about it, and use their credit cards to make a purchase.

The new vending machines designs also enable the retailers to increase the productivity of the machines. Electronic systems in the machines keep track of inventory, cash and other operating conditions. Then radio devices transmit data back to a host computer. These data are analyzed, and communications are sent to route drivers telling them when stock outs and malfunctions occur.

Service Retailing

The retail firms discussed in the previous section sell products to consumers. However, service retailer, firms selling primarily services rather than merchandise, are large and growing part of the retail industry. There are several trends that suggests considerable future growth in services retailing. For example the aging of the population will increase demand for health services. Younger people too are spending increasing amounts of time and money on health and fitness. Parents in two-income families are willing to pay to have their homes cleaned, lawns maintained, cloths washed and pressed, and meals prepared so they can spend more time with their families.

These companies are retailers because they sell goods and services to consumers. However, some of these companies are not just retailers. For example, airlines, banks, hotels and insurance and express mail companies sell their services to businesses as well as consumers. Also, a large number of services retailers such as lawyers, doctors, and dry cleaners are not in the exhibit because they focus on local markets and do not have a national presence.

Many organizations such as banks, hospitals, health spa, legal clinics, entertainment firms, and universities that offer services to consumer traditionally haven't considered themselves as retailers. Due to increased competition these organizations are adopting retailing principles to attract customers and satisfy their needs.

All retailers provide goods and services for their customers. However, the emphasis placed on the merchandise versus the services differs across retail formats. These retail formats consists of self service stores that offer very few services. However, these formats do offer a few services such as check cashing and some assistance from store employees. Moving along the continuum from left to right, we find category specialists, which also emphasize self-service but have employees who can answer questions, demonstrate merchandise, and make recommendations. Next, department and specialty stores provide even higher levels of service. In addition to assistance from sales associates, these stores offer services such as gift wrapping, bridal registries, and alterations.

Optical centers and restaurant lie somewhere in the middle of the merchandise/ service continuum. In addition to selling frames, eyeglasses, and contact lenses, optical centers also provide important services like eye examination and eyeglasses fittings. Similarly, restaurants offer food plus a place to eat, music in the background, a pleasant ambience, and table service. As we move to the right end of the continuum, we encounter retailers and table service. As we more to the right end of the continuum, we encounter retailers whose offering is primarily services. However, even these retailers have some products associated with the services offered, such as a meal on the airplane or a checkbook at a bank. Services retailers are defined as retailers for which the major aspect of their offerings is services versus merchandise.

Difference between Services and Merchandise Retailers

As a retailers falls more to the right on the merchandise/service continuum, service become a more important aspect of the retailers offering. Four important differences in the nature of the offering provided by services and merchandise retailers are (1) intangibility, (2) simultaneous production and consumption, (3) perishability, (4) inconsistency of the offering to customers.

Intangibility: Services are generally intangible-customers cannot see, touch, or feel them. They are performances or actions rather than objects. For example, health care services cannot be seen or touched by a patient. Even after diagnosis and treatment, the patient may not realize the full extent of the service that has been performed.

Intangibility introduces a number of challenges for services retailers. First, since customers can't touch and feel services, it's difficult for customers to evaluate services before they buy them or even after they buy and consume them. Due to the intangibility of their offering, services retailers often use tangible symbol to inform customers about the quality of their services. For example, lawyers frequently have elegant, carpet offices with expensive antique furniture.

Services retailers also have difficulties in evaluating quality of services they are providing. For example, it's hard for a law firm to evaluate how well its lawyers are performing their jobs. To evaluate the quality of their offering, service retailers emphasize soliciting customer evaluations and complaints.

Simultaneous production and consumption: Product are typically made in a factory. Stores and sold by a retailer, and then used by consumers in their homes. Service providers, on the other hand, create and deliver the services as the customer is consuming it. For example, when you eat at restaurant, the meal is prepared and consumed almost at the same time.

The simultaneity of production and consumption creates some special problems for service retailers. First, the customers are present when the service is produced, may even have an opportunity to see it produced, and in some cases may be part of the production process, as in making their own salad at a salad bar. Second, other customers consuming the services at the same time can affect the quality of the service provided. Finally, the services retailer often does not get a second chance to satisfy the needs of its customers. While customers can return damaged merchandise to a store, customers that are dissatisfied with services have limited recourse. Thus, it is critical for services retailers to get it right the first time.

Because services are produced and consumed at the same time, it is difficult to reduce costs through mass production. For this reason, most services retailers are small, local firms. Large national retailers are able to reduce costs by "industrializing" the services they offer. They make substantial investments in equipment and training to provide a uniform service.

Perishability: Because the creation and consumption of services are inseparable, services are perishable. They can't be saved, stores, or resold. Once the airline takes off with an empty seat, the sale is lost forever. This is in contrast to merchandise that can held in inventor until a customer is ready to buy it.

Due to the perishability of services, an important aspect of services retailing is matching supply and demand. Most services retailers have a capacity constraints, and the capacity cannot be changed easily. There are a fixed number of tables in a restaurant, seats in classroom, beds in a hospital, and electricity that can be generated by a power plant. To increase capacity, services retailers need to make major investments such as buying more airplanes or building an addition to increase the size of the hospital or restaurant.

In addition, demand for service varies considerably over time. Consumers are most likely to fly on airplane during holidays and the summer, eat in restaurant at lunch and dinner time, and use electricity in the evening rather than earlier in the day. Thus, services retailers often have times when their services are under utilized and other times when they have to turn customer away because they can't accommodate them.

Services retailer use a variety of programs to match demand and supply. For examples, airlines and hotels set lower prices on weekends when they have excessive capacity because business people aren't traveling. To achieve more capacity flexibility, health clinics stay open longer in the flu season, while tax preparation services are open on weekends during March and April. Restaurant increase staffing on weekends, may not open until dinner time, and use a reservation system to guarantee service delivery at a specific time. Finally, services retailers attempt to make customers' waiting time more enjoyable.

Inconsistency: Merchandise is often produced by machines with very tight quality control so customers are reasonably assured that all boxes of Cheerios will be identical. Because services are performances produced by people (employees and customers), no two service will be identical. Thus, an important challenge for service retailers is providing consistently high-quality services. Many factors determining services quality are beyond the control of the retailers; however, service retailers expand considerable time and effort selecting, training, managing, and motivating their service providers.

Kiosks: freestanding terminal that display products and related information. Shoppers can often touch and feel the product before making the buying decision.

Airport retailing: airport is a major Mecca of retailing. In these shops selling books, magazines, toys, jewellery, food, beverages, liquor, etc. are located at airports, mainly at security check lounges or common areas.

TYPES OF OWNERSHIP

Retailers are classified in terms of their retail mix (the variety and depth of merchandise and services offered to customers) and the merchandise and service they sell (food, general merchandise, and services). Another way to classify retailers is by their ownership. The major classification of retail ownership are (1) independent, single store establishment, (2) corporate chains, and (3) franchises.

Independent, Single-Store Establishments

Retailing is one of the few sectors in our economy where an entrepreneurial activity is extensive. Many such stores are owner-managed. Thus, management has direct contact with customers and can respond quickly to their needs. Small retailers are also very flexible and can therefore react quickly to market changes and customer needs. They aren't bound by bureaucracies inherent in larger retailer organization.

While single store retailers can tailored their offerings to their customers' needs, corporate chains can more effectively negotiate lower prices for merchandise and advertising due to their larger size. In addition, corporate chains have a broader management base, with people who specialize in specific retail activities. Single store retailers typically have to rely on owner-managers' capabilities to make the broad range of necessary retail decisions.

Corporate Retail Chains

A retail chain is a company operating multiple retail units under common ownership and usually has centralize decision making for defining and implementing its strategy. Retail chains can range in size from a drugstore with two stores to retailers with over 1,000 stores. Some retailer chains are division of larger corporation or holding companies.

There has been considerable concern that corporate retail chains drive independent retailers out of business. These stores offer a broader selection of merchandise at much lower prices than previously available from local retailers. Due to scale economies and an efficient distribution system, corporate chains can sell at low prices. This forces some directly competing local retailers out of business and alters the community fabric.

Franchising

Franchising is a contractual agreement between a franchisor and a franchisee that allows the franchisee to operate a retail outlet using a name developed and supported by the franchisor. In a franchise contract, the franchisee pays a lump sum plus a royalty on all sales for the right to operate a store in a specific location. The franchisees also agree to operate the outlet in accordance with procedures prescribed by the franchisor. The franchisor provides assistance in locating and building the store developing the products or services sold, management training, and advertising. To maintain the franchisee's reputation, the franchisor also makes sure that 11 outlets provide the same quality of services and products.

The franchise ownership formats attempts to combine advantage of owner-managed businesses with efficiencies of centralized decisions making in chain store operations. Franchisees are motivated to make their store successful because they receive the profits (after the royalty is paid). The franchisor is motivated to develop new products and systems and to promote the franchise because it receives a royalty on all sales. Advertising, product development, and system development are efficiently done by the franchisor, with costs shared by all franchises.

Types of Retail format in India

Ownership

1. ***Independent retailers:*** E.g. Mom & Pop stores, Kirana stores
2. ***Chains:*** E.g: Shooper's stop, Wave cinemas, PVR, Meena Bazaar, Satya Paul, Koutons, Good Things, Westside, Lifestyle, Reliance Fresh, Bata, CTC Plaza
3. ***Franchising:*** E.g: Mc Donalds, Pizza Hutt, Dominos, Nokia, Sony Erricson, BPL, Godrej, LG, Samsung, Hyundai, Maruti, Honda, Hindustan Petroleum, Indian Oil.

Store Based

E.g: Millennium Shoppe

1. ***Conventional supermarkets:*** E.g: Food Land (Mumbai), store 18
2. ***Combination stores (Hypermarkets):*** E.g: Hypercity (Mumbai), Spencer's Hyper, Le Marche Hypermarket, Reliance Hypermarket (opening shortly)
3. ***Departmental stores:*** E.g: Big Bazaar.
4. ***Factory outlets:*** E.g: Reebok, Adidas, Nike, Woodland
5. ***Convenience stores***
6. ***Flea Markets:*** E.g: Mangal Bazaar, Fashion Street (Mumbai), Janpath
7. ***CSD Canteens***

Non Store Based

1. ***Direct Marketing:*** E.g: Eureka Forbes, Kent Water Purifier
2. ***Direct selling:*** E.g: Credit Cards, Durga Fenile Company
3. ***Vending Machines***

4. ***Web retailing***
5. ***Airport Retailing.***

RETAIL MARKET STRATEGY

The growing intensity of retail competition due to the emergence of new formats and technology plus shifts in customer needs is forcing retailers to devote more attention to long-term strategic thinking. As the retail management decision-making process indicates, retailing strategy is the bridge between understanding the world of retailing, that is, the analysis of the retail environment, and the more tactical merchandise management and store operations activities undertaken to implement the retail strategy. The retail strategy provides the direction retailers need to take to deal effectively with their environment, customers, and competitors.

The first part of this topic defines the term retail strategy and discusses three important elements of retail strategy: the target market segment, retail format, and sustainable competitive advantage. Next we outline approaches for building a sustainable competitive advantage. The topic concludes with a discussion of the strategic retail planning process.

What is Retail Strategy?

The term strategy is frequently used in retailing. For example, retailers talk about their merchandises strategy, promotion strategy, location strategy, and private band strategy. In fact, the term is used so commonly it appears that all retailing decisions are now strategic decisions. But retailer strategy isn't just another expression for retail management.

Definition of Retail Market Strategy

A retail strategy is statement identifying (1) the retailer's target market, (2) the format the retailer plan to use to satisfy the target market's needs, and (3) the bases upon which the retailer plans to build a sustainable competitive advantage. The target market is the market segment(s) toward which the retailer plans to focus its reoccurs and retail mix. A retail format is the retailer's mix nature of merchandise and services offered, pricing policy, advertising and promotion program, approach to store design and visual merchandising, and typical location). A sustainable competitive advantage is an advantage over competition that can be maintained over a long time.

Retail strategies involves (1) selecting a target market segment and retail format and (2) developing suitable competitive advantage that enables the retailer to reduce the level of competition it faces.

Target Market and Retail format

The retailing concept is management orientation that focuses a retailer on determining the needs of its target market and satisfying those needs more effectively and efficiently than its competitors. Successful retailers satisfy the needs of customers in their target segment better than the competition does. The selection of a target market focuses the retailer on a group of consumers whose needs it will attempt to satisfy. The selection of a retail format outlines the retail mix to be used to satisfy needs of those customers. The retail strategy determines the markets in which a retailer will compete. Traditional markets, like a farmer's market, are places where buyers and sellers meet and make transactions-say, a consumer buys corn for years from a farmer. But in modern markets, potential buyers and sellers aren't necessarily located in one place. Transaction can occur without face-to-face interactions. For example, many customers contact retailers and place orders over the Internet using a computer.

We define a retailer market not as a specific place where buyers and sellers meet but as a group of consumers with similar needs (a market segment) and group of retailers using a similar retail format to satisfy those consumer needs. We divide the market into three fashion related segments: Conservative, those who place little importance on fashion and are price-sensitive, traditional, those who want classic styles that are moderately priced; and fashion forward, those who want the most fashionable merchandise.

Retail formats could be expanded to include outlet stores and electronic retailing. Rather than being segmented by fashion orientation, the market could have been segmented using the other approaches.

Building a Sustainable Competitive Advantage

The final element in a retail strategy is the retailers' approach to building a sustainable competitive advantage. Any business activity that a retailer engages it can be a basis for competitive advantage; but some advantages are sustainable over a long period of time, while others can be duplicated by competitors almost immediately. It's hard for retailers to develop a long term advantage by offering a broader or deeper merchandise assortments. If broader and deeper assortments attract a lot of customers, competitors will simply go out and buy the same merchandise for their stores.

Establishing a competitive advantage means that a retailer builds a wall around its position in a retail market. This makes it hard for competitors outside the wall to contact customers in the retainer's target market. If the retailer has built a wall around an attractive market, competitors will attempt to break down the wall. Over time, all advantages will be eroded due to these competitive forces; buy building high, thick walls, retailers can sustain their advantage, minimize competitive pressure, and boost profits for a longer time. Thus, establishing a sustainable competitive advantage is the key to long-term financial performance.

Seven important opportunities for retailers to develop sustainable competitive advantage are (1) customer loyalty, (2) locations, (3) human resource management, (4) distribution and information systems (5) unique merchandise, (6) vendor relations, (7) and customer services.

Customer Loyalty

Customer loyalty means that customers are committed to shopping at the retailer's locations. Many of the bases for maintaining a sustainable competitive advantage discussed in this section also help attract and maintain loyal customers. For instance, having dedicated employees, unique merchandise, and superior customer service all help solidify a loyal customer base. But having loyal customer is, in and of itself, an important method of sustaining an advantage over competitors. Loyalty is more than simply liking one retailer over another. Loyalty means that customers will be reluctant to patronize competitive retailers.

Positioning

A retailer builds customer loyalty by developing a clear, distinctive image of its retail offerings and consistently reinforcing that image through its merchandise and services. Positioning in the customer's mind relative to its competitors.

Positioning emphasizes that the image in the customer's mind (not the retail manager's mind) is critical. Thus, the retailer needs to research what its image is and make sure that its image is consistent with what customers in its target market want. A perceptual map is frequently used to represent the customer's image and preference for retailers.

Loyalty Programs

Loyalty programs are part of an overall customer relationship management (CRM) program that is examined. These programs are prevalent in retailing, from airlines and department stores to the corner pizza shop.

Customer loyalty programs work hand-in-hand with CRM. Members of loyalty programs are identified when they buy because they use some type of loyalty card. Purchase information is stored in a huge data base known as a data warehouse. From this data warehouse, analysts determine what types of merchandise and services certain groups for customers are buying. Using this information, retailer tailor their offerings to better meet the needs of their loyal customers.

Location

The classic response to the question what are the three most important things in retailing? Is "location, location and location." Location." Location is the critical factor in consumer selection of a store. It is also a competitive advantage that is not easily duplicated. Finding great locations is particularly challenging in older urban locations, where space is finite and tenant turnover is relatively slow.

Human Resource Management

Some retailers offer services customers don't necessarily want, such as banking or dry cleaning, yet make customer jump through hoops to return merchandise. Most customers simply want retailers to trust them and tend to basic request. It takes considerable time and effort to build a tradition and reputation for customer services, but good services is a valuables strategic assets. Once a retailer has earned a service reputation, it can sustain this advantage for a long time because it's hard for a competitor to develop a comparable reputation.

Multiple Sources of Advantage

To build a sustainable advantage, retailers typically don't rely on a single approach such as low cost or excellent service. They need multiple approaches to build as high a wall around their position as possible.

GROWTH STRATEGIES

Four types of growth opportunities that retailers may pursue (market penetration, market expansion, retail format development, and diversification). The vertical axis indicates the synergies between the retailer's present markets and growth opportunity markets-whether the opportunity involves markets the retailer is presently pursuing or new markets. The horizontal axis indicates the synergies between the retailer's present retail mix and the growth-opportunity retail mix-whether the opportunity exploits the retailer's present format or requires a new format.

Market Penetration

A market penetration opportunity involves directing efforts toward existing customer by using the present retailing format. The retailer can achieve this growth strategy either by attracting consumers in its current target market who don't shop at its outlets or by devising strategy that induce current customers to visit a store more often or to buy more merchandise on each visit.

Approaches for increasing market penetration include attracting new customers by opening more stores in the target market and keeping existing stores open for longer hours. Other approaches are displaying merchandise to increase impulse purchases and training salespeople to cross sell. Cross-selling means that sales associates in one department attempt to sell complementary merchandise from other department to their customers.

Market Expansion

A market expansion opportunity employs the existing retail format in new market segments.

Retail format development

A retail format development opportunity involves offering a new retail format– a format with a different retail mix– to the same target market.

Diversification

A diversification opportunity is when a retailer introduces a new retail format directed toward a market segment that's not currently served. Diversification opportunities are either related or unrelated.

Related versus unrelated diversification: In a related diversification opportunity, the present target market or retail format shares something in common with the new opportunity. This commonality might entail purchasing from the same vendors, using the same distribution or managements information system, or advertising in the same newspapers to similar target marts. In contrast, an unrelated diversification lack any commonality between the present business and the new business.

Vertical Integration: Vertical Integration is diversification by retailers into wholesaling or manufacturing. Retailers and manufacturers have different customers– the immediate customers for a manufacturer's merchandise are retailers, whereas a retailer's customers are consumers. Thus, a manufacturer's marketing activities are very different from those of a retailer.

Strategic Opportunities and Competitive Advantage

Typically, retailers have the greats competitive advantage in opportunities that are similar to their present retail strategy. Thus, retailers would be most successful engaging in market penetration opportunities that don't involve entering new, unfamiliar markets or operating new, unfamiliar retail formats.

When retailers pursue market expansion opportunities, they build on their strengths in operating a retail format and apply this competitive advantage in a new market. Thus, those retailers that successfully expand globally are able to translate what they do best– their core competencies– to a new culture and market.

Global Growth Opportunities

International expansion is one form of a market expansion strategy. International expansion is risky because retailers using this growth strategy must deal with differences in government regulations, cultural traditions, different supply chain considerations and languages. The types of retailers that successfully compete globally are discussed first, followed by a look at some of the pitfalls of global expansion. Then the key success factors for global expansion are examined. Finally, the strategies for entering a non-domestics market are evaluated.

Who is Successful and Who Isn't

Retailers particularly specialty store retailers with strong brand names. Retailers have a competitive advantage in global market because the culture is emulated in many countries, particularly among young people. Due to the rising prosperity and rapidly increasing access to cable TV with programming, fashion trends are spreading to young people in emerging countries.

Some large retailers have considerable more experience operating retail stores in non-domestic markets. Category killers and hypermarkets retailers may be particularly suited to succeed internationally because of the expertise they've already developed at home. To succeed internationally because of the expertise they've already developed at home. First these retailers are leaders in the use of technology to manage inventories, control global logistical system, and tailor merchandise assortments to local needs. Despite idiosyncrasies in the international environment, category killers and hypermarket retailers have developed unique systems and standardized formats that facilitate control over multiple store. These systems and procedures should work well regardless of the country of operation. The category killer's narrow assortment and focused strategy, communications across national boundaries and cultures are specifically focused, which improve management coordination. Finally at one time, people felt that consumer outside the states were used to high levels of personalized service and would not accept the self- service concept employed by category killers and hypermarket retailers. However, consumer around the globe are willing to forgo the service for lower prices.

Globe expansion is often difficult and full of pitfalls.

Key to Success

Four characteristics of retailer that have successfully exploited international growth opportunities are (1) globally sustainable competitive advantage, (2) adaptability (3) global culture, and (4) deep pockets. A hypothetical evolution of international growth opportunities is described in the appendix to this chapter.

Globally Sustainable Competitive Advantage

Entry into non-domestic markets is most successful when the expansion opportunity is consistent with the retailers' core bases of competitive advantage.

Adaptability

While successful global retailers build on their core competencies, they also recognize cultural differences and adapt their core strategy to the needs of local markets. Colour preference, the preferred cut of apparel, and sizes differ across cultures.

Selling seasons also vary across countries. Stores designs need to be adjusted. In some cultures, social norms dictate that men's and women's clothing cannot be displayed next to each other.

Government regulations and cultural values also affect store operations. Some differences such as holidays, hours of operations, and regulations governing part-time employees and terminations are easy to identify. Other factors require a deeper understandings.

Global Culture

To be global, one has to think globally. It is not sufficient to transplant a home-country and infrastructure into another country. In the early years of its international expansion, it started in each country slowly, which reduced the company's ethnocentrism. Further enriching its global perspective.

Deep Pockets

Expansion into international markets requires a long-term commitment and considerable upfront planning. Retailers find it very difficult to generate short-term profit when they make the transition to global retailing.

Entry Strategies

Four approaches that retailer take when entering non-domestic markets are direct investment, joint ventures, strategic alliance, and franchising.

Direct Investment: Direct investment involves a retail firm investing in and owning a division or subsidiary that builds and operate stores in a foreign country. This entry strategy requires the highest level of investment and exposes the retailer to significant risks, but it has the highest potential returns. One advantage of direct investment is that the retailer has complete control of the operations.

Joint venture: A joint venture is formed when the entering retailer pool its resources with a local retailer to form a new company in which ownership, control and profits are shared.

A joint ventures reduces the entrant's risks. Besides sharing the financial burden, the local partner understand the market and has access to resources- vendors and real estate.

Strategic alliance: A strategic alliance is a collaborative relationship between independent firms.

Franchising: Franchising offers the lowest risk and requires the least investment. However, the entrant has limited control over the retail operations in the foreign country, potential profit is reduced, and the risk of assisting in the creation of a local domestic competitor is increased.

THE STRATEGIC RETAIL PLANNING

The strategic retail planning process is the set of steps a retailer goes through to develop a strategic retail plan. It describes how retailer select target market segments, determine the appropriate retail format, and build sustainable competitive advantages. It is not always necessary to go through the entire process each time an evaluation is performed. For instance a retail could evaluate its performance and go directly to conduct a situation audit.

The following are the steps in Retail Planning:

Step 1: Define the Business Mission

The first step in the strategic retail planning process is to define the business mission. The mission statement is a broad description of a retailers objectives and the scope of activities it plans to undertake.

The objective of a publicly held firm is to maximize its stockholders wealth by increasing the value of its stock and paying dividends. Owners of small, private held firms frequently have other objectives, such as achieving a specific level of income and avoiding risks rather than maximizing income.

The mission statement should define the general nature of the target segments and retail formats that the firm will consider.

In developing the mission statement, managers must answer five question: (1) what business are we in? (2) what should be our business in the future? (3) who are our customers? (4) what are our capabilities? (5) what do we want to accomplish?

Since the mission statement defines the retailers' objectives and the scope of activities it plan to undertake

Step 2: Conduct a Situation Audit

After developing a mission statement and setting objectives, the next step in the strategies planning process is to do a situation audit. A situation audit is an analysis of the opportunities and threats in the retail environment and the strengths and weakness of the retail business relative to its competitors.

The elements in the situation analysis.

Market Factors: Some critical factors related to consumers and their buying patters are market size and growth, sale cyclicality, and seasonality. Market size, typically measured in retail sales dollars, is important because it indicates a retailers' opportunity for generating revenues to cover its investment. Large markets are attractive to large retail firms. But they are also attractive to small entrepreneurs because they offer more opportunities to focus on a market segment. Some retailers, however, prefer to concentrate on smaller markets.

Growing markets are typically more attractive than mature or declining markets. Retail markets for specialty stores are growing faster than those for department stores. Typically, margins and prices are higher in growing markets because competition is less intense than in mature markets. Since new customers are just beginning to patronize stores in growing markets, they may not have developed strong store loyalties and thus might be easier to attract to a new store. Some retailers, however, prefer to locate in mature markets. These locations are attractive when the customer base is stable and competitions is weak.

Firms are often interested in minimizing the businesses cycle's impact on their sales. Thus, retail markets for merchandise affected by economic conditions are less attractive than retail markets unaffected by economic conditions. In general, markets with highly seasonal sales are unattractive because a lot of resources are needed to accommodate the peak season, but then resources are underutilized the rest of the year.

Competitive Factors: The nature of the competitor is retail makers in affected by barriers to entry, bargaining power of vendors, and competitive rivalry. Retail markets are more attractive when competitive entry is costly. Barriers to entry are conditions in a retail market that make it difficult for firms to enter the market. These conditions include scale economies, customer loyalty and availability of great locations.

Scale economics are cost advantage due to a retailer's size. Market dominated by large competitor with scale economies are typically unattractive. Retail market dominated by a well-established retailer that has developed a loyal group of customers offer limited profit potential.

Finally, the availability of locations may impede competitive entry. Entry business are a double-edged sword. A retail market with high entry barriers is very attractive for retailers presently competing in that market, because those barriers limit competition. However, markets with high entry barriers are unattractive for retailers not already in the market. Another competitive factor is the bargaining power of vendors. Markets are less attractive when a few vendors control the merchandise sold in it. In these situations, vendors have an opportunity to dictate prices and to her terms (like delivery dates), reducing the retailers profit.

The final industry factor is the level of competitive rivalry in the retail markets. Competitive rivalry is the frequency and intensity of reaction to actions undertaken by competitors. When rivalry is high, price wars erupt, employee raids occur, advertising and promotion expense sincere, and profit potential falls, conditions that may lead to intense rivalry include (1) a large number of competitors that are all about the same size, (2) slow growth, (3) high fixed costs, and (4) the lack of perceived difference between competing retailers.

Environmental factors: Environmental factors that affect market attractiveness span technological, economic, regulator, and social changes. When a retail market is going though significant changes in technology, present competitors are vulnerable to new entrants that are skilled at using the new technology.

Some retailers may be more affected by economic conditions than others. Government regulations can reduce the attractiveness of a retail market. Trend in demographics, lifestyles, attitudes, and personal values affect retail markets attractiveness.

SUMMARY

Merchandising is the activities which involves in acquiring particular goods and services and make them available to final consumer at right time, right place and adequate quantity. Internal is also new source of finding information about product so most of the retail industry place their product catalogue on the internet. Merchandise than its competitors. The degree to which retailers compete against each other isn't simply based on the similarity of their merchandise. Merchandise management is essential part of any retail industry. The retailing concept is management orientation essential part of any retail industry. The retailing concept is management orientation that focuses a retailer on determining the needs of its target market and satisfying those needs more effectively and efficiently than its competitors. The final element in a retail strategy is the retailers approach to building a sustainable competitive advantage.

PROJECT REPORT

1. Suppose you are a manager of Reliance fresh and your boss asked you to increase the sales volume that what would be the key area which you focus and what would be your course of action?
2. Collect the material regarding to following topic:
   1. Mall Management
   2. Store Management
   3. Merchandise management

SHORT QUESTIONS

1. What is Retailing?
2. What is non store retail format?
3. What is Retail Strategy?
4. What are Growth Strategies?

REVIEW QUESTIONS

1. Explain different characteristics of Retailer with the help of suitable examples.
2. Discuss different types of Retailer.
3. Discuss the mechanism of Merchandising Management.
4. Discuss Retail Marketing Strategy in detail.

GO TO THE NET

1. Using internet search tool prepare a retail strategy of 10 FMCG products.
2. Using internet search tool prepare a report on merchandising management of Vishal Megamart and Big Bazaar.

Caselet

Fine Furnishings Limited is a small chain of distributors of good-quality office furniture, carpets, safes and filling cabinets. Within each category, the company offers a wide variety of products, with great many variations of each product being offered. For example, the company currently offers some 52 different designs of chairs and 33 varieties of office desks. The company keeps in touch with advances made in the office furniture field worldwide and introduces those products, which are in keeping with needs of the market in terms of design, workmanship, value for money and technical specifications.

Fine furnishings trades only in good quality furniture, which is sturdily constructed. Differences between its precuts and cheaper, lower quality ones are well known to those who have several years of experience in the business.

An important features, the company feels, is the availability of a complete list of components of the furniture system. This enables customers to add bits and pieces of matching designs and colour in the maintained in stock by the company for a number of years, and spare parts for chains and other furniture are always available.

The trade is currently witnessing a downward due to the recession. Fine furnishings has also experienced the same over the past two years. In addition, it had to trim its profit margins. Last year, it barely broke even and this year it is heading for a small loss for the first time in the company's twenty-year history.

Questions:

1. Explain the terms product item, product line and product mix in the context of above situation.
2. Advise the company in relation to its product mix. How your recommendation affect the company's image?

CHAPTER 32

merchandise techniques

learning objectives

The objectives of this chapter are to:

- understand role and importance of merchandising management
- discuss the role of Planning of Assortment
- discuss the role and importance of supply chain management.

content outline

- Opening Case
- Merchandise Management
- Planning of Assortments
- The Assortment Plan
- Supply Chain Management
- The Objective of a Supply Chain
- Decision Phases in Supply Chain
- Process View of a Supply Chain
- Strategic Planning in the Real World
- Leveraging Space: In Store Kiosks
- Visual Merchandising
- Do we do Windows?
- Supply Chain Macro Processes in a Firm
- The Importance of Supply Chain Flows
- Summary
- Project Work
- Short Questions
- Review Questions
- Go to the Net
- Caselet

opening case

Twenty five years ago, a multinational company had set up a factory in eastern India. Today, the factory, situated in the heart of the coal belt, is the only industrial unit in the area. Its production caters to about 50 percent of national demand for product vital to the industry. Thus the working of the factory, when disrupted, has considerable impact on the national economy. Over the years, the break-even of the factory has risen to about 85 percent of annual production as pricing of products is controlled by Government.

The factory employs about 2,000 workers 350 general staff and are covered by union management agreements. This apart, there are 110 supervisory staff and about 75 officers. The employees of the factory are easily amongst the better paid in the region/industry both in terms of monetary benefits and welfare amenities.

Historically, the factory has enjoyed satisfactory industrial relations and has a recognized union for the last 15 years. Over the last 10 years, however, another union with a different political affiliation has also come into existence. The last major upheaval (IR wise) in 1987 when following the dismissal of a worker for proven gross negligence, the recognized union called and organized a near total strike. Production being vital, the government intervened and after a fortnight matters were resolved and the union called off the strike. However, at the juncture the unrecognized union succeeded in continuing the strike. Immense pressure from all quarters forced the management to concede some monetary demands. After nearby 40 days, the strike was again called off. This was turning point in Industrial relations in the factory with the recognized union establishing its authority as a bargaining agent. However, in 1990 with the signing of a 4-year long term settlement and also an agreement on production incentive, industrial peace was brought about.

During the last one year danger signals loomed large with fissiparous tendencies in both the unions resulting in weakening of the union structure and loss of union control on the shop floor. A group of self motivated, self styled leaders from among the known destructive elements in the workforce came to the fore. Public meetings became commonplace where employees were provoked, management was abused and hopes were raised on unreasonable and unjustified issues causing repeated pin picks on the shop floor, gheraos, work stoppages and other tactics of confrontation.

On a particular day, a whole shift of about 150 workers in a department (which is the nerve center of production) did not report to their workplace till 2.00 p.m., assembled and went en-masse to the production officer's demanding clarification on an issue. Despite their awareness of the fact that this issue was already under discussion at union management level, the workers demanded that the manager should come and speak to them. Other staff and supervisors were present in and around the officer, when the crowd of workers went outside to wait. The Manager came at about 2.30 p.m. parked his car and was walking towards the office with a supervisor when one worker from the crowd came towards him. The worker, however, caught hold of the arm of the Manager and tried to drag him towards the crowed. On being asked to release his arm, the worker started pelting the Manager with blows. The supervisor remained dumbfounded at this sudden unprecedented development. Meanwhile, four other workers from the crowed joined him and also started hitting the Manager.

The supervisor, along with some other staff, somehow managed to rescue the Manager. The assault caused serous bodily injuries requiring hospitalization of the Manager. Soon, the security and police moved in to control the situation. Therefore, considerable tension prevailed in the area; the concerned 150 workers did not go to their workplace at all and gradually by about 5.00 p.m., all of them left the factory.

After preliminary investigation the Management, at about 9.30 p.m. on the same day, issued charge sheet letters and also suspended five workers pending enquiry. By about 10.00 p.m., small groups of workers split from shop floor in other departments causing major work stoppages in most of the departments. By 6.00 p.m., the nest day, all production came to a halt with only general staff and that of certain essential services, like security. Reporting for duty the bargainable cadre of employees.

The unrecognized union put up a notice expressing its support to the stride by the workers and accused the Manager of having assaulted some workmen. They also demanded withdrawal of the charge sheet and suspension letters.

The very next day Labour Department of the State Government initiated investigations and soon declared the strike as prima-facie illegal and asked workers to resume duty forthwith. Thereafter, in a week's time, the recognized union also advised workers to resume duty. Both these developments, however, did not result in ending the strike. Striking workers organized meetings in the neighbouring villages instigating all to continue with the strike and prevent management from getting an upper hand. Open threats were made to management personnel and those going for work. With peace being threatened, the law and order authorities clamped section 144 in the area.

Management, in preparedness had made arrangements to protect employees coming for duty. Arrangement were also made to get production started with their help by employing casual workers. Meanwhile, a domestic enquiry into the charges agents the Five workers was started. Chargesheets were issued to three more workers for instigating to participate in an illegal strike.

The importance of the factory's products attracted many outside elements including leading local and state level political figures to fish in these troubled waters. They all urged the workers to remain united and carry on the strike.

With general staff reporting for duty, and with the assistance of supervisory staff, management spared no effort service to keep production going. Soon production of essential items crossed 50 percent levels.

A massive campaign mounted to help workers see reason and resume work, only caused the opposite camp to increase their activity more workers for resuming duty and also stop those who were doing so. As a result, round the clock picketing, harassment and intimidation, and even violence were reported in the areas surrounding the factory. Disciplinary action for assault and instigation were initiated against five more employees. Also, as the period of strike neared a month, management decided to take general action and warned workers that their services would be broken. As a vast majority did not respond, break in service was effected in about 40 cases.

Meanwhile, domestic enquiry proceedings continued to be held, without any of the defendant employees participation. Production improved to 75 percent levels. Although Labour Department officials camping at the factory tried best to end the strike, their efforts were unsuccessful due to the unreasonable attitude to the leaders of the strikes. The atmosphere was rife with rumours of all kinds. Management's attempts to dispel these and highlights facts were countered by pamphlets and propaganda by the leaders of the strikers.

The domestic enquiry proceedings concluded ex parte, and the five workmen were dismissed, after fulfilling all requirements as per law. With attendance not showing any marked improvement and production being maintained at unexpectedly high levels, a stalemate was reached.

After nearly six weeks, the labour Minister summoned the parties for discussions at the Capital. Initial rounds of discussions did not lead to any solution. Provocative measured by striking workmen increased some loyal workmen were beaten up and their houses ransacked by striking workmen supported by their wives and children. As a result, depression and tension prevailed in the area. The service of two employees, who had taken a leading role in these acts of violence, were terminated for continuous absence resulting in voluntary abandonment of service as per company's rules. This only heightened the desperation with the result that even casuals were not spared by the striking workers and for a while production showed signs of declining. However, it improved again and touched 80 percent level.

After nearly two months, the Hon'ble Labour Minister using his good office, persuaded the parties to accept this advice regarding the dismissal of the five workers this would be binding on all the parties, with such an understanding being reached, the strike was called off after nearly two months.

TRY YOURSELF

1. By not reporting to their workplace at 2.00 p.m. workers had already struck work. What steps, if any, could have led to defusing the situation before the assault occurred?
2. Although the assault was unprecedented in 24 years, should this possibility have been foreseen?
3. Without any action being taken, work in the department did not start after 2.00 p.m. while work in other departments was stopped only after the charge sheet cum suspension letters were given to the striking workman. What steps takers between 2.30 and 9.30 p.m. could have pre-empted the work stoppage in other departments?
4. Given the background, what was your assessment of the time for which the stride would continue? What solution would be just and fair to both parties? What steps/course of action would you adopt to strengthen your position in order to achieve the above?

5. As a Manager what was your assessment of the time for which the strike would continue? What solution would be just and fair to both parties? What steps/course of action would you adopt to strengthen your position in order to achieve the above?

6. (a) Following due enquiry the five workers were dismissed after nearly a months of the strike, and (b) During the two months, disciplinary action was initiated against workers, break in service given to about forty and abandonment of service resorted to in two cases.

   As a Manager what would you consider to be the plus/minus points of (a) and (b) above?

7. What other steps could management have taken which may have led to a larger number of striking workers resuming duty?

8. Management's strength in facing the strike lay in sustaining high levels of production. Even then the Management agreed to leave the matter to the advice of the Labour Minister. Were there any other alternatives available to the management

9. What in your assessment did the Labour Minister finally advise? What advice would have resulted in a win-win situation for both union and management?

MERCHANDISE MANAGEMENT

Where to look for Merchandise?

There are countless ways to find goods for our store, from reading trade magazines in bed at night to traveling to meet with native suppliers on the floor of the rain forest like Anita Roddick of the Bodyshop. Trade shows, usually held once or twice a year and open only to qualified wholesale buyers, have traditionally been the major source of new lines. In addition to temporary trade show exhibits, market centers in major cities often feature some permanent showrooms. These showrooms are usually open certain days outside of trade show week, which is convenient if we need to place orders right away.

Magazines published especially for our line of retailing will also help us find out who the wholesaler are for our type of merchandise. Once we have made contact with a few manufacturers or importer, the sale representatives (Called sales reps) for these companies may start calling on us. Unless the sales rep works exclusively for one line, he or she will be able to introduce us to many more potential sources. To find out what trade shows and magazines cover the type of goods were/are interested in, check with stores similar to ours in other parts of the country, or call the library.

The Internet is a wonderful new resource for finding product lines especially when we have seen an item we like and need more information. Most companies will send us a catalogue if we request it, but a complete website allows us to pursue their full range of goods immediately. (Wholesale prices, however, may not be given, especially if the site is also available to consumers.) Some composite web sites offer a search option that provides links to individual companies' sites. These would be especially helpful if we had specific need, for example, if we were looking for a source for papier-mache picture frames. Other sites specially aimed at business (called B2B, or business-to-business, sites) feature closeouts or special buys from a number of different vendors, and provide centralized billing and shipping if we choose to place an order.

A wise buyer remains open to new idea from all sources and will give thoughtful consideration to any new merchandise. It is quite surprised that some buyers refuse to see sales reps or to go to trade shows to look for new lines. We should always be on the lookout for new items that fit with our merchandise mix. Shopkeepers without the time energy to find new lines need to delegate some of their other duties, especially if we are ordering factory-made goods. Unless we have an agent working on our behalf in the other country, we will be trusting the company we buy from to send us merchandise in perfect condition. We will need to pay for freight and often customs fees and the services of a broker. Freight claims for merchandise damaged in transit can be difficult to resolve.

Direct importing has two main advantages: paying a lower price gives us a better margin when we set our retail prices, and we sometimes can find merchandise that no other store in our area offers. Another advantage is that there are many trade shows abroad, offering the retailer who can afford it (it may deductible, but it's not free) the opportunity to travel.

Finding lines to direct import can be a challenge for a small shop, especially since most goods with well-developed market in the United States are already brought into the country by large wholesale importers. We once ordered some hand-painted Christmas ornaments at the Frankfurt Trade Show in Germany, only to find out that the exclusive U.S. importer of the line visited the booth a few minutes later and tore up our order. Nevertheless, there are small suppliers in other countries still willing to export to individual shops. We buy dressed in other countries still willing to export to individual shops. We buy dressed felt business every Easter from a woman who lives on an island off the coast of England. Our customers know spring can't be far behind when the English bunnies arrive at Orange Tree Imports. The bunnies come to us a via airmail, so there is no chance of their being lost on sea.

Larger shipments of heavier or more expensive goods are usually shipped by boat and may require a letter of credit in payment and the services of a broker to process them through customs. We may have to pay to truck the merchandise to our shop from the port of arrival, where U.S. Customs may hold the goods for sometime while levying the customs charges. All of these factors and costs need to be taken into account when deciding whether to import a line of merchandise directly from overseas.

If we are buying an item in large quantities through an importer, ask about getting better pricing by doing a direct import of the goods. Some supplier, especially those dealing with department stores and large chains, are set up to assist us with overseas shipments if our order is large enough. A small shop might consider getting together with other retailer to place larger consolidated import order in order to make this economically feasible. A word of caution, however: Be clear about who will pay for what, and when. Goods not paid for on arrival at the port may incur storage costs or shifts in the currency market that can negate any savings.

A professional freight consolidator combines large orders from several stores and arranges to shop them in from overseas. The consolidator brings the goods through customs and then sends them on to the individual businesses. While not practical for small orders such as felt bunnies, the services of a freight consolidator can be the key to doing direct imports of larger items for shops not large enough to do huge order on their own.

Many buyers choose items only on the basis of whether they like them, but, of course, they are not going to be the retail customers buying the merchandise. Our exasperated supplier said, "I'd like to banish the words 'I don't like it' from buyers' vocabulary! It doesn't matter if they like it or not, if it fits well! in their shop, and if it is selling well, they should try it." Another sale person reported that a buyer wouldn't carry cat items in her shop because she didn't like cats. If her customers like cats, and some of them undoubtedly do, she should consider carrying cat items, unless, of course, her shop is called The Dog House. This is not to say that we need to carry merchandise that we find to be in poor taste, or offensive. We draw the line at war toys, for example, and we won't carry Halloween decorations that make irritating electronic noises, no matter how well they might sell.

When considering new merchandise, try to imagine where a line will go in our store and how we will display it. What category will it fit into? Do we need more merchandise in that category? If we use an open-to-buy budget, are there dollars available in that department for the time period in which the order will arrive? Don't rust our buying decisions. We may wish to wait until after we have compared several lines before deciding which one to buy. Try to test new lines in our off-seasons so we can reorder heavily if they sell well.

Determining Quantities

It can be very difficult to determine how many of each item to buy. When my friend, came into business with me, I was shocked by the size of the orders he wrote, and twenty years later, he still sometimes orders by the gross while I order by the dozen. He is often right, so he will have enough of a good seller on hand to break sales records. But when testing a new item or line, I feel safer ordering conservatively. Still, we must order enough of a line to 'make a statement', or present it fairly. If a line has several different items, styles, colours, or price points, consider ordering a variety of a product in order to make a display items, styles, colours, or price points, consider ordering a variety of products in order to make a display. As a rule, order at least two of each item ('one to show and one to go' is an old retail expression). Otherwise we will never know if more than one customer is interested in the product.

It stands to reason that the more merchandise we order, the less frequently we will need to reorder, saving time and effort. Ordering in large quantities will usually also get us better prices and sometimes special invoice terms. Consolidating orders into a few big shipments instead of many small ones helps keep freight costs down. The flip side of ordering in depth, of course, is that we will have to store the additional merchandise until we can sell it and our money will be tied up in the stock. This is referred to as opportunity cost. The fact that the money used to purchase certain inventory is no available to use for some other purpose.

There is also the risk, especially early in our retailing career that we will purchase a large quantity of an item that bomb. Reserve quantity purchases for items we have tested already, or merchandise that is basic to our stock. Avoid size style or fragrance. We might also be able to do our own packaging of items purchased in bulk, such as candle, seeds, beads or soaps. Use a distinctive package, and add a fancy sticker or ribbon giving the store name, which features private label products.

Customizing Merchandise for the Tourist Market

Someone once said that the best souvenir is an item that is a good buy and not readily available back home. As all products become more widely distributed, it gets harder to find something to offer tourists that is not available elsewhere. Locally produced items or regional specialties are often too expensive to be considered a good buy by most tourist.

One solution to this problem is to buy merchandise that has been souvenired, personalized with the name of the area of tourist attraction. The most common souvenir item is, of course, the T-shirt. Many T-shirt manufacturers will add the name of the city or state to any of their designs for a small additional charge. Magnets, ornaments, and mugs can also have the tourist destination added to stock design.

In order to develop a coordinated program of customer souvenir items, Beth Engh, former gift buyer for the Brookfield Zoo in Chicago, suggests designing a logo and one or more visual images and selecting a set colour scheme. Use the same designs and colours on a wide range of impulse items-key rings, pencils, button, T-shirts, mugs, water bottles, and so forth- to create a coordinated look in our souvenir area. The same images can be used on slightly more expensive items, such as embroidered sweatshirts, wooden boxes, and tote bags.

Young customers are a prime market for souvenirs, especially at attraction visited by school groups. Be sure to carry a good selection of impulse items aimed at young buyers. Open acrylic bins, well labeled with price signs, are an effective way to display these small items, although shoplifting can be a problem. Plan to have at least one employee other than the one behind the cash register available to assist young shoppers when a large group comes in store.

Not every tourist wants to buy an inexpensive souvenir. A selection of higher–quality, more expensive items will help make the shop look more sophisticated and can lead to larger sales. Look for merchandise representative of the area, preferably locally made. We may also want to stock guidebooks and other educational material relating to the local attraction. Keep in mind that visitors may have walk some distance to their car, so heavy so bulky items may need to be shipped or delivered to the customer's hotel.

Direct Importing

Goods ordered to be shipped from the country of origin right to our shop or a port of entry nearby are said to be direct imports. Merchandise purchased this way is almost less expensive than goods bought from an importer or dealer, but importing has its own headaches. We must, as a rule, purchase in quantity, buying in quantity just to get a bargain. It's not a bargain unless we can sell the entire shipment, and in a reasonable amount of time.

Buying on Consignment

One way to stretch our inventory in rupees is to purchase on consignment, which means we don't play unless the product sells. The risk of stocking the merchandise is thus placed on the vendor, not the store. Problems may arise, however, if merchandise on consignment is damaged or stolen. And we need to take into account that our shelf space is valuable, so consignment merchandise still carries some overhead cost, despite the fact that these items don't tie up inventory.

Good sold on consignment also usually have a lower markup than merchandise purchased outright, so our profit margin will often be 40 percent or less. A consignment arrangement makes it less risky to try unusual merchandise we are not sure will sell but would like to try. It is a method best used for art, crafts, or expensive items such as antiques. Keep careful track of consignment goods so that at the end of the predetermine period we remember to return the remaining portion of the order and to pay for what we have sold. A price tag with a tear off sub that can be removed at the time of purchase is one way to track consignment merchandise. Another way is to assign a code for each consignment vendor, and to write down purchase information in a journal by the cash register.

Developing our own Products

One way to ensure a unique selection of merchandise in our shop is to arrange to have merchandise produced exclusively for us. If we sell gifts for pet owners, for example, we could contact a local potter to make cat food bowls for our shops, jeweler to create earrings featuring popular breeds of dogs. It is fund to help develop new products, and we (or the craft person) might be able to wholesale them to other stores outside our trading area. We carried a line of silk-screened cards by local artists (and scientist) Vaughn James, and one night I had a dream that Vaughn turned his card designs into T-shirts. Vaughn was happy to follow up on my idea, and has sold thousands of silk-screened T-shirts-the only products I've literally dreamed up.

There are also manufacturers willing to put our store name and logo on their precuts, a process called private labeling. Private label merchandise reinforces our store name and image and gives the consumer the impression that our operation is large enough to include manufacturing. It is also hard for consumers to compare prices on private label products, so extra markup can usually be taken on these items. Chain stores often feature on or more private label brand of clothing and other merchandise, and the profit on these products is considerably greater than on competitive name brands.

Private label manufacturing usually requires placing large orders, if for no other reasons than the expense of printing full colour labels. Look of product that can share the same label, perhaps with a separate sticker indicating the sell down to the last prices of these items or to display them when there are not many left (not one want to see a zodiac display with only Aires, Taurus, Libra!). Some companies' offer a buy-out program for these products, giving credit toward other merchandise if we return a certain percentage of our original order. These programmes are sometimes very profitable, but try to be certain that the product is good, the company is reliable, and our shop has enough traffic to sell it in quantity. It is also difficult to close out products that are seasonal, fashioned-oriented, artsy or edible. Special caution is necessary when buying goods for these categories.

Few items continue to sell well forever. The fluctuation in an item's popularity is called its product life cycle. New merchandise that is well received by our customer may demonstrate a market increase in sales every time we reorder, until suddenly sales drop off. Pay close attention to customer buying patterns, and listen to what sales reps are saying about an item's popularity. When we begin to sense that the sales of an item are slowing down, reorder cautiously or not at all. It is better to brings in new merchandise than to carrying an item just because it has been popular in the past.

Tracking Sales for Reorders

Every store has certain categories of steady sellers, called bread-and-butter items that should never be out of stock. Most other items get reordered a few times, until sale slow down. Still others are ordered once, and then replaced with something new.

A point-of-sales (POS) cash register system will compile records of what merchandise has been sold, alerting us to dangerously low inventory levels. We can set a minimum inventory level for each item; based on how long it usually takes to receive a reorder and how many units we are likely to sell each day or week. The POS system can even generate a reorder; in fact many chain stores use a system called EDI (electronic data interface), which provides a direct link between the store's computer and that of major suppliers. Some day this technology may be practical for smaller stores heavily dependent on a few key vendors.

In a single store location, we can control inventory levels by watching what is selling and doing manual counts. For items we reorder regularly, we use a perpetual inventory to recording the quantity of each item received and the quantity left on hand a few weeks or months later. By tracking the number sold, we know how many to reorder. The quantity left from the first order, plus the quantity received on the reorder, become the new starting figure that we use to compare the amount left on hand the next time we are ready to order. This system can easily be set up as a computer spreadsheet.

A perpetual inventory can be taken weekly, monthly or just whenever stock seems low enough to warrant placing an order. Many vendors have a fairly high minimum reorder, so we can't order just one item that is out of stock. It also helps to reduce freight costs if we order a large number of items at a time. The trick is not to wait so long that a popular item is completely sold out Many countries maintain trade offices in their embassies or consulates in the United States to assist buyers in planning business trips abroad and arranging for direct imports. It is the economic interest of other countries to encourage exports of their goods to the United State, so they are happy to provide information about trade shows, visas, buying offices, export regulations, and so forth. State and federal trade offices here can assist with customs and other import regulations.

Inventory Control

In is easy to make the mistake of buying too much or buying enough through as to whether there is enough customers for certain items. In fact, it is much harder to say no a line, especially when it is presented with a convincing sales pitch, than it is to say yes. New merchandise invariably looks fresher and more exciting that the stock on hand. Learn to stand our ground and turn down good we don't need.

We should also plan to routinely clear out old goods that haven't been selling well so that we will have to money and space for fresh stock. Some experts even recommended budgeting a certain amount for marketing each month. It is certainly helpful to track our markdowns, so we know whether the high sales in a line to table lamps come from the fact that most of them are being sold at 50 percent off. We'll also want to know what we've marked down as clearance so we don't record these items.

There is a saying in retailing that the first markdown is the most importunate. One retailers shop had a rule that anything that hadn't sold in a year went into a trunk in which every item was Rs. 10- no matter what its original price had been. We can bet that its clearance items moved out quickly, since the trunk was the first spot every customer checked on entering the store. Take less Texas-sized discount than this retailer as soon as we realize than an item isn't selling, so that we can regroup our investment and not "sit on dead merchandise", as it is so colourfully described in the trade. Keeping show movers on the move allows us to continue buying new goods with a clear conscience.

Dated price tags will help us determine how long the merchandise has been on our shelf. In order to make this system work, we need to make sure that shipment of merchandise arriving first is displayed before the next reorder of the same items (this is known as FIFO, first in, first out in the trade-as opposed to LIFO, last in, first out). If we notice that an item has been around too long, use a colour-coded sale tag with a date on it to mark it down 10 percent to 20 percent. We can then track how long it's been on display at the sale price before marking it down an additional percentage until it sells.

Consider what we will do if a line doesn't sell well before we place an order. Most items can be marked down a sold, but if we have invested in special fixtures, we may not be able to reuse them. Be especially cautious with programmes that involve stocking items personalized with a range of names, initials, zodiac signs, or months or years of birth. It is notoriously difficult to before the new stock arrives. Keep track of which suppliers ship in a few days and which ones need to receive orders month or more before they can ship.

Another way to track the inventory of certain items is to use a price tag with a detachable stub listing a product description or code number. When an item is sold, the stub is removed and put in a box, to be tallied latter. We use this system to track collectible items such as Department 56's lighted houses. A record book kept by the cash register shows how many pieces of each day or two and marks off those sold. This system gives us a fairly accurate picture at two and marks off those sold. This system gives us a fairly accurate picture at all times of how many pieces are in stock. (We also use detachable stub tickets on our store supplier, removing the stub when, for example, a new case of gift boxes is opened. This helps us reorder these supplies before we run out).

Many stores do not reorder exactly the same item of merchandise more than a time or two in certain categories, so even a simple perpetual inventory system may be more record keeping than is necessary for most lines. There is nothing wrong with checking to see how many teddy bears have been sold by just taking a look at how many bears are on the shelf and in the stockroom.

Seasonal Planning

Long before the first snowfall signal the start of the Christmas season to most shoppers, buyers who order seasonal merchandise will be turning their attention to Easter bunnies and valentines. And while people are anticipating the arrival of spring, retailers who stock seasonal goods will be pondering the ghoulish jack-o-lanterns and wintry Christmas cards. Seasonal buying is somewhat like working in the night shift; we always feel a bit out of step with the rest of the world.

Anyone would find it difficult to remember which Easter candies sold best while ringing up. Halloween treats. If we add to this fact that the buying season for holiday merchandise has gotten so long that Christmas ordering takes place over almost a nine-month period, it becomes clear that it is in an ongoing challenges to keep track of whether there are enough (or too many, which is often worse) gift bags, tree toppers, or jingle bell ornaments on order.

Many shop owners have discovered that some form of seasonal planning is must. There are two real dangers in ignoring this need. The first, and more obvious, is that having too much merchandise on hand leads to excessive inventory at the end of a holiday that may have to be carried over in storage for a year. Some of these goods, of course, can be marked down and sold for cost within a few days of the holiday. Department stores have developed the after Christmas sale into one of their biggest events of the year. But few small shops have the traffic to ensure that all of the post-seasonal merchandise is goods that haven't been sold while the holiday is still on everyone's mind are not likely to sell. I once visited a hospital gift shop in April and Saw Christmas candy still on sale. The bad impression made by these stale boxes of chocolate cast a pall over all the merchandise on display.

What to order?

An exciting, electric selection of merchandise is one of the key components to a successful specialty shop. Customers have the option of spending their rupees at many different places, and to a great extent, the same goods are available in most stores. The specialty store distinguished itself by presenting shoppers with products carefully chosen and enticingly displayed. Stanley Mercus, Chairman emeritus of Neiman-Marcus, pointed out that customers want the specialty shop buyer to edit the options for them and present those they think are the very best, or the best value at a good price.

Specialty shop buyers need to be risk-takers, constantly looking for products unique in their market. As soon as an item turns up in a discount store, the time has come for the small retailer to drop it. Whenever possible, the specialty shop buyer should look for items not available to mass marketers. This help eliminate price competition, which is a game that's hard to win when we don't have the buying clout of a big chain.

Are there still products that are not being sold to the big stores? One way to find out is to shop these stores regularly, paying attention to new merchandise. Ask our customer where else they shop, and look for weakness in the merchandise and services being offered by those stores. Make sure we offer something different-perhaps by doing some direct importing or by commissioning product from crafts people or small manufacturers that will be unique to our store. We can also favour lines whose marketing is focused solely on the independent retailer.

Although specialty shop customers do not tend to focus solely on price, price is an important factor in most buying decision. When I consider a product, I need to determine right away whether it is in a price range appropriate for my store. Since it is very difficult to run a store profitability at only keystone, mark up of 100% on top of the wholesale price, another price consideration is whether the item would be likely to sell at a slightly mark up.

One way to maintain a good margin while still offering attractive prices is to get the lowest possible wholesale price. We are constantly looking for good prices, special discounts, and extended terms from suppliers. Whenever possible, we buy in case packs, which often offer a lower price per piece than broken, or partial or packs. We try to buy directly from the source rather than through a distributor or middleman. As Gary Darwin, former Vice-President of Sales at Cardinal Inc., always reminded us, it never hurts to ask a supplier, "Is this is the best price I can get?"

Other stores band together to form buying groups, combining the orders of many independent small ships into single large orders to get better terms and lower prices. Buying groups, or co-ops, have already proved successful for book stores, pharmacies, and hardware aspirated stores. The idea may work for other types of specialty shops as well. The second, less obvious, problem with not planning for seasonal sale is that we may have to little inventory on hand. We cannot sell twelve Santa figurines if we have only four in stock, unless we are lucky enough to find a supplier who can ship a reorder at the last minute. "We can't sell from an empty cart," the saying goes. Customers want what appears to be a full selection to chose from right up to holiday itself. They usually will not buy the very last item on hand, even at closing time on Christmas Eve.

Creating a Seasonal Planning System

A seasonal planning programme can make life easier for anyone who buys holiday merchandise and should lead to better inventory turns and a more profitable operation. It is especially helpful to new buyers, including the hospital shop's volunteer who is asked to order seasonal goods without having any experience of her own to rely on.

The basic premise behind a seasonal planning system is that the buying patterns of customer can be predicted based on their past patterns. If we sold thirty dozen Valentines in 2005, we are more likely to sell thirty-five dozen in 2006 than we are to sell three dozen – or three hundred dozen. And if hand painted Easter Eggs sold out early this season, we will probably want to make sure us have more on hand next year.

A new store will not have any history to go on, of course, but it is never too early to start keeping records to help plan for future years.

Watching for Change

Although it is generally true that future sales can be predicted based on past sales, a number of factors can alter these predictions, and they should be taken into account when making buying decisions. First the local factors are the store's sales increasing or declining? How is our community's economy and that of our particular mall or shop locations? Do we know of any special factors, such as feature story in the news about our shop, or bad weather that influences our sales figures last year? Do we know of anything that will have in impact on this year's sales? The opening of a competing store or roadwork in front of our shop may influence what we will need to buy.

Look closely at any change in the holiday we are buying for. Easter, for example, can fall in March or in April, and an early Easter is generally an indication of a slightly weaker season because of the shorter sales period. Halloween and Valentine sales are influenced by whether they fall on a weekday or weekend. And finally, be alert to trends in consumer holiday celebration and buying. Fashions in holiday decoration, cards, and gifts all changes to some extent from year-to-year.

Despite these variables- all of which contribute to making retailing a constant challenge, it is possible to significantly increase our chances of doing a good job of holiday through consistent seasonal record keeping.

Setting up Planning Notebook

A large three ring binder works as well as seasonal planning notebook, because it is portable and can expand to fill our needs. Pages can be added easily, and notes can be taken out and copied to take to trade shows. We might also consider keeping the records on a computer, printing out copies of whatever data we need to take with us.

Arrange our records by holiday, subdividing the larger holiday by merchandise category if necessary. We keep our records in chronological order, progressing from one season to the next. Even if we are working in Mother's Day in January, at least Father's Day still comes next. We also have a category for calendars, in increasingly important part of the seasonal mix for many retailers.

The seasonal record book could be used to organized photographs of the store's holiday displays and advertising, along with pictures of display ideas from trade magazines and vendor catalogues. Trade magazines often feature articles with useful ideas for seasonal promotions that can be clipped and saved. We keep a calendar in the front of our seasonal planning notebook with the dates of all the major holidays over the next few years. These are sometimes available in trade magazine, or from the library's reference department.

The Good, the Bad, and the Merely O.K.

The hundreds of items carried seasonally by specialty shops can be followed inasmuch detail as is necessary for the size of the store. The most basic record is simply a listing of three columns: good, bad, and O.K- with our impression of the items that sold most quickly, those that were slow sellers, and those in between.

A more detailed record would include everything ordered for a particular holiday, by company, with notes as to how well each item sold. We could even make copies or the purchase order or invoices and insert them into the notebook for note taking. A simple yes or no next to each item will help us remember what to order more, and less, of the following year. Take a quick count a few days before a holiday to note any items that sold out early enough to warrant an increase for the next year. For example, there may be no Valentine candy hearts left after valentine's day, which means that all twenty four boxes sold. But if there were no candy hearts left four days before Valentine's Day, it is a safe bet that more than twenty-four would have been sold had there been more on hand.

Counting leftover seasonal merchandise when we pack it away at the end of a holiday save time on inventory day. Put a copy of this in the seasonal planning notebook for easy reference when doing future ordering. If we are going to use the inventory for planning, however, list items by company or by category so that we can see at a glance what we carryover is on a certain item.

Planning for Displays and Promotion

Keep display and advertising in mind when we do our buying always staying on the look out for items that will be good draws when featured in ads or store windows? Advertising, promotions, and display should be coordinated, with any item features in an ad prominently displayed in the store. Never have the last one of an item in the window; plan ahead so we will have an adequate quantity of every item being highlighted. We may also wish to order a few oversize items to use mostly as display props, but priced in case a customer want to buy them.

When we order a new line of merchandise or even just a new item, have some idea where we will display it in the store. If special fixtures will be required, order these to arrive at the same time as the goods. In addition to working toward a full and interesting variety, think about how the various lines we order will complemented each other, and look for colours and textures that go well together. The merchandise we order will become the basic material we will use to create in-store and window display to excite customers and make them want to buy.

Working with sales Reps

We see sales reps by appointment only. If a new rep calls without any lines we already buy (this is tough for reps to do; it's called making a cold call, probably referring to the chilly reception they received from most buyers), we ask a few questions before deciding whether to give an appointment. Obviously, this is an easy decision to make if the rep is selling jewelry, but often we really can't say yes or no to new lines without seeing them. However, once a rep is in our store, it's hard to say no to him or her. Ever since we saw death of a Salesman, we've had great sympathy for the trials of the sales rep, and we rarely turn anyone away without some sort of an order. If we think we may have to, we grant the appointment with the qualification that we may just be taking a look this time. That way the rep can decide if it's worth coming to see us. We both know that if we don't order anything, the rep won't get paid for the sales call.

Buying Trips

One of the joys of retailing is being able to travel while scouting out new goods. Even visiting gift shops in some popular resort area can yield samples of items that would sell well in our shop (although the Internal Revenue Services would probably still not consider a day at the beach to be a business trip).

We used to make a game of memorizing the name and address of a supplier before leaving a shop, since it seemed impolite to write it down in front of the shopkeeper. But it would be even better to pay full retailer for a sample of the product- much as this hurts when we are used to getting items wholesale. Unfortunately, not every item is labeled with its source-in some very competitive locations, retailers actually go to the effort of obscuring any information that could give away the sources of an item, and frequently manufacturer neglect to label their product. But we may find some friendly retailer who are willing to look up information and share it with us, as long as it is clear our shop is outside their trading area.

Visiting arts and crafts shows is an excellent way to find small suppliers with handmade wares, which can be wonderful addition to the merchandise selection of many specialty shops and are rarely carried by mass merchants. Artists who have never sold merchandise wholesale may need some help developing special products to sell a store. We ask that artists selling to us not sell the same merchandise directly to the public- for example, at an art fair- at price much lower than our retail prices. This often means they need to decide which item they will sell wholesale to store which they will sell themselves.

There are several special trade fairs of crafts where artist already familiar with selling goods wholesale exhibit their ware for shop buyers. These artisans have already developed a line of crafts that they can produce at low enough prices to be viable when retail mark-up is added.

Most other product categories are also marketed through large wholesale trade shows. These shows are often a combination of temporary exhibits by suppliers and sales reps and permanent showrooms of merchandise, set up like small shops. Trade shows are an excellent source of merchandise display ideas, and contact with fellow shopkeepers. A retailer who does not feel any need to go to trade shows is one, who is not interested in growing a thriving business.

Credit References

The purpose of the credit sheet, or list of credit references, is to establish our creditability and reliability with a new supplier. We are asking the supplier to believe that our business is creditworthy enough to receive valuable merchandise on account and that we will pay for it when the invoice is due. Think of the credit reference sheet as a resume for our store. When we apply for open credit terms from a supplier, we want to make a good impression. The credit reference sheet should be neatly types and present all the pertinent details about our business:

- Name
- Address
- Phone and fax numbers
- Website and e-mail address
- Date the store was established
- The store's legal entity (corporation, partnership, or sole proprietorship)
- The name of the store's owner(s)
- Resale number
- Name and address of the store's bank
- Name of some of the store's major suppliers

The Purchase Order Form

For orders written in our shop, especially those faxed to reps or suppliers, we may want to produce our own purchase order form with the store's name, address, phone and fax number, and other pertinent data already listed. Leave room for the name of the supplier and its address and phone number. It is also useful to leave a space for the name to the sales rep, if the line is new tour store, we will need to send a copy of our credit references. We would then write 'references enclosed' on the line for the account number.

The body of the purchase order form is the space for the quantity, item number, description, and wholesale price of the items being ordered. Since we use the purchase order to check in the merchandise, our form has room to the left of the quantity ordered for checking off the number received. The column to the right of the wholesale prices is used for our retail price and category code, usually written in after the order is placed. We may wish to ask that all orders be written on our customized purchase order form. If this is the case, we will need copies for the sales rep and the vendor. Print a supply on carbonless carbon paper with at least three copies, and remember to take a supply with us to trade shows.

If we send or fax an order to a sales rep, we will often receive a copy back in the mail as a confirmation copy. This copy is usually created when the rep copies the order onto his or her own form in order to get credit of the sales. After comparing the confirmation copy with our copy for accuracy, we may choose to discard it or to staple it behind the original purchase order.

We file purchase orders alphabetically by company name, which sometimes necessitates writing it in above there group's name on the top of a purchase order. Other stores file purchase orders by ship date, especially if they place orders with only a few suppliers.

Placing Purchase Orders

In addition to specifying the items and the quantities being ordered, the buyer specifies when the order should be shipped and the method of shipping to be used. If the merchandise is needed by a certain date, state a ship date a week or two earlier. If the goods will not be of any use to the store if received after a specific time, specify a cancellation date for the order. If the supplier ships the goods after that date, we have the right to refuse the order.

We may also want to place a series of orders, called programme orders with staggered ship dates. In this way we plan our purchases from many months at a time and can cancel orders if the line does not sell as well as expected. Some vendors like having an idea of our needs far in advance; others find the cancellation of orders very problematic. Check with the vendor to find out whether programme orders are welcome.

Suppliers often have a set minimum dollar amount for a wholesale order. His minimum order discourages individuals from buying wholesale for their own use and also assures the vendor that the orders are large enough to be handled efficiently. The minimum order is usually larger on the first order, since the vendor will have to go the trouble of establishing a new customer number and account for the store. Companies also want retailers to order to encourage shops to reorder the best selling items as soon as they have sold. For customer special orders, companies sometimes waive the reorder minimum or allow a small order if we pay an extra charge.

The Laurel Burch designer line, once decided to raise its minimum reorder to $500 at wholesale, thinking that this would encourage stores to offer a complete assortment of Laurel's jewelry, mugs, shirts and stationary. This strategy works well if the initial minimum is high and some lines requires as much as $5,000 for a first order. But it was a real problem when applied to reorders. Customers wanting a pair or earrings in a certain colour or a T-shirt in a certain size had to wait until the store's entire stock had gotten low enough to warrant a $500 order. It was not long before the word came from Laurel Burch that there was no longer any minimum at all on reorders.

Vendors are often out of certain merchandise, especially imported items, and may choose to ship them when they arrive. Items that are out of stock when the first part of the order is shipped are referred to as being on back order. If we don't want to receive any items later, be sure to specify no back orders. We can also set a minimum for the size of the back orders we will accept. Small back orders often have high freight charges, so we tell vendors not to shop back orders of less than $50, unless they are paying for the freight. If we have established special terms for the original order, such as free freight or a 10 percent advertising allowance, these terms should apply to back orders as well. When reordering a line, specify whether we want any items still not shipped from our first order kept on back order or cancelled.

Some suppliers prefer to substitute items that are in stock for those that are out of stock. We specify 'no subs' if we want our selections or nothing at all, especially when it comes to greeting cards. Suppliers, sometimes, ask if a shop uses a purchase order number, and we find that using the date the order is written as the purchase order number helps track the order if there is even any question about it.

If we have already established an account with a company, we maybe asked to specify the terms, when we will pay the invoice. Usually the terms are dictated by the company's policy, and are net 30 or sooner. A discount may be offered for paying earlier than the due date- for example, 2% / 10 net 30 which means we can take 2 percent off the invoice of we pay within ten days of the invoice date. A discount of 2 percent may not seem like much, but when calculated over a long period, these discounts add up. By paying a Rs. 1,000 invoice twenty days before it is due, we save Rs. 20. If we were to invest that Rs. 1,000 in a bank for twenty days instead, we would have to make more than 35 percent interest to get a better return on our money.

After our first new – buyer orientation talk at the Chicago Gift show, a man came up and shyly asked me, "what's dating?" It took me a moment to realize he was asking a legitimate business question. Vendors sometimes offer more than thirty day to pay, especially on seasonal merchandise that they want to ship as soon as soon as they can. IT is not uncommon to find seasonal dating on these lines, with the invoice due close to the holiday or season in question. Delayed dating means we have the merchandise to sell for a long period before we have to pay for it, always a plus.

Terms such as net 30 and beyond give the store a grace period in which to sell the merchandise before paying for it–a great help to the store's cash flow and a nice benefit provided by the supplier. Taking excessive advantage of this situation by paying bills late is called leaning on the trade, and is an unfair way to generate cash flow. Department stores are notorious for not paying bills on time, which gives the specialty shop that is a prompt payer an advantage over these pokey giants in the eyes of a supplier. Many supplier belong to trade associations that share information about delinquent accounts-another reason to stay current on all bills.

Specifying Shipping References

More often than not, our store will pay the freight on an order, so it is our right to determine how it is shipped to us. Freight costs can have a significant impact on the profit margin of our merchandise.

Consider shipping options and distance when selection merchandise. Shipments from companies in our part of the country will almost always have lower freight costs, but some vendors offer to pay part of the freight costs on large orders so that they can compete with companies in other regions. Freight costs will not vary so much on small orders or lightweight merchandise, so the location of the vendor is not as important with jewellery, for example, as it is with jams and jellied. Heavy, inexpensive merchandise such as bottles of lamp oil incur freight costs almost equal to the wholesale price of the merchandise. Ordering a larger quantity at a time helps reduce the freight cost per item.

Many shops simply put 'cheapest and best' under 'ship via'. This allows the supplier the choose whether to send the goods with a less-than-truckload (LTL) trucking company (also called a common carrier) or with a small-package service such as United Parcel Service (UPS) or Federal Express (FedEx) Ground. The size of the cartons and the total shipping weight usually determine which type of service is most economical, although UPS now has a service, UPS Hundredweight, for larger, heavier shipments.

There may be some special considerations to take into account in selection the most economical way to ship merchandise. Small shipments of books, for example, may be sent inexpensively by parcel post's special book rate. Bulky items such as pinatas must be shipped by common carrier, adding two or more dollars in freight costs to each burro or bull. Merchandise that is urgently needed by a customer may require shipment by FedEx or some other overnight services, and customers may be willing to pay extra for this speedy delivery.

To minimize freight costs, try to avoid placing small, fill-in orders for heavy items. Remember to add more markups to the retail prices of items with high freight costs. Look for special shipping terms from suppliers, such as free freight or a partial freight allowance, terms often available when an order reaches a certain size or if it is prepaid. When calculating freight allowances, keep in mind that a 2 percent discount for freight means 2 percent off the invoice total for the merchandise, whereas half freight or full freight refers, respectively, to deducting half or all of the amount of the actual freight charges.

A purchase order sometimes states at what point the shipment becomes the responsibility of the store. The term FOB means that freight costs must be paid by the store after the merchandise has been delivered to the shipping company. FOB stands for 'Free On Board', a throwback to the days when a supplier might actually deliver a bundle of goods shipside instead of just handing the package over to a friendly delivery person.

Setting Retail Prices

Merchandise must be purchased at a considerably lower price than it is sold for if we don't want to fall victim to that old retailing joke: "I', taking a loss on every item, but I'm taking a loss on every item, but I'm making up for it in volume! Traditionally, most merchandise is purchased at a wholesale, or net, price that is half the retail prices. This means there is a 100 percent market-up (or 50 percent margin) on each item. The 100 percent mark-up has been standard for so many years that it is referred to as keystone. Most experts agree, however, that keystone mark-up is no longer enough to keep a store profitable. Some items must be sold at a higher retail, at least at keystone plus a portion of the freight costs. Merchandise that is pre-priced, such as books and greeting cards, allows no fluctuation in retail pricing (and, unfortunately, none of our current card supplier price his cards at higher than keystone markup). Luckily other items can be priced however we wish, providing we don't break our state's minimum markup laws. In Wisconsin, for example, it is illegal to set retail prices below wholesale cost-hardly a practice we would ever consider, but when the law was passed, one of our kind customers asked me with great concern whether this new regulation would hurt our business.

We are always looking for closeouts and other items on sale from our vendors, or available with special terms such as free freight, that will allow us to take markup that is higher than keystone and still offer prices customers will find attractive. We also look for blind items- unique merchandise that customers don't have a preconceived idea of how much it should sell for, so we can price these items slightly higher without hurting sales. One way to create blind items is to bundle several item together, such as soap dish, soap, and scented candle, and sell them as a set. Conversely, we can buy items in sets and then price them separarely at a slightly higher total retail than the set price. Selling items individually that are normally sold prepackaged is a service to the customer, who may not want a large quantity of an item.

Keep markdowns and perishability in mind when setting retail prices. A nursery, for example, will price plants as high as 300 percent above wholesale cost. Plants require high maintenance until sold, and a certain percentage may not survive. Seasonal or trendy fashion apparel often needs to be cleared out a reduced price after just a month or two in the store. Added mark-up is necessary to maintain some profitability when selling a significant amount of merchandise at clearance prices.

We write the retail prices on the purchase order soon after I've written an order, so the merchandise is still fresh in my mind and we can remember which items we feel can be sold for slightly higher than keystone. When we place orders at trade shows, we try to get all the orders retailed before the end of each day. We occasionally catch errors when reviewing orders to price and will contact the rep to make a correction before it is too late.

In determining retail prices, we pay close attention to the even price points such as Rs. 5, Rs. 10, and Rs. 20. If an item wholesales for Rs. 2.50, I almost always keep it at the Rs. 500 price point. An item that wholesales for Rs. 600, however, will sell just as well at Rs. 12.50 as at Rs. 12.00. This type of discretionary pricing requires some customer psychology. We need to look at each item and try to determine how much above keystone we can go without acquiring a reputation for high or, worse yet, unfair prices.

Customer love a bargain, so when we are able to offer a lower price because of a quantity purchase or manufacturer's special offer, we often draw attention to the price by suing a white price tag to indicate the 'regular' price and a red one pre-printed with the words 'special' to flag the lower price.

Competing with discounter will require us to occasionally settle for less than keystone items and to make up the difference on other merchandise. There are also categories, such as books and electronic, that traditionally are sold at a lower standard mark-up. In order to protect our profit margin when going up against a discounter or when featuring low mark-up merchandise, we need to buy very carefully, looking for volume discounts, dating program, and other special offers. It is essential to have a diverse product mix so that some of our merchandise will provide us with a higher potential margin.

Developing Vendor Relations

The suppliers we buy from should be partners in our success. Our store cannot thrive without good quality merchandise for customers to buy, and vendors cannot get their merchandise to the buying public without retailers as the link. Ideally, this partnership work well for both parties.

Retailers help vendors by:

- Ordering conscientiously.
- Not canceling order capriciously.
- Displaying all merchandise well.

- Reporting damage and defective claims fairly.
- Paying invoice promptly.
- Giving the supplier feedback from customers about the merchandise.

Vendors help retailers by:

- Providing quality, fashionable merchandise.
- Communicating regularly with retailer about new merchandise and specials.
- Filling orders completely and on time.
- Settling damage and defective claims quickly.
- Not selling the same goods to discounters and neighboring stores.
- Offering special terms such as free freight or early payment discounts.

It stands to reason that a good retailer will favour suppliers who make a sincere effort to support specially shop accounts. Some stores track vendor compliance to see how many orders are received close to the date specified and how many items are defective, incorrect, or on back order. It is also important to note which suppliers are selling to other stores in our area, especially mass merchandisers, by shopping our competition often. When goods become commonplace or are discounted, they are usually no longer as viable for a specialty shop.

The speed with which a vendor can ship reorders, called the replenishment time, is important in determining how much merchandise we need to keep on hand. If suppliers can furnish us with new goods quickly, we will have fewer rupees tied up in stored inventory. Some suppliers, especially those dealing with imported goods, have great difficulty in shipping promptly and completely, but it stands to reason that we should favour those that make an effort to do so. Our life is certainly easier when goods arrive just when we want them.

Because specialty shop customers expect high quality, the condition of the merchandise when we receive it is also important. We inspect items carefully upon receipt and expect our vendors to take back merchandise that arrives broken or does not meet our reasonable quality standards. IF a customer returns an item as defective, we often contact the supplier for credit. It is usually only by hearing from us about a problem that the vendor will know if the consumer is dissatisfied with a product.

It doesn't hurt to ask if special terms or pricing are available from a vendor, especially if we are placing sizable order. Be sure to ask the supplier's advice about what items in the line are selling well, as well as what items are new. Order – writing should reflect the partnership relationship we are working to establish with each vendor.

How many vendors should we buy from? Having too few vendors puts our store in jeopardy should one of them fail or being selling to mass merchandisers. Too many can be difficult to keep track of and can lead to an unfocused look in the store's merchandising. Some buyers also point out that by concentrating on large orders to a number of key suppliers, stores can become important accounts to these vendors and will receive preferential treatment in return for their loyalty.

We are always looking for new, unique merchandise, so we open many new vendor accounts each year. This become somewhat of a headache for our bookkeepers, but it means we constantly have new good to offer our customers. We favour certain exemplary vendors with larger reorders, but we rarely drop a line of really wonderful merchandise just because of poor performance in shipping or some other aspect of vendor compliance. We want out store to feature the very best selection of merchandise available, and working with many vendors is one way are able to do so.

PLANNING OF ASSORTMENT

All retailers face the fundamental strategic questions of what type of retail format to maintain to achieve a sustainable competitive advantage. A critical component of this decision is determining what merchandise assortment will be carried. Merchandise decisions are constrained by the amount of money available to invest in inventory and the amount of space available in the store. Based on the financial objective that have been set at the top and have tricked through the retail organization, decisions regarding variety. Assortment, and product availability must be trade.

Variety

Variety is the number of different merchandising categories within a store or department. Stores with a large variety are said to have breadth – the terms variety and breadth are often used interchangeably.

Assortment

Assortment is the number of SKUs within a category. Stores with large assortments are said to have good depth – the terms assortment and depth area also used interchangeably.

Product Availability

Product availability defines the percentage of demand for a particular SKU that is satisfied. Product availability is also referred to as the level of support or service level.

Assortment Planning for Service Retailers

Consider health clubs. Some offer a larger variety of activities and equipment from exercise machines to swimming, wellness programs, and new age lectures. Some hospitals, such as big municipal hospitals found in most urban areas, offer a large variety of medical services. Smaller private hospitals often specialize in physical rehabilitation or psychiatry. For service retailers, the level of product availability is a sales forecasting issues.

Trade-offs between Variety, Assortment, and Product Availability

How do retailers make the trade-off between variety, assortment, and product availability? It depends on their particular marketing strategy. A retail strategy identifies (1) the target market toward which a retailer plans to commit its resources, (2) the nature of the retail offering that the retailer plans to use to satisfy the target market's needs, and (3) the bases upon which the retailer will attempt to build a sustainable competitive advantage.

The trade-offs between variety, assortment, and product availability are strategic issues. Of the three issues, variety is the most strategic. Variety is most important in defining the retailer in the customer's eyes. For instance, is 'the retailer perceived to be a category? Variety also defines the retailer's vendor structure. Does it purchase from many different types of manufactures or just a few? Finally, decisions regarding variety are typically made less often and at a higher level in his organization then decisions regarding assortment or product availability. Top manager, for instance, make decisions about whether to delete categories or even departments from the store. Since these decisions have important ramifications, they're made only after serious considerations.

Determining Variety and Assortment

In attempting to determine the variety and assortment for a category like jeans, the buyer would consider the following factors: profitability of the merchandise mix, the corporate philosophy toward the assortment, physical characteristics of the store, layout of the Internet site, balance between too much versus too little assortment, and the degree to which categories of merchandise complement each other.

Profitability of merchandise mix: Since retailers are constrained by the amount o money they have to invest in merchandise and space to put the merchandise in, they're always trying to find the most profitable mix of products.

Corporate strategy and positioning toward the assortment: The corporate strategy toward the assortment helps the buyer determine the number of styles and colours to purchase.

As with stocks, the more diversified the portfolio, the less risk of large losses, the buyer runs the additional risk of breaking sizes, which means running out of stock on particular sizes. Typically retailers take markdowns on assortments with broken sizes since they become harder to sell. Additionally, a large assortment of styles and colours won't enable the buyer to maximize profits by investing a large portion of the budget on the big winners.

Another issue is whether top management wants to grow or shrink a particular merchandise category. Some department stores, for instance, have dropped furniture and major appliances altogether because of low turnover, low profit margins, or lack of space. Many stores, however, have taken a fairly aggressive stance on men's sportswear in recent years. So if a category is shrinking if the retailer's overall strategy is to enlarge the department, the category could be expanded.

Physical Characteristics of the Store and Layout of the Internet Site

Retailers must consider how much space to devote to the category – in terms of both physical space and space on their Internet site. If many styles and colours are in the assortment, much space will be required to properly display and store the merchandise. The display area's physical characteristics are also important in the case of bricks-and-mortar retailers. A rack, for instance, may hold 300 pair of jeans. It wouldn't be aesthetically pleasing to display only 100 units on the rack or to mix the jeans with another merchandise category.

By the same token, websites must be designed so that the customer can easily navigate through them. If there are too many choices, if the merchandiser organized in a less than obvious fashion, if the customer perceives the site to be cluttered, or if the checkout process is difficult, customers click and are off to another site.

Retailers typically divide their chain into A, B, and C stores on the basis of their ability to generate sales. Not only will A stores get the largest total inventory allocation, but they can also handle the largest assortment. C stores, for instance may not receive the extreme sizes or the more avant-grade styles or colours. It's important, however, to assign merchandised that's expected to be best-sellers to the C stores and to judiciously add a assortment to the larger A and B stores.

Balance between too much versus too little assortment: Both traditional retailers and multichannel retailers must contend with the balance between having too much versus too little assortment. In general, retailers must offer enough assortments to satisfy the customer's needs and expectation, but not too much so as to confuse them and turn them off.

An important function of retailers has been to provide a carefully edited selection of merchandise that meets the needs of their target customers. In the past, buyers were able to choose the products they believed were the very best choices for their customers. As they venture into new categories and deeper assortments, they may begin to lose their focus by choosing items that don't have the same appeal to their target customers. They may, for instance, being to lose their customer base if they start carrying new categories like athletic apparel or sweater colours that are not their top choices. Increasing their customers may become confused by the additional choices, resulting in lost sales.

The electronic channel side of multichannel retailer faces a very different set of assortment balance issues than the traditional bricks-and-mortar side. First, the electronic channel side does not have to stock every item that it can, for instance, stock its best selling items in distribution centers and have other items shipped directly form wholesalers or manufactures. If done properly, the customer would not know or care about the shipping point of origin because the item would be delivered in the same amount of time regardless of who is the shipper. Finally, and most important, because the size of store and level of investor investment constraints are relaxed, the Internet business can provide a wider variety, deeper assortment, and higher level of product availability more easily than its bricks-and-mortar counterparts can.

Recent research has show that customers actually buy more if there are modest reductions of redundant items made to assortments such as different sizes of ketchup in a supermarket. Deep cuts in the assortment size, however, lead to sale decline. In the end, size of the assortment depends on the target markets' expectations. Is it to provide customers with a carefully edited assortment or one stop shopping. Second, how effective is the multichannel retailer in guiding customer through its website with tailored and adaptive search engines?

Complementary merchandise when retailers plan to add to their assortment, they must consider whether the merchandise under consideration complements other merchandise in the department. Retailers may decide to carry other merchandise, such as men's underwear and socks, as a service because their customers expect it. Internet retailers have the advantage of being able to easily suggest complementary products.

Determining Product Availability

The third dimension of the assortment planning process is product availability. Recall that product availability defines the percentage of demand for a particular SKU that is satisfied. The higher the product availability, the higher the amount of backup stock necessary to ensure that the retailers won't be out of stock on a particular SKU when the customer demands it. Choosing an appropriate amount of backup stock is critical to successful assortment planning because if the backup stock is too low, the retailer will lose sales, and possibly customers too, due to stock outs. If the level is too high, scarce financial resources will be wasted in needless inventory that could be more profitably invested in more variety or assortment.

Cycle stock, also known as base stick, is inventory that results from the replenishment process and is required to meet demand when the retailer can predict demand and replenishment time (lead times) perfectly, as depicted in orange. In this case, 96 units of SKU are ordered. During the next two weeks, much of the inventory is sold. But before the store is out of stock, the next order arrives. The cycle then repeats in this typical zigzag fashion.

Unfortunately, most retailers are unable to predict demand and replenishment times without errors. As a result, carry backup stock, also known as safety stock or buffer stocks, as a cushion for the cycle stock so they won't run out before the next order arrives.

Several issues determine the level of required backup stock. First, since every SKU shows a demand and lead time pattern, inventory management systems should calculate safety stock requirements of each SKU. That way, SKUs with smooth demand won't be overstocked, and the retailer won't constantly be out of stock on SKUs with erratic demand.

Second backup stocks and therefore, overall inventory investment depend on the product availability the retailers wished to provide.

Third, the higher the fluctuations in demand, the greater need for backup stock. Yet in some weeks, sales are greater or less than the average. When sales are less than average, the retailer ends up carrying a little more merchandise than it needs. But if sales are more than average, there must be some backup stock to ensure that the retailer's doesn't go out of stock.

Fourth, the amount of backup stock also depends on lead time from the vendor. Lead time is the amount of time between recognition that an order needs to be placed and the point at which the merchandise arrives in the store and is ready for sale. The shorter lead times inherent in quick response inventory system result in a lower level if backup stock required to maintain the same level of product availability.

Fifth, fluctuation in lead time also affects the amount of backup stock. But lead time plus or minus one day on one shipment and then plus or minus five days on the next shipment, the store must carry additional backup stock to cover the uncertainty in lead time. Many retailers using quick response inventory system are forcing their vendors to deliver hours- to reduce the fluctuations in lead time and thus the amount of required backup stock.

Finally the vendor's product availability also affects the retailer's backup stock requirements.

THE ASSORTMENT PLAN

After setting financial goals and determining the relative importance of variety, assortment, and product availability, the retailer is ready to determine what merchandise to stock using an assortment plan. An assortment plan describes in general terms what should be carried in a particular merchandise category. The assortment of plan for fashion merchandise doesn't identify specific SKUs since fashions change from year-to-year. The more fashion-oriented the category, the less detail will be found in the assortment plan because the merchandise planner requires more flexibility to adjust to fashion changes.

Historical precedence is the starting point for developing the assortment plan for the current season. The merchandise planner uses the sales, GMROI, and turnover forecast along with the assortment plan from the previous season to develop the plan for the current season. Adjusments are then made based on the merchandise planner's expectations for what items or fashions will be important in the coming season. For instance, if a particular style, such as boot-cut jeans, is expected to be especially popular in the coming season, the merchandise planner will use more of the merchandise budge for that style and cut back on traditional jeans.

The development of an assortment plan can be complicated. In an actual multistore chain, the process is even more complex than in our example. A good assortment plan requires a good forecast for sales, GMROI, and inventory turnover along with a mix of subjective and experienced judgments. A good inventory management system that combines these elements is also critical to successful merchandise management.

SUPPLY CHAIN MANAGEMENT

What is supply chain?

A supply chain consists of all parties involved, directed, directly or indirectly, in fulfilling a customer request. The supply chain not only includes the manufacturer and suppliers, but also transporters, warehouses, retailers and customers themselves. Within each organization, such as manufacturer, the supply chain includes all function involved in receiving and filling a customer request. These function include, but are not limited to, new product development, marketing, operations, distribution, finance, and customer service.

Consider a customer walking into a Wal-Mart store to purchase detergent. The supply chain begins with the customer and their need for detergent. The next stage of this supply chain is the Wal-Mart retail store that the customer visits. Wal-Mart stocks its shelves using inventory that may have been supplied from a finished-goods warehouse that Wal-Mart manager or from a distributor using trucks supplied by a third party. The distribution in turn is stocked by the manufacture (Say Procter & Gamble [P & G] in this case). The P & G manufacturing plant receives raw material from a variety of suppliers who may themselves have been supplied by lower ties suppliers. For example, packaging material may come from Tenneco packaging while Tenneco receives raw material to manufacture the packaging from other suppliers. This supply chain is illustrated in Figure 32.1.

figure 32.1

Stages of a Detergent supply Chain

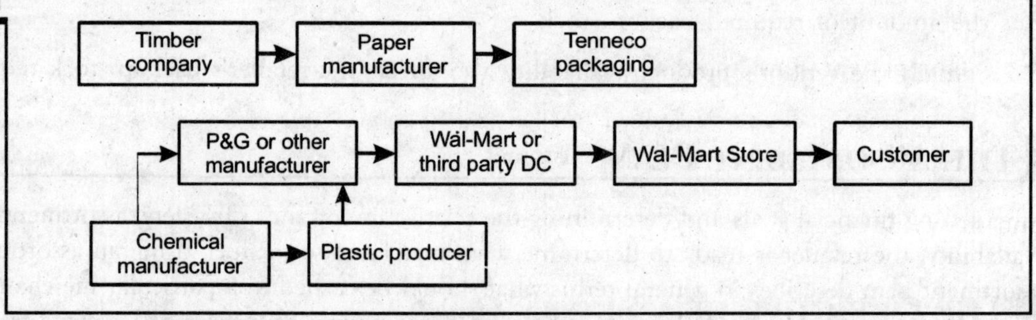

A supply chain is dynamic and involves the constant flow of information, product, and funds between different stages. In our example, Wal-mart provides the product, as well as pricing and availability information, to the customer. The customer transfers fund to Wal-Mart, Wal-Mart conveys point-of-sales data as well as replenishment order to the warehouse or distributor, who transfers the replenishment order via trucks back to the store. Wal-Mart transfers funds to the distributor after the replenishment. The distributor also provides pricing information and send delivery schedules to Wal-Mart. Similar information, material and fund flows take place across the entire supply chain.

These example illustrate that the customer is an integral part of the supply chain. The primary purpose for the existence of any supply chain is to satisfy chain, is to satisfy customer needs, in the process generating profits for itself. Supply chain activities begin with a customer order and end when a satisfied customer has paid for his or her purchase. The term supply chain conjures up images of product or supply moving from suppliers, to manufacturers, to distributors, to retailers, to customers along a chain. It is important to visualize information, funds, and product flows along both directions of this chain. The term supply chain may also imply that only one player is involved at each stage. In reality, a manufacturer may receive material from several suppliers and then supply several distributors.

Thus, most supply chains are actually networks. It may be more accurate to use the term supply network or supply web to describe the structure of most supply chains, as shown in figure 32.2.

figure 32.2

Supply Chain Stages

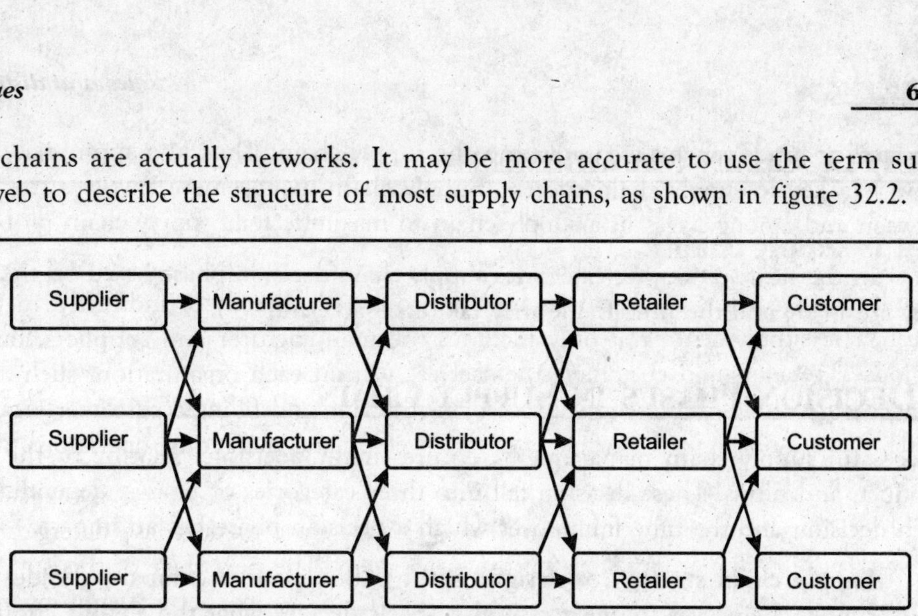

A typical supply chain may involve a variety of stages. These supply chain stages include:

- Customers
- Retailers
- Wholesaler/Distributors
- Manufactures
- Component/Raw material suppliers

Each stage of figure 32.2 need not be present in a supply chain. The appropriate design of the supply chain will depend on both the customer's needs and the roles of the stages involved. In the case of other retail stores, the supply chain may also contain a wholesaler or distributor between the store and the manufacturer.

The Objective of a Supply Chain

The objective of every supply chain is to maximize the overall value generated. The value, a supply chain generates is the difference between what the final product is worth to the customer and the effort the supply chain expends in filling the customer's request. For most commercial supply chains value will be strongly correlated with supply chain profitability, the difference between the revenue generated from the customer and the overall cost across the supply chain. Supply chain profitability is the total profit to be shared across all supply chain stages. The higher the supply chain profitability, the more successful the supply chain. Supply chain success should be measured in terms of the profits at an individual stage. (In subsequent chapters we see that a focus on profitability at individual stages may lead to a reduction in overall supply chain profits.)

Having defined the success of supply chain in terms of supply chain profitability, the next logical step is to look for sources of revenue and cost. For any supply chain, there is only one source of revenue: the customer. At Wal-Mart, a customer purchasing detergent is the only one providing positive cash flow for the supply chain. All other cash flows are simply fund exchanges that occur within the supply chain given that different stages have different owners. When Wal-Mart pays its supplier, it is taking a portion of the funds the customer provides and passing that money on to the supplier. All flows of information, product, or funds generates costs within the supply chain. Thus, the appropriate management of these flows is a key to supply chain success. Supply chain management involves the management of flows between and among stages in a supply chain to maximize total supply chain profitability.

In the next section, we categories supply chain decision phase based on the frequency with which they are made and the time frame they take into account.

DECISION PHASES IN SUPPLY CHAIN

Successful supply chain management requires many decisions relating to the flow of information, product, and funds. These decision fall into three categories or phases, depending on the frequency of each decision and the time frame over which a decision phase has an impact.

1. ***Supply chain strategy or design:*** During this phase, a company decides how to structure the supply chain over the next several years. It decides what the chain's configuration will be, how resources will be allocated, and what processes each stage will perform. Strategic decisions made by companies include the location and capacities of production and warehousing facilities, the products to be manufacture or stored at various locations, the modes of transportation to be made available along different shipping legs, and the type of information system to be utilized. A firm must ensure that the supply chain configuration supports its strategic objectives during this phase. Dell's decisions regarding the location and capacity of its manufacturing faculties, warehouses, and supply sources are all supply chain design or strategic decisions. Supply chain design decision are typically made for the long term (a matter of years) and are very expensive to alter on short notice. Consequently, when companies make these decisions, they must take into account uncertainty in anticipated market conditions over the next few years.
2. ***Supply chain planning:*** For decisions made during this phase, the time frame considered is a quarter to a year. Therefore, the supply chain's configuration determined in the strategic phase is fixed. This configuration establishes constraints within which planning must be done. Companies start the planning phase with a forecast for the coming year (or a comparable time frame) of demand in different markets. Planning includes decisions regarding which markets will be supplied from which location, the subcontracting of manufacturing, the inventory policies to be followed, and the timing and size of marketing promotions. Dell's decisions regarding markets a given production facility will supply and target production quantities at different locations are classified as planning decisions. Planning established parameters within which a supply chain will function over a specified period to time. In the planning phase, companies must include uncertainty in demand, exchange rates, and competition over this time horizon in their decisions. Given a shorter time horizon and better forecasts than the design phase, companies in the planning phase try to incorporate any flexibility built into the supply chain in the design phase and exploit it to optimize performance. As a result of the planning phase, companies define a set of operating policies that govern short-term operations.
3. ***Supply chain operation:*** The time horizon here is weekly or daily, and during this phase companies make decisions regarding individual customer order. At the operation level, supply chain configuration is considered fixed and planning policies are already defined. The goal of supply chain operations is to handle incoming customer orders in the best possible manner. During this phased, firms allocate inventory or production to individual orders, set a date that an order is to be filled, generate pick lists at a warehouse, allocated an order to a particular shipping mode and shipment, set delivery schedules of trucks, and place replenishment orders. Because operational

decisions are being made in the short term (minutes, hours, or days), there is less uncertainty about demand information. Given the constraints established by the configuration and planning policies, the goal during the operation phase is to exploit the reduction of uncertainty and optimize performance.

The design, planning, and operation of a supply chain have a strong impact on overall profitability and success.

We develop concepts and present methodologies that can be used at each of three decision phase described earlier. Most of our discussion addresses the supply chain design and planning phases.

PROCESS VIEW OF A SUPPLY CHAIN

A supply chain is a sequence of processes and flows that take place within and between different stages and combine to fill a customer need for a product. There are two different ways to view the processes performed in a supply chain:

1. *Cycle view:* The processes in a supply chain are divided into a series of cycles, each performed at the interface between two successive stages of a supply chain.
2. *Push/Pull View:* The processes in a supply chain are divided into two categories depending on whether they are executed in response to a customer order or in anticipation of customer orders. Pull processes are initiated by a customer order whereas push processes are initiated and performed in anticipation of customer orders.

Cycle view of Supply Chain Processes

Given the five stages of a supply chain shown in Figure 32.2, all supply chain processes can be broken down into the following four processes cycles, as shown in figure 32.3.

- Customer order cycle
- Replenishment cycle
- Manufacturing cycle
- Procurement cycle

figure 32.3

Cycle view of supply chain processes

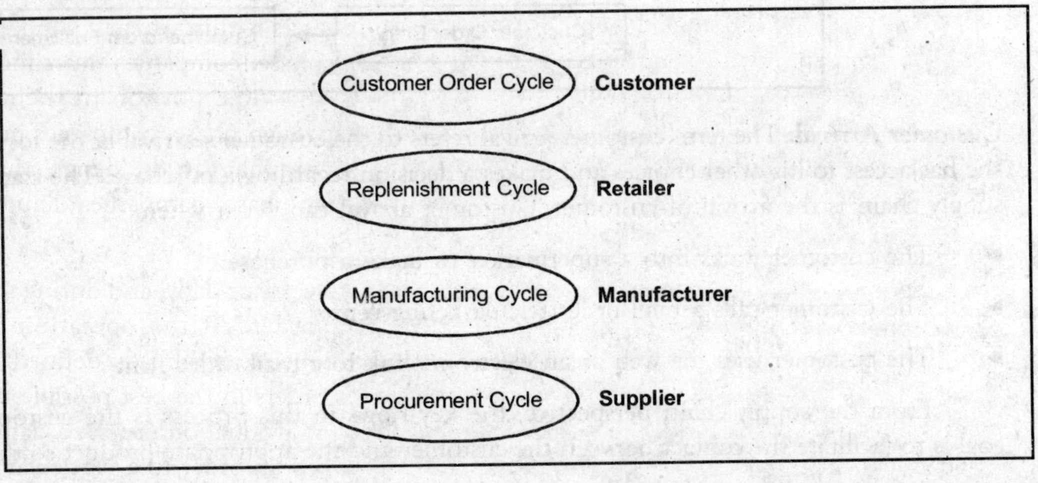

Each cycle occurs at the interface between two successive stages of the supply chain. The five stages thus result in four supply process cycles. Not every supply chain will have all four cycles clearly separated. For example, a grocery supply chain in which a retailer socks finished goods inventories and place replenishment orders with a distributor is likely to have all four cycles separated. Dell, in contrast, sells directly to customers, thus bypassing the retailer and distributor.

A cycle view of the supply chain is very useful when considering operational decision because it clearly specifies the roles and responsibilities of each member of the supply chain. The detailed process description of a supply chain in the cycle view forces a supply chain designer to consider the infrastructure required to support these processes. The cycle view is useful, for example, when setting up information system to support supply chain operations, as process ownership and objectives are clearly defined. We now describe the various supply chain cycles in greater details.

Customer Order Cycle

The customer order cycle occurs at the customer/retailer interface and includes all processes directly involved in receiving and filling the customer's order. Typically, the customer initiates this cycle at a retailer site and the cycle primarily involves filling customer demand. The retailer's interaction with the customer starts when the customer arrives or contact is initiated and ends when the customer arrives or contact is initiated and ends when the customer receives the order. The process involved in the customer order cycle are shown in figure 32.4 and includes:

- Customer arrival
- Customer order entry
- Customer order fulfillment
- Customer order receiving

figure 32.4

Customer Order Cycle

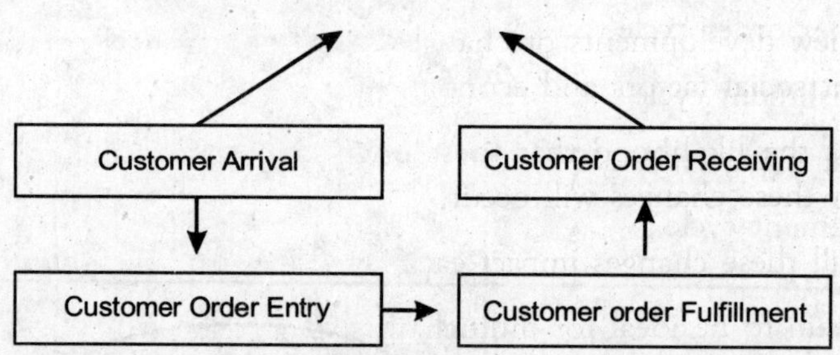

Customer Arrival: The term customer arrival refers to the customer's arrival at the location where he or she has access to his other choices and makes a decision regarding a purchase. The starting point for any supply chain is the arrival of customer. Customer arrival can occur when

- The customer walks into a supermarket to make a purchase
- The customer calls a mail order telemarketing center
- The customer uses the web or an electronic link to a mail order firm

From the supply chain perspective, the key flows in this process is the customers' arrival. The goal is to facilitate the contact between the customer and the appropriate product so that the customer's arrival turns into a customer order. At a supermarket, facilitating a customer order may involve managing customer flows and product displays. At a telemarketing center, it may mean ensuring that customers do not have to wait on hold for too long. It may also mean having systems in a way that turns calls into orders. At a website, a key system may be search capabilities with tools such as personalization that allow customers to quickly locate and view products that may inters them. The objective of the customer arrival process is to maximize the conversion of customer arrivals to customer orders.

Customer order entry: The term customer order entry refers to customer informing the retailer what products they want to purchase and the retailer allocation products to customers. At a supermarket, order entry may take the form of customer loading all items that they intend to purchase onto their carts. At a mail order firm's telemarketing center or Website, order entry may involve customers informing the retailer of the items and quantities they selected. The objective of the customer order entry process is to ensure that the order entry is quick, accurate, and communicated to all other supply chain processes that are affected by it.

Customer order fulfillment: During this process, the customer's order is filled and sent to the customer. At a supermarket, the customer performs this process. At a mail order firm this process generally includes picking the order from inventory, packaging it, and shipping it to the customer. All inventories will need to be updated, which may results in the initiation of the replenishment cycle. In general, customer order fulfillment takes place from retailer inventory. In a build-to-order scenario, however, order fulfillment takes place directly from the manufacturer's production line. The objective of the customer order fulfillment process is to get the correct orders to customers by the promised due dates at the lowest possible cost.

Customer order receiving: During this process, the customer receives the order and took ownership. Records of this receipt may be updated and payment completed. At a supermarket, receiving occurs at the checkout

Retailers need to answer three questions about each environmental factor:

1. What new developments or changes might occur, such as new technologies and regulations or different social factors and economic conditions?
2. What is the likelihood that these environmental changes will occur? What key factors affect whether these changes will occur?
3. How will these changes impact each retail market, the firm, and its competitors?

Gifts seem to be ideal for multichannel retailing. Customers can get ideas by visiting the store or browsing through a catalog. Then they can order the item by visiting the store or browsing through a catalog. They can order the item also over the internet. Since many Gifts To Go customers are buying present for other people, the convenience of placing shipping instruction on the Internet is appealing.

Strengths and weaknesses analysis: The most critical aspect of the situation audit is for a retailer to determine its unique capabilities in terms of its strengths and weakness relative to the competition. A strengths and weakness analysis indicated how well the business can seize opportunities and avoid harm from thieats in the environment.

Step 3: Identify Strategic Opportunities

After completing the situation audit, the next step is to identify opportunities for increasing retail sales. Some of these growth opportunities involve a redefinition of its mission.

Stem 4: Evaluate Strategic Opportunities

The fourth step in the strategic planning progress is to evaluate opportunities that have been identified in the situation audit. The evaluation determines the retailer's potential to establish a sustainable competitive advantage and reap long term profits from the opportunities under evaluation. Thus, a retailer must focus on opportunities that utilize its strengths and its area of competitive advantage. Both the market attractiveness and the strength and weakness of the retailer need to be considered in evaluation strategic opportunities. The greatest investments should be made in market opportunities where the retailers has a strong competitive position.

Step 5: Establish Specific Objectives and Allocate Resources

After evaluating the strategic investment opportunities, the next step in the strategic planning processes is to establish a specific objective for each opportunity. The retailer's overall objective is included in the mission statement. The specific objectives are goals against which progress toward the overall objective can be measured. Thus, these specific objectives have three components: (1) the performance sought, including a numerical index against which progress may be measured, (2) a times frame within which the goal is to be achieved, and (3) the level of investment needed to achieve the objective. Typically, the performance levels are financial criteria such as return on investment, sales, or profits.

Step 6: Develop a Retail mix to Implement Strategy

The sixth step in the planning process is to develop a retail mix for each opportunity in which investment will be made and to control and evaluate performance.

Step 7: Evaluate Performance and Make Adjustments

The final step in the planning process is evaluating the results of the strategy and implementation program, if the retailer is meeting or exceeding its objectives, changes aren't needed. But if the retailer fails to meet its objectives, reanalysis is needed. Typically, this reanalysis starts with reviewing the implementation programs; but it may indicate that the strategy (or even the mission statement) needs to be reconsidered. This conclusion would result in starting a new planning process, including a new situation audit.

STRATEGIC PLANNING IN THE REAL WORLD

The planning process indicates that strategic decisions are made in a sequential manner. After the business mission is defined, the situation audit is performed, strategic opportunities are identified, alternatives are evaluated, objectives are set, resources are allocated, the implementation plan is developed, and, finally, performance is evaluated and adjustments are made. But actual planning process have interactions among the steps. For example, the situation audit may uncover a logical alternative for the firm to consider, even though this alternative isn't included in the mission statement. Thus, the mission statement may need to be reformulated. Development of the implementation plan might reveal that resource allocation to the opportunity is insufficient to achieve the objective. In that case, the objective would need to be changed or the resources would need to be increased, or the retailer might consider not investing in the opportunity at all.

Marketing Strategies of Different Retail Formats

Independent Retailers/Mom & Pop stores/ Kirana Stores

We all are aware of kirana stores and come in contact with them everyday. Though small in size and capital investment, kirana stores adopt various strategies to lure and maintain their customer base.

These strategies are:

Age

The concept of kirana stores is an age long one. They have existed for generations together and served every small and big neighborhood. This very age of independent retailers is used as a strategy to maintain the already formed customer base.

Often kirana stores become family stores and generations after generations of the same families buy their supplies from those stores, hence ensuring a fixed market for the independent retailer.

The prolonged presence of these stores also ensure loyalty of the customers and a sense of belongingness in the customers' minds.

Location

The owner of mom and pop store makes sure that he is located in the center of locality or in the central market of a residential complex. This location works to his advantages as it is convenient for nearby residents to shop at his store.

It has also been observed that a lot of people move into a particular locality on the basis of the number of Kirana store in the neighborhood.

These stores always place themselves such that they are at walking distance from all the homes in the neighborhood. Thus being centrally located, these stores ensure market for themselves.

Free Home delivery

Since a kirana store is located within a colony it is easy for the owner to provide home delivery to his customers. The concept of home delivery also provides convenience to the customer.

Due to short distance, deliveries can be made quickly either by foot or a low cost cycle. Home delivery is a low cost service for the retailer due to cheap unskilled labour and low ownership and maintenance cost of cycles. Thus there is no need to charge extra money for it.

Home delivery not only saves the customers' time but also ensures their loyalty towards the store.

Personal Touch & Relationship Selling

Maintaining a personal touch and a friendly rapport with customers is one of the most effective strategies of a mom and pop store. The owner-cum-operator of the store pleases his customers in a very friendly and folksy way.

A few words of general concern and greeting like "Kaise hain saab" or "Kya haal chaal hain, bade dinon se dikhe nahin" builds a personal bond between the retailer and customer. This bond is cherished by the customer who ensures his loyalty towards the retailer.

Often retailer also call their customer prior to a bank holiday and ask them if they need anything. This gesture make the customer feel that the retailer cares about him and strengthens the bond.

Retailers also remind customer of forthcoming festivals and the various items needed in rituals, thus increasing their own sales.

Adaption to Festivals

It is seen that prior to any festival, kirana store owners stock their stores with the main item of that festival. They normally decorate their store according to the festival and erect stalls outside their store having all the essential of the festival.

This display reminds customers of the various items used in that festival hence increasing the retailer's sales.

Since such goods are non-branded, retailer keep increasing the prices of these goods as the festival come closer.

Festivals goods (crackers for diwali, colours and pichkaris for Holi, rakhis for Rakshabandhan, etc.) are normally sold at wholesale market and thus their availability at kirana stores not only provides convenience to customers but a large profit for retailers.

Presence of Television and Radio

Kirana stores normally have a television or radio fitted in their ships for occasions like cricket matches. People interested in cricket matches flocks to their shops to see the score or even the whole match. In the bargain, they buy eatables from the same store hence increasing the retailer's sale.

Credit Facility

Often mom and pop store offer credit facilities to their fixed home delivery customers. The retailer keeps a track of the products ordered by the customer and send a monthly bill to his/her house.

In doing so, customers do not have to keep ready cash for the product ordered daily (convenience) and the retailer gets a chance to manipulate the accounts and earn a little more.

Availability of a Wide Variety of Goods

While ordering for goods by phone, customer prefer to call a retailer stocked with all kinds of daily-use items. Thus retailers make sure that they are well stocked and also provide a service of buying goods, not available in their store, from another store and delivering them to the customers.

This increases the reliability and popularity of the kirana store.

Joining Hands to form a MULTIPURPOSE Market

Some independent retailers join hands with other retailers and form a large market place catering to one or more large localities.

They adjust their prices according to the income level of people staying in those localities. The retailers prefer sitting together as they get first hand information from other retailers about new products and the customers prefer to shop at such a multipurpose market.

E.g: **INA Market** is the best example of such a conglomerate of independent retailers. The overall prices are high since thy cater to the residents of Hauz Khas, AIIMS, Jor Bagh, etc which are high income localities of New Delhi.

Chains

We all have been exposed to a variety of chains selling different products. All chains have very standardized strategies plans. Some popular strategic adopted by chains are:

Advertising

Retail chains were one of the first users of mass advertising. Many chains use different media to advertise about their product line as well as promotional offers.

Chains advertise on TV, Radio, Newspaper, Magazines, Hoardings, etc.

Information about new stores, discounts, schemes, new products of chains is always conveyed to customers by advertisements.

E.g: McDonald's has come up with an advertising campaign called the "Happy Price Menu" wherein all the products in that sub-menu are prices at Rs. 20. This is to target the lower income segment and regular customer who prefer reasonable pricing.

The slogan of this campaign is "Aap ke Jamane Main Baap ke Jamane ke Daam". It has been endorsed by duplicates of famous bollywood father-son combinations like Dharmendra and Sunny Deol and Amitabh Bachchan and Abhishek Bachchan to convey to its customers that McDonald's, in this high-priced generation, is selling products at the previous generations prices (low prices).

These ads are primary being aired on TV and hoarding also.

Some chains also adopt the strategy of personal advertising wherein shopping-card holders get personalized mails and notifications announcing new discounts and schemes.

E.g: Shopper's Stop and Westside send their card-holders mails announcing different sales and promotional offers.

Membership Cards

It is observed that chains of lifestyle stores, supermarket apparel stores issue frequent-shoppers-cards to their regular customers.

This is advantageous to customers as they get preferential treatment like separate billing lines, free parking, discounts on purchases worth a certain amount and personalized discount notifications. Customers also win points on every purchase and after a certain amount get an opportunity to redeem those points and buy something free of cost.

Chains also issue different categories of cards depending on the amount spent by the customer in the store.

Issuing cards is very profitable for retailers as a card binds person to that store and shopping points lure the customer to buy more goods from there. Being a card holder makes the customer feel important and thus he prefers to shop where he gets importance. This increase the sales of the chain.

E.g: Some chains that offer membership cards are:

- ***Shopper's stop:*** first citizen card
- ***Reliance retail:*** reliance one card
- ***Westside:*** Club west card

Discounts

Chains are very famous for different kinds of discounts. Discounts like end-season discounts, festive discounts, bumper discounts, chain anniversary discounts and republic day discounts are offered to lure customers and maximize sales.

Some chains have discounts all year round. Information regarding discounts is conveyed to customers either by displaying posters outside the stores or by mass advertising.

E.g: Koutons is famous for having perennial discounts. Initially the "Up to 50% discount", later they changed it to "Flat 50%" discounts and the latest one if their "50% + 49% discounts". This perennial discounts has been a very successful since it has made Koutons more popular among its customers.

Due to standardization, all outlets of Koutons offer the same discounts thus making it easy and convenient for customers to avail of the same discount at a store near them.

The strategy behind perennial discounts is to mark up the price in such a manner that customers feel that they are buying heavily discounted goods and at the same the retailer makes a good profit.

A shirt having a marked up price of Rs. 1000 is sold at Rs. 250 after discount fetching the retailer a profit of Rs. 100 on each shirt as the basic cost is only Rs. 150. The cumulative profits are usually large since such discounts lead to very high sales.

Seasons Sales

In plane subjected to extremes of seasons and climatic conditions, retail chains hold season discounts at the end of every seasons.

In places like Delhi, Noida, etc., after winter, chains try to get rid of the left over winter stock by announcing sales and discounts and push the stock out at a very low profit margins. Similarly, monsoon and summer sales are held at the end of the respective seasons.

These sales are beneficial to the customer as they can cater for the future and buy off season goods at half the price.

The retailers benefit from this strategy since they get a chance to flush the left over stock at a profit (even through small) rather than selling their goods back to the manufactures at a huge loss.

E.g.: Woodland: in the month of march, Woodland announced an "Off seasons sale-50% flat" wherein they sold all winter goods like cardigans, jackets, pullovers, warm pants, warm caps, etc. at half the price.

For customers this was a once-in-a-year opportunity and retailers could flush out the left over stocks successfully.

Festive Offers

India, being a national of many festivals, gives retailers chain an opportunity (excuse) to launch festive schemes and thereby increase sales.

Festivals like Diwali, Holi, Raksha Bandhan, Pongal, Ganesh Chaturthi, Dassehra, Karvachauth, Christmas and Valentines Day are used as ideal occasions for discounts, exchange offers and schemes.

Diwali, being the mother of all Indian festivals, is a time of discounts and enhanced shopping all over the country. It is the time when people get their homes done up and buy new things which signifies the start of a prosperous new year.

Retail chains cash in on this festive sentiment and use strategies like mass advertising, discounts, sales, store interior decoration, free product trial, etc. to lure customer and maximize sales.

During festivals retails chains not only increase the investment per store but also increase the sale targets. They go out of their ways to adapt the interior design of stores according to the festivals. This calls for greater investment and hiring of professional designers.

Price Segmentation within Stores

Retail chains catering to different income segments of society usually adopt price segmentation in their stores.

This is done by dividing the complete product mix into categories on the basis of price, quality and brand. Customers prefer this as it caters to their budget. Retailers prefer this strategy as they get a larger customer base which leads to the increase in foot falls in stores.

The introduction of home brands help satisfy this problem. They not only satisfy the brand consciousness of customers but also suit their budgets. The retailer benefits from this as home brands are sold at very good profit margins.

Eg: Mc Donald's has created a sub menu called "Happy Price Menu" containing 4 products prices at Rs. 20, this caters to the middle and lower-middle income group visiting its outlets and increases footfalls, popularity and overall sales.

Birthday and Anniversary Greetings

Retail chains, as a public retaliations move, maintain a database of their regular customers and send them greeting cards on their birthdays and anniversaries. They even offer discounts to them as birthday gifts.

By this the retailer shows that he cares about the customer so much that he even remember his/her birthday. This moves the customer and instills a sense of belongingness in the customers' minds.

However, this is strategy of the retailer to increase daily sales as everyday at least one customer has his/her birthday.

Store Layout

A good store design should be like a good story. Every story has beginning, middle, and end, usually in that order. The entrance sets up the story. It creates expectations and contains promises. As for the first impression, the storefront says, "I'm cheap" or "I'm sophisticated" or "I'm cool." Too often, stores launch right into "Here's what we've got to sell. Don't you love it?" A good entrance should entice, hint, and tease. There should be mystery.

Inside the store comes the middle of the story. It should start off slow. Customers need a few seconds to orient themselves after the entrance. A single message has a far greater chance of sticking then to a dozen products cluttering the way.

Customers need to be led on a journey throughout the store. Using light, motion, and visuals, takes customers down a path of discovery. There should, for instance, be visual destinations at the end of a long aisle.

This chapter is part of the store management section. We start with the objectives of store design. Then we examine the big picture- How should the overall store be laid out? Next we look at how retailers plan and evaluate the location of departments and then merchandise within departments. Finally, we explore specific methods of altering a store's atmosphere.

Objective of a Good Store Design

When designing or redesigning a store, managers must meet five objectives.

Design should be consistent with image and strategy

To meet the first objective, retail managers must define the target customer and then design a store that complements customers' needs. Customers would find it hard to accurately judge value if the physical environment were inconsistent with the merchandise or prices.

Design should positively influence consumer behaviour

To meet the second design objectives of influencing customer buying decisions, retailer concentrate on store layout and space-planning issues. Imagine a grocery store laid out laid a women's specialty store, or an art galley that looked like a tire store. Grocery stores are organized to facilitate an orderly shopping trip and to display as much merchandise as possible. Yet boutiques are laid out in free-form design that allows customers to browse.

Customers' purchasing behaviour is also influenced, both positively and negatively, by the sore's atmosphere. Signs are designed to attract attention more subtle level.

Design should consider costs versus value

Consistent with any retail decision, the third design objectives is to consider the cost associated with each other store design element versus the value received in terms of higher sales and profit. Also, the best locations within a store are "worth" the most, so they're reserved for certain types of merchandise. Retailers develop maps called planograms that prescribe the location of merchandise based on profitability and other factors. Finally, when considering atmospheric issues of store design, retailers must weight the costs along with the strategy and customer attraction issues. For instance, certain types of lighting used to highlight expensive jewelry and crystal cost more than rows of bare fluorescent bulbs.

Design should be flexible

As merchandise changes, so must a store's image. Thus, store planners attempt to design stores with maximum flexibility. Flexibility can take two forms: the ability to physically move store components, and the ease with which component can be modified.

To meet their objectives, retailers must decide which design type to use and how to generate traffic through feature areas.

Types of Design

Today's modern retailers use three general types of store layout design: grid, racetrack, and free-form.

Grid: The gird layout is best illustrated by most grocery and drugstore operations. It contains long gondolas of merchandise and aisles in a repetitive pattern (Fig. 1). The grid isn't the most aesthetically pleasing arrangement, but it's very good for shipping trips in which customer needs to move throughout the entire store and easily located products they want to buy. For instance, when customer move to their weekly grocery shopping, they weave in and out of the specific aisles easily picking up similar products every week. Since they know where everything is, they can minimize the time spent on a task that many don't especially enjoy. The grid layout is also cost-efficient.

Racetrack: One problem with the grid design is that customers aren't exposed to all of the merchandise in the store. This isn't an issue in grocery stores, where most customers have a good notion of what they're going to purchase before they enter the store. But how can a design pull customers through stores that want to encourage them to explore and seek out new and interesting merchandise.

The racetrack layout facilities the goal of getting customer to visit multiple department. The racetrack layout, also known as a loop, is a type of store design that provides a major aisle to facilitate customer traffic, with access to the store's multiple entrances. This aisle loops through the store, providing access to all the departments. The racetrack design encourage impulse purchasing. As customer go around the racetrack, their eyes are forced to take different viewing angles rather than looking down one aisle as in the grid design.

Free form: A free-form layout also known as boutique layout, arranges fixtures and aisles asymmetrically. It's successfully used primarily in small specialty stores or within the departments of large stores. In this relaxed environment, customer feels like they're at someone's home, which facilitates shopping and browsing. A pleasant atmosphere isn't inexpensive, however. For one thing, the fixtures are likely to be expensive custom units. Since the customers aren't naturally drawn around the store as they are in the grid and racetrack layouts, personal selling becomes more important. Also, since sales associates can't easily watch adjacent departments, theft is higher than with the grid design. Finally, the store sacrifices some storage and display space to create the more spacious environment. If the free-form layout is carefully designed, however, the increased costs can be easily offset by increased sales and profit margins because the customer feels at home.

Features Areas

Besides, where most of the merchandise is displayed and stored, there are features areas – areas within a store designed to get the customer's attention. They include end caps, promotional aisles or areas, freestanding fixtures and mannequins that introduce a soft goods department, windows, point-of-sale or cash-warp areas, and walls.

End caps: End caps are display located at the end of an aisle.

Promotional Aisle or area: A promotional aisle or area is an aisle or are used to display merchandise that is being promoted.

Freestanding fixtures and mannequins: Freestanding fixtures and mannequins located on aisles are designed primarily to get customers' attention and bring them into a department. These fixtures often display and store the newest, most exciting merchandise in the department.

Windows: Although windows are clearly external to the store, they can be an important component of the store layout. Properly used, window display can help draw customers into the store. They provide a visual message about the type of merchandise for sale in the store and the type of image the store wishes to portray. Window displays should be tied to the merchandise and other display in the store.

Points of sales areas: Point-of-sales area, also known as point-of-purchase, POP, checkout, or cash wrap area, are places in the store where customers can purchase merchandise. These area can be the most valuable piece of real estate in the store, because the customers often wait there for the transactions to be complete. While waiting in a long checkout lines at a grocery store, notices how these items? Not really, but the wait bored them, so they spent the extra time shopping.

Several department store chains are experimenting with centralized checkout stations. But department stores have traditionally place cash register deep within each department. By centralizing the checkout areas, these department store hope to reduce staff and customer complaints at rising from slow or poor checkout service.

Walls: Since retail space is often scarce and expensive, many retailers have successfully increase their ability to store extra stock, display merchandise, and creatively present a message by utilizing wall space. Merchandise can be stored on shelving and racks. The merchandise can be coordinated with displays, photographs, or graphics featuring the merchandise.

Space Planning

Allocation of space to departments, categories, and finally items is one of store planner's and buyer's most complicated and difficult decisions. They must answer four questions:

1. What items, vendors, categories, and department should be carried?
2. How much of each item should be carried?
3. How much space should the merchandise take?
4. Where should the merchandise be located?

Store planners in conjunction with buyers typically start by allocating space based on sales productivity. For instance, if knit shirts represent 15 percent of the total expected sales for the men's furnishing department, they will initially get 15 percent of the space. Store planers must then adjust the initial estimate on the basis of the following five factors:

1. How profitable is the merchandise? The marginal analysis approach for allocating promotional expenditures to merchandise also works for allocating space. In this situation, a retailer allocates space. In this situation, a retailer allocates space to SKUs to maximize the merchandise category's profitability. Similar analyses can be performed for department. Consider, for instance, allocating space for beer in a supermarket. At first glance, you might think that since Bud Light is the most profitable brand, it should get all the space. But if the store took this approach, it would lose sales on less profitable brands- and it might even lose customers who are loyal to the other brands. Thus, the store should experiment with different shelf space allocations until it find a combination that maximizes profits for the category. Optimal space allocation system are part of the planogramming programme discussed later in this section.
2. How will the planned inventory turnover and the resulting stock-to-sales ratio affect how many SKUs will normally carried in stock? Recognize that (as in the merchandise budget plan) monthly inventory levels vary according to seasonal demand, holidays, and so on. Buyers and store planners must allocates space on the basis of these seasonal needs rather than yearly averages. They must also estimate the proportion of merchandise kept on display versus backup stock. Merchandise kept as backup stock in a storage area takes much less room.
3. How will the merchandise be displayed? Merchandise and fixtures go hand in hand. Store planners design fixtures to go with the merchandise. But once the fixtures in the store, buyers must consider the fixtures' physical limitations when assigning space to merchandise. Will the shirts be displayed on hangers or folded on tales? Customers can more easily examine merchandise on hangers, but this display method takes more space.
4. Will the location of certain merchandise draw the customer through the store, thus facilitating purchase? Notice, for instance, the way the mannequins and fixtures are placed on the perimeter of the department. We examine how retailers locate department and specific merchandise to facilitate purchases of impulse and complementary products.

5. What items does the retailer wish to emphasize? Suppose that a buyer has decided that this season will be particularly strong in knot shirts rather than woven shirts. The buyer purchases accordingly and plans additional advertising. As a result, knit shirts must also receive additional selling and display and space. Retailing examines how some department stores have cut back on their space to designers so they can make room for other merchandise.

We've discussed in general terms how store planners and buyers plan the space requirements for a category like knit shirts or beer. Similar decision are made for larger groups of merchandise like classification, department, and even merchandise groups. Now let's examine how retailers decide where to locate departments and where to locate merchandise within department.

Location of Departments

Mrs. Seema recently went to Connaught place for a haircut. On the way in, she stopped at the cosmetics counter to buy makeup. Then on the escalator she sopped by the lingerie department to browse. Did she simply take a random walk through the store? Probably not. The departments she shopped, like all departments, are strategically located to maximize the entire store's profits. The profit-generating abilities of various locations within a store aren't equal. The more traffic through a department, the better the location will be. Unfortunately, every department can't be situated in the best location. Retailers must consider additional demand-generating factors and the interrelations between departments when determining their locations.

Relative location advantages: The best locations within the store depend on the floor locations, the position within a floor, and its location relative to traffic aisles, entrances, escalators, and so on. In general, in a multilevel store, a space's value decreases the farther it is from the entry-level floor. Since men aren't generally as avid shoppers for clothing for women, many large stores locate the men's department on the entry level floor to make shopping as easy as possible.

The position within a floor is also important when assigning locations to departments. The best locations are those closest to the store's entrance, main aisles, escalators, and elevators. Mrs. Seema spotted the red dress because she could see it from the escalator. Multilevel stores often place escalators so customers must walk around the sales floor to get to the next level. Also, most customers turn right when entering a store or floor, so the right side will be especially desirable space. Finally, most customers won't get all the way to the center of the store, so many stores use the racetrack design to introduce people to move into the store's interior.

Impulse products: impulse products are products that are purchased without prior plans, like fragrances and cosmetics in department stores and magazines in supermarkets. They are almost always located near the front of the store, where they're seen by everyone and may actually draw people into the store.

Mrs. Seema didn't plan her makeup purchase, for example, but decided she wanted some once she saw the displays.

Demand/destination Areas: Children's, expensive specialty goods, and furniture departments as well as customer-service areas like beauty saloons, credit offices, and photography studios are usually located off the beaten path-in corners and on upper floors. A purchase of one these unique, expensive pieces requires thought and concentration. Customers would probably become distracted if the department were adjacent to a high-traffic area. Besides, customer looking for these items will find them no matter where they're located in the store. These departments are known as demand/destination areas because demand for their products or services is created before customers get to their destination. Thus, they don't need prime locations.

Seasonal needs: Some departments need to be more flexible than others. For instance, it's helpful to locate winter costs near sportswear. Extra space in the coat department can be absorbed by sportswear or swimwear in the spring when the bulk of the winter coats have been sold.

Physical Characteristics of Merchandise: Departments that require large amounts of floor space, like furniture, are often located in the less desirable locations. Some department, like curtains, need significant wall space, while others, like shoes require accessible storage.

Adjacent Departments: After trying on the red dress, Mrs. Seema found a complementary scarf and stockings nearby. Retailers often cluster complementary products together to facilitate multiple purchases.

Some stores are now combining traditionally separate departments or categories to facilitate multiple purchase using market-base analysis. Stores are laid out according to the way customers purchase merchandise rather than traditional categories or departments.

The special case of grocery stores: Now consider some of the special departmental location issues in grocery stores. As a customer walks in, there is typically a barricade-checkouts stands and grocery carts-that pushes the customer to the right. The items almost everyone buys- milk, eggs, butter and bread-are the back left-hand corner. To get to them, a shopper tending to turn right must travel half the store's perimeter and go past every aisle.

Most supermarkets steer shoppers immediately into the produce section because they can see and feel and smell the food there. The smell of fresh fruits and vegetables gets a shopper's mouth watering, and the best grocery store customer is a hungry one.

Supermarkets place private-label brands and other higher margin items to the right of national brands. Most languages are read from left to right. So a customer will see the higher –priced national brand first and then see and purchase the lower-priced private-label item on the right.

Evaluating a departmental layout: The firm utilizes lots of hidden video cameras and other high-tech equipment, its most important research tool is a piece of paper called a track sheet in the hands of individual called trackers. Trackers follow shoppers and note everything they do. They also make inferences on consumer behaviour based on what they've observed. Here are jut a few of the things they have learned:

- ***Avoid the butt-brush effect:*** The researcher taped shoppers attempting to reach the rack while negotiating an entrance during busy times. They noticed that after being bumped once or twice, most shoppers abandons their search for neckwear. The conclusion: Shoppers don't like to shop when their personal space is invaded.
- ***Allow a transition zone:*** The first product encountered in a department isn't always going to have an advantage. Sometimes, just the opposite will happen. Allowing some space between the entrance of a store and a product gives it more time in the shopper's eye as he or she approaches it. For instance, cosmetic firms don't usually want to occupy the fist counter inside the entrance of a department store because they know that know that women want a little privacy.

Location of Merchandise within Departments: The use of Planograms

To determine where merchandise should be located within a department, retailers of all types generate maps known as planograms. A planogram is a diagram created from photographs, computer output, or artists' rendering that illustrate exactly where every SKU should be placed. Planograms should be visually appealing, represent the manner in which a consumer shops (or the manner in which the retailer would like the consumer to shop), and embody the strategic objectives of the corporation. There is an art and a science to planogramming. The art is ensuring that the proper visual impact on presentation is maintained; the science is in the financial analysis portion. A planogrammer must be able to balance these two elements in creating a planogram that is best for the store. Technology for computer-generated planograms can be somewhat sophisticated, lending to advanced analysis, or it can be fairly simple.

Electronic planogramming requires the users to input model number or UPC codes, product margins, turnover, sizes of product packaging or actual pictures of the packaging, and other pertinent information into the program. The computer plots the planogram based on the retailer's priorities. For instance, if the retailer wants prime shelf space given to products that produce the highest turns, the computer will locate those products in the best locations. If margin are more important, the computer will determine the shelf space priority and the optimal number of SKUs to stock in that space. Adjustments to the initial planogram can be made to see how additional space or different fixtures would affect the productivity measures.

Planograms are also useful for merchandise that doesn't fit nicely on gondolas in a grocery or discount store.

Recent advances in computer graphics and three- dimensional modeling allow planograms to be designed, tested with consumers, and changed, all in a "virtual" shopping environment can view merchandise on a computer screen that looks like a real store. The shopper can "pick up" a package by touching its image on the monitor. She can turn the package so it can be examined from all sides. If she wants, she can "purchase" the product. In the meantime, the computer tracks the time spent shopping for and examining a particular product and the quantity purchased. Armed with this information, the retailer can test the effectiveness of different planograms.

A productivity measure (the ratio of an output to an input) determines how effectively a retailer uses a resource. Most retailers measure the productivity of space using sales per square foot, since rent and land purchases are assessed on a per-square-foot basis. But sometimes it's more efficient to measure profitability using sales per linear foot. For instance, in a grocery store, most merchandise is displayed on multiple shelves on long gondolas. Since the shelves have approximately the same width, only the length, or linear dimension, is relevant. Sale per cubic foot may be most appropriate for store like wholesale clubs that use multiple layers of merchandise.

When allocating space to merchandise or a department, a retail manager must consider the profit impact on all departments. Remember, the objective is to maximize the profitability of the store, not just a particular department. Since the cosmetic department has a relatively high gross margin per square foot, should management give it more or less space? The answer depends profitability of the entire store would increase if more space were allotted to this department. A department may be achieving its high productivity ratio because it's too small and has only a limited assortment. Conversely, a department may actually be too large- if so, almost as much profit could be generated with a smaller space. The buyer could buy smaller quantities more often, thereby making more productive use of smaller space. If management decides to shrink the cosmetics department more space would be available for, say, female apparel. If the store's overall profitability would be increased by making this move, then the retailer should do it.

LEVERAGING SPACE: IN STORE KIOSKS

In-store kiosks are spaces located within stores containing a computer connected to the store's central offices or to the Internet. In-store kiosks can be used by customers or salespeople to order merchandise through a retailer's electronic channel, check on product availability at distribution centers or other stores, get more information about the merchandise, and scan bar coded to check the prices.

Retailers are interested in installing these kiosks because they create a synergy between the store and the Internet size.

Kiosks can encourage customers to stay in the store longer and, it is hoped to spend more money. For instance allowing customers to check their e-mail is an added service that will endear customers to the store.

Do kiosks cannibalize store sales? Yes, but only initially. Shoppers who purchase in stores and online from an in-store kiosk tend to buy more. When REI installed in-stores kiosks, it found that customers who shop both online and in the store spend 22 percent more than those who buy only from traditional stores. Staples provided an incentive to store managers to push the use of kiosks. Online sales are credited to the stores from which they're placed.

There are downsides to making investments in these kiosks, however from $3,000 to $25,000 per kiosk. Second, once the investment is made, there is no guarantee that customers will use them. Finally, there are significant costs in maintaining the kiosks-making sure they are working properly.

VISUAL MERCHANDISING

Buying for our store can be like shopping for a living, and sharing the exciting new merchandise we have found with our customers is enjoyable and rewarding. But in between these two stages come two tasks crucial to the success of our stores. First, the goods need to be accurately and efficiently checked in, inspected, and priced. Mistakes or delays in the receiving area can be expensive. The merchandise then needs to be displayed in a way that will invite shopper's attention and enhance the appearance of our store.

Checking in Merchandise

Before a shipment of new merchandise can be put on display, it must be checked in and priced. Some, stores hire employees especially for stock work; others add this to the duties of the sales staff. Accuracy in checking in merchandise can have an important financial impact on the store's operations. Not only is it essential that items be priced correctly, but shipping errors on the part of vendors are not unusual; they can be costly if not caught and reported. We must be certain that what we receive is what we ordered and that the vendor's invoice matches the purchase order.

In the front of our file of purchase orders is alined sheet, the arrivals chart, with room to write down which shipments arrive each day, listing the vendor name, our purchase order number (we assign the date the order was placed as the purchase order number), whether the shipment arrived COD (Cash on delivery), and how it was shipped to us. This chart helps us track all packages that come into the store and can be useful, if there is a disagreement later about what we received.

When a shipment arrives, it is entered on the arrivals chart and the purchase orders are pulled. Each purchase order is then labeled with a sticker, printed on our computer, with spaces for the date of arrival, number of boxes received, and the initials of the staff member unpacking the order. Most shipments include a list of contents, the packing list, which we staple to the back of the purchase order. If an actual invoice is enclosed, it is forwarded to the bookkeeper. Invoices and packing lists often look the same, but an invoice has the shipping costs added and is totaled. If an invoice is mistaken for a packing list and is stapled to the back of an order, it may not get paid, so it is important to be sure that this does not happen in future.

Ideally, the wholesale price we wrote on the purchase order is the same price we will be charged for the goods. We calculate retail prices when we write an order and put them on the purchase order forms so that the merchandise can be checked in and priced as soon as it arrived. Other stores wait until the invoice arrived in order to see what the shipping costs are and whether there have been price changes. But some vendors are rather slow in getting their invoices sent, which might mean the merchandise sits in the store for days without being priced and put out to sell. The sooner merchandise is displayed, the better it will be.

Dealing with Back Orders

If we have elected to have back-ordered merchandise shipped to us, when it arrives, we will receive shipments that do not have a purchase order to file. The reason is that the original order was pulled and processed when the first part of the order arrived; it is necessary to find this order and check to see whether the back order is corrected.

We use a special form to check in back orders. When a back order arrives, we being by looking up the original order date and then enter the date the back order arrives. The wholesale and retail information is taken from the original purchase order. This is a rather tedious process, which makes it even more inviting to specify 'no back orders'. Not accepting back orders, however, might mean that we are unable to get certain very popular items that are often out of stock. Most stores put up with some back orders in order to get the choicest merchandise, but it is smart not to allow a supplier to send numerous small back orders instead of consolidating them.

If we have merchandise on back order and are writing a new order with the supplier, be sure to note if we want to keep items on back order.

Dealing with Problems on Shipments

Ideally, we open a shipment to check it in, every item looks exactly the way it did in the showroom or catalogue, and the quantities match those on the purchase order.

Late and Lost orders

Vendors sometimes ship later than the desired ship date, but unless we have stated a cancel date, we can expect the merchandise to eventually arrive on our doorstep. If an order without a cancel date is late and we decide we can no longer use the goods, be sure to notify the vendor in writing that we don't want it shipped. We are under no obligation to accept goods that arrive unreasonably late, if we have specified a cancellation date, or written to cancel the order before it is shipped.

Periodically reviewing all orders still open is a wise idea. Call vendors to find out why merchandise due in the store has not arrived, or fax them a 'when will we ship?' Sometimes a supplier will have no record of receiving an order, and sometimes the supplier will not have been able to ship the merchandise for one reasons or another. Good vendors will notify us of delays, but many do not. Open-to-buy budgeting depends on shipments arriving during the month specified, and unfortunately many of our suppliers are rather hit and miss in their delivery times. Some ship the day after receiving the order, and others take a month or two. Some ship every order complete, and others let the goods dribble in on numerous back orders. Dealing with these variables is one of the challenges in acquiring an optimal selection of merchandise for our specialty store.

Pricing the Merchandise

Once a shipment has been received and checked against the purchase order or invoice, the goods need to be labeled with prices. If we are using a bar code scanning system, this may not be necessary, but we will need to make sure the price on the shelf and in the system are corrected. One of the most frustrating experiences for shoppers is getting stuck in line waiting to check out while someone up ahead is arguing that the scanned price is not the same as the one on the display or in the ad.

Displaying the Merchandise

Now, the merchandise we have purchased is priced and ready to sell, it is time to give some thought to how to display the goods to best advantage. A good display makes the goods look appealing and makes it easy for customers to purchase them. The back store of merchandise needs to be stored in an accessible, safe place. (We use the cardboard tote boxes with handles available at many grocery stores to carry priced merchandise away to be stored and to bring out items to be put out display).

As a general rule, must items should be put in displays that allow customers to handle them. Customers always prefer to touch an item before deciding to buy it. We may choose to put a large quantity of each item on display or to highlight the uniqueness of a piece by displaying just one. During the holiday season, consider putting a few already wrapped boxes of our most popular items on the shelf for quick purchase..

Merchandise that is easily shoplifted or broken can be displayed in locked cases, but customers are often reluctant to ask to see an item that is under glass. Stores with locked cases of merchandise need alert sales staff to offer help as soon as they see someone interested in a closed display.

Focal point displays

Many stores are designed exclusively around fixtures that hold merchandise, with little thought to special areas that can feature changing displays highlighting new or seasonal merchandise. Often the only display that changes from the month to month is the end panel, or end cap, of the traditional freestanding gondola units. When we expanded twenty years ago, we neglected to allow enough space for seasonal displays and for cross merchandising, the technique of displaying merchandise from different departments together, such as placements shown with holiday china, brass candlesticks, green glassware, and a Christmas cracker (a traditional English decorative and amusing table hibiscus tree, was soon pressed into service as a restful area with a bench and a hibiscus tree, was soon pressed into service as a display area. We now change the atrium displays as often as we change the main window, with seasonal merchandise dominating in the fall and spring and features items from one or more departments being highlighted the rest of the year.

Clothing stores often have mannequins or body forms positioned throughout the stores. On platforms or on the walls above the handing rods, showing coordinated outfits and accessories. Other types of specialty shops can make use of small areas of floor or wall space to create displays that can be changed periodically. Our store's regular customers should be rewarded for their loyalty by seeing something, new each time they come into the shop. A focused display, even one using merchandise that is not new, draws customers attention to the featured items.

Displays can be used to give decorating, gift, and use suggestions that customers find very helpful. Showing scented candles with bath salts, for example, evckes the image of a sensuous bath and suggests that candle, which most customers think of as a dining table accessory, are also appropriate for the bathroom. Displaying a number of different apple-related gift items together, such as bags of potpourri, apple-shaped cookie cutters, a apple-corer, and towels silk-screened with an apple design, gives customers the idea of putting together a gift basket of apple merchandise.

Cross merchandising can also be done on the basis of colour, leading to some unusual and interesting display combinations, for instance, red casseroles displayed with red Christmas ornaments and teddy bears with big red bows. Some stores display all their merchandise in cross merchandising setting rather than having a separate are for soap, candles, linens, and other categories. This is perfect for leisurely impulse shopping in a tourists area, but not ideal for shoppers hoping to find a specific item quickly.

The area near any checkout counter, even in the finest specialty shop, is a prime spot for impulse merchandise. (We all know what a strong draw the candy display can be along most grocery checkouts lanes). Leave room near the register for a compact display of add-on accessories, treats, or any small new items to which we wish to draw attention. Because checkout counters can become cluttered with impulse merchandise, it is important to limit and frequently change the items that are features there. These displays may be the final impression that customers have of our store, so be sure that the merchandise on the counter looks as enticing as the goods shown elsewhere in the shop.

Maintaining good Merchandising

It is more work, and less fun, to maintain existing displays than to create new ones. As merchandise sells, it must be replenished. Customers will unfold the folded shirts, move items around, tear packaging, or put merchandise they've changed their mind about in the wrong place. Straightening and dusting the merchandise and shelves is no one's favourite job, but it has to be done regularly, if displays are to look fresh and inviting. Merchandise and display fixtures must be kept clean, and all displays should be kept full. A full display always sells- more than one that is half empty.

We divide up the task of maintain displays by having a staff member in charge of very department. This employee does the merchandise display and also dusts and straightens that area. Standing items are turned to face the same direction, and soiled or damaged merchandise is removed. Folded items get refolded and restacked in a standardized manner. Some stores have employees use a folding board to be sure that all shirts and sweaters are folded uniformly. Ideally, someone are quite, we give employees flexitime away from the counter (but within easy contact, using walkie-talkies) to dust their departments. Which brings to mind another old retailing saying, "If we have time to lean, we have to clean."

The employee in charge of an area in our stores also restocks the displays. We encourage employees to restock from the basement, looking to see what is in back stock and then making sure everything is on display. If the fixture seems full, those who restock from the display may not notice that an item is missing or that a new item has arrived. Staff members in charge of department also do inventories for the buyer of that area, and in many cases they eventually do routine reorders of merchandise and perhaps even new merchandise buying. Even part-time staff members are in charge of a small area, so that maintaining the attractive appearance of the stores is truly a team effort. With many stores offering the same items, we all realize that the way we present our merchandise is an important factor in our store's success.

Using Shop Windows Effectively

The concept of store window displays is not very old; until the invention of plate glass, windows were very small and intended just to allow light to enter the shop premises. Early plate glass window display took advantage of the larger space to cram in a sample of almost everything in the store, and some merchants today still follow this 'more is better' philosophy. Others err to the opposite extreme, with so little in the window that it seems dubious that there is much in the store. Good window displays take a certain amount of artistic talent as well as organized planning.

Window displays should be changed at least once a month, and in high-traffic area, every two to three weeks. Establish a calendar that identifies themes and responsibilities for creating the displays several months in advance, and share this information with the store's buyers in case they need to order any special merchandise for a display. One of the cardinal rules for putting merchandise in a window is that there be a reasonable amount of back stock for customers to buy. A customer who wants to buy something displayed in a window will be frustrated if told it is out of stock. The goal of a window, after all, is to bring customers into the store in order to buy our merchandise.

Laurie Karzen ad Charlotte R. Morrill, experts in design, merchandising, and marketing, recommend keeping a notebook of display plans, with a page for each of the g next twelve months of window and in-store displays. Each planning page contains a description of the proposed theme, sketches, notes about sources for the tools and props to be used, and information about the merchandise to be features, including when it will need to arrive. These pages can be taken along when doing the buying for the season, to be sure that all the items need are ordered. When a window has been completed, Karzen and Morrill suggest, attach a photograph of the finished display to the planning page, along with an evolution of which elements worked well and which one did not.

Sources of Display Ideas

A good window combines the elements of good visual display and creative advertising. There should always be a unifying theme, although the theme can be as simple as a single colour or texture. Other theme might be a season or holiday, a product category, a colour combination, an in-store event, or even an individual new item. Sometimes display themes are small vignettes, or realistic home settings such as a dining room table or a bedroom dresser complete with all accessories. The theme, which is sometimes referred to as the story the window is trying to tell, determines the material, merchandise, and signage to be used.

Where can we find ideas for window displays? A walk through our store should give us some ideas; look for product that are visually exciting or are hot sellers. We keep a photo album of all past window displays to inspire future designs. We also watch for good displays in the wholesale showrooms from which we buy merchandise. Some companies allow retailers to take pictures of trade show and showroom displays they wish to replicate and provide information about the sources of any props or background material used. Trade magazines often feature photographs of successful store windows we can adapt for our own use. There is even a special magazine devoted to display ideas, VS+SD, which stands for Visual Merchandising and Store design (800–421 – 1321 or www. Visualsstore.com). Every year VS+SD conduct an international visual merchandising competition and carries photographs of all the winner both in the magazine and on its website.

We occasionally do a window display that helps a non-profit group publicize a special event or cause. Often we are able to tie some of our merchandise into the display, for example, adding picnic baskets and non-breakable wine glasses to a window promoting American Players Theatre, a nearby outdoor classical theater.

DO WE DO WINDOWS?

In larger cities, there are professional window dressers, or visual merchandisers, who can take our design concept and brings it to life. We may also be able to find an artist who can translate his or her talents into store displays. We have always done our own displays, encouraging staff members to pair up and take turns doing a window. Near our main window is a sing giving the window dressers credit for their work. Some of our employees have turned out to be gifted designer, and it is nice to share the opportunity, and the challenges, of creating a new window display with our entire staff.

Art students, and even floral designers, are taught how to use complementary colours and geometric shape to create a pleasing design-skill that retailers often have to learn on their own in order to do good window displays. Merchandise alone does not make a display. Consider the aesthetics of the display, in addition to the lighting, backdrops, props, and possibly signage. Good window design should take into account five elements: balance (symmetrical or asymmetrical), proportion, contrast, harmony, and focus. The Crabtree & Evelyn display is an excellent illustration of these essential elements.

The Tools of the Trade

Good window displays often create an illusion, for example, an imaginary garden or jungle. A number of material that fool the eye but are lightweight and intensive are ideal for creating this magic. The first of these is Foamcore, a stiff board made of Styrofoam that can be cut into any shape using a sharp blade. Foamcore can be painted and pinned into, and it sill not wrap as easily as other stiff material. It can be used to create a smooth floor, and archway, or a palm tree. Creates a starry night background by punching holes through Foamcore painted dark blue and inserting small Christmas lights from the back. Foamcore is available in large rectangular sheets from most art supply stores and some lumberyards. It comes in different thickness, from ¼ inch sheet to 2-inch, insulation Foamcore that can be carved with a knife. Gatorboar, a much stronger and more expensive synthetic material, is ideal for permanent signs and other display applications. It surface takes pain well, and it will not warp.

Fishing line is an essential tool for window dressers. This study monofilament, available in sporting goods stores, allows items hung in window to appear to be floating. Fish line is also useful for reinforcing standing items, so they don't tip over during the time window is on display.

We are strong believers in the use of small white Christmas lights to outline window displays, especially during the holiday season. We have, in fact, outlined both of our buildings in little white lights, which helps to brighten our streetscape during the long Wisconsin winter evenings. There are other colours of little lights available as well; we have used orange ones in the Halloween window and pastel lights at Easter. Strings of lights can be woven through a glassware display, intertwined in a floral garland, or even used on a Christmas Tree.

Prop Master

"Display and visual presentation are the theater of retailing," write designer Martin M. Pegler, author of the annual stores of the year and store window books (New York: Retail Reporting Corp.). As in the theater, backdrops and props can be used to make a display come alive. These materials need not be items as sell, as long as the focus remains on the merchandise we do stock. We should constantly be on the lookout for inexpensive items that can be used in displays. Buy props at antique stores or rummage sales, or borrow them. Many organizations are willing to loan out items in exchange for a credit in the window. Over the years, we have borrowed customers from the Nutcracker ballet, a cast iron bathtub, an antique table, a bicycle, and a baker's sample of a wedding cake.

It is wonderful to have storage space so window props can be reused. This storage need not be in the store, since it does not need to be accessible on short notice. Over the years, we can build up a useful collection of fabric, window shades, silk flowers, greenery, pedestals, and display props such as fake rocks and mannequins.

Some prop items that can be purchase in expensively or borrowed to make an original window display include:

- Toys, such as beach ball and hoops
- Masks
- Musical instruments
- Theatrical costumes
- Trellises and garden fences
- Terra-cotta pots
- Hammocks
- Ropes, rope ladders
- Standing mirrors
- Shopping bags with the store name and logo
- Silk tree and plants
- Plush animals
- Giftwrapped boxes
- Sporting goods
- Paper or silk kites
- Life-size cardboard cutout figures
- Plastic flamingos or other lawn ornaments
- Natural material (e.g. hay, vines, wood chips)

The Backdrop

The background or the window is not important if the window opens up into the store (although even in this type of window, some kind of railing, net, or gird may be helpful to keep customers out of the window). Closed window's however, allow a backdrop to be an integral part of the display. We often use window shades made of bamboo, rice paper, or pleated fabric as a background, lowering the last share carefully as we back out of the completed window. Fabric panels and woven throws are also useful as focal points the background of a window. We often base an entire display around a background that inspire us.

Many other items can be used to form an interesting background in a display window:

Flags and Banners

- Panels covered with wallpaper of gift wrap
- Posters
- Fishnet
- Sheet music
- Product photographs mounted on foamcore
- Blankets and woven throws
- Window frames, shutter, doorways
- Fireplace mantle
- Large paper fans
- Bull's eye targets
- Enlarged clip art or photographs
- Sheets
- Scarves
- Parachutes
- Maps
- Wood folding screens

Photographs, clip art, and other graphics can be enlarges for use in a window display by a local photographic outlets or printing services. Be sure to have signed permission to reproduce any photographs or art work that is not clip art, which is sold free of copyright restrictions. Dry-mounting the enlargements on Foamcore will keep it from warping, although it may still fade when exposed to direct sunlight.

Mannequins

Fashion in mannequins change along with changes in clothing fashion. Stores selling clothes may choose to display their products on hanging rods or forms, or to invest in a cost of characters that will model the clothing in a more realistic manner. A recent trend is toward modern, faceless mannequins, which circumvents the problem of dated hairstyles and makeup. The question remains, however, whether customers can really relate to these androgynous, anonymous figures.

The futuristic look is appropriate for stores selling cutting –edge, youthful fashion. More traditional stores should invest in mannequins that offer flexibility in hairstyle ad poses and expect to have to replace these figures periodically to avoid a dated look. Never leave mannequins undressed even temporarily in a window or with an arm or leg off. We wouldn't want to give some small child nightmares.

L.L. Bean executes all process in the customer order cycle after the customer arrives. All processes that are part of the customer order cycle are thus pull processes that are part of the customer order cycle are thus pull processes. Order fulfillment takes place from product in inventory that is built up in anticipation of customer orders. The goal of the replenishment cycle is to ensure product availability when a customer order arrives. All processes in the replenishment cycle are performed in anticipation of demand and are thus push processes. The same holds true for processes in the manufacturing and procurement cycle. In fact, raw material like fabric is often purchased six to nine months before customer demand is expected. Manufacturing itself begins three to six months before the point of sale. All processes in the L.L. Bean supply chain break up into pull and push processes, as shown in Figure 32.6.

figure 32.5

Customer order Cycle in L.L. Bean supply chain

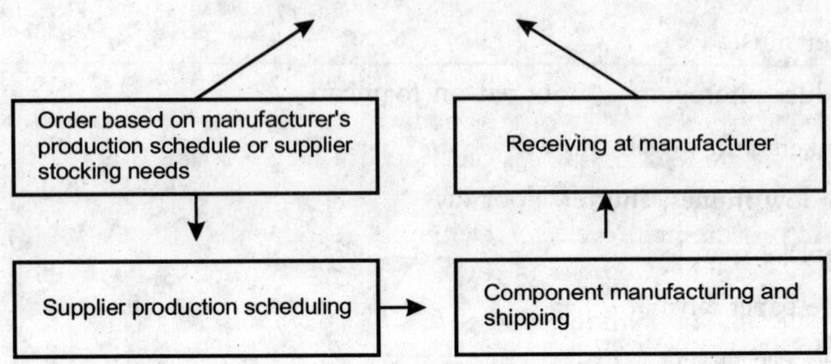

figure 32.6

Push/ Pull Process for the L.L. Bean Supply Chain

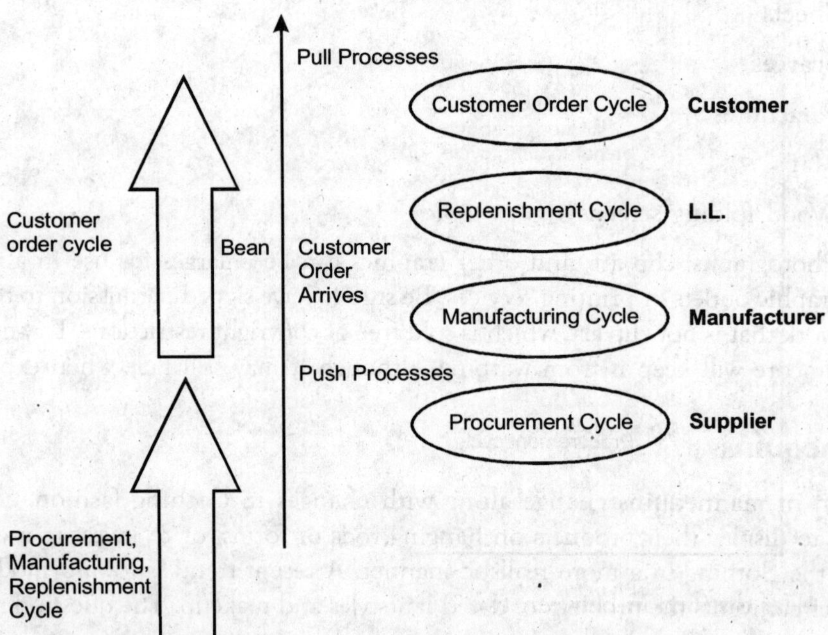

The situation is different for a build-to-order computer manufacture like dell. Dell does not sell through a reseller or distributor but directly to the consumer. Demand is not filled from finished product inventory, but from production. The arrival of a customer order triggers production. The arrival of a customer order triggers production of the product. The manufacturing cycle is thus part of the customer order fulfillment process in the customer order cycle. There are effectively only two cycles in the dell supply chain (a) a customer order and manufacturing cycle in figure 32.5 and (b) a procurement cycle in Figure 32.7.

figure 32.7

Dell Supply Chain

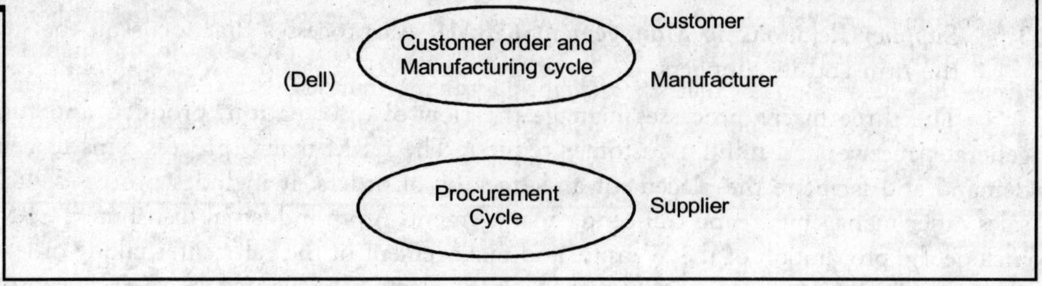

All process in the customer order and manufacturing cycle at Dell are thus classified as pull process because they are initiated by customer arrival. Dell, however, does not place component orders in response to a customer order. Inventory is replenished in anticipation of customer demand. All processed in the procurement cycle for Dell are thus classified as push processes because they are in response to a forecast. The processes in the Dell supply chain break up into pull and push processes as shown in Figure 32.8.

figure 32.8

Push/ Pull Process for the Dell Supply Chain

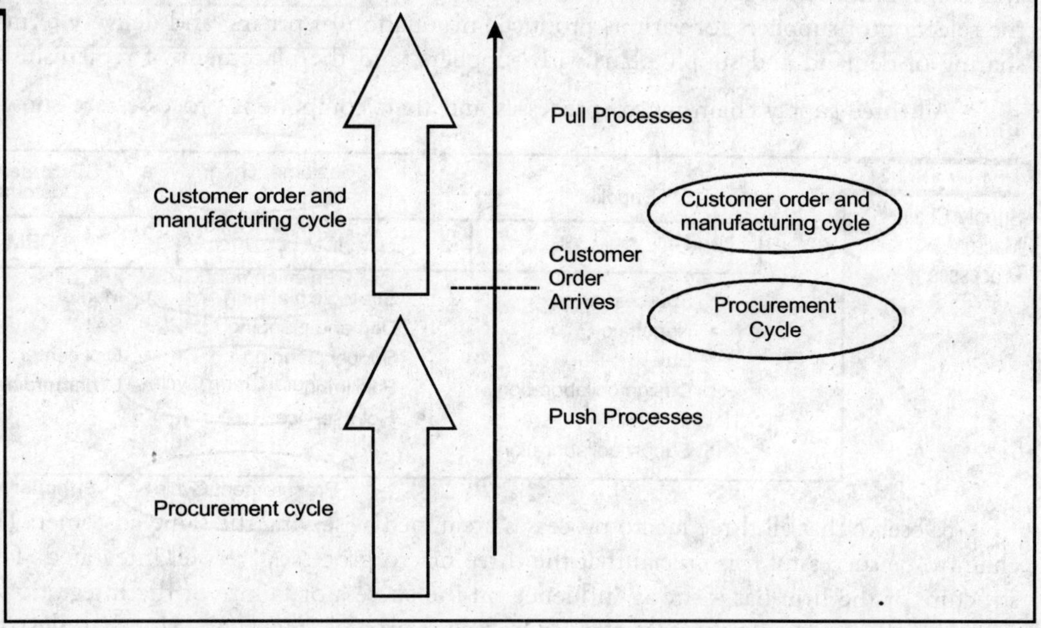

Once clear distinction between two supply chains discussed earlier is that the Dell supply chain has fewer stages and more pull processes the L.L. Bean supply chain. This impact on supply chain performance.

SUPPLY CHAIN MACRO PROCESSES IN A FIRM

All supply chain process in a firm can be classified into the following three macro process as:

1. ***Customer relationship management* (CRM):** All process that focus on the interface between the firm and its customer.

2. ***Internal supply chain management (ISCM):*** All process that are internal to the firm.
3. ***Supplier Relationship Management (SRM):*** All processes that focus on the interface between the firm and its suppliers.

The three macro processes manage the flow of information, product, and funds required to generate, receive, and fulfill a customer request. The CRM macro process aims to generate customer demand and facilitate the placement and tracking of orders. It includes processes such as marketing, sales order management, and call center management. At an industrial distributor, CRM process would include the preparation of the Website, and management of the call center taking orders and providing services. The ISCM macro process aims to fulfill demand generated by the CRM process in a timely manner and at the lowest possible cost. ISCM process includes the planning of internal production and storage capacity, preparation of demand and supply plans, and internal fulfillment of actual orders. ISCM processes would include planning for the location and size of warehousing; planning for which products to carry at each warehouse; preparation of inventory management policies; and the picking, packing, and shipping of actual orders. The SRM macro process aims to arrange for and manage supply sources for various goods and services. SRM process include the evolution and selection of suppliers, negotiation of supply terms, and communication regarding new products and order with supply terms, and communication regarding new products and order with suppliers. SRM processes would include the selection of suppliers for various products, negotiation of pricing and delivery terms with suppliers, sharing of demand and supply plans with suppliers, and the placement of replenishment order.

All three supply chain macro processes and their component processes are show in Figure 32.9.

figure 32.9
Supply Chain Macro Processes

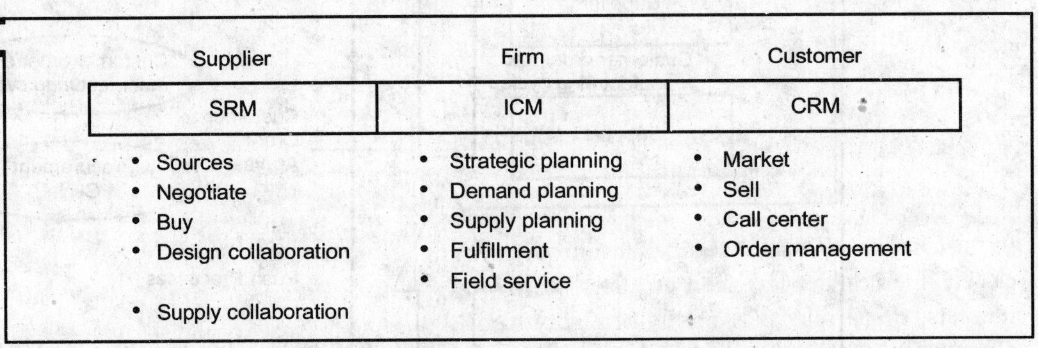

Observe that all three macro processes are aimed at serving the same customer. Thus, for a supply chain to be successful it is crucial that the three macro processes are well integrated. The organizational structure of the firm has a strong influence on the success or failure of the integration effort. In many firms, marketing is in charge of the CRM macro process, manufacturing handles the ISCM macro process, and purchasing overseas the SRM macro process with very little communication between them. It is not unusual for marketing and manufacturing to have two different forecasts when making their plans. This lack of integration hurts the supply chain's ability to match supply and demand effectively, leading to dissatisfied customers and high costs. Thus, firms should structure a supply chain organization that mirrors the macro processes and ensures good communication and coordination between the owners of processes that interact with each other.

THE IMPORTANCE OF SUPPLY CHAIN FLOWS

There is a close connection between the design and management of supply chain flows (product, information, and cash) and the success of a supply chain. Dell computer is an example of a firm that has successfully used good supply chain management of supply chain flows.

Dell has, over a relatively short period of time, become the world' largest PC manufacturer. They have generated margins, profits, and subsequently, market capitalization beyond any of their competitors' PC businesses. Dell has attributed a significant part of its success to the way it manages flows-product, information, and cash-within its supply chain.

Dell's basic supply chain model is direct sales to customers. As distributors and retailers are bypassed, the Dell supply chain has only three stages-customers, manufacturer, and suppliers-as shown in figure 32.10.

Because Dell is in direct contact with its customers, it has been able to finely segment them and analyze the needs profitability of each segment. Close contact with their customers and an understanding of customers' needs also allows Dell to develop better forecasts. To further improve the match between supply and demand, Dell makes an active effort to steer customers in real time, on the phone or via the Internet toward PC configurations that can be built given the components available.

figure 32.10

Dell Supply Chain stages

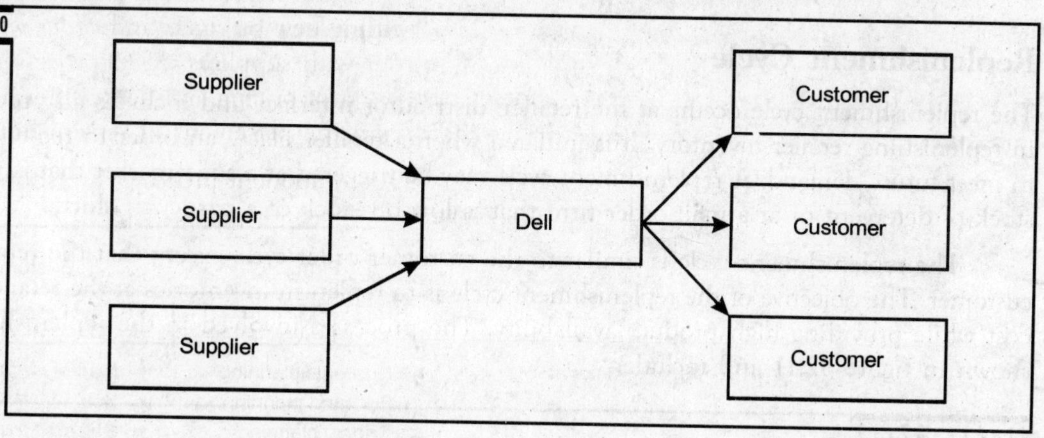

On the operational side, inventory turns is a key performance measure that Dell watches very closely. Dell carries less than ten days' worthy of inventory; in contrast, the competition, selling through retailers, carriers in the vicinity of eighty to one hundred days' worth of inventory. If Intel introduces a new chip, the low level of inventory allows Dell to go to market with a PC containing the chip faster than the competition. If prices suddenly drop, as they often do, Dell has less inventory that losses value relative to its competitors. For some products, such as monitors manufactured by Sony, Dell maintains no inventory. The transportation company simply picks up the appropriate number of computers from Dell's Austin plant and monitors from Sony's factory in Mexico, matches them by customer order, and delivers them to the customers. This procedures allows Dell to save time and money associated with the extra handling of monitors.

The success of Dell supply chain is facilitated by sophisticated information exchange. Dell provides real time data to suppliers on the current state of demand. Suppliers are able to access their components" inventory levels at the factories along with daily production requirements. Dell has created customized web pages so that its major suppliers can view demand forecasts and other customer-sensitive information, thus helping suppliers to that of Dell. The company has production concentrated in five manufacturing centers- Brazil, China, Irelend, Malaysia, and Texas. Because demand at each location is relatively large and stable, suppliers are able o replenish component inventories regularly, allowing for low levels of component inventories to be maintained. In some cases, Dell carries only hours of component inventory at its factory.

Dell's low levels of inventory also help ensure those defects are not introduced into large quantity of product. When a new product is launches, supplier engineers are stationed right in the plant. If customer calls in with a problem, production is stopped and flaws are fixed in real time. As there is no finished product in inventory, the amount of defective merchandise produced is minimized.

Dell also manages its cash flows very effectively. By managing receivables and payables very closely, they are able to collect cash from their customers, on average, ten to fifteen days before they have to pay their suppliers.

Clearly, Dell's supply chain design and their management of product, information and cash flows play a key role in the company's success. This approach has left Dell very well positioned in the PC industry. Given that the PC is to an extent a commodity, the competitive battlefield is more focused on supply chain responsiveness and efficiency. This bodes well for Dell.

The failure of many e-business can be attributed to their inability to manage supply chain flows effectively.

Counter. For a mail order firm, receiving occurs when the product is delivered to the customer.

Replenishment Cycle

The replenishment cycle occurs at the retailer/distributor interface and includes all processes involved in replenishing retailer inventory. It is initiated when a retailer places an order to replenish inventories to meet future demand. A replenishment cycle may be triggered at a supermarket that is running out of stock of detergent or at a mail order firm that is low on stock of a particular shirt.

The replenishment cycle is similar to the customer order cycle except that the retailer is now the customer. The objective of the replenishment cycle is to replenish inventories at the retailer at minimum cost while providing high product availability. The processes involved in the replenishment cycle are shown in figure 32.11 and include:

figure 32.11
Replenishment Cycle

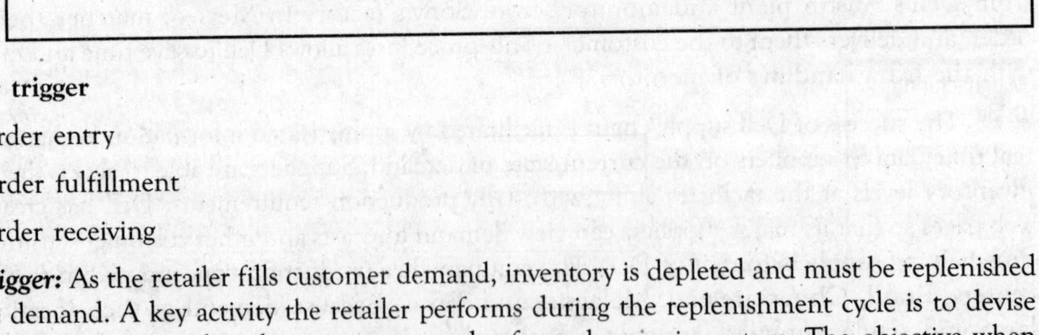

Retailer order trigger

- Retail order entry
- Retail order fulfillment
- Retail order receiving

Retail order trigger: As the retailer fills customer demand, inventory is depleted and must be replenished to meet future demand. A key activity the retailer performs during the replenishment cycle is to devise a replenishment or ordering policy that triggers an order from the previous stage. The objective when setting replenishment order triggers is to maximize profitability by ensuring economies of scale and balancing product availability and the cost of holding inventory. The outcome of the retail order trigger process is the generation of a replenishment order trigger process is the generation of a replenishment order that is ready to be passed on to the distributor or manufacturer.

Retail order entry: This process is similar to customer order entry at the retailer. The only difference is that retailer is now the customer placing the order that is conveyed to the distributor. This may be done electronically or by some other medium. Inventory or production is then allocated to the retail order. The objective of the retail order be entered accurately and conveyed quickly to all supply chain processes affected by the order.

Retail order fulfillment: This process is very similar to customer order fulfillment except that it takes place at the distributor. A key difference is the size of each order as customer orders tend to be much smaller than replenishment orders. The objective of the retail order fulfillment is to get the replenishment order to the retailer on time while minimizing costs.

Retailer order receiving: Once the replenishment order arrives at a retailer, the retailer must receive it physically and update all inventory records. This process involves product flow from the distributor to retailer as well as information updates at the retailer and the flow of funds from the retailer to the distributor. The objective of the retail order receiving process is to update inventories and displays quickly and accurately at the lowest possible cost.

Manufacturing Cycle

The manufacturing cycle typically occurs at the distributor/manufacture (or retailer/manufacturer) interface and includes all processes involved in replenishing distributor (or retailer) inventory. The manufacturing cycle is triggered by customer orders (as is the case with Dell), replenishment orders from a retailer or distributor (War-Mart ordering from P & G), or by the forecast of a customer demand and current product availability in the manufacturer's finished goods warehouse.

Our extreme in a manufacturing cycle is an integrated steel mill that collects orders that are similar enough to enable the manufacturer to produce in large quantities. In this case, the manufacturing cycle is reacting to customer demand (referred to as a pull process). Another extreme is a consumer products firm that must produce in anticipation of demand. In this case the manufacturing cycle is anticipated customer demand (referee to as a push process). The processes involved in the manufacturing cycle are shown in figure 32.11 and include the following:

- Order arrival from the finished-goods warehouse, distributor, retailer, or customer
- Production scheduling
- Manufacturing and shipping
- Receiving at the distributor, retailer, or customer

figure 32.12

Manufacturing Cycle

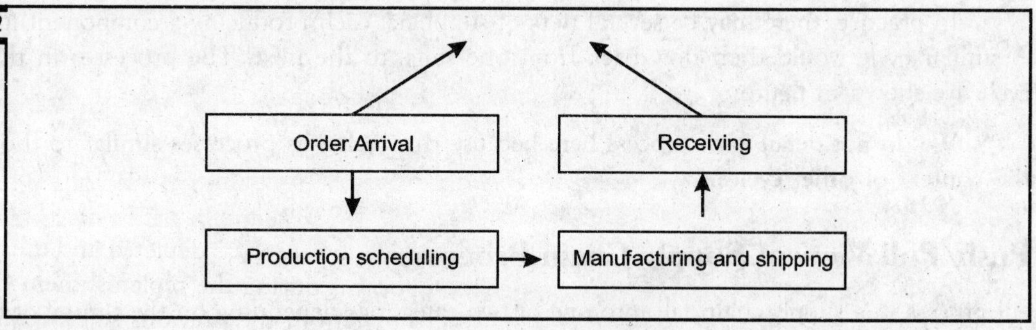

Order arrival: During this process, a finished goods warehouse or distributor sets a replenishment order trigger based on the forecast of future demand and current product inventories. The resulting order is then conveyed to the manufacturer. In some case the customer or retailer may be ordering directly from the manufacturer. In other cases a manufacture may be producing to stock a finished-products warehouse. In the latter situation, the order is triggered based on product availability and a forecast of future demand. This process is similar to the retail order trigger process in the replenishment cycle.

Production scheduling: This process is similar to the order entry process in the replenishment cycle where inventory is allocated to an order. During the production scheduling process, order (or forecasts orders) are allocated to a production plan. Given the desired production quantities for each product, the manufacturer must decide on the precise production sequence. If there are multiple lines, the manufacturer must also decide which products to allocate to each line. The objective of the production scheduling process is to maximize the proportion of orders filled on time while keeping cost down.

Manufacturing and shipping: This process is equivalent to the order fulfillment process described in the replenishment cycle. During the manufacturing phase of the process, the manufacture produces to the production schedule. During the shipping phase of this process, the product is shipped to the customer, retailer, distributor, or finished-product warehouse. The objective of the manufacturing and shipping process is to create and ship the product by the promised due date while meeting quality requirements and keeping costs down.

Receiving

In this process, the product is received at the distributor, finished-goods warehouse, retailer, or customer and inventory records are updated. Other processes related to storage and fund transfers also take place.

Procurement Cycle

The procurement cycle occurs at the manufacturer/supplier interface and includes all processes necessary to ensure that materials are available for manufacturing to occur according to schedule. During the procurement cycle, the manufacturer orders components from suppliers that replenish the component inventories. The relationships is quite similar to that between a distributor and manufacturer with one significant difference. Whereas retailer/distributor orders are triggered by uncertain customer demand, component orders can be determined precisely once the manufacturer has decided what the production schedule will be. Component orders depend on the production schedule. Thus it is important that suppliers be linked to the manufacture' production schedule. Of course, if a supplier's lead times are long, the supplier has to produce to forecast because the manufacture's production schedule may not be fixed that far in advance.

In practice, there may be several tiers of suppliers, each producing a component for the next tier. A similar cycle would then flow back from one stage to the next. The processes in the procurement cycle are shown in figure.

We do not detail each process here because this cycle has processes similar to those discussed in the context of other cycles.

Push/Pull View of Supply Chain Processes

All process in a supply chain fall into one of two categories depending on the timing of their execution relative to end customer demand. With pull processes, execution is initiated in response to a customer order. With push processes, execution is initiated in anticipation of customer orders. Therefore, at the time of execution of a pull process, customer demand is known with certainty whereas at the time of execution of execution of a push process, demand is not known and must be forecast. Pull processes may also be referred to a reactive processes because they react to customer demand. Push processes may also be referred to as speculative processes because they respond to speculated (or forecasted) rather than actual demand. The push/ pull boundary in a supply chain separates push processes from pull process. At Dell, for example, the beginning of PC assembly represent the push/pull boundary. All processes before PC assembly are push processes and all processes after and including assembly are initiated in response to a customer order and are thus pull processes.

A push/pull view of the supply chain is very useful when considering strategic decision relating to supply chain design. This view forces a more global consideration of supply chain processes as they relate to a customer order. Such a view may, for instance, result in responsibility for certain processes being passed on to a different stage of the supply chain if making this transfer allows push process to become a pull process.

Let us consider two distinct supply chains that we have discussed and related them to the push/ pull and cycle views. One supply chain is mail order company like L.L. Bean that receives customer orders through its telemarketing center or Website. The other is to build-to-order computer manufacture like Dell.

SUMMARY

Retailing is the last stage of distribution channel. A retailer is someone who breaks the bulk, makes product or service available to the consumer whenever required. Each retailer survives and prospers by satisfying a group of consumers needs more effectively decisions are constrained by the amount of money available to invest in inventory and the amount of space available in the store. Supply chain management includes all parties involved directly or indirectly in fulfilling a customer request. A supply chain is a sequence of processes and flows that take place within place within and between different stages of distribution channel.

PROJECT WORK

Collect the material regarding to merchandise management of the following companies:

1. Vishal Megamart
2. Big Bazaar
3. Reliance Fresh

Collect the material which is related to application and scope of supply chain management of five automobile companies:

SHORT QUESTIONS

1. What is merchandise management?
2. Define Inventory Control?
3. What is supply chain management?
4. What is assortment?

REVIEW QUESTIONS

1. Discuss the process of planning of assortment.
2. Discuss the role and importance of supply chain management.
3. Explain the nature and objectives of merchandise management.

GO TO THE NET

1. Using the Internet search tool prepare a report on the role and responsibilities of merchandise management.
2. Using the Internet search tool prepare a report in supply chain management of 5 logistics companies.
3. Using Internet search tool prepare a report on the merchandise management of any 3 mall store.

Caselet

Soumitro Ghosh, M.D., Tabeffer India, was convinced his company had developed a product with the potential to be a winner; a tablet base soft drink, branded Larino. The results or the market research that he had commissioned indicated that consumers were not only interested in the concept, but also liked the flavours in which Larino had been test marketed. However, breaking into the soft-drinks market world not be simple.

While the concentrates segment was stagnant, the aerated drinks segment was dominated by global players with enormous financial backing.

The product had two over riding advantages. If did not have the inconvenience of mixing. Sugaring, stirring and disposing of the package unlike tetrapack.

The company had worked out a third party contract distribution arrangement with Gretas which is also distributing soaps, biscuits and hair creams.

Tabeffer India also hired the services of Product Profile, a leading market research firm. The initial research revealed the following facts:

(a) The consumption pattern in volumes was: filter coffee 4.9 percent, malted drinks 3.3 percent, instant coffee 2.8 percent, and soft drinks 2.2 percent. The soft drinks market though of a low volume in comparison was for more impressive in terms of value- Rs. 2,300 crore per annum.

(b) Aerated Soft Drinks (or ASD's) accounted for Rs. 2,200 crore, tetrapacks Rs. 160 crore, concentrates Rs. 80 crore, and branded squashes Rs. 25 crore.

(c) ASDs consisted of Colas (80 percent), lemon drinks (20 percent) and Oranges (10 percent).

(d) There are three brands in the coal segment of ASD; Life, prime and Vic. Life is a 100 year old global brand with a brand image built around fun, youth and group socializing. Prime is a close rival of life in several markets around the world. Vic had a near monopoly position, with a 60 percent share of the Cola market. With its macho image it tried to position itself directly against Prime.

(e) In the lemon segment, Misty was the single largest selling brand in the 70's and 80's. it was initially directly against Prime.

It later projected an anytime drink image highlighting the occasion brand association. Its cloudy appearance was well received. Thus, the following six conclusions were analysed by the company.

1. The brand image projected during the launch will be vital.
2. ASD brands have enormous ad spends.
3. Global brands have been successful only in the cola segment.
4. Tetrapacks have seen the largest number of failures, but also single largest success.
5. Brands targeting several demographic and psychographic segments have not been successful.
6. For five years, the concentrates market has defined all attempts at expansion.

Questions:

1. Highlight the per issues discussed in the case.
2. Develop an "image plan" for Lorino.
3. How will you develop a product concept for Lorino before launching?

[illegible]

[illegible] distribution arrangement [illegible] distributing [illegible]

[illegible] leading market research firm [illegible] following data:

[illegible]

(c) [illegible] 120 percent [illegible] 110 percent.

(d) [illegible] 100 percent [illegible] global brand [illegible]

[illegible]

1. [illegible]
2. [illegible] have [illegible]
3. [illegible] global [illegible] successful [illegible]
4. [illegible] the largest [illegible]
5. [illegible] demographic segment [illegible]
6. [illegible]

Questions

1. Identify the [illegible] discussed in the case.
2. Develop a [illegible] plan for [illegible]
3. How would you develop a product [illegible]?

CHAPTER

33

retail selling

learning objectives

The objectives of this chapter are to:

- understand the meaning of retail selling
- discuss retail selling steps.

content outline

- Introduction
- The Sales Approach
- Proper Attitude
- Making the Sale
- What Goods to Show First?
- Summary
- Project Work
- Short Answer Questions
- Review Questions
- Go to the Net
- Caselet

INTRODUCTION

The distinction between retail selling and other types is not always sharp, and a wide area exists where the distinction is almost non-existent. A lazy speciality sales rep can wait for business to roll in, while an alert retail clerk can go after business. Sellers of such items as electrical appliances and automobiles usually work part time on the floor as store clerks and part time outside as speciality salespeople. There are good and poor salespeople in both groups.

In the late fifties and early sixties a rash of articles appeared in the trade press deploring the low state to which retail selling had fallen. In recent years, this complaint has been tempered with the realisation that the distributive system at the retail level has undergone a fundamental change towards pre-sold merchandising and mass distribution. The basic marketing strategy for a large number of common goods is to move them quickly and cheaply through the retail stage, using low-skilled help who are little more than stock clerks, checkers and wrappers. For many goods, the demand-creation function has shifted from personal selling to advertising.

For the most part, the large retailing organisations have chosen to focus their managerial strategies not on personal selling but on physical assets, financial power, advertising, and operational systems – things they believe they can manage and control.

As one retail executive said, "I put money in a good location, I own it. I put money in people and they leave me for a better job. So we don't invest much in people."

But the large organisation's weakness is the small merchant's opportunity. Salespeople can be a good investment and developing good ones can be a sound strategy.

Much true salesmanship survives in many small speciality shops which are not participating in the mass distributive system. In fact, it is doubtful whether selling in the good old days was as good as it is pictured in nostalgic memories. What critics remember were probably not so much good salespeople as hungry ones – people who had to exert themselves because of a scarcity of customers and other jobs to which they could flee. It was not a time of plenty.

As these words were written, the author and his wife had just returned from a short shopping trip to pick up a graduation present for our son. As had been the case for the past 3 months, "We" had to stop at two yet unvisited plant nurseries to look for two or three indoor plants that were "needed" for the living room. Knowing little about such greenery, we were uncertain about what we wanted or what would thrive in the particular location that they would occupy. Without exception, in each of the dozen nurseries, the customers were largely left alone to select what was wanted and take it to a checkout stand. In a few stores a clerk would answer a few direct questions, but none would really "wait" on you. Finally in one establishment, The Plant Room, a young woman waited on us and escorted us around the premises showing us things that would prosper in our locale.

She knew the plants and was pleasantly helpful and most understanding of what we wanted. She sold us four plants with little effort; it was all so natural and I am sure we'll return there the next time when we are in the market. Moreover, we'll recommend the place to our friends.

Lazy merchants and salespeople like to use self-selection as a cop-out for not helping the customer. True, there are many people who will buy of their own accord, but there are many others who need help.

Destructive criticism is easy to find and easy to offer, but it does not go far towards solving the problem. An effort to discover the reasons for the situation would be more helpful.

Some store managers insist that the public does not want good service – at least, not strongly enough to be willing to pay for it. Customers are now so used to self-service stores with virtually no service from sales clerks that they expect very little from them in any store.

It has also been pointed out that many customers are responsible for the poor treatment they receive. They are unreasonable and unkind in their attitudes, thereby arousing feelings of resentment and dislike on the part of the sales personnel. "If customers would treat us with some degree of courtesy and consideration, we would try much harder to please them" seems to be the reaction of many salespeople, for which there is some basis.

Another reason often assigned is that stores simply cannot afford to pay enough to their sales personnel to attract top-notch people. The managers of the stores study their "cost to sell" figures and see them steadily rising. It costs more to sell a dollar's worth of goods today than it did some years ago. The natural reaction is to cut selling expense wherever possible – and one place is wages of salespeople.

Our retail executives see the marketing process growing more automatic year by year; robots dispense coffee, cigarettes, gum, cold drinks, entire meals, and scores of other items. Self-service stores are taking over one field after another, while department stores are transforming various departments into self-service units. Advertising sells the customers in advance, especially now that television has entered the scene. It is only natural that a retail executive, harried by rising costs of operations, should trim expenses by cutting down on sums spent on salespeople.

This means that many young people are hired who do not regard the job as permanent and who, therefore, are not greatly concerned with trying to climb or advance in it. They therefore put forth a minimum of effort.

Just what would happen if all the retail executives decided to raise the pay of their salespeople and thereby attempt to attract and encourage more efficient personnel is anybody's guess. But a few stores have done precisely this and have discovered that their sales increased and the cost of selling each dollar's worth of goods dropped These stores are chiefly those selling "shopping lines" and catering to the higher-income patrons. If all stores tried to follow their example, there might not be enough good salespeople to go around. So most stores continue to pay a weekly wage appreciably lower than that paid to workers in other lines.

But the problem of poor salesmanship would not be solved by merely offering higher wages to salespeople. Of equal importance is sound training of all sales personnel. If the salespeople sell more, they should be paid more; and this could often be done without increasing the cost of selling each dollar's worth of goods. It might actually decrease it.

It is clear that management is by no means free from blame in this matter of inefficient retail selling. New clerks are too often allowed to struggle along, picking up what ideas they can from colleagues, and many of these ideas do not improve their technique. They deserve better treatment.

Finally, few retail salespeople today perceive themselves as career professionals. Too frequently it is just a job to hold "until something better comes along." With little pride in their work, it is small wonder that their skill at it lies uncultivated.

THE SALES APPROACH

Instead of being obliged to search for customers, retail salespeople rely upon advertising, attractive display windows and counters and numerous services in the store to bring in buyers. A salesperson, actually, is in the position of a host receiving a guest. It devolves upon him or her to make the visitor feel welcome and at ease. A further difference between speciality and retail selling lies in the fact that the prospect for the speciality sales rep is frequently not even interested in the sales offer until learning about its advantages, but the buyer in the retail establishment usually comes into the store with some idea of what is wanted.

Service Approach

- "Have you been attended to?"
- "Have you been waited on?"
- "Do you wish to be served?"

"May I wait on you please?" (This last one is used by a large variety chain and is good for that type of store).

These service approaches are so similar that they may be considered together. They surely indicate a desire to be of service, if asked in the proper tone of voice and with the proper expression and attitude. They would, however, be manifestly out of place in a small speciality store where the customer could be plainly seen as he entered the store. It would be evident that he had not received attention and he might resent such an inquiry as being pointless and inane. In a large department store, it would be more excusable; but even here, where it is possible that the customer has already made a purchase in another department, there is, in it, a suggestion that could frighten away the "looker," who might otherwise be induced to linger, look, and perhaps buy. In other words, it is too easy for the customer to reply "Yes" to the first two questions or "No" to the last two, then move on without becoming interested.

The objection may be made that the assumption is that the customer does not wish to buy, that only the customer who is not a good prospect is considered. This is true. It requires no salesmanship to sell to a person who knows and states exactly what he or she wants. But it does require salesmanship to sell to the person who has little intention of buying. Therefore students of salesmanship are justified in devoting major effort to this type of prospect, as the others are easily cared for.

- "Something for you?"
- "Something special I could show you?"
- "Was there something in particular?"

These questions are typical. The consensus seem to be against them. The reason these greetings are not more popular is their weakness. A petulant customer naturally replies (mentally at least), "Of course there's something, or I wouldn't have come in here". If the customer is not certain just what she does want, such a salutation places her on the defensive and causes her to hurry on to some other part of the store. The inclusion of the word "special" or "particular'" is added as it implies a lack of willingness to display goods unless the customer is able to state precisely what is wanted.

- "What will it be for you?"
- "What can I do for you?"
- "What did you want?"
- "What was it you wanted?"

In this group there is an obvious attempt to utilise the principle of the positive suggestion–that the customer wants something, in which respect they are perhaps better than the previous group. This type of salutation is applicable in a store dealing in convenience goods, as a drugstore. Here it may more safety be assumed that the customer intends to purchase something than in a store handling shopping lines, as jewellery or shoes.

These questions are dangerous ones to be put in the mouths of uninterested clerks, however, as they may so easily be made to sound brusque and abrupt. There is no suggestion of service in any of them except the second, and this has been so frequently inverted to "What can I do for you?" there is danger in its use.

- "Yes, sir," or "Yes, madam "

This greeting is used in some stores as the salesperson steps up to the customer after having been otherwise occupied for a moment. It is best used in the type of store where the counter does not separate the salesperson and manner and tone used by the salesman, but properly handled, it is good. Obviously, it could not be used on the casual shopper roaming through the aisles of a department store.

- "May I serve you?"
- "May I assist you?"
- "May I be of any service, madam?"
- "May I help you?" (Widely used. Best of the four).

These are typical greetings that stress the idea of service. They are adapted to use in a high-class store by salespeople possessing more than the average amount of culture. Many salespeople may not be able to utter such a salutation easily and naturally, and to many customers it would sound forced, almost laughable. In smaller communities where acquaintance exists between customer and salesperson such a salutation would appear little short of ridiculous.

When addressed to the casual shopper, such a salutation may cause the latter to say, "No, thank you," and move on. Much depends on the way the question is asked.

Salutation Approach

- "Good morning, sir, or "Good afternoon, madam".

In case of doubt, this greeting is perhaps the safest to use. Almost any clerk can use it without making it sound brusque, as all of us have been accustomed from childhood to a smile or at least register good humour as we voice such a salutation. It should not be shouted at the customer, on the contrary, many salespeople mumble it almost inaudibly so that it will not appear to call for an answering "Good morning".

When coupled with the customer's name, as "Good afternoon, Mrs Bennett," or "Good Morning, Mr Mclntyre," it is good. In communities where customers are well-known to the salespeople and no social chasm lies between them, the salutation may be familiarized by "Hello, Jim" or "How are you Bertha?" without giving offense.

When this "Good morning" salutation is used, it is important to give it a rising inflection. Used with a falling infection, it starts the sale off wrong. It does not sound friendly - and the big objective is to start the sale in an atmosphere of friendliness. Whether the customer seems friendly or not, the salesperson must be smiling.

And this is important – speak the first word yourself and don't wait for the customer to set the tone of the interview. If you offer a greeting that is genuinely friendly, accompanying it with a smile and a meeting of the eyes, the customer will usually take a cue from you.

Merchandise Approach

Many times it is best not to greet the customer with a salutation or a service approach but rather to use a modification of the product approach discussed in earlier chapters which is referred to in retail circles as a merchandise approach.

The merchandise approach is used largely with two types of customers. It is the best way to approach rather uninterested "lookers" and also to handle someone who is ardently looking at some goods with obvious interest.

Retail clerks quickly learn to detect the person who is just looking, to approach these people with, "May I serve you?" This always prompts the answer, "No, thank you, I am just looking". After this turndown the clerk will find such persons do not want service. It is best not to approach these lookers too quickly or eagerly.

How does one identify "lookers?' They usually are wandering with an obvious aimlessness. They avoid the eyes of the clerks. They try to keep at some distance from clerks, for they do not want to be waited upon.

A clerk should wait until a looker settles down to look at one item before moving in with the merchandise approach. Suppose a "looker" stops and examines some sports shirts, one of the following merchandise approaches could be used: "What size are you interested in?" "Is there a particular colour you have in mind?" "We have some additional stock if you don't find what you like here." "We just received these new Dacron shirts today. We think they are the best buy we have seen for a long time." "These have a more tapered body that gives a better fit for the man who has kept himself trim."

The salesperson walks up and starts talking about the merchandise without asking the customer whether he wants to be waited upon. The comment used in the merchandise approach should be the most appropriate to the situation and should give the "looker" some information that is not apparent to his eye. More will be said about handling "lookers" in a following section.

In other cases, a customer may speed directly for a certain section, obviously bent on buying something. He picks it up and eagerly examines it when the sales clerk walks up. A merchandise approach is indicated in such an instance also. In fact, some clerks approach with a trial close in such cases. Some questions as "Which colour do you like?'' or "What size are you?" may reveal that the person is ready to buy.

A word about asking for the customer's size. The skilled salesperson can judge the prospect's size by observation, thereby demonstrating experience by saying, "The XLs are all on the top shelf", or "The 46-regulars begin here." If the salesperson is in error, no harm is usually done, as the prospect will quickly provide the correct information. Admittedly there are instances where tact requires that the size of the prospect be minimized and not brought out so overtly that it might embarrass the customer. Obese people may be sensitive about their size and not appreciate the salesperson who makes an issue of it.

The merchandise approach is particularly adapted to the "looker," so let's examine it a bit further.

For example, to the customer who pauses before some blouses the saleswoman might say, "Those are splendid values at $15.98. Notice the double stitched seams."

The shirt salesperson might easily offer the comment, "Solid colours seem to be going out this season, don't they? Stripes are good now, though". Such a comment would be more likely to induce the customer to linger and look than a query, "May I show you some shirts today?"

This attitude on the part of the retail salesperson is worth cultivating, as it aids him to sell to many idly curious shoppers who would otherwise pass on without purchasing. A shopper was standing in a bookstore one day looking over a book with the idea of learning if the vocabulary was too difficult for his children to understand, when a clerk bustled up with, "Did you want to buy that book?" The immediate impulse was to deny any such intention, to lay the book down, and leave. The clerk's attitude and words produced an effect similar to that produced upon a loitering vagabond by a blue-coated officer who prods him in the ribs with his club and exhorts him to "move on, you". In striking contrast was the skill displayed by another salesperson in the same store, who under identical circumstances, casually strolled near, rearranging books as he came and finally remarked, "That's a splendid book you have there for children around ten years of ago. Did you happen to hear the talk by Mrs Whittler, of the Detroit Public Library's juvenile department, before the Parent-Teacher Association last week? She specifically mentioned it as one of the very best books for children of this age because...." This salesperson did not frighten his customer away; he sold the book.

The casual attitude, devoid of all signs of selling, has a large part in enabling a salesperson to gain the attention and interest of the undecided shopper.

Sometimes the store has advertised a special offering for the day or week. In this case, the salesperson may ask a question such as "Have you seen the new line of sport shirts we advertised this morning for $18.95?" The prospect, although he may not have any definite intention of buying, usually replies, "No, I haven't, perhaps adding, "What are they like?" This question, which carries scant suggestion of either buying or selling, is more effective than one which makes the prospect feel that he is being importuned to spend his money.

PROPER ATTITUDE

Salespeople's verbal greetings are important, but not so important as their attitudes.

One of the first points in a good approach is promptness. The salesperson must stop a conversation with a fellow salesperson, must stop work with the stock-in short, must show instant willingness to wait on the customer. This point appears self-evident, yet there is a peculiar trait in most of us that makes us like to seem busy. It crops out in the purchasing agent who enjoys keeping sale reps waiting while fussing with papers on the desk and the clerk who exhibits the identical characteristic while diligently rearranging stock after the customer has entered. It is partly mental inertia and partly a desire to appear important. Whichever it may be, no customer likes to wait while the salesperson continues doing something which could easily be suspended.

Promptness is essential in approaching a customer, but this should not be interpreted as meaning haste. The speed of the salesperson's approach will be governed largely by that of the customer. If the latter is hurrying, the salesperson will exhibit more alacrity in an effort to accommodate the customer's mental state. In an open department it is safe to time the approach so that the customer will be met about halfway. At a counter, the sales clerk must walk towards that part of the counter before which the customer has paused.

The importance of promptness is not fully appreciated by many salespeople. One authority ventures the opinion that the prompt salesperson gains 25 to 50 per cent more trade than a slow one who may in other ways be equally efficient. This does not mean that salespeople should engage in a scramble to wait on a customer, but merely that promptness is appreciated by customers.

Some salespeople seem to forget that their main duty is to sell goods. They become so engrossed in other details, such as arranging or dusting stock, that they lost sight of the fundamental fact that they are here to serve the customers. Others are timid about approaching a customer and need to have their courage strengthened. Be alert for the customer's first words, as it places a damper on a sale to ask, "What did you say?" or "I beg your pardon?"

MAKING THE SALE

Those all important first words!

Top-notch retail salespeople try to develop short sentences that will open the sale favourably. These selling sentences state or imply that a customer benefits or gains from buying the item. They are not mere statements of product facts; they interpret such facts in terms of customer benefits.

The late Elmer Wheeler made this technique famous and was called upon to work out what he called "tested sentences that sell' for many products, often with spectacular results.

A few of these tested sentences made famous by Wheeler are:

- It won't nib off (For white shoe dressing).
- How would you like to cut your shaving time in half? (for Barbasol). This sentence was followed with "Use Barbasol – just spread it on – shave it off – nothing else required." Sales in one store increased 300 per cent
- They won't roll (for square clothespins). These three words reminded homemakers of experiences with round clothespins – stepping on them and falling, fishing them out from under tubs and tables where they had rolled.

A sporting goods salesman sold a ski outfit to a reluctant customer who had entered the store for the sole purpose of buying a parka. He opened his sales presentation on a package deal the store was featuring with the words, "These skis and bindings are for men who can't afford a broken leg." He had read the prospect correctly.

WHAT GOODS TO SHOW FIRST?

In an effort to determine the customer's needs, the retail salesperson is often puzzled as to what grade of merchandise to show first. If too cheap a grade is shown, the customer may be offended, whereas if too high a grade is shown, it may scare the shopper away.

This last point is not understood by all salespeople, many of whom reason that showing high-grade goods will flatter a customer and induce the purchase of a better grade. Frequently, however, the customer, who cannot afford to pay such a price and is unwilling to admit poverty, decides to play the role which the sales rep has to play.

SUMMARY

Retail organisations have grown dramatically in the food sector. In urban areas, retailers have tended to move towards large-scale retailing in terms of multiple chains and stores in order to gain from efficiencies and economies of scale. However, small-scale operators do have certain advantages.

The management of retail cannot be divorced from the management of service and quality. The marketing management of retail cannot ignore the primary characteristics which set retail apart form other products.

PROJECT WORK

How do you make prospecting for retail products?

SHORT ANSWER QUESTIONS

1. What do you mean by retail selling?
2. Define service approach.
3. What is mercantile approach?
4. What is sales approach?

REVIEW QUESTIONS

1. Take one component of the four P's and look at it in relation to what a retail company of your choice does.
2. Visit a store when it has embarked upon made models. Try to assess the level and effectiveness of different methods and hold discussion with staff.
3. What are the key changes which you expect in retail markets in the next five years in urban and rural areas?
4. Discuss different types of approach with the help of example

GO TO THE NET

Using Internet sources, study the retail selling approach of four organisations.

Using Internet search tools prepare a report on the nature and scope of the sales approach.

Caselet

CRM – AN APPROACH TO MODERN MARKETING

Customer relationships are now at the forefront of business — breaking all barriers after Liberalisation, Privatisation and Globalisation (LPG). Customer Relationship Management (CRM) has once again gained prominence among management professionals in general and academicians in particular. Relationships are as old as mankind. They have been studied by sociologists, social psychologists, anthropologists, philosophers, theologians and many other people. Businessmen and academicians and researchers of yesteryear relied on relationships for their success. However the modern markets started taking to the fashion only recently.

It is always interesting to look at history to understand the evolution of any discipline. Though marketing as a systematic study subject or an activity may be of recent origin, but the practice of marketing is as old as human civilization. The barter system may be a stepping stone for the discipline of marketing management, which passed through several stages to arrive at the present form. The development of marketing can be chronologized as follows

1. Marketing of the early stages can be termed as traditional marketing which basically refers to the barter system. The starting point for the discipline of marketing lies in human needs and want. Marketing emerged when people decided to satisfy needs and wants through exchange.
2. The effect of successful exchange resulted in the invention of money. Industrial revolution led the seller to engage in mass production, mass distribution and mass promotion or marketing known as mass marketing epitomised by Henry Ford.
3. Formal marketing started with psychologists helping marketers to manipulate customers to their advantage. The heart of modern strategic marketing can be described as STP marketing namely – Segmenting, Targeting, and Positioning. Then it got established as a discipline with its 4Ps – Product, Price, Place, Promotion.
4. Then came value based marketing which emphasised offering better value to the customers' money by constantly improving the quality of products and services offered to customers.
5. Simultaneously, the developments in business -to-business marketing and services marketing emphasised the need for developing long-term relationship with customers. The new paradigm emphasises need for the customer retention through relationship building. Transaction marketing is a part of a larger idea, that of relationship marketing. Smart marketers try to build up long-term trusting, "win-win" relationship with customers, distributors, dealers and suppliers.
6. Another variant of the same is emerging marketing on the Web which leads to one-to-one marketing that emphasises relationship customisation at the individual level.

A model for a marketing cycle is given below

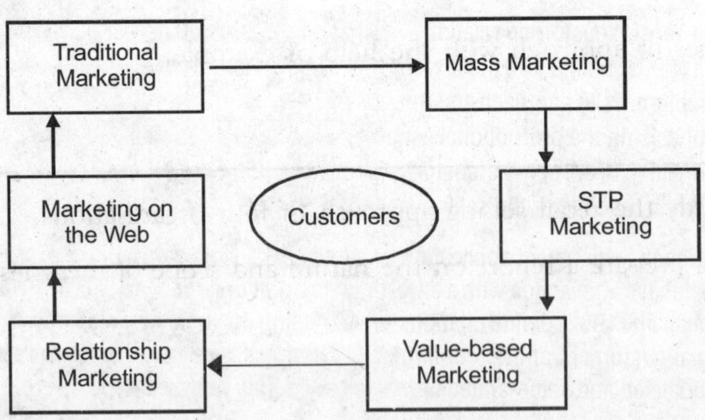

These days marketing is moving from being broad based to a one-to-one relationship with the customer.

In this paper, an attempt has been made to explore the conceptual foundations of CRM by examining the closer relationship with customers which results in better returns to companies. Research issues as well as CRM implementation challenges are discussed with an Indian perspective.

Contd...

Key Words: Customer Relationship Management, Relationship Marketing, One-to-one Marketing, CRM Process, CRM Definition, CRM Strategy, CRM Programmes, CRM Implementation, Wireless Application Protocol.

In the early 90s smart marketers tried to build up long-term trusting "win-win" relationship with customers, distributors, dealers and suppliers. With the recent advent of the era of globalisation, there has been total transformation from sellers' market to buyers' market which has paved the path for customer relationship marketing. Marketers realised, authentic marketing is not the art of selling what you make but knowing what to make. The present-day marketing concepts rest on four main pillars, namely – a market focus, customer orientation, coordinated marketing and profitability. Their focus has shifted towards integrating the three elements – people, service and marketing, which is known today as customer service, quality and marketing in a close alignment. Thanks to government policy on liberalisation, privatisation and globalisation, consumerism has come to India. Today you name any product in consumer durables, you have more than half a dozen brands in each category and there is heavy competition in the field with each company fighting in the market to get a major share.

Customer relationship management has attracted the expanded attention of scholars and practitioners. Many scholars with interest in various sub-disciplines of marketing such as channels, services marketing, business-to-business marketing, advertising and so forth are actively engaged in studying and exploring the conceptual foundations of managing relationship with customers.

Scholars for other academic disciplines, particularly those interested in the area of information system and decision technologies, are also exploring new methodologies and techniques that create efficient Frontline Information System (FIS) to efficiently manage customer interface techniques such as collaborative filtering rules based on expert systems; artificial intelligence and relational databases are increasingly being applied to develop enterprise level solutions for managing information on customer interaction.

The concept of relationship marketing was formally introduced into the field of service marketing. Financial service institution, airlines and other service providers found it more profitable to retain and reward the existing customers rather than running after new customers. It was established that building a closer relationship with customers resulted in better returns to companies through

- Increased use of company services by loyal customers.
- Changing price premiums for customised services.
- Referrals by satisfied customers that brought new customers.

Thus relationship paradigm is accepted as a foundation on which the entire marketing theory can be built.

What is Customer Relationship Management?

In marketing literature the terms 'customer relationship marketing' and 'customer relationship management' are used interchangeably. As Nevin (1990s) points out, these terms have been used to reflect a variety of themes and perspective that is broad and somewhat paradigmatic in approach and orientation. A narrow perspective of customer relationship management is database marketing emphasising the promotional aspects of marketing linked to data-based efforts. Another narrow, yet relevant viewpoint is to consider CRM only as customer retention in which a variety of after marketing lines is used for customer bonding or staying in touch after the sale is made.

A more popular approach, with recent application of infotech, is to focus on individual or one-to-one relationship with customers that integrate database knowledge with a long-term customer retention and growth strategy (Peppers and Rogers 1993). Thus Shani and Chalasam (1992) define relationship marketing as "an integrated effort to identify, maintain and build up a network with individual customers and to continuously strengthen the network for the mutual benefit of both sides, through interactive, individualised and value-added contacts over a long period of time.

Berry (1995), in somewhat broader terms, also has a strategic viewpoint about CRM. He stresses that attracting new customers should he viewed only as an intermediate step in the marketing process. Developing a close relationship with these customers and turning them into loyal ones are equally important aspects of marketing. Thus he proposed relationship marketing as attracting, maintaining, and, in multi-service organisations, enhancing customer relationships."

Contd...

The core theme of all CRM and relationship marketing perspective is to focus on the cooperative and collaborative relationship between the firm and its customers and\or other marketing actors. Dwyer, Schurr and Oh (1987) have characterised such cooperative relationship as being interdependent and long-term oriented rather than being concerned with short-term discrete transactions. The long-term orientation is often emphasised because it is believed that marketing actors will not engage in opportunistic behaviour if they have a long-term orientation and that such relationship will be anchored on mutual gains cooperation (Ganesan 1994). Another important facet of CRM is "customer selectivity". As several research studies have shown, not all customers are equally profitable for an individual company is not to really profitable to its customer base but to identify appropriate programmes and methods that would be profitable and create value for the firm and the customer.

CRM may be defined as a comprehensive strategy and process of acquiring, retaining and partnering selective customers to create superior value for the company and the customer. The purpose of CRM is to improve marketing productivity which is achieved by increasing marketing efficiency and by enhancing marketing effectiveness (Sheth & Sisodia 1995). In CRM, marketing efficiency is achieved because cooperative and collaborative processes help in reducing transaction costs and overall development costs for the company.

CRM Practices

In new age marketing, aimed at winning the customer forever, where companies greet the customers, create products to suit their needs, work hard to develop lifetime customer approval, customer enthusiasm, etc., of ways like sending thank you cards, special discount cards, develop "customer databases for a large storehouse of customers' personal profiles, preferences, intentions, expected purchases, suggestions, etc., customer education, customer invitation on special occasions in the company and so on". Constant improvisation, customisation, shift from marketing myopia to marketing hypermetropia, provision of additional services and giving something special to customers beyond functional utility inclusive of both the tangible and intangible attribute, binds a consumer with the brand and the company itself.

In recent years, however, several factors have contributed to the rapid development and evolution of CRM. These include the disintermediation process in many industries due to the advent of sophisticated computer and telecommunication technologies that allow producers to directly interact with end customers. In many industries such as airlines, banks, insurance, computer programme software, or household appliances and even consumables, the disintermediation is fast changing the nature of marketing and consequently making relationship marketing more popular. Databases and direct marketing tools give them the means to individualise their marketing efforts. As a result, producers do not need those functions formerly performed by middlemen. Even consumers are willing to undertake some of the responsibilities of directly ordering personal merchandise, and product use-related services with little help from the producer.

Thus, relationship marketing is aimed at creating strong, long lasting, fruitful relationships by developing long-term bonds through its various instruments of personal connections. As a result, the customer starts identifying and associating himself with the product, prefers and accepts the company's products and services over competitors offerings, buys again, and recommends others to buy.

A model for customer relationship marketing

Indian marketers have recorded a high score for greeting the customers, paying them due respect, attending to customers promptly, talking in terms favourable to them, informing about the latest in the field, maintaining competitors activity with customers, asking for references from existing customers, promotions or benefits of buying from their company, practicing a two-way communication, listening and recording customer problems and keeping promises made as post-sales strategy, exploring the opportunity to meet new customers and maintaining relationship with existing customers. However "Customer Care" is practiced by some of the leading industries in India. Some examples are recently Reckitt & Coleman Company, for the first time in India, has introduced toll free telephone number to serve its customers better.

Lakme employs 'Computer Touch Screen' to advise customers regarding use of cosmetics on the basis of their skin colour. For the satisfaction of the customers, beauty consultants are also there at the point of purchase to help those who are hesitant.

Pond's Institute has a customer response centre to answer to each and every letter and phone call received. Calls are answered with empathy and responsibility.

Recently HLL- SURF received "open customer feed back" on product defects and suggestions. New product Surf Excel was launched on the basis of suggestions given by customers.

Contd...

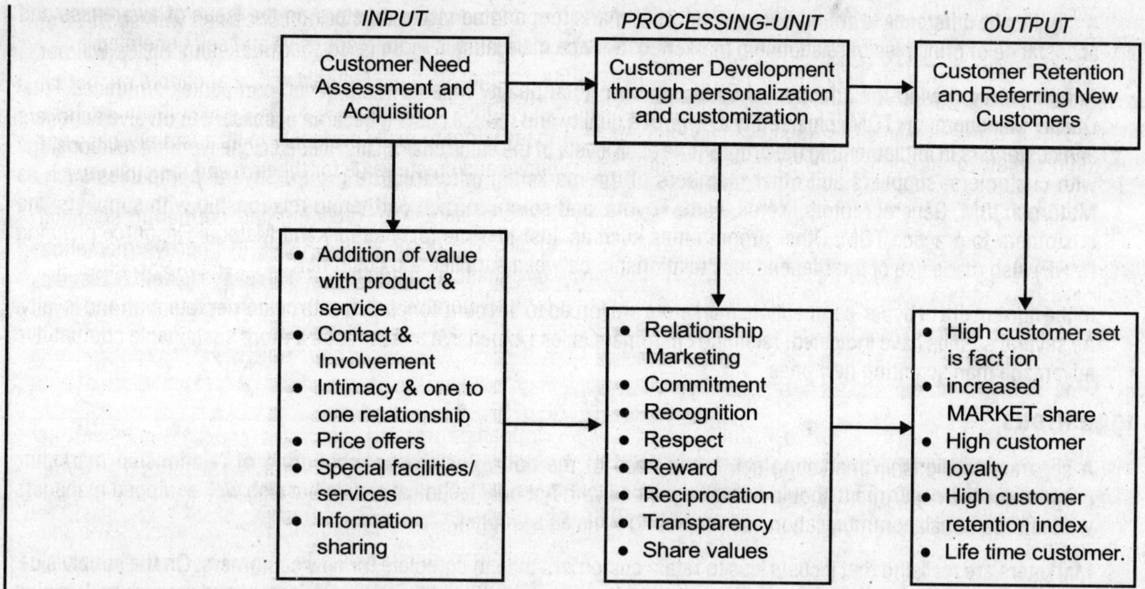

In the consumer durable sector, Godrej - GE has a database of millions of customers. Service personnel regularly contact customers and enquire about complaints. In order to serve the customers better, the company franchises its service to expand its reach.

Executives working with the DHL couriers constantly track the CSI (Customer Satisfaction Index) since their increments are based not on the sales revenue but on CSI.

Baron International (Akai) has set up a 42-Factor Service Centre (FSC) and 18 substations. It employs 536 service technicians and operates 150 vans, which are equipped with cellular phones. Complaints from the customers are redressed within two hours.

Voltas company constantly collects information on future need of potential customers through questionnaires.

Eureka Forbes Ltd — a leading company in direct marketing — is gearing up to meet the challenges in the new millennium. This company follows competitive bench-marking strategy with players like Modi, Philips and BPL.

ICICI and HDFC have, for example, recently announced their mobile banking services on WAP (Wireless Application Protocol). With this service one can request cheque books, check bank balance and even effect a fund transfer. Other interesting features on the service include a restaurant search and the like. It is going to be business at WAP- speed now.

Blue Star Ltd. sets up competitive delivery goals by bench marketing which helps the company to reduce its response time from 6 to 4 months.

Indian companies need call centres to boost their marketing effort. As Indian customers become more aware of the choices available worldwide, a number of companies already use call centres as a marketing tool. It is a learning process that a lot of Indian companies will go through.

The customer relationship space is fast getting crowded. Another entrant into this space is Olive e-business Pvt Ltd. The company, launched in June 2000, aspires to be a fore runner in online client servicing along with customer support modules. Its USP is a 24-hour a day, online client servicing feature, facilitated through interactive chats.

Inferences

In the recent success of online banking, Charles Schwab and Merill Lynch's online investment on programmes, direct selling of books, automobiles, insurance and so on, on the Internet, all attest to the growing consumer interest in laminating a direct relationship with marketers.

▶ The disintermediation process and consequent prevalence of CRM is also due to the growth of the service economy. Since services are typically produced and delivered at the same institution, it minimises the roles of the middlemen.

Contd...

A significant difference is found between product marketers and service marketers on the issue of awareness and acceptance of principles of relationship marketing. Service marketing is more responsive and self generated.

- Another force driving the adoption of CRM has been total quality management. When companies embraced Total Quality Management (TQM) philosophy to improve quality and reduce costs it became necessary to involve suppliers and customers in implementing the programme at all levels of the value chain. This needed close working relationships with customers, suppliers and other members of the marketing infrastructure group. Several companies such as Motorola, IBM, General Motors, Xerox, Ford, Toyota, and so on, formed partnering relationship with suppliers and customers to practice TQM. Other programmes such as Just-in-Time (JIT) supply and Material Resource planning (MRP) also made use of interdependence relationship between supplier and customers.
- In the current era of hyper-competition, marketers are forced to be more concerned with customer retention and loyalty. As several studies have indicated, retaining customers is less expensive and perhaps a more sustainable competitive advantage than acquiring new ones.

Suggestions

1. A separate relationship marketing cell is the need of the hour. For proper monitoring of relationship marketing programme the department should be well equipped with not only technical people but also well equipped managers with interpersonal, communication and marketing tools as a whole.
2. Marketers are realising that it costs less to retain customers than to complete for new customers. On the supply side, it really pays more to develop a closer relationship with customers through people, equipment and procedure. It is high time to re-engineer the marketing department.
3. As customer expectations have rapidly changed over the last two decades, fueled by new technology and growing availability of advanced product features and services, customers' expectations are changing almost on a daily basis. Consumers are less willing to make compromises to trade-off in product and service quality. So companies should continuously search for value building approaches through a system of Total Quality Management (TQM) review process, which will result in value-laden-relationship with customers.
4. In order to keep competitors away from customers, cross selling and up selling can meet the customer requirement. However, the idea seems to predominantly meet with the seller's need and maximise his revenues by exploiting relationship with customer. But CRM techniques should ensure mutual economic values to both customer and companies.
5. Indian companies need call centres to boost their marketing effort. As the Indian consumer starts becoming more aware of the choice available worldwide, a number of companies already use call centres as a marketing tool. It is a learning curve that a lot of Indian companies will go through.
6. If globalisation proceeds as expected, it must surely have a major impact on how firms manage customer relationships. A good training programme for progressing young dynamic international managers is the need of the hour. Global marketing communication, global consumerism and business process re-engineering are three main factors for CRM in the international market. A globalised communication strategy has to be integrated at the business unit level.
7. Managing Customer Relationship around the world calls for external and internal partnering across a firm's worldwide organisation.

CHAPTER

34

distribution of services

learning objectives

The objectives of this chapter are to:

- understand the importance of distribution of services
- describe the different types of participants in services
- discuss channel options.

content outline

opening case

Gupta Rentals – Equipment Hire

Since 1990, Gupta Rentals suffered from cash constraints. The analysis of the performance of the company carried out by Rajesh Jain and Associates highlighted the reasons as under

1. Addition of small petrol engine repair line to the existing business.
2. Increase in manpower to handle engine repair division.
3. Finances required for the purchase of parts and inventory maintenance. Presently this is also managed through existing cashflows and accounts payable.

To overcome the financial constraints, a plan has been made which specifically addresses several methods that will be used to correct the cashflow, profitability and equity deficiencies. Several changes have been initiated which have started showing positive results. The next phase of plan requires changes in two categories: Management and Financial. It is felt that when these changes are introduced, the company will return to industry norm within two years.

In 1985, the family of Guptas thought of starting a family business. Since they had most of their relations at Chandigarh, they started thinking in terms of settling close to their relations. They started exploring the possibilities of potential business opportunities. Gupta was a senior executive with a public limited company which manufactured equipment like generator sets, pumps, etc. He studied the market in and around Chandigarh and found that there were five equipment rental companies. Their equipment was obsolete, sub-standard and the people who hired equipment from them were not satisfied.

Before starting the business venture, the Guptas considered the following points:

- Providing long-term financial opportunity and to provide adequate standards of living.
- To go into business where competition could be and would be limited.
- To be in business with long-term growth.
- To be in business which could ultimately be taken over by the next generation.

After a careful analysis, the Guptas decided to go in for the equipment rentals business. The following issues were quite prominent with regards to these market offerings.

Product and Service Offering/Primary Service Mix

'If you have a job to do, we have a tool to make it easier and quicker. Service to our customers, both professional and "Do-it-yourselves" is a primary part of our daily operation'.

The philosophy of the Guptas was:

- Provide equipment in good working condition
- Provide equipment when it is needed
- Provide "How To" instructions verbally and in writing
- Provide pick up and delivery
- Must be with the customer when he is in problem
- In addition to this, the Guptas provided sale or rent of accessories needed with the equipment
- At a payment of an extra 100%, a damage waiver facility
- Gupta are agents of Raj Equipments Movers, a premier transport company specialising in equipment movement. They could move the complete range of equipment of various dimensions and sizes.

Guptas are dealers of Kirlosker Cummins, HMT, Eicher, Escorts and have inventory of vast tractor and engine lines. Because of this they have a supply contact division catering to the Agricultural and Mining Industry.

Market Potential and Competition

The Guptas have been in business for the past 13 years and have maintained detailed financial information. The company is making its projections and devising the marketing plan based on historical data augmented with the latest charges that are outlined in the plan. In addition, they have maintained complete information on the requests they have not been able to meet and reasons thereof. This gave them knowledge about the market demand forecasts.

Before starting the business, Guptas made an extensive market analysis with the help of a local agency who was conversant with regional needs and locations. This helped them to make up their minds.

Today the Guptas know that the demand is going to be up as many new construction avenues have opened and industrial growth is moving at a fast pace. They see a better future.

Bankers had been considerate to Guptas as their past records were flawless and they helped them by giving attractive refinancing schemes. They accepted these schemes, now finance was no problem to enhance business.

Market Analysis

Gupta Rentals has several areas where they maintain a competitive advantage as they are the only service providers in the area for the equipments sought by the customers. They face competition only in one area where Satish Rentals are providing similar services but are not expanding their territory.

Marketing Strategy

The goal of Gupta Rentals are

- Best service and equipment to our customers.
- Competitive prices to prevent competition at the present business location and surrounding areas.

Target Marketing

Guptas have been concentrating on supplying the equipment on rent to small contractors, the industrial sector and also house owners. The major share of the market is of small contractors who account for fifty-five per cent of business followed by industrial sectors accounting for thirty per cent.

Since most of the business at present is coming from small contractors and the industrial sector, homeowners are not being paid sufficient attention. In the coming year plan, services to homeowners are gaining attention.

Sixty-five per cent and twenty-five per cent of this business is accounted for people moving out of the town, people moving in the town and commercial moves respectively. They have acquired the leaders' position in this segment.

The sales parts division earns a revenue of fifty per cent, fifteen per cent and thirty five per cent from industrial, institutional and homeowner markets respectively.

Sales Plan

The Guptas have made the following plans to enhance sales

- Identifying and targeting the homeowner market to gain ten per cent sale over the previous years.
- Enhance the sales of 'moving needs' by creating more moves.
- Parts division will continue selling parts.

Promotional

To achieve the targeted sales as per market plan for the year 1998, radio and TV advertising shall be dropped and door-to-door flyers and direct mail will be used for homeowners. This decision was taken by Gupta as they had sufficient database about their customers and also about themselves. They propose to direct the mailing to the neighbourhood areas as discount offers to study the effectiveness. They propose to "start a thanks giving scheme" to all the equipment users in the past and with this they will offer a discount of 10% on the next rental. The technical expertise possessed by the Guptas shall be highlighted to create trust about technical capability and back up services. Door-to-door campaigning shall be introduced as a trial to convey the following messages

- Where we are?
- What we have?
- How they can use us to their advantage?

Another scheme which will be introduced in 1999 shall be to make the equipment available **for** rent on the rental outlets of the respective companies' e.g., Kirloskar engine will be available for rent on Kirloskar outlets. For meeting the moving needs, a cash incentive shall be offered to the person bringing the customer to them.

Since the year closing for the company is March 1999, the campaign for the year **1999** shall be completed by middle of May 1999. The campaign shall be budgeted by the type of media used and itemised by the type of equipment and service used for the promotional period. The complete information technology cell, website. Internet and answering machine facilities shall be made available for access of information any time, any where.

TRY YOURSELF

1. What market offerings have the Guptas planned and why?
2. Explain the service mix elements used.
3. What was the competition and how was it outsmarted?
4. Carry out the market analysis for the following
   (i) Market niche selected
   (ii) Marketing strategies used
   (iii) Target market and market share
5. What sales plan was devised to stay competitive?
6. What promotional strategies were used? In your opinion what will bring positive results?

INTRODUCTION

Delivery of services differs significantly from that of the manufactured goods. The production of goods is followed by distribution whereas services usually cannot be separated from the service provider. Because of this inseparability characteristic, the channels for most services is short and simple. The place or distribution of services refers to availability of a service, i.e., when and where it can be purchased. The place or distribution of services is discussed in this chapter in light of

- Location
- Accessibility
- Channels of distribution
- Distribution facilities
- Service inventory/Storage
- Managing channels.

PLACE: DISTRIBUTION OF SERVICES

The special characteristics of services, e.g., intangibility, inventory, inconsistency and inseparability have led to specific forms of distribution. Service products are mostly those where no transfer of ownership takes place and the service is simply rented or consumed. But it is essential that it must be available and accessible before its consumption. This needs a distribution system. The distribution system may be defined as the channels, or means used by which the service provider gains access to potential buyer of the service product.

Before the formulation of channel structure, following aspects of service distribution must be taken into consideration

- There is no actual tangible product which is being distributed.
- It involves consumer's movement to the service location. As consumer is part of the service operation, the method of selling and environment within which service product purchase is made becomes part of the service experience.
- The intermediaries/agents play a key role in recommending services to consumers.
- The service organisation has to devise promotional/distribution strategies which encourage the customer to come directly, through agents or other modes.

LOCATION

Location involves considering where to deliver the service to the customer, and whether the service organisation should be a single location or multi location organisation.

A well located restaurant will be able to pick up passing demand because the consumer will locate the service product easily, quickly. Thus, a well located hotel/restaurant/travel agent may not need any distribution channel.

Key Issues Regarding Location

The importance of location varies with the type of service and marketers should address following issues regarding location of the service. Table 34.1 highlights the considerations for branch location analysis. Poor location leads to postponement or delay.

- **Need of the market**

  If the market requires accessibility and convenience to make a choice of service, poor location will lead to either postponement or delay in service operation or the customer will look for a service available at an arm's length.

- **Technological innovation**

  A number of service sectors are finding that they gain considerable competitive edge through changes of distribution. Technology has facilitated telephone banking and at home shopping. The banks are now expanding their distribution network through ATMs or electronic fund transfer facilities. Now you can book your cinema admission ticket electronically.

- **Convenience**

  Is it obligatory to locate the services at a convenient place? Government hospitals, health care services are located accordingly. The concept of convenience has created services like home delivery, advance reservations of air tickets, train tickets, etc.

  In service operations, the following three situations are generally faced regarding service locations (refer Table 34.1).

table 34.1 **Service Location: Situations and their Impact**

Situation	Impact
1. Customer goes to service provider.	Service providers have to select an appropriate location or multi-locations.
2. Service provider goes to customer.	Location becomes less important because the service provider either provides service at customer's place, e.g., janitorial services, customer lawncare service, lift repair service or decides to do it at his premises, e.g., some mechanics repair the car at owner's premises or they bring the car to the garage for repairs.
3. Service provider and customer transact at arm's length.	Location becomes insignificant, e.g., in case of e-mail, no transaction or interaction is required whereas at ATM, customer is using a service without interacting with people but he may choose to go to a bank for another transaction personally.

ACCESSIBILITY

While designing the service distribution channels, accessibility should clearly be given a special attention. In addition to convenient location, following factors play a significant role in influencing the customer:

- Accessibility to range and choice of service literature and brochures
- Accessibility to components such as visas, traveller's cheques, insurance and cards

- Accessibility to booking points in every main town and cities
- Accessibility to alternative brands
- Accessibility to alternative agents.

For example, electronic distribution has created opportunity to have access to a wide network and now travel agents located at distant locations can make the services accessible at the convenience of the customer.

figure 34.1

Elements of Branch Location Analysis (Typical)

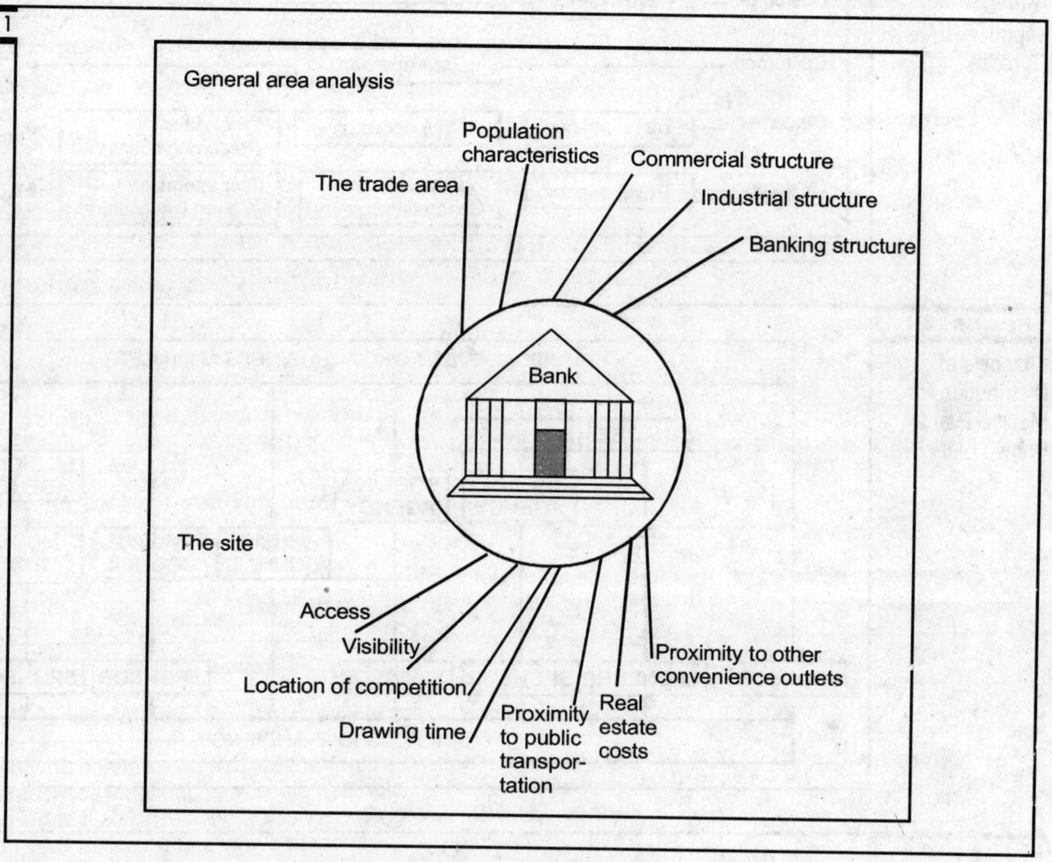

CHANNELS OF DISTRIBUTION OF SERVICES

All the organisations or people participating in the distribution process are known as channels of distribution. There are three types of participants

- The service provider
- Intermediaries
- Customers

It has already been explained that the channel for many services is simple and short because services cannot be separated from its providers. Therefore, it has been argued that the most appropriate form of distribution for services is direct selling. While the direct selling channel of distribution is common for some of the services – firms in other areas of services are looking for additional channels to achieve better growth and to fill unutilised capacity. Intermediaries are now playing an important role in delivering the services. Some typical examples of channels of distributions are given in Figures 34.2, 34.3, 34.4:

figure 34.2

Channels of Distribution-Destination/ Tourism Supplier (Typical)

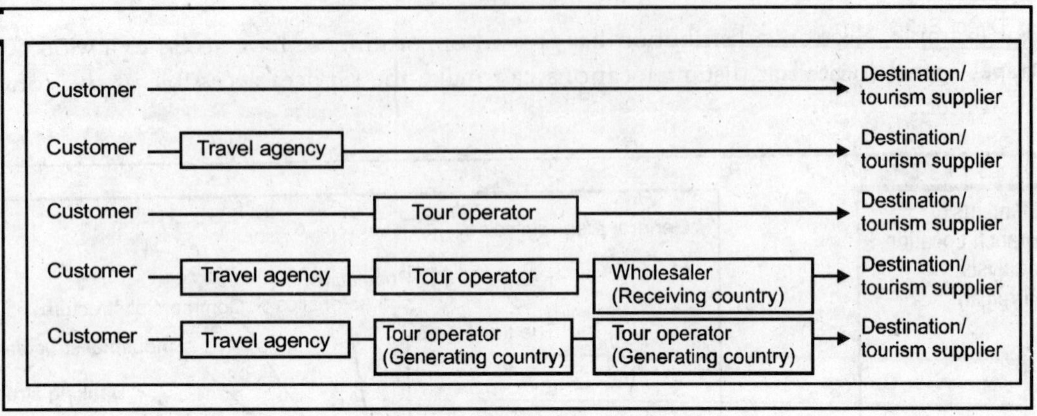

figure 34.3

Channels of Distribution for Musical Event Show

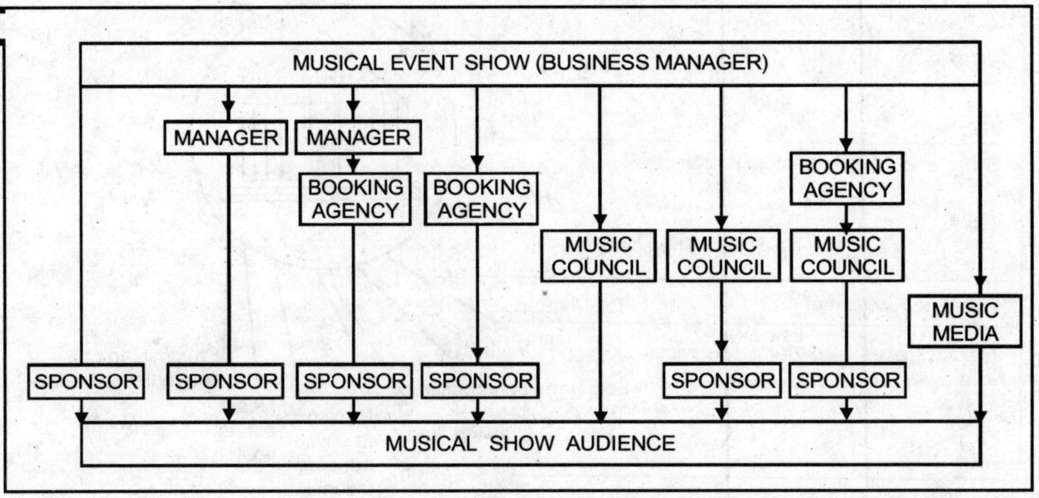

figure 34.4

Channels of Distributions for Airline Services (Typical)

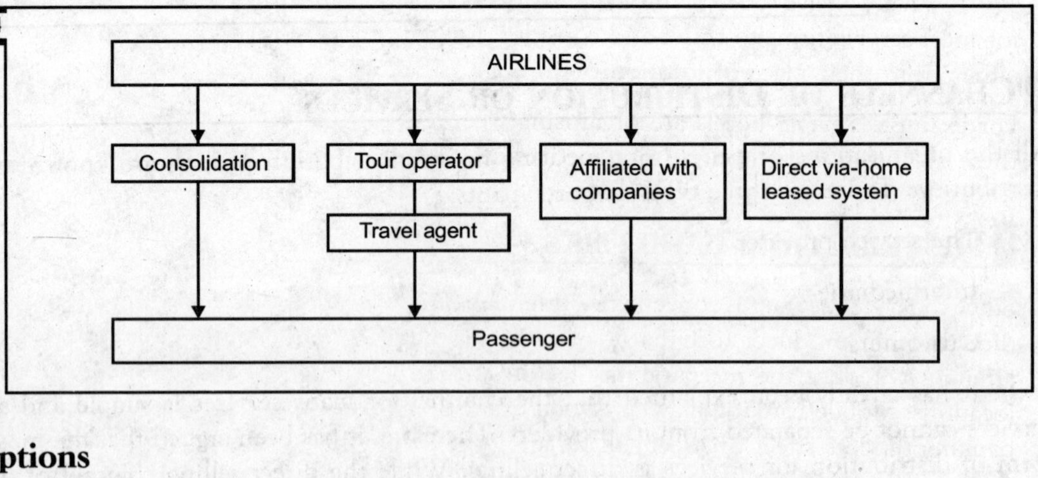

Channel Options

Marketers have been following broad options for the different forms of channels (refer Table 34.2):

table 34.2 Broad Options for the Form of Channel

Form of Channel	Type of Service
Direct Sales	Accounting Services
Producer → Consumer	Management Consuiting Services Design and Technical Services Dieting Services Eyecare Services Hair Fashioning Services Healthcare Services Legal Services
Agents or Brokers	Insurance Services
Producer → Agent → Consumer	Tour and Travel Services Hotel Reservation Services Ticketing Services Advertising Services
Seller and Buyer Agent or Broker	Stocks and Shares Brokers Commodity Brokers Real Estate
Agent → Consumer	Holding and Investment
Franchises and Contracted Services Deliveries	Fast Food Services Car Rental Services Dry Cleaning Services

What we have today is an increasingly competitive marketing environment. It has become necessary for most service firms to think and consider different forms of distribution. Firms are able to sell direct either from their place of location or through direct marketing methods.

For example, several hotels are organising weekend breaks to improve weekend occupancy levels and these are promoted through print media and booked directly with the hotel.

DISTRIBUTION FACILITIES

Since today's consumer is convenience oriented, a good location is essential when the service is distributed directly from producer (originator or service principal) to consumer. Some service marketers, in an attempt to reduce the inseparability factor, have broadened their distribution base by extending their locations. Mobile banking may be a good example if a bank designs an armoured mobile van to provide banking services street to street; ATMs are located at various places at convenient locations, away from the main bank to facilitate service delivery. Many courier companies have opened distribution and collection centres at different parts of the city.

In non-profit marketing, health care organisations provide mobile units for X-rays/ blood examination. Delhi Public Library has set up a mobile library which is covering various parts of Delhi.

The physical surroundings and ambience in the distribution of services play an important role in influencing the customers' perception of that service and its originator. As services are intangible, the customer looks to the service facility and the people providing that service before making a purchase. Because of this, many firms which are facing competition are redesigning or revamping their facilities to reflect a more caring and trusting atmosphere. Service facilities are being upgraded by improvements in interior designs/lighting, music and even the smell in the service facility.

For example, hotels are providing small fountains with perfumed water to give a fragrance. Indian Oil corporation is redesigning its petrol pumps by changing layout and providing soothing colour schemes and also retrofitting the gas delivery systems.

MANAGING CHANNELS

Channel selection is the difficult decision. While choosing a distribution channel, the firms need to consider intensity of market coverage which can be achieved by one of three major types of distribution.

1. **Intensive distribution**

   It is a strategy in which a producer sells products and services at retail and wholesale levels in a particular territory.

2. **Selective distribution**

   It is a strategy in which a producer sells its goods and services through multiple, but not all possible, wholesalers and retailers in a market where a consumer might reasonable look for it.

3. **Exclusive distribution**

   It is a strategy in which a supplier agrees to sell its products and services only to a single wholesaling middleman and/or retailer in a given market.

Table 34.3 summarises the three types of distribution:

table 34.3 **Intensity of Channel Coverage**

	Characteristics	Intensive Distribution	Selective Distribution	Exclusive Distribution
1.	Objectives	Volume sales and corresponding profits, channel acceptance and wide market coverage	Best image, good profit margins, reasonable channel control and loyalty. Moderate market coverage	Exclusive image, high profit margins, price stability and loyalty
2.	Intermediaries' Services	All types of firms, many number of outlets	Well established firms, moderate number of outlets only	Well established sound and reputed firms, few outlets
3.	Customers	Organisational consumer, focus on all types of accounts, many number of customers, services expected from intermediaries	Brand conscious, moderate number of customers, final consumers	Brand loyal Few customers Final consumers
4.	Marketing Focus	Final Consumers ▶ Mass advertising ▶ Convenient outlets ▶ Items in inventory	Final Consumers ▶ Promotion mix ▶ Pleasant ambience ▶ Good service	Final Consumers ▶ Personal selling ▶ Pleasant ambience ▶ Good service

Contd...

		Organisational Consumer ▶ Availability ▶ Continuous ▶ Communication ▶ Superior service	Organisational Consumer ▶ Availability ▶ Continuous ▶ Communication ▶ Superior ▶ Service	Organisational Consumer ▶ Availability ▶ Continuous ▶ Communication ▶ Superior service
5.	Disadvantage	Limited channel control	Difficult to carve out a niche	Limited sales
6.	Examples	Routine services like ▶ Fast foods ▶ Courier services ▶ Home delivery?services	Industrilised services ▶ Repair and maintenance ▶ Electrical appliances ▶ Airconditioners ▶ Refrigerators	Complex services Designer's hair style Specialised training Designers fashioning

Many producers, for achieving a broad market coverage, employ multiple distribution channels which are sometimes called dual distribution channels. The producers use multiple distribution channels to:

- ▶ Reach different types of markets
- ▶ Reach different segments within a single market.

For example, Life Insurance Corporation of India may directly sell group health insurance policies to large business houses and individual life insurance policies indirectly to final consumers through independent insurance agents.

MAJOR INTERMEDIARIES FOR SERVICE DELIVERY

Major intermediaries used in service distribution are given in and discussed next.

figure 34.5

Major Intermediaries in Service Delivery

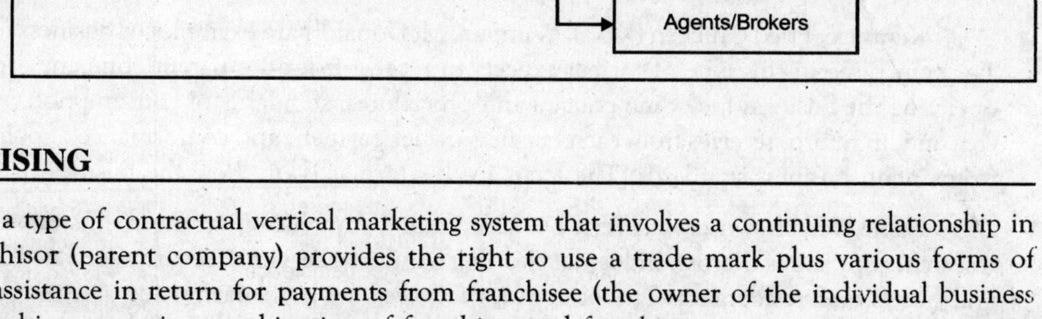

FRANCHISING

Franchising is a type of contractual vertical marketing system that involves a continuing relationship in which a franchisor (parent company) provides the right to use a trade mark plus various forms of management assistance in return for payments from franchisee (the owner of the individual business unit). The franchise system is a combination of franchisor and franchises.

table 34.4 **Some Franchising Examples**

Product/Service Category	Sample Franchises
FAST FOOD	McDonald's Dominos Wimpy's
EDUCATION	Aptech NIIT CMC STG Tulec
COURIER	Overnite Express DHL Fedex
HOTELS	Holiday Inn Radisson
BEAUTY PARLOURS	Shehnaz

There are two types of franchising:

1. Product or Trade Name Franchising

It is a distribution contract under which a franchisor (supplier) authorises the franchisee (dealer/distributor) to sell a product line using the franchisor firm's (parent organisation) trade name for purposes of promotion. The key element in product and trade name franchising is on "what is sold". The franchisee agrees to buy from franchisor and also is bound by the specific policies.

2. Business Format Franchising

For the past three decades, franchising growth has taken place over business format franchising. This format covers the entire method for the business operations. A successful retail business sells rights to operate the same business in different geographical locations.

Kentucky Fried Chicken (KFC), Wimpy's, McDonald's are examples of business format franchising. The franchisee in this type of format expects to receive from the parent company a proven method of operating the business including policies and procedures, standards of consumption, marketing policies, etc., and, in return, receives from each business owner payment and conformance of policy and procedures to maintain business standards. The focus in this format is on 'how the business is run'.

Some well-known commercial business format franchising arrangements are car rentals, market research, copy shops (Xerox), industrial cleaning (janitorial services), security services (Group 4 Securities) and hotels and restaurants. The basic rules followed by both parties for a system to work are given below in Table 34.5.

table 34.5 **Basic Rules for Franchising**

Expectations of Franchisee	Expectations of Franchisor
1. Transfer of know-how by franchisor	No trading of other products
2. Promotional support for the products/services (use of logos/trade names and literature)	Optimum standards of sales and service.
3. Uninterrupted support stocks from the franchisor	The inventory and lead time standards as agreed by franchisee
4. Credit for the supplies	Ambience, maintenance of premises and equipment to agreed operational standards
5. Advisory services for managerial and financial areas	Pricing as per agreed terms of franchise contract. Financial commitment and information on franchisee's operations
6. Identification with franchisee services (e.g., use of logos like yellow arched M of McDonald's)	Display of franchisor's identification and equipment
7. Exclusiveness of rights geographically	Right to purchase of a franchisee business in the event of his disposing it
8. Recruitment and training standards and aids.	Maintenance of service delivery standards through right people rightly trained.

It is always beneficial to consider a franchise provided there is advantage to both the parties. Some of the advantages are listed in Table 34.6.

table 34.6 **Advantages of Franchising**

To Franchisee	To Franchisor
Minimised risk of business of franchisee	High motivation and financial commitment
Fast growth of business and learning curve	Low capital cost and business expansion
Fast build up of reputation due to joint promotion	Knowledge of local markets
Low stocks and financial aids	Compliance to agreed systems
Obtaining an established business format for initiating the business	Low cost expansion of business and also of channels of distribution
Advantage of brand name and marketing.	Maintenance of consistent standards.

Electronic Channels

In the last decade, a number of technological advances have taken place due to immense use of EDI (Electronic data interchange). These advances have led to

- Increased use of self service operations, e.g., many marketing firms have put their services on the Net.
- Providing data bank services, e.g., a service provider may require information to make a mailing list to target a specific audience.
- Electronic banking.
- E-mail and many more.

Distribution of services through electronic channel is without any direct human interaction because services are distributed through a service distribution system. This channel requires a predesigned service and a system to deliver it. Delivery of services through alternate channels like ATMs, Call centres, Internet kiosks is growing at an ever-increasing pace.

For example, Electronic banking involves ATMs and Cards (vehicles of service delivery) for instant delivery of services through electronic processing of data (An application of EDI). The electronic banking services enables customer 24 hrs. banking, seven days a week at convenient locations (banking and non-banking locations). Mobile banking is an example of electronic distribution system .

Advantages

- ***Convenience:*** Customers can have access to services at convenient location on a convenient day and marketers have access to those customers who otherwise are not accessible at the service outlets.

For example, 24 hrs/7 days/365days banking.

- ***Low Cost:*** Reaching a customer through personal selling is quite expensive compared to electronic media. Also the delivery is more efficient as electronic media has introduced the element of speed of service (SOS). The interactive media approach has added credibility to remote encounters.

For example, E-banking, electronic fund transfer.

- ***Wide Distribution:*** The electronic media allows simultaneous interaction directly or through a number of intermediaries, thereby resulting in wide distribution.

For example, installation of electronic terminals at agents/brokers premises or ATMs at different locations has added wide spectrum to distribution.

- ***Customer Choice:*** The electronic media explosion has made many options available with the customer.

For example, the customer can now choose the films of his choice on cable TV network.

- ***Quality Control:*** The service delivery by electronic channel is likely to be of same quality.

For example, the service provided by a bank employee sitting at the drafts counter will not be of same quality every time, whereas service provided by ATM will be same every time in each transaction.

Electronic media, no doubt, has brought in fast revolution in the service business environment but security of data, customer involvement in service delivery, customisation of services is lacking.

Some Examples

Some of the examples of electronic channels include:

- Plastic money
- Selling through online services
- Buying through online services
- Video conferences
- Electronic marketing/E-banking
- Education through satellite/E-MBA

Agents and Brokers

The major part of services business is still transacted through agents and brokers. These channels of distribution are discussed below:

Unlike the merchant wholesaler, agents and brokers do not take title to the merchandise. In the service environment, their primary function is to sell services in return for which they get a commission from the service provider.

▶ ***Agents***

Agents are wholesalers that do not take title of products. They work for commission or fee as payment for their services and are comprised of manufacturers/service provider's agents, selling agents and commission merchants.

▶ ***Services Providers Agents***

They work for two or more related services from non competing service creators in a specific geographic territory.

For example, a travel agent represents Indian Airlines and does the booking for passengers travelling by Indian Airlines for a fee or commission and may also provide booking for tour related services for a tour operator.

A service firm may employ many agents (LIC Agents) each with a unique product-territory mix. Agents have limited association with the marketing programme or price structure of the service.

▶ ***Selling Agents***

Selling agents sell full range of services of a service provider and are responsible for all aspects of marketing of those services under a contractual agreement. In fact, they are empowered to negotiate on behalf of the service providers. They perform the function of wholesaling without taking the title of the product. They mostly work for small firms.

For example, a travel agent who is the authorised selling agent of a hotel may negotiate a block booking on behalf of the hotel under contractual obligation.

▶ ***Brokers***

Brokers do not have any affiliation with any particular service provider. They specialize in certain areas and bring buyers and sellers together to negotiate the contract.

For example, real estate broker does not have the title of the property but brings property owner who wants to sell and a customer who wants to buy together for negotiations. He gets a fee/commission for this deal.

A broker may represent many non-competing brands in a metropolitan area. Brokers are very common in food and financial services industries.

For example, commercial stock brokers are licenced sales representatives who advise business clients, take orders and then acquire stocks for the clients. For these services they get brokerage/commission.

Brokers are well informed about market conditions, prices, potential buyers and sellers, terms of business and possess the negotiating skills. They do not take the title and usually are not allowed to complete the transaction without the approval of the parties involved in negotiations.

Benefits of Using Agents/Brokers

1. The services become widely represented and accessible.
2. The selling and distribution costs are reduced.
3. The marketing strategies can be tailored to suit the local markets as agents/brokers possess expert knowledge of local conditions.
4. Those involved in providing services possess special knowledge and skill and therefore assemble the package of services from the suppliers for the service buyers.
5. They can provide services of the customers choice and they represent multiple providers of services.

SUMMARY

The role of distribution is to make the product/service reach the target market. The assignment of delivering the product to the target market may be direct or through middlemen who perform this task for an interest. A middleman or intermediary is a business organisation rendering the services directly related to sale or purchase of the product as it flows from producer to consumer.

In case of designing the distribution system for a service organisation, marketers face the challenge of selecting the channel of distribution and to provide physical facilities for the distribution of services. The channels of service distribution are created, sold and consumed simultaneously. Therefore direct channel is the most common channel followed by agents or middlemen.

In the present scenario, when consumers are getting highly convenience oriented, marketers must lay emphasis on good, easily accessible location of services particularly when a service is distributed directly from producer to consumer. With the world going electronic at supersonic speed, services distribution has to catch up with this environment. Most services like banking, financing, marketing are using electronic distribution system.

PROJECT WORK

Study the type of distribution applicable for the following services

1. Insurance Services
2. Hospitality Services
3. Banking Services

SHORT ANSWER QUESTIONS

1. What are the channels of distribution for services?
2. What do you mean by selective distribution?
3. Define agents and brokers.

REVIEW QUESTIONS

1. Which of the following institutions are intermediaries in the channel of distribution?

    a. Advertising agency

    b. Bank

   c. Stock broker
   d. Real estate broker
   e. Travel agent
2. Design the distribution channel for and give reasons thereof
   a. An ocean cruise
   b. Image consultancy
   c. Management consultancy
   d. Industrial services
3. Who are the major intermediaries in the service delivery? Discuss their role.
4. a. What is franchising?
   b. Discuss trade name franchising and business format franchising with special reference to service.
5. There are three keys to success of service delivery – location, location and location. Do you agree? Explain.
6. Discuss the use of electronic channels in services distribution. Explain your answer with examples of typical service industry you are familiar with.
7. Write short notes on the following with special reference to services distribution.
   - Intensive distribution
   - Selective distribution
   - Extensive distribution
8. Explain different advantages and disadvantages of electronic channel.

GO TO THE NET

Using Internet websites, study the type of distribution applicable for the following services

1. Hotel Services
2. Telecom Services
3. Social Services

Using Internet search tools prepare a report on too different types of distribution channel.

CHAPTER 35

SAP sales & distribution

learning objectives

The objectives of this chapter are to:

- understand ERP
- familiarize with SAP features
- create master data in SAP
- learn about sales process in SAP
- present reports in SAP.

content outline

- Introduction
- Definition, Scope and Benefits of ERP
- ERP Products in Market
- Systems, Applications & Products in Data Processing (SAP)
- SAP GUI
- Organization Structure in Sales
- Customers and Business Partners
- Material Master
- Sales Process
- Types of Sales Documents
- Sales Document Icons
- Sales Return
- Condition Records
- Reports
- Exporting Data from SAP to MS-Excel
- Frequently Used Transaction Codes
- Annexures

INTRODUCTION

In these competitive global environments, businesses are becoming more complex. For a organization to sustain its competitive advantage, it has to manage its resource in better way.

Over a period of time organizations realized that they have to be flexible enough to change themselves as per the situation demands. Our IT system has to flexible enough to respond to changing needs of global environment.

There has been a paradigm shift in approach towards IT spending in these years. Companies are increasingly looking for IT systems that can value add to the existing business. Today's IT systems are being used as enabler of business and helps in fast decision making.

Here decision making is important because, this is where the whole business scenario changes. For fast and right decision making process, the basic ingredients are accurate information and accessibility on time with little effort. At the same time the IT systems should be cost competitive.

Here comes the role or resources management in organization. All resources are to be managed in such as way so that every one in the organization is accessible and should be participate in whole decision making process. This demands for a enterprise wide systems to handle such complexity and ever growing demands to access information.

DEFINITION, SCOPE AND BENEFITS OF ERP

What is ERP?

ERP is a software architecture that facilitates the flow of information among the different functions within an enterprise. Similarly, ERP facilitates information sharing across organizational units and geographical locations. It enables decision-makers to have an enterprise-wide view of the information they need in a timely, reliable and consistent fashion

Why ERP?

Implementing a solution at the enterprise level allows organizations to get rid of standalone computer systems in finance, HR, manufacturing and the warehouse and replaces them with a software solution with individual sub modules for each department. The key difference is that now finance can look into the warehouse module and check if the pending orders from a day before have been processed or not. This allows interdepartmental monitoring of business processes while allowing the management to correlate reports that provide a clearer picture of the enterprise as information is being used from across all levels and departments of the organization.

Scope of ERP

- Integrate Financial Information
- Integrate Customer Order Information and Store Customer History
- Streamline the manufacturing process
- Standardizing HR Information
- Store and Analyze productivity information for employees and facilities

- Allow interdepartmental process monitoring and reporting
- Reports with data from across the organization
- Allow Marketing and Management to monitor and analyze all stages required to provide the clients with products and services
- Allow users limited and monitored access to data across the organization according to needs.
- Efficiently manage suppliers, business partners, customers.

Benefits of ERP

ERP has many benefits for the Management and Marketing, but a properly designed and implemented system will be appreciated by employees as well for all the benefits it offers to every one in the organization.

The Marketing and Sales of an organization also has a lot of benefits if a robust ERP is being used. They are able to store and analyze information pertaining to Customers'. This could be about the status of orders' or the history of each customer.

By employing Data Mining and Business Intelligence Tools this data can be used to profile customers and come up with future marketing and sales strategies that maximize customer value.

The Management is the biggest beneficiary of a successful ERP system. They are able to monitor and get reports and all aspects of the organizations operations. This allows them to see a clearer picture of the status and direction of the organizations' processes.

The Employees are now able to store their data and productivity centrally. As data access in now limited and secure, there are less chances for data theft, which removes the need for direct monitoring.

ERP PRODUCTS IN MARKET

There are many ERP packages available in market. Some of them are free and open source ERP software where some are Proprietary ERP software

figure 35.1

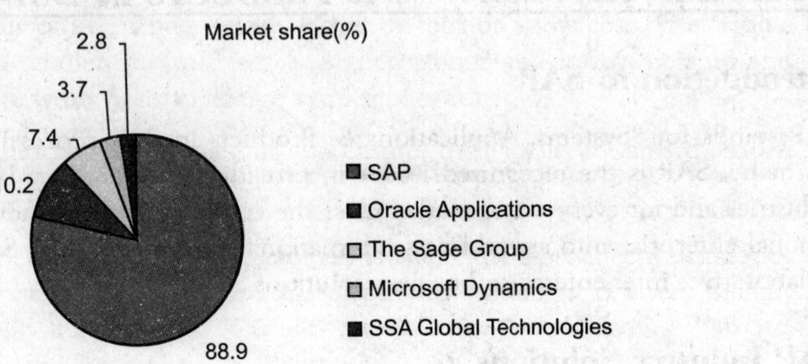

Source: Market share 2005 according to Gartner

Some of the Proprietary ERP software are as below.

- IFS Applications from Industrial and Financial Systems
- JD Edwards EnterpriseOne & JD Edwards World from Oracle

- JustFoodERP.com based on Microsoft Dynamics NAV
- Maximo (MRO) from IBM
- Microsoft Dynamics NAV (formerly Navision) from Microsoft
- Oracle e-Business Suite from Oracle
- PeopleSoft from Oracle
- QAD Enterprise Applications from QAD Inc.
- Ramco On Demand ERP from Ramco Systems
- SAGE ERP X3 from The Sage Group
- SAP R/3 from SAP

Some of Free and Open Source ERP Software

- Adempiere, a Java based ERP-System which started as a fork of Compiere
- BlueErp, a PHP based ERP System
- ERP5, a Python based ERP system
- GNU Enterprise
- OFBiz Apache Java based ERP-System
- Openbravo, a Java based ERP-System
- OpenERP (formerly Tiny ERP)
- OrangeHRM
- SQL-Ledger uses Perl and PostgreSQL
- WebERP is a LAMP based system

SYSTEMS, APPLICATIONS & PRODUCTS IN DATA PROCESSING (SAP)

Introduction to SAP

SAP stands for "Systems, Applications & Products in data processing". Headquartered in Waldorf, Germany, SAP is the recognized leader in providing collaborative business solutions for all types of industries and for every major market Over the course of three decades, SAP has evolved from a small, regional enterprise into a world-class international company. Today, SAP is the global market leader in collaborative, inter-enterprise business solutions.

SAP Industry Solutions

Industry solution is the latest value proposition of SAP to customer. Industry solutions are aimed at addressing the specific business process areas of different industries differently, hence pre-customizing the package for generic industry purpose. Through its industry solutions, SAP addresses the unique core processes of more than 25 distinct industries. Some of the key verticals are listed below:

Manufacturing Industries

- SAP for Automotive
- SAP for Chemicals
- SAP for Consumer Products
- SAP for Engineering, Construction & Operations (SAP for EC&O)
- SAP for High Tech
- SAP for Oil & Gas (SAP for O&G)
- SAP for Apparel and Footwear Industry (AFS)

Service Industries

- SAP for Media
- SAP for Professional Services
- SAP for Retail
- SAP for Telecommunications
- SAP for Utilities

Public Services

- SAP for Healthcare
- SAP for Public Sector

Financial Services

- SAP for Banking,
- SAP for Financial Service Providers
- SAP for Insurance

The SAP R/3 architecture is based on a 3-tier client/server principle

Presentation Server

Application Server

Database Server

Dedicated servers are linked by communication networks. This architecture performs tasks without sacrificing data integration and processes within the system, as a whole

The picture here illustrates a typical R/3 system. Multiple presentation layers from multiple computers communicate with the application servers over the local or wide area network. For a single R/3 system, there may be multiple application servers in order to balance the operational load. All these application servers interact with a single database server and the database server acts as the interface between the external RDBMS and the application servers.

figure 35.2

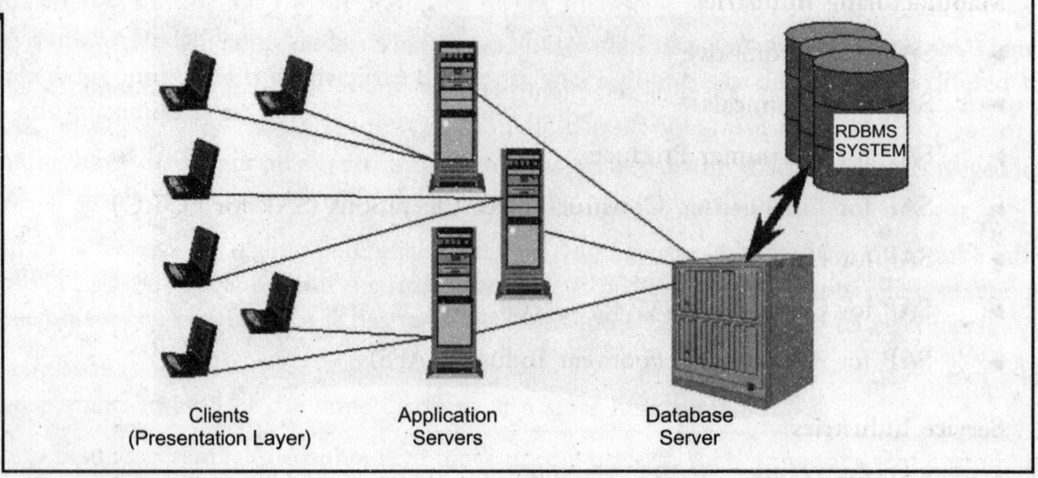

The Concept of Client in SAP

Clients are used to divide data in a SAP System into various data areas for various purposes. If a company, for example, wants to use its SAP System for both test and training purposes, a client is created for each purpose.

A client in R/3 is a 3 digit number with range from 000 to 999 which enables one to maintain multiple independent sets of data within the same R/3 system.

When logging on to the system, the user has to select a client in which he/she wants to work. The users can then only access data in this client. The term "log on client" has nothing to with the Client/Server terminologies.

figure 35.3

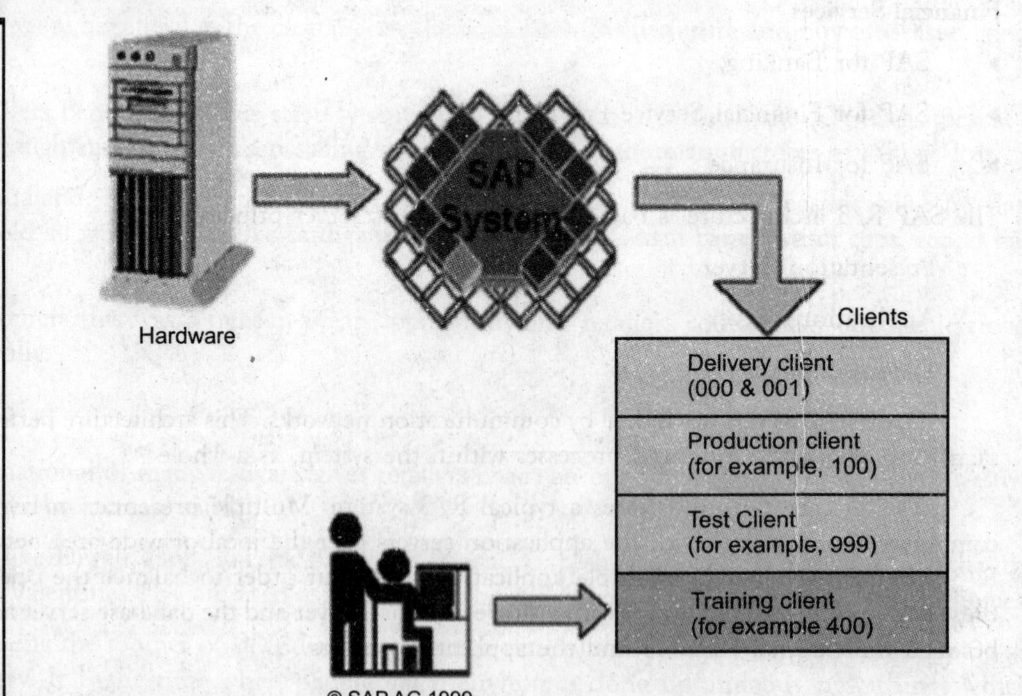

For example, a developer might log in to client 100 to do training, client 200 to review and approve new business logic, and client 500 to conduct actual development activities for the company.

In the same way, an end-user might log in to client 700 in the production system to do his day-to-day work, and occasionally client 950 in the QA or Test system to check on the status on new functionality being developed for production.

SAP Logon

SAP Logon Pad, a simple utility with a straightforward yet powerful interface designed to help you manage your SAP systems and accounts. As seen in fig the SAP Logon Pad enables you to organize the various systems you need to use After you have started the SAP System the first screen you see is the logon screen.

figure 35.4

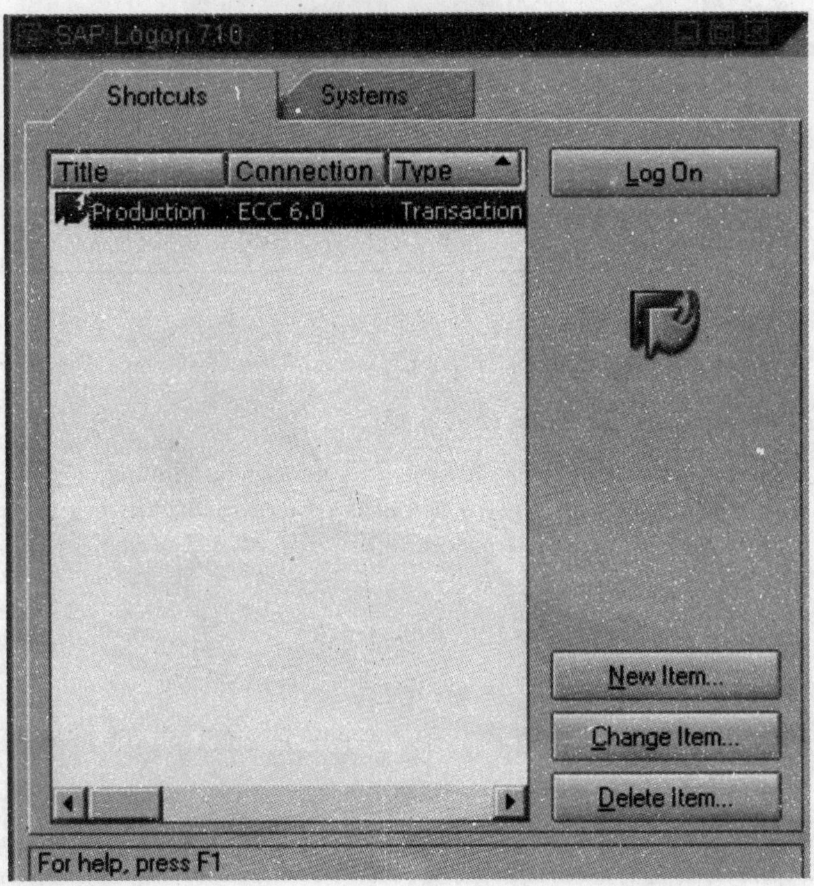

The logon screen is shown above. To log on to the SAP System:

figure 35.5

Steps to logon

- Enter the client number in the **Client** field.
- Enter your user ID in the **User** field.
- Enter the initial password provided by your system administrator in the **Password** field. As you type the initial password, the asterisks remain in the field, and only the cursor moves. As a security measure, the system does not display what you type. In the SAP System, passwords are not case-sensitive.
- Enter the language as EN (English).
- Press **Enter.**

The system automatically displays the new password dialog box. You must change your initial password.

- In the **New password** field, enter a new password.
- In the **Repeat password** field, enter the new password again, exactly as you entered it the first time.
- Choose **Confirm** (or press Enter).

figure 35.6

Logging Off

You can log off from the SAP System from any screen either from menu bar, choose System -> Log off. Alternatively you can click the button at the upper right-hand corner of the screen.

If you are not certain that you have saved all of your data and you do not want to log off, choose No otherwise choose Yes. All of your SAP System sessions close. You have successfully logged off.

Creating a new session

In SAP, you can create a session at any time and from nearly any screen in the system. You do not lose any data in the sessions that are already open with each new session you create, either.

Create a new session by following the menu path System-> Create Session or by clicking the Create Session Button in toolbar. If you want to determine which session you are currently in, check the status bar on the bottom-right side of your screen

figure 35.7

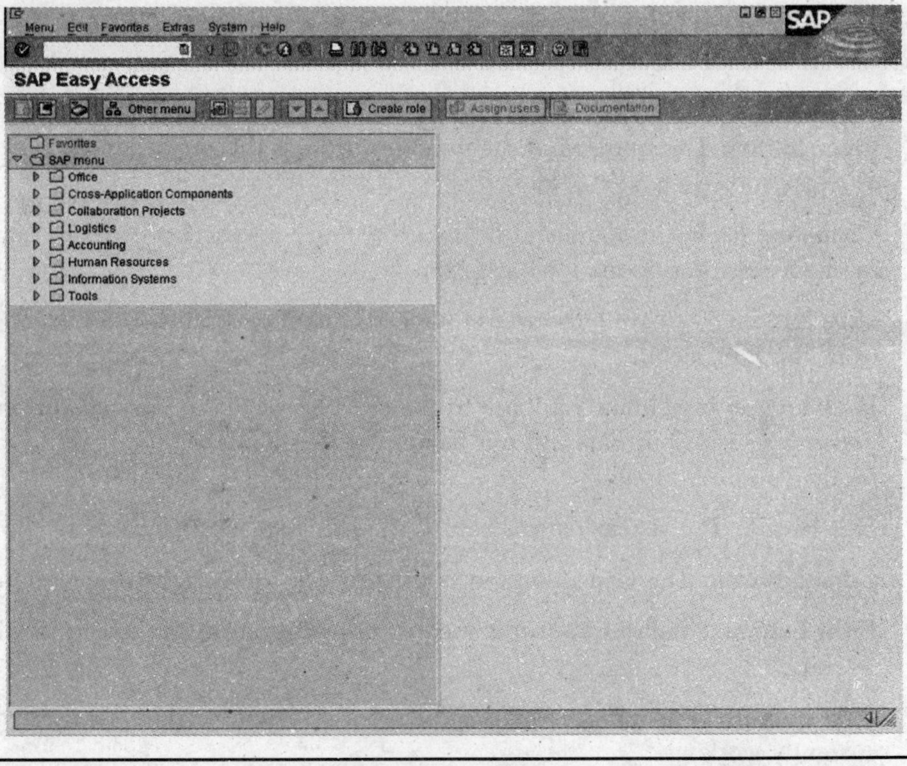

You can create up to nine sessions by default. You can execute different transactions in each session. However more number of sessions if opened may affect to some degree of system performance.

SAP GUI

The SAP GUI window is the user interface to most SAP systems available today. At the top of the window is the title bar, which gives the screen (or transaction) description for the window that is displayed. The standard elements of an SAP GUI window are shown in figure 35.8.

figure 35.8

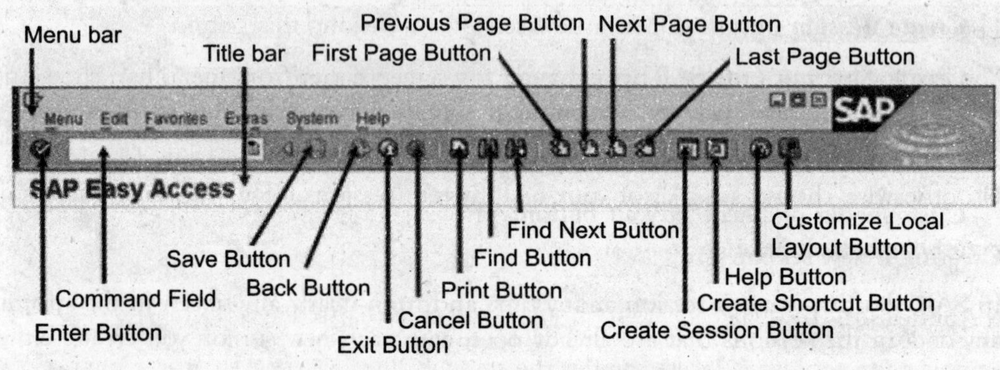

Menu bar: The menus shown here depend on which application you are working in. These menus contain cascading menu options. The menu bar contains all the menu options available. The menu bar changes from screen to screen to match the function module that you are currently processing.

Standard toolbar: The icons in the system function bar are available on all R/3 screens. If you leave the cursor on an icon for a moment, a small flag will appear with the name (or function) of that icon. You will also see the corresponding function key. It contains the following elements:

- ***Enter button:*** This button has the same function as the Enter key on your keyboard and is used to check your entry in a field
- ***Command field:*** The command field used to enter transaction codes to call a task without having to choose menu options for navigation.
- ***Save button:*** The Save button saves your work and performs the same function as selecting Save from the Edit menu.
- ***Back button:*** It will take you back to the previous screen. If you use this button to return to the previous screen, your data will not be saved unless you save it first using the Save button on the toolbar.
- ***Exit button:*** The system returns you to the previous application or to the main menu screen.
- ***Cancel button:*** The Cancel button is used to exit the current task without saving.
- ***Print button:*** The Print button is used to print data from the screen in which you are currently working.
- ***Find button:*** This button is used to perform a search for data on the screen in which you are currently working.

- ***Find Next button:*** This button is used to perform an extended search for data on the screen in which you are currently working.
- ***First Page button:*** It is used to travel to the top of a screen (or page) if the information on the screen is too long to fit on a single screen, generally used in reports
- ***Previous Page (Page Up) button:*** Used for moving one page up.
- ***Next Page (Page Down) button:*** Used for moving one page down
- ***Last Page button:*** It is used to travel to the bottom of a screen (or page) if the information on the screen is too long to fit on a single screen, generally used in reports
- ***Create Session button:*** Open a new session by clicking this button.
- ***Create Shortcut button:*** This is handy for creating a shortcut on a user's desktop for any SAP transaction, report, or other task that is executed frequently.
- ***Help button:*** Displays context sensitive help.
- ***Customizing of Local Layout button:*** This customizing button allows a user to customize SAP GUI display options.

The Application Toolbar

The application toolbar is located under the standard toolbar. This toolbar is application- and in some cases transaction-specific and varies depending on the screen (or transaction) that you are currently processing in.

For example, if you are in the Finance module, Create Rental Agreement screen, your application toolbar will contain buttons that enable you to copy or retrieve master data from SAP.

figure 35.9

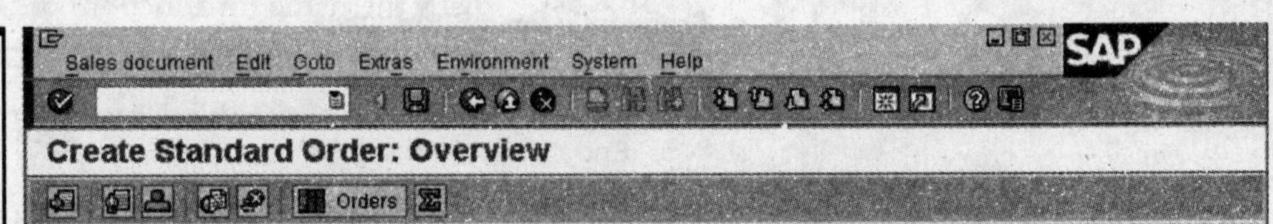

Screen Elements

- ***Title bar:*** The title bar displays your current
- ***Check boxes:*** Check boxes allow you to select several options simultaneously within a group.
- ***Radio buttons:*** Radio buttons allow you to select one option only.
- ***Status bar:*** The status bar displays information on the current system status, for example, warning and error messages.
- ***Tab Page:*** provides a clearer overview of several information screens.
- ***Options:*** You can set your font size, list colors, and so on here.

figure 35.10

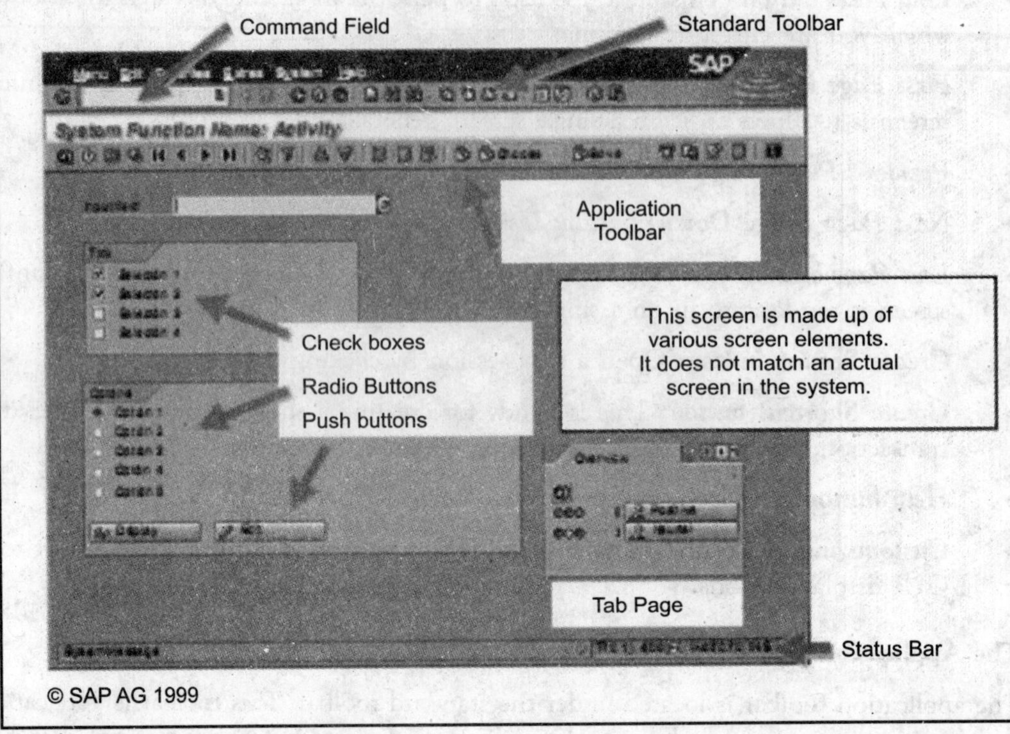

Frequently used Shortcuts

To save time in navigating between screens to call up a transaction, you can use these short cuts below for quick access to desired screen.

Frequently used Shortcuts	
Transaction Code	**Description**
/n	End current Transaction
/I	Delete current session
/o	Generate session list
/oVA01	Opens transaction VA01 in new session
/nva01	Moves to sales order creation screen from anywhere
/nend	Logs off from the system
Function Keys	Description
F1	Help
F3	Back
F4	List possible entries for the field
F8	Execute a transaction
F12	Cancel

SAP Modules

figure 35.11

SAP Modules

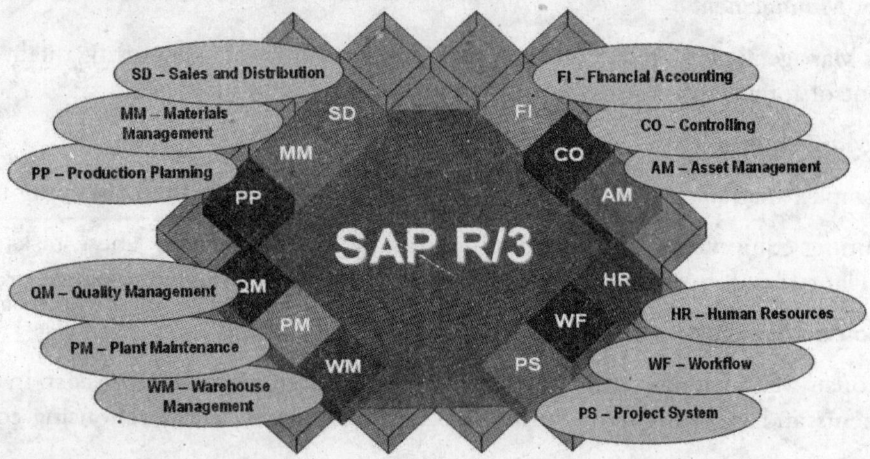

Let us see a few of the R/3 Modules in brief

Financial Accounting

The functionalities of this module are external reporting of General ledger, Accounts receivable/payable, Sub-ledger accounts with a user-defined Chart of Accounts. Key elements are General ledger, Accounts payable, Accounts receivable, Asset Management, Special Purpose Ledger (FI-SL), Legal consolidation, Accounting Information System etc.

Controlling

Controlling represents the company's flow of cost and revenue. It is a management instrument for organizational decisions process. It is also automatically updated as and when events occur.

Assets Management

Asset Management module is designed to manage and supervise individual aspects of fixed assets including purchase and sale of assets, depreciation and investment management.

Sales and Distribution

Sales and Distribution helps to optimize all the tasks and activities carried out in sales, delivery and billing. Key elements of the SD application module include Pre-sales support, Inquiry processing, Quotation processing, Sales order processing, Delivery processing, Warehouse management, Billing, Credit Management , Sales Information system etc

Materials Management

Materials Management supports the procurement and inventory functions occurring in day-to-day business operations such as purchasing,, reorder point processing, etc. Functionalities of this module are Material Procurement, Inventory Management, Batch Management, Goods inspection and Invoice Verification.

Production Planning

Production Planning is used to plan and control the manufacturing activities of a company. This module includes; bills of material (BOM), routings, work centers, sales and operations planning

(SOP), master production scheduling (MPS), material requirements planning (MRP), shop floor control, production orders, product costing, Capacity Evaluations, and QM in production.

Quality Management

Quality Management is a quality control and information system supporting quality planning, inspection, and control for manufacturing and procurement.

Plant Maintenance

In a complex manufacturing process, maintenance means more than sweeping the floors.

Maintaining equipments and servicing periodically is also needed. These tasks affect the production plans. Plant Maintenance module supports and supervises this maintenance process.

Warehouse Management

Warehouse Management provides flexible, automated support to assist in processing all goods movements and in maintaining current stock inventories in the warehousing complex.

Human Resources

Human Resources is a complete integrated system for supporting the planning and control of personnel activities such as payroll processing, time management etc.

Workflow

Workflow is a solution which has been integrated fully in the R/3 System and which enables customer-specific business process flows to be coordinated and controlled on a cross-application and cross-workplace basis.

Project System

Project System is designed to support the planning, control and monitoring of long-term, highly complex projects with defined goals.

Organizational Structure in SAP

figure 35.12

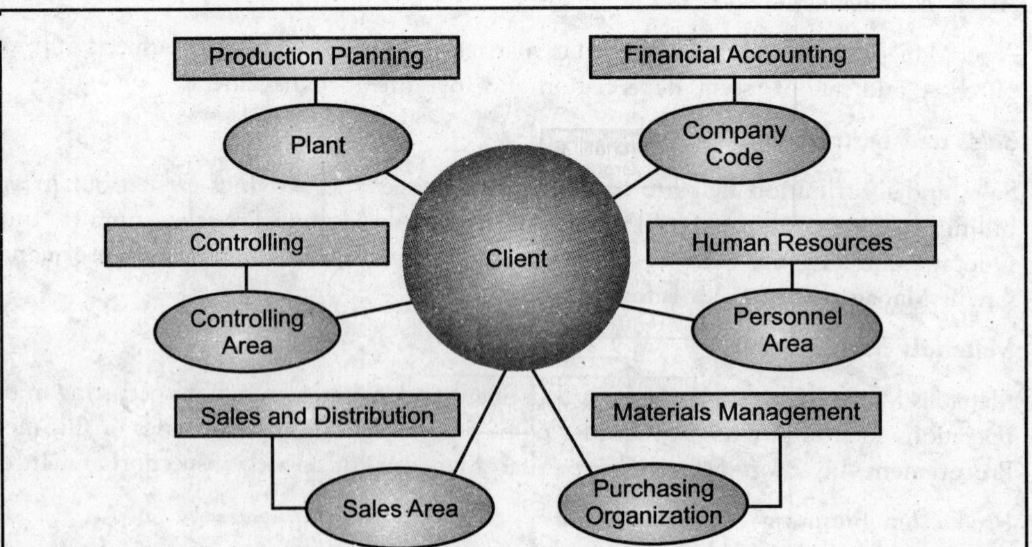

Client: The client is the highest level in the R/3 system hierarchy. Specifications or data which shall be valid for all organizational units in all R/3 applications are entered at the client level, eliminating the need to enter this information more than once (e.g. exchange rates). Each client is a self-contained unit which has separate master records and a complete set of tables and data. Users must enter a client key and have a user master record in the client in order to log on to the system.

Company code: A Company Code is a unit included in the balance sheet of a legally-independent enterprise. It is the central organizational element of Financial Accounting.

Controlling Area: The Controlling Area is the business unit where Cost Accounting is carried out. Usually there is a 1:1 relationship between the controlling area and the company code. For the purpose of company wide cost accounting, one controlling area can handle cost accounting for several company codes in one enterprise

Sales Area: A combination of sales organization, distribution channel, and division

Purchasing Organization: An organizational unit in Logistics, subdividing an enterprise according to the requirements of Purchasing.

Purchasing Organization: A purchasing organization procures materials and services, negotiates conditions of purchase with vendors, and is responsible for such transactions. You specify the form of procurement by assigning purchasing organizations to company codes and plants.

Personnel Area: An organizational unit representing an area in an enterprise delimited according to personnel administration, time management, and payroll accounting criteria.

ORGANIZATION STRUCTURE IN SALES

Sales Organization: In the context of Sales and Distribution, the Sales Organization is central organizational element that controls the terms of sale to the customer. Distribution Channel is the element that describes through what channel goods and/or services will be distributed to the customer

figure 35.13

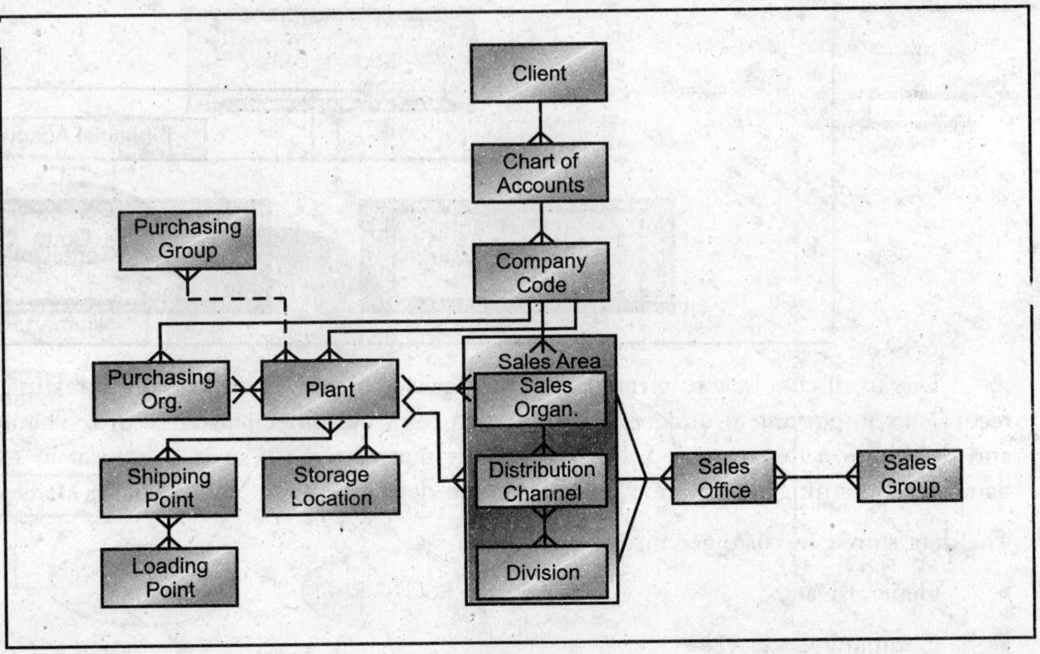

Distribution Channel: defines different ways of reaching customer

Division: Segment responsibility of products

Sales District: Sales territories in an organization

Sales Office: method of representing internal subdivisions

Sales Groups: further internal divisions of people in sales office

Sales Employee: an employee carrying out sales

Shipping Point: Location in a plant from where deliveries happen

Loading Point: Part of a shipping point where physical delivery is handled

Storage Location: A location where a group of materials are physically handled

Purchase Groups: Buyers responsible for purchases who handles specific group of materials or vendors

Organizational units may be assigned to a single application (such as a sales organization assigned to Sales and Distribution, or to several applications (such as a plant assigned to Materials Management and Production Planning).

CUSTOMERS AND BUSINESS PARTNERS

In a business, a company deals with customers with different requirements of each and may spread over a vast geographical area. In some cases company uses forwarding agents to supply goods to customers where company can not deal with customers directly. There may be the various reasons to this. For this process an employee may be assigned inside a company to take care of the business processes. In the same way different people involved with company with different objectives. In SAP R/3 all the customers, forwarding agents, vendors are known as business partner.. The data for each are stored in different master record.

figure 35.14

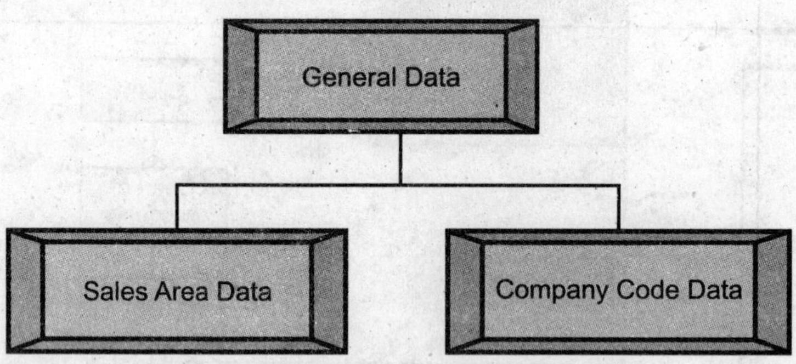

Lets us discuss how to create a customer master. Before going ahead of creating customer master record, it's important to understand the structure of customer master record. The account and sales and distribution department accesses customer master record, so it is natural to expect a common database containing information from both the departments.

The data stored in customer master record are:

- General Data
- Company Code Data
- Sales Area Data

Customer Master Data

Step 1

Select menu path: Logistics-Sales and Distribution-Master Data-Business Partner-Customer-Create-Complete

Transaction Code: **XD01**

figure 35.15

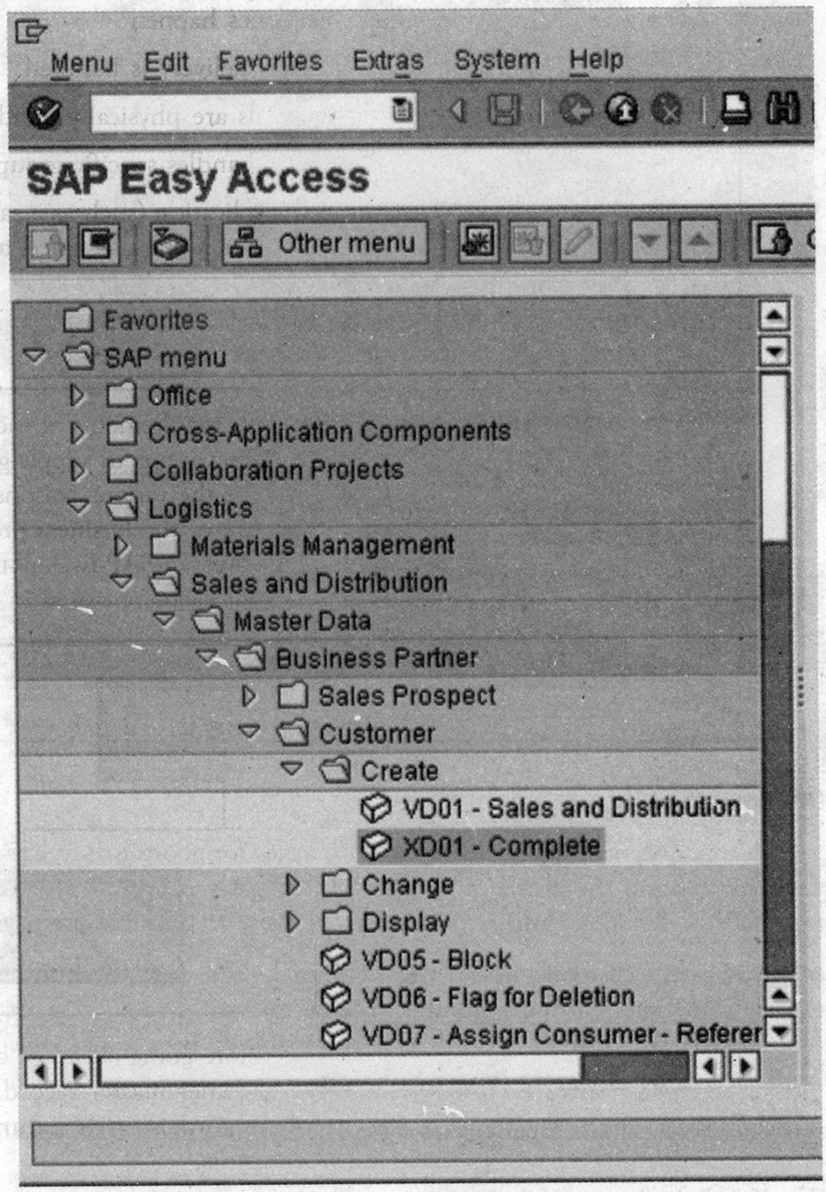

Step 2

Account Group: Each Customer master is assigned to an Account Group. The account group is a classifying feature within the customer master that allow customers to be grouped together

figure 35.16

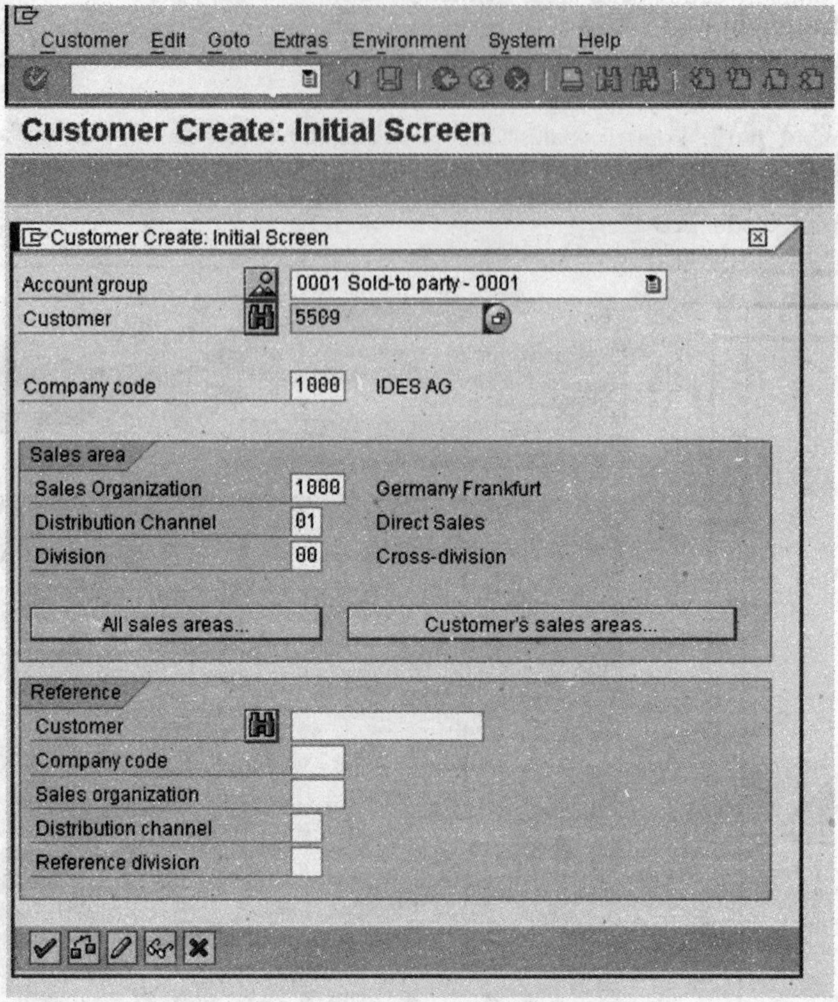

Select 0001 from the List

Sold-to party is a person or company that places an order for goods or services. Ship-to party is a person or company who receives the goods or services. Bill-to party is a person or company who receives the invoice for goods or services. Payer is person or company responsible for paying invoices

Customer No.: Enter a customer no. in this field; make sure that the number you are entering is not created earlier. Sometimes customer number may be internal, in that case system will generate its own customer number as per customization. It is also possible to have a alphanumeric customer number if the customization is done during implementation.

Company Code: Select the company code from the list (example: 1000 taken as shown in picture).

Sales Area

Sales Organization: select sales organization as 1000 as shown in picture.

Distribution Channel: Select direct sales (01)

Division: Select Cross-division (00)

The company codes, sales areas defined by each organization during SAP implementation, it certainly helps to know these before creating customer master. In case you are using IDES for learning, you may choose work any of the standard company codes provided for each country.

Step 3: Address

Select Customer Title. Enter name, address, postal code, country, region (state or province), time zone, telephone and fax numbers.

In the search Item field enter a search word though which you may like to search.

figure 35.17

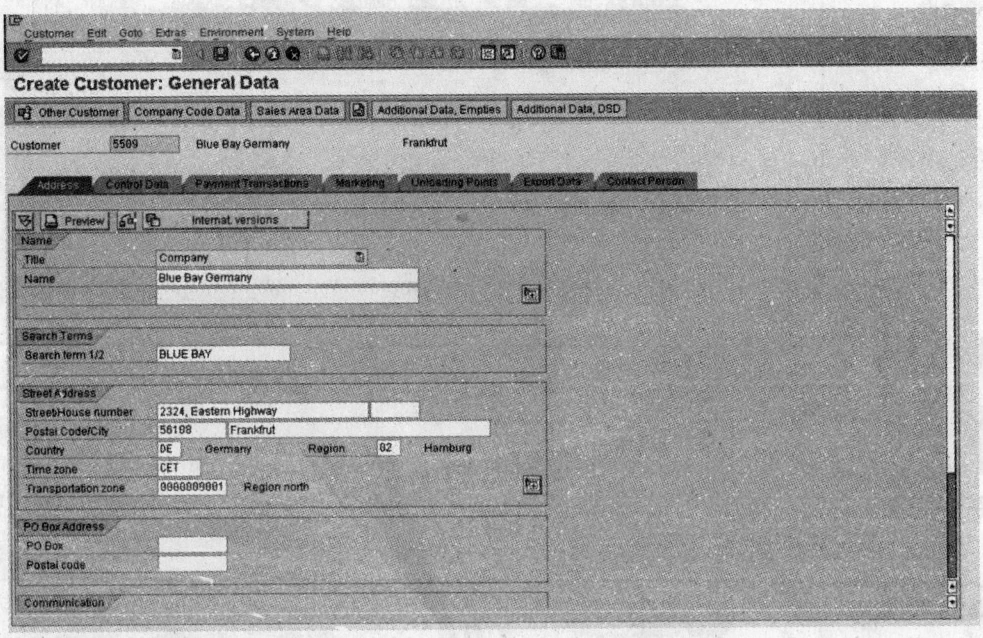

Step 4: Payment Transactions

In the payment transaction TAB, enter the country key, Bank Key, Bank Account no, Account Holder and control key of the customer.

figure 35.18

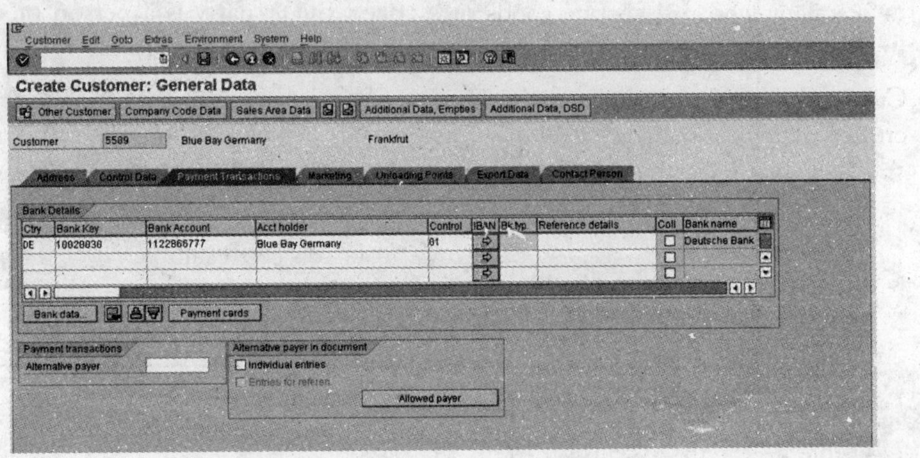

Step 5: Marketing

This tab deals with marketing information. Select customer class, industry type. Enter annual sales turnover of customer, no. of employees of customer etc.

figure 35.19

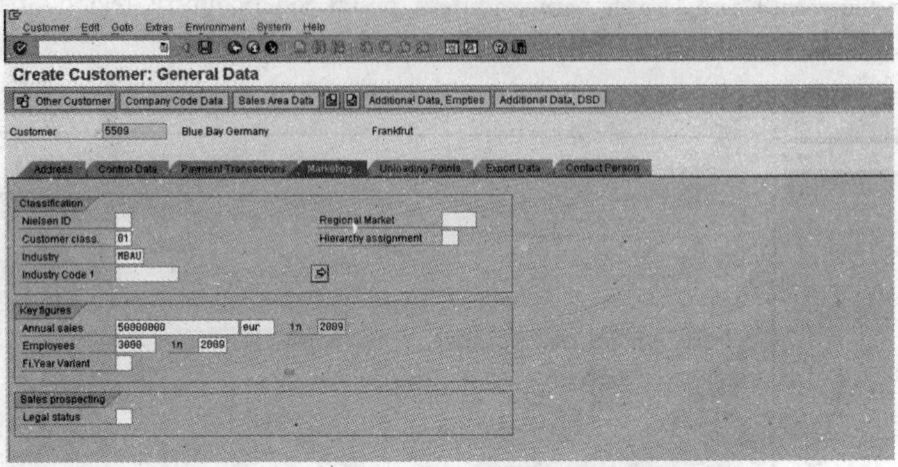

Step 6: Unloading Points

In this tab, enter customer contact points where goods will be delivered. You can also enter goods receiving points along with receiving hours and the concerned department information that deals goods receipt at customer end.

figure 35.20

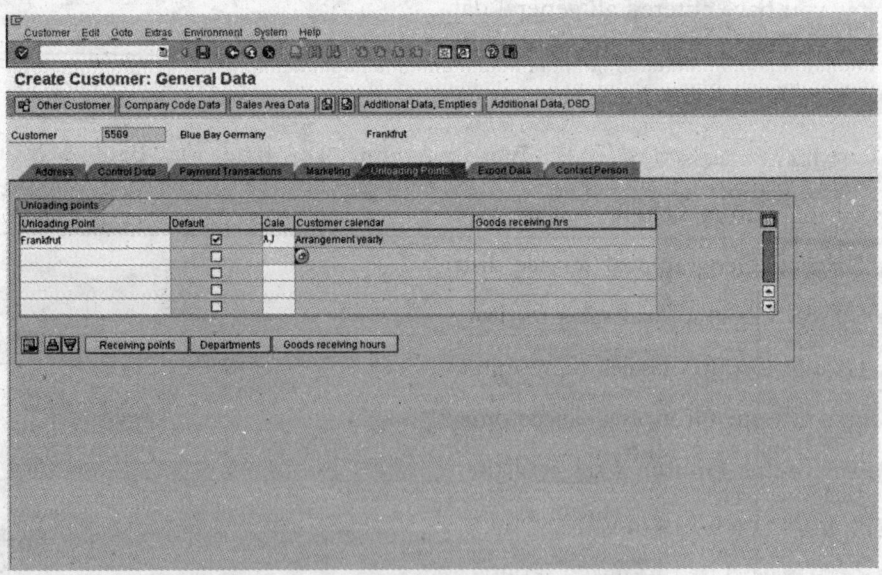

Step 7 Contact Person

In this tab enter the contact person of the customer with their home address, visiting hours, communication details etc.

figure 35.21

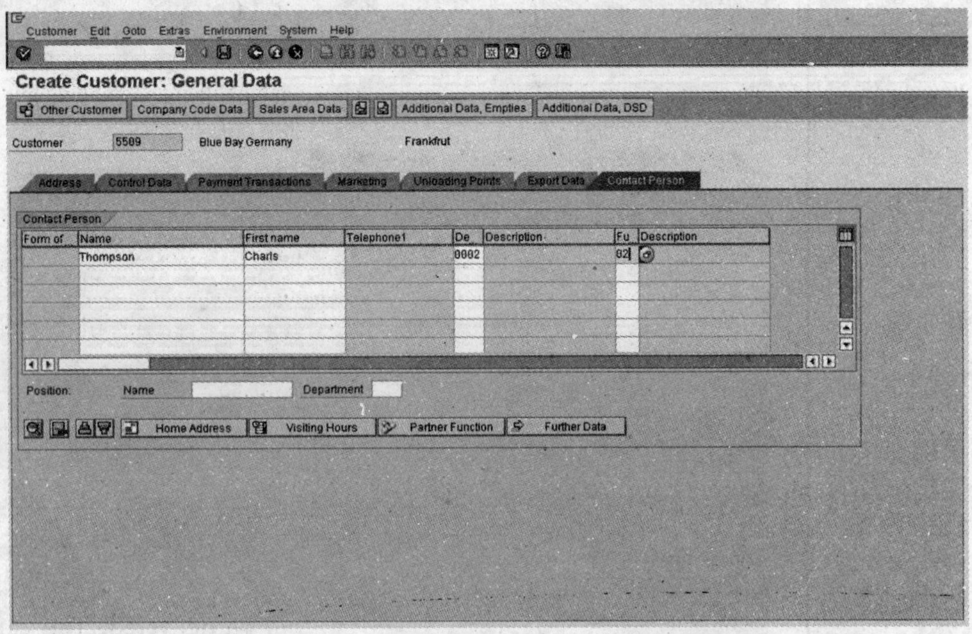

In case, the customer is also a vendor, than you can enter vendor information in control data. If the customer you wish to create is out of your country, you may enter export information in export tab. Now you have entered all general data information, lets move into sales area data. Select the "Sales Area Data" Button on application toolbar.

Sales Area Data: Sales Area data normally deals with sales and shipping information

Step 8: Sales

Enter all mandatory fields

Sales District: Geographical service district.

Sales Office: Geographical sales territory

Sales Group: Group of sales representatives that serving this customer.

Customer Group: Grouping of customers.

Customer Status Group: if selected the customer information will be used for statistical analysis.

Price Group: Used to identify commissionable third party representatives.

Price List Type: Used to give a group of customer the same pricing such as you may have one pricing structure for retail customers and another for wholesale customers.

figure 35.22

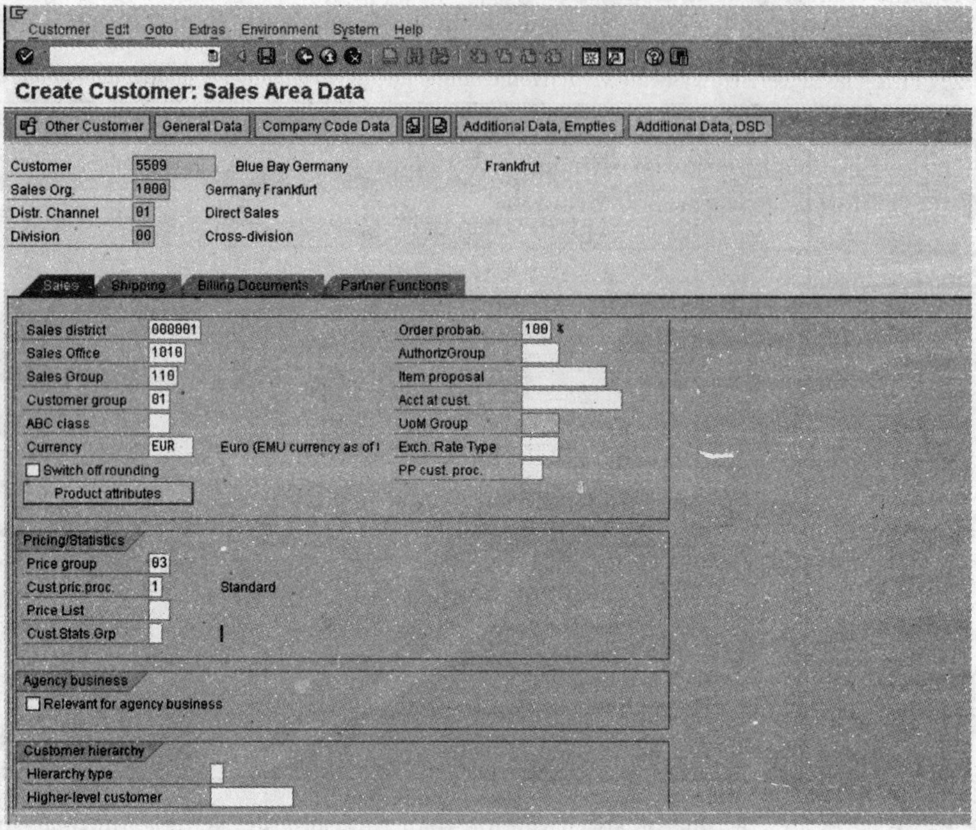

Step 9: Shipping

This tab deals with shipping information.

Select delivery priority, shipping conditions etc

Enter delivery plant from where your material will be shipped to customer. If you check the "Order combination " system will allow you to combine multiple sales orders in one delivery. By default it is unchecked.

Step 10

Incoterms are standard trade definitions most commonly used in international sales contracts. Devised and published by the International Chamber of Commerce.

Part 1: This characteristic contains Incoterms for shipping transactions. If goods are shipped through a port of departure, for example, the appropriate incoterms might be: FOB ("Free On Board").

Part 2: This characteristic contains further details about the incoterms for example, the name of the port: FOB Mumbai.

Enter incoterms details, terms of payment, credit control area. Select account assignment group (01-for domestic revenues). Select tax classification.

figure 35.23

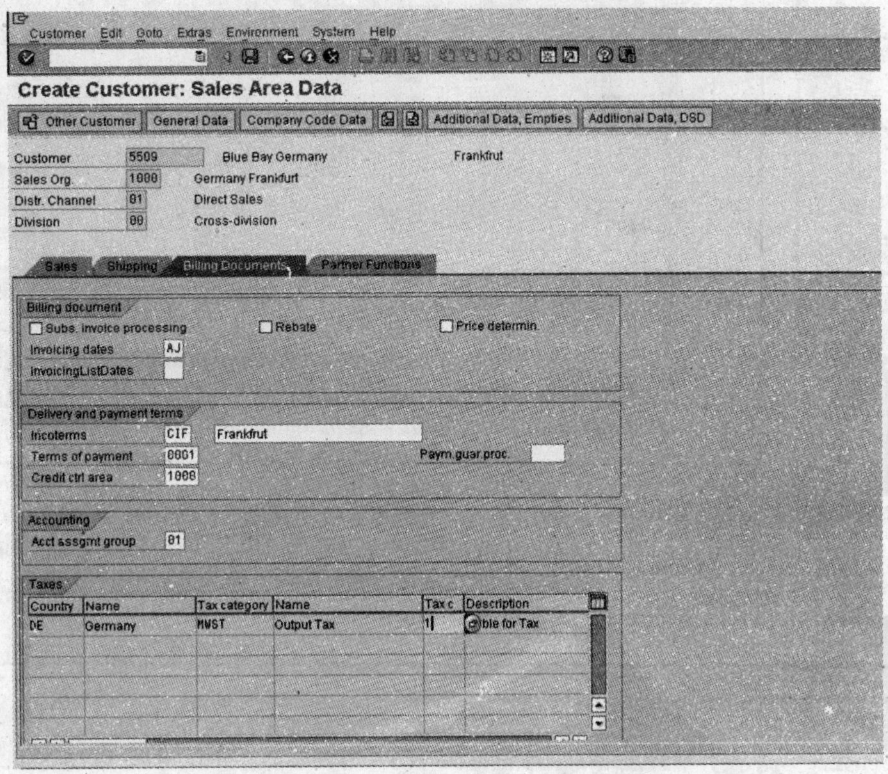

Step 11: Partner Functions

In the Partner function tab you can view all partner functions of customer. Also you can add/delete new partner functions.

Now we will enter company code data. The company code data holds information that are relevant for accounting department.

figure 35.24

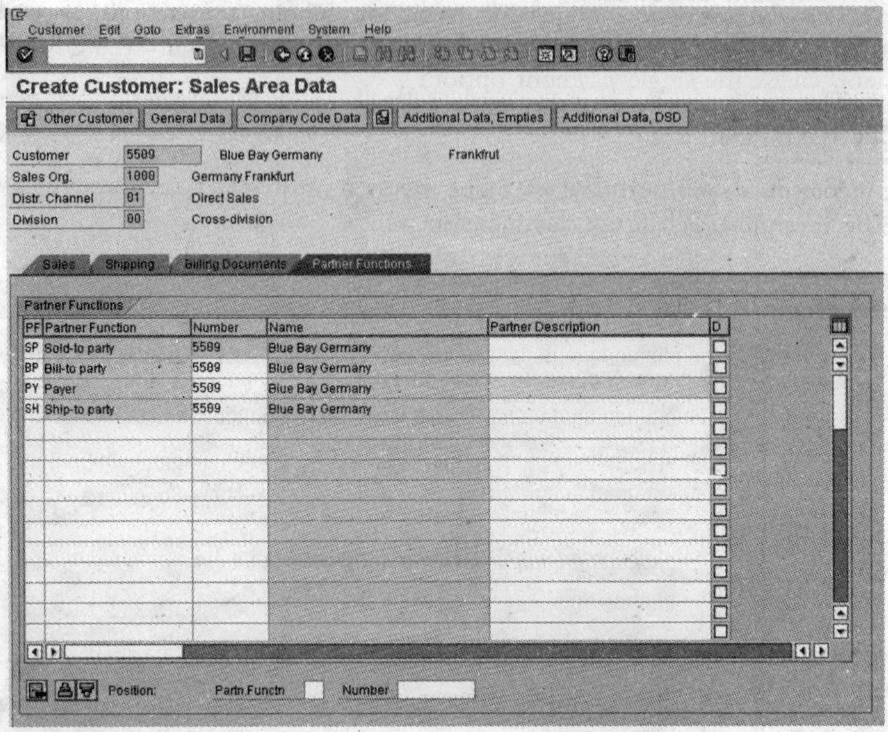

Company Code Data

Step 12: Account Management

Enter recompilation account no. for customer.

figure 35.25

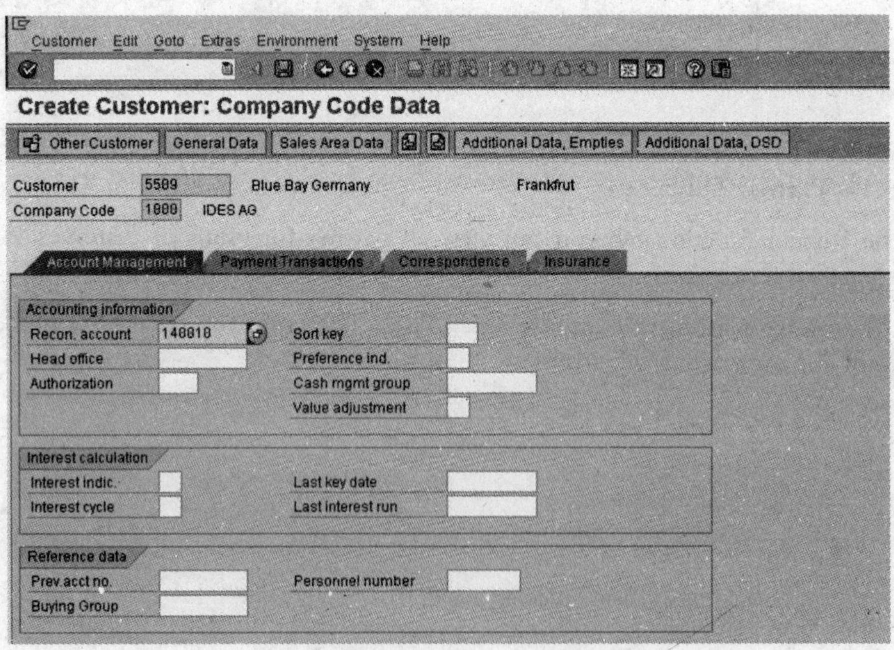

Step 13: Payment Transaction

Enter terms of payment and payment methods. For the customers where you like to receive single payment, check the single payment option.

figure 35.26

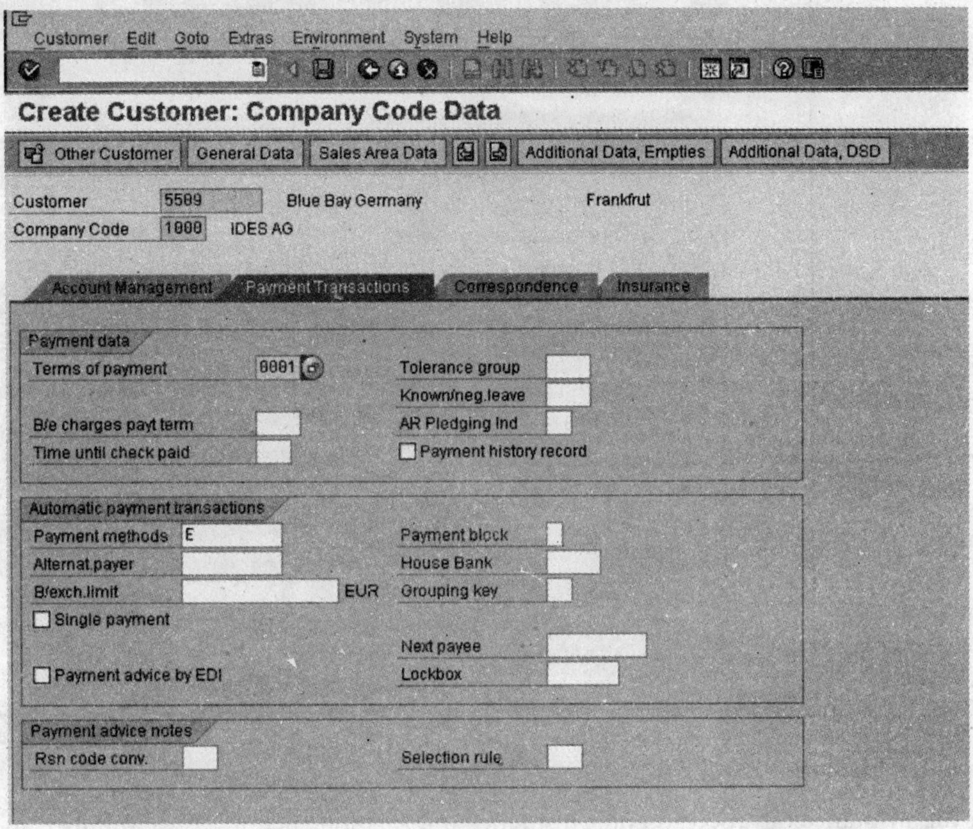

Step 14: Correspondence

Select the dunning procedure from the list. Dunning is the process of sending reminders or making follow ups to customers for outstanding payments. In case the customer is also a vendor, you can adjust the outstanding balance.

figure 35.27

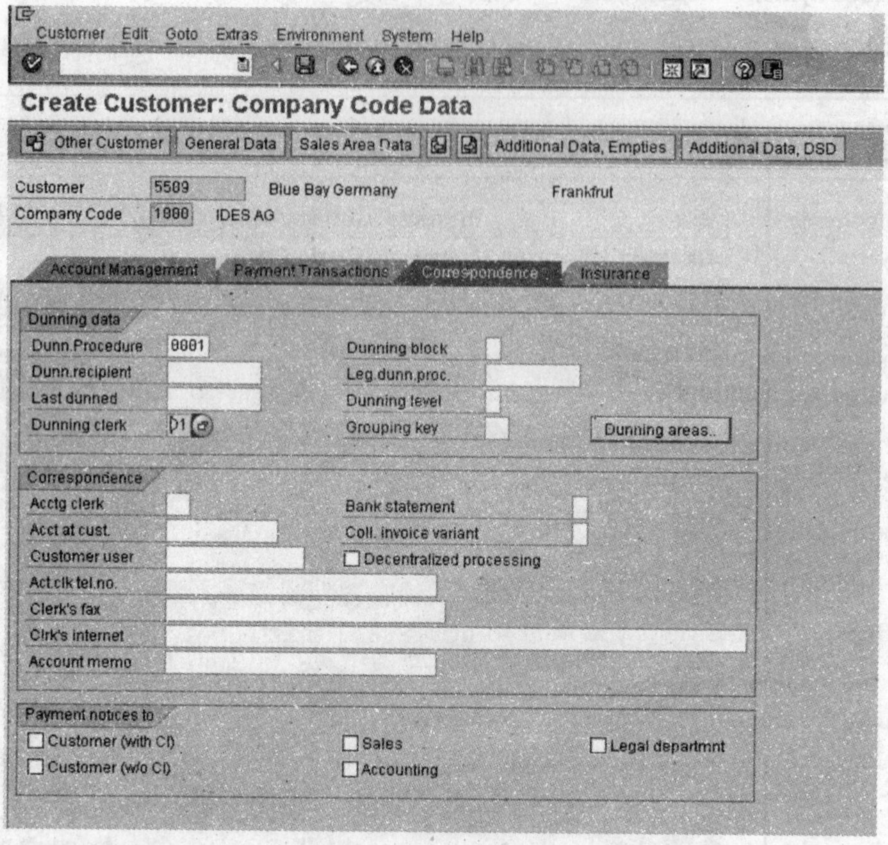

Step 15: Insurance

In the insurance tab you can enter insurance information such as policy number, insured amount and its validity etc.

Now that you have completely entered information for the customer , its time to save the data.

figure 35.28

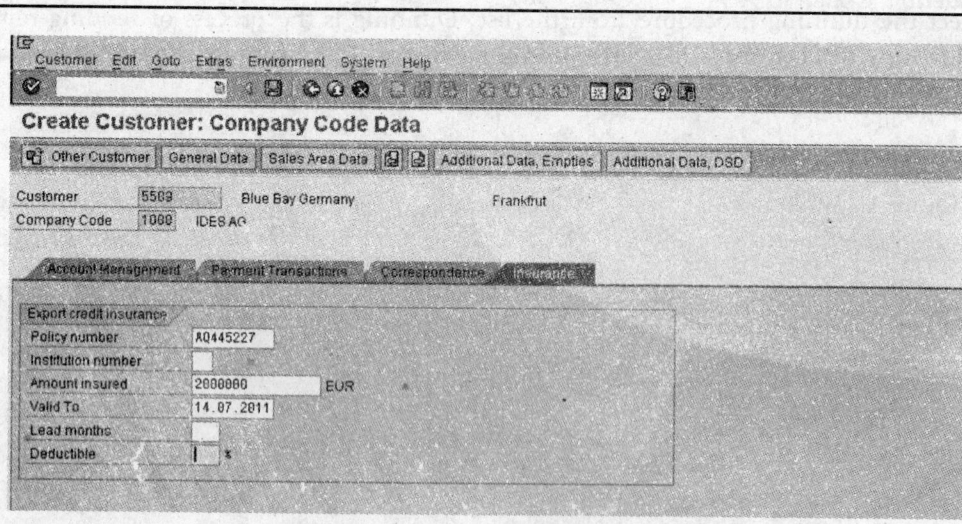

Step 16

Press "Save" button.

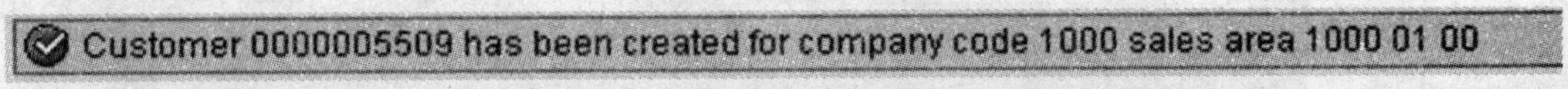

On saving data system will display message as "Customer 00000005509" has been created for company code 1000 sales area 1000 01 00" in status bar as shown above.

Changing Customer Master Record Centrally

The process of changing customer master record is similar to the process of creation. You should know the customer number to access information and further go ahead with changes.

Select menu path: Logistics-Sales and Distribution-Master Data-Business Partner-Customer-Change-Complete

Transaction Code: XD02

Step 1: Select the customer number, company code, sales area in initial screen.

Step 2: Now select the views you want to make changes.

Step 3: Once you have finished changing data, now press save button on toolbar to save the data. After saving data the status bar should display message "Changes have been made" as below.

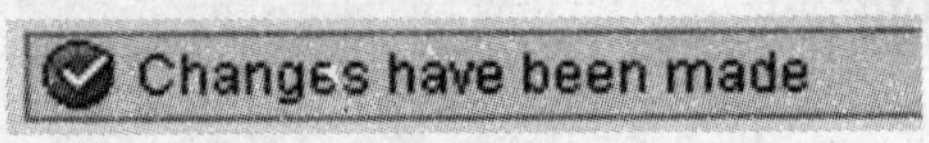

Displaying Customer Master Record Centrally

If you want to display a customer

Select menu path: Logistics-Sales and Distribution-Master Data-Business Partner-Customer-Display-Complete

Transaction Code: XD03

Step 1: Select the customer number, company code, sales area in initial screen.

Step 2: Now select the views you want to make changes.

Blocking Customer Master Record

A customer may be blocked from business transactions for various reasons. If you want to block a customer then transaction code is : XD05 to block customer centrally. Alternatively you can block at sales organization level by using transaction code VD05

Select menu path: Logistics-Sales and Distribution-Master Data-Business Partner-Customer-Block

Select the customer you want to block with appropriate sales area. Further select from blocking options as shown in figure and save it. The customer will no longer accessible to blocked areas.

figure 35.29

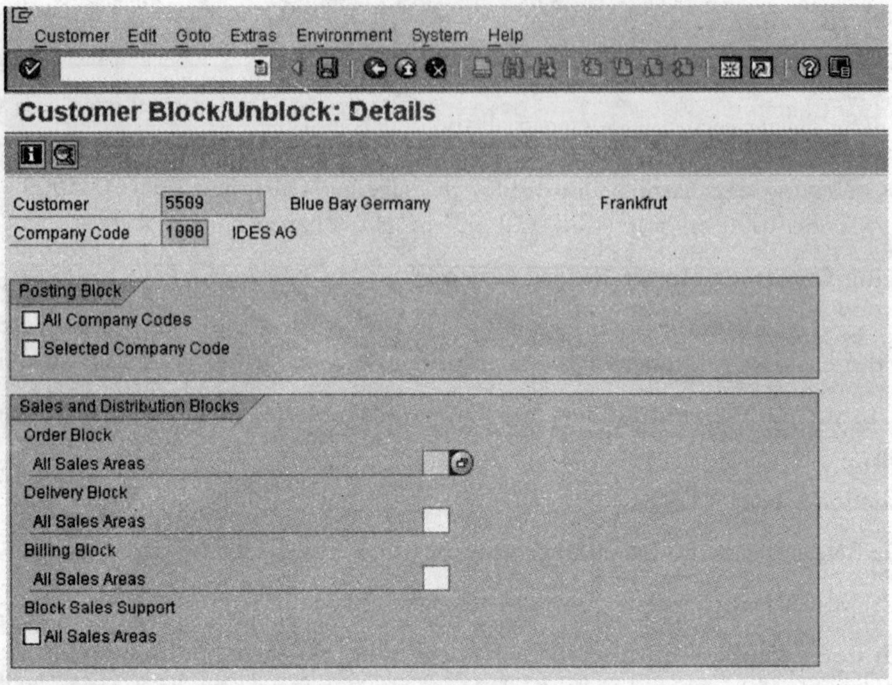

Deleting Customer Master Record

You may want to delete a customer if you are no longer in business relationship with them. To delete a customer record deletion indicators can be set for that customer master record.

figure 35.30

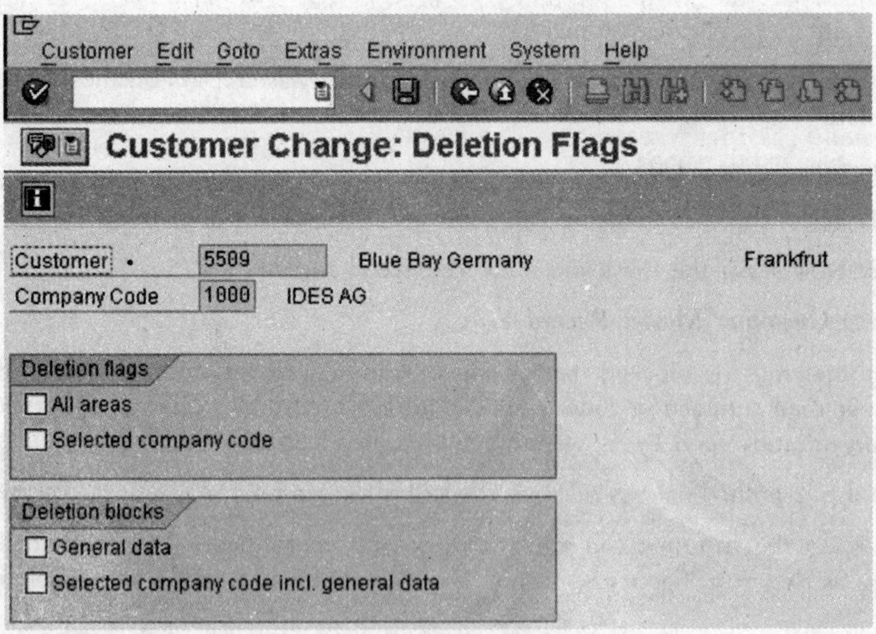

One way is open customer master record in change mode (XD02), select menu Extras-Deletion flags, and check the options for deletion.

Alternatively from SAP easy access menu select menu path ***Logistics-Sales and Distribution-Master Data-Business Partner-Customer-Flag for Deletion***

The master record is deleted if all the dependent data has been deleted. In the same way you can uncheck the deletion flag too.

MATERIAL MASTER

All products and services are combined under the term as material in SAP R/3. All relevant information for the management of material and its stocks as well as its use are maintained in material master record.

The material master is a central repository containing information on all the materials that a company procures, produces, stores, and sells.

It is the company's central source for retrieving material-specific data. The material master is used by all the components in the SAP Logistics System.

The material master may contain huge numbers of different types of materials that are maintained by users in several different industry sectors. The system frequently accesses the material master records during sales processing such as creating enquiry, quotation, sales order.

Let's create a material.

Step 1

Select menu path: Logistics-Sales and Distribution-Master Data-Products-Material-Other Material–Create

Transaction Code: MM01

Industry Sector: By assigning a material to an industry sector, you can take industry-specific factors into account. The industry sectors maybe Chemical, Mechanical, Pharmaceutical, Retailing etc.

Material Types: Each material is assigned to a material type by its use in the company. For example, you can define a material as a raw material, a semi finished product, a finished product, or a service.

The material type has some important control functions such as it

- Determines which user departments can maintain the material.
- Determines the procurement type.
- Helps determine automatic account determination. The stock account in financial accounting is derived with reference to material type.
- Determines the inventory management type in relevant plants

As shown in figure Type the material (can be alphanumeric), Select industry sectors and material type. Then Press Enter.

figure 35.31

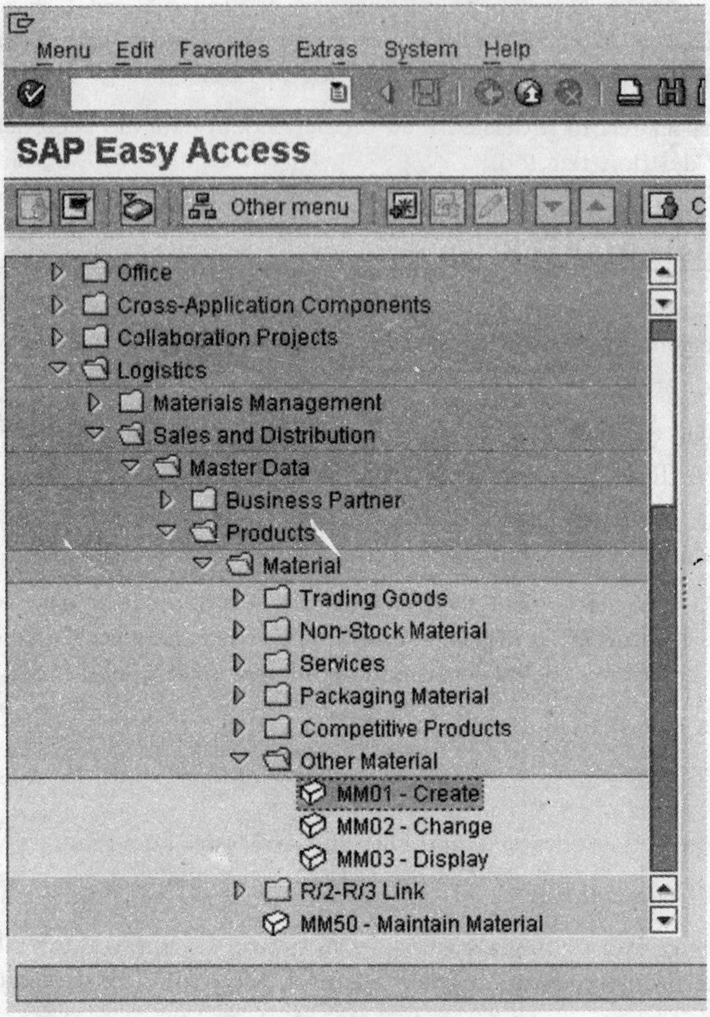

figure 35.32

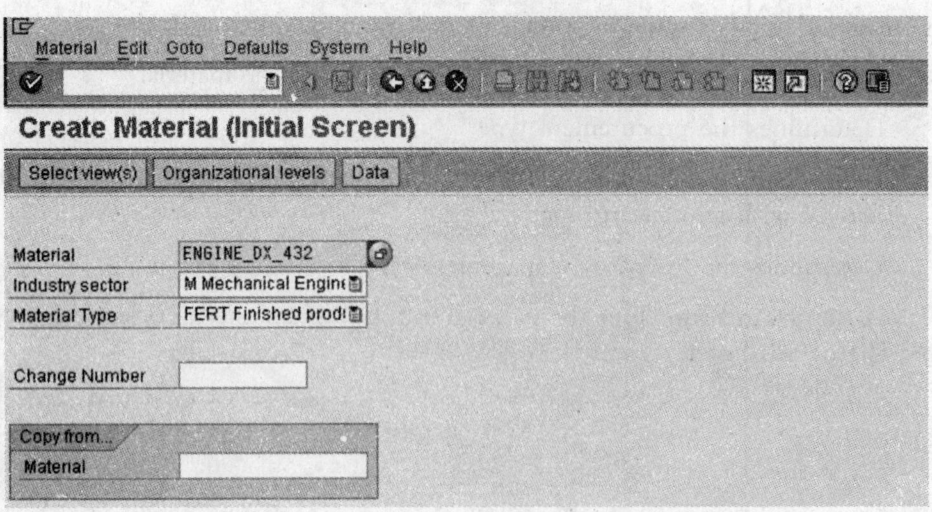

Step 2

Select views as shown in figure. Select following screens from the views.

- Basic Data 1
- Sales: Sales Org. Data1
- Sales: Sales Org. Data2
- Sales: General/Plant Data
- Sales Text
- MRP 1
- Accounting 1

However you can select more views than the above, provided you have relevant information to create material for those respective views. After selecting required views press ✔ button

figure 35.33

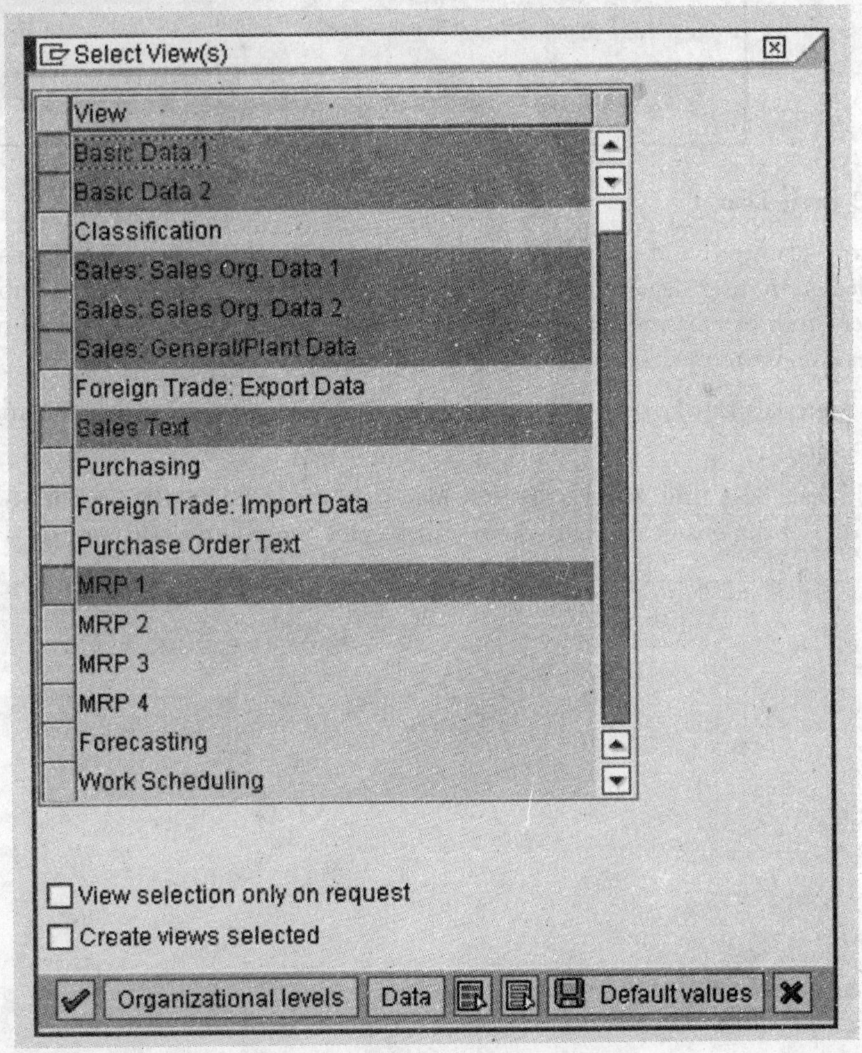

Step 3

Enter Organizational levels information such as Plant, Storage Location, Sales Organization, and Distribution Channel. Then press Enter.

figure 35.34

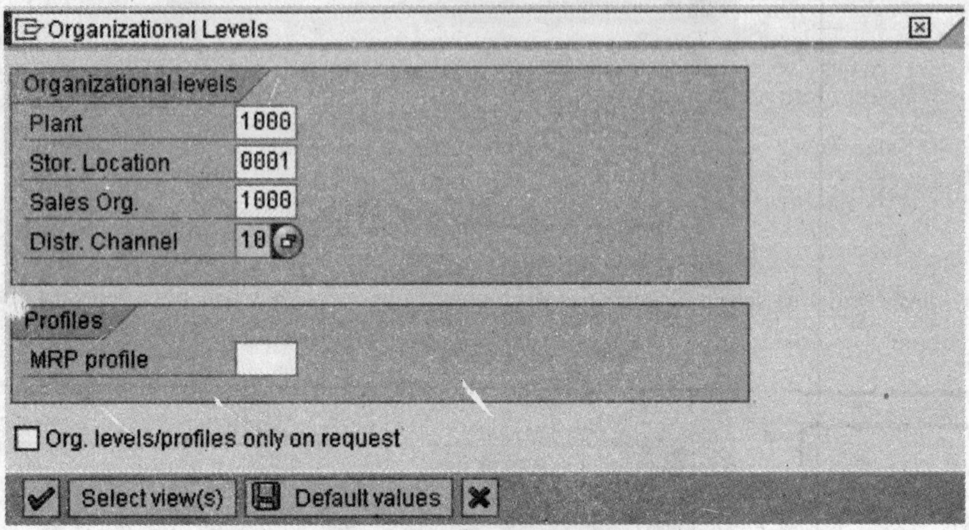

Step 3 Basic Data 1

Unit of Measure: Besides the base unit of measure, in which the system manages stocks and performs all calculation, user departments can use separate units of measure. For example, Purchasing can use a different unit of measure than Sales or Warehouse Management. All unit of measure except base unit of measure are termed as alternative unit of measure.

Materials can be grouped according to different criteria for easier management and evaluation purpose.

Select Base unit of measure and material group. Enter Net weight and Gross weight. In case the material dimensions are in volume then enter the volume with appropriate volume unit.

Further if you are using any packaging material for then enter packaging material data.

figure 35.35

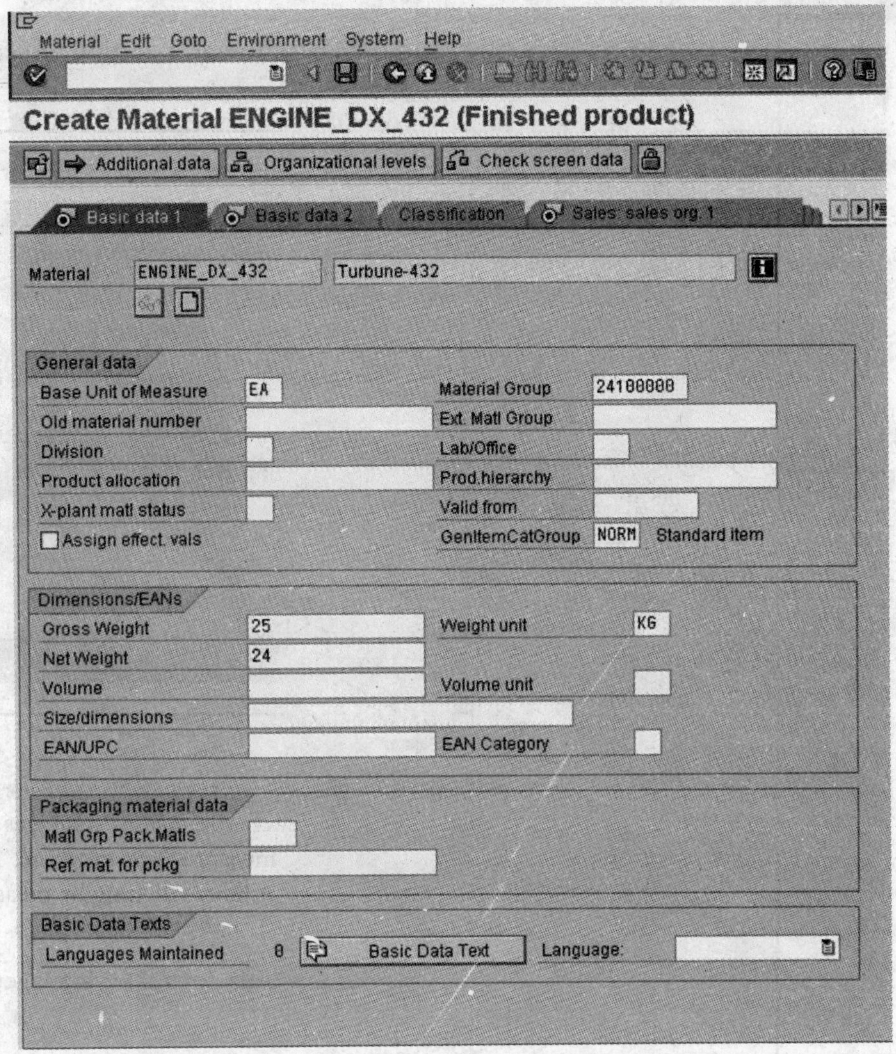

Step 4 Sales Org. 1

The sales unit may be defined as the unit in which the materials are sold to end customers. In this step enter the delivery plant, the plant from where the goods will be delivered. Enter the tax category applicable.

You may enter the Division which your product is in for sales (defaults if entered in the Basic data screen).

Material Group is used to group several materials or services for analysis/reporting as well as search by match code. Cash discount indicator is used for materials, which allow for a cash discount. Also you can set minimum order quantity, minimum delivery quantity and delivery unit in this screen.

figure 35.36

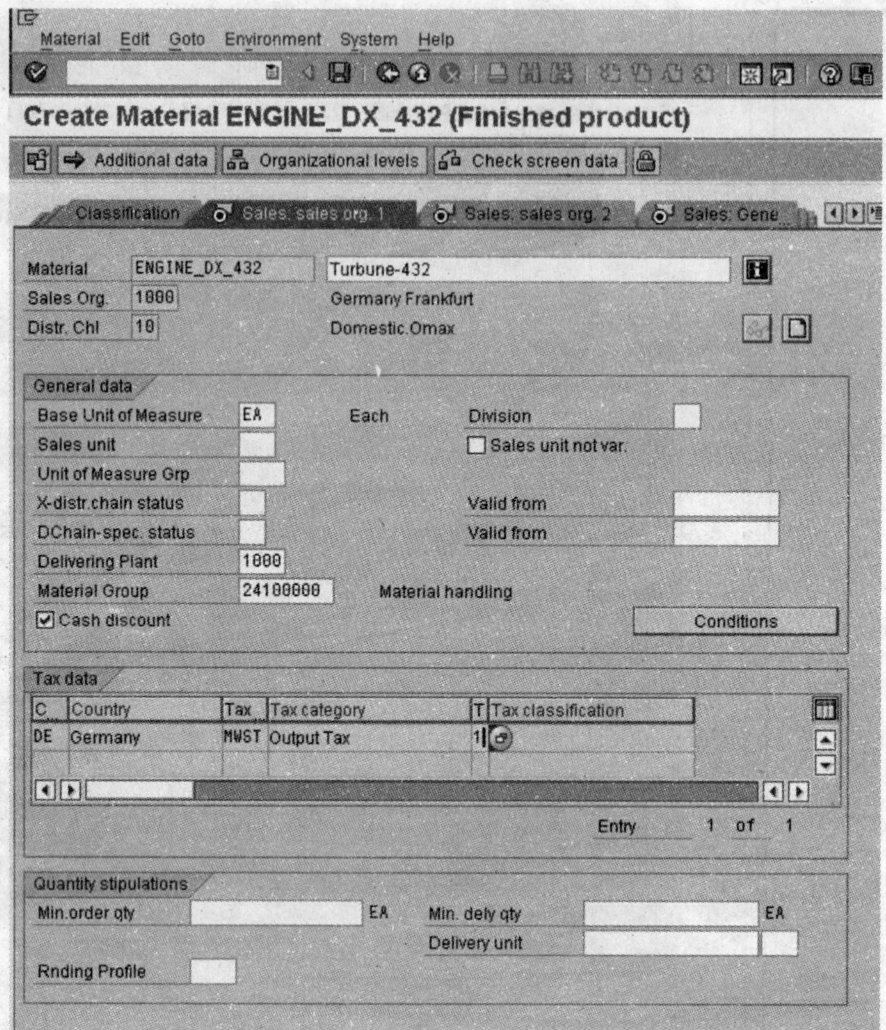

Step 4 Sales Org. 2

Material statistics group helps to determine which data the system updates in the Logistics Information System (LIS).

Materials with similar pricing conditions can be grouped in material pricing group.

You can assign volume rebate group if this material qualifies for rebate.

Account assignment group is used group material with same accounting requirements such as determining sales revenue and sales deductions.

Several materials can be assigned to the same commission group, if the commission sharing between representatives is the same for these materials. Item category group is grouping of materials, that help the system determine the Item Category. Item Category determines how a specific item is processed by system. E.g. a text item is not relevant for pricing.

figure 35.37

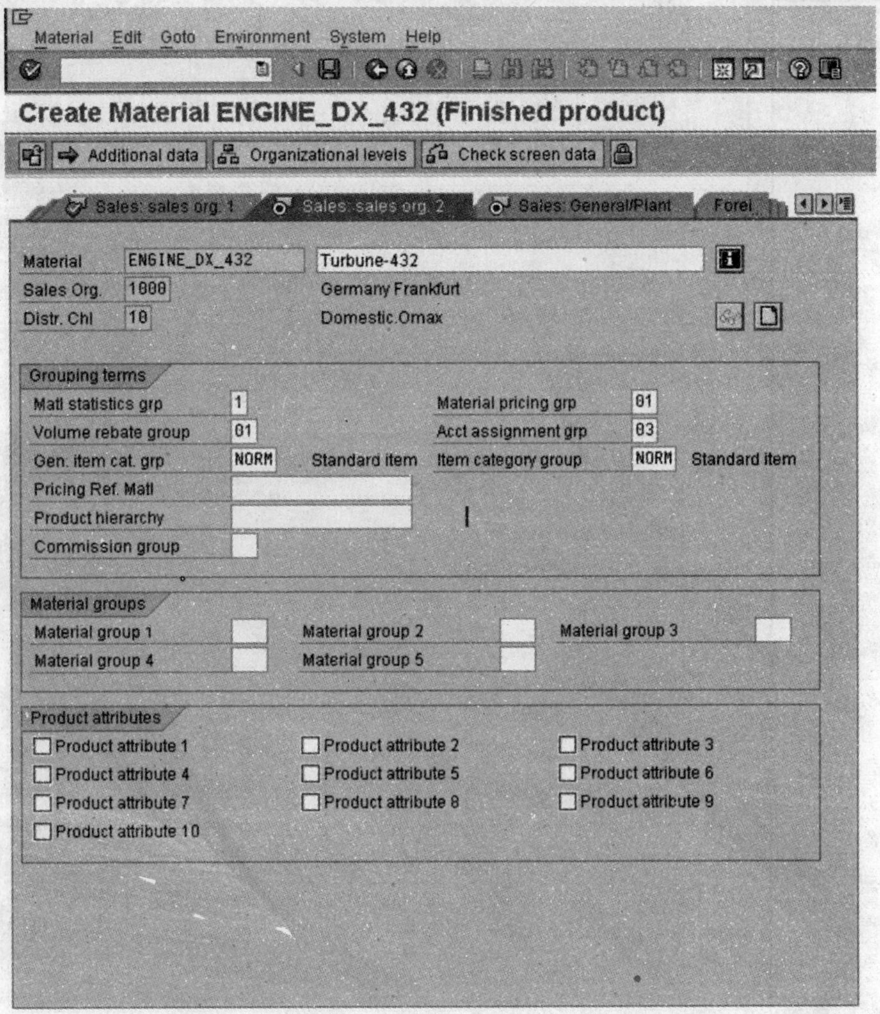

Step 5 Sales: General/Plant

Transportation groups are groups of materials that have the same transportation requirements, for example, all goods that need refrigeration can be of one group. Transportation groups are like containers, pallets etc.

Loading groups define materials that have the same loading requirements, such as forklift truck, crane or manual.

Packaging material data can be entered here provided a packaging material is created for this material. You can create a separate packaging material and refer to that material here for further use.

In case your plant allows carrying negative stocks, you can check the negative stock indicator here.

figure 35.38

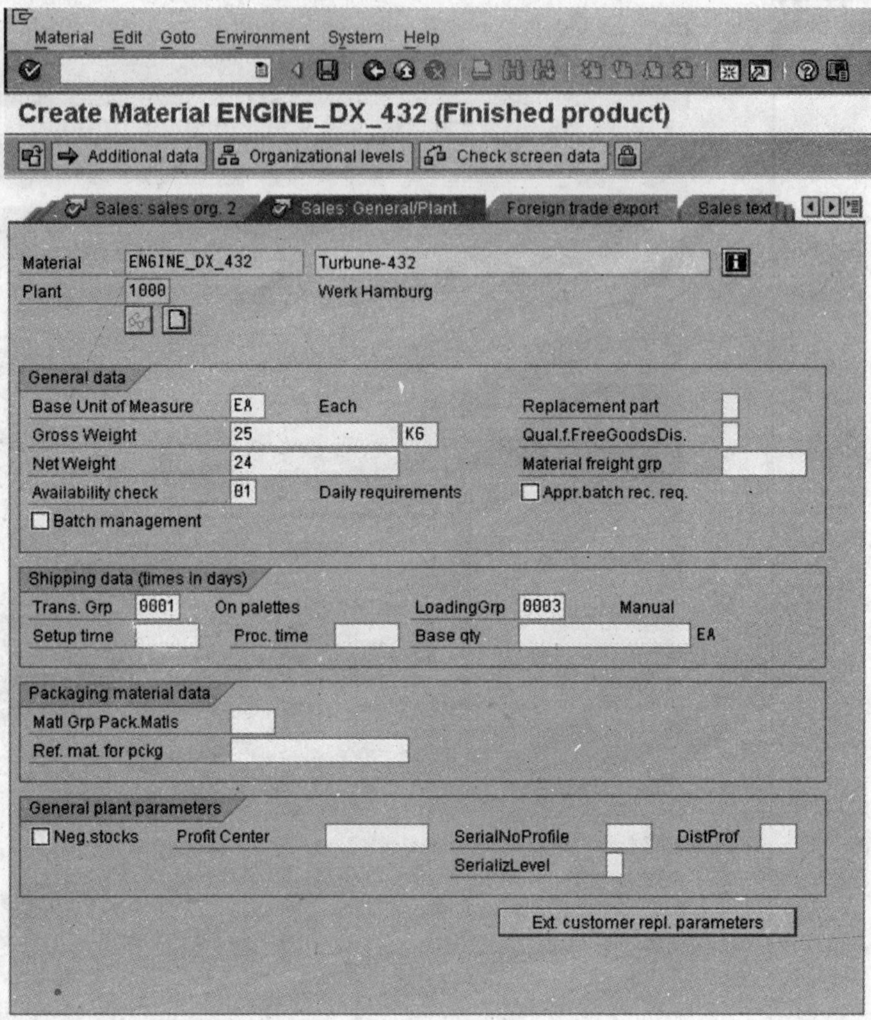

Step 6: Sales Text

Here you can mention text specific to the material and in an appropriate language.

figure 35.39

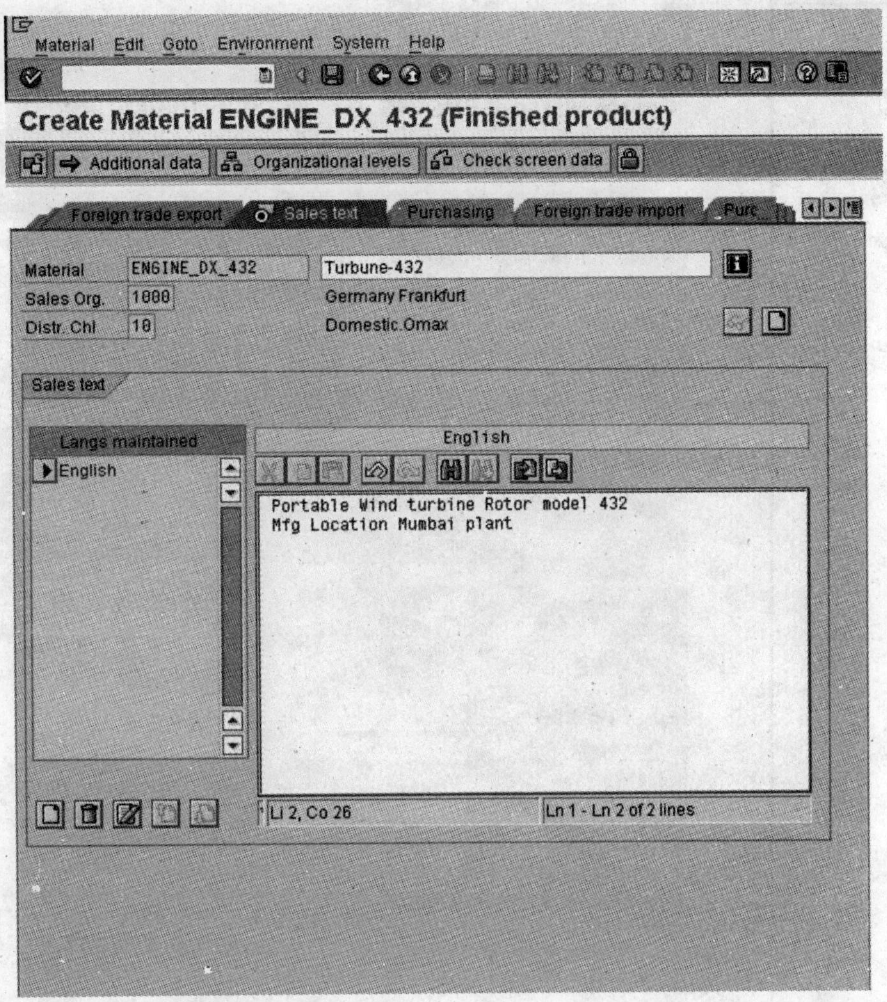

Step 7: MRP 1

This is a screen for material requirement planning (MRP).

MRP has important role in material management and production processes. The main role of material requirement planning is to monitor stocks and generate planned order, purchase requisitions and delivery schedules etc. Planning is usually done at plant level. There exist various types of planning such as consumption based planning, Forecast-based planning, Time-phased planning, and Seasonal MRP etc. The Material Management module of SAP R/3 deals in details about MRP and other related parameters. However for our example we have taken ND-No Planning as a MRP type.

figure 35.40

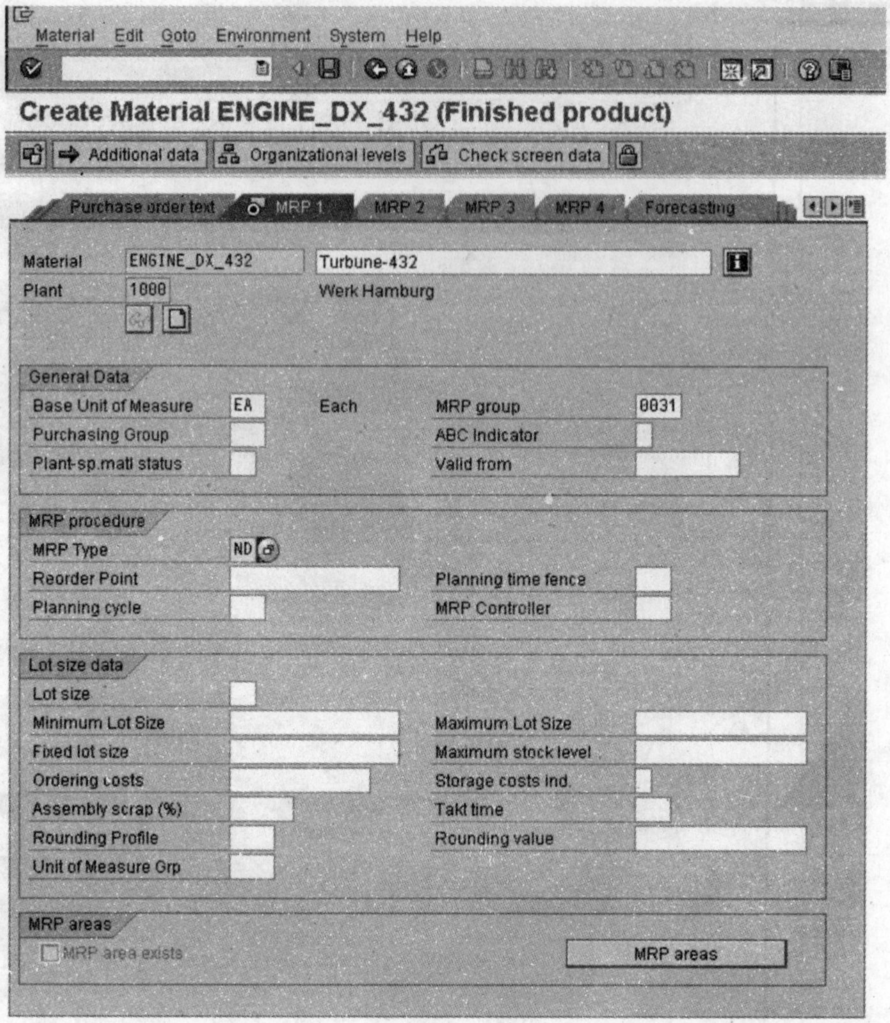

Step 8: Accounting

This tab deals with accounting information. Valuation class is nothing but how your material is valuated and maintained in G/L accounts. Stock values of different materials types can be posted in same G/L account. Also stock values of material with same material type can be posted in different G/L accounts.

Price control is used to valuate the stock material. Price control can be standard or moving average price. Based you the price control you have selected you must enter standard price or moving price in the field.

figure 35.41

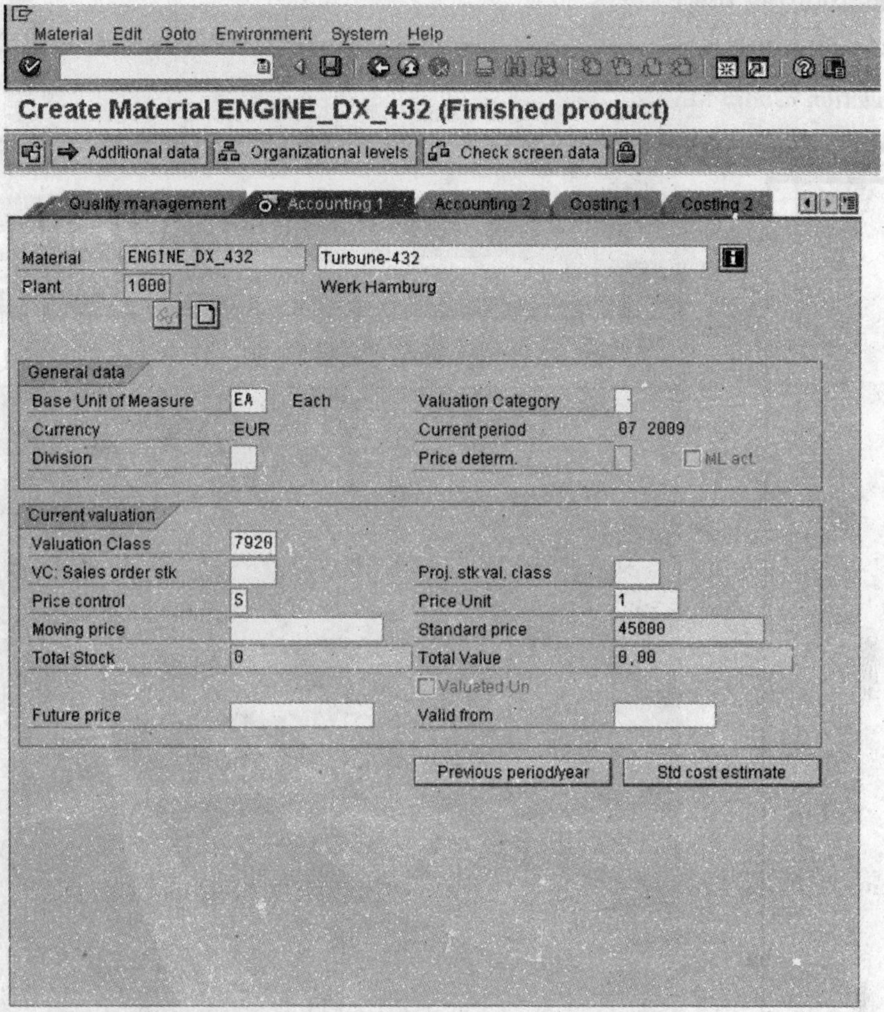

Step 9: Save

Press save button. On saving master record you will see a message flashed in your status bar as below.

With this above information we are almost created a material master record for future use. However for a complete material in real terms other fields in Tabs such as purchasing, costing, Quality management etc may be maintained. From a sales and distribution point of view the information we have entered is quite sufficient to execute a sales process.

Change Material Master

Select menu path: Logistics-Sales and Distribution-Master Data-Products-Material-Other Material—Change

Transaction Code: MM02

figure 35.42

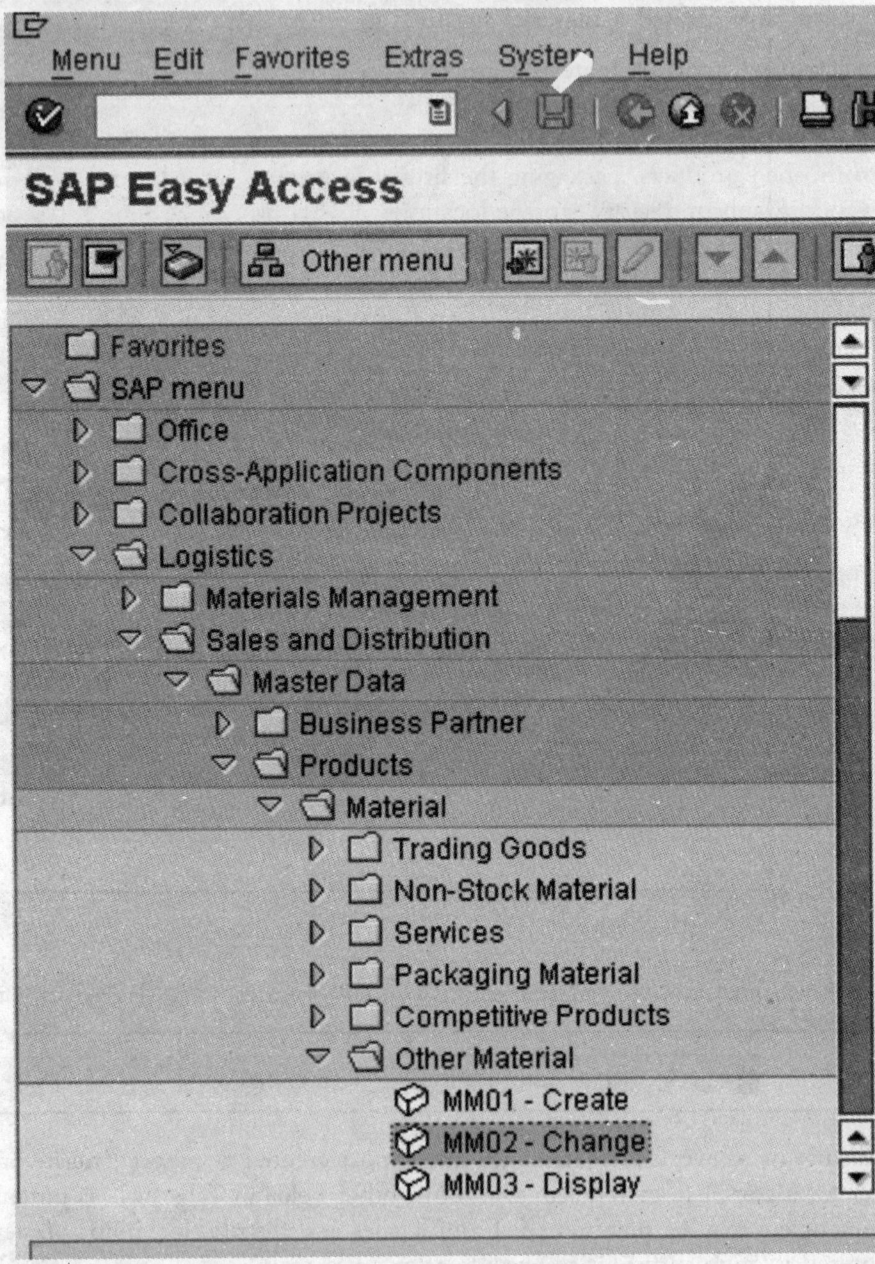

Display Material Master

Select menu path: Logistics-Sales and Distribution-Master Data-Products-Material-Other Material–Display

Transaction Code: MM03

Now that we have created a material master record, we have to add stock to the material.

In a normal practice materials are produced by plants in manufacturing units and then it is moved to specific storage location before available for sale. There exist several stages and processes such as procuring raw materials, processing raw materials to semi-finished goods, assembling semi-finished goods to finished products, packaging the finished products etc. Material movement happens between plants, vendors, subcontractors, storage locations at certain point of time and when requirement arises. SAP R/3 manages all these process by using certain movement types. All these processes mentioned certainly beyond the current focus of discussion.

For this reason we will focus our discussion only within finished goods stocks.

Material Stock Addition

Select menu path: Logistics-Logistics Execution-Inbound Process- Goods Receipt for Purchase Order, Order, Other Transactions- MB1C - Goods Receipt for Other Activities

Transaction Code: MB1C

If the customer complains (for example, that they received the incorrect quantity) you can send them the extra material later free of charge. This free-of-charge subsequent delivery always made with reference to sales order.

figure 35.43

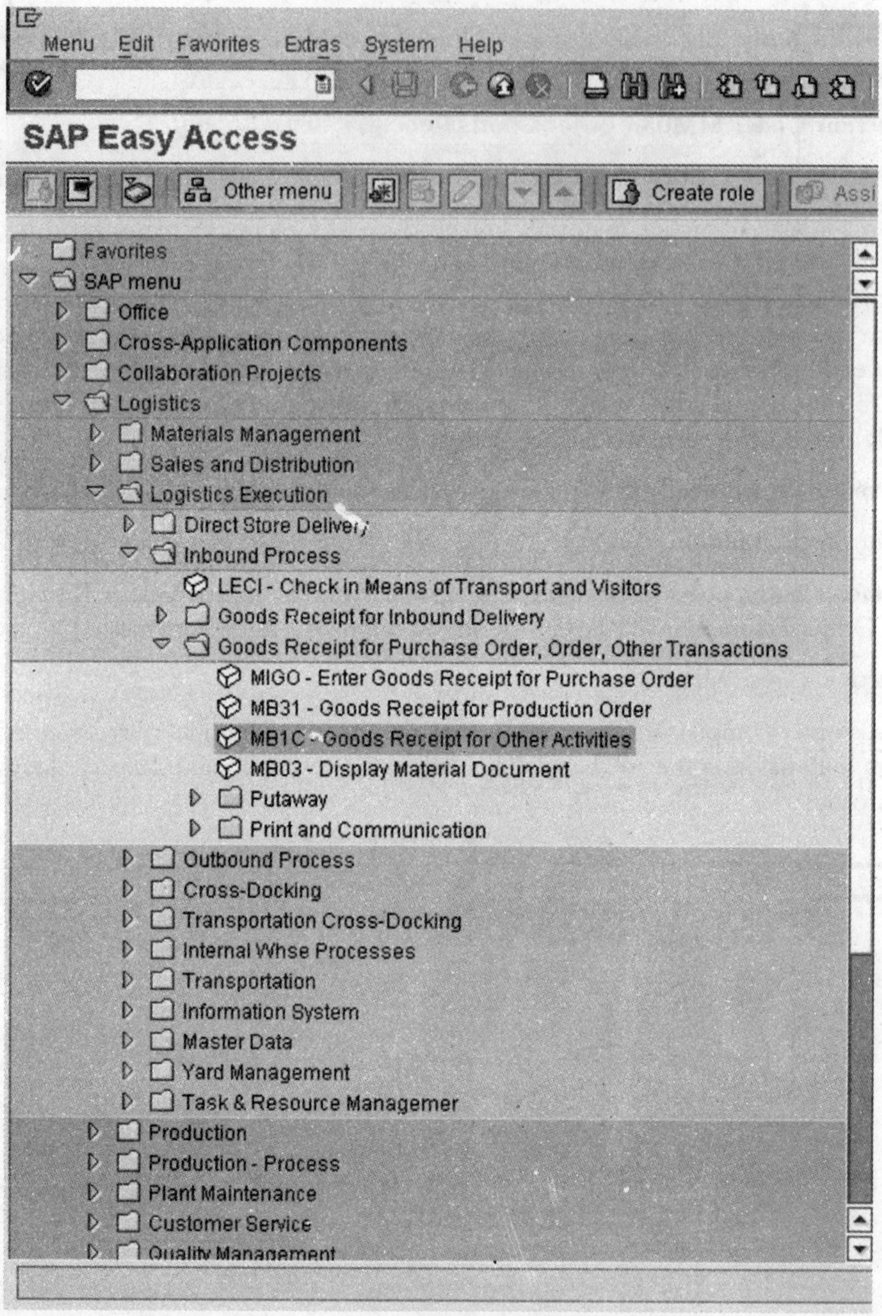

On the goods receipt initial screen, enter movement type 561-Receipt per initial entry of stock balances into unrestricted use

Enter the plant and storage location of the material.

Then press Enter.

figure 35.44

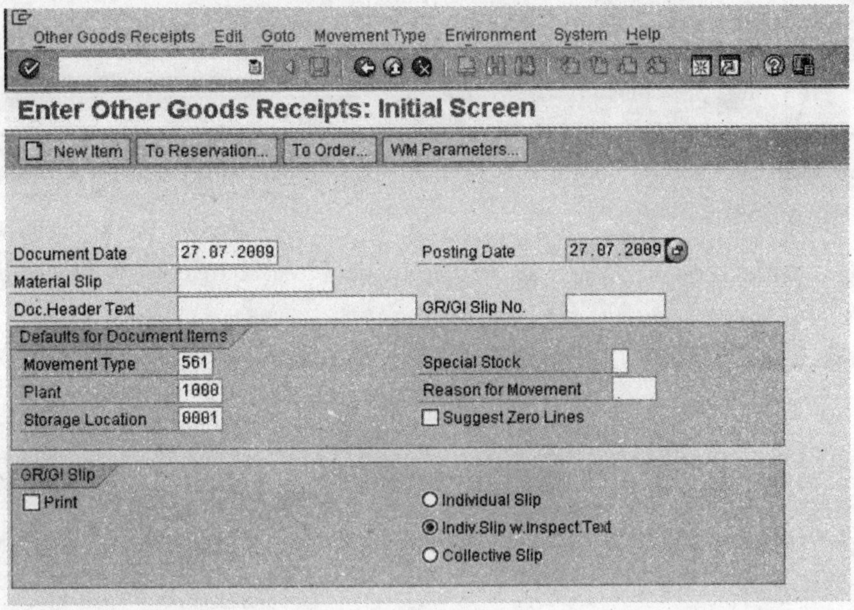

In this screen enter the material number and quantity to be added to stock. Enter storage location too.

You can add stock to multiple materials in different storage location in this screen too provided they belong to same plant.

figure 35.45

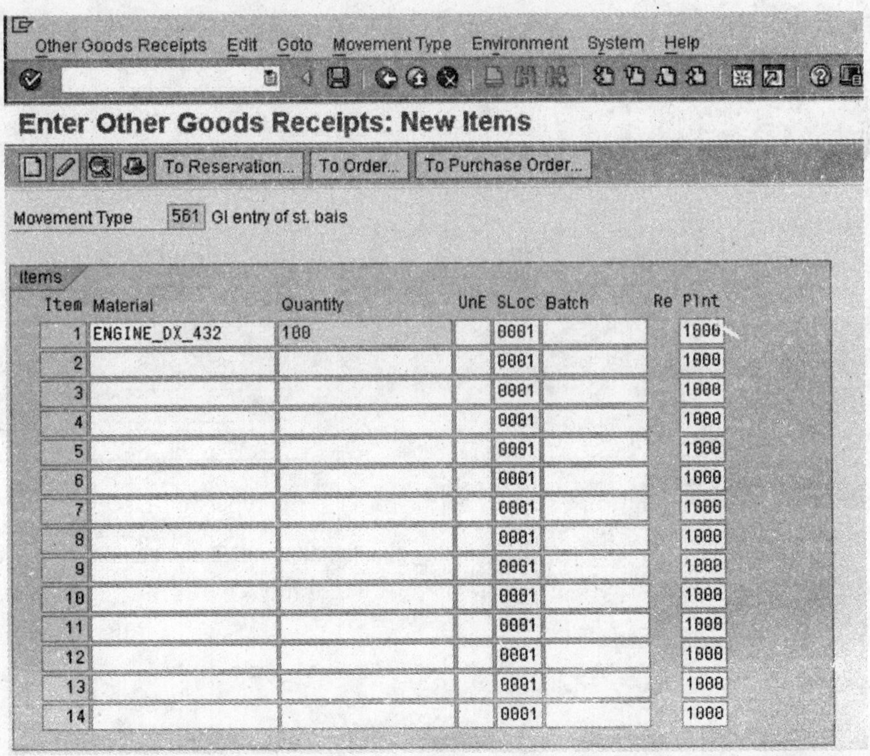

Press Save button

You will see a message flashed on status bar as below.

Now that the stock is added it is time to view the existing stock at storage location.

Material Stock Display

Select menu path: Logistics- Materials Management- Physical Inventory- Environment- MMBE - Stock Overview

Transaction Code: MMBE

figure 35.46

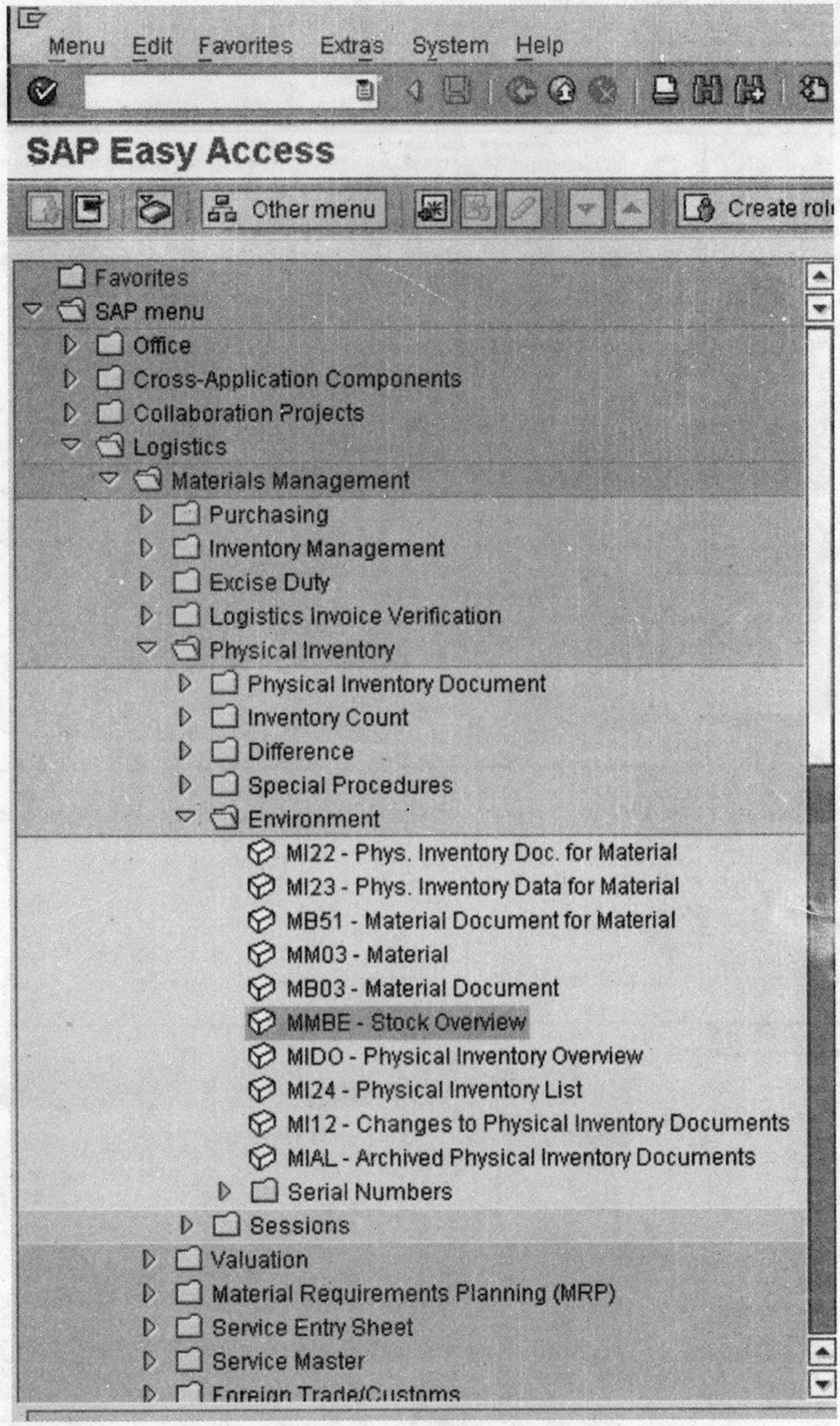
Menu Edit Favorites Extras System Help
SAP Easy Access
Other menu
Create rol
Favorites
SAP menu
Office
Cross-Application Components
Collaboration Projects
Logistics
Materials Management
Purchasing
Inventory Management
Excise Duty
Logistics Invoice Verification
Physical Inventory
Physical Inventory Document
Inventory Count
Difference
Special Procedures
Environment
MI22 - Phys. Inventory Doc. for Material
MI23 - Phys. Inventory Data for Material
MB51 - Material Document for Material
MM03 - Material
MB03 - Material Document
MMBE - Stock Overview
MIDO - Physical Inventory Overview
MI24 - Physical Inventory List
MI12 - Changes to Physical Inventory Documents
MIAL - Archived Physical Inventory Documents
Serial Numbers
Sessions
Valuation
Material Requirements Planning (MRP)
Service Entry Sheet
Service Master
Foreign Trade/Customs

Select the menu path as mentioned above. In the stock overview screen enter the material number, plant, storage location.

figure 35.47

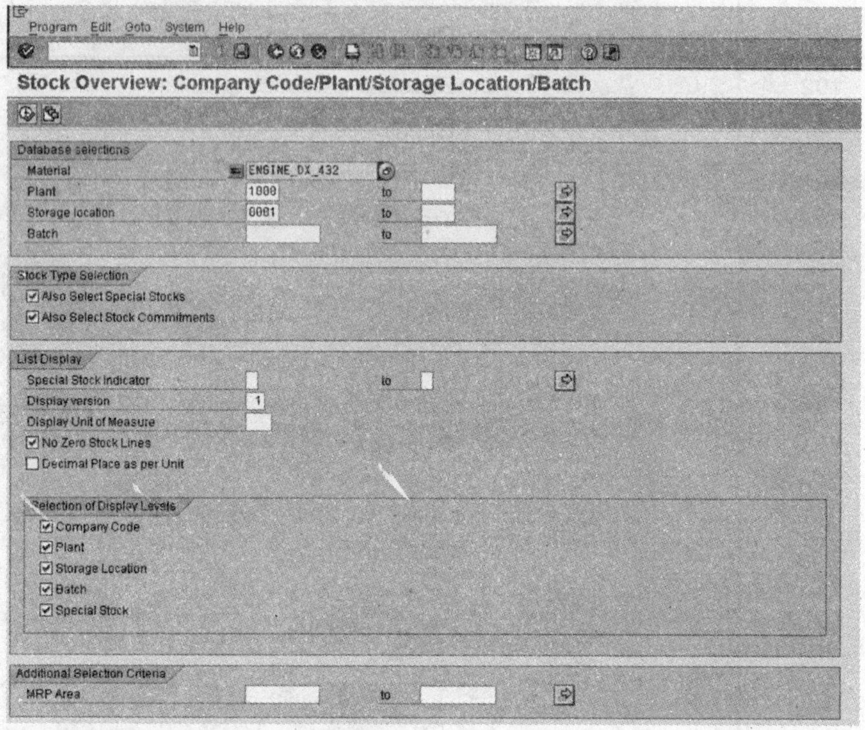

You can also display stock of materials indifferent plants and storage location. For this select the Multiple Selection icon  and enter a list of plants or storage location you want to see.

Then Execute  or press F8

After Execution you will see the stock level as shown in figure below.

figure 35.48

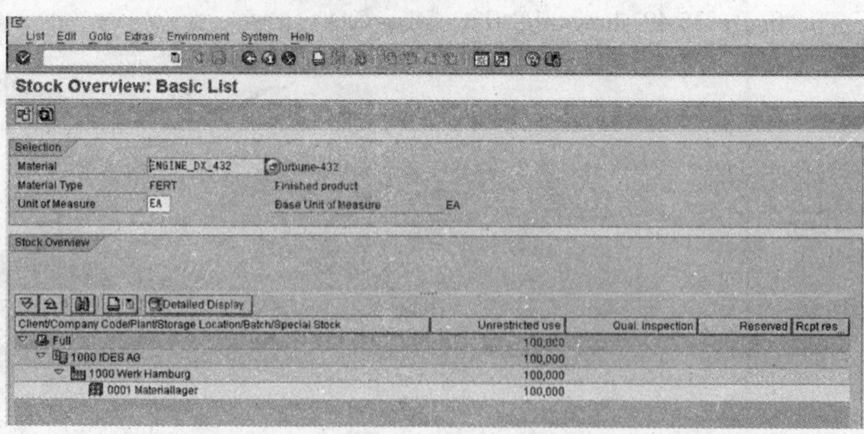

Frequently used Movement types

Below is the table of frequently used movement types.

Movement Type	Description
102	Reversal of Goods Receipt
161	Goods Receipt of returns
231	Goods Issue for sales order
302	Transfer from Plant to Plant
309	Transfer from Material to Material
311	Transfer within Plant (Storage locations to Storage Locations)
322	Transfer from Quality to Unrestricted
343	Transfer From blocked to unrestricted
561	Receipt per initial entry of stock balances into unrestricted use

SALES PROCESS

In the sales process you can execute different business transaction based on sales activity performed. Each sales activity of sales process is recorded as a document in SAP R/3. Broadly these documents can be classified into four types.

Presales: Include customer inquiries, Quotations

Sales: include Sales orders

Agreements: Outline agreements, Contracts and scheduling agreement

Complaints: Returns, credit memo requests, debit memo requests, free of charge deliveries

Further you can create and process delivery and billing documents. However , in some cases such as cash sales and rush order you may not have to create delivery and billing documents as system automatically creates subsequent delivery and billing documents.

The figure 35.49 shows the flow of sales document.

figure 35.49

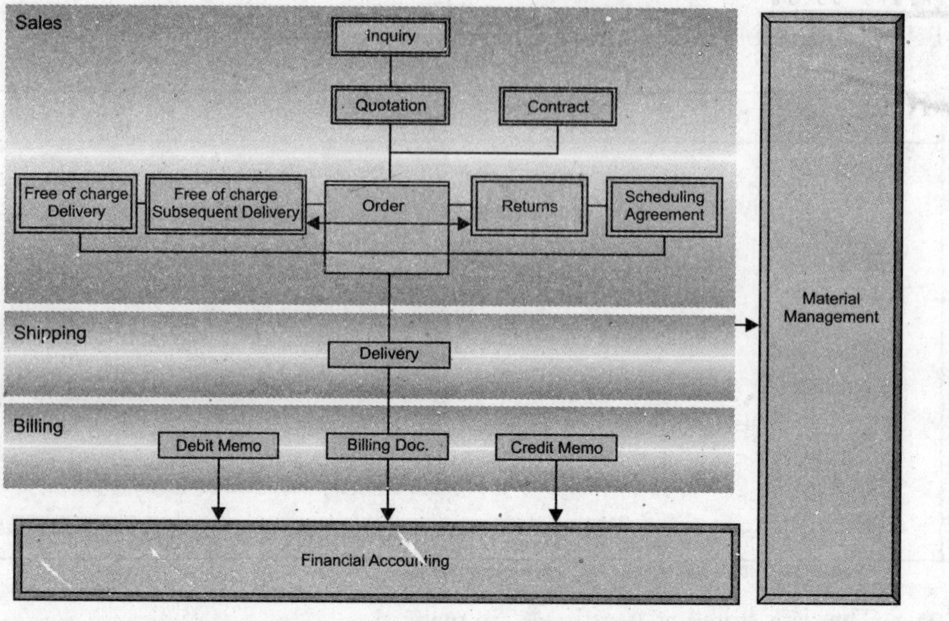

The sales documents you create are individual documents but they can also form part of a chain of interrelated documents. For example, you may receive a customer inquiry over telephone for certain products that is recorded in system. The customer requests for a quotation, which you generate and send to customer. Later the customer places order and subsequently you deliver the order and send a invoice along with the delivery. Its possible that sometimes customer may receive some damaged goods. For that customer claims credit and you may deliver free of charge for the quantity of goods damaged.

The entire chain of documents – the inquiry, the quotation, the sales order, the delivery, the invoice, and the subsequent delivery free of charge – creates a document flow or history. You can always access document flow at any point of the document chain. This particularly helps in keeping track of processes involved and reduces repeat data entry at each step.

System carries out certain basic functions during sales order processing, such as monitoring of sales transactions, availability checking, checking credit limits, calculating prices, surcharges and taxes, delivery scheduling, transferring requirement to planning (MRP) etc. However it depends on your system configuration about how these processes are being handled.

Before going ahead, it is essential to understand the structure of sales documents. Any sales documents are made up of three types of data i.e. header data, item data, schedule line data.

Header data is valid for entire document. The data that is part of header data are sold-to party, ship-to party and the payer, currency and exchange rate, pricing elements for the entire document, delivery date and shipping point.

figure 35.50

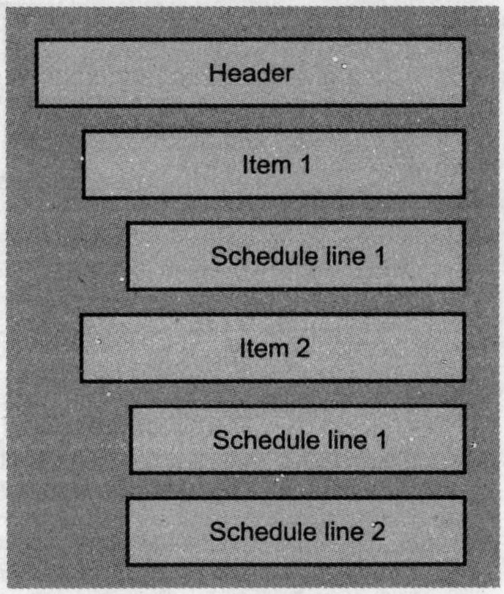

Item data is data that applies only to specific.

The data stored at item levels are material number, target quantity for outline agreements, ship-to party and the payer, plant and storage location specifications, pricing elements for the individual items.

The schedule line contains all the data that is needed for a delivery. Data recorded in the schedule lines includes, Schedule line quantity, delivery date, confirmed quantity.

TYPES OF SALES DOCUMENTS

The standard SAP R/3 System includes a variety of predefined sales document types.

Some or all these document types may be changed during implementation in organization to fulfill particular needs of the organization.

Type of Processing	Sales document type	Abbreviation
Presales	Inquiry	IN
	Quotation	QT
	Free-of-charge delivery	FD
Sales orders	Standard sales order	OR
	Cash sale	BV
	Rush order	SO
Outline agreements	Quantity contract	CQ
	Maintenance contract	WV
	Rental contract	MV
	Scheduling agreement	DS
Complaints	Credit memo request	CR
	Debit memo request	DR
	Subsequent delivery, free-of-charge	SD
	Returns	RE

SALES DOCUMENT ICONS

The figure 35.51 shows the icons with descriptions frequently used during sales press.

figure 35.51

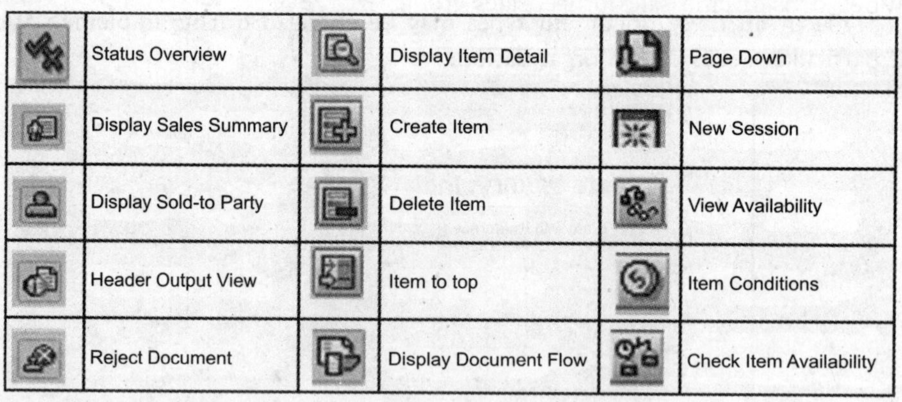

Let's create inquiry and quotation

Create Inquiry

Select menu path: Logistics-Sales and Distribution-Sales-Inquiry-VA11- Create

Transaction Code: VA11

Step 1: Select menu path as mentioned above

figure 35.52

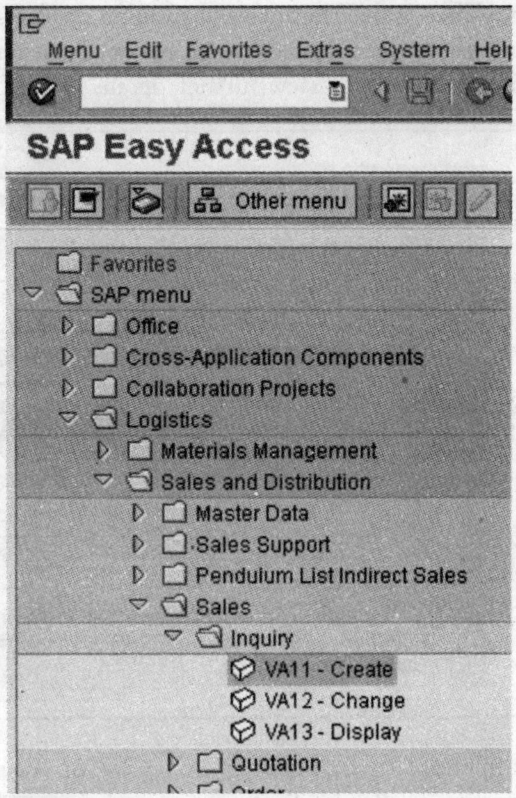

Step 2: In the Initial Screen of inquiry select inquiry type as IN, select sales organization, distribution, channel, division and sales office, sales group if applicable.

figure 35.53

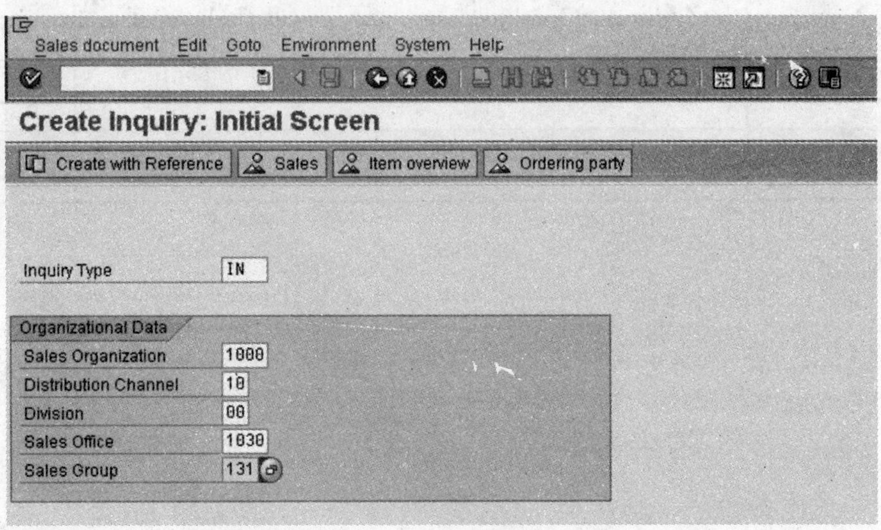

Step 3: In the header enter sold-to- party, ship-to-party. In the Item Overview tab enter PO number and PO date. Enter valid date from and valid date to. This is to ensure the inquiry information is valid for certain period of time. Then enter the material number in the material column and number pieces in quantity column then press enter. This will fetch material master record and display data. You can visit other tabs such as sales, shipping to view further details.

figure 35.54

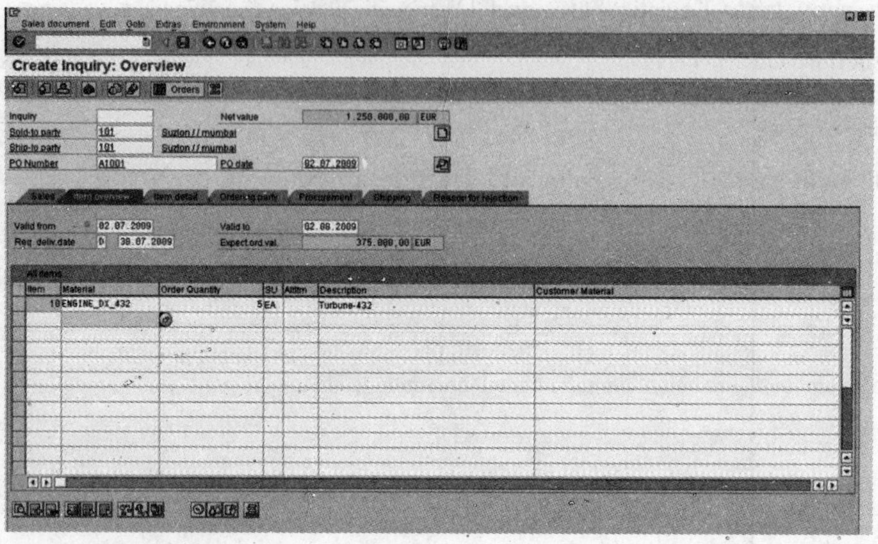

Step 4: Check incompletion log by pressing Ctrl + F8 or from menu Edit-Incompletion Log. If the document is complete system should display message in status bar as below.

Now press save button. Once you save, system will flash message in your status bar with a sales inquiry number as below.

The number shown above is generated internally by system. However in real time implementation this may be customized as per business requirements.

Similarly you can change and display existing enquiry by menu path or by transaction codes as mentioned below.

Change Inquiry

Select menu path: Logistics-Sales and Distribution-Sales-Inquiry-VA12- Change

Transaction Code: VA12

Display Inquiry

Select menu path: Logistics-Sales and Distribution-Sales-Inquiry-VA13- Display

Transaction Code: VA13

Quotation

Quotation is a legally binding document presented by company to its customers for delivering certain products or services with certain fixed condition within a specified time period.

Quotations are normally generated from a sales area with reference to customer enquiry.

It comprises of one or more items that contain the quantity of a material or service being asked by customer.

Create Quotation

Step 1

Select menu path: Logistics-Sales and Distribution-Sales-Quotation-VA21- Create

Transaction Code: VA21

figure 35.55

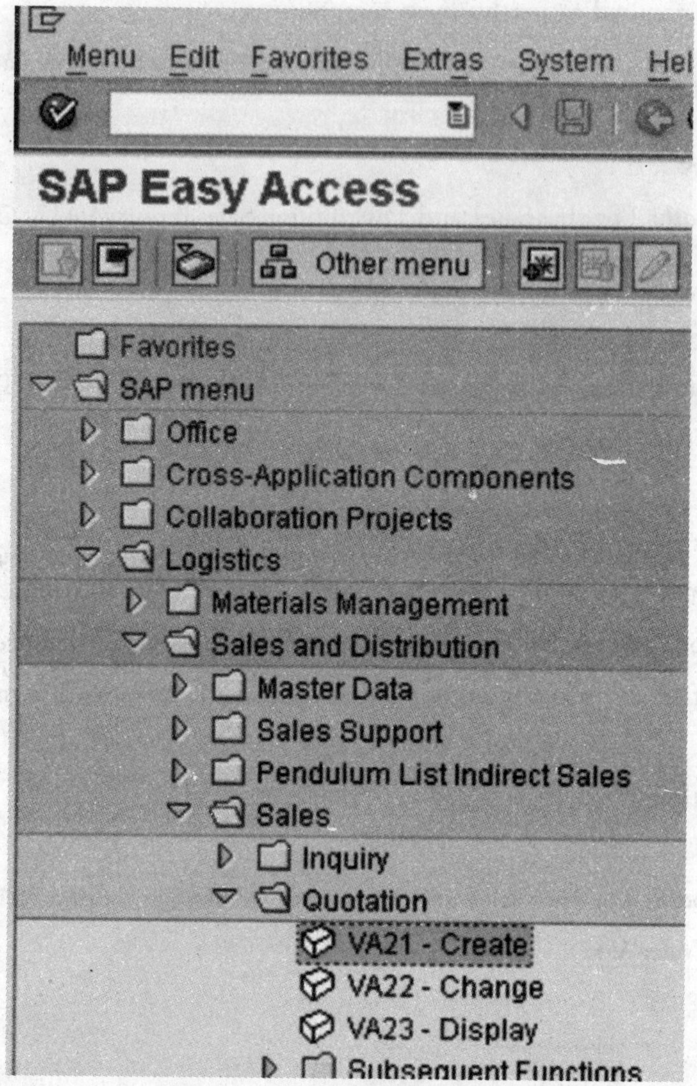

Step 2

Select Quotation type QT , Enter sales area information such as sales organization, distribution channel and division.

To create quotation with reference to inquiry, press "**Create with Reference**" button,

In the "**Create with Reference**" window select Inquiry tab.

You can type the inquiry number or search from existing enquiries here. Once your relevant inquiry number is found, press "**Copy**" button.

figure 35.56

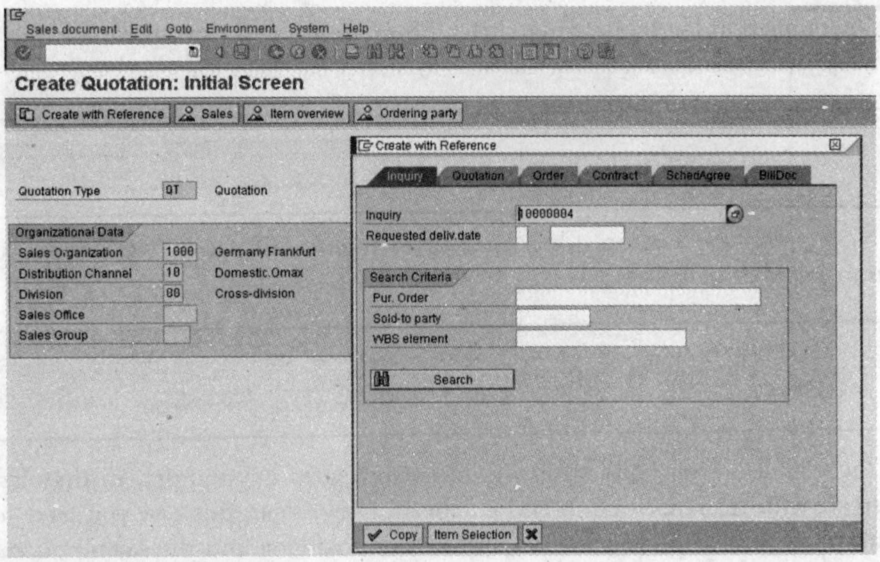

Step 3

Once you select "**Copy**" button, all the information from the selected inquiry will be fetched from system.

figure 35.57

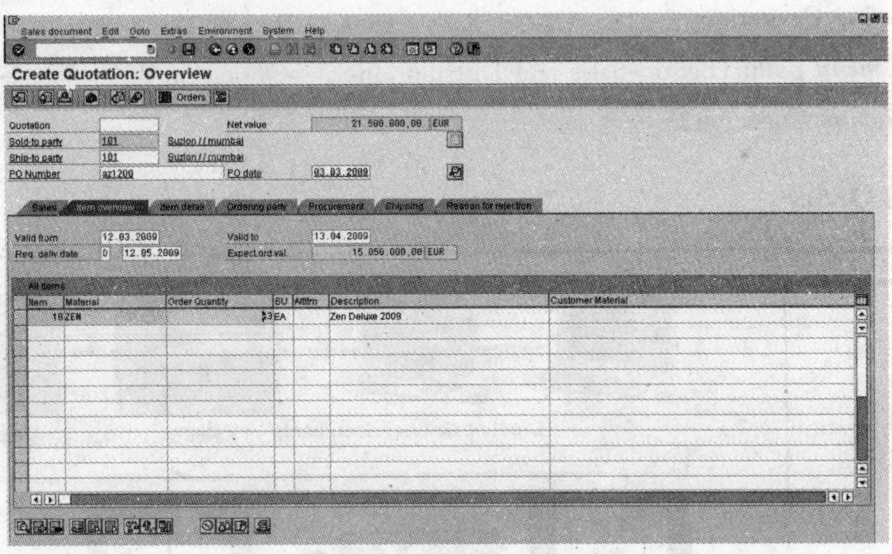

Enter Validity data such as valid from and valid to date for quotation. Here you can change quantity, price of the item. For changing of price select item condition icon and then enter price for each condition. We will be discussing in detail to manage condition master record in later part of this chapter.

Step 4

Check incompletion log by pressing Ctrl + F8 or from menu Edit-Incompletion Log. If the document is complete system should display message in status bar as below.

Document is complete

Now press save button. Once you save, system will flash message in your status bar with a quotation number as below.

Quotation 20000021 has been saved

You can also create quotation without referring to any inquiry, in that case you do not have to select create with reference option and go ahead. However in this case you have to enter all header and item information to complete the document. For changing and displaying quotation, select the below mentioned menu path

Changing Quotation

Select menu path: Logistics-Sales and Distribution-Sales-Quotation-VA22- Change

Transaction Code: VA22

Displaying Quotation

Select menu path: Logistics-Sales and Distribution-Sales-Quotation-VA23- Display

Transaction Code: VA23

Sales Order

figure 35.58

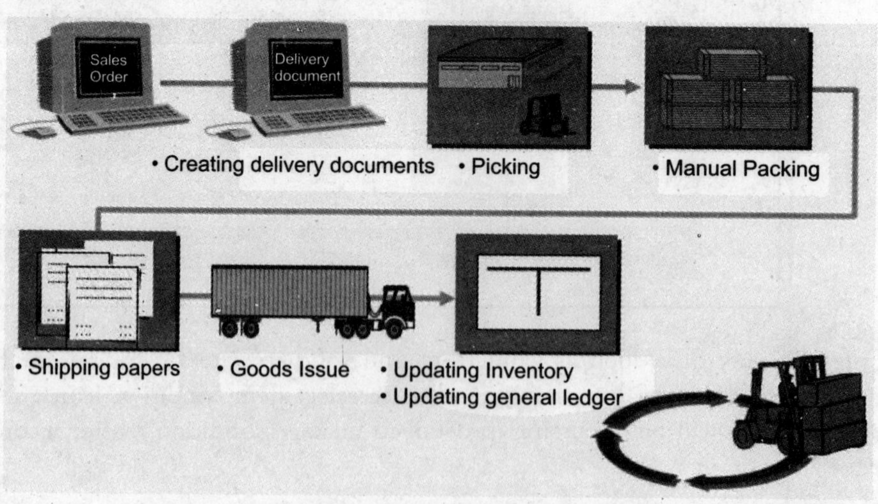

Above figure shows the sales and delivery process. The sales order is a contractual agreement between a sales organization and a sold-to party about delivering products or providing a service for defined prices, quantities and times.

In sales order processing, the system determines various functions such as availability check of material, checking credit limits, pricing, transferring requirements to production, scheduling delivery and generating output. You can also create new sales order with reference to quotation.

Sales order fetches data from customer master and material master for completing the process. Also condition master record is accessed for various pricing, tax defined for that customer and material.

Create Sales Order

Step 1

Select menu path: Logistics-Sales and Distribution-Sales-Order-VA01- Create

Transaction Code: VA01

figure 35.59

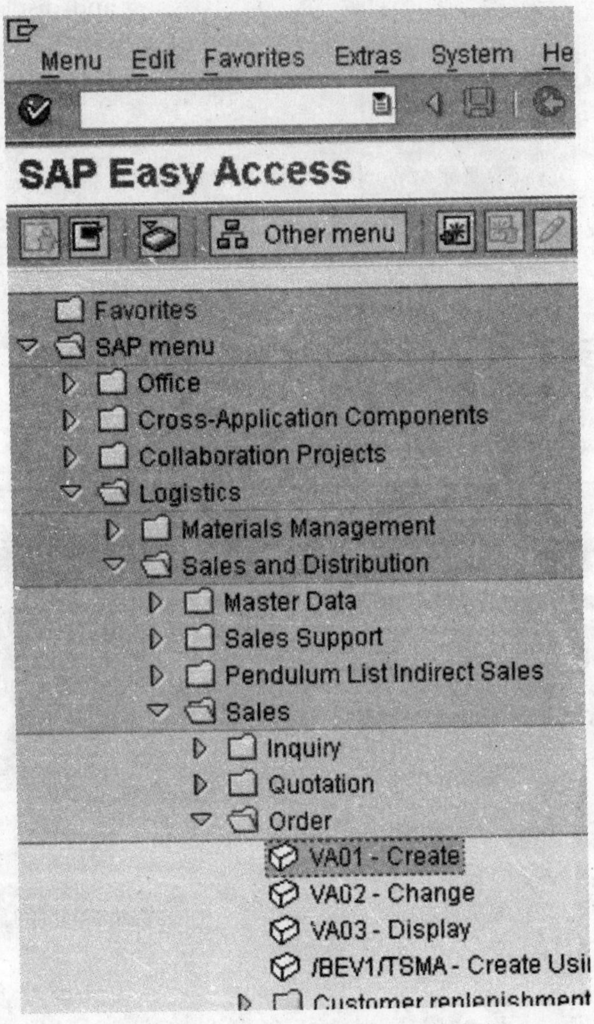

Step 2

In this step select order type OR (standard order) from the list. Enter sales area information such as sales organization, distribution channel and division.

figure 35.60

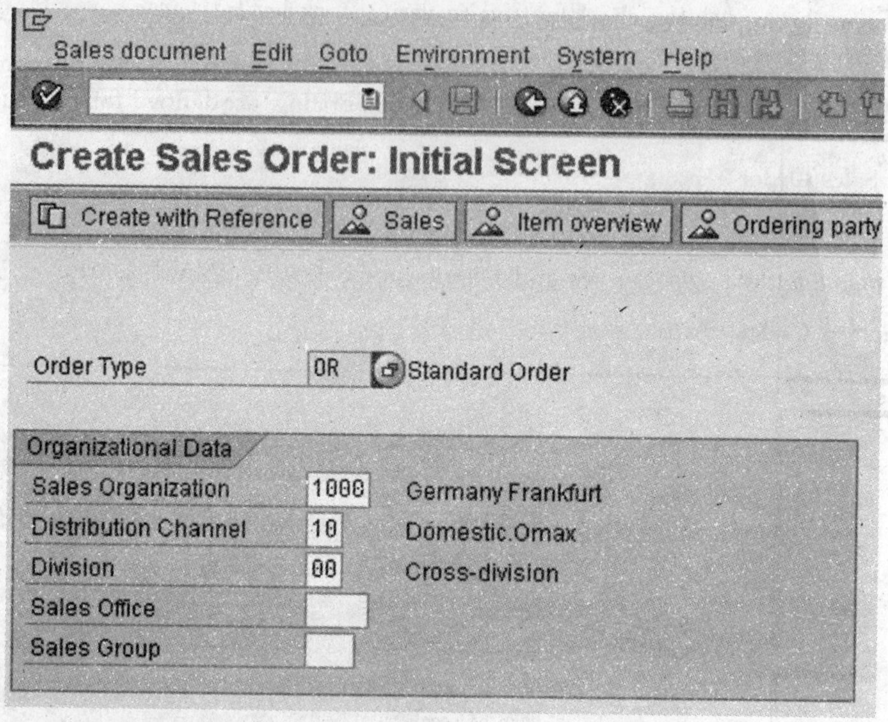

Step 3

Enter sold-to-party, ship-to-party, PO number and PO date in header.

figure 35.61

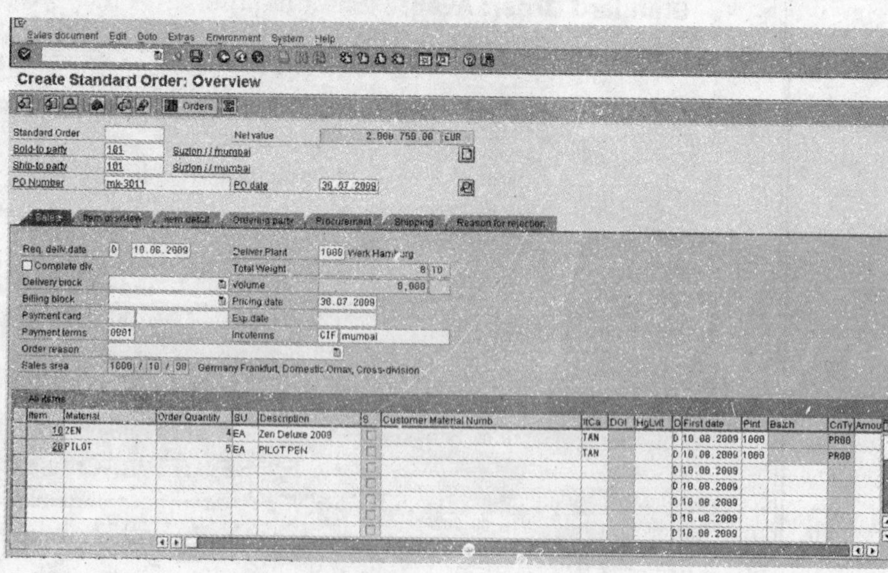

Enter delivery plant, item and quantity in of each item in the sales tab.

Here you can view customer, material and shipping information available in various tabs.

For entering pricing information press item condition button

Press the availability check button to verify stock levels. If you have enough stock available to meet the required quantity is sales order , press complete delivery button to come back to sales screen.

figure 35.62

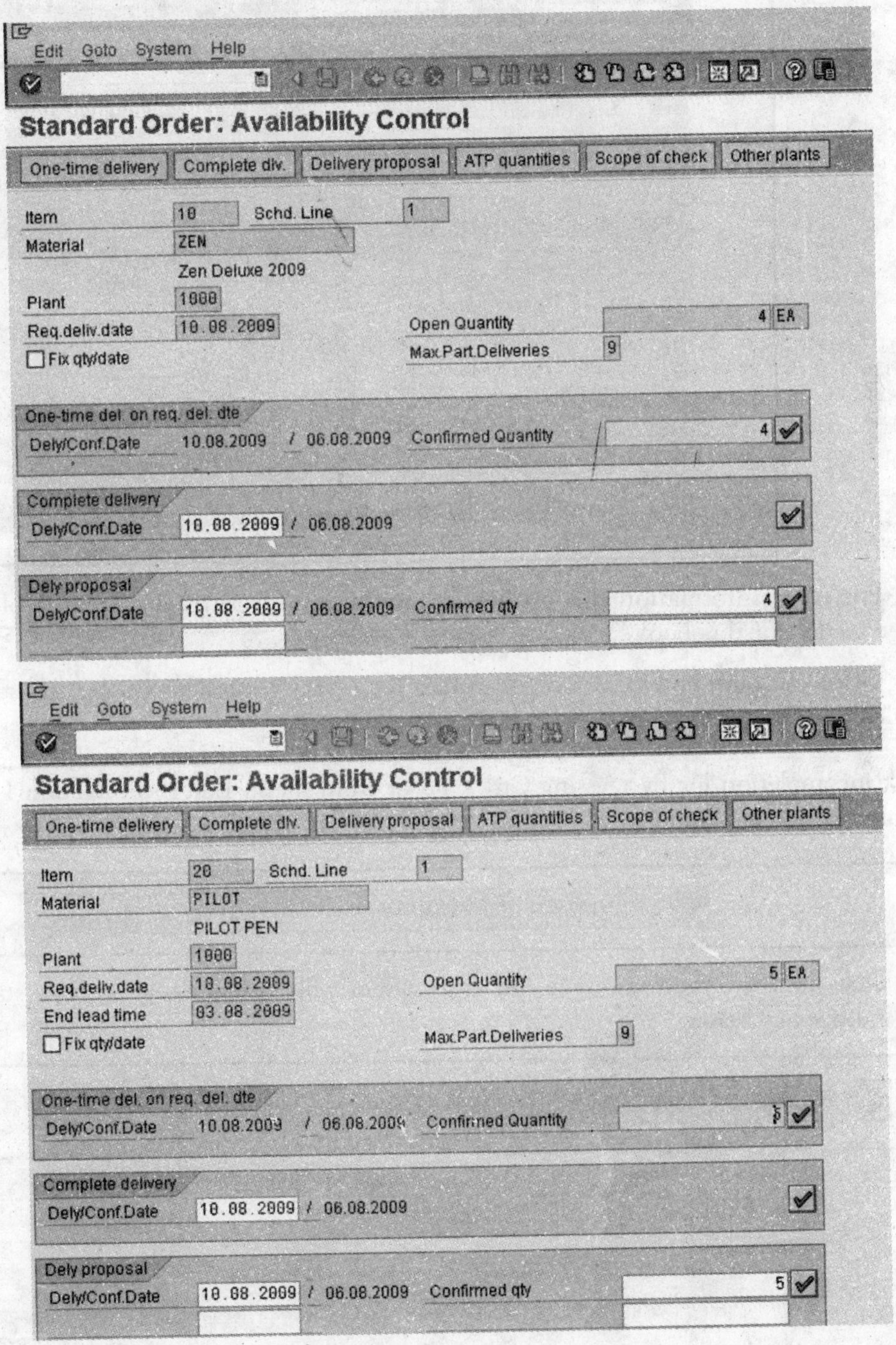

Step 4

Enter Pricing, discount, freight conditions here. As in figure the pricing condition entered as PR00 and value for PR00 is entered.

You can create condition master records for customer; material, certain groups etc, so that all relevant condition information be updated here automatically.

figure 35.63

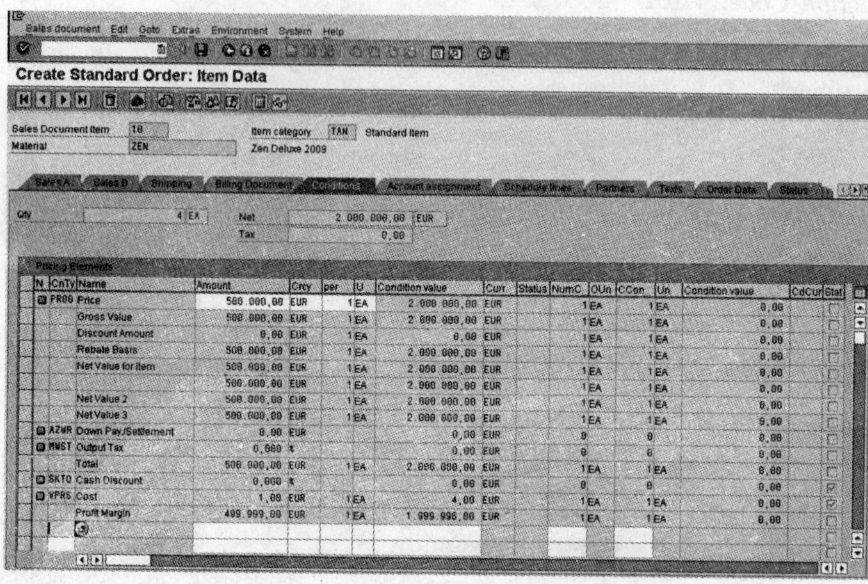

For more information this on how to create condition master records please refer condition master section of this book.

Once you have entered condition values press back button to reach original sales order screen.

Step 5

Check incompletion log by pressing Ctrl + F8 or from menu Edit-Incompletion Log. If the document is complete system should display message in status bar as below.

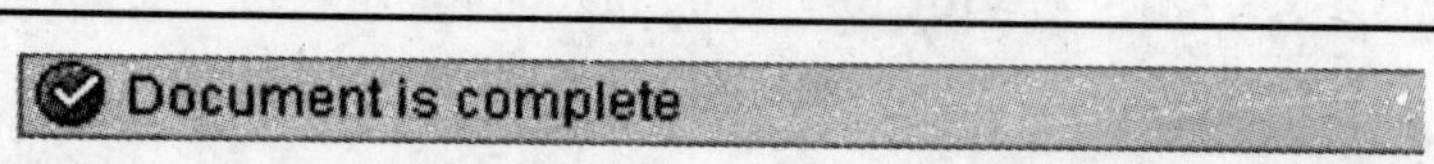

Now press save button. Once you save, system will flash message in your status bar with a sales order number as below.

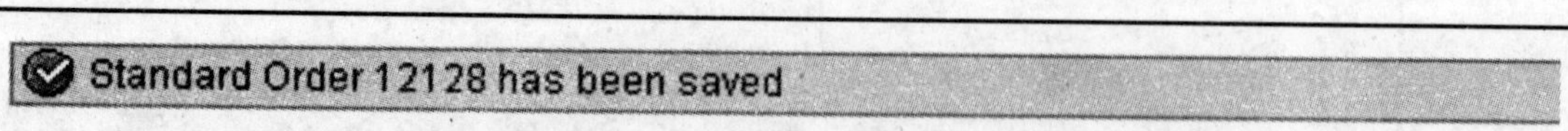

Change Sales Order

When you change a sales order, you can either change the data for individual items in the sales order, or you can make changes simultaneously to more than one item, by using the fast change function. To change sales order proceed as follows

Select menu path: Logistics-Sales and Distribution-Sales-Order-VA02- Change

Transaction Code: VA02

Select sales order form the list or enter sales order number to change. After changes made, you can save the document

Display Sales Order

To change sales order proceed as follows

Select menu path: Logistics-Sales and Distribution-Sales-Order-VA013-Display

Transaction Code: VA03

Select sales order form the list or enter sales order number to display.

Shipping

Shipping is an important part of the logistics In shipping processing, all delivery procedure decisions can be made at the start of the process such as business agreements with customer, recording requested regarding material, shipping conditions and priority.

Delivery is central to goods issue process. The outbound delivery supports all shipping activities including picking, packing, transportation and goods issue. When the outbound delivery is created, the shipping activities, such as picking or delivery scheduling, are initiated, and data that is generated during shipping processing is included in the delivery

Create Delivery

Step 1

Select menu path: Logistics-Sales and Distribution- Shipping and Transportation- Outbound Delivery-Create- Single Document- VL01N - With Reference to Sales Order

Transaction Code: VL01N

figure 35.64

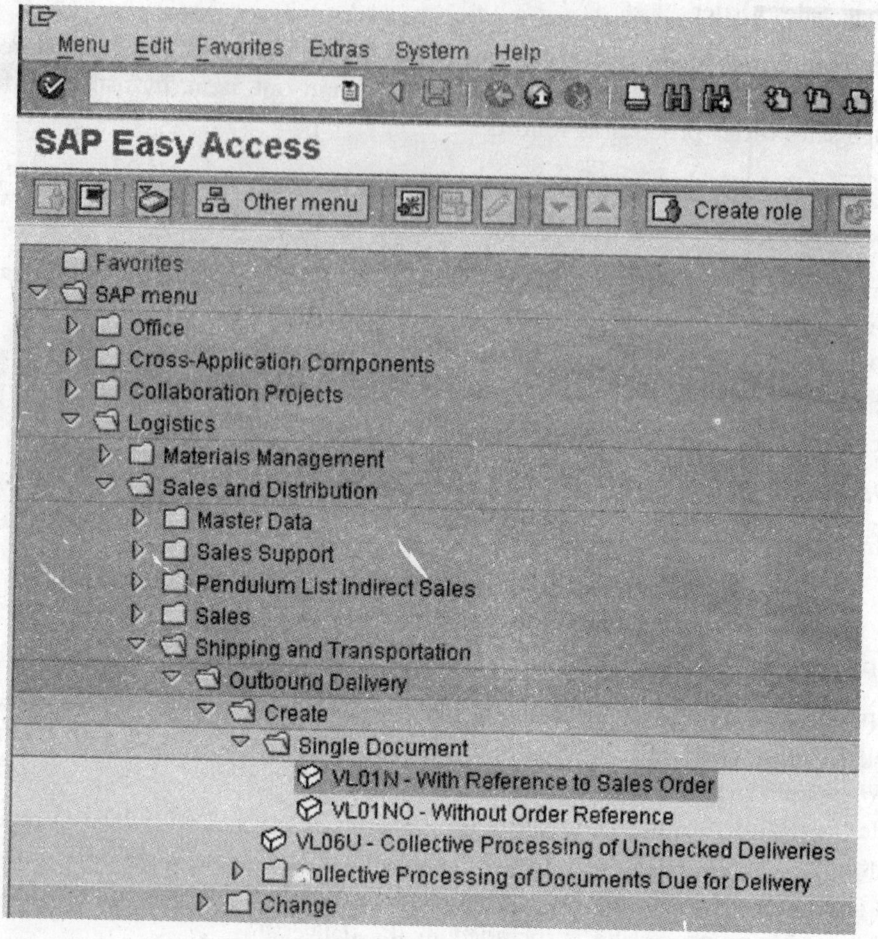

Step 2

Enter Shipping point in this screen.

Enter sales order number, and delivery type LF (outbound delivery).

figure 35.65

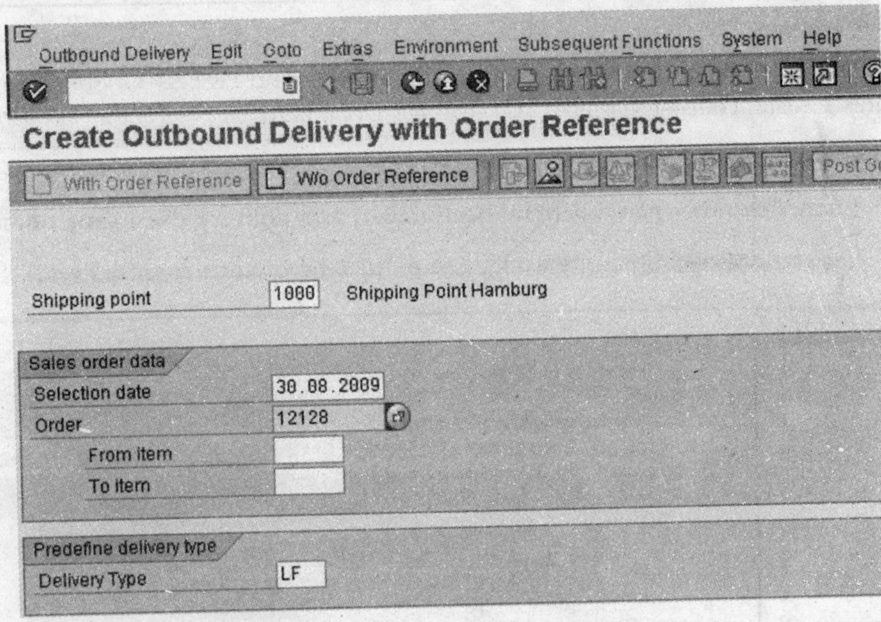

Step 3

In this screen you can view delivery items, item overview tab. All the items have to be picked and packed before goods issue. If you see the picking tab, you will find pick quantity is zero. The next step is to create a transfer order to be sent to warehouse where actual goods are located. To create a transfer order, select menu **Subsequent Function-Create Transfer order.**

System will ask to save your data, press yes to save information. On saving data system will generate a delivery document number as shown in figure.

figure 35.66

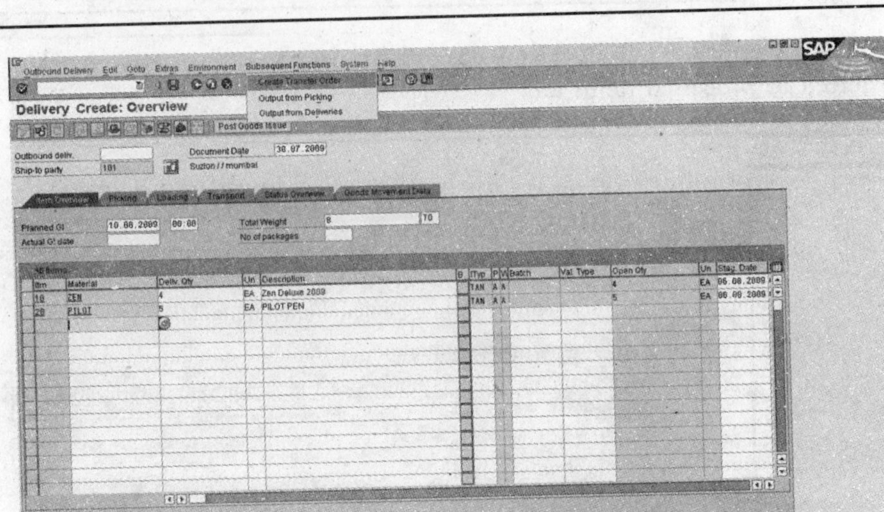

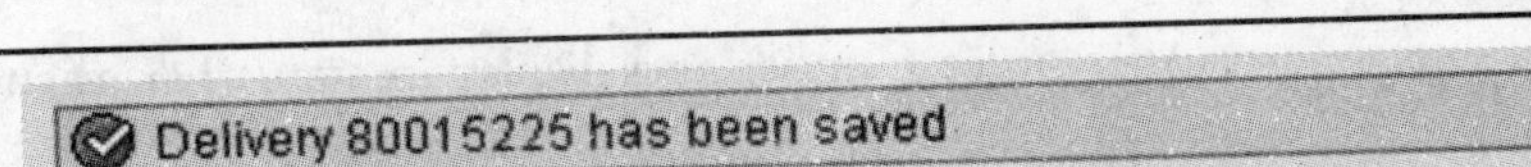

Step 4

Select menu path: Logistics- Logistics Execution- Outbound Process- Goods Issue for Outbound Delivery- Picking- Create Transfer Order- LT03 - Single Document

Transaction code: LT03

Enter delivering plant, warehouse number, and delivery document number.

Select AdoptPickQuantity as 1 (include picking quantities in delivery). Press Enter.

figure 35.67

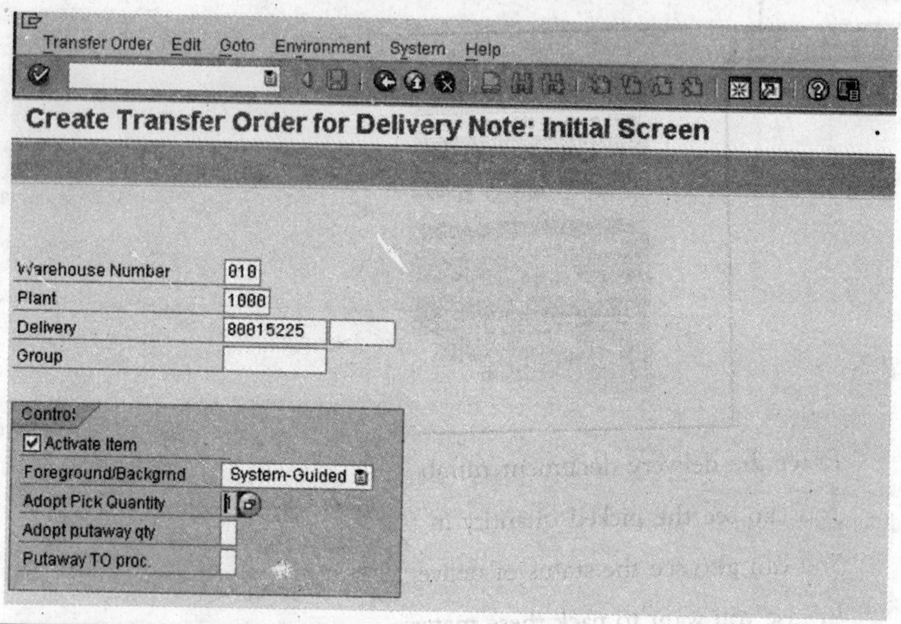

Press **Generate TO Item** button. All the Items in the active worklist will be processed and transferred to processed items tab.

figure 35.68

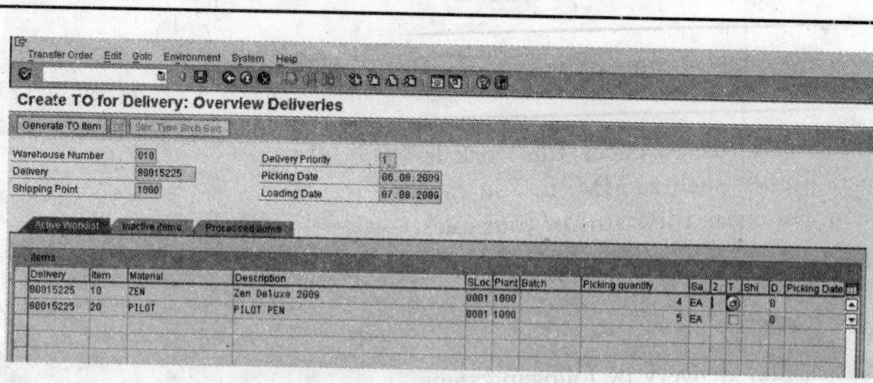

Press **save** button.

System will generate a transfer order number and display in status bar as shown in figure.

Step 5

Select menu path: Logistics-Sales and Distribution- Shipping and Transportation- Outbound Delivery-Change- VL02N - Single Document

Transaction Code: **VL02N**

figure 35.69

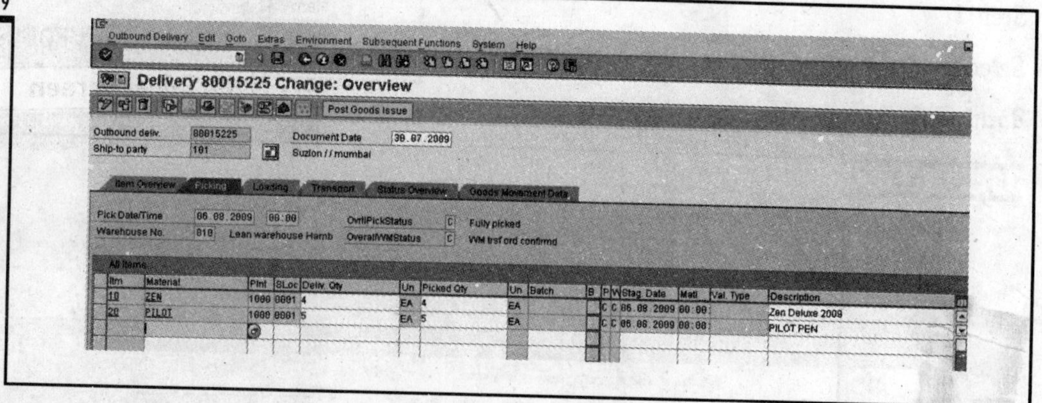

Enter the delivery document number to arrive at this screen.

You can see the picked quantity in the picking tab.

You can also see the status of delivery in **Status Overview** tab.

In case you want to pack these material with special packaging material, that process can be done by pressing packing button.

The next step is to issue goods, for the press "**Post Goods issue**" button. After PGI system will display message in status bar as follows.

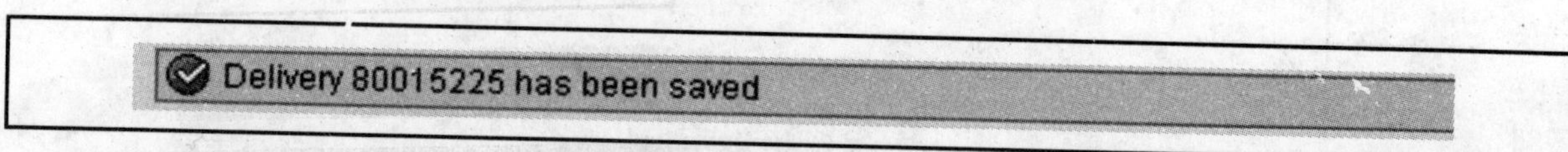

You may like to check the stock level of sold items after PGI by displaying stock report in transaction code such as MMBE. You can see that the stock has been reduced from the earlier level. Also you can check the status of your sales order and goods movement in VL02N –transaction, status tab.

Display Delivery

You can display delivery by following steps

Select menu path: Logistics-Sales and Distribution- Shipping and Transportation- Outbound Delivery-VL03N - Display

Transaction Code: **VL03N**

Enter the delivery document number or select from list. Press enter to view.

Billing

Billing is the final processing stage for a business transaction in Sales and Distribution.

Information on billing is available at every stage of order processing and delivery processing.

The Billing Process includes creation of invoices for delivery or services, creating Pro Forma invoices and issuing credit and debit memos, canceling billing transactions, processing rebates if any and transferring billing data to Financial Accounting (FI).

The billing document can be created with reference to delivery document

Step 1

Select menu path: Logistics-Sales and Distribution- Billing- Billing Document- VF01 - Create

Transaction Code: VF01

figure 35.70

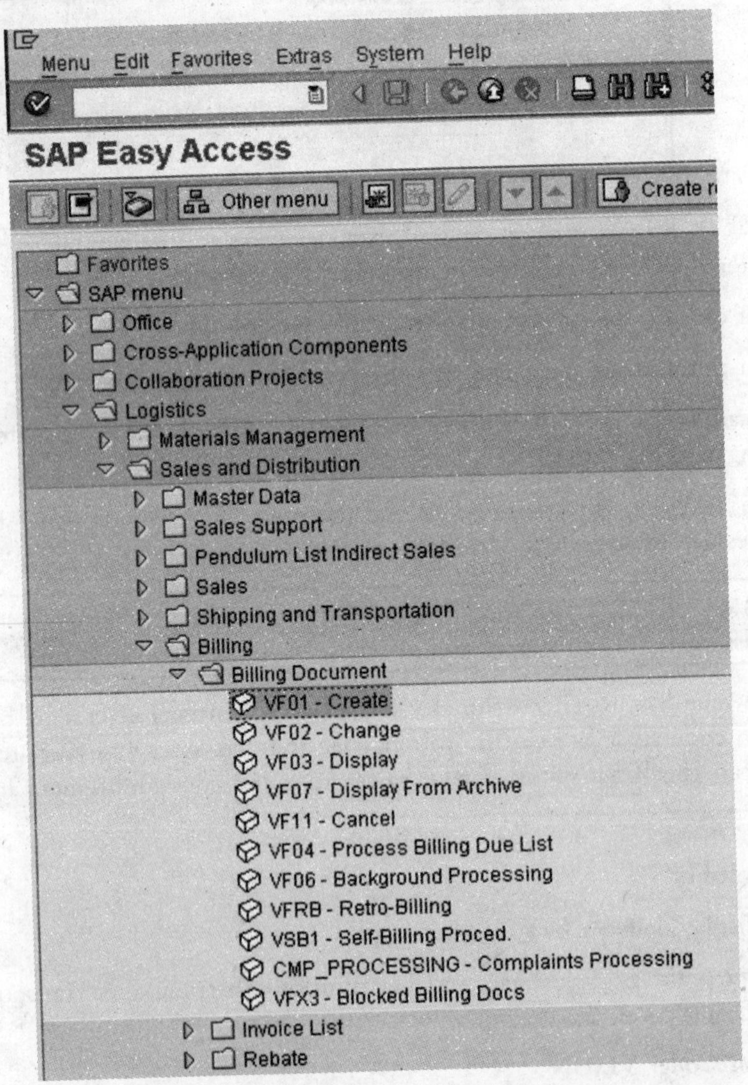

Step 2

Select Billing type as F2, Enter billing date.

Enter Delivery document number for processing and press Enter.

System will process billing, and will take you to next screen where you can see details of individual items.

figure 35.71

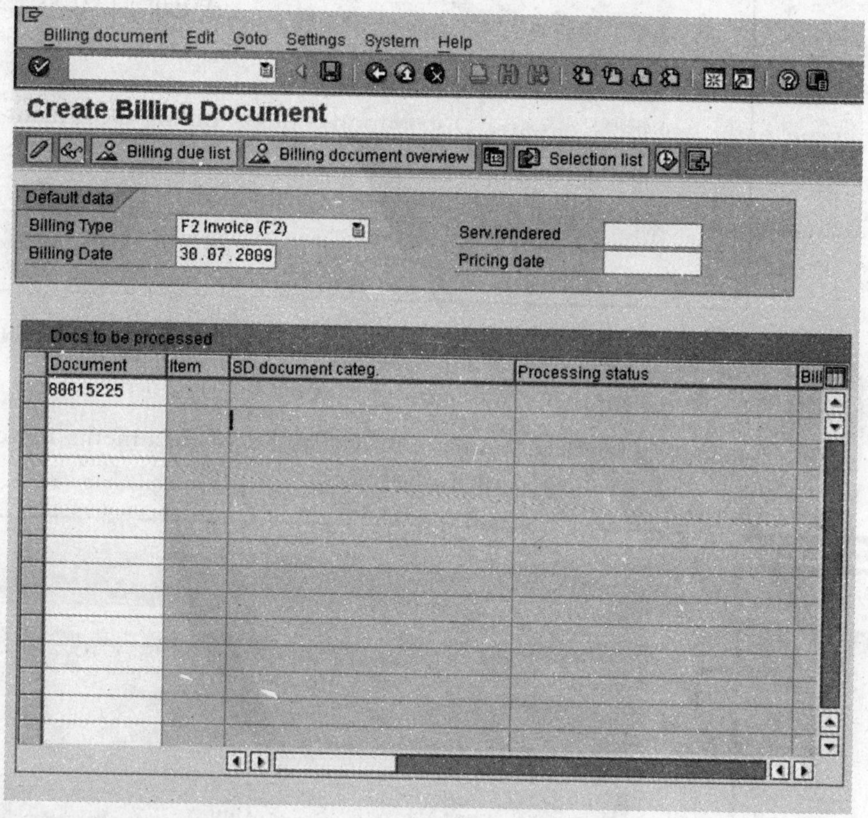

Press Save button, system will generate billing document number and will flash on status bar as below.

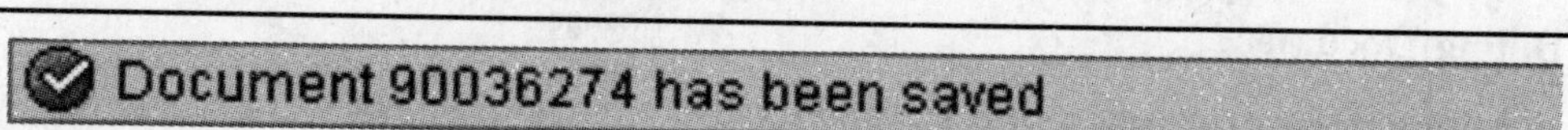

Step 3

Select menu path: Logistics-Sales and Distribution- Billing- Billing Document- VF03 - Display

Transaction Code: VF02

figure 35.72

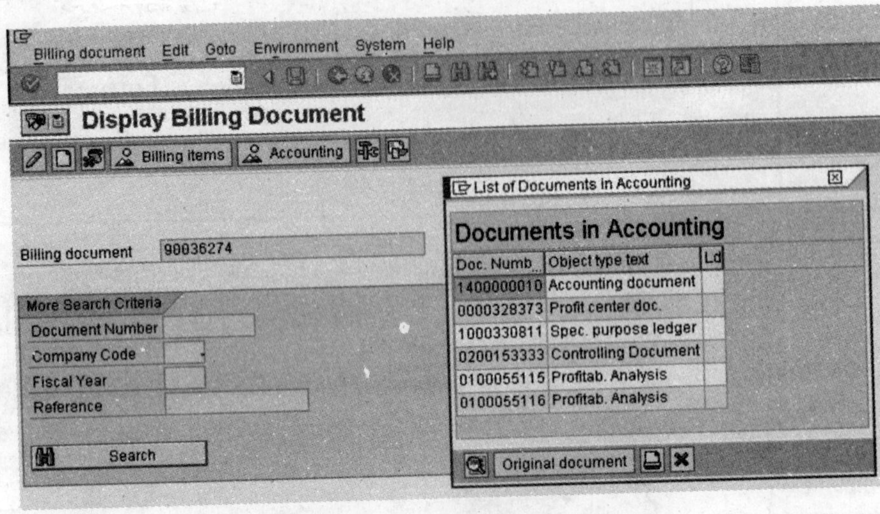

As we discussed earlier billing process transfers data to Financial Accounting (FI).

Select the menu path as mentioned above, enter billing document number.

Press "Accounting" button. System will display list of documents in accounting. You can view each document by double clicking each document.

figure 35.73

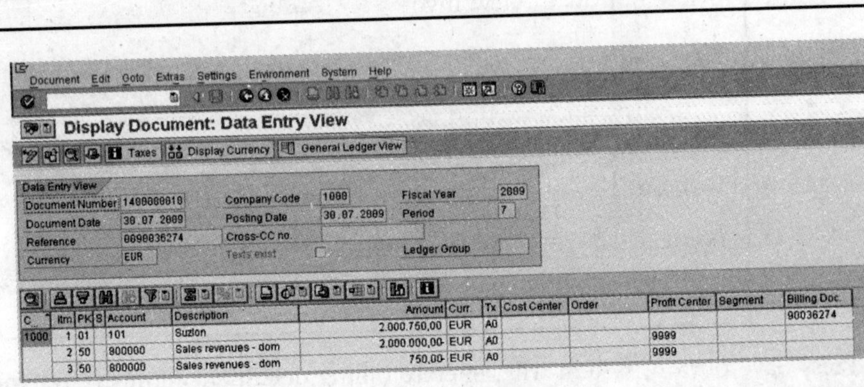

Display Billing Document

To display billing document follow the steps as below.

Select menu path: Logistics-Sales and Distribution- Billing- Billing Document- VF03 - Display

Transaction Code: VF03

Enter the billing document number or select from the list. Press Enter.

Printing Invoice

Select menu path: Logistics-Sales and Distribution- Billing- Billing Document- VF03 - Display

Transaction Code: VF03

figure 35.74

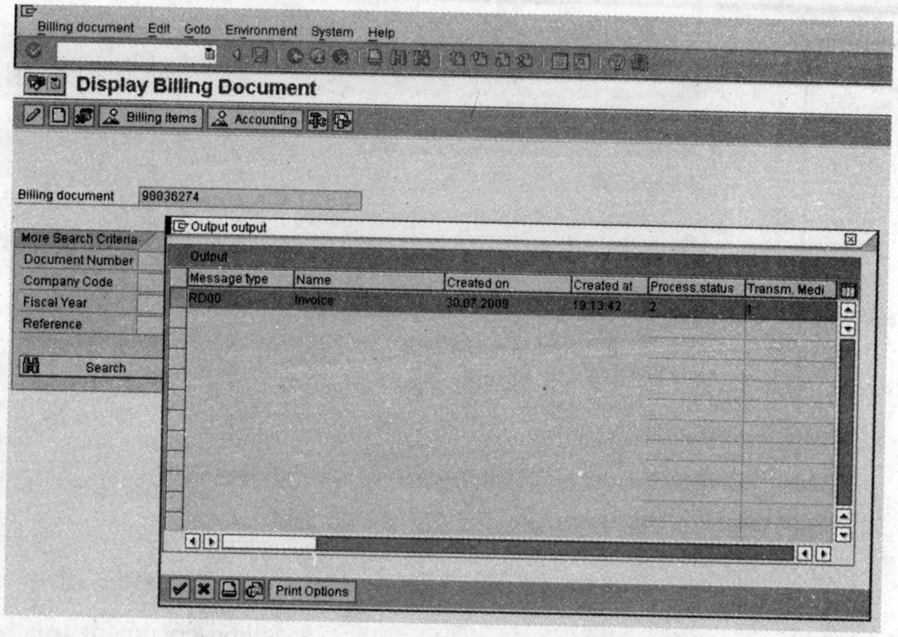

Enter Billing document number. Select Billing Document-Issue Output To from menu bar Press the **Print Preview** button to view invoice and press **Print** button to print invoice.

Payment Processing

The final in the process is Payment execution. After we have created invoice for customer, it is time now to receive payment from customers for the good or services you have delivered. In this Process the customer account is debited and corresponding account will be cleared.

Before processing payment for customers it is prudent to see existing customer balance. For displaying customer balance follow steps below.

figure 35.75

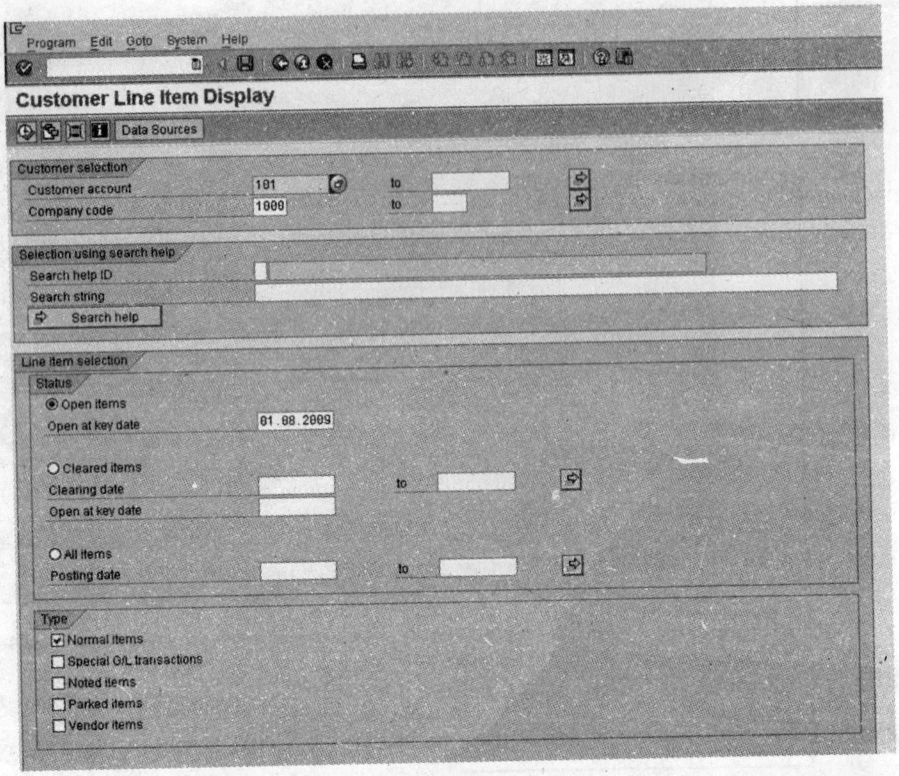

Select menu path: Logistics- Sales and Distribution- Credit Management- Item- FBL5N - Display/ Change

Transaction Code: FBL5N

Enter Customer Account number and company code. Execute by pressing "Execute" button.

You can see a list all transactions being done by this customer. The transaction marked by rectangle is our latest transaction we are discussing with. By double clicking on the transaction line you can view details inside.

figure 35.76

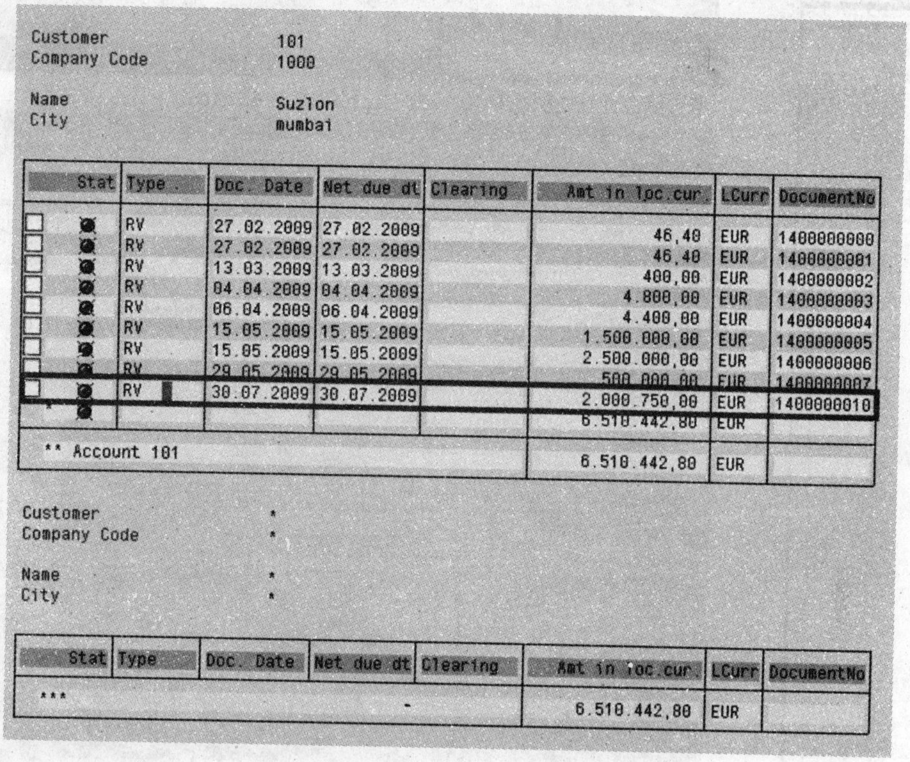

Customer 101
Company Code 1000

Name Suzlon
City mumbai

Stat	Type	Doc. Date	Net due dt	Clearing	Amt in loc.cur.	LCurr	DocumentNo
	RV	27.02.2009	27.02.2009		46,40	EUR	1400000000
	RV	27.02.2009	27.02.2009		46,40	EUR	1400000001
	RV	13.03.2009	13.03.2009		400,00	EUR	1400000002
	RV	04.04.2009	04.04.2009		4.800,00	EUR	1400000003
	RV	06.04.2009	06.04.2009		4.400,00	EUR	1400000004
	RV	15.05.2009	15.05.2009		1.500.000,00	EUR	1400000005
	RV	15.05.2009	15.05.2009		2.500.000,00	EUR	1400000006
	RV	29.05.2009	29.05.2009		500.000,00	EUR	1400000007
	RV	30.07.2009	30.07.2009		2.000.750,00	EUR	1400000010
*					6.510.442,80	EUR	
** Account 101					6.510.442,80	EUR	

Customer *
Company Code *

Name *
City *

Stat	Type	Doc. Date	Net due dt	Clearing	Amt in loc.cur.	LCurr	DocumentNo
***					6.510.442,80	EUR	

Let's start payment posting. Follow these steps below to post payments.

Step 1

Select menu path: Accounting-Financial Accounting-Accounts Receivable-Document Entry-F-28 - Incoming Payments

Transaction Code: F-28

figure 35.77

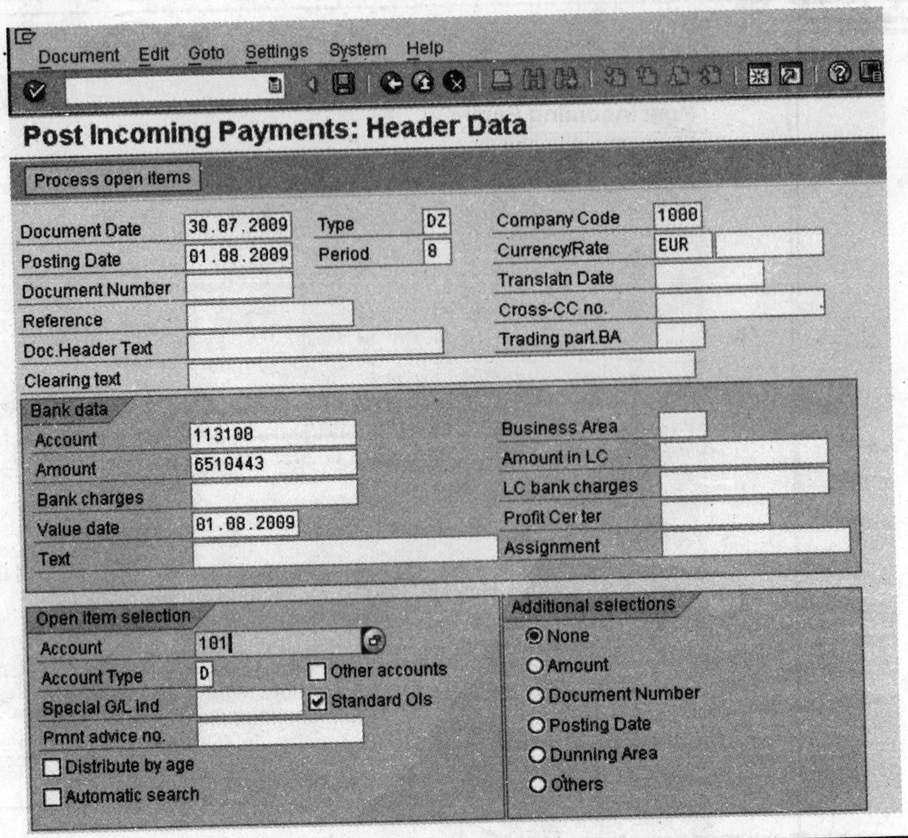

Step 2

Enter the document date, company code, currency. Enter Bank account number. Enter amount of payment. Enter the customer number. Once all relevant information is entered choose the **Process Open Items** or press Enter.

Here you can see again the list of transaction to be cleared. You have a option to clear multiple transacting by selecting them for assigning payment.

You can assign multiple transactions by double clicking each.

Here also you can offer discount to customer for early payment.

Enter the discount amount here in cash discount column for relevant transaction.

figure 35.78

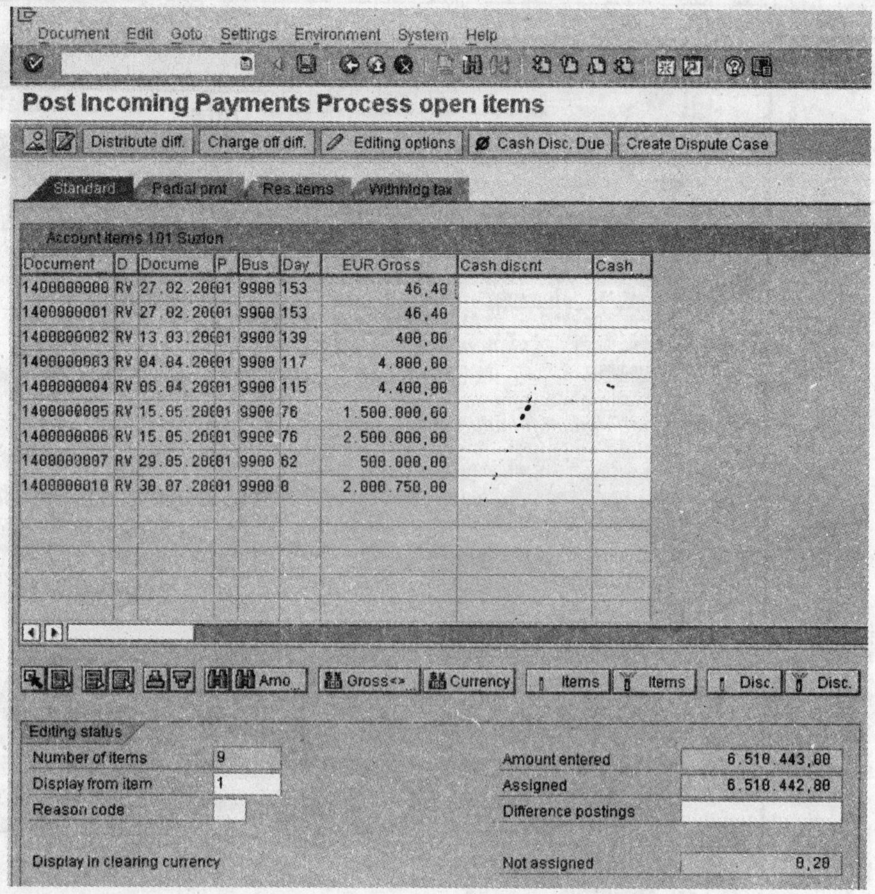

Select Residual items tab in the screen, here you can see your relevant transaction line is reduced by the discount amount and its color is black.

In the residual items filed, double click to cheek difference (Overpayment). It may display a warning message if the payment amount differs than the actual amount to be posted.

Press enter to go ahead if it is a minor difference amount otherwise you may have reassign the payment items.

figure 35.79

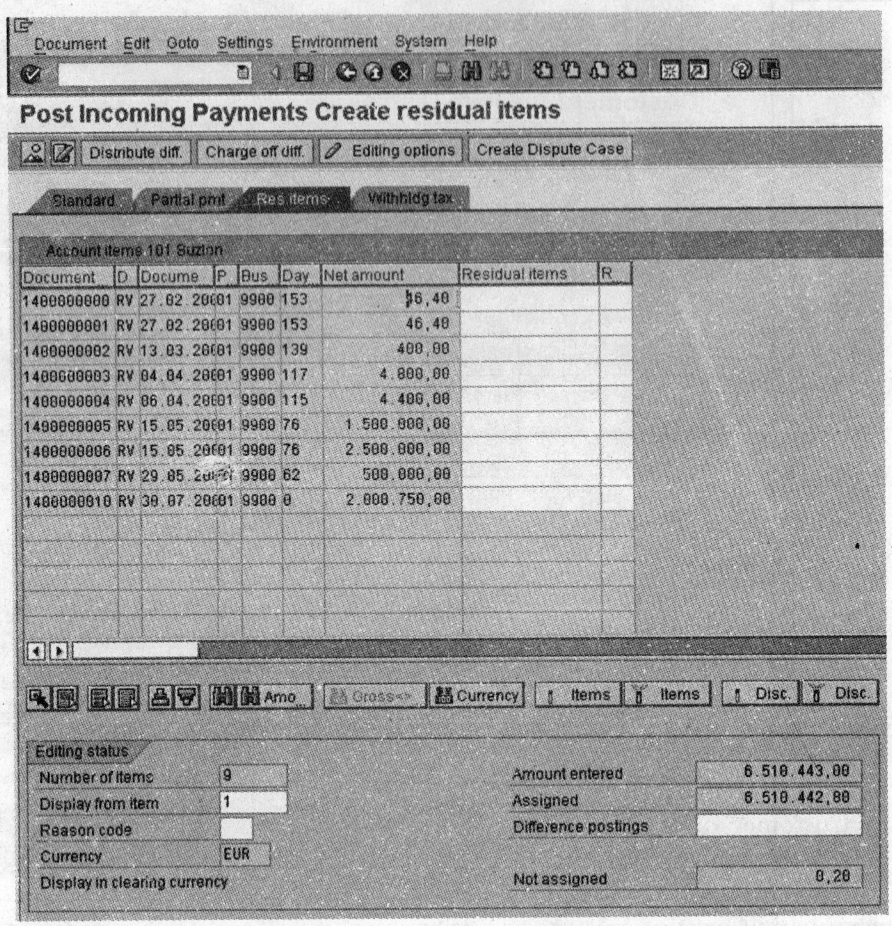

Step 3

Then press **save** button. Your status bar will display a message as below.

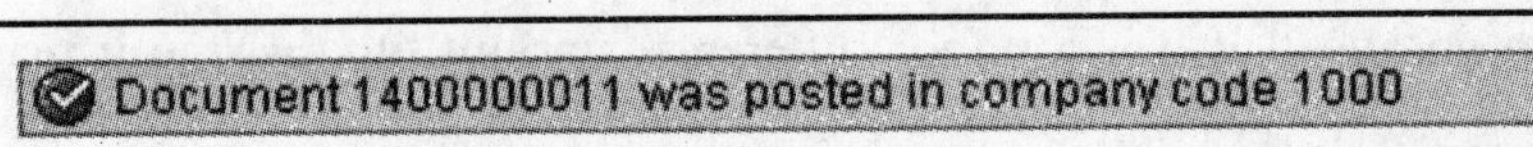

Now you can check the customer balance after posting in transaction FBL5N.

figure 35.80

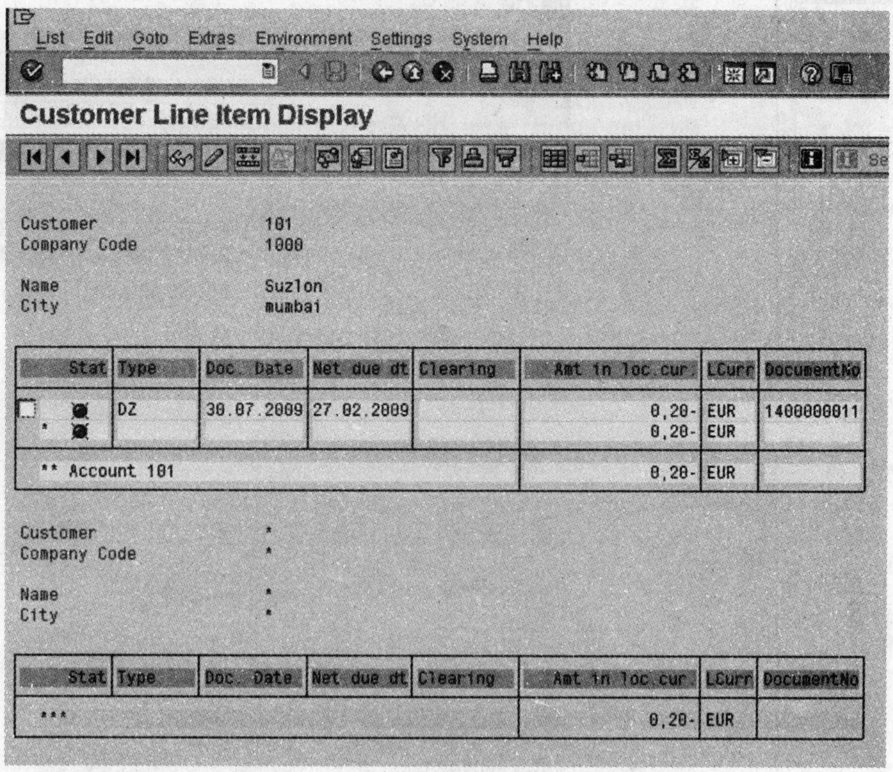

Checking Customer Credit Limit

You can check customer credit limit by following steps.

Select menu path: Logistics- Sales and Distribution- Credit Management- Master data- FD32 - Change

Transaction Code: FD32

figure 35.81

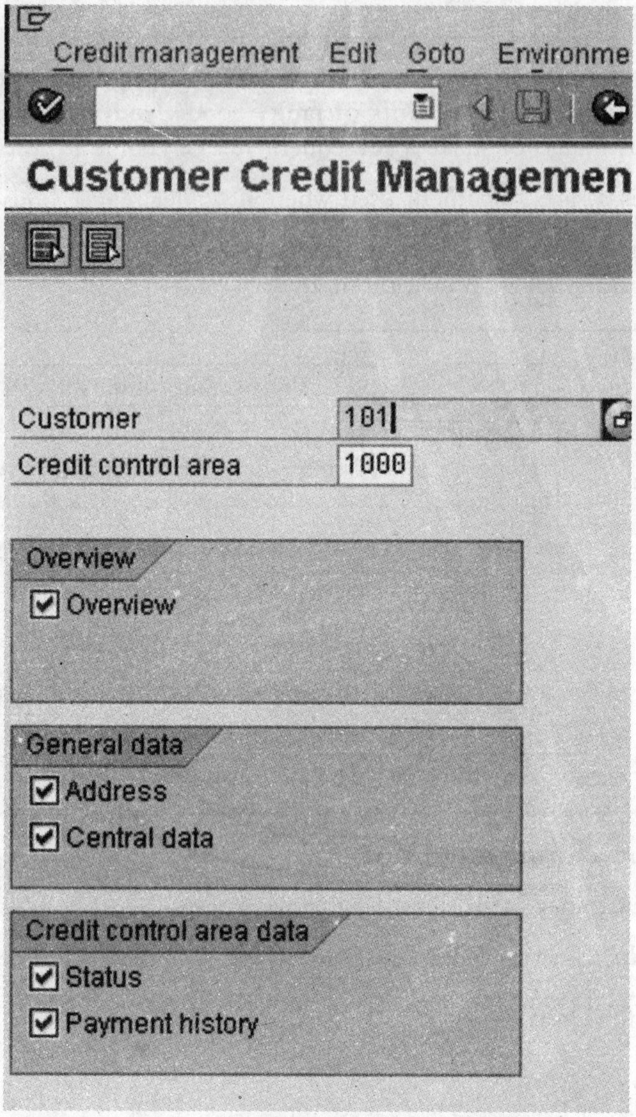

Enter customer number and credit control area. Select the options from checkbox. Press Enter.

You can see, credit limit, credit exposure, risk category, dunning data and payment history of customer. Here you can set new credit limits for customers.

SALES RETURN

It's absolutely normal to receive complaints from customer regarding products or services you are offering. If the customer complaints of faulty goods, you normally take back goods and send the customer a credit memo or make a subsequent free of charge delivery of the goods.

A return is a sales document used when customer sends goods back.

A return is normally created with reference to sales order or billing document no. However you can also create return sales order without any reference.

figure 35.82

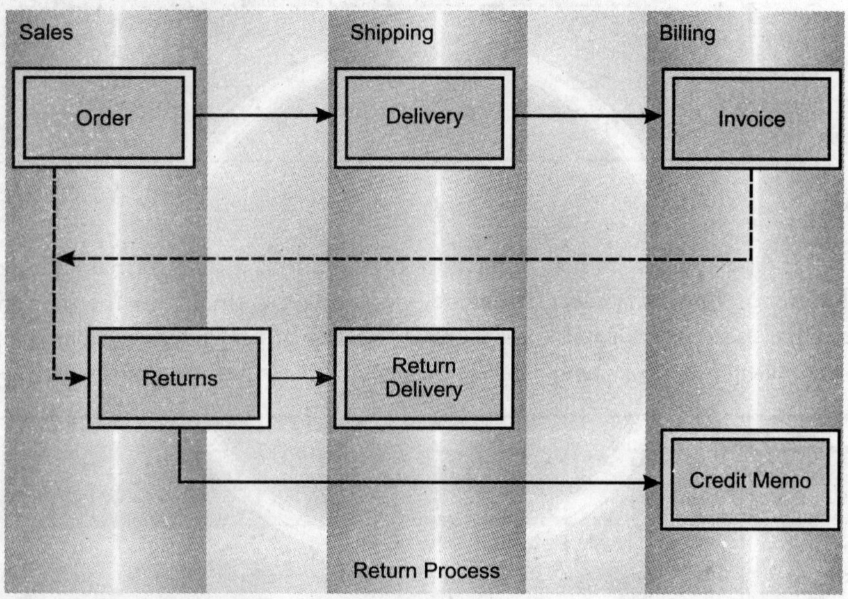

Let's see how return process is being handled in SAP R/3. Follow the steps as below.

Step 1

Select menu path: Logistics-Sales and Distribution-Sales-Order-VA01- Create

Transaction Code: VA01

figure 35.83

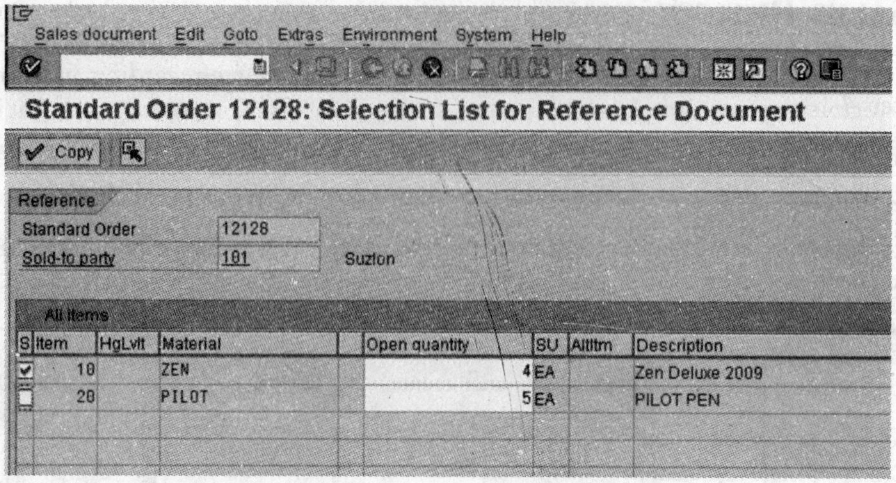

Step 2

Select order type "RE" from list. Enter sales organization, distributional channel, division. Press "Create With Reference Button". Select Order no. or billing document no for reference. Press "Copy" button to access that sales order. In case your order consists of very large number of items then you may press "Item Selection" button, where you can select items for return processing.

figure 35.84

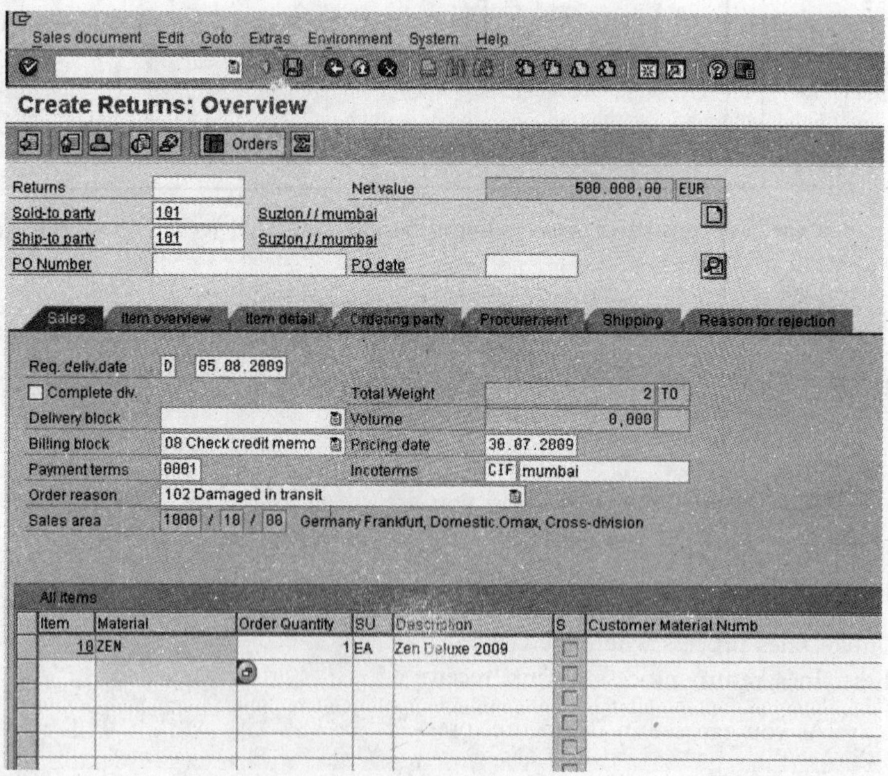

Step 3

Enter the number of quantity for return in order quantity column. Make sure you enter order reason before saving document.

Step 4

Press save button, your status bar will display a return document number as shown in figure

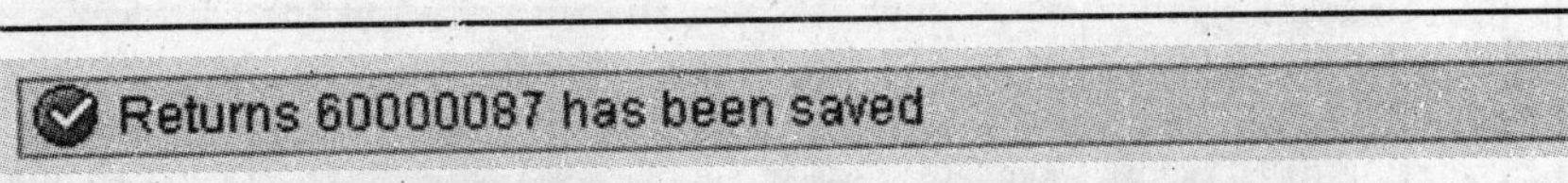

Step 5

After returns order is created, we will create return delivery of goods from customer.

Select menu path: Logistics-Sales and Distribution- Shipping and Transportation- Outbound Delivery- Create- Single Document- VL01N - With Reference to Sales Order

Transaction Code: VL01N

figure 35.85

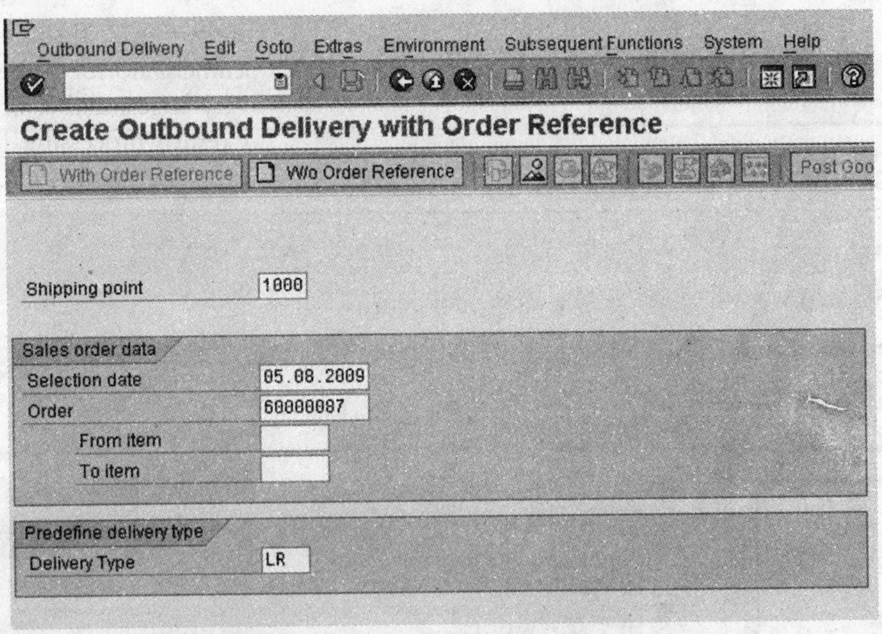

Enter Shipping point where you are going to receive goods, Enter return order number and delivery type "LR". Press Enter.

Step 6

Unlike sales process where we created transfer order and picking, here it's not necessary to create all these. In a return process we just receive goods from customer.

As you can see in the figure, press "Post Goods Receipt" button to complete the return process.

figure 35.86

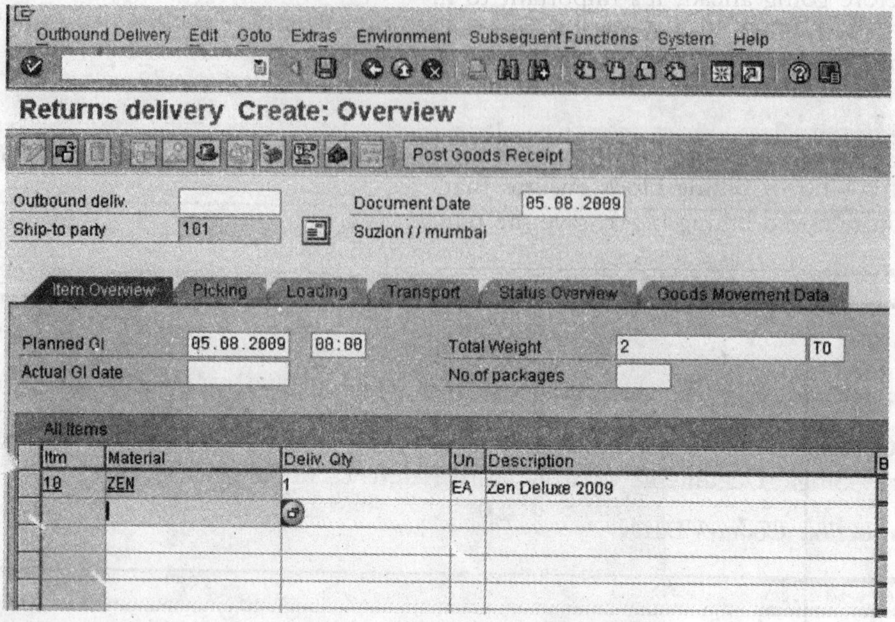

System will display a return deliver document number on your status bar as shown in figure.

Step 7

In this step we will create credit memo for returns.

Select menu path: Logistics-Sales and Distribution- Billing- Billing Document- VF01 - Create

Transaction Code: VF01

figure 35.87

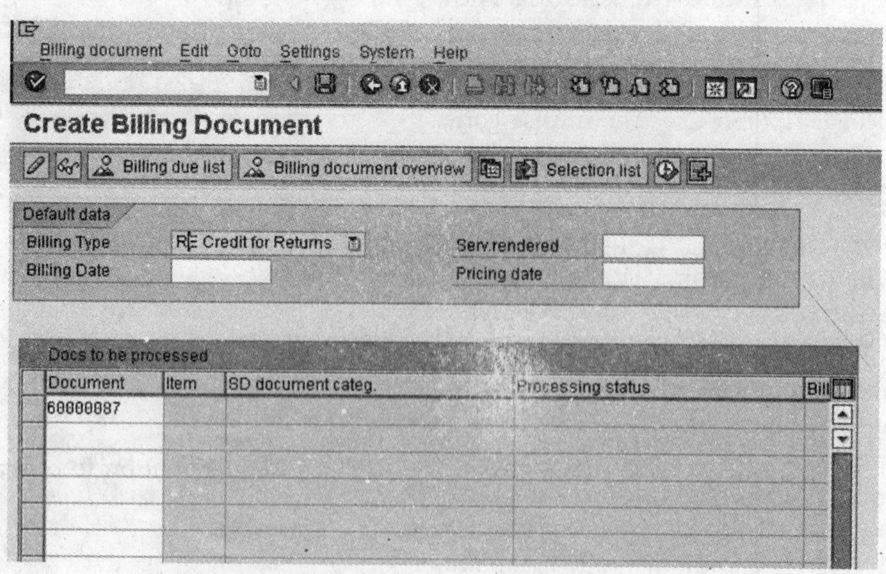

Before going ahead, it's important to make sure you check if the billing is blocked for return delivery. For that you have to open return sales order in change mode (VA02).

Select billings block option to blank.

This will allow you to process credit memo creation.

This kind of billing block ensures that unauthorized credit memo processing to be restricted. Once you removed billing block, save the return sales order and come back to billing screen again.

figure 35.88

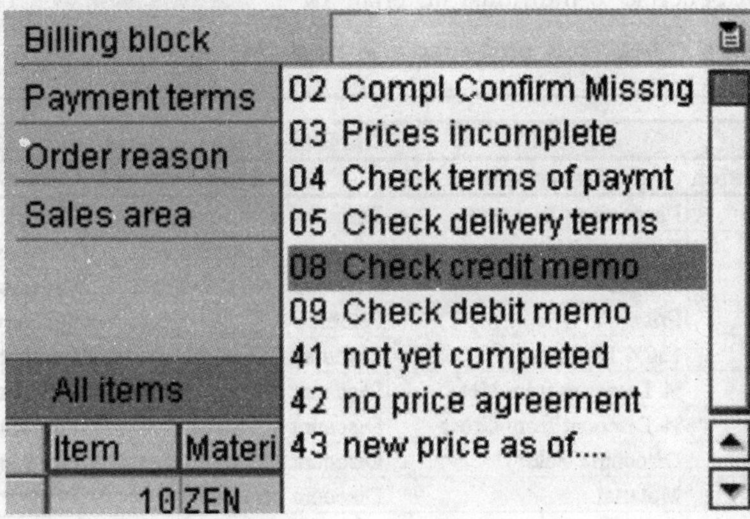

Step 8

Save the billing document, your status bar will display a message as shown in figure.

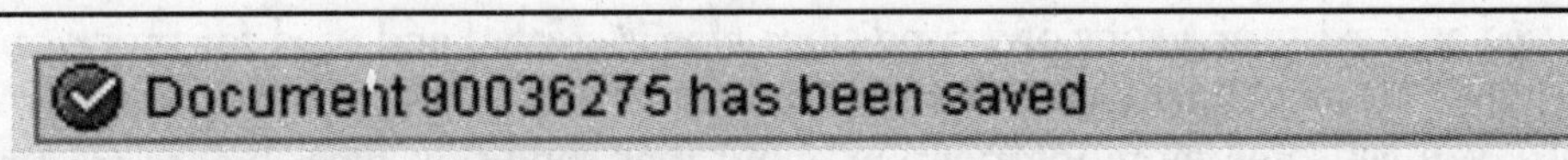

Similarly you can create Debit memo requests, Debit memo request are normally created if the prices calculated is too low. The invoice correction request works in the same way as credit and debit memo requests, but here you enter the price or quantity that should have been calculated. The system then calculates the difference and creates either a debit or a credit memo, depending on whether the difference is negative or positive

If the customer complains (for example, that they received the incorrect quantity) you can send them the extra material later free of charge. This free-of-charge subsequent delivery always made with reference to sales order.

CONDITION RECORDS

The purpose of Condition records is to allow you to store and retrieve pricing data in the system. All the pricing elements of your daily business such as the prices, discounts, and surcharges for freight and taxes can be accessed automatically if condition records are defined for each. You can define as many condition records as you want for the different pricing elements for any validity period. System retrieves condition records for relevant document and determines individual pricing elements such as price, discount, and surcharges during processing.

Pricing elements are usually managed at sales organization level. When you create condition record you have to mention appropriate organizational level for each condition. Apart form this you may define conditions pertaining to certain group level such as product groups or consumer groups.

Conditions may be broadly classified as header condition and item conditions. Header conditions such as freight, insurance are applicable to complete document. Item conditions such as material discount are applicable to individual material.

Below is the list of frequently used condition types.

Condition Types			
Condition	**Description**	**Type**	**Value**
HA00	Percentage Discount	Discount or surcharge	Percentage
HB00	Discount (Value)	Discount or surcharge	Fixed amount
KF00	Freight	Discount	Gross weight dependent
PR00	Price	Prices	Quantity dependent
R100	100% Discount	Discount	Percentage
RA00	% Discount from Net	Discount	Percentage
RA01	% Discount from Gross	Discount	Percentage
RB00	Discount (Value)	Discount	Fixed amount
K004	Material	Discount on Material	Percentage
K005	Customer/Material	Discount on Material	Quantity dependent
K007	Customer Discount	Discount on Material	Percentage
K030	Customer/material group	Discount on Material	Percentage

These conditions types are standard condition types offered by SAP R/3. During implementation these may be used as it exists or a copy of a conditions type is created and used for processing. Generally the condition types created during customization starts with 'Z'. If you encounter any Z condition types, make sure you get some more information about that condition types before creating condition records.

Creating Condition Records

Select menu path: Logistics-Logistics Execution- Master Data- Conditions- Discounts/Surcharges- Others-VK11 Create

Transaction Code: VK11

figure 35.89

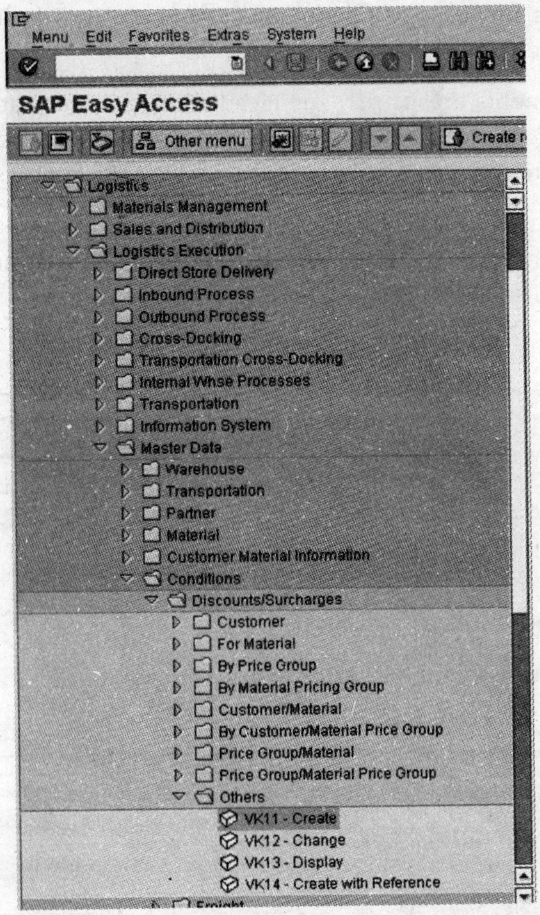

Let's create a condition record for condition type PR00 (Price).

Step 1

In the condition type field, enter condition type as PR00 or select from the list.

Now press "Key Combination" .You will be asked to select from three options as below.

- Customer/Material with release status
- Price list category/currency/material/with release status
- Material with release status

Lets select the third option i.e. Material with release status. This option will let you define condition for material.

figure 35.90

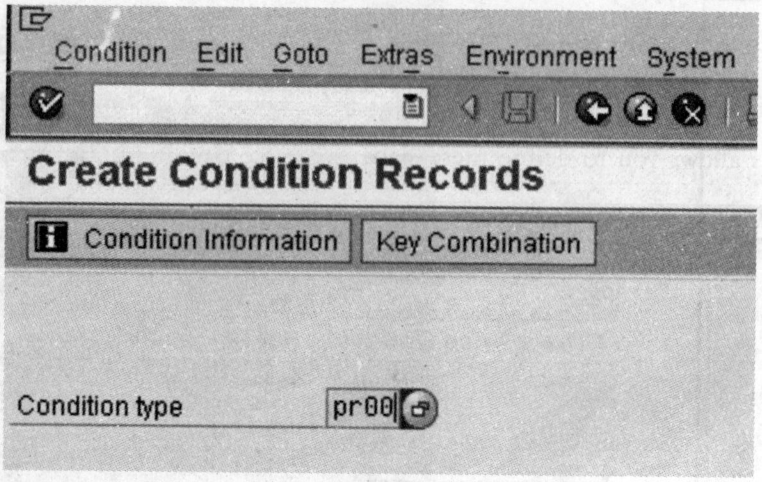

Step 2

Enter sales organization, distribution channel.

Enter the material, and the price in relevant columns. You may enter valid from and valid to dates within which the price is effective for material.

figure 35.91

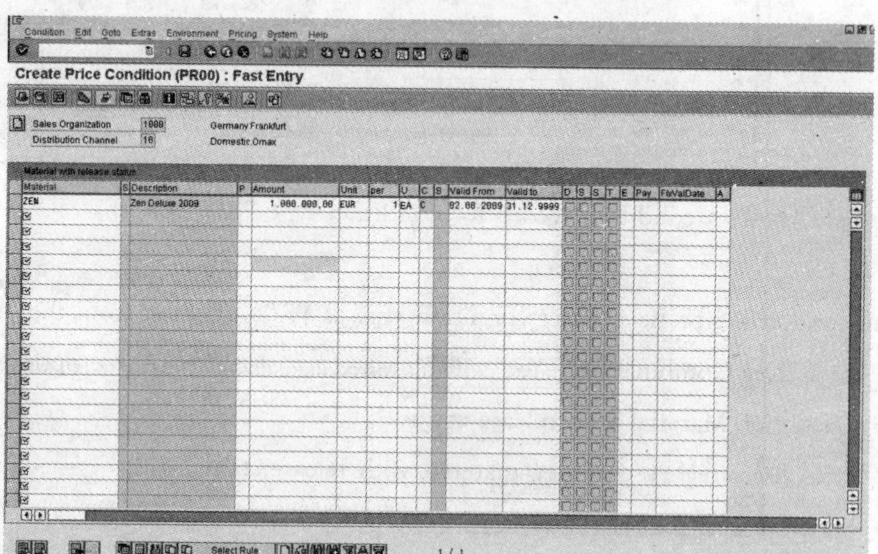

Step 3

Press Save button, your status bar will display message as below.

Defining Scales

You may want to define scales in pricing. For example you may create a price condition for certain quantity of material but you maintain slab for this. If your quantity crosses the slab, you may offer different price structure to customer.

Scales allows you to define these slabs and price condition. The steps are as below.

figure 35.92

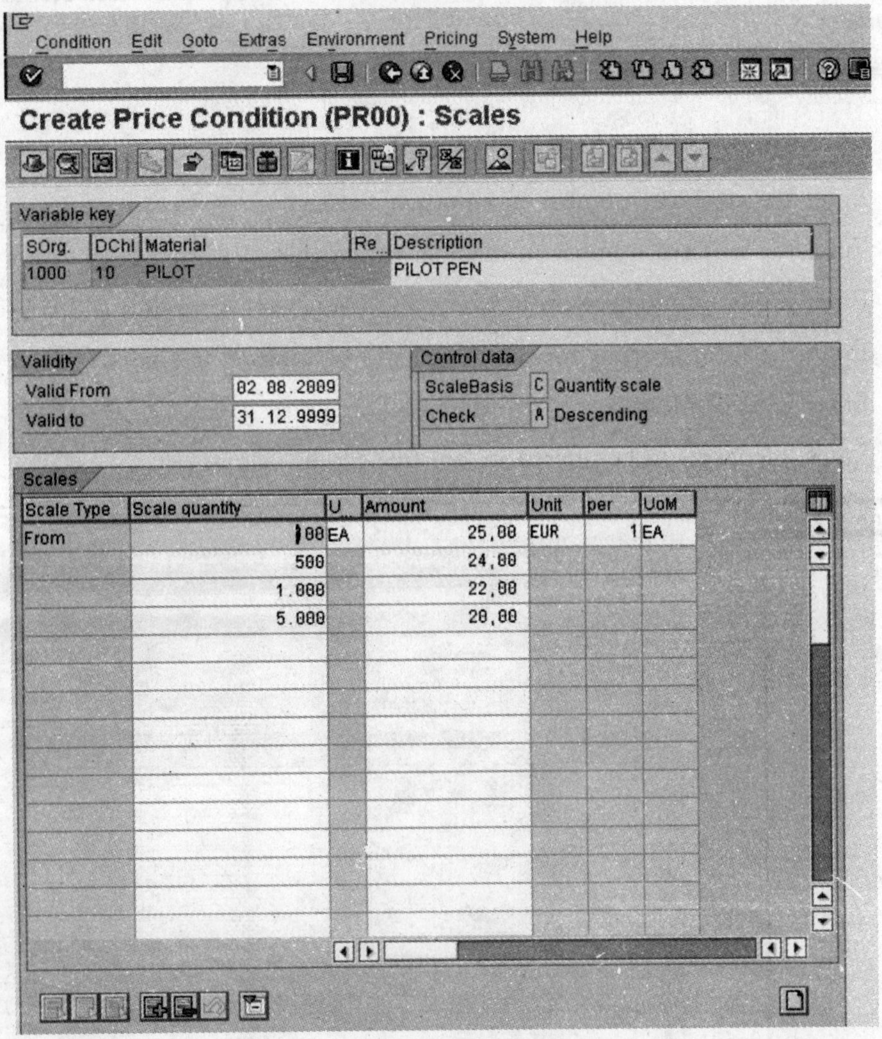

Enter the material number in material column.

Click on scales button toolbar. 

In the scale you can mention the quantity and price as shown in figure.

You can also enter validity dates for this condition.

Press Save Button to save condition record.

You can see its effect during sales order creation. System will fetch price condition as per the quantity entered during sale process.

Creating Free Goods

Free are normally offered for promoting sales where companies offer certain free goods to attract customers.

Below are the steps to create free goods condition.

Click on free goods button from toolbar.

- Enter the customer number in customer field.
- Enter the material number in material column
- Enter minimum quantity from where the free goods condition will trigger.
- Enter the from quantity for which you will be offering free goods.
- Enter Unit of Measure
- Enter free goods to be offered in 'are free goods' column.

figure 35.93

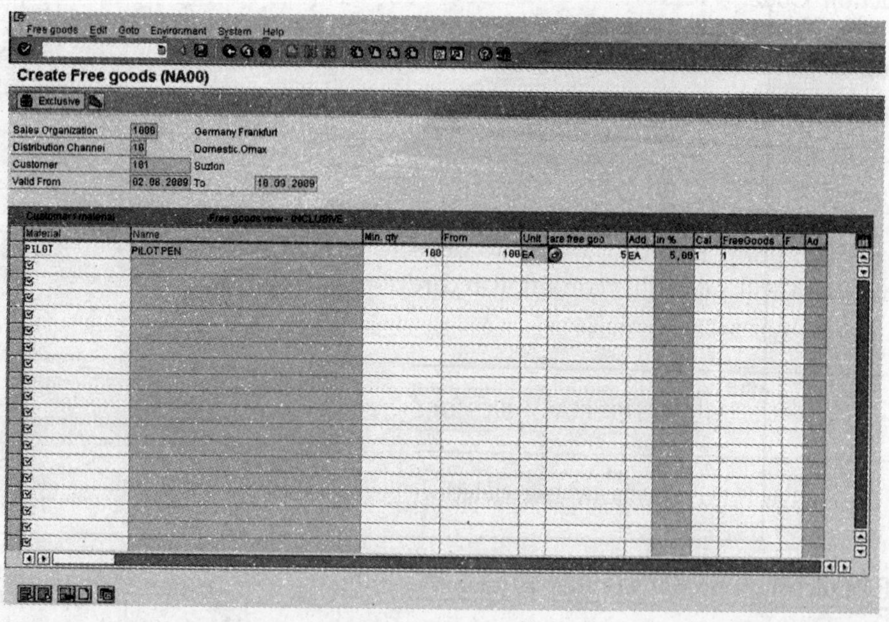

As shown in figure the customer can free goods of 5 units for each 100 units of order placed. And the minimum order quantity here is 100.

As you can see the free goods mentioned is exclusive, means 5 units will be offered for 100 units of order. It means the billing will be done for 100 units of item.

You may also offer free goods in inclusive mode. In that scenario 5 units will be offered for each 100 units order placed, but the billing will be done for 95 units of item.

You may also enter validity period for this condition record.

After entering relevant data press save button to save the condition record.

Change Condition Record

It's a normal practice to maintain current values of condition record in business.

For changing condition record follow the steps as below.

Select menu path: Logistics-Logistics Execution- Master Data- Conditions- Discounts/Surcharges- Others- VK12 - Change

Transaction Code: VK12

Display Condition Record

For displaying condition record follow the menu path as below. Select the condition type and enter the relevant details to display condition record.

Select menu path: Logistics-Logistics Execution- Master Data- Conditions- Discounts/Surcharges- Others- VK13 -Display

Transaction Code: VK13

Deleting Condition Record

Select menu path: Logistics-Logistics Execution- Master Data- Conditions- Discounts/Surcharges- Others- VK12 - Change

Transaction Code: VK12

Open the condition record you want to delete. Select the condition record and press delete button System will mark this condition record for deletion and will display message in status bar as below.

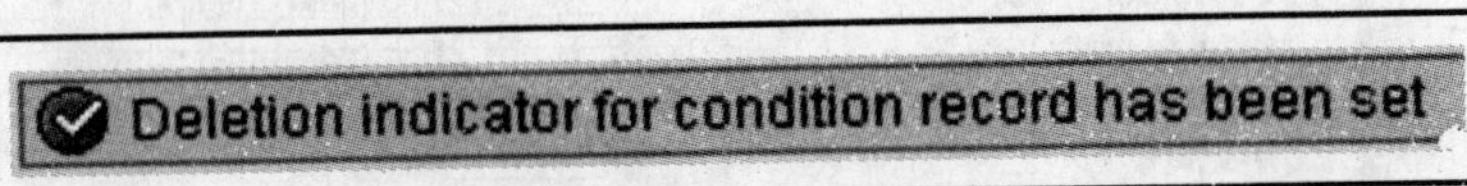

Press save button to complete deletion process.

REPORTS

A report is an executable program which reads data from the database evaluates it and then issues the results. SAP has various in built in the system. However customized reports can be developed by ABAP programming. Exploring reports in details is certainly beyond the scope of our discussion. Lets take a an example of frequently used report in sales and distribution. We will try to familiar with the features provided in SAP R/3 and how we can use it.

Select menu path: Logistics- Sales and Distribution- Sales Support -Information system -VA05 - List Sales Orders

Transaction Code: VA05

figure 35.94

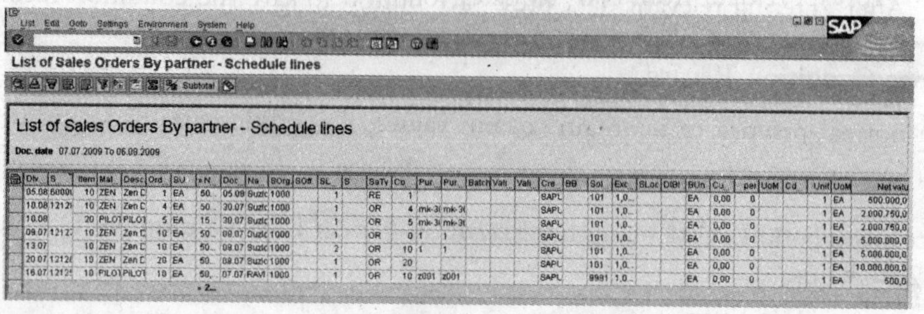

Enter organization details, partner, and date range for generating reports.

The figure above shows a report of list of sales documents.

As you can see there are so many columns are displayed, you can customize as per your requirement. Choose change Layout Button from the tool bar.

figure 35.95

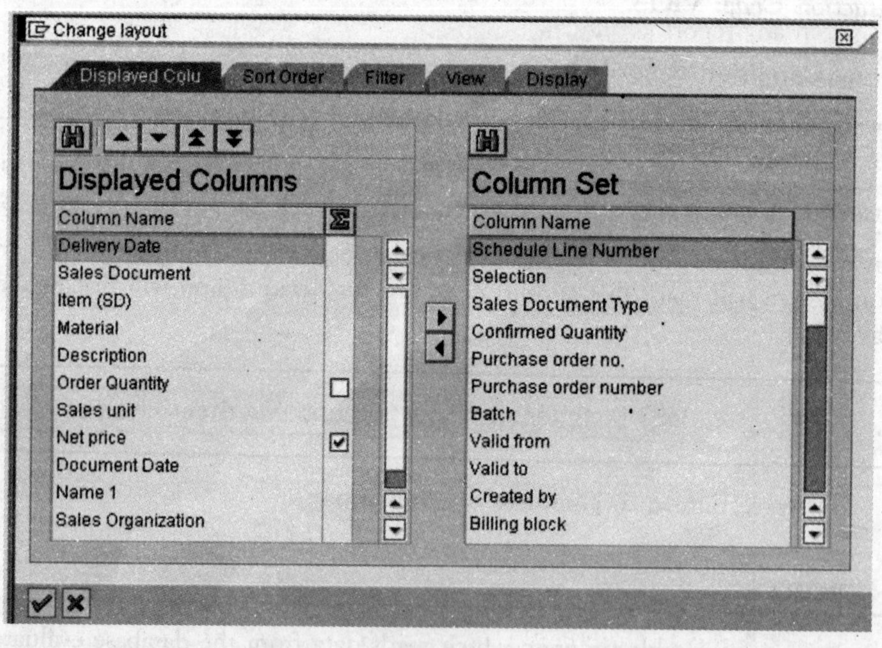

In the change layout window, you can see there are various tabs available for customizing display of your report. You can add/remove any column in report display. Select the column in displayed area and then move to set columns and vice versa.

Similarly you can see many options available to customize your sorting options, filter options and view option.

EXPORTING DATA FROM SAP TO MS-EXCEL

Microsoft Excel provides a user-friendly format and helpful tools to assist you in the process of analyzing and presenting data.

To export data from SAP to Excel follow the steps as below.

figure 35.96

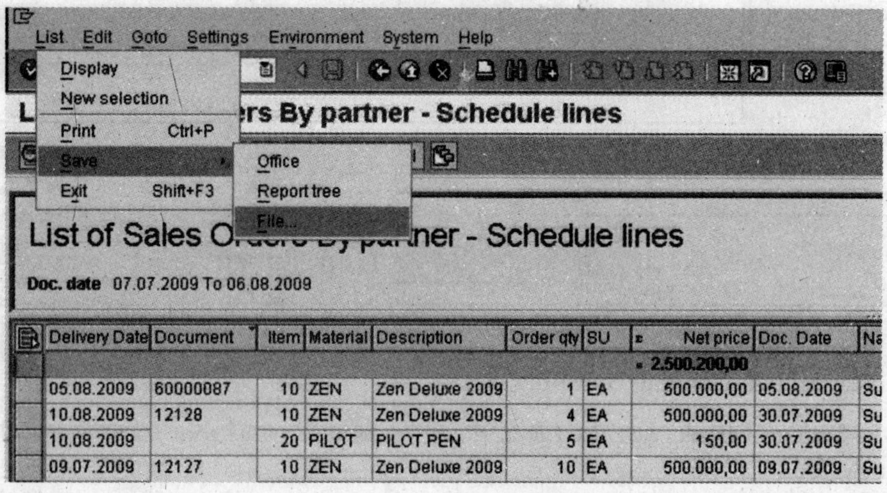

Open any report as shown in figure.

Select List-Save-File option from menu.

figure 35.97

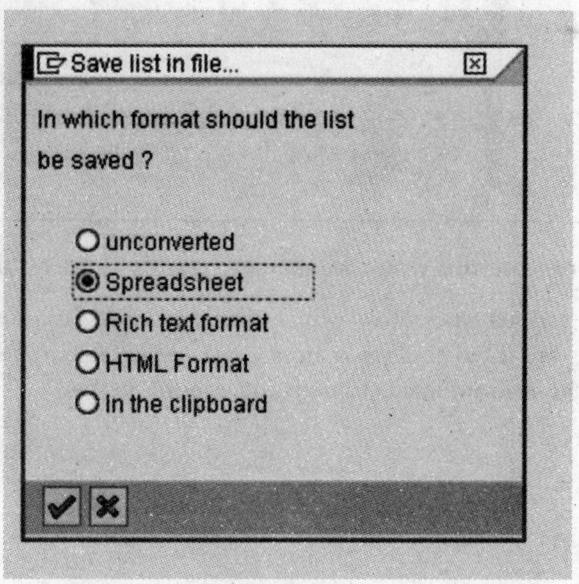

A dialog box will appear as shown in figure,

figure 35.98

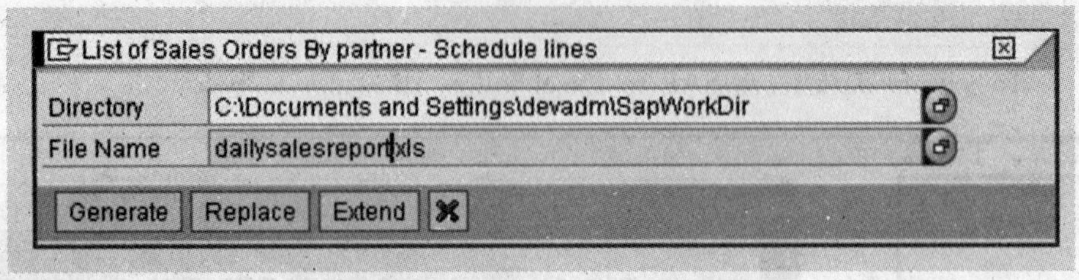

Select **Spreadsheet** option from the options available.

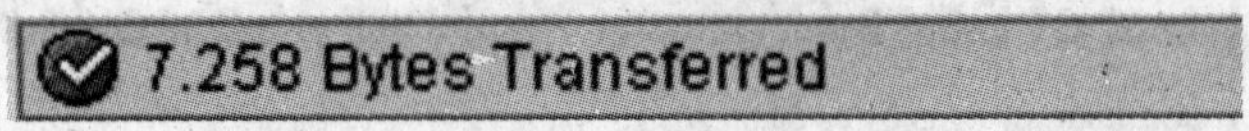

Enter the path where you want to store file and enter the file name of excel worksheet you want to create. Press **Generate** button.

System will generate the file at the given location and your status bar will show a message of bytes transferred.

To check data transferred open the file in MS-Excel.

figure 35.99

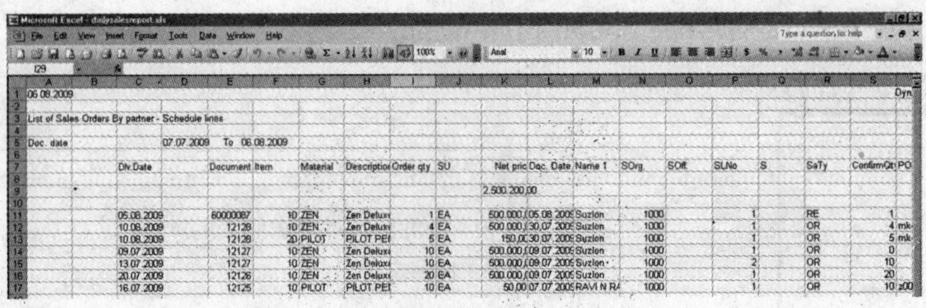

Now you can use this data for analysis, creating chart or almost any purpose.

There are various types of reports available in SAP. Some of the frequently used reports in Sales and Distribution are listed in Transaction Code Table later in this chapter; you may like explore each one and apply the techniques to understand reports better.

Frequently Used Transaction Codes

Transaction Code	Description
Customer Master	
XD01	Create Customer Master
XD02	Change Customer Master
XD03	Display Customer Master
VD05	Block Customer
VD06	Mark Customer for Deletion
XD07	Change Account Group of Customer
Condition Record	
VK11	Create Conditions Record Master
VK12	Change Conditions Record Master
VK13	Display Conditions Record Master
Order Creation	
VA01	Create Sales Orders
VA02	Change Sales Orders
VA03	Display Sales Orders
Outbound Delivery	
VL01N	Create Outbound Delivery
VL02N	Change Outbound Delivery
VL02N	Display Outbound Delivery
VL09	PGI Reversal Process
Billing	
VF01	Create Billing Document
VF02	Change Billing Document
VF03	Display Billing Document
VF11	Cancel Billing Document
VF03	Printing Billing Document
VF31	Output from Billing Document List
Material Master	
MM01	Create Material Master
MM02	Change Material Master
MM03	Display Material Master

Contd...

Reports	
SDQ1	Expiring Quotations
SDQ2	Expired Quotations
SDQ3	Completed Quotations
V.02	List of Incomplete Sales Orders
V.03	List of Incomplete Inquiries
V.04	List of Incomplete Quotations
V.14	Sales Orders Blocked for Delivery
VA05	List of Sales Orders
VA25	Quotations list
VF05	List billing documents
VF07	Display bill. document from archive
VF25	List of Invoice Lists
VFX3	Release Billing Documents for Accounting
VL04	Process Delivery Due List
VL06C	List Outbound Deliveries for Confirmation
VL06F	General delivery list – Outbound delivery
VLO6G	List of Outbound Delivery for Goods Issue
VL06P	List of Outbound Delivery for Picking

annexure 1

FRANCHISING AS NEW TOOL OF DISTRIBUTION

Introduction

Although in a nascent stage, franchising is gaining popularity in the retail segment in India, more particularly in the areas of food products and drinks, restaurant chains, consumers goods, and computer training centers. Franchising is one way in which a company can take advantage of India's vast market with a degree of control that other traditional forms of distribution cannot match.

In a nutshell, franchising is a business system where under the franchisor grants a license to the franchisee to use the franchisor's diverse intellectual property rights, namely, know-how, designs, brands, trade marks, patents, and trade secrets along with the franchisor's proven name, reputation and marketing techniques to market the franchisor's products or services in return for a sum of money. The franchisor provides training and continuous assistance to the franchisee.

Franchising is an entrepreneurial alliance. Much like a commercial business partnership wherein the franchisor provides the brand name, manufacturing/service delivery process and access to the system and the franchising provides the capital and forms the front end of the delivery system. Franchising is based on sound principles of excellent and consistent quality that is associated with a brand name.

Trends in Franchising

Populations and the move toward free market economies, new franchise concepts will come on the scene and the solid, well-managed existing Franchise companies will continue to grow. New business owners the best possible chance of succeeding with the least risk. The major advantage is that the system, the means for distributing goods and or services, has been developed, tested, and associated with the trademark. Within two to three decades or less, franchising will comprise over 50% of the retail economy, and will employ millions of people, and will enable hundreds of thousands to realize their dream of successful business ownership.

In around mid 2006, India's GDP (on a Purchasing Power Parity basis) is going to cross the magical figure of USD 3300. After crossing this figure what can be expected is a sudden growth in demand of consumer durables, mobile phones, better utilities and everything that is needed for a better standard of living.

Food and education sectors are showing promising trends. India is likely to see the addition of at least 400 restaurants, fast food outlets and coffee joints in the coming years. Food chains such as Yum Brands, McDonald's, Dominos and Café Coffee Day have earmarked an estimated investment of over $750 million to expand their retail presence across the country. India currently has more than 900 fast food restaurants and coffee shops. Yum Brands, parent of the KFC and Pizza Hut fast-food chains, plans to add 30- 40 restaurants in the next 12-18 months. Yum operates around 134 Pizza Hut restaurants in India and plans to scale up to 175 by 2010. Pizza Hut serves over 300,000 customers every week in India. It also runs 30 KFC outlets in the country and intends to add 15-20 new restaurants this year. Yum competes with McDonald's, Dominos, Pizza Corner and local brands such as Nirulas and Haldiram in the $280 million organized food and beverage retail sector, which is growing at around 25-30 per cent annually. Dominos Pizza India has announced an investment of $55-58 million in India over the next three years for expanding its retail fast food chain and manufacturing capacities. Like food franchises, the education and training franchise model is a success story in India.

Some experts believe that the real franchising revolution in India started with the emergence of national information technology (IT) education. According to IT magazine Data Quest, the $700 million IT education market in India is growing at 20 percent per year. Currently the IT education sector is seeing a boom, driven by a talent crunch, demand for qualified employable graduates, and an all-round need for trained manpower at all levels.

Contd...

Few Highlights about Franchising in India

- New education concepts are expecting a growth of 30-35 per cent, where as established concepts anticipate one to 15 per cent growth in terms of extending their franchise network in 2010-11.
- Fashion and lifestyle franchising is expected to grow at 27 per cent in 2010-11.
- Food and Beverage Industry Growth is expected 45 per cent for new market penetration through franchising.
- The outlook for healthcare and wellness is at 25 per cent growth in 2010-11.

Franchising World's Top Categories

Established: This category of the survey focuses on the brands which have been into franchising for more then 10 years and are well established. The brands in these categories are well established and are industry leaders and have contributed to the growth of franchising industry in the country. Few brands which features in this categories are Amul, JK tyre, Kwality Raymonds, VLCC, NIIT, Next and Tanishq.

Emerging: The emerging category features the new and vibrant brands that are on the verge of becoming bigger brands. This category comprises the brands which have shown a positive growth in the last couple of years, which include brands from various sectors like F&B, Financial, logistics etc. SAFEXPRESS, ICICI securities, Kodak, Gitanjali, Cox&Kings and Amara Raja are few of the brands which are part of emerging categories.

Debutant: This category feature brands which are relatively new and have new concepts and ideas for growth. These brands are expected to grow exponentially in the future. Most of the brands in these categories were launched in 2009 and have registered a phenomenal growth in a very short span of time. Few of the brands under these categories are Reliance world, NIIT-eGuru, Pidilite, DTDC plus point, 3M etc.

International: This category features some of the international brands which have opted for the franchise model for growth in the country. These brands have their presence in the country for more than 10 years and have a proven success record. Adidas, Pizza Hut, Samsonite, Nokia, Subway, Levi's and Baskin Robbins are few of the brands which are part of the international category of the survey.

Market Entry

With the rapid growth of franchising in India, the U.S. franchisors could appoint a master franchisee for the country, and with the assistance of the master franchisee develop a franchise network. Alternately, the U.S. franchisor could open a subsidiary in the country, and develop the franchise network. The master franchisee will not only be responsible for developing and adapting the foreign prototype to a new and different market in which it has limited recognition, but will also be responsible for implementing the expansion plan of the franchisor for the entire country. Given the large size of the country, U.S. franchisors are advised to appoint regional master franchisee to develop the network. Further, it is vital to conduct a thorough financial and legal due diligence or feasibility report on the potential partner, which includes a check on the owners, directors, financial status, and its availability to invest and expand the business.

India has no specific legislation regulating the franchise arrangements. However, a number of laws affect the franchisor-franchisee relationship. Intellectual property, taxation, labor, competition, property and exchange control regulations all influence the franchising operations in India. The absence of specific regulations or guidelines, coupled with the applicability of several laws, poses a number of challenges for foreign franchisors.

Since 1991, the Government of India has continuously liberalized rules relating to foreign direct investment. The Indian Government permits foreign Franchisors to charge royalties up to 1% for domestic sales and 2% on export sales for use of the foreign franchisor's brand name or trade mark, without transfer of technology. In effect, this means that by lending just their brand name or trademark to an Indian company, a foreign company could receive royalties. A notable example is the franchising of its famous character names and logos by Walt Disney Inc. that are common on various merchandise, and clothes in India.

Contd...

A foreign company must seek the approval of the Reserve Bank of India (RBI), India's banking regulatory authority (which is also responsible for exchange control regulations) if royalties exceeding prescribed limits. If the proposed franchise arrangement involves technology collaboration, the Government permits a lump sum payment of not exceeding US$2 million to the foreign Franchisor. Usually, the Indian franchisee will pay the lump sum in three equal installments. In addition, royalties up to a maximum of 5% on domestic sales and 8% on export sales will be allowed without approval. The Government has specified a formula for calculating royalties that must be followed for transferring funds to the foreign franchisor.

The Government of India's Foreign Investment Promotion Board (FIPB) will review on a case-by-case basis all requests for lump sum and royalty payments beyond the specified limits. The FIPB is the government agency responsible for reviewing and approving foreign investment and technology collaboration proposals.

Taxation, including sales tax, property tax, withholding tax, income tax, is another issue, which deserves to be carefully considered. Further, the structuring of the franchise arrangement and the double taxation avoidance treaties between India and the U.S. may have considerable influence on the franchise operations.

Franchising Legal Issues in India

There is no specific legislation regulating franchise arrangement in India, reason being the complexity of the relationship and the vast areas of law which such relationship involve.

The laws regulating franchising in India includes - law relating to contract, agency, distribution, leasing, assignment, securities, financial investments, intellectual and industrial property, competition, companies, immovable and movable properties, labour, foreign investment, insurance, banking, import-export, technology transfer, and other legislations which may become applicable in particular case. The applicability of laws depends precisely upon the modes of franchising which may be domestic or transborder.

Royalty Remittance

The FEMA and RBI regulate the terms of payment under Franchise Agreements (such as franchise fees, management fees, development fees, administrative fees, royalty fees and technical fees) where one party is a non-Indian entity including the amount to be paid and procedure for remittance of these payments outside India. The RBI prescribes certain requirements such as furnishing of tax clearances and chartered accountant certificate at the time of remittance of royalty payments by the franchisee to franchisor outside India.

The Indian government permits foreign franchisors to charge royalties up to 1% for domestic sales and 2% on exports for use of the foreign franchisor's brand name or trademark, without transfer of technology. The laws in India also permit lump sum and royalty payments to be made by Indian franchisees to their foreign counterparts for use of foreign technology, which includes manuals, systems etc. Lump sum payments up to US$2 million are permitted and royalties of 5% on domestic sales and 8% on exports can be paid to the foreign franchisor. In addition, foreign companies can enter into consulting agreements and receive up to US$ 1 million per project. Amounts in excess of these can also be received but with the permission of the Indian Government. These rules allow a foreign franchisor to structure its business in India in such a way so as to ensure that it can repatriate the maximum amount from India.

The Government has specified formula for calculation of royalties which must be adhered to before the foreign company can remit funds out of India. If the franchise agreement proposes royalties or lump sum fees beyond the specified limits, the approval of the Foreign Investment Promotion Board is required.

Taxation

Taxation is another issue which deserves due consideration. It is important to know the local sales tax, property tax, and withholdings tax applicable in certain area. Further, how the franchise arrangement is structured and the existence of treaties between the countries involved may have considerable influence on the structure adopted.

Contd...

Where the franchisor receives royalties, service or franchise fees, tax has to be paid under the income tax Act (as income arising and accruing in India), whether the franchisor is an Indian or foreign. In case where the foreign franchisor sends training personnel and supervisors to India, the salaries payable to these persons may be subject to personal income tax, whether an arrangement is made to deduct the tax at source or they are taxed as self-employed persons (professionals).

In calculating the amount of tax payable by the franchisor or the franchisee company, the deduction available in tax laws of India can be important for tax planning purposes. Sometimes of these relate to rent, repairs and insurance in respect to premises used for business; depreciation and expenditure on research; and, expenditure of capital nature on acquisition of patent rights or copyrights. However, the availability of tax advantages depends on the type of franchise, the product of the franchise and unit locations.

annexure 2

E-RETAILING IN INDIA: PROSPECTS AND CHALLENGES

Introduction

The recent deal between Bharti and Walmart for investing up to USD 2.5 billion setting up a nationwide chain of supermarkets and retail shops has triggered retail boom in Indian sub-continent. Indian Business Report 2008 predicted the e-commerce industry to touch 9,210 crores (Appendix 1). Organised retailers have begun investing in various compositions to capture market, be it in the form of discounted stores, supermarkets, hypermarkets, etc. A result of strenuous marketing research studies, retailers such as Pantaloons, RPGs, Tatas, etc. have adopted different business models to capture consumers' buying behaviours. One such study carried out revealed that hub and spokes model constituting of cash and carry and neighbourhood stores a more value enhancing proposition.

A large working and earning Indian population has attracted global retailers. Improvised retail activities including logistics, warehousing, merchandising, etc. have given a new meaning to Indian retailing. Price Water House Cooper's N.V. Sivakumar says, "India is a fragmented country and an absence of strong infrastructure and logistics system makes it all the more challenging to reach to consumers." Reliance and Future Group have already invested Rs. 6,000 crores and Rs. 400-500 crores respectively for setting up better logistics patterns in their working cultures. Supply Chain Management is another area which requires remodeling. Studies reveal that 40% of wastage levels of perishables in Indian food and grocery segment is on account of inadequate supply chain management.

Adoption of few laid down operational metrics devised by analysts could greatly help to bridge gaps between Indian and foreign retailing. Efficiency measurement in the form of inventory turns ratio, stock availability, adoption of value added procurement, transportation and storage procedures, and finally technology would drastically alter the retail scenario in India.

A study by Indian Council for Research and International Economic Relations (ICRIER), expects a growth of about 10% p.a. on Indian's unorganised retail sector. The sales figure expects a growth rate from USD 309 billion in 2006-7 to USD 496 billion in 2011-12. Organised retail sector, as per the research study is expected to grow at a comparatively faster rate of 45-50% p.a. Changes in the mindset and lifestyle of the Indian customers have drastically affected the Indian retail Industry. KPMG's report predicts a rise in number of malls in metros to rise to about 450 by the end of 2010.

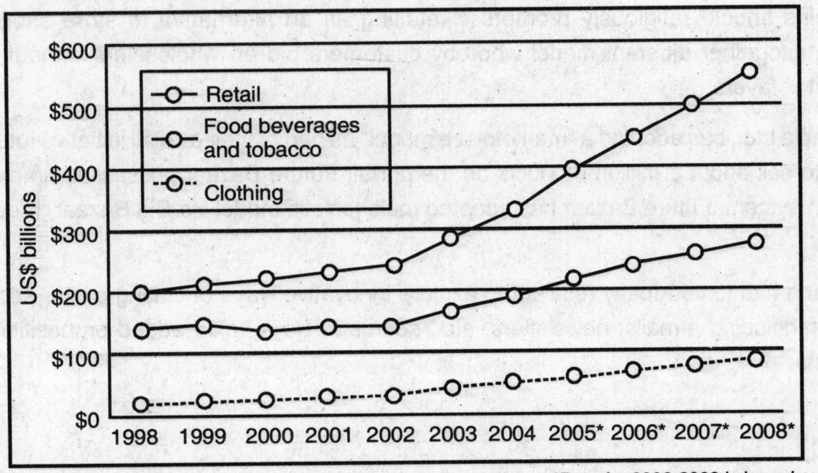

Sources: Economist intelligence unit and A.T. Kearney analysis *Data for 2006-2008 is based on estimates

Contd...

Technology penetration in India has triggered the pace of e-commerce's inception in the retail sector. Better internet facilities and provision of hassle free online-transactions have given a new dimension to e-retailing. Sify's president V.V. Kannan is very optimistic about the trend of online shopping in India on account of better payment options available, more organized supply-chain systems, customer care and internet availability at a cheaper cost.

More and more tech-savvy buyers in India are getting hooked to e-commerce culture, as is evident from the increased online purchases of CD/DVD's, electronic items, books, gifts, flowers etc. The 'convenience' of online shopping has not only attracted major e-stores (futurebazaar.com, HomeShop18, eBay, Indiatimes.com, etc.) but even small retailers. Shalini Gera, GM, Ferns 'N' Petals is of the belief that online retail offers global reach for both buyers and receivers which is absent in case of fixed physical store. She further adds that e-retailing provides round the clock reach and hence there are no market restrictions. Online retail option has enabled a larger target audience through digitized medium with negligible investment in physical infrastructure and other overhead expenses. Pawan Gadia, VP, Ferns 'N' Petals, credits e-commerce for achieving 60% growth every year out of which 10% is totally dependent on online sales.

A path breaking venture in auto-E-retailing in India has been introduced by Tata Steel, Sail and Mjunction Services Ltd. As part of the venture, new cars can be bought simply by logging on to website www.autojunction.in RECC (REVA Electric Car Company) has added feathers to its cap by selling REVA electric car through e-retailing model. Auto-retailing option has ushered a global revolution in automobile industry. With virtual showrooms, transparent supply chain systems and high cost and distribution efficiency. With high growth potential of auto-retailing in India and increased number of internet savvy customers, auto-retail services predict a favourable market opportunity through one stop car shop.

Construction is another sector entering e-retail arena with full swings. One of India's largest e-commerce organisations, "Straightline" has signed up an MoU with two leading construction companies - Patton International Ltd. (PIL) and Lafarge India Ltd., for selling products online initially in eastern part of India.

FabMall.com, India's largest shopping network online, has adopted a model similar to one adopted by Walmart and Shopper's Stop. Rather than holding on with inventory, shelf space is increased on the portal. This enables the consumers with a higher choice of items. However, despite better payment collection and logistic procedures and with more focused goal of "Improving Customer Experience", the model has not produced anticipated outcomes. Fabmall believes that in order for the model to be effective, many small and large retail chains should religiously promote e-retailing as an alternative to store shopping. eBay.in, functions on an altogether different model whereby customers bid on wholesalers without intervention of multiple distributor layers.

Future Bazaar India Ltd., has adopted a "marketplace model" as part of their e-retail initiative futurebazaar.com. With the ability to sell about a million products on the portal, Future Bazaar possesses an excellent end-to-end supply chain system. Future Bazaar has adopted multi-logistic model via Big Bazaar, Blue Dart and Gati courier services.

Ongoing recession has forced many retailers to explore innovative ways of cutting costs. Adoption of online advertising tools including e-mails, newsletters, etc., seems to be a value added proposition of increasing sales at low costs.

Contd...

B2C E-Commerce Sales* in India, 2006-2011 {billions and % change}		
	Sales	%change
2006	INR34.5 ($0.76)	
2007	INR50.6 ($1.23)	46.7%
2008	INR73.1 ($1.90)	44.4%
2009	INR106.3 ($2.84)	45.4%
2010	INR148.6($4.07)	39.8%
2011	INR200.2($5.56)	34.7%

Note: Converted at average annual exchange rate (projected for future years); total B2C e-commerce sales include all purchases made on a retail Website, regardless of device used to complete the transaction; *includes online travel, event ticket and digital download Sales

Source: eMarketer, January 2008

Factors affecting E-retail Penetration in India

Adoption of strong telecommunication channels, hassle-free internet access and comfortable payment options would definitely boost e-commerce penetration into Indian retail. An exhaustive research carried out by I-cube (Internet.in.india) revealed the total Internet population of India to be 55.5 million by 2008. Improvements in telecommunication and increased internet speed and bandwidth have been the prime cause of internet penetration is not only in urban but also in rural India. The study further adds that out of the 55.5 million active users, about 4.24 million urban internet users fall in the age group of 21 to 35 years. Sandra Hanchard, senior analyst, Hitwise, believes that there lies an immense opportunity for e-retailers in Asia Pacific. Studies reveal the internet penetration rate to be 17% compared to 75% in North America and 50% in Europe. According to JuxtConsult's online 2009 report, 91% of all regular online Indians shop online.

(Appendix 2)

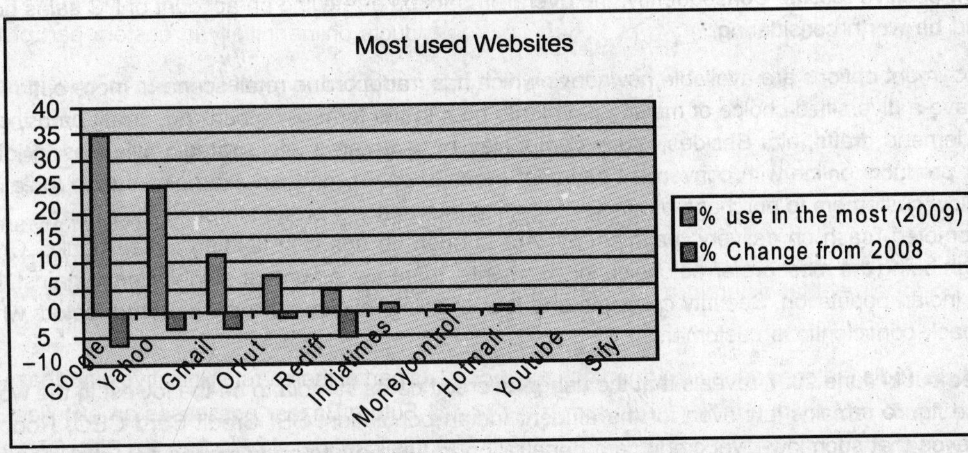

Source: Adapted from JuxtConsult Online 2009 Study

Leading Indian retailers like Pantaloons, Shoppers' Stop and Globus are looking at e-retailing portals to reach small towns where they are yet to open retail outlets. Euromonitor report predicts a contribution of 46% by e-retailing to non-store retailing by 2010. Although statistics indicate a heavy internet usage by 1 out of every 3rd person from the urban Indian population, researchers believe that in order to further intensify internet penetration, users should be convinced to use internet beyond their working hours. The idea is to convert net users to net customers.

As per report released by Manufacturer's Association for Information Technology (MAIT), there has been a registered growth rate of 16% in the PC sales in India by the end of fiscal year 2007-8. MAIT further predicts sales figure to touch 8.5 million by 2008-09.

Contd...

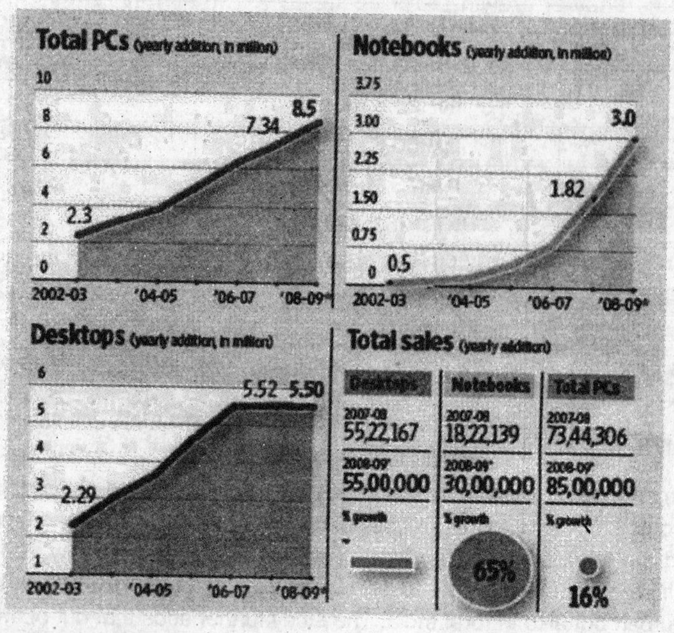

Source: MAIT: IMRB

With India's PC market opening up more for notebook computers, the growth of country's telecom sector seems quite evident. Ravi Bapna, Associate Professor IT at University of Minnesota's Carlson School of Management, is of the opinion that 3G technology is going to have a significant acceleration effect on notebook adoption. By eliminating bandwidth constraints, the quality and functionality of these devices are bound to show positive results. Consequently, the overall impact on e-retailing on account of PC sales boost in India would be worth considering.

A variety of payment options are available nowadays which has made online retail scenario more optimistic. Customers have a diversified choice of making payments be it in the form of netbanking, credit cards, cash on delivery, demand drafts, etc. Besides, many companies have entered into strategic alliances to jointly promote their products online with convenient payment procedures. To give an example, Yahoo India and Rediff.com allow customers to purchase products of leading international brands through their portals. They have also promoted "cash on delivery" payment system through tie ups with leading Indian banks. Credit cards, although being the most preferred choice for payments, there are a number of inhibitions against their use amongst Indian population. Security concerns and fear of being misused are the blocking factors which are holding back conscientious customers.

A study carried out in June 2007 reveals that the usage of credit cards in India to be the lowest in the world. Surprising, the figure remains low even for the affluent Indian population. SBI Credit Card CEO, Roopam Asthana, believes that such low-level credit card penetration in India offers an immense potential for credit card companies. There were approximately 22 million credit cards and 70 million debit cards in India by January 2007. Contrarily, during the same period, the number of credit card transactions compared to debit card transactions was much higher. There exists a need for credit card issuers to capture wider market and expand their customer base more aggressively in India.

Fear of cyber crime is amongst the biggest challenge to e-commerce adoption in India. Although, credit card companies have invested phenomenal amounts to ensure secured online transactions, they are still not able to remove inhibitions against fraudulent cyber activities from consumer's mindset. Pinkerd, Senior VP, VISA at USA strictly believes that consumers do not completely understand the reason and frequency of an internet fraud. As a result major credit card companies have developed password based systems and improved security programs to reduce fraud thereby gaining consumers' confidence levels.

Contd...

Demography dynamics is another growth factor contributing to e-retailing in India. Almost 60% of Indian population falls below the age group of 30 years. This contributes to an overall attitudinal change whereby Indian consumer prefers to be more choice and value oriented. However, majority of the Indian population is traditional as far as buying habits are concerned. Older generation finds greater pleasure in shopping conventionally. With no time constraint, shopping is more or less a socialising activity. Similar is the situation with traditional Indian women for whom conventional shopping seems to be a "social release".

E-Business Models, Theories and Strategies

Business models are methods devised by companies for generating profits. Rise of e-commerce across the globe has given birth to many internet models and theories. Here we will examine few of the commonly used taxonomies on the subject.

The "Dotcom" Theory

This theory forms an integral part of the e-retail business model and has been widely accepted primarily by pure-play e-retailers. The theory emphasises on delivering products directly to the consumers rather than investing huge capital in building massive retail outlets. Online retailers should make use of sophisticated analysis tools for predicting consumer's buying behaviours. Prior to choosing Internet as a distribution channel, internet retailers should develop various strategies through which they would be able to serve their customers more efficiently than through traditional retailing. One such strategy referred to as niche-play strategy identifies those existing niches in the market which are not adequately serviced through catalogue or traditional retailing. E-retailers could thereafter focus on serving those niches in a more efficient manner by using unique product assortment methodologies.

Customer Focused Business Model

This business model proposed by Zeller recognises consumer as the central component of the model. Contrarily, any traditional business model focuses more on maximising shareholder's wealth. Zeller believes that success of any e-commerce based business can be achieved if consumer's needs are adequately identified and serviced. The e-retailer should effectively utilise internet as a medium to present its products to the consumers. Real wealth could then be created through brand recognition for their products.

Utility Business Model

The factors of user necessity, reliability, usability, utilisation, scalability, and exclusivity, when taken together, shape the business model for utility services (M.A. Rappa, 2004). Rappa has used nine major categories to classify different types of identified business models.

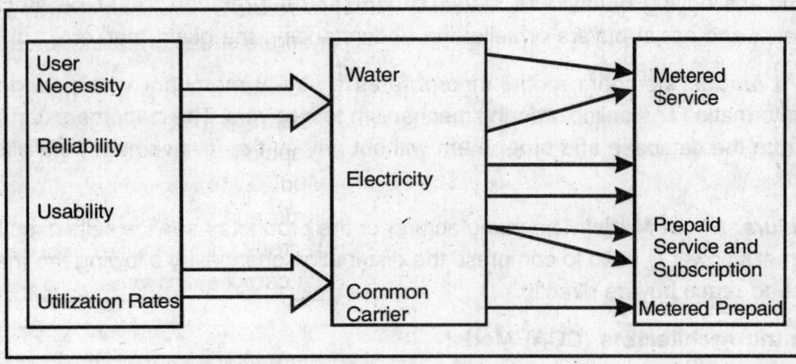

Utility Service Characteristics and Business Model

1. ***Brokerage Model:*** Brokerage Model is a kind of Internet Business Model in which brokers are involved in online transactions between sellers and buyers. They connect either consumer with retailer, business with business or consumer with consumer. Brokers may be classified as online marketplaces, aggregators, metamediaries and intelligent agents.

Contd...

- *Online Marketplaces:* Bring commercial buyers and sellers together online. They provide services such as providing market assessments, negotiations, fulfillments, etc.
  - *Aggregators:* Primarily focus on the concept of group purchasing. They help in providing better rates to businesses or consumers.
  - *Metamediaries:* Provide additional features such as billing and order tracking other than involving in bringing together interested parties.
  - *Intelligent Agents:* Are basically the software programs which individual consumer or business units could use for searching essential information related to product or price.

2. ***Advertising Model:*** This e-commerce model emphasises on utilising advertising as a means of maximising profits by selling online. Organisation's web portals may offer a variety of additional features such as free e-mails, travel services and banner ads in order to capture higher customer base.
3. ***Affiliate Model:*** Affiliate marketing model works on the concept that e-retailers are willing to share their financial incentives with affiliated partners for sharing their products. The affiliates provide purchase-point click through the e-retailers. The model can be regarded as a pay-for-performance model whereby the merchant does not get billed if the affiliate is not able to produce revenue.
4. ***Community Model:*** The community model makes use of various electronic tools to encourage interaction amongst various consumers and business group. Webinars, videoconferences, virtual chats, etc., are some of the techniques of bringing together like-minded people online for sharing business plans.
5. ***Subscription Model:*** Another form of e-commerce business model, the customer is charged a subscription price to access to available products or services online. Subscription model and advertising model are often combined for value interests.
6. ***Utility and Hybrid Model:*** Utility model makes use of "pay as you go" approach wherein customers pay for the internet services as and when they are used. Internet service providers make use of metered services in which customers are charged on the basis of connection minutes. This is unlike subscription model wherein subscription fee is charged by the ISP's irrespective of the actual usage rates.
7. ***Infomediary Model:*** Organisations functioning as information intermediaries collect useful data such as consumer's buying behaviours, detailed company information, real-time stock quotes, product ratings, etc., and assist buyers or sellers in understanding the given market.
8. ***Merchant Model:*** Merchant model incorporates a virtual merchant who provides a data bank of product information and online ordering mechanism to e-buyers. The customers can select the products directly from the database and order them without any sort of involvement from either wholesalers or retailers.
9. ***Manufacturer Direct Model:*** The manufacturer or the product or service sells directly to the customer. The internet's power is used to compress the distribution channel by allowing the maker of the product or service to reach buyers directly.

Customer Centric Architecture (CCA) Model

This is yet another Customer Centric Architecture Business Model which emphasises on being more customers focused rather than product focused. CCA business cycle incorporates attracting, nurturing and retaining customers as the key components of a healthy online customer relationship management (CRM). E-retailers should be able to attract customers by satisfying their needs better than traditional retailers. In present day competitive marketplace, customer service in the biggest differentiator for many organisation. The need of the hour is to provide outstanding service in a much cheaper, safer, reliable and easier way.

Contd...

Incorporating nurturing strategies in the form of cross-selling and up-selling maximise the value of business. The whole idea is to identity customer's requirements before recommending any product.

E-retailers can make to use many strategies to retailing customer loyalty. Regular feedbacks, updated information, bonus points, discounts, privileged shopper programs are some of the means of building a strong customer loyalty.

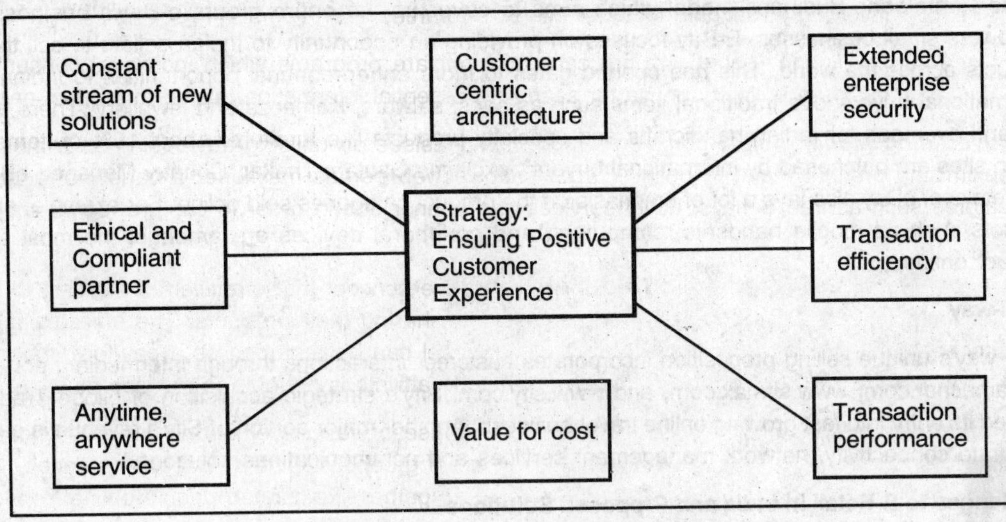

Dimensions of Customer Experience

A key element in the Group's multi-format policy, our convenience stores offer a complementary outlet to urban and rural customers. Each of the Group's convenience store banners stands out for the way it tailors its offering to the needs of its customer base. In France, our convenience stores offer a range of products and services (for example, home delivery, dry cleaning, 48-hour photo development, ticket distribution, photocopying, stamps, newspapers and more). With surface areas that range between 50 and 900 sq.m. convenience stores can be adapted to suit any situation, from urban sites to the most rural locations, where they help to counteract the trend of disappearing services.

Drop-shipping Strategy

Adoption of Drop-ship strategy in an e-Retail business model could prove to be a wonderful means of increasing product selection without increasing inventory investment. E-retailers develop strong relationships with their suppliers that can drop-ship merchandise to retailer's customers. "We're able to sell inventory and not have to pay for it until we take orders from our customers", says Jason Roussos, President, Richlund Ventures.

Adopted Business Models and Strategies by Leading E-retailers in India

Pantaloons India

Although being in its nascent stage, e-business in India has certainly exhibited an upward thrust with powerful organised retailers venturing into e-commerce arena. Pantaloons India has come up with mega plans for its e-commerce initiative, Futurebazaar. The business model adopted by Pantaloons is different from the ones adopted by its competitors in the market. The model envisages covering Pantaloon's entire group constituting Pantaloons, Food Bazaar, Big Bazaar, Central, Depot, ConvergeM, Home Solutions, Electronics Bazaar and E-Zone.

Futurebazaar attempts to cover up geographical boundaries to reach to wider market by leveraging the power of Internet. Anup Seth, Head, e-Retailing, Pantaloons (Retail) India strongly believes that internet power can be used to extend the value proposition of the companies offline formats. By deploying various sophisticated ERP (Enterprise Resource Planning) tools such as SAP R/3 for integration, it supply chain

Contd...

management systems, inventory management and customer handling can be done in a more efficient manner. Seth is of the opinion that Futurebazaar e-retailing functions were in a multi-dimensional delivery format rather than as a content provider. It aims to reach up to its customer's expectations by servicing in a cheaper, faster, easier and trustworthy manner.

e-Bay

Unlike Pantaloons Business model which aims to cover up the entire group, e-Bay's business model empowers small businesses. E-Bay focuses on providing an opportunity to Indian sellers to sell their local products across the world. This has opened gates to more entrepreneurial opportunities to Indian sellers. "International buyers love traditional items such as saris, salwars, Kameezs and jewellery. There is a high demand overseas for Indian handicrafts and specialty products like furniture. About 15% of items on the Indian sites are purchased by international buyers", exclaims Gautam Thakar, Country Manager, eBay India Marketplace. eBay also lays a lot of emphasis on the product categories sold online. For example, electronic gadgets such as mobile handsets, computers, and peripheral devices are amongst the most shopped product online.

Sify I-way

Sify I-way's unique selling proposition incorporates customer interactions through intermediary portals such as Samachar.com, www.sifmax.com, and www.sify.com. Sify's strategic acquisition of Globe Traders has marked its entry into fast growing online travel business. Another major portion of Sify's revenue is generated corporate connectivity, network management services and communications solutions.

Challenges to E-Retail in India and Proposed Solutions

Payment gateway is an e-commerce service that authorises payments for online retailers. The services include credit card processing, billing, reporting, capturing credit card funds between different accounts, etc. Payment gateways charge a percentage of e-merchant's profit share for providing these services. In most of the cases, online retailers give out a considerable share of their revenues (approx. 4-7%) in the form of gateway fees. Besides, the services rendered are also not up to merchant's expectation levels. Some of the common payment gateways functionings in India are CC Avenue, Pay Pal, ICICI Payseal, Verisign and Google Checkout. To enable e-commerce to flourish in India, more number of efficient payment gateway services should be operational who can provide cost effective global platform to e-merchants.

The content of an e-retailing website matters a lot. A huge amount of research is involved prior to populating information online. Most of the existing e-commerce portals in India lack in providing useful information to the customers. The matter is either very primitive to irrelevant. This means that the content information does not contribute towards decision-making of online buyers. It is of utmost importance to provide value-added information in the portal. Technology should be used for presenting appropriate assortment of products based on customer's requirements. Indian buyers are also skeptical about the security aspect associated with transacting online. People are unwilling to use credit cards for making payments. To overcome this hurdle, e-retailers have come up with alternate payment methods such as cash-on-delivery, cheque and demand draft.

Although technology has helped e-retailers in making strategic business decisions related to product, inventory, supply chain systems, etc., one grey area which still remains untapped is price. Most of the e-retailers have adopted traditional pricing strategies such as offering low prices to products compared to brick-and-mortar prices. Such methods are unreliable, time-consuming and costly. Analysts therefore suggest performing "live-tests" on the internet. Live-testing captures extremely vital information related to varying customer demands, perceived market value of a brand, competitor's influence, etc.

annexure 3

INTERNATIONAL RETAILING STRATEGIES

Introduction

Over a decade, there has developed a strong tendency in International Business Studies to discuss the internationalisation of marketing activities. This is not surprising as the ongoing globalisation has pushed corporations to seek entry into foreign markets at a relentless pace. When a firm decides to operate outside domestic market, it has to choose which market to enter, and also the organisational structure. There are varieties of modes which firms might use to enter into foreign markets, and the success of the firm depends on the right choice which in turn depends on several factors. Retailing is one of the favourite choices, especially in consumers industry.

What is retailing? We all know that Wal-Mart, Home Depot, Carrefour, Marks and Spencer's are retailers but so are Avon representatives, Amazon.com, and a doctor seeing patients. Retailing includes all the activities involved in selling products or services directly to final consumers for their personal, non-business use. Many institutions, manufacturers, wholesalers and retailers do retailing. But most retailing is done by retailers: business whose sales constitute primarily from retailing. Although most retailing is done in retail stores, in recent years non-store retailing commonly referred as direct selling through mail, catalogues, internet, TV home shopping, vending machines is also growing, yet the arena of retailing at international level belongs to store retailing. Being so, this paper is a case study on the international retailing strategies of Carrefour in Asia. The case reflects the various issues of international retailing strategies and the unique approach adopted by Carrefour. In the process, the study also investigates what factor - internal or external caused or was responsible for Carrefour's success in Asia. The case clearly indicates that Carrefour as a retailer has excellent international retailing strategies in its armory: background, strategy, vision values and sufficient resources to compete and operate successfully also in Asia.

Case Example

Carrefour Stores

Over the past 40 years, the Carrefour Group has grown to become one of the world's leading distribution groups. The world's second largest retailer and the largest in Europe, the Group currently operates in the below store formats:

- ***Hypermarkets:*** the appeal of the new
- ***Supermarkets:*** making life easier
- ***Hard discount:*** grocery products at low prices
- ***Convenience stores:*** just what you need, right next door
- ***Cash and Carry:*** proximity and accessibility for catering professionals
- E-commerce

The Carrefour Group currently has over 15,000 stores, either company-operated or franchisees.

Hypermarkets: The Appeal of the New

Faithful to the concept of "everything under-one -roof", Carrefour hypermarkets offer an average surface area of 8,400 sq.m. filled with a range of between 20,000 and 80,000 food and non-food items, all at extremely attractive prices. Located in the centre of broad catchment's areas, they will often be important drivers of traffic in the area around them. Carrefour hypermarkets combine choice, quality, innovation and modernity with the best prices around and a pleasurable buying experience. Carrefour's emphasis on price, one of the key elements of the brand's strategy, is complemented by its constant pursuit of improvement in

Contd...

ranges and services. This includes adapting what is on offer to local needs, extending product ranges and developing services for customers with whom Carrefour seeks to form ever-closer ties, with the aim of improving the service it offers them.

In 2007, the Carrefour Group opened 149 hypermarkets a driving force in its conquest of emerging markets and developed the strong potential of its brand in this format.

World leader in the Hypermarket Segment

With 1,163 hypermarkets in 30 countries, the Carrefour Group is widening its No. 1 global position in this format. In 2007, expansion accelerated outside France, particularly in Asia, with the building of 36 new hypermarkets, including 22 in China where the Group broke its record for store openings in a one-year period. In Europe, 51 new hypermarkets came on board, including the 160th in Spain and the 71st in Poland following integration of the 15 Ahold Polska hypermarkets. In Latin America, the Group became the number one food retailer in Brazil after acquiring the 34 Atacadao discount hypermarkets and inaugurating 62 new hypermarkets.

Carrefour Grooms its Brand Image

France adopted a new law on 1st January 2007 authorising the retail sector to advertise on television. In January, Carrefour France launched its first advertising campaign on terrestrial channels with the new promise of "Quality for all". The commercials used Carrefour products to demonstrate the brand's quality commitment and its loyalty programme to illustrate its price commitment. A campaign in the print press highlighted the Carrefour Ligne Alerte Prix (Price Hotline), which guarantees the lowest prices on major brands' products. A range of customer commitments, which is posted in the 218 French hypermarkets, rounded out the Carrefour brand.

Mini Hypermarkets: A Pilot Project

In June 2007, seven Hyper Champion hypermarkets adopted the Carrefour name in France. This pilot project marked a new stage in the Group's multi-format and single-brand strategy. The switch to a single brand could help stores to capitalise on the Carrefour image and develop synergies. The Group may thus introduce a new growth format in France: small hypermarkets of 3,000 to 6,000 sq.m. already adopted in several countries in 2006.

In 2007, Carrefour expanded its selection of non-food products and promoted the Carrefour brand. Tableware, Carrefour Home and Carrefour Selection (gourmet foods) made a grand entrance and drew rave reviews. Carrefour's services are providing new opportunities to customers worldwide. Services include mobile phones, home computer support, travel services, credit cards and savings products. The launch of the Tex by Max Azria women's ready-to wear brand, created exclusively for Carrefour by the world-renowned designer, upgraded the clothing ling in 600 Carrefour hypermarkets in Europe. In the same vein, the exclusive distribution agreement for Europe signed with American personal computer maker Dell added new appeal to the hypermarket offering in France, Spain and Belgium starting on 15th January 2008.

Hypermarket Snapshot

- 1,163 hypermarkets worldwide at 31st December 2007.
- 59.1% of group sales under banners (inclusive taxes) in 2007.
- 123 new hypermarkets worldwide in 2007.
- 3,19,858 employees at 31st December 2007.

Contd...

Supermarkets: Making Life Easier

Carrefour Group supermarkets offer their customers in town and country a wealth of choice close to where they live. Located in town, out of town and in rural areas, with surface areas ranging from 1,000 to over 2,000 sq.m., our supermarkets offer a range of some 10,000 listings, most of them food, at highly competitive prices. Our rural stores are currently developing a broader offering of non-food products, such as clothing and household goods. In 2007, the Carrefour Group opened 326 supermarkets, mainly in Europe, and moved faster to update this format, constantly striving to make the shopping experience easier for its customers.

Setting Course for Eastern Europe

Ten years after the Group first set foot in Poland, the integration of 183 Ahold Polska supermarkets vaulted Carrefour to the second spot in the food retailing sector. In Romania, Carrefour's acquisition of Artima gave the Group a foothold in the supermarket segment, providing visibility to the new Carrefour Express banner the 21 supermarkets will display in 2008. At year-end 2007, the Carrefour Group had 2,708 supermarkets in 10 countries

Single-brand Strategy moves forward

In Spain, all the supermarkets have switched to the Carrefour Express banner and in Brazil to Carrefour Bairro. Customers have come to know and enjoy the Carrefour brand in a format other than the hypermarket. To prove the point, sales have risen by 30% in Spain based on comparable floor area. In Poland, Belgium, Turkey and Argentina, the Carrefour brand has gradually replaced local retailers, including Globi, GB, Gima and Norte. In France, the Group launched the first brand convergence tests in October. Six Champion supermarkets in Brittany switched to the Carrefour Market name, combining Champion's convenience with Carrefour's strength.

More Floor Area, More Choice

In France, 107 new supermarkets opened, 17 were remodeled and 63 were expended to the target size of 2,000 sq.m. totaling an additional 77,000 sq.m. Twenty-three per cent of products were replenished across the year and the offering enhanced with 100 own-brand products promoting the trend towards organic, fair trade and eco-friendly products. Champion also came up with new ideas in its service offering, selling 20,000 mobile phone contracts in 2007 and providing personal services that make life easier for its 5.6 million loyalty card holders.

Hard Discount: Grocery Products at Low Prices

These stores offer a reduced range at discount price around 20% lower than major brands in surface areas ranging from 200 to 1,000 sq.m. for Dia stores with a parking lot. The range mainly comprises Dia-branded food products plus a small selection of established, major brand items. The Group's hard discount stores have extensive expertise in the retailing of fruit and vegetables, offering a range of quality fresh products at attractive prices. Its stores now cover everything a family needs, between, 1,500-18,00 food listings plus a limited number of essential personal care and cleaning products.

Supermarket Snapshot

- 656 stores opened in 2007.
- 9.7% of gross sales under banners (inclusive taxes) in 2007.
- 6,166 stores world wide in 2007.
- 897 Ed stores in France at 31st December 2007.
- 49,891 employees at 31st December 2007.

Contd...

Convenience Stores: Just what you need, right next door

A key element in the Group's multi-format policy, our convenience stores offer a complementary outlet to urban and rural customers. Each of the Group's convenience store banners stands out for the way it tailors its offering to the needs of its customer base. In France, our convenience stores offer a range of products and services (for example, home delivery, dry cleaning, 48-hour photo development, ticket distribution, photocopying, stamps, newspapers and more). With surface areas that range between 50 and 900 sq.m. convenience store can be adapted to suit any situation, form urban sites to the most rural location, where they help to counteract the trend of disappearing services.

Convenience Stores Snapshot

- 4,800 stores worldwide at 2007.
- 3,245 convenience stores in France inclusive Proxi et Sherpa.
- Operating in 7 countries namely: Belgium, France, Greece, Italy, Poland, Spain, Brazil.
- 95% under Franchise Agreements in 2007.

Cash & Carry: Proximity and Accessibility for Catering Professionals

The Carrefour Group includes a " cash & carry" operation serving catering professionals under the Promocash brand in France (2,000-4,000 sq.m.) and under the Docks Market and Gross IPer name in Italy. This division has 154 outlets, 134 of which are in France.

E-commerce

Ooshop: The Online Grocery Store

Ooshop was set up to enable Carrefour to market its food products online. Created in 1999, Ooshop is currently the leading French online supermarket in terms of sales. It allows customers to shop on the Internet, choosing from among 8,000 listings with the added benefit of home delivery.

http://www.ooshop.com/

CarrefourOnline.com: everything you need in non-food, online

In june 2006, Carrefour France hypermarkets launched a new, non-food retail website. This innovative site combines discounted prices with an extensive product selection and a range of services. CarrefourOnline.com has benefit form Carrefour's hypermarket expertise, offering the broadest selection available in the marketplace with over one million listings: leisure products (DVDs, games, software, music, books and more), hi-fi, audio and video, and household electrical goods, as well as music downloads and even flower and bicycle delivery. http://online.carrefour.fr/vente-achaten-ligne.html

Building Strategic Relationships

Growth in mature markets forges ahead, while conquest of emerging markets has just begun. The Group has adopted a proactive strategy for positioning its brand: growth and convergence shape Carrefour's new ambitions plans. Carrefour is thus gaining ground in all markets. It is No. 1 in Europe and No. 2 worldwide - the Carrefour Group being the most international of retailers is boosting business in every market.

Mature Countries: Where Carrefour Stands

The Carrefour Group generates 83% of its sales in Europe and is the leader or co-leader in most of the region's countries. This is the primary reason for its success. This is also why, in 2007, it withdrew from Portugal and Switzerland, where it would not have been able to rise quickly enough to a top-three spot. The four major European markets - France, Spain, Belgium and Italy represent 74% of Carrefour's sales.

Contd...

France alone accounts for 46%. The maturity and intense competition that characterise these countries means we must continually reinvigorate our business to consolidate our leading position. In 2008, the Group will actively pursue two major projects: bringing new energy to the Carrefour brand and continuing to transform its retail models in the food and non-food segments.

Leveraging Emerging Markets

With a 42% increase in activity contribution and a 25.4% rise in sales, growth markets act as an engine for Carrefour's growth and dominance. In Europe, the acquisition of Ahold Polska in Poland and Artima in Romania is accelerating Carrefour's penetration of these two high-potential markets. In 2008, the Group also plans to open stores in Russia, a market of 142 million inhabitants, and in Bulgaria, with the opening of Sofia's first hypermarket. In its two other large markets, Latin America and Asia, the Carrefour Group also benefits from a solid image. As a result, it plans to invest significantly in these regions. Its major growth catalysts are Brazil, China, Indonesia and India.

Asia – A Tremendous Potential

- Asia Contributes 6% of Sales
- 108 hypermarkets
- Tremendous growth opportunities
- Big expansion plans to cover India, Sri Lanka, etc.

	Population 2001 in thousand	Average Annual Growth 2001-2006	GDP Growth in 2001	GDP per capita (US $)	Inflation 2001	Sales under Banners in Pound Million
China	12,71,890	0.80%	7.30%	4,204	1.40%	1,341
South Korea	47,720	0.80%	1.50%	18,129	4.20%	1,244
Indonesia	213,855	1.50%	3.00%	3,086	4.50%	203
Japan	1,27,064	0.10%	–0.60%	26,183	–1.00%	161
Malaysia	23,556	1.90%	0.00%	9,220	1.50%	242
Singapore	3,511	3.40%	–3.50%	27,631	1.50%	86
Taiwan	22,364	0.80%	–2.10%	22,085	0.30%	1,460
Thailand	62,936	0.80%	2.00%	6,535	2.10%	350
Total						**5,087**

Source: Carrefour Annual Report 2001.

As an international, multi-format retail group, Carrefour's growth is based on the expansion of powerful and complementary networks that can meet the needs of local consumers worldwide. Carrefour's strong financial position and competitiveness are built on its facilities in emerging countries that are drivers of growth, and on the strong potential of "all-purpose" store formats, such as supermarkets, hard discount store and convenience stores. As the world's leading hypermarket operator with 731 units, Carrefour has also become, in less than four years and on the strength of its concepts, the European supermarket leader with 2,300 outlets and No. 3 worldwide in hard discount stores with 3,800 units. Carrefour's strategy is to expand its presence in its local markets in each of its formats.

Contd...

A Multi-format Group

For a long time, Carrefour based its growth on the hypermarket concept which it invented. The acquisition of Comptoirs Modernes in 1998, followed by the merger with Promodès in 1999, brought Carrefour strong market positions and real expertise in the supermarket segment, along with a diversified business portfolio. Today Carrefour offers the consumer a full array of store formats and styles, one of which is bound to suit his or her life style and consumption habits.

With a variety of store formats, Carrefour can fine tune its expansion strategy to the specific characteristics of the markets it wishes to serve. For example, Carrefour's expansion into Asia was based primarily on its hypermarket concept in order to gain market share quickly. In Latin America, the Group is focusing on the development of supermarkets and hard discount stores alongside an already dense hypermarket network. Complementary formats become a definite asset to continue to grow in more mature markets such as France, Spain and Italy.

The Most International Retailer

In 2001, for the first time, international sales were slightly higher than sales in France. Well established on three continents, and leader in nine countries, Carrefour is the retailer with the broadest geographical coverage. It operates in 30 countries, including some of the world's largest countries, such as Mexico, Brazil, China, Korea and Japan.

Carrefour's international experience is unequaled. It began to expand to other countries very early, at time when competition was less fierce and modern retailing was not very widespread. Carrefour was the first foreign retailer to establish its presence in a number of countries, such as Spain in 1973, Brazil in 1975, Argentina in 1982, Taiwan in 1989, China in 1995 and Japan in 2000.

An International Group, A Local Operator

If Carrefour is now a world retailer, it is because it has succeeded in establishing itself, country by country, as a local player, close to the consumer and respectful of local lifestyles and cultures. When making acquisitions, the Group has chosen to retain a number of local supermarket names when they enjoyed strong brand name recognition, such as GS in Italy, GB in Belgium, Norte in Argentina. While the Carrefour, Champion and Dia concepts are global, over 90% of their product inventories are local or sometimes regional. The stores adapt their products and arrange their shelves to meet customer needs. In Turkey, for example, there is a very large spice section; the Icerenkoy store sells over ten tons a month. In China, the bicycle department is a major department and, given the size and diversity of the country, the Beijing and Shanghai store do not offer the same local products. In Malaysia, the meat department is designed to respect Muslim religious practices. In Colombia, clothing is a focal point in the stores. The quality lines, which have been developed internationally since 1998, now complete the regional products.

How Does Asia fit into Carrefour's Plans?

Expecting a great deal from this area, since been doing business in Asia since 1989, and we are very familiar with local customs and tends. We believe the rapid charges in consumer patterns in the countries where we do business are promising. Asia is the continent with the greatest potential for long-term growth for the Group through two particularly attractive countries: China which will soon open up a market of over one billion people to international companies through its membership in the World Trade Organisation; and Japan, because the buying power and behaviour of its residents.

Markets Change in 2001

The Asian markets are still suffering form the effects of the Japanese Crisis. The downturn in the US market has had an adverse effect on exporting countries like Taiwan, Malaysia and Japan. The strength of our concept, backed by a policy of differentiation and low prices, has continued to drive growth in all our stores. As on December 31, 2001, sales in Asia, on a constant store basis, grew faster than in any other region. With the exception of Japan, which is in a start-up phase, all the countries in the region made positive contributions to earnings.

Contd...

Base of Growth Exclusively on Hypermarkets

As the leading international retailer in Asia, the Group is also the first to have introduced the hypermarket concept. We are now operating 108 hypermarkets, three quarters of which are located in Taiwan, China and Korea. The advantage of a hypermarket is that it can attract a substantial number of customers. Now, because of the maturity of some countries and our in-depth knowledge of local consumers, we can introduce other Carrefour formats. There is a thought on it; though 6% sales come from 108 hypermarkets in Asia region as shown in Table 1:

table 1 **Country-wise Hypermarkets in Asia**

Serial No.	Country	Number of Hypermarkets
1.	Taiwan	26
2.	China	27
3.	Korea	22
4.	Thailand	15
5.	Indonesia	08
6.	Malaysia	06
7.	Singapore	01
8.	Japan	03

Taiwan

As the leading retailer in Taiwan, Carrefour continued to expand in a sluggish economic environment, as all economic indicators deteriorated in 2001. The company opened two new stores during the year in Kaohsiung and Taipei.

In this context, Carrefour Taiwan gained market share thanks to a determined discount pricing policy. Major promotional campaigns were held to mark the major events of the year, including the Chinese New Year, Carnival, Carrefour's anniversary. This led to a significant increase in customer traffic, especially at the end of the year.

In 2002, Carrefour should continue to improve sales and profitability because of the quality of the stores and the strong image of the banner. The company will continue to keep prices low, renovate the fresh product line, and emphasise low-priced products and products bearing the Carrefour label.

China

Carrefour has been active in China since 1995 and is the country's top foreign retailer. It is now expanding in fifteen of the seventeen major cities. In 2001, a process to reorganise Carrefour's legal structures carried out in cooperation with Chinese authorities slowed our growth in the country temporarily, and delayed some store openings. Solely on the basis of its marketing strategies, the Group increased its sales in local currency by 15% compared with 2000. At the end of the year, Carrefour received the authorisations required to continue its growth. It resumed its expansion projects in January 2002 and has plans to open between seven and ten stores a year.

China's membership in the World Trade Organisation in 2001 opens up new possibilities for medium-term growth for international retailers. Carrefour is in a good position to take advantage of these opportunities.

Korea

The third largest retailer is Korea, Carrefour opened two stores in Seoul in 2001 and posted a 17% increase in sales in local currency, aided by steady consumer spending despite an economic slowdown. At year-end, the "Power Card" was introduced. This is a Visa card co-branded by Carrefour, Cetelem and Shinham Bank, with a permanent credit authorisation. This major marketing and customer loyalty tool for Carrefour has

Contd...

been very successful. By the end of February, more than 1,00,000 people had used it since its introduction on December 12, 2001.

During the year, the Carrefour product line was also expended as 950 food and textile items were added to a product line that now offers 1,850 products. Carrefour received a prize for foreign companies awarded by Korea's Ministry of Commerce and Industry for the quality of its investments in the country and its contribution to job creation. In 2002, Carrefour Korea will continue to adjust its concept to the expectations of Korean consumers.

Thailand

The brand opened four stores in 2001 and increased its presence in the capital. At year-end 2001, it had fourteen stores in Bangkok and a store in Chiang Mai, the country's second largest city. In 2001, the economic slowdown in Thailand weakened consumer spending and affected consumer purchasing power. In this environment, Carrefour's low prices made the difference. The Group's sales rose 20% in local currency, stimulated by an aggressive promotional strategy. The Group continued to expand the number of low-priced and Carrefour brand products. It also initiated a substantial program to achieve differentiation through fresh products and services. In cooperation with Cetelem, Carrefour developed a highly competitive credit offer. A partnership with "Bangkok Bank", the leading local band, will allow Carrefour to offer additional financial services in all its shopping malls.

Carrefour Thailand, in partnership with the Carrefour International Foundation, is assisting the UNESCO programs to educate needy children in Thailand. As part of this program, Princess Maka Chakhty Sirindhorm is sponsoring a local project to establish 60 informal training centre to compensate for a school system that is practically non-existent. Carrefour has made a commitment to fund the entire project. Eleven centres are already in operation, and nine more are being established.

Indonesia

The developments initiated three years ago in Indonesia are now paying off. Carrefour posted a gain in market share of roughly 4%, and a 42.6% increase in sales in local currency. The company implemented a major name recognition program through an intensive promotional campaign in both catalogues and in the press, television and radio. Carrefour opened an eighth store, Lebak Bulus, in Djakarta. In 2002, the Groups plans to expand outside the capital city for the first time by opening two new stores.

Malaysia

Carrefour continues to expand in Malaysia. To counteract the slowdown in consumer spending, it conducted aggressive promotional campaigns to mark Carrefour's seventh anniversary in Malaysia in February, the Carnival in April, and the Group's 38th anniversary in October. Carrefour also developed its position as a discounter by harmonising the prices and product lines in its stores. The company introduces new staple items produced locally and sold exclusively by Carrefour.

Singapore

Carrefour successfully integrated its Singapore store and positioned it to meet the expectations of a multicultural population with substantial buying power. Sales increased 7% with a constant sales area, driven by an intensive sales strategy. The banner conducted a total of twenty advertising campaigns in 2001. Expanding the low-priced line in the stores and increasing the number of items sold in the various departments increased store traffic. More than 450 Carrefour, Reflets de France and Carrefour Bio products imported from France were added to the inventory. Carrefour was planning to increase that number to 500 in 2002.

Japan

In December 2000, Carrefour became the first foreign retailer to enter the Japanese market. The real estate slump provided an opportunity for the Group to move into a country with strong potential thanks to its high standard of living, even in times of economic crisis. The first hypermarket was opened in Makahari, a suburb

Contd...

of Tokyo; two others followed in Tokyo and Osaka in January 2001. This first year was a year in which the banner became familiar with and adapted to local consumer habits. With their small homes, the Japanese have limited storage capacities and tend to shop more frequently and in small quantities. The latest Western products are very popular with the Japanese, who expect a French department store to take them to another country and offer them everything they love about France, from bread to perfume to clothing.

Carrefour redesigned its concept during the year to meet these expectations, doubling the number of French products in its lines and including luxury products in the non-food line. Carrefour also consolidated its retail channels with the support of local partners. A fourth store has opened in Sayama (Tokyo) in 2002.

India

With an office established in Gurgaon-Delhi and probably operating under franchise agreement with plans for extending into other metros.

Strengthening the Positions in Asia

With operations in eight Asian countries, the Group strengthened its positions in the region in 2005. After the agreement concluded with Tesco in September 2005, the Group now has 43 stores in Taiwan. This agreement included 6 hypermarkets and 2 projects. At the same time, the Group signed an agreement with Tesco for the sale of its activities in the Czech Republic (11 hypermarkets) and Slovakia (4 hypermarkets).

In Japan, a franchising agreement was signed in March 2005 with Aeon, according to which the latter acquired 8 Carrefour hypermarkets which will continue to operate under the same name. This partnership calls for the exchange of marketing concepts and the sale of Carrefour products by the Japanese retailers.

Future Snapshot

- 4,25,000 sq. m. acquired
- 606 stores acquired, including:
- 28 Hypermarkets, 150 Supermarkets,
- 155 Hard Discount Stores,
- 271 Convenience Stores,
- 2 Cash & Carry Stores

Looking Ahead Future Strategies

The change of course initiated in 2005 is only a first step. 2006 and the years to come are already shaping up as the beginning of a new era of accelerated growth, which will find expression in new store opening, enlargements, new formats, product innovations and, of course, sales growth. Some major new projects are already underway, such as the development of the non-food product range and the expansion of the services we offer. All our teams are already hard at work.

Targeting Growth

Profitable growth remains the absolute priority of the Carrefour Group in 2006 and for the years to come. This clearly/defined strategy is structured around two key focal points: the customer and growth as shown in Table 2. The new strategy is already producing results. Preliminary results in 2005 offer evidence of the start of an upturn. For the first time since 2000, the Group recaptured grocery market share in France. This increase is the sign of a new dynamic.

Internationally, sales increased by 7.5% at constant exchange rates. Carrefour Group has strengthened its positions everywhere throughout the world. An additional 1.5 million square metres of sales floor area were added, including 4,25,000 through acquisitions. But even though these results portend a better future, much remains to be done.

Contd...

Table 2 Planned Growth

100 hypermarket opening planned per year between 2006-2008
1,000 new retail outlets per year
10 dedicated to organic growth over the period of 2006-2008
Billion euros of investments

Cautious Optimism

The Carrefour Group must face the challenges of both a difficult and changing economic environment, and of stiff competition, with each market participant fiercely defending its market share. Customers are changing as well. It is crucial to keep pace with their changing expectations and needs. Customers are better informed and more vigilant, and have adopted new purchasing behaviours. The least expensive food products or those with a high level of added value have each won favour. The demand for non-food products in increasing and customers are ready to support such products particularly when they are innovative in nature. Technological progress is shortening product life cycles, and product ranges must be constantly updated. In-store services must also be expanded.

Continuing the Effort to win Customers

To ensure customer satisfaction and meet the full range of customer needs, we will continue to emphasise six key points:

- The ongoing implementation of a consistent and determined pricing strategy.
- An extensive and well-positioned range of products and services to set the Group apart from the competition and regain market share. The proposed new "High Turnover Consumer Goods" concept and the creation of so-called "Schools" to redefine the Textile, General Merchandise and Electrical/ Audiovisual are good illustrations of this determination.
- The drawing power of the Group's own brands by further improving their quality and enhancing their added value.
- The development of services to assist customers and facilitate their shopping throughout the stores.
- The Partnership with our suppliers by focusing on the essential: the development of a better balanced selection of brand name products and optimisation of the supply chain.
- Increased knowledge of our customers by finding a harmonious balance between micro-marketing and mass marketing. A more nuanced form of customer relations will be implemented, which will have an impact on all activities (through the sharing of information, local definition of the best product mix, and targeted marketing and pricing).

Leading the Field through Continued Development

Organic growth and acquisitions will continue in the years to come, and the optimisation of the portfolio will continue by seizing all opportunities. Even though pragmatism and expediency will guide this reallocation of resources, the Group will not change course. Investment activities will also continue to be sustained. The nature of the resulting portfolio of stores will be decisive for the future.

Outlook

Over the 2006-08 periods, the Group will maintain this strategy of strong and profitable growth. In 2005, investment activities increased sharply (by 38% compared with the average over the last five years). These investments will continue to be devoted to sustained development, via increasing numbers of store openings and targeted acquisitions. As evidence of this strategy, 100 hypermarkets are scheduled to open in 2006,

Contd...

while the average for previous years was 45 opening per year. The emergence of new ideas will also play an important role in coming years. The Group's ability to transform its stores and invent new formats to respond to specific local situations will be crucial.

A number of new concepts designed to ensure the future success are already under development, including "Tintalito" in Colombia, "Bodega Cluster" in Argentina, "GS Spesa Idea Supermarkets" in Italy, and the "Super Très Urbain" concept in France.

Increased globalisation has put pressure on all retailers to seek entry into foreign regions, as markets are becoming more integrated with one another and countries are becoming more dependent of each other for exchange of resources. Simply put, the gradual decline of national barriers, that is creating accessibility for foreign investments by international competitors. In addition to increased access, major developments in communication and transportation have reduced costs and risks, improved the flow and filtering of information thus making foreign investments more attractive than ever before (Rasheed, 2005; Hill, 2000).

In this globalised market, prices are being bargained down as companies are not just competing with only domestic rivals, instead with foreign rivals. Goods and services are also sourced from one location to another, where costs of production are cheaper. Buyers can easily sort for sellers or vise versa. In this globalised world, transportation of goods and services from one country to another has become much easier due to innovation in telecommunication and transportation technology.

As a consequence of the globalisation of business, world trade has grown faster than world output. Foreign direct investment has surged, imports have penetrated more deeply into the world of industrial nations and competitive pressures have increased from one industry after another. To retaliated to this global pressure, firms started expanding to foreign countries (Hill, 2000; Ekeledo, 1998; Barlet & Ghoshal, 1987; O'Donnell, 2000).

Proper international retailing strategies after entering into foreign market increases both firm market shares and sales. Despite these benefits entry into foreign market is challenging from managerial viewpoint (Lam & White, 1999).

Word of Caution.....

When a firm decides to operate outside the domestic market, it has to choose which market to enter, the organisational structure and the entry mode for entering the new market. Entry mode is an institutional arrangement that a firm uses to market its product in a foreign market for the first three to five years (Ekelodo & Sivakuma, 2003). Or a means of linking a company's product to foreign market (Kwom & Kanopa, 1992).

There are varieties of modes which firms might use to enter into foreign markets, firms, for instance, might choose to use exporting through independent intermediaries to enter to one market, whereas in another market, the firm might choose to export through integrated company-owned channel, or operate overseas either via contractual mode (such as licensing and franchising) or through foreign direct investment (Joint venture and wholly-owned subsidiary) (Eramilli, 1992). The selection of appropriate entry mode plays an important role in determining the success and performance of firm in the new market (Ekeledo & Sivakumar, 2003).

Last Few Words.....

Carrefour has so far been able to play the game very well, with respect to its international retailing strategies, expansion plans, geographical spread and customer's needs.

Retail is Essentially the Art of Bringing People Together......and

Carrefour has made it amply clear that retail involves building relationships.

Carrefour Group plays a leading role in this arena as they build relationships not only with customers, employees and suppliers, but with institutional, financial and non-profit partners as well, trading products and sharing ideas, cooperating with others for a more efficient and responsible world.

Index